CONSUMER BEHAVIOR

SIXTH EDITION

CONSUMER BEHAVIOR
SIXTH EDITION

JAMES F. ENGEL
Wheaton College

ROGER D. BLACKWELL
The Ohio State University

PAUL W. MINIARD
The Ohio State University

The Dryden Press
Chicago · Fort Worth · San Francisco · Philadelphia
Montreal · Toronto · London · Sydney · Tokyo

Acquisitions Editor: Robin Zwettler
Developmental Editor: Jan Richardson
Project Editor: Cate Rzasa
Design Supervisor: Rebecca Lemna
Production Manager: Barb Bahnsen
Permissions Editor: Doris Milligan
Director of Editing, Design, and Production: Jane Perkins

Text and Cover Designer: Vargas/Williams Design
Production Services: Chernow Editorial Services, Inc.
Compositor: Arcata Graphics/Kingsport
Text Type: 10/12 ITC New Baskerville

Library of Congress Cataloging-in-Publication Data

Engel, James F.
    Consumer behavior / James F. Engel, Roger D. Blackwell,
Paul W. Miniard.—6th ed.
        p. cm.
    Bibliography: p.
    Includes index.
    ISBN 0–03–022979–0
    1. Consumer behavior.   2. Marketing research.
I. Blackwell, Roger D.   II. Miniard, Paul W.   III. Title.
HF5415.3.E53   1990
658.8′342—dc20   89-7696

Address orders:
The Dryden Press
Orlando, FL 32887

Address editorial correspondence:
The Dryden Press
908 N. Elm Street
Hinsdale, IL 60521

The Dryden Press
Holt, Rinehart and Winston
Saunders College Publishing

Cover Source: "Ludwigskirche in München," by Wassily
Kandinsky, 1908.
Thyssen-Bornemisza Collection, Lugano, Switzerland.

THE DRYDEN PRESS SERIES IN MARKETING

PREFACE

It seems almost unbelievable as we publish this sixth edition that this text is celebrating its twenty-second anniversary in 1990. The world today is a radically different one from the one we faced in 1965 when the concept of this book was born.

Three of us (James F. Engel, David T. Kollat, and Roger D. Blackwell) on the faculty of marketing at The Ohio State University joined together and offered a seminar on consumer behavior. Little did we realize that a book would emerge from this collaborative effort or that a number of doctoral candidates in this and subsequent seminars would become active leaders in what was just beginning to emerge as a major field of study.

It soon became apparent that a text was necessary to give structure and direction to this infant field. Three years later, the first edition of *Consumer Behavior* was published by Holt, Rinehart & Winston, the parent company of The Dryden Press. A number of graduate students actively contributed to that volume through their ideas and research. We especially remember the impact of Larry Light, Brian Sternthal, Alice Tybout, Orville Walker, C. Samuel Craig, Philip Kuehl, and Beverlee Anderson among others.

Subsequent editions reflecting changes in this newly emerging field appeared in 1973, 1978, 1982, and 1986. One member of the original co-author team, David Kollat, dropped out in 1982 because of pressures he faced as a business executive. Paul W. Miniard joined in 1986 and has become a valued partner.

Now that 22 years have passed, a bookshelf that held our text and one or two specialized books on consumer behavior now has become completely filled with consumer behavior texts alone. It is exciting to see how the field of consumer behavior has grown into a standard subject in business schools and related disciplines.

The conceptual and methodological sophistication of consumer behavior research has burgeoned, making book revision a demanding task indeed. Fields of specialization such as information processing, multi-attribute models, and involvement theory now generate as much or more relevant research than the entire body of marketing-related literature we reviewed for the first edition.

Our basic purposes remain unchanged from the first edition.

1. To explore and evaluate a rapidly growing body of published and unpublished research.

2. To advance generalizations and propositions from the evidence.

3. To assess the practical significance of what has been learned.

4. To pinpoint areas where research has been lacking.

This time, however, we would like to add one more objective:

5. To make the field of consumer behavior exciting, interesting, and relevant to both students and faculty.

Nothing can be more dull than wading through mountains of abstractions and theories. More than ever before, we have infused this edition with examples that illustrate the use of consumer behavior research and theory in marketing strategy. You will find our *Consumer in Focus* sections especially interesting as we attempt to provide a vivid picture of how consumer research is applied and used.

Because of our backgrounds and interests, the primary perspective of this book continues to be marketing. However, we branch out in many other directions as well, reflecting the diversity of application of consumer behavior research. Therefore, those with differing perspectives will find much of value in this edition.

From the outset we have made use of a model of consumer behavior as a basic method of exposition. Although there have been changes since 1968, we still are convinced that a model is helpful in structuring knowledge in the field and guiding applications in both research and strategy. It should be noted that we maintain our conviction that *one* model is sufficient to explain all types of decision-process behavior, ranging from high involvement to low involvement.

NEW TO THIS EDITION

How, then, is this edition different? From the outset we can say this edition is not merely a cosmetic rewrite. It is a thoroughly revised book from beginning to end. We have rethought the model, flow of topics, exposition, and subjects to include and exclude. Here are the major things you will notice:

1. As mentioned above, more than ever before our entire outlook has been shaped by one dominant question: "How helpful is a given concept, theory, or technique in the world beyond the classroom?" As our knowledge and experience have grown over these decades, so has our grasp of applications. Therefore, you will find many examples from the business world, from non-profit organizations, and from many countries beyond North America integrated throughout the text.

2. We keep our long-standing decision-process perspective but there are changes in the way in which we introduce and use the EKB (*E*ngel, *K*ollat, and *B*lackwell) model. We begin with a more encompassing general model of consumer behavior. Only in later chapters is our familiar and more structured EKB model introduced and used.

3. We have made every effort to reflect the growing conviction within the field that sole reliance on a decision-process perspective can be unduly limiting. What about the needs and gratifications in the consumption process itself? This is referred to as the *hedonic* perspective. We welcome this growing emphasis and are convinced it provides some much needed richness.

4. There is a return to our structuring of topics in earlier editions which begins with environmental influences and progressively narrows to individual differences, psychological processes, and decision processes. Those who prefer a differing order, however, will have no difficulty beginning with other sections and topics.

5. We have added three new chapters to this edition and have combined certain topics for more logical exposition. The new ones are Chapter 7 (Situational Influence), Chapter 10 (Knowledge), and Chapter 22 (Market Segmentation). Chapter 8 (Consumer Resources) pulls together our previous discussion of attention, time, and money into an integrated perspective on how these scarce resources shape consumer behavior. Chapter 9 combines coverage of involvement and motivation. These additions necessitated some sacrifices. At the suggestion of various reviewers, we have dropped our chapter on organizational buyer behavior.

6. We have restored the discussion of high and low involvement behavior in response to suggestions from users and reviewers, and we make frequent references to both throughout the text.

7. In keeping with our increased emphasis on the managerial implications of consumer behavior research and theory, we have added opening vignettes and *Consumer in Focus* boxes to each chapter. These demonstrate how companies have applied or could apply consumer behavior theory in developing marketing strategy and action.

8. As in previous editions, we have continued to look to the future in terms of economic, demographic, and sociocultural trends.

9. In recognition of the increasing globalization of consumer markets, we have expanded our coverage of the international dimensions of consumer behavior and marketing.

10. We have added 16 pages of full-color ads that illustrate the use of consumer behavior theory in advertising. The four inserts are coordinated with Parts 2, 3, 4, and 6 of the text.

SUPPLEMENTS

The supplementary material for this edition has been greatly expanded to help meet the needs of instructors. The *Instructor's Manual/Test Bank/Transparency Masters* volume includes teaching suggestions, detailed lecture outlines, answers to discussion questions, approximately 2,000 test questions, and more than 80 transparency masters of new figures and in-class exercises as well as key figures and tables from the text. The Test Bank was written by Edward Laurie of San Jose State University, and the Transparency Masters were prepared by JoAnn Schwinghammer of Mankato State University. The volume is available to adopters of the text. A *Computerized Test Bank,* for use with IBM PC microcomputers, is also available.

In addition, a companion casebook, *Contemporary Cases in Consumer Behavior,* Third Edition, by Blackwell, Talarzyk, and Engel, can be used to great advantage to highlight the practical relevance of the concepts covered in the text.

ACKNOWLEDGMENTS

If we were to go back over past editions and list all of those who have assisted us, this preface would necessarily be longer. All we can do is offer our heartfelt thanks once again. We do, however, wish to acknowledge those colleagues who read the manuscript for this edition through from beginning to end. This group went beyond the call of duty and have interacted with us, responded to questions we asked of them, and diligently worked in partnership to help make this a better text. Our thanks go to:

Gordon Bruner, Southern Illinois University, Carbondale

John Bennett, University of Northern Colorado

Peggy Gilbert, Southwest Missouri State University

Lee Meadow, Bentley College

John Schouten, Iowa State University

JoAnn Schwinghammer, Mankato State University

Tommy E. Whittler, University of Kentucky, Lexington

Other colleagues also provided helpful suggestions for improving this edition through their feedback on the fifth edition and/or their reactions to our plan for the sixth edition. Our appreciation is extended to:

April Atwood, University of Washington

Peter Chadraba, DePaul University

Sayeste Daser, Wake Forest University

Peter Dickson, Ohio State University

Peter DiPaulo, University of Missouri, St. Louis

Betty Harris, University of Southwestern Louisiana

Gail Hudson, Arkansas State University

Inder Khera, Wright State University

Jim Leigh, Southern Methodist University

Larry Lepisto, Central Michigan University

Ken Lord, SUNY, Buffalo

Deanna Mader, University of Louisville

James McNeal, Texas A & M University

Don Norris, Miami University

Dan Sherrell, Louisiana State University

Doug Stayman, University of Texas, Austin

Tillie Voegtli, University of Missouri, St. Louis

Malcolm White, California State University, Sacramento

We also wish to encourage readers of the sixth edition to share with us any ideas or materials they might have for improving the text. Those contributing ideas and/or materials used in the next edition will of course be acknowledged.

We continue to express our appreciation to the staff of Management Horizons, a division of Price Waterhouse, for the help provided over all six editions. We have benefited from use of its excellent library facilities and research resources. William R. Davidson, Cyrus Wilson, and Dan Sweeney deserve our thanks.

The staff at The Dryden Press have been real partners in this edition, and we appreciate all they have done. To Jan Richardson and Rob Zwettler, a special word of thanks. You have provided the kind of working relationships that authors always want but seldom find.

Finally, we acknowledge our wives, Sharon, Ann, and Debbie. You have endured our long hours and frustrations, and we are grateful.

James F. Engel   *Wheaton, Illinois*
Roger D. Blackwell   *Columbus, Ohio*
Paul W. Miniard   *Columbus, Ohio*

ABOUT THE AUTHORS

James F. Engel (Ph.D., University of Illinois, Urbana; B.S., Drake) has a distinguished name in the study of consumer behavior. He was honored by his peers in 1980 as "the founder of a field" when he was named one of the first two Fellows of the Association for Consumer Research. He received a similar citation when he received the prestigious Paul D. Converse Award of the American Marketing Association. These were given in recognition of his pioneering research which first appeared in 1960, his role as senior author of this text, and other forms of leadership. He presently is Professor of Communications Research at the Wheaton College Graduate School (Illinois) where he moved in 1972 from The Ohio State University after founding the consumer behavior faculty there. Professor Engel has shifted his emphasis from consumer goods marketing to the application of nonprofit marketing principles to religious organizations worldwide. He also has published widely in that field and serves as Senior Vice President of Management Development Associates, a consulting group specializing in these applications. In that capacity he has served as a consultant to more than 150 groups in 50 countries.

Roger D. Blackwell (Ph.D., Northwestern; B.S., Missouri) is Professor of Marketing at The Ohio State University where he has served since 1965. He is a well-known author, and his works include several casebooks also published by The Dryden Press. He is in constant demand as a business consultant and speaker in the area of the impact of changing environments on marketing strategy. He was recipient of the Marketing Educator of the Year Award given in 1984 by Sales and Marketing Executives International. Dr. Blackwell has also received a number of awards for outstanding teaching at Ohio State, including the Alumni Award for Distinguished Teaching in 1988.

Paul W. Miniard (Ph.D., M.A., B.S., University of Florida) is Associate Professor of Marketing at The Ohio State University where he has served since 1979. Since joining the faculty, he has won a number of undergraduate and graduate teaching awards, including Marketing Professor of the Year in 1988–1989. He has published articles in the leading marketing and psychological research journals such as the *Journal of Consumer Research, Journal of Marketing Research,* and *Journal of Experimental Social Psychology.* In addition, he has had wide consulting experience in consumer research and strategic planning.

BRIEF CONTENTS

CONTENTS

PART II   ENVIRONMENTAL INFLUENCES   57

CHAPTER 3

CULTURAL AND ETHNIC VALUES   59

CHAPTER 4

SOCIAL CLASS AND STATUS   104

PART IV   PSYCHOLOGICAL PROCESSES   361

PART VII   EPILOGUE   757

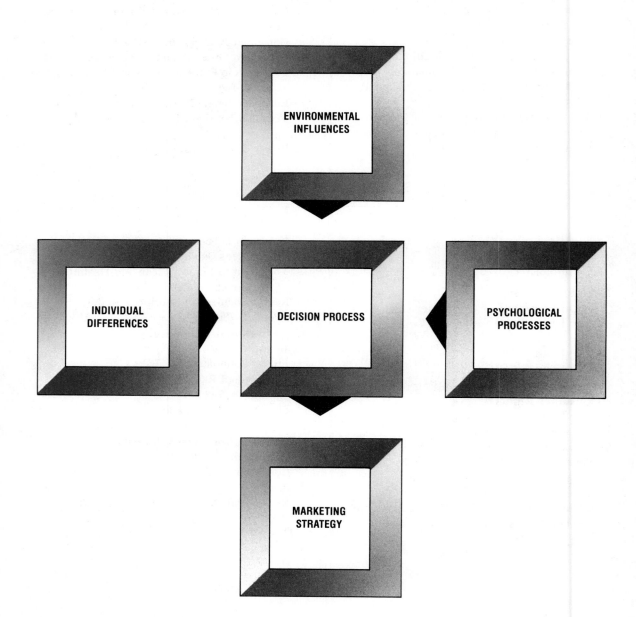

INTRODUCTION AND OVERVIEW

What is consumer behavior all about? Why should it receive growing recognition as an academic discipline and field of research? These and many other questions are considered in the first two chapters, which build a framework of essential concepts.

Of particular importance is Chapter 2, which presents a diagrammatic overview model of consumer behavior and the complex of influences on it, including environmental influences, individual differences, and psychological processes. A review of the contents shows that the book is organized around this model and the set of influences.

THE CONSUMER:
PERSPECTIVES AND
VIEWPOINTS

SHINJINCUI: JAPAN'S YOUNG CONSUMERS

When he commutes across Tokyo to classes, university student Ryoichi Mizutani, 18, carries his books in a $100 black Valentino shoulder bag and his subway pass in a $60 Louis Vuitton wallet. Naomi Matsuoka, 21, a senior at prestigious Waseda University, orders Budweiser or Heineken in restaurants instead of local brands "because of the ambiance of imported beer." For a snack she likes the designer ice cream at Dipper Dan, Baskin-Robbins, or Haagen-Daz.

Japanese youth are heavy on hedonism and light on traditional Confucian values of frugality and hard work. Dubbed the *shinjincui,* which means "new breed of man," they are more individualistic and creative than their elders. Their parents scrimped and saved to rebuild after the war, but they save little and spend extravagantly on what they want. A new phenomenon in Tokyo is the "BMW pauper," a young Japanese who lives in a shabby room and possesses not much else but his BMW.

Indulgent parents give kids generous monthly allowances plus cash gifts at New Year's. Many students work after school too and spend much of what they earn on themselves. Tokyo teenagers have disposable incomes averaging $2000 a year, according to Marplan Japan, the market research subsidiary of the McCann-Erickson Hakuhodo advertising agency.

American products, which older Japanese sometimes view as shoddy, are in particular demand with the *shinjincui.* "I'd rather sell in Japan than in France or Italy," says Robert Wilk, an American who is managing director of Marplan Japan.

"Many older Japanese are ambivalent about the U.S., since it's an enemy turned friend," says Joseph Precker, an American psychology professor at Tokyo's Sophia University who is also a marketing consultant. "But to the young, the U.S. is a paradise."

One surprising hit from the U.S.: stationery. Students especially like American notebooks and binders. Says Keiko Shimizu, 26, a marketing planner at Sony, "Japanese students are fascinated with the IVY League image. They feel American when they buy American stationery."

Source: Adapted from Frederick Katayama, "Japan's Prodigal Young Are Dippy About Imports," *Fortune* (May 11, 1987), 118. © 1987 Time Inc. All rights reserved.

WHAT'S CONSUMER BEHAVIOR ALL ABOUT?

The story of the *shinjincui* is interesting reading, isn't it? This is because all of us are buyers and consumers, and much that we do in this arena is central to our lifestyle and sense of well-being. Therefore, it is not surprising that a large and expanding field of research has emerged focusing on consumer behavior. We define **consumer behavior** as those actions directly involved in obtaining, consuming, and disposing of products and services, including the decision processes that precede and follow these actions.

This subject can be approached from several perspectives, all of which are considered in this book: (1) consumer influence; (2) wholistic; and (3) intercultural. As you will see, these categories overlap to some extent.

A CONSUMER INFLUENCE PERSPECTIVE

Consumer behavior is of particular interest to those who, for various reasons, desire to influence or change that behavior, including those whose primary concern is marketing, consumer education and protection, and public policy.

MARKETING   Prior to World War II, many businesses, but by no means all, operated from a production orientation reflecting the philosophy that "a good product will sell itself."[1] This was the case because there frequently was more demand than supply in some industries. Why ask consumers what they want when they will buy almost anything you produce?

Matters changed after the war, however, when large numbers of businesses discovered that they possessed more productive capacity than the market

---

[1] Ronald A. Fullerton, "How Modern Is Modern Marketing? Marketing's Evolution and the Myth of the 'Production Era,'" *Journal of Marketing* 52 (January 1988), 108–125.

could absorb. It then became imperative to shift the focus from production to **marketing** — the process of planning and executing the conception, pricing, promotion, and distribution of ideas, goods, and services to create exchanges that satisfy individual and organizational objectives.[2]

The key element in this definition is the *exchange* between the customer and the supplier. Each party gives something of value to the other with the goal of satisfying their respective needs. In the normal buying context money is exchanged for a desired good or service.

Notice that the customer lies at the heart of the process. Everything that the supplier does in the way of product, price, promotion, and distribution (the "marketing mix") is adapted to market demand. Hence, customers such as Ryoichi Mizutani and Naomi Matsuoka exercise a dominant influence on everything that is done by the business firm.

The consumer controls the exchange through the pocketbook. In 1954 Peter Drucker sounded the clarion call: "There is one valid definition of business purpose: *to create a customer*" [italics ours].[3] More recently, Peters and Austin isolated the two factors which appear to distinguish the excellent business organization from the also-ran:

> *In the private or public sector, in big business or small, we observe that there are only two ways to create and sustain superior performance over the long haul. First, take exceptional care of your customers . . . via superior service and superior quality. Second, constantly innovate. That's it.*[4]

It is not surprising, then, that the study of consumer behavior had its initial taproot in the field of economics and, more recently, in marketing. The underlying question guiding most of the writing in this field is, as Belk has noted, "What arrangement of the marketing mix will have what effects on the purchase behavior of what types of consumers?"[5] Therefore, the *buying process* is of more concern to marketers than the *consumption process*. And, consumer research must have distinct managerial relevance in this context before it will be considered.

Marketers will take the *shinjincui* seriously and do everything possible to capitalize upon the opportunities they present. Levi Strauss, for example, has cashed in on the demand for jeans in Japan by featuring images of James Dean and proclaiming that "Heroes wear Levi's." Also, Japanese sales of Soloflex exercise equipment exceeded $4 million in the first year on the market.[6]

---

[2] "AMA Board Approves New Marketing Definition," *Marketing News* (March 1, 1985), 1.

[3] Peter F. Drucker, *The Practice of Management* (New York: Harper & Row, 1954), 37.

[4] Tom Peters and Nancy Austin, *A Passion for Excellence* (New York: Random House, 1985), 4.

[5] Russell W. Belk, "ACR Presidential Address: Happy Thought," in Melanie Wallendorf and Paul Anderson, eds., *Advances in Consumer Research* 14 (Provo, Utah: Association for Consumer Research, 1986), 2.

[6] Frederick Katayama, "Japan's Prodigal Young Are Dippy About Imports," *Fortune* (May 11, 1987), 118.

CONSUMER EDUCATION AND PROTECTION   Others also want to shape and influence consumer behavior but do so in an effort to help the consumer *buy wisely.* The consumer economist, in particular, will examine the behavior of Ryoichi, Naomi, and their *shinjincui* counterparts in terms of whether they make the best choices in view of their motivations and goals. Here are some issues that might be raised:

1. Would the overall value received have been higher had there been better information at hand on other purchase alternatives?
2. Are they being misled through advertising to "buy American"?
3. Would these consumers have been better off to buy on the basis of price as opposed to brand name?

Through education the consumer can be taught how to detect the presence of deception and other abuses and be made aware of remedies that exist and opportunities for redress. Also, anyone can benefit from greater insight into money-saving strategies. Educational programs also must be based on research into motivation and behavior if they are to be relevant in the real world of consumer life. Not surprisingly, consumer economists and home economists now rank among the most serious students of consumer behavior.

The marketer and the consumer economist often take adversarial positions when analyzing the same behavior. Nevertheless, both desire to change that behavior when it is perceived as beneficial to do so. The only difference is in their respective agendas.

PUBLIC POLICY   Education alone will not guarantee consumer welfare. The cornerstone of a free-enterprise economy is the right of any consumer to make an informed and unrestricted choice from an array of alternatives. When this right is curtailed because of business abuse, societal consensus affirms that government has the duty to influence consumer choice by restrictions in monopoly power and by curbing deception and other unfair trade practices.

Consumer protection legislation and regulation all too often are based on the opinions of a small group of advocates. The outcome can be ineffective or even counterproductive activity. There now is growing awareness that greater reliance must be placed on consumer research if consumer protection is to function as intended.

A MORE WHOLISTIC PERSPECTIVE

The domain of consumer research goes far beyond the managerial perspective when primary focus is placed on *consumption.* Hirschman and Holbrook, among others, strongly advocate that the purchase decision is only a small component in the constellation of events involved in the consumption experience.[7] Holbrook contends that it is time for consumer researchers to take consumption as the central emphasis and examine "all facets of the value potentially provided when some living organism acquires, uses, or disposes of any product that might achieve a goal, fulfill a need, or satisfy a want."[8] The decision process itself thus assumes a secondary importance.

This broadened perspective has been recently reflected in the literature on research into the aesthetic pleasures acquired from consumption of arts, music, and other nonutilitarian activities. This has come to be known as "hedonic consumption" — that undertaken purely for pleasure.[9] Research often makes use of both questionnaires and human-observation methods in order to achieve a broader understanding of the impact of the consumption event.[10]

If we were to analyze the behavior of the *shinjincui* from this point of view, our goal would be to understand what has taken place without any particular intent to change or influence the process:

1. Why are there such generational differences in outlooks?

2. What values are transmitted by the American products as opposed to Japanese alternatives?

3. How can we understand the deeper meaning of the pleasures offered by the designer ice creams to Japanese youth?

4. Is it ethical for American and European firms to try to make these inroads into a culture with such different traditions?

5. What long-lasting effects will the consumer culture have on traditional Japanese values?

While some of the outcomes may be of managerial significance as well, overall understanding is the goal.

This wholistic perspective is a recent development, and both the number who hold this point of view and the resulting numbers of publications are still relatively small. There is little doubt, however, that it will grow, because

---

[7] Morris B. Holbrook and Elizabeth C. Hirschman, "The Experiential Aspects of Consumption: Consumer Fantasies, Feelings, and Fun," *Journal of Consumer Research* 9 (September 1982), 132–140. Also see Elizabeth C. Hirschman and Morris B. Holbrook, "Hedonic Consumption: Emerging Concepts, Methods, and Propositions," *Journal of Marketing* 45 (Summer 1982), 92–101.

[8] Morris B. Holbrook, "What Is Consumer Research?" *Journal of Consumer Research* 14 (June 1987), 130.

[9] Morris B. Holbrook, "The Dramatic Side of Consumer Research: The Semiology of Consumption Symbolism in the Arts," in Wallendorf and Anderson, *Advances*, 237–240.

[10] See Lawrence J. Marks, Susan Higgins, and Michael A. Kamins, "Investigating the Experiential Dimensions of Product Evaluation," *Advances in Consumer Research* 15 (Provo, Utah: Association for Consumer Research, 1987), 114–121; and Elizabeth C. Hirschman, "Humanistic Inquiry and Marketing Research: Philosophy, Method, and Criteria," *Journal of Marketing Research* 23 (August 1986), 237–249.

of the importance of understanding the nature of human behavior and values in this significant arena of life activity, over and above the pragmatic concerns of marketers.

AN INTERCULTURAL PERSPECTIVE

If one were to examine the literature, it would be easy to assume that consumer research is of primary importance only in North America, Europe, and Japan. Nothing could be further from the truth. On all continents, there is striving toward economic development and greater self-sufficiency. Even in such socialistic countries as China and the USSR, consumer goods are becoming increasingly important. As a consumer-oriented society emerges, an early manifestation is a middle class with disposable income. Unless political restrictions are imposed, a rising standard of living becomes a dominant concern.

A vogue word in China today is *"Huoli* 28," the Chinese pronunciation for "Power 28," which almost instantaneously has become the most popular detergent in this country.[11] Through television, radio, and newspaper advertising, sales increased by ten times between 1986 and 1987, resulting in a substantial profit. Until quite recently such a marketing success would have been unthinkable.

The middle-class counterparts of the *shinjincui* are seen on the streets of Kuala Lumpur, Nairobi, Quito, Beijing, New Delhi, Caracas, and elsewhere in the world. Therefore, marketers have been quick to capitalize on resulting opportunities, as the ad in Figure 1.1 demonstrates.

It is time to broaden horizons beyond the western world and view consumer research as a universal necessity. This is because basic human needs are universal, although there are undeniable and profound cultural differences in their expression.

THE PERSPECTIVE OF THIS BOOK

Since the first edition we have tried to be eclectic in the best sense of the word and to reflect a broad orientation. Nevertheless, we approach the subject of consumer behavior from a marketing point of view. Our primary concern is phasing consumer research into marketing strategy. Increasingly, however, the other perspectives have changed our outlook. We welcome and affirm the enrichment that is taking place.

RIGHT THINKING ABOUT THE CONSUMER

There are four significant principles that underlie all that we say and do in these coming pages.

---

[11] "Detergent Shows Power in Washing Market," *China Daily* (June 13, 1988), 6.

FIGURE 1.1   EVIDENCE OF A GROWING CONSUMER CULTURE WORLDWIDE

Johnson's Baby Jelly, another pure and gentle product for baby's tender skin

For years, mothers have relied on Johnson's baby products to help give their babies all the loving care they need. Because they know that only the purest and gentlest products are suitable for baby's tender and sensitive skin.

So we at Johnson and Johnson have created another pure and gentle baby care product; Johnson's Baby Jelly, specially formulated to protect baby's tender skin, from urine wetness and harmful bacteria that cause nappy rash.

Used after every bath and especially after every nappy change, Johnson's Baby Jelly acts as an effective moisture barrier, that ensures that baby's skin remains baby soft and smooth.

New Johnson's Baby Jelly is available in two versions. The Pink top is scented and the Blue top un-scented, both are pure, gentle and smooth textured.

Johnson & Johnson

"Sea Gull" Watches
The Treasure of Timing in China

THE CONSUMER IS SOVEREIGN

The Cadillac Division of the General Motors Company has been labeled in the automobile industry as a "fallen angel." Take time now to analyze the Cadillac story in our first *Consumer in Focus* case.

Some Cadillac executives apparently made a dangerous assumption. They believed that *the consumer will respond to a product as long as it is backed with sufficient selling firepower.* The primary beneficiaries from such thinking were Lincoln-Mercury and the luxury imports.

The bottom-line issue is failure to recognize that *the consumer is sovereign.* He or she is not an unthinking pawn to be manipulated at will by the commercial persuader. Consumer behavior, as a rule, is purposeful and goal oriented. Products and services are accepted or rejected on the basis of the extent to which they are perceived as relevant to needs and lifestyle. The individual is fully capable of ignoring everything the marketer has to say.

Business history is full of wreckages that can be traced to a defective

CONSUMER IN FOCUS

1.1   CADILLAC — THE FALLEN ANGEL

The onetime "Standard of the World" has been struggling for a decade. In 1982 Cadillac made an abortive bow to youth by attaching its crest to a compact model called Cimarron, which buyers correctly perceived as little more than a gussied-up Chevrolet Cavalier. The nadir came in 1985 when Cadillac introduced slimmed-down versions of its Seville and Eldorado. At around $25,000 a copy, the cars cost several thousand dollars more than their predecessors, but they were smaller and looked like some other General Motors cars that cost significantly less. Sales of the newly styled models fell as much as 50%, forcing Cadillac to cut prices 5% in 1987. In the worst of all possible worlds, it had antagonized its traditional big-car customers without drawing younger small-car aficionados.

Now Cadillac is on an intensive program to get back up to speed. Until the look-alike cars can be reconfigured, designers are hurriedly trying to restore panache any way they can — by adding inches to the rear deck of the Eldorado, for instance. Analyst

Maryann Keller of Furman Selz Mager Dietz & Birney observes tartly: "Attempting to disguise the current models by adding fender extensions will not reverse Cadillac's problems."

General manager John Grettenberger likes to brag that Cadillac has been the luxury leader for 38 years. But its 300,000-car-a-year volume has been stagnant for a decade.

One beneficiary of Cadillac's woes has been Ford's Lincoln–Mercury division. The elephantine Lincoln Town Car ($23,126), a throwback to the land yachts of the 1960s and early 1970s, nevertheless has picked up sales from buyers who did not want pocket-size Cadillacs. The Mark VII LSC ($26,016), a luxury two-door with a sporting flair, is drawing somewhat younger buyers and now accounts for about 75% of Mark VII sales.

Source: Excerpted from Alex Taylor III, "Detroit vs. New Upscale Imports" *Fortune* (April 27, 1987), 72 and 76. © 1987 Time, Inc. All rights reserved.

philosophy on this principle. Purina Homestyle, "the quick dog dinner that's like homemade," was rejected almost as soon as it was introduced.[12] So it's homemade? So what? And the Bristol-Myers Company introduced Small Miracle, which would allow the consumer to shampoo once or twice a week. It achieved only 30 percent of market potential because most women are convinced of the necessity of more frequent shampooing.[13] And on the story goes.

It all comes down to this essential point: *Understanding and adapting to consumer motivation and behavior is not an option — it is an absolute necessity for*

---

[12] Michael M. Miller, "What a Museum! Panda Punch, I Hate Peas, Nutrimate and More," *The Wall Street Journal* (December 15, 1986), 26.
[13] Nancy Giges, "No Miracle in Small Miracle Story Behind Clairol Failure," *Advertising Age* (August 16, 1982), 76.

competitive survival. In the final analysis, the consumer is in control, and the marketer succeeds when the product or service is perceived as offering real benefits.

CONSUMER MOTIVATION AND BEHAVIOR CAN BE UNDERSTOOD THROUGH RESEARCH

As we discover in the coming pages, consumer behavior is a process, and the purchase is only one stage. There are many underlying influences, ranging from internal motivations to social influences of various kinds. Yet, motivation and behavior can be understood, albeit imperfectly, through research. If this were not the case, this book would never have been written. Perfect prediction is never possible, but properly designed and used research efforts can significantly lower the risks of marketing failure.

CONSUMER BEHAVIOR CAN BE INFLUENCED

Consumer sovereignty presents a formidable challenge, but skillful marketing can affect both motivation and behavior *if the product or service offered is designed to meet consumer needs.* A sales success occurs because demand either exists already or is latent and awaiting activation by the right marketing offering.

A case in point is one of 3M's greatest successes, the Scotch Post-it™ Brand Note Pad (Figure 1.2). Quite by accident a researcher in the 3M laboratories discovered an adhesive that would bond two pieces of paper together while allowing quick and total separation with minimal effort. He believed there might be a market for removable, self-stick notes but was greeted with initial skepticism. Perseverance, followed by marketing research, verified his hunch, however.

Why did this new idea succeed so dramatically? Once consumers had a chance to observe it and try it, large numbers quickly saw that it met a need. Notes can be attached to something else without defacing or damage, and there proved to be a multitude of uses both at home and on the job.

It is worth noting that high promotional expenditures do not prevent the failure of most of the new products introduced on the market each year. Once again, consumer relevance is the central issue.

CONSUMER INFLUENCE IS SOCIALLY LEGITIMATE

Consumer needs are real, and there is undeniable benefit from products or services that offer genuine utility. The consumer benefits while, at the same time, the economic system is energized. Remember that the consumer, not the marketer, sets the agenda for the whole process.

There is no question, however, that deception, monopoly power, and

FIGURE 1.2
SCOTCH *POST-IT*
NOTE PADS: **A**
PRODUCT THAT
SUCCESSFULLY
ACTIVATED
CONSUMER
DEMAND

Source: Courtesy of 3M Commercial Supply Division.

other forms of manipulation can and often do short-circuit the benefits received. *The key to social legitimacy is a guarantee that the consumer retains complete and unimpeded freedom throughout the process.* This freedom is manifested when nothing induces the consumer to act in ways that would be regretted and even disavowed after more careful reflection. Improper influence gives rise to serious ethical violations necessitating legislation and other forms of protection activities. More is said on this subject in Chapter 25.

IMPROVING MARKETING EFFECTIVENESS

A central underlying premise of this book is that proper use of consumer research significantly sharpens the effectiveness of marketing efforts. We trust that the examples given here will amply underscore this point.

MARKET SEGMENTATION

The Disney Channel entered the highly competitive cable television market in 1983 and experienced a decidedly shaky start. It took off in 1985, however, when it moved away from children's programs and differentiated itself from Nickelodeon and others by offering new material designed for the whole family.[14] Disney experienced sharp increases in market share by expanding into such segments as those who do not have children under 12 and those who are age 40 or over.

Disney followed the practice of all successful marketers by recognizing that the consumer market for any product or service is likely to be *segmented.* This means that there are various groupings of buyers who may differ from one another in expected benefits. The alert marketer capitalizes on these differences through a strategy of **market segmentation,** in which each segment is viewed as a distinct target with its own requirements for product, price, distribution, and promotion.

So the starting point in marketing planning always is with the consumer. Who are the prospective buyers? How do our offerings stack up against the competition? What needs and motives enter into the decision? Is more than one family member involved? What information is used in the decision? These and other questions provide essential input for successful segmentation.

The Anheuser-Busch company maintains industry dominance by "segmenting the market with a vengeance."[15] The United States is divided into 210 markets, and there are regional strategy variations designed to position Anheuser-Busch products as "everyone's hometown beer." Sponsored events and advertising are specifically aimed at blacks, whites, blue-collar workers, computer buffs, and auto-racing fans, to mention only a few examples. One commercial event saluted waitresses and bartenders by saying, "This Bud's for everyone that serves them up cold."

You will find examples of segmentation strategies in many of the chapters as we unfold the complex of influences on consumer behavior. Segmentation is of such importance that it is the subject of Chapter 21.

THE MARKETING MIX

The term **marketing mix** refers to a unified strategy integrating product, price, promotion, and distribution. Each element of the mix requires the input of consumer research. Research assumes especially crucial importance when marketing expands across cultural boundaries onto the international scene.

PRODUCT POSITIONING   In 1986 Liz Claiborne Inc. moved onto the *Fortune 500 List* of America's largest industrial companies. As an 11-year-old firm, it was one of the youngest ever to be so honored. Read the story of how this

---

[14] Raymond Roel, "Disney's Marketing Touch," *Direct Marketing* (January 1987), 50ff.
[15] Patricia Sellers, "How Busch Wins in a Doggy Market," *Fortune* (June 22, 1987), 99–111.

CONSUMER IN FOCUS

1.2   THE RAG TRADE'S RELUCTANT REVOLUTIONARY: LIZ CLAIBORNE

Her dream was to design clothes for professional women, get her name on the label, and build a small, successful business. Instead Elisabeth Claiborne Ortenberg built an empire.

Claiborne was one of the first designers to steer executive women away from navy-blue-suit-and-bow-tie uniforms. Her comfortable, colorful clothes are fashionable but not faddish, and they fit. Why? Because she designs for the full, sometimes pear-shape bodies that most American women have, not for runway-strutting models. Prices are a bit above moderate, which means $60 blouses, $50 to $100 pants, and $100 to $150 dresses.

Retailers seem to appreciate Liz Claiborne Inc. as much as women shoppers do. For some it is their most profitable account. Besides, they say, Liz Claiborne responds to the consumer better than any other apparel company. It [Liz Claiborne Inc.] offers a constant flow of fresh merchandise — six seasons instead of the traditional four, so that a customer can actually find a summer outfit in July. Ten Liz Claiborne "fashion specialists" spend all their time visiting stores, talking with customers, taking photographs of displays, and giving seminars to salespeople. Most apparel companies track sales by what the retailer buys; Liz Claiborne uses a sophisticated computer system that records what styles, colors, and sizes the consumer buys each week in a cross section of stores.

Expansion has brought mistakes. When it introduced men's clothing (called "Claiborne") in 1985, the company sold pants that were too baggy and poorly fitting; now that division is growing nicely. Claiborne still worries about the children's line, launched in 1983, which brings in only about $15 million in annual sales. The company solved the initial problem: The clothes, scaled-down versions of the women's line, were too sophisticated for youngsters.

Source: Excerpted from Patricia Sellers, "The Rag Trade's Reluctant Revolutionary," *Fortune* (January 5, 1987), 36–37. © 1987 Time, Inc. All rights reserved.

---

company has come to dominate the market for professional women's clothing (*Consumer in Focus 1.2*).

Liz Claiborne, the founder and chief designer, and her staff have an enviable record of new product introduction because of continual touch with the market. *The key is always to find a niche representing unmet consumer desires and to capitalize upon that opportunity aggressively.*

Minit-Lube experienced an 80 percent growth in profits and sales during 1986, with 185 shops and sales of $40 million. President Jeffrey J. O'Neill explains this success by noting that "we want it to be the best eight minutes of the customer's day."[16]

---

[16] "Presto! The Convenience Industry: Making Life a Little Simpler," *Business Week* (April 27, 1987), 92.

Research also can provide the clues for turning a product failure into a success. Toro introduced a lightweight snowthrower, named the Snowpup. It went nowhere on initial introduction, for the reason that it was perceived by many as a "low-power toy."[17] When it later was renamed simply *Toro*, the negative image was reversed and sales were quite adequate.

THE PRICING DECISION   Pricing decisions never have to be left to chance. Skillful research can document consumer price sensitivity. The Disney Channel, for example, found that a lower monthly charge per household increased both its market penetration and retention levels, two of the chronic problems plaguing the other pay-television services.[18]

Also, economists have long hypothesized the existence of a backward-sloping demand curve for certain products. When this is the case, raising the price can *increase* sales. If a brand carries a prestige image, the demand curve often will take this shape. As Chrysler Vice Chairman Bennett Bidwell observed, "Sometimes you have to soar the price to get prestige. A guy driving a $50,000 Mercedes convertible feels it is more desirable than the same car at $40,000."[19]

ADVERTISING AND PROMOTIONAL STRATEGY   In 1981 the Pontiac Division of General Motors decided to concentrate once again on the segment where it historically has done best — the 25 to 44 age group representing 40 percent of the population and 55 percent of the auto-buying power. Image studies showed that the Pontiac was seen as just a traditional American car — very ordinary.[20] A new Pontiac personality was designed into its cars, emphasizing bright colors, stiffer-backed seats, leather-wrapped steering wheels, aluminum wheels, and tighter suspensions.

This revamped image was driven home with the "We build excitement" campaign (Figure 1.3), aired on MTV and such network programs as "Saturday Night Live" and "Late Night with David Letterman." As a result, Pontiac is the only GM division to have increased its market share in this decade.

The "We build excitement" theme was not just the product of fruitful advertising minds. Rather, it reflected the underlying motivations and expected benefits discovered through market research. The results speak for themselves.

SELECTION OF DISTRIBUTION CHANNELS   How and where does the consumer prefer to buy what a company has to offer? This is yet another question that can be readily answered through consumer research, thus minimizing the risk of a faulty distribution decision. It has been discovered, for example, that a large segment of women prefer to buy designer-quality clothing by

---

[17] John Neher, "Toro Cutting a Wide Swath in Outdoor Appliance Marketing," *Advertising Age* (December 4, 1978), 17.
[18] Roel, "Disney's Marketing Touch."
[19] Alex Taylor III, "Detroit vs. New Upscale Imports," *Fortune* (April 27, 1987), 69–78.
[20] "How Pontiac Pulled Away from the Pack," *Business Week* (August 25, 1986), 56–57.

**FIGURE 1.3
"WE BUILD
EXCITEMENT":
MARKETING
RESEARCH
CREATED A NEW
IMAGE FOR
PONTIAC**

*H*ow we pushed
*America's premier road sedan
to the ultimate braking point.* When driving conditions
are less than ideal, Pontiac 6000 STE helps keep you out of a bind with advanced
anti-lock braking. This new system delivers improved braking capability on
almost any surface, wet or dry. Together with superb handling and fuel-injected V6 power,
it gives you a machine with some of the finest performance
credentials going. Or stopping. ▼**PONTIAC 6000
WE BUILD EXCITEMENT**

Source: Courtesy of Pontiac Division; General Motors Corporation.

mail rather than to invest the time in retail-store shopping. As a result, the Spiegel catalogs now are full of such names as Norma Kamali and Ralph Lauren. Spiegel management has discovered through research that there is a market segment who believes that "it's smart to buy from a catalog, but chic to buy from Spiegel."[21] The company has capitalized upon this attitude through both its product offerings and its advertising.

Research has also shown that many consumers scan the shelves in a supermarket instead of using a shopping list. Therefore, consumer research has played a major role in the growing sophistication of retail-store design and display (see Chapter 23).

[21] "Spiegel, Inc. (A) and (B)," in Roger D. Blackwell, W. Wayne Talarzyk, and James F. Engel, *Contemporary Cases in Consumer Behavior*, rev. ed. (Hinsdale, Ill.: Dryden, 1985), 85–94, 191–194.

1.3 WHY PARKER'S GLOBAL MARKETING FOUNDERED

In 1984 the Parker Pen Company was one of the world's best known brands. It sold writing instruments in 154 countries. And it wanted to bring virtually every one of them under the "global-marketing" umbrella: it planned to centralize and standardize everything connected with the selling effort: Packaging, pricing, promotional materials and, especially, advertising.

For the still young and controversial world of global marketing, Parker Pen was to be the grand experience, the classic real-world test. If successful, Parker might serve as a model. And if Parker failed, well, there would be lessons in that as well. Parker Pen's global-marketing attempt did fail, and fast. Parker Pen is now a private company based in England.

The very idea of selling pens the same way everywhere didn't sit well with many Parker subsidiaries and distributors. Pens were indeed the same, as Parker's marketing people incessantly pointed out, but markets were different. France and Italy fancied expensive fountain pens; Scandinavia was a ballpoint market. In some markets, Parker could assume an above-the-fray stance; in others it had to get in the trenches and compete on price.

Nevertheless the word came down, printed and distributed worldwide: "Advertising for Parker pens [no matter model] will be based on a *common* worldwide advertising theme; 'Make your mark with a Parker,' has been adopted." The London-created "Make your mark" campaign finally broke in October, 1984. Except for language, it was essentially the same everywhere: Long copy, horizontal layout, illustrations in precisely the same place, the Parker logo at the bottom and the "Make your mark with a Parker" tag line or local equivalent in the lower right corner.

Observers noted that it was "lowest-common-denominator-advertising that tried to say something to everybody, and it didn't say anything to anybody." They came up with ideas "that sounded good around the table but had nothing to do with the real world." "Wrong thinking led to flawed strategy, and the flawed strategy was rejected by the Parker culture."

Source: Joseph M. Winski and Laurel Wentz, "Parker Pen: What Went Wrong? Why Company Global Marketing Plan Foundered," *Advertising Age* (June 2, 1986), 1+.

INTERNATIONAL MARKETING   Overseas markets always have a special attraction, because the opportunities seem limitless. The easiest strategy is to engage in **global marketing,** where essentially the same strategy is used in all cultural contexts.[22] Certainly this approach, if it works, greatly simplifies the whole process and brings about economies of scale.

The Parker Pen Company found to its dismay, as have others, that it

---

[22] Theodore Levitt, "The Globalization of Markets," *Harvard Business Review* (May–June 1976), 106–118.

can be dangerous to ignore cultural differences. As the case history in *Consumer in Focus 1.3* reveals, cross-cultural consumer research accompanied by substantial marketing adaptation can be a necessity.

A far wiser strategy in nearly all cases is to engage in **contextualized marketing,** a strategy designed to take into account cultural differences in consumer motivation and behavior by adapting marketing efforts, where necessary, so that they are perceived as being culturally relevant.[23]

Recent research has made clear that desired product attributes vary from one Asian country to the next, thereby reflecting significant cultural differences.[24] Based on his research in China, Wang has shown that cultural variations are least when products have high technological content (computers and household appliances are examples). Therefore, it would be appropriate for producers of such items to engage in a high degree of marketing standardization worldwide. Quite the opposite is the case, however, with food and clothing, which usually reflect cultural values.[25]

It was mistakenly thought for a period that European Common Market (EEC) countries would represent a fertile field for uniform global marketing. Only 17 percent of companies competing in the EEC tailored their ads in 1973, but that figure leaped to 50 percent 10 years later and no doubt is even higher today.[26] Even Coca Cola, with a seemingly universal appeal, has introduced 21 versions worldwide of its TV spot featuring children singing the praises of Coke.[27]

It is not unusual to face major problems in what appear to be straightforward and simple translations. An English slogan reading, "It takes a tough man to make a tender chicken" came across in Spanish as, "It takes a sexually excited man to make a tender chicken."[28] Much more is said about these problems in Chapter 24.

THE RETAILER

It is tempting to focus only on the research requirements of marketing strategy at the manufacturing level. Yet, retailers have significant marketing problems of their own. What product mix should be handled? What image should be projected? What happens to sales when prices are raised? Is point-of-sale

---

[23] James F. Engel, "Toward the Contextualization of Consumer Behavior," in Chin Tong Tan and Jagdish N. Sheth, eds., *Historical Perspectives in Consumer Research: National and International Perspectives* (Singapore: National University of Singapore, 1985), 1–4.

[24] See Wang Zhengyuan, "Toward Some Standardized Cross-Cultural Consumption Values: An Empirical Investigation" (unpublished MBA thesis, University of International Business & Economics, Beijing, People's Republic of China); and David K. Tse, John K. Wang, and Chin Tong Tan, "Toward Some Standardized Cross-Cultural Consumption Values," *Advances in Consumer Research* 15 (Provo, Utah: Association for Consumer Research, 1987), 387–395. Both of these sources refer to a common series of studies; hence the nearly identical titles.

[25] Wang Zhengyuan, "Toward Some Standardized Cross-Cultural Consumption Values."

[26] Julie Skur Hill and Joseph M. Winski, "Goodbye Global Ads," *Advertising Age* (November 16, 1987), 16ff.

[27] Hill and Winski, "Goodbye Global Ads."

[28] "Snafus Persist in Marketing to Hispanics," *Marketing News* (June 24, 1983), 3.

display sufficient, or is personal selling needed? It is not unusual to find continuing use of taste tests, surveys of store awareness and image, satisfaction evaluation, and panels of shoppers who evaluate potential new items.

We discussed in *Consumer in Focus 1.1* the problem of slumping sales in the Cadillac Division of General Motors. Obviously, many Cadillac dealers also suffered a sales decline. This was not the case at Sewell Village Cadillac in Dallas, however. Among other things, the owners discovered that postsale service is the dominant consideration in owner loyalty. As a result, each customer is assigned a personal service adviser whose sole job is to relate to the buyer over the life of the car and assure that all service is undertaken quickly and properly.[29] Customer loyalty (and profit) remains high because management has kept its thumb on the consumer pulse.

THE NOT-FOR-PROFIT MARKETER

Marketing concepts have quickly been adopted by not-for-profit organizations established to provide public service in such forms as changed ideas (religion, health, social practices, etc.) and direct help (famine relief, housing assistance, etc.). In many respects the challenges faced are even greater than those of the business firm, because it is necessary to contend with two markets: (1) the market for services and (2) the donor market.

For example, the Coalition for Literacy (Figure 1.4) must find ways to motivate and help the 27 million Americans who are functionally illiterate to do something about this handicap. As if that is not a sufficiently great challenge, funds must be raised to raise public awareness that this problem exists. The potential donor market must be segmented to find those who have the greatest interest in this appeal. Donor research now is finding widespread use.[30]

CAPITALIZING ON CONSUMER RESEARCH: SOME ORGANIZATIONAL NECESSITIES

If marketing opportunities are to be capitalized upon fully, there are two organizational imperatives: (1) commitment to ongoing innovation; and (2) a balanced view of research in decision making.

COMMITMENT TO ONGOING INNOVATION   Recently one of us consulted with two different organizations in the same industry. Each had a nearly identical product idea. Company A invested over $50,000 in research to see if the market would accept the product and still has not built a prototype in spite of a green light from the research. Company B made five prototypes

---

[29] Joseph P. Kahn, "Caddy Shack," *Inc* (May 1987), 80–87.
[30] For a review of donor-related research done in one field of not-for-profit marketing, see James F. Engel, *Averting the Financial Crisis in Christian Organizations: Insights from a Decade of Donor Research* (Wheaton, Ill.: Management Development Associates, 1983).

FIGURE 1.4
MARKETING IS
SIGNIFICANT IN THE
NOT-FOR-PROFIT
ORGANIZATION

and then tested them in homes to gauge potential acceptance. As a result, they will be the first on the market.

Company B has recognized that survival demands market sensitivity and quick response, the keys to innovation. Tom Peters puts it this way:

> *No company's edge is commanding anymore. No transformation, no matter how dramatic, provides each five years' safety against the wildly gyrating forces at work. In today's fast-changing world, where we don't even know the names of next month's competitors, let alone their cost structure, no one has a safe lead. For the forseeable future, organizations must learn to cherish change and to take advantage of constant tumult as much as they have resisted change in the past.*[31]

---

[31] Tom Peters, "There Are No Excellent Companies," *Fortune* (April 27, 1987), 382.

American and European businesses seem to have become blinded by the quickness with which Japanese competitors have outdistanced them repeatedly. Why has this happened? In comparison with their British counterparts, Japanese firms gain advantage in these ways:[32]

1. Their focus is on changing markets and the opportunities presented rather than on production or finance.

2. Market changes are constantly monitored to detect emerging segments and opportunities.

3. Once these opportunities are in view, new models are brought onto the market almost instantly.

4. Decision making is decentralized so that rapid response is possible without endless management review.

The key lies in managerial commitment to adapt quickly to a rapidly changing environment.

A BALANCED VIEW OF RESEARCH IN DECISION MAKING   The Chevrolet Division of General Motors seems to be recouping some of its lost market momentum through the success of its "Heartbeat of America" advertising theme. This theme was the creation of Sean K. Fitzpatrick, an executive vice president at Campbell-Ewald Company, the Chevrolet agency.[33]

As he reviewed marketing research, it was obvious to Fitzpatrick that Chevrolet advertising was no longer of much relevance. His eye was caught by brochure copy that referred to the Chevy small-block V8 engine as the "Heartbeat of America." He mulled over this theme in his mind in the coming months and eventually chose it for the 1986–1987 campaign and had it set to music with an original score. Once it was aired, consumers rated the Chevy ads in the top 12 among all commercials, only the second time since 1978 that an American automaker made that list.

Fitzpatrick and his colleagues used three bases to arrive at this decision, all of which are necessary in strategic planning: (1) intuition (creative insight); (2) experience; and (3) research. There are times, especially in a rapidly changing environment, when intuition and experience fall short. This is when research assumes special importance by shedding needed factual light on potential market response.

Some of the best research comes when executives engage in MBWA (Managing by Wandering Around).[34] Eastman Kodak executive Raymond H. De-

---

[32] Peter Doyle, John Saunders, and Veronica Wong, "A Comparative Investigation of Japanese Marketing Strategies and the British Market," in Robert F. Lusch et al., eds., *1985 AMA Educators' Proceedings* (Chicago: American Marketing Association, 1985), 256–262.

[33] "Those Heartbeat Ads Are a Hit in the Heartland," *Business Week* (February 23, 1987), 107.

[34] Peters and Austin, *A Passion for Excellence*, Chapter 2.

Moulin was in a Tokyo fish market in early morning when he observed a photographer trying to pry open a film container with his teeth while holding his camera. This observation quickly gave rise to a product change so that it now is possible to open containers of Kodak film with one hand.[35]

The intent of MBWA is to remove executives from their desks and keep them in touch with both customers and workers. When this is done sensitively and perceptively, *research becomes an attitude,* and the benefits are real.

MBWA is a major part of the remarkable success of Japanese companies in penetrating the U.S. market. For example, the Kao Corporation dominates the detergent and soap market in Japan by constantly monitoring the consumer environment and providing quick marketing responses when needed.[36] It is not unusual to find top-level management observing and talking with consumers at point of sale to find ways to serve them better. In this way Kao and other manufacturers countered Procter & Gamble, which introduced disposable diapers to Japan, and reduced P&G's market share from 90 percent in the mid-1970s to 8 percent by 1984.

CONSUMER BEHAVIOR AS A FIELD OF ACADEMIC STUDY

Our thrust so far has been on the uses and applications of consumer research, but it is also worth evaluating why it has become a significant academic discipline in its own right. The taproot of the field lies in economics. A more extensive historical review is given in Chapter 2, but it is worth emphasizing here that various theories about the consumer generally were not tested empirically until the middle twentieth century. This distinctly practical emphasis awaited development of the field of marketing in the business curriculum and consumer studies in home economics.

Marketers, of course, always have acknowledged the significance of consumer sovereignty, but consumer research really came into its own after World War II. A natural development at this time was a turning to behavioral sciences in the hopes of finding new insights into consumer behavior.

In the 1950s trained psychologists, often with a Freudian psychoanalytic perspective, found their way into the applied world and launched an era of inquiry known as **motivation research.** Although the outcome of this invasion (discussed in more detail in Chapter 2) was not especially notable, it did serve to stimulate awareness that behavioral sciences have something to contribute.

Consumer behavior emerged as a distinct field of study during the 1960s

---

[35] "Why Kodak Is Starting to Click Again," *Business Week* (February 23, 1987), 134.
[36] Johnny Johansson and Ikujiro Nonaka, "Market Research the Japanese Way," *Harvard Business Review* (May–June 1987), 16–23.

through the influence of such writers as Katona,[37] Ferber,[38] and Howard.[39] Suddenly, the behavioral sciences became the "in thing" in the schools of business. Marketers, in particular, borrowed rather indiscriminately from social psychology, sociology, anthropology, or any other field that might relate to consumer behavior in some way, no matter how remotely.

Although this borrowing process was counterproductive at times, it also was necessary in a field of study in its infancy. Soon this unfocused inquiry gave way to something far different, however, with publication of what Holbrook has referred to as the "landmark syntheses."[40] Serious attempts were made by Nicosia,[41] Howard and Sheth,[42] Engel, Kollat, and Blackwell[43] and others to integrate what was known about consumer motivation and behavior in the form of systematic diagrammatic models.

Courses in consumer behavior quickly burgeoned throughout the Western world. The numbers of active researchers increased geometrically from the initial handful. A major catalytic influence was formation of the Association for Consumer Research in 1969. Membership now exceeds 1,000, and the growing maturity of the field is reflected in its annual conference proceedings, entitled *Advances in Consumer Research*. You will sense the importance of these volumes by the frequency of citation in our footnotes.

The outcome is that consumer research is now an important field of study in its own right. The literature has grown sharply,[44] with the *Journal of Consumer Research* (first published in 1974) standing as a premier source. The field has grown from infancy to a healthy state of maturity in its 30-year life. With the onset of the wholistic perspective discussed earlier, it is safe to say that its impact will widen even further in the coming years.

---

[37] George Katona, *The Powerful Consumer* (New York: McGraw-Hill, 1960).

[38] Robert Ferber's writings ranged from advanced statistical techniques to applications of principles of psychology and economics to various phases of consumer behavior. He was coeditor with Hugh G. Wales of an important early book, *Motivation and Market Behavior* (Homewood, Ill.: Richard D. Irwin, 1958).

[39] John A. Howard, *Marketing Management Analysis and Planning,* rev. ed. (Homewood, Ill.: Richard D. Irwin, 1963).

[40] Holbrook, "What Is Consumer Research?" 130.

[41] Francesco M. Nicosia, *Consumer Decision Processes* (Englewood Cliffs, N.J.: Prentice-Hall, 1966).

[42] John A. Howard and Jagdish N. Sheth, *The Theory of Buyer Behavior* (New York: John Wiley & Sons, 1969).

[43] James F. Engel, David T. Kollat, and Roger D. Blackwell, *Consumer Behavior,* 1st ed. (New York: Holt, Rinehart and Winston, 1968).

[44] See especially Henry Assael, *Consumer Behavior and Marketing Action,* 3d ed. (Boston: Kent Publishing Co., 1987); Gilbert Harrel, *Consumer Behavior* (New York: Harcourt Brace Jovanovich, 1987); John C. Mowen, *Consumer Behavior* (New York: Macmillan, 1987); J. Paul Peter and Jerry C. Olson, *Consumer Behavior — Marketing Strategy Perspectives* (Homewood, Ill.: Richard D. Irwin, 1987); Thomas S. Robertson, Joan Zielinski, and Scott Ward, *Consumer Behavior* (Glenview, Ill.: Scott Foresman, 1984); William L. Wilkie, *Consumer Behavior* (New York: John Wiley & Sons, 1986); and Gerald Zaltman and Melanie Wallendorf, *Consumer Behavior: Basic Findings and Management Implications* (New York: John Wiley & Sons, 1979). An especially noteworthy theoretical contribution is James R. Bettman, *An Information Processing Theory of Consumer Choice* (Reading, Mass.: Addison-Wesley, 1979).

Summary

Research into consumer motivation and behavior has assumed significance in contemporary societies worldwide. In the past 30 years a large and growing multidisciplinary field of study has emerged. The central concern of businesses, consumer economists, and others is to find more effective strategies to influence and shape that behavior. As a result, consumer research is of premier importance in this applied world.

Others have a more wholistic perspective and are focusing efforts on studies of consumption in order to understand how humans think and behave in this important life activity. When we factor in the more recent expansion of inquiry across cultural borders, the result is a rich and growing field of research and inquiry.

The perspective of this book is primarily, though not exclusively, that of the field of marketing. As a result, our central concern is the practical relevance of principles and findings to business strategies. Everything done by marketers and others attempting to influence consumer behavior rests on four essential premises:

1. *The consumer is sovereign.* He or she has full capability to screen out all attempts at influence, with the outcome that everything done by the business firm must be *adapted* to consumer motivation and behavior.

2. *Consumer motivation and behavior can be understood through research.* Perfect prediction is not possible, but strategic outcomes are notably improved through properly undertaken and utilized research.

3. *Consumer behavior can be influenced through persuasive activity that takes the consumer seriously as being sovereign and purposeful.*

4. *Consumer persuasion and influence has socially beneficial outcomes as long as legal, ethical, and moral safeguards are in place to curb attempts at manipulation.*

When these premises are disregarded, the consequences almost always are negative. We gave examples of the outcomes of both right and wrong thinking about the consumer. We further demonstrated that consumer research, properly conceived and interpreted, provides essential input for marketing strategies in both the for-profit and not-for-profit organization. Finally, research also serves as the basis for consumer education and protection, and furnishes important information for public policy decisions.

REVIEW AND DISCUSSION QUESTIONS

1. Contrast the consumer influence and wholistic perspectives in consumer research. How would the agendas of researchers from these two perspectives differ in an analysis of the decision processes and consumption behavior undertaken by new home purchasers?

2. Now, assume that new home buyers are studied in Chicago; New Orleans; Nairobi, Kenya; and São Paulo, Brazil. In each case, the target market segment is the upper middle class. What differences would you anticipate from one culture to the next?

3. Which of the following decisions should be considered legitimate topics of concern in the study of consumer behavior? (a) selecting a college, (b) purchasing a life insurance policy, (c) smoking a cigarette, (d) selecting a church to join, (e) selecting a dentist, (f) visiting an auto showroom to see new models, or (g) purchasing a college textbook.

4. Examine current advertisements for consumer products and select one for a new product. Will this product succeed in the long run in the consumer marketplace? What factors determine success?

5. A family has just come into the local office of a lending agency, asking for a bill consolidation loan. Payments for a new car, television, stereo, bedroom set, and central air conditioning have become excessive. The head of the family does not have a steady source of income, and real help is now needed. Is this an example of purposeful consumer behavior, or has this family been manipulated into making unwise purchases?

6. If it is true that motivations and behavior can be understood through research, is it also true that the marketer now has greater ability to influence the consumer adversely than would have been true in an earlier era?

7. What contributions does the analysis of consumer behavior make to the field of finance? of production? of real estate? of insurance? of top management administration?

8. Would it be equally necessary to understand consumer behavior if the economic system were not one of free enterprise? In other words, is the subject matter of this book only of interest to those in capitalistic systems, or does it also have relevance for socialism and communism?

9. Consumer protection is an important issue. What areas of consumer behavior appear to be most in need of increased regulation and/or consumer education?

UNDERSTANDING THE CONSUMER

THE WATKINS: REAL-LIFE CONSUMER DECISIONS

Philip and Carolyn Watkins live in Manley, Australia, a short commute by water from Sydney. Philip is a computer information specialist with a leading bank, and Carolyn is a registered nurse. They are the same age (35) and have been married for 8 years. While they do not yet have any children, they are considering adopting. When asked to state their major shared goals in life, both responded quickly. They agreed that the priority is to find a workable balance between commitment to one another and to professional success. Both enjoy the "good life" Sydney offers and love to spend weekends sailing. Also, they are connoisseurs of fine wines and European cuisine, especially French.

During the past few weeks, the Watkins have made a number of buying and consumption decisions, both individually and as a couple. Here are some examples:

1. Philip and Carolyn have never owned their own sailing yacht. After several months of deliberation, they purchased a new fiberglass yacht from a Manley distributor for $18,500 (Australian dollars).

2. They attended a movie in downtown Sydney the previous Friday night. After identifying two interesting comedies from the newspaper movie ads, they chose the film they would see; a friend's earlier recommendation was the deciding factor.

3. On his way home Philip picked up a bottle of petit sirah red table wine. The brand he chose was inexpensive and unknown to him, but he wanted to try something different for a change.

4. While he was in the wine shop, Philip also noticed a display featuring a new type of cocktail peanuts. Because the can cost only a few dollars, he thought, "Why not try it?" and added one to his purchases.

5. Their Saab 9000 Turbo was serviced and tuned up at a garage located at the far end of Sydney specializing in imported cars. Philip indicated how much he has trusted their workmanship.

6. While shopping in the grocery, Carolyn turned to the cereal shelves because she noted on her shopping list that they were out of muesli (a high-fiber cereal). Because she thinks all brands are pretty much the same, she stayed with the brand they have been using, despite some heavy advertising by competitors.

———

Philip and Carolyn Watkins made six purchase decisions, each of which revealed major differences in decision-making processes and the psychological and social influences that shape behavior. These processes and influences can range from simple to complex.

This chapter has two purposes: (1) to help you understand the variables and processes at work in consumer decision making and (2) to provide an overview of the remaining chapters. We demonstrate, first of all, that many consumer actions reflect different stages on a decision-making continuum ranging from **extended problem solving** (EPS) at one end to **limited problem solving** (LPS) at the other. These are in contrast to repeat-purchase decisions, which reflect different dynamics.

Then we illustrate the important ways in which *environmental influences*, *individual differences*, and *psychological processes* shape and influence decisions. A diagrammatic model is utilized to show how this complex set of variables fits together.

CONSUMER DECISION PROCESSES

Many attempts have been made to explain human choice behavior. John Dewey's conceptualizations of decision-process behavior as problem solving have been especially influential.[1] By **problem solving** we refer to thoughtful, reasoned action undertaken to bring about need satisfaction. Many factors can shape the final outcome, including internal motivations and such external

---

[1] John Dewey, *How We Think* (New York: Heath, 1910).

influences as social pressures and marketing activities. Consider these words by Ajzen and Fishbein:

> *Generally speaking . . . human beings are usually quite rational and make systematic use of the information available to them . . . people consider the implications of their actions before they decide to engage or not engage in a given behavior.*[2]

At times, problem solving in a consumer behavior context involves careful weighing and evaluation of *utilitarian* (or functional) product attributes. Often the term **rational decision making** is used when this is the case.[3] At other times, concern for so-called **hedonic benefits** will dominate, and the consumption object is viewed *symbolically,* in terms of emotional responses, sensory pleasures, daydreams, or aesthetic considerations.[4] It is to be expected that most buying and consuming actions reflect a mixture of both the utilitarian and the hedonic.

The problem-solving perspective, then, encompasses all types of need-satisfying behavior and a wide range of motivating and influencing factors. Broadly speaking, consumer decision making takes the form shown in Figure 2.1 and has the following steps:

1. Need recognition — the consumer perceives a difference between the desired state of affairs and the actual situation sufficient to arouse and activate the decision process.

2. Search for information — the consumer searches for information stored in memory (internal search) or acquires decision-relevant information from the environment (external search).

3. Alternative evaluation — the consumer evaluates options in terms of expected benefits and narrows the choice to the preferred alternative.

4. Purchase — the consumer acquires the preferred alternative or an acceptable substitute if necessary.

5. Outcomes — the consumer evaluates whether or not the chosen alternative meets needs and expectations once it is used.

The extent to which each of these steps is followed rigorously can vary, however, from one decision situation to the next. In this section we show that problem-solving behavior represents a continuum ranging from extended problem solving at one end to limited problem solving at the other. We also take account of the fact that the majority of consumer purchases are made on a repeated basis. When this is the case, buying routines are established to simplify and reduce the complexity of the problem-solving process.

---

[2] Icek Ajzen and Martin Fishbein, *Understanding Attitudes and Predicting Social Behavior* (Englewood Cliffs, N.J.: Prentice-Hall, 1980).

[3] John C. Mowen, *Consumer Behavior* (New York: Macmillan, 1987), 19.

[4] Elizabeth C. Hirschman and Morris B. Holbrook, "Hedonic Consumption: Emerging Concepts, Methods, and Propositions," *Journal of Marketing* 46 (Summer 1982), 92–101.

FIGURE 2.1
A PROBLEM-
SOLVING
PERSPECTIVE ON
THE FIVE STEPS IN
CONSUMER
DECISION MAKING

Need Recognition
▼
Search for Information
▼
Alternative Evaluation
▼
Purchase
▼
Outcomes

THE PROBLEM-SOLVING CONTINUUM

It is helpful to visualize a continuum anchored on the one end by *extended problem solving* and on the other by *limited problem solving*. Buying decisions can range anywhere between these extremes; for convenience we refer to situations falling toward the center as *mid-range problem solving*.

EXTENDED PROBLEM SOLVING (EPS)   When the decision process is especially detailed and rigorous, as it was when Philip and Carolyn purchased the yacht, it is referred to as **extended problem solving.** EPS also is commonly seen in purchases of automobiles, expensive clothing, stereo equipment, and other instances where it is perceived as essential to make the "right choice."

When this is the case, all of the steps in Figure 2.1 are followed, although not necessarily in any precise order. It is likely that many alternatives will be evaluated and a wide variety of information sources consulted. Furthermore, the decision on how and where to make the purchase also may require additional search and evaluation.

The process does not cease following purchase, because expectations often are clear and rigorous. If the item purchased is perceived as falling short, the outcome can be substantial and often vocal dissatisfaction. The desired outcome, of course, is satisfaction expressed in the form of positive recommendations to others and intention to repurchase should the occasion arise.

LIMITED PROBLEM SOLVING (LPS)   We now approach the other extreme of the decision-making continuum (LPS) and arrive at what Kassarjian has humorously depicted as the "muddling through consumer."[5] Few consumers

---

[5] Harold E. Kassarjian, "Consumer Research: Some Recollections and a Commentary," in Richard J. Lutz, *Advances in Consumer Research* 13 (Provo, Utah: Association for Consumer Research, 1986), 6–8.

have the resources or motivation to engage in EPS very frequently. It is far more common to simplify the process and reduce the number and variety of information sources, alternatives, and criteria used for evaluation. All of the stages in Figure 2.1 still may be followed, but there is a major difference in both extent and rigor.

Consumers recognize, for example, that most brands of gasoline, detergent, and toilet tissue are largely similar in their characteristics. Therefore, choice can be made following such a simple rule as "buy the cheapest brand."[6]

The so-called **impulse purchase** (a spur-of-the-moment action triggered by product display or point-of-sale promotion) is the least complex form of LPS and represents the extreme on the continuum. When Philip saw the peanut display, for example, he bought a package with little or no deliberation. His only thought was "Why not try it?" and hence the purchase was made. There was no information search, and the only real alternative evaluation took place *after purchase,* when the peanuts were consumed, and not before.

It is commonly accepted that a majority of supermarket purchases are made in this way, especially if prior exposure to advertising has built some brand recognition. Point-of-sale display now plays a major role, as exposure to the product itself or promotional materials triggers recall, builds interest, and stimulates buying action.

MID-RANGE PROBLEM SOLVING   As we have noted, EPS and LPS are extremes on a decision-process continuum, but many decisions range somewhere in between. The category of mid-range problem solving is used here in recognition that most buying decisions cannot be neatly pigeonholed.

An example is Philip and Carolyn's choice of the movie. A certain minimum amount of information was required to know what was playing, and this was easily found in the daily paper. Because there were several promising options, there was a need to evaluate which comedy to choose. They were helped, of course, by the friend's recommendation. All of this was accomplished quickly and was far different from the deliberations required to purchase the yacht or the spur-of-the-moment decision to buy the peanuts.

FACTORS INFLUENCING THE EXTENT OF PROBLEM SOLVING

Extended problem solving is most likely when three major conditions are met: (1) the alternatives are differentiated in relevant ways; (2) there is sufficient time available for deliberation; and (3) there is a high degree of *involvement* (personal relevance) accompanying the purchase. When involvement is high, the product is seen as being important in the context of basic motivations and felt needs.[7]

---

[6] Wayne D. Hoyer, "Variations and Choice Strategies Across Decision Contexts: An Examination of Continent Factors," in Lutz, *Advances,* 23–26.

[7] James R. Bettman, "A Functional Analysis of the Role of Overall Evaluation of Alternatives and Choice Processes," in Andrew Mitchell, ed., *Advances in Consumer Research* 8 (Ann Arbor, Mich.: Association for Consumer Research, 1982), 87–93.

DIFFERENTIATED ALTERNATIVES   Philip and Carolyn engaged in EPS in their purchase of the yacht because alternatives differed in such important respects as size, maneuverability, durability in open seas, price, and so on. Also, many information sources were available to them, including published ratings, ads, point-of-sale information, and recommendations from friends. The more similar the alternatives are perceived to be, on the other hand, the greater the likelihood of LPS or some form of mid-range problem solving.

It is important, however, to stress once again that alternative evaluation encompasses more than objective or utilitarian considerations. There can be a wide range of subjective factors that, while more intangible, can be of equal or greater importance in the decision. Examples are such hedonic benefits as happiness and self-expression. Therefore, product and brand symbolism can outweigh the more easily measurable objective considerations.[8]

TIME AVAILABILITY   Extended problem solving is inhibited by time pressures. Philip and Carolyn might have acted differently in their yacht purchase if they had been forced by circumstances to make a quick decision. Certainly they would not have engaged in much search and alternative evaluation. Perhaps they would have shifted to an LPS strategy such as "choose one that's recommended by our champion racer friend."

INVOLVEMENT   It is apparent that EPS is not always followed, even when alternatives are differentiated and there is no time pressure. Philip and Carolyn did not engage in EPS when they chose the movie they were to see or when Philip tried the unknown brand of red wine. There is little incentive to engage in this decision-making effort unless there is a high degree of **involvement** — the degree of perceived relevance and personal importance accompanying the product and brand choice within a specific situation.[9] When involvement is high, it is important to make the "right choice."

Involvement and perceived relevance are highly personalized matters. The choice of color becomes a central issue for an artist, whereas it is of less significance to others. Therefore, involvement can have complex and diverse underlying roots, which are discussed in more detail in Chapter 9.

---

[8] Morris B. Holbrook and Elizabeth C. Hirschman, "The Experiential Aspects of Consumption: Consumer Fantasies, Feelings, and Fun," *Journal of Consumer Research* 9 (September 1982), 132–140.

[9] John Antil, "Conceptualization and Operationalization of Involvement," in Thomas Kinnear, ed., *Advances in Consumer Research 11* (Provo, Utah: Association for Consumer Research, 1984), 204; Herbert Krugman, "The Impact of Television Advertising: Learning Without Involvement," *Public Opinion Quarterly* 29 (Fall 1965), 349–356; John R. Rossiter and Larry Percy, "Advertising Communication Models," in Elizabeth C. Hirschman and Morris B. Holbrook, eds., *Advances in Consumer Research* 12 (Provo, Utah: Association for Consumer Research, 1985), 510–524; Joel B. Cohen, "Involvement and You: One Thousand Great Ideas," in Richard Bagozzi and Alice Tybout, eds., *Advances in Consumer Research* 9 (Ann Arbor, Mich.: Association for Consumer Research, 1983), 325–328; and David W. Finn, "Low Involvement Isn't Low Involvement," in Bagozzi and Tybout, *Advances,* 419–424.

Research has shown the following factors to be major determinants of high involvement and subsequent EPS:[10]

1. Ego relationship — This occurs when the choice is perceived to reflect one's self-image. Common examples are clothing or jewelry items and, of course, such big-ticket items as expensive yachts. The brand of muesli, however, is much less likely to have this degree of significance for most people.

2. Perceived risk of negative consequences — Everyone at times fears that the outcomes of a purchase will not live up to expectations. Much greater care will be devoted to the decision, for example, when the purchase requires substantial financial outlay or there may be some danger in use. Because of the risks of danger, it is likely that the Watkins placed importance on trial of yachts in open water under varying climatic conditions. Moving to the opposite extreme, it is hard to imagine Philip or anyone else subjecting peanuts to exacting trial.

3. Social sanctions — There are times when social acceptance is affected by choice of products or services, thus underscoring the need to make the right choice. It is possible that this would be a major factor to Philip and Carolyn if they belonged to an exclusive yacht club, whereas social acceptance is not usually a determinant of one's choice of ordinary table wine.

4. Hedonic significance — Here the item or service purchased assumes importance by offering significant ability to provide pleasure. This could have been of considerable importance to Philip and Carolyn, given their love of yachting. Also, although this was not the case with the Watkins, such factors as taste also could elevate such items as cereal or wine into a higher involvement category.

Involvement is a highly personalized consideration and varies from one person to the next. Furthermore, it varies in extent of transiency or permanence. In some cases it is stable over time, but it also can be situation-specific and less enduring.

REPEAT PURCHASES

Thus far, we have not addressed the issue of what happens when the buying process is repeated over time. There are two decision-making possibilities: (1) **repeated problem solving** (EPS or LPS) and (2) **habitual decision making.**

REPEATED PROBLEM SOLVING   Repeat purchases often require continued problem solving. Several factors can lead to this outcome. One of the most important is dissatisfaction with the previously bought alternative. A brand

---

[10] Gilles Laurent and Jean-Noel Kapferer, "Measuring Consumer Involvement Profiles," *Journal of Marketing Research* 12 (February 1985), 41–53.

switch is likely. But this also happens when retail stock has been depleted. Now the buyer must weigh the consequences of investing time and energy in shopping elsewhere.

It also is not unusual to switch brands simply because of **variety seeking.**[11] This is another "Why not try it?" response and is most often seen when there are many similar alternatives.[12] Philip probably tried the unfamiliar brand of red wine just to experience a change, a commonly expressed buying motivation. If it proves to be satisfactory, he might buy it again when the occasion arises.

Finally, in many consumer product categories, a large share of repeat-purchase decision making is based on the LPS decision rule of "buy the cheapest." Hence, there is a high degree of market share volatility as consumers make use of price-off coupons and are constantly on the outlook for the best "deal." This requires constant search activity in the form of price monitoring.

HABITUAL DECISION MAKING   Repeat purchases also can be based on habits that are formed to simplify decision-process activity and enable the consumer to cope more effectively with the pressures of life. EPS, in particular, requires allocation of scarce time and energy and hence is usually avoided as much as possible. Now the decision-process behavior will take the form of the diagram in Figure 2.2.

Purchasing habits differ sharply, however, depending upon the degree of product involvement. Therefore it is necessary to contrast buying habits based on **brand loyalty** and those based on **inertia.**

Brand Loyalty.   Philip consistently uses the same mechanic for his expensive imported car. Hence it would not be surprising to discover that he has had some bad experiences with mechanics in the past. Now that he has a $45,000 (Australian dollars) car, he is unwilling to face the risk that the job will not be done right. Replacement of an improperly serviced turbo mechanism can be costly indeed. Also, it is a matter of high involvement to Philip to have a well serviced, properly performing car.

Given these circumstances, Philip made his initial choice of a mechanic by following EPS. Once he discovered that these people could be trusted, this became important information to him. So he has no incentive whatsoever to switch. He returns each time the need arises and is loyal to this dealer, even though this requires more time and expense because of inconvenience of location.

---

[11] For a review of the literature, see Leigh McAlister and Edgar Pessemier, "Variety Seeking Behavior: An Interdisciplinary Review," *Journal of Consumer Research* 9 (December 1982), 311–322.

[12] Wayne D. Hoyer and Nancy M. Ridgway, "Variety Seeking as an Explanation for Exploratory Purchase Behavior: A Theoretical Model," in Kinnear, *Advances*, 114–119.

**FIGURE 2.2
REPEAT
PURCHASES CAN
SIMPLIFY DECISION
MAKING: THE
STAGES IN A
HABITUAL DECISION
PROCESS**

Brand loyalty, then, can reflect a motivated and difficult-to-change habit because it is rooted in high involvement. One of the most helpful research indicators is to ask, "Which other brands (or options) would you consider if your favorite were not available?" Entrenched loyalty is revealed when the answer is "None — I'll shop further."

Inertia.   Carolyn's cereal purchase reflected a purchasing habit of quite a different nature. She, along with most others, has little or no involvement in this product category. Even though she feels that all brands are pretty much the same, she does not switch very often unless there are price specials.

Her buying habit reflects little more than inertia. She has no particular incentive to switch but might do so if prices are lowered or she sees something bannered as being "new." Hence, this habit is nonstable, reflecting little or no brand loyalty. Even though there is repeat purchase of the same brand, this reflects indifference more than anything else. Given a reason, she will switch again.

CAPITALIZING ON CONSUMER DECISION-PROCESS RESEARCH

Faulty assumptions about the nature of consumer decision processes in target markets can have some unfortunate consequences. For a relevant and timely example, read the story of the Kodak Disk Camera in *Consumer in Focus 2.1*.

Kodak marketing strategy was based on the mistaken presupposition that most customers would follow a particular decision process in their camera purchase: Buy an inexpensive camera that is 'goof proof' and gives OK pictures." Unfortunately for Kodak, it appears that too few prospects proceeded in this way. The result was failure to capitalize on the growing mass market for a more sophisticated camera that, while being somewhat more expensive,

2.1 DOUBTS ABOUT THE DISK: EASTMAN KODAK

Eastman Kodak has suspended production of its compact disk camera, hailed when introduced in 1982 as the "new engine that will drive amateur photography." Camera industry specialists had anticipated the Kodak action, citing problems with picture quality from the disks as well as the increasing popularity of easy-to-use 35mm cameras.

Kodak estimates that it has sold 30 million disk cameras since 1982, when it launched the camera with the largest advertising campaign in its history. The small cameras fit in the palm of a person's hand. Film for the camera is mounted in 15 frames on a disk that clicks automatically to the next frame each time an exposure is made.

Alta Cools, publisher of an industry newsletter, said that although millions of disk cameras were sold, the camera didn't do as well as planned. The main flaw with it was the size of the negatives. She said: "The negatives were too small to give a good quality picture." "Now you can buy a 35mm camera almost as cheaply as a disk and with better results," said Ms. Cools.

Former Kodak Chairman Walter A. Fallon believed that the disk would be the camera of the 1980s. But while the company concentrated on the easy-to-use inexpensive, but lower quality disks, other camera makers were simplifying the high quality 35mm camera.

"I think Kodak misread the market when they introduced the disk," said Eugene Glazer, an analyst with Dean Witter Reynolds Inc. "Kodak always viewed cameras as a mass market product, which by nature means very low prices. They failed to see customers are willing to pay significantly higher prices to get higher quality."

Source: Clare Ansberry, "Kodak Suspends Its Production of Disk Camera," *The Wall Street Journal* (February 2, 1988), 4.

offers greater versatility and picture quality. Other manufacturers such as Olympus have caught this trend (see Figure 2.3).

CONSUMER PROBLEM SOLVING AND MARKET-PENETRATION STRATEGIES

We learned from *Consumer in Focus 2.1* that a majority in the mass camera market no longer will settle for average picture quality. They expect more options, such as built-in flash, automatic focus and aperture setting, and auto film wind. In short, photography is a relatively high involvement activity for many, with the result that even an inexpensive camera is expected to offer the basic features of higher-priced 35mm models. Consumers will follow EPS and compare options until they find what they want within an acceptable price range.

In this type of situation, a proper strategic response begins with an understanding of the attributes consumers expect, followed by designing a product

**FIGURE 2.3
A PRODUCT
MARKETED WITH A
CORRECT
UNDERSTANDING
OF CONSUMER
DECISION
PROCESSES: THE
OLYMPUS CAMERA**

Source: Courtesy of Olympus Corporation, Consumer Products Group.

line that offers these features. It is to be expected that some information search will be undertaken by most prospects. Therefore, ads should present hard information on product characteristics (see Figure 2.3).

Information search also can carry over to point-of-sale, where demonstration may be needed. This, of course, requires skilled salespeople. Furthermore, there may be some latitude for price variation, depending on the features that are offered. "Buy the cheapest" may not be the determining consideration, as it often is when buyers are following an LPS strategy.

The alert marketer, however, should anticipate LPS in the majority of new product introductions and adapt strategy accordingly. To illustrate this point, stop and list those buying situations in the past month in which you have gone to the effort of intensive search and alternative evaluation. For most of us, the majority of our purchases are "everyday and mundane." This fact was clearly noted some years ago by advertising strategist Leo Bogart:

2.2 THE SHAME OF SMELLY CLOTHES: LEVER BROTHERS

Lever Brothers Co. seems to have a real talent for selling laundry detergent by showing how humiliating dirty clothes can be. First there were the "ring-around-the-collar" ads that irritated people but made Wisk one of the top-selling detergents. Now a body-odor campaign is turning a new Lever detergent called Surf into the No. 2 brand in the country.

Largely because of this odor-fighting claim, Surf has managed to clean up in the $3.3 billion detergent market. Surf's 8% market share now is second only to the 23% share held by Procter & Gamble Co.'s Tide.

So what's the big deal about odor removal? It sounds like an obvious benefit of any detergent. Strangely enough, however, it's a novel claim. While detergents have long been promoted for making clothes smell fresh and fragrant, none has stressed odor elimination. A unique selling proposition like odor removal is especially critical in the detergent business where product differences are very slight. In a 1986 study by the BBDO ad agency, 55% of consumers said all detergents are "about the same."

Surf's success hasn't come cheaply. So far, the company has invested well over $100 million for ads and promotions. Introductory advertising has been running at an annual rate of $30 million, plus. Free samples have also helped fuel Surf's fast take-off. Lever claims no household product has ever had as extensive a sampling program as Surf, which is being distributed free to 80% of households at a cost of nearly $50 million.

Source: Ronald Alsop, "The Shame of Smelly Clothes Makes Lever Detergent a Hit," *The Wall Street Journal* (July 2, 1987). Reprinted by permission of The Wall Street Journal, © Dow Jones & Company, Inc. 1987. All Rights Reserved Worldwide.

Perhaps the main contribution that advertising research can make to the study of communications is in the domain of inattention to low-key stimuli, as exemplified by the ever increasing flow of unsolicited and unwanted messages to which people are subject in our over communicative civilization. [13]

Marketing strategy takes different forms when LPS, especially impulse buying, is the norm. Here is a case in point. In 1983 Lever Brothers Company introduced the first new powdered laundry detergent since Colgate–Palmolive's Fresh Start in 1978. A venerable brand name, Surf, was resurrected after being pulled from the market in the 1970s. Surf was designed to offer odor removal as the benefit, and it made significant market inroads. This successful product launch is detailed in *Consumer in Focus 2.2.*

Notice that Lever Brothers spent heavily on advertising. Executives knew full well that there was minimal consumer processing of these ads. The best that could be hoped was that widespread exposure would succeed in some

---

[13] Leo Bogart, "Where Does Advertising Research Go from Here?" *Journal of Advertising Research* 9 (March 1969), 6.

low-level, often nonconscious, awareness of the brand name and its benefit. The best possible outcome occurs when a detergent buyer *recognizes* the brand and is willing to try it. Trial was stimulated, in turn, by price cuts and extensive product sampling.

In this case, heavy point-of-sale promotion built effectively on the foundation laid by consumer advertising. The bright orange, dayglow color package certainly helped catch the potential buyer's attention. When offered a free sample plus a substantial price cut, large numbers of consumers responded with, "Why not? What have I got to lose?" And when it was found to perform satisfactorily as claimed, Surf qualified as a brand worth using again.

MARKETING RESPONSE TO REPEAT PURCHASING

When there is continual product repurchase, the challenge for marketers is to retain market share. The ideal situation, of course, is to have a high degree of consumer loyalty. When a purchase is based on strong involvement, the probability of brand switching is sharply minimized.

Inertia-based loyalty, on the other hand, presents a different challenge:

> *When generic products were coming on strong a few years ago, J. Walter Thompson, the New York-based ad agency, gauged consumers' loyalty to brands in 80 product categories. It found that the leader in market share was not necessarily the brand-loyalty leader. At that time, Bayer aspirin was the market share leader among headache remedies, but Tylenol had the most loyal following.*
>
> *Thompson measured the degree of loyalty by asking people whether they'd switch for a 50 percent discount. Cigarette smokers most often said no, making them the most brand-loyal of consumers (see table). Film is the only one of the top five products that the user doesn't put in his mouth — so why such loyalty? According to Edith Gilson, Thompson's senior vice president of research, 35-mm film is used by photography buffs, who are not your average snapshooter: "It's for long-lasting, emotionally valued pictures, taken by someone who has invested a lot of money in his camera." Plenty of shoppers will try a different cola for 50 percent off, and most consumers think one plastic garbage bag or facial tissue is much like another."[14]*

The results of Thompson's research appear in Table 2.1.

TABLE 2.1 "WHO CAN BE LOYAL TO A TRASH BAG?"	**High-Loyalty Products**	**Medium-Loyalty Products**	**Low-Loyalty Products**
	Cigarettes	Cola drinks	Paper towels
	Laxatives	Margarine	Crackers
	Cold remedies	Shampoo	Scouring powder
	35-mm film	Hand lotion	Plastic trash bags
		Furniture polish	Facial tissues

Source: "Coke's Brand Loyalty Lesson," *Fortune* (August 5, 1985), 46. Used by special permission.

---

[14] "Coke's Brand Loyalty Lesson," *Fortune* (August 5, 1985), 46.

No doubt there could be some disagreement with the classifications provided in Table 2.1, but the point is made that only a subset of purchase habits reflect loyalty. The primary differentiating factor, we feel, is the extent of product involvement experienced by purchasers in each category.

Any marketer covets high loyalty and does everything possible to maintain it. Any who tries to dislodge loyal purchasers of a brand of 35mm film, let's say those who prefer Fuji, faces a tough challenge indeed. This loyalty is often based on both the high involvement nature of photography to many and a belief that Fuji offers the truest color and picture quality. Such buyers have no incentive to change unless there is a real and demonstrable competitive breakthrough.

Such loyalty can quickly erode, however, when it is taken for granted. Marketing research consistently shows that the key to maintenance of market share is pervasive and continuing commitment to customer satisfaction.[15] Quality standards must be maintained at all costs, with any failure to perform as expected followed by immediate retribution. Furthermore, a premium must be placed on innovation to maintain competitive superiority.

Manufacturers of paper towels, on the other hand, do not enjoy much loyalty based on high involvement. Towels are a household necessity and the brands are pretty much alike, regardless of what advertisers say. So, why not switch?

Any manufacturer offering a competitive distinction, no matter how small, can gain temporary advantage. Hence, the most commonly used advertising word is *NEW*. Market share often is dictated more by winning the battle of advertising recall than anything else.[16]

Heavy point-of-sale sampling, display, couponing, and other devices also are used to trigger a brand switch. Yet, instability of preference rather than loyalty is the most common outcome. Marketers with products in this category have no choice but to push for innovation, no matter how trivial, fully expecting to be matched or exceeded competitively.

PROPER DEFINITION OF THE DECISION-MAKING UNIT

Thus far we have referred only to the individual consumer as being the decision-making unit. It is common, however, for many people to take part and play differing roles. Therefore, the decision-making unit can range from an individual to a complex extended family. Here are the major roles that can be performed (see Chapter 6 for a more thorough discussion):

1. Initiator — an initiator of the buying process.
2. Influencer — an individual whose opinions weigh heavily in the options that are evaluated and chosen.

---

[15] "Rediscovering the Customer," Research and Development Department, The Forum Corporation, 1988.

[16] Scott Hume, "Market Leaders Also Dominate in Recall of Ads," *Advertising Age* (February 1, 1988), 6.

2.3   KNOWING YOUR CONSUMER: THE IMPORTANCE OF DEFINING THE DECISION-MAKING UNIT CORRECTLY

Several years ago the product-design staff of a well-known manufacturer of electric razors proposed several new product options. An important but unresolved issue was the number and types of colors to be featured. Marketing research was undertaken to discover color preferences among prospective buyers, and these findings led to the offering of three different options.

Once initial sales results were tallied, it became obvious that there was a serious discrepancy between marketing research predictions and actual sales. Specifically, the color predicted to be most popular by market researchers turned out to be last in sales,

whereas the reverse proved to be true with the color expected to have least popularity. Researchers were called on the carpet to explain the differences.

Further analysis disclosed that the chief researcher had mistakenly assumed that the male user also made the purchase. This proved to be false — wives account for the majority of purchases through gift buying for their husbands. It was their color preferences, not those of the husband, that influenced the choice. In short, the problem came from failure to distinguish between buyer and user.

---

3. Decider — one with the financial authority or power to dictate the final choice.
4. Buyer — the purchasing agent.
5. User — the actual consumer.

When the buying unit is an individual making choices for his or her personal consumption, the individual will generally perform all roles, although there always can be influences of various types from friends and relatives. In the extended family, however, five or more people could perform entirely different roles.

We can make serious marketing mistakes if strategy is concentrated only on the individual as buyer and consumer. For an example, read *Consumer in Focus 2.3*.

THE UNDERLYING INFLUENCES ON CONSUMER BEHAVIOR

Thus far we have focused only on variations in decision process but have said little about the underlying determinants of these variations in behavior. These fall into three categories: (1) environmental influences; (2) individual differences and influences; and (3) psychological processes.

A summary follows of each of the many variables that illuminates consumer behavior. The model in Figure 2.1 is expanded as we progress, to help provide an overview. While each of these factors is covered in depth in later chapters, some are discussed at greater length here in order to help trace the main stages in the history of consumer research and some major landmarks along the way.

ENVIRONMENTAL INFLUENCES

As Figure 2.4 indicates, consumers live in a complex environment. Their decision-process behavior is influenced by (1) culture; (2) social class; (3) personal influence; (4) family; and (5) situation. Figure 2.4 indicates the flow from broad (culture) to the specific (situation) influences.

CULTURE   In parts of East Africa one of the worst curses a woman can face is to be slim. In short, "fat is beautiful," and reducing aids face a nonreceptive market. What a contrast to the Western world! This is a vivid example of how cultural values shape consumer behavior.[17] **Culture,** as used in the study of consumer behavior, refers to the values, ideas, artifacts, and other meaningful symbols that help individuals communicate, interpret, and evaluate as members of society. Chapter 3 illustrates vividly that a marketer with a defective knowledge of culture is doomed.

From a different perspective, however, all forms of marketing are a channel through which cultural meanings are transferred to consumer goods.[18] Hence, marketing is a value transmitter that simultaneously shapes culture and is shaped by it.

Unfortunately, the field of consumer research until very recently has been almost solely oriented to Western culture. The single exception has been some recognition of ethnic subcultural differences in the United States. The rapid economic development in many parts of the world, however, is quickly changing this outlook. The Association for Consumer Research held its first truly international meeting in 1985.[19] As we saw in Chapter 1, it is increasingly evident that cultural anthropology is finding growing use in conceptualizing and understanding marketing problems.

SOCIAL CLASS   **Social classes** are divisions within society composed of individuals sharing similar values, interests, and behaviors. They are differentiated by socioeconomic status differences ranging from low to high. Social

---

[17] See Martin S. Roth and Christine Moorman, "The Cultural Content of Cognition and the Cognitive Content of Culture: Implications for Consumer Research," in Michael J. Houston, ed., *Advances in Consumer Research* 15 (Provo, Utah: Association for Consumer Research, 1988), 403–410.

[18] Grant McCracken, "Advertising: Meaning or Information?" in Melanie Wallendorf and Paul Anderson, eds., *Advances in Consumer Research* 14 (Provo, Utah: Association for Consumer Research, 1987), 121–124.

[19] See Chin Tong Tan and Jagdish N. Sheth, eds., *Historical Perspectives in Consumer Research: National and International Perspectives* (Singapore: National University of Singapore, 1985).

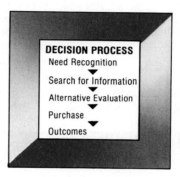

class status often leads to differing forms of consumer behavior (e.g., the types of alcoholic beverages served, the make and style of car driven, and the styles of dress preferred).

Some of the earliest contributions to the study of consumer behavior used social class differences as a major variable in explaining consumer differences.[20] While social class differences are blurring somewhat in the United States, this certainly is not the case in emerging countries of the world. Therefore, the concepts reviewed in Chapter 4 still are of significance for the student of consumer behavior.

PERSONAL INFLUENCE   As consumers, our behavior often is affected by those with whom we closely associate. We may respond to perceived pressure to conform with the norms and expectations provided by others. Also, we value those around us for their counsel on buying choices. This can take

---

[20] See, for example, Lee Rainwater, Richard P. Coleman, and Gerald Handel, *Workingman's Wife* (Dobbs Ferry, N.Y.: Oceana Publications, 1959).

the form of observation of what others are doing, with the result that they become a comparative reference group. When we actively seek advice from another, however, that person serves as an **opinion leader.** All of these forms of personal influence are discussed in Chapter 5.

Personal influence has been an important subject in consumer research ever since it became a serious field of study. Such names as Katz[21] and Rogers[22] appear prominently in the literature because of their significant research on word-of-mouth behavior and other forms of influence.

FAMILY   Since the field of consumer research was founded in the post–World War II era, the family has been a focus of research.[23] The family often is the primary decision-making unit, of course, with a complex and varying pattern of roles and functions. Chapter 6 unfolds the significance of the family in shaping buying and consumption decisions.

SITUATION   It is obvious that behavior changes as situations change. Sometimes these changes are erratic and unpredictable. At other times they can be predicted by research and capitalized upon in strategy. An obvious example is the peak in flower purchases during the popular gift-buying seasons. Following the initiative of Belk and others in the 1970s,[24] the situation now is treated as a research variable in its own right, as you discover in Chapter 7.

INDIVIDUAL DIFFERENCES

Now we move from the external environment to those internal factors that affect and influence behavior. The diagram of influences on consumer behavior is expanded (Figure 2.5) by including five important ways in which consumers can differ: (1) consumer resources; (2) motivation and involvement; (3) knowledge; (4) attitudes; and (5) personality, lifestyle, and demographics.

CONSUMER RESOURCES   Each person brings three resources into every decision-making situation — (1) time, (2) money, and (3) attention (information reception and processing capabilities). Generally there are distinct limits on the availability of each, thus requiring some careful allocation.

---

[21] See Elihu Katz, "The Two Step Flow of Communication: An Up to Date Report on an Hypothesis," *Public Opinion Quarterly* 21 (Spring 1957), 61–78.

[22] A significant early book was Everett M. Rogers, *Diffusion of Innovations* (New York: Free Press, 1962). Also, important work on this subject in marketing has been done by Thomas Robertson. See Thomas S. Robertson, Joan Zielinski, and Scott Ward, *Consumer Behavior* (Glenview, Ill.: Scott, Foresman, 1984).

[23] An important early source was James N. Morgan, "Household Decision Making," in Nelson Foote, ed., *Household Decision Making* (New York: New York University Press, 1961).

[24] For significant early writings on this subject, see Russell W. Belk, "An Exploratory Assessment of Situational Effects in Buyer Behavior," *Journal of Marketing Research* 11 (May 1974), 156–173; and Russell W. Belk, "Situational Variables and Consumer Behavior, *Journal of Consumer Research* 2 (December 1975), 157–164. Also Gordon R. Foxall, *Consumer Choice* (London: MacMillan, 1983), 86–97.

FIGURE 2.5
INDIVIDUAL
INFLUENCES ON
CONSUMER
BEHAVIOR: THE FIVE
WAYS IN WHICH
CONSUMERS CAN
DIFFER

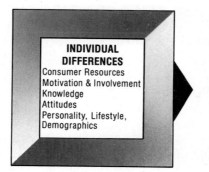

INDIVIDUAL DIFFERENCES
Consumer Resources
Motivation & Involvement
Knowledge
Attitudes
Personality, Lifestyle,
Demographics

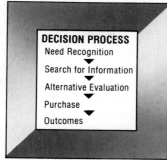

DECISION PROCESS
Need Recognition
▼
Search for Information
▼
Alternative Evaluation
▼
Purchase
▼
Outcomes

To take an example, the busy career woman who also is a wife and mother may have an income sufficiently ample to enable frequent purchases of expensive clothing and furnishings. Yet there are restrictions on the time available for shopping and the ability to allocate attention to the information gathered in the process. As a result, many women are resorting to purchase of high-fashion items from catalogs. The so-called "upscale busy woman" is the primary target for leading catalog marketer Spiegel Inc.[25] These and other issues are discussed in Chapter 8.

MOTIVATION AND INVOLVEMENT   Psychologists and marketers alike have always been concerned about explaining what takes place when goal-directed behavior is energized and activated. This is what we mean by motivation, the subject of Chapter 9.

Consumer involvement has been discussed earlier in this chapter, and you saw how its presence or absence affects decision-process behavior. Because it is such a potent directive factor, we believe that it is best conceived as a primary motivating influence. Therefore, it is covered in depth in Chapter 9.

Turning to the subject of motivation as traditionally conceived, a central variable has always been **motive** — an enduring predisposition that arouses and directs behavior toward certain goals. Researchers still debate the issues of how consumer motives can be classified and the extent to which they are conscious or unconscious.

Classification of Consumer Motives.   In the 1920s, marketing scholar Melvin Copeland introduced the classification of rational versus emotional

[25] "Spiegel, Inc.(A)," in Roger D. Blackwell, W. Wayne Talarzyk, and James F. Engel, *Contemporary Cases in Consumer Behavior* (Hinsdale, Ill.: Dryden, 1985), 85–94.

2.4 SYMBOLS, ICONS, AND SEMIOTICS: SNUGGLE FABRIC SOFTENER

In just a few years, Lever Brothers Co. built a $300 million fabric softener brand through the charms of a huggable teddy bear named Snuggle. Most marketers only dream of creating such a powerful advertising symbol, and Lever didn't want to do anything to jeopardize this little gold mine. It felt it needed to know more about why Snuggle was so successful and how the bear should be used in ads. So Snuggle got psychoanalyzed.

Carol Moog, a psychologist turned advertising consultant, did an analysis of Snuggle that went way beyond cuddliness. "The bear is an ancient symbol of aggression, but when you create a teddy bear, you provide a softer, nurturant side to that aggression," she says. "As a symbol of tamed aggression, the teddy bear is the perfect image for a fabric softener that tames the rough texture of clothing."

Lever had other questions about Snuggle: Should the bear be a boy or girl? Should it interact with humans in the ads? How about blinking its eyes, wiggling its ears and sniffing the laundry? Blinking, wiggling and sniffing were all deemed suitable behavior, but Ms. Moog recommended that Snuggle remain genderless and that people not be included in ads. "To keep the magic, it has to be just Snuggle and the viewer communicating," she says. "The teddy bear acts as a bridge between the consumer's rational and more instinctual, emotional side."

Ms. Moog calls her analysis of signs and symbols in advertising "psychological semiotics." Some people refer to it simply as semiotics; others prefer "iconology" or image decoding. Whatever academic jargon they use to describe it, more marketers are turning to social scientists to help them understand the many messages their advertising is transmitting to consumers on both a conscious and subconscious level. Ads have always been rich with psychological imagery, but advertisers now are trying harder to control and manipulate the symbols. Even the penguins in a new Diet Coke commercial

motives.[26] If we were to use this system, we would classify as rational motives such preferred utilitarian vacuum cleaner features as lightweightness, ease of handling, and convenience of storing.[27]

Yet we also recognize that products have *symbolic* values that go far beyond economic considerations. This is what Copeland meant by emotional motives, but that term is seldom used today. In a landmark contribution to consumer behavior in 1959, Sidney Levy stated:

---

[26] Melvin Copeland, *Principles of Merchandising* (Chicago: A. W. Shaw, 1924), Chapters 6–7.
[27] "New Vacuum Addresses Consumer Trends," *Marketing News* (November 21, 1986), 24.

aren't there just for humorous effect. SSC&B, an ad agency that practices semiotics, notes that the birds symbolize coolness, refreshment and friendliness.

"It's mind boggling to try to control all the non-verbal symbols in our creative work," says Elissa Moses, a research executive at the BBDO ad agency. "But if advertisers aren't aware of subtleties, they may inadvertently communicate the wrong message." Consider an ad for Grey Flannel cologne. The marketer was startled to learn from a psychologist that the ad showing only a man's back could be perceived as "rudely giving the consumer the cold shoulder."

Some ad agencies, though, are skeptical of semiotics. They question whether social scientists read too much into commercials, and they chafe at efforts to transform the creative process from an art to a science. "These psychologists tend to be overly intellectual and a little tutti-frutti," says George Lois, chairman of Lois Pitts Gershon Pon/GGK, an ad agency.

Even companies that do semiotic research sometimes take it with a grain of salt. That was the case with executives at American Cyanamid Co., when Ms. Moog, the psychologist, studied a commercial for Pierre Cardin men's fragrance. The ad was designed to show men who are aggressive and in control, but Ms. Moog saw a conflict in an image of the cologne gushing out of a phallic-shaped bottle. She said it symbolized male ejaculation and lack of control. "We recognized that she probably was right," says a marketing official who worked with Ms. Moog, "but we kept the shot of the exploding cologne in the commercial anyway. It's a beautiful product shot, plus it encourages men to use our fragrance liberally."

Source: Ronald Alsop, "Agencies Scrutinize Their Ads for Psychological Symbolism," *The Wall Street Journal* (June 11, 1987), 25. Reprinted by permission of *The Wall Street Journal*, © Dow Jones & Co., Inc. 1987. All rights reserved.

The things people buy are seen to have personal and social meanings in addition to their functions. Modern goods are recognized as psychological things, as symbolic of personal attributes and goals, as symbolic of social patterns and strivings.[28]

While Levy was giving a broad, eclectic viewpoint, those from a more psychoanalytic persuasion soon began to find hidden symbolism. An example would be the sexual connotations of changing the design of a bar of hand soap from a square to a round shape. Small wonder that Vance Packard seized the opportunity in 1959 to write his best-seller, *The Hidden Persuaders*,[29]

---

[28] Sidney J. Levy, "Symbols by Which We Buy," in Lynn H. Stockman, ed., *Advancing Marketing Efficiency* (Chicago: American Marketing Association, 1959), 410.
[29] Vance Packard, *The Hidden Persuaders* (New York: McKay, 1957).

which was to trigger great interest in the press and among the general public.

While the psychoanalysts and others may have gone to the extreme, symbolism cannot be ignored. Certainly it is an important part of everyday life. Do you agree with the conclusion in *Consumer in Focus 2.4* that the teddy bear, Snuggle, offers symbolism that triggers emotions leading to purchase of the fabric softener by that name?

The concept of motive is helpful in understanding consumer preferences because criteria used in alternative evaluation are best conceived as product-specific manifestations of motives. A wide range of motives is presented in Chapter 9, including variety seeking and risk avoidance.

The Motivation-Research Era.   Borrowing from the Freudian-oriented clinical psychology of that time, a group of psychologists entered the marketing field in the 1950s and attempted to explain behavior on the basis of unconscious motivations. The most famous by far was Ernest Dichter, who was to be a dominant voice during that period.[30]

"Women bake cakes because of an unconscious desire to give birth." This was one of the findings that marketers found most intriguing. Pillsbury soon introduced the legendary advertising theme, "Nothing says lovin' like something from the oven." This was followed by the Pillsbury Doughboy (Figure 2.6) who took first place in 1987 as the favorite commercial character. What do you think he symbolizes?

KNOWLEDGE   Knowledge, the outcome of learning, can be defined simply as the information stored in memory. As discussed in Chapter 10, consumer knowledge encompasses a vast array of information, such as the availability and characteristics of products and services, where and when to buy, and how to use products.

Recently, the importance of understanding consumer knowledge or expertise has been stressed anew within the consumer research field.[31] One major outcome of advertising and selling is simply to provide relevant knowledge and information, especially under extended problem solving. Certainly our Australian friends, the Watkins, were motivated to acquire as much knowledge as possible before spending $18,000 for their yacht. Therefore, stimulation of awareness often is an important and necessary marketing objective.

ATTITUDES   Once Philip and Carolyn Watkins finished their search for information and considerable evaluation of various possibilities, the outcome was the formation of an attitude toward the considered alternatives. We define **attitude** as an overall evaluation that enables one to respond in a consistently

---

[30] Ernest Dichter, *The Strategy of Desire* (New York: Doubleday, 1960).
[31] Joseph W. Alba and J. Wesley Hutchinson, "Two Dimensions of Consumer Expertise," *Journal of Consumer Research* 13 (March 1987), 411–454.

FIGURE 2.6
THE PILLSBURY
DOUGHBOY—A
POTENT SYMBOL?

favorable or unfavorable manner with respect to a given object or alternative. All things being equal, people usually behave in a manner consistent with their attitudes and intentions.

Judging by the literature in social psychology and related fields, at least until recently, attitude is the most important variable utilized in the study of human behavior. For the last half century, much of marketing persuasion has been undertaken to change attitudes. Yet, as recently as the first edition of this text in 1968, there was little agreement on how to define attitudes, let alone measure and change them. Indeed, there was even an unresolved controversy over the issue of whether a change in attitude would lead to a change in behavior.[32]

Fortunately, needed clarification was introduced in the 1960s by Milton

---

[32] A. J. Vogl (quoting Charles A. Ramond), "Advertising Research — Everybody's Looking for the Holy Grail," *Sales Management* (November 1, 1963), 43.

Rosenberg,[33] Martin Fishbein,[34] and others. Soon it was possible to demonstrate a positive relationship between knowledge (beliefs), attitudes, intentions, and behavior.[35]

Furthermore, attitude was conceptualized as a positive or negative feeling toward brands and viewed as the outcome of brand ratings along important evaluative criteria or attributes. Hence, multi-attribute models found their way into the consumer research literature and exerted dominant influence on the directions of the field for the next 20 years. The yield from this effort is generally positive, as our discussion on this subject in Chapter 11 reveals.

PERSONALITY, LIFESTYLE, AND DEMOGRAPHICS   For convenience we are combining three significant and frequently related variables into our diagrammatic model (see also Chapter 12). All three are useful in defining various objective and subjective characteristics of consumers in target market segments.

Personality.   Personality research has always been important in clinical psychology, but an interesting concept was introduced by Pierre Martineau in the 1950s when he hypothesized that products also have personalities in the form of brand images.[36] A logical deduction at that point was that marketing strategy should focus on matching consumer personalities with product personalities.

An intriguing theory? Yes, but researchers chasing this dream for the next 15 years or so found it to be illusory.[37] While the personality-matching effort proved largely fruitless, the literature did reveal that some personality traits, such as venturesomeness, predict certain types of consumer behavior. As a result, personality scales still are in the arsenal of the consumer researcher, as Chapter 12 demonstrates.

Lifestyle.   Perhaps the greatest yield from the personality-research era was a broadening of the focus to encompass **lifestyle** — patterns by which people live and spend time and money. Such researchers as William Wells[38] devised extensive inventories of Activities, Interests, and Opinions (AIO measures) that measure some personality traits, values, beliefs, preferences, and

---

[33] Milton J. Rosenberg, "Cognitive Structure and Attitudinal Effect," *Journal of Abnormal and Social Psychology* 53 (1956), 367–372.

[34] Martin Fishbein, "An Investigation of the Relationships Between Beliefs About an Object and the Attitude Toward the Object," *Human Relations* 16 (1963), 233–240.

[35] Icek Ajzen and Martin Fishbein, *Understanding Attitudes and Predicting Social Behavior* (Englewood Cliffs, N.J.: Prentice-Hall, 1980).

[36] Pierre Martineau, *Motivation in Advertising* (New York: McGraw-Hill, 1957).

[37] Franklin B. Evans, "Psychological and Objective Factors in the Prediction of Brand Choice: Ford Versus Chevrolet," *Journal of Business* 32 (1959), 340–369.

[38] See William D. Wells and Douglas J. Tigert, "Activities, Interests, Opinions," *Journal of Advertising Research* 11 (August 1971), 27–35.

behavior patterns. As it grew, this line of inquiry soon became labeled as **psychographics.**

Psychographic research was quickly recognized as providing highly practical input to marketing strategy. For example, knowing that heavy users of eye makeup differed from nonusers in fashion consciousness, cosmopolitanism, and future orientation affected advertising, packaging, and distribution.[39]

Demographics.   One of the most discussed (and condemned) phenomena in the Western world during the 1980s has been the so-called yuppie (young, upwardly mobile, professional) and his or her uniquely hedonic lifestyle. As a subset of the 77 million "baby boomers" born between 1946 and 1964, it is often jokingly said that you can always spot yuppies by their BMWs, their Jacuzzis, and their Perriers.

This is an example of what can be learned from the field of **demography,** where the objective is to describe segments of consumers in such terms as age, income, and education. The emphasis always is on trends in behavior and expenditures. When accompanied with psychographic research, demographics can shed much light on the nature and composition of markets. Indeed, demographics has been the bread and butter of marketing research since the 1920s.

PSYCHOLOGICAL PROCESSES

Human information processing, learning, and attitude change all have been of major interest to consumer researchers (Figure 2.7). In fact, it is here that some of the greatest contributions have been made to the understanding of consumer behavior.

INFORMATION PROCESSING   Communication is the bottom-line marketing activity. Therefore, consumer researchers have long been interested in discovering how people receive, process, and make sense of marketing communications. Studies during and since World War II have underscored one crucial principle: *people see and hear what they want to see and hear.*

Information processing research addresses ways in which information is transformed, reduced, elaborated, stored, recovered, and used. This is of such importance to marketing communication that information processing dominated the consumer research field for nearly 20 years beginning in the late 1960s.[40] Chapter 13 gives a comprehensive grasp of this important subject.

---

[39] Edgar A. Pessemier and Douglas J. Tigert, "Personality, Activity, and Attitude Predictors of Consumer Behavior," in John S. Wright and Jack S. Goldstrucker, eds., *New Ideas for Successful Marketing* (Chicago: American Marketing Association, 1966), 332–347.

[40] Two important conceptual works on information processing are James R. Bettman, *An Information Processing Theory of Consumer Choice* (Reading, Mass.: Addison-Wesley, 1979) and Flemming Hansen, *Consumer Choice Behavior* (New York: Free Press, 1972). For textbooks written from this perspective see J. Paul Peter and Jerry C. Olson, *Consumer Behavior* (Homewood, Ill.: Richard D. Irwin, 1987); Brian Sternthal and C. Samuel Craig, *Consumer Behavior: An Information Processing Perspective* (Englewood Cliffs, N.J.: Prentice-Hall, 1979); and William L. Wilkie, *Consumer Behavior* (New York: John Wiley & Sons, 1986).

FIGURE 2.7
PSYCHOLOGICAL PROCESSES: THE IMPORTANCE OF INFORMATION PROCESSING, LEARNING, AND ATTITUDE CHANGE

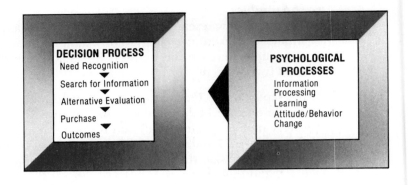

LEARNING   Anyone attempting to influence the consumer is trying to bring about **learning** — the process by which experience leads to changes in knowledge, attitude, and/or behavior. The marketing significance of learning theory became apparent when one of its leading proponents, John B. Watson, entered the advertising field in the 1930s.[41] He popularized a view that we come into this world with nothing other than a capacity to learn. His philosophy was that constant repetition would reinforce a response and build purchasing habits. Today's emphasis on repetitive advertising rests on this foundation, as does consumer research devoted to discovering appeals that stimulate the best short-run response.

Learning processes must be understood, therefore, if the marketer is to persuade. Some European researchers and writers have gone so far as to place learning as *the* central variable in understanding consumer behavior.[42] Although we would not concur with this more extreme view, there is no question that the discussion of learning processes in Chapter 14 is important if consumer behavior is to be understood and influenced.

ATTITUDE AND BEHAVIOR CHANGE   Changes in attitude and behavior are a common marketing objective. This process reflects basic psychological influences that have been the subject of decades of intensive research. Chapter 15 reviews this literature from the perspective of designing effective promotional strategies.

---

[41] See John B. Watson, *Behaviorism* (New York: The People's Institute Publishing Company, 1925).

[42] See Andrew S. C. Ehrenberg and G. J. Goodhardt, *Consumer Attitudes* (New York: J. Walter Thompson and MRCA, 1980) and Gordon R. Foxall, *Models of Consumer Choice* (London: Macmillan, 1983).

Consumer Decision Processes and Behavior

This chapter has provided only a brief overview of the nature and functions of various types of consumer decision processes. We return to this important subject in Part V of the book.

Chapter 16 builds upon the model presented here and clarifies how the complex of variables presented here interact to shape decision-process behavior. It establishes that a model, properly used, can be of real significance in diagnosing consumer behavior for purposes of strategic marketing planning.

The subsequent three chapters discuss the major stages in consumer decision processes: (1) need recognition and search (Chapter 17); (2) alternative evaluation (Chapter 18); and (3) purchase and its outcomes (Chapter 19). Each is designed to provide a rich grasp of strategic implications.

Consumer Analysis and Marketing Strategy

We have made repeated reference to the way in which consumer research impacts marketing strategy. Basic marketing courses are designed to cover product development, pricing, promotion, and distribution. Therefore, we do not cover that ground in this book. Nevertheless, each chapter offers a rich yield of insights into the implications of consumer research for strategy development.

Chapters in Part VI, however, are written to address certain strategic marketing issues from the perspective of consumer research. Chapter 20 returns to the subject of demographic and psychographic differences but concentrates on future trends and their relevance for strategic marketing. Chapter 21, on the other hand, pulls together our many references to possible ways to segment and market with sharper focus on segmentation bases and methods.

Chapter 22 introduces a new subject, diffusion of innovations, and gives important insights into new product development and promotion. Chapter 23 broadens our perspective by clarifying the unique applications of consumer research in distribution and retailing. Finally, Chapter 24 builds on and expands the discussion of culture in Chapter 3 and shows the key role of consumer research in marketing across cultural boundaries.

No discussion of consumer research and marketing strategy would be complete without a serious analysis of the moral and ethical dimensions of consumer-oriented marketing from the consumer's perspective. This important issue is the subject of Chapter 25.

Summary and Plan of the Book

The purpose of this chapter has been to introduce you to the nature of consumer decision making and the influences upon this process. A general model of consumer decision processes was introduced that depicts the following phases in problem-solving activity: (1) need recognition; (2) search for information; (3) alternative evaluation; (4) purchase; and (5) outcomes (especially degree of satisfaction).

When there is a high degree of search for information in an initial purchase decision, followed by rigorous alternative evaluation, the consumer is engaging in extended problem solving (EPS). It is most often undertaken when (1) alternatives are differentiated in significant ways; (2) there is an absence of restricting time pressures; and (3) there is a high degree of involvement — perceived relevance of the purchase in the context of important needs and motivations.

EPS can be viewed as one end of a problem-solving continuum. The opposite end of this continuum is anchored by limited problem solving (LPS). Here there is far less motivation to search widely for information and to engage in alternative evaluation. A common form of LPS is the impulse purchase, in which the buyer acts on a "Why not try it?" response. We see this most often when alternatives are essentially similar, there is unwillingness to devote time to the process, and involvement is low. In short, there is little perceived risk of doing the wrong thing.

When the occasion arises for repeat purchases, however, many consumers quickly develop habitual decision processes. On occasion they are brand loyal and stay with their initial choice. This occurs mainly when there is high perceived involvement. When this is not the case, however, habits are built on inertia. If there is no reason to switch, a repurchase will be made. But the consumer also is prone to switch if there is incentive to do so. Once again there is low involvement and little commitment to one alternative versus another.

We demonstrated, therefore, that there are two major types of decision processes, depending upon degree of involvement and the extent of habit: (1) a problem-solving continuum ranging from EPS to LPS; and (2) repeated behavior taking the form of brand loyalty and inertia. The respective marketing strategies differ sharply from one to another.

We systematically expanded our basic model of consumer decision processes to reveal the complexity of factors that influence and shape decision-process behavior. The first of these is environmental influences, including (1) culture; (2) social class; (3) personal influence; (4) family; and (5) situation. The second is the complex of important individual differences: (1) consumer resources; (2) motivation and involvement; (3) knowledge; (4) attitudes; and (5) personality, lifestyle, and demographics. The last component consists of the basic psychological processes of (1) information processing; (2) learning; and (3) attitude and behavior change. A complete model appears in Figure 2-8.

We could begin our concentrated study of consumer behavior anywhere in this model, and we have tried different approaches in our previous editions. Experience over the years has shown, however, that it often is best to move from the general to the specific. Therefore, our starting point in the next section (Part II) is with environmental influences.

FIGURE 2.8   A COMPLETE OVERVIEW MODEL OF CONSUMER DECISION-MAKING BEHAVIOR AND THE INFLUENCES ON IT

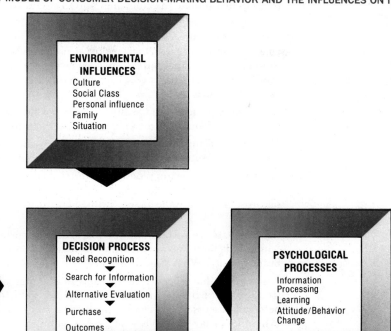

Part III concentrates on individual differences, and we move from there to psychological processes in Part IV. Once we have this comprehensive grasp of the ways in which behavior is shaped and influenced, we return once again to the subject of consumer decision processes in Part V. And the book concludes in Parts VI and VII with discussions of marketing strategies and organizational ethics.

REVIEW AND DISCUSSION QUESTIONS

1. There are some who argue that consumers really do not pursue any kind of decision process but make their selections more or less randomly without any apparent reasoning. What is your position on this issue? Why?

2. In speaking of the problems that might result from psychological analysis of consumer behavior, Vance Packard stated many years ago, "Much of it seems to represent regress rather than progress for man in his struggle to become a rational and self-guiding

being."[43] His point is that marketing persuaders now have new tools that enable them to manipulate the consumer and to circumvent his or her processes of reasoning. Comment.

3. Define the terms *extended problem solving* and *limited problem solving*. What are the essential differences? What type of decision process would you expect most people to follow in the initial purchase of a new product or brand in each of these categories: toothpaste, flour, men's cologne, carpeting, toilet tissue, bread, light bulbs, a 35mm camera, a sports car?

4. Referring once again to Question 3, is it possible that decision-process behavior could differ widely from one consumer to another in purchasing each of these items? Explain.

5. How might a manufacturer of automatic washers and dryers use a decision-process approach to better understand how consumers purchase these products?

6. Which of the following types of products do you think are most likely to be purchased on the basis of brand loyalty? Or on the basis of inertia? Laundry detergent, motor oil, lipsticks, shoe polish, soft drinks, lawn care products (fertilizers, etc), and spark plugs.

7. Assume you are responsible for marketing a new and previously unknown brand of 35mm slide film. You are up against Kodak and Fuji, both of which have built substantial brand loyalty. What strategies could you suggest to make market inroads?

8. Assume you have been called in as a marketing consultant to suggest an advertising strategy for a new brand of dry cat food. Which of the types of decision-process behavior discussed in this chapter do you feel is likely with most prospective buyers? Why do you say this? What difference will this make in marketing strategy?

---

[43] Packard, *The Hidden Persuaders*, 6.

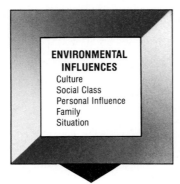

**ENVIRONMENTAL
INFLUENCES**
Culture
Social Class
Personal Influence
Family
Situation

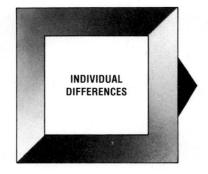

**INDIVIDUAL
DIFFERENCES**

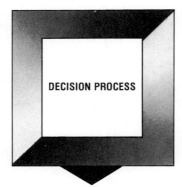

DECISION PROCESS

**PSYCHOLOGICAL
PROCESSES**

**MARKETING
STRATEGY**

ENVIRONMENTAL INFLUENCES

No person is an island. This statement is certainly true in the study of consumer behavior. Consumers are both created by their environment as well as operate within an environment. The following chapters analyze these influences.

You have just completed an introduction, providing an overview of consumer decisions and marketing influences. To begin a more intensive analysis, a choice must be made. Should the next stage be an in-depth analysis of individuals or an in-depth analysis of the environmental influences that affect individuals? There are merits to both approaches. In this edition of *Consumer Behavior,* the first stage is understanding the environmental influences that shape and constrain individuals in their consumption decisions. In later sections, the focus is on individual differences and psychological processes.

Consumer behavior was once concerned mostly with goods and services. Today, consumer behavior increasingly includes other activities and a broader view of the resources given up to obtain benefits. Decisions to watch television or visit a museum, to participate in holidays, to support a charity or to volunteer for community service are now important topics in the study of consumer behavior. Clothing not only covers our bodies. Today, clothing is recognized as communication to others about our bodies and how we perceive ourselves. There is major interest in moving toward a better understanding of business signs and symbols, reflected in new ways of understanding the meanings of goods and services, consumption choices and experiences, advertising, retail settings, corporate imagery and culture, business negotiations, global marketing and product design and planning.

Controlling images and messages in the marketplace requires both a broad and an intensive understanding of the environment. Most fundamental, perhaps, is an understanding of the nature and meaning of culture. That is the topic in Chapter 3. Also important is an understanding of social class, personal influence, family, and consumption situations, topics covered in Chapters 4, 5, 6, and 7. These chapters cover the basics. Trends and specialized topics such as diffusion of new products and global environments are covered in later sections of the book.

Why are you who you are? Why do you do what you do? Is your behavior caused mostly by genetic predisposition, by the environment, or by some combination that is uniquely you? Scientists from many disciplines disagree radically on the answers to such questions so you should not expect the answers from a book on consumer behavior. However, we can develop a thorough understanding of the basic concepts and explore how they are related to consumption.

Life chances and their influence on consumption is the topic of the next five chapters. These chapters serve as a foundation for understanding individual consumers — the target for marketing programs of business firms and many other organizations. Hopefully, you will also find these chapters useful in better understanding yourself and your consumption choices.

CULTURAL AND ETHNIC VALUES

W

RESPONDING TO VALUES: THE LESSON OF LOW-CALORIE BEER

hen Gablinger introduced a low-calorie beer in 1968, it was a spectacular failure. Miller Brewing Co. did the same thing seven years later with huge success. In fact, Miller changed the very nature of beer drinking. By the early 1990's, light beers will constitute 33% of all beer consumption in the United States. Miller did a lot of things right that Gablinger didn't: positioning, distribution, advertising. But what Miller did best was to gauge the changing role of beer in consumers' redefined values about health.

Source: Joseph T. Plummer, "Changing Values," *Futurist* 23 (January–February, 1989), 8–13, at 10.

CULTURE AND CONSUMPTION: WHY WE DO WHAT WE DO AND BUY WHAT WE BUY

Products have function, form, and meaning. When consumers buy a product, they expect it to perform a function — clean clothes in the case of laundry detergent or provide nutrition in the case of food. Consumers continue buying products only if their expectation for the product performing the function is met fairly well. But more than function determines success in marketing products.

Successful products must also meet expectations about form. Nutritional requirements in food might be met in many ways, but some forms are much preferred by customers. Foods are expected to be "hot" or "cold" or "crisp" or "tender" or "microwavable." Sometimes the form of the product acts as a symbol of the function, as the addition of "blue crystals" may do for a detergent that gets clothes "whiter."

Products also have significance beyond their function and form. Products sometimes are used in *ritual behavior* — as when certain foods are eaten during holidays or by candlelight for special occasions. Products may provide *symbols of meaning* in a society. Spinach may be associated with strength, possibly enticing children to eat an otherwise unenforceable choice. Foods may be symbols of family relationships, as in the case of a special recipe handed down through the generations or associated with one's national or ethnic identity. Occasionally, products become so much of a symbol in a society that they are an *icon*, as in the case of foods eaten especially in religious observances.

As you read this chapter, it may be helpful to think of the major ways culture affects products you buy and use. At least three major effects may be studied. First, culture affects the *structure of consumption* — the institutions available for marketing, for example. Second, culture *affects how individuals make decisions*. Third, culture is a major variable in the *creation and communication of meaning* in products.

THE STRUCTURE OF CONSUMPTION

Societal and ethnic structure determines much of what an individual consumer purchases and uses. The legal and governmental system is part of a nation's culture. It determines what suppliers can offer, the ways products can be marketed, and the degree to which consumers are allowed to act on their preferences. Shall countries put their resources into military, industrial, or consumer goods? Shall a nation produce good cars or good tanks? Good education or good health? Good computers or good music? And, because insatiability of demand dictates there will never be enough for all, should these products be most available to the old or to the young? To which ethnic or religious groups? To the persons who are the best educated or to the members of the "right" families or to persons of the ruling party? Such choices are heavily impacted by the culture of which an individual is a part.

INDIVIDUAL DECISION MAKING

Culture, along with other elements of the environment, impacts all stages of consumer decision making. As you read the first two chapters, describing how consumers make decisions, perhaps you wondered why some individuals make decisions in one way and other people make decisions in quite different ways. The study of culture, especially ethnicity, answers some of the "why" people vary in the manner in which they make decisions.

Culture affects the drives that motivate people to take further action — even for motives as diverse as liberty, literacy, or lascivity. The culture of a society determines what forms of communication are permitted about these problems and often the nature and degree of search behavior that an individual considers appropriate. The American culture may emphasize individual, competitive behavior, for example, while the Japanese culture may emphasize cultural conformity in consumption and production rather than individual achievement.

Consumers place more weight on some product attributes than on others when they choose between competing brands. The cause for such weights is often the culture to which the individual belongs. For example, a wealthy individual may attach great importance to low price, not because of lack of money but because of cultural values to which he or she subscribes. Conversely, a poor consumer may purchase an expensive pair of shoes because of personal or group values. During the purchase process, the amount of price negotiation expected by both seller and buyer is culturally determined. The amount of complaint behavior or expressions of satisfaction may also be affected by cultural variables. Almost all elements of marketing strategy will be affected by cultural expectations, some of which become laws or voluntary regulations. Thus, culture is a major determinant of how consumer decisions are made.

MEANING TO PRODUCTS

Culture gives meaning to goods and services. The marketing literature recently has focused on cognitive meanings, symbolic functions, and cultural histories of products,[1] emerging in a concept called **product semantics** or **semiotics,** the study of the symbolic qualities of products in the context of their use. An ad, for example, may include a singing jingle that implies a "country" or natural quality in a product; or it may use an Australian accent, or male–female voices, to give an Australian or male–female flavor.

IDEOLOGY OF CONSUMPTION   The culture of a nation includes an **ideology of consumption** defined as the social meaning attached to and communicated by products. Research by Belk and his associates[2] reveals that culture provides meaning not only to the advertising or communications about a product but also to acts of consumption. We can define consumer decision making

---

[1] Ruby R. Dholakia and Sidney J. Levy, "Effect of Recent Economic Experiences on Consumer Dreams, Goals and Behavior in the U.S.," *Journal of Economic Psychology* 8 (1987).

[2] Russell Belk, "Worldly Possessions: Issues and Criticisms," in Richard P. Bagozzi and Alice M. Tybout, eds., *Advances in Consumer Research* 10 (Ann Arbor, Association for Consumer Research, 1983), 514–519; and Russell Belk and Richard W. Pollay, "Images of Ourselves: The Good Life in Twentieth Century Advertising," *Journal of Consumer Research* 12 (June 1985), 887–897.

broadly enough so we can understand not only why people purchase products but also why people enjoy attending museums and participating in athletic events, and the kinds of meaning that people attach to plots and character development when attending movies.[3]

The ideology of consumption can be understood with an example from the research of Hirschman. She found that television programs communicate many forms of consumption, which vary in binary opposition between secular and sacred.[4] Secular consumption refers to the acquisition of man-made products, typically those resulting from technological process and those sought after by consumers in a competitive fashion. Consumption of secular products is typically associated with greed, avarice, and envy and is sought as an end in itself. In contrast, sacred consumption places primary importance on virtues such as love, honor, and integrity. Sacred consumers display little interest in acquiring technologically produced material goods. They are not fashion conscious and do not use products in a competitive manner. Sacred consumers in the media are usually involved in productive or natural careers rather than management, and they often are portrayed as upholding values of family nurturance, friendship, loyalty, and honesty. Secular women characters dress in expensive couture apparel and fur coats, with jewelry, makeup, and highly styled hair. Secular men characters invariably wear conservative business suits, have closely trimmed hair, and often wear black tie and a dinner jacket, reflecting a symbolic commitment to capitalism and the management of technology. In contrast, sacred consumption is portrayed with work clothes and cowboy gear or products constructed from inexpensive natural materials (flannel, denim, leather), obtainable from low-status sources. Food, residences, leisure activities, services, and many other aspects of consumption reflect the sacred–secular dichotomy in the ideology of consumption. In the TV series "Dallas," Cliff Barnes and April Stevens symbolize the secular, Ray Krebs and Miss Ellie symbolize the sacred, and Bobby Ewing and Donna Krebs are mediating characters representing a synthesis of the two.

Meaning moves first from the culture of a nation or group to consumer goods and then from these goods to individual consumers. From the culture, products absorb meaning through advertising, fashion systems, retailing presentation, and many other ways not influenced by marketers. The individual consumer develops meaning through possession, exchange, grooming, and divestment rituals. McCracken explains:

---

[3] David Glen Mick, "Consumer Research and Semiotics: Exploring the Morphology of Signs, Symbols, and Significance," *Journal of Consumer Research* 13 (September 1986), 196–213. See also Morris B. Holbrook and Mark W. Grayson, "The Seminology of Cinematic Consumption: Symbolic Consumer Behavior in *Out of Africa*," *Journal of Consumer Research* 14 (December 1987), 374–381.

[4] Elizabeth C. Hirschman, "The Ideology of Consumption: A Structural-Syntactical Analysis of 'Dallas' and 'Dynasty'," *Journal of Consumer Research* 15 (December 1988), 344–359.

Culture constitutes the phenomenal world in two ways. First, culture is the "lens" through which the individual views phenomena; as such, it determines how the phenomena will be apprehended and assimilated. Second, culture is the "blueprint" of human activity, determining the co-ordinates of social action and productive activity, and specifying the behaviors and objects that issue from both. As a lens, culture determines how the world is seen. As a blueprint, it determines how the world will be fashioned by human effort. In short, culture constitutes the world by supplying it with meaning.[5]

Culture determines consumption of such important activities as what, when, where, and with whom we eat. Culture, therefore, determines what is appropriate and effective for marketers to do in providing goods and services. It is a logical starting point for examination of consumer behavior.

WHAT IS CULTURE?

Culture refers to a set of values, ideas, artifacts, and other meaningful symbols that help individuals communicate, interpret, and evaluate as members of society. Culture does not include instincts, nor does it include idiosyncratic behavior occurring as a one-time solution to a unique problem.

Culture provides people with a sense of identity and an understanding of acceptable behavior within society. Some of the more important attitudes and behaviors influenced by culture are the following:[6]

1. Sense of self and space
2. Communication and language
3. Dress and appearance
4. Food and feeding habits
5. Time and time consciousness
6. Relationships (family, organizations, government, etc.)
7. Values and norms
8. Beliefs and attitudes
9. Mental process and learning
10. Work habits and practices

Macroculture refers to the sets of values and symbols that apply to an entire society. Social scientists ordinarily use the term *society* to refer to very large and complex, yet organized, social systems, such as a nation or perhaps

---

[5] Grant McCracken, "Culture and Consumption: A Theoretical Account of the Structure and Movement of the Cultural Meaning of Consumer Goods," *Journal of Consumer Research* 13 (June 1986), 71–81.

[6] Phillip R. Harris and Robert T. Moran, *Managing Cultural Differences* (Houston: Gulf Publishing Company, 1987), 190–195.

even Western civilization. **Microculture** refers to the sets of values and symbols of a more restrictive group, such as a religious, ethnic, or other subdivision of the whole. (In older textbooks, microcultures are usually called *subcultures,* but some observers have voiced concern that identifying ethnic groups as subcultures may connote inferiority. In this book, we use the term *microculture* to avoid any connotation of inferiority that the term *sub-* may imply.) In this chapter, we look at the American macroculture and some of the ethnic microcultures of North America. In Chapter 24, which deals with global marketing, we examine cultures throughout the world.

Culture includes both abstract and material elements. **Abstract elements** include values, attitudes, ideas, personality types, and summary constructs, such as religion. **Material components** include such things as books, computers, tools, buildings, and specific products, such as a pair of Levi's 501 jeans. Material elements of culture are sometimes described as **cultural artifacts** or the material manifestation of culture, thereby restricting the use of *culture* to abstract concepts.

SOCIALIZATION

The processes by which people develop their values, motivations, and habitual activity is called **socialization,** the process of absorbing a culture. From the time a baby looks up and begins cooing and smiling, he or she starts forming values through socialization. The process continues throughout a lifetime, causing people to adopt values that influence consumption — such as thrift, pleasure, honesty, and ambition. These life forces also produce specific preferences — relating to choices of color, packaging, convenience, hours of shopping, and characteristic interactions with salespeople and many others. Recently, considerable attention has been focused on **consumer socialization,** the acquisition of consumption-related cognitions, attitudes, and behavior. Earlier studies in consumer socialization focused on this process among young people, but increasingly the emphasis is on the lifelong development of such skills.[7]

Values are shared beliefs or group norms that have been internalized by individuals, perhaps with some modification. **Norms** are beliefs held by consensus of a group concerning the behavior rules for individual members. Although it is correct to speak of an individual's values, and we do so in Chapter 12, marketers more often study the values of groups, usually groups large enough to be important market targets.

WHERE DO CONSUMERS GET THEIR VALUES?

No human exists without values, yet babies are not born with them. An examination of how people are socialized reveals some of the basic elements of the concept of culture.

---

[7] George P. Moschis, *Consumer Socialization* (Lexington, Mass.: Lexington Books, 1987), 9.

CULTURE IS LEARNED   Unlike animals, whose behavior is more instinctive, humans are not born with norms of behavior. Instead, humans learn their norms through imitation or by observing the process of reward and punishment in a society of members who adhere to or deviate from the group's norms. Norms learned early in life may be highly resistant to promotional effort by marketers. When an advertiser is dealing with deeply ingrained, culturally defined behavior (about food, sex, basic forms of clothing, etc.), it is nearly impossible to change the marketing mix to conform with cultural values than to try to change the values through advertising. As an example, eating dogs, horses, sheep eyes, or even fish served with heads is normal and healthy behavior in some cultures. It is doubtful, however, that advertising would be successful in convincing most people in the United States to buy any of these forms of products.

CULTURE IS INCULCATED   Culture is passed from one generation to the next, primarily by institutions such as the family, religion, and schools. Early lifetime experiences and peers also transmit values; this process is shown in Figure 3.1. An understanding of future cultural proscriptions on behavior requires analysis of how these institutions are changing.

CULTURE REWARDS SOCIALLY GRATIFYING RESPONSES   Culture develops and exists almost as if it were an entity in itself. Some anthropologists

FIGURE 3.1
ENVIRONMENTAL INFLUENCES ON CONSUMER DECISION AND MARKETING STRATEGY: INTERGENERATIONAL TRANSMISSION OF VALUES

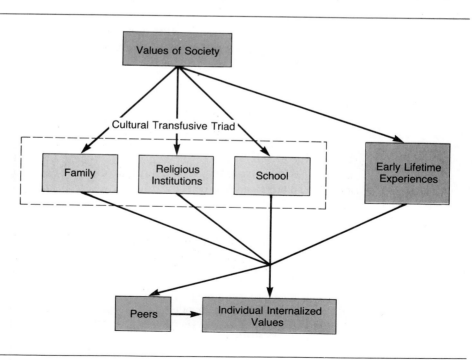

(known as **cultural functionalists**) view culture as an entity serving humans in their attempts to meet the basic biological and social needs of the society. For example, wearing ties is a cultural norm in many societies, even though it appears to provide no physical benefit. The need for "right behavior" or social status may be the only reward for wearing ties. In a nation such as Israel, where neither social nor physical needs are gratified by wearing ties, even members of the Knesset and other government leaders frequently do not wear ties except when dealing with international audiences.

When norms no longer provide gratification in a society, the norms are extinguished. To understand consumers, it is important to consider what "gratifying response," physical or social, is provided by a cultural norm. It may be possible to associate a product or brand with that cultural value or benefit. If that value is no longer gratifying in society, sales will suffer. For example, "meat and potatoes" used to be a desired food in the mass American culture. When most consumers worked on the farm or in strenuous manufacturing and labor jobs, high-energy and high-calorie foods were valued and gratifying. As those jobs were replaced increasingly by white-collar and other sedentary careers, the beef industry had to change its appeal to "Light cooking with beef."[8]

CULTURE IS ADAPTIVE   Culture is adaptive. Marketing strategies based upon values of society must also be adaptive. Why culture adapts is a controversial topic, reflecting the varied perspectives of cultural anthropologists and others who study society.[9] As change occurs in the traits that represent a society's ability to function, trends develop that provide marketing opportunities to those who spot the traits before competitors. How to spot these trends and maximize marketing opportunities is among the topics discussed in Chapter 20.

CORE VALUES OF A SOCIETY

Successful retailers know that a basic group of products is essential to the store's traffic, customer loyalty, and profits. These products are known as **core merchandise.** A group of values also exists basic to understanding the behavior of people. These values are called **core values.**

---

[8] W. Wayne Talarzyk, "California Beef Council," Cases and Exercises in Marketing (Hinsdale, Ill.: Dryden, 1986), 11–12.

[9] According to **cultural functionalism,** culture adapts to provide survival of the group, in what has been called social Darwinism. Another view, **dialectical materialism,** believes culture moves in a determined direction through a process of exchange and social interaction in competition for scarce resources. In the view of leading dialectical materialists such as Hegel and Marx, the direction is inevitably toward a classless society or communism. Other observers, known as **structuralists** and **historicalists,** believe culture follows some logic all its own based on patterns of the human mind. Structuralists are impressed more with the similarities between cultures than with differences. Marvin Harris, *Cultural Anthropology* (New York: Harper & Row, 1968), especially 320–329.

FIGURE 3.2
ADVERTISING
ADDRESSED TO
CORE VALUES AND
PRODUCT-SPECIFIC
VALUES

In the competition
for better value
in employee health,
life, and disability benefits...
Now there is

Victory

Central Benefits
Mutual Insurance Company
Blue Cross of Central Ohio

Source: Courtesy of Central Benefits Mutual Insurance Co.

Core values help explain consumer behavior in several ways. Core values frequently are *incorporated into advertising,* along with product benefits. In Figure 3.2, an insurance company advertisement (selling health insurance to businesses) appeals to the core American values of competition and victory while incorporating the product benefits and value of employee health.

Core values *define how products are used in a society.* Not only do core values determine what foods should be eaten but they also determine with what other foods are they appropriate, how they are prepared, and the time of day to eat them.

The core values of a nation *provide positive and negative valences for brands and for communications programs.* "As American as apple pie" communicated well in America for Chevrolet, but negative valences would surely result from associating cars with other foods such as bird nest soup or monkey gland stew (which have positive valences in China or Africa, respectively). Many marketers have used the Olympics to give positive valences to their company or product, appealing both to sports/health valences and to national pride.

The core values of a nation also *define acceptable market relationships.* In Japan, the relationships between groups of firms — dating back to east and west dynasties — are so rigid and complex that outsiders have difficulty obtaining distribution unless they form a joint venture with one of the groups.

People in rich economies tend to assume that transactions probably will be completed as specified. If problems arise, they have agencies such as the Better Business Bureau, and consumer protection agencies, and access to the legal system. In contrast, in poor countries, very little of this support structure may exist, and people may have little faith in trading with distant partners. Even when liberal laws exist, the social resources to protect economic transactions may not be available.

In peasant marketplaces, people develop long-term trading partnerships to provide reciprocating values to both buyers and sellers. These values include assured supply, reliable quality, employment of family members and neighbors, and price stability. In Haiti, trading partnerships are known as *pratik*. A buying *pratik* who knows that her selling counterpart is coming will wait at the proper place and time, refusing to buy from others stock that she is sure her *pratik* is carrying. Similarly, a selling *pratik* will refuse to sell to others until she has met her *pratik* buyer. In Nigeria, similar partnerships are called *onibara* relationships; in Jamaica, they are "customers" rather than "higglers"; in the Philippines, such relationships are called *suki*. In Guatemala, growers bargain vigorously in the marketplace with middlemen with whom they do not have personal relationships. A *cliente* middleman, in contrast, will pay the prevailing price with no bargaining and will almost always buy the products unless he has absolutely no use for them. In return, the agricultural producer is expected to deliver the best produce to the *cliente* middlemen.[10]

Core values affect these and many other marketing functions. We look in more detail in Chapter 24 at the core values of various nations around the world. There are, however, core values of the American society that affect consumption patterns and the marketing programs directed to American consumers. Most of these also affect Canadian markets, especially the Western provinces and Ontario, although the distinctive Canadian culture is more related on some dimensions to European than United States values.

AMERICAN VALUES AND THEIR INFLUENCE ON CONSUMPTION

In the United States, core values can be observed that permeate most aspects of the society. This is true even in a country as large as America. The United States reflects diverse values, however, because America is so young compared to Asian and European countries. The United States culture also reflects many national origins.

America was an agrarian nation only two generations ago. Although it

---

[10] Stuart Plattner, "Equilibrating Market Relationships" (paper presented to Society for Economic Anthropology Conference, Universiy of California-Davis, April 6–7, 1984).

is now primarily urbanized and suburbanized, many core values are still traceable to the agrarian base. Daily living is now regulated more by the clock and the calendar than by the seasons or degree of daylight. Most people are employees of large, complex organizations rather than farmers or shopkeepers. Goods and services are purchased rather than produced, with money or plastic rather than property as the denominator of exchange.

The origin of American values is described by Arensberg and Niehoff:

> *Where does this American character come from? . . . The values derived from life on the frontier, the great open spaces, the virgin wealth, and the once seemingly limitless resources of a "new world" appear to have affected ideas of freedom. Individualism seems to have been fostered by a commitment to "progress" which in turn was derived from expansion over three hundred years. Much of the religious and ethical tradition is believed to have come from Calvinist (Puritan) doctrine, particularly an emphasis on individual responsibility and the positive work ethic. Anglo-Saxon civil rights, the rule of law, and representative institutions were inherited from the English background; ideas of egalitarian democracy and a secular spirit sprang from the French and American Revolutions. The period of slavery and its aftermath, and the European immigration of three centuries, have affected the American character strongly.*[11]

Sometimes advertisers are accused of appealing mostly to fear, snobbery, and self-indulgence. Would advertisers be effective if they continually based their advertising on such appeals? Such an approach would be limited to special situations and specific groups. Notice in Figure 3.3 how an insurance company tries to identify itself with conservative values visually, while recognizing everyone's desire to grow. The values orientation in the copy is clear, however: "A new house. A promotion. A growing family," and the promise: "We'll be there when you need us. Helping you keep the commitments you make."

What are the core values that provide appeals for advertising and marketing programs? Eight of the most basic are described in the following pages.

MATERIAL WELL-BEING

Americans believe in the marvels of modern comforts: swift and pleasant transportation, central heating, air conditioning, instant hot and cold water, labor-saving devices of unending variety. It is almost a right to have such material things.

A familiar statement of core values says, "Cleanliness is next to godliness." As a consequence, marketers who expect to sell hotel space, food, or gasoline had better provide sanitary toilets and soft tissue. Proctor and Gamble and DuPont Textile Fibers Division both earn large profits from the continual stream of products essential to well-scrubbed and cleanly dressed Americans.

---

[11] Conrad M. Arensberg and Arthur H. Niehoff, "American Cultural Values," in James P. Spradley and Mihale A. Rykiewich, eds., *The Nacirema: Readings on American Culture* (Boston: Little, Brown and Company, 1980), 363–379. This section of the chapter is abstracted from Arensberg and Niehoff.

FIGURE 3.3
APPEAL TO CORE
VALUES IS
ESSENTIAL IN
SUCCESSFUL
ADVERTISING

Source: CNA Insurance Company.

Sewell Cadillac in Texas has become one of America's most successful Cadillac dealers. One of the keys of this success is a service area with floors scrubbed several times a day, literally clean enough to eat lunch off of.[12]

Achievement and success are measured to a large degree by the quantity and quality of material goods. There is little display value in the size of one's paycheck or bank account but plenty of prestige in articles that others can see: designer clothes, luxury personal cars, swimming pools, 200-watt equalized compact disc stereos, and personal computers for the children. Although some rebellion against such values was expressed in the 1960s and 1970s, it appears that material well-being is fundamental to the American value system — one that marketers can count on year after year. As the popular movie *Wall Street* opined, "In America, greed is good."

---

[12] Tom Peters and Nancy Austin, *A Passion for Excellence* (New York: Random House, 1985).

TWOFOLD MORALIZING

Americans believe in polarized morality. Twofold judgments are the rule: moral–immoral, legal–illegal, civilized–primitive, secular–sacred. This is not the yin-and-yang duality of the Chinese but a classification of actions as good or bad. Consequently, the evaluation that public officials do "bad" things causes enormous problems, whereas this behavior would be accepted as normal in other parts of the world. Most Americans may personally accept nonmonogamous sexual relationships, but accusations against former Senator Gary Hart ended his presidential campaign. Lt. Col. Oliver North was accused of breaking laws and taking money, but when in front of a congressional committee he was perceived to be honest and patriotic and generated widespread public support. Public personalities are considered ethical or unethical — not a little of both.

Marketing strategy is affected in many ways. Advertising that is "a little deceptive" is considered bad even if the overall message is largely correct. Salespeople in many countries are expected to give gifts to managers of client firms, but in North America, most corporations have policies that severely restrict or totally exclude the acceptance of gifts, even small holiday greetings. In many countries of the world, it would be considered immoral for a manager not to give preference in hiring to members of the manager's family or ethnic group. In North America, managers are expected to give jobs to the best-qualified person with severe sanctions against preference toward family or ethnic members, even though such preference may be common in the manager's social relationships. Gambling is "wrong" and often a criminal activity but "right" if organized as a state lottery to benefit a good cause.

WORK IS MORE IMPORTANT THAN PLAY

Work is serious, adult business. People are judged by their work. When strangers meet, often the first topic of conversation is the kind of work each does. People are supposed to "get ahead" and "make a contribution" to society through their work. What women have done in homes for centuries may be much more valuable than what has been done in factories and offices, but society appears to value women more when they perform work in offices and factories as men have traditionally done.

While work is associated in American values with high or necessary purpose and grim effort, play is associated with frivolity, pleasure, and children. In other cultures, festivals and holidays and children having fun are the most important events in the society. In America, even socializing is often work-related. Advertisements for most products appeal more to work situations than to having fun or "play." Saturday morning television ads, however, appeal to play values because they are for children.

TIME IS MONEY

Americans' view of time is different from that of many other cultures. In many countries, people actually distinguish between *hora Americana* versus *hora Mexicana* or *among Amelikan* versus *among Lao*. In doing so, they mean that American time is exact — that people are punctual, activities are scheduled, time is apportioned for separate activities, and the measure is the mechanical clock. Americans are often irritated when other people miss appointments or delivery schedules for promised orders. In some cultures, people have difficulty understanding the values that produce a felt need to keep hours or appointments precisely.

Time is closely related to work in American core values. Work is paid for in money-related time periods. In America, people work for 8 or 10 hours a day. If more time is worked, more money is expected, probably as "overtime." Although Americans may complain about the necessity of routine and the tyranny of the clock, they are thoroughly accustomed to such strictures, especially among the middle classes.

As the American business system has increased in influence throughout the world, the American concept of time (as well as its language and other core values) has influenced other cultures to some extent. But American businesspeople still must be sensitive to the distinctive American values relating to time.

EFFORT, OPTIMISM, AND ENTREPRENEURSHIP

Americans believe that problems should be identified and effort should be expended to solve them. With proper effort, one can be optimistic about success. Europeans sometimes laugh at their American friends who believe that for every problem there is a solution. When Americans find a problem, they form a committee or start a fund to solve it.

This thinking is based upon the concept that the universe is mechanistic, people are their own masters, and all is perfectible almost without limit. Thus, with enough effort, people can improve themselves and manipulate the part of the universe around themselves. This also produces a certain intolerance for people who have failed to do so by those who have succeeded. A failure in life is a person who "didn't have the guts" to "make a go of it" and "get ahead." American heroes are "can-do" people.

In the American culture, effort is rewarded, competition is enforced, and individual achievement is paramount. Activist, pragmatic values rather than contemplative or mystical ones are the basis of the American character. In America, only 6 percent of millionaires were born wealthy; most started very poor. For the American overseas, it is often difficult to accept the fact that those in authority have achieved their position by means other than their own effort. Americans may become angered or cynical by such situations or may make activist judgments and try to remedy the situation, using the American code of values. Entrepreneurship is one result of American values of effort and optimism.

In such a competitive society, some people win and some people lose. And that is fine. Being the best is morally acceptable; more than acceptable, it is the goal. Football reflects American values, and Vince Lombardi said it well: "Winning is not everything; it is the only thing." In business, excellence and being number one is the goal. Lee A. Iacocca, Chairman of the Board and Chief Executive Officer of Chrysler Corporation, gained the cooperation of the unions, fought the government, and fought the competitors. He won the admiration of Americans more than any business leader in recent years. His philosophy to become the best is the theme of Chrysler's advertising, as shown in Figure 3.4. Even when his company was found guilty of tampering with odometers, Iacocca accepted personal responsibility and fit in with American values by offering, along with extensions of warranties on the affected cars, an apology to the American public, saying, "We goofed up. It was dumb. I apologize. It won't happen again."

MASTERY OVER NATURE

American core values produce a conquering attitude toward nature. In Buddhism and Hinduism, people and nature are one, and people work with nature rather than attempt to conquer it. In America, lack of water to grow crops is conquerable by irrigation. Chemicals are used to kill bugs and weeds with little regard for nature's balance. This conquering attitude toward nature appears to rest on at least three assumptions: that the universe is mechanistic,

FIGURE 3.4
CHRYSLER ADVERTISING THEME "TO BE THE BEST": AN EXAMPLE OF EFFORT, OPTIMISM, AND ENTREPRENEURSHIP IN AMERICA

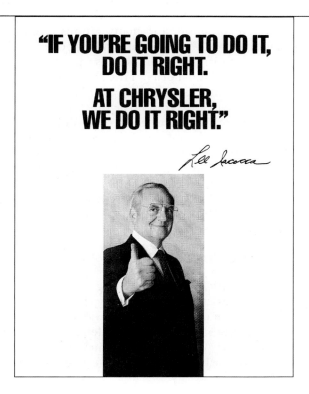

Source: Courtesy of Chrysler Corporation.

that people are the masters of the earth; and that people are qualitatively different from all other forms of life.

This Western view of life (shared by other cultures such as Israel and South Africa, and increasingly by Korea and other countries) has produced enormous agricultural productivity and industrial might. It also produces some blunders, such as when American military equipment designed for solid ground becomes bogged down in the soggy fields and marshes of Vietnam and Laos, or when helicopters fail to work in the blowing sands of Iran.

American advertising usually shows that people are in command of the natural environment. It is the exception that proves the rule when an advertiser deviates from core values by saying, "It's not nice to fool Mother Nature." There are always people waiting to buy the latest product to reverse nature's battle to make men bald, old people wrinkled, and people overweight. The ability to challenge nature is shown in Figure 3.5. Bosley Medical Group has become a major national provider of professional medical services by challenging nature.

EGALITARIANISM

American core values support the belief that all people should have equal opportunities for achievement. This is more of a moral imperative than an actual condition, and many groups face discrimination by other groups and individuals. Yet the core values, codified legislatively and judicially, favor equality of all people, if those people accept the core values and behaviors of the social majority. This effect on behavior is also supported by the value of humanitarianism, described below.

Americans often favor the "underdog," a trait that is difficult for people raised in some other cultures to understand. Open patterns of subordination, deference to royalty, or prestige based on variables other than personal achievement bother most Americans. People who get advantages without "earning" them are objects of ridicule. Persons of inherited wealth are subjects of such ridicule in both advertising and television programming. Lee Iacocca became a folk hero in America partly because of his immigrant background and underdog "fighting the big boys" positioning, even though he and his family were wealthy.[13]

HUMANITARIANISM

An American trait of coming to the aid of the less fortunate is widespread. It expresses itself in the giving of donations to unknown individuals and groups; in the outpouring of aid to Ethiopians or Armenians and other victims of famines, floods, and epidemics; in contributions of time and money to the Heart Association and countless other causes (with the exception, initially, of AIDS, which conflicted with other mainstream values); and in the rebuilding

---

[13] Lee Iacocca, *Iacocca* (New York: Bantam Books, 1984).

FIGURE 3.5
THE BOSLEY
MEDICAL GROUP:
SUCCESS THROUGH
MASTERY OVER
NATURE

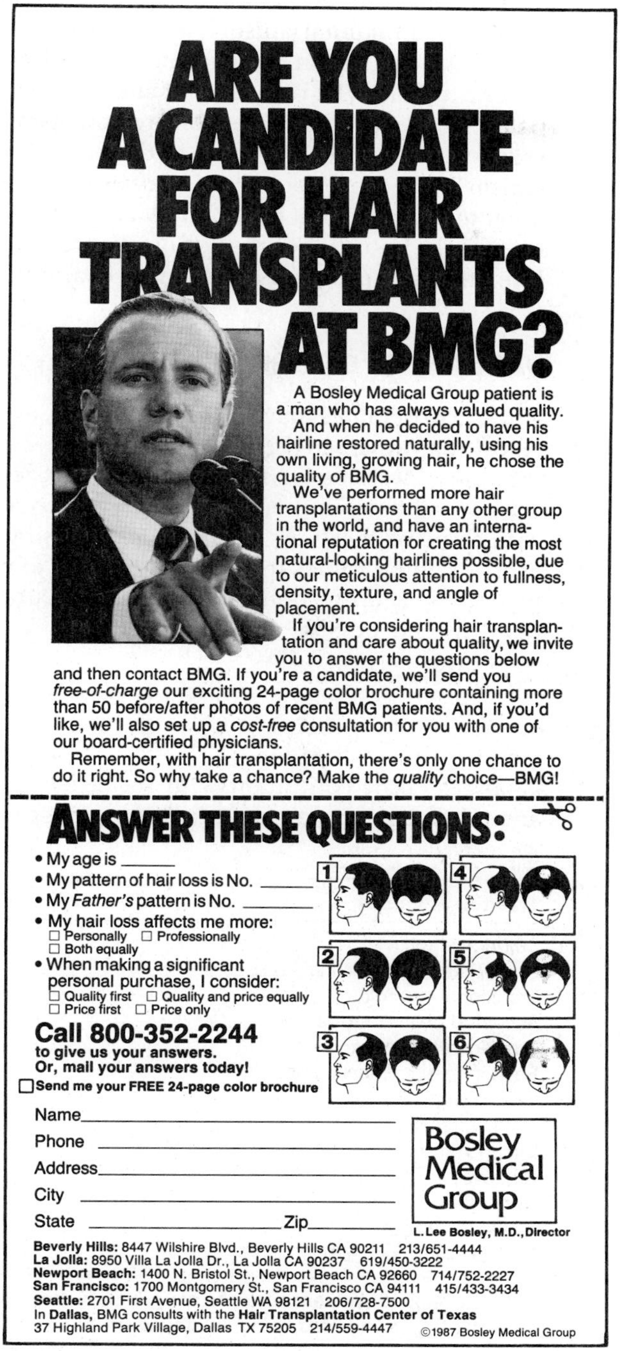

Source: Courtesy of Bosley Medical Group, Beverly Hills, California.

of factories and homes of conquered enemies after world wars. In some countries, humanitarianism is more personal and related to kinship obligations, but in America, giving is more organized and depersonalized. In India and other countries, the recipients of almsgiving are usually seen with outstretched palm; in the United States, the recipients are more likely to be unseen and reached though a committee or a direct mailing list. For marketers, humanitarianism has become not only a social responsibility but an important communications and marketing program. McDonald's, with its sponsorship of Ronald McDonald houses, youth organizations, and other community and national humanitarian programs, is a prime example.

VARIABILITY OF CORE VALUES

These core values have been described as typical of American society by cultural anthropologists and other observers. Not every American holds all the values described, and the further you are from being the "typical" middle-class or mainstream person, the more likely you are to hold values at variance with some of these. As you study advertising and marketing programs, however, examine values to see how they are expressed. When you prepare such programs, keep in mind that those that stray very far from core values are risky in their effects.

CHANGING VALUES

Changes occur continuously in society's values even though the core values are relatively permanent. Marketers must pay special attention to values in

TABLE 3.1 CHANGING VALUES IN WESTERN CIVILIZATION	Traditional Values	New Values
	Self-denial ethic	Self-fulfillment ethic
	Higher standard of living	Better quality of life
	Traditional sex roles	Blurring of sex roles
	Accepted definition of success	Individualized definition of success
	Traditional family life	Alternative families
	Faith in industry, institutions	Self-reliance
	Live to work	Work to live
	Hero worship	Love of ideas
	Expansionism	Pluralism
	Patriotism	Less nationalistic
	Unparalleled growth	Growing sense of limits
	Industrial growth	Information/service growth
	Receptivity to technology	Technology orientation

Note: Developed Western societies are gradually moving away from traditional values, and toward the emerging new values being embraced on an ever-widening scale.

Source: Joseph T. Plummer, "Changing Values," *The Futurist* 23 (January–February 1989), 10.

transition because they affect the size of market segments. Changes in values may alter responses to advertising as well as responses to service offerings and preferred formats for retailing. Some of the changes that are occurring in the 1990s have been identified in research at Young & Rubicam, shown in Table 3.1. They represent what Plummer calls a paradigm shift or a fundamental reordering of the way we see the world around us.[14]

Two types of forces explain both constancy and change in values. The first source of values is the triad of institutions: families, religious institutions, and schools. The second source is early lifetime experiences. Such experiences include wars, civil rights movements, economic realities, and many other factors. Institutions such as government and the media are important in transmitting influences on values. Individuals internalize values transmitted by these influences in a process affected by peers as well as an individual's own decision and learning process, as you saw in Figure 3.1.

CHANGING INSTITUTIONS

The triad of institutions known as family, religion, and education plays a key role in understanding the values of a society. As long as these institutions are stable, the values transmitted are relatively stable. When these institutions change rapidly, the values of consumers change, creating the need for corresponding changes in marketing and communications programs.

Some of the dislocative changes in these institutions are described in the next few pages. Although described in the context of the United States, similar trends are occurring in Canada, Europe, Japan, Australia, and other areas of the world.

DECLINING FAMILY INFLUENCES

Family is the dominant transfusive agent of values in most cultures. Many changes are occurring in the family, which we examine more closely in Chapter 6. We look at only a few basic influences on values now.

Less time for in-home or parent–child influence is available for children. This is partly due to increased enrollments in preschool or day-care facilities. Among 3 to 4 year olds, only 5.7 percent were enrolled in schools in 1965. Today tha number is approaching 60 percent. In the past, children spent the formative years up to 6 with their parents. Now children must increasingly learn their values outside the family. "Weekend parents" also cause values to be transmitted to children by substitute parents such as babysitters, schools, and media. Today's parents may have extensive travel responsibilities and longer, irregular working hours. With both parents gone from the home much of the time,

---

[14] Joseph T. Plummer, "Changing Values," *The Futurist* 23 (January–February 1989), 8–13.

especially among the higher social classes, the values of future leaders depend more heavily on sources outside the family.

Increasing divorce rates contribute to decreased family influence as children are socialized in one-parent households. The divorce rate has more than doubled in the past 20 years and in 1986 stood at 5.2 divorces per 1,000 people; current estimates are that about half of all marriages formed in recent decades will end in divorce.[15] The majority of children are now raised for part of their lives in single-parent households. Divorced men typically remarry younger women. Therefore, the husband's children from his first marriage are likely to be older than the wife's first children, causing problems for reconstituted families of different ages.[16]

The *isolated nuclear family* or geographical separation of the nuclear family from grandparents and other relatives (extended family) contributes to decline in family influences on value transmission. Much greater proportions of young people attending college cause higher percentages of families to take jobs geographically separated from where the family grew up and from the influence of the extended family. This removes an important stabilizing or traditionalizing influence on values. The result may be lack of heritage or a yearning for roots.

Communications and travel companies may benefit from geographical separation, provided they have effective marketing programs. Delta Airlines has developed a senior citizen program with ads that proclaim, "Attend weddings and family reunions and be sure to allow enough time to visit the grandchildren."

How should businesses respond to the diminished influence of family? Some companies are reviewing their policies about job interference with family life, providing quality day-care centers for employees, encouraging families to travel out of town with executives, involving spouses in company seminars and newsletters, providing scholarships for children of employees, providing marital counseling, and in other ways recognizing the changing role of the family.

CHANGING RELIGIOUS INFLUENCES

Judeo-Christian religious institutions historically played an important role in shaping the values of Western cultures. In recent years, these institutions have changed substantially.

Religious groups necessarily grow at the expense of others. Catholics have risen from tiny levels in 1776 to a quarter of the U.S. population largely

---

[15] Daphne Spain and Suzanne M. Mianchi, "How Women Have Changed," *American Demographics* 5 (May 1983), 19–25.

[16] Karhyn A. Lond and Barbara F. Wilson, "Divorce," *American Demographics* 10 (October 1988), 23–26.

because of European immigration in the early 1900s and current immigration from Hispanic countries. Baptists have replaced Anglicans (Episcopalians) as the dominant Protestant group. More recently, rapidly growing groups, such as the Latter Day Saints (Mormons), have become a major influence on many of the values of their members. Other non-Christian religions have been gaining influence in the United States, including many of the traditional Oriental religions and the New Age Movement.

Groups declining in membership currently include moderate and liberal groups (Lutherans, Methodists, Presbyterians, Episcopalians, and others). The greatest gains in religious preference currently in America are among fundamentalists and among those with no religious preference, according to the General Social Survey conducted by the National Opinion Center at the University of Chicago.[17] Catholics are gaining, but Hispanic fertility rates, cohort succession, and immigration are more important factors than conversion.[18] These trends are shown in Table 3.2, which also shows the inheritance and conversion ratios of each religious group. Conversions occur mostly among the young.

Current trends in religous affiliation and attitudes are associated with the secularization of religious institutions — or loss of religious function. According to a thesis developed by Francis Schaeffer, religion has become compartmentalized and has lost some of its capacity to judge secular values and structure.[19] Although religion has weakened as an institutional influence in American society, it may still be very important for individuals. Recent research concludes that religion influences life in private areas more than in the public realm. Specifically, religious influence is quite strong on family life, moderate on work life, and minimal on political action.[20] Among fundamentalists, the influence is more pervasive in all areas of life. Religion is especially important for families, but among people with no historical institutional affiliation, religious involvement may serve as a surrogate for family involvement for divorced, widowed, and unmarried consumers.[21]

There is some evidence that a new sense of religious commitment and understanding is emerging in the United States, Canada, and some other

---

[17] Tom W. Smith, "America's Religious Mosaic," *American Demographics* 6 (January 1984), 19–23.

[18] Smith, "America's Religious Mosaic," 19–23.

[19] Francis A. Schaeffer, *How Should We Then Live?* (Old Tappan, N.J.: Fleming H. Revel Company, 1976).

[20] Joseph B. Tamney and Stephen D. Johnson, "Consequential Religiosity in Modern Society," *Review of Religious Research* 26 (June 1985), 367–375.

[21] Kevin J. Christiano, "Church as a Family Surrogate: Another Look at Family Ties, Anomie, and Church Involvement," *Journal of Scientific Study of Religion* 25 (September 1986), 339–354.

TABLE 3.2
RELIGIOUS TRENDS

	Part 1 / Religious Composition by Birth Cohort				
	Year of Birth				
	Prior to 1907	1907–1923	1924–1940	1941–1957	1958–1965
Fundamentalists	11.8%	7.8%	9.2%	9.7%	12.0
Southern Baptists	12.3	13.7	13.9	12.4	14.4
Misc. Protestants	1.1	0.9	0.9	0.8	0.5
Other Baptists	6.7	6.7	7.5	7.8	7.2
Lutherans	9.5	9.4	8.3	7.1	5.7
Methodists	15.9	16.1	11.6	9.1	7.7
Inter/non-denominational	3.2	3.1	3.3	3.4	2.8
Liberals	3.4	3.3	2.5	1.5	0.8
Presbyterians	6.6	5.6	4.8	3.5	3.0
Episcopalians	3.3	2.9	3.0	2.2	1.8
Catholics	19.4	23.2	26.4	27.5	28.7
Jews	3.1	3.1	2.1	2.1	0.8
None	3.0	3.4	5.2	10.8	13.0
Other	0.6	0.8	1.2	2.0	1.5

	Part 2 / Religious Conversions	
	Percent of Current Members Raised in Same Faith	Ratio of Converts/ Disaffiliators[a]
Fundamentalists	52.0%	1.53
Southern Baptists	86.0	0.53
Misc. Protestants	40.5	1.15
Other Baptists	77.3	0.65
Lutherans	75.7	0.81
Methodists	72.4	0.57
Inter/non-denominational	27.8	2.74
Liberals	49.5	1.03
Presbyterians	59.8	0.81
Episcopalians	54.0	1.29
Catholics	89.7	0.57
Jews	93.3	0.40
None	16.1	3.32
Other	46.9	2.07
All	69.7	

[a] *A ratio greater than one means the religion gains more through conversion than it does through disaffiliation.*
Source: Tom W. Smith, "America's Religious Mosaic," *American Demographics*, 6 (June 1984), 22–23. Reprinted by permission.

countries. In the Gallup Poll, about one out of every three Americans now indicates being a born-again Christian, and among families with children present, the following religious practices are reported:

42 percent of parents pray before meals with their children.

38 percent attend church services with their children.

28 percent attend church-related activities with their children.

17 percent read the Bible with their children.

44 percent talk about God and religion with their children.

31 percent pray or meditate with their children.

23 percent watch or listen to religious programs with their children.[22]

What are the effects of changing religious institutions upon marketing? The answer seems to be that values of consumers in coming years will be more personal, diversified, and pluralistic. Retailers report more inventory shrinkage if religious institutions decline because employees may no longer think stealing is wrong. If the traditional Judeo-Christian value system declines, firms need to recruit more selectively and develop programs such as those of IBM that inculcate values among employees.[23]

Religious values are major influences on marketing, but what about the ability of marketing to affect religion? Can religious institutions use marketing methods to enhance effectiveness? The answer is yes. Much of the material presented in this text has been developed by Engel into a text specifically designed for religious organizations.[24] Religious institutions are doing consumer research and applying the results to marketing plans.[25]

A successful application of consumer research by a religious organization is the Garden Grove Community Church in California. Started in a drive-in theater, the church now has thousands of members attending consecutive services each week in the multimillion-dollar Crystal Cathedral and a top-rated electronic ministry in the United States, Canada, and Australia. The church also supports hospitals, senior citizen centers, youth music schools, and relief programs throughout the world and produces a television program that has survived the problems of other television evangelists in the late 1980s. The basic approach of the church is to do research to determine felt needs or areas of life where people need help and then develop a "shopping center for God — a part of the service industry to meet those needs."[26] The Crystal Cathedral, shown in Figure 3.6, serves not only as a highly visible landmark to attract customers but also as a logo or symbol for the many ministries and programs.

---

[22] George Gallup and David Poling, *The Search for America's Faith* (Nashville: Abingdon, 1980), 51.

[23] F. G. Buck Rogers, *The IBM Way* (New York: Harper & Row, 1986).

[24] James Engel, *Contemporary Christian Communications* (Nashville: Thomas Nelson, 1979).

[25] James F. Engel and H. Wilbert Norton, *What's Gone Wrong with the Harvest?* (Grand Rapids: Zondervan Publishing House, 1975); Donald McGavran, *Understanding Church Growth* (Grand Rapids: William B. Eerdmans, 1970).

[26] Robert H. Schuller, *Your Church Has Real Possibilities!* (Glendale, Calif.: Regal Book, 1974). Also see "Possibility Thinking and Shrewd Marketing Pay Off for a Preacher," *The Wall Street Journal* (August 26, 1979), 1ff.

FIGURE 3.6 THE CRYSTAL CATHEDRAL: AN EXAMPLE OF SUCCESSFUL MARKETING BY A RELIGIOUS ORGANIZATION

Source: Courtesy of Robert Schuller Ministries.

CHANGING EDUCATIONAL INSTITUTIONS

The third major institution that transmits values to consumers is education. The influence of education appears to be increasing, due partly to the increased participation of Americans in formal education and partly to the vacuum left by families and religious institutions.

A dramatic rise in formal education has occurred at all levels. The result is a highly educated work force. By 1988, one in four workers in the United States was a college graduate, up from about one in eight in 1970. Fewer women workers are college graduates compared to men, but currently more women are enrolled in colleges and universities than are men.[27] Weekend MBA programs, "Night Owl" and "Early Bird" programs, and other innovations in university continuing education departments encourage higher levels of education, even among those beyond the "normal" college age.

Other factors also change the influence of educational institutions on values and lifestyles. Prior to World War II, teachers originated mostly from the middle class and taught middle-class values. During the 1950s a new breed of teacher emerged as college enrollments from all social classes soared. Although the middle classes still dominate teaching, teachers now come to some extent from the entire spectrum of society. Students can expect to encounter teachers with values different from their own — in some cases radically different.

Another trend in education involves the emergence and proliferation of new teaching methods. Previously, teaching often emphasized description and memorization. This approach to learning implicitly, if not explicitly, says, "This is the way things are; just learn it," with no latitude for questioning. More recently, there has been a gradual but steady trend away from these methods toward analytical approaches emphasizing questioning of the old and the formulation of new approaches and solutions. There is no one correct answer; new horizons are encouraged. The case method in business schools is an example of this analytical, questioning approach. Another effect is described in *The Closing of the American Mind,* in which Bloom argues persuasively that American universities no longer provide much knowledge about values that arise from the great traditions of philosophy and literature.[28]

Consumers socialized in the new teaching environment may reject rigid definitions of right or wrong. Individuals, particularly younger consumers, are no longer willing to lead unexamined lives. This leads to aggressive consumerism, a topic examined later in this text. Marketing organizations must develop sales programs and product-information formats that give answers when customers ask about market offerings. Consumers may not complain to the firm but tell friends instead. Firms need complaint-management programs that seek out such complaints rather than just passively accept them. In a society where new consumers are increasingly scarce it may be profitable to compensate complaints of existing customers, even when compensation exceeds the product's profit margin.[29] Nordstrom and Stew Leonard's grocery stores are examples of firms that prosper with liberal refunds and complaint handling.

These three institutions — family, religion, and school — all contribute to transmitting traditional values as well as creating receptivity for changed lifestyles.

---

[27] Bryant Robey and Cheryl Russell, "A Portrait of the American Worker," *American Demographics* 6 (March 1984), 17–21.

[28] Allan Bloom, *The Closing of the American Mind* (New York: Simon and Schuster, 1987).

[29] Claes Fornell and Birger Wernerfelt, "Defensive Marketing Strategy by Customers' Complaint Management: A Theoretical Analysis," *Journal of Marketing Research* 24 (November 1987), 337–346.

INTERGENERATIONAL MOTIVATING FACTORS

Consumers are products of their environment. People strive as adults to achieve what they feel they were deprived of in early stages of life. As a result, consumer analysts can further understand the socialization process by studying early lifetime influences of groups of people who experience similar influences while growing up.

Cohort analysis is a method for investigating the changes in patterns of behavior or attitudes of groups called **cohorts.** A cohort is any group of individuals linked as a group in some way — usually by age. Cohort analysis focuses on actual changes in the behavior or attitudes of a cohort, the changes that can be attributed to the process of aging and that are associated with the events of a particular period, such as the Great Depression or the Watergate events.[30] Many marketing organizations, for example, have focused on the "Baby Boomers," a group of consumers of similar age and experiences.

PRE–WORLD WAR II CONSUMERS

Mature consumers experienced the Great Depression of the 1930s. Even more experienced World War II. The severity of these two events profoundly and indelibly affected the lives of consumers who lived through them. The effect of these events was so pervasive that it impacted on values of security, patriotism, and the acquisition and protection of material goods. Such values reflect the deprivations experienced during the depression and war.

INTERPERSONAL GENERATION

The cohort of consumers who were children in the 1950s and 1960s — the Interpersonal Generation — express awareness and concern for other people. This manifests itself in social concern on issues of civil rights and equal opportunity but also makes fashion more important. Not fashion in the sense of keeping up with the Joneses, as had been true of their parents, but fashion that emerged because of so much social contact and interpersonal awareness.

Vinson and Munson measured values of students and compared them to similar measures of values of parents, particularly as they relate to automobiles. The researchers concluded that parents emphasized attributes signifying utilitarian or functional characteristics associated with automobile ownership (e.g., quality of warranty, service required, handling), whereas students were more concerned with aesthetic and socially observable features (styling, prestige, luxury interior).[31]

---

[30] Norval D. Glenn, *Cohort Analysis* (Beverly Hills: Sage Publications, 1977).

[31] Donald Vinson and J. M. Munson, "Personal Values: An Approach to Market Segmentation," in Kenneth Bernhardt, ed., *Marketing: 1776–1976 and Beyond* (Chicago: American Marketing Association, 1976), 313–317.

THE "SELF-VALUES" GENERATION

The values of the most recent cohort of new consumers emphasize the self — self-expression, self-realization, self-help, do-it-yourself. Critical influences on this cohort include the energy crisis, inflation, feminism, Watergate, and an expanding tax and Social Security burden. Concern of the previous cohort was how to help others achieve the good life, but the most recent cohort is more concerned with the problem of maintaining the good lifestyle. You can see many of these values, likely to affect the 1990s, reflected in Table 3.1 at the beginning of this section.

An emerging mainstream value is egoism (not to be confused with egotism) or the moral philosophy that when people take care of themselves and leave others to do the same, society is most likely to thrive. The elections of U.S. Presidents Reagan and Bush reflected beliefs that good job prospects and the maintenance of consumers' preferred lifestyles were more likely under individualistic policies than those that emphasize welfare programs and centralized planning. Recent economic analyses reinforce the belief that welfare programs create rather than reduce poverty.[32]

The new consumer values are described by a marketing research firm that does much research in this area in the following manner:

> *The cornerstone of the new values is a shift from the concept of self-denial to a new focus-on-self. The new focus-on-self subsumes, "I have a duty to myself;" and more specifically: self-understanding, self-expression, self-fulfillment, concern with physcial self, etc. It means putting yourself, either on par with, or a little above the others that perhaps you once considered before yourself.*

On campus, more students in recent years have chosen business majors and other pragmatic subjects likely to bring financial success. The economy gets its strength more from entrepreneurship than from the large corporations and governmental programs typical of the immediate post–World War II era.[33]

On a personal basis, people with the new values must take responsibility for their own success. Among other things, this places a great emphasis upon nutrition and health. About 40 percent of Americans work out every day; a quarter take part in more than one sport, and wellness programs are increasingly supported by organizations as well as by individuals.[34] As a consequence, advertising frequently features such themes. Identification with healthy foods, personal appearance, and sports have surged in advertising usage for a broad array of products and services.

---

[32] Greg J. Duncan, *Years of Plenty* (Ann Arbor: Institute for Social Research, 1984).

[33] Peter F. Drucker, "An Entrepreneurial Economy," *Harvard Business Review* 62 (January–February 1984), 1ff.

[34] Doris Walsh, "A Healthy Trend," *American Demographics* 6 (July 1984), 4–6.

ETHNIC INFLUENCES ON CONSUMER BEHAVIOR

The norms and values of specific groups within the larger society are called **ethnic patterns.** Individual consumers may be influenced slightly or extensively by an ethnic group. Ethnic groups may be formed around nationality, religion, physical attributes, geographic location, or other factors. "Bikers" or the Grey Panthers might even be an important ethnic group for some.

Ethnicity is a process of group identification in which people use ethnic labels to define themselves and others. A "subjectivist" perspective reflects ascriptions people make about themselves. An "objectivist" definition is derived from sociocultural categories. In consumer research, ethnicity is best defined as some combination of these, including the strength or weakness of affiliation which people have with the ethnic group.[35] To the degree that people in an ethnic group share common perceptions and cognitions that are different from those of other ethnic groups or the larger society, they constitute a distinct ethnic group or market segment.[36]

The values of an ethnic microculture may conflict with the values of the macroculture. Individuals exhibit a synthesis of the macroculture and perhaps more than one microculture. As an example, the lifestyles and consumption patterns of a black person living in the western states may reflect both black and western microcultures and perhaps a religious group, as well as the values of the American macroculture. Keep in mind also that specific individuals may not reflect the values of the ethnic group with which they are commonly identified. A black or Hispanic consumer may, intentionally or otherwise, not reflect the culture that color or surname might indicate, and an Anglo consumer might assimilate and reflect the music, language, foods, or other aspects of an ethnic microculture.

NATIONALITY GROUPS

America is a montage of nationality groups. It has been called the greatest genetic pool of malcontents in the world, composed mostly of people or the descendants of people who were dissatisfied in their original nation and sought something better. Of the 226 million people counted in the 1980 census, more than 118 million traced their origins to one foreign nation, while nearly 70 million more listed multiple ancestry. England is the background nation for 26.34 percent of Americans, followed closely by Germany with 26.14 percent. The 50-million figure for "English" Americans is higher than the current population of England. The Irish are the third largest, with 17.77

[35] Rohit Deshpanae, Wayne D. Hoyer, and Naveen Donthu, "The Intensity of Ethnic Affiliation: A Study of the Sociology of Hispanic Consumption," *Journal of Consumer Research* 13 (September 1986), 214–219.

[36] Elizabeth C. Hirschman, "An Examination of Ethnicity and Consumption Using Free Response Data," in AMA *Educators' Conference Proceedings* (Chicago: American Marketing Association, 1982), 84–88.

percent, followed by Afro-Americans at 11.13 percent. Other significant nationality groups include French, Italian, Scottish, Polish, and Mexican, but recent census figures register 54 countries represented with 100,000 or more American residents.

Some immigrants identify with much of their culture of origin. Others do not. A variable closely associated with national ethnic identity is the language spoken at home. Even though the Chinese are usually not as recent immigrants as other nationality groups, 81 percent speak Chinese at home, indicating the great importance of cultural identity among Chinese. About 43 percent of Americans who speak a language other than English are Hispanics. Cuban-Americans speak Spanish at home at a frequency of 92 percent, compared to Mexican-Americans, who speak Spanish at home in 77 percent of the households.[37]

RELIGIOUS ETHNIC GROUPS

Religious groups have important influences on consumption. Mormons, for example, may refrain from purchasing tobacco, liquor, and other stimulants but are prime prospects for fruit juices endorsed by Marie and Donnie Osmond. The *Christian Science Monitor* is not the best place for ads for Anacin or Tylenol. Seventh-Day Adventists limit their purchases of meat but may be prime targets for vegetable-based foods.

Born-again Christians are less materialistic and less interested in consumer goods than other Americans, have low use of credit, and weaker-than-average preferences for national brands. They have higher per capita consumption, however, of automobiles and motorcycles, groceries and fast food, apparel stores, sporting goods, insurance, and products from hardware stores, and fabric and pattern stores.[38]

Jewish ethnicity is both religious and national and is an attractive market for many firms. Food products provide specific identification for kosher certification. Maxwell House Coffee and Tetley Tea have tried to give their brands special appeal to Jewish consumers by featuring bagels in their ads. Star-Kist says, "Beautify a bialy with Star-Kist tuna salad surprise." Chef Boy-Ar-Dee promotes its macaroni shells with the line, "Treat your macaroni mayvin to real Italian taste."

Recent research has concentrated on differences in cognitive processing and other variables related to ethnicity. Hirschman found that Jewish norms create more childhood information exposure than among other groups, more adult information seeking, consumption innovativeness, consumption information transfer, and more active memory capacity. Jewish consumers are

---

[37] Edith McArthur, "What Language Do You Speak?" *American Demographics* 6 (October 1984), 32–33).

[38] Brad Edmondson, "Bringing in the Sheaves," *American Demographics* 10 (August 1988), 28–32.

more disposed toward sensory gratification and arousal compared to other nationality groups, as evidenced by the types of leisure activities they prefer and their motives for engaging in these activities. Jewish (and also Hispanic) consumers appear more oriented toward sensual behavior (e.g., making love) in leisure activity than do other nationality groups that have been examined, and differ substantially from Christians in product salience rankings. The research by Hirschman clearly indicates that ethnicity (Jewish or otherwise) is a variable of large potential influence. The more an individual consumer identifies with the ethnic group, the greater the influence is likely to be.[39]

GEOGRAPHIC CULTURE

Geographic areas in a nation sometimes develop their own culture. The Southwest area of the United States is known for casual lifestyles featuring comfortable dress, outdoor entertaining, and active sports. The Southwest may also appear to be more innovative toward new products such as cosmetic surgery when compared to conservative, inhibited attitudes that characterize some areas of the nation. Climate, religious affiliations of the population, nationality influences, and other variables are interrelated to produce a core of cultural values in a geographic area.

Nine Nations of North America, as conceived by Joel Garreau,[40] cuts across national, state, and provincial borders of North America. This conceptualization incorporates the culture of each area, as well as its climate, institutions, business organizations, and resources such as mineral and water. In Garreau's system North America is described as consisting of the following areas: The Foundry (industrial Northeast), Dixie, Ectopia (northern Pacific rim), Mexamericana (Southwest wealthy area), Breadbasket, Quebec, The Empty Quarter (Northwest Canada), the Islands, and New England.

The application of geographic values to marketing is explained by Kahle:

> *Contemporary marketing managers must also know that marketing activities often vary from one place to another. Because the underlying causes of success and failure in various places may not always be evident, understanding the values of various regions may provide an important clue to deciphering what sometimes seems like a regionally random pattern of successful experiences in marketing both new and established products. For example, an advertisement promoting the capacity for self-fulfillment (e.g., "Set yourself free with Stouffer's") of a product may be more successful in the West than in the South. Security, on the other hand, may be a more successful appeal*

---

[39] Findings in this paragraph are summarized from Elizabeth C. Hirschman, "American Jewish Ethnicity: Its Relationship to Some Selected Aspects of Consumer Behavior," *Journal of Marketing* 45 (Summer 1981), 102–109; and Elizabeth C. Hirschman, "Ethnic Variation in Leisure Activities and Motives," in AMA *Educators' Conference Proceedings* (Chicago: American Marketing Association, 1982), 93–98.

[40] Joel Garreau, *The Nine Nations of North America* (Boston: Houghton Mifflin Company, 1981).

in the South than in comparably urbanized areas of the West (e.g., "Protect your home from break-ins with Electronic Touch Alarm"). For personal computers, an advertising campaign emphasizing how computers can help one accomplish his/her goals or emphasizing the computer attributes that facilitate accomplishment will probably be more effective in the East than in the South, and particularly in the West South Central.[41]

ASIAN AMERICAN CULTURE

Asian-Americans are rapidly increasing in attractiveness as a target for marketing organizations for two reasons. First, they are growing in number. Second, Asian-Americans have higher incomes, more education, and are more likely to own a business than other minorities.[42] Asian-Americans are usually defined to include Chinese, Japanese, Koreans, Vietnamese, Cambodians, Laotians, Filipinos, Asian Indians, Pakistanis, Hawaiians, Samoans, Guamanians, Fiji Islanders, and other Asians and Pacific Islanders living in the United States. Some immigrants from Hong Kong, looking for safety and refuge before the 1997 change of control, bring substantial amounts of capital to the United States and Canada.

The Asian-American culture is characterized by hard work, strong family ties, appreciation for education, and other values that lead to success in entrepreneurship, technical skills, and the arts. The success also may bring conflict with more entrenched immigrants and other consumers.

The socioeconomic characteristics of the Asian-American market attract marketers, but success in marketing programs hinges on understanding the distinctions of the microculture. Consumer-in-Focus 3.1 shows how a dentist — perhaps more sensitive to ethnic influence than others would be because of his own ethnic identity — achieved success in selling to Asian-American consumers. Careful reading of this box serves to indicate other details of most Asian microcultures.

Retailing and advertising are two areas of marketing directly affected by national ethnic groups. Many cities contain large groups of relatively homogeneous ethnic groups, creating the opportunity for stores featuring ethnic foods and other products. Staff may need to be bilingual. National- and language-oriented media may promote greater loyalty among the readers and listeners, as well as provide excellent "cost-per-thousand" of concentrated market targets. Korean-Americans have substantially more education than other groups and may respond better to communications than less educationally oriented groups.

---

[41] Lynn R. Kahle, "The Nine Nations of North America and the Value Basis of Geographic Segmentation," *Journal of Marketing* 50 (April 1986), 37–47, at 44.
[42] Wendy Manning and William O'Hare, "Asian-American Businesses," *American Demographics* 10 (August 1988), 35–39.

3.1 CAN AN ETHNIC DENTIST FIND HAPPINESS SELLING GERMAN CARS TO THE CHINESE?

San Francisco has long been the capital of Asian America. But Ron Greenspan, an orthodontist in a comfortable San Francisco neighborhood, had a small practice that had changed from 70 percent white in 1969 to 70 percent Asian a decade later.

Straightening teeth, however, was never Greenspan's great love — cars were. In 1981, he bought one of San Francisco's two Volkswagen dealerships for $250,000. At the time, this was a business going nowhere. The flocks of youthful, white San Franciscans, who once bought "Bugs" by the boatload, now were opting for more expensive German imports or cheaper cars from Japan.

It was natural that Greenspan would find former patients among his new customers. What was not so predictable is that this Jewish dentist from Cleveland could build a booming trade selling German cars to the Chinese. That required a good deal of ingenuity.

Greenspan started out by placing ads in such outlets as the *Asian Yellow Pages*. He mailed fliers into middle-class Asian neighborhoods such as the Richmond section of San Francisco, and the nearby suburb of Daly City, with its large concentration of Filipinos. Taking his cue from his salesman father, Nat, who had encouraged him as a youth to sell everything from shoe polish to toilet deodorizers door-to-door, Greenspan sent his salespeople out into the streets of the city to visit shops and hangouts frequented by the Asian bourgeoisie.

Bringing Asian customers into the showroom, however, was the easy part. Persuading them to buy was where the real challenge began. Most intimidating was the Chinese penchant for tough bargaining over price. To the Chinese, this is simply a normal part of the business culture. But to someone more accustomed to American business — even a car salesperson — the exchange can seem downright cutthroat. "When the guy comes in here and makes a ridiculous offer on a car, you don't get mad," Greenspan instructed his sales force. "You come back with something equally ridiculous and have a good laugh. Then start your real negotiation."

Another facet of Greenspan's "Asian Sensitivity Training" focused on dealing with the family. The Chinese prefer shopping in large family groups, with buying decisions usually made by the family elders. Greenspan explained to his salespeople that while the car might be for a teenage schoolgirl or a middle-aged engineer, the successful sales pitch may have to be directed to the grandfather or elderly uncle. To help things along, 75-year-old Nat Greenspan is often on hand to make the generational connection.

Largely as a result of sales to Asian-Americans, Greenspan has now boosted car sales from only 20 a month to more than 100, ranking among the top few VW dealers in America.

Source: Excerpted from Joel Kotkin, "Selling to the New America," *Inc.* (July 1987), 46–47. Reprinted with permission, *Inc.* magazine. Copyright © 1987 by Goldhirsh Group, *Inc.*, 38 Commercial Wharf, Boston, MA 02110.

BLACK CULTURE

Black culture refers to a common heritage rather than to a skin color. In the United States, the black heritage is conditioned by an American beginning in slavery, a shared history of discrimination and suffering, confined housing opportunities, and denial of participation in many aspects of the majority culture. Greater homogeneity in black markets than among white markets has been historically a valid assumption, although that may be challenged as well-educated blacks achieve substantial separation in income and social status from other blacks.[43]

The black market is worthy of serious marketing attention. It has a population base of over 26 million (and growing faster than whites) and buying power estimated as high as $140 to $150 billion. If U.S. black consumers were considered a separate country, that country would rank as eleventh largest in the free world. The black middle class is emerging as an important source of consumer buying power and influence. We look more closely at demographic changes occurring in black and other ethnic groups in Chapter 20.

Structural influences shape black ethnic markets. They also inhibit some black consumer preferences or intentions. These structural influences include low income, educational deprivation, different family characteristics, and, of course, discrimination.

INCOME DEPRIVATION

The black culture is sometimes associated with the low-income culture. This confusion is not difficult to understand because black consumers average much less income than white consumers. About 30 percent of black families are below the poverty level, as defined by the U.S. Department of Commerce, compared to only about 10 percent of white families. There are more white families below the poverty level in absolute terms, but the percentage of black families is larger.[44]

Two factors related to low income among black families are significant in the study of consumer behavior. First, there is the direct effect derived from reducing spending power. Consumers often must buy from stores that welcome food stamps; many products are not financially within the reach of poor consumers; income must be spent on the basics of life to a large degree.

The second factor is the methodological complexity of separating effects due to low income from those due to being black. Some studies attempt to correct for the income differences when reporting black–white differences, but many report "differences" between black and white consumers that are

[43] Reynolds Farley and Suzanne M. Bianchi, "The Growing Gap Between Blacks," *American Demographics* 5 (July 1983), 15–18.
[44] U.S. Department of Commerce, *Current Population Reports*, Series P-20 (Washington, D.C.: U.S. Government Printing Office, 1988).

mostly differences in income levels. If marketers do not recognize this problem, it is easy to minimize the importance of middle- and higher-income black market targets. There are more similarities than differences in black and white spending. Most of the differences are linked to blacks' lower incomes and their concentration in central cities.[45]

EDUCATIONAL DEPRIVATION

Inadequate education places black consumers at a disadvantage not only in earning income but in acquiring consumer skills. Such skills must be learned "on the street" if not at school. Because of inadequate resources or by design, schools have often failed in helping black consumers master the educational skills needed for full participation in the market system.

Quality education can also provide "a way out" for black consumers. Some advertisers sponsor contests in which the prizes are scholarships. Ads showing consumer durables and other expensive goods often use models portraying occupations that require education, knowing that many black customers recognize this is the best way to upward mobility and the middle-class lifestyle.

FAMILY CHARACTERISTICS

The black culture is influenced by unique family characteristics, primarily a highly mobile family structure. There also is a high proportion of families headed by females, perhaps twice as high as for whites. This gives more importance to females in influencing purchases, as well as creating subtleties of relationships an advertiser must understand and consider in the execution of creative strategy.

The black family is much younger than the typical white family. The median age is about 5 years younger, a factor accounting for differences in preferences for clothing, music, shelter, cars, and many other products and activities.[46]

DISCRIMINATION

The effects of discrimination on the black culture are so massive and enduring that they cannot be ignored in the analysis of consumer behavior. Discrimination has been particularly restrictive on black consumption decisions in the area of housing.

Black consumers, as a result of years of discrimination, should have substantial skepticism toward white businesses. Many businesses contributed to segregated residential patterns and limited employment opportunities. They

---

[45] William O'Hare, "Blacks and Whites: One Market or Two?" *American Demographics* 9 (March 1987), 44–48.
[46] A collection of articles on this topic is found in Harriette Pipies McAdoo, ed., *Black Families* (Newbury Park, Calif.: Sage Publications, 1988).

FIGURE 3.7
KENTUCKY FRIED
CHICKEN USES ITS
ADS TO IMPROVE
ITS RAPPORT WITH
THE BLACK
COMMUNITY

Source: Courtesy of Kentucky Fried Chicken.

supported invisibility of blacks in the media until recent years. Today, firms that make a special effort to show sensitivity to the black culture, use black media wisely, and stand against discrimination may be able to turn a problem into an opportunity. Notice how Kentucky Fried Chicken (Figure 3.7) attempts to build rapport with black consumers. The black franchisee reflects a common value in the black microculture: that black individuals who succeed have an obligation to help others, to "put something back." This ad appeared in *Ebony* magazine.

BLACK CONSUMPTION PATTERNS

Do blacks differ much in their consumption patterns from other market segments? The similarities are much greater than the differences, especially among middle-income groups. Many differences in consumption are explained by income differences.

Many factors must be considered in developing marketing programs for the black market. Numerous studies provide guidelines for developing effective programs.[47] Marketers must consider both cultural and structural elements. A fast-food chain, for example, completed a marketing research project among black consumers and found lower per capita purchases of hamburgers among black than among white consumers. The chain's stores located in black, inner-city areas, however, had the highest volume of any stores in the nation — apparently in conflict with the market research report. At first, executives were bewildered by the research findings. The answer lies, however, in the population-density ratios of the areas surrounding the store. While the average per capita consumption was lower, so many people living in the neighborhood bought hamburgers that the store's total volume was very high.

Consumer research has focused on similarities and differences between whites and blacks in the United States, starting with early reviews by Bauer and Cunningham and others.[48] For the most part, these studies failed to control for socioeconomic status or other structural variables.[49] Often they were conducted in a single city, quite a few years ago. Thus, for the consumer researcher a dilemma exists. Which of the many studies are still valid? Which were valid to begin with? It would be incorrect to disregard all of them because some — such as the finding that blacks are very loyal to specific brands — have been reported repeatedly.[50]

Our solution to the dilemma is to report findings about black and white differences in Table 3.3, which describes findings from many studies, organized by Moschis around the topic of black consumer socialization. As you read through these findings, remember that some are based upon early research that may not be true today. There is no easy way to determine which findings are still valid or which need modification. Nevertheless, they provide propositions about black consumer behavior and ways to reach black markets. The propositions can be considered as hypotheses helpful in the design of marketing programs. When you are in the position of responsibility for developing marketing programs, you may want to repeat the studies underlying the propositions and extend them to your specific product or situation before investing large amounts of resources.

---

[47] D. Parke Gibson, *$70 Billion in the Black* (New York: Macmillan, 1978); B. G. Yovovich, "The Debate Rages On: Marketing to Blacks," *Advertising Age* (November 29, 1982), M-10; David Astor, "Black Spending Power: $140 Billion and Growing," *Marketing Communications* (July 1982), 13–18; P. A. Robinson, C. P. Rao, and S. C. Mehta, "Historical Perspectives of Black Consumer Research in the United States: A Critical Review," in C. T. Tan and J. Sheth, eds., *Historical Perspectives in Consumer Research* (Singapore: National University of Singapore, 1985) 46–50.

[48] Raymond A. Bauer and Scott M. Cunningham, *Studies in the Negro Market* (Cambridge, Mass: Marketing Science Institute, 1970). Also Donald Sexton, "Black Buyer Behavior," *Journal of Marketing* 36 (October 1972), 36–39.

[49] Thomas E. Ness and Melvin T. Stith, "Middle-Class Values in Blacks and Whites," in Robert E. Pitts, Jr., and Arch G. Woodside, *Personal Values and Consumer Psychology* (Lexington, Mass.: Lexington Books, 1984), 255–270.

[50] Alphonziz Wellington, "Traditional Brand Loyalty," *Advertising Age* (May 18, 1981), S-2.

**TABLE 3.3
BLACK CONSUMER
BEHAVIOR**

Sixteen Propositions Summarizing Literature

1. Socioeconomic deprivation leads black youths to behave differently than whites in an effort to upgrade their status. Black youths, in relation to their white counterparts, are more likely to:
   a. have higher occupational aspirations
   b. have stronger desires for conspicuous consumption
   c. be more impatient regarding acquisition of socially conspicuous items
   d. be less likely to defer consumption gratifications
2. Black youths, compared to their white counterparts, are more likely to respond favorably to marketing stimuli. They tend to:
   a. have more positive attitudes toward marketing stimuli
   b. be more susceptible to marketing practices
3. Black youths are more likely than white youths to use brand names when purchasing low involvement products.
4. The black youth's propensity to use brand name as a criterion in purchasing products declines with socioeconomic status.
5. White youths are more likely than their black counterparts to use price as a criterion when purchasing low involvement products.
6. Black girls in comparison with white girls are more likely to:
   a. acquire greater independence than boys
   b. participate more in family purchasing decisions than boys
7. Black youths are more likely to have favorable orientations toward television than their white counterparts. Black youths are more likely than white youths to:
   a. watch television
   b. evaluate television stimuli as being realistic
   c. use television for consumer information
   d. model after television characters
8. White youths are more likely than black youths to use newspapers for information about consumption.
9. Black youths are less likely than white youths to interact with parents about consumption matters.
   a. Black youths discuss consumption less frequently than white youths.
   b. Black youths are less likely to model after their parents' consumer behavior than white youths.
10. White youths are socialized into the consumer role earlier than black youths.
11. Different socialization processes operate among black and white youths.
12. Black adult consumers are more likely than their white counterparts to emphasize consumption. Blacks are more likely than whites to:
    a. hold materialistic values
    b. spend a larger proportion of their available income on items of social status and social significance
    c. be innovators of socially conspicuous products
    d. have higher occupational aspirations
13. Blacks are more likely than whites to trade goods and services among family members.
14. Black consumers are not likely to interact with the marketplace as effectively and efficiently as white consumers. Blacks are less likely than whites to:
    a. seek information
    b. consider a larger number of alternatives
    c. evaluate alternatives on a large number of objective attributes
15. Black/white differences in consumer behavior are contingent on the adult person's socioeconomic status. When social class is taken into account:
    a. Blacks are more likely to hold egalitarian sex role perceptions about household decisions.
    b. Black/white differences in consumer behaviors are greater among lower-class than higher-class adults.
16. With increasing age, older black consumers are more likely to experience declining activity in consumption than older white consumers.

Source: George P. Moschis, *Consumer Socialization* (Lexington, Mass.: Lexington Books, 1987), 247–258. Reprinted by permission of the publisher.

HISPANIC CULTURE

Hispanics are the fastest-growing ethnic market in the United States. Although the 1980 census reported 14.6 million, the actual number is higher, with some estimates as high as 20 million. Sometime close to the year 2000, most experts believe Hispanics will outnumber blacks because of immigration and higher birth rates. The Hispanic market is 88 percent concentrated in cities, an attractive feature for media plans, distribution facilities, and other elements of marketing programs.

WHO IS HISPANIC?

The key element in the Hispanic culture is language and identity rather than national origin. *Chicano* is sometimes used to refer to persons born in the United States of Mexican descent. *Latino* is a more general term, used to identify those of Latin-American origin. *Hispanic* is the term used by the Census Bureau, and includes those of Spanish surname and Spanish origin.

Hispanic consumers are often segmented into four groups. *Mexicans* are the largest segment, about 60 percent of all Hispanics. They are concentrated in the Southwest, and 53 percent were born in the United States. They tend to be young and have large families. *Puerto Ricans* are about 15 percent of all Hispanics. They are concentrated in the Northeast, especially New York City. Most have arrived in the past 25 years, and many are now in middle age, with young children born in the United States. *Cubans* are about 7 percent of all Hispanics and are concentrated in the Southeast. Only 7 percent were born in the United States. Cubans are the oldest group, have few children, and are the "aristocracy" in terms of occupation, education, and income. *Other Hispanics* constitute 18 percent, heavily from Central America, and are dispersed geographically. They are 93 percent foreign-born and mostly young adults with few children.[51]

The diversity provides differences in values and motivations. Mexican-Americans are more likely to be assimilated into the U.S. culture, with less desire to return home. Cubans are more likely to consider themselves stranded in the host country. Although they may not want to return home, they are more likely than are other Hispanics to think of themselves as Hispanic first and American second.[52] Cuban income is also much higher than for any other Hispanic group, roughly at or above the average American income. Puerto Ricans have the lowest average of any Hispanic group.

Language is often described as a unifying factor, but even this is not always true. An advertiser describing brown sugar in Spanish would need to say *azucar negra* in New York, *azucar prieta* in Miami, *azucar cafe* in California,

---

[51] Daniel Yankelovich, *Spanish USA* (New York: Yankelovich, Skilly & White, Inc., 1981). Also see reports on a repetition in 1984 of the same study in "Homogenized Hispanics," *American Demographics* 7 (February 1985), 16.
[52] Yankelovich, *Spanish USA*.

azucar morena in South Texas, and *azucar pardo* in other places. In New York, an insecticide company advertised to Puerto Ricans that its product would kill all *bichos* (bugs), without understanding that the colloquial understanding to Puerto Ricans for *bichos* is a reference to male genitals.

Culturally unaware marketers might assume that because Hispanics are bilingual, it would be adequate to communicate with them in English. About 94 percent speak Spanish in the home, and studies show that Hispanics think in Spanish — creating the need for marketers to communicate in Spanish-based forms to be most effective.[53]

MARKETING TO CULTURAL VALUES

The Hispanic culture provides high value on quality. Many Hispanics emigrated from poorer countries. They seek status symbols that demonstrate that they have "arrived." For example, Bulova watches had an image in the Hispanic market of a "cheap American product." To counter this image, Hispanic media were used to position Bulova as an expensive but affordable piece of jewelry. Emphasis was placed upon the fact that Bulova had an extensive line of 18-karat gold watches, because Hispanics view 14-karat as synonymous with gold-plated. These efforts achieved for Bulova a 40 percent share in the Spanish-speaking market.

When Liggett & Myers Tobacco targeted a new cigarette toward Hispanics, it faced a major problem. Brand-loyal Hispanics preferred Marlboro and Winston. Rather than do a superficial adaptation by translating one of their brands into Spanish, Liggett conducted a major study involving personal interviews with Hispanic families in New York, Miami, San Antonio, and Los Angeles. Based on that study, Liggett introduced an entirely new cigarette. It had to be a full-flavored blend, because low-tar products and menthols would not be well accepted. To convey status and machismo, the package was designed with gold letter on paper with a rustic rosewood look. Names with a slight Latin ring, such as Dorado, tested well, as did L&M Superior. However, if the cigarette were identified as an Hispanic cigarette, rather than for Anglos as well, the cigarette might also be rejected.[54]

Coupons are thought to be not as effective with Hispanics as with Anglos or with blacks because of the stigma coupons have for people who came to this country poor. Hispanics are proud that they are now making a better living. They may not want to use coupons that are "for people who can't afford to pay the full price."[55]

Some products have made successful adaptations to the Hispanic market. Cudahy established a premium bacon called Rex based on the strategy that

---

[53] Jim Sondheim, Rodd Rodriquez, Richard Dillon, and Richard Parades, "Hispanic Market: The Invisible Giant," *Advertising Age* (April 16, 1979), S-20.

[54] Ronald Alsop, "Liggett Tests a New Cigarette Developed for Hispanic Tastes," *Wall Street Journal* (July 12, 1984), 29.

[55] Examples are for Luiz Diaz-Altertini, "Brand-Loyal Hispanics Need Good Reason for Switching," *Advertising Age* (April 16, 1979), SX-23.

a lean, premium bacon could sell in a 12-ounce size for prices comparable to the biggest competitor's (Farmer John) 16-ounce package. The package shouts the message, *"Vale su peso en carne."* Beers such as Budweiser and Miller have battled to sponsor community celebrations such as *Cinco de Mayo* and the Independence Day Fair because of their importance in the Spanish culture.

The family is very important in Hispanic culture, differing from Anglos not only in values but also in size (larger) and age (younger).[56] Look at Figure 3.8 and see how Ford Motor has adapted its advertising theme to this important value in the Hispanic culture.

AVOIDING MARKETING BLUNDERS

Failure to understand the Hispanic culture can lead to marketing blunders. Three major types are common and have been identified by Humberto Valencia as translation blunders, culture misunderstandings, and Hispanic idiosyncrasies.[57]

TRANSLATION BLUNDERS   Translation blunders occur in Hispanic markets just as they often do in global markets. One cigarette advertisement wanted to say "less tar," but the translation actually said the brand claimed to have "less asphalt." A beer company found that the radio commercial they hoped would say, "less filling, delicious" incorrectly came across in Spanish as "filling, less delicious" merely because of the way it was sung. Even market researchers blunder when they ask for the *"dama de la casa"* (madam of the house) rather than the *"señora de la casa"* (lady of the house).

CULTURE MISUNDERSTANDINGS   Serious misunderstandings occur when marketers use stereotypes of their own self-reference criteria for designing strategies. A telephone company commercial portrayed a wife saying to her husband, "Run downstairs and phone Maria. Tell her we'll be a little late." Two serious culture errors were committed. First, it is socially unacceptable for a Latin wife to order her husband around. Second, Hispanics do not normally call to say they will not be on time; it is customary to arrive a little late.

A radio station ran a contest in which the prize was two tickets to Disneyland, but there were few Hispanics interested. Giving away two tickets was not enough for the family-oriented Hispanic. When the number was increased, much more interest was generated.

HISPANIC IDIOSYNCRASIES   Marketing blunders sometimes occur from failure to understand the idiosyncrasies of each segment of the total Hispanic

---

[56] Lisa Penaloza Alaniz and Marcy C. Gilly, "The Hispanic Family — Consumer Research Issues," *Psychology and Marketing* (Winter 1986), 291–303.

[57] Humberto Valencia, "Point of View: Avoid Hispanic Market Blunders," *Journal of Advertising Research* 23 (January 1984), 19–22.

FIGURE 3.8   THE FORD ADVERTISEMENT RECOGNIZES THE IMPORTANCE OF THE FAMILY IN HISPANIC CULTURE

Source: Courtesy of Ford Motor Company, Agency: Hispania.

market. Just as the British, Canadians, South Africans, and Americans have some differences even though English is the language of all, so there are differences between Mexican-Americans, Puerto Rican–Americans, Cuban-Americans, and other Hispanics. A radio advertisement in Miami used the term *banditas,* which is a Puerto Rican term for Band-Aids. The ad failed because Miami's largely Cuban population did not recognize the term. Domino planned to add papaya flavor into its line of tropical-flavored drinks but dropped the idea because of the vulgar connotations papaya has for Cubans in Miami. A beer company filmed a Hispanic advertisement using San Antonio's Paseo del Rio (Riverwalk) as a background. The ad was well received among west coast Hispanics who liked the Spanish atmosphere. In San Antonio itself, Hispanics did not like the ad because they considered the Paseo del Rio to be for Anglo tourists rather than for Hispanic residents.

The Hispanic market is being assimilated into older Anglo markets, and

3.2 MARS MARKET IN EL MONTE, CALIFORNIA

The New America has arrived in the Los Angeles suburb of El Monte, California. To the owner of the local Mars Market, the transition from predominantly white to predominantly Hispanic was a transition the owner wanted no part of. "The guy simply wanted no Mexican trade," recalls Mark Roth, who purchased the failing business in 1969 for $72,000.

To appeal to this market, Roth started by hiring local Spanish-speaking employees, both as a way to facilitate communication with non–English-speaking customers and to tie the market to the community. Today, about two thirds of the employees at Mars Market are Spanish speaking. And the community ties are more than simply commercial: a former box boy once counted relations to 52 different families in the area.

The focus on family has been the key to Roth's marketing efforts. Because Hispanics spend relatively more of their free time with their extended families, shopping is often a group affair, not a lonesome chore. Using television celebrities and a local mariachi band to attract attention, the store provided balloons and prizes for the kids. Mars Market's sales doubled.

Fiestas are regularly featured. The store takes on the feel of a Mexican town square instead of the sterile American supermarket. Aisles are gaily decorated in bright colors and customers mingle at the complimentary salsa and chips table. Roth is a friendly and familiar presence with employees and customers.

Product selection is geared toward Hispanics, who now account for nearly three out of every four customers. Next to the lettuce and onions in the vegetable section are cactus leaves, hot chillies, and other Mexican ingredients. The meat department has long since stopped pushing high-priced meats, such as porterhouse and London broil, in favor of large displays of the chuck steak and neck bones used in many traditional Mexican dishes.

Roth installed a *tortilleria* — a bakery for making tortillas — just inside the main entrance to the store. By producing hot, fresh corn tortillas, the staple of the Mexican diet, Roth gave every Mexican family in El Monte a reason to shop in his store. Fresh burritos, tamales, enchiladas, and other Mexican specialties soon followed and continue to give him an edge even as large supermarket chains have also added Hispanic products.

Although most of the techniques for marketing to Hispanics are fairly obvious, Roth has found that nuances are also important. Early on, for instance, Roth thought it would be a great idea to put up posters and fliers for the stores in Spanish for his growing clientele of non–English-speaking customers. But to his surprise, this offended not only his Anglo clients, but also many Mexican-Americans who had already been in the United States for a generation and resented being lumped in with the recent arrivals. His solution: print fliers in English, but use large pictures to illustrate the items on sale.

Source: Excerpted from Joel Kotkin, "Selling to the New America," *Inc.* (July 1987), 44–47. Reprinted with permission, *Inc.* magazine. Copyright © 1987 by Goldhirsh Group, Inc., 38 Commercial Wharf, Boston, MA 02110.

many assumptions — such as higher brand loyalty, lower coupon usage, more shopping enjoyment, and so forth — are increasingly questionable or need to be qualified.[58] Brand loyalty is increasingly questioned as typical of Hispanics, although price, product quality, and shopping ease appear to be important attributes to Hispanics.[59] The reason findings about Hispanic or other ethnic groups are often confusing is because research fails to take into consideration the strength or weakness of identification with the ethnic group.[60] Consumer in Focus 3.2 shows, however, how one firm adapted successfully to the needs of the Hispanic market.

FRENCH-CANADIAN CULTURE

One of the largest and most distinct cultures in North America is the French-Canadian area of Canada, mostly in Quebec. This might be considered a nationality group or a geographic culture. The province of Quebec accounts for over 27 percent of the Canadian population and about 25 percent of income and retail sales.[61] For years, the French culture was somewhat ignored by English-oriented advertisers, thereby creating a social problem as well as limiting the potential effectiveness of communications to the French market. Some of the differential treatment may have been due to different social class groupings compared to Anglo markets.[62]

Marketing strategists need to be concerned with the question of whether advertising is transferable between the French-Canadian (FC) culture and the English-Canadian (EC) or Anglophone culture. Some marketers believe that separate advertising material must be developed to be effective in the FC subculture. Others believe materials can be developed that are effective with both groups. A minimum of verbal material is used, with emphasis on the visual.

Tamilia's research comparing communications with FC and EC consumers on a cross-cultural basis indicates the potential for increasing effectiveness in advertising communications. This is built upon some previous research by Tigert that indicated the French are more responsive to people-oriented than to message-oriented advertisements.[63] Tamilia's research led to the

---

[58] Robert E. Wilkes and Humberto Valencia, "Shopping-Related Characteristics of Mexican-Americans and Blacks," *Psychology and Marketing* 3 (Winter 1986), 247–259.

[59] Joel Saegert, Robert J. Hoover, and Marye Tharp Hilger, "Characteristics of Mexican American Consumers," *Journal of Consumer Research* 12 (June 1985), 104–109.

[60] Deshpande, 1986.

[61] Clarkson Gordon, *Tomorrow's Customers in Canada* (Toronto: Woods Gordon, 1984).

[62] Pierre C. Lefrancois and Giles Chatel, "The French-Canadian Consumer: Fact and Fancy," in J. S. Wright and J. L. Goldstrucker, eds., *New Ideas for Successful Marketing* (Chicago: American Marketing Association, 1966), 705–717; Bernard Blishen, "Social Class and Opportunity in Canada," *Canadian Review of Sociology and Anthropology* 7 (May 1970), 110–127.

[63] Robert Tamilia, "Cross-Cultural Advertising Research: A Review and Suggested Framework," in Ronald C. Curhan, ed., *1974 Combined Proceedings of the AMA* (Chicago: American Marketing Association, 1974), 131–134.

3.3 MARKET INFORMATION SOURCES IN FRENCH CANADA

Market information can come from various sources including friends, family members and the mass media. Where do French Canadians obtain their information? A recent study on the purchase of a car showed that, contrary to expectations, English Canadians used personal sources to a greater extent than French Canadians. Other interesting findings showed that:

—French Canadians considered fewer cars than did English Canadians

—French Canadians devoted less time to search

—English Canadians made three times as many test drives as French Canadians

—Overall, English Canadians generally seem to conduct a more extensive information search than French Canadians, at least as it applies to the purchase of a new car

French Canadians traditionally have showed affinity for mass media preferences quite unlike their English counterparts. As a result, brand images, brand attitudes, product attributes, and positioning strategies in general may not achieve similar re-sponse patterns among the two groups. Language affects media choice and obviously the marketing information contained therein impacts on the quantity and quality of the information received. For example, Quebec lags behind all other provinces and the United States in newspaper production per capita. The daily newspaper is not standard reading material for French Canadians as it is for the rest of Canadians. TV viewing is also heaviest among French Canadians, the heaviest in the world according to a source. Radio listening is also heaviest in Canada with listening and television viewing habits showing marked contrast between Montreal and Quebec City, as an example, or between French Canadians working vs non-working viewers and listeners, or between business executives living in Quebec City and Montreal. There is no doubt that media buying in Quebec is a complex decision process.

Source: Robert D. Tamilia, "The Duality of Canadian Culture: Toward an Understanding of the Quebec and French Canadian Markets," Working Paper No. 01–88 (Montreal: University of Quebec, Department of Administrative Sciences, 1988), 59–60.

conclusion that French-Canadians do react more to the source of the advertise-ment than do English-Canadians, who are more message-oriented.

Because of the size and importance of the French-Canadian market, it has attracted the attention of many marketers. The process of understanding communications in a cross-cultural setting, however, is applicable to other situations where diverse ethnic groups are the target for marketing programs.

SUMMARY

Culture is the complex of values, ideas, attitudes, and other meaningful symbols that serve humans to communicate, interpret, and evaluate as members of society. Culture and its values are transmitted from one generation to another.

The core values of a society define how products are used. They also provide positive and negative valences for brands and for communications programs.

Important or core values in America include material well-being, twofold moralizing, work is more important than play, time is money, effort-optimism-entrepreneurship, mastery over nature, egalitarianism, and humanitarianism.

The fundamental forces forming values include the cultural transfusive triad and early lifetime experiences. The former refers to the influence of the institutions of the family, religion, and schools. The latter refers to basic intergenerational influences, such as depressions, wars, and other major events.

The norms and values of specific groups are called microcultures, in contrast to the macroculture of the nation. Ethnic groups may be formed around nationality, religion, physical attributes, or geographic location. Ethnicity is a process that may be defined objectively, based on sociocultural characteristics, or subjectively, based on identification that a person makes for self or others. Major microcultures in North America include Asian-Americans, blacks, Hispanics, and French Canadians.

REVIEW AND DISCUSSION QUESTIONS

1. What is meant by the term *culture?* Why does this term create confusion about its meaning?

2. What is meant by the term *idology of consumption?* Why should this concept be of concern to marketers?

3. Where do consumers get their values?

4. Examine the American core values described in this chapter. Consider how they might influence a marketer of consumer electronics products.

5. Select the topics of family, religious institutions, or schools, and prepare a report documenting the changes that are occurring in these institutions.

6. Describe ways in which advertising directed to consumers brought up during the Depression era might differ compared to that directed at consumers of the post–World War II era. What do you consider to be the most important changes that will occur in the future?

7. Asian Americans are a small proportion of the total population of the United States. Why should they be given much importance in marketing strategies? What adaptations in a marketing plan should be made to reach Asian Americans?

8. Assume that a soft drink marketer wanted to increase penetration in the Hispanic market. Prepare a set of recommendations for doing so.

9. Assume that a major retailer of shoes was considering a market program to make a special appeal to black consumers. Would you suggest such an approach? If so, what would be your recommendations?

10. Assume that a French manufacturer of women's apparel is seeking to expand markets by exporting to Canada. What marketing program should be recommended for maximum effectiveness?

SOCIAL CLASS AND STATUS

SOCIAL CLASS BRAND PERCEPTIONS

Consumers associate brands of products and services with specific social classes. The great variations in believed associations between branded products and social class segments have important managerial implications.

In the case of beer, Heineken is primarily believed to be an upper/upper-middle class product, while Old Style is perceived as being an "every-man" product consumed by people from the middle and lower classes. Beer was perceived to be a lower class beverage in the past. Beer has seemingly increased in social prestige over the years, perhaps as a result of heavy marketing efforts. In the "good old days," beer was more of a working class, blue collar drink.

Marshall Field is primarily believed to be a store for the upper/upper-middle classes, while K mart is mainly perceived as being a store for the lower classes. Among restaurants, Burger King and Denny's are seemingly more downscaled than is Wendy's.

Source: Kjell Gronhaug and Paul S. Trapp, "Perceived Social Class Appeals of Branded Goods," *The Journal of Consumer Marketing* 5 (Fall 1988), 25–30.

Social Stratification

Social classes and status systems exist in every country of the world. In England and other countries of Europe, the concept is so important to understanding consumer behavior that the European Society for Opinion and Marketing Research (ESOMAR) set up a working group to devise questions so that research about social class would be comparable from one country to another. Japan is a country with rigid expectations about social class, even though a large proportion of consumers are middle class. In Latin America, many countries have huge numbers of poorer classes struggling for existence, while the small but wealthy classes purchase a wide array of products that serve as visible symbols of class membership. Even in Marxist societies, officially classless, the best of the available consumer products go to privileged classes, based upon party affiliation, athletic ability, or educational attainment. In the United States, many Americans *believe* that class has become less important but *act* as if class were quite important. Research indicates that Americans perceive effects of social class even more than in England, a country known for class importance.[1]

Even animals other than humans divide themselves into stratified societies. One famous study concerned a barnyard society in which it was found that each hen tends to maintain a definite position in the "peck" order of the group.[2] This is where the term "pecking order" apparently originated. Ries and Grout, in their influential book on positioning, extend this principle: "Consumers are like chickens. They are much more comfortable with a pecking order that everybody knows and accepts."[3]

Brands and stores also have a pecking order. Consumers believe one brand is higher or lower than others and that some stores are more appropriate for people higher in social status than others. The customer base of Bloomingdales department store does not overlap much with that of Wild Woody's Bargain Barn. Nor is there much confusion about the different status value of a Cadillac and a Chevette. For other brands and stores, however, differences in status are more subtle and multidimensional.

Brands and stores seek to establish a position or location in the minds of customers, consistent with the values and beliefs of one social stratum or another. Consumers' mental stratification of brands and stores leads to cognitive consistency between their various attributes and consumers' perceptions of their own social position. This allows consumers to say, "This brand (or store) is for me."

---

[1] Robert V. Robinson, "Explaining Perceptions of Class and Racial Inequality in England and the United States of America," *The British Journal of Sociology* 34 (1983), 344–363.

[2] T. Schjelderup-Ebbe, "Social Behavior of Birds," in C. Murchison, ed., *A Handbook of Social Psychology* (Worcester, Mass.: Clark University Press, 1935).

[3] Al Ries and Jack Grout, *Positioning: The Battle for Your Mind* (New York: McGraw-Hill, 1981), 53.

Social class positioning is illustrated by beer, a product purchased heavily by middle and lower social classes, in contrast to wine. Miller once positioned its brand as "the champagne of bottled beer." Later, Miller changed to the slogan "When you've got the time, we've got the beer," also targeted to the busy, active leisure activities of the upper classes. More recently, Miller switched to "the workingman's beer" to try to emulate the success Budweiser has always maintained with the mass classes. Budweiser ads show people who don't have much fun on their jobs but relax with "The King of Beers" to forget their jobs. Budweiser's symbol of Clydesdale horses appeals to the strong, physical, working nature of lower- and middle-class life, controlled by other people.

You may find this chapter unsettling because American traditions emphasize equality. This leads some people to deny that classes exist. But the traditions concern more what ought to be than what actually exists. Few constructs are better documented in the sociological literature than social inequality and the differential prestige or **deference** (granting of social honor) paid by some in society to members of higher classes. Most sociologists accept class inequality as a proven fact, regardless of what idealists believe should be.

Americans may hope that every person has equal opportunity to gain access to products and services. Yet, the empirical evidence indicates otherwise. Social class determines **life chances,** a term used by Max Weber to emphasize the fundamental aspects of an individual's future possibilities. Life chances range from the infant's chances for decent nutrition to the adult's opportunities to purchase the goods and services that students of consumer behavior market.

Understanding the development of social class is important in understanding consumption for two additional reasons. First, consumers adopt lifestyles acquired in their original class, even though people move up or down in the class structure. Secondly, the lifestyles of the upper-middle class tend to filter down and become generally accepted by the rest of society.

WHAT IS SOCIAL CLASS?

Social class refers to grouping of people who are similar in their behavior based upon their economic position in the market place. Class membership exists and can be described as a statistical category whether or not individuals are aware of their common situation. **Status groups** reflect a community's expectations for style of life among each class as well as the positive or negative social estimation of honor given to each class. Max Weber, who along with Karl Marx, might be regarded as the father of social class theory, clarified the distinction:

> With some over-simplification, one might thus say that "classes" are stratified according to their relations in the production and acquisition of goods, whereas "status groups"

are stratified according to the principles of their consumption of goods as represented by special "styles of life."[4]

For marketers, status systems are of primary interest because they exert a major influence on what people buy and consume. However, the determinant of what consumers are *able* to buy is determined by social class — namely the income or wealth of the consumer — and thus, our empirical emphasis in marketing research is on social class variables. For practical purposes, it is usually adequate in the study of consumer behavior to treat the terms *status* and *class* interchangeably, as we do in this chapter, although recognizing that the word *status* may be used in other contexts to describe differential respect given to an individual within a group.

INEQUALITY SYSTEMS

All countries, except the very smallest and most primitive, are stratified or have formal systems of inequality. Social class systems rank *families* rather than individuals. A family shares many characteristics among its members that affect relationships with outsiders, such as the same house, the same income, the same values, and thus much of the same buying behavior. *When a large group of families are approximately equal in rank to each other and clearly differentiated from other families, they form a social class.*

The *caste* system is more rigid. Only relatively controlled interaction is found or permitted between castes. Mobility between groups is especially limited. Caste is based upon hereditary status and, especially as it was traditionally found in India, upon religion.

The *estate* system, prevalent in medieval Europe, was founded upon power and alliances — mainly the power of the lords and their warriors to offer protection from violence. Force was the basis of power, status, and a share of the land's produce. An extension of this system of inequality in contemporary societies is the power and deference given to people in the media, professional athletics, and organizations such as labor unions, political parties, and government agencies. Certain corporations — IBM, General Electric, Mitsubishi and so forth — give such status regardless of the other characteristics of the people who are employed by "status corporations."

SOCIAL CLASS VARIABLES

Stratification occurs in order to develop and preserve collective social identity in a world characterized by pervasive economic inequality.[5] Social identity is

---

[4] Max Weber, In H. H. Gard and C. Wright Mills, *From Max Weber: Essays in Sociology* (New York: Oxford University Press, 1946), 193.

[5] Max Haller, "Marriage, Women and Social Stratification: A Theoretical Critique," *American Journal of Sociology* 86 (1981), 766–795.

FIGURE 4.1
A CONCEPTUAL
MODEL OF SOCIAL
INSTITUTIONS AND
SOCIAL STRATA IN
AMERICAN SOCIETY

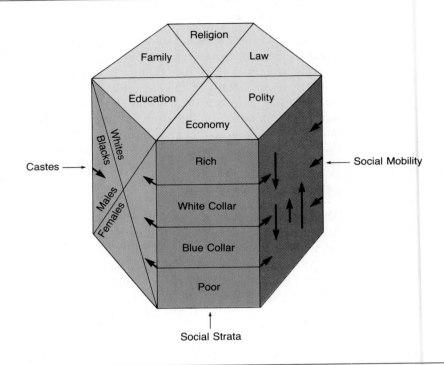

Source: Leonard Beeghley, *Social Stratification in America* (Santa Monica, Calif.: Goodyear Publishing Company, Inc., 1978), 102. Reprinted by permission.

achieved by establishing boundaries on interactions between people of unequal status.

Stratification involves many variables. An attempt to conceptualize these is shown in Figure 4.1, a model you can examine vertically or horizontally. By looking down on the top of the model, you can identify the social institutions that generate the goal-oriented activities of the society. The vertical dimension of the model can be seen by looking at its side, where various levels of inequality, called strata or classes, are located. Individual consumers can be studied by examining their economic, political, legal, religious, familial, and educational characteristics. Social mobility can be studied by examining rates of intra- and intergenerational mobility in the population or market segments. The patterns of convergence among the variables create social classes. The patterns are tendencies or ideal types that, though not fully realized in any one situation, are discernible when one steps back from detail to think about the underlying forces.

NINE VARIABLES OF SOCIAL CLASS RESEARCH

The scientific study of social stratification in the United States began in the 1920s and 1930s with descriptions of social classes in small towns of New England and the South. Research continues today with thousands of studies dealing with the measurement of social class in large cities and nationally, movement between social classes, the interactions of social class with other variables such as gender, race, ethnicity, and education, and the effects of social class on poverty and economic policy.

Nine variables have emerged as most important in the stream of sociological and other research concerned with social class. These nine variables were identified in an influential synthesis of social class research by Gilbert and Kahl, grouped in the following manner.

Economic variables.   *Occupation, income, and wealth* are of critical importance because what a person does for a living not only determines how much the family has to spend, but is extremely important in determining the deference given to family members. [Occupation and income are such an important variable, they will be given substantial discussion in a later part of this chapter.] Wealth is usually a result of an accumulation of past income. In certain forms such as ownership of a business or of stocks and bonds, wealth is the source of future income which may enable a family to maintain its [high] social class from generation to generation.

Interaction variables.   *Personal prestige, association, and socialization* are the essence of social class. People have high prestige when other people have an attitude of respect or deference to them. *Prestige* is a sentiment in the minds of people who may not always recognize it is there. For consumer analysts, prestige is studied in two ways: by asking people about their attitudes of respect toward others and by watching their behavior in such things as imitation of lifestyles and product usage.

Association is a variable concerned with everyday relationships. People have close social relationships with people who like to do the same things they do, in the same ways, and with whom they feel comfortable.

Socialization is the process by which an individual learns the skills, attitudes, and customs to participate in the life of the community. Much of the sociological research has concluded that social class behavior and values are learned early in the life cycle. The class positions of the parents are clearly differentiated in children by the time they have reached adolescence, not only for basic behavior patterns but personality variables that vary by social class such as self-esteem.[6]

Political variables.   *Power, class consciousness, and mobility* are important to understanding the political aspect of stratification systems. *Power* is the potential of individuals or groups to carry out their will over others. While

---

[6] David H. Demo and Ritch C. Savin-Williams, "Early Adolescent Self-Esteem as a Function of Social Class,"*American Journal of Sociology* 88 (1983), 763–773.

this variable is central in the analysis of many theorists of social class, it is of less direct interest to marketers.

Class consciousness refers to the degree to which people in a social class are aware of themselves as a distinctive group with shared political and economic interests. As people become more group conscious, they are likely to organize political parties, trade unions, and other associations to advance their group interests. Americans often state they are not class conscious and thus, advertising with a direct class appeal may not be well received. However, empirical sociological research as well as observation of marketing patterns reveals that Americans behave with a great deal of class consciousness.

Mobility and *succession* is a dual concept related to the stability or instability of stratification systems. Succession refers to the process of children inheriting the class position of their parents. Mobility refers to the process of moving up or down relative to their parents. When mobility occurs in an upward direction, the possibility exists that consumers will need to learn a new set of consumption behaviors — products and brands that are consistent with their new status. This possibility is sufficiently intriguing that we will examine the question of mobility in more detail later in this chapter.[7]

WHAT DETERMINES SOCIAL CLASS?

What causes your social status? The family in which you were raised is an important factor. Your father's occupation probably had a significant effect upon your social class because a man's occupation is the most important determinant, followed closely by the wife's occupation.[8] The primary role of the father may be less true in the future, especially among the 6 million or more families in the United States in which wives earn more than their husbands do.[9] But what, besides your family's occupation, determines status or your social class? The answer, based on variables originally identified by sociologist Joseph Kahl, also includes personal performance, interactions, possessions, value orientations, and class consciousness.[10]

It is important to recognize that social class is not directly determined by income. A senior garbage collector, for example, might earn considerably more than the typical assistant professor. The professor typically would be

---

[7] Reprinted with permission of Wadsworth, Inc. From *The American Class Structure: A New Synthesis*, 3/e by Dennis Gilbert and Joseph A. Kahl. © 1982, 1987 by Dennis Gilbert and Joseph A. Kahl. Although not cited in each instance, this excellent book has influenced the content of this chapter in numerous other points.

[8] Stephen L. Nock, "Social Origins as Determinants of Family Social Status" (paper presented to the Mid-South Sociological Association, 1980).

[9] Suzanne M. Bianchi, "Wives Who Earn More Than Their Husbands," *American Demographics* 6 (July 1984), 18–23.

[10] Joseph A. Kahl, *The American Class Structure* (New York: Holt, Rinehart and Winston, 1957), 8–10. A more recent emphasis centers on the ownership of capitalistic assets and the role of occupations. See Dennis Gilbert and Joseph A. Kahl, *The American Class Structure: A New Synthesis* (Homewood, Ill.: The Dorsey Press, 1982).

ascribed higher social class, however. You can probably think of more examples of how income and social class differ.

OCCUPATION

When strangers meet, a question often asked is, "What kind of work do you do?" This question provides a good clue to the social class of the individual. Consumer analysts consider occupation the best single indicator of social class. The work consumers do greatly affects their lifestyles and is the single most important basis for according prestige, honor, and respect.

Physicians, for example, are accorded respect and usually high financial reward in most cultures. As information occupations — television anchorpersons, computer programmers, and so forth — have increased in importance to the society, so has the status of the individuals in those occupations. Capitalist or entrepreneur is one of the occupations with a more lasting effect upon the family's social class because of the possibility of building a store of capital that will continue the income for future generations.

PERSONAL PERFORMANCE

A person's status can also be influenced by her or his success relative to that of others in the same occupation — by an individual's personal performance. Statements such as "She is the finest trial lawyer in town," or "Frank is the only programmer that I trust to do it right," or "That professor is doing the most significant research in the field" are examples of evaluations of personal performance.

Even though income is not a good indicator of overall social class, it may serve as a gauge of personal performance within an occupation. The top 25 percent of income producers in any occupation are also likely to be the most highly respected as personally competent in their field.

Personal performance also involves activities other than job-related pursuits. Perhaps your father has a low-status occupation. Your family may still achieve more status if your father is perceived as one who helps others in need, is unusually kind and interested in fellow workers, or is a faithful worker in civic or religious organizations. The president of a corporation who serves as chairperson of the United Way or a trustee of a university may achieve higher social status than the president of a similar corporation not involved in such activities. A reputation as a good mother or a good father may contribute to one's status.

INTERACTIONS

People feel most comfortable when they are with people of similar values and behavior. Sociologists who emphasize analyses of social interactions are sometimes called the "who-invited-whom-to-dinner" school. In such an approach, group membership and interactions are considered a primary determinant of a person's social class.

Although interactions are probably the best validity check in social class research, they are not as useful a variable in consumer research as occupation, because of the difficulty in measuring social interactions. Social intimacy is an expression of social equality even though the interactions may be difficult to measure.

Social interactions ordinarily are limited to one's immediate social class, even though opportunities exist for broader contact. Most marriages occur within the same or adjacent social classes. In public schools, open contact may be encouraged by the institution, but children usually reveal definite patterns of restricted association. Sometimes these groups have their own names — the "straights," the "grubbies," the "cheerleaders," and so forth. One of the most obvious examples of restricted social interaction is the *Social Register,* which contains rigid criteria for gaining and maintaining admission and which in 1980 was changed from a series of local editions to a national edition listing socially prominent people throughout the United States.

POSSESSIONS

Possessions are symbols of class membership — not only the number of possessions, but the nature of the choices made. Thus, a middle-class family may choose wall-to-wall carpeting, whereas an upper-class family is more likely to choose Oriental rugs, even if the prices are equal. Thornston Veblen referred to such symbols as "conspicuous consumption."

The most important possession decision reflecting a family's social class is the choice of where to live. This includes both the type of home and the neighborhood. Another very important "possession" is the university one attends. Upper-class individuals select the "best" schools, which in turn reinforces class consciousness and cohesion.[11] Other possessions that serve as indicators of social status include club memberships (which also reflect interactions), preferred furniture styles, clothing, appliances, and types of vacations chosen.

People who lack the possessions or knowledge of them but who aspire to a higher social class may study diligently to learn more about the possessions of that class. Business students and others interested in making it "to the top," for example, may be prime prospects for books and courses that teach how to "dress for success" or the secrets "they didn't teach you in business school."

Products and brands often seek to be positioned as symbols of status — as the products used by upper-middle or upper classes. For people who are striving to become associated with those classes, the purchase of such brands may be partially based upon the desire for such affiliation or identification. Consumer in Focus 4.1 describes such status symbols, based upon a list prepared for consumers who may have been raised in classes lower than their improved status.

---

[11] Michael Useem and S. M. Miller, "The Upper Class in Higher Education," *Social Policy* 7 (January–February 1977), 28–31.

4.1 THE BRANDS TO BUY TO REFLECT INCREASING SOCIAL STATUS

THE WATCH: Rolex, for its Swiss accuracy, respectable name and gold-link band. THE RAINCOAT: Burberry. Check out the coatroom where the rich and powerful lunch and you'll find a sea of Burberry trench coats. THE SUIT: Armani. While the traditional status-conscious male may continue to have suits tailor-made, the new breed of businessmen will plunk down as much as $1,500 for one of Giorgio Armani's couture suits. THE ATTACHE CASE: Mark Cross, because what's on the outside can be as important as what's on the inside. THE PEN: Montblanc. This top-dollar writing utensil starts at $12 for the ballpoint and reaches the $6,500 mark for a solid-gold fountain pen. THE CAR: Porsche, for those who are serious about power, performance and being out in front on the road. THE SUNGLASSES: Porsche, an extension of the car.

THE SNEAKERS: Reeboks. Averaging about $55 a pair, these leather aerobic shoes are gracing the most graceful to work out in the trendiest health spas. THE RIGHT CREDIT: American Express platinum card. For $250 a year, the user gets a choice of billing dates, 24-hour customized travel service and more. THE GOOD SOUND: Front row orchestra seats at a Wynton Marsalis or Sade concert. THE SWEET SMELL OF SUCCESS: For women, Giorgio, at $150 an ounce; for men, Lagerfeldt, at $30 for the four-ounce spray cologne. MAN'S BEST FRIEND: The Akita. They resemble German shepherds, but they're really Japanese guard dogs who will be your constant companion if you're willing to pay $750 to $2,000 for one.

Source: Monique Greenwood, "Status Symbols," *Black Enterprise* 16 (May 1986), 65.

VALUE ORIENTATIONS

Values — shared beliefs about how people should behave — indicate the social class to which one belongs. When a group of people share a common set of abstract convictions that organize and relate a large number of specific attributes, it is possible to categorize an individual in the group by the degree to which he or she possesses these values.

Consumer analysts must ask the question, "What values characterize specific market segments?" These beliefs may refer to general values about political ideals, religious practices, work motivation, the capitalistic economic system, and so forth. Also included are more specific activities such as child rearing, family structure, sexual behavior, abortion, and impulsiveness in decision making.

Figure 4.2 shows ads that might appeal to upper social classes. Notice how these ads — which cover products as diverse as cars and cigarettes, airlines, and blinds — contain common themes or values. The ads speak of the "high goals" and the "loneliness at the top" of the "privileged few." The cigarette ad hopes to achieve the same relative status as the St. Moritz ski resort. The

FIGURE 4.2   SUCCESSFUL ADVERTISEMENTS APPEAL TO THE VALUES OF PARTICULAR SOCIAL CLASSES. THE SYMBOLS IN THESE ADVERTISEMENTS WERE CREATED TO APPEAL TO UPPER-CLASS VALUES

Source: Courtesy of TransWorld Airlines, Inc., American Express, Inc.   Source: Courtesy of Cadillac Motor Car-Division of General Motors Corporation.

vertical-blind ad shows furnishings, art, clothing, and even a dog, all aimed at "those who live well," while making the point that the rest of society cannot afford to acquire the product.

CLASS CONSCIOUSNESS

A person's social class is indicated to some extent by how conscious that person is of social class in a society. Individuals who are relatively conscious of class differences are more likely to be from higher classes, although lower social class individuals may be more aware of the reality of social class overall. This suggests that marketing organizations with market targets in the upper

classes need to study social class and build marketing strategies on finer distinctions of social class more than companies appealing to lower social classes.

How to Measure Social Class

Many methods have been developed to measure and describe social class. For consumer researchers, the purpose is usually to relate dependent variables such as product usage, brand preference, attitudes, store image and patronage, to the independent variable of social class. With such research, it may be possible to define market segments on the basis of social class and to understand consumption and buying patterns of those segments.

Social class research methods are of two types: methods used for *theoretical or validity* research or methods especially appropriate to practical *marketing research* issues. A specific method might be used for either purpose, but the theoretical methods are usually so costly and time consuming that market researchers do them on a day-to-day basis. They are valuable for consumer researchers to understand the theory and concepts of social class and to serve as a validity check on the practical techniques used regularly in marketing research.

Research methods may also be classified as **objective,** in that they involve quantitative variables of socioeconomic status (SES) measures such as occupation, education, and income. Methods may also be **subjective** when they involve reports by individuals of their perceptions of other people, perhaps interpreted additionally by the subjective insights or theories of the researchers. Marketing researchers prefer objective methods because of the availability of data from census or representative surveys as well as the greater ease of using computerized, quantitative analytical techniques. Although objective methods are the most preferred in business research, the choice is sometimes at the expense of the richer insights and understanding provided by subjective methods.

THEORETICAL AND VALIDITY METHODS

Reputational methods involve asking people to rank the social position or prestige of other people. The reputational method was developed by Lloyd Warner, one of the pioneers in the study of social class in the United States.[12] This work was extended by Burleigh Gardner and his associates in the Deep South[13] and in the Midwest by Hollingshead.[14] These studies also include **association** or **sociometric measures** which count the number and nature of personal contacts of people in their informal relationships. These studies are also called **evaluative participation studies,** because the researchers use not only the data they collect from respondents but the researchers' own observations gained from living in the community and participating in the informal networks and formal organizations of the community.

Warner and his colleagues developed the *Index of Status Characteristics* based upon the need for more objective and less laborious research techniques. After years of work with reputational, associational, and evaluative participation methods, which established the validity of social class, researchers concluded

---

[12] W. Lloyd Warner and Paul S. Lunt, *The Social Life of a Modern Community* (New Haven, Conn.: Yale University Press, 1941). Also see the classic book by W. Lloyd Warner, *Yankee City* (New Haven, Conn.: Yale University Press, 1963).

[13] Allison Davis, Burleigh B. Gardner, and Mary R. Gardner, *Deep South: A Social-Anthropological Study of Caste and Class* (Chicago: The University of Chicago Press, 1941).

[14] August B. Hollingshead, *Elmtown's Youth* (New York: John Wiley & Sons, 1949).

that, once the evaluated rankings were established, they could accurately predict such rankings on the basis of a family's *occupation, source of income, house type,* and *residential area.* By establishing the validity of these objective measures in social class research, marketing researchers can use updated and readily quantifiable methods.

The theoretical research provided a stream of empirical data and concepts

---

TABLE 4.1   TRADITION SOCIAL CLASS BEHAVIOR IN AMERICA

Upper Upper. Upper uppers are the social elite of society. Inherited wealth from socially prominent families is the key to admission. Children attend private preparatory schools and graduate from the best colleges.

Consumers in the upper-upper class spend money as if it were unimportant, not tightly but not with display either, for that would imply that money is important. For some products a trickle-down influence may exist between social classes. The social position of these individuals is so secure that they can deviate from class norms if they choose to without losing status.

Lower Upper. Lower uppers include the very high-income professional people who have earned their position rather than inherited it. They are the *nouveaux riches*, active people with many material symbols of their status. They buy the largest homes in the best suburbs, the most expensive automobiles, swimming pools and other symbols of conspicuous consumption, making them innovators and good markets for luxury marketing offerings.

Upper Middle. The key word for upper middles is career. Careers are based on successful professional or graduate degrees for a specific profession or the skill of business administration. Members of this class are demanding of their children in educational attainment.

The *quality* market for many products is the upper-middle class and gracious living in a conspicuous but careful manner characterizes the family's lifestyle. The home is of high importance and an important symbol of the family's success and competence.

Lower Middle. Lower-middle class families are typical Americans, exemplifying the core of respectability, conscientious work habits, and adherence to culturally defined norms and standards. They believe in attending church and obeying the law and are upset when their children are arrested for law violations. They are not innovators.

The *home* is very important to the lower-middle family and they want it to be neat, well-painted, and in a respected neighborhood. They may have little confidence in their own tastes and adopt standardized home furnishings—perhaps from Levitz or similar furniture stores. This is in contrast to the upper-middle consumer who feels freer to experiment with new styles and new arrangements and with the upper-lower consumer who is not very concerned about the overall plan for furnishing the home: The lower-middle consumer reads and follows the advice of the medium-level shelter and service magazines in an attempt to make the house pretty.

The lower-middle class consumer works more at shopping than others and considers purchase decisions demanding and tedious. He/She may have a high degree of price sensitivity.

Upper Lower. Upper-lower social classes—exhibit a routine life, characterized by a day-to-day existence of unchanging activities. They live in dull areas of the city, in small houses or apartments. The hard hats are included in this class, with many members working at uncreative jobs requiring manual activity or only moderate skills and education. Because of unions and security, many may earn incomes that give them considerable discretionary income.

The purchase decisions of the working class are often impulsive but at the same time may show high brand loyalty to national brands. Buying them is one way to prove knowledge as a buyer, a role in which he/she feels (probably correctly) that he/she has little skill. This consumer has little social contact outside the home and does not like to attend civic organizations or church activities. Social interaction is limited to close neighbors and relatives. If he/she takes a vacation, it will probably be a visit to relatives in another city. Upper lowers are concerned that they not be confused with the lower lowers.

Lower Lower. The lower-lower social class contains people who may try to rise above their class but usually fail to do so. An individual in the lower-lower class often rejects middle class morality and gets pleasure wherever possible— and this includes buying impulsively. This lack of planning causes purchases that cost too much and may result in inferior goods. This person pays too much for products, buys on credit at a high interest rate and has difficulty obtaining quality or value. This group includes highly distressed families, some who have habitual legal problems and the homeless.

that are central to our present efforts to relate social class to consumption. It was Warner, Gardner and their colleagues who described the six basic social classes found in the United States, detailed in Table 4.1.

MARKETING RESEARCH METHODS FOR MEASURING SOCIAL CLASS

Marketing researchers measure social class as an independent variable in order to determine its association with dependent variables of interest in marketing. Objective methods assign status on the basis of respondents' possessing some value of a stratified variable. The most often used variables are occupation, income, education, size and type of residence, ownership of possessions, and organizational affiliations. Objective methods can be divided into those that are single indexes and those that are multiple indexes.

Subjective or self-reporting methods ask respondents to rate themselves on social class. Such methods, although occasionally used, are of limited value to consumer analysts for two reasons: (1) respondents tend to overrate their own class position, and (2) respondents avoid the connotative terms of upper and lower classes and, thus, exaggerate the size of the middle class.

SINGLE-ITEM INDEXES   Occupation is the best single proxy indicator of social class. People who have similarly ranked (in prestige) occupations often share similar access to the means of achieving a lifestyle. Leisure time, income independence, knowledge, and power are often common to occupational categories. They interact with one another. The observations of Barth and Watson indicate the importance of this for consumer analysts:

> *The products of such occupational interaction are likely to be an increased consensus concerning the types of activities, interests, and possessions that are important; some agreement as to how, in general, family resources should be allocated in order to implement the achievement of these goals; and the development of a shared set of norms of evaluation.*[15]

Occupation is used in consumer research by asking respondents to write in their exact occupation, which can later be coded numerically according to its social class or status value. These values are established in one of two ways. One method is to use surveys of people asked to rank the prestige of people in various occupations or of the occupations themselves. A second method is to use objective measures, such as ranking of the average educational level and/or income of occupational groups.

There is a long history of studies of occupational prestige. Much of this history evolved around the need of the U.S. Census Bureau to establish occupa-

[15] Ernest A. Barth and Walter B. Watson, "Social Stratification and the Family in Mass Society," *Social Forces* 45 (March 1967), 394.

CONSUMER IN FOCUS

4.2 AN EARLY UNDERSTANDING OF OCCUPATION AND CONSUMER BEHAVIOR

"The most nearly dominant single influence in a man's life is probably his occupation. More than anything else, perhaps, a man's occupation determines his course and his contribution in life. And when life's span is ended, quite likely there is not [one?] other single set of facts that will tell so well the kind of man he was and the part he played in life as will a detailed and chronological statement of the occupation, or occupations, he pursued. Indeed, there is no other single characteristic that tells so much about a man and his status — social, intellectual, and economic — as does his occupation. A man's occupation not only tells, for each workday, what he does during one-half of his waking hours, but it indicates, with some degree of accuracy, his manner of life during the other half — the kind of associates he will have, the kind of clothes he will wear, the kind of house he will live in, and even, to some extent, the kind of food he will eat. And usually, it indicates, in some degree, the cultural level of his family."

Source: Alba M. Edwards, *Comparative Occupation Statistics for the United States, 1870 to 1940* (Washington: U.S. Government Printing Office, 1943).

tional categories, resulting in the major categories still used by most governmental studies: professional and technical workers, managers, sales workers, clerical workers, artisans, transport workers, laborers (nonfarm), farmers, farm laborers, service workers, private household workers, and unemployed persons. Much of this research was inspired by Alba Edwards of the Census Bureau, whose opinion on occupation is quoted in Consumer in Focus 4.2, one of the most cited references in the social science literature.

A major study by the National Opinion Research Center (NORC) was originally conducted in1947, ranking 100 occupations. Updates of this study disclose the stability of ratings over time. High correlations between nations are also found in the prestige rankings of occupations, regardless of cultural differences among nations. Research by Hollingshead, Duncan, and others indicates that the key variables causing occupations to have prestige are the amount of education required as a prerequisite for entering the occupation and the typical income earned, a measure of the reward that society bestows on the occupation.[16]

Today, governmental data relating to occupations uses the Standard Occu-

[16] Robert W. Hodge, Paul M. Siegel, and Peter H. Rossi, "Occupational Prestige in the United States: 1925–1963," *American Journal of Sociology* 70 (1956), 286–302. Otis D. Duncan, "A Socioeconomic Index for All Occupations, in A. J. Reiss et al., *Occupations and Social Status* (New York: Free Press, 1961).

pational Classification, or SOC.[17] The Classification provides a coding system and nomenclature for identifying and classifying occupations in a system that can be used for marketing purposes as well as standard categories used by diverse governmental agencies. Information is solicited about the company and type of business or industry in which the individual works, the kind of work and job duties as well as occupational title, and the classification of work as public, private, or self-employed. Expert coders review all of these data and assign a number or letter code for the industry and a separate number or code for the individual.

One of the easiest scales for marketing researchers to use was developed by Nam and Powers and provides a precise, numerical status score for 589 occupations.[18] This scale is similar to but more precise than the Trieman scale, which has been widely used to compare occupations on an international basis.[19] An example of the scores that are assigned to occupations using the Nam and Powers scale is shown in Table 4.2.

MULTIPLE-ITEM INDEXES   Multiple-item indexes combine several indicators of social class into one index to provide a richer measure of social status. Using the Nam and Powers occupational status scores, such as those shown in Table 4.2, an additional score is added for both the educational category and the income level of the respondent. These scores are based upon census data and can be updated to reflect inflationary increases in income. The three scores (occupation, education, income) are then summed and divided by 3 to provide a multiple-item SES score. This provides an easy-to-use, numerical score of social class which can then be related to product purchase, brand preference, media processing, or other variables of interest to marketing researchers.

COLEMAN'S CSI   Coleman's Computerized Status Index (CSI) is an index developed by Social Research, Inc., that has been extensively used in commercial consumer research. Figure 4.3 shows the format for administering the CSI. In this particular version, occupation is weighted double when computing the total scale. Other versions include an occupation scaling specifically for employed women, to be used whether they are the spouse or the household head. The status for conventional married couples with male household head between 35 and 64 years age is as follows: Upper American, 37 to 53; Middle

---

[17] U.S. Department of Commerce, *Standard Occupational Classificational Manual* (Washington, D.C.: U.S. Government Printing Office, 1980).

[18] Charles B. Nam and Mary G. Powers, *The Socioeconomic Approach to Status Measurement* (Houston: Cap and Gown Press, 1983).

[19] D. J. Trieman, *Occupational Prestige in Comparative Perspective* (New York: Academic Press, 1977). Also, see the Fifth Edition of *Consumer Behavior* (1986) for an example of the Trieman scale.

**TABLE 4.2
OCCUPATIONAL
STATUS SCORES OF
OCCUPATIONS**

Occupation	Status Score
Accountants	89
Architects	97
Engineers	
Aeronautical	96
Industrial	93
Mechanical	93
Librarians	75
Physicians	
Chiropractors	95
Medical and Osteopathic	99
Registered Nurses	66
Clergymen	77
Social Scientists	
Economists	96
Sociologists	94
Social Workers	82
Teachers	
Chemistry	97
Business and Commerce	95
Elementary School, Public	80
Secondary School, Public	86
Sales Managers, Retail Trade	74
Sales Managers, Except Retail	94
Bank Tellers	49
Cashiers	29
Keypunch Operators	49
Typists	46
Mechanics	
Aircraft	72
Automotive	45
Office Machine	69
Bottling and Canning Operatives	22
Dry Wall Installers	51
Coal Mine Operatives	35
Bus Drivers	40
Taxicab Drivers	35
Farm Managers	52
Farm Laborers, Wage Workers	04
Bartenders	42
Busboys	12

Source: Excerpts from Table A1 of Charles B. Nam and Mary G. Powers, *The Socioeconomic Approach to Status Measurement* (Houston: Cap and Gown Press, 1983). See this source for a complete list of occupations.

Class, 24 to 36; Working Class, 13 to 23; and Lower American, 4 to 12. Additional refinements include adjustment for unusual income levels or abnormalities in occupation or neighborhood ratings.[20]

---

[20] Richard P. Coleman, "The Continuing Significance of Social Class to Marketing," *Journal of Consumer Research* 10 (December 1983), 265–280.

FIGURE 4.3
EXAMPLE OF A
COMPUTERIZED
STATUS INDEX (CSI)

Interviewer circles code numbers (for the computer) which in his/her judgment best fit the respondent and family. Interviewer asks for detail on occupation, then makes rating. Interviewer often asks the respondent to describe neighborhood in own words. Interviewer asks respondent to specify income—a card is presented to the respondent showing the eight brackets—and records R's response. If interviewer feels this is overstatement or under, a "better-judgment" estimate should be given, along with explanation.

Education:	Respondent	Respondent's Spouse
Grammar school (8 yrs or less)	−1 *R's*	−1 *Spouse's*
Some high school (9 to 11 yrs)	−2 *age:*	−2 *age:*
Graduated high school (12 yrs)	−3	−3
Some post high school (business, nursing, technical, one yr college)	−4	−4
Two, three years of college—possibly Associate of Arts degree	−5	−5
Graduated four-year college (B.A./B.S.)	−7	−7
Master's or five-year professional degree	−8	−8
Ph.D. or six/seven-year professional degree	−9	−9

Occupation Prestige Level of Household Head:

Interviewer's judgment of how head of household rates in occupational status.
   (Respondent's description—ask for previous occupation if retired, or if R. is widow, ask husband's: _____)

Chronically unemployed—"day" laborers, unskilled: on welfare	−0
Steadily employed but in marginal semiskilled jobs: custodians, minimum-pay factory help, service workers (gas attendants, etc.)	−1
Average-skill assembly-line workers, bus and truck drivers, police and firefighters, route deliverymen, carpenters, brickmasons	−2
Skilled craftsmen (electricians), small contractors, factory foreman, low-pay sales-clerks, office workers, postal employees	−3
Owners of very small firms (2–4 employees), technicians, salespeople, office workers, civil servants with average level salaries	−4
Middle management, teachers, social workers, lesser professionals	−5
Lesser corporate officials, owners of middle-sized businesses (10–20 employees), moderate-success professionals (dentists, engineers, etc.)	−7
Top corporate executives, "big successes" in the professional world (leading doctors and lawyers), "rich" business owners.	−9

Area of Residence:

Interviewer's impressions of the immediate neighborhood in terms of its reputation in the eyes of the community.

Slum area: people on relief, common laborers	−1
Strictly working class: not slummy but some very poor housing	−2
Predominantly blue-collar with some office workers	−3
Predominantly white-collar with some well-paid blue-collar	−4
Better white-collar area; not many executives, but hardly any blue-collar either	−5
Excellent area: professionals and well-paid managers	−7
"Wealthy" or "society"-type neighborhood	−9

FIGURE 4.3
continued

Total Family Income per Year:

					Total Score ____
Under $5,000	−1	$20,000 to $24,999	−5		
$5,000 to $9,999	−2	$25,000 to $34,999	−6		
$10,000 to $14,999	−3	$35,000 to $49,999	−7	**Estimated**
$15,000 to $19,999	−4	$50,000 and over	−8	**Status** ____

(Interviewer's estimate: _____ and explanation: _____)

R's Marital Status:

Married _____ Divorced/Separated _____ Widowed _____ Single _____
(Code _____)

Source: Richard P. Coleman, "The Continuing Significance of Social Class to Marketing," *Journal of Consumer Research* 10 (December 1983), 265–280.

ZIP CODE MEASURES   A number of scales are being developed currently that measure social status by assigning a status value to the zip postal code or other geographic designation of a respondent's residence. These have been developed mostly by commercial research firms specializing in zip or geodemographic data based on the distribution of occupations, educational characteristics, income, condition of housing, and so forth, in zip code areas. (An example applied to media selection is described in Table 4.5.)

Zip methods are valuable because of their ability to measure status without the need to collect additional data from respondents beyond their addresses, which can then be related to variables such as the class of customers that will be attracted to a shopping center or a specific store, or the type of people that may respond to types of merchandise offered by a direct-mail organization.

WHICH SCALE IS BEST?

Social class is a rich, multidimensional variable. Social status has many subtle nuances that can be valuable to creative strategies in marketing but that may be missed unless the right measure is used. At a basic research level, there is much to be discovered about the relationships of social class to consumption of products and services, offering substantial opportunities for theory construction and conceptual development. These opportunities require independent measures of social class that can provide a high quality of data.

An ideal scale would satisfy the criteria offered by Dominquez and Page:

1. Validated Criterion Variable: The scale should be measured against the actual class or status rank of individuals, ascertained by independent means.

2. Appropriate Universe: Scales are validated against community or national samples. A community scale is not strictly applicable to different types of communities or to national samples.

3. Objective Predictors: Variables such as house type or dwelling area involve subjective, time-consuming, and potentially inaccurate evalua-

tions by raters and should be avoided. Variables such as a subject's own perceived class membership are prone to serious biases and should also be avoided. Objective variables such as income, education, or occupation are preferred.

4. Detailed Fit: Because is is comparatively easy to separate the extremely high- and low-ranked cases, a scale will overstate its ability to order a class or status hierarchy. The acid test of a scale's goodness of fit is its ability correctly to order closely ranked cases.

5. Split Sample Validation: Ultimately the most critical test of a scale is its ability to rank cases correctly in a second sample.

6. Contemporaneousness: Major social and economic shifts, such as the baby boom, the movement to suburbia, increased educational levels, and the consequences of inflation and the energy crisis may render obsolete scales that were devised prior to the occurrence of those phenomena.[21]

STATUS CRYSTALIZATION

One further complexity in measuring social class, as if any more were needed, is the problem of status inconsistency, or consideration of people who rate high on one variable but low on another. Status inconsistencies are logical consequences of the normal growth processes in status hierarchies.

Lenski developed an index of status crystalization and as a result of his studies concluded that people with low degree of status crystalization — people such as a black physician, a poorly educated but wealthy businessperson, or a low-paid professor — are subject to pressures from the social order. This is likely to make them more liberal and willing to support programs of social change.[22] The consequences will probably be greatest when the status inconsistency has high social visibility. The Nam and Powers Scale recognizes this problem and makes provisions for measuring the consistency of the status variables of occupation, income, and education.

ARE SOCIAL CLASSES CHANGING?

Are social classes as prevalent as they once were? Maybe social class is vanishing among working-class and middle-class people. This theory is sometimes called the *embourgeoisment* of society or the **massification theory.** Perhaps the prevalence of mass media and increasing income as well as dissemination of economic and political power on a wider basis have eliminated many of the differences

---

[21] Louis V. Dominquez and Albert L. Page, "Stratification in Consumer Behavior Research: A Re-Examination," *Journal of the Academy of Marketing Science* 9 (Summer 1981), 257–258.

[22] Gerhard E. Lenski, "Status Crystalization: A Non-Vertical Dimension of Social Status," *American Sociological Review* 21 (August 1956), 458–464.

between working-class and middle-class people. This issue is usually addressed by examination of economic indicators such as income and wealth. A major controversy exists concerning whether or not the middle class is shrinking in America,[23] but this topic will be discussed later, in Chapter 18.

An extensive review of factors such as power, income, wealth, status, and participation in the political process by Kriesberg concluded:

Personal wealth has probably become more equally distributed in the past fifty years, but wealth in the form of corporate shares has not; concentration in ownership of the means of production has increased, as is reflected in the decline of self-employment.[24]

The Duncan studies at the University of Michigan indicate much more economic mobility than was generally thought to be true in the past.[25] These studies are based upon analysis of movement between quintiles of income and show that between 1971 and 1978 only about half of those who started out in the lowest income quintile ended up there. Conversely, of the individuals in families in the highest quintile, fewer than half stayed there. Thus, "riches to rags" is about as common in the United States as "rags to riches."

Perhaps most surprising in the Duncan studies — and important for consumer researchers — is the finding that consumers below the poverty line do not stay there. In the 10-year period of the study (the 1970s), with average poverty levels about 12 percent, about 25 percent of Americans were below the poverty line for at least 1 year, but only 2.6 percent stayed there. In their book *Years of Poverty, Years of Plenty*, Duncan and his fellow researchers reported that the 2 percent chronically below the poverty level tend to be heavily dependent on welfare, to live in rural areas, and to be black, elderly, disabled, or in households headed by women with limited job opportunities. For most consumers, economical mobility is as probable as is geographic mobility.

Except for the 2 to 3 percent that are chronically poor, marketers can conclude from these studies, however, that poor consumers who have little purchasing power in one year may be individuals whom marketers may seek as valued customers in later years. Social class has not been eliminated in the United States, just changed a little. After an exhaustive review of the literature in this field, two of the most influential commentators on social class, Gilbert and Kahl, concluded:

---

[23] Dick Stevenson, "The Middle Class Comes Undone," *Ad Forum* 5 (June 1984), 32–39; Neal H. Rosenthal, "The Shrinking Middle Class: Myth or Reality," *Monthly Labor Review* 108 (March 1985), 3–10; McKinley L. Blackburn and David F. Bloom, "What Is Happening to the Middle Class?" *American Demographics* 7 (January 1985), 19–25; Patrick J. McMahon and John H. Tschetter, "The Declining Middle Class: A Further Analysis," *Monthly Labor Review* 109 (September 1986), 22–26.

[24] Louis Kriesberg, *Social Inequality* (Englewood Cliffs, N.J.: Prentice-Hall, 1979), 77–78.

[25] Greg J. Duncan, ed., *Years of Poverty, Years of Plenty* (Ann Arbor: Institute for Social Research, 1984).

Proportionately, the working class is declining while the upper-middle and middle classes, working poor, and the underclass are expanding. The blue-collar/white-collar distinction has lost force, and the fundamental cleavage in the class structure has moved upward. More generally, Americans in the top half of the class structure appear to be gaining privilege and power at the expense of those in the bottom half.[26]

HOW LIKELY ARE YOU TO CHANGE YOUR SOCIAL CLASS?

You may change your occupation and income, but can you change them enough to attain a social class different from your parents? How often is such change likely to occur? These are issues of intergenerational mobility.

The answer seems to be that, while it is possible to climb upward (or downward) in the social order, the probabilities of this actually happening are not very high.[27] Both men and women are affected by the low probability of change in social class, although women may have a bit more mobility through marriage than do men through occupations, since a man is more likely to inherit his father's status.[28] Women are also more likely to be lowered in status by divorce than are men. Upper-class people are more likely to believe that poverty is a result of equity or wasting money, while lower-class people tend to believe that the rich would resist social change that might end poverty.[29] Parental wealth is very important in determining the social class of the next generation, not only because of its direct effect but also because parental wealth has such a strong effect on the quality of education an individual receives.[30]

After reviewing the literature, Snarey and Vaillant concluded:

Children's social class is a stubborn predictor of their social class as adults. Only 1.8% of the children of manual laborers, for instance, entered the professions. Research to date has impressively documented factors that derail lower- and working-class individuals from upward social mobility. Among these are restricted access to educational and employment opportunities; high school tracking; class-biased career counseling; residential segregation by social class; class-biased achievement and IQ tests; lower teacher expectations for lower-class youth; and, perhaps most serious of all, racial prejudice.[31]

---

[26] Gilbert and Kahl, *The American Class Structure*, 340.

[27] Andrea Tyree and Robert W. Hodge, "Five Empirical Landmarks," *Social Forces* 56 (March 1978, 761–769. Some of the methodological issues in these studies are discussed in C. Matthew Snipp, "Occupational Mobility and Social Class: Insights from Men's Career Mobility,"*American Sociological Review* 50 (August 1985), 475–492.

[28] Ivan D. Chase, "A Comparison of Men's and Women's Intergenerational Mobility in the United States," *American Sociological Review* 40 (August 1975), 483–505.

[29] Robert L. Leahy, "Development of the Conception of Economic Inequality: Explanations, Justifications, and Concepts of Social Mobility and Change," *Developmental Psychology* 19 (1983), 111–125.

[30] Russell W. Rumberger, "The Influence of Family Background on Education, Earnings, and Wealth," *Social Forces* 61 (March 1983), 755–770.

[31] John R. Snarey and George E. Vaillant, "How Lower- and Working-Class Youth Become Middle-Class Adults: The Association Between Ego Defense Mechanisms and Upward Social Mobility," *Child Development* 56 (1985), 904–908.

HOW LARGE ARE SOCIAL CLASSES?

There is no unqualified answer to the question of how large specific social classes are. Table 4.3 shows some recent estimates, using measures of class used in contemporary marketing research.

The Gilbert and Kahl definitions shown in Table 4.3 emphasize economic distinctions, especially the recent emphasis on capitalism and entrepreneurship, whereas the Coleman-Rainwater approach emphasizes how people interact with each other as equals, superiors, or inferiors, especially in their work relationships.

TABLE 4.3
SOCIAL CLASSES IN AMERICA

Two Recent Views of the American Status Structure	
The Gilbert-Kahl New Synthesis Class Structure: A situations model from political theory and sociological analysis[a]	**The Coleman-Rainwater Social Standing Class Hierarchy: A reputational behavioral view in the community study tradition**[b]
Upper Americans	**Upper Americans**
The Capitalist Class (1%)— Their investment decisions shape the national economy: income mostly from assets earned inherited: prestige university connections Upper Middle Class (14%)—Upper managers, professionals, medium businessmen: college educated: family income ideally runs nearly twice the national average	Upper-Upper (0.3%)—The "capital S society" world of inherited wealth, aristocratic names Lower-Upper (1.2%)—The newer social elite drawn from current professional corporate leadership Upper-Middle (12.5%)—The rest of college graduate managers and professionals: life style centers on private clubs, causes, and the arts
Middle Americans	**Middle Americans**
Middle Class (33%)—Middle level white-collar, top level blue-collar: education past high school typical: income somewhat above the national average Working Class (32%)—Middle level blue-collar: lower level white-collar: income runs slightly below the national average: education is also slightly below	Middle Class (32%)—Average pay white-collar workers and their blue-collar friends: live on the "the better side of town," try to "do the proper things" Working Class (38%)—Average pay blue-collar workers: lead "working class lifestyle" whatever the income, school background, and job
Marginal and Lower Americans	**Lower Americans**
The Working Poor (11–12%)—Below mainstream America in living standard, but above the poverty line: low-paid service workers, operatives: some high school education The Underclass (8–9%)—Depend primarily on welfare system for sustenance: living standard below poverty line: not regularly employed: lack schooling	"A lower group of people but not the lowest" (9%)—Working not on welfare: living standard is just above poverty: behavior judged "crude," "trashy" "Real Lower-Lower" (7%)—On welfare, visibly poverty-stricken, usually out of work (or have "the dirtiest jobs"): "bums," "common criminals"

[a] Abstracted by Coleman from Gilbert, Dennis and Joseph A. Kahl, "The American Class Structure: A Synthesis." Chapter 11 in *The American Class Structure: A New Syntheses.* Homewood, Ill.: The Dorsey Press, 1982).
[b] This condensation of the Coleman-Rainwater view is drawn from Chapters 8, 9, and 10 of Coleman, Richard P. and Lee P. Rainwater, with Kent A. McClelland, *Social Standing in America: New Dimensions of Class* (New York: Basic Books, 1978).

SOCIAL CLASS DYNAMICS

Social class behavior is dynamic because it reflects the changing environment. Particularly important was the "counterculture" that emerged during the Vietnam era and the decade of the 1970s, which created attempts to display nonclass symbols and behavior.

Parody display is a term used to describe the mockery of status symbols and behavior, such as when the well-to-do wear blue jeans, even worn and threadbare ones, to proclaim their distaste for class and/or their own security in the social status system. The "youth culture" of the 1960s and 1970s caused greater importance to be placed on symbols and behavior of young people who exhibited parody display, both because of counterculture attitudes and the economic reality of limited income.

As those groups evolved through the 1980s and into the 1990s, social class symbols regained importance. The Reagan/Bush administrations and a new wave of entrepreneurial capital accumulation, as well as the influence and affluence of yuppie (Young Urban Professionals) consumers during the 1980s, contributed to display social class status symbols in the possession and use of consumer goods.

Today, there is also more individualism or "doing your own thing" among the middle social classes, possibly as another example of the emulation of the same trend among the upper classes in earlier years. Coleman describes this situation:

> Through the 1960s and 1970s, the lifestyles and self-conceptions of people identified with the upper sixth of the nation appear to have changed more than those of people in the classes below. The life-style variations that have emerged exist vertically within Upper America, crossing the substrata and combining people from several status layers into one consumer group with common goals that are differentiated internally mainly by income. . . . The result is that Upper America is now a vibrant mix of many lifestyles, which may be labeled post-preppy, sybaritic, countercultural, conventional, intellectual, political, and so on. Such diversions are usually of more importance for targeting messages and goods than are the horizontal, status-flavored, class-named strata.[32]

MARKETING TO SOCIAL CLASS SEGMENTS

After you have read through the preceding pages, you should have a good grasp of what is meant by social stratification, how it is measured, how it is changing — both for individual consumers and in the society as a whole — and some reasonably specific descriptive ideas of how people in one social stratum differ in their behavior from people in higher or lower strata. Now

---

[32] Richard P. Coleman, "The Continuing Significance of Social Class in Marketing," *Journal of Consumer Research* 10 (December 1983), 263–280, at 270.

it is time to bring this all together and ask, "How are buying decisions affected by social class? What does this mean for a marketing organization?"

Most stratification studies in the consumer behavior literature have been concerned with the influence of social class on product choice rather than brand choice. Brand choice studies are often proprietary in nature. Consequently, these studies are not as available in the published literature.

MARKET SEGMENTATION

Social class is often applied to the problem of market segmentation, the process of defining homogeneous customer groups and making an especially strong offering to them. Social class was found to be a useful concept for the segmentation of markets in pioneering work by people such as Pierre Martineau (marketing researcher at the *Chicago Tribune*), Sidney Levy of Northwestern University, and Richard Coleman of Social Research Inc.[33]

The procedures for market segmentation include the following steps:

1. identification of social class usage of product
2. comparison of social class variables for segmentation with other variables (income, life cycle, etc.)
3. description of social class characteristics identified in market target
4. development of marketing program to maximize effectiveness of marketing mix based upon consistency with social class attributes

An example of this process is illustrated by the AT&T marketing of telephones. Figure 4.4 shows the socioeconomic/life cycle grid used to identify market targets. In this instance, another variable was found useful in conjunction with social class — life cycle, a topic examined in depth in Chapter 6 on family. Notice how AT&T has identified in quantitative terms the number of families in each cell, considered on the axes of life cycle and socioeconomic class. The next stage in this strategy is describing the social class characteristics of each cell. Some indication of how this is done is shown in Table 4.4, which is from another study by AT&T.

Notice that social class segments can be described with two types of variables: general profile information, and product-specific information. Table 4.4 contains both types of information. Other forms of marketing research can be conducted to build a comprehensive understanding of each segment.

Analysis of market segments by socioeconomic profile allows a marketer to develop a comprehensive marketing program to match the socioeconomic characteristics of the market target. This would include product attributes, media strategy, creative strategy, channels of distribution, and pricing.

---

[33] Classic publications that in the 1990s are still valuable reading for consumer analysts include Pierre Martineau, "Social Classes and Spending Behavior," *Journal of Marketing* 23 (October 1958), 121–130; Sidney Levy, "Social Class and Consumer Behavior," in Joseph W. Newman, ed., *On Knowing the Consumer* (New York: John Wiley & Sons, 1966), 146–160; Richard P. Coleman and Bernice L. Newgarten, *Social Status in the City* (San Francisco: Jossey-Bass, 1971).

FIGURE 4.4
IDENTIFYING
SOCIOECONOMIC
MARKET SEGMENTS

Socioeconomic/Life Cycle Grid
Population _____   Characteristic _____

			Socioeconomic Class				Life Cycle Totals
			Lower	Lower Middle	Upper Middle	Upper	
Life Cycle Category	*Younger Households*	*No Children*	1.5	5.7	6.8	2.9	16.9
		Younger Children	0.9	6.2	8.1	4.3	19.5
		Older Children	1.4	8.7	10.8	4.8	25.7
	Older Households		12.5	13.5	8.8	3.1	37.9
	SES Class Totals		16.3	34.1	34.5	15.1	100.0

Composite Totals

SES	Life Cycle		Total
Middle Class*	Family Households†	Younger Households	Middle-Class Family Households
68.6	45.2	62.1	33.8

* Lower-middle and   † Younger households—
upper-middle classes   younger and older children

Source: R. B. Ellis, "Composite Population Descriptors: The Socio-Economic/LIfe Cycle Grid," in M. J. Schlinger, ed. *Advances in Consumer Research II* (Chicago: Association for Consumer Research, 1975), 490. Reprinted by permission.

INCOME OR SOCIAL CLASS?   Is social status a better variable for market segmentation than income? The controversy has been debated in the marketing literature for years. Generally the conclusion is that income is adequate for some products, but that social class is superior for others.

Schaninger thoroughly reviewed the income versus social class issue and the conduct of empirical research measuring frequency of use, and found that social class is superior to income in segmenting food and nonsoft-drink/ nonalcoholic beverage markets, as well as shopping behavior and evening television viewing. Income is superior to social class for segmenting markets for major appliances, soft drinks, mixers, and alcoholic beverages. The combi-

TABLE 4.4 DESCRIPTIONS OF SOCIOECONOMIC MARKET SEGMENTS

A General Psychographic Profile of Customer's Socioeconomic Status

Style/Color Statements	Lower Class Agreement (%) (n = 25)	Lower-Middle Class Agreement (%) (n = 108)	Upper-Middle Class Agreement (%) (n = 202)	Upper Class Agreement (%) (n = 105)
I am generally willing to try even the most radical fashion at least once.	32	25	42	37
When I must choose between the two, I usually dress for fashion not for comfort.	9	15	24	29
Our home is furnished for comfort, not style.	96	87	79	79
I have more modern appliances in my home than most people.	17	23	41	48
I prefer colored appliances.	57	73	87	92
I enjoy the better things in life and am willing to pay for them.	36	70	70	82

Note: All significant levels are based on x^2 with $p < .05$, 3 d.f.

A Product-Specific Psychographic Profile of Customer's Socioeconomic Status

Style/Color Statements	Lower Class Agreement (%) (n = 25)	Lower-Middle Class Agreement (5) (n = 108)	Upper-Middle Class Agreement (%) (n = 202)	Upper Class Agreement (%) (n = 105)
Phones should come in patterns and designs as well as colors.	60	80	63	58
A telephone should improve the decorative style of a room.	47	82	73	77
Telephones should be modern in design.	58	85	83	89
A home should have a variety of telephone styles.	8	46	39	51
You can keep all those special phones. All I want is a phone that works.	83	67	68	56
The style of a telephone is unimportant to me.	86	54	58	51

Source: A. Marvin Roscoe, Jr., Arthur LeClaire, Jr., and Leon G. Schiffman, "Theory and Management Applications of Demographics in Buyer Behavior," in Arch G. Woodside, Jagdish N. Sheth, and Peter D. Bennett, eds., *Consumer and Industrial Buying Behavior* (Amsterdam: North-Holland, 1977), 74–75. Reprinted by permission.

nation of income and social class is superior for determining markets for makeup and clothing, as well as for automobile and television ownership.[34]

In the analysis of consumer behavior, we should not expect major differences between social classes as much as subtle differences in consumption of products. What counts in contrasts between social classes are the small

---

[34] Charles M. Schaninger, "Social Class Versus Income Revisited: An Empirical Investigation," *Journal of Marketing Research* 18 (May 1981), 192–208.

4.3   SOCIAL CLASS INFLUENCES ON APPEARANCE PRODUCT: YOU ARE WHAT YOU WEAR

There is an elite look in this country. It requires women to be thin, with a hairstyle dating back eighteen or twenty years or so. (The classiest women wear their hair for a lifetime in exactly the style they affected in college.) They wear superbly fitting dresses and expensive but always understated shoes and handbags, with very little jewelry. They wear scarves — these instantly betoken class, because they are useless except as a caste mark. Men should be thin. No jewelry at all. No cigarette case. Moderate-length hair, never dyed or tinted, which is a middle-class or high-prole sign. . . . Never a hairpiece, a prole usage. Both women's and men's elite looks are achieved by a process of rejection — of the current, the showy, the superfluous. Thus the rejection of fat by the elite. It pays to be thin.

"Layering" is obligatory. It has generally been true that the more clothes someone has on, the higher his or her status; it is a fine way of displaying a large wardrobe. The upper-middle-class woman will appear almost invariably in a skirt of gray flannel, Stuart plaid, or khaki; a navy-blue cardigan, which may be cable stitched; a white blouse with Peter Pan collar; hose with flat shoes; hair preferably in a barrette. When it gets cold, she puts on a blue blazer, or for business, a gray flannel suit. But the color toward which everything aspires is really navy.

If navy is the upper-middle-class color, purple is the prole equivalent. The purple polyester pantsuit offends two principles that determine class in clothes: the color principle and the organic-materials principle. Navy blue aside, colors are classier the more pastel or faded, and materials are classier the more they consist of anything that was once alive. That means wool, leather, silk, cotton, and fur. Only. All synthetic fibers are prole, partly because they're cheaper than natural ones, partly because they're not archaic, and partly because they're entirely uniform and hence boring — you'll never find a bit of straw or sheep excrement woven into an acrylic sweater. (The organic principle also determines that in kitchens wood is classier than Formica, and on the kitchen table a cotton cloth "higher" than plastic or oilcloth.)

nuances that give products higher appeal to some classes than to others.[35] These nuances, however small, are often the key to yielding higher margins for some products than for others.

NEED RECOGNITION AND EVALUATIVE CRITERIA

Social class research reveals many insights into usage patterns of consumers that may create need recognition leading to decision making about purchases. These patterns also reveal criteria for evaluating the product or services that

---

[35] Q. J. Munters, "Social Stratification and Consumer Behavior," *The Netherlands Journal of Sociology* 13.

So important for genuine upper-middle-class standing is the total renunciation of artificial fibers that the elite eye becomes skilled in detecting even, as *The Official Preppy Handbook* has it, "a small percentage of polyester in an Oxford-cloth shirt" — a sad middle-caste mark. The same invaluable book praises young Caroline Kennedy unreservedly — "on technical points Preppier than Mummy" — because "during four years at Harvard Square, an unnatural fiber never went near her body."

If you can gauge people's proximity to prole status by the color and polyester content of their garments, legibility of their dress is another slight. The messages may be simple, like BUDWEISER or HEINEKEN'S, or they may be complex and often lewd. As you move up the classes, the words gradually disappear, to be replaced, in the middle and upper-middle classes, by mere emblems. Once, ascending further, you've left all such trademarks behind, you may correctly infer that you are entering the purlieus of the upper class itself.

The tweed jacket is indispensable to the upper-middle-class trick of layering. A man signals that he's classy if, outdoors, he comes on in a tweed jacket, with vest or sweater (or two), shirt, tie, long wool scarf, and overcoat or raincoat. Since sweaters are practically obligatory for layering, it's important to know that the classiest is the Shetland crewneck pullover, and in "Scottish" colors — heather and the like, especially when a tieless Oxford-cloth shirt (palpably without artificial fibers) just peeps over the top. Add a costly tweed jacket without shoulder padding and no can tell you're not upper-middle at least. The V-neck sweater, designed to prove conclusively that you're wearing a necktie, is for that reason middle-class or even high prole. It's hard to believe that sometimes people tuck pullovers into the top of their trousers. If this does happen, it's a very low sign.

Source: Paul Russel, *Class* (New York: Ballantine Books, 1983).

---

meet consumer needs. The final portion of this chapter describes some of these findings. [Consumer in Focus 4.3 describes some of these symbols, reflected in the clothes and other appearance items purchased by consumers.]

CLOTHING   The kind, quality, and style of clothing a person wears is closely linked to that person's social class, as Consumer in Focus 4.3 so vividly describes. Clothing furnishes a quick, visual cue to the class culture of the wearer.

The greatest interest in fashion is usually found in upper social classes, although high interest may be found among all social classes. Clothing serves well as a symbol of social differentiation because of its high visibility. When adolescent girls are asked to describe the characteristics of the popular girls, "dressed well" is the response most frequently given — that is, linked to social class characteristics.

A 14-year-old student, attending a private high school in an upper-middle-class suburb, described the other students in the following manner:

> There are three types of kids in our school. The rich kids wear Guess Jeans or Forenza from the Limited. They have their parents' credit cards or their own, so they are used to getting what they want. They have to go to the bathroom after lunch to put on their makeup. They have seven Swatch watches, one for each day of the week. Their hair is curly or bobbed in a wave. At home they have waterbeds. The lower class kids don't dress as well. They don't hang around the cooler groups. They get made fun of a lot. They may have styles from the Limited but you know they bought them at T. J. Max. The lower class (at this school) have more money than the kids at public schools, but they don't dress well or act right. The middle class kids have money and dress nice but they are not really cool and they don't talk about themselves as much as the upper class kids.

For business students, clothing has become more complicated in recent years, because of the high amount of sex-typing that also accompanies the clothing of career women. Although more related to occupational classes than social class, it appears to be true that if a woman wants to succeed in a man's world, she had better not look too feminine. Psychologists Cash and Janda asked personnel consultants to judge businesswomen groomed in two different ways. One way was very feminine, with longer hair, soft sweaters, low necklines, dangling jewelry, and heavy makeup. The other was with tailored clothes with a jacket, subtle makeup, and either short hair or hair swept away from the face. The less feminine the appearance, the more competent they were rated by the personnel consultants.[36]

HOME FURNISHINGS   Criteria used by families to furnish a home are closely related to social class. Laumann and House carefully observed the contents and characteristics of a living room, using a 53-item checklist inventory. Using a cluster technique called Smallest Space Analysis (SSA), the researchers were able to arrange the 53 variables into the two-dimensional space on the axes of social status and modern/traditional. The modern respondents were generally upwardly mobile within this generation; they were frequently *nouveaux-riches*.[37]

The *nouveaux-riches* may have a strong need to validate their newly found status. Yet they may not have been accepted socially by the traditional upper classes, so they turn to conspicuous consumption, or display of the products that are symbols of their position. This is done with taste in order to validate

---

[36] Thomas F. Cash and Louis H. Janda, "The Eye of the Beholder," *Psychology Today* 18 (December 1984), 46–52.

[37] Edward O. Laumann and James S. House, "Living Room Styles and Social Attributes: The Patterning of Material Artifacts in a Modern Urban Community," *Sociology and Social Research* 54 (April 1970), 326.

their claim to high status rather than to mere possession of money. The researchers concluded that the evaluative criteria used by this mobile class reflect the chic norms of tastemakers, observed by personal interactions by the upper classes and by other classes by reading the pages of *The New Yorker* or *Architectural Digest*.

The criteria used to purchase products for a home and display them can also be discerned in Figure 4.5, based on status of household products. This is an updated version of a classic study by F. Stuart Chapin and is presented somewhat tongue-in-cheek. Careful consideration of the items in the scale, however, serves to help marketers understand what consumers in each social class will buy and what should be included or avoided in the advertising and sales presentations for household products.

LEISURE   Social class affects leisure in a variety of ways. The type of leisure preferred is based upon activities that occur primarily with people in the same or closely adjacent status levels. The influence to adopt new leisure activities will be from people with the same or slightly higher status than the adopters.[38]

The proportion of family income spent on leisure may not vary a great deal between social classes, but the type of recreation varies greatly. Polo is upper class; bridge is a middle- to upper-class game, whereas bingo is lower class. Squash is upper class, tennis and racquetball are middle to upper class, boxing is predominantly lower class. Opera is upper class, Roller Derby is lower class.

Prestige leisure time activities (jogging, swimming, tennis, etc.) involve fairly rapid movement, with extreme use of arms and legs, suggesting a compensatory form of leisure for the otherwise sedentary life of many prestige occupations. Most of these pursuits do not require much time to the degree that activities such as hunting, fishing, or boating would — typical leisure-time pursuits of lower social class. Time is a critical element in the prestige classes' use of leisure. Members of lower social classes tend to participate in team sports, whereas people of higher socioeconomic status tend to participate in individual or dual sports.[39] The heaviest users of both commercial leisure and public facilities (such as parks, museums, and swimming pools) are the middle classes, since upper classes frequently have their own facilities and the lower classes often cannot afford them or do not have the propensity to participate in them.

Chief executives of major corporations may have little time for leisure because of their long hours, typically 59 hours a week at work and increasing. Most senior managers enjoy leisure pursuits on a daily basis, however. Many

---

[38] Patrick C. West, "Status Differences and Interpersonal Influence in the Adoption of Outdoor Recreation Activities," *Journal of Leisure Research* 16 (1984), 350–354.

[39] Susan L. Greendorfer, "Social Class Influence on Female Sport Involvement," *Sex Roles* 4 (August 1978), 619–625.

FIGURE 4.5   THE LIVING ROOM SCALE

(Revised)

(An early primitive form of this was promulgated in 1935 by F. Stuart Chapin in his book *Contemporary American Institutions.*)

Begin with a score of 100. For each of the following in your living room (or those of friends or acquaintances) add or subtract points as indicated. Then ascertain social class according to the table at the end.

Hardwood floor	add 4	*Town and Country*	add 2
Parquet floor	add 8	*New York Review of Books*	add 5
Stone floor	add 4	*Times Literary Supplement*	
Vinyl floor	subtract 6	(London)	add 5
Wall-to-wall carpet	add 2	*Paris Match*	add 6
Working fireplace	add 4	*Hudson Review*	add 8
New Oriental rug or carpet	subtract 2 (each)	Each family photograph (black-	
Worn Oriental rug or carpet	add 5 (each)	and-white)	subtract 2
Threadbare rug or carpet	add 8 (each)	Each family photograph (color)	subtract 3
Ceiling ten feet high, or higher	add 6	Each family photograph (black-	
Original paintings by		and-white or color) in sterling-	
internationally recognized		silver frame	add 3
practitioners	add 8 (each)	Potted citrus tree with midget fruit	
Original drawings, prints, or litho-		growing	add 8
graphs by internationally recog-		Potted palm tree	add 5
nized practitioners	add 5 (each)	Bowling-ball carrier	subtract 6
Reproductions of any Picasso paint-		Fishbowl or aquarium	subtract 4
ing, print, or anything	subtract 2 (each)	Fringe on any upholstered furni-	
Original paintings, drawings, or		ture	subtract 4
prints by family members	subtract 4 (each)	Identifiable Naugahyde aping	
Windows curtained, rods and draw		anything customarily made of	
cords	add 5	leather	subtract 3
Windows curtained, no rods or draw		Any item exhibiting words in an	
cords	add 2	ancient or modern foreign lan-	
Genuine Tiffany lamp	add 3	guage (Spanish excluded)	add 7
Reproduction Tiffany lamp	subtract 4	Wooden venetian blinds	subtract 2
Any work of art depicting cowboys	subtract 3	Metal venetian blinds	subtract 4
"Professional" oil portrait of any		Tabletop obelisk of marble, glass,	
member of the household	subtract 3	etc.	add 9
Any display of "collectibles"	subtract 4	No periodicals visible	subtract 5
Transparent plastic covers on furni-		Fewer than five pictures on walls	subtract 5
ture	subtract 6	Each piece of furniture over 50	
Furniture upholstered with any me-		years old	add 2
tallic threads	subtract 3	Bookcase(s) full of books	add 7
Cellophane on any lampshade	subtract 4	Any leather bindings more than	
No ashtrays	subtract 2	75 years old	add 6
Refrigerator, washing machine, or		Bookcase(s) partially full of books	add 5
clothes dryer in living room	subtract 6	Overflow books stacked on floor,	
Motorcycle kept in living room	subtract 10	chairs, etc.	add 6
Periodicals visible, laid out flat:		Hutch bookcase ("wall system")	
National Enquirer	subtract 6	displaying plates, pots, porce-	
Popular Mechanics	subtract 5	lain figurines, etc., but no books	subtract 4
Reader's Digest	subtract 3	Wall unit with built-in TV, stereo,	
National Geographic	subtract 2	etc.	subtract 4
Smithsonian	subtract 1	On coffee table, container of	
Scientific American	subtract 1	matchbooks from funny or	
New Yorker	add 1	anomalous places	add 1

FIGURE 4.5 *continued*

Works of sculpture (original, and not made by householder or any family member)	add 4 (each)	Each "Eames chair"	subtract 2
Works of sculpture made by householder or any family member	subtract 5 (each)	Anything displaying the name or initials of anyone in the household	subtract 4
Every item alluding specifically to the United Kingdom	add 1	Curved moldings visible anywhere in the room	add 5

CALCULATING THE SCORE	
245 and above	Upper class
185–245	Upper-middle
100–185	Middle
50–100	High prole
Below 50	Mid- or low prole

Any item alluding, even remotely, to Tutankhamen	subtract 4
Each framed certificate, diploma, or testimonial	subtract 2
Each "laminated" ditto	subtract 3
Each item with a "tortoiseshell" finish, if only made of Formica	add 1

Source: Paul Fussell, *Class* (New York: Ballantine Books, 1983), 230–233. Copyright © *1983 by Paul Fussell. Reprinted by permission of Summit Books, a division of Simon & Schuster, Inc.*

take part in recreational sports; others paint, play musical instruments, photograph nature and family, or escape into the world of literature. Reading work-related books and listening to music are among the favorite pursuits of highest-ranking executives, with social class backgrounds reflected in their preferences. Executives with middle-class backgrounds prefer classical music more than those with upper-class backgrounds do.[40]

CREDIT CARDS   Credit card acceptance and usage appear to be related to some extent to social class. Slocum and Mathews concluded that the lower classes prefer to use bank cards for durable and necessity goods (appliances, furniture, clothing) in contrast to the upper class, who charge luxury items (travel, luggage, restaurants).[41] Earliest use of credit or bank cards was associated with higher income, better education, middle age, and professional occupations.[42]

SEARCH PROCESSES

The amount and type of search undertaken by an individual varies by social class as well as by product and situation category. Unfortunately, the lowest social classes have limited information sources, and they are at a disadvantage

---

[40] Louis E. Boone, David L. Kurtz, and C. Patrick Fleenor, "Games CEOs Play," *American Demographics* 11 (January 1989), 43–45.

[41] John W. Slocum and H. Lee Mathews, "Social Class and Income as Indicators of Consumer Credit Behavior," *Journal of Marketing* 34 (April 1970), 71–78.

[42] Joseph T. Plummer, "Life Style Patterns and Commercial Bank Credit Card Usage," *Journal of Marketing* 35 (April 1971), 35–41; Douglass K. Hawes, Roger D. Blackwell, and W. Wayne Talarzyk," Attitudes Toward Use of Credit Cards: Do Men and Women Differ?" *Baylor Business Studies* 110 (January 1977), 57–71.

TABLE 4.5
MAGAZINE
EFFECTIVENESS
FOR SOCIAL
CLASS TARGETS

Domestic Airplane Travel

Zip-Market Cluster	Percent of Population	Percent of Market	Index
1. Blue Blood Estates	0.61	3.26	537
2. Furs and Station Wagons	2.07	9.85	475
3. Young Influentials	3.08	9.45	306
4. Two More Rungs	1.60	4.83	301
5. Money and Brains	1.41	3.15	225

Better Homes and Gardens

Correlation with the Target Market: .306

Zip-Market Cluster	Percent of Population	Percent of Audience	Index
1. Furs and Station Wagons	2.07	2.96	143
2. Coalburg and Corntown	3.77	4.80	127
3. Money and Brains	1.41	1.77	126
4. Grain Belt	1.93	2.34	121
5. Pools and Patios	3.79	4.57	121

Glamour Magazine

Correlation with the Target Market: .658

Zip-Market Cluster	Percent of Population	Percent of Audience	Index
1. Urban Gold Coast	0.33	0.82	248
2. Hispanic Mix	0.51	0.75	148
3. Young Influentials	3.08	4.52	147
4. Money and Brains	1.41	2.06	147
5. Two More Rungs	1.60	2.34	146

National Enquirer

Correlation with the Target Market: −.284

Zip-Market Cluster	Percent of Population	Percent of Audience	Index
1. Old Brick Factories	3.18	5.11	161
2. Norma Rae-video	2.09	3.29	158
3. Marlboro Country	3.33	4.86	146
4. Shotguns and Pickups	2.31	3.37	146
5. Bohemian Mix	0.78	1.06	136

The New Yorker Magazine

Correlation with the Target Market: .712

Zip-Market Cluster	Percent of Population	Percent of Audience	Index
1. Urban Gold Coast	0.33	2.40	726
2. Blue Blood Estates	0.61	2.95	485
3. Money and Brains	1.41	6.71	478
4. Bohemian Mix	0.78	3.02	388
5. Young Influentials	3.08	9.63	312

Source: Hugh Cannon and Gerald Linda, "Beyond Media Imperatives: Goedemographic Media Selection," *Journal of Advertising Research* 22 (June/July 1982), 34. Copyright 1982 by The Advertising Research Foundation.

in filtering out misinformation and fraud in a complex, urbanized society. To compensate, working-class consumers often rely on relatives or close friends for information about consumption decisions. Middle-class consumers put more reliance upon media-acquired information and actively engage in external search from the media. As the level of social class increases, so does access to media information.

Media and messages can be tailored to specific social classes. The language and appearance, as well as how the product is used, communicate to each social class whether or not "this product is for me." At different times, some TV networks have had stronger appeal in some social classes than in others, and many firms forego direct commercial messages for the soft sell of "Funding provided by . . ." that can be placed upon the Public Broadcasting Service stations directed to upper-class audiences.

Magazines offer the possibility of detailed social class positioning. An example is shown in Table 4.5 in which social class variables are combined with zip codes to provide a very specific evaluation of the effectiveness of magazines for different classes. Using one firm's definitions of neighborhoods, markets can be classified as Blue Blood Estates, Furs and Station Wagons, Urban Gold Coast, and Old Brick Favorites.

The profiles of these groups provide useful insights into the nature of the audience and types of creative appeals that may be most effective. When the usage of a brand is correlated with purchase in these groups, zip code information can then be obtained to measure the strength of various magazines in reaching each group.

In the example of domestic airplane travel shown in Table 4.5, *Better Homes & Gardens* includes two of the top five air travel categories, but *Glamour* and *The New Yorker* contain three and the *National Enquirer* none. When the percentage of population reached is combined with the percentage of audience using air travel, *The New Yorker* becomes the best vehicle, with an index of correlation with the market of .712, compared to scores of .658 for *Glamour* and .306 for *Better Homes & Gardens*, and a negative index of −.284 for *National Enquirer*.[43]

SOCIAL LANGUAGE

The language patterns of individuals are closely correlated with their social class. In one set of experiments, the social classes of respondents were first measured before they were asked to make a 40-second recording of the fable, "The Tortoise and the Hare." These short recordings were played to groups of 15 to 30 regionally diverse college students who served as judges. The average ratings of social class by these judges correlated 0.80 with the speakers' social classes.[44]

---

[43] Hugh M. Canon and Gerald Linda, "Beyond Media Imperatives: Geodemographic Media Selection," *Journal of Advertising Research* 22 (June/July 1982), 31–36.
[44] Dean S. Ellis, "Speech and Social Status in America," *Social Forces* 45 (March 1967), 431–437.

**FIGURE 4.6
SOCIAL CLASS
INFLUENCE ON
ADVERTISING COPY
INCLUDES
LANGUAGE
PATTERNS**

When speakers were asked in role playing to alter their voices to sound upper class, the student judges' correlation with measured actual class was still 0.65. All of the subjects used proper grammar, but their choice of vocabulary, sentence length, sentence structure, and fluency varied by social class. In still another approach, speakers were asked to count from 1 to 20, and even in this situation, college students' rankings correlated 0.65 with social class of speakers.

The importance of language can be understood by analysis of the copy used in advertisements. Expensive cars such as Mercedes and Cadillac use longer words, fewer euphemisms, and more abstract language. Lower- and middle-class car ads speak more of physical attributes, emphasize pictures rather than words, and are more likely to use slang or street language.

FERRELL
REED
MAKES
SHIRTS

FERRELL REED LTD., 5571 ARAPAHOE AVENUE, BOULDER, COLORADO 80303 TELEPHONE (800) 421-6119

A practical application of social language is shown in Figure 4.6. An ad for a middle-class shirt typically contains copy describing benefits of the product. The ad for an upper-class shirt is a masterpiece of understatement and directness: "Ferrell Reed makes shirts."

PURCHASING PROCESSES

Social status influences where and how people feel they should shop. Lower-status people prefer local, face-to-face places where they get friendly service and easy credit — often in the neighborhood. Upper-middle consumers feel more confident in their shopping ability. They will venture to new places to shop and will range throughout a store to find what they want.

The discount store traditionally appeals to the middle classes because they are careful and economy-minded in their buying. In their early years, discount stores frequently did not carry prestige or designer brands, but as the middle classes' income grew and information influences broadened, firms such as J. C. Penney, K mart, and Target have added more designer brands. K mart expanded this concept to a new chain, called Designer Depot. Major retail organizations no longer do well by serving only one social class; many develop a portfolio of stores to appeal to the variety of social classes and lifestyles that exist in industrialized societies such as Canada and the United States.[45]

Consumers have an image of what social class a store attracts and have an understanding of what shopping should be like in a store that appeals to their own social class. People in upper classes want a pleasant store atmosphere featuring exciting displays; lower classes emphasize acquiring household things or clothing as the enjoyable part of shopping. Historically, upper classes shop more frequently than middle or lower classes but may be shopping more in the future with catalogues or videotex offerings such as CompuServe or other forms of direct marketing because of the time pressures felt by so many dual-income families. The greatest propensity for family members to shop together is among lower, white-collar, skilled, and semiskilled occupational classes. Shopping for many middle-class families, however, is a form of recreation. They are the ones willing to visit regional shopping malls. They are also most likely to experiment with store brands and respond most to variations in price offerings.

A CONCLUDING NOTE

Social class is essential to positioning — the creating of perceptions in consumers' minds about the attributes of a product or organization. Positioning is difficult, however, if those in charge of marketing strategies do not understand the class characteristics desired for the product or the class characteristics of the target market.

Beer companies have not usually maintained long-term relationships with Madison Avenue ad agencies. The beer companies have often gone to agencies outside of Manhattan. The reason, some veteran advertising observers have commented, is that there are too many martini drinkers on Madison Avenue. Whether that is true or not may be questioned, but the conclusion to draw is that if you are selling to market targets of social classes different from your own, be sure you do your homework to understand well the social class characteristics of your market target.

Among industrialized societies the market for people who aspire to higher social classes is increasing even faster than the numbers of consumers in upper-middle or upper classes. Their level of affluence is high enough to permit them to satisfy their aspirations on some occasions, as the concluding

---

[45] Roger Blackwell and Wayne Talarzyk, "Lifestyle Retailing: Competitive Strategies for the 1980's, *Journal of Retailing* 59 (December 1983), 7–27.

CONSUMER IN FOCUS

4.4 THE HIGH-LIVING MIDDLE CLASS

Some 3.3 million American households have incomes that enable them to live affluent or rich lives. But far more — some 26 million — partake of the good life some of the time, treating themselves to Godiva chocolates, Giorgio Armani cologne, and long weekends in St. Thomas and Jamaica. They are the Joneses of the Eighties, and most have incomes of less than $40,000.

Market researchers at Grey Advertising interviewed people across the country between the ages of 21 and 50 with household incomes of more than $25,000 a year, a slice representing about a quarter of the adult population. Of those surveyed, just over half said they bought the top of the line whenever they could afford it. Only 5% of these ultra consumers had incomes above $75,000, Fortune's minimum for an affluent lifestyle.

The vast majority of these folks obviously aren't in the market for Rolls-Royces or complete designer wardrobes. But they do *rent* limos from time to time and are devotees of designer label accessories like Hermes scarves and Gucci loafers. "This is more an attitude of the mind than the pocketbook," says Barbara Feignin, an executive vice president at Grey.

Wanting it all has long been a hallmark of the middle class. Ultra consumers also want the best. Buying the best is a way to set themselves apart and bolster their self-image. Madison Avenue strives to reinforce that desire. Ads for premium-priced products as varied as Ultress hair coloring and Mitsubishi cars have a cloying sameness: sensual, provocative, and elegant, no matter what's for sale.

Source: Jaclyn Fierman, "The High-Living Middle Class," *Fortune* 115 (April 13, 1987), 27.

Consumer in Focus 4.4 demonstrates. Middle-class consumers respond to the "pull" of wanting upward mobility more than do the lower or working classes because the lower classes do not revere the upper class as much as does the middle class.[46] Consequently appeals with higher-class nuances may be effective with middle-class consumers but not with lower-class ones.

SUMMARY

Social classes are relatively permanent and homogeneous groupings of people in society, permitting groups of people to be compared with one another. These groups are recognized as having inferior or superior positions by the individuals who comprise the society, often based upon economic position in the marketplace.

[46] F. Russell and F. LeMasters, *Blue Collar Aristocrats: Life Style at a Working Class Tavern* (Madison: University of Wisconsin Press, 1975).

Social classes are discrete groups in theory, but in practice they are usually analyzed as continuous-status variables. Status is a multidimensional concept and is best measured as such. Occupation is the single most important measure of an individual's social class. Other important variables are the personal interactions a person has with other individuals, possessions, value orientations, and class consciousness.

Social classes in the United States were traditionally divided into six groups: upper upper, lower upper, upper middle, lower middle, upper lower, and lower lower or marginal classes. Newer classification systems emphasize the enlarged capitalist or professional classes in the upper-middle or lower-lower classes. Social classes are always in transition, however, causing status and its symbols to be dynamic. Each group displays characteristic values and behaviors that are useful to consumer analysts in designing marketing programs. It is necessary to analyze need recognition, search processes, evaluative criteria, and purchasing patterns of various social classes to match products and communications correctly to actual and aspiring social classes.

REVIEW AND DISCUSSION QUESTIONS

1. What variables determine an individual's social class? In what order of importance should they be ranked?

2. In what way does income relate to social class? Why is it used so little as an indicator of social class? What should be its proper value as an indicator?

3. Prepare an outline of the major problems involved in the measurement of social classes. How would your outline differ for academic researchers compared to business practitioners?

4. Some observers of contemporary America believe that social classes have declined in importance and presence, but others disagree. Outline your analysis of what has happened in recent years to social classes in the United States or other countries.

5. A marketing researcher is speculating on the influence of upper classes on the consumption decisions of the lower classes for the following products: automobiles, food, clothing, baby care products. What conclusions would you expect for each of these products? Describe a research project that could be used to answer this question.

6. The leisure products group of a large conglomerate is constantly seeking additional products for expanding markets and additional penetration for existing products. What conclusions that would be helpful in the design of marketing strategy might be reached concerning social class and leisure?

7. The operator of a large discount chain is contemplating a new store in an area of upper-lower class families. He asks for a consulting report defining the precautions he should take to ensure patronage among this group. What would you place in such a report? Assume that the area is mostly lower-lower class families. Would you recommend entry?

8. Prepare a research report comparing the search process of the major social classes of consumers in the United States or other countries.

9. Assume that you are preparing the advertisements for a home furnishings store. How would you vary the ads if the target segments are lower middle rather than if they were upper middle?

PERSONAL INFLUENCE

PERSONAL INFLUENCE AS MARKETING STRATEGY: THE MARY KAY MODEL

Prior to the late 1980s, you never saw any product manufactured by Mary Kay Cosmetics, Inc. on the shelves of a retail store. This is because 150,000 "Beauty Consultants" working exclusively through a "Home Beauty Show" lie at the heart of Mary Kay marketing strategy.

Part of the reason for this strategy is that skin care products must be adjusted for each person's skin conditions and applied personally. Each consultant is carefully trained in how to diagnose skin care needs through use of the Mary Kay Beauty Profile. Then all phases of the "Five Steps to Beauty" are actually used and demonstrated so that each potential customer can see the outcomes.

The Home Beauty Show strategy offers some potent additional advantages, however. This alone creates a sense of obligation to buy at least something. Friends and relatives are invited by a hostess to participate in a social event in her home. When the hostess is viewed as credible, her endorsement of Mary Kay products does much to influence the receptivity of those who attend. Furthermore, the positive reactions of satisfied customers can stimulate the buying interest of others. In short, direct personal social influence is both activated and used to the benefit of the company.

The social influence does not stop once the home showing concludes. Every effort is made to recruit future hostesses from those who attend. Thus a new customer is encouraged to become an opinion leader for others. It is worth her while to do so, because the hostess is guaranteed 10 percent of actual product sales. And this percentage increases to 15 percent if one additional home showing is booked and 20 percent if there are two or more.

Source: Mary Kay Cosmetics, Inc., (A), (B), in James F. Engel and W. Wayne Talarzyk, *Cases in Promotional Strategy*, rev. ed. (Homewood, Ill.: Richard D. Irwin, 1984), 3–18; 226–230.

Wise marketers have long realized that personal influence often exceeds the power of company promotional efforts. As Mary Kay Cosmetics, Inc. has successfully demonstrated, marketing strategy can be designed both to activate and stimulate personal influence and to capitalize on it where it presently exists.

This chapter first discusses the ways in which consumer beliefs, attitudes, and behavior are affected when other people are used as reference groups. At times individual actions are constrained by conformity pressures. In other instances the impact is primarily informational.

The second purpose is to explore an especially prominent type of personal impact that comes through word-of-mouth communication initiated or supplied by an influential person known as an opinion leader. It has been demonstrated frequently that information from this source can either make or break a marketing campaign. We discuss many ways in which word-of-mouth communication, if properly understood, can be used advantageously in marketing strategy.

An important determining variable in personal influence is involvement. High product involvement and social influence are related in two ways. First, involvement increases when the choices made affect one's social status and acceptance. Equally important, high involvement often triggers a search for information from credible people. Therefore, personal influence is both a cause and outcome of high involvement and is rarely of much importance when involvement is low.

REFERENCE GROUP INFLUENCE

The term **reference group** was first introduced several decades ago by Hyman[1] and is defined as "a person or group of people that significantly influences an individual's behavior."[2] Reference groups provide standards (norms) and values that can become the determining perspective for how a person thinks and behaves.

---

[1] Herbert H. Hyman, "The Psychology of Status," *Archives of Psychology* 38 (1942).
[2] William O. Bearden and Michael J. Etzel, "Reference Group Influence on Product and Brand Purchase Decisions," *Journal of Consumer Research* 9 (September 1982), 184.

The impact of personal influence was clearly demonstrated by Asch's classic study.[3] In this experiment, subjects were required to choose which of three lines differing in length matched the length of a fourth line. Each person was seated with a group of confederates, all of whom were strangers, who were instructed to make an incorrect choice. When exposed to the incorrect opinion of confederates, the experimental subjects made a substantial number of errors consistent with group consensus. This was not the case, however, when other people were not present. This finding demonstrated the extent to which people are reluctant to voice an opinion that differs from group consensus.[4]

A similar study demonstrated the same personal influence pattern within a consumer behavior context. Venkatesan presented subjects with three identical suits and asked them to select the one they considered to be of highest quality.[5] Confederates always chose the suit labeled "B," and the experimental subjects gave the same response. Suit B was chosen least often, however, when other people were not present.

TYPES OF REFERENCE GROUPS

Social groups can take many forms, depending upon degree of personal interrelationships, structure, and intended purpose. The classifications introduced here reflect standard terminology, but no category is mutually exclusive. It is possible, for example, for a person to be part of a formal, primary group.

PRIMARY VERSUS SECONDARY

The Primary Group.   The greatest influence and impact usually is exerted by primary groups,[6] defined as a social aggregation that is sufficiently small to permit and facilitate unrestricted face-to-face interaction. They exist because "like attracts like." There is cohesiveness and motivated participation. Members demonstrate marked similarities in beliefs and behavior.[7]

As we see in Chapter 6, the family is the most obvious example of a primary group, especially in the non-Western world, in which the extended family and clan exercise dominant influence on individual choice.

---

[3] Solomon E. Asch, "Effects of Group Pressure on the Modification and Distortion of Judgments," in H. Guetzkow, ed., *Groups, Leadership, and Men* (Pittsburgh, Pa.: Carnegie Press, 1951).

[4] Lee Ross, Gunter Bierbrauer, and Susan Hoffman, "The Role of Attribution Processes in Conformity and Dissent: Revisiting the Asch Situation," *American Psychologist* (February 1976), 148–157.

[5] M. Venkatesan, "Experimental Study of Consumer Behavior Conformity and Independence," *Journal of Marketing Research* 3 (November 1966), 384–387.

[6] Charles H. Cooley, *Social Organization* (New York: Schoken, 1962).

[7] Robert E. Witt and Grady D. Bruce, "Group Influence and Brand Choice," *Journal of Marketing Research* 9 (November 1972), 440–443.

The Secondary Group.   This type of reference group also has face-to-face interaction, but it is more sporadic, less comprehensive, and less influential in shaping thought and behavior. Examples of secondary groups are professional associations, trade unions, and community organizations.

ASPIRATIONAL VERSUS DISSOCIATIVE

The Aspirational Group.   In this type of reference group there is a desire to adopt the norms, values, and behavior of others. On occasion there is anticipation of acceptance into membership and motivation to behave accordingly, although membership aspirations are not always present. The influence, while often indirect, can play a significant role in product choices.

The ad in Figure 5.1 ran in Nairobi, Kenya, a typical non-Western urban center characterized by predominance of families living at or only slightly

FIGURE 5.1
**THIS AD IS
DESIGNED TO
CAPITALIZE ON THE
CONSUMER
DREAMS AND
ASPIRATIONS OF A
NON-WESTERN
URBAN MARKET**

Omo gives a brightness you can see

You can always spot the people who really care about their clothes.
They're the families that use New Blue Omo in their washing. They know Omo makes whites whiter, and colours brighter.

That's because only Omo has a special active brightener to give all your washing a brightness you can see.
No wonder the bright people all over Kenya prefer Omo to any other kind of washing product.

New blue Omo washes brightest and it shows!

Source: Colgate-Palmolive Company. Reprinted with permission.

above the poverty line. The lifestyle depicted here accurately reflects their dreams and aspirations, and it is not surprising that New Blue Omo has achieved significant market penetration.

The Dissociative Group. Influence also can be exerted by others when the individual is motivated to *avoid* association. Many so-called "Baby Boomers" (born between 1946 and 1964), for example, have turned their backs on the exaggerated materialistic lifestyle of a segment in their age cohort known as "yuppies." Ever since the October 1987 stock market slump and the evidence of widespread stock manipulation there has been a decline in some of the more extreme forms of conspicuous consumption. You can read more about "boomer" lifestyles in later chapters.

FORMAL VERSUS INFORMAL

The Formal Group. Formal groups are characterized by a defined, known list of members, and the organization and structure are codified in writing. Examples are churches, fraternal bodies, and community service organizations. The influence exerted on behavior varies, depending upon the motivation of the individual to accept and comply with the group's standards. Also, there are wide latitudes in the degree to which specific conformity is expected and enforced.

The Informal Group. As would be expected, informal groups have far less structure and are likely to be based on friendship or collegial association. Norms can be stringent, but they seldom appear in writing. The affect on behavior can be strong if individuals are motivated by social acceptance. There also is a high degree of intimate, face-to-face interaction, which further strengthens the power with which expectations and sanctions are expressed and enforced.

THREE FORMS OF REFERENCE GROUP INFLUENCE

There are three principal ways in which reference groups affect consumer choice — utilitarian influence, value-expressive influence, and informational influence.

UTILITARIAN (NORMATIVE) INFLUENCE Reference group influence can be expressed through pressures for compliance with group norms; therefore it also is common to refer to **normative influence.** (**Group norms** are stable expectations arrived at by consensus concerning behavioral rules for individual members.) Conformity pressures become most potent when there is both positive motivation to maintain group identity through compliance and the motivation of threats of sanctioning power in the form of rewards and punishments.

Sociologist George Homans has shed useful light on why there is normative compliance.[8] He has put forth an equation of human exchange that is built on the relationship between the rewards of compliance as compared with the costs. Symbols of esteem or approval can provide rewards and incentives, thereby reinforcing that behavior and encouraging its repetition. There also are costs, however, such as association with certain undesirable people, lost time, or restriction on freedom of choice.

The outcomes will be determined by an individual's perception of the *profit* inherent in the interaction (i.e., rewards minus costs). Examples would be a college fraternity member who perceives that the rewards of acceptance outweigh the costs of not wearing a high school letter jacket; or the marketing manager who willingly endures the sometimes abusive responses of dissatisfied customers, knowing full well that future advancement is based on high customer retention.

Normative influence can occur even when others do not control tangible outcomes. People are concerned with what others *think* of them. Therefore, their decisions often will be affected by beliefs about the attributions that others will make about them.

Mason Haire's classic 1950 study is a case in point.[9] Haire showed that perceptions of users of regular coffee were evaluated favorably, whereas purchasers of instant coffee (a new product at that time) were perceived as lazy. Calder and Burnkrant provided further evidence demonstrating the ways in which product choices can evoke positive or negative attributions about the user.[10]

A number of marketing studies over the years have demonstrated that conformity pressures do impact buying decisions,[11] and this is especially true when the product is conspicuous in its purchase and use and when group social acceptance is a strong motivator.[12] Marketers have learned the potency of appealing to the "in thing," and this is not confined to North America, as the German ad in Figure 5.2 demonstrates ("calories are out, slim is in").

Conspicuousness is not a fixed product characteristic but depends on how the product is used. Consequently, the impact of personal influence varies depending upon the usage situation. Miniard and Cohen found, for

---

[8] George Homans, *Social Behavior: Its Elementary Forms* (New York: Harcourt, 1961).

[9] Mason Haire, "Projective Techniques in Marketing Research," *Journal of Marketing* 14 (April 1950), 649–656.

[10] Bobby J. Calder and Robert E. Burnkrant, "Interpersonal Influence on Consumer Behavior, An Attribution Theory Approach," *Journal of Consumer Research* 4 (June 1977), 29–38.

[11] Paul W. Miniard and Joel E. Cohen, "Modeling Personal and Normative Influences on Behavior," *Journal of Consumer Research* 10 (September 1983), 169–180. Also, Bearden and Etzel, "Reference Group Influence;" C. Whan Park and V. Parker Lessig, "Students and Housewives: Differences in Susceptibility to Reference Group Influence," *Journal of Consumer Research* 4 (September 1977), 102–109; George P. Moschis, "Social Comparison and Informal Group Influence," *Journal of Marketing Research* 13 (August 1976), 237–244; and M. Venkatesan, "Consumer Behavior: Conformity and Independence," *Journal of Marketing Research* 3 (November 1966), 384–387.

[12] Bearden and Etzel, "Reference Group Influence."

FIGURE 5.2
AN APPEAL TO CONFORM TO THE "IN-THING": THE PRESSURE FOR SOCIAL ACCEPTANCE IS STRONG THROUGHOUT THE WORLD

Source: Courtesy of the Coca-Cola Company.

example, that normative influence on brand choice is important when beer is to be served to friends but not when it is consumed privately.[13]

It is interesting to note, however, that normative compliance seems to be declining in its impact in much of the Western world.[14] A major factor, we feel, is the worldwide growth of urbanization, which leads to greater social isolation and individualism. Grandparents, uncles, aunts, and other members of the extended family have far less face-to-face influence. Also, urban living arrangements, often in high-rises, minimize the social interaction that takes place much more readily when living in the country or the bush. Finally, television and other mass media open windows to the world and thereby broaden horizons and interests beyond normal social circles. A clear demonstration of this growing reality appears in *Consumer in Focus 5.1.*

---

[13] Miniard and Cohen, "Modeling Personal and Normative Influence."
[14] "31 Major Trends Shaping the Future of American Business," *The Public Pulse* 2 (1986), 1; Park and Lessig, "Students and Housewives"; and Robert E. Burnkrant and Alan Cousineau, "Informational and Normative Social Influence in Buyer Behavior," *Journal of Consumer Research* 2 (December 1975), 206–215.

5.1 A VANISHING SENSE OF COMMUNITY: BOLINGBROOK, ILLINOIS

THE BUSINESS OF LIFE IS TO GO FORWARD. SAMUEL JOHNSON

For many years, the residents of Ottawa Drive in Bolingbrook, Ill., did just that.

In the townhouses of this suburban Chicago street, families shared in the heritage of the middle class: the guarantee of progress. Most would be promoted at work; most would buy more and better products for their homes. One longtime resident remembers the neighborhood surrounding Ottawa Drive as a nest of young families who shared in wine-tasting parties, spaghetti dinners and block dances. Neighbors, she says, were the best of friends.

Today, however, neighbors hardly know one another, and progress — when it comes — benefits individuals, not the community. "We used to have a lot of fun in this neighborhood," says Debie Weingarden, who has lived here for 14 years. "But now everybody's going his own way."

Ottawa Drive and its families reflect some of the changes that have splintered the middle class. Where upward mobility was once a given, middle-class households here and elsewhere now find themselves heading both up and *down* the economic ladder.

At the same time, the life styles of the people on the block have become as varied as their bank accounts. At one home, the wife is the breadwinner and works the night shift. Next door, three unmarried people share a house. Another address down, a young woman lives by herself. And, across the street, one family is building an addition for their 20-year-old son. As they come and go, most people here barely see or talk to each other.

The result, among other things, is a disappearing sense of community. Neighbors no longer share common aspirations or values. Though it still has the appearance of a traditional middle-class neighborhood, Ottawa Drive has become a site of differing expectations, values and financial prospects.

Unlike the families who first lived here in the 1960s, most residents now find little agreement on what constitutes success, how they should live their lives or how they should raise their children. "Everybody's rushing around trying to do their own thing, trying to get their own life settled."

Source: Alex Kotlowitz, "Changes Among Families Prompt a Vanishing Sense of Community," *The Wall Street Journal* (March 11, 1987), p. 33. Reprinted by special permission of *The Wall Street Journal,* © Dow Jones & Company, Inc. 1987. All rights reserved worldwide.

Another factor leading to diminished normative compliance is a weakened respect for social norms rather than a complete denial of their existence or impact. This is referred to by sociologists as **anomie.**[15] People so affected

[15] Emile Durkheim, *Suicide,* trans. by George Simpson (New York: Free Press, 1951). For a cultural perspective, see Robert Merton, "Anomie, Anomia, and Social Interaction: Contexts of Deviate Behavior," in M. B. Clinard, ed., *Anomie and Deviate Behavior* (New York: Free Press, 1964).

FIGURE 5.3
AN EXAMPLE OF
HOW ONE COMPANY
IS FIGHTING
NORMATIVE SOCIAL
INFLUENCE

Source: Courtesy of Ally & Gargano, Inc. for Saab-Scania of America.

are apt to conform grudgingly or, in certain instances, to engage in motivated evasion and failure to conform. The ad in Figure 5.3 is a good example of how Saab-Scania has capitalized upon anomie and turned it into an effective appeal.

It is also interesting to observe ways in which some people seek to reverse the effects of anomie by deliberately seeking relationships in which others invoke rewards and sanctions designed for a person's own good. Alcoholics Anonymous and Weight Watchers are two examples in which membership is sought in recognition that changes in undesirable behavior can be nearly impossible to accomplish without stringent social pressure.

VALUE-EXPRESSIVE INFLUENCE   Reference groups also can perform a value-expressive function, whereby a need for psychological association with a group is evidenced by acceptance of its norms, values, or behavior and a conforming response is made, even though there is no motivation to become a member. One desired outcome is enhanced image in the eyes of others.

FIGURE 5.4
IN THIS AD, CUTTY SARK IS CAPITALIZING ON VALUE-EXPRESSIVE SOCIAL INFLUENCE

Source: Courtesy of the Buckingham Wile Company.

Another is identification with people who are admired and respected. Both of these benefits are captured in an advertising campaign by Cutty Sark (see Figure 5.4).

INFORMATIONAL INFLUENCE   Consumers often accept the opinions of others as providing credible and needed evidence about reality.[16] This is most apparent when it is difficult to assess product or brand characteristics by observation. They will then perceive usage or recommendation by others as thoughtful and valid.[17] We have more to say about the role of friends and relatives in the next section of the chapter.

A commerical spokesperson's ability to exert informational influence will be affected by his or her perceived expertise. Woodside and Davenport varied the expertise of a music store salesperson, who encouraged customers to

---

[16] Burnkrant and Cousineau, "Informational and Normative Social Influence."
[17] Bobby Calder and Robert Burnkrant, "Interpersonal Influence on Consumer Behavior: An Attribution Theory Approach," *Journal of Consumer Research* 4 (June 1977), 29–38.

**FIGURE 5.5
APPEALS TO
EXPERTISE AFFECT
CONSUMER
OPINION**

purchase a tape-deck cleaning kit.[18] When the salesperson was seen as knowledgeable, two thirds bought the product, but this dropped to only 20 percent when there was admission of unfamiliarity with the product.

This study illustrates the facilitating effect of perceived expertise on compliance, a fact that marketers have long recognized. Rigorous sales-training programs provide help in answering customers' questions and complaints. Ads often feature an expert spokesperson as a primary persuasive appeal or make reference to recommendations by groups of experts (Figure 5.5).

---

[18] Arch G. Woodside and William Davenport, Jr., "The Effect of Salesman Similarity and Expertise on Consumer Purchasing Behavior," *Journal of Marketing Research* 11 (May 1974), 198–203. Also see Paul Busch and David T. Wilson, "An Experimental Analysis of a Salesman's Expert and Referent Bases on Social Power in the Buyer-Seller Dyad," *Journal of Marketing Research* 13 (February 1976), 3–11.

DETERMINANTS OF REFERENCE GROUP IMPACT

We have already stressed that social visibility is a factor in receptivity to the views of others. In other words, all things being equal, we expect greater social influence when the product is publicly displayed or consumed as opposed to its being privately displayed and used. Bearden and Etzel, however, have added one additional factor — whether the product is a luxury or necessity — the hypothesis being that luxuries are more susceptible to social influence than necessities.

These two hypotheses were tested in a direct-mail survey of 800 households. Respondents were asked to consider 16 products which differed along the private–public and necessity–luxury dimensions. For each product they rated the extent of informational, value-expressive, and utilitarian reference group influence on both the choice of the product class and a brand. A summary of these results appears in Figure 5.6.

Figure 5.6 contains some interesting findings. Look at the upper left quadrant, for example. Here we encounter public consumption of a necessity in which there is weak reference group influence on choice of the *product* but strong influence on selection of the *brand*. A wristwatch is worn out of necessity, and it is of little consequence what others do. But brand choice is

**FIGURE 5.6
REFERENCE GROUP
INFLUENCE AS A
FUNCTION OF
PRODUCT TYPE AND
CONSUMPTION
SITUATION**

COMBINING PUBLIC–PRIVATE AND LUXURY–NECESSITY DIMENSIONS WITH PRODUCT AND BRAND PURCHASE DECISIONS

	Publicly consumed	
Product / Brand	Weak reference group influence (−)	Strong reference group influence (+)
Strong reference group influence (+)	*Public necessities* Influence: Weak product and strong brand Examples: Wristwatch, automobile, man's suit	*Public luxuries* Influence: Strong product and brand Examples: Golf clubs, snow skis, sailboat
Weak reference group influence (−)	*Private necessities* Influence: Weak product and brand Examples: Mattress, floor lamp, refrigerator	*Private luxuries* Influence: Strong product and weak brand Examples: TV game, trash compactor, icemaker

Necessity — Luxury

Privately consumed

Source: William O. Bearden and Michael J. Etzel, "Reference Group Influence on Product and Brand Purchase Decisions," *Journal of Consumer Research* 9 (September 1982), 185. Used with permission.

quite different, an example being the high social acceptability in some quarters signified by wearing a Rolex. As you read through these four quadrants, you gain helpful insights into the ways in which social influence becomes expressed.

WORD-OF-MOUTH INFLUENCE

As we have already stated, consumers frequently turn to others, especially friends and family members, for opinions about products and services. The transmitter of this information is referred to as an **influential.** Over the years, the influential also has been labeled as an *opinion leader,* but we prefer to avoid this term because of the connotation that the transmitter has a dominant position over a so-called "follower." As you will see, word-of-mouth influence usually is not expressed in such a hierarchical pattern.

When are consumers most likely to accept and respond to word-of-mouth communication? Based on more than 30 years of research, it is safe to conclude that personal influence in the form of opinion leadership is most likely when one or more of these conditions and situations are present:

1. The consumer lacks sufficient information to make an adequately informed choice.
2. The product is complex and difficult to evaluate using objective criteria. Hence the experience of others serves as "vicarious trial."[19]
3. The person lacks ability to evaluate the product or service, no matter how information is disseminated and presented.
4. Other sources are perceived as having low credibility.
5. An influential person is more accessible than other sources and hence can be consulted with a saving of time and effort.
6. Strong social ties are in existence between transmitter and receiver.[20]
7. The individual has a high need for social approval.

MODELS OF THE PERSONAL INFLUENCE PROCESS

Personal influence has been theorized as working in three different ways: (1) trickle down; (2) a two-step flow; or (3) multistage interaction.

THE TRICKLE-DOWN THEORY   The oldest theory of personal influence alleges that lower classes often emulate the behavior of their higher-class counterparts.[21] In other words, influence is transmitted vertically through

---

[19] William L. Wilkie, *Consumer Behavior* (New York: Wiley, 1986), 160.

[20] Jacqueline Johnson Brown and Peter H. Reingen, "Social Ties and Word-of-Mouth Referral Behavior," *Journal of Consumer Research* 14 (December 1987), 350–362.

[21] Thorstein Veblen, *The Theory of the Leisure Class* (New York: Macmillan, 1899); and George Simmel, "Fashion," *International Quarterly* 10 (1904), 130–155.

social classes, especially in the area of new fashions and styles. Presumably those in the higher classes express wealth through "conspicuous consumption," and their behavior is copied, when possible, by those in lower social strata.

The trickle-down theory is rarely seen demonstrated today in economically developed countries. The reason is that new fashions are disseminated overnight through mass media and quickly copied on a mass-merchandise basis. It still is observed, however, in underdeveloped tribal economies when access to the mass media is restricted. Even here, however, it is rapidly disappearing.

It is far more common for this type of influence to occur among peers. This has come to be known as **homophilous influence,** a term that refers to information transmission between those who are similar in social class, age, education, and other demographic characteristics.[22] As we have demonstrated, reference group impact is often greatest when there is at least some degree of prior association and relationship.

A TWO-STEP FLOW   In 1948 Lazarsfeld and his colleagues observed that new ideas and other influences flow from the mass media to influentials who, in turn, pass them on through word of mouth to others who are more passive in information seeking and far less exposed to the mass media and other sources.[23]

Although this model was an historic breakthrough for its time, there is ample reason now to question its accuracy. The primary reason is the audience is not as passive as the theory assumes. It is apparent, first of all, that the mass media have a widespread impact that is not confined to the influential. Furthermore, the initiative does not necessarily lie with the influential, as the theory assumed. Word-of-mouth communication is equally if not more often initiated by the receiver who is seeking the advice of a credible friend or relative.

A MULTISTAGE INTERACTION   Extensive research on the diffusion of innovations has largely invalidated the two-step flow model by demonstrating that both influential and seeker are affected by the mass media. In fact, mass media can motivate the seeker to approach someone else for advice rather than vice versa. Rarely does the influential mediate the flow of mass media content, as the two-step theory assumes.

At one time it was accepted that advertisers and other commercial persuaders would achieve greatest impact by concentrating only on influential people. It was assumed, of course, that they would pass on what they learned from the media. Current understanding shows that *both* the influential and the seeker are legitimate targets.

---

[22] Paul F. Lazarsfeld and Robert K. Merton, "Friendship as Social Process: A Substantive and Methodological Analysis," in Monroe Berger, et al, eds., *Freedom and Control in Modern Society* (New York: Octagon, 1964).

[23] Paul F. Lazarsfeld, Bernard R. Berelson, and Hazel Gaudet, *The People's Choice* (New York: Columbia University Press, 1948), 151.

THE INFLUENTIAL

How do we find the influentials? What type of people are they? What motivates them to share their experience? These questions have stimulated extensive research over the years in many countries of the world,[24] and it now is possible to advance some valid generalizations.

RESEARCH METHODS   There are three basic ways to identify the influential person:

1. *The sociometric method* — people are asked to identify other people they seek out for advice or information in making a particular type of decision.

2. *The key-informant method* — knowledgeable people are used to identify the influentials within a social system.

3. *The self-designation method* — people are asked to evaluate the extent to which they are sought out for advice.

The first two methods do not find widespread use in marketing research because of the focus on a specific, identifiable existing group. There are times, however, when a high-rise apartment complex or neighborhood is the focus. When that is the case, the key-informant method is usually preferred because of greater ease of administration.

When many groups are targeted, the self-designation method is preferred. It is designed to be used on a wide scale, and it appears to have acceptable validity.[25] The objective is to identify whether certain types or categories of people serve as influentials and not to designate the individuals themselves by name. If they can be identified and isolated from others as a distinct market segment, then it is possible to direct marketing efforts their way. An example of a multi-item scale designed for this purpose appears in Table 5.1.

CHARACTERISTICS   Extensive research on the characteristics of the influential is summarized in Table 5.2. It is safe to conclude that source and receiver are similar to one another in terms of demographic characteristics and lifestyle (i.e., they are homophilous).[26] Evidence also shows that the person who provides the information also is a seeker in other situations.[27]

---

[24] See, especially, Everett M. Rogers, *Diffusion of Innovations*, 3rd ed. (New York: Free Press, 1983). Also most of the pertinent references have been cited in the first five editions of this book.

[25] The relative strengths and problems of alternative methods are reviewed in George Brooker and Michael J. Houston, "An Evaluation of Measures of Opinion Leadership," in Kenneth L. Bernhardt, ed., *Marketing 1776–1976 and Beyond* (Chicago: American Marketing Association, 1976), 561–564.

[26] See Brown and Reingen, "Social Ties and Word-of-Mouth."

[27] Feick, Price, and Higie, "People Who Use People."

TABLE 5.1 **A SELF-** **DESIGNATING** **SCALE USED FOR** **ISOLATING AN** **INFLUENTIAL** **PERSON**	(1) In general, do you like to talk about _____with your friends? Yes _____—1 No _____—2 (2) Would you say *you give very little information, an average amount of information, or a great deal of information* about _____ to your friends? You give very little information _____ —1 You give an average amount of information _____ —2 You give a great deal of information _____ —3 (3) During the *past six months,* have *you told anyone* about some _____? Yes _____ —1 No _____ —2 (4) Compared with your circle of friends, are you *less likely, about as likely,* or *more likely* to be asked for advice about _____? Less likely to be asked _____ —1 About as likely to be asked _____ —1 More likely to be asked _____ —3 (5) If you and your friends were to discuss _____, what part would *you* be most likely to play? Would you *mainly listen* to your friends' ideas or would *you try to convince them* of your ideas? You mainly listen to your friends' ideas _____ —1 You try to convince them of your ideas _____ —2 (6) Which of these happens more often? Do *you tell your friends* about some _____, or do *they tell you* about some _____? You tell them about _____ —1 They tell you about _____ —2 (7) Do you have the feeling that you are generally regarded by your friends and neighbors as a good source of advice about _____? Yes _____ —1 No _____ —2

Source: Charles W. King and John O. Summers, "Generalized Opinion Leadership in Consumer Products: Some Preliminary Findings," paper no. 224 (Lafayette, Indiana: Institute for Research in the Behavioral, Economic and Management Sciences, Krannert Graduate School of Industrial Administration, January 1969), 16. Reprinted by permission.

TABLE 5.2
CHARACTERISTICS
OF THE INFLUENTIAL
	Demographic
	There is wide variation from one product category to another:
	  Young women dominate for fashions and movie-going.
	  Women with many children are consulted about self-medication.
	  Demographics usually show low correlation and are not a good predictor.
	
	Social Activity
	Gregariousness is the most frequently found predictor of opinion leadership.
	
	General Attitudes
	Opinion leaders are innovative and positive toward new products.
	
	Personality and Lifestyle
	Personality measures generally do not correlate with opinion leadership.
	Opinion leaders tend to be more socially active, fashion conscious, and independent.
	
	Product Related
	Opinion leaders are more interested in the topic under discussion than others are. Fashion is an example.
	They are active searchers and information gatherers, especially from the mass media.

One issue of importance is whether the influence process is product-specific (**monomorphic**) or overlapping into other product areas (**polymorphic**). While much of the earlier literature supported the monomorphic hypothesis, there now is evidence that word-of-mouth influence is quasi-generalized, in that most serve as influentials for related products but not for all products in general.[28]

MOTIVATIONS   Generally speaking, people will not share their experience with products or services unless the conversation produces some type of gratification. The motivations that drive such interactions fall into one or more of the following categories: (1) product involvement; (2) self-enhancement; (3) concern for others; (4) message intrigue; and (5) dissonance reduction.

Product Involvement.   First, the tendency to initiate conversations is directly proportional to the extent of interest or involvement in the topic under consideration. A young executive is the first among his/her peers to have a new high-resolution television set complete with a built-in VCR. Telling others can serve as an outlet for pleasure or excitement caused by or resulting from purchase and use.

Self-Enhancement.   Dichter showed that word-of-mouth initiation often performs such functions as gaining attention, showing connoisseurship, suggesting status, giving the impression of possessing inside information, and asserting superiority.[29] It is not uncommon for this to take the form of "insider information"—"I've just discovered the greatest Ethiopian restaurant."

Concern for Others.   Conversation also is precipitated simply by a genuine desire to help a friend or relative make a better purchase decision. Old-fashioned altruism is not at all uncommon, especially when social ties are strong.

Message Intrigue.   Some people find it entertaining to talk about certain ads or selling appeals. Who can deny the word-of-mouth that occurs when jokes are made of the Jolly Green Giant, Mr. Whipple, or the many sufferers of "ring around the collar"?

Dissonance Reduction.   Finally, research suggests that word of mouth is sometimes used to reduce cognitive dissonance (doubts) following a major purchase decision.[30] As we discover in Chapter 19 and other chapters, dissatis-

---

[28] James H. Myers and Thomas S. Robertson, "Dimensions of Opinion Leadership," *Journal of Marketing Research* 9 (February 1972), 41–46; Charles W. King and John O. Summers, "Overlap of Opinion Leadership Across Consumer Product Categories," *Journal of Marketing Research* 7 (February 1970), 43–50; and Edwin J. Gross, "Support for Generalized Marketing Leadership Theory," *Journal of Advertising Research* (November 1969), 49–52

[29] Ernest Dichter, "How Word-of-Mouth Advertising Works," *Harvard Business Review* (November–December 1966), 147–166.

[30] Hubert Gatignon and Thomas S. Robertson, "A Propositional Inventory for New Diffusion Research," *Journal of Consumer Research* 11 (March 1985), 849–867.

fied customers can be dangerous. It is not unusual for them to vent anger by disparaging the product or brand. Marketers worldwide are discovering that negative information of this type can have a decided impact on potential buyers.

THE IMPACT OF WORD-OF-MOUTH COMMUNICATION

Here is what we know about the effects of personal influence on consumer behavior.

COMPARISON WITH OTHER MEDIA   First, research consistently demonstrates that personal influence generally has a more decisive role in influencing behavior than advertising and other marketer-dominated sources.[31] The issue of greater perceived credibility is most often the deciding factor. It is common to assume that another consumer has no ulterior or commercially motivated reasons for sharing information.

SOURCE-VERSUS SEEKER-INITIATED CONVERSATION   Word-of-mouth can be initiated by either the source or the receiver, and the impact usually is strongest when the receiver plays this role.[32] The difference no doubt arises from the fact that a seeker is motivated to attend to and process the information, whereas that may not be the case when the source is the initiator.

NEGATIVE VERSUS POSITIVE INFORMATION   More than a third of all word-of-mouth information is negative in nature, and evidence indicates that it usually is given higher priority and assigned a greater weight in decision making.[33] No doubt this occurs because marketer-dominated communication will be uniformly positive, thus making the potential buyer all the more alert to anything that provides a different perspective. Also, the dissatisfied buyer is more motivated to share.[34]

VERBAL VERSUS VISUAL INFORMATION   Information can be passed interpersonally in either verbal or visual form. To the extent that information can be given visually, through observation or actual product demonstration, the greater will be the impact in terms of awareness and stimulation of interest. On the other hand, verbally communicated information has a stronger effect

---

[31] For a review of relevant research see Linda L. Price and Lawrence F. Feick, "The Role of Interpersonal Sources and External Search: An Informational Perspective," in Kinnear, ed., *Advances,* 250–255. An example of a current study is Theresa A. Swartz and Nancy Stephens, "Information Search for Services: the Maturity Segment," in Kinnear, ed., *Advances,* 244–249.

[32] Gatignon and Robertson, "A Propositional Inventory."

[33] Marsha L. Richins, "Word of Mouth Communication as Negative Information," in Kinnear, ed., *Advances,* 697–702. Also Richard W. Mizerski, "An Attribution Explanation of the Disproportionate Influence of Unfavorable Information," *Journal of Consumer Research* 9 (December 1982), 301–310.

[34] John H. Holmes and John D. Lett, Jr., "Product Sampling and Word of Mouth," *Journal of Advertising Research* 17 (October 1977), 35–40.

on thinking and evaluation.[35] Ideally, both visual and verbal will work in combination.

MARKETING STRATEGY IMPLICATIONS OF PERSONAL INFLUENCE

Positive word of mouth can be one of the marketer's greatest assets, whereas the opposite can be true when the content is negative. Personal influence, of course, cannot be directly controlled by a business firm, but it can be stimulated and channeled in many ways.

MONITORING THE CONTENT OF WORD OF MOUTH   At the very least it is necessary to monitor whether or not word-of-mouth communication is occurring and the impact it is having. For example, Coca-Cola examined the communication patterns undertaken by those who had complained to the company.[36] Here are some of the major conclusions:

1. More than 12 percent told 20 or more people about the response they had received from the company.
2. Those who were completely satisfied with the response told a median of 4 to 5 others about their positive experience.
3. Nearly 10 percent who were completely satisfied increased their purchases of company products.
4. Those who felt they were not treated adequately communicated this fact to a median of 9 to 10 other people.
5. Nearly a third who felt their complaints were not dealt with adequately refused to buy any more company products, and another 45 percent reduced their purchases.

Although involvement is usually a predisposing factor for social influence, this example shows how extensive word of mouth can be, even for a low-involvement product such as a soft drink. This was further demonstrated during the now legendary "cola war," in which consumers overwhelmingly rejected "New Coke" and let their feelings be known (for more detail, see Chapter 19).

Focus-group research is often the best method for monitoring influence. From eight to twelve people are brought together and guided by a moderator to discuss appropriate issues. When personal influence is taking place, its nature and impact quickly become evident because most people are willing to talk about products and their experiences. This is especially true when involvement is high.

SOLE RELIANCE ON WORD OF MOUTH   On some occasions it is possible to rely only on word-of-mouth communication to influence a product's sales

---

[35] Gatignon and Robertson, "A Propositional Inventory."
[36] *Measuring the Grapevine: Consumer Response and Word-of-Mouth,* the Coca-Cola Company, 1981.

5.2 IS IT POSSIBLE TO MOVE A PRODUCT WITH WORD-OF-MOUTH ONLY? ANHEUSER-BUSCH

Anheuser-Busch is introducing into test markets a new "ultrapremium" beer, and it's going to see whether the new brand can make it without advertising.

The new beer, called Anheuser, is getting no marketing support from the nation's largest brewer and none is planned, said a source close to St. Louis-based A-B. That strategy is part of the test.

"There is no real marketing plan for [Anheuser], and there won't be one," the source said. "A-B wants to have an entry in this [ultrapremium] category, but it also wants to see what happens to its sales without advertising and without promotion.

"It's just there, on shelves, in two small markets and in very limited quantities to give it a bit of a mystique. Maybe word-of-mouth advertising can do for Anheuser what it did for Corona."

Sales of Corona Extra, imported from Mexico by Barton Beers, Chicago, last year increased 170% to 13.5 million cases, making it the No. 2 import behind Heineken, the trade publication *Impact* reported.

Media advertising for Corona — print and radio handled by HCM Dawson Johns & Black — began only after word-of-mouth had made the beer a hit among young urbanites.

A-B's new Anheuser is positioned and priced above its Michelob superpremium beer. Superpremiums are positioned above premium brands, such as Budweiser, and below imported beers like Heineken.

The test brand is in two undisclosed markets — one in the Southwest and the other in the Northeast.

Anheuser reportedly is a heavier-tasting, European-style beer.

Limited advertising and limited availability are parts of the allure of many imports or so-called "specialty" beers such as Anchor Steam beer from San Francisco's Anchor Brewing, industry observers noted.

If Anheuser succeeds without marketing support, it could cause one of the nation's largest advertisers to scrutinize more closely the approximately $600 million it spent last year advertising and promoting its established brands.

It is doubtful that a mainstream beer could survive without advertising; the tactic works primarily with "niche" products, observers noted.

once it is launched. An interesting experiment of this type has been undertaken by Anheuser-Busch, and it is detailed in *Consumer in Focus 5.2*.

USING THE INFLUENTIAL AS A MARKET TARGET   Although the two-step flow has largely been abandoned, it cannot be denied that influentials are sensitive to various sources of information, including advertising.[37] It is at least theoretically feasible to view them as a distinct market segment, *if they can be identified.* You will recall that identification can present quite a research challenge because of the similarity (homophily) between sender and receiver.

Even if they can be identified, however, their media exposure patterns often do not differ in any meaningful ways from those of receivers. Hence, it may be impossible to mount strategies that reach only this segment. The only exception is when certain types of social or organizational leaders are known to play the role of influentials. Examples are coaches, physicians, pharmacists, and pastors.

When identification is feasible, there are several possible strategies. One of the most common is to establish them as the target of space advertising, direct mail, and publicity releases aimed at them. As we discuss in Chapter 23, it is possible to buy mailing lists for coaches, teachers, and other specialized professions. Another option is to use the general media, knowing full well that there will be waste resulting from the large number of nonprospects. Sometimes there is no other option.

STIMULATING WORD OF MOUTH   At times there is benefit in either loaning or giving known influentials a product to display and use. The Ford Motor Company used this approach as part of its strategy to promote the 1984 Thunderbird.[38] Invitations were mailed to over 406,000 executives and professional people, giving them the opportunity to drive the car for a day, and about 15,000 took advantage. While only 10 percent became buyers, 84 percent indicated they would recommend the Thunderbird to a friend.

CREATING INFLUENTIALS   Next, it is sometimes possible to hire or directly involve those who seem to have the characteristics of an influential. Department stores and other clothing retailers, for example, have experimented with hiring the most popular young people, who then receive substantial discounts on clothing they purchase.

Hospitals have used this strategy to cope with excess capacity by forming alliances with physicians, who often hold the key to which hospital is chosen. This very interesting strategy is described in *Consumer in Focus 5.3*

Yet another possible approach is to provide incentives for new customers to attract others to the point of sale. Sometimes this is done by offering attractive product premiums or even outright financial rebates.

At times it is possible to activate information seeking through word of mouth. This can be done through ads that capture imagination and intrigue, especially through phrases or characters that become part of the everyday

---

[37] Jonathan Gutman and Michael K. Mills, "Fashion Lifestyle and Consumer Information Usage: Formulating Effective Marketing Communications," in Bruce J. Walker, et al., eds., *An Assessment of Marketing Thought and Practice* (Chicago: American Marketing Association, 1982), 199–203.
[38] Meg Cox, "Ford Pushing Thunderbird with VIP Plan," *The Wall Street Journal* (October 17, 1983), 37.

5.3 MOTIVATING PHYSICIANS TO INFLUENCE THE HOSPITAL CHOICES OF THEIR PATIENTS

Growing numbers of doctors have banded together to provide diagnostic testing or refer patients to free-standing diagnostic centers, thereby cutting into hospitals' business. "Hospitals' best defense is to approach physicians and form joint ventures; to take a proactive stance," says Glen Kollen, director — marketing and planning, HCA Physician Services.

"There's been a swing in the pendulum," he says. "Hospitals had tried to stiff-arm them. Now they view physicians as distributors of brands and products." Mr. Kollen agrees that about a year ago most hospitals were emphasizing consumer marketing programs and not promoting their physician relationship. "Hospitals alienated physicians by asking for their patients to be sent to them, but also taking their patients whenever they could."

The scenario has changed, he says. "There is a transition from consumer to physician. Our success lies in combining efforts with physicians. They are our key players." And their survival is key to keeping hospitals off the critical list.

This helps explain why physician referral was a hot product for hospitals in 1986. "The emphasis on physician referral will be even more marked in 1987," Mr. Kollen says, because it is a primary element physicians assess in selecting hospitals with which to affiliate. Also, 66% of consumers will follow their physician's recommendation in selecting a hospital.

More hospitals are looking at ways to lock the gatekeepers into long-term commitments. They are offering physicians a managing role, high quality nursing staffs and elaborate ancillary services —"anything that helps increase his efficiency, reduce his overhead and market himself better," Mr. Kollen says.

Source: Ed Fitch, "Healthcare Marketing: More Than the Dr. Ordered." Reprinted with permission from *Advertising Age* (December 15, 1986), S-1. Copyright Crain Communications, Inc. All rights reserved.

---

vernacular. A famous early example is the "thousands of tiny time pills" theme used when Contac was first introduced as a cold remedy. This phrase in itself stimulated a great deal of conversation. More recently, Wendy's Clara Peller and the spokesmen for Bartle & Jaymes wine coolers have frequently been the subject of amused conversations.

Another tactic is to use ads asking consumers to seek information. "Ask the person who owns one" is an example of this approach.

Demonstrations, displays, and trial usage also are helpful methods. For example, color television manufacturers sell their sets to hotels and motels at low prices partly because it can help generate consumer interest and information seeking. And automobile manufacturers make deals with rental companies on cars like the Lincoln Continental featured at Budget Rent-a-Car.

CURBING NEGATIVE WORD OF MOUTH   You have started your car and suddenly it surges, out of control, forward or backward. This is exactly what happened with the 1986 Audi 5000S, according to more than 500 complaints made to the National Highway Traffic Safety Administration. Audi management initially refused to acknowledge any culpability for this problem, even after a "60 Minutes" exposé on TV activated public outrage. It took a drastic drop in sales to induce acknowledgment of a problem, product recall, and remedial repair.[39]

What can be done in an instance like this? Certainly stonewalling (denying the problem) is not the answer. The Toshiba Corporation found out that resignation and public disgrace of top management did little to mitigate U.S. public outrage over the release of important military secrets in product sales to Russia. The company decided to take the major face-losing step of running ads in several major papers which were headlined: "Toshiba Corporation Extends Its Deepest Regrets to the American People." This was a step in the right direction, but it may have been too little and too late.

The best strategy usually is an immediate acknowledgment of a problem by a credible company spokesperson. It is important to recognize that negative word of mouth rarely goes away by itself. If matters are not dealt with promptly, the financial results could be immediate and catastrophic. We return to this issue Chapter 19.

Summary

Personal influence often plays an important role in consumer decision making, especially when there are high levels of involvement and perceived risk and the product or service has public visibility. This is expressed both through reference groups and through word-of-mouth communication.

Reference groups are any type of social aggregation that can influence attitudes and behavior, including primary (face-to-face) groups, secondary groups, and aspirational groups. The influence occurs in three ways: (1) utilitarian (pressures to conform to group norms in thinking and behavior); (2) value-expressive (reflecting a desire for psychological association and a willingness to accept values of others without pressure); and (3) informational (beliefs and behaviors of others are accepted as evidence about reality). When there is motivation to comply with group norms, it is important to make this a feature in marketing appeals.

Personal influence also is expressed through what has traditionally been referred to as "opinion leadership." What this means is that a credible person, referred to as an "influential," is accepted as a source of information about purchase and use. Usually the influential and the seeker are similar in characteristics, and both are influenced by mass media. The greater the credibility of the influential, the greater his or her impact upon other people.

Marketers can capitalize on personal influence by monitoring word of

---

[39] John E. Pluennecke and William J. Hampton, "Can Audi Fix a Dented Image?" *Business Week* (November 17, 1986), 81–82.

mouth and attempting to curb it when it is negative. Other strategies include creating new influentials, stimulating information seeking through this source, relying entirely on interpersonal influence to promote products, and combating negative word of mouth.

REVIEW AND DISCUSSION QUESTIONS

1. For which of the following products would you expect personal influence to be a factor in buying decisions? Soft drinks, motor oil, designer jeans, eye liner, house paint, breakfast cereals, wine, carpeting, a dishwasher, and a 35mm camera. What are your reasons in each case?

2. For each of the products listed in Question 1 do you think there could be a variation between personal influence on product choice and on brand name? Why do you say this?

3. Would any of the products in Question 1 be subject to personal influence coming from normative compliance? From value expression? From informational influence?

4. Assume that you are a consultant for a manufacturer of men's clothing. How would you go about identifying influentials on the college campus?

5. Recall the last time you volunteered information to someone about a brand or product that you purchased. What caused you to share in this way? How does your motivation compare with the motivations mentioned in the text?

6. In what ways do influentials differ from those who are information seekers?

7. Defend the conclusion mentioned in the text that influentials, as a rule, have a greater impact on consumer decision than advertising or personal selling.

8. Your company manufactures a full line of mobile homes in all price ranges. Several studies have indicated that word-of-mouth communication plays a role in the buying decision. Prepare a statement indicating the alternative strategies that can be utilized to harness and capitalize upon this source of consumer influence. Which strategy do you think would be most effective?

9. Assume that you are a public relations consultant for a state medical society concerned about public attitudes toward malpractice claims. The problem is to counteract a point of view, picked up through word-of-mouth monitoring, that filing a malpractice claim against a doctor is an easy way to pay medical bills or to get something for nothing. What can be done to attack this way of thinking?

FAMILY AND HOUSEHOLD INFLUENCES

WHICH HOUSEHOLD ARE YOU IN?

If your household has a combined income of over $65,000 to spend, you are most likely to be married, white, and aged 45 to 54. Furthermore, you most likely live in the suburbs of the Northeast or West and work as a manager or administrator. In spending power, your family ranks in the top 5 percent of the nation. If your family has less than $20,000 a year to spend, there is probably one wage earner, possibly a female head of household; you may live in the city or in the South, and there is a high probability that you are black or Hispanic.

If you earn less than $5,000, you are probably a university student! But cheer up. You are also the most likely to have over $60,000 in the future, especially if you attain postgraduate education.

FAMILIES AND THE STUDY OF CONSUMER BEHAVIOR

The study of families and their relationship to buying and consumption is important, but often neglected in the analysis of consumer behavior. The importance of the family arises for two reasons.

First, *many products are purchased by multiple consumers acting as a family unit.* Homes are an example of products purchased by both spouses, perhaps with involvement from children, grandparents, or other members of the extended family. Cars are usually purchased by families, with both spouses and often a teenager involved in various stages of the decision. A favorite form of leisure for many families is visiting a regional shopping mall. The visit often involves multiple family members buying a variety of household items, clothing, and perhaps groceries. The trip may also involve all members in deciding at which fast-food outlet to spend the family's disposable income.

Second, even when purchases are made by an individual, *the buying decision of the individual may be heavily influenced by other members of the family.* Children may buy clothing that is financed and sanctioned by parents. The influence of a teenager may also be substantial on the clothing purchases of a parent. Spouses and siblings compete with each other in the decision of how the family's income will be allocated to their individual desires. The person responsible for buying and preparing the family's food may act as an individual in the supermarket but be influenced by the preferences and power of the other family members. Even when people are "on their own" as individual households, they may prefer the same furniture style (or perhaps the opposite) as the family in which they were raised. The consumer may like the same foods and leisure activities, and drive the same brand of car as other family members. The influence of family on consumer decisions is pervasive.

The study of family consumer decisions is less common than the study of individuals as consumers. The reason for neglect in studying family buying is the *difficulty of studying the family as an organization.* Surveys and other marketing research methodologies are easier to administer to individuals than to families. Administering a questionnaire to an entire family requires access to all members at approximately the same time (difficult in today's environment), using language that has the same meaning to all family members (difficult with discrepancies in age or education), and interpreting results when members of the same family report conflicting opinions about what the family buys or relative influence in the decision (a common finding in family research).

WHAT IS A FAMILY?

A **family** is a group of two or more persons related by blood, marriage, or adoption who reside together. The **nuclear family** is the immediate group of father, mother, and child(ren) living together. The **extended family** includes the nuclear family, plus other relatives, such as grandparents, uncles and aunts, cousins, and in-laws. The family into which one is born is called the **family of orientation,** whereas the one established by marriage is the **family of procreation.**

WHAT IS A HOUSEHOLD?

Household is another term frequently used by marketers when describing consumer behavior. Household differs from family in that household describes all the persons, both related and unrelated, who occupy a housing unit. For both households and families, data can be used by marketing organizations for both macro and marketing analyses. Haverty has identified the major variables that are involved in such analyses:

A. Household Production Functions
   1. Purchasing Function
   2. Household Production
   3. Consumption Function
   4. Labor Market Function
   5. Family Maintenance Function

B. Household Stocks (Resources)
   1. Information
   2. Financial Resources
   3. Market Goods
   4. Characteristics
   5. Time

C. Exogenous or Predetermined Variables
   1. Data
   2. Labor Market Opportunities
   3. Product Market Opportunities
   4. Household Structure
   5. Satisfaction.[1]

Most, if not all, of these variables are concerns in this chapter.

Although *household* and *family* are sometimes used interchangeably when analyzing how purchase decisions are made, it is important to distinguish between these terms when examining data. Household is becoming a more important unit of analysis for marketers because of the rapid growth in nontraditional families and nonfamily households. Among nonfamily households, the great majority consist of people living alone. The remaining nonfamily households include those consisting of elderly people living with nonfamily members and the relatively new census term POSSLQ, "Persons of Opposite Sex Sharing Living Quarters."

Marketers think not only about families, the largest category of households, but also of nonfamily households, which are growing faster. In the first part of the chapter, we look mostly at how families make purchase decisions, although such conclusions sometimes apply to nonfamily households. In the latter part of the chapter, we examine the fastest growing types of households. Some retain the traditional family structure and decision-making style, although many do not.

VARIABLES AFFECTING FAMILY/HOUSEHOLD PURCHASE

Families have higher median incomes than do households because of the greater number of employed individuals in families. For both families and

---

[1] John L. Haverty, "A Model of Household Behavior," in Russell W. Belk et al., 1987 *AMA Winter Educators' Conference* (Chicago: American Marketing Association, 1987), 284–289.

households, the four structural variables that impact purchasing decisions most and that are therefore of primary interest to marketers are the age of head of household or family, marital status, presence of children, and employment status.

Families are like corporations; they are organizations formed to accomplish particular functions more effectively than individuals on their own. The most obvious function that two people can accomplish better than one is to have children. Although consumer analysts may have no opinion on whether or not families should have children, they have enormous interest in whether or not they do. The economic consequences of children create the demand structure for clothing, food, furniture, homes, medical care, education, and other products. Children in a family cause decreased demand for other products, such as travel, some restaurants, adult clothing, and many discretionary items.

SOCIOLOGICAL VARIABLES AFFECTING FAMILIES

Marketers also need to analyze noneconomic variables in order to predict buying behavior. How families make decisions can be better understood by considering sociological dimensions such as cohesion, adaptability, and communication. **Cohesion** is the emotional bonding that family members have toward one another. It is a measure of how close to each other family members feel on an emotional level. Cohesion reflects a sense of connectedness to or separateness from other family members.

Family adaptability is the ability of a marital or family system to change its power structure, role relationships, and relationship rules in response to situational and developmental stress. Family adaptability is a measure of how well a family can meet the challenges presented by changing needs.

Communication is a facilitating dimension, critical to movement on the other two dimensions. Positive communication skills (such as empathy, reflective listening, supportive comments) enable families to share with each other their changing needs and preferences as they relate to cohesion and adaptability. Negative communication skills (such as double messages, double binds, criticism) minimize the ability of a family to share feelings, thereby restricting movement on the dimensions of cohesion and adaptability. Understanding whether or not family members are satisfied with the products their families have purchased may require understanding communication within the family.

Families vary in their amount of cohesion and adaptability. In a major study of normal families in America, Olson and his associates found the 16 types of families shown in Figure 6.1, classified by whether couples are balanced, midrange, or extreme in cohesion and adaptability. The actual percentage of adults and adolescents falling into each of the 16 types is shown in the numbers in Figure 6.1. (The percentages for adolescents in the families studied are shown in parentheses.) The four center cells represent the balanced

FIGURE 6.1
THIS CLASSIFICATION OF FAMILIES BY COHESION AND ADAPTABILITY IS USEFUL TO MARKETERS, BECAUSE THESE FACTORS INFLUENCE CONSUMPTION DECISIONS

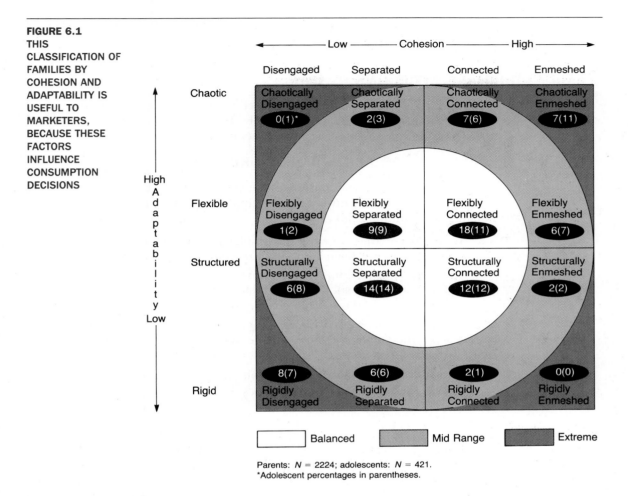

Parents: $N = 2224$; adolescents: $N = 421$.
*Adolescent percentages in parentheses.

Source: David H. Olson, Hamilton I. McCubbin, et. al, *Families: What Makes Them Work?* (Beverly Hills: Sage Publications, 1983), p. 90. Copyright 1983 by Sage Publications. Reprinted by permission.

types and the four corner cells, the extreme types. The mid-range types are represented by the other eight cells.[2]

Consumption decisions are influenced by the type of family in which an individual is a member. When cohesion levels are high (enmeshed systems), there is a high identification with the family. Such families do most things together and probably choose the same brands, colors, type of homes, and so forth. At the other extreme (disengaged systems), high levels of autonomy are encouraged and family members "do their own thing," with limited attachment or commitment to their family. In the central area of Figure 6.1 (sepa-

---

[2] David H. Olson, Hamilton I. McCubbin et al., *Families: What Makes Them Work?* (Beverly Hills: Sage Publications, 1983).

rated and connected), individuals are able to experience and balance being independent from and connected to their family.

FAMILY PURCHASE DECISIONS

The family is a "buying center" reflecting the activities and influences of the individuals who make up the family. Individuals buy products for their own use and for use by other family members.

INDIVIDUAL ROLES IN FAMILY PURCHASES

Family consumption decisions involve at least five definable roles. These roles may be assumed by the husband, wife, children, or other members of a household. Both multiple roles and multiple actors are normal.

1. *Gatekeeper.* Initiator of family thinking about buying products and the gathering of information to aid the decision.
2. *Influencer.* Individual whose opinions are sought concerning criteria the family should use in purchases and which products or brands most likely fit those evaluative criteria.
3. *Decider.* The person with the financial authority and/or power to choose how the family's money will be spent and the products or brands that will be chosen.
4. *Buyer.* The person who acts as purchasing agent: who visits the store, calls the supplier, writes the check, brings the products into the home, and so on.
5. *User.* The person or persons who use the product.

Marketers need to communicate with occupants of each role. Children, for example, are users of cereals, toys, clothing, and many other products but may not be the buyers. One or both of the parents may be the decider and the buyer, although the children may be important as influencers and as users. Parents may act as gatekeepers by preventing children from watching some TV programs or attempting to negate their influence by saying, "Toys don't really work like they appear on TV, you know."

Influencer roles may be taken by those with the most expertise. For example, a parent may be the decider about which car to purchase, but teenagers often play a major role as gatekeepers of information and as influencers because of greater knowledge about performance, product features, or social norms.

ROLE BEHAVIOR

Families and other groups also exhibit what sociologist Talcott Parsons called instrumental and expressive role behavior. **Instrumental roles,** also known as functional or economic roles, involve financial aspects, performance characteristics, and other "functional" attributes such as conditions of purchase.

Expressive roles involve support to other family members in the decision-making process and expression of aesthetic or emotional needs of the family, including upholding norms of the family. Choosing the color, product features, and retailer that fits most closely to the family's needs will be the outcome of role performance. Various family members may fulfill both instrumental and expressive roles, depending upon the type of purchase decision and individual characteristics of the family member.

Marketing communications should be directed to an individual's preferences and evaluative criteria. This is complicated, however, because of the influence of the other family members. For example, as Davis explains, "a husband may buy a station wagon, given the reality of having to transport four children, despite his strong preference for sports cars. . . . A housewife bases product and brand decisions to some extent on orders or requests from family members and on her judgment of what they like or dislike and what is 'good for them.' "[3]

SPOUSAL ROLES IN BUYING DECISIONS

Which spouse is most important in family buying decisions? How does this vary by product category? How does this vary by stage of decision making? Generally, the following role-structure categories are used to analyze these questions:

1. Autonomic, when an equal number of decisions is made by each spouse, but each decision is individually made by one spouse or the other.
2. Husband dominant.
3. Wife dominant.
4. Syncratic, when most decisions are made by both husband and wife.

These categories are sometimes simplified to "husband more than wife," "wife more than husband," "both husband and wife," or simply "husband only," "wife only," or "children only." Which situation is likely to exist is influenced by the type of product, the stage in the decision process, and the nature of the situation surrounding the decision.

A landmark study investigating husband–wife influences was conducted by Harry Davis and Benny Rigaux.[4] Their findings are usually presented in the familiar triangular configuration shown in Figure 6.2 and have greatly influenced thinking about the relative influence of husbands and wives upon decision making and the extent of role specialization. This study was recently updated by Management Horizons, a division of Price Waterhouse, for

---

[3] Harry L. Davis, "Decision Making within the Household," *Journal of Consumer Research* 2 (March 1976), 241–260.

[4] Harry L. Davis and Benny P. Rigaux, "Perception of Marital Roles in Decision Processes," *Journal of Consumer Research* 1 (June 1974), 5–14.

FIGURE 6.2
HUSBAND-WIFE INFLUENCES IN DECISION MAKING: MOVEMENT FROM INFORMATION SEARCH TO FINAL DECISION

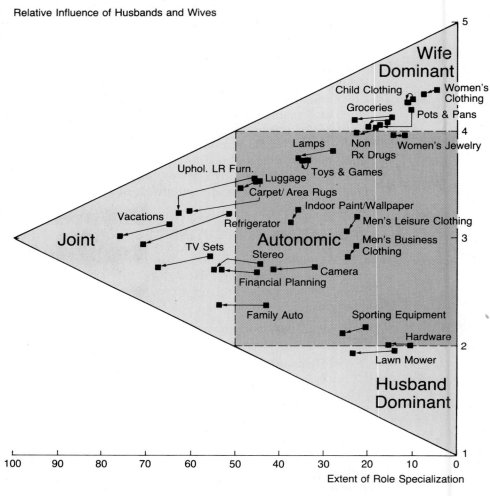

Relative Influence of Husbands and Wives

use by businesses selling a wide variety of goods.[5] The results are shown in Figure 6.2

Overall Influence.   The top and bottom portions of Figure 6.2 present overall measures of husbands' and wives' perceptions of their relative influence upon decision making across all decision stages.

Some product/service categories are wife-dominant. They include women's

---

[5] Mandy Putnam and William R. Davidson, *Family Purchasing Behavior: II Family Roles by Product Category* (Columbus, Ohio: Management Horizons Inc., a Division of Price Waterhouse, 1987).

clothing, children's clothing, pots and pans, toiletries, groceries, and nonprescription drugs. Two categories that are husband-dominant include lawn mowers and hardware.

Joint decisions tend to be made about vacations, television sets, refrigerators, upholstered living room furniture, carpet/area rugs, family autos, and financial planning services. Autonomic decision making tends to be present in decisions about categories that include women's jewelry, men's leisure clothing, men's business clothing, sporting equipment, lamps, cameras, toys and games, indoor paint/wallpaper, luggage, and stereos.

Influence by Decision Stage.   The lower portion of Figure 6.2 shows variation in the influence of spouses by stages in the decision-making process. This movement may be minimal in the case of many low-involvement goods but more pronounced for goods that are risky or have high involvement for the family.

The decision process tends to move toward joint participation and away from autonomic behavior as a final decision nears. This movement is shown in the triangular presentation in the lower portion of Figure 6.2 and is most pronounced for products and services such as family autos, refrigerators, television sets, toys and games, paint and wallpaper, vacations, and financial planning. Vacations are perhaps the most democratic of a family's purchase decisions.

Information-search stage is autonomic more than joint participation. Marketing plans thus require specialized use of media—such as magazines or other media having a strong appeal to either husbands or wives rather than both. Product or store design must reflect the evaluative criteria of both, however, as consensus on these must be achieved in the final decision. Separate campaigns may be timed to coincide with specialized interests, especially for products with a long planning cycle such as vacations and major purchases.

DECLINE OF GENDER DIFFERENCES

Changes in family structure over time are causing husband and wife decisions increasingly to be made jointly or syncratically. Qualls recently studied family decisions concerning vacations, automobiles, children's education, housing, insurance, and savings. These were all products that had been studied extensively in prior decades and generally were reported to involve a minority of joint decisions. Qualls found overwhelmingly that joint decisions are now the norm for children's education and housing in 80 percent or more households. The majority shared decisions for the other products as well, although not as dramatically.[6] The Management Horizons Family Purchasing Study

---

[6] William J. Qualls, "Changing Sex Roles: Its Impact upon Family Decision Making," in Andrew Mitchell, ed., *Advances in Consumer Research* 9 (Ann Arbor: Association for Consumer Research, 1982), 267–270.

FIGURE 6.3
EXAMPLE OF MULTIPLE ROLES OF FAMILY MEMBER: GENDER DIFFERENCES ARE BECOMING LESS IMPORTANT IN FAMILY BUYING DECISIONS

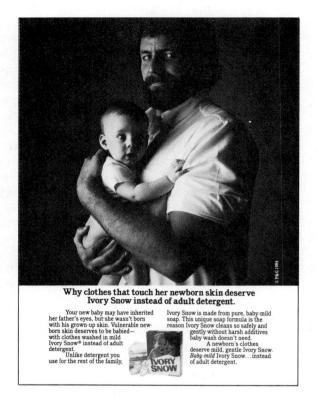

Why clothes that touch her newborn skin deserve Ivory Snow instead of adult detergent.

Your new baby may have inherited her father's eyes, but she wasn't born with his grown-up skin. Vulnerable newborn skin deserves to be babied—with clothes washed in mild Ivory Snow® instead of adult detergent.
Unlike detergent you use for the rest of the family, Ivory Snow is made from pure, baby-mild soap. This unique soap formula is the reason Ivory Snow cleans so safely and gently without harsh additives baby wash doesn't need.
A newborn's clothes deserve mild, gentle Ivory Snow. *Baby-mild* Ivory Snow…instead of adult detergent.

Source: Courtesy of the Proctor & Gamble Company.

also found that increasing resources of women and shifts toward egalitarianism are producing more joint decision making in product/service categories of perceived high risk. In contrast, however, time pressures, brought about by larger numbers of dual-worker families, may produce more autonomic decisions in categories of perceived low risk.

Consumer researchers must recognize that gender differences, despite movement away from sex-role dominance, still exist for some products and in some situations.[7] Additionally, advertising still includes sex-role dominance, perhaps by companies insensitive to such issues.

Literature reviews of these areas are available in Jenkins,[8] Burns and

---

[7] For research on this topic from a wide variety of disciplines, see Beth B. Hess and Myra Marx Ferree, *Analyzing Gender* (Newbury Park, California: Sage Publications, 1987).

[8] Roger Jenkins, "Contributions of Theory to the Study of Family Decision-Making," in Jerry Olson, ed., *Advances in Consumer Research* 7 (Ann Arbor: Association for Consumer Research, 1980), 207–211.

Granbois,[9] and Gupta, Hagerty, and Myers.[10] But psychological gender differences in household decision making today is a low-yield area of research. Roberts explains: "It has never been very productive, and it will be even less productive in the future."[11]

There are many causes for the demise of gender differences in family buying decisions. Most have to do with the changing employment status and roles of women. The resource-contribution theory suggests that the greater the relative contribution of an individual, the greater the influence in decision making. A variation of this theory is called the "least interested partner" hypothesis, which states that the greater the value of one partner relative to the other as valued by society, the greater influence that partner will have. Whatever the reasons, marketing strategies must be built upon the new realities of role structures and family buying decisions. Notice the ad for Ivory Snow in Figure 6.3, reflecting the role of the father in a product category for which he previously would have been ignored.

FAMILY LIFE CYCLES

Families change over time, passing through a series of stages. This process is called the **family life cycle (FLC).** Although the concept has been used in the literature since 1931, it received its widest influence in marketing research by Wells and Gubar,[12] and later in a book by Reynolds and Wells, showing how life cycle affects consumer behavior.[13]

TRADITIONAL FLC

Passages through life are described by the traditional family life cycle (FLC). The FLC describes patterns found among families as they marry, have children, leave home, lose a spouse, and retire. These stages are described in Table 6.1, along with consumer behavior associated with each stage. Other versions, such as Murphy and Staples', recognize contemporary developments of divorce, smaller sizes of families, and delayed age of marriage.[14] The FLC

---

[9] Alvin Burns and Donald Granbois, "Advancing the Study of Family Purchase Decision Making," in Olson, *Advances in Consumer Research*, 221–226.

[10] Sunil Gupta, Michael R. Hagerty, and John G. Myers, "New Directions in Family Decision Making Research," in Alice M. Tybout, ed., *Advances in Consumer Research* 10 (Ann Arbor: Association for Consumer Research, 1983), 445–450.

[11] Mary Lou Roberts, "Gender Differences and Household Decision-Making: Needed Conceptual and Methodological Developments," in Thomas C. Kinnear, ed., *Advances in Consumer Research* 11 (Provo: Association for Consumer Research, 1984), 276–278.

[12] William D. Wells and George Gubar, "The Life Cycle Concept," *Journal of Marketing Research* 2 (November 1966), 355–363.

[13] Fred D. Reynolds and William D. Wells, *Consumer Behavior* (New York: McGraw-Hill, 1977).

[14] Patrick E. Murphy and William Staples, "A Modernized Family Life Cycle," *Journal of Consumer Research* 6 (June 1979), 12–22.

**TABLE 6.1
TRADITIONAL LIFE
CYCLES AND
BUYING BEHAVIOR**

Single Stage
Although earnings are relatively low, they are subject to few rigid demands, so consumers in this stage typically have substantial discretionary income. Part of this income is used to purchase a car and basic equipment and furnishings for their first residence away from home—usually an apartment. They tend to be more fashion and recreation oriented, spending a substantial proportion of their income on clothing, alcoholic beverages, food away from home, vacations, leisure time pursuits, and other products and services involved in the mating game.

Newly Married Couples
Newly married couples without children are usually better off financially than they have been in the past and will be in the near future because the wife is usually employed. Families at this stage also spend a substantial amount of their income on cars, clothing, vacations, and other leisure time activities. They also have the highest purchase rate and highest average purchase of durable goods, particularly furniture and appliances, and other expensive items, and appear to be more susceptible to advertising in this stage.

Full Nest I
With the arrival of the first child, some wives stop working outside the home, and consequently family income declines. Simultaneously, the young child creates new problems that change the way the family spends its income. The couple is likely to move into their first home, purchase furniture and furnishings for the child, buy a washer, dryer, and home maintenance items, and purchase such products as baby food, chest rubs, cough medicine, vitamins, toys, wagons, sleds, and skates. These requirements reduce family savings and the husband and wife are often dissatisfied with their financial position.

Full Nest II
At this stage the youngest child is six or over, the husband's income has improved, and the wife often returns to work outside the home. Consequently, the family's financial position usually improves. Consumption patterns continue to be heavily influenced by the children as the family tends to buy food and cleaning supplies in larger sized packages, bicycles, pianos, and music lessons.

Full Nest III
As the family grows older, its financial position usually continues to improve because the husband's income rises, the wife returns to work or enjoys a higher salary, and the children earn money from occasional employment. The family typically replaces several pieces of furniture, purchases another automobile, buys several luxury appliances, and spends a considerable amount of money on dental services and education for the children.

Empty Nest I
At this stage the family is most satisfied with their financial position and the amount of money saved because income has continued to increase, and the children have left home and are no longer financially dependent on their parents. The couple often make home improvements, buy luxury items, and spend a greater proportion of their income on vacations, travel, and recreation.

Empty Nest II
By this time the household head has retired and so the couple usually suffers a noticeable reduction in income. Expenditures become more health oriented, centering on such items as medical appliances, medical care products that aid health, sleep, and digestion, and perhaps a smaller home, apartment, or condominium in a more agreeable climate.

The Solitary Survivor
If still in the labor force, solitary survivors still enjoy good income. They may sell their home and usually spend more money on vacations, recreation, and the types of health-oriented products and services mentioned above.

The Retired Solitary Survivor
The retired solitary survivor follows the same general consumption pattern except on a lower scale because of the reduction in income. In addition, these individuals have special needs for attention, affection, and security.

has been shown to be a helpful explanation of consumer behavior even at such basic levels as how much energy is consumed by families.[15]

Adding economic data helps in using the traditional FLC to explain consumer behavior. Wagner and Hanna[16] found that FLC does not predict decisions about products such as clothing as well as socioeconomic variables, especially income.

CONSUMER MARKET MATRIX OF LIFESTAGES

The Consumer Market Matrix can be used to analyze how consumers choose products and stores. This matrix blends the FLC with income data in the manner shown in Figure 6.4. The Consumer Market Matrix was developed by Management Horizons, a division of Price Waterhouse, to understand the interaction of income and lifestages on consumer behavior. It recognizes the increasing importance of aging of the population as well as the increased tendency for women either to delay having children to a later age or to choose not to have children.[17]

The major lifestages of households represent important market segments and are described as follows:

Younger Singles: Head of household single and under 45 with no children present.

Younger Couples: Married couple with head of household under 45 and no children present.

Younger Parents: Head of household under 45, with child(ren).

Mid-Life Families: Head of household between the ages of 45 and 64 with child(ren) either present in or financially supported by the household.

Mid-Life Households: Head of household between the ages of 45 and 64 with no child(ren) either present in or financially supported by the household.

Older Households: Head of household age 65 or older or retired.

The lifestage segments in the matrix are divided by income into:

Down Market: The lower quartile of household income for a specific lifestage.

Middle Market: The two middle quartiles of household income for a specific lifestage.

Up Market: The upper quartile of household income for a specific lifestage.

---

[15] David J. Frirtzche, "An Analysis of Energy Consumption Patterns by State of Family Life Cycle," *Journal of Marketing Research* 18 (May 1981), 227–232.

[16] Janet Wagner and Sherman Hanna, "The Effectiveness of Family Life Cycle Variables in Consumer Expenditure Research," *Journal of Consumer Research* 10 (December 1983), 281–291.

[17] Mandy Putnam, Sharyn Brooks, and William R. Davidson, *The Expanded Management Horizons Consumer Market Matrix* (Columbus, Ohio: Management Horizons, A Division of Price Waterhouse, 1986).

FIGURE 6.4   DISTRIBUTION OF U.S. HOUSEHOLDS BY LIFE STAGE, 1985 (000'S)

	Down Market		Middle Market		Up Market			
Younger Singles	2,780	3.2%*	5,730	6.6%	2,950	3.4%	11,460	13.2%
Younger Couples	1,300	1.5%	2,780	3.2%	1,390	1.6%	5,470	6.3%
Younger Parents	6,770	7.8%	12,150	14.0%	6,600	7.6%	25,520	29.4%
Mid-Life Families	2,340	2.7%	4,510	5.2%	2,780	3.2%	9,630	11.1%
Mid-Life Households	3,210	3.7%	6,160	7.1%	3,300	3.8%	12,670	14.6%
Older Households	4,690	5.4%	11,710	13.5%	5,640	6.5%	22,040	25.4%
	21,090	24.3%	43,040	49.6%	22,660	26.1%	86,790	100.0%

* Read as: 2,780,000 households are Down Market Younger Singles, 3.2% of all U.S. households.

Source: U.S. Department of the Census, and MANAGMENT HORIZONS, A Division of Price Waterhouse; reproduced with permission.

These definitions permit quantitative analysis of the size of each market, as shown in Figure 6.4, for the approximately 87 million households of the United States. Surveys, which can be accomplished efficiently with mail-panel data, provide information about the preferences, expenditures, and shopping behavior of each segment.

Strategic planning to reach core segments is an important application of the Consumer Market Matrix of Lifestages. Manufacturers and retailers can determine the position or "location in the minds of consumers" of the firm's offering. The objective is to attract core customers in the lifestage most profitable as the firm's target market. Close examination of the firm's marketing mix might reveal, for example, lack of a clearly defined offer, suggesting that the current marketing mix may be aimed at fringe rather than core customers.

Once a consumer segment has been identified along with its lifestyles and buying patterns, a coherent and well-coordinated marketing strategy will emphasize attributes most important to that segment. The plan must also specify the media to which the core consumers are most exposed, as well as the retailing facilities where they primarily shop. *Consumer in Focus 6.1* provides information that could be used for successful marketing programs by manufacturers or retailers of men's or women's apparel.

The FLC helps explain how a specific family changes over time. But the basic structure of families and households is changing in the United States and other industrialized countries. In the next section, we examine trends in family and household structure. Many of these changes greatly affect marketing strategies and tactics.

CHANGING FAMILY AND HOUSEHOLD STRUCTURE

What is the structure of contemporary families? How is that structure changing? How does structure affect consumption? Are the developing realities of family structure a problem or an opportunity for marketing organizations? These are some of the questions that consumer researchers try to answer. Many of the answers involve data from the decennial census and interim reports by the Bureau of Census.[18]

MARRIED OR SINGLE?

Marriage: To be or not to be? That is the question. The answer is that marriage is in the cards for most consumers. Approximately 93 percent of American adults marry at some time in their lives, although in the 1990s this may be only about 90 percent.[19] People are marrying at later ages and experiencing more divorces. Thus, the proportion of consuming households composed of nonmarried individuals is increasing rapidly. Table 6.2 gives the projected number of households by type in 1990 and 2000.

The number of marriages in the United States in 1986 was 2.4 million, and declining at the rate of 25,000 a year compared to previous years, according to the Census Bureau. That represents a national marriage rate of 10.0 per 1,000 people, also a decline from previous years and the lowest rate since 1977, when it was 9.9. In 1932, the bottom of the Great Depression, the marriage rate was at its all time low of 7.9 per 1,000 people.

HOUSEHOLD SIZE

Average household size is falling in most industrialized countries. In the United States it dropped from 3.11 in 1970 to 2.75 in 1980. One-person households are now about 23 percent of the total, compared to 18 percent in 1970, and households with six or more persons dropped from 19.5 percent of all households to less than 6 percent today. *Consumer in Focus 6.2* shows how a marketer such as Stouffer Foods adapts to these changes.

---

[18] Data in this chapter are mostly from U.S. Bureau of the Census, Current Population Reports, Series P-20, No. 410. *Marital Status and Living Arrangements: March 1985*, U.S. Government Printing Office, Washington, D.C., 1986.

[19] Martha Farnsworth Riche, "The Postmarital Society," *American Demographics* 10 (November 1988), 23–26 ff.

6.1 SHOPPING PATTERNS FOR CLOTHING BY LIFESTAGE AND INCOME

MEN'S CASUAL AND DRESS APPAREL

The analysis of shopping for men's apparel is presented for both casual and dress apparel and for both males and females shopping for the category.

The analysis of shopping behavior for men's casual apparel indicates that preferred store type is influenced strongly by household income:

Down Market segments tend to prefer discount stores and national chains and identify good value, wide selection, and low prices as reasons for selecting preferred store types.

Middle Market segments are more likely to mention department stores and national chains as preferred store types. These segments also identify good value, low prices, and wide selection as important reasons for their store choice.

Up Market segments are much more likely to mention department stores and specialty stores as preferred store type. The Up Market segments identify good value, wide selection, and quality as important reasons for shopping their preferred store.

Females shopping for men's casual apparel have similar shopping preferences, but exhibit less intense differences in their shopping preferences for the various store types. The females shopping for the category are also more likely to cite good sales as an important reason influencing their store choice.

Males' shopping behavior for men's dress apparel varies widely by lifestage segment and household income. Generally:

Up Market and Younger Singles segments indicate a preference for department stores and specialty stores and identify good value, high quality, and wide selection as important reasons for shopping preferred store type.

The remaining Down and Middle Market segments for the other lifestage groups are more likely to identify national chains, and particularly among the Down Market segments, discount stores as the store type shopped most often. These segments mention good value, wide selection, and low prices as key reasons for selecting their preferred store type.

Females' shopping behavior for men's dress apparel is somewhat different than males' shopping behavior for the category:

Females shopping for men's dress apparel in Up Market segments indicate a preference for department stores and cite good value, wide selection, and quality as reasons for their store preference.

National chains enjoy strong store patronage among females shopping for men's dress apparel among Down Market segments and Middle Market Younger Parents and Middle Market Mid-Life Household segments. These segments are more likely to mention low prices and good sales, in addition to good value and wide selection, as important reasons affecting their store patronage.

WOMEN'S CASUAL AND DRESS APPAREL

Shopping behavior for women's apparel is analyzed for both casual and dress apparel. For women's casual apparel:

Department stores are the preferred store type for all Up Market and Younger Singles segments.

Discount stores have strong store patronage among Down Market Younger Couples, Younger Parents, and Mid-Life Families.

Remaining segments indicate similar levels of store preferences for national chains, discount stores, and department stores.

Generally, off-price outlets enjoy slightly higher levels of store preference for women's casual apparel than for other merchandise categories. This preference is somewhat stronger among the Up Market segments in the younger lifestages.

Good value and wide selection are key reasons for store preference among most segments. In addition, good sales and low prices are important factors among Down and Middle Market segments, while high quality emerges in the Up Market segments as an important reason influencing store preference.

For women's dress apparel:

Department stores are dominant as preferred store for all Up Market segments and for Younger Singles. They also lead as preferred store type among Middle Market Mid-Life Families, Younger Couples, and Older Households. These segments mention good value, wide selection, and high quality as key reasons for store preferences.

National chains lead as the preferred store type in all remaining segments. These segments tend to mention low prices in addition to good value and wide selection as factors influencing their preferred store types.

Source: Mandy Putnam, Sharyn Brooks, and William R. Davidson, *The Expanded Management Horizons Consumer Market Matrix* (Columbus, Ohio: Management Horizons, a Division of Price Waterhouse, 1986), Executive Summary. Used with permission.

TABLE 6.2 HOUSEHOLDS BY TYPE—1990–2000 PROJECTIONS	1990	2000	% Change 1990–2000
All households	95.2[a]	110.2	15.8
Family households	65.9	70.0	13.8
Married couples	51.7	52.3	1.1
Male householder	2.7	3.8	40.7
Female householder	11.5	13.9	20.9
Nonfamily households	29.3	40.2	37.2
Male householder	13.0	19.5	50.0
Female householder	16.3	20.7	27.0

[a] Numbers refer to millions.
Source: U.S. Bureau of the Census, Current Population Reports, Series P-25, No. 986, Series A assumptions (reflecting recent changes in marriage and divorce trends).

LATER MARRIAGES

The median age at which people get married has increased substantially. Among males, the median age at first marriage was 22.8 in 1950 but increased to 25.8 by 1987. For women, the median age increased from 20.3 to 23.6. In older marriages, consumers may have to buy fewer of the basic furnishings and products needed for housekeeping but are able to buy better merchandise — higher-quality furniture, designer services, and so forth. Older marriages produce more extensive travel capabilities, a higher probability of owning two cars, and probably firmer preferences for styles, colors, and design of products.

SINGLES BOOM

There are more singles in the United States than ever before. In 1987, according to Census Bureau reports, the percentage of men aged 30 to 34 who had never married was 23.1 percent, up from 9.4 percent in a 1970 Census Report. Among women in the 30 to 34 age group, 14.6 percent had never married, compared with 6.2 percent in 1970. When those who are also single because of divorce or death are considered, singles are growing twice as fast as married couples and represent 25 percent of households or about 40 percent of the adult population, up from 32 percent in 1960. By 1990, it is projected that one of every four occupied dwelling units will have only one person in it.

One of the reasons for more singles is the increasing time between divorce and remarriage. Divorced women wait an average of 3.6 years before remarrying and divorced men wait an average of 3.2 years, figures that are both more than a year longer than in prior decades.[20]

---

[20] Ibid.

CONSUMER IN FOCUS

6.2   STOUFFER FOODS ADAPTS TO CHANGED FAMILY SIZE

For 30 years, Stouffer Foods provided frozen prepared food with quality, taste, and variety at an economical price. Layered onto those traditional marketing variables, in more recent years Stouffer added Lean Cuisine in one- and two-serving packages for today's smaller families and the increasing number of single-person households.

The company believes that women in a previous era had guilt feelings about serving prepared food instead of cooking for their families, but that today's woman — who is a significant contributor to the family's financial well-being — feels it proper to buy the best-prepared food available and can afford to do so. In the 1960s, Stouffer's research indicated that larger families — those with two or more children — accounted for a significant sales volume. The company introduced the Family Casserole line, frozen food packages that served four or more people. It was unsuccessful because even larger families have such active lifestyles that they are unable to eat together and preferred split menus and split meals. When Stouffer reintroduced products such as lasagne in smaller packages, the product was successful.

DIVORCE AND CONSUMER BEHAVIOR

The number of divorces increased for many years in the United States and most other countries. Very recently, however, the trend has changed. In 1986, there were 1,159,000 divorces, down from the 1985 total of 1,187,000. That represented a drop from 5.0 divorces per 1,000 people to 4.8 for the most recent year. This was the lowest divorce rate since 1975, when it was also 4.8. The record high divorce rate was in 1979 at 5.3. Recent declines in the divorce rate are attributed to various causes, such as later ages of marriage or the possibility that the pent-up demand of previous decades has simply been satisfied.

Divorce contributes an added dimension to analysis of consumer decision making. Consumer behavior in "never-married" households may be analyzed in ways similar to that of individuals, but people who have been previously married, sometimes called the "single again" market, carry with them preferences and shopping patterns learned in a family situation. They often carry financial problems that restrict their ability to buy the things that married couples or never-married singles might.[21] In spite of the recent declines in divorce rate, 51.6 percent of today's marriages are ending in divorce.[22] If a couple completes 10 years of marriage, the odds of divorce fall to 30 percent.

---

[21] For a thorough analysis of the financial and other decisions of these families, see Frank Furstenbert and Graham B. Spanier, *Recycling the Family* (Beverly Hills: Sage Publications, 1984).
[22] "The Life of a Marriage," *American Demographics* 11 (February 1989), 12.

Thus, while most people live most of their lives married, about half live part of their lives divorced.

Divorce creates markets. One family unit becomes two — with two households and two sets of household equipment. There are fewer divorced men because more men than women remarry and because men remarry sooner. Studies show that a man's income usually rises after a divorce while a woman's income usually falls, especially if she gets custody of children. For this reason, some divorced adults spend freely while others are forced into frugality. Both parties learn new patterns of consumer behavior.[23]

COHABITING SINGLES

Cohabiting singles are the fastest-growing segment of the singles market, although their numbers are small in proportion to the total number of households. The number of unmarried couples tripled from 523,000 in 1970 to 1.6 million in 1980, or about 4 percent of all couples in the United States. About half a million have at least one child; most are young and likely to have much less income than married couples; 8 percent are married to someone other than the person with whom they are cohabiting.[24]

A study financed by the National Institute of Health found that almost half of all Americans 25 to 35 have lived with an individual of the opposite sex outside of marriage, with a prediction that in the 1990s this practice will be a majority experience.[25]

MARKETING TO SINGLES

Most singles (61 percent) are women, and of the 12 million women who live alone, the median age is 66. For the men the median age is 45. The demographics of single men and women are dramatically different because they are single for different reasons. Women live alone principally because their husbands have died. Men live alone because they have not yet married or they are divorced.

The gap in life expectancy between men and women (78.9 for white females compared to 71.8 for white males and 73.6 for black women compared to 65.5 for black men in 1987) means that the largest fraction of singles in the foreseeable future will be elderly widows — with a median income of $8,000. Single men aren't exactly wealthy, either; their median annual income is only $14,000, but it is more likely to be from wages and salaries, whereas single women are more likely to receive monies from Social Security, other pensions, interest, and dividends.

Consumer analysts will find most of the "booming singles market" buying

---

[23] Kathryn A. London and Barbara Foley Wilson, "Divorce," *American Demographics* 10 (October 1988), 23–26.

[24] Graham B. Spanier, "Living Together in the Eighties," *American Demographics* 4 (November 1982), 17–31.

[25] Alan A. Otten, "People Patterns," *The Wall Street Journal* (June 14, 1988), 33.

6.3 MARKETING TO SINGLE CONSUMERS

Thanks to Hallmark Cards, the unmarried can now commiserate by mail about the ups and downs of dating. Campbell Soup Company, whose Le Menu frozen dinners for one have been a hit since their 1983 debut, is following up this summer with Swanson's Homestyle Recipe Entrees, and Pillsbury has high hopes for its pint-size cake, microwavable in 10 minutes. There are miniaturized appliances for the condominium-size kitchen, and Corning Glass Works' small microwaveproof bowls for the cook who eats alone. Don't want to wait till the wedding to collect china and crystal? Singles can list preferred gifts in the Bloomingdale's Self Registry, which works as any bridal registry does.

Home builders are paying attention, too, since singles account for a fourth of first-time home buyers. "We're seeing a lower number of bedrooms, decreasing dining-room space and an increase in kitchen area, which is becoming a living room to the single," says Robert Burchell, director of the Center for Urban Policy Research at Rutgers University. Master bedrooms will be more luxurious, he predicts, bathrooms more spa-like and living space better equipped for high-tech entertainment. En-

trepreneurs are seizing some of the action as well. "I'm the next-door neighbor who was there when you were a kid," says Judith Cills of Robbins-Cills Associates in Philadelphia, one of a swarm of personal-service agencies springing up to manage the lives of those too busy to do it themselves. Half of her clients — who pay her to take pets to the vet and clothes to the cleaner, run to the florist and wait for deliveries — are single.

"The world is not set up for people doing things on their own," says Bobbe Wolf, a single photographer in Chicago who relies on Personalized Services owner Lois Barnett for shopping help and errand running, and once for a last-minute passport renewal. Perhaps not yet. But as America's singles find strength in numbers, society is granting them more respect. There's no question that scything one's own path through life can be lonely and backbreaking work, but it can be rewarding and exhilarating, too.

Source: "Living Alone and Loving It," *U.S. News and World Report* (August 3, 1987), 56. Copyright 1987, U.S. News & World Report.

home-security devices, treatment for chronic health problems, congregate care facilities, and perhaps a sedate Caribbean cruise. Magazines such as *Living Single,* cars such as Pontiac's Fiero, resorts such as Club Med, Nautilus equipment, VCRs, and restaurants such as TGI Friday are often associated with the booming singles market. They hardly fit, however, the majority of the single market. Some of the ways that marketing organizations are adapting to both the problems and the priorities of the single life are described in *Consumer in Focus 6.3.*

REMARRIAGES

Most divorced people remarry. Markets in total, therefore, remain mostly married. Consumers who remarry, however, are more complex to analyze because they are often subject to the family influences from stepchildren. Also, there is potential conflict between siblings of the multiple families as well as continuing influences from former spouses on the children of their own households.

The problem of analyzing resource distribution and other consumption problems can make analysis of consumer behavior complex:

> When a person enters into a remarriage, financial decision-making becomes more complex. After having spent some time in independent households, remarried partners must find some compatible way to handle their two economies. This may necessitate incorporating people from two separate households and two different generations who have different and/or opposing earning, spending, and saving habits. An additional factor complicates the family economy . . . financial responsibilities after remarriage may involve three or four adults across several households. In addition, the remarried family may be experiencing several different family stages simultaneously (for example, the newly married couple stage and the adolescent child stage). These two stages may conflict in their demands for resource distribution. That means problems may arise over whether to spend money for new household items versus a teenage child's request for a used car.[26]

CHANGING ROLES OF WOMEN

Marketing managers have always been interested in women because women buy so many products. Interest in women has intensified in recent years because of greater numbers of women, improved purchasing and employment status, and changed roles of women.

The female population is growing faster than the male population due to a higher survival rate for women. Life expectancy has increased more for women than for men. Controversy exists about why women live so much longer than men. Many observers thought that when women have equal representation in high-stress jobs, such as corporate executive, their life expectancy would be similar to men's. In fact, women handle stress much better than men, possibly because estrogen may be better adapted than testosterone for the flight-or-fight situations of modern life. Whatever the reasons, females now exceed males by 6.5 million. This figure is expected to be 7.5 million in 2000.

More women attend colleges or universities than do men, in sharp contrast

---

[26] Marilyn Ihinger-Tallman and Kay Pasley, *Remarriage* (Newbury, California: Sage Publications, 1987), 70.

TABLE 6.3 DIFFERENCES BETWEEN WOMEN AND MEN	**Remarkable Differences**
	Between 130 and 150 males are conceived for every 100 females. About 105 boys are born for every 100 girls. But by the time they reach the age of 20, there are only about 98 males per 100 females. And among those 65 and older, just 68 men survive for every 100 women.
	Females have a better sense of smell than males from birth onward. They are also more sensitive to loud sounds. But males are more sensitive to bright light—and can detect more subtle differences in light.
	It is physiologically more difficult for women than for men to maintain a desirable weight and still meet their nutritional needs.
	Women on average spend 40 percent more days sick in bed than do men.
	Sexual perversions—foot fetishes, for instance—are an almost exclusively male phenomenon.
	Boys get more than 90 percent of all perfect scores of 800 on the math section of the Scholastic Aptitude Test. And the gap between SAT math scores for boys and girls is greatest—about 60 points higher for males—among students who are in the top 10 percent of their class.
	Infant girls show a strong, early response to human faces—at a time when infant boys are just as likely to smile and coo at inanimate objects and blinking lights.
	Boys are far more likely than girls to be left-handed, nearsighted and dyslexic (more than 3 to 1). Males under 40 are also more likely than females to suffer from allergies and hiccups.

Source: "Men Vs. Women," *U.S. News and World Report* 105 (August 8, 1988), 52. Copyright U.S. News & World Report.

to the past. The principal reason females outnumber males on college campuses today is the greater number of women over 25 returning to campus.

Women now have much higher rates of employment outside the home than in past eras. Women have left hearth and home to bring home some of the bacon. By 1987, about 54 percent of married women were employed, in contrast to less than 25 percent in 1950. When movement in and out of the labor force is considered, the proportion of women working within a 2-year period may be as high as 80 percent. Among women with children, over 57 percent have jobs, and by 1990 the 25 to 34 age group is expected to have a labor participation rate of 80 percent.[27]

Feminine roles are of great concern today to consumer analysts and marketers. A **role** specifies what the typical occupant of a given position is expected to do in that position in a particular social context.[28] Consumer analysts are especially concerned with sex roles of women in the family and in their position as purchasing agents for the family.

Many other differences exist between women and men, some culturally determined and some genetically determined. Table 6.3 reviews a few of

[27] Elizabeth Waldman, "Labor Force Statistics from a Family Perspective," *Monthly Labor Review* (December 1983), 16–20.

[28] David Wilson, "Role Theory and Buying-Selling Negotiations: A Critical Review," in Richard Bagozzi, ed., *Marketing in the 1980s* (Chicago: American Marketing Association, 1980), 118–121.

these differences. If you examine sense of smell, ability to maintain body weight, illness, sexual perversions, or other differences, it is easy to explain why the markets for perfume are greater for women, why men read more "sophisticated" magazines, why health care organizations have women as their primary market target, and many other common differences in marketing to women and to men.

FEMALE EMPLOYMENT

Participation in the labor force affects consumption in several ways. Most importantly, families with two earners have far higher spending power — more than $5,000 average additional income compared to families where only the husband works. Working women contribute heavily to the rapidly growing affluent markets of over-$50,000 families, considered to be the "premium" market.

The chief limitation in the purchasing power of women is that they face a "dual labor market," the term used to describe the situation in which women receive less for the same work than do men. Barbara Bryant of Market Opinion Research hypothesizes the cause for this discrepancy may be both discrimination and the choices that working women make about their careers. Specifically, the largest group (46 percent) of women move in and out of the labor force, often remaining at home when children are young. Women are disproportionately represented in mathematics, science, and engineering, and have other historically lower-paid jobs such as nursing and teaching.[29] Some change is occurring, and among dual-income families, about 6 million women earn more than their husbands.[30]

CAREER ORIENTATION

Working women may be classified by their orientation toward their careers. Rena Bartos finds two groups of working women: those who think of themselves as having a career and those to whom work is "just a job." There are also two categories of housewives: those who prefer to stay at home and those who plan to work in the future. Bartos found that in many ways the "plan to work" housewives are like the working women, especially in the purchase of cosmetic and apparel products. The homemakers and "just a job" women are more likely to read traditional women's magazines, whereas the other women are more likely to read general-interest and business-oriented magazines and newspapers.[31]

---

[29] Barbara E. Bryant, "Women, and the 59-Cent Dollar," *American Demographics* 5 (August 1983), 28–31.

[30] Suzanne M. Bianchi, "Wives Who Earn More Than Their Husbands," *American Demographics* 6 (July 1984), 18–23.

[31] Rena Bartos, *The Moving Target: What Every Marketer Should Know About Women* (New York: Free Press, 1982).

WOMEN AND TIME

Married working women experience many time pressures. They often have two jobs: household responsibilities plus their jobs in the marketplace. Studies show they have significantly less leisure time than either their husbands or full-time homemakers.[32] This would suggest that working wives would buy more time-saving appliances, use more convenience foods, spend less time shopping, and so forth. Actually, Weinberg and Winer found that working and nonworking wives are similar in such behavior if income, life cycle, and other situational variables are held constant.[33] Bellante and Foster report that, although understanding employment effects is complex, working-wife families appear to spend more on food away from home, child care, and some services.[34]

Today's retail facilities must be open longer hours, not only because of so many women working but also because they frequently work different shifts than their spouses. One study found that among mothers who work full time, 45 percent work different shifts than their spouse. Among part-time working women, 57.4 percent work different shifts than their husbands.[35] Split shifts may cause retailers to be open longer hours but also aid the marketing programs of direct marketers with "800" numbers as well as the newer technologies of videotex and other time-flexible forms of shopping.

Role Overload.   **Role overload** exists when the total demands on time and energy associated with the prescribed activities of multiple roles are too great to perform the roles adequately or comfortably.[36] Much of the role overload felt by contemporary women occurs when they work more in total than men. This creates the possibility of their solving the problem by purchases of products or services from marketing organizations.[37]

Data from three major studies of families, classified by gender and employment, are shown in Table 6.4. These studies examined paid work versus family work and disclosed that employed women work more hours each day than husbands who are employed, and wives who are not employed. Sex-role ideology, especially found in feminism, and other forces are creating pressures toward more equality in work loads between men and women.

---

[32] Marianne Ferber and Bonnie Birnbaum, "One Job or Two Jobs: The Implications for Young Wives," *Journal of Consumer Research* 8 (December 1980), 263–271.

[33] Charles B. Weinberg and Russell S. Winer, "Working Wives and Major Family Expenditures: Replication and Extension," *Journal of Consumer Research* 7 (September 1983), 259–263.

[34] Don Bellante and Ann C. Foster, "Working Wives and Expenditure on Services," *Journal of Consumer Research* 11 (September 1984), 700–707.

[35] Alan Otten, "People Patterns," *The Wall Street Journal* (June 14, 1988), 33.

[36] Patricia Voydanoff, *Work and Family Life* (Newbury Park, California: Sage Publications, 1987), 83.

[37] Alvin C. Burns and Ellen Foxman, "Role Load and Its Consequences on Individual Consumer Behavior," in Terence A. Shimp et al., *1986 AMA Educators' Proceedings* (Chicago: American Marketing Association, 1986), 18.

TABLE 6.4
EMPLOYED
HUSBANDS' AND
WIVES' TIME USE
(HOURS/DAY) IN
PAID WORK, FAMILY
WORK, AND ALL
WORK

Study	Time Use Category	Employed Husbands		Wives	
		Wife Employed	Wife Not Employed	Employed	Not Employed
Walker &	Family Work	1.6	1.6	4.8	8.1
Woods (1976)	Paid Work	6.3	7.8	5.3	.5
	All Work	7.9	9.4	10.1	8.6
Robinson	Family Work	1.1	1.0	4.0	7.6
(1977a)	Paid Work	5.8	6.5	5.3	0
	All Work	6.9	7.5	9.3	7.6
Meissner	Family Work	.6	.6	2.3	4.6
et al.	Paid Work	7.1	7.7	6.5	1.9
(1975)	All Work	7.7	8.3	9.0	6.5

Source: Joseph H. Pleck, *Working Wives/Working Husbands* (Beverly Hills: Sage Publications, 1985), 30.

There is some evidence, especially among younger families, of a shift in attitudes toward work and housework that is causing a move toward more household equality between the sexes.[38]

Marketers must find ways of communicating with women who feel role overload. Figure 6.5 shows such an ad, by Whirlpool. The ad recognizes the increasing number of employed women and their perceptions of lives that are busier than ever. Yet the ad avoids referring to employed women. To do so might alienate nonemployed women. Whirlpool makes products of high quality, targeted especially to families with the income to purchase quality — a situation most likely to occur among families with employed women. The ad is positioned to this target market, both in copy and illustration.

Employed women may feel the pressure of too little discretionary time, but not all of them are in high-income families. If they do not have more income, they find ways of coping with problems that cause their behavior to be not too different from that of full-time homemakers. Differences in store patronage and other buying decisions may be more meaningfully understood by looking at type of employment (professional versus nonprofessional, for example, or satisfaction-seeking versus income-seeking) to find the best explanations of behavior.[39]

[38] F. Thomas Juster, "A Note on Recent Changes in Time Use," in F. Thomas Juster and Frank P. Stafford, *Time, Goods, and Well-Being* (Ann Arbor: Institute for Social Research, 1985), 313–332.

[39] Mary Joyce and Joseph Guiltinan, "The Professional Women: A Potential Market Segment for Retailers," *Journal of Retailing* 54 (Summer 1978), 59–70.

FIGURE 6.5
THIS AD WAS DESIGNED TO APPEAL TO EMPLOYED WOMEN WITHOUT ALIENATING NONEMPLOYED WOMEN

Source: Courtesy of Whirlpool Corporation.

FEMININE ROLES

The differences in feminine roles can be observed in a study by Venkatesh, who collected a large bank of lifestyle data about women, categorized on the basis of traditionalists, moderates, and feminists.[40] Feminists and moderates were younger than traditionalists and generally more educated and more likely to be employed full time. More traditionalists labeled themselves as

---

[40] Alladi Venkatesh, "Changing Roles of Women: A Life-Style Analysis," *Journal of Consumer Research* 7 (September 1980), 189–197.

6.4 WOMEN AS AUTO BUYERS

By 1990, Women will represent more than half the automobile buyers in this country, says the Motor Vehicle Manufacturers Association. Among other efforts to target this audience, training programs are being conducted to help dealers better service the female market. Training videotapes teach dealers how to attract and work with women customers, and individual dealers are sponsoring special events to bring women into the showroom, says MVMA. Overall, manufacturers are looking hard at their marketing efforts and *making dramatic changes* directed toward gaining the female car buyer's attention.

Television and Print ads reflect new lifestyles and interests of women, and advertisements directed towards women no longer appear exclusively in home-related magazines. Automakers are also offering mail-in credit applications in print ads in order to *counteract the feeling* of discrimination women have felt in relation to financing, says the association.

Source: *American Marketplace* 9 (February 18, 1988), 25. For additional information see Frieda Curtindale, "Marketing Cars to Women," *American Demographics* 10 (November 1988), 29–31.

"housewives," and more feminists were likely to label themselves as "co-head of household."

From a larger amount of data, Venkatesh was able to reduce the topics into ten factors. Space does not permit reproduction of all of them, but two factors, "sex stereotyping" and "fashion and personal appearance," are displayed in Table 6.5. Look at the factor on sex stereotyping and you will see that responses to every statement are statistically significant between groups. Look at the fashion and appearance factor, however, and you will see that no statistically significant differences exist between groups of women in the study except one concerning beauty parlors.

Marketers can use such information to make themselves sensitive to the topics that can be the same or must be different for different segments. An ad appearing in *Ms.* appealing to feminists might show boys playing with dolls, but the same illustration would have little appeal to traditionalists. Concerning fashion, however, about 90 percent of all types of women say, "I like to feel attractive." Ads with such an appeal are likely to cut across almost all types of women.[41]

[41] Donald Sexton and Phyliss Habertman, "Women in Magazine Advertisements," *Journal of Advertising Research* 14 (April 1974), 41–46; Ahmed Belkaoui and Janice Belkaoui, "A Comparative Analysis of the Roles Portrayed by Women in Print Advertisements: 1958, 1970, 1972," *Journal of Marketing Research* 13 (May 1976).

Environmental Influences

Part II explores the role played by environmental influences on consumer behavior. The manner by which such information affects marketing strategy and tactics is illustrated by the following set of full-color ads. Each ad is accompanied by a brief description of the specific environmental factor at work.

An effective advertising approach is one that appeals to a nation's cultural values. In this advertisement Xerox Corporation expresses its support of egalitarianism, an important core value in American society.

Source: Courtesy of Xerox Corporation.

The study of social class enables marketers to develop products, services, and communication approaches that target specific market segments. In this advertisement promoting a unique travel experience Cunard combines a classy illustration with a headline and copy designed to attract the upper class market.

Source: Courtesy of Cunard Line Limited.

The personal influence of reference groups often shapes consumer attitudes and product-choice decisions. This advertisement promoting Levi's® jeans for boys capitalizes on young people's desire to comply with group norms.

Source: Courtesy of Levi-Strauss & Company.

Show this ad to your friends.

We built the TW200 with only one thing in mind.

Pure, unadulterated fun.

That's why we gave it a knobby rear tire that's not just fat, it's obese. And that's why we gave it fun stuff like Monocross rear suspension, five-speed gearbox and a high-torque, 196cc engine.

All of which makes the TW200 the most righteous, on-road, off-road, off-the-wall example of very un-basic transportation you can buy. But, as the next page shows, your parents will like it anyway.

YAMAHA
We make the difference.

12 month limited warranty. Warranty terms are limited. See your Yamaha dealer for details. Dress properly for your ride with a helmet, eye protection, long sleeved shirt, long trousers, gloves and boots. Yamaha and the Motorcycle Safety Foundation encourage you to ride safely and respect the environment.

Show this ad to your parents.

We built the TW200 with only one thing in mind.

Pure, unadulterated practicality.

That's why we gave it a built-in luggage rack, to carry your lunch box safely. And that's why we gave it electric starting and a low seat, to carry you easily to your meeting of the Concerned Young People Against Rock Lyrics.

All of which makes the TW200 the most practical, functional, plain-old-common-sense example of basic transportation you can buy. But you'll like it anyway.

YAMAHA
We make the difference.

For further information regarding the MSF rider course please call 1-800-447-4700. Do not drink and drive. It is illegal and dangerous. Rear view mirror(s) standard equipment. Models sold in California equipped with evaporative emission control device. Specifications subject to change without notice.

Consumer buying decisions are often heavily influenced by family members. Yamaha recognized the role parents play in purchasing products for their children by creating this humorous two-part advertisement that ran on separate magazine pages.

Source: Courtesy of Yamaha International Corporation.

CHUCKS & TUX
OK guys, loosen up. All Stars, now suitable for All Occasions.

By understanding the situational influences on consumer buying behavior, marketers can expand the usage of their products and services. This advertisement for Converse hightops illustrates that the shoes are not limited to athletic purposes but also can be used as a fashion accessory on prom night.

Source: Courtesy of Converse Inc.

TABLE 6.5
FEMININE ROLES

Factor Analysis of Life-Style Variables

Extracted Factor	Percent in Each Group Who Agree with the Statements		
	Traditionalists	Moderates	Feminists
Sex Stereotyping			
American advertisements picture a woman's place to be in the home.	38[a]	64	89[b]
American advertisements seem to have recognized the changes in women's roles.	48	33	22[b]
American advertisements depict women as sexual objects.	44	56	81[b]
American advertisements depict women as independent without needing the protection of men.	14	8	4[b]
I would like to see more and more young girls play with mechanical toys.	18	42	75[b]
I would like to see boys playing with dolls just the way girls do.	10	30	66[b]
Boys and girls should play with the same kind of toys.	30	64	80[b]
Fashion and Personal Appearance			
An important part of my life and activities is dressing smartly.	39	38	38
I like to feel attractive.	86	92	90
I would like to go to the beauty parlor as often as I can.	17	12	5[c]
I enjoy looking through fashion magazines to see what is new in fashions.	60	63	57
I like to do a lot of partying.	26	39	38
I love to shop for clothes.	49	46	47

[a] Based on Chi-square tests results.
[b] Significant at 0.01 level.
[c] Significant at 0.05 level.
Source: Alladi Venkatesh, "Changing Roles of Women: Life-Style Analysis," *Journal of Consumer Research* 7 (September 1980), 192–193.

WOMEN AND ADVERTISING

Advertising has often portrayed women in limited, stereotyped roles. Generally, women were shown as purchasers of low-unit-price items and as homemakers rather than career persons. However, Duker and Tucker report that advertisers who change their appeals "to be with it" may appeal to only a small group of moderns rather than to the larger group of consumers. Advertisers must create messages with deeply rooted values.[42] Contemporary women

---

[42] Jacob M. Duker and Lewis Tucker, Jr., "Women's Libbers Versus Independent Women: A Study of Preferences for Women's Roles in Advertisement," *Journal of Marketing Research* 14 (November 1977), 469–475.

are increasingly oriented toward self-realization, self-expression, and personal fulfillment.

The "New Traditionalist" is a term used by some advertisers to describe the career woman of the 1990s. *Good Housekeeping* used this concept to redesign their magazine. After examining Yankelovich Monitor studies, *Good Housekeeping* concluded that the American contemporary woman feels strongly about building a strong family, and a strong commitment to her husband, her home, and the values her mother had. These traditional values are synthesized with an emphasis on individuality and on tolerance for diverse ideas, lifestyles, and beliefs. While many marketers have accepted this concept of the "New Traditionalist," other observers and women's scholars see the repetition of "traditional values" as reviving former stereotypes of the dependent housewife. Feminist Betty Friedan warns that this new "feminine mystique" defines women once again in terms of their husband, family, and home. Other feminists see such efforts of marketers as antifreedom, antiliberty, and anti–self-actualization.[43]

FEMINIST ORIENTATION

Consumer researchers need research tools to examine the extent to which women hold feminist attitudes and values. The goal is to relate consumer behavior, reaction to communications, or other variables to feminist orientation. Fortunately, there exist many excellent tests and measures about feminism and related topics.

A typical feminist scale used in consumer research is the Smith and Self scale used to divide women into feminist or traditionalist categories based upon "agree" and "disagree" statements.[44] The scale consists of 21 items, such as the achievements of women in history have not been emphasized as much as those of men; in general, men tend to have more common sense than women do; and women have just as strong a biological drive for sex as men do. Using the Smith and Self scale with more specific behaviors than other studies, Koch found that attitudes toward clothing and the way a woman dresses is significantly related to feminist orientation.[45]

CHANGING MASCULINE ROLES

The roles of men in families are also changing substantially. As women increasingly participate in the labor force and as values shift in society, men are taking on new roles in consuming and purchasing products. In a survey of

---

[43] Connie Koenenn, "New Women's Ad Causes Stir," from the *Los Angeles Times*, in the *Columbus Dispatch* (January 15, 1989), 5F.

[44] M. D. Smith and G. D. Self, "Feminists and Traditionalists: An Attitudinal Comparison," *Sex Roles* 7 (1981), 182–188.

[45] Kathryn E. Koch, "Dress-Related Attitudes of Employed Women Differing in Feminist Orientation and Work Status: Emphasis on Career Apparel" (unpublished Ph.D. dissertation, The Ohio State University, Columbus, 1985).

1,000 American males by the advertising agency Cunningham & Walsh, more and more men could be observed as househusbands. The privately published survey disclosed that 47 percent of men vacuum the house, 80 percent take out the garbage, 41 percent wash dishes, 37 percent make beds, 33 percent load the washing machine, 27 percent clean the bathroom, 23 percent dust, 23 percent dry dishes, 21 percent sort laundry, 16 percent clean the refrigerator, and 14 percent clean the oven.

Over 50 percent of men take part in regular shopping trips, suggesting that men are important targets for marketing activity for many types of household products. Supermarkets may profit by giving special assistance to men shoppers. Even for a role so traditionally rooted in mother dominance as taking care of a baby, it is possible to see recognition of the need for male roles, as can be observed in the Ivory Snow ad (Figure 6.3) earlier in this chapter.

Men not only participate in household and consumption activities but apparently are increasing their rate of participation. Men now do one fifth of the cooking, cleaning, and laundry, and married men now do more housework than unmarried men. Fathers are doing more than they once did, and mothers are doing less than previously (although still more than men).[46]

Not all researchers accept the finding that the "new father" is widespread nor even beneficial.[47] Much literature, however, is focusing on new roles of men.[48] One of the primary contributors to this literature, Joseph Pleck, concludes that while some of these images reflect hype, there is also much of substantive change:

> *A new image, summed up in the term "the new father," is clearly on the rise in print and broadcast media. This new father differs from older images of involved fatherhood in several key respects: he is present at the birth; he is involved with his children as infants, not just when they are older; he participates in the actual day-to-day work of child care, and not just play; he is involved with his daughters as much as his sons.*[49]

RESEARCH METHODOLOGY FOR FAMILY DECISION STUDIES

When you prepare an analysis of family influences on buying or the consumption decisions of families, most of the research techniques will be similar to other marketing research studies. There are a few unique aspects of family decisions that should be considered, however, in these final pages of the chapter.

---

[46] John P. Robinson, "Who's Doing the Housework," *American Demographics* 10 (December 1988), 24–28 ff.

[47] Charlie Lewis and Margaret O'Brien, eds., *Reassessing Fatherhood* (Newbury Park, California: Sage Publications, 1987).

[48] Michael S. Kimmel, ed., *Changing Men: New Directions in Research on Men and Masculinity* (Newbury Park, California: Sage Publications, 1987).

[49] Joseph H. Pleck, "American Fathering in Historical Perspective," in Kimmel, loc. cit., 93.

DECISION-PROCESS FRAMEWORK

Role-structure studies have often viewed purchasing as an act rather than a process and have based findings on questions such as "Who usually makes the decision to purchase?" or "Who influences the decision?" Yet, the evidence indicates that the role and influence of family members varies by stage in the decision process. An example of process methodology is provided by Wilkes, who found useful the following questions for measuring family influence:

1. Who was responsible for initial problem recognition?
2. Who was responsible for acquiring information about the purchase alternatives?
3. Who made the final decision as to which alternative should be purchased?
4. Who made the actual purchase of the product?[50]

Better results using this methodology were obtained than with more global measures. Husbands and wives are more likely to hold similar perceptions about their relative influence for a given phase than when questioning fails to ask about decision stages.

ROLE-STRUCTURE CATEGORIES

The relevant role-structure categories in a research project depend on the specific product or service under consideration, but in many product categories only the husband or wife is involved. In other categories it is useful to measure the amount of influence in different roles. Spiro found that influence strategies or persuasion depend on several variables, especially stage in the life cycle and lifestyles.[51] Children are involved in many types of purchase situations, but the nature of their influence has often been ignored.

INTERVIEWER BIAS

The sex of the interviewer or observer may influence the roles husbands and wives say they play in a purchase situation. To overcome this bias, either self-administered questionnaires should be used or the sex of the observer should be randomly assigned to respondents.

RESPONDENT SELECTION

In measuring family buying, it is necessary to decide which member(s) of the nuclear family should be asked about the influence of family members. Results often vary considerably depending on which family members are

---

[50] Robert E. Wilkes, "Husband-Wife Influence in Purchase Decisions: A Confirmation and Extension," *Journal of Marketing Research* 12 (May 1975), 224–227.
[51] Rosann L. Spiro, "Persuasion in Family Decision-Making," *Journal of Consumer Research* 9 (March 1983), 393–401.

TABLE 6.6 INFLUENCE STRUCTURE IN THE VACATION AND LODGING DECISIONS PROCESS

Subdecision: In What Proportion Did the Husband/Wife/Children Influence Your Family's Decision	Influence as Perceived by	Family Respondents (n = 234)							Couple Respondents (n = 306)			
		Influence of			Statistical Significance of Differences in Influence of			Statistical Significance of Differences in Perceptions of	Influence of		Statistical Significance of Differences in Influence of	Statistical Significance of Differences in Perceptions of
		(1) Husband (H)	(2) Wife (W)	(3) Children (C)	H-W (1-2)	H-C (1-3)	W-C (2-3)	H-W (4-5)	(7) Husband (H)	(8) Wife (W)	H-W (7-8)	H-W (4-5)
(1) ... to take a vacation this year	(4) Husband	42.1	40.8	17.1	0.63	—[a]	—[a]	0.18 (H)	51.6	48.4	0.23	0.79 (H)
	(5) Wife	45.4	35.8	18.8	—[a]	—[a]	—[a]	0.02 (W)	52.1	47.9	0.12	0.08 (W)
	(6) Both	43.7	38.3	18.0	—[a]	—[a]	—[a]	0.49 (C)	51.9	48.1	0.08	—
(2) ... to take a vacation this summer	(4) Husband	41.7	38.5	19.9	0.27	—[a]	—[a]	0.29 (H)	52.4	47.4	0.07	0.79 (H)
	(5) Wife	44.4	35.6	19.9	—[a]	—[a]	—[a]	0.18 (W)	52.9	47.1	0.02	0.80 (W)
	(6) Both	43.0	37.1	19.9	—[a]	—[a]	—[a]	0.94 (C)	52.6	47.4	0.01	—
(3) ... concerning exactly when you take this vacation	(4) Husband	59.5	28.4	11.6	—[a]	—[a]	—[a]	0.82 (H)	57.1	43.0	—[a]	0.55 (H)
	(5) Wife	58.8	27.1	14.1	—[a]	—[a]	—[a]	0.19 (W)	61.4	38.6	—[a]	0.38 (W)
	(6) Both	59.2	28.0	12.8	—[a]	—[a]	—[a]	0.36 (C)	60.2	39.8	—[a]	—
(4) ... concerning the length of this vacation	(4) Husband	61.6	30.2	8.1	—[a]	—[a]	—[a]	0.69 (H)	59.1	40.9	—[a]	0.38 (H)
	(5) Wife	63.0	26.4	10.6	—[a]	—[a]	—[a]	0.19 (W)	61.4	38.6	—[a]	0.38 (W)
	(6) Both	62.3	28.3	9.3	—[a]	—[a]	—[a]	0.30 (C)	60.2	39.8	—[a]	—
(5) ... concerning the amount of money to be allocated to your vacation budget	(4) Husband	64.0	33.0	2.2	—[a]	—[a]	—[a]	0.57 (H)	65.1	34.9	—[a]	0.26 (H)
	(5) Wife	65.9	31.8	2.4	—[a]	—[a]	—[a]	0.71 (W)	62.1	38.0	—[a]	0.21 (W)
	(6) Both	64.9	32.4	2.3	—[a]	—[a]	—[a]	0.78 (C)	63.6	36.4	—[a]	—
(16) ... concerning the particular hotel/motel in which you are staying	(4) Husband	49.1	39.9	11.0	—[a]	—[a]	—[a]	0.38 (H)	55.0	45.0	0.01	0.89 (H)
	(5) Wife	46.4	48.8	12.8	0.09	—[a]	—[a]	0.74 (W)	54.8	43.2	0.01	0.89 (W)
	(6) Both	47.8	40.3	11.9	0.01	—[a]	—[a]	0.51 (C)	54.9	45.1	—[a]	—
(17) ... concerning the choice of your particular hotel room	(4) Husband	47.5	41.4	11.4	0.17	—[a]	—[a]	0.65 (H)	53.8	47.4	0.01	0.53 (H)
	(5) Wife	49.0	39.8	11.2	0.01	—[a]	—[a]	0.68 (W)	55.4	41.8	—[a]	0.52 (W)
	(6) Both	48.2	40.5	11.3	0.01	—[a]	—[a]	0.89 (C)	54.6	44.6	—[a]	—

[a] Indicates level of significance less than 0.01.

Source: Pierre Filiatrault and J. R. Brent Ritchie, "Joint Purchasing Decisions: A Comparison of Influence Structure in Family and Couple Decision-Making Units," *Journal of Consumer Research 7* (September 1980), 131–140. Reprinted by permission.

interviewed. Most often, wives are the ones interviewed, but the percentage of couples whose responses agree is often so low as to make interviewing only one member unacceptable.

Granbois and Summers found husbands' responses concerning purchase intentions to be better than those of their wives as predictors of total planned cost and number of items planned from joint responses, although wives predicted better for certain products such as appliances, home furnishings, and entertainment-equipment plans.[52] The researchers concluded that joint responses are more likely to uncover more plans of the family.

An example of a decision-process approach and the consideration of multiple roles in the influence and purchase process is provided by Table 6.6. In this study of vacation decisions by Filiatrault and Ritchie, the influence of the children was measured, as well as that of each parent. The study also included a wide variety of decision-making units, validity checks on the response of an individual by asking for similar information from family members, and the use of a 100-point constant-sum scale that permits more sophisticated analyses than do Likert scales, which are more typically found in family studies.[53] It shows the differences in influence on different stages of decisions about vacations. It also shows differences that exist in perception of influence by husbands and wives.

Although this table includes only a small proportion of the total study, by looking closely at the data you can see the type of research needed to understand the complex roles and relationships in family decisions about consumer behavior.

SUMMARY

The family is of critical importance in the study of consumer behavior for two reasons. First, it is the unit of usage and purchase for many consumer products. Second, the family is a major influence on the attitudes and behavior of individuals.

A family is a group of two or more persons related by blood, marriage, or adoption who reside together. Household differs from family by describing all the persons, both related and unrelated, who occupy a housing unit. There are currently about 87 million households in the United States, 20 million more than families. The decision-making process may be similar in each category, although the category of households includes nontraditional groups that are growing much more rapidly than families.

Family (or household) members occupy various roles, which include gate-

---

[52] Donald H. Granbois and John O. Summers, "Primary and Secondary Validity of Consumer Purchase Probabilities," *Journal of Consumer Research* 1 (March 1975), 31–38.

[53] Pierre Filiatrault and J. R. Brent Ritchie, "Joint Purchasing Decisions: A Comparison of Influence Structure in Family and Couple Decision-Making Units," *Journal of Consumer Research* 6 (September 1980), 131–140.

keeper, influencer, decider, buyer, and user. The influence of spouses, children, or other family members varies depending on the resources of family members, type of product, stage in the life cycle, and stage in the buying decision. These variables are more important in understanding family decisions than traditional roles that have been ascribed to one gender or the other.

The family life cycle (FLC) describes how families change over time. Traditional approaches of analyzing FLC have been updated with a consumer market matrix of lifestages that emphasizes the relative income of a family in each stage. This matrix is built upon six stages: younger singles, younger couples, younger parents, mid-life families, mid-life households, and older households.

Families and households are changing in their structure and composition. Among more important recent changes are increases in the number of single households, smaller average family size, and increases in the number of divorced and remarried households. The increasing number of employed women has resulted in role overload for employed women, who work more hours (combining paid work and family work) each week than their husbands or nonemployed women.

Study of family buying involves marketing research techniques useful in many other studies. Special consideration must be given to the decision-process framework, questioning techniques, role-structure categories and relative influence, interviewer bias, and respondent selection that considers that husbands and wives often differ in their responses to questions about how their families buy consumer goods and services.

REVIEW AND DISCUSSION QUESTIONS

1. What is meant by the term *family*? What is the importance of studying families to the understanding of consumer behavior?

2. Some studies of consumer behavior maintain that the family rather than the individual should be the unit of analysis in consumer behavior. What are the advantages and disadvantages of using the family as the unit of analysis?

3. Do husbands or wives have the most influence on buying decisions? Outline your answer.

4. How might an advertisement be designed that would appeal to the differences in instrumental and expressive roles within families?

5. Will there be more or fewer women employed outside the home in the future? What variables should be considered in answering this question? How does the answer affect demand for consumer products?

6. "Working women buy products and services essentially the same as nonworking women." Analyze this statement.

7. What is meant by the "singles" market? How would a food company appeal to the singles market?

8. Assume that an airline has asked for a research project to understand how families make vacation decisions. You are asked to prepare a research design for the project. What would you suggest?

SITUATIONAL INFLUENCE

SONY: LISTENING TO ITS LISTENERS

here's a Sony for every person's life," is the philosophy that guides product development for Sony Electronics. It all started with the Walkman. By 1987 there were 256 versions of the Walkman — one for every lifestyle imaginable.

One of the most recent models is for swimmers. Totally immersible, the latest "Swimman" allows the swimmer to reduce the boredom of daily laps in the swimming pool by listening to the sounds of a favorite radio station. Other models are marketed especially with joggers in mind, while still others are designed with a more sedentary lifestyle, featuring ultra-high quality stereo for tape and radio.

Listening to the customer is the key at Sony. In addition to conventional marketing research, executives at Sony constantly talk to distributors and retailers. "How are customers using our products? Where do they use the products? What keeps customers from using them more or in other situations?" The answers to these questions lead to constantly changing products that are built for very particular market segments and adapted to the specific needs of their lifestyles and usage situations.

Source: William Trepner, "Sony Adapts to Today's Lifestyles," *Inc* 9 (May 1987), 52–54, and Johny Johanssen and Ikujiro Nonaka, "Market Research the Japanese Way," *Harvard Business Review* 3 (June 1987), 16–22.

Our opening example provides a rather compelling demonstration of how marketers can benefit from understanding the variety of settings in which their product may be used. Sony has been able to develop new sources of demand for the Walkman by modifying their product offering to meet the situational needs of potential users.

This chapter focuses on the role of situational influences as a determinant of consumer behavior and therefore marketing strategy. Indeed, situations exert some of the most pervasive influences in the realm of consumer behavior for one simple reason — behavior always occurs within some situational context. This is not to say that behavior is always shaped by situational influences. Die-hard Budweiser drinkers, for instance, might always buy a Bud regardless of whether they are out partying with friends or sitting alone at home watching TV. In many, if not most cases, however, situational factors will exert important influences.

Before proceeding any further, let us define what we mean by the term *situational influence*. Because consumer situations also involve people and objects (e.g., a product or advertisement), it is necessary to distinguish between influences due to consumers and objects from those that are unique to the situation itself. Accordingly, **situational influence** can be viewed as the influence arising from factors that are particular to a specific time and place which are independent of consumer and object characteristics.[1]

What are these situational factors or characteristics? Belk has suggested that consumer situations may be defined along the lines of five general characteristics, which are summarized in Table 7.1.[2] Although you can probably

---

TABLE 7.1 CHARACTERISTICS OF CONSUMER SITUATIONS

1. *Physical surroundings:* the tangible properties comprising the consumer situation. These features include geographical location, decor, sounds, aromas, lighting, weather, and visible configurations of merchandise or other material surrounding the stimulus object.
2. *Social surroundings:* the presence or absence of other people in the situation.
3. *Time:* the temporal properties of the situation such as the particular moment when behavior occurs (e.g., time of day, weekday, month, season). Time may also be measured relative to some past or future event for the situational participant (e.g., time since last purchase, time until payday).
4. *Task:* the particular goals or objectives consumers have in a situation. For instance, a person shopping for a wedding gift for a friend is in a different situation than when shopping for one's own personal use.
5. *Antecedent states:* the temporary moods (e.g., anxiety, pleasantness, excitement) or conditions (e.g., cash on hand, fatigue) which the consumer *brings* to the situation. Antecedent states are distinguished from those momentary states which occur in response to a situation as well as from more enduring individual traits (e.g., personality).

Source: Russell W. Belk, "Situational Variables and Consumer Behavior," *Journal of Consumer Research* 2 (December 1975), 157–164. Used with permission.

---

[1] Russell W. Belk, "An Exploratory Assessment of Situational Effects in Buyer Behavior," *Journal of Marketing Research* 11 (May 1974), 156–163.
[2] Russell W. Belk, "Situational Variables and Consumer Behavior," *Journal of Consumer Research* 2 (December 1975), 157–164.

remember how each of these factors has, at one time or another, affected your own behavior as a consumer, additional examples of their influence can be found throughout the chapter.

TYPES OF CONSUMER SITUATIONS

The Walkman example described in the chapter opening centered around a very important type of consumer situation — namely, the consumption or usage situation. Consumer situations can in fact be separated into three main types: communication, purchase, and usage situations.[3] Each of these are discussed in the sections following.

THE COMMUNICATION SITUATION

Communication situations can be defined as those settings in which the consumer is exposed to either personal or nonpersonal communications. Personal communications would encompass conversations consumers might have with others, such as salespeople or fellow consumers. Nonpersonal communications would involve a broad spectrum of stimuli, such as advertising and consumer-oriented programs and publications (e.g., *Consumer Reports*).

To illustrate the potential impact of the communication situation, let us consider how it might determine the effectiveness of television advertising. We focus on this particular form of communication for two reasons. First, expenditures on TV advertising often receives a significant share of the promotion budget. Moreover, TV ads have often been employed in empirical investigations of the influences arising from the communication setting.

In the context of television advertising, a number of situational characteristics are likely to surface as potential determinants of an ad's effectiveness. The presence of others during message exposure may easily undermine the likelihood that the ad will receive much, if any, attention. Viewers often use commercial breaks as a time to interact with others in the immediate audience. Similarly, factors such as an ad's position within a commercial "string" (i.e., a series of consecutive ads) or program might also be important. Reductions in audience size have been found to be greater for commercials in the middle of a string versus ads at the beginning or end.[4]

The sheer number of ads that are processed during television viewing

---

[3] Flemming Hansen, *Consumer Choice Behavior: A Cognitive Theory* (New York: Free Press, 1972), p. 53.
[4] Burke Marketing Research Inc., "Viewer Attitudes Toward Commercial Clutter on Television and Media Buying Implications" (paper presented at the 18th Advertising Research Foundation Conference, New York, 1972).

can have an adverse impact on a given ad's effectiveness.[5] Given the recent trend toward shorter commercials (the industry standard has been shifting from 30 seconds to 15 seconds), which permits broadcasting more messages in a given time period, marketers have become increasingly concerned about the potential effects of advertising clutter.[6] *Clutter* refers to the problem of simply too many ads in the viewing environment. This increase in the number of ads can interfere with the consumer's ability to process an ad's selling points.

Situational influences may also arise from the particular program in which an ad appears. Indeed, several studies have reported such effects. In one investigation, viewers' mood states while watching commercials were affected by the surrounding program. Happy programs induced happier moods during commercial exposure compared to sad programs. This more favorable mood state led subjects to have more positive thoughts while processing the ads, as well as better recall of the commercial information.[7] The impact of the TV program, however, may depend on the type of commercial. A recent study reports that a happy program produced greater recall than a sad one for a happy ad, whereas the program had no significant effect on recall for a sad ad.[8]

Similarly, consumers' interest or involvement with a program may partly determine an ad's effectiveness. Recall of the advertised brand and ad copy was lower for ads shown during a more involving program compared to a less involving program. Moreover, attitudes toward the ads were often more favorable when ad exposure occurred during the less involving program.[9]

Practitioners are very aware of the potential influences that a program may exert on the effectiveness of their advertising. Coca-Cola, for instance, avoids advertising during TV news programs because "there's going to be

---

[5] Peter H. Webb, "Consumer Initial Processing in a Difficult Media Environment," *Journal of Consumer Research* 6 (December 1979), 225–236.

[6] See, for example, "Emotional Impact Can Cut Clutter of 15-second Spots," *Marketing News* 20 (December 5, 1986), 13; Michael L. Ray and Peter H. Webb, "Three Prescriptions for Clutter," *Journal of Advertising Research* 26 (February/March 1986), 69–77.

[7] Marvin E. Goldberg and Gerald J. Gorn, "Happy and Sad TV Programs: How They Affect Reactions to Commercials," *Journal of Consumer Research* 14 (December 1987), 387–403. For an arousal explanation of programming effects, see Surendra N. Singh and Gilbert A. Churchill, Jr., "Arousal and Advertising Effectiveness," *Journal of Advertising* 16 (1987), 4–10.

[8] Robert E. Burnkrant, H. Rao Unnava, and Kenneth R. Lord, "The Effects of Programming Induced Mood States on Memory for Commercial Information," (Working Paper Series, The Ohio State University, October 1987).

[9] Gary F. Soldow and Victor Principe, "Response to Commercials as a Function of Program Context," *Journal of Advertising Research* 21 (April 1981), 59–65. Also see Kenneth R. Lord and Robert E. Burnkrant, "Television Program Elaboration Effects on Commercial Processing," in Michael J. Houston, ed., *Advances in Consumer Research*, 15 (Provo, Utah: Association for Consumer Research, 1988), 213–218; C. Whan Park and Gordon W. McClung, "The Effect of TV Program Involvement on Involvement with Commercials," in Richard J. Lutz, ed., *Advances in Consumer Research*, vol. 13 (Provo, Utah: Association for Consumer Research, 1986), 544–548.

7.1 PROGRAMMING INFLUENCES ON ADVERTISING EFFECTIVENESS: THE INFLUENCE OF THE COMMUNICATION SITUATION

One of the most popular, yet controversial mini-series to hit the airwaves during 1987 was ABC's "Amerika." This 14½ hour film, three years in the making at a cost of nearly $40 million, centers around the life of an American family living in a United States that has been peacefully taken over by the Soviet Union. The Chrysler Corporation had initially purchased roughly $7 million of air time for its commercials that pronounced "The Pride is Back — Born in America." However, shortly before the program aired, Chrysler withdrew its ads, a decision supported by Lee A. Iacocca, the chairman of Chrysler, after viewing six hours of the film. The reason? According to a Chrysler spokesperson:

> We have concluded that the subject matter and its portrayal are so intense and emotional that our upbeat product commercials would be both inappropriate and of diminished effectiveness in that environment.

Source: Peter J. Boyer, "Chrysler Pulls Ads From 'Amerika,'" *The New York Times* (January 28, 1987), C26.

some bad news in there and Coke is an upbeat, fun product."[10] Similar concerns led to Chrysler's withdrawal of its advertising from ABC's miniseries "Amerika," the topic of *Consumer in Focus 7.1.*

While the prior discussion has focused on television advertising, recognize that the communication situation is also an important consideration for other forms of advertising. Outdoor billboards, for instance, must be designed to accommodate the fact that exposure will be quite brief in most instances. This communication situation is quite different from, say, being exposed to ads while seated in a theater. In the latter setting, consumers have far less stimuli competing for their attention, thereby diminishing the need for including attention-getting properties within the advertisement. The importance of gaining attention is considered further in Chapter 8.

THE PURCHASE SITUATION

Purchase situations refer to those settings where consumers acquire products and services. Situational influences are very prevalent during purchasing. As a simple example, consider the tremendous change in consumers' price sensitivity across purchase situations. A grocer would find it extremely difficult to charge the prices that consumers pay for soda and snacks at a movie theater or ballpark.

---

[10] "GF, Coke Tell Why They Shun TV News," *Advertising Age* (January 28, 1980), 39.

Situational influences can manifest themselves in a variety of ways during purchasing. Several major forms are described subsequently.

THE INFORMATION ENVIRONMENT   **Information environment** refers to the entire array of product-related data available to the consumer.[11] The nature of the information environment will be an important determinant of marketplace behavior when consumers engage in some form of nonhabitual decision making. Some of the major environmental characteristics include the availability of information, the amount of information load, and the modes in which information is presented and organized.

Information Availability.   The availability of information is extremely important. The absence of information about the performance of competing brands on some attribute will preclude its use during decision making. Sometimes the availability of information will depend on the consumer's ability to retrieve the information from memory (the topic of memory and retrieval is considered more fully in the Chapter 14 discussion of cognitive learning). Research suggests that choice may depend on the extent to which product information is externally present during decision making versus being available only in memory (e.g., a consumer at Sears trying to decide whether to buy the microwave in front of him or the one he examined yesterday at a competitive store). In one study, subjects were more likely to select the "best" brand when information about the brand was externally available than when they had to rely on their ability to recall this information, which had been presented previously but removed at the time of choice.[12]

Note that the issue of information availability is particularly relevant to those concerned with providing an information environment that allows consumers the opportunity to make well-reasoned and informed choices. In this regard, researchers have considered the potential value of providing consumers with information such as the energy consumption costs of appliances,[13] a product's life cycle cost (i.e., purchase price plus operating costs),[14] unit price information,[15] and nutritional information.[16]

[11] James R. Bettman, "Issues in Designing Consumer Information Environments," *Journal of Consumer Research* 2 (December 1975), 169–177.

[12] Gabriel Biehal and Dipankar Chakravarti, "Information Accessibility as a Moderator of Consumer Choice," *Journal of Consumer Research* 10 (June 1983), 1–14.

[13] Dennis L. McNeill and William L. Wilkie, "Public Policy and Consumer Information: Impact of the New Energy Labels," *Journal of Consumer Research* 6 (June 1979), 1–11.

[14] R. Bruce Hutton and William L. Wilkie, "Life Cycle Cost: A New Form of Consumer Information," *Journal of Consumer Research* 6 (March 1980), 349–360.

[15] J. Edward Russo, "The Value of Unit Price Information," *Journal of Marketing Research* 14 (May 1977), 193–201; J. Edward Russo, Gene Krieser, and Sally Miyashita, "An Effective Display of Unit Price Information," *Journal of Marketing* 39 (April 1975), 11–19.

[16] Bettman, "Issues in Designing Consumer Information Environments"; J. Edward Russo, Richard Staelin, Catherine A. Nolan, Gary J. Russell, and Barbara L. Metcalf, "Nutrition Information in the Supermarket," *Journal of Consumer Research* 13 (June 1986), 48–70.

Information Load.   The information load of a choice environment is determined by the number of choice alternatives and the number of attributes per alternative. Increases in the number of choice alternatives can alter the type of decision rule consumers employ during decision making,[17] a topic further explored in Chapter 18. Some have also argued that, beyond a certain level, information load may exceed consumers' ability to accurately process the information (i.e., they become "overloaded") and, consequently, reduce their accuracy during decision making.[18] We return to this issue of information overload in Chapter 8.

Information Format.   The format of information (i.e., the manner in which it is organized) can also influence the behavior of consumers. As described in *Consumer in Focus 7.2*, consumers' use of unit price information may depend on how it is organized.[19] Research also indicates that format can influence the order in which information is acquired or processed, and the amount of time taken to reach a decision.[20]

Information Form.   Even the form of the information can play an important role. For some attributes (e.g., gas mileage, nutritional properties), product information can be presented either numerically or semantically (e.g., excellent, good, average, etc.). Numerical product ratings enable consumers to more easily estimate differences among products. Consequently, consumers are more inclined to compare brands on an attribute-by-attribute basis when brand information is presented in numerical rather than semantic form.[21]

THE RETAIL ENVIRONMENT   The physical properties of the retail environment, often referred to as **store atmospherics,** are of particular interest to marketers for two fundamental reasons. First, unlike many situational influences that are beyond the marketer's control, marketers have the ability to create the retail environment. Secondly, this influence is brought to bear on consumers at just the right place—inside the store.

---

[17] Denis A. Lussier and Richard W. Olshavsky, "Task Complexity and Contingent Processing in Brand Choice," *Journal of Consumer Research* 6 (September 1979), 154–165.

[18] Jacob Jacoby, Donald Speller, and Carol Kohn, "Brand Choice as a Function of Information Load," *Journal of Marketing Research* 11 (February 1974), 63–69.

[19] Also see Valarie A. Zeithaml, "Consumer Response to In-Store Price Information Environments," *Journal of Consumer Research* 8 (March 1982), 357–369.

[20] James R. Bettman and Pradeep Kakkar, "Effects of Information Presentation Format on Consumer Information Acquisition Strategies," *Journal of Consumer Research* 3 (March 1977), 233–240; James R. Bettman and Michel A. Zins, "Information Format and Choice Task Effects in Decision Making," *Journal of Consumer Research* 6 (September 1979), 141–153. Also see Scott Painton and James W. Gentry, "Another Look at the Impact of Information Presentation Format," *Journal of Consumer Research* 12 (September 1985), 240–244.

[21] J. Edward Russo and Barbara Dosher, "Strategies for Multiattribute Binary Choice," *Journal of Experimental Psychology: Learning, Memory, and Cognition* 9 (1983), 676–696.

7.2 ENHANCING CONSUMERS' USE OF UNIT PRICE INFORMATION

During the 1970s there was considerable debate over the value of unit price information. Although consumer activists were calling for the posting of unit price information in the retail environment, there was considerable uncertainty as to whether the costs incurred by posting this information were worthwhile, particularly since many consumers did not appear to use it during shopping.

Russo and his colleagues argued that consumers' use of unit price information depends not only on its availability, but on its "processability" as well. They reasoned that consumers would find it easier to use unit price lists, which rank-ordered the relative cost of competing brands on a single piece of paper, than the standard practice of posting unit price tags on the shelves. A field study was, therefore, undertaken in which both the presence and format of unit price information was varied for a set of grocery items.

The results indicated that unit price tags produced an average savings in consumer expenditures of 1%. However, unit price lists led to an additional 2% savings beyond that incurred by the tags. Thus, presenting the information in a form more easily processed resulted in greater use of the information. An examination of the particular brands and sizes purchased by consumers was also quite informative. When tags were present, consumers continued to buy the same brands but switched to the larger, more economical sizes. In contrast, the lists led consumers to switch from their previous brand to the cheaper house brands (i.e., brands marketed by the grocer). This latter finding carries obvious implications for retailers wishing to enhance the sales of their less expensive offerings.

Source: J. Edward Russo, "The Value of Unit Price Information," *Journal of Marketing Research* 14 (May 1977), 193–201; J. Edward Russo, Gene Krieser, and Sally Miyashita, "An Effective Display of Unit Price Information," *Journal of Marketing* 39 (April 1975), 11–19.

From the marketer's perspective, a store's atmospherics can have a number of desirable effects on consumers.[22] First, it can help shape both the direction and duration of consumers' attention, thereby enhancing the odds of purchase for products that otherwise might go unnoticed. Second, the retail environment can express various aspects about the store to consumers, such as its intended audience and positioning (e.g., the clothing store wishing to attract upscale customers with a fashion image). Finally, the store setting can also elicit particular emotional reactions from consumers (e.g., pleasure and arousal). Research

---

[22] Philip Kotler, "Atmospherics as a Marketing Tool," *Journal of Retailing* 49 (Winter 1973–1974), 48–65.

suggests that these feelings can influence the amount of time and money consumers spend while shopping.[23]

The retail environment is comprised of a variety of elements, including store layout, aisle space, placement and form of displays, colors, lighting, presence and volume of in-store music, smells, and temperature. Although much of the research documenting the influence of these factors is of a proprietary nature, published studies have gradually accumulated in this area.

Music.   Some of the more interesting findings have involved the influence of music. In an early study, the *volume* of music played by supermarkets was varied from loud to soft. Consumers exposed to the loud music took less time shopping but spent the same amount of money relative to those exposed to the soft music.[24] More recently, the effect of music *tempo* (slow versus fast) has been examined in a supermarket setting. Slow-tempo music increased both shopping time and expenditures compared to fast-tempo music.[25] Similar effects due to tempo have also been observed in a restaurant setting. Patrons spent nearly 25 percent more time and nearly 50 percent more on bar purchases when the tempo was slow rather than fast.[26]

Layout and In-Store Location.   Store layout and product location can be used to enhance the likelihood of consumers coming into contact with products. A supermarket, for instance, might design a layout that encourages a traffic flow that guides shoppers into particular areas. Similarly, the bakery department might be located close to the entrance and/or checkout lines in the hope that the aromas of fresh-baked items will entice shoppers. Department stores will place product displays in high-traffic areas, such as at the end of an escalator. Vendors are extremely sensitive to a product's location because they recognize the incremental sales that can result from shelf position. And convenience stores strategically place impulse items near the checkout in the hope that consumers will succumb to the buying urge.

Colors.   The colors within the store are sources of potential influence on both consumers' perceptions and behavior. Warm colors, such as red and yellow, appear more effective in physically attracting people, relative to the

---

[23] Robert J. Donovan and John R. Rossiter, "Store Atmosphere: An Environmental Psychology Approach," *Journal of Retailing* 58 (Spring 1982), 34–57; Elaine Sherman and Ruth Belk Smith, "Mood States of Shoppers and Store Image: Promising Interactions and Possible Behavioral Effects," in Melanie Wallendorf and Paul Anderson, eds., *Advances in Consumer Research*, vol. 14 (Provo, Utah: Association for Consumer Research, 1987), 251–254.

[24] Patricia Cane Smith and Ross Curnow, "Arousal Hypotheses and the Effects of Music on Purchasing Behavior," *Journal of Applied Psychology* 50 (June 1966), 255–256.

[25] Ronald E. Milliman, "Using Background Music to Affect the Behavior of Supermarket Shoppers," *Journal of Marketing* 46 (Summer 1982), 86–91.

[26] Ronald E. Milliman, "The Influence of Background Music on the Behavior of Restaurant Patrons," *Journal of Consumer Research* 13 (September 1986), 286–289.

cooler colors of green and blue. In one study where subjects were allowed to determine how close they sat to a colored wall, the distance was much shorter for warm than cool colors. Nonetheless, subjects rated retail interiors using cool colors as more positive, attractive, and relaxing than those employing warmer colors. The researchers concluded that warm colors were most suitable for a store's exterior color or display windows as a means of drawing customers into the store.[27] Additional support of color's behavioral impact comes from the finding that the shade of brown used in coloring walls altered the speed at which people moved through a museum.[28]

POP Materials.   Point-of-purchase (POP) materials can serve as very powerful stimuli. Displays and signs can enhance the odds of capturing the consumer's attention, and thereby stimulate purchasing. Consistent with this, POP materials have been shown to increase sales.[29] It is likely that marketers will place greater emphasis on POP materials given that they are relatively inexpensive compared to other forms of promotion. In addition, informative and easy-to-use POP materials can partly help offset the recent declines in the quantity and quality of retail salespeople.[30]

Salespeople.   Although our discussion of the retail environment thus far has focused on nonpersonal stimuli, it is important to recognize the role of salespeople. The potential to influence consumers during shopping can be strongly affected by the retailer's frontline staff. Indeed, a store's image and ability to build loyalty can heavily depend on the availability and characteristics (e.g., attentiveness, expertise, friendliness, how they dress) of salespeople.

Crowding.   Another aspect of the retail setting that may affect shopping behavior is the perceived level of crowding due to the density of shoppers within the store. High levels of crowding can lead to reductions in shopping time, postponement of unnecessary purchases, and less interaction with sales personnel.[31]

---

[27] Joseph A. Bellizzi, Ayn E. Crowley, and Rondla W. Hasty, "The Effects of Color in Store Design," *Journal of Retailing* 59 (Spring 1983), 21–45.

[28] Rajendra K. Scrivastava and Thomas S. Peel, *Human Movement as a Function of Color Stimulation* (Topeka: Environmental Research Foundation, 1968).

[29] V. Kumar and Robert P. Leone, "Measuring the Effect of Retail Store Promotions on Brand and Store Substitution," *Journal of Marketing Research* 25 (May 1988), 178–185; Gary F. McKinnon, J. Patrick Kelly, and E. Doyle Robison, "Sales Effects of Point-of-Purchase In-Store Signing," *Journal of Retailing* 57 (Summer 1981), 49–63; Arch G. Woodside and Gerald L. Waddle, "Sales Effects of In-Store Advertising," *Journal of Advertising Research* 15 (June 1975), 29–33.

[30] John A. Quelch and Kristina Cannon-Bonventre, "Better Marketing at the Point of Purchase," *Harvard Business Review* 61 (November–December 1983), 162–169.

[31] Gilbert D. Harrell, Michael D. Hutt, and James C. Anderson, "Path Analysis of Buyer Behavior Under Conditions of Crowding," *Journal of Marketing Research* 17 (February 1980), 45–51.

The Influence of Time. As noted in Table 7.1, time represents an important aspect of situational influence. This is particularly true for purchase situations. The demand for many products is highly time-sensitive. The Christmas season is vitally important for many products, especially toys. Consumers' purchases of soft drinks, which peak during the summer, slow down considerably during the winter months (with the exception of the temporary spurts brought on by holidays such as Christmas and New Year). Moreover, products may be positioned differently depending on the time of year. As reflected by the promotional piece appearing in Figure 7.1, Sanka attempted to overcome the sales lag typically experienced during warmer months by promoting a different way of consuming coffee.

The amount of time available for decision making can also be an important situational influence. A consumer whose refrigerator has broken down beyond repair will typically experience greater pressure to make a speedy decision than consumers shopping to replace an old but still working refrigerator.

Time pressure can affect consumer decision making in a couple of ways. First, it may "force" consumers to rely on existing knowledge and experience in making their decisions, rather than collecting additional information. Even if time pressures are not so great as to preclude some use of external information during decision making, they can still lead consumers to adopt simpler product-evaluation strategies, such as relying on fewer attributes in comparing alternatives.[32] Time pressure has been found to reduce both the purchasing of products that consumers had initially planned to buy (i.e., before time pressure manifested itself) and the frequency of unplanned purchases (i.e., products that are acquired even though they were not on the shopping list).[33]

Time relative to prior events can also affect purchase behavior. A classic example is the effect of food deprivation (i.e., time since last meal) on grocery shopping. The food expenditures of many consumers grow larger as the time since their last meal increases.[34] For this reason, home economists often recommend food shopping on a full stomach, so as to decrease the impulse buying hunger often motivates.

Finally, recent evidence suggests that advertising effectiveness can be affected by the particular time of day when consumers encounter an advertisement.[35] Shoppers at a suburban mall were shown a segment of a television news program containing six new 30-second TV commercials. Sessions were conducted in either the morning, afternoon, or early evening. When ad retention was measured immediately after the program, learning

---

[32] Peter L. Wright and Barton Weitz, "Time Horizon Effects on Product Evaluation Strategies," *Journal of Marketing Research* 14 (November 1977), 429–443.

[33] Easwar S. Iyer, "The Effects of Situational Factors on In-Store Grocery Shopping Behavior: The Role of Time Pressure and Knowledge of Store Layout," working paper (1988).

[34] R. E. Nisbett and D. E. Kanouse, "Obesity, Food Deprivation, and Supermarket Shopping Behavior," *Journal of Personality and Social Psychology* 12 (August 1969), 289–294.

[35] Jacob Hornik, "Diurnal Variation in Consumer Response," *Journal of Consumer Research* 14 (March 1988), 588–591.

FIGURE 7.1
TIME-DEPENDENT
PRODUCT
POSITIONING: AN
EXAMPLE OF OFF
SEASON SELLING

Source: SANKA is a registered trademark of General Foods Corporation and is used with permission, © 1985, General Foods Corporation.

was best for the morning sessions and worst in the evening sessions. However, just the opposite pattern was observed when learning was not tested until nearly 2 hours had elapsed since viewing the commercials.

THE USAGE SITUATION

The remaining type of consumer situations considered here are **usage situations,** which refer to those settings where consumption occurs. In many instances, purchase and usage situations are virtually the same (e.g., consumers who eat their meals at a fast-food restaurant). But product consumption often occurs in settings that are quite removed, both physically and temporally, from the setting in which the product is acquired.

Even when purchase and usage situations are distinct, the latter can still have a powerful influence as consumers take into account the *intended* usage situation during decision making.[36] Consider consumers purchasing rice, who might choose a brand based on whether they were planning to serve the rice as a stand-alone side dish, as an ingredient in recipes, or both.

The *social surroundings* that characterize a usage situation can have an important influence on consumer behavior. In today's increasingly anti-smoking environment, the presence of nonsmokers will often serve as an impediment to smokers' "lighting up." Beer sales are particularly sensitive to whether consumption occurs in public versus private settings. Between 80 and 90 percent of import beer sales is "on premise" (e.g., in bars and restaurants) where others can see the type of beer one consumes. In contrast, 70 percent of domestic brands' sales are generated by in-home consumption.[37]

The *time* at which usage occurs may also affect consumer behavior. For example, food consumption depends very heavily on the time of day. We rarely eat spaghetti for breakfast or cereal for dinner. Figure 7.2 shows how college students' preferences for various fruits depended on the time of day and context in which consumption occurred. Peaches were the most preferred fruit for breakfast or a daytime snack but were replaced by strawberries for a supper dessert.

In order to understand *why* behavior is affected by usage situations, it is useful to examine how the importance consumers attach to product attributes and their beliefs about a product's performance may change across various settings. Consider, for example, Miller and Ginter's findings that patronage of a particular fast-food restaurant often depended on the usage situation.[38] While McDonald's had a market share of nearly 40 percent for leisurely evening meals with the family, its share of weekday lunches was less than 30 percent. This fluctuation in share was driven by two factors. First, consumers gave McDonald's its lowest convenience ratings when it was to be used for a weekday lunch. Second, convenience was viewed as more important in this situation.

USAGE SITUATIONS AND MARKETING STRATEGY   Marketing strategy and tactics are affected by usage situations in several ways. First, it may often be vital that market segmentation schemes reflect the variety of usage situations. The apparel market, for instance, can be segmented in terms of the situation in which clothing is to be worn (e.g., formal dinners, work, sports, casual). Targeting each of these segments will obviously necessitate changes in the

[36] John L. Stanton and P. Greg Bonner, "An Investigation of the Differential Impact of Purchase Situation on Levels of Consumer Choice Behavior," in Jerry C. Olson, ed., *Advances in Consumer Research*, vol. 7 (Ann Arbor: Association for Consumer Research, 1980), 639–643.

[37] Kevin T. Higgins, "Beer Importers Upbeat about Future, Despite Warning Signs," *Marketing News* (October 25, 1985), 1 ff.

[38] Kenneth E. Miller and James L. Ginter, "An Investigation of Situational Variation in Brand Choice Behavior and Attitude," *Journal of Marketing Research* 16 (February 1979), 111–123.

FIGURE 7.2
STUDENTS' FRUIT PREFERENCES BY EATING OCCASION ILLUSTRATES THE IMPORTANCE OF TIME IN CONSUMPTION DECISIONS

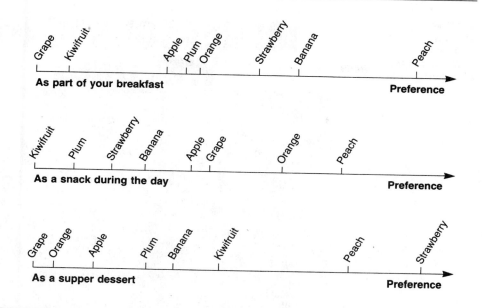

Source: Peter R. Dickson, "Person-Situation: Segmentation's Missing Link," *Journal of Marketing* 6 (Fall 1982), 56–64.

product offering. Another, more detailed, example of segmentation based on the usage situation involving suntan lotion is presented in the next section of the chapter.

The usage situation may often assume an important part in the positioning of a product. The advertising campaign that promotes the theme "The night belongs to Michelob" represents an attempt to position this beer as the one to use in nighttime social settings. Similarly, Wet Ones, a premoistened towelette, introduced itself to the marketplace with a series of ads similar to the ad appearing in Figure 7.3, which depicted the variety of situations in which the product would come in handy.

The discovery or development of new usage settings can be a vital source of new sales, and often represents an important strategic option for revitalizing mature products.[39] Arm and Hammer baking soda is one product that has successfully broadened its appeal by promoting a variety of uses, ranging from dental care to a deodorizer for carpets and refrigerators. Orange juice producers attempted to enhance the product consumption through an advertising campaign that claimed "It's not just for breakfast anymore." Even the

---

[39] Jagdish Sheth and Glenn Morrison, "Winning Again in the Marketplace: Nine Strategies for Revitalizing Mature Products," *Journal of Consumer Marketing* 1 (1984), 17–28.

FIGURE 7.3
WET ONES
PROMOTES ITS
PRODUCT BY
SHOWING A USAGE
SITUATION

Source: Courtesy of Lehn & Fink Products Group. Agency: Jordan McGrath Case Taylor.

refrigerator has benefited from an expansion of potential usage situations by the development of very small models that easily fit into the office.

PERSON–SITUATION INTERACTIONS

Thus far our discussion has implicitly assumed that all consumers respond in the same manner to a particular situation. Yet this need not be so. While some consumers may be highly influenced by situational variations, others may often prove to be rather insensitive.

FIGURE 7.4 PERSON–SITUATION SEGMENTATION MATRIX FOR SUNTAN LOTION

Persons: Situations	Young Children		Teenagers		Adult Women		Adult Men		Situation Benefits/Features
	Fair Skin	Dark Skin	Fair Skin	Dark Skin	Fair Skin	Dark Skin	Fair Skin	Dark Skin	
Beach/boat sunbathing	Combined insect repellent				Summer perfume				a. Windburn protection b. Formula and container can stand heat c. Container floats and is distinctive (not easily lost)
Home-poolside sunbathing					Combined moisturizer				a. Large pump dispenser b. Won't stain wood, concrete, or furnishings
Sunlamp bathing					Combined moisturizer and massage oil				a. Designed specifically for type of lamp b. Artificial tanning ingredient
Snow skiing					Winter perfume				a. Special protection from special light rays and weather b. Antifreeze formula
Person "Benefits"/ Features	Special protection a. Protection critical b. Nonpoisonous		Special protection a. Fit in jean pocket b. Used by opinion leaders		Special protection Female perfume		Special protection Male perfume		

Source: Peter R. Dickson, "Person–Situation: Segmentation's Missing Link," *Journal of Marketing* 6 (Fall 1982), 56–64. Used with permission.

As an illustration of person–situation interactions, let us return to the previously discussed finding that consumers' grocery purchases escalated as the time since their last meal increased.[40] Whereas this effect was observed for average-weight consumers, it did not occur for overweight consumers.

---

[40] Nisbett and Kanouse, "Obesity, Food Deprivation, and Supermarket Shopping Behavior."

Thus, the situational influence of time since their last meal depended on the type of consumer.[41]

The notion that consumers are not homogeneous in their response to situational factors has important implications for market segmentation. Because different consumers may seek different product benefits, which can change across different usage situations, Dickson has argued that marketers may often need to employ **person–situation segmentation.**[42] An example of this form of segmentation in the context of suntan lotions appears in Figure 7.4. The columns represent different types of people who are consumers of suntan lotion. The rows identify various settings in which the product may be used. The benefits desired by a particular group or sought within a given usage situation are listed at the bottom of the column and at the end of the row. These are the benefits that the product should deliver in courting a specific person–situation segment. In addition, some person–situation segments seek unique benefits (e.g., a scented winter lotion for female skiers), which are listed within that cell of the matrix. A suntan manufacturer interested in targeting dark-skinned adult women who use the product while snow skiing, for instance, should include ingredients that will provide special protection from the light rays and weather, an antifreeze formula, and a winter perfume scent that appeals to women.

UNEXPECTED SITUATIONAL INFLUENCES

Marketers sometimes ask target consumers their purchase intentions in order to forecast future demand for products. Although purchase intentions can, under the right conditions (see Chapter 11), be predictive of future behavior, one major threat to their predictive power is the disruption caused by unexpected situational influences.[43] For example, a consumer may fully anticipate buying a particular brand of potato chips during the next visit to the grocer. Yet this purchase intention may not be fulfilled if the product is out of stock or if another brand of similar quality is on sale. Conversely, a consumer may lack any interest in buying a product when surveyed at a particular point in time. Subsequently, however, purchase may occur because of some

---

[41] The manner in which situational influences vary across consumers and products has been examined in several studies. A review of this literature can be found in Belk, "Situational Variables and Consumer Behavior." Also see Girish N. Punj and David W. Stewart, "An Interaction Framework of Consumer Decision Making," *Journal of Consumer Research* 10 (September 1983), 181–196.

[42] Peter R. Dickson, "Person–Situation: Segmentation's Missing Link," *Journal of Marketing* 6 (Fall 1982), 56–64.

[43] For an empirical demonstration of how unexpected situations affect the intention-behavior relationship, see Joseph A. Cote, James McCullough, and Michael Reilly, "Effects of Unexpected Situations on Behavior-Intention Differences: A Garbology Analysis," *Journal of Consumer Research* 12 (September 1985), 188–194.

unanticipated event (e.g., a noncoffee drinker who buys coffee for her visiting, coffee-drinking parents).

From a marketing perspective, the important point here is simply that one must recognize the potential for unexpected situational influences to undermine the accuracy of forecasts based on purchase intentions. While it is often hoped that such effects will tend to be counterbalancing (i.e., the number of customers lost because of unexpected situational influences will be offset by the number gained for the same reasons), this may not be the case.

Summary

This chapter has focused on the influences that may arise from situational properties. The physical and social surroundings, time, task, and antecedent states are the major characteristics that comprise a given consumer situation.

In consumer behavior, it is useful to consider the potential impact of environmental factors in three main areas: communication, purchase, and usage situations. The effectiveness of marketing messages may often depend on the communication setting. The impact of a TV ad, for example, may in part be determined by the program in which it appears.

The purchase situation can have a strong influence on consumer behavior. Properties of the information environment, such as the availability, amount, format, and form of information, can affect decision making. Similarly, features of the retail environment, including music, layout, colors, POP materials, and crowding, will influence shopping and purchase behaviors.

The situation in which product consumption occurs can exert a major influence on consumer behavior. Consumers may often alter their purchasing patterns depending upon the usage situation. What is an acceptable brand of beer in one setting may be unacceptable in another. An understanding of the usage situation can be invaluable for segmenting markets and developing appropriate product positionings.

REVIEW AND DISCUSSION QUESTIONS

1. What are the five basic characteristics of a consumer situation?

2. What are the three main types of consumer situations?

3. A recent test of advertising effectiveness has revealed that your television advertising was more effective when shown during program A than program B. How could you explain this finding?

4. A grocery chain has recently developed a set of private-label brands. These brands are comparable in product quality to their competition but offer the consumer a substantial price savings. How might this grocer structure the information environment so as to best convey this price differential to consumers?

5. What is meant by *store atmospherics,* and why is it important to marketers?

6. Many consumers will switch from one brand of rice to another depending on the usage situation. What explanations can you offer as to *why* this switching may occur?

7. Describe how the concept of the usage situation could be useful to a snack-food manufacturer.

8. Returning to Figure 7.4, suppose a suntan lotion manufacturer was interested in targeting fair-skinned teenagers who use the product while sunlamp bathing. What benefits and features should the product deliver in courting this segment?

ENVIRONMENTAL INFLUENCES

INDIVIDUAL DIFFERENCES
Consumer Resources
Motivation & Involvement
Knowledge
Attitudes
Personality, Lifestyle,
Demographics

DECISION PROCESS

PSYCHOLOGICAL PROCESSES

MARKETING STRATEGY

INDIVIDUAL DIFFERENCES

No two people are created the same. If you do not believe this statement, examine their fingerprints. In the study of consumer behavior, however, there are far more important differences than fingerprints.

Measured by effects on consumer behavior, possibly the most important differences among individuals is the differences in resources. A consumer with an income of $25,000 will have substantially different buying behavior than a consumer with $50,000. In addition to economic resources, consumers vary in other resources as well. The effects of such differences are examined in Chapter 8 of this part of the book.

Individuals differ in other fundamental ways that affect consumer behavior. Chapter 9 examines the topics of involvement and motivation. Chapter 10 examines the topic of knowledge, and Chapter 11 examines the basic concept of attitudes and their relationship to consumer behavior.

The final section in Part III, Chapter 12, deals with a summary concept — lifestyle. Lifestyles are the patterns of living that result from many other influences. Personality, a concept that describes the characteristic ways an individual responds to the environment, is also described in Chapter 12.

CONSUMER RESOURCES

WHO BENEFITS FROM BAD ECONOMIC NEWS?

On October 19, 1987, the Dow Jones Index plunged over 500 points, the largest decline ever recorded in the stock market. What is the effect of such news on consumer behavior? Do the marketers of some companies benefit from bad economic news?

In a nationwide study of 500 adults, 32 percent said they are staying home more since the decline. Carol Hess, research consultant at Decision Research Corporation which conducted the study, commented, "Many people are focusing on their own household and their personal finances but also the level of concern about the overall economy has not dropped off." On a scale of 1 to 10, 10 indicating most concern, an average of 6.38 was registered in April 1988 when asked about the state of the national economy, compared to 6.28 in the fall of 1987.

Parents under 40 years old earning less than $40,000 annually were most likely to stay at home. Only 7 percent of older respondents with yearly incomes higher than $40,000 indicated they are staying home more. Nine percent of respondents before the stock market crash said they had changed plans regarding major expenditures such as homes and vacations because of economic worries, but that figure increased to 17 percent six months after the crash.

Two-thirds of consumers in the poll reported that their spending habits changed since the crash. Items being purchased more include gourmet food (perhaps because people are eating at home more) and home improvement gadgets.

Source: Associated Press, excerpted from the *Columbus Dispatch* (April 16, 1988), 7D. Reprinted with permission.

CONSUMERS AND THE EXCHANGE PROCESS

You may have seen varied definitions of the word *marketing*. Such definitions differ in format and comprehensiveness, but the one element usually present in all is the word *exchange*. Marketing involves the exchange of something of value given by the customer for something of value received from the seller. In traditional marketing situations, consumers may exchange money (or plastic substitutes) for products. In political marketing, consumers exchange their votes for the election of a candidate. In other organizations, consumers may exchange their time as a volunteer or money donations for the accomplishments of the Heart Association, a religious group, or a student government. But in all of these transactions, consumer behavior is determined, indeed constrained, by the resources available to exchange for the goods and services that an organization intends to sell.

In this chapter, three consumer resources are examined: economic, temporal, and cognitive. Practically speaking, this means that marketers are competing for consumers' money, time, and attention. Other resources, such as energy, may be needed for shopping and consuming, but money, time, and attention are primary. It is not only the amount of time and economic resources that determines consumer behavior. A consumer's *perception of available resources*, or what will be available in the future, is also important in spending decisions, as the opening vignette of this chapter indicates about the effects of a stock market decline. In spite of the widespread effects on perception, in the 1987 stock market crash only 3 percent of households suffered a loss greater than 5 percent of their net worth.[1]

ECONOMIC RESOURCES

Consumer decisions concerning products and brands are heavily influenced by the amounts of economic resources which they have or may have in the future. It takes money to be a consumer. Credit cards also suffice. In an

---

[1] "Stock Answers," *American Demographics* 11 (February 1989), 11.

FIGURE 8.1
FAMILY
EXPENDITURES AS
PERCENT OF
AVERAGE INCOME,
1917–1919 AND
1985: THE LARGER
THE "OTHER"
CATEGORY, THE
MORE DYNAMIC
MARKETING
BECOMES

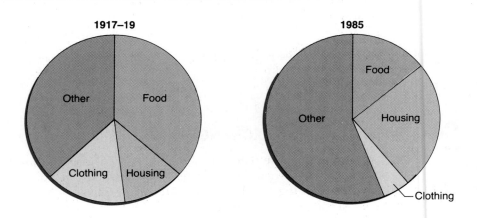

Note: Expenditure composition is not exactly comparable for the different time periods, but the data reflect differences in expenditures of the two time periods.
Sources: Bureau of Labor Statistics and Bureau of the Census.

earlier era, barter—the trading of goods for goods—was common. Barter is still important in less developed societies and to a degree in the underground economies of advanced societies. We concentrate our analysis in this chapter on money. There exists, however, a substantial "informal economy" in which people barter or purchase goods and services in ways that often escape record keeping and perhaps taxation. The "heavy users" of the informal economy are affluent, well educated, and comparatively young.[2]

Economic resources—such as income or wealth—were the first variables to be analyzed in the study of consumer behavior, with studies traced back as far as 1672. The first with a reasonable statistical basis was published by Ernest Engel in 1857. The relationships between income and expenditures became popularized as "Engel's Laws of Consumption." They contained four propositions about the relationship between family income and the proportion spent on categories such as food, clothing, lodging, and "sundries" (education, health, recreation, and so forth).[3]

Substantial changes occur over time in the basic expenditures of families, depending on the economic development or income of the family. Notice in Figure 8.1 the comparison in the United States between the early part of this century and recent years. The proportion of the budget spent on food and clothing has dropped dramatically, leaving money for upgraded housing

[2] Kevin F. McCrohan and James D. Smith, "Consumer Participation in the Informal Economy," *Journal of the Academy of Marketing Sciences* 13 (Winter 1987), 62–67.
[3] Ernest Engel, "Die Productions und Consumptionsverhaltnisse des Konigreichs Sacksen," *Zeitschrift des Statistischen Bureaus des Koniglich Sachsischen Ministeriums des Innern,* Nos. 8–9 (November 22, 1857), 8.

and for the broad category of "other," similar to Engel's "sundries." It is this latter category that makes marketing dynamic and understanding the consumer a challenge of critical importance. Less developed countries of the world are likely to have a pattern of consumer expenditures more like the left side of Figure 8.1.

CONSUMER CONFIDENCE

Consumer expectations about future income have become an important variable in the prediction of consumer behavior. While an individual's current income determines what is possible to buy, expectations about future income often influence what is actually purchased, especially when analyzing purchases of automobiles, major appliances, and other durable goods.

Measures of consumer confidence are reported periodically by various data services, such as the Conference Board. These data are very important to marketers making inventory decisions. During late summer, for example, major retailers examine closely consumer confidence about future economic conditions in order to place inventory orders for the holiday selling season. The months of November and December account for over half of the sales or profits of many types of retailers. If inventories are too low, sales will be missed. If inventories are too high, price cuts may be needed so early in the season and so deep that few profits will be realized. Thus, consumer confidence is an important variable in the marketing decisions of retailers and their suppliers.

WHOSE INCOME?

It is sometimes a bit unclear whose income is the critical variable affecting buying. Most of the research about consumer behavior focuses on individuals, yet economic resources are usually shared with others, in families or households. Consumer surveys often deal entirely with individual behavior, except in the demographic section, where resource questions ask about family or household income. This is a matter of expediency in data collection, since the proportion is small of people whose income can be separated from family or household income. Recall some of the problems involved in this issue from Chapter 6. Although the trend is toward more emphasis on households, many surveys still ask resource questions with terminology such as "your family income last year before taxes."

The concept of per capita income is used to develop a better understanding of the role of income in determining aggregate expenditures for various products. In marketing research per capita income, adjusted by the number of family members, may improve the predictability of buying as it is related to income. Table 8.1 contains such figures, reported for a recent year for each state. The Bureau of Economic Analysis reports that average per capita income for Americans was $15,340 in 1987. Income in the richest state, Connecticut, was more than twice that of the poorest state, Mississippi.

	Rank	State	1987 PCI	Rank	State	1987 PCI
TABLE 8.1 **1987 PER CAPITA** **PERSONAL INCOMES** **BY STATE, RANKED** **BY AMOUNT**	1	Connecticut	$20,980	26	Iowa	$14,191
	2	New Jersey	20,067	27	Georgia	14,098
	3	Massachusetts	18,926	28	Vermont	14,061
	4	New York	18,055	29	Arizona	14,030
	5	Alaska	17,886	30	Oregon	13,887
	6	Maryland	17,722	31	Indiana	13,834
	7	California	17,661	32	Texas	13,764
	8	New Hampshire	17,133	33	Maine	13,720
	9	Illinois	16,347	34	North Carolina	13,155
	10	Virginia	16,332	35	North Dakota	13,061
	11	Delaware	16,238	36	Wyoming	12,759
	12	Nevada	15,958	37	Tennessee	12,738
	13	Colorado	15,862	38	Oklahoma	12,520
	14	Minnesota	15,783	39	South Dakota	12,511
	15	Washington	15,444	40	Montana	12,255
	16	Hawaii	15,366	41	Kentucky	11,950
	17	Rhode Island	15,355	42	South Carolina	11,858
	18	Michigan	15,330	43	Idaho	11,820
	19	Florida	15,241	44	Alabama	11,780
	20	Pennsylvania	14,997	45	New Mexico	11,673
	21	Kansas	14,952	46	Louisiana	11,362
	22	Wisconsin	14,659	47	Arkansas	11,343
	23	Ohio	14,543	48	Utah	11,246
	24	Missouri	14,537	49	W. Virginia	10,959
	25	Nebraska	14,347	50	Mississippi	10,204

Source: Bureau of Economic Analysis.

SPENDING AND INCOME

Buying is closely related to income. Table 8.2 shows how expenditures for major categories of consumer goods vary greatly by income level. Knowing the general level of expenditures and relating this to the income level of a firm's market target could provide estimates of the market potential within that product category. From other sources (such as Census of Retailing, Census of Services, and so forth), the number of suppliers can be obtained in order to assess the sales performance of an individual firm or to forecast sales that might be obtained by entry to the market.

The most comprehensive source of data on spending habits is the Consumer Expenditure Survey of the Bureau of Labor Statistics (BLS), which has been conducted periodically since 1968. Using consumer diaries, two types of data are collected. Inexpensive, frequently purchased products (food and beverages, personal care products, household supplies, and so forth) are measured for 2 weeks. A separate survey is collected on a quarterly basis asking consumers to recall expenditures of the past 3 months on relatively expensive items such as home appliances, property, automobiles, rent, and so forth. In addition to income, the data can be classified by age of householder, place of purchase (restaurant or grocery store, for example), and other social,

TABLE 8.2 SPENDING AND INCOME

(Average annual expenditures in 1982–83, by quintiles of income before taxes, in dollars)	Lowest 20%	Second 20%	Third 20%	Fourth 20%	Highest 20%
Total expenditures	$8,324	$12,155	$16,733	$22,425	$35,171
Food	1,753	2,333	2,877	3,606	4,834
At home	1,228	1,664	1,929	2,298	2,828
Away from home	525	669	958	1,308	2,006
Alcoholic beverages	134	196	273	359	468
Housing	2,980	3,994	5,032	6,466	10,188
Shelter	1,730	2,203	2,832	3,635	5,824
Owned	582	833	1,322	2,230	4,462
Rented	1,028	1,250	1,325	1,112	636
Other	120	120	185	293	725
Fuels, utilities, public services	901	1,223	1,388	1,662	2,116
Household operations	124	154	197	292	578
House furnishings and equipment	225	414	616	877	1,669
Apparel and apparel services	429	612	870	1,174	2,054
Transportation	1,231	2,259	3,451	4,604	6,950
Vehicles	356	707	1,242	1,707	2,895
Gasoline and motor oil	429	763	1,062	1,351	1,692
Other vehicle expenses	341	640	971	1,324	1,901
Public transportation	105	149	176	222	461
Health care	514	807	825	882	1,074
Entertainment	284	429	710	1,123	1,851
Personal care	84	122	152	197	303
Reading	59	86	116	156	219
Education	267	126	136	208	548
Tobacco	126	186	221	260	246
Miscellaneous	130	162	237	342	527
Cash contributions	141	272	533	701	1,361
Personal insurance, pensions and Social Security	191	570	1,301	2,347	4,548
Life insurance and other personal insurance	79	119	193	308	546
Retirement, pensions and Social Security	112	451	1,108	2,038	4,002

People spend their money differently depending on their income level.

Source: "Consumer Expenditures Survey Results from 1982–84," (Interview Survey) Bureau of Labor Statistics, Tables 1 and 2, 1983

demographic, or economic variables describing families. In recent decades, the amount spent for housing and transportation has increased slightly, with small declines in the amounts spent for food and apparel. The share of expenditures devoted to life insurance, pensions, and other personal insurance has remained fairly constant.[4]

MARKET FORECASTS BY SUBMARKETS   Demand by product categories can be forecast by partitioning aggregate data into submarkets. Forecasting

---

[4] David E. Bloom and Sanders D. Korenman, "Spending Habits of American Consumers," *American Demographics* 8 (March 1986), 22–25.

methods simulate future markets by assuming that the purchase behavior of individuals in a submarket remains constant over time but that the number of people in the submarket changes over time. Under the assumption of **behavioral consistency,** a 45-year-old man in the future is likely to have similar basic needs to a 45-year-old man of today. Thus, by knowing the spending patterns of submarkets today and forecasting numbers of submarkets in the future by age or other relevant variable, useful forecasts or at least simulations are possible for aggregate demand by product category in the future. McCann and Reibstein have developed models helpful in making such forecasts.[5]

WHO HAS THE INCOME?

It is much easier to hit a bull's-eye when one can see the target. That is why marketers place so much emphasis on knowing who has money and whose share is increasing. In Chapter 18, "Consumer Trends," we discuss most of these demographic variables and changes that are occurring in them. Table 8.3, however, shows how incomes vary by classification.

The young have less buying power, with average household income of $15,000 in 1985, less than half of that of 35 to 44 year olds, who have median income of $31,000, or the 45 to 55 year olds, with income of $33,200. In addition to higher salaries, the higher age groups have higher proportions of married couples, who may have more than one income per household.

Age, household type, and education are the three most important factors that affect income, although there are attractive market targets in every category. When forecasting demand or selecting market targets, other variables may yield even more precise information, however. Such measures include after-tax income, discretionary income, per capita income, personal income, and income per household member as well as net worth or other measures of wealth.[6]

THE AFFLUENT MARKET   An increasing number of marketers are targeting affluent households, also called the "Up Market," generally defined as the upper income quartile of the population. This 25 percent of households controls over 40 percent of spending power. The Up Market is likely to be dual-income households, time constrained (especially where children are present), and emphasizing quality in their product preferences. A special report on this target by Management Horizons, a Division of Price Waterhouse, concluded that large percentages of purchases are made by this group for products such as men's wear, furniture, electronic and home entertainment,

---

[5] John M. McCann and David J. Reibstein, "Forecasting the Impact of Socioeconomic and Demographic Change on Product Demand," *Journal of Marketing Research* 22 (November 1985), 413–423.

[6] Thomas G. Exter, "Where the Money Is," *American Demographics* 9 (March 1987), 26–32.

TABLE 8.3
WHO HAS THE
MONEY?

	Households in 1986	Median income in 1985	Median income in 1980	Percent change 1980–85
All Households	88,458	$23,600	$23,100	2.2%*
Age of Householder				
Under 25	5,503	$15,000	$16,600	−9.6%*
25 to 34	20,410	25,100	25,200	−0.4
35 to 44	17,997	31,100	30,800	1.0
45 to 54	13,099	33,200	32,800	1.2
55 to 64	12,852	25,600	25,500	0.4
65 and over	18,596	13,300	11,500	15.7*
Type of Household				
Family households	63,558	$27,700	$27,400	1.1%*
Married couples	50,933	31,100	30,200	3.0*
With children <18 at home	24,630	32,400	31,700	2.2*
Without children <18 at home	26,304	29,400	28,300	3.9*
Other family, female head	10,211	14,200	14,100	0.7
With children <18 at home	6,105	10,800	11,000	−1.8
Without children <18 at home	4,106	20,100	18,900	6.3*
Other family, male head	2,414	24,100	24,500	−1.6
Nonfamily households	24,900	13,700	12,300	11.4*
Person living alone	21,178	12,000	10,700	12.1*
Male householder	8,285	16,100	15,000	7.3*
Female householder	12,893	9,700	8,700	11.5*
Person living with nonrelatives	3,722	28,700	26,400	8.7*
Male householder	2,363	30,000	27,700	8.3*
Female householder	1,359	27,300	23,900	14.2*
Educational Attainment				
All householders aged 25+	82,942	$24,700	$24,000	2.9%*
Less than high school	22,314	13,900	12,600	10.3*
High school graduate	339	24,300	25,600	0.1*
One to three years college	11,991	28,800	28,400	1.4
Four years college	10,436	37,500	35,700	0.0*
Five or more years of college	7,369	45,900	40,000	14.7*

(Median household income by age of householder, household type, and education; 1986 households in thousands; income in constant 1985 dollars)

* Significant at the 95 percent level.
Source: Thomas G. Exter, "Where the Money Is," *American Demographics* 9 (March 1987), 26–32. Reprinted with permission.

home furnishings, tableware, domestics, fine jewelry and tools, hardware, and building materials.[7]

Where Does the Up Market Shop?   The Management Horizons study found a consistent preference across many product categories for department

---

[7] Mandy Putnam, "The Up Market." (Columbus, Ohio: Management Horizons, a Division of Price Waterhouse, 1988).

FIGURE 8.2   ADS ARE INCREASINGLY TARGETED TO APPEAL TO THE "UP MARKET"

stores, off-price stores, and specialty stores. Department stores are particularly strong competitors for apparel purchases. Specialty sporting goods stores are also beneficiaries of the purchasing power of the Up Market. Airport retailing provides a unique opportunity to reach the upscale, normally time-impoverished consumers in a unique situation where they have excess time to spend. Bloomie's Express, a Bloomingdale's branch at New York's Kennedy Airport, for example, grosses an average of $1,000 per square foot annually with items like $375 denim jackets and $100 infant overalls.[8]

Communicating to the Up Market is more print oriented than to other market segments. Readership of local weekday and Sunday newspapers is higher, creating effectiveness for ads such as that shown in Figure 8.2. The Up Market watches television less and listens to radio less, although they

---

[8] "Airport Retailing," *The Wall Street Journal* (December 29, 1988), A1.

have a higher proportion subscribing to cable television than lower-income segments.

The affluent market is substantial. The "super affluents" are defined in various levels such as over $50,000, over $75,000, or even over $100,000. The "super affluents" have grown rapidly in number in recent years. In the future, these markets are expected to become even more important.[9] We examine this topic in more depth in Chapter 18.

A most major implication of affluence in consumer resources is the rising importance of service marketing. The affluent can buy a wide variety of services that other consumers only wish they might buy—at beauty salons, dry cleaning shops, lawn care companies, and so forth. Many of the growth opportunities for marketing organizations are therefore in services. Additionally, excellence in service becomes especially important for many traditional marketers of a wide variety of products. The importance of such service was a major conclusion of the best-seller by Albrecht and Zemke, *Service America.*[10] Retailers such as Nordstrom have achieved enviable rates of growth and profitability by providing almost legendary levels of service.

OTHER ECONOMIC RESOURCES

Other economic resources than income affect consumer behavior. The most important are wealth (net worth) and credit.

Wealth, measured by assets or net worth, is correlated with income. The primary variation is that older consumers tend to have a larger proportion of wealth than younger consumers. In 1980 there were 574,342 millionaires in the United States, and the total has grown substantially since then. The average millionaire is 57 years old, and more than 95 percent have attended college for at least one year, with about 4 out of 10 having advanced degrees.[11] Wealthy families spend their money on services, travel, interest, and investments more than do their more plebian neighbors. Their expenditures on home furnishings, appliances, entertainment equipment, and similar products are not particularly high because wealthy families are usually in later stages of the life cycle and not concerned with furnishing new homes or making additional purchases of major equipment.

Credit extends the income resource, at least for a period of time. Actually, because the cost of credit must be subtracted from the consumer's total resource availability, credit reduces ability to buy goods and services in the long run.

---

[9] William Lazer, *Handbook of Demographics for Marketing and Advertising* (Lexington, Massachusettts: Lexington Books, 1987), 29–40.

[10] Karl Albrecht and Ron Zemke, *Service America* (Homewood, Illinois: Dow Jones-Irwin, 1985).

[11] Thomas J. Stanley and George P. Moschis, "America's Affluent," *American Demographics* 6 (March 1984), 28–33.

8.1 CONSUMER BEHAVIOR OF AFFLUENT MARKETS

As affluence increases, many households, particularly those with two earners, will place a premium on time. Improved customer service, immediate availability, trouble-free operation of products, and dependable maintenance and repair services will be valued. There will be a new willingness to pay the price for services that assure product performance and limit inconvenience.

In general, these income projections suggest that marketers should upgrade their focus and concentrate on higher-quality, higher priced goods and services. Goods and services in demand will include:

Products that ease drudgery and household maintenance, automate homemaking chores, save time, demonstrate quality, reliability, durability, and luxury.

Improved housing, including single-family homes and condominiums, that will appeal to more affluent middle-aged and pre-retirement husband–wife households. Included here are quality furniture, fixtures, appliances, and household services.

Products and services designed to enhance the physical self, particularly those perceived as maintaining and restoring youthfulness: cosmetics, skin care products, health foods, vitamins, cosmetic surgery, spas, hair stylists, clothing consultants, exercise facilities, and diet and health programs.

Products and services that support the psychological self: counseling, education, skills analysis, stress management training, cultural activities, and self-improvement books and courses.

Products that support mobility and immediate gratification: instant photography, all-night restaurants, portable telephones and computers, emergency health centers, world-wide product services, rentals, 800 numbers, home entertainment centers, automated tellers, and instant credit.

Products and services that will secure and protect individuals and property: sensing devices, home protection systems, security guards, protected residential areas, insurance of various kinds, fire and burglar protection, financial security plans, air and water purifiers, and sanitation products.

Entertainment and leisure activities, including services as varied as participatory and spectator sports, travel, and gambling.

Products that permit us to differentiate ourselves and that appeal to the snob in all of us; products associated with taste, breeding, graceful lifestyles, culture, and the so-called "markets of the mind." Included are gourmet foods, wines, decorator and designer products and services, paintings, sculpture, and performing arts such as ballet, opera, symphony concerts, and drama.

Source: William Lazer, "How Rising Affluence Will Reshape Markets," *American Demographics* 6 (February 1984).

TABLE 8.4 CONSUMER WILLINGNESS TO BORROW

	Boats and Hobby Purchases	Auto Purchases	Expenses Due to Illness	Educational Expenses	Furniture Purchases	Vacation Expenses	Living Expenses When Income Is Cut	Consolidation of Bills	Fur Coat or Jewelry
All households	19%	82%	82%	79%	49%	13%	46%	48%	5%
Household Income									
Under $10,000	10%	63%	77%	65%	39%	11%	54%	53%	3%
$10,000–19,999	14	86	81	81	49	13	46	52	4
$20,000–29,999	24	91	84	87	55	15	49	50	5
$30,000–39,999	32	93	84	88	58	15	41	48	6
$40,000–49,999	25	91	84	85	55	15	40	44	5
$50,000 and over	37	90	89	90	59	17	45	47	10
Age of Householder									
<25	27%	88%	91%	89%	56%	18%	68%	66%	8%
25–34	28	90	84	88	57	17	52	55	6
35–44	26	90	83	87	52	15	46	48	5
45–54	17	84	82	82	50	12	42	50	5
55–64	14	82	80	76	47	10	45	44	4
65+	5	61	74	58	33	9	37	35	2

(percent of householders who feel it is all right to use installment debt for different types of purchases, 1983)

Source: David E. Bloom and Todd P. Steen, "Living On Credit," *American Demographics* 9 (October 1987), 22–29, at 25. Reprinted with permission.

Nevertheless, Americans are increasingly willing to use credit for temporary expansion of their economic resources. Younger householders are more likely to favor borrowing than older householders. About 90 percent of those younger than 45 feel it appropriate to borrow for an automobile purchase, compared to only 60 percent of those aged 65 and older. These data are shown in Table 8.4. Americans are most willing to borrow for cars, for medical bills, or for educational reasons. Younger households and those with higher incomes are more willing to borrow, no matter what the reason.[12]

Many other effects of income on buying can be observed. When studying the family in Chapter 6, you may recall more examples of the "Up Market" or "Down Market," with profound effect within each lifestage. In Chapter 4, "Social Class," you were able to observe that economic resources are major variables affecting social class and its association with consumer behavior. Consumers who have the least amount of economic resources are a concern, both in Chapter 18 on "Consumer Trends" and Chapter 25 about "Consumerism."

---

[12] David E. Bloom and Todd P. Steen, "Living on Credit," *American Demographics* 9 (October 1987), 22–29.

8.2 BLUE-BLOOD BUYERS

Where do the affluent shop? At chain speciality stores like the Limited and Benetton, according to Management Horizons of Dublin, Ohio. Among people who shop chain speciality stores at least once a month, 22 percent have household incomes of $50,000 or more, compared with 17 percent of all U.S. households. Catalog showrooms, home-improvement centers, and local specialty stores trail close behind: 20 percent of their customers are in this income bracket, compared with 18 percent of department-store customers and 17 percent of off-price store shoppers.

At national chain stores such as Sears or JCPenney, and also at drugstores, only 14 percent of shoppers are in the affluent group. Twelve percent of regular convenience-store shoppers (at least three visits a month) have household incomes of $50,000 or more. The affluent share is lowest (11 percent) among monthly visitors to discount stores like K-Mart.

Source: "Blue-Blood Buyers," *American Demographics* 10 (May 1988), 20.

TEMPORAL RESOURCES

Time is becoming an increasingly important variable in understanding consumer behavior because of the increasing time poverty of Americans. The hours spent at work each week (including commuting time, housework, and schoolwork) increased from 40.6 hours in 1973 to 47.3 in 1984. At the same time, the median number of hours available for leisure dropped from 26.2 to 18.1 hours per week.[13]

One of the most individual variables of human behavior is concerned with how a person spends her or his time budget. Most is spent on work, sleep, and other required activities. A portion, however, is spent on very personal activities called **leisure,** reflecting both personality and lifestyle preferences.

Consumer resources consist of two budget constraints: money budget and time budget. Income is a critical variable, as we have just seen. Now, however, we want to look at the time budget consumers have to spend to reflect their personal lifestyle preferences.[14] Although rising incomes might

---

[13] Martha Riche, "The Importance of the Arts," *American Demographics* 7 (July 1985), 42.

[14] This section is drawn from Justin Voss and Roger Blackwell, "Markets for Leisure Time," in Mary Jane Slinger, ed., *Advances in Consumer Research* (Chicago: Association for Consumer Research, 1975), 837–45; and Justin Voss and Roger Blackwell, "The Role of Time Resources in Consumer Behavior," in O. C. Ferrell, Stephen Brown, and Charles Lamb, eds., *Conceptual and Theoretical Developments in Marketing* (Chicago: American Marketing Association, 1979), 296–311.

FIGURE 8.3
CONCEPTUALIZATIONS
OF CONSUMER TIME
BUDGETS AND
LEISURE: ONLY
"DISCRETIONARY"
TIME IS TRULY
LEISURE TIME

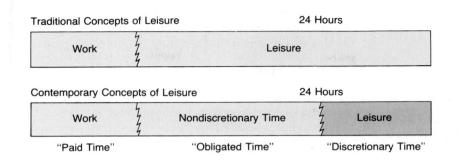

allow consumers to *buy* more of everything, they cannot conceivably *do* more of everything. Doing more things, as opposed to buying more things, requires an additional resource: time. Whereas money budgets have no theoretical expansion limits, time has an ultimate restraint.

As discretionary income continues to increase in a society, markets for time-related goods or services become more important. Scarcity creates value. For affluent consumers, the chief concern becomes buying more time rather than more products. The value of time increases as money budgets increase, thereby increasing the possibility that a marketer may enhance the value of products (and the corresponding price) more than the additional cost of doing so.

Historically, the consumer's time budget naively has been regarded as having two components: work and leisure. This conceptualization is shown in the upper portion of Figure 8.3. A more contemporary conceptualization is shown in the lower portion. Here, consumer time budgets are divided into three blocks: "paid time," "obligated time," and "discretionary time." Lane and Lindquist use a similar classification system including income-producing time, committed (obligated and nonobligated) time, and uncommitted (planned and unplanned) time.[15] It is only the latter block of discretionary or uncommitted time that can be truly regarded as leisure time. Voss concludes: "Leisure is a period of time referred to as discretionary time. It is that period when an individual feels no sense of economic, legal, moral, or social compulsion or obligation, nor of physiological necessity. The choice of how to utilize this time period belongs solely to the individual."[16]

An additional complication in defining leisure occurs when individuals are paid for activities they might otherwise choose as discretionary activities.

[15] Paul M. Lane and Jay D. Lindquist, "Definitions for the Fourth Dimension: A Proposed Time Classification System," in Kenneth D. Bahn, ed., *Developments of Marketing Science* 11 (Blacksburg, Virginia: Academy of Marketing Science, 1988), 38–46.
[16] Justin Voss, "The Definition of Leisure," *Journal of Economic Issues* 1 (June 1967), 91–106.

Artists, professors, and professional athletes may be examples of individuals who are fortunate to be paid for activities they would otherwise choose as leisure activities. Perhaps students might even view reading textbooks such as this one as leisure rather than obligated or paid activities!

TIME GOODS

A contemporary conceptualization of consumer time budgets leads to the recognition that goods and services have important time properties. Products and services classified by their time properties may be called **time goods,** and the time properties of goods have important marketing implications.

TIME-USING GOODS
One category of products and services is that which requires the use of time with the product. Examples would be watching TV, skiing, fishing, golfing, or playing tennis, all of which are usually classified as leisure-time activities. They would normally fall in the portion of time called "discretionary time" or leisure.

To understand the nature of time-using purchased goods of the discretionary type, we must examine what is happening to the other categories of time usage in a typical 24-hour day. Contrary to popular opinion, there has been no substantial decline in the work week since the end of World War II.[17] The only increases in leisure time have been associated with an increased number of holidays, length of vacations, and earlier retirement.

Nondiscretionary, or "obligated time," includes physical obligations (sleeping, commuting, personal care, and so forth), social obligations (which seem to increase with urbanization and the rising proportion of professional and white-collar occupations), and moral obligations. It appears that nondiscretionary activities are also not declining; instead, at least in consumer perceptions, they are increasing. Thus, the net effect of trends in time usage leads to a feeling by many consumers of less leisure rather than more.

When the effect of increased money budgets is considered, the conclusion must be that consumers will be willing to pay more money to enjoy their limited leisure time. In such an economy, it could be predicted that consumers would be willing to pay more and more of the dollars required (in travel, skiing, expensive sports equipment, and so forth) to enjoy their leisure time, and would be likely to switch from less intense or active leisure activities

---

[17] Geoffrey H. Moore, "Measuring Leisure Time," *The Conference Board Record* (July 1971), 53–54. Belief in a reduced work week may be due to confusion in statistics, which as typically reported are usually based on manufacturers' payrolls. As such, they usually include both full-time and part-time workers, which distorts the averages for all workers in decades of increasing proportions of part-time workers. Also, manufacturers' payroll records do not include second jobs, which are part of the work week from the consumer's perspective. It is also misleading to consider only manufacturing statistics in an era when a rising proportion of workers are technical, professional, and managerial—and may have longer work weeks than manufacturing employees do.

such as golf to more intense or active ones such as tennis. This was shown in a study of leisure-time satisfactions in which highly educated and high-income men (presumably busier) were more likely to derive satisfaction from tennis than from golf.[18]

TIME-SAVING GOODS   One way for consumers to obtain increased discretionary time (leisure) is to decrease nondiscretionary time. Frequently, this may be achieved through the purchase of goods and services.

Services represent the obvious offering that provides additional discretionary time. The purchase of lawn-mowing or lawn-fertilizing services (such as ChemLawn) may free the consumer for true leisure activities. Much of the restaurant and frozen-food industry can be considered to be selling time. Convenience goods and disposable products of many types are ways in which the consumer can buy time. Jet airplanes may cost more money but save time, thereby providing more time for leisure. Finally, many so-called labor-saving devices or consumer durable goods (such as dishwashers) are also valued for their time-saving properties.

More and more marketing organizations are capitalizing on the desire to save time. New products such as microwave ovens and retort pouch cooking are the result. Positioning strategies in which time properties are featured in communications about the product are also possible. It is a contemporary recognition of the principle Benjamin Franklin in 1748 told a young tradesperson, "Remember that time is money." Franklin also commented, "Dost thou love Life? Then do not squander Time; for that's the stuff Life is made of."

Time Prices.   Some advertisers feature the "time price" of the product. This is done by advertising that the product requires only 2 hours to install. Convenience due to a nearby location is also an attempt to reduce the time price. Some shopping malls have become so congested that they are losing customers because the time price of shopping at that mall is less than at malls that might be less attractive otherwise. Many product innovations have been built on the desire to reduce the time price of the product. Examples include new "dry" deodorants, quick-dry paint, higher horsepower lawn mowers, and the Concorde airplane, which, although it has a high price in economic resources, is the cheapest plane in the air in temporal resources.

Some marketers offer a **time guarantee** (TG), defined as a promise by the seller that assures customers that they will not have to devote an unreasonable amount of time to getting product and service problems resolved. Any unusual problems would be handled at locations and times convenient to the customer. Koerner Ford in Rochester, New York, offers a TG which assures customers that if a problem with the vehicle is not fixed right the first time, the dealership will send a mechanic to the home or work location

---

[18] Douglass K. Hawes, W. Wayne Talarzyk, and Roger D. Blackwell, "Consumer Satisfaction from Leisure Time Pursuits," in Mary J. Slinger, *Advances*, 822.

at times convenient to the customer to solve the problem. In a study of this offer, 63 percent of customers of the dealership rated the TG as very important, although most wanted it as an included service rather than something for which customers would pay extra.[19]

SHOPPING TIME   Of the 168 hours in a week, Americans now spend about 6 hours in shopping-related activities. That is about 6 percent of their waking hours and 40 minutes a week more than in 1975.[20] The higher amounts of time spent today reflect consumers' higher incomes, cheaper gasoline, and more abundant shopping opportunities. About half of people's shopping time goes for buying groceries, clothing, and other basics. Traveling to and from stores takes roughly one third of shopping time, about 5 percent goes for shopping for larger durables such as cars, and the remaining 12 percent is spent on services such as banks, hair salons, and post offices. Marketers need to install equipment, training, and systems to assist the shoppers who feel harried. Harried consumers—those who feel rushed and pressured for time—visit fewer stores and make few comparisons by considering fewer brands and attributes than those who are relaxed shoppers.[21]

Time is increasingly recognized as an important part of consumers' decisions about products.[22] Fox suggests that important attributes of time include performance time (actual and perceived), flexibility or fixity of carrying out activities, frequency, regularity, duration, disruption/simultaneity, and monitoring time (how much effort is required to remember to carry out the activity).[23] It was originally believed that a consumer's decisions about time expenditures would be determined by personal characteristics, but recent research indicates that situational variables determine how people spend their time, especially for leisure as opposed to obligatory activities.[24]

Consumer researchers are giving more attention to how consumers spend their time. At AT&T, time-use diaries are collected from a nationally representative sample of 1,900 households. In the diaries, respondents describe each activity they participated in on their diary day, the time and place of the activity, its duration, how enjoyable the activity was, whether other people were there, and whether the respondent participated in any other activities

---

[19] Eugene H. Fram and Andrew J. DuBrin, "The Time Guarantee in Action: Some Trends and Opportunities," *Journal of Consumer Marketing* 5 (Fall 1988), 53–60.

[20] John P. Robinson, "When the Going Gets Tough," *American Demographics* 11 (February 1989), 50.

[21] Aida N. Rizkalla, "Consumer Temporal Orientation and Shopping Behavior: The Case of Harried vs. Relaxed Consumers," in Robert L. King, ed., *Retailing: Its Present and Future* 4 (Charleston, South Carolina: Academy of Marketing Science, 1988), 230–235.

[22] Jacob Jacoby, George J. Szybillo, and Carol Kohn Berning, "Time and Consumer Behavior: An Interdisciplinary Overview," *Journal of Consumer Research* 2 (March 1976), 320–339.

[23] Karen Fox, "Time as a Component of Price in Social Marketing," in Richard P. Bogozzi, ed., *Marketing in the 80's* (Chicago: American Marketing Association, 1980), 464–467.

[24] Jacob Hornik, "Situational Effects on the Consumption of Time," *Journal of Marketing* 46 (Fall 1982), 44–55.

at the same time. AT&T uses the diary data to identify market segments with more or less discretionary time. People without discretionary time may respond differently than those with free time to products or services that give them more time, that allow them to shift times, or that permit them to do two things at once.[25]

The way time is spent by consumers of various age categories has changed during the past decade. While some activities are stable, there are some major changes, especially in the area of communications, such as interpersonal conversations. For men between 25 and 44, Juster found that time on the telephone has almost doubled recently, and the gap between the sexes has narrowed. In other areas of time budgets, television viewing was increasing in prior years but now appears to be declining.[26] In a major study comparing time budgets in 1984 with those in 1973, Hawes found that men are spending more time doing things around the home, while women are spending more of their time in the work world.[27]

The importance of time must be recognized when developing marketing strategies, as well as in communications programs. *Consumer in Focus 8.3* describes how the food industry is being dramatically changed, with requirements of millions of dollars in capital, facilities, and technology, as a result of consumers' increased actual or perceived time poverty.

COGNITIVE RESOURCES

Thus far our discussion has focused on how the availability of time and money can shape consumer behavior. Another type of resource considered here is cognitive in nature. This cognitive resource represents the mental **capacity** available for undertaking various information-processing activities.

Capacity is a limited resource. We are able to process only a certain amount of information at a time. Capacity size is often described in terms of a **chunk,** which represents a grouping or combination of information that can be processed as a unit. Depending upon which source one chooses to draw upon, capacity varies from four or five chunks to as many as seven.[28]

---

[25] Jonathan McAdams, "How to Use Time-Use Diaries," *American Demographics* 9 (January 1987), 46–48.

[26] F. Thomas Juster, "A Note on Recent Changes in Time Use," in F. Thomas Juster and Frank P. Stafford, eds., *Time, Goods, and Well-Being* (Ann Arbor: University of Michigan, 1985), 316–317.

[27] Douglass K. Hawes, "Time Budgets and Consumer Leisure-Time Behavior: An Eleven-Year-Later Replication and Extension," in Melanie Wallendorf and Paul Anderson, eds., *Advances in Consumer Research,* Vol. 14 (Provo, Utah: Association for Consumer Research, 1987), 543–547.

[28] Herbert A. Simon, "How Big Is a Chunk?" *Science* 183 (February 1974), 482–488; George A. Miller, "The Magical Number Seven, Plus or Minus Two: Some Limits on Our Capacity for Processing Information," *Psychological Review* 63 (March 1956), 81–97.

8.3 HOW THE FOOD INDUSTRY IS CATERING TO CONSUMERS WHO WANT IT *NOW*

Call it a sign of the times. "The Living Section" of the *New York Times* usually features lengthy recipes for saddle of wild boar with wild juniper berries and rabbit in mustard sauce. You know, the kind of dishes that take four hours to make—not including the time spent hunting. But now the *Times* offers a monthly column called "Microwave Cooking." John C. Webber, director of marketing research at General Foods Corp., says, "The baby boomers have been raised on instant gratification. People want what they want, wherever they are and whenever they want it."

With nearly $500 billion in total food spending at stake, the battle for consumers' stomachs is blurring the distinctions between restaurant, grocery store and manufacturer. Companies such as Geo. A. Hormel & Co. are testing shelf-stable entrees that can sit at room temperature for at least 18 months. Campbell Soup Co. is wrapping fresh fruit and vegetables and selling them as snacks. Because such offerings are typically aimed at higher-income households and often carry high prices, convenience must be accompanied by high quality and variety.

The fast-food giants were the first to capitalize on the rise of working women and one-person households, and the resulting decline of traditional home-cooked meals. This year, meals eaten away from home will account for 40.5% of all food spending, up from 36.3% in 1983. In the food business, where overall growth is a plodding 2%, such shifts are seismic upheavals. Grocers, fed up with losing customers to fast-food outlets, are responding with convenience-driven efforts of their own. Giant and other supermarket chains are adding take-out dishes such as prepared salads, sandwiches, soup and hot foods.

Technology is giving food companies new weapons. Some 60% of U.S. kitchens now have microwave ovens, and Pillsbury Co. believes that proportion will reach 90% by 1990. Most food companies are developing products that can be heated in either conventional or microwave ovens. Pillsbury is developing microwave-only products, such as a cake mix that takes a scant 10 minutes to mix and bake.

Golden Valley Microwave Foods Inc. is devoted solely to microwave popcorn and pancakes. Net income at the nine-year-old company leaped 188% last year on sales up 107%. "I think the definition of convenience is five minutes," says James. D. Watkins, the founder and chief executive of Golden Valley

And now five minutes is looking slow. Shelf-stable foods such as Hormel's may be the ultimate in convenience—if consumers can accept the idea of getting a meal from an unrefrigerated package. Hormel's 10 entrees, including lemon filet of cod, need only two minutes in the microwave. Burger King has launched a new line of bite-sized Burger Bundles, small enough to be eaten one-handed while driving, and recently began advertising its offerings as "the best food for fast times."

Source: *Business Week* (April 27, 1987), 88–89.

It has been rumored that the phone company selected seven-digit phone numbers because of the difficulties many consumers would have with more numbers. Consistent with this, learning declines as the number of words in a sentence increases beyond seven.[29]

The allocation of cognitive capacity is known as **attention.** Attention consists of two dimensions: **direction** and **intensity.**[30] Direction represents the *focus* of attention. Because consumers are unable to process all of the internal and external stimuli available at any given moment, they must be selective in how they allocate this limited resource. Some stimuli will gain attention, others will be ignored.

Intensity, on the other hand, refers to the *amount* of capacity focused in a particular direction. Consumers will often allocate only the capacity needed to identify a stimulus (e.g., another car ad) before redirecting their attention elsewhere. On other occasions, consumers may pay enough attention to understand the basic gist of the ad. Sometimes consumers may give the ad their complete concentration and carefully scrutinize the message, such as a consumer in the market for a new car who is reading an automobile ad.

The fact that capacity is a limited resource carries a number of important implications concerning how consumers process information and make product choices. Some of these are discussed subsequently.

GAINING ATTENTION

Gaining the consumer's attention represents one of the most formidable challenges a marketer may face. Consumers are bombarded continually by a substantial number of stimuli that compete for their limited capacity. Estimates of the number of ads consumers encounter in a typical day range in the hundreds, and are likely to increase as marketers continue to develop new avenues for reaching consumers (e.g., the use of ads in rental videos). A major determinant of an ad's success, then, is the likelihood of its gaining the consumer's attention.

Gaining attention at the point of purchase can be equally important. The use of eye-catching displays can be instrumental in helping a product stand out from the clutter of brands squeezed onto a retailer's shelf (see *Consumer in Focus 8.4*). Packaging can serve a similar function. Achieving a "louder voice on store shelves" was a major consideration in designing the cans for the various Coca-Cola brands.

Consequently, it is very important for marketers to understand what factors may influence the focus of attention. As we see in Chapter 13 ("Information Processing"), there are a number of stimuli at the marketer's disposal for gaining attention.

---

[29] Alexander J. Wearing, "The Recall of Sentences of Varying Length," *Australian Journal of Psychology* 25 (August 1973), 156–161.

[30] Scott B. MacKenzie, "The Role of Attention in Mediating the Effect of Advertising on Attribute Importance," *Journal of Consumer Research* 13 (September 1986), 174–195.

8.4 GAINING ATTENTION WITH POINT-OF-PURCHASE DISPLAYS: OLYMPIA BREWING COMPANY

Point-of-purchase (POP) displays are often used by marketers for attracting consumers' attention in a retail environment that is increasingly "cluttered" with new products. The Olympia Brewing Company conducted a study to determine the effects of POP displays on purchase behavior. The research involved both food and liquor stores located within two California cities. Some of the stores received a display while others did not (these latter stores provided a baseline for comparing the results for stores with displays). In addition, two types of POP displays were tested: motion displays (those with some movement being generated by the display) versus static displays (those without movement).

Sales in the stores were then monitored over a four-week period. The results (numbers represent the increase in sales over stores without displays) are presented as follows:

	Static Display	Motion Display
Food Store	18%	49%
Liquor Store	56%	107%

These findings clearly reveal the effectiveness of POP displays in generating sales. The presence of a display produced an average sales increase of more than 50%. The greater effectiveness observed for liquor stores relative to food stores suggests that the impact of POP displays is facilitated when consumers are already inclined toward purchasing the product (it seems safe to believe that those visiting the liquor store were so inclined). Further, the use of movement generated nearly three times the sales of the static display in food stores and nearly twice the sales in liquor stores.

SHALLOW ATTENTION

Another reality of the marketplace is that many products are simply not that important to consumers (see the concept of product involvement in Chapter 9) to warrant a "large" investment of their limited cognitive resources. In many respects, consumers are "cognitive misers" as they attempt to find acceptable rather than optimal solutions for many of their consumption needs. Thus, the cognitive demands required by an elaborate decision-making process are such that consumers will devote the needed capacity (as well as the time) for only a limited number of products. Simplistic decision strategies (as discussed in Chapter 17) that lower the demands on capacity are more common.

This same barrier occurs for marketing communications. Even if one can succeed in gaining attention, consumers may not devote the amount of attention desired. Research indicates that failure to achieve an adequate degree of attention can reduce learning. For example, in a typical "shadowing" study, subjects wearing headphones receive a different message in each ear.[31] Subjects are then asked to "shadow" one of the messages: that is, repeat aloud the content. Despite hearing two different messages simultaneously, subjects can easily shadow one of them, although this task requires nearly all of their cognitive capacity.

The interesting question is what can be recalled about the message that is not shadowed. Some aspects of this message are absorbed, such as whether it contained human speech versus a nonspeech sound (e.g., buzzing), or when the sex of the speaker changed during the message. However, recall of message content is nonexistent. Even changes from normal speech to a nonsense speech-sound (e.g., normal speech played backward) escape detection. These findings suggest that stimuli that fail to receive a sufficient amount of capacity are unlikely to leave a lasting impression on the consumer.

Persuasion as well as learning can depend on the amount of capacity allocated to a communication.[32] If consumers are unwilling or unable to devote the attention necessary for carefully evaluating an ad's claims, then persuasion can depend more heavily on reactions to the ad's executional features.[33] However, such features may have little influence when the claims receive the attention necessary for a thoughtful evaluation of their validity. We return to this issue in Chapter 15.

THE DANGER OF EXCEEDING COGNITIVE CAPACITY

Because capacity is limited, it is possible that the demands of the information environment (see Chapter 7) may sometimes exceed this capacity. In 1974, for instance, the Federal Trade Commission developed a proposal for increased disclosure of nutritional information within food advertisements. A fundamental flaw with the proposal was that it required the presentation of more information than could be processed within the time made available.[34]

What happens when the demands of the information environment exceed cognitive capacity? This question has led to a considerable amount of research and debate concerning the potential for **information overload.** Some have speculated that increased disclosure of product information may have undesirable effects. If the information "load" (i.e., the amount of information) in a choice environment exceeds capacity, then consumers might become confused and make poorer choices.

---

[31] For example, see E. C. Cherry, "Some Experiments on the Recognition of Speech with One and Two Ears," *Journal of the Acoustical Society of America* 25 (1953), 975–979.

[32] Anthony G. Greenwald and Clark Leavitt, "Audience Involvement in Advertising: Four Levels," *Journal of Consumer Research* 11 (June 1984), 581–592.

[33] See, for example, Scott B. MacKenzie and Richard J. Lutz, "An Empirical Examination of the Structural Antecedents of Attitude-Toward-the-Ad in an Advertising Pretesting Context," *Journal of Marketing* 53 (April 1989) 48–65; Richard E. Petty and John T. Cacioppo, *Communication and Persuasion: Central and Peripheral Routes to Attitude Change,* (New York: Springer/Verlag, 1986).

[34] James R. Bettman, "Issues in Designing Consumer Information Environments," *Journal of Consumer Research* 2 (December 1975), 169–177.

In an early study of overload by Jacoby and his colleagues, they concluded that

It would appear that increasing package information load tends to produce: (1) dysfunctional consequences in terms of the consumer's ability to select that brand which was best for him, and (2) beneficial effects upon the consumer's degree of satisfaction, certainty, and confusion regarding his selection. In other words, our subjects felt better with more information but actually made poorer purchase decisions.[35]

This study and a similar investigation sparked a heated controversy.[36] Critics contended that the Jacoby studies overstated their findings and suggested that the data did not reflect overload as a result of increased product information, a conclusion with which we agree. This is not to say that overload cannot occur, only that the Jacoby studies did not demonstrate that more product information led to poorer decisions.

The information-overload controversy has continued, although with somewhat different players.[37] Jacoby now maintains that information overload, while possible, is unlikely because consumers will stop processing information before they are overloaded.[38] However, a recent study suggests that consumers may be unable to stop short of overloading themselves when faced with a sufficiently rich information environment.[39]

<u>S</u>UMMARY

Consumers possess three primary resources which they use in the exchange process through which marketers provide goods and services. These resources

---

[35] Jacob Jacoby, Donald Speller, and Carol Kohn Berning, "Brand Choice Behavior as a Function of Information Load," *Journal of Marketing Research* 11 (February 1974), 63–69.

[36] Jacob Jacoby, Donald Speller, and Carol Kohn Berning, "Brand Choice Behavior as a Function of Information Load: Replication and Extension," *Journal of Consumer Research* 1 (June 1974), 33–42; J. Edward Russo, "More Information Is Better: A Reevaluation of Jacoby, Speller, and Kohn," *Journal of Consumer Research* 11 (November 1974) 467–468; William L. Wilkie, "Analysis of Effects of Information Load," *Journal of Marketing Research* 11 (November 1974), 462–466; Jacob Jacoby, Donald E. Speller, and Carol A. K. Berning, "Constructive Criticism and Programmatic Research: Reply to Russo," *Journal of Consumer Research* 1 (September 1975), 154–156; Jacob Jacoby, "Information Load and Decision Quality: Some Contested Issues," *Journal of Marketing Research* 15 (November 1977), 569–573.

[37] Debra L. Scammon, "Information Load and Consumers," *Journal of Consumer Research* 4 (December 1977), 148–155; Naresh K. Malhotra, "Information Load and Consumer Decision Making," *Journal of Consumer Research* 8 (March 1982), 419–430; Naresh K. Malhotra, Arun K. Jain, and Stephen W. Lagakos, "The Information Overload Controversy: An Alternative Viewpoint," *Journal of Marketing* 46 (Spring 1982), 27–37; Naresh K. Malhotra, "Reflections on the Information Overload Paradigm in Consumer Decision Marking," *Journal of Consumer Research* 10 (March 1984), 436–440.

[38] Jacob Jacoby, "Perspectives on Information Overload," *Journal of Consumer Research* 10 (March 1984), 432–435.

[39] Kevin Lane Keller and Richard Staelin, "Effects of Quality and Quantity of Information on Decision Effectiveness," *Journal of Consumer Research* 14 (September 1987), 200–213.

are economic, temporal, and cognitive. Practically speaking, this means that marketers are competing for consumers' money, time, and attention. A consumer's perception of available resources may affect the willingness to spend time or money for products. Thus, measures of consumer confidence may be useful in forecasting future sales by product category.

Buying is affected greatly by consumers' income. Affluence is a variable of major interest to marketers. About 25 percent of households control over 40 percent of spending power. This group makes proportionately high purchases of products such as apparel, furniture, electronic and home entertainment, home furnishings, tableware, domestics, fine jewelry, tools, hardware, and building materials. Department stores are particularly strong competitors for affluent customers but so are some off-price retailers and specialty stores. These customers are reached relatively more effectively with print media, although they also have higher ownership of cable television. Americans have expressed a high propensity to use credit, which extends the income resource, at least for a period of time.

The second major consumer resource is time. Products and services classified by their time properties may be called time goods. Time-using goods require the use of time with the product and include products such as attending a museum, watching television, and other activities often classified as leisure activities. Time-saving products allow consumers to increase their discretionary time, often through the purchase of services or goods that reduce the time required in other activities. A contemporary conceptualization is time budgets, which include paid time, obligated time, and discretionary time.

The third major type of consumer resource is cognitive capacity. The allocation of cognitive capacity is known as attention. Because this capacity is limited, people must be selective in what they pay attention to and how much attention is allocated during information processing. Gaining the consumer's attention will often represent a major hurdle for marketers. Similarly, gaining "enough" attention can be equally challenging, particularly when the product is of limited importance. Finally, there is the possibility of consumers becoming "overloaded" when the information environment exceeds their cognitive capacity.

REVIEW AND DISCUSSION QUESTIONS

1. Why is "perception" of economic resources a variable as important in explaining consumer behavior as actual resources? Analyze the opening vignette to explain the research results reported as a result of a drop in stock market prices.

2. Describe the relationships that can be expected between income and the purchase of major product categories.

3. When conducting marketing research, how should income be measured?

4. If a consumer goods manufacturer is seeking growth opportunities that may be expected from rising affluence, what advice would you provide?

5. What is meant by the term "Frontier Consumerism"? How might it affect the marketing programs of a major retailer?

6. How might the relationship between time budgets and economic budgets affect the marketing strategy of a major retailer?

7. A retailer has just completed a study of the effects due to the amount of shelf space given a product and where the product is located in the store. Whereas both the amount of space and location had significant effects on the sales for some items (e.g., cookies), such effects were not observed for other items (e.g., milk). How can you explain these differences?

8. Consider the manufacturer interested in determining which of two alternative ads would be most effective. Initially, target consumers were shown one of the ads along with several other ads and later tested for recall. The results revealed no difference in recall between the ads. However, in a later field test where target consumers encountered the ads in a "real world" setting, major differences were observed in the ads' effectiveness. How can you account for these inconsistencies between the two studies?

9. What is your opinion about the information-overload controversy? Do you believe overload can occur? Do you believe it will occur?

INVOLVEMENT AND MOTIVATION

ANTI-PLAQUE TOOTHPASTE: DEMISE OF A "SURE THING"

Three years ago, Noxell Corp. thought it had a great idea—introduce a toothpaste to fight plaque, the bacterial film that clings to the teeth and causes gum disease. But when Noxell's Periogene made its debut, it bombed. The company soon pulled the toothpaste from the market.

The short life of Periogene was a sign of things to come for plaque fighters, a product that the dental-care industry was convinced would be the hottest thing since fluoride. With so many baby boomers headed for middle-age—and 90% of them likely to develop gum problems—the potential for plaque fighters seemed enormous.

Instead, manufacturers have stumbled over a variety of problems. They have found that consumers don't really understand what plaque is. One reason anti-plaque toothpastes haven't sold well is that they were introduced at the same time as the new anti-tartar toothpastes. Buyers quickly decided that they would rather get rid of tartar, which is strictly a cosmetic problem, than plaque. Plaque isn't "as easy to understand" as tartar, says Daniel Meade, an analyst at First Boston Corp. "People can see tartar. Plaque is different. It's been a very hard message to get across."

Source: Andrea Rothman, "Anti-Plaque Toothpaste, Once Considered a Breakthrough Product, Stumbles Badly," *The Wall Street Journal* (October 10, 1988), B1. Reprinted by permission of *The Wall Street Journal,* © Dow Jones & Company, Inc. 1988. All rights reserved worldwide.

All marketers and others who want to shape and influence human behavior start with the question faced by Noxell Corporation management—*what motivates the consumer?* The marketing challenge is to discover the primary influences and to design strategies that both activate and satisfy felt needs. In this situation marketing success was severely hampered by the fact that the cosmetic benefit of tartar reduction was a more important motivator than plaque control.

A person can be said to be motivated when his or her system is energized (aroused), made active, and behavior is directed toward a desired goal. In short, the system is "turned on" and triggered to engage in need-satisfying activity.

In this chapter we explore some foundational concepts and theories of motivation. We begin with a discussion of the dynamics of the motivation process and the central importance of need activation and satisfaction.

Next, we demonstrate how the degree of involvement (perceived relevance) accompanying the purchase and consumption situation serves as an important motivating construct. When we are involved we respond in an entirely different manner than when this is not the case.

The remainder of the chapter focuses on some major needs that affect consumer behavior, various approaches to measurement and evaluation, and the primary implications for marketing strategy.

THE MOTIVATION OF HUMAN BEHAVIOR[1]

Motivated behavior is initiated by need activation (or need recognition—see Chapter 17). A need or motive (these terms often are used interchangeably) is activated when there is a sufficient discrepancy between the actual state and a desired or preferred state of being. As this discrepancy increases, the outcome is activation of a condition of arousal referred to as **drive.** The stronger the drive, the greater the perceived urgency of response.

Over time certain behavior patterns are recognized as more effective than others for need satisfaction, and these come to function as **incentives.** An incentive is an anticipated reward from a course of action that offers need-satisfying potential.

To take a simple example, a college student studying for a final examination says to her roommate, "I'm thirsty." First she perceives discomfort (felt need) that is recognized as thirst. This activated need leads to drive (arousal). A can of Diet Coke (her favorite beverage) from the machine down the hall is the incentive, and she behaves accordingly.

---

[1] For useful background on theories of motivation see David C. McClelland, *Personality* (New York: William Sloane, 1951), 474.

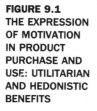

FIGURE 9.1
**THE EXPRESSION
OF MOTIVATION
IN PRODUCT
PURCHASE AND
USE: UTILITARIAN
AND HEDONISTIC
BENEFITS**

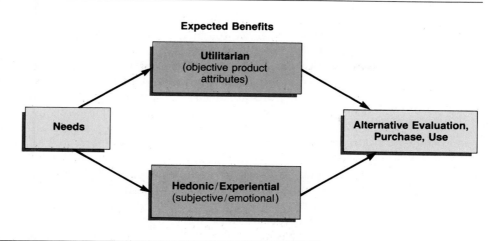

DYNAMICS OF THE MOTIVATION PROCESS

Felt need can be activated in different ways, one of which is entirely physiological, thirst or hunger being examples. The human being also possesses the capacity for thinking about a person or object not present at the immediate time or imagining the desirable consequences of a particular action. This thought process in itself can be arousing. All of us, for example, can feel hunger at times just by thinking about a favorite food. Finally, arousal can be triggered by outside information. You become hungry when your eye is stopped by a point-of-sale display announcing a special low price for Dove Bars.

Activated need ultimately becomes expressed in buying behavior and consumption in the form of two types of expected benefits illustrated in Figure 9.1–(1) **utilitarian benefits** and (2) **hedonic/experiential benefits.**[2]

Utilitarian benefits are objective, functional product attributes. Hedonic benefits, on the other hand, encompass emotional responses, sensory pleasures,

[2] See T. C. Srinivasan, "An Integrative Approach to Consumer Choice," in Melanie Wallendorf and Paul Anderson, eds., *Advances in Consumer Research* 14 (Provo, Utah: Association for Consumer Research, 1987), 96–101; William J. Havlena and Morris B. Holbrook, "The Varieties of Consumption Experience: Comparing Two Typologies of Emotion and Consumer Behavior," *Journal of Consumer Research* 13 (December 1986), 394–404; Roberto Friedman and V. Parker Lessig, "A Framework of Psychological Meaning of Products," in Richard J. Lutz, ed., *Advances in Consumer Research* 13 (Provo, Utah: Association for Consumer Research, 1986), 338–342; and Morris B. Holbrook and Elizabeth C. Hirschman, "The Experential Aspects of Consumption: Consumer Fantasies, Feelings, and Fun," *Journal of Consumer Research* 9 (September 1982), 132–140.

daydreams, and esthetic considerations.[3] The criteria used when considering hedonic benefits are subjective and *symbolic*, centering on appreciation of the product or service for its own sake apart from more objective considerations. Both types of benefits become expressed as *evaluative criteria* used in the process of weighing and selecting the best alternative (see Chapter 18).

It is common for utilitarian and hedonic benefits to function simultaneously in a purchase decision. For example, a potential buyer compares European luxury cars on such objective dimensions as headroom, rear seat room, acceleration, and automatic locking systems. These attributes are stressed in specific terms in advertising and personal selling.

Hedonic benefits, on the other hand, can include experiential considerations such as a sense of status and prestige derived from owning a top-of-line car and the sheer sense of pleasure in driving. Alternative evaluation now becomes more spontaneous and wholistic, focusing on overall symbolism, as opposed to specific features.[4] The concern now lies with the joy and experience of *consumption and use*. This often is best captured pictorially. Could words ever explain the emotions expressed in the "A diamond is forever" ad in Figure 9.2?

Our concern here is to broaden your horizons beyond those of the objective and utilitarian, which have dominated the consumer behavior research journals for more than a decade. The emotional and symbolic dimensions were in vogue during the so-called "motivation-research" era discussed in Chapter 2. These have tended unfortunately to become de-emphasized in the literature in favor of a more utilitarian information-processing perspective (see Chapter 13). We are merely stressing once again Copeland's balanced and influential 1924 perspective that consumers are motivated by both rational (utilitarian) and emotional (hedonic) considerations.[5]

THE UNITY AND STABILITY OF MOTIVE PATTERNS

One of the fundamental premises of human behavior is that people behave in a purposeful and consistent manner. This implies that motives are integrated in some way. Over the course of this century authorities agree that the **self-concept** provides this unification.[6]

The self-concept is an organized structure of perceptions of one's self,

---

[3] Elizabeth C. Hirschman and Morris B. Holbrook, "Hedonic Consumption: Emerging Methods and Propositions," *Journal of Marketing* 46 (Summer 1982), 92–101; and Holbrook and Hirschman, "The Experiential Aspects of Consumption."

[4] Srinivasan, "An Integrative Approach to Consumer Choice."

[5] Melvin Copeland, *Principles of Merchandising* (Chicago: A. W. Shaw, 1924), Chapters 6–7.

[6] See, for example, Lynn R. Kahle, "The Relationships Among Consumer Attitudes, Self-Concept, and Behaviors: A Social Adaptation Approach," in Jerry Olson and Keith Sentis, eds., *Advertising and Consumer Psychology* 3 (New York: Praeger, 1986), 121–131; and Keith Sentis and Hazel Markis, "Brand Personality and the Self," in Olson and Sentis, *Advertising and Consumer Psychology*, 132–148.

FIGURE 9.2
THE EXPRESSION OF HEDONIC BENEFITS IS OFTEN CAPTURED BEST IN A PHOTOGRAPH

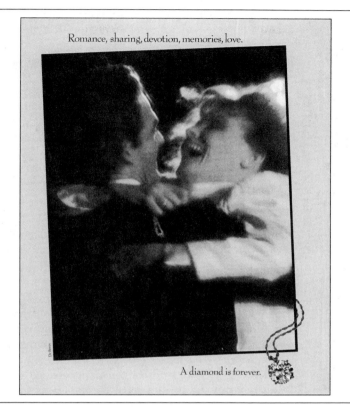

Romance, sharing, devotion, memories, love.

A diamond is forever.

and it becomes a part of active memory. It is comprised of perceptions of abilities and characteristics and perceptions of one's self in relationship to the external environment. A central motive is to enhance this view of one's self. As a result, it has a direct influence on values, ideas, goals, and objectives.[7]

It is generally agreed that consumers engage in buying behavior that is consistent and congruent with their self-image.[8] Often there is a perceived difference between *ideal* self and *actual* self. When this is the case, there can be strong and persistent motivation to reduce the discrepancy. There have been many published attempts to measure self-concept and relate it to aspects

[7] Carl R. Rogers, *Client-Centered Therapy* (Boston: Houghton-Mifflin, 1951), 492.
[8] For a thorough review of studies in the marketing literature, see J. Paul Peter, "Some Observations on Self-Concept in Consumer Behavior Research," in Jerry C. Olson, ed., *Advances in Consumer Research* 7 (Ann Arbor, Michigan: Association for Consumer Research, 1980), 615–616.

of buying behavior.[9] Most have confirmed that there usually is consistency between self-concept and behavior, but the actual correlations are relatively low.[10] Low correlations are a consequence of methodological difficulties in measuring self-concept and do not reflect that people commonly behave in ways contradictory to self.[11]

Of greater importance, however, has been a failure until recently to take account also of meanings attached to material possessions. As Tuan states, "Our fragile sense of self needs support, and this we get by having and possessing things because, to a large degree, we are what we have and possess."[12] In most societies possessions play the important role of helping us learn and define our sense of the past, who we are, and where we are going. This is referred to by Belk as the *extended self*.[13]

CAN NEEDS BE CREATED?

Here is a question that has been debated in marketing classrooms probably since the first course was taught in 1904 at the University of Michigan: *Can marketers create needs?* If so, some serious ethical questions are raised, and we must be very clear on this issue.

We contend that a purchase will never be made unless underlying needs (or motives) are activated and satisfied. Buying action, in turn, is not undertaken until an alternative is viewed positively in these terms. The need must already exist even though it may be dormant and largely unrecognized; *it is not created by the marketer*. It is true that marketing communication stimulates desire to buy a product or service to satisfy that need, but the need itself lies beyond the influence of the business firm.

As a broad generalization, we may conclude that a major role of marketing efforts is to position a product or service in the most favorable possible light in terms of potential to satisfy need. For example, many women no longer make homemade jam because of the effort required and the necessity of using large amounts of sugar to ensure the right jelling consistency. Now Sure-Jell presents the option of Sure-Jell Light (Figure 9.3), which assures perfect homemade jam with one third less sugar and no artificial sweeteners.

---

[9] M. Joseph Sirgy, "Self Concept in Consumer Behavior: A Critical Review," *Journal of Consumer Research* 9 (December 1982), 287–300; and Sak Onkvisit and John J. Shaw, "Image Congruence and Self Enhancement: A Critical Evaluation of the Self-Concept," in Robert F. Lusch, et al, eds., *1985 AMA Educators' Proceedings* (Chicago: American Marketing Association, 1985), 6.

[10] Sentis and Markus, "Brand Personality and Self." Also see Nancy Giges, "Buying Linked to Self-Esteem," *Advertising Age* (April 13, 1987), 68.

[11] See, for example, Hazel Markus, "Self-Knowledge: An Expanded View," *Journal of Personality* 51 (1983), 543–565.

[12] Yi-Fu Tuan, "The Significance of Artifact," *Geographical Review* 70 (1980), 472, as cited in Russell W. Belk, "Possessions and the Extended Self," *Journal of Consumer Research* 15 (September 1988), 139.

[13] Belk, "Possessions and the Extended Self."

FIGURE 9.3
NEED *ACTIVATION,*
NOT NEED
CREATION: **SURE-**
JELL MEETS REAL
NEEDS OF ITS
CONSUMERS

Source: Reprinted courtesy of General Foods Corporation.

This ad effectively tackles the obstacles and assures the buyer of success while reducing sugar as a significant way for meeting felt needs connected with nutrition and health.

INVOLVEMENT

You will recall from Chapter 2 that the concept of *involvement* is of major significance in understanding and explaining consumer behavior (also see Chapter 16). This term was first popularized in marketing circles by Krugman[14] in 1965 and has generated considerable interest since that time.[15]

---

[14] Herbert Krugman, "The Impact of Television Advertising: Learning Without Involvement," *Public Opinion Quarterly* 29 (Fall 1965), 349–356.

[15] See Joel B. Cohen, "Involvement and You: One Thousand Great Ideas," in Richard Bagozzi and Alice Tybout, eds., *Advances in Consumer Research* 9 (Ann Arbor, Michigan: Association for Consumer Research, 1983), 325–328; and David W. Finn, "Low-Involvement Isn't Low Involving," in Bagozzi and Tybout, *Advances,* 419–424.

Although it has been defined in many ways,[16] we like the following conceptualization put forward by Antil after careful consideration of multiple points of view: "Involvement is the level of perceived personal importance and/or interest evoked by a stimulus (or stimuli) within a specific situation."[17] To the extent that it is present, the consumer acts with deliberation to minimize risks and to maximize the benefits gained from purchase and use.

Involvement is best conceived as a function of *person, object,* and *situation.* The starting point always is with the person—underlying motivations in the form of needs and values, which, in turn, are a reflection of self-concept. Involvement is activated when the object (a product, service, or promotional message) is perceived as being instrumental in meeting important needs, goals, and values. But, as we will see, the perceived need-satisfying significance of the object will vary from one situation to the next. Therefore, all three factors (person, object, and situation) must be taken into account.

Involvement, then, is a reflection of strong motivation in the form of high perceived personal relevance of a product or service in a particular context.[18] Depending upon the perceived linkage between the individual's motivating influences and the benefits offered by the object, it is a continuum ranging from low to high.[19] It becomes activated as felt involvement when intrinsic personal characteristics (needs, values, self-concept) are confronted with appropriate marketing stimuli within a given situation.[20]

SOME ANTECEDENTS OF INVOLVEMENT

Research on the factors that generate high or low involvement is extensive.[21] Therefore, we will only highlight some main points here.

---

[16] See especially James A. Munch and Shelby D. Hunt, "Consumer Involvement: Definition Issues and Research Directions," in Thomas C. Kinnear, ed., *Advances in Consumer Research* 11 (Provo, Utah: Association for Consumer Research, 1984), 193–196; Michael L. Rothschild, "Perspectives on Involvement: Current Problems and Future Directions," in Kinnear, 216–217; Rajeev Batra and Michael L. Ray, "Operationalizing Involvement as Depth and Quality of Cognitive Response," in Bagozzi and Tybout, 309–313; Peter H. Bloch, "An Exploration into the Scaling of Consumers' Involvement with a Product Class," in Kent B. Monroe, ed., *Advances in Consumer Research,* 8 (Ann Arbor, Michigan: Association for Consumer Research, 1981), 61–65; Robert N. Stone, "The Marketing Characteristics of Involvement," in Kinnear, 210–215; and Richard Vaughn, "The Consumer Mind: How to Tailor Ad Strategies," *Advertising Age* (June 9, 1980), 45–46.

[17] John H. Antil, "Conceptualization and Operationalization of Involvement," in Kinnear, *Advances,* 204.

[18] Antil, "Conceptualization and Operationalization."

[19] Rothschild, "Perspectives on Involvement," and Rothschild, "Advertising Strategies."

[20] Richard L. Celsi and Jerry C. Olson, "The Role of Involvement in Attention and Comprehension Processes," *Journal of Consumer Research* 15 (September 1988), 210–224.

[21] See Giles Laurent and Jean-Noël Kapferer, "Measuring Consumer Involvement Profiles," *Journal of Marketing Research* 22 (February 1985), 41–53; and Judith L. Zaichkowsky, "Measuring the Involvement Construct," *Journal of Consumer Research* 12 (December 1985), 341–352.

PERSONAL FACTORS   Without activation of need and drive, there will be no involvement, and it is strongest when the product or service is perceived as enhancing self-image.[22] When that is the case, it is likely to be enduring, as opposed to situational or temporary.

Richins and Bloch have shown, for example, that some consumers are auto enthusiasts, who attend races and rallies and subscribe to car magazines.[23] Others use their car continually but demonstrate low involvement through indifference to cars in general, including their own (unless perhaps it starts to self-destruct prematurely).

PRODUCT FACTORS   Products are not involving in and of themselves. Rather, it is how consumers respond to products that will determine their level of involvement. Nonetheless, product characteristics can shape consumer involvement. In general, involvement is greater for products that fulfill important needs and values. In addition, involvement can increase as choice alternatives are seen as more differentiated in their offerings.[24]

Products or brands also become involving if there is some perceived risk in purchase and use. In 1960 the late Raymond Bauer advanced this important proposition: "Consumer behavior involves risk in the sense that any action of a consumer will produce consequences which he cannot anticipate with anything approximating certainty, and some of which are likely to be unpleasant."[25]

Many types of perceived risk have been identified, including physical (risk of bodily harm), psychological (especially a negative effect on self-image), performance (fear that the product will not perform as expected), and financial (risk that outcomes will lead to loss of earnings).[26]

As one would logically expect, the greater the perceived risk, the greater the likelihood of high involvement.[27] When perceived risk becomes unacceptably high, there is motivation either to avoid purchase and use altogether or to minimize risk through the search and alternative evaluation stages in extended problem solving.

[22] Meera P. Venkatraman, "Investigating Differences in the Roles of Enduring and Instrumentally Involved Consumers in the Diffusion Process," in Houston, *Advances*, 299–303.

[23] Marcia L. Richins and Peter H. Bloch, "After the New Wears Off: The Temporal Context of Product Involvement," *Journal of Consumer Research* 13 (September 1986), 280–285.

[24] Laurent and Kapferer, "Measuring Consumer Involvement Profiles."

[25] Raymond A. Bauer, "Consumer Behavior as Risk Taking," in *Dynamic Marketing for a Changing World* (Chicago: American Marketing Association, 1960), 389.

[26] See George Brooker, "An Assessment of an Expanded Measure of Perceived Risk," in Kinnear, *Advances*, 439–441; and John W. Vann, "A Multi-Distributional, Conceptual Framework for the Study of Perceived Risk," in Kinnear, *Advances*, 442–446.

[27] Michael L. Rothschild, "Advertising Strategies for High and Low Involvement Situations," in Maloney and Silverman, *Attitude Research*, 74–93.

Finally, the hedonic value of the product also is a determining factor—i.e., its emotional appeal and its perceived ability to provide pleasure quite apart from its objective benefits.[28] To the extent that these subjective considerations are important, involvement will increase.

SITUATIONAL FACTORS   Whereas enduring involvement can be considered as a stable trait, situational (or instrumental) involvement changes over time. It is operational on a temporary basis and wanes once purchasing outcomes are resolved.[29] This is often the case with fads such as trendy clothing items where involvement is high initially but quickly diminishes once the item is worn and fashions begin to change.

There also are times when an otherwise uninvolving product takes on a differing degree of relevance because of the manner in which it will be used.[30] For example, there can be a big difference between the perceived importance of a brand of hand soap purchased for home use as opposed to that given as a gift.

Finally, involvement also can increase when social pressures are felt.[31] Zaichkowsky demonstrated, for example, that consumers react quite differently when they purchase wine for ordinary personal consumption as opposed to that which will be served at a dinner party.[32]

THE FORMS OF INVOLVEMENT AND THE OUTCOMES

Figure 9.4 shows the forms that involvement can take and the way it becomes expressed in consumer behavior. Notice, first of all, that consumers are motivated to search for relevant information and to process it more thoroughly when involvement is high (see Chapter 13).[33] Also, they are more likely to be influenced by strength of argumentation as opposed to the way in which the appeal is expressed and visualized (see Chapter 15). This is represented in Figure 9.4 as message involvement.

Consumers also can become involved with the product (or brand). They are more likely to notice differences in the attributes offered by various products or brands, and a common outcome is greater loyalty when preference is grounded on high felt involvement.

---

[28] Laurent and Kapferer, "Measuring Consumer Involvement Profiles."

[29] Ibid.

[30] Russell W. Belk, "Effects of Gift-Giving Involvement on Gift Selection Strategies," in Andrew Mitchell, ed., *Advances in Consumer Research* 9 (Ann Arbor, Michigan: Association for Consumer Research, 1981), 408–411.

[31] Houston and Rothschild, "Conceptual and Methodological Perspectives."

[32] Zaichkowsky, "Measuring the Involvement Construct."

[33] J. Craig Andrews, "Motivation, Ability, and Opportunity to Process Information: Conceptual and Experimental Manipulation Issues," in Michael J. Houston, ed., *Advances in Consumer Research* 15 (Provo, Utah: Association for Consumer Research, 1988), 219–225; and Richard E. Petty, John T. Cacioppo, and David Schumann, "Central and Peripheral Routes to Advertising Effectiveness: The Moderating Role of Involvement," *Journal of Consumer Research* 10 (September 1983), 135–144.

FIGURE 9.4
A CONCEPTUAL-IZATION OF THE INVOLVEMENT CONCEPT AS EXPRESSED IN CONSUMER BEHAVIOR

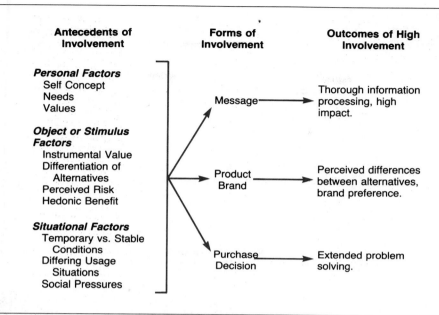

Antecedents of Involvement	Forms of Involvement	Outcomes of High Involvement
Personal Factors Self Concept Needs Values	Message	Thorough information processing, high impact.
Object or Stimulus Factors Instrumental Value Differentiation of Alternatives Perceived Risk Hedonic Benefit	Product Brand	Perceived differences between alternatives, brand preference.
Situational Factors Temporary vs. Stable Conditions Differing Usage Situations Social Pressures	Purchase Decision	Extended problem solving.

Source: Adapted from Judith L. Zaichkowsky, "Conceptualizing Involvement," *Journal of Advertising* 15 (1986), p. 6.

Finally, there is a greater likelihood of extended problem solving when involvement is high, whereas low involvement leads to the more simplified choice tactics of limited problem solving.[34] This is expressed in the amount of effort expended in search for information and alternative evaluation.

MEASURING INVOLVEMENT

Largely because of definitional disagreement,[35] many ways have been proposed to measure involvement. Ideally, any measurement should encompass the richness of the three categories of antecedents summarized in Figure 9.4. Laurent and Kapferer have come the closest to doing so.[36] Interestingly, their scale was first designed for use in France, and it measured these dimensions (notice that they have used different wording and categorization):

1. Importance of negative consequences—scale items evaluated both product importance and perceived risk of negative consequences.
2. Subjective probability of a mispurchase—the risk of making a bad choice.

[34] Wayne D. Hoyer, "Variations in Choice Strategies Across Decision Contexts: An Examination of Contingent Factors," in Lutz, *Advances,* 32–36.
[35] For a good critique, see Carolyn L. Costley, "Meta Analysis of Involvement Research," in Houston, *Advances,* 554–562.
[36] Laurent and Kapferer, "Measuring Consumer Involvement Profiles."

TABLE 9.1 INVOLVEMENT PROFILES OF 14 CONSUMER PRODUCTS		Importance of Negative Consequences	Subjective Probability of Mispurchase	Pleasure Value	Sign Value
	Dresses	121	112	147	181
	Bras	117	115	106	130
	Washing machines	118	109	106	111
	TV sets	112	100	122	95
	Vacuum cleaners	110	112	70	78
	Irons	103	95	72	76
	Champagne	109	120	125	125
	Oil	89	97	65	92
	Yogurt	86	83	106	78
	Chocolate	80	89	123	75
	Shampoo	96	103	90	81
	Toothpaste	95	95	94	105
	Facial soap	82	90	114	118
	Detergents	79	82	56	63

Source: Giles Laurent and Jean-Noël Kapferer, "Measuring Consumer Involvement Profiles," *Journal of Marketing Research* 22 (February 1985), 45. Used with special permission.

3. Pleasure value—the hedonic value of purchase and use.

4. Sign value—the extent to which purchase and use makes a psycho/social statement about the person.

Table 9.1 shows you how 14 different products ranked on these four dimensions. As you would expect, dresses and bras rate at the top on all four dimensions, whereas detergents are quite low. The importance of using four dimensions is clearly demonstrated with vacuum cleaners and facial soap. The vacuum cleaner is not evaluated as having high pleasure or sign value; yet the perceived risk of purchase is high. Hence, there is relatively high involvement, whereas we see an exactly opposite situation with facial soap. Few had high concerns on product performance or risk, but pleasure and sign value were much higher.

Zaichkowsky also has designed a useful Involvement Inventory (Figure 9.5).[37] You might try this Inventory yourself across a variety of products. Notice that her scale items mostly measure the product importance dimension. Follow the scoring directions at the bottom—the higher the score the greater the involvement. A maximum possible score is 140. Zaichkowsky found a mean score of 89.55 across 15 categories, with automobiles and calculators emerging as most involving and instant coffee, bubble bath, and breakfast cereals as least.

---

[37] Zaichkowsky, "Measuring the Involvement Construct."

**FIGURE 9.5
THE PERSONAL
INVOLVEMENT
INVENTORY**

(insert name of object to be judged)

important __: __: __: __: __: __: __	unimportant*
of no concern __: __: __: __: __: __: __	of concern to me
irrelevant __: __: __: __: __: __: __	relevant
means a lot to me __: __: __: __: __: __: __	means nothing to me*
useless __: __: __: __: __: __: __	useful
valuable __: __: __: __: __: __: __	worthless*
trivial __: __: __: __: __: __: __	fundamental
beneficial __: __: __: __: __: __: __	not beneficial*
matters to me __: __: __: __: __: __: __	doesn't matter*
uninterested __: __: __: __: __: __: __	interested
significant __: __: __: __: __: __: __	insignificant*
vital __: __: __: __: __: __: __	superfluous*
boring __: __: __: __: __: __: __	interesting
unexciting __: __: __: __: __: __: __	exciting
appealing __: __: __: __: __: __: __	unappealing*
mundane __: __: __: __: __: __: __	fascinating
essential __: __: __: __: __: __: __	nonessential*
undesirable __: __: __: __: __: __: __	desirable
wanted __: __: __: __: __: __: __	unwanted*
not needed __: __: __: __: __: __: __	needed

* Indicates item is reverse scored.

Items on the left are scored (1) low involvement to (7) high involvement on the right. Totaling the 20 items gives a score from a low of 20 to a high of 140.

Source: Judith L. Zaichkowsky, "Measuring the Involvement Construct," *Journal of Consumer Research* 12 (December 1985), 350. Used by special permission.

Appealing to Consumer Needs

Need (or motive) is a variable of central importance to those whose goal is to influence consumer behavior. If needs can be measured and understood, it is possible to position marketing efforts more effectively in the context of consumer goals.

THE CHALLENGE OF MEASUREMENT

Several methodological approaches to measurement are possible, including standardized research inventories, scaled AIO (Activity, Interest, and Opinion) questions, motivation-research methods, and focus groups.

STANDARDIZED RESEARCH INVENTORIES   Needs can be measured by standardized research inventories used in clinical counseling and psychotherapy.[38] This methodology found its way into marketing in the motivation-research era discussed subsequently, but experience soon demonstrated that tools designed for individualized diagnosis (an example being the Rorschach inkblot test) are not applicable in large-sample marketing research. Responses are subjective and require additional background and insight to interpret properly. This can be done only in a therapeutic session over time.

SCALED AIO QUESTIONS   Another approach is to use a series of scaled agree–disagree questions covering varying areas of possible motivation and interest. Often these are referred to as AIO questions (see Chapter 12). Basic needs are often uncovered by searching for a common pattern of interest across various questions. This approach was used in a study of American college students, and here are three concerns that proved to be strongly correlated, in the sense that all three were mentioned by many people:[39]

How to overcome performance stress here on the campus

How to get better grades

How to be free from financial worries when I graduate

The common denominator here is a fear of future financial insecurity, which is expressed by strong motivation to get better grades (mentioned as being of major importance by over half of the students). It was found that over 10 percent of students responded positively to direct marketing appeals for a book offering help in getting better grades—an unusually high direct-marketing response.

MOTIVATION-RESEARCH METHODS   Chapter 2 introduced you to an interesting era in marketing history—the motivation-research era. As we noted earlier in this chapter, much use was made of research methods designed initially for individualized diagnosis of needs and personality disorders. One of the most commonly borrowed methods was the so-called **depth interview.** Only a small sample is interviewed (50 or less) one at a time in a lengthy, unstructured session. Attempts are made to probe below the surface to uncover the wealth of possible motivating influences.

As you may recall from Chapter 2, some early advocates contended that the depth interview enables researchers to plumb all levels of consciousness and even the unconscious, thus moving beyond the scope of conventional marketing research methods. Advocates allege that the marketer has much

---

[38] See, for example, David C. McClelland, "Methods of Measuring Human Motivation," in John W. Atkinson, ed., *Motives in Fantasy, Action and Society* (Princeton, New Jersey: Van Nostrand, 1958), 7–42; C. N. Cofer and M. H. Appley, *Motivation Theory and Research* (New York: Wiley, 1964); and Albert Mehrabian and James Russell, *An Approach to Environmental Psychology* (Cambridge, Massachusetts: MIT Press, 1974).

[39] Unpublished survey undertaken by Management Development Associates, Wheaton, Illinois, 1987.

to gain by appealing to motivating influences that cannot be consciously expressed. We still hear this claim, and here is an example.

A clinically trained researcher contended that people in one European country disdain consumption of fluid milk because of unfavorable childhood imagery. The proposed solution, supposedly based on depth interviews, was to associate milk with motherhood. This was accomplished by naturelike packaging and advertising imagery, complete with rolling hills, suggesting a most obvious part of the female anatomy as viewed at the time of birth. Plausible? Well, sales *did* increase. Perhaps a more logical explanation is that greatly increased advertising enhanced name recognition.

Few today would contend that depth interviewing has such magic qualities. After all, how much can be learned in a 1-hour interview? But the use of unstructured, probing questions has survived to this day and is a helpful tool in the research arsenal.

The motivation researcher also made use of **projective tests**—questioning techniques that allowed the respondent to reply in third person. An example is, "What would your next-door neighbors think if someone down the street suddenly showed up with a new Yugo?" Or the question could be asked in pictorial form. An example appears in Figure 9.6.

**FIGURE 9.6
A PICTORIAL
PROJECTIVE
QUESTION ALLOWS
RESPONSES IN THE
THIRD PERSON**

The theory of projective testing is that third-person reply would overcome reluctance to give a true response to a first-person direct question (i.e., What do *you* think?). Although there is proven validity in clinical counseling uses, Engel and others found that this type of projective test produces exactly the same pattern of responses as direct questioning.[40] When projective questions are used today, they are viewed far more as an interesting methodological variant than as a way to "probe the depths of the psyche."

FOCUS GROUPS   Other times, people are asked to discuss their motivations and behavior in small groups referred to as **focus groups.** Groups of about ten people are brought together for a session that usually does not exceed 1 hour in length. The interviewer, a skilled discussion leader, lets conversation flow naturally but guides it in such a way that pertinent issues are covered. The group setting provides a relaxed atmosphere, and the thoughts of one person stimulate those of others. Participants soon find themselves talking freely about their concerns. The outcome is often a richer yield of information that cannot be gathered through structured questionnaires.

CLASSIFICATION OF NEEDS

For more than 60 years, psychologists and marketers alike have tried their hand at classifying needs. Some of their lists are quite lengthy and exhibit creative ingenuity. It is still common today to find detailed enumeration of needs as classified by Murray in 1938,[41] Maslow,[42] McClelland,[43] Cofer and Appley,[44] McGuire,[45] and others.

Unfortunately, such lists, especially from an earlier period, often reflected opinion more than empirical analysis. More recently, the literature has concentrated on specific needs that can be isolated and explained empirically. Hence we find such needs as variety seeking.

Rather than succumb to the usual textbook tendency of walking through endless lists, we have found it more useful to classify needs into the broad underlying categories which are most helpful in understanding consumer behavior. These appear in Table 9.2, and each is then discussed in more detail. It should be noted that we have not attempted to make this classification exhaustive.

It is helpful before proceeding further to refer to the concept of **prepotency,** most often attributed to the late Abraham H. Maslow.[46] He hypothesized

---

[40] James F. Engel and Hugh G. Wales, "Spoken Versus Picture Questions on Taboo Topics," *Journal of Advertising Research* 2 (March 1962), 11–17.
[41] A. H. Murray, *Explorations in Personality* (New York: Oxford University Press, 1938).
[42] Abraham H. Maslow, *Motivation and Personality,* 2nd ed. (New York: Harper & Row, 1970).
[43] McClelland, *Personality.*
[44] Cofer and Appley, *Motivation Theory.*
[45] William J. McGuire, "Psychological Motives and Communication Gratification," in J. G. Blumer and C. Katz, eds., *The Uses of Mass Communications: Current Perspectives on Gratification Research* (New York: Sage, 1974), 167–196.
[46] Maslow, *Motivation and Personality.*

TABLE 9.2 A SUMMARY CLASSIFICATION OF CONSUMER NEEDS	1. *Physiological:* the fundamentals of survival, including hunger, thirst, and other bodily needs. 2. *Safety:* concern over physical survival and safety. 3. *Affiliation and Belongingness:* a need to be accepted by others, to be an important person to them. 4. *Achievement:* a basic desire for success in meeting personal goals. 5. *Power:* a desire to gain control over one's destiny as well as that of others. 6. *Self-expression:* the need to develop freedom in self-expression and to be perceived by others as significant. 7. *Order and Understanding:* the desire to achieve self-actualization through knowing, understanding, systematizing, and constructing a system of values. 8. *Variety Seeking:* maintenance of a preferred level of physiological arousal and stimulation often expressed as variety seeking. 9. *Attribution of Causality:* estimation or attribution of the causality of events and actions.

that needs are organized in such a way as to establish priorities and hierarchies of importance. According to his theory, there are five levels of needs ranging in priority from lowest order to highest order. These fall into three basic categories: (1) survival and safety; (2) human interaction, love, and affiliation; and (3) self-actualization (competency, self-expression, and understanding). Each higher-order need, according to Maslow, is largely dormant until lower-level needs are satisfied.

A distinguished pioneer in consumer research, George Katona, showed that prepotency does affect consumer behavior to the extent that previously ignored desires exert themselves most frequently after purchases have satisfied a predominant (and perhaps lower-order) need.[47] This can help explain why an older, successful business or professional person in his or her 50s can move away from status as a dominant motive into a more leisurely pursuit of art and music.[48]

Few researchers today would accept that lower-order needs somehow cease functioning once there is a satisfactory level of fulfillment in the sense that Maslow implied. Furthermore, actions can be impelled by a combination of needs across the hierarchy. Therefore, prepotency is accepted more as a helpful general principle than a determining rule of behavior.

APPEALING TO CONSUMER NEEDS

PHYSIOLOGICAL NEEDS   We accept Maslow's contention that physiological needs usually will be satisfied before others, especially if survival is at stake. These needs often dominate and receive priority in information processing. Have you ever noticed how differently you react in a grocery store when you are hungry? In fact, retailers gain by attracting shoppers in and around mealtimes.

---

[47] George Katona, *The Powerful Consumer* (New York: McGraw-Hill, 1962), 132.
[48] George Booker, "The Self-Actualizing Socially Conscious Consumer," *Journal of Consumer Research* 3 (September 1976), 107–112.

FIGURE 9.7
APPEALING TO A
SAFETY MOTIVE:
CONSUMERS ARE
INCREASINGLY
CONCERNED WITH
NUTRITION

SAFETY NEEDS   Caution is sometimes thrown to the wind when survival is the issue. After some degree of need satisfaction, safety can become a priority issue. Who, for example, counts calories when they have not had enough food for some period of time? An abundance of high-caloric food, on the other hand, is now a proven cause of heart disease and other ailments. Hence the "Health Nut" theme of the California avocado ad in Figure 9.7 now stands a much better chance of triggering action than in an earlier era.

AFFILIATION AND BELONGINGNESS   Little need be said about the importance of love and acceptance. Indeed, these needs seldom are fully satisfied. Once a society moves past a focus solely on physical survival, priorities quickly

9.1   GETTING AN EDGE ON LIFE: THE U.S. ARMY

Since the end of the Vietnam War and the draft, the United States Army has faced the challenge of recruiting sufficient numbers to staff an all-volunteer army. In the mid-1970s, in particular, military service was rarely seen as an attractive option in a decidedly antimilitary environment. Was there any way to convince young men and women to consider the army in spite of these negative factors?

Extensive marketing research led to positioning of Army service as a natural, beneficial step for many between high school and adulthood—not just something done in wartime. The goal was to show the Army as something one does as part of life, to test oneself, to grow mentally and in other ways, and to present a way to serve one's country while serving one's self. Hence the theme, "Today's Army Wants to Join You." Aided by the 1974 recession, the numbers of recruits jumped.

The strategy of the 1970s gave way to an all new theme ten years later reflecting the change in motivation of potential recruits. Now the appeal became "Army. Be All That You Can Be." Here was an opportunity to gain specialized training and grow in life-relevant professional skills.

A departure from the "Be All You Can Be" theme began in mid-1987 with a TV spot called "Sentry" which premiered on a July 4 ABC-TV special, "A Star-Spangled Celebration." The campaign goal was to attract new recruits as the pool of 18-year-olds begins hitting new post–World War II lows into the 1990s. The Army wants to lure those who would not ordinarily consider enlisting, such as people who have attended college.

"Sentry" touts the Army's traditional, benefits-oriented theme of dollars for college, skill training, and experience.

The spot opens with "Germany 1987" on the screen, then cuts to a shot of a soldier walking from a vehicle to a checkpoint at a mock-up of the Berlin Wall.

The soldier's voice narrates the spot, as if he were talking to himself. Several bold-type messages flash on the screen, interrupting the video with split-second shots of the words "Maturity," "Self-discipline," "Character," "Freedom" and "America."

The overall theme? "GET AN EDGE ON LIFE."

Source: Adapted from "The United States Army Recruiting Program," in Roger D. Blackwell, James F. Engel, and W. Wayne Talarzyk, *Contemporary Cases in Consumer Behavior* (Hinsdale, Illinois: Dryden Press, 1984) 53–60; and William F. Gloede, "Army Expands Its Sights," *Advertising Age* (July 6, 1987), 7.

shift in this direction. A perusal of advertising themes in such popular Western magazines as *Vogue, Mademoiselle,* and *Elle* will quickly show that sexual attraction, belongingness, and love are dominant themes.

ACHIEVEMENT   What motivates a young person to join the U.S. Army? This was the question leading to extensive research followed by a series of successful advertising campaigns. Read *Consumer in Focus 9.1.*

HERE'S TO OVER-ACHIEVEMENT!

The ultimate recognition from your banker. A gold MasterCard card.

The achievement motive has been researched extensively by McClelland and found to be far-reaching in its impact.[49] Certainly it has been capitalized upon effectively over the years by the U.S. Army.

Achievement, of course, is a basic and universal motivation, although it is expressed in varying ways from one culture to the next. It is evident that products and services providing ways to fulfill life goals stand an excellent chance of success. A good example appears in Figure 9.8.

POWER   Power as a motive stimulates some people to seek solutions to problems, to favor alternatives offering promise of real impact in gaining control. One can be motivated by achievement but be acquiesent on this dimension.

---

[49] David C. McClelland, "Achievement and Entrepreneurship: A Longitudinal Study," *Journal of Personality and Social Psychology* 1 (April 1965), 389–392.

FIGURE 9.9
SELF-EXPRESSION
IS A MOTIVE FOR
BUYING "GOURMET"
COFFEES

Not many years ago, a manufacturer introduced a lawnmower with a muffler that really worked. There was only minimal noise as the mower did its job. What do you think happened? It was later withdrawn from the market and the standard noisy motor reinstated. The reason was that many potential buyers ignored it on the belief that a quiet mower cannot possibly do the job. Noise was associated with power and potency in problem solution.

Continuing with a lawn care example, one of the greatest frustrations is a mower that will not start. Here the power-motivated person is defeated by an inanimate object. Therefore, Toro now guarantees a start each time. Not only is power gained in that manner, but ads show a dad achieving victory over his reluctant son, who now has no choice but to mow the lawn.

SELF-EXPRESSION   A common consumer motive is the need to express uniqueness—to make a statement to oneself and the world that "I am a person of significance." Notice the ad for Maxwell House Private Collection Coffees in Figure 9.9. The theme is, "A variety of coffees for when you're feeling confident, indulgent, calm, civilized—or not." The coffee, in short, "helps

9.2 MAXWELL HOUSE SERVES UP A YUPPIE BREW

Several years ago, executives at the Maxwell House Div. of General Foods Corp. discovered a serious image problem. Cigarette smokers, nervous types, and older people were coffee drinkers. Active, sexy, fun-loving folks preferred other beverages.

That's hardly a pleasing customer profile, and the nation's largest coffee roaster is working hard to change it. Through livelier ads and new products, Maxwell House is aggressively wooing younger customers. Its strategy: Move upscale. Under the Maxwell House Private Collection label, the company now sells whole beans and premium ground coffees in selected supermarkets. Because Private Collection is expensive, Maxwell House isn't selling it everywhere. The brand is available in only one-tenth of the nation's 36,000 supermarkets, stores that cater to young, affluent consumers.

"A lot of us around here thought a gourmet product with Maxwell House on it would not fly," says Mary B. Seggerman, category manager for Maxwell House. But consumer polls proved otherwise.

Private Collection is being advertised through magazines such as *Bon Appetit* and direct mail. The ad and promotion budget is $20 million. The ads show people using the product while they're relaxing. "Premium products are partly emotional. So the concept of the ads is "private coffee for private moods," says Stephen B. Morris, president of Maxwell House.

Source: Amy Dunkin, "Maxwell House Serves Up a YUPPIE Brew," *Business Week* (March 2, 1987), 62.

you to be you." As *Consumer in Focus 9.2* shows, this theme was not arrived at by accident.

ORDER AND UNDERSTANDING   If one accepts the concept of prepotency as put forth by Maslow, **self-actualization** is the highest-order motive. This encompasses the desire to know, understand, systematize, prioritize, and construct a system of values. Therefore, those whose lower-order motives have been largely met will often turn to music, literature, the arts, travel, and other means to help fulfill this striving.

VARIETY SEEKING   Consumers often will express satisfaction with their present brand of such items as potato chips or toothpaste but still engage in brand switching. Why does this take place? There are several plausible explanations, all of which postulate that variety seeking is a fairly common consumer motive.[50] It is seen most often when there are many similar alternatives,

---

[50] For a review of the literature see Leigh McAlister and Edgar E. Pessemier, "Variety Seeking Behavior: An Interdisciplinary Review," *Journal of Consumer Research* 9 (December 1982), 311–322.

low involvement, and high purchase frequency.[51] Variety seeking often leads to innovativeness and active information seeking.[52]

A number of years ago Venkatesan argued in a pioneering paper that boredom is often the root cause of variety seeking.[53] In later years it became apparent that the theory of optimal stimulation provides a better explanation.[54] This theory assumes that everyone needs a certain degree of stimulation. When the expected or optimum stimulation level is not reached, then exploratory behavior is triggered.

Further light has been shed by Mehrabian and Russell, who have identified some people described as **sensation seekers.**[55] They are motivated by continued high-level stimulation and disdain anything that suggests boredom. Hence, we see the popularity of new and trendy restaurants offering exotic food and drink and highly stimulating lighting and music. Sensation seekers tend to be the first to adopt the new and the "trendy."

There is good reason to hypothesize that both boredom and sensation seeking are plausible explanations for brand shifting undertaken without any dissatisfaction with existing choices and preferences.[56] A growing body of research shows that using one brand repeatedly can create a satiation effect and decreases its utility.

When stimulation levels get too high, however, quite the opposite occurs. A television commercial shows a harried baseball umpire reaching the end of his tolerance. Then the music—"I need a vacation"—and we see him comfortably on his way 35,000 feet above sea level, saying "I'm out of there." This is a potent way to cope with overstimulation. Many such options are available for the popularly expressed malady of "burnout."

Pessimier and Handelsman have suggested some additional marketing implications based on variety-seeking research to date:

1. Brand loyalty will be attained only among a modest proportion of buyers. Therefore, brand loyalty is not always an attainable marketing objective.

2. Multiple product and brand offerings are preferable in view of variety-motivated brand switching, as compared with a single brand strategy.

---

[51] Wayne D. Hoyer and Nancy M. Ridgway, "Variety Seeking as an Explanation for Exploratory Purchase Behavior: A Theoretical Model," in Kinnear, *Advances,* 114–119.

[52] Erich A. Joachimsthaler and John L. Lastovicka, "Optimal Stimulation Level—Exploratory Behavior Models," in *Journal of Consumer Research* 11 (December 1984), 830–835; and Linda L. Price and Nancy M. Ridgway, "Development of a Scale to Measure Use Innovativeness," in Bagozzi and Tybout, *Advances,* 679–684.

[53] M. Venkatesan, "Cognitive Consistency and Novelty Seeking," in Scott Ward and Thomas S. Robertson, eds., *Consumer Behavior: Theoretical Sources* (Englewood Cliffs, New Jersey: Prentice-Hall, 1973), 354–384.

[54] Pessemier and Handelsman, "Temporal Variety"; Joachimsthaler and Lastovicka, "Optimal Stimulation Level."

[55] Mehrabian and Russell, *Environmental Psychology.*

[56] Hoyer and Ridgway, "Variety Seeking."

3. Manufacturers and distributions should adopt a regular cycle on which products are replaced to satisfy needs for variety and stimulation.[57]

ATTRIBUTION OF CAUSALITY   A consumer has recently bought an expensive, top-of-the-line television set featuring new high-resolution picture technology. Within 2 weeks after purchase, it no longer is possible to receive sound with the picture. All of us will ask, "Why did this happen?" as we try to bring order into our world. Did I do something wrong? Is this set a lemon? Has something gone wrong with the antenna system? In other words, we try to attribute causes to events.

Various theories have been proposed attempting to explain this process, which fall under the broad category of **attribution theory.**[58] According to this theory, there is motivation to ascertain whether the causal influence is *internal* to the object or something *external*. In this situation, it is not unreasonable to assume that this particular set is a lemon (an internal attribution). The other two possible causes represent external attributions in that the fault is not inherent within the product itself.

You will find frequent reference to attribution theory throughout this book. It often gives clues needed to understand aspects of both motivation and behavior.

SOME ADDITIONAL CLUES FOR MARKETING STRATEGY

Our central objective has been to establish and reinforce the principle that marketers must accept needs as given. They are not likely to be created or modified by any type of marketing effort. Therefore, the goal always is to position a product or service within a target market as a valid and useful alternative for need satisfaction. This, of course, is the cardinal tenet of consumer sovereignty. There are several additional ways, however, to sharpen marketing impact.

INTERPRET RESEARCH WITH CAUTION   People have a tendency to give socially acceptable answers to questions probing their motivations. Where possible, make every attempt to determine whether or not actions match the words. Here is a benefit of using projective techniques. As we have already stated, focus groups also can be useful in this context. Consumers often have a tendency to be more open when they sense that others are being candid. Analysis of response patterns thus allows a researcher to infer the true state of affairs. Unless this can be done, there always is the possibility of being misled by surface answers.

BE ALERT TO THE POSSIBILITY OF MOTIVATIONAL CONFLICT   It is common for several motives to function in a given situation. Kurt Lewin put forth

---

[57] Pessemier and Handelsman, "Temporal Variety," 442.

[58] For a useful introduction to attribution theory, see Richard Mizerski, Linda Golden, and Jerome Kernan, "The Attribution Process in Consumer Behavior," *Journal of Consumer Research* 6 (September 1979), 123–140.

FIGURE 9.10
A WAY TO HELP OVERCOME APPROACH-AVOIDANCE CONFLICT IS WITH GOOD SERVICE AND MONEY-BACK GUARANTEES

Source: © Lands' End, Inc. Reprinted courtesy of Lands' End Catalog.

the theory that some forces produce movement toward a goal object (he refers to this as **approach**), whereas others bring about **avoidance.**[59] Hence conflicts can occur, especially when involvement is high, and a skillful marketer often can anticipate and overcome them.

Here is an example. A female executive is attracted to a previously unknown brand of leisure clothing advertised in a catalog received through direct mail. While she is very interested in purchasing several items (*approach*), she is fearful about sizes and quality (*avoidance*). Her action will be dictated by a trade-off between these two forces, and one outcome may be no purchase. This conflict could easily be anticipated and diminished by a personalized service backed by a money-back guarantee. Notice how Lands' End has made use of this strategy (Figure 9.10).

---

[59] Kurt Lewin, *A Dynamic Theory of Personality* (New York: McGraw-Hill, 1935).

THE MERCEDES-BENZ 190 CLASS: THE SUBTLE DIFFERENCE BETWEEN MASTERING THE ROAD AND MERELY COPING WITH IT.

The road passes beneath you as always, but the sensations are markedly different. So is your state of mind. This is your first experience with a 190 Class sedan, but already you are driving with calm confidence. The car has earned your trust.

It feels resolutely stable, going precisely where you steer it, refusing to waver off course or wallow over potholes. Even the severest bumps seem only a minor disturbance as the suspension gently quells the violence underneath. Negotiating a run of switchback turns seems more routine business than high drama as the car shifts direction nimbly in response to your steering commands. Sports sedans might occasionally handle this adroitly, but they seldom feel this composed.

Suddenly the pavement deteriorates into washboard gravel, but the car tracks steadfastly ahead, curiously unfazed by the change in terrain. It occurs to you that you have yet to hear a squeak or rattle. The engine remains almost subliminally quiet, wind noise a faint whisper when you hear it at all. You normally feel an urge to stretch your legs after sitting for so long, but now you feel the urge to keep driving.

Even if you chose the automatic transmission, you still find it easy to shift manual-style when the mood strikes, locating each gear by feel without glancing downward. Your driving has become pleasurably instinctive, as driving at its best should be.

This ostensibly mystical exaltation of the driving experience springs from such technological advances as "the most sophisticated steel suspension ever put into volume production" (Britain's *Car* Magazine). And the simple fact that a 190 Class sedan is built like every Mercedes-Benz—not one ergonomic or safety principle sacrificed for the sake of cosmetic luxury or digital showmanship. Every detail of construction and assembly meeting universally envied standards.

The result is a sedan that does not "challenge" you in the macho sports-sedan tradition, but rather serves as a congenial and supremely capable ally—at once exciting and obedient, responsive and considerate. The road provides challenge enough.

Engineered like no other car in the world

BE PREPARED TO PROVIDE SOCIALLY ACCEPTABLE REASONS FOR CHOICE The most important buying motive may be one which for varying reasons the consumer does not want to consciously acknowledge. When that is the case, it can be wise to give a set of reasons that are more acceptable. The consumer thus is allowed to attribute a greater degree of objectivity or rationality to the choice.

Do you feel that the mechanical and technical details mentioned in the Mercedes-Benz 190 Class ad in Figure 9.11 are of central importance for all who buy a luxury car? Certainly there are some who base their actions, knowingly or unknowingly, more on the statement made to the world by Mercedes ownership about the driver and his or her lifestyle.

EXERCISE CAUTION WHEN MARKETING CROSS-CULTURALLY   In a general sense needs are universal, but priorities and means of expression and satisfaction can vary sharply. In many parts of Africa, for example, overly conspicuous consumption is frowned upon. While this may change as the middle class and affluence grow, less conspicuous means of satisfaction can be more appropriate. We discuss this issue in much more detail in Chapter 24.

Summary

This chapter examines, albeit briefly, the complex subject of involvement and motivation. Our purpose has been to identify the ways in which consumer behavior is activated, energized, and directed.

Need is a central variable in motivation. We defined need as a perceived difference between an ideal state and the present state, sufficient to activate behavior. When need is activated, it gives rise to drive (energized behavior), which is channeled toward certain goals that have been learned as incentives.

Involvement (perceived relevance or pertinence) is an important factor in understanding motivation. Involvement refers to the degree of perceived relevance in the act of purchase and consumption. When it is high, there is motivation to acquire and process information and a much greater likelihood of extended problem solving.

There are two types of involvement: (1) enduring (existing over time because of self-concept enhancement) and (2) situational (temporary involvement stimulated by perceived risk, conformity pressures, or other considerations).

Classification of needs is always a challenge, and we utilized eight summary categories without an attempt to be fully exhaustive (see Table 9.2).

1. Physiological—fundamental bodily needs.
2. Safety—concerns over survival.
3. Affiliation and belongingness—love and acceptance by others.
4. Achievement—desire for success in goal attainment.
5. Power—gaining control over one's destiny as well as that of others.
6. Self-expression—freedom in expressing one's uniqueness.
7. Order and understanding—the desire to know and understand.
8. Variety seeking—exploratory behavior undertaken to maintain a desired state of arousal.
9. Attribution of causality—estimation or attribution of the causality of events or actions.

The most important strategy is to accept these motivations as given and find ways to present a product or service as a valid means of motive satisfaction. Many examples were given of how to identify needs through research and then capitalize upon them through skillful use of the marketing mix.

REVIEW AND DISCUSSION QUESTIONS

1. Can needs be changed by marketing efforts? Why or why not?

2. Differentiate between utilitarian and hedonic benefits. How might these be expressed in purchase and use of a compact disc player? An electric can opener? Expensive perfume?

3. For which of these product categories would you expect high involvement for most buyers? A moped? Dry dog food? Lawn care products? A home computer? Dishwashing detergent? What reasons can you give?

4. What is meant by the concept of prepotency? Contrast the economies of West Germany and Haiti. What differences would you expect in priorities within the need hierarchy?

5. Self-concept is said to be the source of motive integration and prioritizing. What is the self-concept? What is meant by the principle of congruence?

6. Would it be helpful for the marketing manager of a new line of detergents to have some insight into the self-concept of the average consumer, assuming this were possible through research?

7. Do you think there are intergenerational differences in the Western world in terms of sensation seeking? In other words, is this more a characteristic of the under-30 generation?

8. Using variety seeking as a need, to what extent do you think it influences the following types of buying behavior: soft drinks, lawn care products, eye makeup, motor oil, wine, choice of restaurant, and ballpoint pens?

9. Based on your own experience, would you agree that categories of needs are the same everywhere in the world? If so, how do you explain the widespread differences in buying behavior?

10. A survey was taken on college campuses throughout Scandanavia asking for beer brand preferences. When asked for the reasons, the most common answers were "flavor" and "price." If you were the brand manager for a brewery marketing in these countries, would you accept these findings as valid?

KNOWLEDGE

AVON'S SKIN SO SOFT: EXPANDING CONSUMER KNOWLEDGE

As discussed in Chapter 7, one option for increasing sales is to expand a product's usage situations. Avon has recently pursued this strategy for its bath oil called Skin So Soft by informing consumers about the various ways in which the product can be used. Sales reps delivered small samples of the product to their customers along with a description of twelve "fun and true uses." Some of these are listed below:

1. It's a bath oil and an after-shower moisturizer.
2. It can be used to remove makeup and is a great tanning oil.
3. Use as a hot-oil treatment to soften cuticles and as an oil massage for tired muscles.
4. It's an insect repellent for people and pets — helps relieve itching caused by insect bites and dry skin.
5. It cleans off tape marks left from bandages on skin, and cleans ink from skin, most vinyl surfaces, and painted surfaces. Use Skin So Soft instead of turpentine to remove paint from skin.
6. It removes lime and hard water deposits from fixtures, tile, shower doors and windows, and removes soap scum from shower doors, shower curtains, windows, bathroom and kitchen fixtures.
7. Tar spots on automobiles can easily be removed without damage to the paint.

10.1 THE INFLUENCE OF KNOWLEDGE ON PRODUCT EVALUATIONS

In a recent study by Alba and Marmorstein, subjects were given descriptions of three fictitious brands of 10-speed bicycles. Brand A was described as possessing four features as standard equipment: pump, tire irons, reflectors, and water bottle. Brand B was described as also possessing these features plus four others. Brand C had the same features as brand B plus four more.

Importantly, the additional features of brands B and C represented undesirable characteristics associated with poor quality bicycles. Consequently, it was expected that "experts" would prefer brand A the most but would be least favorable toward brand C. Just the opposite pattern was predicted for "novices." Because they lacked the knowledge to understand the true signifi-cance of the additional features, novices should be more likely to follow a "more is better" decision rule.

The results strongly confirmed these predictions. Experts (bicycle shop employees) evaluated brand A the highest and brand C the lowest. Novices (undergraduate students enrolled in marketing courses) preferred brand C the most and brand A the least. Thus, the same brand was perceived very differently depending on the person's level of knowledge.

Source: Joseph W. Alba and Howard Marmorstein, "The Effects of Frequency Knowledge on Consumer Decision Making," *Journal of Consumer Research* 14 (June 1987), 14–25.

As illustrated by the Avon example, influencing consumers' knowledge is a frequent objective of many marketing activities. The introduction of major product innovations will typically require considerable efforts to "educate" consumers about the new offering. Even if a new product is simply another brand within an established category, it will often be necessary to influence consumers' knowledge about the brand's existence and how the brand differs from its competition.

More fundamentally, it is essential for marketers to examine what consumers know, since this knowledge is a major determinant of consumer behavior. What consumers buy, where they buy, and when they buy will depend on the knowledge relevant to these decisions. Consumers who believe that generic pharmaceuticals contain the same ingredients as their branded counterparts, for instance, are unlikely to pay the additional price for the brand name. A demonstration of the influence knowledge can exert on the favorability of consumers' product preferences is presented in *Consumer in Focus 10.1*.[1]

---

[1] A similar demonstration is provided by Mita Sujan, "Consumer Knowledge: Effects on Evaluation Strategies Mediating Consumer Judgment," *Journal of Consumer Research* 12 (June 1985), 31–46.

10.2   CONSUMER KNOWLEDGE AND PUBLIC POLICY

Since 1965 the cigarette industry has been required to display a standard warning label on their packages and advertisements that states "The Surgeon General has determined that cigarette smoking is dangerous to your health." The intent of this warning was to provide consumers with sufficient information so as to make an informed choice.

In the mid-1980s, the government commissioned several surveys to assess the American public's knowledge about the dangers of smoking. While 90% of those surveyed did agree that smoking is dangerous to one's health, many people were unaware of the specific dangers (e.g., threats to pregnancy) associated with this consumption behavior. Consequently, the cigarette industry was required to replace the old warning label with a series of warnings describing specific dangers that are rotated periodically. Some of these new warnings appear below:

"Smoking by pregnant women may result in fetal injury, premature birth, and low birth weight."

"Cigarette smoke contains carbon monoxide."

"Smoking causes lung cancer, heart disease, emphysema, and may complicate pregnancy."

An understanding of consumer knowledge is also important to public policy makers. Governmental agencies such as the Federal Trade Commission may commission a survey of consumer knowledge to help guide policies aimed at protecting the "uninformed" consumer. When consumers are judged to lack sufficient information to make an "informed choice," policy makers may enact legislation that requires the disclosure of appropriate information. A recent example of this is presented in *Consumer in Focus 10.2.* At other times, consumers may hold inaccurate knowledge as a result of deceptive or misleading advertising. Corrective advertising may then be ordered by government agencies in order to remedy this erroneous knowledge.[2]

At a general level, **knowledge** can be defined as the information stored within memory. The subset of total information relevant to consumers functioning in the marketplace is called **consumer knowledge.** This chapter addresses three basic questions about consumer knowledge: What do consumers know? How is knowledge organized in memory? and How can knowledge be measured? Questions concerning the processes and factors that govern how external information is transferred to memory (i.e., becomes knowledge) and retrieved are deferred until later chapters on information processing

---

[2] William L. Wilkie, Dennis L. McNeill, and Michael B. Mazis, "Marketing's 'Scarlet Letter': The Theory and Practice of Corrective Advertising," *Journal of Marketing* 48 (Spring 1984), 11–31.

(Chapter 13) and learning (Chapter 14). Similarly, the role played by knowledge during the cognitive processes that shape consumer decision making is described in subsequent chapters as well.[3]

THE CONTENT OF KNOWLEDGE

A fundamental question that arises in a proper consumer analysis is "What do consumers know?" The answer to such a question rests upon understanding the contents of memory. Cognitive psychologists have suggested that there are two basic types of knowledge: declarative and procedural.[4] **Declarative knowledge** involves the subjective facts that are known, while **procedural knowledge** refers to the understanding of how these facts can be used. These facts are subjective in the sense that they need not correspond to objective reality. For instance, a consumer may believe price is an indicator of quality even when they are truly unrelated.

Declarative knowledge is divided into two categories: episodic and semantic.[5] **Episodic knowledge** involves information that is bounded by the passage of time. It is used for answering the question, "When did you last buy some clothes?" **Semantic knowledge,** on the other hand, contains generalized knowledge that gives meaning to one's world. It is the knowledge you would use, for example, in describing a videocassette recorder.

While these distinctions provide a general basis for categorizing knowledge content, a more useful typology is needed for the marketing practitioner. Although consumer researchers have largely ignored the development of such a typology,[6] our experience suggests that marketers will often find it useful to examine consumer knowledge within three general areas: product knowledge, purchase knowledge, and usage knowledge.

PRODUCT KNOWLEDGE

Product knowledge is itself a conglomerate of many different types of information. It would encompass:

1. Awareness of the product category and brands within the product category.

---

[3] A comprehensive and advanced discussion of how knowledge affects various cognitive processes can be found in Joseph A. Alba and J. Wesley Hutchinson, "Dimensions of Consumer Expertise," *Journal of Consumer Research* 13 (March 1987), 411–454.

[4] John R. Anderson, "A Spreading Activation Theory of Memory," *Journal of Verbal Learning and Verbal Behavior* 22 (1983), 261–295.

[5] Endel Tulving, "Episodic and Semantic Memory," in Endel Tulving, ed., *Organization of Memory* (New York: Academic Press, 1972).

[6] For an exception, see Merrie Brucks, "A Typology of Consumer Knowledge Content," in Richard J. Lutz, ed., *Advances in Consumer Research* 13 (Provo, Utah: Association for Consumer Research, 1986), 58–63.

2. Product terminology (e.g., "floppy disk" in computers).
3. Product attributes or features.
4. Beliefs about the product category in general and about specific brands.

In general, marketers are most interested in consumers' knowledge about their brand and competitive offerings. This information is obtained by analyzing consumers' awareness and image of available brands.

AWARENESS ANALYSIS   A common approach to assessing brand awareness is the "top-of-the-mind" awareness measure. As the name suggests, consumers are asked to recall all of the brands that are applicable to the probe. The probe might be very general, such as a question asking you to name all of the toothpaste brands you can remember. Alternatively, the probe might limit the set of relevant brands by defining a particular benefit or usage situation (e.g., the brands that would be best suited for someone going on a date).

Those brands familiar to the consumer comprise the **awareness set.** Obviously, it is difficult to sell an "unknown" product. Consequently, an important marketing objective would be to move the brand name into the awareness set. Enhancing awareness is a primary objective of the ad appearing in Figure 10.1.

IMAGE ANALYSIS   Marketers are also concerned with the beliefs consumers hold that determine a brand's image. A toothpaste brand, for instance, may attempt to position itself as a superior cavity fighter relative to the competition. By examining consumers' beliefs about the brand's cavity-prevention abilities (as well as beliefs regarding competitive brands), it is possible to determine whether a product has achieved the desired positioning within the consumer's mind. The examination of consumers' knowledge about an object's properties is known as an **image analysis.**

One approach to image analysis consists of asking consumers to rate the product on a series of scales representing the properties of interest. Typically, these properties are expressed in the form of product attributes or benefits. As an example, suppose we were commissioned by bank A to assess the images consumers hold of their bank and two competitors. For simplicity, we will focus on four attributes, although in practice many more attributes may be used.

Figure 10.2 contains the results of the image analysis for the three banks. Rather than aggregating the data across all respondents, it is typically useful to separate the respondents into different groups. First, we would want to consider the findings based on bank A's customers. These are presented in the top half of the figure. In an absolute sense, the results indicate that bank A's customers generally hold favorable beliefs about the bank. Even so, there is room for improvement (assuming of course that consumers desire a bank to fall in the extreme left response category of each attribute scale), particularly in the areas of the speed of service and the personnel's friendliness

FIGURE 10.1
ENHANCING BRAND
NAME AWARENESS
MAKES IT EASIER TO
SELL THE PRODUCT

Why you should invest your hard earned money with a company you've never heard of.

You shouldn't.
That's why we're running this ad. To tell you who we are. To tell you we're one of the largest investment organizations in the world with a capital base of over 566 million dollars. And managing assets over 8 billion dollars. To tell you we have hundreds of investments to help you not only keep more of what you earn but earn more on what you keep.

So, while you may not have heard of us, it's obvious someone else has. 175,000 someones to be exact.

If you think those numbers were impressive, you should try these.
1-800-255-5550 ext. 600.

Integrated Resources
Because there's money to be made.
Circle No. 209 on Reader Service Card.

toward customers. To the extent these attributes are important, improvements in them should enhance the bank's ability to retain customers.

A comparison of the three banks' ratings also carries implications for customer retention. For example, bank B receives very poor ratings. Consequently, this bank would pose little threat to bank A's customer base without substantial changes in its image. Bank C, on the other hand, represents a much more serious competitive threat, as it receives very similar ratings to bank A. Further, those areas where bank C is deficient might easily be improved. Bank A should, therefore, be much more sensitive to the threat posed by bank C and may wish to undertake activities that would help further differentiate the two banks within the minds of their current customers.

The benefits of this image analysis extend beyond their implications for customer-retention concerns. Indeed, it can also assist the development of customer-recruitment programs that focus on converting competitive users

FIGURE 10.2
IMAGE ANALYSIS FOR THREE BANKS: HOW CONSUMERS VIEW THE COMPETITORS

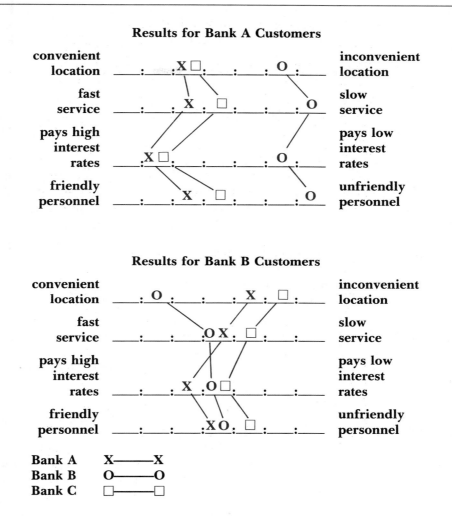

Results for Bank A Customers

Results for Bank B Customers

Bank A	X———X
Bank B	O———O
Bank C	□———□

into our users. For this, we need to examine the findings based on competitive users. Ideally, this would be done for each competitor's customer base, as different competitive customers may hold very different beliefs. In our example, we consider the results based on bank B's customers, which are summarized in the bottom half of Figure 10.2.

These results indicate both opportunities and constraints for bank A in attempting to attract bank B's customers. Bank B holds a substantial location advantage. If this perceived advantage is false, in the sense that these customers hold a misperception of bank A's convenience (e.g., they may be unaware of a nearby branch office), then correcting this misperception would be critical.

On the other hand, if this disadvantage is real, bank A may be forced into building one or more branch offices in order to successfully attract these customers. Alternatively, bank A may try to offset this location disadvantage by building their image on other attributes.

The approach used in our bank example is incomplete in that it does *not* provide needed information about the importance consumers place on the various attributes. There are, however, other approaches at the marketer's disposal that yield such information. Indeed, some of these techniques can even identify a brand's "ideal" positioning or image. These alternative approaches are presented in Chapter 11.

It is of course possible to assess consumers' brand knowledge at a more general level. Rather than measuring beliefs about each brand's quality, we could simply ask consumers whether they agree that all brands possess the same quality. However, when important differences exist between brands within the consumer's mind, measures of general knowledge are unable to identify the precise nature of these differences (e.g., which brand is seen as having the best quality).

PRODUCT MISPERCEPTION   As suggested previously, marketers must also be alert to inaccuracies in consumers' knowledge. It is quite common to discover that consumers hold incorrect beliefs that represent significant barriers to success. For example, many people overestimate the number of calories in a potato, a very unfavorable belief for this industry in today's calorie-conscious marketplace. The ad appearing in Figure 10.3 is designed to combat such beliefs.

PRICE KNOWLEDGE   One aspect of product knowledge that deserves to be singled out is that involving product prices. An examination of what consumers know about an absolute price (e.g., the price of a 1-pound can of Maxwell House coffee) and a relative price (e.g., whether this brand costs more than another or whether one store charges more than another for the same item) can provide important information for guiding marketing actions.

One example comes from a proprietary study undertaken by a consumer service firm. Consumers were asked to estimate the price of this service. As expected, users of the service gave very accurate estimates. This was not the case for nonusers. Their average price estimate was *twice* the actual price, and many nonusers exaggerated the price by a factor of three or four. This information resulted in a change in the company's advertising strategy, which previously had avoided price information.

Marketing executives' pricing decisions may also depend on their perceptions of how well informed consumers are about prices.[7] As suggested by

---

[7] Joel E. Urbany and Peter R. Dickson, "Consumer Information, Competitive Rivalry, and Pricing in the Retail Grocery Industry" (working paper, University of South Carolina, 1988).

FIGURE 10.3
COMBATING
PRODUCT
MISPERCEPTIONS:
CORRECTING
ERRORS IN
CONSUMER
KNOWLEDGE

Source: Courtesy of the National Potato Promotion Board.

the study reported in *Consumer in Focus 10.3,* marketers will be more motivated to hold prices down and respond to competitive price cuts when they believe consumers are knowledgeable about the prices charged in a market.

Low levels of price knowledge, on the other hand, enable marketers to be less concerned about significant price differences relative to the competition. If consumers are largely ignorant of relative price differences, marketers may exploit this ignorance through higher prices.

PURCHASE KNOWLEDGE

Purchase knowledge encompasses the various pieces of information consumers possess that are germane to acquiring products. The basic dimensions of purchase knowledge involve information concerning the decisions of *where* the product should be purchased and *when* purchase should occur.

10.3 THE DEPENDENCY OF PRICING DECISIONS ON PERCEPTIONS OF CONSUMERS' PRICE KNOWLEDGE

In an interesting field study, comparative retail grocery prices were published in the Sunday editions of local newspapers in four cities for three months. The price of a market basket of goods was then tracked over time. Compared to a set of matched control cities, prices in the test markets declined when the price information was published, but rose after the publishing was discontinued.

What is particularly intriguing about these results is that the publication of comparative prices seemingly had a small effect on consumers. Less than one-fourth of them reported noticing and using the published information in their shopping. Moreover, the percentage of consumers patronizing the lowest priced store was virtually unaffected by the information. Apparently, the grocers believed that publishing comparative prices would enhance consumers' price knowledge, and this belief alone was sufficient to prompt them into lowering their prices.

Source: Robert D. Boynton, Brian F. Blake, and Joe N. Uhl, "Retail Price Reporting Effects in Local Food Markets," *American Journal of Agricultural Economics* 65 (February 1983), 20–29.

WHERE TO BUY   A fundamental issue consumers must address during decision making is where they should purchase a product. Many products can be acquired through very different channels. Cosmetics, for example, may be purchased by visiting a retail store, ordering from a catalog, or contacting a field representative of a cosmetic firm that utilizes a sales force (e.g., Avon, Mary Kay).

Because a given channel may consist of multiple competitors, the consumer must further decide which one to patronize. A consumer who has chosen to buy her cosmetics from a retailer can pick from a number of different department stores, mass merchandisers, and specialty stores.

Decisions of where to buy are determined largely by purchase knowledge. As in our prior discussion of product knowledge, awareness and image are important components of purchase knowledge. Low levels of patronage, for instance, may simply be due to a lack of store awareness among target consumers. Alternatively, it may reflect deficiencies in store image. The store may be seen as inferior to the competition in one or more key areas (e.g., breadth of offering, price, convenience, availability of salespeople). Recognize that the image analysis described earlier can be easily adapted to examining consumers' knowledge about retailers.

Purchase knowledge also includes the information consumers have about the *location* of products within the retail environment. One aspect of this location knowledge involves the consumer's information about which stores carry which products. Another dimension concerns the knowledge about where the product is actually located within a store. In a study of the latter, shoppers were shown floor plans of a supermarket and asked to identify the location of various products.[8] Shoppers were more accurate for products placed on peripheral or exterior aisles than for those items located along central or interior aisles. Accuracy was also greater for smaller stores and shoppers reporting higher levels of store patronage.

Knowledge about the location of products in a store can affect purchase behavior.[9] When consumers are unfamiliar with a store, they have to rely more heavily on in-store information and displays for identifying product locations. This increased processing of in-store stimuli may activate needs or desires previously unrecognized, thereby leading to unplanned purchases.

WHEN TO BUY   Consumers' beliefs about when to buy is another relevant component of purchase knowledge. Consumers who know that a product is traditionally placed on sale during certain times of the year may delay purchasing until such times. Knowledge about when to buy can be a very important determinant of purchase behavior for new innovations. Many consumers will not immediately acquire new products because they believe that prices may drop over time.

An ad aimed at influencing purchase knowledge appears in Figure 10.4. AT&T is attempting to modify the purchase behavior of college students by informing them of the price differences that result from when they place their phone calls.

USAGE KNOWLEDGE

Usage knowledge represents our third category of consumer knowledge. Such knowledge encompasses the information available in memory about how a product can be used and what is required to actually use the product. A consumer might know what a power saw can be used for but still lack the knowledge about how to operate the product.

The adequacy of consumers' usage knowledge is important for several reasons. First, consumers are certainly less likely to buy a product when they lack sufficient information about how to use it. Marketing efforts designed to educate the consumer about how to use the product are then needed. The ad appearing in Figure 10.5 is one example of enhancing usage knowledge by providing consumers with step-by-step information on how the product can be used.

A similar barrier to purchase occurs when consumers possess incomplete information about the different ways or situations in which a product can

---

[8] Robert Sommer and Susan Aitkens, "Mental Mapping of Two Supermarkets," *Journal of Consumer Research* 9 (September 1982), 211–215.
[9] Easwar S. Iyer, "Unplanned Purchasing: Knowledge of Store Layout and Time Pressure" (working paper, University of Massachusetts, 1988).

QUESTION #4.

WHEN SHOULD THE COLLEGE STUDENT CALL FAMILY AND FRIENDS?

a) **During weekends until 5 pm Sunday, and from 11 pm to 8 am Sunday through Friday, to save over 50% off AT&T's weekday out-of-state rates.**

b) **The minute your bank statement reveals a negative $60 balance.**

c) **Between 5 pm and 11 pm, Sunday through Friday, to save 38% off AT&T's weekday out-of-state rate.**

d) **With AT&T, any time you want a clear long distance connection.**

e) **When you hear they've removed the mysterious "Venetian Blind" ritual from your fraternity initiation.**

You've just aced the calculus exam that you'd been dreading like the plague. Your date last night told you she had an "out-of-body" experience. Your roommate's joined a new cult that worships luncheon meats.

When you're away at school, there are a million reasons to stay in touch with the people you miss. And there's no easier way to do it than with AT&T Long Distance Service.

Between our discount calling periods and our everyday high quality service, the best time to call with AT&T Long Distance Service is any time you want to say "Hello," or "Guess what?" or "You won't believe this, but..."

For more information, give us a call at 1...

CALL NOW!

AT&T
The right choice.

© 1987 AT&T

---

be used. The discovery of aspirin's ability to reduce heart attack risks prompted Bayer to inform consumers of this new use (see Figure 10.6). Such efforts are quite common, as marketers often identify and promote new product uses to enhance demand, particularly in the case of mature products.

Note, however, that care must be taken in selecting new uses. A major concern is that a new use may in fact lower a product's attractiveness to consumers. For instance, one potential concern with Avon's multiple-usage positioning of its bath oil (described in the chapter opener) is that consumers

FIGURE 10.5
ENHANCING
CONSUMERS'
KNOWLEDGE ABOUT
HOW TO USE A
PRODUCT

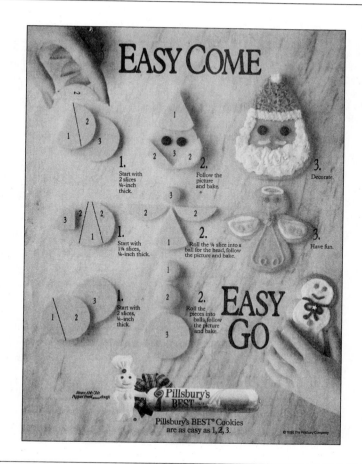

may be less than enthusiastic about using a skin moisturizer that can also remove tar from a car.

Even if inadequate usage knowledge does not prevent product purchase, it can still have detrimental effects on consumer satisfaction. A misused product may not perform properly, causing the customers to feel dissatisfied. Even worse, misuse may lead to bodily injury, such as the frequent accidents involving hand-held power saws.[10]

---

[10] For an example of research concerning product safety knowledge, see Richard Staelin, "The Effects of Consumer Education on Consumer Product Safety Behavior," *Journal of Consumer Research* 5 (June 1978), 30–40.

**FIGURE 10.6
EXPANDING
CONSUMERS'
KNOWLEDGE ABOUT
PRODUCT USES:
BAYER DEVELOPED
THIS AD TO INFORM
CONSUMERS OF A
NEW USE FOR
ASPIRIN**

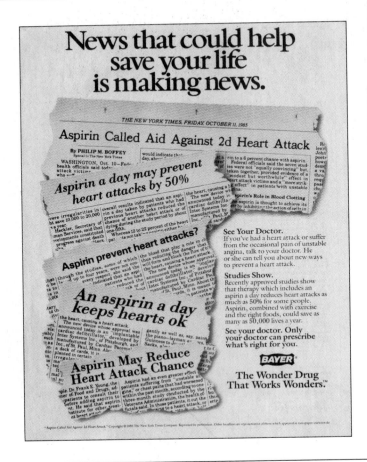

THE ORGANIZATION OF KNOWLEDGE

In this section we consider how the various pieces of information within memory are structured or organized. Although there are many theories about memory organization, the literature largely favors the view of memory being organized in the form of an **associative network**.[11] According to this associative network concept, memory consists of a series of nodes (representing concepts) and links (which represent associations between nodes). Figure 10.7 displays

---

[11] John R. Anderson, *The Architecture of Cognition* (Cambridge, Massachusetts: Harvard University Press, 1983).

FIGURE 10.7
AN ASSOCIATIVE
NETWORK OF
KNOWLEDGE FOR
THE IBM PERSONAL
COMPUTER

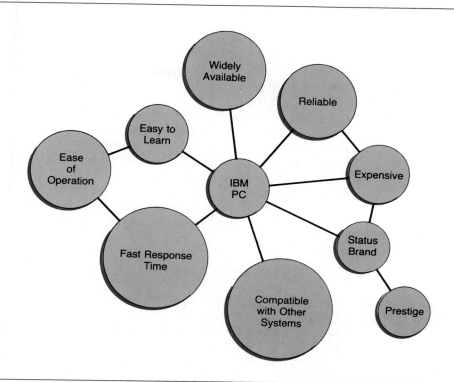

a simplified associative network that might exist for an IBM personal computer.

The combination of various nodes within memory leads to more complex units of knowledge. A link between two nodes forms a **belief** or **proposition,** such as "IBM is an expensive brand." These beliefs will differ in the strength of the association between the two nodes. Thus, the consumer may strongly believe that IBM is an expensive brand but be far less convinced about the ease of learning how to operate an IBM.

These propositions or beliefs, in turn, can be combined to create a high-order knowledge structure called a **schema.**[12] Schemata are likely to exist for most brands familiar to the consumer. Schemata can also occur at various levels of abstraction. For example, consumers may possess a schema for a specific brand of automobile (e.g., Mercedes-Benz) as well as the general concept of automobile.

---

[12] For an evaluation of the schema concept, see Joseph W. Alba and Lynn Hasher, "Is Memory Schematic?" *Psychological Bulletin* 93 (March 1983), 203–231.

One type of schema, known as a **script,** contains knowledge about the temporal action sequences that occur during an event.[13] Most of us have scripts for activities such as making a bank deposit, dining in a restaurant, or getting a prescription filled at a drug store. Schemata and scripts play an important role during information processing. In essence, activation of schemata or scripts during the processing of an incoming stimulus reduces the cognitive effort necessary for identifying what the stimulus is and how the person should respond to it.

One aspect of knowledge organization that has been examined in the research literature is whether product information is organized around brand names or product attributes. The associative network depicted in Figure 10.7 assumes a brand-based structure. Alternatively, the central node of such a network might involve a product attribute with surrounding nodes representing various brands within the product category. Research on this issue will typically expose subjects to a set of new information about the attributes of fictitious brands.[14] Later, subjects are asked to recall the information. The order in which this information is retrieved from memory is used to infer memory organization.[15]

The weight of current evidence supports a brand-based organizational structure.[16] Some have argued that this is to be expected, since most of consumers' product experiences are brand specific (e.g., an ad discussing only one brand).[17] Consistent with this, research has shown a tendency to organize

[13] Research on consumer scripts can be found in George John and John C. Whitney, "An Empirical Investigation of the Serial Structure of Scripts," in *AMA Educators' Conference Proceedings* (Chicago: American Marketing Association, 1982), 75–79; Ruth Ann Smith and Michael J. Houston, "A Psychometric Assessment of Measures of Scripts in Consumer Memory," *Journal of Consumer Research* 12 (September 1985), 214–224; John C. Whitney and George John, "An Experimental Investigation of Intrusion Errors in Memory for Script Narratives," in Alice M. Tybout and Richard P. Bagozzi, eds., *Advances in Consumer Research* 10 (Ann Arbor, Michigan: Association for Consumer Research, 1983), 661–666.

[14] An example of studying memory structure for existing knowledge can be found in J. Edward Russo and Eric J. Johnson, "What Do Consumers Know About Familiar Products?" in Jerry C. Olson, ed., *Advances in Consumer Research* 7 (Ann Arbor, Michigan: Association for Consumer Research, 1980), 417–423.

[15] For an excellent discussion of the methodological limitations of this approach and alternative methods for testing memory structure, see John G. Lynch, Jr., and Thomas K. Srull, "Memory and Attentional Factors in Consumer Choice: Concepts and Research Methods," *Journal of Consumer Research* 9 (June 1982), 18–37.

[16] Gabriel Biehal and Dipankar Chakravarti, "Information — Presentation Format and Learning Goals as Determinants of Consumers' Memory Retrieval and Choice Processes," *Journal of Consumer Research* 8 (March 1982), 431–441; Russo and Johnson, "What Do Consumers Know About Familiar Products?".

[17] Eric J. Johnson and J. Edward Russo, "The Organization of Product Information in Memory Identified by Recall Times," in H. Keith Hunt, ed., *Advances in Consumer Research* 5 (Chicago: Association for Consumer Research, 1978), 79–86.

information within memory in a manner similar to how it is processed.[18] Thus, if information is presented one brand at a time (e.g., all of the attributes for one brand are provided before turning to other brands), a brand-based memory structure is more likely to emerge. The fact that brand-based structures are also more likely to occur for subjects high rather than low in their knowledge provides further support for this experience explanation.[19]

THE MEASUREMENT OF KNOWLEDGE

Consumer researchers have employed a variety of approaches for measuring consumer knowledge. Some studies have relied on the amount of purchase or usage experience as an indicator of knowledge.[20] The assumption is that greater experience translates into great knowledge. Although product experience is obviously a rich source of information, consumers can possess some level of knowledge even though they have never used a particular product. Further, different types of experiences can create different types of knowledge. For these reasons, then, experience represents an imprecise indicator of knowledge.[21]

Perhaps the most obvious manner of measuring knowledge is to directly assess the contents of memory. Measures of **objective knowledge** are those

---

[18] Biehal and Chakravarti, "Information — Presentation Format and Learning Goals as Determinants of Consumers' Memory Retrieval and Choice Processes"; Johnson and Russo, "The Organization of Product Information in Memory Identified by Recall Times"; Thomas K. Srull, "The Role of Prior Knowledge in the Acquisition, Retention, and Use of New Information," in Richard P. Bagozzi and Alice M. Tybout, eds., *Advances in Consumer Research* 10 (Ann Arbor, Michigan: Association for Consumer Research, 1983), 572–576.

[19] Eric J. Johnson and J. Edward Russo, "Product Familiarity and Learning New Information," *Journal of Consumer Research* 11 (June 1984), 542–550.

[20] Examples of experience-based measures can be found in James R. Bettman and C. Whan Park, "Effects of Prior Knowledge and Experience and Phase of the Choice Process on Consumer Decision Processes: A Protocol Analysis," *Journal of Consumer Research* 7 (December 1980), 234–248; Jacob Jacoby, Robert W. Chestnut, and William A. Fisher, "A Behavioral Process Approach to Information Acquisition in Nondurable Purchasing," *Journal of Marketing Research* 15 (November 1978), 523–544; Kent B. Monroe, "The Influence of Price Differences and Brand Familiarity on Brand Preferences," *Journal of Consumer Research* 3 (June 1976), 42–49; Joseph W. Newman and Richard Staelin, "Prepurchase Information Seeking for New Cars and Major Household Appliances," *Journal of Marketing Research* 9 (August 1972), 249–257.

[21] See Merrie Brucks, "The Effects of Product Class Knowledge on Information Search Behavior," *Journal of Consumer Research* 12 (June 1985), 1–16; Catherine A. Cole, Gary Gaeth, and Surendra N. Singh, "Measuring Prior Knowledge," in Richard J. Lutz, ed., *Advances in Consumer Research* 13 (Provo, Utah: Association for Consumer Research, 1986), 64–66; Fred Selnes and Kjell Gronhaug, "Subjective and Objective Measures of Product Knowledge Contrasted," in Richard J. Lutz, ed., *Advances in Consumer Research* 13 (Provo, Utah: Association for Consumer Research, 1986), 67–70.

that tap what the consumer actually has stored in memory.[22] This is by no means an easy task, given the vast array of relevant knowledge that consumers may possess. Indeed, our prior discussion of knowledge content provides some indication of the different pieces of information that may comprise consumer knowledge.

Figure 10.8 lists some of the questions that might be used in measuring consumers' objective knowledge. These questions represent various aspects of consumers' product, purchase, and usage knowledge. Which of them should be used will depend on the objective of the research. A study focusing on whether advertising has been successful in communicating a new product use would focus on usage knowledge. Research intended to aid pricing decisions, on the other hand, would focus on consumers' price knowledge.

A final option for assessing knowledge is to use measures of **subjective knowledge.**[23] These measures, as reflected by those appearing in Figure 10.9, tap consumers' perceptions of their own knowledgeability. In essence, consumers are asked to rate themselves in terms of their product knowledge or familiarity.

Unlike measures of objective knowledge, which focus on specific pieces of information that may be known to consumers, subjective knowledge measures center around the consumers' impressions of their total knowledge and familiarity. Thus, a consumer may feel very familiar with aspirins and still be unaware of the product's benefits in reducing the risks of heart attacks.

Research has revealed that subjective and objective knowledge measures, while related, are not substitutable.[24] That is, some people overestimate their knowledge, while others underestimate what they know. Apparently, subjective measures are affected by one's self-confidence such that people who are self-confident may overreport their level of knowledge.

In general, marketers will be most interested in what consumers actually know. As we have already seen, information about consumers' brand awareness

[22] Examples of objective knowledge measures can be found in Brucks, "The Effects of Product Class Knowledge on Information Search Behavior"; Richard L. Celsi and Jerry C. Olson, "The Role of Involvement in Attention and Comprehension Processes," *Journal of Consumer Research* 15 (September 1988), 210–224; Akshay R. Rao and Kent B. Monroe, "The Moderating Effect of Prior Knowledge on Cue Utilization in Product Evaluations," *Journal of Consumer Research* 15 (September 1988), 253–264; Selnes and Gronhaug, "Subjective and Objective Measures of Product Knowledge Contrasted"; Sujan, "Consumer Knowledge: Effects on Evaluation Strategies Mediating Consumer Judgments."

[23] Examples of subjective knowledge measures can be found in Brucks, "The Effects of Product Class Knowledge on Information Search Behavior"; Johnson and Russo, "Product Familiarity and Learning New Information"; Arno J. Rethans, John L. Swasy, and Lawrence J. Marks, "Effects of Television Commercial Repetition, Receiver Knowledge, and Commercial Length: A Test of the Two-Factor Model," *Journal of Marketing Research* 23 (February 1986), 50–61; Selnes and Gronhaug, "Subjective and Objective Measures of Product Knowledge Contrasted."

[24] Brucks, "The Effects of Product Class Knowledge on Information Search Behavior"; Cole, Gaeth, and Singh, "Measuring Prior Knowledge"; Selnes and Gronhaug, "Subjective and Objective Measures of Product Knowledge Contrasted."

**FIGURE 10.8
MEASURING
OBJECTIVE
KNOWLEDGE**

Product Knowledge Measures

1. *Terminology*
   What is meant by the following terms?
   a. Basic
   b. Terminal
   c. CPU

2. *Attributes*
   What product features are important to you in deciding which brand of refrigerator to buy?

3. *Brand Awareness*
   List all of the brands of coffee you can remember.

4. *Product Beliefs*
   How fattening are potatoes?
   Which tastes better, Coke or Pepsi?
   How much does a McDonald's Big Mac cost?

Purchase Knowledge Measures

1. *Store Beliefs*
   Which stores carry JVC televisions?
   Which grocer offers lower prices, Big Bear or Krogers?

2. *Purchase Timing*
   Are some times better than others during the year for buying a new car?

Usage Knowledge Measures

1. *Usage operation*
   Describe the steps involved in creating a data file on a personal computer.

2. *Usage situations*
   What are the different ways a person can use baking soda?

and how they perceive the brand (i.e., its image) can be very useful in formulating marketing activities. Implications for marketing action are also afforded by understanding the contents of consumers' purchase and usage knowledge.

This is not to say that measuring consumers' subjective knowledge is worthless. Subjective measures may be preferable when one is interested in anticipating the likelihood that consumers will search the environment for

**FIGURE 10.9
MEASURING
SUBJECTIVE
KNOWLEDGE**

1. **How knowledgeable are you about personal computers?**
   very knowledgeable__:__:__:__:__:__:__very unknowledgeable

2. **Rate your knowledge of personal computers, as compared to the average consumer.**
   one of the most   one of the least
   knowledgeable__:__:__:__:__:__:__knowledgeable

3. **How familiar are you with personal computers?**
   very familiar__:__:__:__:__:__:__very unfamiliar

4. **If you were going to buy a personal computer today, how comfortable would you feel making such a purchase based on what you know about personal computers?**
   very comfortable__:__:__:__:__:__:__very uncomfortable

new information during decision making. This is because external search is less likely when consumers perceive themselves as possessing adequate amounts of information, regardless of how much they truly know (see Chapter 17). Conversely, even consumers who actually possess a high level of knowledge may search if they believe their knowledge is inadequate. Thus, subjective measures may outperform objective measures in forecasting consumers' propensity to acquire new information from their environment.[25]

SUMMARY

Consumer knowledge consists of the information stored within memory. Marketers are particularly interested in understanding consumer knowledge. The information consumers hold about products will greatly affect their purchasing patterns. Awareness and image analyses are very useful for exploring the nature of product knowledge. Marketers should also consider purchase knowledge in terms of the beliefs consumers hold about where and when purchase should occur. Usage knowledge is another content area worthy of consideration. Expanding such knowledge can be a significant avenue for increasing sales.

Some attention has been given to understanding how consumer knowledge is organized within memory. Present findings suggest that memory is organized in the form of an associative network, with brand names serving as a central node for structures involving product knowledge.

Finally, consideration was given to alternative methods for measuring knowledge. Purchase or usage experience, while certainly related to knowledge, does not necessarily provide an accurate indication of just how much information consumers possess. Objective knowledge measures attempt to assess the actual contents of memory. Subjective knowledge measures, on the other hand, ask people to indicate how knowledgeable they perceive themselves to be.

REVIEW AND DISCUSSION QUESTIONS

1. What is meant by the terms *product knowledge, purchase knowledge,* and *usage knowledge?* Give an example of how each might influence consumer behavior.
2. Consider the following set of results from an image analysis in which the customers of a competitive food product (brand A) rated their own brand, your brand (B), and another competitor (brand C).

---

[25] Selnes and Gronhaug, "Subjective and Objective Measures of Product Knowledge Contrasted."

good tasting $\underline{C}$:$\underline{A}$:$\underline{B}$:__:__:__:__ **poor tasting**

high in nutrition $\underline{C}$:__:__:$\underline{A}$:$\underline{B}$:__:__ **low in nutrition**

expensive $\underline{C}$:__:__:$\underline{A}$:__:$\underline{B}$:__ **inexpensive**

easy to cook __:$\underline{B}$:$\underline{A}$:__:__:__:$\underline{C}$ **difficult to cook**

What conclusions can you make based on this information?

3. Describe how advertising strategies may differ depending on consumer knowledge.

4. A grocer recently completed a study of consumers who patronize the store. One of the more intriguing findings was that the amount spent during a shopping trip depended on the number of times a consumer had shopped at the store. Consumers spent significantly more money when it was only their first or second trip. How can you explain this finding?

5. You have been asked to develop some brochures that describe a fairly sophisticated and technically oriented product. Results of market research indicate that the two primary target markets hold very different beliefs about how much product knowledge they possess. One segment perceives itself as very knowledgeable, while the other feels it is quite ignorant about the product. What implications does this difference in perceived knowledge carry for developing the brochures?

6. A recent market study suggests that consumers have very limited knowledge about the prices charged by your product and competitors. When asked to give a specific price, the majority were unable or unwilling to do so. Moreover, the average error of those giving a price was plus or minus 25 percent. What conclusions can you draw from these results about consumers' price sensitivity during decision making?

7. A recent survey of various target markets reveals important differences in both their level of product knowledge and use of friends' recommendations during decision making. Consumers having limited knowledge relied heavily on others' recommendations, while knowledgeable consumers did not. How can you explain this difference?

ATTITUDES

IDENTIFYING POTENTIAL PURCHASERS WITH ATTITUDE SURVEYS

A company was interested in examining the attitudes of consumers who did not buy their product, even though they "qualified" for purchase (i.e., they possessed the basic need which the product could satisfy and the income necessary for purchase). A national survey was therefore undertaken which included attitude measures that focused on a nonuser's likelihood of becoming a product user (e.g., their agreement with statements such as "I would never buy this type of product"). Based on how they responded to the measures, nonusers were classified into one of the following segments:

"Best prospects" — segment members possess attitudes that indicate a very good chance of product purchase in the immediate future.

"Potentially convertibles" — members hold attitudes that indicate a good chance of product purchase at some point, but not in the near future.

"Neutrals" — members have attitudes that neither favor or oppose product purchase.

"No Ways" — members hold attitudes that indicate they are opposed to product purchase.

It was expected that consumers categorized as best prospects would be more likely to become product users, while those classified as no ways should be the least likely to do so. In order to validate this presumption, a follow-up survey was undertaken a year later in which respondents were now asked to report whether they had purchased the product during the interim.

The results clearly supported the classification procedure. While a significant percentage of best prospects became users, very few of the no ways did so. Findings such as these provide encouraging support for the potential to use attitudes as a means of identifying consumers who are most inclined toward product purchase.

As illustrated by our opening example, attitudes usually play a major role in shaping behavior. In deciding which brand to buy, or which store to patronize, consumers will typically select the brand or store that is evaluated most favorably. Consequently, enhancing attitude can be a worthy marketing objective.

Attitudes are useful to marketers in many ways. For example, they are often used for judging the effectiveness of marketing activities. Consider an advertising campaign designed to increase sales by enhancing consumers' attitudes. Relying solely on sales for evaluating the campaign's success can be potentially misleading, as sales are affected by many factors beyond advertising (e.g., a competitor who slashes prices in response to the campaign). Consequently, it is possible for advertising to have a positive impact on attitudes without influencing sales. If, however, the ads failed to have the desired effect on attitudes, then it would probably be necessary to revise the campaign.

Attitudes can also help evaluate marketing actions before they are implemented within the marketplace. A packaging decision is one example. Establishing which version of several alternative packages evoked the most favorable attitudes from consumers could prove quite useful in making the final selection.

Attitudes can also be very useful in segmenting markets and choosing target segments. One approach to segmentation involves slicing a market based on how favorable consumers are toward the product (as was done in the opening vignette of this chapter). All other things being equal, a firm would target the segment holding favorable attitudes, since these consumers should be more responsive to the product offering than those possessing less favorable attitudes. Even if some other base is used to segment a market (e.g., geographic), one should still attempt to examine the relative favorability of various segments toward the product. The barriers to success become smaller as a segment's liking for a product increases.

Product attitudes are, of course, but one of many different types of attitudes that marketers must concern themselves with. As shown later in the chapter, the attitudes held by consumers toward various product attributes (e.g., attitudes toward the alternative colors, materials, and styles that might be used in clothing) play an important role in determining product attitudes. The attitudes formed toward an advertisement should also be considered as they can determine the ad's persuasive power (see Chapter 15).[1] Attitudes toward health and fitness can carry potent implications for many industries, including cigarettes, exercise equipment, and diet foods. Although the chapter discussion and examples focus heavily on product attitudes, you should remember that these are only a part of the total picture.

In sum, an understanding of consumer attitudes can be beneficial in a number of ways. Fortunately, decades of attitude research have yielded a wealth of information, upon which we can draw. Unfortunately, the amount of information necessary for even a basic appreciation of attitudes cannot fit within the constraints of a conventional textbook chapter. Consequently, we have devoted two chapters to this topic. In this initial chapter, we explore some fundamental issues relevant to attitudes, such as their properties, their relationship with behavior, and their measurement. Chapter 15, on the other hand, builds upon this foundation and focuses on the variety of tactics available for influencing attitudes.

THE PROPERTIES OF ATTITUDES

Although attitude has been defined in a variety of ways, we prefer viewing attitude as simply an overall evaluation. This evaluation can range from extremely positive to extremely negative. For example, a consumer may have a very favorable attitude toward Pepsi, a slightly favorable attitude toward Coke, a neutral attitude toward RC cola, and a mildly negative attitude toward Shasta cola. Thus, attitudes vary in their **intensity** (i.e., strength) and **favorability.**

An important property of attitudes is the **confidence** with which they are held. Some attitudes may be held with strong convictions, while others may exist with a minimal degree of confidence. Although intensity and confidence are related, they are not the same. A consumer may, for example, be equally confident that he or she really likes Pepsi but is only slightly favorable toward Coke.

Understanding the degree of confidence associated with an attitude is important for two basic reasons. First, it can affect the strength of the relationship between attitudes and behavior.[2] Confidently held attitudes will usually

---

[1] Scott B. MacKenzie, Richard J. Lutz, and George E. Belch, "The Role of Attitude Toward the Ad as a Mediator of Advertising Effectiveness: A Test of Competing Explanations," *Journal of Marketing Research* 23 (May 1986), 130–143; Andrew A. Mitchell and Jerry C. Olson, "Are Product Attribute Beliefs the Only Mediators of Advertising Effects on Brand Attitudes?" *Journal of Marketing Research* 18 (August 1981), 318–332; Paul W. Miniard, Sunil Bhatla, and Randall L. Rose, "On the Formation and Relationship of Ad and Brand Attitudes: An Experimental and Causal Analysis" (working paper, The Ohio State University, 1988).

[2] Russell H. Fazio and Mark P. Zanna, "On the Predictive Validity of Attitudes: The Roles of Direct Experience and Confidence," *Journal of Personality* 46 (June 1978), 228–243; Robert E. Smith and William R. Swinyard, "Attitude-Behavior Consistency: The Impact of Product Trial Versus Advertising," *Journal of Marketing Research* 20 (August 1983), 257–267.

be relied upon more heavily to guide behavior. When confidence is low, consumers may not feel comfortable with acting upon their existing attitudes. Instead, they may search for additional information before commiting themselves.

Second, confidence can affect an attitude's susceptibility to change. Attitudes become more resistant to change when they are held with greater confidence.[3]

Another important property of attitudes is that they are *dynamic* rather than static. That is, many attitudes will change over time. This dynamic nature of attitudes is largely responsible for the changes in consumers' lifestyles (see Chapter 12). The clothing industry is highly sensitive to the reality that consumers' fashion attitudes are constantly changing. Manufacturers and retailers have often been left "holding the bag" after an abrupt shift in fashion preferences. Similarly, changes in consumers' health attitudes have been bad news for some industries (e.g., cigarettes, liquor), but great news for others (e.g., exercise and sporting equipment and clothing). Consequently, businesses can benefit from tracking consumer attitudes over time as one way of anticipating potential changes in product demand and shopping behavior.[4]

Finally, it is important to understand the extent to which attitude is based on the perceived utilitarian versus hedonic properties (see Chapter 9) of the attitude object.[5] For some products, attitude will depend very heavily on their utilitarian properties. Consumers' attitudes toward toothpaste, for instance, are likely to be driven primarily by their perceptions about the brand's functional benefits, such as reducing cavities. For other products, however, hedonic factors may dominate attitudes. Amusement parks, ballets, movies, music, and sporting events are valued for their ability to influence consumers' emotions. Understanding the relative influence of these utilitarian and hedonic properties on attitude provides useful guidance in developing effective product appeals (see Chapter 15).

ATTITUDE FORMATION

The attitudes that consumers currently hold are, of course, a result of their prior experiences. Consumers who lived through the Depression era in the

---

[3] Lawrence J. Marks and Michael A. Kamins, "The Use of Product Sampling and Advertising: Effects of Sequence of Exposure and Degree of Advertising Claim Exaggeration on Consumers' Belief Strength, Belief Confidence, and Attitudes," *Journal of Marketing Research* 25 (August 1988), 266–281.

[4] For a discussion of different ways to track attitudes, see Mathew Greenwald and John P. Katosh, "How to Track Changes in Attitudes," *American Demographics* 9 (August 1987), 46–47.

[5] Rajeev Batra and Olli T. Ahtola, "The Measurement and Role of Utilitarian and Hedonic Attitudes" (working paper, University of Denver, 1987). Also see Elizabeth C. Hirschman and Morris B. Holbrook, "Hedonic Consumption: Emerging Concepts, Methods and Propositions," *Journal of Marketing* 46 (Summer 1982), 92–101.

early 1930s, for example, typically have less favorable attitudes toward buying on credit. The origins of many attitudes can be traced back to childhood experiences, such as shopping trips with mom and dad. Thus, the family has a major influence on the development of attitudes during the consumer's early years. More generally, the environmental factors described in Part II of the text will have a strong influence on attitude formation by shaping the type, amount, and quality of information and experience available to consumers.

THE ROLE OF DIRECT EXPERIENCE

Attitudes are frequently formed as a result of direct contact with the attitudinal object. Consumers who enjoy a pleasant shopping trip to a retailer are likely to develop favorable attitudes toward the retailer. In contrast, a product that fails to perform as expected can easily lead to negative attitudes.

Recognize, however, that attitudes can be formed even in the absence of actual experience with an object. For example, many consumers have never driven a Mercedes-Benz or vacationed in Hawaii, but they still hold favorable attitudes toward this car and state. Similarly, product attitudes may be formed even when consumers' experience with the product is limited to what they saw in an ad.

An important characteristic of attitudes based on direct experience is that they are usually held with more confidence.[6] Consistent with this, research has shown that consumers have much stronger convictions about their product attitudes when based on actual product usage than when based on advertising alone.[7]

In order to more effectively develop strategies and activities that will create, reinforce, or modify consumer attitudes, it is important to understand the processes that govern attitude formation. Space constraints prevent us from doing so here. Instead, these processes are explored in our discussion of information processing (Chapter 13) and learning (Chapter 14).

THE ATTITUDE–BEHAVIOR RELATIONSHIP

In many situations, marketers are concerned with forecasting purchase behavior. Suppose your company had just developed a new product and was interested in determining whether there is sufficient demand in the marketplace to warrant introduction. One approach to making this determination involves

---

[6] Fazio and Zanna, "On the Predictive Validity of Attitudes: The Roles of Direct Experience and Confidence."

[7] Marks and Kamins, "The Use of Product Sampling and Advertising: Effects of Sequence of Exposure and Degree of Advertising Claim Exaggeration on Consumers' Belief Strength, Belief Confidence, and Attitudes"; Smith and Swinyard, "Attitude-Behavior Consistency: The Impact of Product Trial Versus Advertising."

CONSUMER IN FOCUS

11.1   PREDICTING CONSUMER BEHAVIOR WITH ATTITUDES: OLD CROW AND JIM BEAM

Attitude surveys have often provided accurate forecasts of future purchase behaviors. Many years ago a study was undertaken of consumers' attitudes toward various brands of bourbon. At the time, Old Crow was the market leader, while Jim Beam was a relatively minor brand. The attitude study, however, suggested that this state of affairs was unlikely to continue. Consistent with its name, Old Crow was perceived as being "old," an image less than appealing to younger consumers. Younger consumers, on the other hand, held a much more favorable image of Jim Beam. The study also suggested that lighter spirits such as vodka and rum were likely to take business away from bourbon sales.

Some fifteen years later, these forecasts materialized. Old Crow drifted into obscurity, while Jim Beam became the leading brand of bourbon. The entire bourbon category had also shrunk thanks to the lighter spirits.

Source: " 'Attitude Share of Market' Predicts Better Than Behavioral Measures," *Marketing News* (May 16, 1980), 7.

---

introducing the product into one or more test markets. Depending on these results, you could then make a more informed judgment about the product's potential. Such a test can also cost millions of dollars, a very expensive price for discovering that a product has little appeal.

Alternatively, you could examine whether the product even merits the opportunity to go to test market by first considering consumers' attitudes toward the product. This approach is quite straightforward. Consumers from the target market would be asked to indicate their interest in buying the product. If few consumers express an interest, the product should be abandoned or modified and retested. On the other hand, if consumers are strongly attracted to the product, then it's time to consider a test market. Recognize that the costs of this attitude study will run thousands of dollars. Even so, such a price is far short of the millions you might spend on test markets, only to discover that your "star" was a "dog."

The use of attitudes to forecast demand is not limited to new products. Producers of existing products are also interested in predicting future sales (see *Consumer in Focus 11.1*). Indeed, knowledge about future consumption can be a critical determinant of many business decisions. For example, how interested would manufacturers operating at full capacity be in expanding their production facilities if they knew that sales were going to increase sharply? Conversely, discovering that demand was about to level off after several years of strong growth would reveal the need to begin exploring alternative avenues for achieving sales growth (e.g., stealing competitors' customers).

The use of attitudes to predict behavior does, of course, presume that attitudes are related to behavior. The strength of the attitude–behavior relationship has long been a major area of inquiry within the social sciences. One of the first published studies on this topic was undertaken by LaPiere.[8] In the early 1930s, LaPiere traveled across the United States with a married Chinese couple. They were refused admittance by only one of the more than 200 restaurants and hotels patronized during their travels. After the trip, LaPiere mailed a questionnaire to these establishments asking if they would serve "members of the Chinese race." Nearly half of the businesses replied, and over 90 percent said they would *not* serve Chinese people.

This finding sparked a battle in the field of social psychology over attitude's predictive power. Hundreds of investigations have been undertaken on this issue, some supporting the attitude–behavior relationship but many others confirming LaPiere's findings. In a review article published 35 years after LaPiere's study, the author concluded that "it is considerably more likely that attitudes will be unrelated or only slightly related to overt behaviors than that attitudes will be closely related to actions."[9]

Despite this pessimistic assessment, research has continued to explore the attitude–behavior relationship. It is now recognized that, under the proper circumstances, attitudes can predict behavior. Nonetheless, it has become evident that certain factors, as described subsequently, can affect the strength of this relationship.

MEASUREMENT FACTORS

Suppose you wanted to measure consumers' attitudes toward some product (e.g., Mercedes-Benz automobile). Figure 11.1 summarizes some of the possible ways in which this could be done. Although these measures differ in their wording and response scales, each of them focuses on consumers' overall evaluation of some *object* (in this case, a car).

Note, however, that these measures of attitude toward a product are limited in their ability to predict future behavior. This limitation is reflected by the fact that although most students will give favorable responses to the measures in Figure 11.1, very few of those who buy a car upon graduation will purchase a Mercedes. Before reading further, stop and think about what changes in the measures would lead to a better prediction of students' auto purchases following graduation.

The basic problem with the measures is their *lack of correspondence* with the behavior of interest. The extent to which a measure matches or corresponds to a behavior, which in turn determines the measure's predictive power, will

---

[8] Richard Tracy LaPiere, "Attitudes vs. Actions," *Social Forces* 13 (December 1934), 230–237.
[9] Allan W. Wicker, "Attitudes vs. Actions: The Relationship of Verbal and Overt Behavioral Responses to Attitude Objects," *Journal of Social Issues* 25 (Autumn 1969), 41–78.

FIGURE 11.1
ALTERNATIVE
MEASURES OF
PRODUCT
ATTITUDES

1. **How much do you like Mercedes-Benz automobiles?**
   like very much__:__:__:__:__:__:__dislike very much
2. **How favorable is your overall opinion of Mercedes-Benz automobiles?**
   very favorable__:__:__:__:__:__:__very unfavorable
3. **Mercedes-Benz automobiles are:**
   good__:__:__:__:__:__:__bad
   favorable__:__:__:__:__:__:__unfavorable
   pleasant__:__:__:__:__:__:__unpleasant
4. **Indicate how strongly you agree with the following statement:**
   "I really like Mercedes-Benz automobiles"

strongly agree	agree	neither	disagree	strongly disagree

depend on how well it captures four possible behavioral elements: action, target, time, and context.[10]

ACTION   This element refers to the *specific* behavior of interest (e.g., buying, using, borrowing). It is imperative that attitude measures accurately represent the action element, since failure to do so can be very detrimental to their predictive accuracy. Indeed, the lack of an action element in the measures presented in Figure 11.1 is largely responsible for their limited predictive power. A student can have a very favorable attitude toward a Mercedes-Benz but still hold a very unfavorable attitude toward *buying* such a car, due to a lack of need (e.g., the student just bought a new car) or ability (e.g., the student can't afford it). Consequently, better predictions can be expected from measures that assess students' attitudes toward buying a Mercedes-Benz. In general, measures of attitude toward an object (i.e., measures omitting the action element) will be *inferior* to measures of attitude toward a behavior (i.e., measures that specify the action element) in forecasting behavior.

Although measures of attitude toward the behavior are preferrable to those that assess attitude toward an object, **behavioral intention measures** are most appropriate when the objective is to maximize prediction.[11] Intention

[10] The literature is greatly indebted to the following article for its contribution concerning the importance of measurement correspondence: Icek Ajzen and Martin Fishbein, "Attitude-Behavior Relations: A Theoretical Analysis and Review of Empirical Research," *Psychological Bulletin* 84 (September 1977), 888–918. For an empirical demonstration, see James Jaccard, G. William King, and Richard Pomazal, "Attitudes and Behavior: An Analysis of Specificity of Attitudinal Predictors," *Human Relations* 30 (September 1977), 817–824.

[11] For research on the intention–behavior relationship, see Donald H. Granbois and John O. Summers, "Primary and Secondary Validity of Consumer Purchase Probabilities," *Journal of Consumer Research* 4 (March 1975), 31–38; Paul W. Miniard, Carl Obermiller, and Thomas J. Page, Jr., "A Further Assessment of Measurement Influences on the Intention–Behavior Relationship," *Journal of Marketing Research* (May 1983), 206–212; David J. Reibstein, "The Prediction of Individual Probabilities of Brand Choice," *Journal of Consumer Research* 5 (December 1978), 163–168; Paul R. Warshaw, "Predicting Purchase and Other Behaviors from General and Contextually Specific Intentions," *Journal of Marketing Research* 17 (February 1980), 26–33.

measures attempt to capture the perceived likelihood that a particular behavior will occur.[12] For example:

How likely is it that the first car you buy after graduation will be a Mercedes-Benz?

very likely__:__:__:__:__:__:__very unlikely

We return to this distinction between intention and attitude in our later section on behavior intention models.

TARGET   Target elements can be very general (e.g., buying *any* automobile) or very specific (e.g., buying a Mercedes). The degree of target specificity depends upon the behavior of interest. For instance, the trade association for the automobile industry is primarily concerned with purchases of all automobiles. In contrast, General Motors would be more interested in purchases of its own models.

Returning to the LaPiere study, we can now understand the reported inconsistency between attitude and behavior. LaPiere's attitude measure involved a very general target (members of the Chinese race). In contrast, the actual behavior consisted of serving a married Chinese couple accompanied by a European male. This discrepancy, along with other problems (such as whether the person who answered the survey was the same one who served them), probably explains LaPiere's unsupportive findings.

TIME   This element focuses upon the time frame in which the behavior is to occur. Suppose that on Monday you were asked about your attitude toward buying soft drinks. You report a very favorable attitude because you plan to purchase soft drinks on Wednesday, your normal day for grocery shopping. However, on Tuesday, you are asked to indicate which, if any, soft drinks you purchased since the day before. The apparent inconsistency between attitudes and behavior that would occur is simply due to the failure to specify this important timing factor. A more appropriate measure would have assessed your attitude toward buying soft drinks within the next 24 hours.

CONTEXT   The remaining element, context, refers to the setting in which the behavior is to occur. Soft drinks, for example, can be purchased in a variety of settings, such as a grocery store, vending machine at school, restaurant, and movie theater. If one is interested in predicting vending machine purchases, the attitude measure must incorporate this contextual element.

---

[12] Research indicates that it is usually better to measure the perceived likelihood of performing a behavior than the intention to perform a behavior. See Paul R. Warshaw and Fred D. Davis, "Disentangling Behavioral Intention and Behavioral Expectation," *Journal of Experimental Social Psychology* 21 (1985), 213–228.

TIME INTERVAL

A very strong relationship between attitudes and behavior should occur whenever attitudes are measured just prior to actual purchase. Marketers, however, are interested in using today's attitudes to forecast behaviors that are somewhat distant in time. Retailers, for instance, place their orders for the Christmas buying season many months in advance.

The need to assess attitudes well in advance of actual behavior works against the strength of the attitude–behavior relationship. Attitudes are not static. They can easily change as a result of unexpected circumstances and situational influences.[13] A sudden budget crunch can lead to the postponement of a previously planned purchase, or an unanticipated increase in financial resources can result in purchases that were not seriously contemplated prior to this increase. The subsequent introduction of new products and brands can also influence previously formed attitudes.

This potential for change suggests that the strength of the attitude–behavior relationship will be affected by the time interval between the measurement of attitude and performance of the behavior. As this time interval increases, the opportunity for change becomes greater. Generally speaking, the shorter the time interval, the stronger the attitude–behavior relationship.[14]

Even a relatively short time interval does not necessarily ensure a strong relationship between attitude and behavior. Once again, unanticipated circumstances, such as out-of-stock conditions or an attractive in-store promotion by an alternative brand, can intervene. In such situations, it is unreasonable to expect that attitudes measured prior to this "new information" will provide a strong prediction of behavior.

EXPERIENCE

As noted earlier, attitudes based on actual experience are likely to be more related to behavior than those based on "indirect" experience. Consequently, the attitudes of consumers who have purchased and consumed a product should prove more predictive of their future purchase behaviors than those lacking such experiences. Similarly, attitudes should be more indicative of a new product's potential when consumers are allowed to actually use the product as opposed to only being shown pictures or nonfunctional prototypes of the product. New product research may require the production of prototypes,

---

[13] For research on how unexpected situations can influence the attitude–behavior relationship, see Joseph A. Cote, James McCullough, and Michael Reilly, "Effects of Unexpected Situations on Behavior–Intention Differences: A Garbology Analysis," *Journal of Consumer Research* 12 (September 1985), 188–194.

[14] Icek Ajzen and Martin Fishbein, *Understanding Attitudes and Predicting Social Behavior* (Englewood Cliffs, New Jersey: Prentice-Hall, 1980), Chapter 4; E. Bonfield, "Attitude, Social Influence, Personal Norms, and Intention Interactions as Related to Brand Purchase Behavior," *Journal of Marketing Research* 11 (November 1974), 379–389.

even at high cost, and a simulated shopping context to achieve the greatest success in forecasting demand.

SOCIAL INFLUENCES

Behavior is sometimes more affected by pressures from the social environment than by personal attitudes. We have all probably experienced a situation where we did something not because of our personal desires but because of social influences (e.g., smokers who try to avoid "lighting up" when accompanied by nonsmokers). Consequently, as we see later in our discussion of behavioral intention models, attitude measures are often accompanied by measures of social influence for predicting behavior.

SUMMARY

Attitudes offer marketers a powerful predictive tool when used properly. By understanding the factors that influence the strength of the attitude–behavior relationship, we are better able to avoid pitfalls and situations that undermine attitude's predictive accuracy. While the marketer's needs may necessitate using attitude measures under less than optimal conditions (e.g., forecasting behavior in the distant future), some potential problems can be easily minimized, such as avoiding the error of measuring the wrong attitude.

MULTIATTRIBUTE ATTITUDE MODELS

While it is certainly important for marketers to know whether consumers hold favorable or unfavorable attitudes toward their products, it is also imperative for them to understand the basis or reasons for these attitudes. Knowing that consumers dislike your product does not tell you why this is so, or how you might go about overcoming this unfavorable evaluation.

Traditionally, consumer researchers have focused on the cognitive foundations for explaining attitudes. From this perspective, attitude is seen as depending on knowledge about the attitude object. Consequently, emphasis is placed on ascertaining the important beliefs a person holds about the attitude object.

Multiattribute attitude models represent a valuable approach to examining the relationship between consumers' product knowledge (Chapter 10) and their product attitudes in terms of product features or attributes.[15] After

---

[15] For a review of multiattribute models, see Richard J. Lutz and James R. Bettman, "Multi-Attribute Models in Marketing: A Bicentennial Review," in Arch G. Woodside, Jagdish N. Sheth, and Peter D. Bennett, eds., *Consumer and Industrial Buying Behavior* (New York: North-Holland, 1977), 137–149; William L. Wilkie and Edgar A. Pessemier, "Issues in Marketing's Use of Multi-Attribute Models," *Journal of Marketing Research* 10 (November 1973), 428–441.

describing two major types of multiattribute models, we discuss some of the benefits they can offer marketers.[16]

THE FISHBEIN MODEL

Fishbein's formulation is perhaps the most well known multiattribute model.[17] Symbolically, it can be expressed as

$$A_0 = \sum_{i=1}^{n} b_i e_i$$

where:

A_0 = attitude toward the object
b_i = the strength of the belief that the object has attribute i
e_i = the evaluation of attribute i
n = the number of salient attributes.

The model therefore proposes that attitude toward a given object (e.g., brand) is based on the summed set of beliefs about the object's attributes weighted by the evaluation of these attributes. In order to illustrate the model's properties and operations, consider the situation where the model is used to understand consumers' preferences for three brands of running shoes. The first step would be to discover the target market's salient attributes. Assume that the following attributes are identified:

- whether the shoe is shock absorbent to permit running on hard surfaces;
- whether it is priced under $50;
- the durability of the shoe;
- how comfortable it is to wear;
- whether it is available in a desired color;
- the amount of arch support.

Next, the appropriate b_i and e_i measures would be developed. The e_i component, representing the evaluation of an attribute, is typically measured

---

[16] There are additional multiattribute models beyond the two discussed here. See, for example, Frank A. Bass and W. Wayne Talarzyk, "Attitude Model for the Study of Brand Preference," *Journal of Marketing Research* 9 (February 1972), 93–96; Jagdish N. Sheth and W. Wayne Talarzyk, "Perceived Instrumentality and Value Importance as Determinants of Attitudes," *Journal of Marketing Research* 9 (February 1973), 6–9; Milton J. Rosenberg, "Cognitive Structure and Attitudinal Affect," *Journal of Abnormal and Social Psychology* 53 (November 1956), 367–372; Olli T. Ahtola, "The Vector Model of Preferences: An Alternative to the Fishbein Model," *Journal of Marketing Research* 12 (February 1975), 52–59.

[17] Martin Fishbein, "An Investigation of the Relationships Between Beliefs About an Object and the Attitude Toward That Object," *Human Relations* 16 (August 1963), 233–240; Martin Fishbein and Icek Ajzen, *Belief, Attitude, Intention, and Behavior: An Introduction to Theory and Research* (Reading, Massachusetts: Addison-Wesley, 1975); Ajzen and Fishbein, *Understanding Attitudes and Predicting Social Behavior.*

on a 7-point evaluative scale ranging from "very good" to "very bad." For instance:

Buying running shoes priced under $50 is:

very good___:___:___:___:___:___:___very bad
$$+3 \quad +2 \quad +1 \quad 0 \quad -1 \quad -2 \quad -3$$

This would be done for each of the six salient consequences identified previously.

The b_i component represents how strongly consumers believe that a particular brand of running shoes possesses a given attribute. Beliefs are usually measured on a 7-point scale of perceived likelihood ranging from "very likely" to "very unlikely." For example:

Brand A running shoes are priced under $50.

very likely___:___:___:___:___:___:___very unlikely
$$+3 \quad +2 \quad +1 \quad 0 \quad -1 \quad -2 \quad -3$$

For each brand, it would be necessary to assess consumers' beliefs for each attribute. Given three brands and six attributes, a total of eighteen belief measurements would be necessary.[18]

Let us further assume that a survey containing these measures is administered to a sample of white-collar males earning more than $50,000. An average response could then be calculated for each b_i and e_i measure. A set of hypothetical results appear in Table 11.1. It is important to keep in mind while interpreting these results that the b_i and e_i scales range from a maximum score of $+3$ to a minimum of -3.

In this example, durability and comfort are evaluated as the most desirable product attributes, followed by shock absorbent and arch support, with color a relatively minor although still salient consideration. Unlike the remaining attributes, low price (under $50) receives a negative score for this high-income sample. This does not mean that price is unimportant. Rather, it indicates that low price is viewed as an undesirable characteristic. This result is quite possible for a sample that perceives a price–quality relationship.

Findings involving brand beliefs suggest that brand A is viewed favorably by the sample because it receives a positive rating on all desired attributes. Indeed, brand A attains maximum ratings on both durability and arch support. The sample also believes that it is very unlikely (-3) that brand A costs less than $50. Given that low price is undesirable, this perception works in favor of brand A.

As a rule of thumb, marketers want consumers to perceive their brand as (1) possessing desirable attributes (i.e., when e_i is positive, b_i should be

---

[18] Evidence suggests that the order in which beliefs are measured (by attribute across brands versus by brand across attributes) can be important. See Eugene D. Joffe and Israel D. Nebenzahl, "Alternative Questionnaire Formats for Country Image Studies," *Journal of Marketing Research* 21 (November 1984), 463–471.

			Beliefs (b_i)		
Attribute	Evaluation (e_i)	Brand A	Brand B	Brand C
Shock absorbent	+2	+2	+1	−1
Price under $50	−1	−3	−1	+3
Durability	+3	+3	+1	−1
Comfort	+3	+2	+3	+1
Desired color	+1	+1	+3	+3
Arch support	+2	+3	+1	−2
Total $\Sigma b_i e_i$ score		+29	+20	−6

TABLE 11.1 HYPOTHETICAL RESULTS FOR FISHBEIN'S MULTIATTRIBUTE MODEL

positive) and (2) not possessing undesirable attributes (i.e., when e_i is negative, b_i should be negative). Both strategies are commonly employed in advertising for creating favorable attitudes. The ad presented in Figure 11.2 attempts to convince consumers that the product contains desirable ingredients, while

FIGURE 11.2 COMMUNICATING THE PRESENCE OF DESIRABLE ATTRIBUTES CREATES POSITIVE CONSUMER ATTITUDES

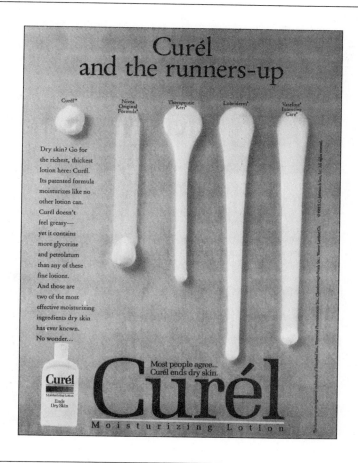

the ad in Figure 11.3 announces the absence of an ingredient that many consumers wish to avoid.

Although brand B outperforms brand A on comfort and color in Table 11.1, it is perceived as inferior to brand A on the remaining dimensions. Brand C is viewed as low-priced, a perception that undermines attitude, given the negative evaluation of low price. The sample also believes that brand C is unlikely to absorb shock, be durable, or provide arch support. On the positive side, the brand is seen as somewhat comfortable and having a desired color.

To estimate the attitude toward each brand using the $\Sigma b_i e_i$ index, each belief score must first be multiplied by the corresponding evaluation score. For example, the brand A belief score of +2 for shock absorbency is multiplied by the evaluation of +2, which produces a value of +4 for this attribute. This same process is repeated for each of the five remaining attributes. This

FIGURE 11.3
COMMUNICATING THE ABSENCE OF UNDESIRABLE ATTRIBUTES ALSO IMPROVES CONSUMER ATTITUDES

produces a total $\Sigma b_i e_i$ score of +29 for brand A. For brands B and C, the $\Sigma b_i e_i$ values are +20 and −6, respectively.

The score for brand A is very good, considering that the maximum score, given the current set of evaluations, is +36. The maximum score is derived by assuming the "ideal" belief score (i.e., +3 or −3, depending upon whether the attribute is positively or negatively evaluated) and combining it with the existing evaluation scores.

We should note that market researchers who undertake a multiattribute analysis are typically much more interested in how a product is rated on various attributes than in the total $\Sigma b_i e_i$ score. Indeed, if one is only interested in consumers' overall product evaluations, then this information can be collected more easily by using the product attitude measures presented earlier, in Figure 11.1.

THE IDEAL-POINT MODEL

A unique and important aspect of the ideal-point model is that it provides information concerning an "ideal brand" as well as information concerning how existing brands are viewed by consumers.[19] The model can be represented symbolically as

$$A_b = \sum_{i=1}^{n} W_i |I_i - X_i|$$

where:

A_b = attitude toward brand B
W_i = the importance of attribute i
I_i = the "ideal" performance on attribute i
X_i = the belief about the brand's actual performance on attribute i
n = the number of salient attributes.

Under the ideal-point model, consumers are asked to indicate where they believe a brand is located on scales representing the various degrees or levels of salient attributes. Consumers would also indicate where the "ideal" brand would fall on these attribute scales. According to the model, the closer a brand's actual rating is to the ideal rating, the more favorable the attitude.

As an illustration, suppose we were to apply the model to soft drinks. Assume that the following attributes are identified as salient dimensions underlying soft drink evaluations:

- the sweetness of taste;
- the degree of carbonation;

---

[19] Examples of model application can be found in James L. Ginter, "An Experimental Investigation of Attitude Change and Choice of a New Brand," *Journal of Marketing Research* 11 (February 1974), 30–40; Donald R. Lehmann, "Television Show Preference: Application of a Choice Model," *Journal of Marketing Research* 8 (February 1972), 47–55.

• the number of calories;
• the amount of real fruit juices;
• the price.

Next, we would develop a scale representing various levels of an attribute for each salient dimension. Using sweetness as an example, the scale could look like:

very sweet taste____:____:____:____:____:____:____**very bitter taste**

           1   2   3   4   5   6   7

Consumers would then indicate their ideal or preferred taste by placing an "I" in the appropriate response category. This would be followed by ratings of where various brands fall along this taste continuum (i.e., the X_i from the model equation). Consumers would also provide ratings of attribute importance on a scale such as:

not at all   **extremely**

important____:____:____:____:____:____:____**important**

          0   1   2   3   4   5   6

Unlike the bipolar coding scheme used for the Fishbein multiattribute model, unipolar coding is used for quantifying responses to the ideal-point model scales. Unipolar coding is necessary for importance measures, since a brand's performance on an unimportant attribute should not affect attitude. For this reason, we assign a zero to the "not at all important" response category. On the other hand, bipolar coding could be used for the ideal and actual brand ratings. Given that the difference between the ideal and actual brand ratings is converted to an *absolute* value, either coding scheme will produce the same results. We prefer unipolar coding since most people find it easier to work with mathematically.

Continuing our soft drink example, suppose we found the results presented in Table 11.2. The first column specifies the attributes and the continuum (e.g., sweet to bitter) along which the ideal (the third column) and actual brand (the fourth and fifth columns) ratings were taken. Attribute-importance ratings appear in the second column.

In this example, taste is the most important attribute, while carbonation is the least important. The ideal-point ratings indicate that the ideal soft drink would be sweet tasting, somewhat carbonated, fairly low in calories, very high in fruit juices (in actuality we would probably use a scale of juice content ranging from 0 percent to 100 percent), and toward the low side on price (again we might use a different scale, such as one containing specific price points). Brand A is perceived as being very close to the ideal brand. Brand B also performs well on some attributes (e.g., calories) but suffers on others (e.g., carbonation).

Total brand attitude scores are estimated by first taking the difference between the ideal and actual brand ratings on an attribute. For taste, brand A has a difference of 0 (2 − 2), while the difference for brand B is −1 (2 − 3).

TABLE 11.2 HYPOTHETICAL RESULTS FOR THE IDEAL-POINT MULTIATTRIBUTE MODEL	Attribute	Importance (W_i)	Ideal-Point (I_i)	Beliefs (X_i)	
				Brand A	Brand B
	Taste: sweet (1)–bitter (7)	6	2	2	3
	Carbonation: high (1)–low (7)	3	3	2	6
	Calories: high (1)–low (7)	4	5	4	5
	Fruit juices: high (1)–low (7)	4	1	2	2
	Price: high (1)–low (7)	5	5	4	3
	Total $\Sigma W_i|I_i + X_i|$ score			16	29

This difference is converted to an absolute value as indicated by the symbol surrounding $I_i - X_i$ in the model equation, and multiplied by the importance score. This operation would produce scores of 0 for brand A (0×6) and 6 for brand B (1×6) on the taste attribute. We would then repeat this process for the remaining attributes and sum the scores. For brand A, the total score is 16, while brand B's score is 29. Unlike Fishbein's multiattribute model where higher scores are preferred, lower scores are better under the ideal-point model. In fact, the best score a brand can receive is zero, which would indicate that the brand matches perfectly the ideal attribute configuration.

BENEFITS OF A MULTIATTRIBUTE ANALYSIS

A multiattribute analysis can be a rich source of useful information for market planning and action. One illustration is provided by the simultaneous impor-tance-performance grid presented in Figure 11.4.[20] A brand is classified into one of eight cells. This classification depends on the attribute's importance (high versus low), the brand's performance on the attribute (good versus poor), and a competitive brand's performance on the attribute (good versus poor). Marketing implications are then drawn for each cell. For example, poor performance by all brands on an important attribute signals a "neglected opportunity." By enhancing our brand's performance on this attribute, we could turn this into a competitive advantage. Poor performance by all brands on an unimportant attribute, however, represents little opportunity. Improv-ing the brand's performance would have little, if any, impact on consumer choice.

A multiattribute analysis can also provide the information necessary for some types of segmentation (see Chapter 22). For example, one might find

---

[20] Alvin C. Burns, "Generating Marketing Strategy Priorities Based on Relative Competitive Position," *Journal of Consumer Marketing* 3 (Fall 1986), 49–56.

FIGURE 11.4
THE SIMULTANEOUS
IMPORTANCE-
PERFORMANCE
GRID

Attribute Importance	Our Performance	Competitor's Performance	Simultaneous Result
High	Poor	Poor	Neglected Opportunity
		Good	Competitive Disadvantage
	Good	Poor	Competitive Advantage
		Good	Head-to-Head Competition
Low	Poor	Poor	Null Opportunity
		Good	False Alarm
	Good	Poor	False Advantage
		Good	False Competition

Source: Alvin C. Burns, "Generating Marketing Strategy Priorities Based on Relative Competitive Position," *Journal of Consumer Marketing* 3(Fall 1986).

it useful to segment consumers based on the importance they place on various attributes. Marketing activities will differ considerably when target consumers are primarily concerned with buying at a low price rather than buying the highest quality.

Another benefit of a multiattribute analysis is its implications for new product development.[21] Discovering that current offerings fall short of the ideal brand would reveal an opportunity for introducing a new offering that more closely resembles the ideal. A multiattribute model has also been used successfully to forecast the market shares of new products (see *Consumer in Focus 11.2*)

ATTITUDE CHANGE IMPLICATIONS

A multiattribute approach can provide the marketer with some guidance in the development of appropriate attitude-change strategies. The Fishbein multiattribute model, for example, suggests two fundamental ways of changing

[21] For research on the model's usefulness in new product development, see Morris B. Holbrook and William J. Havlena, "Assessing the Real-to-Generalizability of Multiattribute Attitude Models in Tests of New Product Designs," *Journal of Marketing Research* 25 (February 1988), 25–35.

11.2 LEVER BROTHERS: A MARKETING APPLICATION OF THE MULTIATTRIBUTE ATTITUDE MODEL

Lever Brothers has added the multiattribute model to its array of market research techniques. In concept, their model closely resembles the ideal-point model described in the text, although additional information is collected about the highest and lowest acceptable performance on an attribute. For instance, consumers would be asked to indicate the highest and lowest levels of carbonation that are acceptable to them. The width of this range reflects how "tolerant" a consumer would be on this attribute.

Using this multiattribute data, Lever Brothers examined how well they could pre-

dict a brand's market share. When tested for Lever's bar soaps, a brand's "attitude share" was found to closely resemble its actual market share. This approach was then extended to new products. Attribute-performance ratings of two new soaps, Tone moisturizing soap and Coast deodorant soap, were used to forecast market shares. These attitude-based estimates came very close to the brands' actual shares of the soap market.

Source: "Lever Brothers Uses Micromodel to Project Market Share," *Marketing News* (November 27, 1981).

---

attitudes.[22] One approach is to influence the salience of evaluative criteria. Sometimes this involves trying to create salience for an attribute that is currently unimportant. For example, flame broiling is unimportant to many consumers in selecting a fast-food burger restaurant, although Burger King's advertising has attempted to alter this feeling.

At other times, it may be desirable to change the evaluation of attributes that are currently salient. Research has supported the possibility of enhancing the salience of an attribute already viewed as somewhat important.[23] Much more difficult is changing an attribute's desirability, such as the attempt by Curtis-Mathis to persuade consumers that high price is a desirable, rather than undesirable, attribute in selecting a television based on the price–quality relationship. However, it is usually very difficult to have a major impact on consumer's evaluative criteria, and, in general, these should be taken as a given.

The second approach is to alter consumers' beliefs. The ad for Eastern Airlines in Figure 11.5 is designed to change consumers' perceptions about the product. The extent to which product modification is actually necessary

---

[22] Richard J. Lutz, "Changing Brand Attitudes Through Modification of Cognitive Structure," *Journal of Consumer Research* 1 (March 1975), 49–59.
[23] Scott B. MacKenzie, "The Role of Attention in Mediating the Effect of Advertising on Attribute Importance," *Journal of Consumer Research* 13 (September 1986), 174–195.

FIGURE 11.5   EASTERN AIRLINES DESIGNED THIS AD TO CHANGE CONSUMERS' BELIEFS ABOUT ITS PRODUCT AND SERVICES

for changing consumers' beliefs will depend on the accuracy of these beliefs. When consumers hold undesirable beliefs because they have misperceived the offering (e.g., consumers who overestimate product price), then efforts should focus on bringing these beliefs into harmony with reality. If, however, consumers are accurate in their perceptions of a product's limitations, then it may be necessary to implement product changes.

To better illustrate the model's use in developing attitude-change strategies, let us return to Table 11.1. Obviously, some major changes are necessary if brand C is to survive within the target market. But what changes? Without the information in Table 11.1, answering this question is a formidable, if not impossible, task.

With the information in hand, however, several options are easily developed. Enhancing the brand's durability is certainly an important option, given the high value attached to this attribute. The same holds true for the arch support attribute, where the brand is rated quite poorly.

Note that the former option offers the greatest potential improvement in attitude. For example, suppose we were able to alter consumers' beliefs from their current unfavorable positions to the most favorable one (i.e., +3) for both durability and arch support. For arch support, this would result in a contribution of +10 to overall attitude: from $(-2) \times (+2)$ to $(+3) \times (+2)$. For durability, the contribution is +12: from $(-1) \times (+3)$ to $(+3) \times (+3)$. Consequently, focusing on durability would be a superior option, assuming that all other things were equal (such as the cost and feasibility of executing these changes).

Are there any other changes that are even more attractive than the durability option? There is one (before reading on, stop and see if you can identify it). If possible, brand C should attempt to change the current negative evaluation of low price to a positive evaluation. If the low-price evaluation were to be changed to a score of +3, this would result in the same contribution (+12) to overall attitude that occurs for the change involving durability. However, unlike changes in belief, changes in evaluation of an attribute can influence the attitude score of all alternatives. Given that brands A and B are not perceived as low-priced, making low price a positive attribute would *lower* the attitudes toward these brands. Thus, if possible (remember that changes in attribute salience are very difficult to accomplish), the ideal change for brand C is to make low price more desirable. This would increase consumers' attitudes toward its brand while lowering attitudes toward the competition.

BEHAVIORAL INTENTION MODELS

Earlier in the chapter we noted that the attitude–behavior relationship may be weaker when behavior is susceptible to social influences. Behavioral intention models represent one approach to examining the relative effects of attitudes and social influences. We again focus on Fishbein's formulation, which is the most widely known behavioral intention model.[24]

The Fishbein model postulates that intention, which is viewed as the immediate antecedent of behavior, is determined by an attitudinal or personal component, and a normative or social component.[25] This model can be expressed as

$$B \sim BI = W_1 (A_B) + W_2 (SN)$$

where:

---

[24] Alternative behavioral intention models can be found in Paul W. Miniard and Joel B. Cohen, "Modeling Personal and Normative Influences on Behavior," *Journal of Consumer Research* 10 (September 1983), 169–180; Paul R. Warshaw, "A New Model for Predicting Behavioral Intentions: An Alternative to Fishbein," *Journal of Marketing Research* 17 (May 1980), 153–172.

[25] Ajzen and Fishbein, *Understanding Attitudes and Predicting Social Behavior;* Fishbein and Ajzen, *Belief, Attitude, Intention, and Behavior: An Introduction to Theory and Research.*

$$B = \text{behavior}$$
$$BI = \text{behavioral intention}$$
$$A_B = \text{attitude toward performing behavior } B$$
$$SN = \text{subjective norm}$$
$$W_1 \text{ and } W_2 = \text{empirically determined weights representing the}$$
$$\text{components' relative influence.}$$

Note that the model assumes that attitudes (A_B) and social influences (SN) do *not directly* affect behavior. Rather, their influence operates through intention, which directly determines behavior.

The attitude component, A_B, is the same construct we covered earlier in the chapter. The normative component, SN, represents a new concept. SN is intended to represent the influence of "important others." It is typically operationalized as the person's perception of what important others think the person should do with respect to a specific behavior. An example of how SN is measured follows:

Most people who are important to me think

I should ____: ____: ____: ____: ____: ____: ____ I should not perform behavior B.

The attraction of behavioral intention models stems from their ability to estimate the relative influence of behavioral determinants, thereby giving guidance to behavioral influence strategies. For example, when social pressures are a dominant force, then influencing behavior might require altering beliefs about referent expectations. Such efforts would hold little promise, however, if social others have minimal influence on behavior.

Research on the Fishbein intention model has been very extensive.[26] In many respects, the evidence has been quite supportive. Perhaps the strongest challenge to the model's validity has come from questions about how to isolate the influence of attitudes and social others.[27]

SUMMARY

An analysis of consumer attitudes can yield both diagnostic and predictive benefits. Identifying receptive market segments, evaluating current and poten-

---

[26] For a review of research from the consumer behavior literature, see Michael J. Ryan and E. H. Bonfield, "The Fishbein Extended Model and Consumer Behavior," *Journal of Consumer Research* 2 (September 1975), 118–136.

[27] Paul W. Miniard and Joel B. Cohen, "Isolating Attitudinal and Normative Influences in Behavioral Intentions Models," *Journal of Marketing Research* 16 (February 1979), 102–110; Paul W. Miniard and Joel B. Cohen, "An Examination of the Fishbein-Ajzen Behavior Intention Model's Concepts and Measures," *Journal of Experimental Social Psychology* 17 (July 1981), 309–339; Miniard and Cohen, "Modeling Personal and Normative Influences on Behavior"; Michael J. Ryan, "Behavioral Intention Formation: A Structural Equation Analysis of Attitudinal and Social Influence Interdependency," *Journal of Consumer Research* 9 (December 1982), 263–278.

tial marketing activities, and forecasting future behaviors are some of the major ways in which attitudes can assist marketing decision making.

Attitudes are defined as an overall evaluation. Intensity, favorability, and confidence are important properties of attitude. Each of these properties will depend on the nature of a consumer's prior experiences with the attitude object. As the consumer accumulates new experiences, attitudes can change.

The extent to which attitudes provide accurate forecasts of behavior will depend on a number of factors. The attitude–behavior relationship should grow stronger when (1) attitude measurements specify correctly the action, target, time, and context components, (2) the time interval between attitude measurement and behavior becomes shorter, (3) attitudes are based on direct experience, and (4) behavior becomes less affected by social influences.

One approach to examining the basis for consumers' product attitudes in terms of product attributes is the multiattribute attitude model. Both the Fishbein and ideal-point models provide information about consumers' perceptions of existing products, but only the latter identifies consumers' preferred or ideal configuration of product attributes. Behavioral intention models, on the other hand, permit estimation of the relative impact of attitudes and social influences on behavioral intentions.

REVIEW AND DISCUSSION QUESTIONS

1. A marketing research study undertaken for a major appliance manufacturer disclosed that 30 percent of those polled plan on purchasing a trash compactor in the next three months and 15 percent plan on purchasing a new iron. How much confidence should be placed in the predictive accuracy of these intention measurements? More generally, will predictive accuracy vary across products? Why or why not?

2. You are interested in predicting whether a person will purchase a new Chrysler from the Bob Caldwell dealership in the next month. Someone suggests the following phrasing for the intention measure: "How likely is it that you will buy a new automobile soon?" Why is this measure unlikely to predict the behavior of interest?

3. In January 1987, prior to market introduction, Mr. Dickson conducted a survey of consumers' attitudes toward his new product. The survey revealed that 80 percent of those interviewed have favorable attitudes toward the product. The product was introduced in June 1988, and product sales have been very low. What explanations can you offer for this discrepancy between the attitude survey and product sales?

4. In order to determine which of two alternative celebrities should be used as the endorser for an upcoming ad campaign, a company assessed how much target consumers liked each celebrity. Based on these results, one of the celebrities was selected and the campaign was launched. Shortly thereafter, the campaign was withdrawn, as it proved ineffective. Interestingly, when the campaign was reintroduced using the celebrity who was liked less, it was found to be quite effective. How can you explain the greater effectiveness of the less-liked endorser?

5. Consider the following results for a TV set, based on Fishbein's multiattribute model:

Attribute	Evaluation	Brand Belief
Clear picture	+3	+2
Low price	+2	−1
Durable	+3	+1
Attractive cabinet	+1	+3

First, calculate the overall attitude score. Second, calculate the maximum overall score a brand could receive *given* the current set of attribute evaluations. Third, describe the product's strengths and weaknesses as perceived by consumers.

6. Using the multiattribute results presented in question 5, identify all possible changes that would enhance brand attitude. Which change would lead to the greatest improvement in attitude?

7. Discuss the trade-offs between multiattribute models, measures of attitude toward a product, and intentions to purchase in terms of (a) their relative predictive power and (b) their usefulness in understanding consumer behavior.

8. Assume a company is trying to decide which consumer segments represent its best bet for future expansion. To help in this decision, the research department has collected information about segment members' product attitudes. The results show the following average attitude scores on a 10-point scale ranging from "bad product" (1) to "good product" (10):

Segment A	8.2
Segment B	7.5
Segment C	6.1

Which segment would you pick as being the most receptive to the company's offering? Why?

INDIVIDUAL DIFFERENCES IN BEHAVIOR:
PERSONALITY, VALUES, AND LIFESTYLE

MAUNA LOA MACADAMIA NUTS: HILLERMAN CATCHES THE CONSUMER

ncreasing sales for snack foods might be a task that would drive many marketers nuts but not those responsible for advertising Mauna Loa Macadamia nuts. "VALS (a technique for measuring values and lifestyles) makes it possible to personalize marketing and to understand the target we're trying to reach better than any other piece of research," says Jerry Hamilton, senior vice president and director of marketing research at Ketchum Advertising in San Francisco. "Sure, it may oversimplify. No matter what classification system you use, you're distorting everybody's individuality. But the alternative is to tailor advertising to 80 million individual households. We're no longer the only cobbler in the community who knows everyone and what kind of shoes they want."

We've moved away from the world of individual contact with the customer, but VALS restores some of that personalization, according to Hamilton. For example, knowing that young, college-educated professionals are 60 percent Societally Conscious (compared to 12 percent of the adult population) and 30 percent Achievers explodes the myth that young professionals are interested only in selfish pursuits and materialistic success.

Hamilton credits the insights derived from VALS for much of the success of Ketchum's advertising campaign for Mauna Loa Macadamia Nuts, which have seen a 20 percent increase in sales in the past two years. The agency identified Achievers and Societally Conscious as its two major targets. The challenge was to find an approach that would succeed with these groups, who are demographically similar but attitudinally different. Ketchum used as a spokesperson John Hillerman, the snobbish sidekick on "Magnum P.I.," a television program with both Achievers and Societally Conscious viewers. Hamilton says the Hillerman character appealed to Achievers because of his "upscaleness," and at the same time to the inner-directed Societally Conscious because of the tongue-in-cheek quality of his snobbery. The basic theme of the Hillerman commercials was also designed for dual appeal: "Mauna Loa Macadamia Nuts are almost too good to share."

Source: Bickley Townsend, "Psychographic Glitter and Gold," *American Demographics* (November 1985), 22–29.

No one is like anyone else. A fingerprint check will quickly cure all doubts should there be any. Even for such behaviors as choosing the clothing one wears, decorating a home, or pursuing leisure activities, few if any people have exactly the same preferences.

Personality, values, and lifestyles constitute an important building block in understanding why people exhibit differences in consumption of products and preferences for brands. These variables are not necessarily more important than other variables that you have just studied—resources, motivation, attitudes, and so forth. However, lifestyles and the underlying personality or values they reflect are frequently more visible. Even personality is more visible than is motivation or knowledge. It is not uncommon in daily language to speak of the nature of an individual as his or her "personality."

Personality, while understood in common language, has proved difficult empirically to relate to consumer behavior. A more comprehensive concept has developed called *lifestyle,* encompassing personal, social, and demographic variables that may also influence a consumer's behavior.

Products and marketing communications are often built upon the assumption of individuality in the personality or lifestyle of consumers. Notice in Figure 12.1 the explicit recognition of such assumptions. In the Sally Hansen ad, women are recognized as having distinctive differences that require substantial variation in the basic product because, as the ad says, "we know all women's need are simply not the same." In Figure 12.1, you also see assumptions that a Mercury Sable is for the type of man for whom music is "melodic, mellifluous, mellow, yet full of energy and surprise. A signature of the man himself."

As you saw in the previous chapter, some people place more weight or importance on an attribute (or have a different "ideal point") than other people. While attitude measures allow the determination that such differences exist, they generally provide little insight into the reasons people have such differences. In this chapter, we examine some of these individual differences and, where possible, how they relate to consumer behavior. Altogether, individ-

FIGURE 12.1   THESE ADS RECOGNIZE THE NEED TO APPEAL TO INDIVIDUAL DIFFERENCES

Source: (left) Courtesy of Ford Motor Company; (right) Courtesy of Sally Hansen.

ual variables influence decision stages of need recognition, information search, alternative evaluation, and purchase, topics examined in the next part of the book. They are particularly important, however, in understanding the perceptions that consumers have of their needs.

Personality

The term *personality* has many meanings. In consumer behavior, **personality** is defined as consistent responses to environmental stimuli.[1] The state of

------

[1] H. H. Kassarjian, "Personality and Consumer Behavior: A Review," *Journal of Marketing Research* (November 1971), 409–418.

organization in an individual, referred to as personality, provides for orderly and coherently related experiences and behavior. It also provides the particular pattern of organization that makes the individual unique and different from all others. The consistency of responses is derived from an understanding that personality is based upon *rather enduring, inner psychological characteristics*.

Three major theories or approaches to the study of personality have been used in consumer research: psychoanalytic, social-psychological, and trait-factor. Personality is sometimes related to the self-concept or the ideal self that individuals would like themselves to be, including Maslow's hierarchical theory in which people seek to achieve their fullest potential of self-actualization.[2]

PSYCHOANALYTIC THEORY

The **psychoanalytic theory** posits that the human personality system consists of the id, ego, and superego.[3] The id is the source of psychic energy and seeks immediate gratification for biological and instinctual needs. The superego represents societal or personal norms and serves as an ethical constraint on behavior. The ego mediates the hedonistic demands of the id and the moralistic prohibitions of the superego. The dynamic interaction of these elements results in unconscious motivations that are manifested in observed human behavior.

The psychoanalytic theory served as the conceptual basis for the motivation-research movement that was described in Chapter 9 but which was also the forerunner of lifestyle studies. According to the philosophy of motivation researchers such as Dr. Ernest Dichter, consumer behavior is often the result of unconscious consumer motives, which can be determined through the indirect assessment methods described in Chapter 9 such as projective and related psychological techniques.

The motivation-research movement has produced some extraordinary findings.[4] Typical of the psychoanalytical explanations of consumer purchase motivations are these often-related examples: A man who buys a convertible sees it as a substitute mistress; a woman is very serious when baking a cake because, unconsciously, she is going through the symbolic act of birth; and men want their cigars to be odoriferous to prove their masculinity.

---

[2] For descriptions of major personality theories, see Walter Mischel, *Introduction to Personality: A New Look* (New York: CBS College Publishing, 1986) and Larry Hjelle and Daniel Ziegler, *Personality Theories: Basic Assumptions, Research and Applications* (New York: McGraw-Hill, 1987).

[3] For a marketing view of psychoanalytic theory, see W. D. Wells and A. D. Beard, "Personality and Consumer Behavior," in Scott Ward and T. S. Robertson, eds., *Consumer Behavior: Theoretical Sources* (Englewood Cliffs, New Jersey: Prentice-Hall, 1973).

[4] The classic example of this literature is Ernest Dichter, *Handbook of Consumer Motivations* (New York: McGraw-Hill, 1964). For a recent example of motivation research by Dr. Dichter, see the "Steinman Dry Cleaners" case in Roger D. Blackwell, James F. Engel, and W. Wayne Talarzyk, *Contemporary Cases in Consumer Behavior* (Chicago: Dryden, 1984).

These examples are interesting and perhaps even useful. They are subject to serious questions of validity, however. Certainly one must go further to gain a thorough, in-depth understanding of personality and consumer decision making. A consumer's personality is a result of more than subconscious drives. Yet a great deal of advertising is influenced by the psychoanalytic approach to personality, especially its heavy emphasis on sexual and other deep-seated biological instincts.

SOCIO-PSYCHOLOGICAL THEORY

Socio-psychological theory differs from psychoanalytic theory in two important respects.[5] First, social variables rather than biological instincts are considered to be the most important determinants in shaping personality. Second, behavioral motivation is directed to meet those needs.

A representative example of socio-psychological personality theory is the Horney paradigm. This model suggests that human behavior results from three predominant, interpersonal orientations: compliant, aggressive, and detached.[6] The Horney theory has been used in marketing research in a form called the CAD scale, developed by J. B. Cohen and consisting of a 35-item scale. It has been applied in situations where the desire is to relate specific consumer choices to personality.[7]

TRAIT-FACTOR THEORY

Trait-factor theory represents a quantitative approach to the study of personality. This theory postulates that an individual's personality is composed of definite predispositional attributes called traits. A **trait** is more specifically defined as any distinguishable, relatively enduring way in which one individual differs from another. Traits can alternatively be considered individual difference variables.[8]

---

[5] Socio-psychological personality theory specifically recognizes the interdependence of the individual and society. The individual strives to meet the needs of society, while society helps the individual to attain his or her goals. The theory is therefore not exclusively sociological or psychological but rather the combination of the two. This theoretical orientation is most widely associated with Adler, Horney, Fromm, and Sullivan. For a more complete explanation of this approach see C. S. Hall and G. Lindzey, *Theories of Personality* (New York: John Wiley & Sons, 1970), 154–155.

[6] Compliant people are dependent on other people for love and affection and are said to move toward others. Aggressive people are motivated by the need for power and move against others. Detached people are self-sufficient and independent and move away from others. See J. B. Cohen, "An Interpersonal Orientation to the Study of Consumer Behavior," *Journal of Marketing Research* 4 (August 1967), 270–278; J. B. Cohen, "Toward an Interpersonal Theory of Consumer Behavior," *California Management Review* 10 (1968), 73–80.

[7] Jon P. Noerager, "An Assessment of CAD: A Personality Instrument Developed Specifically for Marketing Research," *Journal of Marketing Research* (February 1979), 53–59.

[8] A good introduction to the theory and techniques of this approach is found in A. R. Buss and W. Poley, *Individual Differences: Traits and Factors* (New York: Halsted Press, 1976).

TABLE 12.1 **TEST ITEMS IN THE** **MODIFIED** **PERSONALITY** **INSTRUMENT**	*Sociable* I am always glad to join a large gathering. I consider myself a very sociable, outgoing person. I find it easy to mingle among people at a social gathering. When I am in a small group, I sit back and let others do most of the talking. I have decidedly fewer friends than most people. I am considered a very enthusiastic person. *Relaxed* I get tense as I think of all the things lying ahead of me. Quite small setbacks occasionally irritate me too much. I wish I knew how to relax. I shrink from facing a crisis or a difficulty. *Internal Control* Sometimes I feel that I don't have enough control over the direction my life is taking. Many times I feel that I have little influence over the things that happen to me. What happens to me is my own doing. Becoming a success is a matter of hard work; luck has nothing to do with it. Getting a good job depends mainly on being in the right place at the right time.

Source: Kathryn E. A. Villani and Yoram Wind, "On the Usage of 'Modified' Personality Trait Measures in Consumer Research," *Journal of Consumer Research* 2 (December 1975), 223–228. Reprinted by permission.

Three assumptions delineate the trait-factor theory. It is assumed that traits are common to many individuals and vary in absolute amounts among individuals. It is further assumed that these traits are relatively stable and exert fairly universal effects on behavior regardless of the environmental situation. It follows directly from this assumption that a consistent functioning of personality variables is predictive of a wide variety of behavior. The final assumption asserts that traits can be inferred from the measurement of behavioral indicators.

A widely used measurement technique is the standard psychological inventory, such as the California Psychological Inventory or the Edwards Personal Preference Scale (EPPS). But borrowing standard scales that were designed for clinical purposes may produce poor results when applied to marketing.[9] A better practice is to modify standard tests for marketing usage. An example of such a test to measure traits of sociable, relaxed, and internal control is shown in Table 12.1. The research of Villani and Wind indicates that such scales can reliably measure these types of traits.[10]

Trait-factor theory has been the primary basis of marketing personality research. The typical study attempts to find a relationship between a set of personality variables and assorted consumer behaviors such as purchases, media choice, innovation, fear and social influence, product choice, opinion leadership, risk taking, and attitude change. Personality has been found to

---

[9] Raymond L. Horton, "The Edwards Personal Preference Scheduie and Consumer Personality Research," *Journal of Marketing Research* 11 (August 1974), 335–337.

[10] Kathryn E. A. Villani and Yoram Wind, "On the Usage of 'Modified' Personality Trait Measures in Consumer Research," *Journal of Consumer Research* 2 (December 1975), 223–226.

relate to specific attributes of product choice.[11] Research also indicates that people can make relatively good judgments about other people's traits and how these relate to such choices as automobile brands, occupations, and magazines.[12]

PREDICTING BUYER BEHAVIOR

Predicting consumer behavior has been the objective of most personality research, at least until very recently. The rich literature on personality in psychology and other behavioral sciences has enticed many researchers to theorize that personality characteristics should predict brand or store preference and other types of buyer activity. These studies generally fall into two classifications: (1) susceptibility to social influence, and (2) product and brand choice.

Much of the consumer researchers' interest in personality was stimulated by Evans, who attempted to test the assumption that automobile buyers differ in personality structure.[13] A standard personality inventory, the Edwards Personal Preference Scale, was administered to owners of Chevrolets and Fords. There were only a few statistically significant differences between the two groups. Using a discriminant analysis, he was able to predict correctly a Ford or Chevrolet owner in only 63 percent of the cases, not much better than the 50 percent that would be expected by chance. Using 12 objective variables, such as age of car, income, and other demographics, he made a correct prediction in 70 percent of the cases. Evans concluded that personality is of relatively little value in predicting automobile brand ownership.

A number of studies investigated the hypothesis that personality could be directly related to product choice. A few of these reported some relation between product use and personality traits.[14] Most found only very small amounts of variance in product choice explained by personality.[15] Looking back from today's vantage point, it is not surprising that these studies found little relationship between personality and product choice. After all, personality is but one variable in the process of consumer decision making. If any re-

---

[11] Mark I. Alpert, "Personality and the Determinants of Product Choice," *Journal of Marketing Research* 9 (February 1972), 89–92.

[12] Paul E. Green, Yoram Wind, and Arun K. Jain, "A Note on Measurement of Social-Psychological Belief Systems," *Journal of Marketing Research* 9 (May 1972), 204–208.

[13] F. B. Evans, "Psychological Objective Factors in the Prediction of Brand Choice: Ford Versus Chevrolet," *Journal of Business* 32 (1959), 340–369.

[14] M. J. Gottlieb, "Segmentation by Personality Types," in L. H. Stockman, ed., *Advancing Marketing Efficiency* (Chicago: American Marketing Association, 1959), 148–158; W. T. Tucker and J. J. Painter, "Personality and Product Use," *Journal of Applied Psychology* 45 (1961), 325–329; D. M. Ruch, "Limitations of Current Approaches to Understanding Brand Buying Behavior," in J. W. Newman, ed., *On Knowing the Consumer* (New York: John Wiley & Sons, 1966), 173–186.

[15] Ralph Westfall, "Psychological Factors in Predicting Product Choice," *Journal of Marketing* 26 (1962), 34–40; F. B. Evans, "Ford Versus Chevrolet: Park Forest Revisited," *Journal of Business* 41 (1968), 445–459; A. Koponen, "Personality Characteristics of Purchasers," *Journal of Advertising Research* 1 (1960), 6–12; W. F. Massy, Ronald Frank, and T. Lodahl, *Personal Behavior.*

lationship were to be established, dependent variables such as intention would be better candidates than would behavior.

Even if personality traits were found to be valid predictors of intentions or behavior, would they be useful as a means of market segmentation? A positive answer would require that the following circumstances prevail:

1. People with common personality dimensions must be homogeneous in terms of demographic factors such as age, income, or location so that they can be reached economically through the mass media. This is necessary because data are available on media audiences mostly in terms of demographic characteristics. If they show no identifiable common characteristics of this type, there is no practical means of reaching them as a unique market segment.

2. Measures that isolate personality variables must be demonstrated to have adequate reliability and validity. The difficulties in this respect have been extensive.

3. Personality differences must reflect clear-cut variations in buyer activity and preferences, which, in turn, can be capitalized upon meaningfully through modifications in the marketing mix. In other words, people can show different personality profiles yet still prefer essentially the same product attributes.

4. Market groups isolated by personality measures must be of a sufficient size to be reached economically. Knowledge that each person varies on a personality scale is interesting but impractical for a marketing firm, which, of necessity, must generally work with relatively large segments.

The evidence to date falls short of these criteria, and personality has not been demonstrated convincingly as a useful means of market segmentation. There is no reason to assume, for example, that individuals with a given personality profile are homogeneous in other respects; nor does it seem reasonable to expect that they have enough in common to be reached easily through the mass media without attracting a large number of nonprospects.

Research on personality has failed to explain more than about 10 percent of variance in behavior, even in the most conclusive studies. Proctor & Gamble conducted many studies in the 1970s using personality as a segmentation variable. They approached these studies with care, diligence, and the best resources available. After 3 years of effort, the attempt was abandoned because the brand and advertising managers could not generate results that allowed them to develop marketing strategies any more effectively than with other methodologies.

Research with the greatest ability to predict consumer behavior usually involves specific scales. Specific scales are developed for specific products or buying behavior. Naturally they will predict behavior better because they are so closely related to the behavior. Unfortunately, this causes such scales to lack generalizability—not to be useful for other products or other buying situations. More generalized scales or "pure" scales are derived from psychological tests with a history of validity and reliability evidence to support them. Although they have better support for use from a theoretical and methodological perspective, they generally do not predict consumer behavior as well as more specific scales.

The failure of personality measures to predict consumer behavior has stimulated development of more recent approaches. One approach is to study the personality of brands, rather than of people. The second approach is to relate personality measures to mediating variables or stages within the decision process, such as need recognition. The third approach is to develop broader, more behavioral concepts that are likely to be better targets for market segmentation — namely lifestyles, discussed later in the chapter.

BRAND PERSONALITY

For marketing applications, a more effective use of the concept of personality may be to describe brands. The assumption is dropped that people have consistent patterns (drives or traits) that guide their decisions to all brands or consumption situations. Rather, brands have consistent responses evoked to them, not based upon assumptions about the personality of the consumers responding to the brands, although such responses will be stronger in some types of consumers or personalities than among others. Brand personality is a portion of the brand's overall image, understood perhaps by many consumers but more attractive (or repulsive) to some consumers than to others.

Brand personality refers to the communication goals concerning the attributes inherent in a product as well as the profile of perceptions received by consumers about specific brands.[16] Brands have three dimensions. One dimension is *physical attributes,* such as the color, price, ingredients, and so forth. Tang is an orange powder that costs 89 cents, for example. A second dimension is *functional attributes,* or the consequences of using a brand. Lemon-fresh Pledge polishes the consumer's furniture and repels dust. Both of these types of attributes are objectively verifiable.

The third dimension of brands is their *characterization,* their personality as perceived by consumers. Brands may be characterized as modern or old-fashioned, or lively or exotic, just as people are characterized. The Obsession brand of fragrance may be erotic to some consumers or pornographic to others, while the Poison brand of fragrance may evoke a perception of danger. These elements, mediated by the information processing of individuals interacting with the brand, are transformed into a consumer's head as making the brand "appropriate for me" or "not appropriate for me," or possibly, "me for it."[17] *Consumer in Focus 12.1* illustrates how this approach affected the marketing of Dr Pepper in the cola wars of recent years.

---

[16] Joseph T. Plummer, "How Personality Makes a Difference," *Journal of Advertising Research* 24 (January 1985), 27–31.
[17] Plummer, ibid., 29.

12.1 THE DR PEPPER PERSONALITY

Dr Pepper is a brand of soft drink in the difficult strategic position of facing Coke, Pepsi, 7-Up, and Royal Crown with larger market shares and larger media budgets. Research conducted at Young and Rubicam indicated that the Dr Pepper brand had high awareness but was often misperceived, with consumers believing it was made from prune juice, contained peppers or pepper sauce, or was in some way medicinal, and had a weak personality.

A campaign was developed to develop a new personality for Dr Pepper, as "America's Most Misunderstood Soft Drink." Dr Pepper's personality was developed as an underdog fighting to gain awareness, using fun, irreverent, and larger-than-life situations. The campaign was successful not only in building a bright new characterization for Dr Pepper, but also a growth rate double that of the industry.

The campaign was so successful that Dr Pepper was no longer misunderstood.

Therefore, the personality was no longer appropriate and had to be changed. The new campaign developed the personality of a contender, more positive and aggressive and sure of its self. Since the physical attributes gave Dr Pepper the most distinctive taste, the campaign was changed to "the Most Original Soft Drink Ever," and later to a brash, assertive personality of "Be a Pepper." Through the cola wars of Coke and Pepsi and considerable research at Y & R, the strategy evolved to a personality for Dr Pepper that would be integrated with the type of people who favored Dr Pepper. The brand personality was one appealing to fun, off-beat underdogs, transmitted through advertising expressed in radical, changing, fresh, creative approaches.

Source: Adapted from Joseph T. Plummer, "How Personality Makes a Difference," *Journal of Advertising Research* 24 (January 1985), 27–31.

You might consider how fragrances or colognes have brand personalities. The fragrance you use says a lot about the person you are (or want to be.)[18] Which brand personality appeals most to you? Charlie or Cher? Poison or Obsession? Wild Musk or Old Spice?

EMOTIONAL RESPONSES

Brand or product personalities may be further understood by focusing upon the emotional responses that are evoked among consumers. Such responses may be closely related to the drives or motives discussed in Chapter 9. Rather than speak of individual traits or drives that influence behavior, it may be useful to consider the categories of emotional responses that are evoked from the consumption of a product or a specific brand.

---

[18] Patrice Serrani, *Gentlemen's Quarterly* (December 1987), 320–322.

When consumers buy products, they often want more than functional or tangible attributes provided by the product. They also want a good experience, a good emotional response from usage of the product. This is described as "hedonic" benefits of consumption, as we saw in Chapter 9. Although subjective and intangible, emotional responses also evoke physiological reactions that can be measured with physiological research methods.[19]

A battery of psychological tests are used to understand emotional response to brands. Some of these are standard psychological approaches, such as focus groups and interviews. Some are more innovative. The Foote, Cone & Belding ad agency uses a technique in which consumers are given stacks of photographs of people's faces and asked to sort them into types of consumers who might be typical users of certain brands. Each face represents a different emotional reaction to a product.

At the McCann-Erickson ad agency, consumers are asked to draw pictures about products and write stories about their sketches. For example, the agency was advising a client in the development of a new insecticide. To determine how people relate to roaches, the agency interviewed some low-income women about the insecticide brands they used. The women strongly believed a new brand of roach killer sold in little plastic trays was far more effective and less messy than traditional bug sprays. Yet they had never bought it, sticking stubbornly with their old sprays. Further research suggested that the women viewed roaches as symbolizing men whom the women said had abandoned them and left them feeling poor and powerless. The researchers concluded that killing the roaches with a bug spray and watching them squirm and die allowed the women to express their hostility toward men and have greater control over the roaches.[20]

In addition to these techniques, McCann-Erickson asks consumers to write newspaper obituaries for brands. The obituaries are interpreted depending on whether people describe the brand as young and virile and the victim of a tragic accident, or as a worn-out product succumbing to old age.

Are there categories of emotional responses found among consumers just as there are traits in their personalities? Several systems for this purpose have been developed. At least two are being applied in consumer research.

The Mehrabian-Russell category of emotions represents three dimensions. The constructs of *pleasure, arousal,* and *dominance* define emotions in terms of continuous dimensions; this is called the **PAD paradigm.** A more extensive list was developed by Plutchik to include fear, anger, joy, sadness, disgust, acceptance, expectancy, and surprise.[21] Although the indices of these approaches are correlated, research by Havlena and Holbrook indicates that

---

[19]James A. Muncy, "Psychological Responses of Consumer Emotions: Theory, Methods and Implications for Consumer Research," in Susan P. Douglas et. al., *1987 AMA Educators' Conference Proceedings* (Chicago: American Marketing Association, 1987), 127–132.

[20]Ronald Alsop, "Advertisers Put Consumers on the Couch," *The Wall Street Journal* (May 13, 1988). 17.

[21]Robert Plutchik, *Emotion: A Psychoevolutionary Synthesis* (New York: Harper & Row, 1980).

the Mehrabian-Russell PAD approach explains more about the emotional character of consumption experiences than does the approach of Plutchik.[22]

PERSONALITY AND DECISION MAKING

Personality can be used to explain intermediate stages in the decision process. Consumer researchers increasingly recognize that prediction of intermediate stages is better than attempting to explain behavioral outcomes with personality. The most promising of these attempts has been research focusing on the relationship between personality and information-processing variables.

The personality variable of **need for cognition** has been investigated and found to be related to how advertisements may influence the formation of attitudes toward a consumer product. Need for cognition (Ncog) is a measure of an individual's tendency to enjoy thinking. Marketing experiments by Haugtvedt, Petty, Cacioppo, and Steidley indicate that individuals high in Ncog are more influenced by the quality of arguments contained in an ad than are individuals low in Ncog. Individuals low in Ncog are more influenced by peripheral advertising stimuli such as endorser attractiveness than are individuals high in Ncog.[23]

Understanding personality variables such as need for cognition may be useful in several ways. Individuals with low need for cognition (Ncog) may require more repetitions before an ad is more effective. Individuals with high Ncog may need fewer repetitions but may need longer ads or ones with higher amounts of information. Individuals with high Ncog may rely more on newspapers and magazines for news, with television perhaps more useful for low Ncog individuals. While it is difficult to segment the market by the Ncog variable, understanding the type of individuals attracted may help design the communications program with greater effectiveness than not considering personality variables.

Risk taking is another variable that may improve our understanding of consumer decision making. As we saw in Chapter 9, there are risks in buying products that may be minimized by some types of marketing activities. But are there some types of individuals who are characteristically risk takers or avoiders? The answer seems to be yes.

Risk, as defined in personality research, is more than just uncertainty about outcomes. It is a personal expectation that a loss will occur. The greater a person's certainty for the loss, the more that person is a risk taker, a condition

---

[22] William J. Havlena and Morris B. Holbrook, "The Varieties of Consumption Experience: Comparing Two Typologies of Emotion in Consumer Behavior," *Journal of Consumer Research* 13 (December 1986), 394–404.

[23] Curt Haugtvedt, Richard E. Petty, John T. Cacioppo, and Theresa Steidley, "Personality and Ad Effectiveness: Exploring the Utility of Need for Cognition," in *Advances in Consumer Research* 16 (Provo, Utah: Association for Consumer Research, 1988).

FIGURE 12.2
APPEAL TO RISK TAKERS: ALTHOUGH A SMALL GROUP, MANY ADS ARE DESIGNED FOR TYPE T PERSONALITIES

Source: Courtesy of Coty Wild Musk.

that may affect attitudes in the multiattribute models you read about in Chapter 11.[24]

Some consumers can be described on a personality profile as "Type T," for "Thrillseekers." Individuals high in Type T have a higher than average need for stimulation and become bored very easily. They are predisposed to pursue adventure. People who look for positive thrills are call T+ individuals, whereas persons who seek thrills that are negative and destructive are T− personalities. Type T personalities are likely to list success and competence

---

[24] Robert N. Stone and Frederick W. Winter, "Risk: Is It Still Uncertainty Times Consequences?" in Russell W. Belk et. al., ed., *1987 AMA Winter Educators' Conference Proceedings* (Chicago: American Marketing Association, 1987), 261–265.

as their goals in life in contrast to risk avoiders, who list happiness as their first choice.[25] Risk takers are more likely to end up with health hazards such as those involving alcohol, drugs, and reckless driving, but are more likely to be self-motivated and well adjusted. It is easy to find advertisements directed to these people, who are believed to be about 25 percent of the American population. See Figure 12.2 for one example. Although such people are in the minority, some car ads emphasize the adventure and risk that appeal to Type T personalities, whereas most of the other car ads exhibit a less risky appeal.

Future consumer research seems headed toward more emphasis upon understanding the perceptions and responses of consumers in the consumption experience. Such research is focusing upon variables such as consumers' arousal-seeking tendencies and the manner in which they interact with sales personnel, especially as a determinant of planned and impulse purchasing and product/store situations.[26] This appears more effective than attempts to relate buying to the older, more general variables of personality based upon assumptions of pervasive traits or temperaments. Fortunately, as we see in the next few pages, more comprehensive concepts are available that were developed for the managerial interests of marketing organizations.

PERSONAL VALUES

Individuals possess values based upon the core values of the society in which they live but modified by the values of other groups to which they belong and individual life situations or personality. Within organizational settings, values have been recognized as very important to the long-term success of the organization.[27] The reality that personal values have always had a place in corporate settings has been incorporated as an appeal in advertising for the computer firm shown in Figure 12.3.

Personal values answer the question, "Is this product for me?" They are particularly important in the need-recognition stage of consumer decision making. Values are also used by consumers in determining evaluative criteria, answering the question, "Is this brand for me?" Values also have an influence on the effectiveness of communications programs as consumers ask, "Is this situation (portrayed in the ad) one in which I would participate?"

Consumer research relating to values has been influenced by the work of Milton Rokeach. In his book, *The Nature of Human Values*, Rokeach defines a **value** as an enduring belief that a specific mode of conduct or end-state

---

[25] Frank Farley, "The Big T in Personality," *Psychology Today* 20 (May 1986), 44 ff.

[26] Patricia M. Anderson, "Personality, Perception and Emotional-State Factors in Approach-Avoidance Behavior in the Store Environment," in Terence A. Shimp et. al., eds., *1986 AMA Educators' Conference Proceedings* (Chicago: American Marketing Association, 1986), 35–39.

[27] Kennedy, *Corporate Cultures*, 1986.

FIGURE 12.3   APPEAL TO PERSONAL VALUES: SELLERS RECOGNIZE THE IMPORTANCE OF PERSONAL VALUES IN THE CORPORATE ENVIRONMENT

Source: Courtesy of Acer Technologies Corporation.

of existence is personally or socially preferable to an opposite or converse mode of conduct or end-state of existence.[28] Stated alternatively, values are relatively stable but not completely static, as are beliefs (with cognitive, affective, and behavioral components) about what a person should or ought to do (but does not always do), both concerning the goals (end-state or terminal elements) and the ways of behaving (instrumental components) to obtain goals.

Personal values are usually measured as instrumental or terminal. The easiest way to understand the difference is to examine Table 12.2. Rokeach has surveyed American values and classified them by market segmentation

---

[28] Milton Rokeach, *The Nature of Human Values* (New York: Free Press, 1973), 5.

variables such as age, income, race, and gender. The median ranks of importance for instrumental and terminal values by gender are shown in Table 12.2.

Values research in consumer behavior can be used for market segmentation studies. Although the product studied most frequently has been automobiles, as in studies by Vinson, Scott, and Lamont,[29] family influences may be more important in such high-involvement purchases than in the buying of routine or low-involvement purchases such as cereal or deodorants. In a study of deodorants by Pitts and Woodside, for example, individuals who preferred Right Guard over Arrid were consumers with high importance on the Rokeach value scale measuring "mature love."[30] Other scales exist that can be used for measuring personal values in consumer research. Research is being conducted currently in Europe, Africa, and other regions that appears promising in relating personal values to consumer behavior, especially for purposes of market segmentation.

Laddering is a recently developed technique useful in understanding product attributes. **Laddering** refers to in-depth probing directed toward uncovering higher-level meanings at both the benefit (attribute) level and at the value level. Laddering seeks to uncover the linkages between product attributes, personal outcomes (consequences), and values that serve to structure components of the cognitive network in a consumer's mind.[31]

Figure 12.4 shows the attributes provided by wine coolers (carbonation, crisp, expensive, label, bottle, less alcohol, filling, smaller size) and how the consequences of those benefits (refreshing, thirst-quenching, more feminine, avoid negatives of alcohol, impress others, etc.) relate to the values (self-esteem, accomplishment, belonging, family life) of varying market segments. Any of these perceptual maps of the value structures could lead to developing alternative marketing strategies. Although the attributes might be the same, the image that should be developed for those with the self-esteem value would emphasize impressing others, perhaps with a sophisticated image — while the other image would be developed for the family life, emphasizing socializing without the negatives of alcohol. Additional analysis may indicate the size of segments, the degree of overlap between segments or appeals that can be used to appeal to the widest number of consumers, as well as the level of abstraction that should be used in advertising and other elements of advertising strategy.[32]

---

[29] Donald E. Vinson, Jerome E. Scott, and Lawrence M. Lamont, "The Role of Personal Values in Marketing and Consumer Behavior," *Journal of Marketing* 41 (April 1977), 44–50.

[30] Robert E. Pitts and Arch G. Woodside, "Personal Values and Market Segmentation: Applying the Value Construct," in Pitts and Woodside, 1984, 55–67.

[31] Thomas J. Reynolds and Jonathan Gutman, "Advertising Is Image Management," *Journal of Advertising Research* 24 (February/March 1984), 27–36.

[32] Thomas J. Reynolds and Jonathan Gutman, "Laddering Theory, Method, Analysis, and Interpretation," *Journal of Advertising Research* 28 (February/March 1988). 11–31.

TABLE 12.2
ROKEACH'S PERSONAL VALUE COMPONENTS CLASSIFIED BY GENDER

Terminal Value Medians and Composite Rank Orders for American Men and Women

N =	Male 665	Female 744	p
A comfortable life	7.8 (4)	10.0 (13)	.001
An exciting life	14.6 (18)	15.8 (18)	.001
A sense of accomplishment	8.3 (7)	9.4 (10)	.01
A world at peace	3.8 (1)	3.0 (1)	.001
A world of beauty	13.6 (15)	13.5 (15)	—
Equality	8.9 (9)	8.3 (8)	—
Family security	3.8 (2)	3.8 (2)	—
Freedom	4.9 (3)	6.1 (3)	.01
Happiness	7.9 (5)	7.4 (5)	.05
Inner harmony	11.1 (13)	9.8 (12)	.001
Mature love	12.6 (14)	12.3 (14)	—
National security	9.2 (10)	9.8 (11)	—
Pleasure	14.1 (17)	15.0 (16)	.01
Salvation	9.9 (12)	7.3 (4)	.001
Self-respect	8.2 (6)	7.4 (6)	.01
Social recognition	13.8 (16)	15.0 (17)	.001
True friendship	9.6 (11)	9.1 (9)	—
Wisdom	8.5 (8)	7.7 (7)	.05

Instrumental Value Medians and Composite Rank Orders for American Men and Women

N =	Male 665	Female 744	p
Ambitious	5.6 (2)	7.4 (4)	.001
Broadminded	7.2 (4)	7.7 (5)	—
Capable	8.9 (8)	10.1 (12)	.001
Cheerful	10.4 (12)	9.4 (10)	.05
Clean	9.4 (9)	8.1 (8)	.01
Courageous	7.5 (5)	8.1 (6)	—
Forgiving	8.2 (6)	6.4 (2)	.001
Helpful	8.3 (7)	8.1 (7)	—
Honest	3.4 (1)	3.2 (1)	—
Imaginative	14.3 (18)	16.1 (18)	.001
Independent	10.2 (11)	10.7 (14)	—
Intellectual	12.8 (15)	13.2 (16)	—
Logical	13.5 (16)	14.7 (17)	.001
Loving	10.9 (14)	8.6 (9)	.001
Obedient	13.5 (17)	13.1 (15)	—
Polite	10.9 (13)	10.7 (13)	—
Responsible	6.6 (3)	6.8 (3)	—
Self-controlled	9.7 (10)	9.5 (11)	—

Figures shown in the first two columns are median rankings and, in parentheses, composite rank orders. Figures in the last column represent the level of significance between male and female rankings.
Source: Reprinted with permission of The Free Press, a Division of Macmillan, Inc. from Milton Rokeach, *The Nature of Human Values*, 57–58. Copyright 1973 by The Free Press.

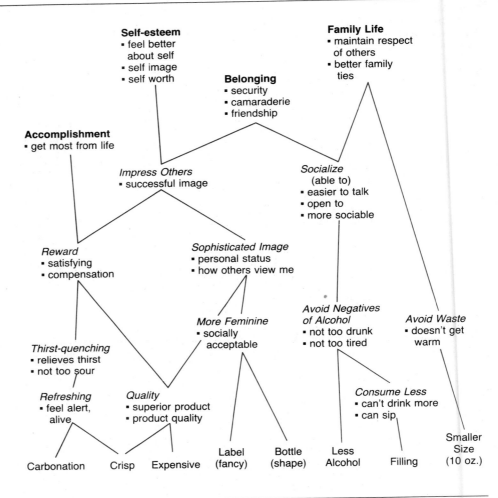

FIGURE 12.4
HYPOTHETICAL HIERARCHICAL VALUE OF MAP OF WINE COOLER CATEGORY

Source: Thomas J. Reynolds and Jonathan Gutman, "Laddering Theory, Method, Analysis, and Interpretation," Reprinted from *Journal of Advertising Research* 28 (February/March 1988), 19. © 1988 by the Advertising Research Foundation.

LIFESTYLE CONCEPTS AND MEASUREMENT

Lifestyle goes beyond personality. Lifestyle is a concept more contemporary, more comprehensive, and more useful than personality. For these reasons, considerable attention has been devoted to understanding the construct or word called *lifestyle,* how it is measured, and how it is used.

Lifestyles are defined as patterns in which people live and spend time and money. They are a function of consumers' motivations and prior learning, social class, demographics, and other variables. Lifestyle is a summary construct reflecting the values of consumers.

**FIGURE 12.5
APPEAL TO
CURRENT
LIFESTYLES: THIS
CONDOM AD
REFLECTS THE
CHANGING NEEDS
OF SOCIETY**

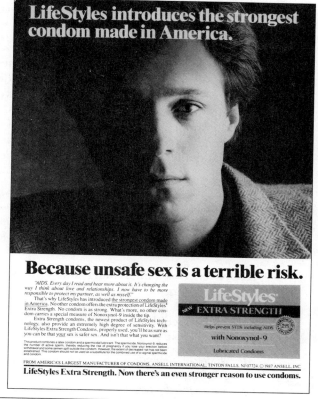

Source: Courtesy of Ansell, Inc.

Consumers develop a set of constructs that minimize incompatibilities or inconsistencies in their values and lifestyles. People use constructs such as lifestyles to construe the events happening around them and to interpret, conceptualize, and predict events. George Kelly has noted that such a construct system is not only personal but also continually changes in response to a person's need to conceptualize cues from the changing environment to be consistent with his or her own values and personality.[33] Values are relatively enduring; lifestyles change more rapidly. Lifestyle researchers must, therefore, place attention on currency and flexibility in research methods and marketing strategies.

---

[33] George A. Kelly, *The Psychology of Personal Constructs,* vol. 1 (New York: W. W. Norton, 1955). Also see Fred Reynolds and William Darden, "Construing Life Style and Psychographics," in William D. Wells, ed., *Life Style and Psychographics,* (Chicago: American Marketing Association, 1974), 71–96.

Products and their communications are often designed for specific life-styles. Notice Figure 12.5 in which condoms, a product that has existed for a long time, is positioned to reflect changing concerns about AIDS.

PSYCHOGRAPHICS

Psychographics is the principal technique used by consumer researchers as an operational measure of lifestyle. It provides quantitative measures with large samples in contrast to soft or qualitative research techniques such as focus-group interviews or in-depth interviews.

Psychographics moves beyond the views of consumers expressed in demo-graphic, behavioral, and socioeconomic measures. Emanuel Demby, a re-searcher generally credited with inventing the term, provides an expanded definition:

> *The use of psychological, sociological, and anthropological factors, such as benefits desired (from the behavior being studied), self-concept, and lifestyle (or serving style) to determine how the market is segmented by the propensity of groups within the market — and their reasons — to make a particular decision about a product, person, ideology, or otherwise hold an attitude or use a medium.*[34]

AIO, a term used interchangeably with psychographics, refers to measures of activities, interests, and opinions. Some researchers use the *A* to stand for attitudes, but activities are a better measure of lifestyles because they measure what people do. AIO components are defined by Reynolds and Darden as follows:

> *An activity is a manifest action such as viewing a medium, shopping in a store, or telling a neighbor about a new service. Although these acts are usually observable, the reasons for the actions are seldom subject to direct measurement. An interest in some object, event, or topic is the degree of excitement that accompanies both special and continuing attention to it.*
>
> *An opinion is a spoken or written "answer" that a person gives in response to stimulus situations in which some "question" is raised. It is used to describe interpreta-tions, expectations, and evaluations — such as beliefs about the intentions of other people, anticipations concerning future events, and appraisals of the rewarding or punishing consequences of alternative courses of action.*[35]

Examples of each category are shown in Table 12.3. Demographics are also included in most psychographic or AIO studies.

AIO STATEMENTS

AIO statements in psychographic studies may be general or specific. In either type, consumers are usually presented with Likert scales (named after the

---

[34] Emanuel H. Demby, "Psychographics Revisited: The Birth of a Technique," *Marketing News* (January 2, 1989), 21.
[35] Reynolds and Darden, "Construing Life Styles," 87.

TABLE 12.3	Activities	Interests	Opinions	Demographics
AIO CATEGORIES OF LIFESTYLE STUDIES	Work	Family	Themselves	Age
	Hobbies	Home	Social issues	Education
	Social events	Job	Politics	Income
	Vacation	Community	Business	Occupation
	Entertainment	Recreation	Economics	Family size
	Club membership	Fashion	Education	Dwelling
	Community	Food	Products	Geography
	Shopping	Media	Future	City size
	Sports	Achievements	Culture	Stage in life cycle

Source: Joseph T. Plummer, "The Concept and Application of Life Style Segmentation," *Journal of Marketing* 38 (January 1974), 34. Reprinted from the *Journal of Marketing* published by the American Marketing Association.

researcher who popularized the method of response) in which people are asked whether they strongly agree, agree, are neutral, disagree, or strongly disagree. Statements can be administered in person, by phone, or by mail, often in mail panels such as those operated by Market Facts of Chicago or NFO of Toledo. Examples of the Likert statements used in a study on leisure and time usage patterns are shown in Table 12.4.

GENERAL AND SPECIFIC AIOs   AIO statements may refer to general activities and motivations of individuals or they may be specific. The specific approach focuses on statements that are product-specific and that identify benefits associated with the product or brand.

One study concerned with health care services included both general and specific statements.[36] The study was concerned with predicting what types of consumers were likely to bring malpractice suits. Because attitude theory indicates that consumers try to behave in a way that will achieve consistency between their behavior and attitudes, it was necessary to determine specific attitudes toward physicians as well as toward malpractice. Thus, statements such as the following were included: I have a great deal of confidence in my own doctor; about half of the physicians are not really competent to practice medicine; most physicians are overpaid; and in most malpractice suits, the physician is not really to blame.

In this study, respondents who indicated that they have a great deal of confidence in their doctors also reported a much lower likelihood of bringing a malpractice suit. Respondents agreeing with the statements that physicians are not really competent and that they are overpaid and disagreeing with the statements that physicians are not really to blame in malpractice suits were more likely to file a malpractice suit.

Analysis of this study also showed that respondents who agreed with general AIO statements such as "I generally do exercises" and "I am sick a

---

[36] This research is summarized from Roger Blackwell and Wayne Talarzyk, *Consumer Attitudes Toward Health Care and Malpractice* (Columbus, Ohio: Grid Publishing, 1977), Chapter 5.

TABLE 12.4 AN EXAMPLE OF AIO QUESTIONS, CLASSIFIED BY SEX

Activity Statements	Females (N = 594)					Males (N = 490)				
	SA	A	N/O	D	CD	SA	A	N/O	D	CD
Vacation Related										
Our family travels together quite a lot.	38%	30%	7%	16%	9%	37%	33%	7%	15%	8%
A cabin by a quiet lake is a great place to spend the summer.	44	28	10	11	7	45	30	9	11	5
On a vacation, I just want to rest and relax.	31	30	7	23	9	34	30	4	21	11
I like to spend my vacations in or near a big city.	6	13	12	30	39	4	10	11	28	47
On my vacations, I like to get away from mechanization and automation.	23	33	16	19	9	28	37	14	16	5
Vacations should be planned for children.	17	39	16	20	8	18	38	19	18	7
Entertainment Related										
Television is our primary source of entertainment.	26%	26%	6%	23%	19%	24%	31%	6%	19%	20%
I would rather spend a quiet evening at home than go out to a party.	24	30	8	25	13	30	31	8	23	8
We do not often go out to dinner or the theater together.	20	22	8	19	31	15	25	6	22	32
Sporting Related										
The best sports are very competitive.	13%	21%	31%	21%	14%	28%	28%	20%	15%	9%
I prefer to participate in individual sports more than team sports.	11	18	39	18	14	16	29	25	17	13
Whenever possible, I prefer to participate in sporting activities, rather than just watch them.	15	27	15	19	24	25	29	12	18	16
I like to go and watch sporting events.	18	40	13	15	14	34	37	10	12	7

Leisure Time Related

	SA	A	N/O	D	CD	SA	A	N/O	D	CD
I have enough leisure time.	14%	23%	8%	28%	27%	13%	14%	8%	31%	34%
I tend to spend most of my leisure time indoors.	16	35	6	29	14	7	22	7	32	32
Basically, I'm satisfied with my present leisure time activities.	21	45	7	29	7	25	39	7	22	7
My leisure time tends to be boring.	4	14	8	26	48	4	12	8	27	49

Specific Activity Related

	SA	A	N/O	D	CD	SA	A	N/O	D	CD
I do a lot of repair work on my car.	1%	4%	23%	7%	65%	24%	24%	5%	16%	31%
I often work on a do-it-yourself project in my home.	37	34	15	7	7	36	31	13	11	9
I am active in one or more service organizations.	12	11	19	17	41	8	10	23	18	41

General Statements

	SA	A	N/O	D	CD	SA	A	N/O	D	CD
When it comes to my recreation, time is a more important factor to me than money.	23%	29%	17%	21%	10%	25%	30%	15%	19%	11%
When it comes to my recreation, money is a more important factor to me than time.	9	19	16	34	22	10	20	18	34	18
I watch television more than I should.	21	28	7	23	21	20	29	9	24	18
My major hobby is my family.	49	30	9	9	3	35	32	14	14	5

Note: SA = Strongly agree; A = Agree; N/O = Undecided or no opinion; D = Disagree somewhat; CD = Completely disagree.

Source: Douglass K. Hawes, W. Wayne Talarzyk, and Roger D. Blackwell, "Consumer Satisfactions from Leisure Time Pursuit," in M. J. Schlinger, ed., Advances in Consumer Research (Chicago: American Marketing Association, 1975), 833. Reprinted by permission.

lot more than my friends are" were found also to be more likely to bring malpractice suits. Such findings demonstrate how both general and specific AIOs can be used to profile consumers and relate their lifestyles to behavior.

MARKET SEGMENTATION

Psychographic studies are used to develop an in-depth understanding of market segments. Sometimes marketers use psychographics to define segments, but a better practice is to avoid definition of the segments through AIOs in favor of using AIOs to better understand segments that have been defined with more traditional variables.

AIO statements can be analyzed by cross-tabulating each statement on the basis of variables believed important for market segmentation strategies, such as gender, age, and so forth. Factor analysis or other multivariate techniques may be used to group the statements into a more parsimonious format. Factor analysis is a mathematical technique for examining the intercorrelation between statements in an attempt to determine common or underlying factors that explain observed variation.[37] Various hierarchical clustering techniques, relying on interobject distance measures, can be used, although factor analysis, especially Q (rather than R correlation), may reveal more of the interrelationship between factors.[38]

Such techniques often reveal factors such as the "traditional" segment or the "modern" segment or perhaps the "frugal" segment or the "natural" segment or group within a segment defined by other variables. General Foods identified a health-conscious segment of consumers through psychographics to reposition its Sanka brand of decaffeinated coffee. Previously, decaffeinated coffee was associated with elderly people. Through psychographics, General Foods targeted active achievers of all ages, using advertising appealing to interests of adventurous lifestyles. The ads featured people in lifestyles such as running the rapids in a kayak with the copy line that Sanka "Lets you be your best."

The purpose of psychographic analysis is to understand consumer lifestyles of the core customers in order to communicate more effectively with people in that segment. The analysis may also lead to efforts to position new or existing products closely to consumers in a lifestyle segment, perhaps more effectively than if the segment were described only by demographics. The idea is to go beyond standard demographics to position the product in line with the activities, hopes, fears, dreams, and so forth of the product's best customers.

An advantage of psychographic studies is the ability to define very precise

---

[37] Introductions to factor analysis are available in Joseph Hair et al., *Multivariate Data Analysis* (Tulsa: PPC Books, 1979); and George H. Dunteman, *Introduction to Multivariate Analysis* (Beverly Hills: Sage Publications, 1984).

[38] Alfred S. Boote, "Interactions in Psychographics Segmentation: Implications for Advertising," *Journal of Advertising* 13 (1984), 43–48.

FIGURE 12.6
APPEAL TO PSYCHOGRAPHICALLY DEFINED MARKET TARGET: THIS RANGE ROVER AD IS DESIGNED FOR A PARTICULAR TARGET MARKET

Source: Courtesy of Range Rover of North America, Inc.

activities and interests, as well as opinions of target markets. Figure 12.6 provides a very precise example. There exists high interest in activities that involve four-wheel drives. This activity and interest probably started among younger consumers, perhaps even those with a "counterculture" viewpoint. Many of those people have now become affluent and a little older. While they want the fun of four-wheel drive, they also want luxury. The Range Rover shown in Figure 12.6 provides an ideal solution. This segment may even have an opinion that is favorable for "braking for animals" and, thus, the juxtaposition of the headline is appealing.

In recent years, some general lifestyle methodologies for market segmentation, described subsequently, have gained widespread acceptance among marketing organizations.

VALS AND THE NINE AMERICAN LIFESTYLES

One of the most widely popularized approaches to lifestyle research for market segmentation is the VALS program, developed by Arnold Mitchell at SRI in California. The "nine American lifestyles" defined in this program, together with typical demographics and buying patterns, are shown in Table 12.5.

TABLE 12.5   VALS LIFESTYLE SEGMENTATION

Percentage of Population (Age 18 and Over)	Consumer Type	Values and Lifestyles	Demographics	Buying Patterns
Need-Driven Consumers				
4%	*Survivors*	Struggle for survival Distrustful Socially misfitted Ruled by appetites	Poverty-level income Little education Many minority members Many live in city slums	Price dominant Focused on basics Buy for immediate needs
7	*Sustainers*	Concern with safety, security Insecure, compulsive Dependent, following Streetwise, determination to get ahead	Low income Low education Much unemployment Live in country as well as cities	Price important Want warranty Cautious buyers
Outer-Directed Consumers				
35	*Belongers*	Conforming, conventional Unexperimental Traditional, formal Nostalgic	Low to middle income Low to average education Blue-collar jobs Tend toward noncity living	Family Home Fads Middle and lower mass markets
10	*Emulators*	Ambitious, show-off Status conscious Upwardly mobile Macho, competitive	Good to excellent income Youngish Highly urban Traditionally male, but changing	Conspicuous consumption "In" items Imitative Popular fashion
22	*Achievers*	Achievement, success, fame Materialism Leadership, efficiency Comfort	Excellent incomes Leaders in business, politics, etc. Good education Suburban and city living	Give evidence of success Top of the line Luxury and gift markets "New and improved" products
Inner-Directed Consumers				
5	*I-Am-Me*	Fiercely individualistic Dramatic, impulsive Experimental Volatile	Young Many single Student or starting job Affluent backgrounds	Display one's taste Experimental fads Source of far-out fads Clique buying
7	*Experiential*	Drive to direct experience Active, participative Person-centered Artistic	Bimodal incomes Mostly under 40 Many young families Good education	Process over product Vigorous, outdoor sports "Making" home pursuits Crafts and introspection

continued

TABLE 12.5 *continued*

Percentage of Population (Age 18 and Over)	Consumer Type	Values and Lifestyles	Demographics	Buying Patterns
8	*Societally Conscious*	Societal responsibility Simple living Smallness of scale Inner growth	Bimodal low and high incomes Excellent education Diverse ages and places of residence Largely white	Conservation emphasis Simplicity Frugality Environmental concerns
2	*Integrated*	Psychological maturity Sense of fittingness Tolerant, self-actualizing World perspective	Good to excellent incomes Bimodal in age Excellent education Diverse jobs and residential patterns	Varied self-expression Esthetically oriented Ecologically aware One-of-a-kind items

Source: Reprinted with permission of Macmillan Publishing Company from Arnold Mitchell, *Nine American Lifestyles: Who We Are and Where We Are Going* (New York: Macmillan, 1983). Copyright © 1983 by Arnold Mitchell.

Another approach, called Monitor, is available from Yankelovich, Skelly, and White, although the SRI or VALS approach appears to be used more by marketers.[39] We will examine VALS more closely.

The VALS system defines a typology of three basic categories of consumer values and lifestyles, with nine more detailed types. SRI describes consumer market segments as Need-Driven, Outer-Directed, or Inner-Directed.

Need-Driven consumers exhibit spending driven by need rather than preference and are subdivided into survivors and sustainers, the former among the most disadvantaged people in the economy.

Outer-Directed consumers, who are divided into three subgroups, are the backbone of the marketplace and generally buy with awareness of what other people will attribute to their consumption of that product.

Inner-Directed consumers are divided into four subgroups. They comprise a much smaller percentage of the population (see Table 12.5). Their lives are directed more toward their individual needs than toward values oriented to externals. Although their numbers are small, they may be important as trend setters or groups through whom successful ideas and products trickle up. This segment is growing rapidly, whereas the number of Need-Driven consumers is declining and Outer-Directed is holding steady. Many ads (as

[39] Rebecca Holman, "A Values and Lifestyles Perspective on Human Behavior," in Pitts and Woodside, 1984, 35–54; Sonia Yuspeh, "Syndicated Values/Lifestyles Segmentation Schemes: Use Them as Descriptive Tools, Not to Select Targets," *AMA Marketing News* 18 (May 25, 1984), 1ff; James Atlas, "Beyond Demographics," *Atlantic Monthly* (October 1984), 49–59.

FIGURE 12.7
APPEAL TO INNER-DIRECTED CUSTOMER: THE BEEF INDUSTRY WANTS CONSUMERS TO MAKE THEIR OWN DECISIONS ABOUT BEEF

"Make ends meat!"

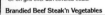

Slow Cooker Tex-Mex Beef Stew

2 lbs. beef for stew, cut in 1-inch pieces, 1 can (16 oz.) whole tomatoes, 3 to 4 carrots, cut in 1-inch pieces, 2 med. onions, quartered, 1 pkg. (1¼ oz.) chili seasoning mix, 1 T. flour, 1 can (16 oz.) kidney beans, drained, 1 green pepper, cut in strips

Break up tomatoes and drain, reserving liquid. Place carrots and onions in slow cooker. Arrange beef cubes on top of vegetable mixture. Combine chili seasoning mix and flour with tomato liquid; pour over meat. Cover tightly and cook on high 3½ hours. Add tomatoes, kidney beans and green pepper strips and continue cooking, covered, 30 minutes. 6 servings.

To prepare on top of the range, brown beef cubes in 2 tablespoons oil in Dutch oven. Pour off drippings. Sprinkle chili seasoning mix over meat; add reserved tomato liquid and ½ cup water. Cover tightly and cook slowly 2 hours. Add reserved tomatoes, carrots, onions, kidney beans and green pepper strips and continue cooking, covered, 30 minutes or until meat and vegetables are done.

Top Round Steak au Poivre

2 lbs. beef top round steak, cut 1¼ inches thick, ½ C. rosé wine, ¼ C. water, 2 T. oil, 2 tsp. instant beef bouillon, ½ tsp. thyme leaves, crushed, ½ tsp. rosemary leaves, crushed, 1 clove garlic, minced, 1 T. crushed black peppercorns

Combine wine, water, oil, instant beef bouillon, thyme, rosemary and garlic in small saucepan; simmer 5 minutes, stirring occasionally. Cool. Place steak in utility dish or plastic bag; pour marinade over meat, turning to coat. Cover dish or tie bag securely; marinate in refrigerator 6 to 8 hours (or overnight). Remove steak from marinade; pat dry with absorbent paper. Press crushed peppercorns into surface of both sides of meat. Cover with waxed paper and refrigerate 30 minutes. Place steak on rack in broiler pan* so surface of meat is 4 to 5 inches from heat. Broil at a moderate temperature to rare or medium (25 to 35 minutes), turning occasionally. Carve steak in thin slices.
*Or on grill over ash-covered coals.

Brandied Beef Steak'n Vegetables

1½ lbs. boneless beef chuck steak, cut ¾ to 1-inch thick, ½ C. water, ¼ C. cider vinegar, 2 T. brandy or apple juice, 1 T. sugar, 1 T. oil, ¾ tsp. salt, ½ tsp. dill weed, ¼ tsp. crushed allspice, ¼ tsp. coarse ground pepper, 1 clove garlic, minced, 4 large carrots, 1½ C. thinly sliced celery, 1 large onion, cut in wedges, ⅓ C. water, 1 T. flour, 3 T. butter or margarine

Combine ½ cup water, vinegar, brandy or apple juice, sugar, oil, salt, dill weed, allspice, pepper and garlic in small saucepan and cook slowly 10 minutes. Cool. Cut steak into fingers 1 x 3½ inches; place meat in utility dish or plastic bag. Pour marinade over beef, turning to coat. Cover dish or tie bag securely; marinate in refrigerator 6 to 8 hours (or overnight). Using vegetable parer, cut carrots lengthwise into thin strips 3 to 4 inches long. Place carrots, celery, onion, ⅓ cup water, 3 tablespoons marinade from meat and ½ teaspoon salt in saucepan and cook slowly 15 minutes. Remove fingers from marinade and pat dry with absorbent paper; sprinkle with flour. Quickly brown meat in butter or margarine in large frying pan to rare or medium, turning to brown evenly. Allow 2 to 3 minutes for each side. Drain vegetables. Arrange beef fingers on cooked vegetables and serve immediately. 4 servings.

We've always loved the taste of beef.

But with the kids growing up, our budget gets pretty tight. And I thought serving beef was a luxury we couldn't really afford.

So I did a little homework. And I found out that beef can still be one of the best buys around.

I didn't know there were so many economical ways to use it! Without having to cut back on taste.

Now we get more variety in our meals. Plenty of nutrition, too. Because beef is our favorite source of protein. With lots of iron and B vitamins.

And the economical cuts I buy give us the same high-quality nutrition as cuts that are higher in price.

These days, it's nice to know we can treat ourselves to one of our favorite foods.

Even on our budget, we can still make ends meat. With beef.

With the great taste of Beef.

Beef Industry Council of the Meat Board.

Source: Courtesy of Beef Industry Council.

in Figure 12.7) are designed to appeal to the "I Am Me" market segment. The ad for the Beef Industry probably appeals to several portions of the inner-directed group with its emphasis on making one's own decisions about beef rather than going along with the outer-directed others.

Advertising agencies and marketing organizations are using the VALS system in a variety of ways. At one time, Merrill Lynch Pierce Fenner & Smith used an advertising campaign, featuring a herd of galloping bulls with the slogan "Bullish on America." With the help of Young & Rubicam advertising agency, the theme was shifted to reach the Achievers target audience, who are upwardly mobile and self-motivated. As a result, the thundering herds were replaced in the ads by a lone bull that wandered through the canyons of Wall Street or huddled in a cave where it found shelter while Merrill Lynch and its Achiever customers were described as "A breed apart."

At Clairol, ads were developed for the Inner-Directed segment to make them feel in charge of their own lives with the theme "Make it happen" and for the Outer-Directed group the reassurance of "Sells the most, conditions the most." At General Foods, the Belonger woman was the target for Jell-O ads that show women in the provider role who don't make Jell-O for their families, they "Make some fun."

GLOBAL LIFESTYLES

Marketing strategy is conducted increasingly on a global basis, as we have seen throughout this book. Consumer research on topics as important as lifestyles, therefore, requires consideration of how lifestyle segments vary between countries. Table 12.6 displays such findings for several major markets of the world. As firms develop sophisticated, global strategies, increasingly they will need to use typologies such as this to develop products that appeal to segments of markets in many countries. Both the print and electronic media are reaching throughout the world as people subscribe to magazines on a worldwide basis and listen to satellite television. Thus, product design and communications strategies might be developed for the Achievers of several countries to reach affluent and growing segments. By 1992 in Europe, segments may be defined on the basis of lifestyles throughout Europe rather than the country specific approach of the past.

LIMITATIONS AND EXTENSIONS

VALS has gained rapid acceptance and widespread usage in marketing.[40] Nevertheless, it has its limitations. Consumers are not "pure" in their type of lifestyle. Respondents are given a score that reflects the degree to which they share similar responses on lifestyles other than their primary lifestyle.

---

[40] Rebecca Holman, "A Values and Life Styles Perspective on Human Behavior," in Pitts and Woodside, 1984, 35–54.

TABLE 12.6 VALS LIFESTYLE SEGMENTS IN GLOBAL MARKETS

Comparison of European/U.S. Lifestyle Types	Survivor	Sustainer	Belonger	Emulator
United States	Old; intensely poor; fearful; depressed; despairing; far removed from the cultural mainstream; misfits.	Living on the edge of poverty; angry and resentful; streetwise; involved in the underground economy.	Aging; traditional and conventional; contented; intensely patriotic; sentimental; deeply stable.	Youthful and ambitious; macho; show-off; trying to break into the system, to make it big.
France	Negligible number, but attributes as in U.S., some older. Belongers and Sustainers share characteristics	Old peasant women and retireds; poor; little education; fearful; live by habit; unable to cope with change.	Aging; need family and community; concerned about financial security, appearance, surroundings, health; able to cope with change, but avoid it.	Youthful, but older and quieter than in the U.S.; better educated; entertain at home rather than outside; consider ideologies to be dangerous; concerned about health.
Italy	Similar to U.S. survivors; live in northern urban slums.	Aging; uneducated; uprooted from agrarian society; dependent; concerned with health and appearance; escapist.	Aging; poorly educated; strongly authoritarian; self-sacrificing for family or church; fearful of change; fatalistic; save rather than spend; reject industrial society and its problems.	Youthful; mostly male; highly educated; reject family ties; highly materialistic; insensitive to nature; read more than average.
Sweden	Two categories: an older group similar to U.S.; a very young group of unemployed school dropouts who are alienated, apathetic.	Wealthier than others; fearful of children's economic future; concerned with own economic security and pensions; afraid of big government and big business.	As in the U.S., but more suspicious of government and big business.	Slightly older than others; concerned with prestige; want beautiful homes; prefer quieter lifestyles.
United Kingdom	Two groups similar to those in Sweden; older group is very similar to that in the U.S. The younger, unemployed, are more aggressive than those in Sweden—form cliques.	Working-class values; concerned about economic security; family centered; afraid of government and big business; mainly women; the youngest group is 35 years and over.	Two groups: one as in the U.S., with addition of wanting more satisfying work; the other traditional but more active, complaining; more concerned about education, creativity, emotions.	Older than others; mostly female; more interested in social status than job status; sacrifice comfort and practicality for fashion.
West Germany	Survivors in a psychological sense, not economic or demographic; fearful, envious, and alienated; concerned about social position, physical appearance; antibusiness; many are women.	Sustainers in a psychological sense only; negative feelings toward all aspects of life; resigned and apathetic; avoid risks; high level of hypochondria.	As in the U.S., although wealthier and better educated; more concerned about prestige and social standing.	Fairly young; well educated; mostly male; conscious about job status and social standing; concerned about physical safety.

Source: Arnold Mitchell, "Nine American Lifestyles: Values and Societal Change," *The Futurist* 18 (August 1984), 4–13.

Achiever	I-Am-Me	Experiential	Societally Conscious	Integrated
Middle-aged and prosperous; able leaders; self-assured; materialistic; builders of the "American dream." Two groups: older, more mature are similar to U.S.; younger are more intuitive; both groups less materialistic than U.S. Achievers; both concerned about ecology, environment, etc.	Transition state; exhibitionistic and narcissistic; young; impulsive; dramatic; experimental; active; inventive. Older (20–30); well educated; contemplative; little concern for financial security, social success, or materialism; enjoy their work.	Youthful; seek direct experience; person-centered; artistic; intensely oriented toward inner growth. Young; predominantly male; highly educated; not fulfilled by work, but by leisure; enjoy the present; hedonistic.	Mission-oriented; leaders of single-issue groups; mature; successful; some live lives of voluntary simplicity. Too few to be statistically significant, although most people have stronger Societally Conscious tendencies than in the U.S.	Psychologically mature; large field of vision; tolerant and understanding; sense of fittingness. Same as in U.S.
Middle-aged; predominantly female; links to family and religion; indifferent to self-fulfillment from work; want success and prestige, but otherwise escapist.	Highly educated; middle- to upper-class; 25–35 age; reject both traditional and consumer/industrial societies; political extremists; live now; bored; take light drugs.	Too few to be statistically significant, although some I-Am-Me's exhibit Experiential characteristics.	Well-educated; generally fairly young; led by protagonists of 1968 protests; satisfied; want more education; socially committed.	Same as in U.S.
As interested in status as in money; save more than U.S. Achievers, buy valuables for their children to inherit; this group is the most middle-class of all.	Older than in the U.S.; entrepreneurial; self-expressive; concerned about self-improvement; reject drugs and alcohol; seek rich inner and emotional life, warm relationships.	Hedonists; risk-takers; crave experience and excitement; enjoy dangerous pursuits.	Want simpler, more basic ways of life; active in communities; questioning and critical; concerned about physical environment and impersonality of large organizations.	Same as in U.S.
Too few to be statistically significant; status geared to social position; wealthy become more inner-directed; older people are unwilling to change.	Too few to be statistically significant; exhibit self-expressive characteristics, but are more Societally Conscious.	Highly educated; want excitement and adventure; risk-takers; creative and self-expressive; want meaningful work; want to demonstrate abilities.	Family-oriented, young; well educated; creative; want personal growth and meaningful, satisfying work; question authority and technology.	Same as in U.S.
As in the U.S., although more are politically active and more concerned about the environment.	Older than in the U.S.; find work meaningful and self-fulfilling; want to have an impact on society; have a high level of anxiety; emotional vacuum, looking for ideologies.	Too few to be statistically significant.	Too few to be statistically significant.	Same as in U.S.

12.2 MAX & ERMA'S CUSTOMERS

Max & Erma's is a chain of dinner restaurants based in the Midwest with locations in Indianapolis, Dayton, Detroit, Columbus, Lexington, and Pittsburgh. The business of the firm is defined as a concept for when the customer seeks a casual, contemporary, sophisticated, adult dining experience which is conducive to relaxation and fun. Major competitors include T.G.I.Friday's, Dalts, Houlihan's, Bennigans, Chi-Chi's, and others.

The firm grew rapidly in the late seventies and the early eighties, along with rapid growth in the restaurant industry. Losses were experienced in 1984, 1985, and 1986, however, and the restaurant undertook extensive research to understand better its core customers and to develop a more effective marketing program.

Customers had previously been defined as the "18 to 45" age group with an emphasis on singles, but the firm felt the need for additional variables that would explain the individuals who were the core customers.

A survey of 400 frequent customers (more than twice a month) was conducted to measure demographics, lifestyle variables (specifically VALS categories), and situation variables.

Using VALS categories, the Max & Erma core customer was described as 38 percent "inner directed" in contrast to only 20 percent of the population. They typically hold managerial or professional jobs, often with two professional incomes. They eat out a lot, will try anything, are sophisticated and nonconformist. They care more about their personal tastes than status or what other people think. They like a wide choice of offbeat menu items that would make a "belonger" really uncomfortable.

The Max & Erma segment also contains more (38 percent) "achievers" than the population (31 percent). They are success oriented with high education. They work hard, are motivated by good service, view value more in terms of quality than price, and have a high level of self-confidence. "Be-

Because VALS is a proprietary data base, some consumer researchers also criticize the fact that researchers do not have full information on the factor loadings or rotations or the explained variance.

Although VALS is clearly useful to marketing organizations, other approaches might be better if they were more widely investigated. Kahle, Beatty, and Homer compared VALS with the List of Values (LOV) approach based on the Rokeach theories. These researchers found that the LOV approach predicted consumer behavior better than VALS, possibly indicating better theoretical support for alternatives to VALS.[41]

Some marketing organizations have developed their own measurement

---

[41] Lynn R. Kahle, Sharon E. Beatty, and Pamela Homer, "Alternative Measurement Approaches to Consumer Values: The List of Values (LOV) and Values and Life Style (VALS)," *Journal of Consumer Research* 13 (December 1986), 405–409. See also S. M. Burgess, "Personal Values and Consumer Behaviour: An Historical Perspective." Working Paper #89/7 (Johannesburg: Business Economics Research Group of the University of Witswatersrand, 1989.

Individual Differences

Individual differences, the topic of Part III, are a major determinant of consumer behavior. The following full-color ads help demonstrate how individual differences shape marketing activities. Each one is accompanied by a short description of the relevant individual characteristic depicted by the ad.

Marketers' awareness of how buying decisions are influenced by consumers' temporal resources has resulted in a wave of time-saving products and services. In this advertisement Speed Queen points out the time-saving properties of its electronic washers and dryers.

Source: Courtesy of Speed Queen, a Raytheon Company, Ripon, WI/Ad Agency: Albright Street, Brookfield, WI.

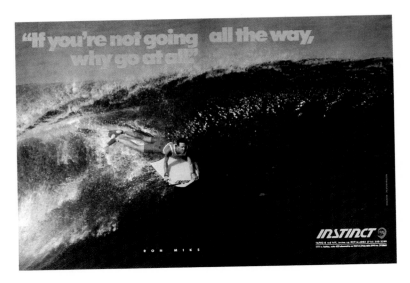

Consumers are motivated by both rational and emotional factors. In this advertisement Instinct seeks to stimulate an emotional response by encouraging the consumer to imagine the exhilaration of riding a bodyboard.

Source: Courtesy of Instinct Sportswear.

Innovations require marketers to create consumer knowledge about product features and attributes. Sony used an eye-catching visual to convey the advanced technology incorporated in its new small and lightweight video camcorder.

Source: © 1988 Sony Corporation of America. Sony, Handycam Pro, Fly Erase, and The One and Only are trademarks of Sony.

LIVE OFF THE LOW FAT OF THE LAND

Or the low salt of the earth.

When you enjoy Dorman's Light cheeses you can indulge in the delectable pleasures of a whole array of fine natural cheeses. And still cut down where you want to. Because some are reduced in fat. And others are low in salt. All are absolutely delicious. Discover Dorman's® Light in your dairy or deli department.

And live it up.

© 1988 Dorman-Roth Foods, Inc.

Attitudes play a major role in shaping buying behavior. Recognizing that some consumers have an unfavorable attitude toward "light" foods, Dorman-Roth created this advertisement to emphasize the quality and good taste of its low-fat, low-salt cheese products.

Source: Courtesy of Dorman-Roth Foods, Inc.

When Was The Last Time You Felt This Strongly About Anything?

Wake up in the morning, and life picks up where it left off. You do what has to be done. Use what it takes to get there. And what once seemed exciting has now become part of the numbing routine. It all begins to feel the same.

Except when you've got a Harley-Davidson.® Something strikes a nerve. The heartfelt thunder rises up, refusing to become part of the background. Suddenly,

things are different. Clearer. More real. As they should have been all along.

The feeling is personal. It affects everyone a little differently. For some, owning a Harley® is a statement of individuality. For others, owning one means being a part of a home-grown legacy that was born in a tiny Milwaukee shed in 1903. Regardless of the reason, more people

are getting to know the feeling. Harley-Davidson has reemerged as the number one selling brand of super heavyweight motorcycles in the U.S.A.*

To the uninitiated, a Harley-Davidson motorcycle is often associated with a certain look, a certain sound. Anyone who owns one will tell you it's much more than that. Riding a Harley changes you from within.

The effect is permanent. Maybe it's time you started feeling this strongly.

Things Are Different On A Harley®

We support the AMA and recommend you wear a helmet and protective gear while riding.
*New motorcycle registrations over 850cc, as per R.L. Polk and Co., Sept. 1987 YTD.

The personality of a product brand can influence consumer buying decisions. As this advertisement illustrates Harley-Davidson motorcycles have a strong brand personality — a certain look, sound, and feeling — that appeals to the soul of the serious biker.

Source: Courtesy of Harley-Davidson Motor Company.

longers" were more likely to choose the traditional offerings of Shoney's, Bob Evans, and other restaurants than Max & Erma's.

Individuals were also described by the situation in which they choose Max & Erma's. These occasions were convenience (24.8 percent), fun (20.4 percent), dates (19.6 percent), regulars (12.4 percent), fast (9.7 percent), families (7.9 percent), and business (4.2 percent). Max & Erma's was much stronger in the fun, dates, and regulars categories and much lower than other restaurants in the fast, families, and business situations.

A marketing plan was implemented during 1986 targeted toward the key segments. The menu was tailored to inner-directed customers with "name your own burger," "top your own pasta," and "build your own sundae" items. Individualized local store programs of special promotions, coupons, and direct mail were used. The achievers were targeted for less formal occasions. An extensive TV advertising program was developed featuring a well-known achiever attorney and his respected but more inner-driven wife, who is also an attorney. They both are shown in TV ads eating frequently at Max & Erma's. Appeals emphasized time convenience, relaxed fun, and quality menu items. An extensive training program for store management and waiters was also implemented to ensure high levels of customer satisfaction.

The results: The firm achieved a 14.5 percent increase in same-store sales in 1987 at a time when industry sales were declining. Sales in 1988 were 16 percent higher and growing even more in 1989. Profits were dramatically higher, even during the summer, a time when the chain had never achieved a profit in its history. The company attributed the success to its total marketing and operational program based upon a thorough understanding of the individual characteristics of its target of core customers.

---

systems that, while similar to VALS, attempt to be more specific to the organization's products and customers. ABC developed its own system to classify viewers into clusters relevant to television viewing, based more upon personality or fundamental psychological attributes than the attitudes and demographics they felt typified the VALS approach. They found, for example, a group called Family Oriented and another group called Rigid and Resistants. While both groups had similar demographics, the Families watch a great deal of situation comedies, but the Rigids watch more action-adventure shows.[42] Many other companies are extending the basic lifestyle profiles to reflect their special interests or marketing problems. The VALS typology has been used very successfully to segment Canadian markets in a study reported by Ian Pearson.[43]

---

[42] Bickley Townsend, "Psychographic Glitter and Gold," *American Demographics* (November 1985), 22–29.

[43] Ian Pearson, "Social Studies," *Canadian Business* 58 (1985), 67–73.

Multiple Measures of Individual Behavior

As you have seen in this chapter, multiple measures of individual behavior are used in the analysis of consumer behavior. Personality has an effect upon buying; lifestyles have more. Certainly economic resources such as income and time, described in Chapter 8, are also very important. Which is best in the development of marketing strategy?

An eclectic approach to lifestyles is the most practical for developing marketing strategy. The goal is to understand consumers as thoroughly as possible. *Consumer in Focus 12.2* illustrates how this was done by one company to achieve a turnaround in its market success. Rather than define its market segment as a specific income or age group or even a specific lifestyle, Max & Erma's Restaurants defined their segment as the "Max & Erma's customer" and conducted research using a variety of measures—demographics, lifestyles, and situation. With a comprehensive data base for each of these variables, management was able to develop multiple marketing strategies to enhance the appeal of the restaurant to a number of segments of core customers in ways that would not have been possible by focusing on only one of the individual influences on the behavior of its customers.

Summary

Purchase decisions vary between individuals because of unique characteristics possessed by each individual. One such variable is called personality. Personality is defined as consistent responses to environmental stimuli. Three major theories or approaches to the study of personality include psychoanalytic, socio-psychological, and trait-factor. Newer approaches to the use of personality include brand personality and more recent attempts to relate personality to elements of consumer decision making and information processing, such as the need for cognition.

Personal values also explain individual differences among consumers. Rokeach has identified such values as terminal and instrumental, or the ends to which behavior is directed and the means of attaining those ends. A promising approach of relating values to attributes of products is called laddering and appears to be useful in segmenting markets and the development of product and communications strategies to reach those markets.

Lifestyles are patterns in which people live and spend time and money. Lifestyles are the result of the total array of economic, cultural, and social life forces that contribute to a person's human qualities.

People develop constructs with which to interpret, predict, and control their environment. These constructs or patterns result in behavior patterns and attitude structures which minimize incompatibilities and inconsistencies in a person's life. Psychographics or AIOs measure the operational form of lifestyles. AIO stands for activities, interests, and opinions, and may be either general or product-specific.

The practical solution to marketing mix problems often involves looking at multiple measures of individual characteristics. In addition to personality and lifestyle, such measures include economic resources such as money and time, as well as demographic measures such as age or nature of the household. All of these variables may interact with the usage situation for the product.

REVIEW AND DISCUSSION QUESTIONS

1. Clearly distinguish between the following terms: lifestyles, psychographics, AIO measures, personality, benefits.

2. Explain the difference between a general lifestyle measure and a specific lifestyle measure. Give two examples of each for a research project involving a soft drink.

3. What is the basis for the VALS system? How might it be used by a marketing organization?

4. Describe the trait-factor theory of personality, and assess its importance in past and future marketing research.

5. Should a restaurant segment its market by lifestyle, income, situation, or some other variable? Explain your answer.

6. Assume that you have recently been employed by a large department store and have been asked to prepare an analysis of the market for furniture in your city. The president of the store is interested in doing a psychographic study and has asked you to prepare a questionnaire. Be sure to indicate the specific content of the questionnaire, some sample questions, the method of data collection, and methods of analysis.

7. Assume that you are developing an advertising program for an airline. How would you use laddering to assist in the development of the program?

8. How might personal values be used to segment markets for financial services? Could similar approaches be used in less developed countries as well as industrialized markets?

ENVIRONMENTAL
INFLUENCES

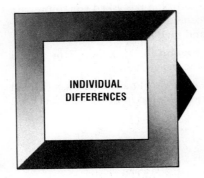

INDIVIDUAL
DIFFERENCES

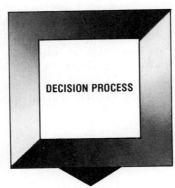

DECISION PROCESS

PSYCHOLOGICAL
PROCESSES
Information
Processing
Learning
Attitude/Behavior
Change

MARKETING
STRATEGY

PSYCHOLOGICAL PROCESSES

Now our focus shifts to three central psychological processes that shape all aspects of consumer motivation and behavior: information processing, learning, and attitude and behavior change.

The information-processing arena has attracted droves of behavioral science researchers in the last two decades, including those specializing in consumer behavior. This interest is understandable, because information processing clarifies the ways in which people receive information, interpret it, and use it in daily life. Chapter 13 covers a wide range of topics and issues in this field. You will find rewards from perseverance here, because the concepts developed are used extensively in chapters which follow.

Chapter 14 addresses the subject of learning. Certainly no single chapter can do justice to such a broad field of research, but you are introduced to various theories and concepts that have the greatest relevance for understanding the consumer.

Can consumer attitudes and choices be influenced? The answer obviously is yes, and much of the key lies in an understanding of persuasion. This is the subject of Chapter 15. An enormous literature is reviewed from the context of principles and strategies which offer the greatest practical payout.

INFORMATION PROCESSING

INFORMATION PROCESSING AND SELLING CLOTHING

Suppose it is your first day on the job as a salesclerk for a clothing store. A consumer walks in and asks to look at a sweater and a three-piece suit. Which one would you try to sell first?

Some might be tempted to start with the sweater. The logic for this approach is that the customer may be more reluctant to spend much more on a sweater if he or she has already purchased the suit. But clothing stores know better and often instruct their sales personnel to sell the more expensive item first.

The basis for starting with the more expensive item is grounded in an understanding of information processing. As we see later in this chapter, the interpretation of a stimulus (such as a product's price) can be affected by many factors. In the present situation, perceptions of a product's expensiveness can be enhanced or reduced by the price of the product initially purchased. By starting with the suit, the sweater will seem less expensive. A man might balk at spending $75 for a sweater, but if he has just bought a $300 suit, a $75 sweater might not seem excessive. In contrast, starting with the sweater can make the price of a suit appear all the more expensive.

Source: Adapted from Robert B. Cialdini, *Influence: How and Why People Agree to Things* (New York: William Morrow, 1984).

Encountering stimuli relevant to their functioning as consumers is a daily experience for most people. Ads, products, brand names, and prices are just some of the stimuli that continually impinge upon us. Estimates of the number of ads a typical consumer might encounter during a single day, for instance, range in the hundreds.

Because consumers' reactions to such stimuli, which will depend on how the stimuli are processed, can greatly shape their attitudes and behavior, an understanding of information processing can be very useful. **Information processing** refers to the process by which a stimulus is received, interpreted, stored in memory, and later retrieved. As you will see, an appreciation of information-processing principles and findings can yield some important lessons for the practice of marketing. Although advertising is perhaps the greatest beneficiary of what we know about how people process information, these lessons can be applied to many areas of communication, including personal selling, package design, branding, training of salespeople, and even consumer behavior classrooms.

STAGES OF INFORMATION PROCESSING

Information processing can be broken down into five basic stages. These stages, shown in Figure 13.1, are based on the information-processing model developed by William McGuire.[1] These stages can be defined as follows:

1. *Exposure:* the achievement of proximity to a stimulus such that an opportunity exists for one or more of a person's five senses to be activated.

2. *Attention:* the allocation of processing capacity to the incoming stimulus.

3. *Comprehension:* the interpretation of the stimulus.

4. *Acceptance:* the degree to which the stimulus influences the person's knowledge and/or attitudes.

5. *Retention:* the transfer of the stimulus interpretation into long-term memory.

Figure 13.1 indicates that a stimulus must be present and available for processing in order for the first stage of information processing, exposure, to occur. Following exposure, the consumer may pay attention to or "process" the stimulus. During this processing, the consumer will attach meaning to the stimulus, which is the comprehension stage.

The next stage, acceptance, is of critical concern in the realm of persuasive communication. Although the consumer may accurately understand what a

---

[1] William J. McGuire, "Some Internal Psychological Factors Influencing Consumer Choice," *Journal of Consumer Research* 2 (March 1976), 302–319.

**FIGURE 13.1
STAGES OF
INFORMATION
PROCESSING**

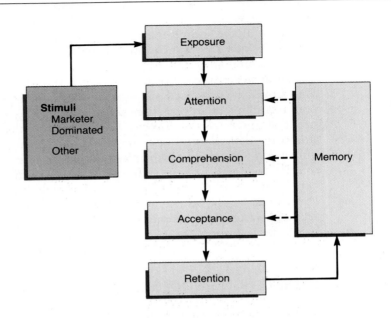

salesperson or advertisement is saying, the critical question addressed at this stage is whether the consumer actually believes this information.

The final stage, retention, involves the transfer of information into long-term memory. Note, however, that memory also influences prior stages as well. For example, the consumer who remembers an upcoming birthday of a family member is more likely to pay attention to gift ads. Similarly, the interpretation of stimuli depends upon stored knowledge and prior experiences.

An important implication of this information-processing model is that a stimulus must pass through each of the stages before it reaches memory. Consequently, the effectiveness of persuasive communications will hinge on their ability to survive all of the information-processing stages. This is not an easy task. In one study involving 1,800 TV commercials, only 16 percent of those exposed to an ad could remember the advertised brand.[2] Similarly, according to the Burke day-after recall test (described in Chapter 14), an average of only 24 percent of those people exposed to a TV ad can give a sufficient response to reflect that retention of the ad has occurred 24 hours after exposure.[3] One benefit you should derive from this chapter is a better

---

[2] Harry W. McMahan, "TV Loses the 'Name Game' but Wins Big in Personality," *Advertising Age* 51 (December 1, 1980), 54.
[3] "To Burke or Not to Burke?" *TV Guide* 29 (February 7, 1981), 3.

appreciation of the factors that influence the likelihood of a stimulus, such as an ad, passing through the separate stages of information processing.

EXPOSURE

Information processing begins when patterns of energy in the form of stimulus inputs reach one or more of the five senses. **Exposure** occurs from physical proximity to a stimulus that allows the opportunity for one or more senses to be activated. This requires the communicator to select media, either interpersonal or mass, that reach the target market.[4]

THRESHOLD LEVELS   Given exposure to a stimulus of sufficient strength, a person's sensory receptors are activated and the encoded information is transmitted along nerve fibers to the brain. This activation is called a **sensation,** which is affected by the following three thresholds:[5]

1. *Lower or Absolute Threshold:* the minimum amount of stimulus energy or intensity necessary for sensation to occur.
2. *Terminal Threshold:* the point at which additional increases in stimulus intensity have no effect on sensation.
3. *Difference Threshold:* the smallest change in stimulus intensity that will be noticed by an individual.

Many consumer researchers maintain that stimuli must attain at least the lower or absolute threshold before they can have an impact on the person. Others argue that stimuli below the lower threshold can be influential. This controversial concept has become known as **subliminal persuasion.**

SUBLIMINAL PERSUASION   Much of the interest in subliminal persuasion can be traced back to the late 1950s when Jim Vicary, the owner of a failing research business, claimed that he had discovered a way of influencing consumers without their conscious awareness. He reported Coca Cola sales increased by 18 percent and popcorn sales grew by 52 percent when the words DRINK COKE and EAT POPCORN were flashed on a movie theater screen at speeds that escaped conscious detection. However, when an independent replication of the study failed to show any effects, Vicary confessed to fabricating the results in the hope of reviving his business.[6]

For years the subject lay dormant until Wilson Bryan Key contended in a popularized book that erotic subliminal cues are implanted in advertisements (e.g., the juxtaposition of ice cubes in a liquor ad) designed to appeal to

---

[4] For a detailed review of the principles of media selection, see James F. Engel, Martin R. Warshaw, and Thomas C. Kinnear, *Promotional Strategy*, 4th ed. (Homewood, Illinois: Richard D. Irwin, 1979), Chapter 13.

[5] See W. N. Dember, *The Psychology of Perception* (New York: Holt, Rinehart and Winston, 1961), Chapter 2.

[6] Walter Weir, "Another Look at Subliminal 'Facts'," *Advertising Age* (October 15, 1984), 46.

subconscious sex drives.[7] Today, the use of subliminal stimuli is quite prevalent. The market is filled with audiocassette tapes containing subliminal messages that offer consumers the hope of overcoming their problems and anxieties. Similarly, some retailers have implanted subliminal messages within their in-store music that are designed to enhance employee performance and undermine a shopper's inclination toward shoplifting. Claims of a 20 to 40 percent reduction in shoplifting losses are not uncommon.

Despite their prevalent use, the power of subliminal stimuli is still a strongly contested issue. There is some research to suggest that subliminal stimuli can be influential, such as the work of Zajonc and his colleagues.[8] In a typical study, subjects are exposed to stimuli for very brief amounts of time (in the milliseconds). Exposure is so brief that subjects are unable to identify these stimuli in subsequent recognition tasks. Even so, subjects evaluate these previously seen but unrecognized stimuli more favorably than similar stimuli encountered for the first time. Such findings suggest the possibility of influencing attitudes without conscious cognitive activity.

Others, however, have challenged the effectiveness of subliminal stimuli. As stated by Moore:

> *A century of psychological research substantiates the general principle that more intense stimuli have a greater affect on people's behavior than weaker ones. . . . Subliminal stimuli are usually so weak that the recipient is not just unaware of the stimulus but is also oblivious to the fact that he/she is being stimulated. As a result, the potential effects of subliminal stimuli are easily nullified by other on-going stimulation in the same sensory channel whereby attention is being focused on another modality.*[9]

Stated differently, why should one choose a weak method of persuasion when much more effective methods exist?

---

[7] Wilson Bryan Key, *Subliminal Seduction: Ad Media's Manipulation of a Not-So-Innocent America* (Englewood Cliffs, New Jersey: Prentice-Hall, 1972). Also see Wilson Bryan Key, *Media Sexploitation* (Englewood Cliffs, New Jersey: Prentice-Hall, 1976). Key's claims have been strongly challenged. See Jack Haberstroh, "Can't Ignore Subliminal Ad Charges," *Advertising Age* (September 17, 1984), 3, 42, 44; Weir, "Another Look at Subliminal 'Facts.'" Research continues in this area and can be found in Ronnie Cuperfain and T. Keith Clark, "A New Perspective on Subliminal Advertising," *Journal of Advertising* 14 (July 1985), 36–41; Myron Gable, Henry T. Wilkens, Lynn Harris, and Richard Feinberg, "An Evaluation of Subliminally Embedded Sexual Stimuli in Graphics," *Journal of Advertising* 16 (1987), 26–31; Philip M. Merikle and Jim Cheesman, "Current Status of Research on Subliminal Perception," in Melanie Wallendorf and Paul Anderson, eds., *Advances in Consumer Research* 14 (Provo, Utah: Association for Consumer Research, 1987), 298–302.

[8] Robert B. Zajonc and Hazel Markus, "Affective and Cognitive Factors in Preferences," *Journal of Consumer Research* 9 (September 1982), 123–131. Also see Chris Janiszewski, "Preconscious Processing Effects: The Independence of Attitude Formation and Conscious Thought," *Journal of Consumer Research* 15 (September 1988), 199–209; Carl Obermiller, "Varieties of Mere Exposure: The Effects of Processing Style and Repetition on Affective Response," *Journal of Consumer Research* 12 (June 1985), 17–31; Yehoshua Tsal, "On the Relationship Between Cognitive and Affective Processes: A Critique of Zajonc and Markus," *Journal of Consumer Research* 12 (December 1985), 358–362.

[9] Timothy E. Moore, "Subliminal Advertising: What You See Is What You Get," *Journal of Marketing* 46 (Spring 1982), 38–47.

WEBER'S LAW   It is often important to understand whether a change in some marketing stimulus (such as price) will be perceived by consumers. A retailer who promotes a special sale, for instance, will be disappointed unless consumers perceive the discounted price to be sufficiently lower than the normal price. Similarly, claims of product improvement will be ineffective when consumers fail to perceive a difference between the old and new versions.

In these situations, the **difference threshold,** representing the smallest change in stimulus intensity that will be noticed by an individual, is quite relevant. This threshold must be met in attempting to generate perceptions of change. According to *Weber's law,* as expressed in the following equation, the actual amount of change necessary to reach the difference threshold will depend on the initial starting point.

$$K = \frac{\Delta I}{I}$$

where:

K = a constant that differs across the various senses,
ΔI = the smallest change in stimulus intensity necessary to produce a just noticeable difference (jnd),
I = the stimulus intensity as the point where the change occurs.

Weber's law suggests that, as the strength of the initial stimulus intensity increases, a greater amount of change is necessary to produce a just noticeable difference. Suppose that, in the area of price changes, K equals 10 percent. A discount of at least $5 would therefore be needed for a $50 item before consumers would perceive a real cost savings. This same $5 discount, however, would not be effective for a $150 item. In this instance, a discount of at least $15 would be necessary.

Note that businesses are sometimes interested in changing their products or prices *without* consumers noticing such changes. Price increases and reductions in product size (such as the shrinking candy bar) are changes that, if possible, should be undertaken without activating the just noticeable difference.

ATTENTION

Attention can be defined as the allocation of processing capacity to the incoming stimulus. Because capacity is a limited resource (see Chapter 8), consumers are very selective in how they allocate their attention. The reality of selective attention means that, while some stimuli will receive attention, others will be ignored. The marketer's job is to achieve the former. Consequently, it is important to understand the factors that determine attention. Such factors can be grouped into two major categories: personal or individual determinants, and stimulus determinants.

PERSONAL DETERMINANTS OF ATTENTION   **Personal determinants** refer to those characteristics of the individual that influence attention. For the most part, these factors are not under the marketer's control. Rather, their existence should be recognized and viewed as constraints against which strategy should be evaluated.

Need/Motivation.   Everyone is well aware from daily life that physiological needs have a strong influence on those stimuli that receive attention and those that do not. Hungry people, for example, are far more receptive to food stimuli than they would be on other occasions. Consumer economists have long contended that the worst time for food shopping is when one is hungry, because of the sharp increase in purchasing.

The nature of consumers' need states at the time of exposure to advertising should affect the emphasis placed on an ad's attention-getting properties. If it is possible for an ad to reach consumers when their needs are activated, then less emphasis on enhancing an ad's ability to gain attention is warranted, since the consumer is already motivated to process the ad. Unfortunately, this can be difficult to achieve because the time span of consumer decision making is often quite small.[10] More often than not, it will be advantageous to develop advertising that contains stimuli (such as those described shortly) that enhance attention.

Attitudes.   According to cognitive consistency theories, such as balance theory and congruity theory, people strive to maintain a consistent set of beliefs and attitudes (hence the name **cognitive consistency**).[11] Inconsistency in this cognitive system is believed to induce adverse psychological tension. Consequently, people are viewed as being receptive to information that maintains or enhances consistency, while avoiding information that challenges their beliefs and attitudes.

The principle of cognitive consistency suggests that attitudes may also influence the attention given to marketing communications. Consumers possessing unfavorable attitudes may allocate little attention, such as an avid antismoker exposed to the cigarette industry's campaign of "smokers' rights." On the other hand, smokers should be much more attentive to these messages. Thus, attitude can be a facilitator when consumers hold favorable feelings toward the product but may serve as a barrier when consumers are negative.

Adaptation Level.   An important tendency people share is to become so habituated to a stimulus that it is no longer noticed—that is, they develop an **adaptation level** for the stimulus. Consider, for example, the couple who moves from a quiet, small town to an apartment in the middle of New York City. Initially, they will find the noise levels to be very disturbing and will suffer through many nights of restless sleep. Eventually, however, they will grow accustomed or become adapted to the noise.

---

[10] National Advertising Bureau, *How America Shops and Buys* (June 1983), 23.

[11] For a discussion of cognitive consistency theories, see William J. McGuire, "The Current Status of Cognitive Consistency Theories," in Joel B. Cohen, ed., *Behavioral Science Foundations of Consumer Behavior* (New York: Free Press, 1972), 253–274.

This same phenomenon occurs in marketing. Advertising is especially likely to fall victim to adaptation. Many products are familiar, and it is often difficult to say much that is really new. This can place some real demands on the design and format of the message. Similarly, repeated exposure to an ad may not be effective as consumers become habituated to this stimulus. A strategy of repetition must, therefore, be carefully conceived because of the danger of habituation.

Although adaptation level frequently represents a barrier between marketers and consumers, marketers can also employ it to their advantage. The use of unique product packaging, for instance, can help a product stand out on the shelf. Similarly, an advertising tactic for gaining attention is to include stimuli within an ad that deviate from the consumer's adaptation level. The use of the phrase "A bad ad" in the advertisement appearing in Figure 13.2 is contrary to what consumers expect to see in an ad. As described subsequently, some of the stimulus factors that help capture attention do so because they capitalize on adaptation.

FIGURE 13.2
DEVIATING FROM CONSUMERS' ADAPTATION LEVEL CAN HELP CAPTURE THEIR ATTENTION

Source: Reprinted with the permission of The Little Tikes Company © 1987.

Span of Attention.   The amount of time we can focus our attention on a single stimulus or thought is quite limited. You can easily demonstrate this to yourself by testing just how long you are able to concentrate on a particular thought before your mind begins to "wander." This limited span of attention may partly explain the increasing use of shorter commercials.

STIMULUS DETERMINANTS OF ATTENTION   The second set of factors influencing attention, **stimulus determinants,** are characteristic of the stimulus itself. They represent "controllable" factors in the sense that they can be used for gaining and/or increasing attention.

Size.   In general, the larger the stimulus, the more likely it will attract attention. Increasing a print ad's size will enhance the odds of gaining the consumer's attention.[12] A similar relationship holds for the size of the illustrations or pictures within an ad.[13]

The likelihood of a product being noticed in a store can depend upon the size or amount of shelf space allocated to the product. This can be particularly important for impulse items, whose sales may depend partly on how much space they receive.[14]

Color.   The attention-attracting and holding power of a stimulus may be sharply increased through the use of color.[15] Companies placing ads in the Yellow Pages, for instance, are encouraged to use the color red as a means of attracting the consumer's attention. In a field study involving newspaper advertising, one-color ads produced 41 percent more sales than did their black-and-white counterparts.[16] Color ads cost more, so their incremental effectiveness must be weighed against the additional expense.

Intensity.   Greater stimulus intensity often produces more attention. Loud sounds and bright colors, for instance, can enhance attention. Radio and television commercials often begin with a loud noise to attract attention. Brightly colored print ads are also quite common.

Contrast.   People have a tendency to attend more closely to those stimuli that contrast with their background. The presentation of stimuli that are inconsistent or contrast with one another creates a perceptual conflict that

---

[12] Adam Finn, "Print Ad Recognition Readership Scores: An Information Processing Perspective," *Journal of Marketing Research* 25 (May 1988), 168–177.

[13] Ibid.

[14] Keith K. Cox, "The Effect of Shelf Space upon Sales of Branded Products," *Journal of Marketing Research* 7 (February 1970), 55–58.

[15] Finn, "Print Ad Recognition Readership Scores: An Information Processing Perspective."

[16] Larry Percy, *Ways in Which the People, Words and Pictures in Advertising Influence Its Effectiveness* (Chicago: Financial Institutions Marketing Association, July 1984), 19.

enhances attention. An example of the use of contrast in print advertisement appears in Figure 13.3.

Techniques based on the contrast principle appear in a variety of forms in advertising. For example, a black-and-white ad preceded by color ads may be more noticed because of contrast. Similarly, a TV ad that is louder than the programming that preceded it may also attract greater attention. Note that both examples follow from adaptation level: that is, the person becomes adapted to color ads only or to a certain volume which, when violated, attracts their attention.

Position. Stimuli may also be more noticeable simply because of certain locational properties. Grocery vendors know this very well and compete for such prime grocery locations as the end of aisle and shelves located near eye level. Similarly, impulse items are strategically located near cash registers.

Position can also be important for print media. A recent study reports greater attention for ads located in the front rather than back part of the

**FIGURE 13.3
THE USE OF
CONTRAST IN
ADVERTISING
INCREASES
CONSUMER
ATTENTION**

FIGURE 13.4
AN AD DESIGN THAT MAY ENCOURAGE IMPROPER EYE MOVEMENT

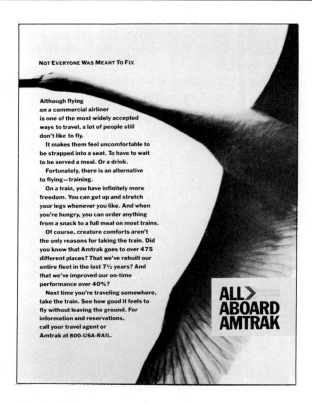

magazine, on right-hand pages rather than left-hand pages, and on the inside front, inside back, and outside back covers.[17] Presumably, these effects are due to the manner in which consumers typically flip through magazines.

Position in broadcast advertising has received less attention in research, although it is a generally accepted rule that commercials perform better when included as part of the regular program rather than during the "clutter" of a program break.[18] Commercials at the beginning and end of a program suffer from the clutter of announcements and other distracting nonprogram material.

[17] Finn, "Print Ad Recognition Readership Scores: An Information Processing Perspective."

[18] For research on advertising clutter, see Peter H. Webb, "Consumer Initial Processing in a Difficult Media Environment," *Journal of Consumer Research* 6 (December 1979), 225–236. Also see Michael L. Ray and Peter H. Webb, "Three Prescriptions for Clutter," *Journal of Advertising Research* 26 (February/March 1986), 69–77.

Directionality.   The eye will tend to follow any signs within the stimulus that indicate directionality. Examples would be arrows or pointing devices. Examine the ad in Figure 13.4. Does it direct the eye to the brand name and pertinent copy? The answer is pretty obvious. The eye goes into the "left field" rather than downward to the Amtrak name. Surprisingly, this commonsense principle is often violated.

Movement.   Stimuli in motion attract greater attention than stationary stimuli. Even quasi or perceived motion, as illustrated by the ad in Figure 13.5, can enhance attention.

Isolation.   Isolation involves presenting a small number of stimuli in a relatively barren perceptual field. For example, a single object in the middle of a large space or a couple of words in the middle of a blank page (see Figure 13.6) attract attention.

Novelty.   Unusual or unexpected stimuli (e.g., those that deviate from one's adaptation level) attract attention. Advertisers understand the value of

FIGURE 13.5   ATTRACTING ATTENTION WITH QUASIMOTION

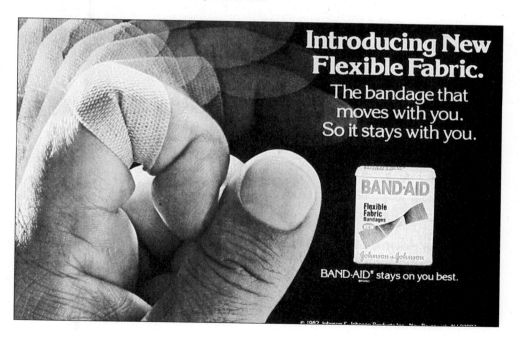

FIGURE 13.6
GAINING ATTENTION
WITH ISOLATION

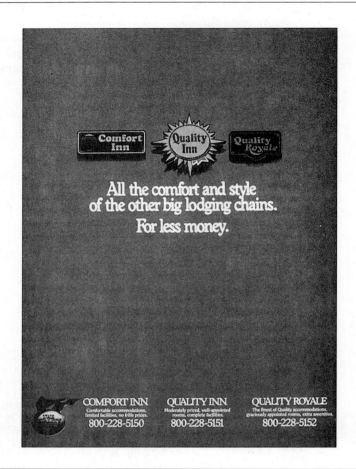

novelty and frequently rely upon it for gaining attention, as illustrated by Figure 13.7. Recent applications include pop-up ads (such as the Dodge ad that showed three views of the Dakota pickup truck), 3-D ads (remember the Coke commercial during the halftime show of the 1989 Superbowl?), and print ads that play music thanks to microchip technology (such as a two-page whiskey ad containing a musical microchip activated by opening the ad).[19]

---

[19]Joe Agnew, "Musical Whiskey Ad to Chime in Time for Christmas," *Marketing News* 21 (October 9, 1987), 24–25; "Oh, What a 3-D Feeling from Toyota," *Marketing News* 21 (October 23, 1987), 9.

**FIGURE 13.7
ATTRACTING
ATTENTION WITH
NOVELTY**

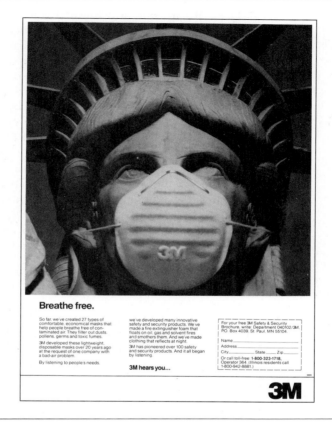

Breathe free.

So far, we've created 27 types of comfortable, economical masks that help people breathe free of contaminated air. They filter out dusts, pollens, germs and toxic fumes.

3M developed these lightweight, disposable masks over 20 years ago at the request of one company with a bad-air problem.

By listening to people's needs,

we've developed many innovative safety and security products. We've made a fire extinguisher foam that floats on oil, gas and solvent fires and smothers them. And we've made clothing that reflects at night.

3M has pioneered over 100 safety and security products. And it all began by listening.

3M hears you...

For your free 3M Safety & Security Brochure, write: Department 040102/3M, P.O. Box 4039, St. Paul, MN 55104.

Name_____
Address_____
City_____ State_____ Zip_____
Or call toll-free: **1-800-323-1718,**
Operator 364. (Illinois residents call
1-800-942-8881.)

3M

"Learned" Attention-Inducing Stimuli.   Some stimuli attract our attention because we have been taught or conditioned to react to them. A ringing phone or doorbell, for example, typically elicits an immediate response from the person. Ringing phones or wailing sirens are sometimes included in the background of radio and TV ads to capture attention.

Attractive Spokesperson.   A common attention-grabbing device is to employ an attractive model or celebrity as a spokesperson.[20] It is nearly impossible

---

[20] For research in this area, see M. Wayne Alexander and Ben Judd, Jr., "Do Nudes in Ads Enhance Brand Recall?" *Journal of Advertising Research* 18 (February 1978), 47–50; Michael J. Baker and Gilbert A. Churchill, Jr., "The Impact of Physically Attractive Models on Advertising Evaluations," *Journal of Marketing Research* 14 (November 1977), 538–555; M. Steadman, "How Sexy Illustrations Affect Brand Recall," *Journal of Advertising Research* 9 (March 1969), 15–18; Lynn R. Kahle and Pamela M. Homer, "Physical Attractiveness of the Celebrity Endorser: A Social Adaptation Perspective," *Journal of Consumer Research* 11 (March 1985), 954–961.

to watch TV for any length of time or flip through most magazines without encountering at least one ad with an attractive person. One company, in an effort to break through the clutter of products on supermarket shelves, has developed a line of common grocery products (e.g., cereal, trash bags, light bulbs) named Star Pak, which features the faces of some very famous movie stars (Marilyn Monroe, Clark Gable) on the product packaging.[21]

One danger of using a spokesperson is that it can backfire when consumers perceive it as inappropriate for the product being advertised. Models attired in bathing suits, while seen as appropriate endorsers for suntan products, may evoke unfavorable reactions when used to promote furniture.

Scene Changes.   A new technique for capturing attention is the use of rapid-fire scene changes, which can cause an involuntary increase in brain activity.[22] In some Pontiac commercials, the viewer is exposed to a large number of scenes that last no longer than 1½ seconds, with some scenes as short as ¼ of a second. This same approach was used in the Goodyear commercials featured so prominently during the broadcast of the 1988 Summer Olympics.

ATTRACTING ATTENTION: A PRECAUTION   As we have already pointed out, capturing the consumer's attention represents a major challenge to marketers. This will only become more difficult as consumers are bombarded with increasing numbers of products and promotions. Very often, marketers will have little choice but to rely on stimulus factors as bait for the consumer's attention.

We must be sensitive, however, to the fact that the use of stimulus factors is not without risk. A stimulus that dominates viewers' attention, while leaving the remaining message ignored, is self-defeating. The marketer must try to use stimuli that capture attention initially but that do not inhibit processing of the entire message. Whenever possible, stimuli should be employed that help reinforce the brand name or product positioning as well as gain attention. In this regard, the ad presented in Figure 13.3 provides an excellent illustration of using a stimulus that attracts attention while communicating the benefits of product use.

COMPREHENSION

Comprehension, the third stage of information processing, is concerned with the interpretation of a stimulus. It is the point at which meaning is attached to the stimulus. This meaning will depend on how a stimulus is categorized and elaborated in terms of existing knowledge.

---

[21] Joe Agnew, "Shoppers' Star Gazing Seen as Strategy to Slash Supermarket Shelf Clutter," *Marketing News* 21 (January 16, 1987), 1, 16.
[22] David H. Freedman, "Why You Watch Some Commercials — Whether You Mean To or Not," *TV Guide* (February 20, 1988), 4–7.

STIMULUS CATEGORIZATION   **Stimulus categorization** involves classifying a stimulus using concepts stored in memory.[23] Consumers' behavior can be affected by how they categorize marketing stimuli. Toro introduced a light-weight snowthrower named Snow Pup, which proved unsuccessful because the name led consumers to categorize the product either as a toy or as not powerful enough for the job. Changing the name (to first Snowmaster and then Toro) reversed this problem and made the product a success.[24]

Thus, influencing stimulus categorization can often be quite important. Consider, for example, the ad appearing in Figure 13.8. Note how it attempts to broaden the product's appeal by encouraging consumers to employ several categories during the categorization process.

STIMULUS ELABORATION   In addition to classifying a stimulus, compre-hension also involves the degree of elaboration that occurs during stimulus processing. **Elaboration** refers to the amount of integration between the new information and existing knowledge stored in memory or, as some have de-scribed it, the number of personal connections made between the stimulus and one's life experiences and goals.[25] Elaboration falls along a continuum ranging from low to high (or shallow to deep).[26]

Consumer researchers have typically focused on elaboration in the form of semantic or verbal elaboration. The amount and nature of elaboration during ad processing, for example, is often measured by asking subjects to write down the thoughts that occur while viewing the ad.[27] As discussed under the acceptance stage, these thoughts can determine the persuasive impact of a stimulus.

Recently, however, there has been a growing interest in the amount of **imagery** that occurs during information processing. Imagery is a process by which sensory information and experiences are represented in working

---

[23] Excellent discussions of categorization in the context of consumer information processing can be found in Joseph W. Alba and J. Wesley Hutchinson, "Dimensions of Consumer Expertise," *Journal of Consumer Research* 13 (March 1987), 411–454; Joel B. Cohen and Kunal Basu, "Alterna-tive Models of Categorization: Toward a Contingent Processing Framework," *Journal of Consumer Research* 13 (March 1987), 455–472.

[24] J. Neher, "Toro Cutting a Wide Swath in Outdoor Appliance Marketing," *Advertising Age* 50 (February 25, 1979), 21.

[25] Herbert Krugman, "The Measurement of Advertising Involvement," *Public Opinion Quarterly* 30 (March 1966), 583–596.

[26] Fergus I. M. Craik and Robert S. Lockhart, "Levels of Processing: A Framework for Memory Research," *Journal of Verbal Learning and Verbal Behavior"* (December 1972), 671–684; Anthony G. Greenwald and Clark Leavitt, "Audience Involvement in Advertising: Four Levels," *Journal of Consumer Research* 11 (June 1984), 581–592.

[27] For example, see Jerry C. Olson, Daniel R. Toy, and Philip A. Dover, "Do Cognitive Responses Mediate the Effectiveness of Advertising Content on Cognitive Structure?" *Journal of Consumer Research* 9 (December 1982), 245–262; Peter Wright, "The Cognitive Processes Mediating Accep-tance of Advertising," *Journal of Marketing Research* 10 (February 1973), 53–62.

**FIGURE 13.8
ENCOURAGING
MULTIPLE PRODUCT
CATEGORIZATIONS
CAN BROADEN A
PRODUCT'S APPEAL**

Source: Courtesy of Champion Motor Coach Inc., a subsidiary of Champion Enterprises, Dryden, Michigan.

memory.[28] An image may range from a single sensory dimension (e.g., visualize a chocolate cake) to a combination of sensory dimensions (e.g., imagine the smell and taste of the cake).

STIMULUS ORGANIZATION   Are there principles or rules governing the manner in which people organize incoming stimuli? This question is the domain of an area known as **Gestalt psychology,** which focuses on how people organize or combine stimuli into a meaningful whole. Three principles of stimulus organization are considered here.

Simplicity.   First, people have a strong tendency to organize their perceptions into "simple" patterns. That is, people will opt for simple perceptions even when more complex perceptions can be derived from the stimulus.

---

[28] Deborah J. MacInnis and Linda L. Price, "The Role of Imagery in Information Processing: Review and Extensions," *Journal of Consumer Research* 13 (March 1987), 473–491.

FIGURE 13.9
AN EXAMPLE OF
SIMPLICITY

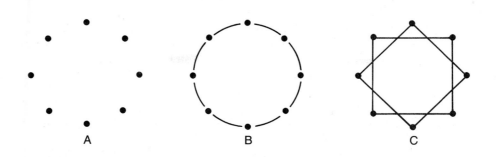

A   B   C

This principle is illustrated in Figure 13.9. Suppose you were asked to connect the dots in stimulus A. Most people would form a circle (B), even though the more complex pattern of two squares (C) can also be derived. This drive toward simplicity partly explains why consumers often perceive only a subset of the copy points contained in an ad.

Figure and Ground.   People tend to organize their perceptions into two major patterns. The first is **figure,** which represents those elements within a perceptual field that receive the most attention. The remaining, less meaningful elements that comprise the background are referred to as **ground.** Many interesting experiments have been undertaken to determine what will be figure and what will be ground. Previous experience exerts a strong effect. The more familiar object tends to stand out. A familiar face, for example, can usually be recognized in a crowd. Similarly, the familiar brand symbol will stand out, thus underscoring the value of repetitive advertising.

The importance of the figure–ground principle in an advertising context is illustrated by consumers' reactions to the series of television commercials featuring James Garner and Mariette Hartley for the Polaroid One Step camera. The commercials built upon verbal sparring by a married couple, and there was no question that people liked them. However, many of those surveyed named Kodak as the brand being advertised. For these consumers, Garner and Hartley became the figure while the product became ground, just the reverse of the advertiser's intent.

Closure.   One of the more important principles from Gestalt psychology is **closure,** which refers to our tendency to develop a complete picture or perception even when elements in the perceptual field are missing. Because of this drive to "fill in" the missing parts, the presentation of an incomplete stimulus provides marketers with a mechanism for increasing the effort and involvement that occur during information processing.[29]

---

[29] James T. Heimbach and Jacob Jacoby, "The Zergarnik Effect in Advertising," in M. Venkatesan, ed., *Proceedings of the Third Annual Conference* (Urbana, Illinois: Association for Consumer Research, 1972), 746–758.

Closure is a very popular technique in advertising. A classic example is the Salem musical jingle of "You can take Salem out of the country, but you can't take the country out of Salem." In the initial stages of the campaign, this jingle was strongly established in the consumer's mind. Subsequently, a new ad was developed that ended with that part of jingle up to the word *but*. According to all reports, the campaign was quite successful.

Closure can be used in many other ways. Kellogg's, for instance, has developed ads as well as billboards in which either the bottom portion or last couple of letters of their name is missing. The ad appearing in Figure 13.10 employs the closure principle by obscuring some of the letters in the claim "Tastes cream-m-mier." Sometimes ads will present a partial picture of the product itself. Playing the soundtrack of well-known TV commercials may also evoke closure as the listener reproduces the visual portion. Heavy viewers of MTV probably have a similar experience when the song from a familiar music video is played on the radio.

FIGURE 13.10 THE USE OF CLOSURE IN ADVERTISING

PERSONAL DETERMINANTS OF COMPREHENSION   Comprehension, like attention, is influenced by many stimulus and personal factors. We first consider how personal factors can affect comprehension.

Motivation.   Just as a person's motivational state during information processing can influence attention, so too can it exert an affect on comprehension. In a classic study, subjects who differed in the amount of elapsed time since their last meal were asked to describe what they saw in an "ambiguous" picture. As expected, subjects were more likely to categorize the stimulus as some type of food-related object the longer it had been since they had last eaten.[30]

Motivation can also influence the elaboration that occurs during comprehension.[31] When a stimulus is perceived as personally relevant (i.e., the stimulus is seen as having some usefulness for need satisfaction), more elaborate processing should occur. An ad featuring a product that is irrelevant to a consumer's needs will typically be processed in a very shallow fashion. The relatively few thoughts that are generated during processing will focus more on the ad (e.g., thoughts about the ad's executional properties) than the product. In contrast, when consumers are more motivated during ad processing, they will engage in more thinking, especially about the advertised product (e.g., thoughts about the benefits of owning the product).

Knowledge.   The knowledge stored in memory is obviously a major determinant of comprehension.[32] Categorization of a stimulus depends heavily on knowledge. The novice perceives a gold coin, the expert sees a rare and valuable St. Gaudens $20 gold coin in MS-65 condition (a grade reflecting a coin in near perfect shape).

Knowledge also enhances consumers' ability to understand a message. Unlike the expert, the novice may have difficulty with understanding the terminology (Did you know what MS-65 meant?) and the significance of message claims. This beneficial effect on understanding is accompanied by a reduction in miscomprehension. Knowledge can help consumers to recognize faulty logic and erroneous conclusions and to avoid incorrect interpretations. Knowledgeable persons are also more likely to elaborate on message claims, whereas unknowledgeable consumers may focus on nonclaim cues (e.g., background music, pictures) within the message.[33]

Expectation or Perceptual Set.   Comprehension will often depend on prior conceptions or expectations of what we are likely to see. Suppose that

---

[30] Robert Levine, Isidor Chein, and Gardner Murphy, "The Relation of the Intensity of a Need to the Amount of Perceptual Distortion," *Journal of Psychology* 13 (January 1942), 283–293.

[31] Richard L. Celsi and Jerry C. Olson, "The Role of Involvement in Attention and Comprehension Processes," *Journal of Consumer Research* 15 (September 1988), 210–224.

[32] Alba and Hutchinson, "Dimensions of Consumer Expertise."

[33] Richard E. Petty and John T. Cacioppo, "The Elaboration Likelihood Model of Persuasion," in Leonard Berkowitz, ed., *Advances in Experimental Social Psychology*, vol. 19 (New York: Academic Press, 1986), 123–205.

FIGURE 13.11
THE "BROKEN B"
STIMULUS: PRIOR
CONCEPTIONS
AFFECT CURRENT
PERCEPTIONS

you were asked to identify the stimulus shown in Figure 13.11. Many people would probably perceive the number *13,* whereas others may interpret it as the letter *B.* However, what if prior to encountering this stimulus you first viewed either four different capital letters or four pairs of digits? Research shows that those led to expect digits will report "13," whereas those who are primed to anticipate letters will report "B."[34]

This same phenomenon is often observed in marketing. In a classic study, consumers were asked to taste and rate various beers. These ratings were attained under both "blind" (no brand identification) and "labeled" (brands were identified) conditions. When the brands were unlabeled, the ratings were essentially the same for all brands. That is, consumers did not differentiate among the brands. However, significant rating differences emerged when the brands were labeled. Thus, the expectation created by the brand label was powerful enough to alter consumers' perceptions of the products.[35]

Expectations have recently been shown to influence how consumers process information provided by a salesperson. Subjects engaged in much more careful consideration of the information supplied by a salesperson who deviated from their expectations of the "typical" salesperson than in that supplied by one who matched their expectations.[36]

STIMULUS DETERMINANTS OF COMPREHENSION   The actual physical properties of a stimulus play a major role in shaping how it is interpreted (see *Consumer in Focus 13.1*). The Apple computer company learned the hard way about the importance of size. Many consumers found it difficult to believe that the Apple IIc, a trimmer version of the Apple IIe, was more powerful, because of its smaller size. A new promotional program was developed to combat this perception (the basic theme being "It's a lot bigger than it looks"), and sales increased.

Similarly, comprehension can depend on a product's packaging and brand

---

[34] Jerome S. Bruner and A. Leigh Minturn, "Perceptual Identification and Perceptual Organization," *Journal of General Psychology* 53 (July 1955), 21–28.

[35] Ralph I. Allison and Kenneth P. Uhl, "Influence of Beer Brand Identification on Taste Perception," *Journal of Marketing Research* 1 (August 1964), 36–39.

[36] Mita Sujan, James R. Bettman, and Harish Sujan, "Effects of Consumer Expectations on Information Processing in Selling Encounters," *Journal of Marketing Research* 23 (November 1986), 346–353.

13.1   COLOR AND PERCEPTION

Color can serve as an important cue in consumers' perceptions. Color is often used to evoke certain moods or feelings. Blue and green are seen as cool and elicit feelings of security, while red and yellow are viewed as warm and associated with cheerfulness. Consistent with this, advertisements for menthol cigarettes often rely quite heavily on blues and greens.

A product's color can also be used to the marketer's advantage. Appliance manufacturers, for instance, have discovered that they can reduce the consumer's perception of a product's weight such as a vacuum cleaner by using pastel rather than darker colors. Similarly, manufacturers of laundry soaps and cold capsules recognize the benefits of including colored granules as a visual reinforcement for product claims.

A recent study has reported the power of color in consumers' taste perceptions. Consumers were asked to taste a pudding and indicate their reactions to the product. The pudding, although vanilla in flavor, was chocolate colored. Interestingly, no one detected that the pudding was vanilla flavored. In addition, the pudding with a chocolate coloring was rated as having a better chocolate flavor than lighter colored puddings.

Sources: Gail Tom, Teresa Barnett, William Lew, and Jodean Selmants, "Cueing the Consumer: The Role of Salient Cues in Consumer Perception," *Journal of Consumer Marketing* 4 (Spring 1987), 23–28; Maryon Tysoe, "What's Wrong with Blue Potatoes?" *Psychology Today* 19 (December 1985), 6ff.

name. A grocery store discovered that the practice of prepackaging fresh fish with a plastic wrap undermined consumers' perceptions of the product's freshness. Many consumers interpreted the packaging to mean that the fish had been frozen. Consequently, a seafood bar was added where unwrapped fish were displayed on crushed ice. Sales for the wrapped fish remained constant, while total sales, including those generated by the seafood bar, nearly doubled.

The importance of brand name is illustrated by Wendy's single hamburger. Although their single contains as much meat as a Whopper or Quarter Pounder and more than the Big Mac, its name fails to convey its size. Wendy's recent introduction of The Big Classic hamburger is intended to overcome this problem.[37]

Linguistics.   A rather substantial body of literature comprises the area known as **psycholinguistics,** the study of psychological factors involved in the perception of and response to linguistic phenomena. Listed next are

---

[37] " 'Classic' Marketing Meets Whopper of a Challenge," *Marketing News* 21 (June 5, 1987), 22ff.

findings that reflect the potential contribution psycholinguistics can make to understanding and enhancing message comprehension:[38]

1. Words used frequently in everyday language are more easily comprehended and remembered.[39]

2. Negative words such as *not* or *never* are less easily comprehended.[40]

3. The potential for misunderstanding is greater for passive sentences (e.g., "The product was developed by Company X") than for active sentences (e.g., "Company X developed the product").[41]

Psycholinguistics can also play a useful role in the development of brand names. *Consumer in Focus 13.2* describes one such application.

Order Effects.   Suppose that you and a friend were each given a list of the same personality traits describing a hypothetical individual, but the order of the traits on the lists were exactly opposite. Would different orderings cause a difference in how much you and your friend liked this person? According to Asch's research, the answer is yes.[42]

Two major types of order effects have been discussed in the research literature. One is **recency,** in which stimuli appearing at the end of a sequence are given more weight in the resulting interpretation. Alternatively, a **primacy** effect can occur. Primacy is consistent with the notion of "first impression" such that stimuli appearing at the beginning are given more weight. Unfortunately, it is presently impossible to predict which effect will emerge in a particular situation.

Context.   The context, or surrounding situation in which the stimulus occurs, will in part determine what is comprehended. In Chapter 7, we considered how the program in which a TV ad appears can exert context effects. For this reason, some companies, such as General Foods and Coca-Cola,

---

[38] For a general discussion of the role of psycholinguistics in advertising copy, see Larry Percy, "Psycholinguistic Guidelines for Advertising," in Andrew Mitchell, ed., *Advances in Consumer Research* 9 (Ann Arbor: Association for Consumer Research, 1982), 107–111. Also see Karen Ann Hunold, "Verbal Strategies for Product Presentation in Television Commercials," in Michael J. Houston, ed., *Advances in Consumer Research* 15 (Ann Arbor: Association for Consumer Research, 1988), 256–259.

[39] Leo Postman, "Effects of Word Frequency on Acquisition and Retention Under Conditions of Free-Recall Learning," *Quarterly Journal of Experimental Psychology* 22 (May 1970), 185–195.

[40] Philip B. Gough, "The Verification of Sentences: The Effect of Delay on Evidence and Sentence Length," *Journal of Verbal Learning and Verbal Behavior* 5 (October 1966), 492–496; Dan I. Slobin, "Grammatical Transformation and Sentence Comprehension in Childhood and Adulthood," *Journal of Verbal Learning and Verbal Behavior* 5 (June 1966), 219–227.

[41] Percy, "Psycholinguistic Guidelines for Advertising."

[42] Solomon E. Asch, *Social Psychology* (Englewood Cliffs, New Jersey: Prentice-Hall, 1952), Chapter 8.

13.2   THE BRAND NAME GAME

The development of brand names has become big business. Today there are a number of companies, such as Name Lab, Interbrand, and The Name Works, that specialize in picking the right name. This service is not cheap. A typical client can easily pay $50,000 for around five weeks work if a suitable name is found.

Name Lab has developed such names as Acura, Compaq, Sentra, and Zapmail through the use of "constructional linguistics," a method where basic word parts or morphemes (the smallest meaningful unit in a language) are combined to form the desired meaning. The development of the Compaq name is an interesting example of this process.

In the early 1980s, two engineers from Texas Instruments founded a company to sell portable computers. At that time, Gateway was the leading candidate for naming the product. Company investors, however, were less than enchanted with the name. Name Lab was contacted, and Compaq was selected from a set of names (others included Cortex, Cognipak, and Suntek). The name Compaq is composed of two morphemes. One implies computers and communications, the other a small, integral object. While we will never know just how much the name contributed to the product's success, Compaq sales during the initial 12 months totaled $111 million, a U.S. record for first-year sales.

Source: Robert A. Mamis, "Name-Calling," *Inc.* 6 (July 1984), 67–74.

will not advertise during news programs because of concerns about the impact of "bad" news on the perception of their products.[43]

The retail environment also represents a potential source of context effects. In the early 1980s, Levi jeans expanded distribution into mass merchandisers (e.g., Sears, Penney's). Department stores viewed the move as damaging the brand's fashion image and threatening to their markups. Consequently, many stores turned to other jean manufacturers for a replacement, and Lee jeans benefited considerably.

MISCOMPREHENSION   Before turning to the acceptance stage, it is important to stress the potential for miscomprehension during information processing. Indeed, the meanings consumers attach to stimuli may differ considerably from those desired by marketers. For example, research suggests that a substantial number of people have some misunderstanding of what they view on

---

[43] "GF, Coke Tell Why They Shun TV News," *Advertising Age* 51 (January 28, 1980), 39.

TV, whether it is news, a regular program, or advertising.[44] Consequently, accurate comprehension of a message, even a relatively simple one, cannot be assumed.

ACCEPTANCE

Suppose that an advertisement successfully captures attention and is accurately understood by viewers. Will persuasion occur? Not necessarily. The simple fact is that message comprehension is *not* the same as message acceptance. Consumers may understand perfectly all that is being communicated, but they may not agree with the message for any number of reasons. Indeed, many if not most consumers are very skeptical of advertising claims. One study reports that over 70 percent of consumers do not believe ads that use test results to support claims of product superiority.[45]

A key question, then, is what determines how much, if any, acceptance will occur during information processing. Research has shown that acceptance may heavily depend on the thoughts that occur during the comprehension stage.[46] Such thoughts are often referred to as **cognitive responses.**

COGNITIVE RESPONSES   Consider a knowledgeable consumer who is highly motivated while processing an ad that contains a number of claims

---

[44] Jacob Jacoby and Wayne D. Hoyer, "Viewer Miscomprehension of Televised Communication: Selected Findings," *Journal of Marketing* 46 (Fall 1982), 12–26. Also see in this same journal issue: Gary T. Ford and Richard Yalch, "Viewer Miscomprehension of Televised Communication: A Comment," 27–31; Richard W. Mizerski, "Viewer Miscomprehension Findings Are Measurement Bound," 32–34; Jacob Jacoby and Wayne D. Hoyer, "On Miscomprehending Televised Communication: A Rejoinder," 35–43. For an update, see "Warning: This Story Will Be Miscomprehended," *Marketing News* 21 (March 27, 1987), 1, 34.

[45] This figure comes from a study by Needham, Harper, and Steers as cited by Stephen J. Hoch and Young-Won Ha, "Consumer Learning: Advertising and the Ambiguity of Product Experience," *Journal of Consumer Research* 13 (September 1986), 221–233.

[46] Rajeev Batra and Michael L. Ray, "Affective Responses Mediating Advertising Acceptance," *Journal of Consumer Research* 13 (September 1986), 234–249; George E. Belch, "The Effects of Television Commercial Repetition on Cognitive Response and Message Acceptance," *Journal of Consumer Research* 9 (June 1982), 56–63; Amitava Chattopadhyay and Joseph W. Alba, "The Situational Importance of Recall and Inference in Consumer Decision Making," *Journal of Consumer Research* 15 (June 1988), 1–12; Anthony G. Greenwald, "Cognitive Learning, Cognitive Response to Persuasion and Attitude Change," in Anthony G. Greenwald, Timothy C. Brock, and Thomas M. Ostrom, eds., *Psychological Foundations of Attitudes* (New York: Academic Press, 1968), 147–170; Jerry C. Olson, Daniel R. Toy, and Philip A. Dover, "Do Cognitive Responses Mediate the Effects of Advertising Content on Cognitive Structure?" *Journal of Consumer Research* 9 (December 1982), 245–262; Arno J. Rethans, John L. Swasy, and Lawrence J. Marks, "Effects of Television Commercial Repetition, Receiver Knowledge, and Commercial Length: A Test of the Two-Factor Model," *Journal of Marketing Research* 23 (February 1986), 50–61; Daniel R. Toy, "Monitoring Communication Effects: A Cognitive Structure/Cognitive Response Approach," *Journal of Consumer Research* 9 (June 1982), 66–76; Peter Wright, "The Cognitive Processes Mediating Acceptance of Advertising," *Journal of Marketing Research* 10 (February 1973), 53–62.

about a product that the consumer anticipates buying very soon. This consumer may engage in considerable thinking about the claims' validity. The nature of these cognitive responses will determine the acceptance of the claims. Of particular importance are those responses called support arguments and counterarguments. **Support arguments** are thoughts that are favorable to the claims. **Counterarguments** are thoughts that oppose the message claims. Acceptance is enhanced as support argumentation increases but is reduced by greater counterargumentation.

Of course, consumers may often be unmotivated or unable to carefully consider an ad's claims about the product. When this occurs, then acceptance may depend more heavily on the cognitive responses evoked by an ad's executional elements.[47] A recent study reports that when subjects processed an ad in anticipation of a subsequent product choice, acceptance depended on the favorability of their thoughts about the advertised brand. However, when subjects did not anticipate a choice, acceptance now depended on their thoughts about the appropriateness of the pictures used in the ad.[48]

Cognitive responses provide a valuable complement to standard attitude measures in evaluating communication effectiveness. Although standard attitude measures can reveal whether a communication leaves a favorable or unfavorable impression on the viewer, they often fail to reveal the *reasons* for this impression. If an ad flops, is it because of an ineffective spokesperson, the absence of compelling arguments, or poor visuals? Standard attitude measures may not answer such questions. Cognitive responses can give insights into these various concerns.

Nonetheless, cognitive responses are not without their limitations. There are some reasonable questions about the extent to which cognitive responses or, more generally, verbalizations of mental processes can fully reflect the content and activities that occur during processing.[49] A second concern is that focusing solely on cognitive thoughts is overly restrictive. This latter concern has led researchers to explore the role of affective responses.

---

[47] Scott B. MacKenzie and Richard J. Lutz, "An Empirical Examination of the Structural Antecedents of Attitude-Toward-the-Ad in an Advertising Pretesting Context," *Journal of Marketing,* forthcoming; Petty and Cacioppo, "The Elaboration Likelihood Model of Persuasion."

[48] Paul W. Miniard, Kenneth R. Lord, and Peter R. Dickson, "An Examination of Some Process and Outcome Predictions of the Elaboration Likelihood Model of Persuasion" (working paper, The Ohio State University, 1988).

[49] Richard E. Nisbett and Timothy D. Wilson, "Telling More Than We Can Know: Verbal Reports on Mental Processes," *Psychological Review* 84 (May 1977), 231–259; Peter Wright, "Message-Evoked Thoughts: Persuasion Research Using Thought Verbalizations," *Journal of Consumer Research* 7 (September 1980), 151–175; Raymond J. Smead, James B. Wilcox, and Robert E. Wilkes, "How Valid Are Product Descriptions and Protocols in Choice Experiments?" *Journal of Consumer Research* 8 (June 1981), 37–42.

AFFECTIVE RESPONSES   **Affective responses** represent the feelings and emotions that are elicited by a stimulus.[50] It is these types of "hot" responses, rather than the "cold" cognitive responses, that are emphasized by much of today's advertising. The musical and visual elements within the "We build excitement" television advertisements for Pontiac are designed to elicit feelings of exhilaration and excitement.

As one example of the diversity of feelings that ads may elicit, consider those appearing in Table 13.1. In a recent study, subjects were exposed to a variety of television commercials and asked to indicate how strongly they experienced these feelings. The results indicated that this assortment of affective responses could be simplified into three primary dimensions: upbeat, negative, and warm. Some have recommended a larger set of primary emotions consisting of fear, surprise, sadness, disgust, anger, anticipation, joy, and acceptance.[51]

The role of affective responses has become a topic of considerable interest in the recent research literature. The findings thus far have been very supportive of the importance they play during the acceptance stage of information processing. For example, one study reports that both cognitive and affective responses were useful in predicting the attitudes formed after ad exposure.[52]

Although advertisers cannot directly control the cognitive and affective responses consumers have during information processing, they can try to influence these reactions through certain elements of the communication (e.g., the type of message, message source). The impact of a communication's properties on acceptance and persuasion is explored in Chapter 15.

RETENTION

The final stage of information processing is **retention,** which involves the transfer of information to long-term memory. Although much current knowledge about memory comes from the cognitive psychology literature, consumer researchers have become very interested in this area over the past decade.

---

[50] David A. Aaker, Douglas M. Stayman, and Michael R. Hagerty, "Warmth in Advertising: Measurement, Impact, and Sequence Effects," *Journal of Consumer Research* 12 (March 1986), 365–381; Batra and Ray, "Affective Responses Mediating Acceptance of Advertising"; Julie A. Edell and Marian C. Burke, "The Power of Feelings in Understanding Advertising Effects," *Journal of Consumer Research* 14 (December 1987), 421–433; Meryl Paula Gardener, "Mood States and Consumer Behavior: A Critical Review," *Journal of Consumer Research* 12 (December 1985), 281–300; Morris B. Holbrook, "Emotion in the Consumption Experience: Toward a New Model of the Human Consumer," in Robert A. Peterson, Wayne D. Hoyer, and William R. Wilson, eds., *The Role of Affect in Consumer Behavior* (Lexington, Massachusetts: Heath, 1986), 17–52; Morris B. Holbrook and Rajeev Batra, "Assessing the Role of Emotions as Mediators of Consumer Responses to Advertising," *Journal of Consumer Research* 14 (December 1987), 404–420; Patricia A. Stout and John D. Leckenby, "Measuring Emotion Response to Advertising," *Journal of Advertising* 15 (1986), 35–42; David M. Zeitlin and Richard A. Westwood, "Measuring Emotional Response," *Journal of Advertising Research* 26 (October/November 1986), 34–44.

[51] Zeitlin and Westwood, "Measuring Emotional Response."

[52] Batra and Ray, "Affective Responses Mediating Acceptance of Advertising,"

TABLE 13.1 TYPES OF FEELINGS	Upbeat	Negative	Warm
	Active	Angry	Affectionate
	Adventurous	Annoyed	Calm
	Alive	Bad	Concerned
	Amused	Bored	Contemplative
	Attentive	Critical	Emotional
	Attractive	Defiant	Hopeful
	Carefree	Depressed	Kind
	Cheerful	Disgusted	Moved
	Confident	Disinterested	Peaceful
	Creative	Dubious	Pensive
	Delighted	Dull	Sentimental
	Elated	Fed-up	Touched
	Energetic	Insulted	Warmhearted
	Enthusiastic	Irritated	
	Excited	Lonely	
	Exhilarated	Offended	
	Good	Regretful	
	Happy	Sad	
	Humorous	Skeptical	
	Independent	Suspicious	
	Industrious		
	Inspired		
	Interested		
	Joyous		
	Lighthearted		
	Lively		
	Playful		
	Pleased		
	Proud		
	Satisfied		
	Stimulated		
	Strong		

Source: Julie A. Edell and Marian Chapman Burke, "The Power of Feelings in Understanding Advertising Effects," *Journal of Consumer Research* 14 (December 1987), p. 424, Table 1.

Indeed, articles relevant to memory issues are appearing at an increasing rate in the major consumer research journals and conferences.

PHYSIOLOGICAL PROPERTIES OF THE HUMAN BRAIN   The human brain is divided into left and right hemispheres, which are connected by a large fiber tract known as the corpus callosum.[53] It is now believed that these two hemispheres are responsible for different types of cognitive activity. The left brain is viewed as the center for logical, abstract, and conceptual thinking, whereas the right brain focuses on creative, intuitive, and imaginal thinking. In addition, the left brain is responsible for the processing of verbal or semantic

---

[53] Flemming Hansen, "Hemispheral Lateralization: Implications for Understanding Consumer Behavior," *Journal of Consumer Research* 8 (June 1981), 23–36.

information, whereas the right brain is involved with the processing of pictorial or visual information.

Evidence for these distinctions comes primarily from "split-brain" persons (those who have lost the corpus callosum). In such cases, the two hemispheres operate as independent units. Consequently, it is possible to present stimuli so that only one hemisphere "receives" the information. If, for instance, a pair of scissors is processed by only the left hemisphere and the person is asked to identify the object, he or she can easily respond with the semantic concept of "scissors." However, when this same object is processed by the right hemisphere, the person is unable to give the answer.

People differ in the relative dominance of the two hemispheres. Some people are left-brain dominated, while others are right-brain dominated. In one test of hemispheric dominance, people are visually presented the word *red* in blue letters. They are then asked to verbalize the color of the letters. The left brain says red, whereas the right brain says blue. Whatever response finally emerges gives an indication of the hemispheres' relative dominance.

Research in this area, particularly with respect to its practical implications, is still in its infancy. One possibility is that, depending upon the relative dominance of the left and right hemispheres within a target market, different advertising messages may be desirable for enhancing persuasion. Some personnel consultants have recently been advocating the value of understanding hemispheric dominance in the recruitment and utilization of employees, although there are important questions as to how far this can or should be taken.[54]

MULTIPLE-STORE THEORY OF MEMORY   In addition to these physiological characteristics of memory, many believe that important psychological differences exist in the structure and functioning of memory. One influential viewpoint is that memory consists of three different storage systems: (1) sensory memory, (2) short-term memory, and (3) long-term memory.[55] This is shown graphically in Figure 13.12. Briefly, memory is assumed to work in this way:

1. The stimulus enters and is processed first in sensory memory. Information is extracted about color, contour, and so on. No meaning is attributed at this stage.

2. The input then goes to short-term memory, where it is held briefly and analyzed for meaning. Unless rehearsed, it will then fade from short-term storage.

---

[54] Kevin McKean, "Of Two Minds: Selling the Right Brain," *Discover* 5 (April 1985), 30–40.

[55] Lyle E. Bourne, Roger L. Dominowski, and Elizabeth F. Loftus, *Cognitive Processes* (Englewood Cliffs, New Jersey: Prentice-Hall, 1979); Donald A. Norman, *Memory and Attention* (New York: John Wiley and Sons, 1969); Peter H. Lindsay and Donald A. Norman, *Human Information Processing* (New York: Academic Press, 1972); A. Newell and H. A. Simon, *Human Problem Solving* (Englewood Cliffs, New Jersey: Prentice-Hall, 1972).

FIGURE 13.12
THE MULTIPLE-STORE MODEL OF MEMORY: THE THREE STORAGE SYSTEMS

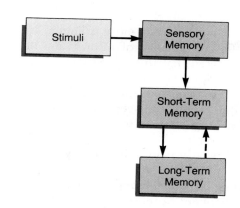

3. Rehearsed information is then transferred to long-term memory where it is stored permanently and may be retrieved later if certain conditions are met.

Some researchers reject this traditional formulation in favor of a "depth of processing" view.[56] Under this approach, there is one basic memory with various levels of information processing. The "deeper" the processing, the greater the retention. In principle, however, both approaches appear similar, and our discussion will focus on the more traditional perspective.

Sensory Memory.   In sensory memory, incoming information receives an initial analysis based largely on such physical properties as loudness, pitch, and so on. Visual processing at this stage is referred to as **iconic** and auditory processing as **echoic**. It takes place virtually instantaneously, wich iconic processing requiring only one quarter of a second.[57]

Short-Term Memory.   Once the stimulus passes through sensory processing, it enters short-term memory, which is viewed as the "workbench" for information-processing activities. In effect, it combines sensory input with

[56] Fergus I. M. Craik and Robert S. Lockhart, "Levels of Processing: A Framework for Memory Research," *Journal of Verbal Learning and Verbal Behavior* 11 (December 1972), 671–684; Jerry C. Olson, "Encoding Processes: Levels of Processing and Existing Knowledge Structures," in Jerry C. Olson, ed., *Advances in Consumer Research* 7 (Ann Arbor, Michigan: Association for Consumer Research, 1980), 154–160.

[57] For more background, see Bourne, Dominowski, and Loftus, *Cognitive Processes;* Ulrich Neisser, *Cognitive Psychology* (New York: Appleton, 1966); Robert G. Crowsers, *Principles of Learning in Memory* (Hillsdale, New Jersey: Lawrence Erlbaum, 1976); and Hershel W. Leibowitz and Lewis O. Harvey, Jr., "Perception," *Annual Review of Psychology* 24 (1973), 207–240.

the contents of long-term memory so that categorization and interpretation can take place.

Short-term memory is limited in several respects. First, it can hold only a limited amount of information at any given point in time. It has been estimated that this capacity is limited to as little as four and perhaps up to seven units of information.[58]

Short-term memory is also limited in how long information can exist without efforts to keep it activated. Suppose you were shown a phone number just long enough to process it and then were prevented from rehearsing the number. How much time would have to elapse before the number faded away? Information is typically lost in 30 seconds or less without rehearsal.[59]

Long-Term Memory.   Long-term memory is viewed as an unlimited, permanent storehouse containing all of our knowledge. We have already examined two key properties of long-term memory, content and organization, in Chapter 10.

Given that marketers often attempt to implant information within the consumer's mind, it is very important for us to understand *how* retention takes place. That is, what factors influence the amount of retention that occurs during information processing? The answer to this question is presented in the following chapter, under the topic of cognitive learning.

Summary

A model of the stages information passes through while being processed by consumers is presented in this chapter. This information-processing model consists of five stages: exposure, attention, comprehension, acceptance, and retrieval.

Exposure can be defined as the achievement of proximity to a stimulus such that an opportunity exists for activation of one or more of the five senses. Such activation results when a stimulus meets or exceeds the lower threshold: the minimum amount of stimulus intensity necessary for sensation to occur. Efforts to influence consumers with stimuli below the lower threshold are known as subliminal persuasion. Current evidence indicates that subliminal stimuli have, at best, minimal effects and suggests that fears of their persuasiveness are unfounded.

Attention represents the allocation of processing capacity to the incoming stimulus. Because of definite limitations in this capacity, consumers are very

---

[58] Herbert A. Simon, "How Big Is a Chunk?" *Science* 183 (February 1974), 482–488; George A. Miller, "The Magical Number Seven, Plus or Minus Two: Some Limits on Our Capacity for Processing Information," *Psychological Review* 63 (March 1956), 81–97.

[59] Richard M. Shiffrin and R. C. Atkinson, "Storage and Retrieval Processes in Long-Term Memory," *Psychological Review* 76 (March 1969), 179–193.

selective in what they pay attention to. Gaining the consumer's attention will often be a major hurdle.

An understanding of what factors influence attention can be very useful in jumping this hurdle. Attention is affected by two major types of determinants: personal and stimulus. Personal determinants are individual characteristics such as motivation, attitudes, adaptation, and span of attention. The net effect of personal influences is to make attention highly selective. Personal determinants are best viewed as constraints and barriers against which strategy should be evaluated.

Stimulus factors are characteristics of the stimulus itself. Size, color, intensity, contrast, position, directionality, movement, isolation, novelty, learned attention-inducing stimuli, attractive spokesperson, and scene changes can influence attention. These factors can be used by marketers in competing for the consumer's valuable attention.

Comprehension is concerned with the interpretation of the stimulus. Successful marketing will often depend on understanding the meaning consumers attach to stimuli such as price, packaging, brand names, as well as on advertising.

Gestalt psychology has uncovered several important principles about how people organize stimuli into a meaningful whole: simplicity, figure and ground, and closure. The most basic level of comprehension involves stimulus classification. Once classified, further elaboration may occur in the form of semantic or imaginal processing.

Comprehension is influenced by a number of factors. A consumer's level of knowledge and motivation or involvement and her or his expectations are critical determinants. Stimulus factors, such as the linguistic characteristics of a stimulus or the order in which stimuli are processed, can also affect comprehension.

The acceptance stage of information processing focuses on the extent to which persuasion occurs in the form of new or modified knowledge and attitudes. Acceptance will depend on the particular cognitive and affective responses experienced during processing. Acceptance is more likely as these responses become more favorable.

The final stage of information processing, retention, involves the transfer of information to long-term memory. Memory consists of three different storage systems: (1) sensory memory, (2) short-term memory, and (3) long-term memory.

REVIEW AND DISCUSSION QUESTIONS

1. How can the concept of information processing be useful in understanding why ads are "successful" or "unsuccessful"?

2. Do you believe there are situations in which advertisers should consider the use of subliminal cues? Why or why not?

3. Many critics contend that too much advertising today is gimmicky and cute. The argument is that creative people are carried away by flashy attention-attracting devices

and are forgetting that good advertising must sell. How would you respond to this criticism?

4. How does adaptation level create a barrier for advertising? How can it be used to increase advertising effectiveness?

5. A recent study reveals that a particular ad was much more effective in magazine A than in magazine B, even though the readership of the two magazines is virtually identical. How can you explain this finding?

6. A retailer of computer goods is puzzled by consumers' response to her recent fall sale. There was only one purchase of the $3,000 model (sale priced at $2,750). The $1,000 model (sale priced at $875), despite having only half the $250 savings offered by the more expensive model, sold out. How can you explain these results?

7. Two consumers are exposed to the same ad. One is in the market for this product, while the other is not. How might these two consumers differ in their processing of this ad?

LEARNING

**$95 BILLION IN
FORGETTABLE ADS**

What advertising had the highest top-of-mind recall in 1985?

Don't know?

That's correct.

That may sound like an Abbott & Costello routine, but "don't know" or "none" were the answers most often given to the unaided question "Of all the advertising you've heard, seen or read in the past 30 days, which ad first comes to mind?" In 1985, ADVERTISING AGE's monthly adWatch survey polled a total of 13,265 adults and more than half (53%) were unable to recall any specific advertiser or advertisement.

That figure seems astonishing, given the estimated $95 billion spent on advertising in 1985 and Americans' general addiction to the media. If you're an advertiser or an agency executive, you may have other words to describe it. Words like "frightening."

Any respondent able to come up with an advertiser off the top of his head most often named Coca-Cola, which got 7% of first mentions. Rival Pepsi-Cola's advertising was named first by 3% of those surveyed, good for second place. Tied for third with 2% of first mentions each was advertising for McDonald's and Miller/Miller Lite.

Eight advertisers managed 1% shares over the course of the year, keeping their advertising from among the ranks of the dreaded "Other." They are AT&T, Anheuser-Busch's Budweiser/Bud Light, Burger King, General Motors' Chevrolet, Ford, Pizza Hut, Proctor & Gamble's Tide and Wendy's.

Survey respondents did much better with aided questions. When asked to recall the first soft-drink advertising that came to mind, for example, only 14% said "none" and 4% responded "don't know." Only the tobacco-advertising question drew a higher percentage of "none" or "don't know" answers (64%) than did the initial, unaided recall question.

Coke and Pepsi's shares of first mentions, when consumers were asked specifically to recall soft-drink advertising, began the year neck and neck at 27%. Pepsi gained early on Coke, peaking at 32.6% in March behind its Lionel Richie ads. But the national ruckus over Coke's reformulation popped its share of first mentions to 53.4% in July, which was almost double its score in April before its marketing coup.

Source: Adapted from Julie Franz, "$95 Billion for What? Ads Remembered as 'Forgettable' in 1985," *Advertising Age* 57 (March 3, 1986), 4ff.

Why do consumers appear to have such a poor memory for advertising? Does failure to remember advertising mean that the advertising is ineffective? Are there ways to enhance the memorability of advertising?

Answers to these and other important questions must be founded in an understanding of how consumers learn. The significance of learning is captured by one simple but powerful observation: Consumer behavior is learned behavior. The tastes, values, beliefs, preferences, and habits that strongly influence consumers' shopping, purchase, and consumption behaviors are the result of prior learning. Consequently, an understanding of learning is an essential prerequisite for those responsible for diagnosing and influencing consumer behavior.

Learning may be viewed as the process by which experience leads to changes in knowledge, attitudes, and/or behavior. This definition is quite broad in that it reflects the position of two major schools of thought about learning. One perspective on learning is known as the **cognitive approach.** Under this perspective, learning is reflected by changes in knowledge. Consequently, the focus is on understanding the mental processes that determine how people learn information (i.e., how information is transferred to long-term memory).

In contrast, the **behaviorist approach** to learning is solely concerned with observable behaviors. Mental processes, which cannot be observed and, thus, must be inferred, are ignored under this approach. Rather, learning is shown by changes in behavior due to the development of associations between stimuli and responses.

Both approaches to learning are explored in this chapter. We begin with cognitive learning. This discussion is followed by an examination of two primary types of learning from the behaviorist perspective: classical and operant conditioning. Finally, we examine a hybrid type of learning, called vicarious learning, which combines elements of both the cognitive and behaviorist approaches.

COGNITIVE LEARNING

As indicated previously, mental processes are the focus under cognitive learning. These mental processes include a variety of activities ranging from the learning of information to problem solving. From this perspective, much of decision making can be viewed as cognitive learning in that such decisions essentially involve finding an acceptable solution to a consumption problem. Where should I spend my vacation? How should I go about selecting a doctor for the surgery I require? What is the best strategy for allocating my savings across the numerous investment options in today's financial markets? All of these represent problems that consumers must solve. Problem solving can also be important even after a purchase decision has been made. Trying to decipher the "easy-to-follow" instructions while assembling a product and understanding why a product breakdown occurs (Did I do something wrong or is this another instance of inferior craftsmanship?) are examples of postpurchase problem-solving activities in the consumer domain.

While acknowledging the importance of problem solving, this section focuses instead on the learning of information for a very important reason.[1] Quite simply, the objective of many marketing activities is to "implant" particular information within the consumer's mind. Sometimes this information takes the form of a brand name, store location, or upcoming sale. At other times marketers are interested in consumers retaining a particular image of their offering along one or more important dimensions (e.g., the brand that claims to be the fastest and safest nonprescription relief available on the market).

Consequently, it is useful for us to understand how people learn information. Knowledge about those factors that influence cognitive learning can help marketers develop effective strategies for implanting the seeds of information within the garden of the mind. Two main determinants of learning are rehearsal and elaboration.

REHEARSAL

Rehearsal involves the mental repetition of information or, more formally, the recycling of information through short-term memory. Some have described it as a form of inner speech.

Rehearsal serves two main functions. First, it allows for the maintenance

---

[1] For research on more complex forms of cognitive learning, see Robert J. Meyer, "The Learning of Multiattribute Judgment Policies," *Journal of Consumer Research* 14 (September 1987), 155–173; Peter Wright and Peter Rip, "Product Class Advertising Effects on First-Time Buyers' Decision Strategies," *Journal of Consumer Research* 7 (September 1980), 151–175.

of information in short-term memory. An example would be the rote repetition of a telephone number just acquired from a directory. Rehearsal is undertaken in order to keep the information activated long enough for the person to dial the number. The second function of rehearsal involves the transfer of information from short-term memory to long-term memory. Greater rehearsal will increase the strength of the long-term memory trace, thereby enhancing the likelihood that the trace can be later retrieved.

ELABORATION

The degree of elaboration (i.e., the amount of integration between the stimulus and existing knowledge) that occurs while a stimulus is processed will influence the amount of learning that takes place. At low levels of elaboration, a stimulus is processed in much the same form in which it is encountered. For instance, a person who wanted to remember a license plate numbered AJN-268 might encode this stimulus without any elaboration by simply repeating "A-J-N-2-6-8."

A more elaborate encoding of this license plate number could involve rearranging the letters into the name JAN, adding the numbers (which total 16), and then visualizing a 16-year-old girl named Jan. This in fact was the strategy a person reported using for remembering the license number of a car he witnessed leaving the scene of a bank robbery. After realizing he had seen the getaway car, he telephoned the police and gave them the license number. The suspects were apprehended, and he received a $500 reward.

Greater elaboration will generally lead to greater learning.[2] That is, the more a person elaborates upon a piece of information (or the more "deeply" it is processed), the greater the number of linkages that are formed between the new information and information already stored in memory. This in turn increases the number of avenues or paths by which the information can be retrieved from memory. In essence, the memory trace becomes more accessible given the greater number of pathways (linkages) that are available for retrieval. Many of the techniques suggested by memory experts and performers rely upon the benefits of elaboration.

The amount of elaboration that occurs during processing will depend

---

[2] Terry L. Childers and Michael J. Houston, "Conditions for a Picture-Superiority Effect on Consumer Memory," *Journal of Consumer Research* 11 (September 1984), 643–654; Fergus I. M. Craik and Endel Tulving, "Depth of Processing and the Retention of Words in Episodic Memory," *Journal of Experimental Psychology: General* 104 (September 1975), 268–294; Fergus I. M. Craik and Michael J. Watkins, "The Role of Rehearsal in Short-Term Memory," *Journal of Verbal Learning and Verbal Behavior* 12 (December 1973), 599–607; Meryl Paula Gardner, Andrew A. Mitchell, and J. Edward Russo, "Low Involvement Strategies for Processing Advertisements," *Journal of Advertising* 14 (1985), 4–12; Joel Saegert and Robert K. Young, "Comparison of Effects of Repetition and Levels of Processing in Memory for Advertisements," in Andrew A. Mitchell, ed., *Advances in Consumer Research* 9 (St. Louis: Association for Consumer Research, 1982), 431–434.

on two primary factors: motivation and ability.[3] Each of these is discussed below.

MOTIVATION   A person's motivational state at the time of exposure to new information will have a considerable influence on what is remembered. Consider, for example, an automobile advertisement that is viewed by two consumers, one of whom is currently in the market for a new car. He or she would more actively process the ad, resulting in greater elaboration. Typically, the consumer more highly motivated during message processing will demonstrate greater learning than the less interested one.

This difference in learning depending on the level of motivation has been referred to as **directed** versus **incidental learning**.[4] Directed learning occurs when learning is the primary objective during information processing (e.g., the student reading this text in preparation for the upcoming exam). Incidental learning, on the other hand, represents learning that occurs even when learning is not a processing objective (e.g., the student flipping through a campus newspaper while waiting for class to begin). Research has consistently shown that increasing subjects' motivation to learn enhances their retention of material.

ABILITY   Knowledge is an important determinant of learning, as it enables the person to undertake more meaningful elaboration during information processing. In a classic study of how prior knowledge enhances learning, chess masters and novices were shown chess games in progress.[5] The masters generally held a substantial advantage over novices in remembering the board positions of the chess pieces. Interestingly, this superiority disappeared when subjects were exposed to games in which the pieces were randomly organized. Thus, the beneficial effect of knowledge materialized only when the information conformed to the person's organizational rules (i.e., when the pieces' placement "made sense").

Even when knowledge is high, ability to process may still be low. This is

---

[3] Richard E. Petty and John T. Cacioppo, "The Elaboration Likelihood Model of Persuasion," in Leonard Berkowitz, ed., *Advances in Experimental Social Psychology*, vol. 19 (New York: Academic Press, 1986), 123–205.

[4] Gabriel Biehal and Dipankar Chakravarti, "Information-Presentation Format and Learning Goals as Determinants of Consumers' Memory Retrieval and Choice Processes," *Journal of Consumer Research* 8 (March 1982), 431–441; Eloise Coupey and Kent Nakamoto, "Learning Context and the Development of Product Category Perceptions," in Michael J. Houston, ed., *Advances in Consumer Research* 15 (Provo, Utah: Association for Consumer Research, 1988), 77–82; James H. Leigh and Anil Menon, "Audience Involvement Effects on the Information Processing of Umbrella Print Advertisements," *Journal of Advertising* 16 (1987), 3–12; Barry McLaughlin, "Intentional and Incidental Learning in Human Subjects: The Role of Instructions to Learn and Motivation," *Psychological Bulletin* 63 (May 1965), 359–376.

[5] William G. Chase and Herbert A. Simon, "Perception in Chess," *Cognitive Psychology* 4 (January 1973), 55–81. For a more general discussion, see Joseph W. Alba and J. Wesley Hutchinson, "Dimensions of Consumer Expertise," *Journal of Consumer Research* 13 (March 1987), 411–454.

because ability depends on both individual and environmental factors.[6] A knowledgeable consumer, for example, may be unable to engage in much elaboration of an ad appearing on TV if the room is filled with distractors (e.g., a newborn crying for milk). Similarly, the aging process apparently reduces our learning abilities as suggested by a study reporting learning deficiencies among elderly consumers.[7]

METHODS FOR ENHANCING RETENTION

When consumers are both motivated and able to engage in elaboration during information processing, life for the marketer is much simpler. Efforts need be directed only toward ensuring that consumers are exposed to and accurately comprehend the information. However, consumers are often unwilling or unable to engage in much elaboration of marketing stimuli. When this occurs, efforts are needed for enhancing elaboration. Some of the ways in which this may be achieved are described subsequently.

PICTURES   Researchers have only recently begun to examine the impact of stimuli that evoke mental imagery. While imagery can take many forms (e.g., sight, smell, taste), visual imagery has been the focus of research thus far.[8] One obvious approach to activating visual imagery is the use of pictures. Two examples of providing visual representations of semantic concepts (in this case, brand names) are presented in Figure 14.1. The wisdom of this technique has been supported by research that indicates that the learning of brand names is greater when accompanied by pictorial representations.[9]

Why do stimuli that elicit visual imagery have a facilitating effect on retention? One explanation rests upon the proposition that knowledge can be stored in both semantic and visual forms.[10] According to this perspective,

---

[6] Rajeev Batra and Michael Ray, "Situational Effects of Advertising: The Moderating Influence of Motivation, Ability and Opportunity to Respond," *Journal of Consumer Research* 12 (March 1986), 432–445; Danny L. Moore, Douglas Hausknecht, and Kanchana Thamodaran, "Time Compression, Response Opportunity, and Persuasion," *Journal of Consumer Research* 13 (June 1986), 85–99; James M. Munch and John L. Swasy, "Rhetorical Question, Summarization Frequency, and Argument Strength Effects on Recall," *Journal of Consumer Research* 15 (June 1988), 69–76.

[7] Catherine A. Cole and Michael J. Houston, "Encoding and Media Effects on Consumer Learning Deficiencies in the Elderly," *Journal of Marketing Research* 24 (February 1987), 55–63. Also see Gary J. Gaeth and Timothy B. Heath, "The Cognitive Processing of Misleading Advertising in Young and Old Adults," *Journal of Consumer Research* 14 (June 1987), 43–54.

[8] For a recent review of this literature, see Deborah J. MacInnis and Linda L. Price, "The Role of Imagery in Information Processing: Review and Extensions," *Journal of Consumer Research* 13 (March 1987), 473–491.

[9] Jose Biron and Stewart J. McKelvie, "Effects of Interactive and Noninteractive Imagery on Recall of Advertisements," *Perceptual and Motor Skills* 59 (May 1984), 799–805; Childers and Houston, "Conditions for a Picture-Superiority Effect on Consumer Memory"; Kathryn A. Lutz and Richard J. Lutz, "Effects of Interactive Imagery on Learning: Application to Advertising," *Journal of Applied Psychology* 62 (August 1977), 493–498.

[10] Allan Paivio, "Mental Imagery in Associative Learning and Memory," *Psychological Review* 76 (May 1969), 241–263; Allan Paivio, *Mental Representations: A Dual Coding Approach* (New York: Oxford University Press, 1986).

FIGURE 14.1   VISUAL REPRESENTATIONS INCREASE RETENTION OF BRAND NAMES

information stored in both forms essentially doubles the pathways that can be traveled within memory for retrieving the information, relative to storage in only one form. While certainly plausible, there currently exists substantial controversy over the validity of this explanation.[11] Nonetheless, the fact remains that stimuli that evoke imagery provide marketers with a potent tool for enhancing learning.

An ad that capitalizes on visual imagery is presented in Figure 14.2. The woman's clothing, sofa pillows, as well as the material bordering the picture provide visual representations of the semantic concept *satin*. Similarly, the television ad for Blue Polly car wax shows the product resting on the hood of a shiny blue automobile next to a blue parrot. Arctic Lights cigarette ads contain a cigarette package made out of ice. Ads for Firestone's Stones tires depict the brand name carved out of stone.

The research literature is less clear about how the type of picture and its relationship to the copy affect learning. In one study of brand name recall, the facilitating effect of pictures was found only for **interactive** pictures (i.e., both the product class and brand name were represented visually). In contrast, **noninteractive pictures** (i.e., either product class or brand name, but not both, are shown visually) did not enhance learning.[12] Another study, however,

---

[11] See, for example, Childers and Houston, "Conditions for a Picture-Superiority Effect on Consumer Memory"; MacInnis and Price, "The Role of Imagery in Information Processing: Review and Extensions."

[12] Lutz and Lutz, "Effects of Interactive Imagery on Learning: Application to Advertising." Also see Michael J. Houston, Terry L. Childers, and Susan E. Heckler, "Picture-Word Consistency and the Elaborative Processing of Advertisements," *Journal of Marketing Research* 24 (November 1987), 359–369.

FIGURE 14.2
AN AD THAT
ENCOURAGES
VISUAL IMAGERY
RELEVANT TO THE
BRAND NAME

failed to replicate this difference, as both interactive and noninteractive pictures increased brand name recall.[13]

Similar inconsistencies have been reported by research focusing on the learning of the information contained within an ad. Recall of information about the product described in an advertisement has been reported to be superior for **framed ads** (i.e., those in which the message relates the picture to the product) relative to **unframed ads** (i.e., those in which the message does not relate the picture to the product).[14] In contrast, others have predicted and found that recall of ad copy was greater when the picture suggested one attribute while the copy discussed a different attribute.[15] Presumably, this discrepancy prompted more elaborative processing, which led to greater learning. Further work is needed to help clarify the role of pictures during learning.

[13] Biron and McKelvie, "Effects of Interactive and Noninteractive Imagery on Recall of Advertisements."

[14] Julie A. Edell and Richard Staelin, "The Information Processing of Pictures in Print Advertisements," *Journal of Consumer Research* 10 (June 1983), 45–61.

[15] Houston, Childers, and Heckler, "Picture-Word Consistency and the Elaborative Processing of Advertisements."

CONCRETE WORDS   A less obvious approach to activating visual imagery is through the use of **concrete words.** Concrete words, such as *tree* or *dog,* are those that can be visualized easily. In contrast, **abstract words,** such as *justice* or *equality,* do not lend themselves to a visual representation. Research has found that subjects exposed to a list of both concrete and abstract words will demonstrate greater retention of concrete words.[16]

The retention advantage of concrete words carries an important message for marketers. Far too often new products are introduced with rather abstract names. Consider, for instance, product names such as Actifed, Advil, Encaprin, and Nuprin, versus more concrete names such as Head and Throat, Easy Off, or Scrub Free. This lesson was learned by the Matex Corporation with its Rusty Jones rust-inhibitor product. Initially introduced as Thixo-Tex, the subsequent renaming of the product was a major reason for sales climbing from $2 million in 1976 to about $100 million in 1980.[17]

SELF-REFERENCING   Research in cognitive psychology indicates that learning is greater when subjects engage in **self-referencing** during processing. Self-referencing involves relating the information to one's own self and experiences. In a typical study, subjects are exposed to a series of words and asked whether each word describes them. These subjects exhibit greater recall than others who perform different tasks during information processing (e.g., identify a synonym for the word).[18]

This facilitating effect of self-referencing is attributed to a more elaborate encoding of the stimulus information. The representation of the self in memory is believed to be a complex, highly organized structure that is activated by self-referencing. The use of this richer structure during encoding should enhance the number and strength of potential linkages that can be made between memory and the stimulus, which in turn increases the likelihood of retrieval.

A 1987 study suggests the potential for encouraging self-referencing through advertising copy. This activation of self-referencing was achieved by using the word *you* and copy that prompted subjects to retrieve prior relevant product experiences. As expected, recall of the information from the ad was greater when the copy encouraged self-referencing.[19]

---

[16] Roberta L. Klatzky, *Human Memory: Structures and Processes* (San Francisco: W. H. Freeman, 1975), 230.

[17] Hooper White, "Name Change to Rusty Jones Helps Polish Product's Identity," *Advertising Age* (February 18, 1980), 47–48.

[18] See, for example, T. B. Rogers, N. A. Kuiper, and W. S. Kirker, "Self-Reference and Encoding of Personal Information," *Journal of Personality and Social Psychology* 35 (September 1977), 677–688; Polly Brown, Janice M. Keenan, and George R. Potts, "The Self-Reference Effect with Imagery Encoding," *Journal of Personality and Social Psychology* 51 (November 1986), 897–906.

[19] Robert E. Burnkrant and H. Rao Unnava, "Self-Referencing: A Strategy for Increasing Processing of Message Content," (working paper, The Ohio State University, 1987). Also see Kathleen Debevec, Harlan E. Spotts, and Jerome B. Kernan, "The Self-Reference Effect in Persuasion: Implications for Marketing Strategy," in Melanie Wallendorf and Paul Anderson, eds., *Advances in Consumer Research* 14 (Provo, Utah: Association for Consumer Research, 1987), 417–420.

**FIGURE 14.3
ENHANCING
BRAND NAME
MEMORABILITY
THROUGH
MNEMONICS**

MNEMONIC DEVICES   Quite often elaboration may be encouraged through simple mnemonic devices such as the use of rhymes. Brim coffee tells us to "fill it to the rim with Brim," while Shout stain remover asks us to "Shout it out." Similarly, B & B liqueur has encouraged elaboration of the brand name in advertisements that play on the name with phrases such as "B & Bewitch" and "B & Beloved" (see Figure 14.3).

TIME-COMPRESSED SPEECH   Technological advances have enabled advertisers to "compress" radio ads without distortion in speech or sound characteristics. For example, a 30-second ad can be reduced to 24 seconds. Initial research indicated that time-compressed ads can yield higher levels of recall than their longer counterparts, presumably because viewers are less likely to divert their attention elsewhere at this higher rate of information transmission.[20] More recent research, however, has been less supportive.[21] These studies have found time-compressed ads to be either equally or less effective than normally paced ads. Additional work is necessary to establish if and when time compression will be beneficial.

REPETITION   When consumers are motivated and able to engage in meaningful elaboration during message processing, then only a single exposure to an advertisement may be necessary for the desired effect. Additional exposures will be desirable, however, if either motivation or ability is low. By continually repeating the message, marketers are increasing the odds that consumers will encounter it under more favorable circumstances.

A heavy reliance on repetition can be very desirable under a couple of conditions. When the communication conveys a large or complex set of information, consumers may be unable to fully comprehend the message during a single exposure, although this can depend on the type of medium in which the ad appears. Unlike radio and television ads, print ads can be processed at one's own rate and reprocessed if necessary. Thus, the additional opportunities for elaboration afforded by repetition may be more useful for ads appearing in broadcast than print media.

Repetition will also be more useful for some product categories than others. Many of the products consumers purchase at the grocery store, for instance, engender relatively low levels of involvement. Consequently, motivation to intensively process an ad will typically be quite limited. Marketers therefore employ repetition as a form of externally imposed rehearsal.

For these reasons, then, repetition is an important tool for enhancing learning. Indeed, a particular ad may heavily rely on repetition as reflected by the number of times the brand name or some other copy point is repeated throughout the ad. Ralston-Purina uses cats in TV commericals, for example, to repeat over and over the Meow Mix brand name. And remember the Rolaids television commercials? How many times did you hear someone "spell relief" as R-O-L-A-I-D-S?

---

[20] Priscilla LaBarbera and James MacLachlan, "Time-Compressed Speech in Radio Advertising," *Journal of Marketing* 43 (January 1979), 30–36; James MacLachlan and Michael H. Siegel, "Reducing the Cost of TV Commercials by Use of Time Compressions," *Journal of Marketing Research* 17 (February 1980), 52–57.

[21] Moore, Hausknecht, and Thamodaran, "Time Compression, Response Opportunity, and Persuasion"; Mary Jane Rawlins Schlinger, Linda F. Alwitt, Kathleen E. McCarthy, and Leila Green, "Effects of Time Compression on Attitudes and Information Processing," *Journal of Marketing* 47 (Winter 1983), 79–85.

The facilitating effect of repetition has been well substantiated.[22] The standard research finding is that message learning will grow with additional exposures, although at a diminishing rate (i.e., each successive exposure adds less than the preceding one). However, it is also evident that too much repetition can have adverse effects. That is, after a certain number of repetitions, additional repetitions may *reduce* advertising effectiveness. This phenomenon is called **advertising wearout**.[23]

Wearout can occur for two reasons. First, consumers may simply quit attending to an ad after a certain number of exposures. Alternatively, consumers may continue to pay attention, but they become more argumentative as a result of the tedium of seeing the same ad over and over.[24]

A simple solution to the wearout problem is the use of ads that differ in their executional strategies but which carry the same basic message.[25] Rather than showing the same ad twenty times, two different versions may be repeated ten times each. While additional expenses are incurred from the production of multiple ads, this cost may easily be offset by the enhanced effectiveness of this approach.

The benefit of repetition may also depend on the level of competitive advertising. A 1988 study found that repetition enhanced recall when competitive advertising was minimal or nonexistent. This effect disappeared, however, under higher levels of competitive advertising.[26]

---

[22] For a general review, see Alan G. Sawyer, "The Effects of Repetition: Conclusions and Suggestions About Experimental Laboratory Research," in G. D. Hughes and Michael L. Ray, eds., *Buyer/Consumer Information Processing* (Chapel Hill: University of North Carolina Press, 1974), 190–219. Research on repetition effects can be found in Batra and Ray, "Situational Effects of Advertising Repetition: The Moderating Influence of Motivation, Ability, and Opportunity to Respond"; George E. Belch, "The Effects of Television Commercial Repetition on Cognitive Response and Message Acceptance," *Journal of Consumer Research* 9 (June 1982), 56–65; Arno J. Rethans, John L. Swasy, and Lawrence J. Marks, "Effects of Television Commercial Repetition, Receiver Knowledge, and Commercial Length: A Test of the Two-Factor Model," *Journal of Marketing Research* 23 (February 1986), 50–61; Surendra N. Singh, Michael L. Rothschild, and Gilbert A. Churchill, Jr., "Recognition Versus Recall as Measures of Television Commercial Forgetting," *Journal of Marketing Research* 25 (February 1988), 72–80; Esther Thorson and Rita Snyder, "Viewer Recall of Television Commercials: Prediction from the Propositional Structure of Commercial Scripts," *Journal of Marketing Research* 21 (May 1984), 127–136.

[23] For research on advertising wearout, see Bobby J. Calder and Brian Sternthal, "Television Commercial Wearout: An Information Processing View," *Journal of Marketing Research* 17 (May 1980), 173–186.

[24] Richard E. Petty and John T. Cacioppo, "Effects of Message Repetition and Position on Cognitive Responses, Recall, and Persuasion," *Journal of Personality and Social Psychology* 37 (January 1979), 97–109; Rethans, Swasy, and Marks, "Effects of Television Commercial Repetition, Receiver Knowledge, and Commercial Length: A Test of the Two-Factor Model."

[25] Robert E. Burnkrant and Hanumantha R. Unnava, "Effects of Variation in Message Execution on the Learning of Repeated Brand Information," in Melaine Wallendorf and Paul F. Anderson, eds., *Advances in Consumer Research* 14 (Provo, Utah: Association for Consumer Research, 1987), 173–176.

[26] Raymond R. Burke and Thomas K. Srull, "Competitive Interference and Consumer Memory for Advertising," *Journal of Consumer Research* 15 (June 1988), 55–68.

FORGETTING

Before reading past this sentence, stop and write down all of the brands of toothpaste you can remember. Once you have done this, consider the following set of toothpaste brands: Aim, Aquafresh, Check Up, Close Up, Colgate, Crest, Gleem, Pearl Drops, Pepsodent, Sensodyne, Topco, Topol, Ultrabrite, and Zact. It is probably safe to wager that you did not recall all of the brands just listed. It is also probably a safe bet that you did not write down some brands that you in fact "know" as reflected by your recognition of these names while reading the list.

Why, then, did you forget brands that are familiar to you? Two explanations have been offered for the lack of **retrieval,** defined as the process by which knowledge stored in long-term memory is activated.

THE ROLE OF DECAY   It is well known that forgetting and time go hand in hand. The ability to retrieve learned information declines with the passage of time. According to **decay theory,** the strength of a memory trace will fade over time.[27] Retrieval failure will occur when the trace lacks sufficient strength.

However, research has shown that forgetting may differ even when the influence of time is held constant. For example, forgetting will be much lower when the time is spent sleeping than if the person spends the same time awake.[28]

THE ROLE OF INTERFERENCE   According to **interference theory,** forgetting is due to the learning of new information over time.[29] This form of interference, where recently learned information inhibits the retrieval of previously learned information, is known as **retroactive inhibition.** Interference can also take the form of **proactive inhibition,** where prior learning hinders the learning and retrieval of new information. Both forms of inhibition have been demonstrated in a 1988 advertising study. Recall of the information presented in an ad was impaired when subjects were also exposed to ads for competitive products that either preceded (proactive inhibition) or followed (retroactive inhibition) the ad to be remembered.[30]

---

[27] Donald Olding Hebb, *The Organization of Behavior* (New York: John Wiley, 1949); Donald Olding Hebb, "A Neuropsychological Theory," in Sigmund Koch, ed., *Psychology: A Study of Science,* vol. 1 (New York: McGraw-Hill, 1959), 622–643.

[28] John G. Jenkins and Karl M. Dallenbach, "Oblivescence During Sleep and Waking," *American Journal of Psychology* 35 (October 1924), 605–612.

[29] For a thorough analysis of interference and related topics, see the collection of articles in William Kaye Estes, ed., *Handbook of Learning and Cognitive Processes: Attention and Memory,* vol. 4 (Hillsdale, New Jersey: Halstead Press, 1976). For a concise description of interference, see Winfred F. Hill, *Psychology: Principles and Problems* (Philadelphia: Lippincott, 1970), 312–321.

[30] Burke and Srull, "Competitive Interference and Consumer Memory for Advertising."

From this perspective, information can be available in memory (i.e., the memory trace is of sufficient strength) and yet not be retrieved because of limitations in its accessibility. All of us have experienced situations where we have tried unsuccessfully to remember something, only to have it "pop" into our mind some time later. Similarly, hypnosis has been used to facilitate the retrieval of "lost" memories. This distinction between availability and accessibility has been supported by research showing that information which appeared to be forgotten could, in fact, be subsequently retrieved when subjects were provided with certain retrieval cues.[31]

The issue of information accessibility is particularly important to marketers. The influence of advertising, for instance, can depend on the consumer's ability to retrieve information from an ad seen some time ago while shopping at a store. More generally, research has suggested that consumers' product attitudes[32] and choices[33] may heavily depend on what information is retrieved from memory.

Two major determinants of information accessibility are (1) the amount of information stored in memory within the same "content domain" and (2) the particular retrieval cues available at the time.[34] The more brand names a consumer "knows," for instance, the more difficulty he or she will have in retrieve a particular name due to the greater number of competing responses.

Retrieval can be enhanced by the cues that are present at the time of such activity. Retrieval cues can be either self-generated or externally generated. In trying to retrieve a particular brand name, one might try to reconstruct the situation in which the product was last seen or used. A picture of the celebrity spokesperson who is strongly associated with the product may also trigger retrieval of the brand name. The role of retrieval cues for enhancing advertising effectiveness is the topic of *Consumer in Focus 14.1.*

---

[31] Endel Tulving and Zena Pearlstone, "Availability Versus Accessibility of Information in Memory for Words," *Journal of Verbal Learning and Verbal Behavior* 5 (August 1966), 381–391.

[32] Amitava Chattopadhyay and Joseph W. Alba, "The Situational Importance of Recall and Inference in Consumer Decision Making," *Journal of Consumer Research* 15 (June 1988), 1–12; Jolita Kisielius and Brian Sternthal, "Detecting and Explaining Vividness Effects in Attitudinal Judgments," *Journal of Marketing Research* 21 (February 1984), 54–64; Jolita Kisielius and Brian Sternthal, "Examining the Vividness Controversy: An Availability-Valence Explanation," *Journal of Consumer Research* 12 (March 1986), 418–431; Barbara Loken and Ronald Hoverstad, "Relationships Between Information Recall and Subsequent Attitudes: Some Exploratory Findings," *Journal of Consumer Research* 12 (September 1985), 155–168.

[33] Gabriel Biehal and Dipankar Chakravarti, "Information Accessibility as a Moderator of Consumer Choice," *Journal of Consumer Research* 10 (June 1983), 1–14; Gabriel Biehal and Dipankar Chakravarti, "Consumers' Use of Memory and External Information in Choice: Macro and Micro Perspectives," *Journal of Consumer Research* 12 (March 1986), 382–405.

[34] John G. Lynch, Jr., and Thomas K. Srull, "Memory and Attentional Factors in Consumer Choice: Concepts and Research Methods," *Journal of Consumer Research* 9 (June 1982), 18–37.

CONSUMER IN FOCUS

14.1   INCREASING CONSUMERS' MEMORY FOR ADVERTISING

One of the challenges to advertising effectiveness is the time delay that typically occurs between ad exposure and product choice. An ad may elicit a very positive reaction from consumers sitting in their living rooms but have little influence on consumers who fail to remember the ad when making their choices at the point of purchase. In such cases, enhancing the retrieval of the ad information would be desirable.

One possible method for increasing consumers' memory for advertising is the use of retrieval cues at the point of purchase. An example of this comes from the popular Quaker Oats' "Mikey" commercial for its Life brand of cereal. For many years, the company placed a picture of one of the commercial's scenes in the lower right-hand corner of the product package. This cue would presumably serve as a prompt to help the consumer remember the ad.

The wisdom of this strategy was supported in both laboratory and field settings. As expected, the presence of such cues led to a greater recall of an ad's claims than when the cue was absent. Moreover, given the favorable nature of the recalled information, the cues also led to more positive brand evaluations. Similarly, the Campbell Soup Company reports that sales increased by 15 percent when point-of-purchase materials were directly related to television advertising.

Sources: Kevin Lane Keller, "Memory Factors in Advertising: The Effect of Advertising Retrieval Cues on Brand Evaluations," *Journal of Consumer Research* 14 (December 1987), 316–333; Joseph O. Eastlack, Jr., "How to Get More Bang for Your Television Bucks," *Journal of Consumer Marketing* 1 (1984), 25–34.

Marketers may sometimes wish to interfere with the retrieval of information. Consider, for example, the situation where a consumer might normally consider four alternative brands during decision making. One approach a brand might adopt for gaining a competitive advantage would entail inhibiting the consumer's ability to recall the remaining brands. How could this inhibition be achieved?

Research has revealed that increasing the salience of a brand (i.e., its prominence in short-term memory) will interfere with the retrieval of other brands within the same product category.[35] For instance, increasing a brand's

---

[35] Joseph W. Alba and Amitava Chattopadhyay, "Effects of Context and Part-Category Cues on Recall of Competing Brands," *Journal of Marketing Research* 22 (August 1985), 340–349; Joseph W. Alba and Amitava Chattopadhyay, "Salience Effects in Brand Recall," *Journal of Marketing Research* 23 (November 1986), 363–369. Also see Paul W. Miniard, H. Rao Unnava, and Sunil Bhatla, "Investigating the Recall Inhibition Effect: A Test of Practical and Theoretical Considerations," working paper, The Ohio State University, 1988.

salience by exposure to an ad for that brand was found to lower the number of recalled brands. Further, this interference occurred even for brands that consumers would consider buying.

MEASURES OF COGNITIVE LEARNING

The two major approaches to measuring cognitive learning are **recognition** and **recall.** Whereas recognition measures provide the person with some type of cue to prompt memory, this is not the case for recall measures. For example, asking a student on an exam to define the concept of elaboration would represent a recall measure. A recognition measure would involve asking the student to identify the correct definition from a set of possible answers.

Recognition tests generally reflect greater learning than recall measures, although there are exceptions.[36] Similarly, forgetting appears to occur more slowly when measured by recognition. This "superiority" of recognition measures is attributable to the additional retrieval cues inherent in such measures.

THE USE OF LEARNING MEASURES IN ADVERTISING   Recognition and recall are often used to evaluate advertising's effectiveness. There are a number of measurement versions that pose different degrees of retrieval difficulty.

Simple recognition measures involve presenting ads to people and asking them whether or not they remember seeing the ad previously.[37] This measure will yield the highest estimate of learning, since the presence of the original stimulus is a very strong retrieval cue. One problem with this approach is the potential for overestimating the amount of retention. People have been found to claim recognition of bogus ads that they could not possibly have seen before.[38]

Forced-choice recognition measures, on the other hand, offer a more realistic and informative appraisal of ad memory.[39] This approach focuses on the memorability of particular ad and brand elements, thus allowing a more detailed analysis of what is retrieved. In addition, respondents are forced

---

[36] Endel Tulving and Donald M. Thompson, "Encoding Specificity and Retrieval Processes in Episodic Memory," *Psychological Review* 80 (September 1973), 352–373.

[37] For a review of the literature on recognition measures, see Surendra N. Singh and Catherine A. Cole, "Forced-Choice Recognition Tests: A Critical Review," *Journal of Advertising* 14 (1985), 52–58.

[38] Eric Marder and Mort David, "Recognition of Ad Elements: Recall or Projection?" *Journal of Advertising Research* 1 (December 1961), 23–25. For an interesting discussion of recognition measures, see Adam Finn, "Print Ad Recognition Readership Scores: An Information Processing Perspective," *Journal of Marketing Research* 25 (May 1988), 168–177.

[39] Surendra N. Singh and Gilbert A. Churchill, Jr., "Using the Theory of Signal Detection to Improve Ad Recognition Testing," *Journal of Marketing Research* 23 (November 1986), 327–336; Singh and Cole, "Forced-Choice Recognition Tests: A Critical Review"; Surendra N. Singh and Michael L. Rothschild, "Recognition as a Measure of Learning from Television Commercials," *Journal of Marketing Research* 20 (August 1983), 235–248; Singh, Rothschild, and Churchill, Jr., "Recognition Versus Recall as Measures of Television Commercial Forgetting."

to choose among a set of fixed answers in responding to questions about a specific element, much like a multiple-choice exam.

Alternatively, recall measures may be used as indicators of learning.[40] Recall measures differ in their use of retrieval cues. **Aided recall measures** (e.g., "Do you remember the brand of soft drink advertised during last night's broadcast of the Academy Awards?") provide such cues. **Unaided recall measures** (e.g., "Name all of the brands you have seen advertised during the past 24 hours") do not.

One of the most frequently used recall measures is the **demonstrated recall measure** developed by Burke, a major marketing research firm. The day after an ad has aired, households in the area are contacted by phone until 200 "qualified" persons (i.e., those watching the program) are located. Each person is then asked to recall both the name of the advertised product and one copy point. The average Burke score is around 24 percent.[41]

LEARNING MEASURES: ARE THEY APPROPRIATE INDICATORS OF ADVERTISING EFFECTIVENESS?

In the early stages of the product life cycle, establishing brand name awareness is a major objective of the promotion mix. Measures that tap brand name learning are very useful in determining whether this objective is being achieved. Similarly, cognitive learning measures are valuable indicators for evaluating advertising aimed at educating consumers about the brand's properties or uses.

In contrast, cognitive learning measures may have very little to say about an ad's impact on consumer attitudes. The fact that consumers can *remember* the claims made in an ad does not mean that they *believe* the claims. Obnoxious ads can be very memorable, but they may also have a negative effect on viewers' attitudes. Research has shown that recall alone may have very little relationship with attitude.[42] Thus, when an important objective of advertising is to influence product preferences, it is necessary to go beyond cognitive learning measures and assess brand attitudes.

Another concern with the validity of ad memory measures as indicators of ad effectiveness is the implicit assumption reflected in the chapter opener: an ad must be remembered before it can have an influence. If a person is unable to recall any recent advertising, has the advertising been wasted? We don't think so. It seems quite possible for advertising to have an effect without establishing a strong link in the consumer's mind between the product and

---

[40] There has been some criticism of recall measures' ability to provide an accurate assessment of the learning that occurs from emotional or feeling ads. See Hubert A. Zielske, "Does Day-After Recall Penalize 'Feeling' Ads?" *Journal of Advertising Research* 22 (February-March 1982), 19–22.

[41] "To Burke or Not to Burke?" *TV Guide* 29 (February 7, 1981), 3ff.

[42] Chattopadhyay and Alba, "The Situational Importance of Recall and Inference in Consumer Decision Making"; Loken and Hoverstad, "Relationships Between Information Recall and Subsequent Attitudes: Some Exploratory Findings."

the ad itself. Certainly all of us retain certain bits and pieces of product knowledge as a result of prior advertising, and yet, cannot identify the source of such knowledge.

This is not to say that having such a linkage is undesirable. Indeed, as reported in *Consumer in Focus 14.1,* activating this linkage through retrieval cues can be very beneficial. We are saying that the "jury is still out" on the role of ad memory as a necessary prerequisite for ad impact.

RECOGNITION OR RECALL: WHICH ONE? When learning measures are appropriate, one is faced with the choice of whether to rely on recognition or recall measures. It has been suggested that this choice should be based on whether brand recognition or brand recall is the important retrieval process during decision making.[43] Very often consumers make their choices within a retail environment filled with retrieval cues (e.g., the product's packaging). However, when recognition is not a viable option, such as decision making that occurs at home (e.g., the consumer deciding which restaurant to patronize), then brand name recall must be the focus.[44]

This decision can have a strong impact on the efficiency of advertising expenditures.[45] Dollars are likely to be wasted if only brand recognition is needed and brand recall is used as the advertising objective. This is because it will typically require fewer exposures (and hence dollars) to achieve a certain level of recognition than needed to reach the same level of recall.

CLASSICAL CONDITIONING

As noted in the beginning of the chapter, cognitive learning is but one of the ways in which learning occurs. The building of stimulus–response associations can also lead to learning. The development of these associations is the focus of classical conditioning.

For many, the term **classical conditioning** elicits thoughts of Pavlov and his dogs. Pavlov, the father of classical conditioning, demonstrated this type of learning through the following procedures. First, an existing stimulus–response relationship is selected, such as food (referred to as the **unconditioned stimulus** [US]), which elicits salivation (referred to as the **unconditioned response** [UR]). A new stimulus (called the **conditioned stimulus** [CS]), such

---

[43] James R. Bettman, *An Information Processing Theory of Consumer Choice* (Reading, Massachusetts: Addison-Wesley, 1979).

[44] For a discussion of advertising tactics to enhance brand recognition and recall, see John R. Rossiter and Larry Percy, "Advertising Communication Models," in Elizabeth C. Hirschman and Morris B. Holbrook, eds., *Advances in Consumer Research* 12 (Provo, Utah: Association for Consumer Research, 1985), 510–524.

[45] Singh, Rothschild, and Churchill, Jr., "Recognition Versus Recall as Measures of Television Commercial Forgetting."

FIGURE 14.4
THE CLASSICAL
CONDITIONING
APPROACH TO
INFLUENCING
PRODUCT
ATTITUDES

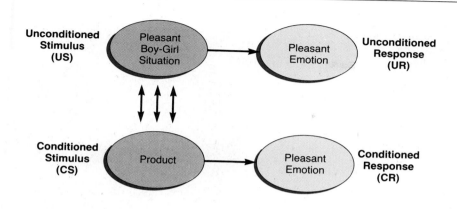

as a bell, is then paired repeatedly with the food. Eventually, the conditioned stimulus will elicit a response (called the **conditioned response** [CR]) that is quite similar to the response originally generated by the unconditioned stimulus.

Figure 14.4 presents the basic classical conditioning framework within a product context.[46] In this example, a boy–girl situation which elicits a pleasant emotion is paired with a product in the hope that these favorable feelings can be conditioned to the product. Thus, classical conditioning represents one mechanism by which attitude formation follows an affective-based rather than cognitive-based process. This basic framework is illustrated by the ad appearing in Figure 14.5.

This simple principle of association between two objects or stimuli underlies much of today's advertising. A prime example is a scene from a Pepsi television commercial featuring a young boy playing with a pack of exuberant puppies. The pleasurable and warm emotions elicited by this scene will presumably generalize by association to the product. Similarly, retailers recognize the value of playing Christmas carols in order to evoke feelings that help overcome sales resistance.[47] A further example of how marketers can use stimuli to elicit desired behaviors is described in *Consumer in Focus 14.2.*

In product markets where competitive brands are virtually the same, it may be impossible to achieve brand differentiation through emphasizing product attributes. Differentiation may be possible, however, by conditioning brand

[46] For an excellent translation of this literature into the marketing domain, see Frances K. McSweeney and Calvin Bierley, "Recent Developments in Classical Conditioning," *Journal of Consumer Research* 11 (September 1984), 619–631.

[47] Walter R. Nord and J. Paul Peter, "A Behavior Modification Perspective on Marketing," *Journal of Marketing* 44 (Spring 1980), 36–47.

FIGURE 14.5
USING CLASSICAL
CONDITIONING IN
ADVERTISING TO
CREATE A
FAVORABLE
ATTITUDE TOWARD
THE PRODUCT

TO SEND THE GIFT OF ROMANCE NATIONWIDE (EXCEPT WHERE PROHIBITED BY LAW), PHONE 1-800-BE-THERE.

attitudes through stimuli that evoke favorable responses. Accordingly, advertising in product categories comprised of fairly homogeneous offerings (e.g., beer, cigarettes, liquor) often rely on a classical conditioning approach.

DETERMINANTS OF CLASSICAL CONDITIONING

Simply pairing a US with a product (i.e., CS) does not guarantee that classical conditioning will occur. Indeed, as described subsequently, there are a number of factors that will influence the effectiveness of any efforts to induce conditioning.[48]

US STRENGTH   The strength of the US will partly determine the amount of conditioning. By strength, we refer to the intensity of the feelings elicited

[48] For a more detailed discussion of conditioning determinants, see Werner Kroeber-Riel, "Emotional Product Differentiation by Classical Conditioning," in Thomas C. Kinnear, ed., *Advances in Consumer Research* 11 (Provo, Utah: Association for Consumer Research, 1984), 538–543; McSweeney and Bierley, "Recent Developments in Classical Conditioning."

CONSUMER IN FOCUS

14.2   INFLUENCING CONSUMER BEHAVIOR THROUGH STIMULUS–RESPONSE ASSOCIATIONS

One of the authors can still remember his parents preaching the evils of using credit cards. "If you can't pay cash for it," they would say, "don't buy it." "Credit cards only cost you more money in the long run." As usual, mom and dad were right.

Recent evidence suggests that credit cards can have a very strong influence on spending. In one experiment, subjects were asked how much they were willing to pay for a black and white TV. Some subjects made this estimate in the presence of credit cards that were placed on the table at which they were seated. Others made the estimate without the credit cards being present. In the absence of credit cards, subjects indicated they would pay an average of $67 for the TV. Subjects were willing to pay nearly $137 for the *same* product, however, following exposure to credit cards.

A similar result was observed even in situations where actual money was involved. Restaurant patrons left larger tips when they paid their tab with a credit card rather than cash. Charitable donations were also greater when contributors were exposed to credit cards.

Why do credit cards have such an effect? One explanation is that credit cards become conditioned stimuli due to their prior association with spending and the positive feelings that often occur from acquiring a new product. As a result of this prior conditioning, "credit card stimuli acquire the ability to elicit spending behavior as a conditioned response."

These findings suggest another way for separating consumers from their money. A retailer, for instance, may find it advantageous to display prominently (perhaps on or near the front door) the all too familiar signs of which credit cards are accepted by the establishment. On the other hand, the lesson for consumers is also clear. Paying in cash will probably save money.

Source: Richard A. Feinberg, "Credit Cards as Spending Facilitating Stimuli: A Conditioning Explanation," *Journal of Consumer Research* 13 (December 1986), 348–356.

by the US. A stronger US can enhance conditioning. When the US is weak, it may not be possible to induce conditioning.

There is, of course, considerable diversity among stimuli in their strength. In an interesting study of "thrills" (tingling sensations that occur in response to emotionally arousing stimuli), respondents were asked to indicate how often they experienced thrills for a variety of stimuli. Virtually everyone reported thrills for music, two thirds had experienced thrills while viewing a beautiful painting, while parades elicited thrills from only one fourth of the respondents.[49]

[49] Avram Goldstein, "Thrills in Response to Music and Other Stimuli," *Physiological Psychology* 8 (September 1980), 126–129.

NUMBER OF PAIRINGS   Just as repetition can play a major role in cognitive learning, it will also influence the degree of classical conditioning. Conditioning has been found for product preferences after a single CS–US pairing.[50] Even so, additional pairings are likely to be needed for maximum effectiveness. It has been suggested that as many as 30 pairings may be required for conditioning product preferences.[51]

CS–US ORDER   Conditioning can also depend on the order in which the CS and US are presented.[52] There are three possible orders. **Forward conditioning** is when the CS precedes the US. **Backward conditioning** is when the US precedes the CS. Finally, presenting the CS and US at the same time is known as **simultaneous conditioning.**

Although conditioning may occur using any of these orders, forward conditioning appears to be the most effective.[53] This carries several implications for advertising practice. Suppose you were developing a TV ad that includes a well-liked musical tune. When should this tune (US) appear relative to the product (CS)? Superior results are expected when product presentation precedes rather than follows the tune or when the product is presented simultaneously with the tune.

It has also been suggested that some media are better suited for classical conditioning advertising because they allow more control of the order in which the US and CS are processed.[54] Broadcast channels (TV, radio) provide such control, while print media (magazines, billboards) do not. Simply because the product is positioned at the top of a page with the US appearing at the bottom does not guarantee that the viewer will process these stimuli in the desired order. The US may easily be viewed first. For this reason, then, print media may be less effective avenues for classical conditioning advertising.

FAMILIARITY   Prior familiarity or experience with a stimulus can undermine conditioning.[55] A well-known song, for instance, may be less effective than a tune created specifically for the product (although this weakness in

---

[50] Gerald J. Gorn, "The Effects of Music in Advertising on Choice Behavior: A Classical Conditioning Approach," *Journal of Marketing* 46 (Winter 1982), 94–101; Elnora W. Stuart, Terence A. Shimp, and Randall W. Engle, "Classical Conditioning of Consumer Attitudes: Four Experiments in an Advertising Context," *Journal of Consumer Research* 14 (December 1987), 334–349. Also see Chris T. Allen and Thomas J. Madden, "A Closer Look at Classical Conditioning," *Journal of Consumer Research* 12 (December 1985), 301–315; James J. Kellaris and Anthony D. Cox, "The Effects of Background Music in Advertising: A Reassessment," *Journal of Consumer Research* 16 (June 1989), 113–118.

[51] Kroeber-Riel, "Emotional Product Differentiation by Classical Conditioning."

[52] McSweeney and Bierley, "Recent Developments in Classical Conditioning."

[53] Ibid.; Stuart, Shimp, and Engle, "Classical Conditioning of Consumer Attitudes: Four Experiments in an Advertising Context."

[54] McSweeney and Bierley, "Recent Developments in Classical Conditioning."

[55] Ibid.

using a popular song may be more than offset by other considerations, such as greater liking for the music).

Similarly, classical conditioning may be more effective for new than existing products. Tentative support for this proposition comes from a recent study that varied subjects' prior exposure to a fictitious brand before pairing the brand with a favorable US. The results indicated greater conditioning for those subjects not previously exposed to the brand.[56]

ELABORATION   It has also been suggested that the degree of cognitive elaboration during message processing will moderate the impact of classical conditioning.[57] Classical conditioning is believed to occur only under low levels of issue-relevant thinking, such as when consumers are relatively uninvolved during message processing. Presumably, the presence of extensive issue-relevant thinking will override any possible effects of classical conditioning. Currently, however, this prediction has not been examined empirically.

EXTINCTION

Extinction occurs when the conditioned stimulus no longer evokes the conditioned response. A classically conditioned response does not simply disappear over time. Rather, it will disappear when the relationship between the CS and US is broken.

How is the CS–US relation broken? One way is for the CS to be encountered *without* the US. Suppose a company uses classical conditioning in an ad by pairing music with the product. Encountering the product without the music will reduce the effectiveness of this ad. Accordingly, advertising that does not pair the product with the US will undermine advertising that does.

Many products, such as cars and clothing, are seen more frequently outside of commercials than other types of products, such as soaps and laundry detergents. These encounters encourage extinction since the CS (product) is seen without the US. Classical conditioning should therefore be better for less frequently encountered products.

Just as contact with the CS without the US will enhance extinction, so too will contact with the US without the CS. The Pepsi commercials featuring Michael Jackson and his music suffer from this limitation. That is, many consumers will encounter Michael Jackson and his music in situations where Pepsi is not present. This will encourage extinction. Consequently, "novel" unconditioned stimuli may often be preferable to familiar or popular ones, since the former are less likely to be encountered without the CS. Despite

---

[56] Stuart, Shimp, and Engle, "Classical Conditioning of Consumer Attitudes: Four Experiments in an Advertising Context."

[57] Anthony G. Greenwald and Clark Leavitt, "Audience Involvement in Advertising: Four Levels," *Journal of Consumer Research* 11 (June 1984), 581–592; Richard E. Petty and John T. Cacioppo, "The Elaboration Likelihood Model of Persuasion," in Leonard Berkowitz, ed., *Advances in Experimental Social Psychology*, vol. 19 (New York: Academic Press, 1986), 123–205.

this limitation, the use of Michael Jackson is very appropriate when we consider his strength as a US (i.e., he can elicit very strong favorable reactions from many young consumers). Indeed, it is important to keep in mind that a stimulus, while deficient on one factor, can be very effective for inducing conditioning because of other factors that more than offset some limitation.

GENERALIZATION

Generalization occurs when, for an existing stimulus–response relationship, a new stimulus that is very similar to the existing one elicits the same response. In Pavlov's experiments, for instance, a noise that was very similar to the bell would evoke the salivation response.

Companies sometimes use generalization in the form of **family branding** by placing the same brand name on its different products. General Electric does so in the hope that consumers will generalize the favorable feelings developed toward one GE product to another.

There is currently a trend toward positioning new products as product-line extensions rather than developing separate brand identities.[58] Examples of this strategy include Crest Tartar Control, Duncan Hines cookies, Ivory Shampoo, and Liquid Tide. Similarly, Nabisco Brands transformed their Apple Bars cookies into Apple Newtons so as to encourage generalization with their highly successful Fig Newtons. This trend is driven primarily by financial considerations. It is typically more expensive to create a new product identity than to build upon an established one.

Recognize, however, that a family branding strategy may not always be the best course of action. Separate brand identities are desirable for a company wishing to market products of varying quality. Gallo was concerned about the possibility that their new line of wine coolers would dilute the quality image of their wines. Consequently, the wine coolers were given a separate identity — Bartles & Jaymes.

In some cases, manufacturers try to encourage generalization through product packaging that is very similar to a leading competitor's packaging. This is the so-called **me-too product.** A soup manufacturer may produce a red and white can that is very similar to the Campbell's soup can. This use of generalization is intended to evoke the same favorable response that is typically associated with the Campbell's brand. Indeed, it is surprising just how often this form of generalization happens in the marketplace.

Consumers may also generalize between competitive products that possess very similar names (e.g., Muffler King versus Speedy Muffler King, Country Inn versus Cross Country Inn). Legal battles often result in such situations. The Adolph Coors Brewing Company brought suit against the soft drink manufacturer of Corr's Natural Beverages on grounds that the names are in-

---

[58] "Firm: Consumers Cool to New Products," *Marketing News* 20 (January 3, 1986), 1ff.

distinguishable to a substantial number of consumers.[59] Similarly, McDonald's has recently filed suits against McTravel Travel Services and McSleep Hotels for infringing on the company name.[60]

DISCRIMINATION

Discrimination is the process whereby an organism learns to emit a response to one stimulus, but avoids making the same response to a similar stimulus. Using classical conditioning, discrimination can be encouraged by pairing a positive US with one CS but not another CS. Conditioning should occur only for the CS paired with the US. Even greater discrimination could be encouraged by pairing the second CS (e.g., a competitor's product) with a negative US.

Discrimination is obviously an important concept in marketing. Marketers usually want consumers to distinguish between their products and those of competitors. When discrimination is desired, it is typically best achieved through endowing the product with unique benefits or features. While this may often be possible, sometimes it is not. As indicated by the beer label study described in the information-processing chapter, consumers could not distinguish between various brands in blind taste tests.[61] When brands are fairly homogeneous, marketers must search for other means of differentiating their products.

A classic marketing example of discrimination on dimensions other than the product's benefits is the Goodrich advertising campaign of many years ago. Goodrich had discovered that many consumers did not distinguish between its name and that of a major competitor, Goodyear. Indeed, when exposed to Goodrich advertising, some consumers mistakenly perceived it as advertising for Goodyear. Consequently, it became critical for Goodrich to combat this confusion. This was accomplished by using the well-known Goodyear blimp in the campaign slogan "We're the one without the blimp."

Discrimination is also very important in the domain of brand name protection. Marketers that fail to encourage brand name discrimination run the risk of losing their trademarks. Courts can rule that a name has passed into the public domain (i.e., the trademark is revoked) when it has become so common or generic that it has lost its specific meaning. Examples of lost trademarks include: aspirin, cellophane, corn flakes, cube steak, dry ice, escalator, kerosene, linoleum, raisin bran, shredded wheat, shuttle, thermos, and yo-yo.[62] Firms are sometimes hired to monitor a name's use in public and

---

[59] "Coors vs. Corr's," *Time* 123 (February 6, 1984), 51.

[60] Diane Schneidman, "Use of 'Mc' in Front of Travel Firms' Names Leads to Lawsuits," *Marketing News* 21 (November 20, 1987), 17.

[61] R. I. Allison and K. P. Uhl, "Influence of Beer Brand Identification on Taste Perception," *Journal of Marketing Research* 1 (August 1964), 36–39.

[62] Julia Keller, "These Are Not Q-Tips," *The Columbus Dispatch* (April 10, 1987), G1.

**FIGURE 14.6
FEDERAL EXPRESS
IS ENCOURAGING
BRAND NAME
DISCRIMINATION**

PLEASE DON'T FOOL AROUND WITH OUR NAME.

Every now and then, the most confusing
conversation in the world takes place. Here it is.
"Let's Federal Express it."
"Okay. Who should we use?"
"Let's just Federal Express it."
"Okay. Who should we use?"
Please. "Federal Express" is not a phrase
that refers to anybody and everybody in the over-
night package business.
Federal Express is a name. Our name. In
fact, our trademark. Which is why when you ask
for Federal Express, you should get no one but
Federal Express. A single, specific air express com-
pany that happens to deliver more packages to
more places overnight than any other air express
company. And, for the last ten years, has earned
its reputation as the most reliable in the business.
So, let's make a deal.
We'll try not to lose your packages.
Please try not to misplace our name.

FEDERAL EXPRESS
WHY FOOL AROUND WITH ANYONE ELSE?

"Federal Express" is a registered trademark of the Federal Express Corporation.
©1984 Federal Express Corporation.

take appropriate actions when potential problems arise (e.g., one firm reports
writing a letter to Johnny Carson about the difference between cat-box filler
and Kitty Litter). The Federal Express ad appearing in Figure 14.6 encourages
consumers to discriminate between their company and competitors by not
using their name in a generic sense.

OPERANT CONDITIONING

While shopping at the grocery store, a consumer notices a new brand of
cereal and decides to buy it. The next morning she gives it a try and is very
satisfied with the taste. She likes it so much that she makes a mental note to
pick up another box during her next shopping.

This simple example illustrates how learning can occur as a result of

operant conditioning. This form of conditioning, also called **instrumental learning,** is concerned with how the *consequences* of a behavior will affect the frequency or probability of the behavior being performed again. The satisfaction experienced by the consumer while eating the cereal increased the odds of repeat purchase. On the other hand, repeat purchasing would be unlikely if the cereal failed to satisfy the consumer.

Figure 14.7 reveals that consequences can affect behavior (called the operant behavior in the jargon of this literature) in one of three ways. To illustrate these distinctions, consider a typical operant conditioning experiment where a pigeon is placed in a cage containing a bar that, when pressed, produces some consequence. Under **positive reinforcement,** pressing the bar (the operant behavior) leads to receiving some positive stimulus (e.g., food). Under **negative reinforcement,** bar pressing leads to the removal of some adverse stimulus (e.g., stopping a low-level electrical shock). In both cases, the pigeon

**FIGURE 14.7
THREE FORMS
OF OPERANT
CONDITIONING**

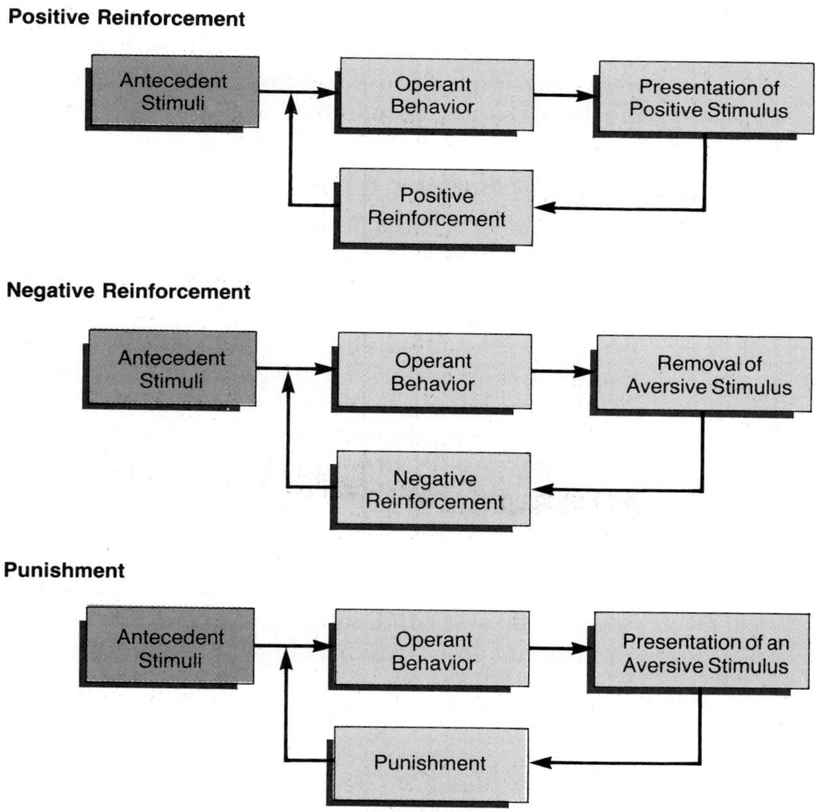

Positive Reinforcement

Antecedent Stimuli → Operant Behavior → Presentation of Positive Stimulus → Positive Reinforcement → (back to Operant Behavior)

Negative Reinforcement

Antecedent Stimuli → Operant Behavior → Removal of Aversive Stimulus → Negative Reinforcement → (back to Operant Behavior)

Punishment

Antecedent Stimuli → Operant Behavior → Presentation of an Aversive Stimulus → Punishment → (back to Operant Behavior)

Source: Adapted from Stanley M. Widrick, "Concept of Negative Reinforcement Has Place in Classroom," *Marketing News* 20 (July 18, 1986), 48–49.

is more likely to repeat the behavior in the future. In contrast, **punishment** would reduce the odds of the behavior occurring again. In this case, pressing the bar would cause the appearance of an adverse stimulus (e.g., a shock).

Although there may be occasions where marketers will employ punishers (e.g., revoking a product warranty for failing to adhere to the maintenance schedule), reinforcement is the major focus of interest from a marketing perspective. In the following sections we examine the various reinforcers available for modifying consumer behavior and factors that influence their effectiveness.

REINFORCEMENT FROM PRODUCT CONSUMPTION

The degree to which reinforcement occurs as a result of product consumption is a critical determinant of whether the product will be purchased again. Products that deliver reinforcement are more likely to be repurchased. Repeat purchasing is unlikely when product use does not reinforce the consumer or, even worse, punishes the consumer (e.g., a lighter that explodes during use). The level of reinforcement provided by products can, and should, be monitored through the use of satisfaction measures, a topic considered in our later chapter on purchase and its outcomes.

TYPES OF PRODUCT REINFORCEMENT   Products differ in whether they provide positive or negative reinforcement.[63] For example, a consumer may eat candy because of the positive sensory experiences that result from this action. In contrast, eye drops might be used to remove the adverse feelings due to burning, irritated eyes. It is possible for a product to deliver both positive and negative reinforcement. An air freshener can replace odors (negative reinforcement) with a refreshing smell (positive reinforcement).

The type of reinforcement provided by a product can influence consumer behavior. Consumers are less likely to enjoy buying and using negative reinforcement products. Consequently, they will often spend less time and effort in buying these products.[64] This in turn limits a product's opportunity to break through the clutter of competitive brands and gain the consumer's consideration.

Marketers of negative reinforcement products should recognize the existence of three distinct consumer segments for their product. Obviously, consumers currently experiencing the problem solved by the product are the

---

[63] Stanley M. Widrick, "Concept of Negative Reinforcement Has Place in Classroom," *Marketing News* 20 (July 18, 1986), 48–49; Stanley Widrick and Eugene H. Fram, "Identifying Negative Products: Do Customers Like to Purchase Your Products?" *Journal of Consumer Marketing* 1 (Fall 1983), 59–66.

[64] Widrick, "Concept of Negative Reinforcement Has Place in Classroom."

primary segment. Consumers who formerly suffered from the problem comprise a segment that may be receptive to appeals that encourage product use to ensure that the problem will not recur. Even consumers who have not faced the problem may be a viable segment. It might be possible to encourage product use as a means of reducing the odds that consumers would ever experience the problem, such as the consumer who takes aspirin daily because of its potential for reducing heart problems.

THE ROLE OF FREE SAMPLES   Fortunately, the reinforcement delivered by a product need not wait until the consumer purchases the product. Instead, a free sample can be given to consumers so that they may experience the reinforcement of product consumption without actually buying the product. Once having experienced this reinforcement, consumers should then be more likely to buy the product.

Free samples, although typically a very expensive method of promoting

FIGURE 14.8
PROVIDING
CONSUMERS AN
OPPORTUNITY OF
PRODUCT TRIAL
WITHOUT PURCHASE

Source: Reprinted by permission of Apple Computer, Inc. Apple and the Apple logo are registered trademarks of Apple Computer Inc. Macintosh is a trademark licensed to Apple Computer, Inc.

FIGURE 14.9
THE IMPACT OF
FREE SAMPLES ON
PURCHASE BEHAVIOR

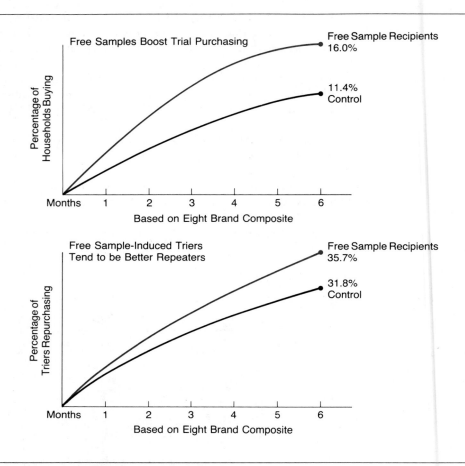

Source: *Insights,* NPD Research, Inc., 1979–1982.

the product, are often used by marketers, particularly when introducing new offerings to the marketplace. Duncan Hines, for example, sent small boxes of their new cookies to selected target households. Similarly, Coca-Cola delivered packages containing single cans of their various brands to the consumer's doorstep. This approach is not feasible, however, for many products, such as high-ticket items. Even so, the benefits of product trial can still be enjoyed by allowing consumers to "test drive" the product. Apple, for instance, has offered consumers the opportunity to take home and try a Macintosh computer (see Figure 14.8).

Evidence concerning the impact of free samples on purchasing behavior is summarized in Figure 14.9. These findings are based on eight new product-introduction tests conducted by National Panel Diary, a market research firm, in which one group of consumers received a free sample while another group did not.[65] The impact of free samples is reflected by a comparison of the two groups. The top graph in Figure 14.9 represents the results involving initial or trial purchasing. As can be seen, nearly 50 percent more households receiving a free sample engaged in initial purchasing relative to control households (i.e., those not receiving a free sample). Moreover, as represented by the bottom graph in Figure 14.9, those who purchased after receiving the free sample were slightly more likely to buy it again. Overall, free samples yielded a penetration level of 5.7 percent after 6 months (trial rate of 16.0 percent times the repurchase rate of 35.7 percent) compared to a level of 3.6 percent when free samples were not used.

NONPRODUCT REINFORCEMENT

While the degree of reinforcement a consumer experiences from using the product is critical, reinforcement can also be delivered in many other forms (see *Consumer in Focus 14.3*). Fast-food restaurants often employ the tactic of including a small gift in children's meals for reinforcing the child who, in turn, influences Mom and Dad. MCL, a cafeteria-style restaurant, provides parents with a token that the child can use in a machine which dispenses small toys. Even adults can be the target of such reinforcers. The Sunflower Chinese restaurant in Columbus often bestows complimentary chocolate mints to their regular patrons.

REINFORCING THE HEAVY USER

To the extent that a company has decided to supplement the reinforcement from product consumption with additional reinforcers, special emphasis should be placed on heavy users when this segment exists. Heavy users are those consumers who account for a disproportionate amount of product consumption. All other things being equal, it is more desirable to attract and retain such consumers than moderate or light users.

The money-back program recently implemented by Harley Hotels, in which the consumer receives $25 for every seven nights of usage, is aimed at the heavy user (see Figure 14.10). Similarly, the Zayre Corporation has introduced the "Frequent Z" points-for-purchase program. Customers earn points for their purchases, which can then be redeemed for catalog gift items. According to Stanley M. Adler, president, "We believe this program will attract new shoppers to our stores while building greater loyalty among current customers."[66]

---

[65] *Insights,* NPD Research, Inc., 1979–1982.
[66] "Zayre Launches 'Frequent Z' to Make Points with Shoppers," *Marketing News* 21 (November 20, 1987), 1.

CONSUMER IN FOCUS

14.3 THANKS FOR THE BUSINESS

Perhaps one of the most underappreciated forms of reinforcement is to simply thank customers for their patronage. Many companies show this concern by sending new customers "thank you" notes. Similarly, the phrase "We thank you for your support" has become a common component of the Bartles & Jaymes wine cooler commercials.

Evidence of the effectiveness of thank you notes comes from a recent study of new life insurance purchasers. Following each monthly payment, some of the customers received a letter thanking them for their recent payment. Less than 9 percent of this customer group cancelled their policy during the 6-month test period. In contrast, the cancellation rate of those customers not receiving this reinforcement was 23 percent.

Additional testimony to the power of thanking customers comes from a jewelry store that employed this tactic. After experiencing a considerable drop in sales, some of the store's prior customers were contacted by phone and thanked for their business, whereas other customers were not. Although sales did not increase among those customers not receiving this verbal reinforcement, the customers who did receive the phone call responded quite favorably. In fact, the store was able to completely reverse the sales decline during the test month.

Adapted from: Blaise J. Bergiel and Christine Trosclair, "Instrumental Learning: Its Application to Customer Satisfaction," *Journal of Consumer Marketing* 2 (Fall 1985), 23–28; J. Ronald Carey, Steven H. Clicque, Barbara A. Leighton, and Frank Milton, "A Test of Positive Reinforcement of Customers," *Journal of Marketing* 40 (October 1976), 98–100.

SCHEDULES OF REINFORCEMENT

Different schedules of reinforcement produce different patterns of behavior. Laboratory studies of animal behavior suggest that learning occurs most rapidly when the desired response is always reinforced (**total reinforcement**). However, when the response is reinforced only part of the time (**partial reinforcement**), learning is more lasting (i.e., more resistant to extinction). A partial reinforcement schedule can be either systematic (e.g., every third response is reinforced) or random (e.g., the first and second responses are reinforced, the third is not, the fourth is, etc.).

The relative effectiveness of total versus partial reinforcement has been examined in the context of bus ridership.[67] Coupons offered as rewards were just as effective in enhancing ridership when given on a partial (every third person) schedule as when given on a continuous schedule (every person). Since it was much cheaper to offer the coupons only part of the time, considera-

---

[67] Brian C. Deslauriers and Peter B. Everett, "The Effects of Intermittent and Continuous Token Reinforcement on Bus Ridership," *Journal of Applied Psychology* 62 (August 1977), 369–375.

**FIGURE 14.10
ONE WAY OF
REINFORCING THE
HEAVY USER IS A
MONEY-BACK
PROGRAM**

ble savings resulted from understanding the effectiveness of alternative reinforcement schedules.

This is not to say that partial reinforcement will always be the optimal strategy. Indeed, some have argued that partial reinforcement schedules may not work in many settings, because the consumer may switch to another brand during the periods when the reinforcement is unavailable.[68] The best course of action is to examine empirically which schedule is best suited for a particular marketing situation.

---

[68] Michael L. Rothschild and William C. Gaidis, "Behavioral Learning Theory: Its Relevance to Marketing and Promotions," *Journal of Marketing* 45 (Spring 1981), 70–78.

SHAPING

Shaping refers to the reinforcement of successive approximations of a desired behavior pattern or of behaviors that must be performed before the desired response can be emitted.[69] An animal that was expected to perform a complex trick would never succeed if the trainer waited for the animal to do the complete trick before rewarding it. Instead, the trainer rewards the animal for each step leading to the trick.

Shaping principles can be used to a marketer's advantage.[70] A retailer can offer door prizes or loss leaders to encourage store entry, a behavior that must occur before the desired response of buying the retailer's products can be achieved. Similar tactics can be employed by a car dealer offering free coffee and doughnuts for those visiting the showroom. The dealer might then give selected visitors a financial incentive for taking a test drive. Whatever the situation may be, shaping encourages marketers to think about what behaviors must precede the ultimate action of purchase and how these antecedent behaviors can be encouraged through appropriate reinforcements.

DISCRIMINATIVE STIMULI

As a result of prior association with reinforcers, **discriminative stimuli** can influence behavior even though they themselves do not provide reinforcement. Rather, they serve as cues about the likelihood that performing a particular behavior will lead to reinforcement. In marketing, discriminative stimuli can take the form of a brand or store name where the consumer has learned from prior experience that purchase behavior will be rewarded only when the distinctive cue is present. Examples of discriminative stimuli include things such as distinctive brandmarks (e.g., the Levi tag), store signs (e.g., 50 percent-off sale), and store logos (e.g., K mart's big red K).[71]

VICARIOUS LEARNING

A special type of learning that incorporates aspects of both cognitive and behavioral learning theories is vicarious learning. **Vicarious learning** (or **modeling**) refers to a process that attempts to change behavior by having an individual observe the actions of others (i.e., models) and the consequences of those behaviors.[72] This form of learning underlies much of today's advertis-

---

[69] Nord and Peter, "A Behavior Modification Perspective on Marketing."

[70] There has been some controversy over the application of shaping principles. See Nord and Peter, "A Behavior Modification Perspective on Marketing"; Rothschild and Gaidis, "Behavioral Learning Theory"; J. Paul Peter and Walter R. Nord, "A Clarification and Extension of Operant Conditioning Principles in Marketing," *Journal of Marketing* 46 (Summer 1982), 102–107.

[71] Nord and Peter, "A Behavior Modification Perspective on Marketing."

[72] Ibid.

ing. Household products commonly promote themselves through ads that show the consumer receiving positive outcomes from product purchase and usage. Laundry detergent ads, for example, show a homemaker being drowned in praise from her family because their clothes are bright and clean. Similarly, dishwashing detergent ads offer users the promise of being noticed for young-looking and smooth hands.

Advertising will sometimes promote the product by focusing on negative consequences that may occur from using the competitive brand. In one of Wendy's advertisements, competitors are shown asking their customers to "step aside" and wait in long lines. Similarly, the ad in Figure 14.11 shows that the punishment (in the form of social disapproval) from not using the product disappears after consumption.

FIGURE 14.11
VICARIOUS
LEARNING IN
ADVERTISING

SUMMARY

In this chapter, we examined four main types of learning. Cognitive learning is concerned with the mental processes that determine the retention of information. Classical conditioning focuses on learning through association. Operant conditioning considers how behavior is modified by reinforcers and punishers. Vicarious learning deals with learning through observation.

The retention of information will depend on the degree of rehearsal and elaboration that occurs during information processing. These in turn are affected by a number of individual (e.g., motivation and ability) and stimulus (e.g., pictures, concrete words, repetition, mnemonic devices, and time-compressed speech) characteristics. The fact that retention has occurred does not necessarily mean that the information can be retrieved. Retrieval failure may be due to either decay or interference in the form of proactive or retroactive inhibition.

Marketers often rely on classical conditioning, particularly in advertising, for influencing consumer preferences. The effectiveness of conditioning depends on a host of variables, including the strength of the US, the number of CS–US pairings, the order of the CS–US pairing, familiarity with the CS and US, and the amount of elaboration during stimulus processing. Extinction, on the other hand, will occur when the CS–US association is broken.

Operant conditioning emphasizes the importance of reinforcement as a tool for influencing consumer behavior. The degree of reinforcement consumers experience during consumption strongly determines future purchase behavior. Marketers can also provide additional reinforcers to consumers through tokens of appreciation (e.g., gifts, thank you notes) for their patronage.

REVIEW AND DISCUSSION QUESTIONS

1. Suppose you were developing a TV ad containing three main stimuli: (1) the product, (2) an attractive model, and (3) a well-liked musical jingle. Based upon classical conditioning principles, what order would you recommend for structuring these stimuli within the commercial?

2. Develop an advertisement containing your product and a competitor's product that would encourage discrimination.

3. A coffee producer is planning a new promotion to cover a 6-week period in which a small gift is attached to the outside of the package. Should this gift be offered every week or every other week?

4. When is classical conditioning most appropriate for promoting products? What factors are likely to limit the effectiveness of classical conditioning advertising?

5. Find advertising examples for the following concepts: (a) vicarious learning, (b) generalization, and (c) discrimination.

6. Are all reinforcers equally effective? If not, which are most effective?

7. The product manager for a new brand of skin softener is considering two possible names: Soft Skin versus Dickson's Skin Moisturizer. What name would you select? Why?

8. In this chapter we discuss many factors that can influence the memorability of ads. What do you perceive as the important principles that can be learned from this chapter for making ads more effective?

9. A company is trying to decide which of two alternative print ads should be adopted for an advertising campaign to be used during the market-introduction phase for a new ice cream product called "Snowball." The only difference between the two ads is the type of picture that appears at the top of the ad. The picture for ad A shows the product sitting on top of snow and surrounded by a mound of snowballs. The picture for ad B shows a cute little girl consuming the product.

   To help decide which ad should be used, a study was undertaken in which target consumers were exposed to either ad A or ad B. (Assume that the method used to expose consumers to the ad was both valid and realistic.) The results indicated that ad A produced greater brand recall, but ad B generated more favorable product attitudes.

   Given these results, which ad would you recommend be used for introducing the product to the market, and why? Second, how can you explain that one ad is better for recall while the other is better for attitude given that the ads differed only in their picture?

INFLUENCING ATTITUDES AND BEHAVIOR

O MAKING RAISINS "IN"

One of the most memorable advertising campaigns to hit the airwaves in 1986 was the California Raisin Advisory Board's television ads featuring raisins dancing to the sounds of Marvin Gaye's classic song "Heard It Through the Grapevine." The original idea behind the campaign was to enhance the product's appeal by emphasizing the nutritional value of raisins. This approach seemed quite sensible given the trend toward greater health consciousness that has swept the country during the past decade or so.

However, research revealed that consumers already appreciated the nutritional properties of raisins. The problem was that consumers viewed raisins as plain and ordinary. As explained by Alan Canton, the board's advertising and promotions manager, "Nutritionally, they were appealing; emotionally, they were not appealing." It was hoped that the feelings evoked by the music and animated raisins would help overcome this limitation.

Did it work? Prior to the campaign, raisin sales had fluctuated between flat and declining. Sales jumped 5% after the campaign began.

Source: Diane Schneidman, "Perception-Altering Ads for Generic Foods Are Spread on the Grapevine," *Marketing News* (June 5, 1987), 15ff.

Influencing consumers' attitudes and behavior is one of the most fundamental and yet challenging tasks confronting businesses. Companies invest billions of dollars each year in efforts designed to modify or reinforce how consumers think, feel, and act in the marketplace. Consequently, knowing how to influence consumers' attitudes and behavior is one of the most valuable skills a marketer can possess.

This chapter attempts to provide a foundation for such knowledge. You will discover that many of the concepts and ideas presented in previous chapters are very germane to this discussion. We begin our journey with a consideration of the persuasive power of marketing communications.

PERSUASION THROUGH COMMUNICATION

Marketing communications, whether in the form of advertising, a salesperson's "pitch," a point-of-purchase brochure, or product packaging, represent a significant means for persuading consumers. The processes that underlie the persuasive impact of such communications are described in Chapters 13 ("Information Processing") and 14 ("Learning"). Little attention, however, has been given to understanding how persuasion can depend on certain elements of the communication, such as the source, types of claims, and so on. The persuasive impact of various message elements is explored in this section. But first, we consider a conceptualization of the role played by various communication elements during persuasion, known as the Elaboration Likelihood Model.

THE ELABORATION LIKELIHOOD MODEL OF PERSUASION

According to the **Elaboration Likelihood Model** (ELM) developed by Petty and Cacioppo, the influence exerted by various communication elements will depend on the elaboration (i.e., issue-relevant thinking) that occurs during processing.[1] When elaboration is high, the **central route** to persuasion is followed, where only those message elements (called **arguments**) relevant to forming a "reasoned" opinion are influential. Conversely, the **peripheral route** to persuasion occurs under low levels of elaboration as elements (called **peripheral cues**) that are irrelevant to developing a reasoned opinion become influen-

---

[1] For recent summaries of the ELM and associated literature, see Richard E. Petty and John T. Cacioppo, *Communication and Persuasion: Central and Peripheral Routes to Attitude Change* (New York: Springer/Verlag, 1986); Richard E. Petty and John T. Cacioppo, "The Elaboration Likelihood Model of Persuasion," in Leonard Berkowitz, ed., *Advances in Experimental Social Psychology*, vol. 19 (New York: Academic Press, 1986), 123–205. A similar conceptualization is offered by Shelly Chaiken, "Heuristic Versus Systematic Information Processing and the Use of Source Versus Message Cues in Persuasion," *Journal of Personality and Social Psychology* 39 (November 1980), 752–766. Also see Shelly Chaiken and C. Stangor, "Attitude and Attitude Change," *Annual Review of Psychology* 38 (1987), 575–630.

tial. Both arguments and peripheral cues may have an effect under moderate levels of elaboration.

Elaboration, in turn, depends on the person's motivation and ability during message processing (see Chapter 13). A person motivated and able to elaborate will take the central route. The peripheral route is traveled when motivation or ability is lacking.

Research on the ELM has been largely supportive of its validity.[2] In one such study, for example, subjects were exposed to a series of print ads.[3] The properties of one of these ads, featuring a fictitious razor product, were systematically manipulated. Some versions of the razor ad listed strong arguments (i.e., claims about the product), while others contained weak arguments. Different endorsers were also used in the ad versions. Some contained celebrity endorsers; other versions featured noncelebrity endorsers. Finally, subjects' involvement was also manipulated in order to vary the amount of elaboration that occurred while processing the razor ad. Only those subjects assigned to a "high-involvement" condition were told that they would eventually make a choice among razors.

The results involving postcommunication attitudes are presented in Figure 15.1. As prescribed by the ELM, the influence of the message elements varied across involvement. The attitudes of high-involvement subjects were affected only by the differences in the message arguments. In contrast, low-involvement

---

[2] For research and critiques beyond those cited in the preceding footnote, see Charles S. Areni and Richard J. Lutz, "The Role of Argument Quality in the Elaboration Likelihood Model," in Michael J. Houston, ed., *Advances in Consumer Research* 15 (Ann Arbor: Association for Consumer Research, 1988), 197–201; Mary J. Bitner and Carl Obermiller, "The Elaboration Likelihood Model: Limitations and Extensions in Marketing," in Elizabeth C. Hirschman and Morris R. Holbrook, eds., *Advances in Consumer Research* 12 (Ann Arbor: Association for Consumer Research, 1985), 420–425; Curt Haugtvedt, Richard E. Petty, John T. Cacioppo, and Theresa Steidley, "Personality and Ad Effectiveness: Exploring the Utility of Need for Cognition," in Michael J. Houston, ed., *Advances in Consumer Research* 15 (Ann Arbor: Association for Consumer Research, 1988), 209–212; Lynn R. Kahle and Pamela M. Homer, "Physical Attractiveness of the Celebrity Endorser: A Social Adaptation Perspective," *Journal of Consumer Research* 11 (March 1985), 954–961; Paul W. Miniard, Peter R. Dickson, and Kenneth R. Lord, "Some Central and Peripheral Thoughts on the Routes to Persuasion," in Michael J. Houston, ed., *Advances in Consumer Research* 15 (Ann Arbor: Association for Consumer Research, 1988), 204–208; Paul W. Miniard, Kenneth R. Lord, and Peter R. Dickson, "An Examination of Some Process and Outcome Predictions of the Elaboration Likelihood Model of Persuasion," working paper, The Ohio State University, 1988; Richard E. Petty and John T. Cacioppo, "The Effects of Involvement on Responses to Argument Quantity and Quality: Central and Peripheral Routes to Persuasion," *Journal of Personality and Social Psychology* 46 (January 1984), 69–81; Richard E. Petty, John T. Cacioppo, and David Schumann, "Central and Peripheral Routes to Advertising Effectiveness: The Moderating Role of Involvement," *Journal of Consumer Research* 10 (September 1983), 135–146; Richard F. Yalch and Rebecca Elmore-Yalch, "The Effect of Numbers on the Route to Persuasion," *Journal of Consumer Research* 11 (June 1984), 522–527.

[3] Petty, Cacioppo, and Schumann, "Central and Peripheral Routes to Advertising Effectiveness: The Moderating Role of Involvement."

FIGURE 15.1
**BRAND ATTITUDE
FAVORABILITY AS A
FUNCTION OF
INVOLVEMENT,
ARGUMENT
STRENGTH, AND
ENDORSER STATUS**

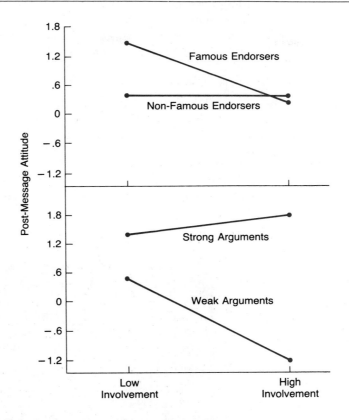

Note: Top panel shows interactive effect of involvement and endorser status on attitudes toward Edge razors. Bottom panel shows interactive effect of involvement and argument quality on attitudes toward Edge razors. Source: Richard E. Petty, John T. Cacioppo, and David Schumann, "Central and Peripheral Routes to Advertising Effectiveness: The Moderating Role of Involvement," *Journal of Consumer Research* 10 (September 1983), 135–146. Used with permission.

subjects' attitudes were influenced by both the arguments (although to a lesser extent than the attitudes formed under high involvement) and endorser.

The ELM provides a very useful perspective for understanding why research has often obtained seemingly inconsistent results concerning the influence of a persuasion variable. The fact that source (endorser) attractiveness, for instance, affects persuasion in one study but not another may simply reflect differences in the amount of elaboration that occurred within each study and, thus, the reliance on peripheral cues in forming attitudes.

The ELM also highlights the importance, in developing persuasive communications, of anticipating how much elaboration is likely to occur during message processing. If elaboration is likely to be high, then more emphasis on including compelling arguments which support the advocated position is appropriate. When this is not the case, other techniques less dependent on the degree of message processing may be desirable. Ads employing classical conditioning or an attractive spokesperson are examples.

SOURCE EFFECTS

Although marketers cannot directly control the responses consumers make while processing persuasive communications, they can try to influence these reactions through certain elements of the communication. One such aspect is the message source.

You might remember the notable series of ads for ENERGIZER® brand batteries featuring Jacko, an athlete turned celebrity from Australia (see Figure 15.2). Jacko's energetic manner during these commercials certainly comple-

FIGURE 15.2
ENHANCING
PERSUASION
THROUGH THE
MESSAGE SOURCE:
CELEBRITY
ENDORSEMENTS
CAN INFLUENCE
CONSUMERS

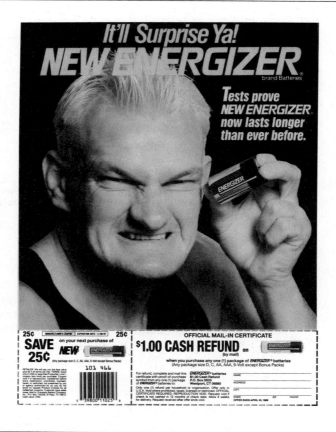

Source: Courtesy of Eveready Battery Company, Inc.

mented the intended product image as well as enhancing the ads' attention-getting abilities. Similarly, mega-rockers such as Michael Jackson, Tina Turner, David Bowie, and Lionel Richie have sung their tunes to the beat of the Pepsi generation. Celebrities from the athletic field, the stage, and the movie and television screen are frequently used to endorse products, either explicitly (e.g., by telling you it's a good product) or implicitly (e.g., by simply appearing in the ad).

CREDIBILITY   A long-standing principle of persuasion is that a credible source will usually facilitate persuasion.[4] According to the theory of cognitive responses (see Chapter 13), greater credibility should inhibit counterarguing with the message (i.e., unfavorable thoughts about the message), which will lead to greater acceptance. This inhibition should be most beneficial, then, in situations where counterargumentation is likely, such as when the audience opposes the advocated position.

An effective demonstration of source credibility's influence comes from research examining how a salesperson's expertise would affect the purchase behavior of music store shoppers.[5] In this study, the salesperson asked customers if they were interested in purchasing a cleaning product for stereo equipment. The number agreeing to buy the item heavily depended on the expertise conveyed by the salesperson. Whereas two-thirds of the consumers bought the product when the salesperson acted knowledgeable about the product, only one-third of them did so when the salesperson admitted to being unfamiliar with the product.

As suggested, the source's level of knowledge or expertise is a primary determinant of credibility. Yet expertise alone is not sufficient. The source must also be perceived as trustworthy. If the receiver questions the source's trustworthiness, then the source will lack credibility regardless of how knowledgeable he or she may be.

---

[4] For a general review, see Brian Sternthal, Lynn Phillips, and Ruby Dholakia, "The Persuasive Effect of Source Credibility: A Situational Analysis," *Public Opinion Quarterly* 42 (Fall 1978), 285–314; Brian Sternthal and C. Samuel Craig, *Consumer Behavior: An Information Processing Perspective* (Englewood Cliffs, New Jersey: Prentice-Hall, 1982), 295–304. Recent empirical investigations can be found in Danny L. Moore, Douglas Hausknecht, and Kanchana Thamodaran, "Time Compression, Response Opportunity, and Persuasion," *Journal of Consumer Research* 13 (June 1986), 85–99; Chenghuan Wu and David R. Shaffer, "Susceptibility to Persuasive Appeals as a Function of Source Credibility and Prior Experience with the Attitude Object," *Journal of Personality and Social Psychology* 52 (1987), 677–688. We should note that less credible sources have on occasion been found to induce more persuasion. See Robert R. Harmon and Kenneth A. Coney, "The Persuasive Effects of Source Credibility in Buy and Lease Situations," *Journal of Marketing Research* 19 (May 1982), 255–260; Brian Sternthal, Ruby Dholakia, and Clark Leavitt, "The Persuasive Effect of Source Credibility: Tests of Cognitive Response," *Journal of Consumer Research* 4 (March 1978), 252–260.

[5] Arch G. Woodside and J. William Davenport, Jr., "The Effect of Salesman Similarity and Expertise on Consumer Purchasing Behavior," *Journal of Marketing Research* 11 (May 1974), 198–202.

ADDITIONAL SOURCE CHARACTERISTICS   Research has shown greater persuasion when the source is physically attractive,[6] likable,[7] a celebrity,[8] or is similar to the target audience.[9] Remember, however, that such effects may be most likely to occur when consumers engage in little elaboration during message processing (see Figure 15.1).

MESSAGE EFFECTS

Additional characteristics of the message beyond the source can play a significant role in the persuasion process. Of particular interest here are the claims and executional elements that comprise the communication.

STRENGTH OF CLAIMS   The strength of message claims will strongly determine how much yielding occurs under the central route to persuasion. Strong claims will inhibit negative thoughts while encouraging positive thoughts. Just the opposite holds for weak claims.

What makes a claim strong? *Relevancy* is critical. Claims that focus on dimensions that carry little or no weight in the decision process lack relevancy. One industry study reports that relevancy was the most important determinant of new product advertising's success in persuading consumers to try the product.[10]

Another important characteristic is a claim's *objectivity*. *Objective* claims focus on factual information that is not subject to individual interpretations. *Subjective* claims, on the other hand, are ones that may evoke different interpretations across individuals. Consider a product's price or weight. Claims such as "low-priced" or "lightweight" would be considered subjective, inasmuch as what is low or light for one person may not be for the next. These same attributes could be expressed objectively by giving the actual price and weight.

Objective claims are preferred by consumers over subjective claims because they are more precise and more easily confirmed. Research has shown that objective claims are perceived as more believable, reduce counterargumenta-

---

[6] Michael J. Baker and Gilbert A. Churchill, Jr., "The Impact of Physically Attractive Models on Advertising Evaluations," *Journal of Marketing Research* 14 (November 1977), 538–555; Shelly Chaiken, "Communicator Physical Attractiveness and Persuasion," *Journal of Personality and Social Psychology* 37 (August 1979), 752–766; Kahle and Homer, "Physical Attractiveness of the Celebrity Endorser: A Social Adaptation Perspective."

[7] Kahle and Homer, "Physical Attractiveness of the Celebrity Endorser: A Social Adaptation Perspective."

[8] Petty, Cacioppo, and Schumann, "Central and Peripheral Routes to Advertising Effectiveness: The Moderating Role of Involvement."

[9] Woodside and Davenport, "The Effect of Salesman Similarity and Expertise on Consumer Purchasing Behavior."

[10] David Olson, "The Characteristics of High-Trial New-Product Advertising," *Journal of Advertising Research* 25 (October/November 1985), 11–16.

TABLE 15.1 CLAIMS THAT DIFFER IN THEIR OBJECTIVITY AND VERIFIABILITY		Objective	Subjective
	Search	• We offer five styles of cedar chests • Our brand has no cholesterol	• We offer an extraordinary collection of jewelry • There are a variety of attractive styles
	Experience	• Our tent keeps you dry • Our test gives you results in 30 min.	• We offer delicious meals • Easy to use with professional results
	Credence	• We invested over $5 billion in our long-distance network • Our polish is used by 77 leading galleries and museums	• Our tire has been extensively tested • Our wine is naturally fermented

Source: Gary T. Ford, Darlene B. Smith, and John L. Swasy, "Are Consumers More Skeptical of Advertising They Can't Evaluate? Empirical Perspectives on the Economics of Information," working paper, American University, 1988.

tion while increasing the number of support arguments, and create more favorable product beliefs and attitudes.[11]

The *verifiability* of claims can also be significant. **Search claims** are those that can be accurately evaluated prior to purchase. **Experience claims** are those that can be fully evaluated only after product consumption. **Credence claims** differ from the prior two types in that accurate evaluation is beyond the consumer's capabilities. Table 15.1 presents some examples of claims differing in their verifiability and objectivity.

Consumers will presumably be less skeptical of a message when the claims lend themselves to confirmation. A recent study has shown that consumers perceive search claims to be much more truthful than either experience or credence claims.[12] Consumers' skepticism differed very little, however, between these latter two types of claims.

Substantiation of claims is also important. Consider the experience claim of great taste. This claim is more likely to be accepted if supported by credible taste-test findings than when such substantiation is lacking.

NUMBER OF CLAIMS   The quantity, as well as the strength or quality, of the claims made in a message can influence persuasion. Petty and Cacioppo have reasoned that whereas claim quality is critical under the central route to persuasion, claim quantity might serve as a persuasion cue under the periph-

---

[11] See Julie A. Edell and Richard Staelin, "The Information Processing of Pictures in Print Advertisements," *Journal of Consumer Research* 10 (June 1983), 45–61; Gary T. Ford, Darlene B. Smith, and John L. Swasy, "Are Consumers More Skeptical of Advertising They Can't Evaluate? Empirical Perspectives on the Economics of Information," working paper, American University, 1988; Morris B. Holbrook, "Beyond Attitude Structure: Toward the Informational Determinants of Attitude," *Journal of Marketing Research* 15 (November 1978), 545–556.

[12] Ford, Smith, and Swasy, "Are Consumers More Skeptical of Advertising They Can't Evaluate? Empirical Perspectives on the Economics of Information."

eral route.[13] Consistent with this, they report that variations in the number of message claims affected yielding when the message was processed under low-involvement conditions. Claim quantity was unimportant, however, when message processing occurred during high involvement.

MESSAGE SIDEDNESS   What may come as a surprise is that including some weak claims along with strong claims can enhance a message's persuasiveness. **Two-sided messages** (those including pros and cons) increase perceptions of advertiser truthfulness and believability relative to **one-sided messages** (those presenting only pros).[14]

COMPARATIVE MESSAGES   Claims can also vary in their use of brand comparisons. **Comparative advertising** is often employed by new brands seeking to take business away from existing brands. It also is used by established brands, as evidenced by the advertising campaigns during the burger and cola wars. Although comparative ads have been shown to outperform noncomparative ads,[15] even in terms of producing greater sales,[16] this is not always the case. Sometimes comparative ads are no better or even worse than their noncomparative versions.[17]

AFFECTIVE MESSAGES   As noted in Chapter 13, affective responses represent the feelings that are elicited by a communication. It is these types of "hot" responses, rather than "cold" cognitive responses, that are emphasized by what is called **transformational** (as opposed to **informational) advertising.** Transformational ads attempt to "make the experience of using the product richer, warmer, more exciting, and/or more enjoyable, than that obtained

---

[13] Petty and Cacioppo, "The Effects of Involvement on Responses to Argument Quantity and Quality: Central and Peripheral Routes to Persuasion." Also see Joseph W. Alba and Howard Marmorstein, "The Effects of Frequency Knowledge on Consumer Decision Making," *Journal of Consumer Research* 14 (June 1987), 14–25.

[14] For recent investigations on message sidedness, see Linda L. Golden and Mark I. Alpert, "Comparative Analysis of the Relative Effectiveness of One- and Two-Sided Communication for Contrasting Products," *Journal of Advertising* 16 (1987), 18–25; Michael A. Kamins and Lawrence J. Marks, "Advertising Puffery: The Impact of Using Two-Sided Claims on Product Attitude and Purchase Intention," *Journal of Advertising* 16 (1987), 6–15; Michael A. Kamins and Henry Assael, "Two-Sided Versus One-Sided Appeals: A Cognitive Perspective on Argumentation, Source Derogation, and the Effect of Disconfirming Trial on Belief Change," *Journal of Marketing Research* 24 (February 1987), 29–39.

[15] Cornelia Droge and Rene Y. Darmon, "Associative Positioning Strategies Through Comparative Advertising: Attribute Versus Overall Similarity Approaches," *Journal of Marketing Research* 24 (November 1987), 377–388; Gerald J. Gorn and Charles B. Weinberg, "The Impact of Comparative Advertising on Perception and Attitude: Some Positive Findings," *Journal of Consumer Research* 11 (September 1984), 719–727; Mita Sujan and Christine Dekleva, "Product Categorization and Inference Making: Some Implications for Comparative Advertising," *Journal of Consumer Research* 14 (December 1987), 372–378.

[16] Z. S. Demirdijian, "Sales Effectiveness of Comparative Advertising: An Experimental Field Investigation," *Journal of Consumer Research* 10 (December 1983), 362–364.

[17] A brief review of these findings is presented in Gorn and Weinberg, "The Impact of Comparative Advertising on Perception and Attitude: Some Positive Findings."

15.1 IMAGE AND EMOTIONAL ADVERTISING: A CRESTING WAVE?

As the glistening, sporty two-door sedan with its distinctively sloping and rounded lines glides down the highway, a voice-over promises that Sable's aerodynamic design holds the road and ensures good performance. This is the latest television commercial for Mercury's Sable automobile. The quality of light, the angle of the photography, the wet curving road and the gentle, mellow music blend carefully into an unmistakable image: sleek, sophisticated styling and harnessed energy.

Contrast this new Mercury campaign with the one that it replaced. As rock star Rod Stewart crooned "Tonight's the Night," a pretty blonde drove off down a wet and smoky street in a sporty white car. The dreamy spot made no obvious reference to design, performance or any other concrete advantage this car might have over another.

The difference between the two commercials, both created by Young & Rubicam/Detroit, represents the cresting of a wave that has come to dominate advertising in the 1980s: the use of image and emotion to sell products. The trend now seems to be moving somewhat the other way. That

is, to blend powerful image ads with the more traditional form, which relied on specific selling points to hammer home particular and perhaps even unique product benefits.

The now-abandoned Mercury image spots helped lower the median age of customers of some models by ten years, a key objective for a line long identified with big, luxury automobiles for an older market. But now Mercury is pursuing a slightly different objective: trying to create advertising that will look different from that of competing products.

Nobody thinks that image advertising is finished — demonstrably it works. But like any good idea, it may become overdone. "Some categories are already saturated with image ads, and many others are getting there," says Gary Stibel, a management consultant with the New England Consulting Group. "There's too much puff, not enough substance, in a lot of advertising."

Source: Edward F. Cone, "Image and Reality," *Forbes* (December 14, 1987), 226, 228. Adapted by permission of *Forbes* Magazine. © Forbes, Inc., 1987.

solely from an objective description of the advertised brand."[18] These ads "transform" the value derived from product consumption by influencing consumers' perceptions of the product's emotional and symbolic features.

The use of emotional appeals, such as in the California raisin ads described in the chapter opener and the ad appearing in Figure 15.3, has become a focal point for much of today's advertising. Whether this emphasis has begun to moderate is the topic of *Consumer in Focus 15.1*.

Figure 15.4 contains the findings from a recent study of the emotionality

---

[18] Christopher Puto and William D. Wells, "Informational and Transformational Advertising: The Differential Effects of Time," in Thomas C. Kinnear, ed., *Advances in Consumer Research* 11 (Provo, Utah: Association for Consumer Research, 1984), 638–643.

FIGURE 15.3
CREATING FAVORABLE
ATTITUDES WITH
"FEELING" ADS

evoked by television commercials.[19] It is not surprising that the positive emotions of joy, acceptance, and anticipation were observed most frequently. The results also revealed considerable diversity among the ads in their emotional intensity. Some ads evoked very little emotion from viewers, although all ads elicited at least some level of emotional response. This latter observation indicates that even so-called "informational" ads are likely to evoke some degree of emotional response.

Ray and Batra have suggested several potential advantages of affective or emotional advertising.[20] People may pay greater attention to emotional ads because of affect's role in guiding attention. Emotional ads may also increase the viewer's arousal, which, as discussed later, can enhance message processing. Affective executions can lead to more favorable attitudes than might otherwise be obtained.[21] The March of Dimes departed from their

---

[19] David M. Zeitlin and Richard A. Westwood, "Measuring Emotional Response," *Journal of Advertising Research* 26 (October/November 1986), 34–44.

[20] Michael L. Ray and Rajeev Batra, "Emotion and Persuasion in Advertising: What We Do and Don't Know About Affect," in Richard P. Bagozzi and Alice M. Tybout, eds., *Advances in Consumer Research* 10 (Ann Arbor: Association of Consumer Research, 1983), 543–548.

[21] For additional citations of research on the role of affective responses in persuasion, see footnote 50 in Chapter 13.

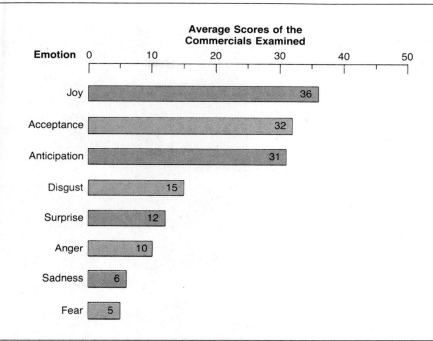

Source: David M. Zeitlin and Richard A. Westwood, "Measuring Emotional Response," *Journal of Advertising Research* 26 (October/November 1986), 34–44, Table 3.

traditional institutional-style advertising in favor of "emotional response" ads for targeting less literate segments.[22] These new ads contained powerful visuals (e.g., a liquor label on a baby bottle filled with alcohol) with little or no copy.

EXECUTIONAL ELEMENTS   Although persuasion may often depend on what you say in your message, how you say it can be equally, if not more, important in many situations. Message execution must therefore be carefully considered in the development of persuasive communications. Indeed, **executional elements** such as visuals, sounds, colors, and pace can play a critical role during persuasion, particularly for ads designed to elicit emotional responses.

Existing research has largely focused on the persuasive impact of pictorial elements. Pictures can also influence consumers' perceptions of the product.[23]

---

[22] "Emotional Response Is Evoked for March of Dimes Campaign," *Marketing News* 20 (November 21, 1986), 6.

[23] Andrew A. Mitchell and Jerry C. Olson, "Are Product Attribute Beliefs the Only Mediators of Advertising Effects on Brand Attitudes?" *Journal of Marketing Research* 18 (August 1981), 318–332.

FIGURE 15.5
WHAT DOES THIS PICTURE CONVEY ABOUT THE PRODUCT?

The fluffy cat resting comfortably on the recliner in Figure 15.5 is intended to enhance beliefs about the product's softness and comfort. Similarly, the Armstrong Tire Company includes pictures of "Tuffy the Rhino" in its advertising to reinforce perceptions of the product's strength, durability, and toughness.[24]

Research has also shown that the use of an attractive or unattractive picture in an ad can change product attitudes without affecting product beliefs.[25] One explanation for this result is that the affective responses evoked by the picture are transferred directly to the product.

---

[24] "Armstrong Retreads 'Tuffy the Rhino,'" *Marketing News* 21 (November 20, 1987), 16.
[25] Miniard, Lord, and Dickson, "An Examination of Some Process and Outcome Predictions of the Elaboration Likelihood Model of Persuasion"; Andrew A. Mitchell, "The Effect of Verbal and Visual Components of Advertisements on Brand Attitudes and Attitude Toward the Advertisement," *Journal of Consumer Research* 13 (June 1986), 12–24.

THE INFLUENCE OF ATTITUDES TOWARD THE AD

The ability of advertising to create favorable attitudes toward a product may often depend on consumers' attitudes toward an ad itself. Ads that are liked or evaluated favorably can lead to more positive product attitudes. Disliked ads may lower consumers' product evaluations. Research has demonstrated repeatedly that attitudes toward an ad serve as a significant predictor of product attitudes.[26]

This is not to say that consumers must always like an ad in order for it to be effective.[27] There can be ads that are disliked but still successful. Indeed, advertisers sometimes make ads deliberately annoying in the hope that the message can break through the clutter. A good example is the "Mr. Whipple" commercials for Proctor & Gamble's Charmin toilet tissue that began in 1968 and ran for 14 years.[28] Consumers reported that they couldn't stand watching the ads. Even so, the campaign was very effective in communicating the brand's softness positioning and certainly helped it become the dominant brand in its category.

---

[26] Interest in this area was largely sparked by the following two articles: Mitchell and Olson, "Are Product Attribute Beliefs the Only Mediator of Advertising Effects on Brand Attitudes?"; Terence Shimp, "Attitude Toward the Ad as a Mediator of Consumer Brand Choice," *Journal of Advertising* 10 (1981), 9–15. Recent research can be found in Marian C. Burke and Julie A. Edell, "Ad Reactions over Time: Capturing Changes in the Real World," *Journal of Consumer Research* 13 (June 1986), 114–118; Scot Burton and Donald R. Lichtenstein, "The Effect of Ad Claims and Ad Context on Attitude Toward the Advertisement," *Journal of Advertising* 17 (1988), 3–11; Dena S. Cox and Anthony D. Cox, "What Does Familiarity Breed? Complexity as a Moderator of Repetition Effects in Advertisement Evaluation," *Journal of Consumer Research* 15 (June 1988), 111–116; Edell and Burke, "The Power of Feelings in Understanding Advertising Effects"; Meryl P. Gardner, "Does Attitude Toward the Ad Affect Brand Attitude Under a Brand Evaluation Set?" *Journal of Marketing Research* 22 (May 1985), 192–198; Larry G. Gresham and Terence A. Shimp, "Attitude Toward the Advertisement and Brand Attitudes: A Classical Conditioning Perspective," *Journal of Advertising* 14 (1985), 10–17; Scott B. MacKenzie and Richard J. Lutz, "An Empirical Examination of Affective and Cognitive Antecedents of Attitude Toward the Ad," working paper, University of Florida, 1987; Scott B. MacKenzie, Richard J. Lutz, and George E. Belch, "The Role of Attitude Toward the Ad as a Mediator of Advertising Effectiveness: A Test of Competing Explanations," *Journal of Marketing Research* 23 (May 1986), 130–143; Thomas J. Madden, Chris T. Allen, and Jacquelyn L. Twible, "Attitude Toward the Ad: An Assessment of Diverse Measurement Indices Under Different Processing 'Sets,' " *Journal of Marketing Research* 25 (August 1988), 242–252; Paul W. Miniard, Sunil Bhatla, and Randall L. Rose, "On the Formation and Relationship of Ad and Brand Attitudes: An Experimental and Causal Analysis," working paper, The Ohio State University, 1988; Mitchell, "The Effect of Verbal and Visual Components of Advertisements on Brand Attitudes and Attitude Toward the Advertisement"; Whan C. Park and S. Mark Young, "Consumer Response to Television Commercials: The Impact of Involvement and Background Music on Brand Attitude Formation," *Journal of Marketing Research* 23 (February 1986), 11–24.

[27] For an interesting discussion of consumers' irritation with advertising, see David A. Aaker and Donald E. Bruzzone, "Causes of Irritation in Advertising," *Journal of Marketing* 49 (Spring 1985), 47–57.

[28] John R. Rossiter and Larry Percy, *Advertising and Promotion Management* (New York: McGraw-Hill, 1987), 235.

REPETITION EFFECTS

Research on the persuasive effects of message repetition has produced a mixed set of findings. Indeed, the literature has reported that repetition has a positive,[29] negative,[30] null,[31] or inverted-U[32] (i.e., attitude increases up to some point, beyond which attitude declines) relationship with persuasion.

Perhaps the most promising explanation for how repetition affects persuasion is the two-stage attitude-modification process proposed by Cacioppo and Petty.[33] Early exposures are believed to provide the person with additional opportunities to evaluate the position advocated by the message. Once the person has fully evaluated the message's implications for her or his attitudes, the second stage takes over and tedium with the message becomes dominant. This tedium will lower message acceptance.

This view carries several implications about the persuasive role of repetition. First, additional repetitions are needed only if the person is unable or unwilling to fully evaluate the message's position after a single exposure.[34] For example, an informationally complex television ad may require several exposures, especially when the consumer is not highly motivated to carefully process the ad.

---

[29] J. Lee McCullough and Thomas Ostrom, "Repetition of Highly Similar Messages and Attitude Change," *Journal of Applied Psychology* 59 (June 1974), 395–397; Carl Obermiller, "Varieties of Mere Exposure: The Effects of Processing Style and Repetition on Affective Response," *Journal of Consumer Research* 12 (June 1985), 17–30.

[30] John T. Cacioppo and Richard E. Petty, "Central and Peripheral Routes to Persuasion: The Role of Message Repetition," in Linda F. Alwitt and Andrew A. Mitchell, eds., *Psychological Processes and Advertising Effects* (Hillsdale, New Jersey: Lawrence Erlbaum, 1985), 91–111.

[31] Belch, "The Effects of Television Commercial Repetition on Cognitive Response and Message Acceptance"; Rethans, Swasy, and Marks, "Effects of Television Commercial Repetition, Receiver Knowledge, and Commercial Length: A Test of the Two-Factor Model."

[32] John T. Cacioppo and Richard E. Petty, "Effects of Message Repetition and Position on Cognitive Response, Recall, and Persuasion," *Journal of Personality and Social Psychology* 37 (January 1979), 97–109; Bobby J. Calder and Brian Sternthal, "Television Commercial Wearout: An Information Processing View," *Journal of Marketing Research* 17 (May 1980), 173–186; Gerald J. Gorn and Marvin E. Goldberg, "Children's Responses to Repetitive Television Commercials," *Journal of Consumer Research* 6 (March 1980), 421–424.

[33] Cacioppo and Petty, "Central and Peripheral Routes to Persuasion: The Role of Message Repetition." For discussions of alternative explanations, see Calder and Sternthal, "Television Commercial Wearout: An Information Processing View"; Obermiller, "Varieties of Mere Exposure: The Effects of Processing Style and Repetition on Affective Response"; Rethans, Swasy, and Marks, "Effects of Television Commercial Repetition, Receiver Knowledge, and Commercial Length: A Test of the Two-Factor Model"; Alan G. Sawyer, "Repetition, Cognitive Response and Persuasion," in Richard E. Petty, Thomas Ostrom, and Timothy Brock, eds., *Cognitive Responses in Persuasion* (Hillsdale, New Jersey: Lawrence Erlbaum, 1981), 237–261; Robert B. Zajonc and Hazel Markus, "Affective and Cognitive Factors in Preferences," *Journal of Consumer Research* 9 (September 1982), 123–131.

[34] Also see Rajeev Batra and Michael L. Ray, "Situational Effects of Advertising Repetition: The Moderating Influence of Motivation, Ability, and Opportunity to Respond," *Journal of Consumer Research* 12 (March 1986), 432–445; Moore, Hausknecht, and Kanchana, "Time Compression, Response Opportunity, and Persuasion."

Moreover, when additional repetitions are required, the effect of repetition will depend on the strength of the message. More repetition should produce a greater amount of positive cognitive responses for messages using strong claims. Just the opposite should occur for weak claims, where repetition will increase the number of negative cognitive responses.

The point at which tedium begins will depend on the amount of processing that occurs during prior exposures. If the ad is fully evaluated after one exposure, tedium will set in immediately. If such thinking does not occur until after many exposures, the negative impact of tedium is delayed.

Evidence germane to this view has been largely supportive.[35] Cacioppo and Petty's initial study focused on the acceptance of a message containing strong arguments in favor of increasing university expenditures.[36] Subjects were exposed to the message a low (once), moderate (three), or high (five) number of times. Agreement with the message increased from one to three exposures but then decreased after five exposures. This pattern was consistent with the cognitive response data. Favorable thoughts followed the same pattern, while unfavorable thoughts moved in the opposite manner (i.e., negative thoughts decreased from one to three exposures and increased after five exposures).

The role of message strength as a moderator of repetition effects has also been demonstrated. Whereas acceptance was greater after three exposures for a message presenting strong claims, acceptance was lower after three exposures for a message based on weak claims.[37] Finally, responses reflecting tedium have been found to increase in intensity and frequency with greater amounts of repetition.[38]

CONSUMER CONSIDERATIONS

Although marketers are able to enhance the persuasiveness of their communications by bringing together the appropriate blend of source and message elements, the ultimate impact of any communication will depend heavily on how consumers respond to it. These responses, in turn, are shaped by a multitude of consumer characteristics, such as the person's motivation or knowledge at the time of exposure. Consequently, the characteristics of the consumer at the time of exposure to a persuasive communication should be

---

[35] For a dissenting point of view, see Belch, "The Effects of Television Commercial Repetition on Cognitive Response and Message Acceptance"; Rethans, Swasy, and Marks, "Effects of Television Commercial Repetition, Receiver Knowledge, and Commercial Length: A Test of the Two-Factor Model."

[36] Cacioppo and Petty, "Effects of Message Repetition and Position on Cognitive Response, Recall, and Persuasion."

[37] Cacioppo and Petty, "Central and Peripheral Routes to Persuasion: The Role of Message Repetition."

[38] Rethans, Swasy, and Marks, "Effects of Television Commercial Repetition, Receiver Knowledge, and Commercial Length: A Test of the Two-Factor Model."

taken into account in designing the communication. In this section we examine some of the more important consumer characteristics.

MOTIVATION   There is a tremendous diversity in consumers' motivational states when they are receiving marketing communications. Sometimes consumers will be highly motivated to carefully process and evaluate such communications. Quite often, however, this is not the case, as consumers either ignore or expend little cognitive effort during processing.

The importance of the consumer's motivational state during message processing was illustrated earlier in the chapter by the research of Petty, Cacioppo, and Schumann (see Figure 15.1).[39] Recall that when subjects were more strongly motivated to process the ad (i.e., the high-involvement condition), persuasion depended solely on the strength of the message claims. However, when this motivation was lacking (i.e., low involvement), the celebrity status of the endorser featured in the ad became influential.

The extent to which the product is purchased because of utilitarian versus hedonic considerations (see Chapter 9) is another important consideration in developing persuasive communications. If the product is purchased primarily for its utilitarian benefits (e.g., its ability to solve current problems or eliminate potential problems), informational appeals (e.g., how the product solves the problem and why it should be chosen over others) should be emphasized. Products that are bought primarily for their hedonic benefits (e.g., those that provide sensory gratification or intellectual stimulation) should rely more heavily on affective appeals.[40]

It is, of course, possible that both types of appeals will be necessary for promoting the product. Automobiles are a good example. Print ads are typically filled with considerable amounts of details and facts about the car's characteristics that can be processed at the consumer's leisure. Television ads, on the other hand, may focus on the sensory pleasures that can be obtained by driving the car.

AROUSAL   Physiological **arousal,** representing a person's degree of alertness along a continuum ranging from extreme drowsiness to extreme wakefulness, can moderate the persuasion process. Arousal presumably has both facilitating and inhibiting effects on the amount of elaboration during message processing. Little processing can occur when the person is drowsy. A certain level of arousal is, therefore, desirable. However, increases in arousal lead

---

[39] Petty, Cacioppo, and Schumann, "Central and Peripheral Routes to Advertising Effectiveness: The Moderating Role of Involvement." Also see Gerald J. Gorn, "The Effects of Music in Advertising on Choice Behavior: A Classical Conditioning Approach," *Journal of Marketing* 46 (Winter 1982), 94–101.

[40] For an expanded discussion of how persuasion tactics may depend on the type of motivation, see John R. Rossiter and Larry Percy, "Advertising Communication Models," in Elizabeth C. Hirschman and Morris B. Holbrook, eds., *Advances in Consumer Research* 12 (Provo, Utah: Association for Consumer Research, 1985), 510–524; Rossiter and Percy, *Advertising and Promotion Management.*

to more processing of internal cues sent by the nervous system, thereby reducing the cognitive capacity available for message elaboration. These considerations suggest an inverted-U relationship between arousal and elaboration. Elaboration should be stronger at moderate levels of arousal than when arousal is very low or very high.

Research has supported the persuasive role of arousal.[41] When arousal was moderate, attitudes formed following message processing depended only on the strength of the message claims. In contrast, attitudes formed under high arousal were based more heavily on the celebrity status of the product endorser.

Such findings indicate the need to consider the arousal level of consumers when exposed to persuasive communications. Message elements other than the product claims may play a much greater role in determining persuasion when arousal is very high. High arousal may characterize a number of situations in which consumers receive persuasive communications, such as sporting events, action-packed movies, and workout shows where viewers actively participate.

KNOWLEDGE   As discussed in Chapter 10, consumer knowledge is a major determinant of consumer behavior. The same holds true in the realm of persuasion. When consumers are knowledgeable about the topic of some persuasive communication, they are better able to evaluate the strengths and weaknesses of the message claims. Consistent with this, knowledgeable consumers have been shown to respond more favorably as advertising content becomes more technical.[42] Just the opposite was observed for unknowledgeable consumers.

This line of reasoning carries important implications for the content of a communication.[43] Because knowledgeable consumers already know the benefits of product ownership and usage, less emphasis on benefits relative to more technical features may be desirable. Camera ads aimed at experts, for instance, often emphasize technical product features. However, when target consumers lack such knowledge, communications that focus on easily understood product benefits are likely to be more successful.

Similarly, knowledgeable consumers are more likely to focus on information most relevant for evaluating a product's strengths and weaknesses. Those less informed may be more persuaded by information that is peripheral or less relevant. In one study, experts' evaluations of a camera were strongly

---

[41] David M. Sanbonmatsu and Frank R. Kardes, "The Effects of Physiological Arousal on Information Processing and Persuasion," *Journal of Consumer Research* 15 (December 1988), 379–385. Also see Surendra N. Singh and Gilbert A. Churchill, Jr., "Arousal and Advertising Effectiveness," *Journal of Advertising* 16 (1987), 4–10.

[42] Rolph E. Anderson and Marvin A. Jolson, "Technical Wording in Advertising: Implications for Market Segmentation," *Journal of Marketing* 44 (Winter 1980), 57–66.

[43] Joseph W. Alba and J. Wesley Hutchinson, "Dimensions of Consumer Expertise," *Journal of Consumer Research* 13 (March 1987), 411–454.

affected by a description of the product's attributes but were unaffected by a label of the camera type (i.e., 110 or 35mm SLR). The opposite was true for novices, as their product evaluations depended only on the product type label.[44]

MOOD   Another consumer characteristic that can influence persuasion is the consumer's mood state at the time of exposure to a communication. Moods refer to transient feelings (e.g., sadness, anticipation) that exist at a particular time and place.[45] Research suggests that favorable moods can enhance persuasion, while unfavorable moods reduce persuasion.[46]

How can a communicator encourage favorable moods? One approach is to include within the communication certain executional elements that tend to evoke the desired mood state, as is commonly done in affective messages. A second approach is to place the communication in a context that encourages favorable moods. For example, as noted in Chapter 7, the program in which a commercial appears can affect the moods consumers bring to the communication situation.[47]

PERSONALITY TRAITS   As noted in Chapter 12, a consumer's personality may also shape her or his responsiveness to persuasive communications. A person's **need for cognition,** representing an individual's tendency to undertake and enjoy thinking, is one such personality trait.[48] Persons scoring high on need for cognition measures are more influenced by message claims, while those having a low need for cognition display greater sensitivity to peripheral message cues such as source attractiveness.[49]

Self-monitoring has also been linked to persuasion. High self-monitoring persons are very sensitive to situational and interpersonal considerations. They are quite willing and adept at modifying their behavior in order to be the "right person in the right place at the right time." At the other end are low self-monitoring individuals who do not try to modify their behavior to fit

[44] Mita Sujan, "Consumer Knowledge: Effects on Evaluation Strategies Mediating Consumer Judgments," *Journal of Consumer Research* 12 (June 1985), 31–46. Also see Alba and Marmorstein, "The Effects of Frequency Knowledge on Consumer Decision Making."

[45] Meryl Paula Gardener, "Mood States and Consumer Behavior: A Critical Review," *Journal of Consumer Research* 12 (December 1985), 281–300.

[46] Thomas R. Srull, "Memory, Mood, and Consumer Judgment," in Melanie Wallendorf and Paul Anderson, eds., *Advances in Consumer Research* 14 (Provo, Utah: Association for Consumer Research, 1987), 404–407.

[47] Marvin E. Goldberg and Gerald J. Gorn, "Happy and Sad TV Programs: How They Affect Reactions to Commercials," *Journal of Consumer Research* 14 (December 1987), 387–403.

[48] John T. Cacioppo and Richard E. Petty, "The Need for Cognition," *Journal of Personality and Social Psychology* 42 (1982), 116–131.

[49] Haugtvedt, Petty, Cacioppo, and Steidley, "Personality and Ad Effectiveness: Exploring the Utility of Need for Cognition." Also see Danny Axson, Susan Yates, and Shelly Chaiken, "Audience Response as a Heuristic Cue in Persuasion," *Journal of Personality and Social Psychology* 53 (1987), 30–40.

circumstantial situations. Rather, they rely more heavily on their own internal feelings and attitudes to guide behavior.[50]

The relative effectiveness of appeals based on a product's image versus claims about a product's quality can depend on self-monitoring.[51] High self-monitors have been found to respond more favorably to image advertising, whereas advertising of product quality was received more favorably by low self-monitors. Similar differences were also observed between high and low self-monitors in their willingness to try and how much they would pay for products associated with either an image or quality appeal. It is interesting to note that low self-monitors are the primary target for the new Mercury car ads described in *Consumer in Focus 15.1.*

EXISTING ATTITUDES   The success of a persuasive communication will also depend on the attitudes presently held by the target audience. A fundamental distinction is whether persuasion takes place under **attitude formation** or **attitude change** conditions. When the person has yet to develop an attitude toward the topic of the message, then we are dealing with attitude formation. Attitude change characterizes settings in which the person holds a pre-existing attitude that differs from the position advocated by the message.

This distinction is important because of its implications for persuasion. In general, persuasive communications will be more successful at creating attitudes than in changing attitudes. Changing attitudes is more difficult simply because of the additional resistance that results from the commitment to the existing attitude. The stronger this commitment, the greater the resistance, as reflected by greater counterargumentation with the message.

Commitment will be stronger for attitudes anchored in a person's sense of self-worth or ego.[52] Similarly, attitudes based on actual product consumption will be held more firmly than those formed through indirect product experience (e.g., advertising).[53]

A recent study provides an interesting demonstration of how existing attitudes moderate persuasion.[54] Initial attitudes were formed toward a brand

---

[50] For a general review of self-monitoring, see Mark Snyder, "Self-Monitoring Processes," in Leonard Berkowitz, ed., *Advances in Experimental Social Psychology*, vol. 12 (New York: Academic Press, 1979), 85–128.

[51] Mark Snyder and Kenneth G. DeBono, "Appeals to Image and Claims About Quality: Understanding the Psychology of Advertising," *Journal of Personality and Social Psychology* 49 (September 1985), 586–597.

[52] C. W. Sherif, M. Sherif, and R. E. Nebergall, *Attitude and Attitude Change* (New Haven: Yale University Press, 1961).

[53] Robert E. Smith and William R. Swinyard, "Attitude-Behavior Consistency: The Impact of Product Trial Versus Advertising," *Journal of Marketing Research* 20 (August 1983), 257–267. Also see Lawrence J. Marks and Michael A. Kamins, "The Use of Product Sampling and Advertising: Effects of Sequence of Exposure and Degree of Advertising Claim Exaggeration on Consumers' Belief Strength, Belief Confidence, and Attitudes," *Journal of Marketing Research* 25 (August 1988), 266–281.

[54] Wu and Shaffer, "Susceptibility to Persuasive Appeals as a Function of Source Credibility and Prior Experience with the Attitude Object."

of peanut butter by either providing subjects with some product information or allowing them to actually taste the product. Afterward, they were exposed to a communication favoring the product delivered by either a high- or low-credibility source. The impact of source credibility depended on the method of initial attitude formation. Source credibility affected postcommunication attitudes only when subjects did not first taste the product. These findings suggest that a message's peripheral cues may have little effect when the message is attempting to change firmly held attitudes.

Consumers' general attitudes about the truthfulness of marketing communications can also influence the persuasion process. An awareness of the persuasive intent of such communications and past experiences with misleading messages have led consumers to be quite skeptical of product claims. One study reports that over 70 percent of consumers do not believe ads that use test results to support claims of product superiority.[55] Indeed, it has been suggested that one reason for the diminishing use of product claims in advertising is "because no one can think of a claim that anyone will believe."[56] While this position seems a bit extreme, there is little doubt that widespread skepticism characterizes the marketplace.

The tentative nature with which opinions formed solely from advertising are held has been documented by research. In one study, consumers exposed only to an ad for Ford automobiles that emphasized the company's concern with quality showed little change in their beliefs about the product's reliability.[57] However, when the ad was followed by information from *Consumer Reports* about the frequency of repair for different car models, consumers displayed a favorable change in their product beliefs. The repair information apparently provided a confirmation of the ad's claims necessary to sway consumers' opinions.

PRODUCT CONSIDERATIONS

Thus far our discussion has largely neglected how characteristics of the product can affect persuasion strategy. However, just as characteristics of the target consumers can affect the form and effectiveness of persuasion strategy, so too must various aspects of the product be taken into account.

STAGE IN THE PRODUCT LIFE CYCLE   Advertising strategy will vary over a product's life cycle. Gaining awareness and product trial are primary objectives for new products. Whereas building favorable brand attitudes is critical

---

[55] This figure comes from a study by Needham, Harper, and Steers as cited by Stephen J. Hoch and Young-Won Ha, "Consumer Learning: Advertising and the Ambiguity of Product Experience," *Journal of Consumer Research* 13 (September 1986), 221–233.

[56] "Pitches We Love to Catch," *Newsweek* (May 23, 1988), 77.

[57] John Deighton, "The Interaction of Advertising and Evidence," *Journal of Consumer Research* 11 (December 1984), 763–770; also see Hoch and Ha, "Consumer Learning: Advertising and the Ambiguity of Product Experience."

Psychological Processes

Efforts to influence consumer behavior should be grounded in an understanding of the psychological processes that shape learning, attitudes, and behavior. Part IV examines these processes and how attitudes and behavior can be modified. The following full-color ads illustrate how psychological processes are considered in developing persuasive communications. Each one is accompanied by a brief description of the psychological process that shapes the ad.

A major challenge to marketers is capturing consumers' attention, the second stage of information processing. Volvo uses an unusual image, which deviates from what consumers expect to see, to capture attention and reinforce its brand name.

Source: © 1988 Volvo North America Corporation.

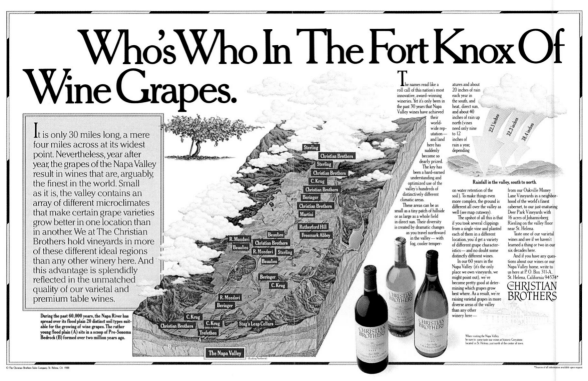

This advertisement takes a cognitive learning approach. Christian Brothers uses a cutaway diagram and informational copy to help consumers understand how different soil and climate conditions affect the growing of different wine grapes.

Source: Courtesy of The Christian Brothers Sales Company.

This advertisement illustrates the classical conditioning approach to learning. Kenwood associates the quality performance of its audio products with a number of stimuli that evoke desirable perceptions of excellence.

Source: Courtesy of Kenwood USA Corporation.

DOESN'T HE DESERVE A DINNER THAT LOOKS AS GOOD AS YOURS?

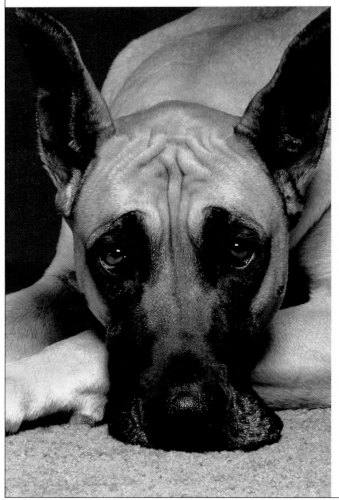

He's put up with your moods for years. When you needed a friend, he was always there.

Loyalty like this deserves new Grand Gourmet.®

The dog food that looks like people food.

It's got tender beefy strips in a rich savory sauce. And it's 100% nutritionally complete.

One look will tell you it's no ordinary dog food. But then, your dog is no ordinary dog.

Grand Gourmet
BEEF DINNER FOR DOGS
100% Nutritionally Complete

People food for dogs.

Marketers frequently employ emotional advertising appeals to influence consumer attitudes and buying behavior. This advertisement uses a heart-tugging photograph and copy that focuses on the loyalty of man's best friend to persuade dog owners to buy gourmet rather than ordinary pet food.

Source: Courtesy of Carnation Company.

during the growth stages, maintaining or reinforcing these attitudes is paramount when the product reaches maturity.

PRODUCT EXPERIENCE   The impact of persuasive communications will depend on consumers' subsequent experiences with the product. A poor tasting beverage is unlikely to be favorably evaluated, no matter how much advertising claims otherwise.

In some cases, however, consumers are limited in their ability to assess product performance accurately. Can the consumer truly evaluate the benefits that may arise from taking a vitamin a day? And how do we know whether the person who repaired our car or TV took advantage of us by unnecessarily replacing parts that were in working condition?

Research suggests that the "ambiguity" of product experiences can shape the impact of prior advertising. In one study, advertising's potential to affect perceptions of product quality was examined for two products — polo shirts and paper towels.[58] Following ad exposure, subjects were allowed to either visually inspect different brands of polo shirts or actually test the water absorption properties of various paper towel brands. The water test yielded clear evidence about the paper towels. Consequently, subjects based their product quality perceptions on this evidence alone and ignored the advertising. In contrast, the ambiguous information provided by visually inspecting the shirts enabled advertising to exert a favorable influence.

PRODUCT POSITIONING   A major determinant of persuasion strategy is the particular positioning desired for a product. That is, what product image does the marketer wish to create in the consumer's mind? The answer to this question will strongly dictate the type of message one uses to influence consumers. A product built around a status positioning will use very different messages than the product that competes based on price.

RELATIVE PERFORMANCE   Attention must also be given to the product's performance relative to competitive products in the areas representing the desired positioning. When the product is demonstrably superior to competitors, this advantage can be a potent selling point. In the absence of such superiority, other tactics must be employed for communicating the product offering.

The two ads appearing in Figure 15.6 illustrate this point. The apparent superiority of Zact over Topol in removing stains permits Zact to employ a comparative ad making strong claims along this dimension. In contrast, the Topol ad attempts to convey the desired positioning without reference to competitors. Instead, an appropriate visual image (the model dressed completely in white, with shining teeth) is combined with the claim that Topol "works more effectively."

---

[58] Hoch and Ha, "Consumer Learning: Advertising and the Ambiguity of Product Experience."

FIGURE 15.6   THE INFLUENCE OF RELATIVE PRODUCT PERFORMANCE ON ADVERTISING STRATEGY

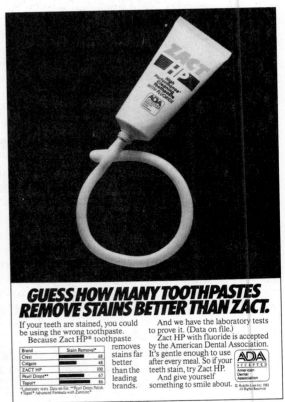

The attractiveness of affective and informational appeals is also linked to the relative performance of competing brands. Informational appeals may be of limited value when consumers perceive competing brands to be homogeneous in their product characteristics. Affective appeals may represent a more promising means for achieving differentiation in such settings. This issue is further explored in *Consumer in Focus 15.2*.

THE QUEST FOR SIMPLE ANSWERS

A great deal of evidence has been reviewed in this section on persuasive communications, and the reader may be bothered by the absence of firm generalizations. But should there be definitive decision rules? The words of distinguished advertising practitioner Harry W. McMahan are of value here:

15.2   INFLUENCING PRODUCT CHOICE THROUGH PERIPHERAL ADVERTISING CUES

Recent research has supported the potential for peripheral advertising cues to influence product choice. Subjects were initially exposed to a set of print ads. One of the ads featured a fictitious brand of soft drink called Sunburst. Two versions of this ad were used which differed in the type of picture included in the ad. One version contained an attractive picture of a tropical sunset. The other version contained an unattractive picture of some very ugly iguanas.

After viewing the ads, subjects were given the results of a taste test in which consumers had tasted and rated Sunburst and two other brands. The results given to some subjects reported virtually the same ratings for all brands. The remaining subjects received ratings that clearly favored one of the other brands over Sunburst. Sub-jects were then told that they would receive a six pack of the brand they preferred.

As expected, the influence of the peripheral cue on product choice strongly depended on the degree of brand differentiation. Sunburst was rarely chosen when the taste ratings favored another brand. However, the type of picture in the Sunburst ad strongly affected how frequently subjects chose Sunburst when the taste ratings were equivalent for the three brands. Little more than half of the subjects exposed to the attractive picture chose Sunburst, whereas only one-quarter did so when they viewed the ad containing the unattractive picture.

Source: Paul W. Miniard, "Peripheral Persuasion and Brand Choice," working paper, The Ohio State University, 1988.

Examples can help. Guidelines can help. But rules often only lead the advertising novice astray. In our 20,000 commercials we can disprove almost any "rule." Why? Because . . . different product fields require different handling in communication and persuasion.[59]

Thus, decisions always must be made on several bases: experience, creativity and intuition, and research. None of these by itself is usually sufficient.

BEHAVIOR MODIFICATION TECHNIQUES

Persuasive communications represent but one of the many weapons in the marketer's arsenal for influencing consumers' attitudes and behavior. In this section we explore a number of additional techniques that have been successfully employed for modifying human behavior.

[59] Harry W. McMahan, "Advertising: Some Things You Can't Teach — and Some You Can," *Advertising Age* (November 8, 1976), 56.

PROMPTING

Prompting is nothing more than simply requesting some action from the person. Probably everyone who has ordered from a fast-food restaurant has encountered a prompt. Requests such as "Would you like to try our new Philly Beef and Cheese?" or "Would you also like a side order of french fries?" are examples. Similarly, shoe salespeople will often ask the female customer preparing to purchase shoes if she is interested in a matching handbag. Prompts require the consumer to at least consider the product. Product purchase is thus more likely than it would be if the product were never considered.

MULTIPLE REQUEST TECHNIQUES

Research suggests that compliance with a "critical" request can be enhanced when the person is first asked to comply with an initial request. There are two major types of multiple-request procedures: foot-in-the-door and door-in-the-face.[60]

FOOT-IN-THE-DOOR   **Foot-in-the-door** (FITD) represents a technique where compliance with a critical request is increased if an individual first agrees to an initial small request. This paradigm was introduced by Freedman and Fraser, who examined its effectiveness in getting homeowners to temporarily display a large, ugly sign reading "Drive Carefully" in their front yards.[61] They found a substantial increase in compliance with this request among those who were first asked to do a smaller task, such as to place a small sign advocating safe driving in their front windows.

The typical explanation offered for the FITD effect is derived from **self-perception theory,**[62] which maintains that individuals come to know their own attitudes, emotions, and other internal states partially from inferring them from observations of their own behavior. The individual is viewed functionally as being in the same position as an outside observer who relies on external cues to infer one's own inner state.

---

[60] A recent synthesis of research on multiple request techniques can be found in Edward F. Fern, Kent B. Monroe, and Ramon A. Avila, "Effectiveness of Multiple Request Strategies: A Synthesis of Research Results," *Journal of Marketing Research* 22 (May 1986), 144–152.

[61] Jonathan L. Freedman and Scott C. Fraser, "Compliance Without Pressure: The Foot-in-the-Door Technique," *Journal of Personality and Social Psychology* 4 (August 1966), 195–202.

[62] Daryl J. Bem, "Self-Perception Theory," in Leonard Berkowitz, ed., *Advances in Experimental Social Psychology,* vol. 6 (New York: Academic Press, 1972), 1–62. Also see William DeJong, "An Examination of Self-Perception Mediation of the Foot-in-the-Door Effect," *Journal of Personality and Social Psychology* 37 (December 1979), 2221–2239. For a dissenting point of view, see Peter H. Reingen, "On Inducing Compliance with Requests," *Journal of Consumer Research* 5 (September 1978), 96–102; Alice M. Tybout, Brian Sternthal, and Bobby J. Calder, "Information Availability as a Determinant of Multiple Request Effectiveness," *Journal of Marketing Research* 20 (August 1983), 280–290.

The self-perception explanation for FITD is as follows. Getting a person to comply with an initial request produces a behavior that indicated favorableness toward the behavioral domain. For instance, agreeing to display a small sign may suggest that a person approves of behaviors of this type. This favorableness results in greater compliance with a second request involving the same behavioral domain. In contrast, those asked to comply only with the second request have not undertaken the behavior generated by the first request. Consequently, they are less likely to do what is asked of them.

Marketing investigations of foot-in-the-door's usefulness for enhancing compliance have focused on behaviors such as answering surveys and donating to charity. Results have been largely supportive. Most studies have found FITD to be more effective than a straight request,[63] although a few have not.[64] The amount of delay between the first and second request, the extent of the requests, whether the person actually undertakes the initial request or only agrees to do so, the similarity in topics between the first and second request, as well as many other factors may influence the effectiveness of FITD.[65] Further research is needed to identify precisely those conditions that limit its usefulness.

DOOR-IN-THE-FACE   **Door-in-the-face** (DITF) is the flip side of foot-in-the-door. Under this approach, the person is first asked to do something that is substantially more complex than the second, critical request. In fact, this initial request is designed to be so extreme that the person will refuse. Following this refusal, the second request is proposed. Research has shown DITF will often increase compliance relative to simply asking the second request alone.

Why does DITF work? One reason is perceptual contrast. The second, small request is made to look even smaller when preceded by the initial, large request.

---

[63] Chris T. Allen, Charles D. Schewe, and Gosta Wijk, "More on Self-Perception Theory's Foot Technique in the Pre-Call/Mail Survey Setting," *Journal of Marketing Research* 17 (November 1980), 498–502; Robert A. Hansen and Larry M. Robinson, "Testing the Effectiveness of Alternative Foot-in-the-Door Manipulations," *Journal of Marketing Research* 17 (August 1980), 359–364; Peter H. Reingen, "On Inducing Compliance with Requests"; Peter H. Reingen and Jerome B. Kernan, "Compliance with an Interview Request: A Foot-in-the-Door, Self-Perception Interpretation," *Journal of Marketing Research* 14 (August 1977), 365–369; Carol A. Scott, "Modifying Socially Conscious Behavior: The Foot-in-the-Door Technique," *Journal of Consumer Research* 4 (December 1977), 156–164.

[64] David H. Furse, David W. Stewart, and David L. Rados, "Effects of Foot-in-the-Door, Cash Incentives, and Followups on Survey Response," *Journal of Marketing Research* 18 (November 1981), 473–478; Peter H. Reingen and Jerome B. Kernan, "More Evidence on Interpersonal Yielding," *Journal of Marketing Research* 16 (November 1979), 588–593; Carol A. Scott, "The Effects of Trial and Incentives on Repeat Purchase Behavior," *Journal of Marketing Research* 13 (August 1976), 263–269.

[65] Fern, Monroe, and Avila, "Effectiveness of Multiple Request Strategies: A Synthesis of Research Results."

A second reason is the principle of **reciprocity,** which essentially says that we should try to repay what others have done for us.[66] Thus, when someone makes a concession to us, we should reciprocate. The dramatic reduction between the first and second request is intended to create the perception that the requester is making a concession. In return, it is hoped that the person will reciprocate by now agreeing to the second request. Research indicates that such concession making is a necessary prerequisite for the DITF effect.[67]

The basic DITF strategy of large-then-smaller-request sequence underlies the retail-store sales practice of "talking the top of the line."[68] The shopper is first shown the deluxe model. If the shopper buys this model, so much the better. If not, then the salesperson can counteroffer with a less expensive model. When Brunswick used this approach by first showing customers the most expensive pool table, followed by the rest of the product line, the average sale was over $1,000. However, starting customers with the least expensive table and working up produced an average sale of $550.[69]

THE PRINCIPLE OF RECIPROCITY

As just noted, the principle of reciprocity provides an important point of leverage for those attempting to influence behavior.[70] Religious groups, including the Hare Krishnas, have used this technique to enhance compliance with their requests for donations by first offering the person some gift, such as a flower. It also applies to marketing. A company that sells through in-home demonstrations, for instance, contacts prospects and offers some gift or cash prize to be delivered by the salesperson. Sometimes the gift comes in the form of a free product sample. Food companies often hire someone to stand in supermarket aisles and offer shoppers a taste of the product. Many consumers find it difficult to accept the sample without feeling a sense of obligation to buy the product (see *Consumer in Focus 15.3*).

---

[66] Robert B. Cialdini, Joyce E. Vincent, Stephen K. Lewis, Jose Catalan, Diane Wheeler, and Betty Lee Darby, "Reciprocal Concessions Procedure for Inducing Compliance: The Door-in-the-Face Technique," *Journal of Personality and Social Psychology* 31 (February 1975), 206–215. For an alternative explanation, see Tybout, Sternthal, and Calder, "Information Availability as a Determinant of Multiple Request Effectiveness."

[67] John C. Mowen and Robert B. Cialdini, "On Implementing the Door-in-the-Face Compliance Technique in a Business Context," *Journal of Marketing Research* 17 (May 1980), 253–258.

[68] Robert B. Cialdini, *Influence: How and Why People Agree to Things* (New York: William Morrow, 1984), 57. This book is highly recommended reading for those interested in a well-written, interesting, and informative discussion of influence techniques.

[69] John Vollbrecht, "To Get Volume Up, Sell Down," *Sales Management* (July 22, 1974), 29.

[70] Also see Dennis T. Regan, "Effects of a Favor and Liking on Compliance," *Journal of Experimental Social Psychology* 7 (1971), 627–639.

CONSUMER IN FOCUS

15.3 AMWAY'S USE OF RECIPROCITY

A different version of the free-sample tactic is used by the Amway Corporation, a rapid-growth company that manufactures and distributes household and personal-care products in a vast national network of door-to-door neighborhood sales. The company, which has grown from a basement-run operation a few years ago to a one and a half billion-dollar yearly sales business, makes use of the free sample in a device called the BUG. The BUG consists of a collection of Amway products — bottles of furniture polish, detergent, or shampoo, spray containers of deodorizers, insect killers, or window cleaners — carried to the customer's home in a specially designed tray or just a polyethylene bag. The confidential Amway Career Manual then instructs the salesperson to leave the BUG with the customer "for 24, 48, or 72 hours, at no cost or obligation to her. Just tell her you would like her to try the products. . . . That's an offer no one can refuse." At the end of the trial period, the Amway representative returns and picks up orders for those of the products the customer wishes to purchase. Since few

customers use up the entire contents of even one of the product containers in such a short time, the salesperson may then take the remaining product portions in the BUG to the next potential customer down the line or across the street and start the process again. Many Amway representatives have several BUGs circulating in their districts at one time.

The customer who has accepted and used the BUG products has been trapped into facing the influence of the reciprocity rule. Many such customers yield to a sense of obligation to order those of the salesperson's products that they have tried and thereby partially consumed. And, of course, by now the Amway Corporation knows that to be the case. Even in a company with as excellent a growth record as Amway, the BUG device has created a big stir.

Source: Robert B. Cialdini, *Influence: How and Why People Agree to Things* (New York: William Morrow, 1984), 39–40.

THE ROLE OF COMMITMENT

The very act of making a commitment can have a strong influence on subsequent behavior. This effect is aptly demonstrated by research asking subjects to estimate the length of various lines.[71] One group was required to write down their estimates, sign their names, and turn the form in to the experimenter. A second group wrote their estimates on a "magic" writing pad that

---

[71] Morton Deutsch and Harold B. Gerard, "A Study of Normative and Informational Social Influences upon Individual Judgment," *Journal of Abnormal and Social Psychology* 51 (November 1955), 629–636.

could be erased before others could see what they had written. A final group kept their judgments in their mind.

Subjects were then given new evidence that challenged their initial estimates. The group who had turned in their original estimates to the experimenter showed the least amount of opinion change. The simple act of publicly committing themselves made them less willing to change their minds. Interestingly, the second group who made a private commitment also displayed less change than those who only made a mental note of their original estimates. Thus, the very act of writing something down, even though it was not made publicly available, induced a sense of commitment that carried over.

Gaining a person's commitment to an opinion or action is a very good way of enhancing the odds that he or she will behave in a consistent manner. Gaining commitment is the key element of the unethical **"lowballing"** procedure.[72] A car dealer, for example, might use this procedure by offering customers a great deal in order to gain their commitment to buying the car. Once the customer has agreed to do so, the deal is then changed. This can be done in a variety of ways. The salesperson might claim that he or she "forgot" to include the price of some option. Another story line is that the boss has cancelled the deal because "we would be losing money." Some customers may walk away. Unfortunately, others will not. The act of committing to the purchase will lead them to complete the transaction despite this change in terms.

Earlier we noted that the simple act of writing something down can enhance one's commitment. This observation helps explain the attractiveness of contests that require consumers to submit essays on "Why I like this product." Door-to-door sales companies have also discovered the magic of written commitment. They are able to reduce their cancellation rates (i.e., customers who void the contract during the "cooling-off" period guaranteed by law) by simply having the customer, rather than the salesperson, complete the sales agreement form.[73]

LABELING

Labeling involves attaching some description to a person, such as "You are kind." Labels presumably lead people to view themselves in the manner implied by the label. This, in turn, should increase the likelihood that they will undertake behaviors that are consistent with the label. Research in this area has been very supportive across a number of behavioral domains, including voting, littering, and charitable actions.[74] However, the influence of labeling may

---

[72] Cialdini, *Influence: How and Why People Agree to Things*, 102–103.

[73] Ibid., 86.

[74] For research on this topic, see Chris T. Allen, "Self-Perception Based Strategies for Stimulating Energy Conservation," *Journal of Consumer Research* 8 (March 1982), 381–390; Trudy Kehret-Ward and Richard Yalch, "To Take or Not to Take the Only One: Effects of Changing the Meaning of a Product Attribute on Choice Behavior," *Journal of Consumer Research* 10 (March

be fairly short-lived. In one study, labeling had an effect on voting behavior that occurred 1 week after the label was attached but not on voting behavior 8 months later.[75]

Labeling appears to hold considerable promise, although further research is needed, particularly with respect to its effects on purchase behavior. Labeling could prove to be very useful in the realm of personal selling. The encyclopedia salesperson might describe prospective buyers with children as "concerned parents." Similarly, charitable organizations might wish to label potential donors as "generous and compassionate." Recent evidence also supports the usefulness of advertising as a mechanism for labeling consumers.[76]

INCENTIVES

Incentives encompass a broad range of promotional tools, such as price discounts, premiums, contests, sweepstakes, rebates, and coupons. Incentives typically represent an important component of the overall product-promotion strategy. Indeed, expenditures in this area have reached incredible levels. Companies spent over $13 *billion* on promotional activities during 1986.[77]

Incentives in the form of small toys have commonly been used by cereal manufacturers to encourage purchase. Recently, however, Ralston-Purina dramatically increased the size of such incentives by placing ten models of red Chevrolet Corvettes that could be redeemed for the real thing (worth $29,000) in boxes of its various cereal brands.[78] The rationale for this strategy was to enhance the odds of product purchase by placing something in the package that would appeal to adults.

Coupons often command a substantial share of the promotion budget. In 1987, 220 billion coupons were distributed through print media.[79] Evidence concerning the impact of coupons on purchasing behavior is presented in Figure 15.7. These results are based on four new product-introduction tests undertaken by the National Panel Diary marketing research firm.[80] The impact of coupons is reflected by a comparison of those consumers who were sent coupons versus those who were not sent coupons.

The top graph in Figure 15.7 represents the findings involving initial

1984), 410–416; Robert Kraut, "Effects of Social Labeling on Giving to Charity," *Journal of Marketing Research* 14 (November 1977), 509–516; Ellen M. Moore, William O. Bearden, and Jesse E. Teel, "Use of Labeling and Assertions of Dependency in Appeals for Consumer Support," *Journal of Consumer Research* 12 (June 1985), 90–96; Alice M. Tybout and Richard F. Yalch, "The Effect of Experience: A Matter of Salience," *Journal of Consumer Research* 6 (March 1980), 406–413.

[75] Tybout and Yalch, "The Effect of Experience: A Matter of Salience."

[76] Allen, "Self-Perception Based Strategies for Stimulating Energy Conservation."

[77] *Incentive Marketing*, December 1986.

[78] Monica Gonzales, "A Box of Surprises," *American Demographics* (September 1988), 18.

[79] "Coupon Distribution Seen Leveling Off," *Adweek's Marketing Week* (March 14, 1988), 22.

[80] *Insights*, NPD Research, Inc., 1979–1982.

FIGURE 15.7
THE IMPACT OF COUPONS ON PURCHASE BEHAVIOR

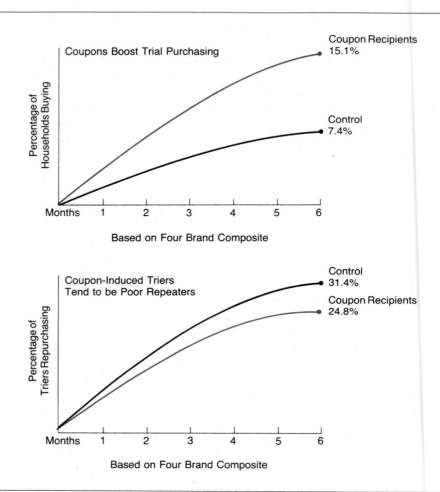

Based on Four Brand Composite

Source: *Insights,* NPD Research, Inc., 1979–1982.

or trial purchasing. As can be seen, coupons had a very strong effect on trial purchasing. Over twice as many households receiving a coupon engaged in product trial compared to those households not receiving the coupon.

What may come as a surprise are the findings involving repeat purchasing. The bottom graph in Figure 15.7 indicates that coupon-induced triers were *less* likely to repurchase the product than those who tried the product without the coupon inducement.[81] Does this finding argue against the use of coupons?

---

[81] A similar finding is reported by Joe A. Dodson, Alice M. Tybout, and Brian Sternthal, "Impact of Deals and Deal Retraction on Brand Switching," *Journal of Marketing Research* 15 (February 1978), 72–78.

Not necessarily. In the present situation, coupons yielded a penetration level of 3.7 percent (trial rate of 15.1 percent times the repurchase rate of 24.8 percent), compared to a level of 2.3 percent when coupons were not used. The lower repurchase rates of coupon-induced triers is more than offset by the substantial boost in trial purchasing when coupons were used. However, this may not always be the case. Furthermore, even when coupons provide greater market penetration, this increase must be weighed against the costs of such gains.

Why do coupons undermine repurchase rates? One possibility is that coupon users tend to be less brand loyal (and hence less likely to be repeat purchasers) than nonusers. Another possibility is suggested by self-perception theory.

SELF-PERCEPTION THEORY   According to self-perception theory, external forces or reasons for performing a behavior work against the person attributing behavioral performance to internal motivation. Incentives represent an external reason for product purchase. Consumers who purchase a product accompanied by some incentive are less likely to attribute the purchase to favorable product attitudes than consumers who purchase without an incentive. This undermining of product attitude is reflected by the decrease in repeat-purchase rates.

Self-perception theory's predictions concerning the impact of external factors have been largely supported.[82] Research has shown that grocery stores introducing new house brands at the regular price enjoyed greater long-run sales than did stores introducing the same brands at a lower-than-normal price for a short time before raising prices to their normal levels.[83] Such findings suggest that incentives can lower brand loyalty and, thus, be detrimental in the long run. Some have argued, however, that self-perception theory, which assumes fairly elaborate cognitive activity, may not be applicable to relatively unimportant purchase decisions that involve low levels of cognitive activity.[84]

SINGLE VERSUS MULTIPLE APPLICATIONS   "Single-shot" incentives may often be inadequate for modifying long-run behavior. Rather, a series of

---

[82] Dodson, Tybout, and Sternthal, "Impact of Deals and Deal Retraction on Brand Switching"; Scott, "Modifying Socially Conscious Behavior: The Foot-in-the-Door Technique"; DeJong, "An Examination of Self-Perception Mediation of the Foot-in-the-Door Effect"; Reingen and Kernan, "Compliance with an Interview Request: A Foot-in-the-Door, Self-Perception Interpretation"; Anthony N. Doob, J. Merrill Carlsmith, Jonathan L. Freedman, Thomas K. Landauer, and Soleng Tom, "Effect of Initial Selling Price on Subsequent Sales," *Journal of Personality and Social Psychology* 11 (April 1969), 345–350. Mixed support is reported by Scott, "The Effects of Trial and Incentives on Repeat Purchase Behavior."

[83] Doob, Carlsmith, Freedman, Landauer, and Tom, "Effect of Initial Selling Price on Subsequent Sales."

[84] Michael L. Rothschild and William C. Gaidis, "Behavioral Learning Theory: Its Relevance to Marketing and Promotions," *Journal of Marketing* 45 (Spring 1981), 70–78.

FIGURE 15.8
A MULTIPLE-APPLICATION APPROACH INVOLVES MORE THAN ONE SALES TECHNIQUE

Source: Reprinted by permission of the Coca-Cola Company.

incentives or multiple applications may be necessary to produce more lasting effects on purchasing behavior.

The Coca-Cola promotional program used for introducing their new Coke formula was based on a multiple-application approach. Consumers were given both free samples (single cans of the product) and coupons (reproduced in Figure 15.8). Note that the coupon with the largest discount has the earliest expiration date, while the smallest discount coupon has the latest expiration date. This decline in the size of the price discount is very desirable. First, it enhances the proportion of reinforcement received from the product versus that stemming from the coupon. The gradual reduction also enhances the similarity of each purchase to the behavior ultimately desired (i.e., buying at regular price).

Existing evidence, although extremely limited, supports the relative effectiveness of a multiple-incentive program versus the single-shot approach. For example, free samples with coupons have been shown to generate higher initial purchase rates than samples without the coupon.[85] Similarly, in-package coupons have been found to enhance repeat purchasing compared to media coupons and price discounts.[86] This observed superiority is consistent with the notion that incentives that help modify behavior over time will outperform those that do not. Further research is desperately needed to clarify the short- and long-run effects of alternative incentive programs.

OVERUSE   Marketers must be sensitive to the potential overuse of incentives. As Rothschild and Gaidis point out:

> *Purchase may become contingent upon the presence of a promotional tool. Removal of the promotion may lead to the extinction of purchase behavior. If long-term behavior toward the product is desired, promotional tools should not overshadow the product. In a marketing situation, it is paramount that reinforcement for purchase be derived primarily from the product, lest purchase become contingent upon a never ending succession of consumer deals.*[87]

PRODUCT FOCUS   Rothschild and Gaidis also argue that the extent to which incentives focus on the product is another important consideration.[88] According to them, incentives that center on the product are superior to those that do not. For this reason, price discounts and rebates are considered poor incentives because of their financial emphasis. Free samples, on the other hand, are superior because they focus on product value.

"THAT'S NOT ALL" TECHNIQUE   An interesting use of incentives to gain compliance is the "That's not all" technique. This procedure involves offering the product at one price and then sweetening the deal before the person responds to the initial offer.

The effectiveness of this technique has been demonstrated in the context of a bakery sale at a local university.[89] Cupcakes are displayed without prices. When people ask about their price, some are told they cost 75 cents, which also includes the cost of two cookies. Others are initially told the price of 75 cents, followed by a brief pause, and then informed that two cookies will also be included. Whereas over 70 percent bought the cupcakes when the deal was sweetened, only 40 percent did so when the cookies were initially included in the price. This same pattern was found when a price reduction was used. If the price of the cupcakes was reduced from 1 dollar to 75 cents, over 70 percent purchased the cupcakes. Only 43 percent did so when offered a price of 75 cents.

---

[85] This finding comes from a proprietary study undertaken by Ogilvy and Mather as reported by Rothschild and Gaidis, "Behavioral Learning Theory," 74.

[86] Dodson, Tybout, and Sternthal, "Impact of Deals."

[87] Rothschild and Gaidis, "Behavioral Learning Theory," 72.

[88] Ibid.

[89] J. M. Burger, "Increasing Compliance by Improving the Deal: The That's-Not-All Technique," *Journal of Personality and Social Psychology* 31 (1986), 277–283.

Summary

This chapter has attempted to convey some sense of the richness and complexity of the vast literature concerning how one might influence attitudes and behavior. A substantial amount of attention has been given to understanding persuasion through communication. From an information-processing perspective, persuasion (i.e., the degree of acceptance) depends on the cognitive (thoughts) and affective (feelings) responses that occur during message processing. These responses in turn are affected by a number of communication (e.g., source, message, repetition) and consumer (e.g., motivation, knowledge, prior attitudes) characteristics.

According to the Elaboration Likelihood Model, persuasion can be characterized as following one of two basic routes. Under the central route, consumers rationally evaluate the position advocated in a message. Consequently, the strength of message claims will determine the amount of yielding. Persuasion in the absence of issue-relevant thinking is called the peripheral route. Other communication elements (i.e., peripheral cues) now become important determinants of persuasion.

Characteristics of both the consumer and the product should be taken into account in developing communication strategy. Consumers' motivation, knowledge, arousal, moods, personality traits, and existing attitudes can strongly affect the impact of persuasive communications. Similarly, the product's life cycle stage, the desired positioning, and the product's performance relative to competition will play major roles in shaping such activities.

In addition to persuasive communications, consumers' attitudes and behavior can be influenced through any one of a number of behavior modification techniques. Single (prompts) and multiple (foot-in-the-door and door-in-the-face) requests can be effective devices for shaping behavior. Evoking the principle of reciprocity (e.g., through a free gift) or commitment (e.g., through the lowballing procedure) can also be very useful in modifying behavior. Incentives such as coupons are often employed by marketers to encourage purchase behavior.

REVIEW AND DISCUSSION QUESTIONS

1. What is meant by central and peripheral routes to persuasion?

2. When is the source most likely to enhance the persuasive power of an advertisement?

3. Suppose you were faced with the choice between an ad that attempts to create favorable attitudes by making several strong claims about the product versus an ad devoid of such claims but filled with attractive visuals and favorable music. How might your preference for using a particular ad depend on: (a) consumer's involvement at the time of ad exposure, (b) consumer's product knowledge at the time of ad exposure, and (c) the product's performance relative to competition?

4. A pretest of two alternative commercials found that consumers liked commercial A better than commercial B but that commercial B produced more favorable product attitudes. Why might this difference occur? Which commercial would you select, and why?

5. In a laboratory study it is discovered that a foreign make of automobile is regarded more favorably when advertising messages feature positive selling points as well as the fact that problems have existed in the past with respect to brake fade, door leaks and rattles, faulty ignition, and spark plug fouling. Would you, as the director of advertising research, recommend that this company use a two-sided campaign? What arguments might be advanced?

6. A cable TV company is trying to increase the number of new subscribers. One proposal under consideration is to provide interested consumers with free service for 2 weeks before asking them to subscribe. Would this enhance the likelihood of a person subscribing? What effect would you expect if receiving the free service was made contingent upon first completing an extensive survey of viewing habits?

7. A local charitable organization is planning its annual door-to-door fund-raising campaign. What suggestions would you make as to how the organization might enhance the effectiveness of its solicitors?

8. A recent study reveals that 20 percent of target households receiving a discount coupon tried the product compared to a 10 percent trial rate among those target households not receiving the coupon. Repeat-purchase rates, however, were far greater among noncoupon trier households (30 percent) relative to coupon-induced triers (15 percent). First, how can you explain this pattern of results? Second, do these results support the use of coupons as a means for increasing the customer base? Justify your position.

9. Consider the following proposals for using price-off coupons during the market introduction of a new food snack purchased weekly:

Proposal	Week			
	1	2	3	4
A	50% off	No coupon	No coupon	No coupon
B	50% off	50% off	50% off	50% off
C	50% off	35% off	20% off	5% off
D	5% off	20% off	35% off	50% off

Under proposal A, for instance, consumers would be supplied with a 50 percent discount coupon in the first week but no coupons in the second, third, and fourth weeks. Which proposal is likely to generate the greatest number of customers in week 5 when coupons are no longer available? Why?

ENVIRONMENTAL
INFLUENCES

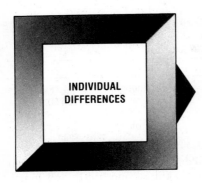

INDIVIDUAL
DIFFERENCES

DECISION PROCESS
Need Recognition
▼
Search for Information
▼
Alternative Evaluation
▼
Purchase
▼
Outcomes

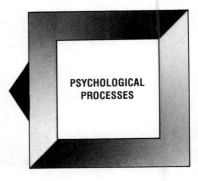

PSYCHOLOGICAL
PROCESSES

MARKETING
STRATEGY

CONSUMER DECISION PROCESSES AND BEHAVIOR

We now have completed our review of the various internal and external processes and influences that shape consumer behavior. It is necessary to return once again to the central component of our diagrammatic model on the facing page — the *consumer decision process.*

Each of the chapters in this section is designed to build on and greatly expand the decision-process overview in Chapter 2. Our major objective here is to integrate the content of previous chapters so that you will have a comprehensive grasp of the complexities of decision processes and the many resulting implications for strategies of consumer influence.

Chapter 16 provides a more complex model of consumer behavior, which will give you a sharper picture of what actually happens in extended problem solving (EPS), limited problem solving (LPS), and in habitual behavior, which takes the form of either brand loyalty or inertia. You will recall that these four variations of decision processes were introduced briefly in Chapter 2.

Chapter 17 focuses on the first two stages in decision process — *need recognition* and *search for information.* The nature and determinants of need recognition are discussed first. Then our focus shifts to the role and characteristics of internal and external search.

The acquisition of information, of course, is just an initial step in *alternative evaluation* — the subject of Chapter 18. The central component of this process is comparison of alternatives against *evaluative criteria* (desired product attributes). This chapter describes how these criteria are formed and the ways in which the evaluation process is undertaken in EPS, LPS, and habitual decision making.

Chapter 19 continues this section by concentrating on the *purchase and its outcomes.* The purchase can be made in many different ways ranging from use of interactive video to an instore visit. The variety of purchasing alternatives has grown rapidly in recent years, and there are many options for marketing strategy. But the decision process continues beyond purchase into outcomes once the product or service is bought and used. Satisfaction and intention to repurchase are the ideal outcomes, and much of our discussion centers on how to build a satisfied customer.

DIAGNOSIS OF DECISION-PROCESS BEHAVIOR

ADVERTISING VERSUS SALES PROMOTION: IMPACT ON DECISION MAKING

The newly appointed senior marketing manager for a major oil and gasoline products chain was perplexed by the fact that retail sales of motor oil at the pump island had been stagnant for many years. In fact, sales actually declined during the first few months of the current year.

About $2.5 million was being spent for consumer advertising in the form of television and radio spots. Furthermore, the advertising budget had increased nearly 25 percent over the last 5 years. The ads stressed the long-wear qualities of this premium brand. This message had changed very little, although various forms of creative execution had been used.

A careful sales analysis confirmed the manager's suspicion that advertising had little or no apparent impact on the consumer. But this analysis uncovered a major surprise — *retail motor oil sales increased only when there were special displays featuring a price reduction of some type.* When such promotions were not run, volume promptly went back to the lower level. Three consumer focus groups were also held to uncover the major dynamics in the motor oil purchase. The conclusion was simple and to the point: *all brands are about the same; I look for the cheapest.*

This also came as a surprise to the current motor oil brand manager. It became obvious that he and his predecessors had proceeded on the mistaken assumption that advertising is more important than sales promotion.

Everyone has a *model* of consumer behavior — that is, a conception of how this behavior takes place and is shaped. If this model is accurate, then it is possible to design effective strategies to influence that behavior. When it is inaccurate, however, quite the opposite can occur.

The basic issue in the example you have just read is that the brand managers apparently assumed that most consumers undertake extended problem solving (EPS) when motor oil is purchased. Hence, it was decided that "reason why" advertising copy stressing long-wear qualities would be actively attended to, processed, and used in making a choice.

It became clear, however, that the basic assumptions were wrong. Motor oil is not an item of such personal importance to the consumer that he or she is motivated to search out and discover the "best" choice. In other words, involvement is low. Furthermore, there are many premium brands, all of which differ very little in essential respects. Hence, nearly everyone would follow limited problem solving (LPS). Display and price incentives serve as a reminder of need and often trigger a "why not try it" response.

Unfortunately, a wrong decision-process diagnosis led to a substantial waste of marketing dollars. The purpose of this chapter is to sharpen your ability to diagnose consumer decision processes in a variety of situations and develop appropriate strategic insights. We return to our five-step decision-process model, which was first introduced in Figure 2.1 and used many times throughout in the book. We expand it systematically to reveal more clearly what happens as we move from EPS to LPS and to habitual behavior. Therefore, this chapter also provides an overview for the other chapters in this part.

DIAGNOSING CONSUMER MOTIVATION AND BEHAVIOR

Our motor oil management team could have benefited from taking time to reflect more deeply on consumer decision processes. By asking the right questions, it is likely that they could have avoided erroneous conclusions.

Table 16.1 gives you some suggested diagnostic questions grouped under the five major phases in consumer decision processes. You will quickly discern that one pattern of answers signifies EPS, another LPS, and so on.

When these diagnostic questions are used in strategic marketing planning, several cautions should be noted:

1. Remember that there is a continuum of initial purchase decision-process possibilities ranging from full-scale EPS on the one extreme to impulse buying (a "why not try it" response reflecting LPS) on the other. Similarly, habitual decision making also is a continuum, with brand loyalty on one end and inertia on the other. People can be anywhere on these continuua.

2. There will be differences from one consumer to the next. One may be motivated by high involvement to engage in EPS, whereas this is

TABLE 16.1
DIAGNOSING THE
CONSUMER
DECISION-MAKING
PROCESS
	Motivation and Need Recognition
	1. What needs and motivations are satisfied by product purchase and usage? (i.e., What *benefits* are consumers seeking?)
	2. Are these needs dormant or are they presently perceived as felt needs by prospective buyers?
	3. How involved with the product are most prospective buyers in the target market segment?
	
	Search for Information
	1. What product- and brand-related information is stored in memory?
	2. Is the consumer motivated to turn to external sources to find information about available alternatives and their characteristics?
	3. What specific information sources are used most frequently when search is undertaken?
	4. What product features or attributes are the focus of search when it is undertaken?
	
	Alternative Evaluation
	1. To what extent do consumers engage in alternative evaluation and comparison?
	2. Which product and/or brand alternatives are included in the evaluation process?
	3. Which product evaluative criteria (product attributes) are used to compare various alternatives.
	  a. Which are most salient in the evaluation?
	  b. How complex is the evaluation (i.e., using a single attribute as opposed to several in combination)?
	4. What kind of decision rule is used to determine the best choice?
	  a. Which are most salient in the evaluation?
	  b. How complex is the evaluation?
	5. What are the outcomes of evaluation regarding each of the candidate purchase alternatives?
	  a. What is believed to be true about the characteristics and features of each?
	  b. Are they perceived to be different in important ways, or are they seen as essentially the same?
	  c. What attitudes are held regarding the purchase and use of each?
	  d. What purchasing intentions are expressed, and when will these intentions most likely be consummated by purchase and use?
	
	Purchase
	1. Will the consumer expend time and energy to shop until the preferred alternative is found?
	2. Is additional decision-process behavior needed to discover the preferred outlet for purchase?
	3. What are the preferred modes of purchase (i.e., retail store, in the home, or in other ways)?
	
	Outcomes
	1. What degree of satisfaction or dissatisfaction is expressed with respect to previously used alternatives in the product or service category?
	2. What reasons are given for satisfaction or dissatisfaction?
	3. Has perceived satisfaction or dissatisfaction been shared with other people to help them in their buying behavior?
	4. Have consumers made attempts to achieve redress for dissatisfaction?
	5. Is there an intention to repurchase any of the alternatives?
	  a. If no, why not?
	  b. If yes, does intention reflect brand loyalty or inertia?

not the case with others. Always recognize that there can be multiple segments with differing motivations and decision-process behavior.

3. In some instances you may not have sufficient information to answer the questions completely. When this is the case, you have an indication that marketing research probably is needed. Be sure, however, that

TABLE 16.2	**Extended Problem Solving (EPS)**	**Limited Problem Solving (LPS)**
CHARACTERISTICS OF DECISION-PROCESS BEHAVIOR	*Motivation and Need Recognition*	
	1. High involvement and perceived risk.	1. Low involvement and perceived risk.
	Search for Information	
	1. Strong motivation to search.	1. Low motivation to search.
	2. Multiple sources used including media, friends, and point-of-sale communication.	2. Exposure to advertising is passive, and information processing is not deep.
	3. Information processed actively and rigorously.	3. Point-of-sale comparison likely.
	Alternative Evaluation	
	1. Rigorous evaluation process.	1. Nonrigorous evaluation process.
	2. Multiple evaluative criteria used, with some more salient than others.	2. Limited number of criteria, focus on most salient.
	3. Alternatives perceived as significantly different.	3. Alternatives perceived as essentially similar.
	4. Compensatory strategy where weakness on given attributes can be offset by others.	4. Noncompensatory strategy, eliminating alternatives perceived to fall short on salient attribute(s).
	5. Beliefs, attitudes, and intentions strongly held.	5. Beliefs, attitudes, and intentions not strongly held.
		6. Purchase and trial can be a primary means of evaluation.
	Purchase	
	1. Will shop many outlets if needed.	1. Not motivated to shop extensively.
	2. Choice of outlet may require a decision process.	2. Often prefer self-service.
	3. Point-of-sale negotiation and communication often needed.	3. Choice often prompted by display and point-of-sale incentives.
	Outcomes	
	1. Doubts can motivate need for postsale reassurance.	1. Satisfaction motivates repurchase because of inertia, not loyalty.
	2. Satisfaction is crucial and loyalty is the outcome.	2. Main consequence of dissatisfaction is brand switching.
	3. Motivated to seek redress if there is dissatisfaction.	

this information is not already available elsewhere before taking this step.

4. The questions given here are suggestive and not complete. It may be necessary to expand the list and provide more detail.

Table 16.2 gives you a guide for interpretation of the answers you will receive through marketing research. It describes those patterns that reflect *EPS* and *LPS*. Therefore, it serves as a helpful summary overview for the discussion that follows.

AN EXPANDED DECISION-PROCESS MODEL

We move now to an expanded perspective in the form of a more detailed model of the decision-making process. This will give you a more comprehensive frame of reference for the discussion in the next four chapters.

We are using the same basic model for both EPS and LPS. The differences between these two extremes on the decision-process continuum do not lie in the stages of the process per se. Rather, EPS and LPS vary in the *extent and rigor to which each stage is observed and followed.*

A model is nothing more than a replica of the phenomena it is designed to represent. It specifies the building blocks (variables), the ways in which they are interrelated (a solid arrow for a direct relationship and a broken arrow for an indirect or feedback relationship), and the outcomes when the model is set in motion by various forces.

Models of this type offer several advantages:

1. *Explanations are provided for behavior.* It is possible to grasp visually what happens as variables and circumstances change.

2. *A frame of reference is provided for research.* Gaps in knowledge and understanding become readily apparent, and it is possible to establish research priorities.

3. *A foundation is provided for management information systems.* As we have seen, proper use of a model discloses the kinds of information required to understand differing consumer decision processes and provides essential insights for marketing strategy.

EXTENDED PROBLEM SOLVING (EPS)

The model introduced here has been refined over 2 decades and has seen many changes from its original 1968 version. It is helpful to make use of a specific decision-making case to help understand the model and its implications. Be certain to read *Consumer in Focus 16.1* before proceeding further.

NEED RECOGNITION   Turn now to Figure 16.1, which depicts *need recognition* as the initial stage. This figure shows three determinants of need recognition: (1) information stored in memory, (2) individual differences, and (3) environmental influences. Any of these working individually or in combination can trigger need recognition.

Because involvement is high, EPS generally is initiated by activation of motives centrally related to self-concept. Also, normative social influence can become relevant in those buying situations in which the response of others assumes importance. Therefore, need recognition is likely to be multifaceted and complex.

The decision-process actions of the Saab 900 Turbo buyer, for example, could have been shaped by a motive to "stand out in the crowd by having

16.1 THE "SWEDISH TINKERTOY" TAKES OFF

Few have ever heard of Svenska Aeroplan Aktiebolager until it is referred to by its more familiar name, Saab-Scania A.B. This $3 billion corporation located in Linopinag, Sweden, experienced a 42.1 percent sales increase in the American luxury/sport automobile market during 1983. And it did so with some sharp marketing tactics based on a thorough understanding of its target market.

The 900 Turbo accounted for about half of Saab's 1983 U.S. sales, and it was a $20,000 car competing against such top-of-line makes as Volvo, BMW, Mercedes-Benz, and Audi. A direct outgrowth of unusual technological sophistication, it no longer bears its 1960s "Swedish Tinkertoy" label.

The average Saab buyer is a male, 30 to 40, and more than 90 percent have attended college. Most are managers and professionals with household incomes in the $50,000 to 80,000 range. They are careful, knowledgeable buyers who follow systematic reasoning and evaluation.

Sales in 1976 were only 40 percent of 1983 levels. This was the direct result of some bad word of mouth when there were not enough trained mechanics and delays in getting parts were exorbitant. These problems were overcome, and the 900 line was introduced in 1979. Initial ads featured the headline: "A Saab is exactly what you want. . . . The question is, 'What is a Saab?'" The copy gave a direct blow-by-blow competitive comparison.

Consumer awareness steadily improved. Initially, few outside the core market (described as a bearded, pipe-smoking professor) had any awareness. By 1983, 75 percent in the target segment were aware, and this was accomplished with a $5.5 million expenditure in auto magazines and news weeklies, plus about $2.3 million in local cooperative dealer ads.

Saab interviews current and prospective owners to determine their wants and needs, likes, and dislikes. In targeting the "upscale" segment for the 900 Turbo, Saab found that individuals in this group wanted a maximum of creature comforts. Every conceivable option was included as a standard feature, with the exceptions of a luggage/ski rack and fog lights. In addition, it was found that safety is not an important feature because the 25-year commitment of Saab to safety is taken for granted. Apparently Saab did something right, because 75 percent planned on buying another Saab.

The Saab prospect is reported to spend hours in the showroom. In fact, management indicates that some know more about Saabs than salespeople. This is because detailed information is provided about gear ratios, peak torque, camshaft bearings, and other details care buyers usually ignore. This is followed by giving each buyer an extensive maintenance kit, complete with manual and tools.

Saab-Scania has overcome its parts and service problems. Now it ranks near the top of all car manufacturers, domestic or import, in satisfaction with dealer. The Swedish Tinkertoy days are gone for good.

Bernie Whalen, "'Tiny' Saab Drives Up Profits with Market-Niche Strategy, Repositioning," *Marketing News* (March 16, 1984), 14–16.

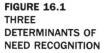

FIGURE 16.1
THREE
DETERMINANTS OF
NEED RECOGNITION

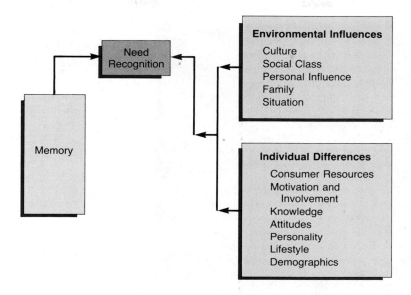

the latest 'in car.' " Or a motivation to achieve power over others could stimulate a favorable response to the speed and acceleration benefits offered by a turbocharger.

Figure 16.2 shows one of the ads run by Saab-Scania. A primary objective here no doubt was to create a new standard of automotive design and performance. Need recognition is stimulated when there is a perceived difference between perception of "what might be" as compared with the present state of affairs. Do you think this ad has that kind of impact?

SEARCH FOR INFORMATION   The next step following need recognition is **internal search** into memory to determine whether enough is known about available options to allow a choice to be made without further information search. This often proves sufficient in low-involvement situations, but **external search** usually will be required when this is not the case. Internal and external search are depicted in Figure 16.3.

Most prospective buyers of the Saab will make use of a variety of outside information resources. Recall how much time is spent in the showroom consulting technical information materials. It also is quite likely that word of mouth from satisfied Saab owners plays a major role.

Figure 16.3 shows that propensity to engage in external search is affected by individual differences and environmental influences. For example, some potential buyers have the characteristic of being cautious and unwilling to act without extensive and detailed information, whereas this is not so much the case with others.

FIGURE 16.2 THE SAAB 900 TURBO: THE AD STIMULATES NEED RECOGNITION

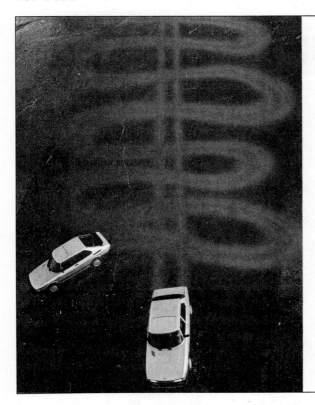

TEST DRIVE A SAAB. IT WILL TELL YOU A LOT ABOUT YOURSELF.

Thirty minutes in the driver's seat of a Saab 900 can be more revealing than a session on a psychiatrist's couch.

What you like or don't like or ignore on a Saab is indicative of whether you're ruled by your intellect or your emotions or whether you've achieved a serene balance.

Example: Saab's front-wheel drive.

Will you look at it as a way to get through the winter and the foul weather parts of the other seasons? Our guess is that you're ruled by your intellect.

Or will you look at front-wheel drive as the means to give a sedan the road-hugging, toe-curling, hair-raising cornering ability of a sports car? Our guess is that you're ruled by your emotions.

But wait a second. Maybe you see front-wheel drive as both. In that case, you're ruled neither by your intellect nor your emotions. You are ruling them. (And, we make a great presumption here, you would enjoy owning a Saab.)

The ego and the id.

The id, the repository of your instinctual impulses, will want to know, on a test drive, how good a Saab is at, well, burning rubber.

Don't repress that feeling. All the practical considerations for buying a Saab (economy,

the reasonableness of its price, the active and passive safety features, the durability in a world where disposability is a perverse virtue) are just as real and just as practical after testing its acceleration as they were before.

But they start to remind one of the classes and textbooks and lectures and schematic diagrams of intersections you had to endure in Driver's Ed before they let you get behind the wheel, turn the key, hear the engine start, and see what the experience of driving could be like.

1985 SAAB PRICE LIST*	
900 3-door	*$11,850*
900 4-door	*$12,170*
900S 3-door	*$15,040*
900S 4-door	*$15,510*
Turbo 3-door	*$18,150*
Turbo 4-door	*$18,620*
Automatic transmission $400 additional.	

Sure, a car's reason for being is to get from Point A to Point B. But a Saab's reason for being is to do that as responsibly as possible without ignoring the romance in the possibilities of Points Q, R, S, T, not to mention X, Y, and Z.

An interpretation of your dreams.

Is the Saab 900 the car of your dreams? Of course, we don't know that.

We do know it's the car of our dreams. At least, our engineers' and designers' dreams.

There are seemingly disparate elements on a Saab. Elements not unlike those on other automobiles.

We'll list them now in no particular order: rack-and-pinion steering, disc brakes on all four wheels, front-wheel drive, 53 (!) cubic feet of cargo space, aerodynamic body, incredible fuel efficiency considering its performance.**

Somehow, in some way, on a Saab, those elements add up to a whole that's greater than its parts. They add up to what's known around here as the driving experience: Saabs somehow feel better to Saab owners than other cars they've owned.

For the first time, they got hold of a car that presented no conflict between what was the most practical thing and the most pleasurable thing.

They got the performance car they always wanted with the responsible car they knew they always needed.

They discovered that even a trip to the supermarket to get some dog food could be a kick if the driving experience was right.

They found out the joy of not following the crowd, but of starting a crowd of their own.

Truth is, a 30-minute test drive may not be able to tell you all this. But we'll bet that three years owning one will.

SAAB 900
The most intelligent car ever built.

*Manufacturer's suggested retail prices. Not including taxes, license, freight, dealer charges or options. **Saab 16-valve Turbo 5-speed: 19 EPA estimated city mpg. 25 estimated highway mpg. Use estimated mpg for comparison only. Mileage varies with speed, trip length and weather.

Source: Courtesy of Ally & Gargano, Inc. for Saab-Scania of America.

Family influence can enter through conflict between the primary influencer of the purchase and spouse over colors and optional features. External search can be used to buttress conflicting positions. Finally, situational influence often *inhibits* search, an example being the urgent need for a refrigerator when the current one breaks down and is not repairable.

Saab management was able to achieve a 75 percent awareness among those in the target market over a short period of time. Use was made of two different types of marketer-dominated stimuli: print ads and TV commercials. In addition, many prospects were exposed to positive word of mouth from satisfied buyers. This information then was processed and stored following the information-processing stages discussed in Chapters 13 and 14. Figure 16.4 expands the decision-making model through the addition of information processing.

FIGURE 16.3
SEARCH FOR INFORMATION IN THE DECISION-MAKING MODEL

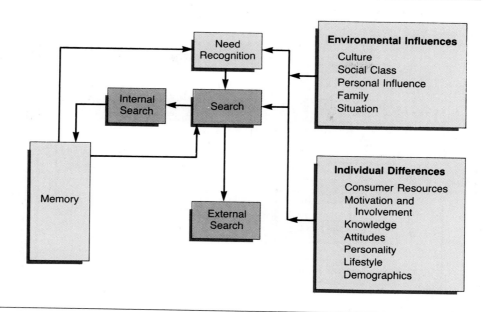

You will remember the distinction made in Chapter 15 between central and peripheral routes in information processing. The central route consists of careful weighing of message content, with the outcome being changes in beliefs, attitudes, and intentions. It is most common when involvement is high and no doubt was utilized by the majority of Saab buyers. This means that information was processed deeply so that it could be stored, recalled, and used during decision making.

ALTERNATIVE EVALUATION   The most common chain of effects of processed information on alternative evaluation begins with formation and change in *beliefs* about the product or brand and its attributes, followed by a shift in *attitude toward the act of purchase.* All things being equal, this leads to an *intention* to act consistently with attitude and finally to the act of purchase itself (Figure 16.5).

Alternative evaluation makes use of **evaluative criteria** — the standards and specifications used by consumers to compare different products and brands. In other words, these are the desired outcomes from purchase and consumption and are expressed in the form of preferred attributes.

Evaluative criteria are shaped and influenced by individual differences and environmental influences. For example, such self-concept–related motives as a need to stand out among peers could lead to a premium being placed on such features as avant-garde design, unusual trim, and a rear window spoiler. Cultural color taboos limit the color options. Harsh winters lead to

FIGURE 16.4   INFORMATION PROCESSING IN THE DECISION-MAKING MODEL

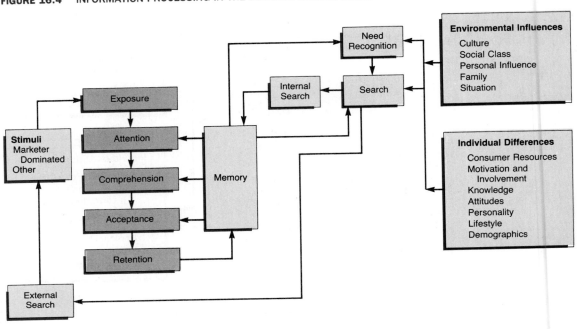

a premium placed on quick starts, a powerful heating system, and handling characteristics. Many other examples could be given.

As alternatives are compared against these standards, judgments are formed and changed regarding the extent to which various options measure up. In turn, there will be corresponding changes in beliefs (what consumers judge to be true about each alternative), attitudes toward the act of purchase, and intentions.

You will learn in Chapter 18 that rigorous alternative evaluation is a distinguishing characteristic of EPS. A common procedure is to process information one brand at a time, weighing each against the most important (salient) attributes. This is done following a **compensatory strategy** in which perceived weakness on one attribute can be compensated for or offset by strength on others. The Saab prospect, for example, may well overlook the unavailability of a preferred paint color because of a strong favorable response to interior comfort and convenience of instrumentation.

The management team at Saab-Scania used marketing research effectively as the basis of the features built into the 900 Turbo. Advertising highlighted Saab's distinctiveness on such salient attributes as swift acceleration and response under harsh winter conditions. The resulting sales increase suggests

FIGURE 16.5   ALTERNATIVE EVALUATION IN THE DECISION-MAKING MODEL

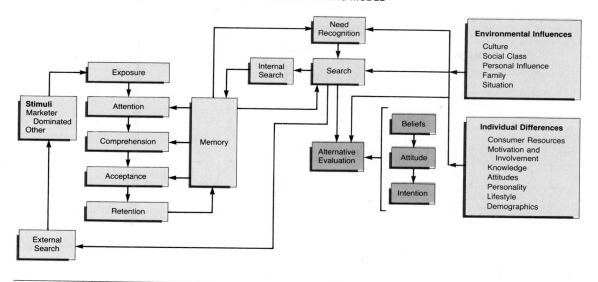

that this advertising apparently was effective in changing beliefs, attitudes, and intentions.

PURCHASE AND ITS OUTCOMES   Figure 16.6 completes the decision-process model by depicting purchase and its outcomes. Purchase most often takes place in some type of retail outlet, although our discussion in Chapter 19 demonstrates the remarkable growth of home shopping of various types. The automobile showroom will retain its present role, however, because salespeople and point-of-sale materials are a significant part of search behavior for most buyers. Often a high level of sales skill is required. Saab has invested heavily in building its dealer and service network, and this strategy appears to have been successful.

Alternative evaluation does not cease once the purchase is made. Remember that an important activator of EPS is the perceived necessity to make the "right choice." Product use provides new information, which is compared against existing beliefs and attitudes. If expectations are matched, the outcome, of course, is *satisfaction*. The broken feedback arrow in Figure 16.6 shows how satisfaction strengthens future purchase intentions.

When the alternative is perceived as falling short in significant ways, **dissatisfaction** is the result. It is common to experience such doubts even before trial simply because of the presence of unchosen alternatives with

FIGURE 16.6   A COMPLETE MODEL OF CONSUMER BEHAVIOR SHOWING PURCHASE AND OUTCOMES

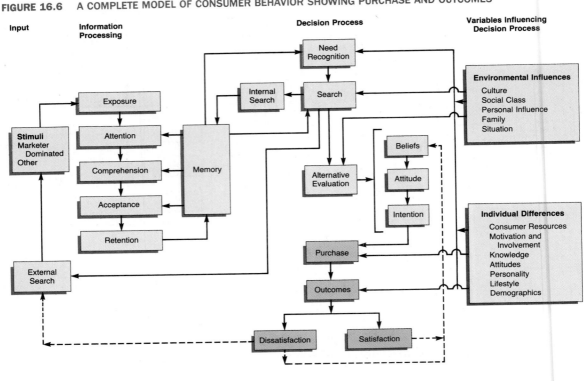

desirable features. Often known as postdecision regret, this can be an incentive for further information search, as the broken arrow in Figure 16.6 indicates.

A true failure to perform, however, will not be taken lying down by many because of the high perceived importance of the purchase. Complaints and efforts to achieve redress are common. The quality of postsale service can make a great difference. This need was recognized at Saab, and major efforts were made to beef up the quality of dealer service. As you read earlier, this was not the situation during the so-called "Swedish Tinkertoy" era.

Satisfaction and dissatisfaction, of course, represent extreme points on a continuum. High satisfaction or dissatisfaction also is a motivation for sharing with others. The discussion in the next chapter underscores that this type of influence is both trusted and used by others. Many companies are finding that negative word of mouth is exceedingly difficult, if not impossible, to overcome.

LIMITED PROBLEM SOLVING (LPS)

We move toward the other end of the problem-solving continuum and approach the extreme point (LPS) when consumers are not highly involved with the alternative. Usually the available options are similar in essential characteristics, and there is less need for comparative shopping.

To take an example, a plaintive cry is heard, "Mom, we're out of toilet tissue!" Mom promptly notes this fact on the shopping list she will use tonight after work when she stops at the supermarket. When she faces the toilet tissue display, she is unlikely to evaluate each brand, carefully considering such factors as "squeezability," the number of sheets per foot, and so on. Also, any brand preferences she might have are not sufficiently strong to prevent a brand switch if the situation warrants it. Her decision rule may be a very simple one such as, "Buy the cheapest brand I can find."

Under low-involvement conditions most buyers are less motivated to search extensively and engage in rigorous alternative evaluation. EPS and LPS are not different decision processes per se, because both involve the same stages, ranging from need recognition to outcomes. The difference lies in the *extent to which time and effort are devoted to external information search and alternative evaluation.* Often this takes place as the buyer scans the shelves.

Consumer in Focus 16.2 underscores the fact that LPS is far more common in consumer shopping and buying than EPS. In fact, two-thirds of all purchases are made by impulse. This means that the marketing strategy battle often is won or lost at the point of sale.

NEED RECOGNITION   Need recognition often is straightforward — "We're out of mouthwash. Pick up something on the way home." Out-of-stock conditions of this type are a primary purchase initiator. And, as we discussed in Chapters 2 and 9, a desire for variety also is common, especially with food items.

SEARCH FOR INFORMATION   Motivated information search prior to shopping, if undertaken at all, is often confined to such strategies as scanning the grocery ads for price specials. Yet, the POPAI study reported in *Consumer in Focus 16.2* indicates that even this is decreasing.

It would be a mistake to conclude, however, that advertising and other types of sales effort are without influence. The strategy becomes one of increasing *share of mind* — relative familiarity of competitive brand names.

All of us are passively exposed to advertising many times daily. We encounter ads in the process of doing something else such as driving, watching TV, and so on. When attention is attracted under these conditions, the content usually receives minimal information processing. While we may be unaware of what happens, the primary outcome often is simple learning in the form of strengthened brand familiarity. This familiarity, in turn, can be an essential precondition for a "why not try it" response. A totally unfamiliar brand is at a competitive disadvantage.

16.2 SHOPPERS GOVERNED BY IMPULSE

A new study shows that more than half of all supermarket purchases are completely unplanned — made with no specific brand or product in mind. A total of 52.6% of grocery store purchases are "specifically unplanned," up 5.8 percentage points from 1977, according to the study undertaken by the Point-of-Purchase Advertising Institute (POPAI), Englewood, N.J.

Another 10% of consumers plan to purchase from a specific product category but not a specific brand name, and nearly 3% substitute another brand when the planned purchase is not available. Taking these figures together, two out of every three supermarket purchases are impulse buys.

Brand loyalty in package goods is most keen in baby products, coffees and teas, pet foods, alcoholic beverages, soft drinks, laundry supplies, soaps and detergents, with the percentage of specifically planned purchases of at least 42% in each category.

At least 80% of buying decisions were made in-store for candy and gum, snacks, pickles and relishes, pasta, cookies and crackers and condiments and sauces. Largely because of time constraints, 69% of grocery consumers do not prepare shopping lists, up 9 points in 1977; 75% ignore newspaper ads before shopping, up 13 points.

The increase in in-store buying decisions is fostering a growth in point-of-purchase advertising, a medium that rose 14.2% in 1986 to $10.8 billion.

Source: Judann Dagnoli, "Impulse Governs Shoppers," *Advertising Age* (October 5, 1987), 93.

ALTERNATIVE EVALUATION   As we have stressed, alternative evaluation is limited, probably consisting of little more than some assurance that each competitive alternative "qualifies" in terms of the expected benefit. You will recall that "meets or exceeds car manufacturer's standards" is a central expected benefit when motor oil is purchased. We now see **noncompensatory** alternative evaluation in which an option will be eliminated if it falls short. This is commonly done at the point of sale.

PURCHASE AND OUTCOMES   The purchase usually is made with minimum deliberation and further decision making. Trial serves as a principal method of alternative evaluation. If it meets or exceeds expectations, the outcome is an intention to repurchase. Such an intention, however, does not necessarily lead to brand loyalty. There are other acceptable options as well.

Dissatisfaction, of course, will most likely lead to brand switching. Yet the low-risk nature of the purchase does not make dissatisfaction such a crucial outcome as it would be if the consequences were greater. Complaint and seeking for redress may not be worth the time and expense.

HABITUAL DECISION MAKING

One of the ways in which consumers cope with demands on their time and energy is to routinize the process. Therefore, repetitive behavior quickly can become habitual, characterized by absence of external information search and alternative evaluation. Need recognition triggers a "buy the same thing" response.

BRAND LOYALTY VERSUS INERTIA   It is helpful to distinguish between the major types of habitual buying. Two women executives always buy the same brand of quality blush table wine. One does so because she is convinced it has a smoother, more full-bodied flavor than anything else at this price. Also, her friends comment appreciatively when it is served. Because it is important to serve the "right thing," involvement is high and her buying habit reflects brand loyalty.

The other consumer is far less committed to her choice, however, and feels that most blush wines are about the same. But she also feels that this brand provides a sufficient value to warrant repurchase unless she sees something else at a lower price. For her the habit reflects inertia and avoidance of brand switching unless she has reason to do so.

Ellen Goodman vividly underscores in *Consumer in Focus 16.3* why inertia-based habits are so common in buying behavior.

THE IMPLICATIONS OF STRONG LOYALTY   A high degree of brand loyalty is one of the greatest assets a marketer can possess. This is because strongly favorable attitudes resist change, thus making competitive inroads both difficult and expensive.

When deregulation opened the doors for new companies to enter the long-distance telephone field, it was quickly discovered that "Ma Bell" could not be dislodged easily. After a lifetime of service, many long-distance customers refused to consider switching despite the significant price savings that were offered.

When loyalty is strong, the challenge is to find ways of "kicking" consumers out of this routine and back into active decision making. It will take time, however. Inroads are most likely, of course, when a significant and demonstrable benefit can be offered, but this is not always possible. Therefore, it is often necessary to offer strong financial incentives in the form of lower price or rebates.

Loyalty must be both earned and cultivated, however, through continuing commitment to customer satisfaction. The Coca-Cola Company's recent experience in changing the traditional Coke formula is illustrative of the problems that can occur when the strength of consumer loyalty is either underestimated or taken lightly.

Archcompetitor Pepsi Company introduced its Pepsi Challenge taste tests and consistently claimed taste superiority. In response, Coca-Cola reformu-

16.3 FREEDOM OF CHOICE ENSLAVED DAZED CONSUMER

The woman is standing in the drugstore suffering from acute "consumeritis." This attack has been brought on by the excess of choices on the shelf before her. Its chief symptom is mental paralysis, the total inability to make a decision.

She came here on a quest for a refill of shampoo. But when her usual brand was no longer available, she was tossed willy-nilly into the chaos of the modern day world of shampoos.

What did she want after all? Which of the three-dozen options lined up before her would make the dead follicles that grow out of her busy head come alive? A moisturizing formula? A body-building protein? A mysterious chemical soup of Elastin? Collagen? Keratin? Balsam?

She was compelled by the labels to ask herself some penetrating questions. Was she the sort of person who needed her pH balanced? Or would she prefer her pH a bit off of kilter? Should she put essential fatty acids in her scalp? Did she want shampoo with a pectin extract? Or isn't that what she uses to make jelly?

This proliferation of personal products had turned shopping into a decision-making marathon. The competing claims of manufacturers had produced an information glut.

Informed consumers are propelled into examining their bodies in ever more minute detail. Does my skin need intensive care or not? Do I have plaque on my teeth or not? Ridges on my nails? Split ends on my hair? Am I normal or dry?

One thing is clear to the woman lathering the body-building protein into her scalp: What the advertisers call brand loyalty is a low-level consumer protest movement. It's our way of cutting through the bouts of decision-making, avoiding the barrages of useless information. It's a defense against the need to waste energy differentiating things that barely differ.

Source: Ellen Goodman, "Freedom of Choice Enslaves Dazed Consumer," *The Columbus Dispatch* (October 9, 1987), 13A. © 1987, The Boston Globe Newspaper Company/Washington Post Writer's Group. Reprinted with permission.

lated its flavor and tested it with nearly 200,000 present and prospective customers, usually without any indication of brand name. Impressed by the overwhelming vote in favor of this new formulation, the old formulation was dropped in favor of the new in 1985.

The change sparked a tremendous uproar from consumers, many of whom boycotted new Coke and petitioned for the return of the old formula. Little did management realize the extent of loyalty to the tried-and-true formulation. Disaster was averted by retaining the new formula and reintroducing the old under the name "Coca-Cola Classic," and market share increased.

OVERCOMING INERTIA-BASED BUYING HABITS Inertia-based habitual buying presents a less potent competitive obstacle, because brand switching can be stimulated relatively easily. This type of habit is maintained without strong commitment and hence is susceptible to change. Couponing, price reductions, two-for-one sales, and end-aisle displays are just a few of the ways that trial can be stimulated when there are not strong incentives to remain loyal. Unfortunately, the ground gained at one period can quickly be lost at the next as competitors counterattack. The goal always is to increase and retain market share.

SUMMARY

This chapter builds upon the overview of consumer decision processes provided in Chapter 2. The primary difference is that a sharpened and clarified decision-process model was introduced, showing more clearly how essential variables and influences interact to shape how the consumer thinks and behaves.

An accurate model is essential if consumer behavior is to be diagnosed properly. A checklist of questions was provided to guide marketing research undertaken for strategic planning.

REVIEW AND DISCUSSION QUESTIONS

Since this chapter is an expansion and integration of material discussed in Chapter 2 and other chapters, additional questions are of less value. Instead, we suggest that you refer to the diagnostic questions in Figure 16.1 and use them in a variety of situations. Ask friends or acquaintances how they make buying decisions. Here are some suggested products and services which cover a wide range of decision-process options: cassettes, shaving lotion, ties, women's lingerie, portable stereos, used cars, movies, toilet paper, nail polish, pencils, and airline tickets.

NEED RECOGNITION AND SEARCH

H COURTING THE CUSTOMER AT RUBBERMAID

ow do you make a silk purse out of a sow's ear? Rubbermaid does it all the time by lavishing on its homely products — dishdrainers, platescrapers, microwave utensils, and the like — the attention a crown jeweler would devote to the royal diadem. The company listens intently to customers and retailers, and spends millions on consumer research, product development, and new designs.

Its reward: lush profits from a business with slow market growth. Like a medieval knight, Rubbermaid pursues its mission with a religious fervor. The Holy Grail: boosting sales and earnings per share 15% a year.

Such single-mindedness has made Rubbermaid remarkably adept at searching out ways to grow. Designers continually tweak mature products to provide incremental sales. Revising the plastic composition and design of ice trays, for instance, made it easier to remove the cubes. Garbage container sales accelerated 20% when a slate-blue model was added.

When Rubbermaid brings out a new product, it's almost always a hit. The company claims a success rate of 90%. It maintains that enviable record by making a fetish of keeping in touch with customers. For instance, it tests color preferences year round through consumer focus groups in five cities, then confirms the results by quizzing people in shopping malls.

Most executives read customer letters to find out how people like the products, and sometimes glean new ideas. One was a compact one-piece dish drainer, prompted by customers in small households who found the traditional rack-and-mat set too bulky to store easily.

To avoid tipping off competitors, Rubbermaid never test-markets. Instead it generates reams of consumer research through user panels, brand awareness studies, and diaries that consumers fill with notions about product lines. Says Chairman Stanley Gault, "Our formula for success is very open: We absolutely watch the market, and we work at it 24 hours a day." That wouldn't be a bad formula even in the royal diadem business.

Source: Alex Taylor III, "Why the Bounce at Rubbermaid?" *Fortune* (April 13, 1987), 77–78.

Decision-process behavior always commences with **need recognition** — defined here as perception of a difference between the desired state of affairs and the actual situation sufficient to arouse and activate the decision process. Researchers and decision makers at Rubbermaid Incorporated are well aware that a key to marketing success is to detect when consumers recognize a need and to offer realistic and affordable solutions. Another strategy is to create need recognition through new product designs. Is it any wonder that those living in cramped space grabbed up the dish drainer designed especially for them? The 90 percent new product success rate attests to the benefits gained from continually monitoring the market.

When need recognition occurs, the human system is energized and goal-oriented behavior begins. Activities now become directed toward satisfying this need state. In other words, the system is turned on and activated to engage in purposeful behavior.

This chapter has two basic objectives. The first is to explore what happens during need recognition. The second is to examine the nature and role of consumer search.

NEED RECOGNITION

The simple diagram appearing in Figure 17.1 illustrates what happens during need recognition. Need recognition essentially depends on how much discrepancy exists between the actual state (i.e., the consumer's current situation) and the desired state (i.e., the situation the consumer wants to be in). When this discrepancy exceeds a certain level or threshold, a need is recognized. For example, a consumer currently feeling hungry (actual state) and wanting to eliminate this feeling (desired state) will experience need recognition if

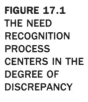

FIGURE 17.1
THE NEED
RECOGNITION
PROCESS
CENTERS IN THE
DEGREE OF
DISCREPANCY

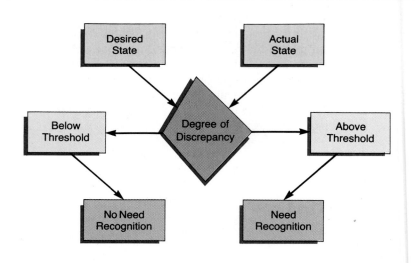

the discrepancy between the two states is of sufficient magnitude. However, if the discrepancy is below the threshold level, then need recognition will not occur.

It is necessary to point out that the presence of need recognition does *not* automatically activate some action. This will depend on a couple of factors. First, the recognized need must be of sufficient importance. A hungry consumer may not feel that the rumblings in his stomach merit action at this point in time. Second, consumers must believe that a solution to the need is within their means. If need satisfaction is beyond a consumer's economic or temporal resources (see Chapter 8), for instance, then action is unlikely.

NEED ACTIVATION

A need must first be *activated* before it can be *recognized*. A host of factors will influence the likelihood that a particular need will be activated. Such factors operate by altering the person's actual and/or desired states.

CHANGED CIRCUMSTANCES   Needs will often be activated due to changes in one's life. The employee who is relocated to another geographic region will recognize the need to find new living quarters. A salary increase may lower the attractiveness of one's present automobile relative to what is now affordable. Changes within the family can also trigger need recognition. The birth of a child, for instance, results in modified requirements for food, clothing, furniture, and housing.

PRODUCT ACQUISITION   The acquisition of a product may, in turn, activate the need for additional products. It is not uncommon to find that acquiring new furnishings will affect perceptions of the desirability of existing carpeting, wall coverings, and so on. Similarly, buying a new home will usually require the purchase of additional products, particularly for first-time buyers. It is for this reason that new home buyers are an important target market for many companies.

PRODUCT CONSUMPTION   Actual consumption itself can trigger need recognition. In many buying situations, a need is recognized simply because of an out-of-stock situation. The last slices of bread were toasted for breakfast, and more bread will be needed for tonight's dinner. Thus, need recognition occurs because of an *anticipated* need in the immediate future resulting from a change in the actual situation.

The extent to which the product lives up to consumers' expectations during consumption can also affect need recognition (as well as satisfaction — see Chapter 19).[1] When a product meets these expectations, then the actual and desired states will be in harmony. However, a product that falls short of consumers' expectations (i.e., the actual state is less than the desired state) will trigger need recognition when repurchase in the product category is anticipated.

MARKETING INFLUENCES   We noted in Chapter 9 that marketers are unable to "create" needs in the marketplace. Rather, their influence is constrained to activating needs that already exist within consumers. A basic objective of many advertisements, then, is to stimulate consumers' awareness of their needs. This stimulation may be either primary or selective in nature. An example of the former is the meat industry's recent campaign using celebrity endorsers such as James Garner and Sybil Sheppard to strengthen the primary demand for meat. Marketing activities that focus on primary demand are, in essence, attempting to elicit **generic need recognition.**

Selective need recognition, on the other hand, occurs when the need for a specific brand within a product category is stimulated. Consider the person holding a 13 percent loan and feeling quite satisfied with this rate. He then sees the ad appearing in Figure 17.2. Suddenly, he feels a bit uncomfortable. His perceptions of the desired state begin to change. He wonders why he should pay his current bank 13 percent when someone else is offering a lower rate. Thus, the ad has prompted both a redefinition of the desired state and selective need recognition for the advertised brand.

Sometimes need recognition can be prompted by marketing materials at the point of purchase. Consumers browsing a retailer's aisles may encounter a display that reminds them of a previously recognized but unfulfilled purchase

---

[1] Sirgy has employed the concept of congruity between perceived and expected product performance to predict the strength of need recognition. See M. Joseph Sirgy, "A Social Cognition Model of Consumer Problem Recognition," *Journal of the Academy of Marketing Science* 15 (Winter 1987), 53–61.

FIGURE 17.2
AN AD DESIGNED
TO STIMULATE
SELECTIVE NEED
RECOGNITION

need. Alternatively, the display may directly activate a need that leads to a previously unintended purchase.

Product innovations are another source of need recognition. The Black & Decker automatic shut-off iron (see Figure 17.3) should evoke need recognition among consumers wishing to reduce the anxiety and potential dangers that come from forgetting to turn off their electric iron. Similarly, the innovative designs from Kohler (see Figure 17.3) could make the traditional bathroom sink seem obsolete by providing an entirely different concept of what is now possible.

INDIVIDUAL DIFFERENCES   Bruner has recently proposed that consumers may often differ in whether need recognition results from changes in the

FIGURE 17.3 STIMULATING SELECTIVE NEED RECOGNITION THROUGH PRODUCT INNOVATION

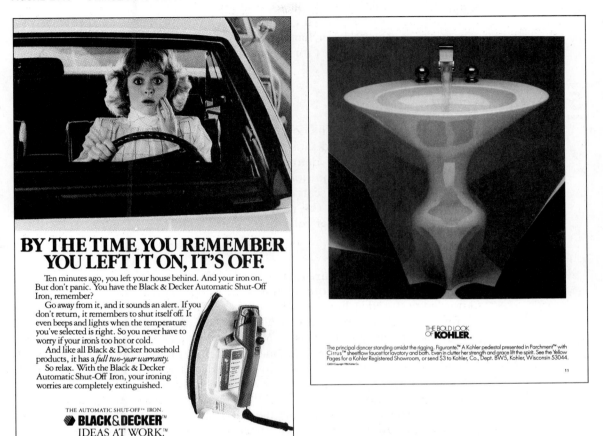

Source: (left) Courtesy of Black & Decker Corporation; (right) Courtesy of Kohler Co.

actual state versus the desired state.[2] At one extreme are consumers (called **Actual State Types**) for whom need recognition is triggered typically by changes in the actual state. Consumers at the other extreme (called **Desired**

---

[2] Gordon C. Bruner II, "The Effect of Problem Recognition Style on Information Seeking," *Journal of the Academy of Marketing Science* 15 (Winter 1987), 33–41; Gordon C. Bruner II, "Problem Recognition Styles and Search Patterns: An Empirical Investigation," *Journal of Retailing* 62 (1986), 281–297; Gordon C. Bruner II, "Recent Contributions to the Theory of Problem Recognition," in Robert F. Lusch, Gary T. Ford, Gary L. Frazier, Roy D. Howell, Charles A. Ingene, Michael Reilly, and Ronald W. Stampfl, eds., *1985 AMA Educators' Proceedings* (Washington, DC: American Marketing Association, 1985), 11–15.

State Types) usually experience need recognition produced by changes in the desired state. For example, Actual State Types tend to recognize a need for clothing only when their clothing does not perform satisfactorily. Desired State Types, on the other hand, will frequently experience need recognition as a result of their desires for something new.

Search

Once need recognition has occurred, the consumer may then engage in a search for potential need satisfiers. **Search,** the second stage of the decision-making process, can be defined as the motivated activation of knowledge stored in memory or acquisition of information from the environment. This definition suggests that search can be either internal or external in nature. Internal search involves the retrieval of knowledge from memory, whereas external search consists of collecting information from the marketplace.

INTERNAL SEARCH

Search of an internal nature first occurs following need recognition (see Figure 17.4). Internal search is nothing more than a memory scan for decision-relevant knowledge stored in long-term memory (see Chapter 10).[3] If this scan reveals sufficient information to provide a satisfactory course of action, then external search is obviously unnecessary. Many times a past solution is remembered and implemented. For example, one study reports that many consumers needing an auto repair service relied on their existing knowledge in making their choice.[4] Only 40 percent turned to external search.

Whether consumers rely solely on internal search will heavily depend on the adequacy or quality of their existing knowledge. First-time buyers are obviously unlikely to possess the necessary information for decision making. Even experienced buyers may need to undertake external search. Experienced buyers may find their knowledge to be inadequate for product categories characterized by large interpurchase times (the amount of time between purchase occasions) during which there are significant product changes in terms of prices, features, and new brands and stores. Even if product changes have been minimal, internal search is hindered by large interpurchase times due to problems of forgetting. Nor may existing knowledge be sufficient when

---

[3] Internal search has received relatively little attention in the consumer behavior literature. For exceptions, see James R. Bettman, *An Information Processing Theory of Consumer Choice* (Reading, Massachusetts: Addison-Wesley, 1979), 107–111; Gabriel J. Biehal, "Consumers' Prior Experiences and Perceptions in Auto Repair Choice," *Journal of Marketing* 47 (Summer 1983), 87–91. For research on how the adequacy of internal search will affect external search, see Girish Punj, "Presearch Decision Making in Consumer Durable Purchases," *Journal of Consumer Marketing* 4 (Winter 1987), 71–82.

[4] Biehal, "Consumers' Prior Experiences and Perceptions in Auto Repair Choice."

FIGURE 17.4
THE INTERNAL
SEARCH PROCESS

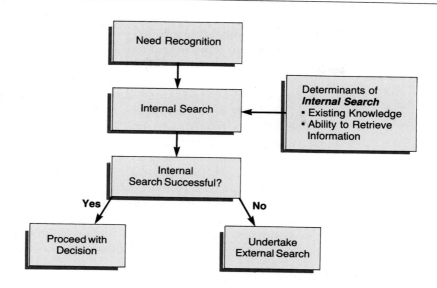

the present consumption problem is perceived to be different from those in the past.

The degree of satisfaction with prior purchases will also determine the consumer's reliance on internal search. If the consumer has been satisfied with the results of previous buying actions, then internal search may suffice.[5] Such is the case for habitual decision making, where the consumer simply remembers to buy the same brand as before.

EXTERNAL SEARCH

When internal search proves inadequate, the consumer may decide to collect additional information from the environment. External search that is driven by an upcoming purchase decision is known as **prepurchase search.** This type of external search can be contrasted with another type called **ongoing search,** where information acquisition occurs on a relatively regular basis regardless of sporadic purchase needs.[6] For example, a consumer subscribing to automotive magazines would reflect an ongoing search activity. These same magazines might also be examined during prepurchase search, but only when the consumer is in the market for a new car. The fact that the same activity

---

[5] Geoffrey C. Kiel and Roger A. Layton, "Dimensions of Consumer Information Seeking Behavior," *Journal of Marketing Research* 18 (May 1981), 233–239.
[6] Peter H. Bloch, Daniel L. Sherrell, and Nancy M. Ridgway, "Consumer Search: An Extended Framework," *Journal of Consumer Research* 13 (June 1986), 119–126.

(e.g., looking at a magazine) can occur during prepurchase and ongoing search, as well as the difficulty in establishing just when the decision process begins, pose significant problems for researchers attempting to distinguish between these two types of external search.

The primary motivation behind prepurchase search is the desire to make better consumption choices. Similarly, ongoing search may be motivated by desires to develop a knowledge base that can be used in future decision making. Ongoing search, however, may also occur simply because of the enjoyment derived from this activity. There is no denying that many consumers enjoy ongoing search for its own sake. Consumers may browse through a mall, without having specific purchase needs, simply because it is "fun" to them. A study reports that enjoyment was the driving force behind consumers' ongoing search for both clothing and personal computers.[7]

Note that ongoing search should affect the need for prepurchase search. Consumers active in ongoing search seem likely to possess greater amounts of decision-relevant information in memory, thereby lowering the amount of prepurchase search necessary for decision making.

DIMENSIONS OF SEARCH

Table 17.1 indicates that consumer search can be characterized along three main dimensions: degree, direction, and sequence. **Degree** represents the total amount of search. Search degree is reflected by the number of brands, stores, attributes, and information sources considered during search as well as the time taken in doing so. **Direction** represents the specific content of search. The emphasis here is on the particular brands and stores involved during search rather than simply the number. The third dimension, **sequence**, represents the order in which search activities occur.

DEGREE OF SEARCH   A common research finding is that many consumers engage in very little external search prior to purchase, even for major purchases involving furniture, appliances, and automobiles.[8] Indeed, these studies have found that significant numbers of consumers make major purchases after shopping at a single retailer and/or considering only one brand.

The fact that consumers sometimes engage in minimal search has led some to suggest that purchase can occur without being preceded by a decision process.[9] The problem with this view is that it fails to consider the role of

---

[7] Bloch, Sherrell, and Ridgway, "Consumer Search: An Extended Framework."

[8] John D. Claxton, Joseph N. Fry, and Bernard Portis, "A Taxonomy of Prepurchase Information Gathering Patterns," *Journal of Consumer Research* 1 (December 1974), 35–42; David H. Furse, Girish N. Punj, and David W. Stewart, "A Typology of Individual Search Strategies Among Purchasers of New Automobiles," *Journal of Consumer Research* 10 (March 1984), 417–431; Joseph W. Newman, "Consumer External Search: Amount and Determinants," in Arch G. Woodside, Jagdish N. Sheth, and Peter D. Bennett, eds., *Consumer and Industrial Buyer Behavior* (New York: North-Holland, 1977), 79–94.

[9] Richard W. Olshavsky and Donald H. Granbois, "Consumer Decision Making — Fact or Fiction?" *Journal of Consumer Research* 6 (September 1979), 93–100.

**TABLE 17.1
DIMENSIONS OF
CONSUMER
SEARCH**

Degree of Search
- How many brands are examined?
- How many stores are visited?
- How many attributes are considered?
- How many information sources are consulted?
- How much time is spent on search?

Direction of Search
- Which brands are examined?
- Which stores are visited?
- Which attributes are considered?
- Which information sources are consulted?

Sequence of Search
- In what order are brands examined?
- In what order are stores visited?
- In what order is product attribute information processed?
- In what order are information sources consulted?

internal search. As noted earlier, internal search alone may sometimes suffice in making purchase decisions. That consumers choose to rely on their existing knowledge would seem to provide inadequate grounds for suggesting that decision making has not occurred.

The degree of search is directly related to the type of decision-making process. Differences in search as a function of the decision process are summarized in Table 17.2. An extended problem-solving process will usually entail a considerable amount of search. The consumer may consider a number of brands, visit a number of stores, consult friends, and so on. At the other extreme is the habitual decision process. Here the consumer minimizes search time and effort by considering only one brand (the brand last purchased) and one attribute (brand name). Other sources of information are ignored. Uncertain, however, is the number of stores shopped, which may range from one (e.g., if the consumer is also store loyal) to several. Search under a limited problem-solving process falls between these two extremes.

The amount of search related to a particular product can greatly vary from one consumer to the next. Consequently, it is possible to segment consumers based on their level of search. A study of new car purchasers, for instance, identified the following six segments:[10]

1. A low-search group, representing 26 percent of the respondents, with below-average activity on all search dimensions, especially out-of-store search activities.

---

[10] Furse, Punj, and Stewart, "A Typology of Individual Search Strategies Among Purchasers of New Automobiles." Also see David F. Midgley, "Patterns of Interpersonal Information Seeking for the Purchase of a Symbolic Product," *Journal of Marketing Research* 20 (February 1983), 74–83.

TABLE 17.2		Decision-Making Process		
DIFFERENCES IN THE DEGREE OF SEARCH AS A FUNCTION OF THE DECISION-MAKING PROCESS	**Nature of Search**	**Extended Problem Solving**	**Limited Problem Solving**	**Habitual**
	Number of brands	Greater	Fewer	One
	Number of stores	Greater	Fewer	Unknown
	Number of attributes	Greater	Fewer	One
	Number of external information sources	Greater	Fewer	None
	Amount of time	Larger	Smaller	Minimal

2. A purchase-pal-assisted search group, representing 19 percent of the respondents.

3. A high-search group, with only 5 percent of the respondents, characterized by above-average activity on all search factors.

4. A high-self-search group, representing 12 percent of the respondents, who are above average on all out-of-store search activities in addition to the total number of visits to different car dealers.

5. A retail-shopper group comprising about 5 percent of respondents.

6. A moderate-search group, accounting for 32 percent of the respondents, characterized by moderate activity on all search factors, although slightly above average on out-of-store search activities and slightly below average on number of visits to car dealers.

Segmentation based on the degree of search can provide some insight into how search affects purchase behavior. Suppose that a car maker found that the segment characterized by very high levels of search was much more likely to buy one of the company's cars than segments which undertake less search. What implications does this finding suggest? Obviously, this segment would represent an attractive target relative to the remaining segments, given its demonstrated propensity to buy the company's products. Moreover, the company should also consider the possibility of enhancing consumers' search efforts, perhaps through advertising the potential advantages of search activity, since doing so will increase the likelihood that consumers will buy one of the company's offerings.

Even when markets are segmented on some other basis (see Chapter 22), it is still desirable to understand the search behavior of each segment. Segments that engage in considerable external search generally will be easier to reach. Marketers can feel more confident about the potential payoff of investments in advertising and in-store information. In contrast, such investments can be wasted on segments that rely on internal search. For these segments, free samples or substantial and well-publicized price discounts may be required to attract consumers.

CONSUMER IN FOCUS

17.1   THE INFLUENCE OF COMPARISON SHOPPING ON PRICE SETTING

Imagine that you are responsible for setting the prices charged by a supermarket. You have just discovered that a competitor has lowered prices on selected items. How might your response to the competitor's action depend on the level of comparison shopping undertaken by consumers? Would you be more likely to retaliate and cut prices when comparison shoppers constitute a majority of the market?

This basic issue was examined in a recent study of nearly 200 grocery executives responsible for making such pricing decisions. The executives reviewed a case situation where a competitor has cut prices for eight products and they must now decide how to respond. They are also given information about the reactions (or inactions) of other competitors as well as a recent survey of comparison shoppers. Some are told that few consumers compare prices. The rest are informed that most consumers comparison shop.

The findings revealed that the influence of consumers' comparison shopping on the executives' pricing decisions varied across the eight products. The executives recommended lower prices for "high visibility" items (e.g., soda, milk, bananas) as the amount of comparison shopping increased. In contrast, the level of comparison shopping was largely irrelevant in setting new prices for less visible items (e.g., bologna, orange juice, mayonnaise). The pricing decisions for these products were more strongly influenced by the competitors' reactions to the initial price cut.

Source: Joel E. Urbany and Peter R. Dickson, "Consumer Information, Competitive Rivalry, and Pricing in the Retail Grocery Industry," working paper, 1988.

DIRECTION OF SEARCH   While it is important to understand how much consumers search before purchase, it is equally if not more vital to examine the direction of search. Knowing which brands consumers considered during decision making would be very useful in understanding the consumer's view of a firm's competitive set. Distribution decisions could benefit from information about which stores are visited.

Marketers are especially interested in the specific product attributes that consumers examine during search. Attributes receiving considerable attention might be emphasized more strongly in promotional materials, unless, of course, they represent areas of product weaknesses. The emphasis placed on price during search can affect pricing strategies, as described in *Consumer in Focus 17.1*.

The particular information sources used during search will also influence marketing strategy. Table 17.3 indicates that information sources can be classified in terms of their source (personal versus impersonal) and type (commercial

TABLE 17.3		Impersonal	Personal
SOURCES OF INFORMATION	Commercial	Advertising In-store information	Salespeople
	Noncommercial	General purpose media	Social others

versus noncommercial). Each of these major sources is discussed subsequently.

Advertising.   Once consumers recognize a need, they generally become more receptive to advertising, which they previously might have ignored completely. Ads are then often consulted for informational purposes. Although the informative role of advertising varies between products and consumers, the following are illustrative findings:

1. Consumers make considerable use of TV ads for information on style and design.[11]

2. About 50 percent of those interviewed in one study actually purchased a product after seeing a magazine ad or a commercial for it. Information on price reduction was a major sales trigger.[12]

3. There is a distinct segment of the American public that relies heavily on advertising. They are likely to be male, young, single, and employed.[13]

4. Print and TV ads were found to be the primary information sources used in the purchase of small electrical appliances and outdoor products.[14]

The effects of advertising can be difficult to discern through questioning. People typically do not remember much about advertising unless it clearly stands out as decisive. A more definitive test is to do a field experiment, such as advertising in one market and not in another. This is expensive and methodologically demanding, but many companies will do it simply because there is no better way.

---

[11] Michael A. Houston, "Consumer Evaluations and Product Information Sources," in James H. Leigh and Claude R. Martin, Jr., eds., *Current Issues and Research in Advertising* (Ann Arbor: University of Michigan Graduate School of Business, 1979), 135–144.

[12] *A Study of Media Involvement* (New York: Magazine Publishers' Association, 1979).

[13] "Whirlpool Corporation," in Roger D. Blackwell, James F. Engel, and W. Wayne Talarzyk, *Contemporary Cases in Consumer Behavior*, rev. ed. (Hinsdale, Illinois: Dryden Press, 1984), 365–388.

[14] "Study Tracks Housewares Buying, Information Sources," *Marketing News* (October 14, 1983), 16.

In-Store Information.   As noted in Chapter 16 (see *Consumer in Focus 16.2*), many buying decisions are actually made at the point of purchase. Consequently, in-store information can have a strong influence on consumer behavior. For example, at least 40 percent of the buyers of housewares mentioned using in-store displays.[15] The informativeness of displays should increase sharply in the future as computerization becomes more common. Revlon and Estee Lauder introduced computerized displays several years ago, as it was found that consumers often want answers to questions that might be embarrassing to raise with a frequently ill-informed sales clerk. Hence, the display allows immediate feedback to these questions.

Package labels are often consulted, and, at times, the effects of this information source can be substantial. For example, nutritional labeling tends to improve consumer perception of such attributes as "wholesome" and "tender."[16] It has also been found that strictly promotional terms such as "sweet" and "succulent" leave people with an assurance of quality comparable to that of the more detailed nutritional data. This shows how easy it is for deception to take place.

On the other hand, there is growing evidence that labels are not used as thoroughly as was previously thought. At times, they are misperceived, used only in part, or disregarded altogether.[17] This is a particularly disturbing finding when the content consists of safety warnings or precautions. Moreover, consumers with lower socioeconomic status make less use of package information and vice versa — just the opposite of what policy makers usually intend.[18] Figure 17.5 contains an ad that may affect consumer search by encouraging consumers to read the product label.

Salespeople.   A number of situations exist in which personal selling still plays an important role, even in this era of mass merchandising. It becomes especially crucial when there is the necessity of some type of point-of-sale negotiation and information exchange between buyer and seller. The energy-use labeling program for major appliances, for instance, was found to be ineffective without the input from sales personnel to explain just what the

---

[15] "Study Tracks Housewares Buying, Information Sources."

[16] Edward H. Asam and Louis P. Bucklin, "Nutritional Labeling for Canned Goods: A Study of Consumer Response," *Journal of Marketing* 37 (April 1973), 32–37.

[17] Gary T. Ford and Philip G. Kuehl, "Label Warning Messages in OTC Drug Advertising: An Experimental Examination of FTC Policy-Making," in James H. Leigh and Claude R. Martin, Jr., eds., *Current Issues and Research in Advertising* (Ann Arbor: University of Michigan Graduate School of Business, 1979), 115–128; Lorna Opatow, "How Consumers 'Use' Labels of OTC Drugs," *American Druggist* 177 (March 1978), 10ff; and Jo-Ann Zybtniewski, "Keeping Pace with the Nutrition Race," *Progressive Grocer* 59 (July 1980), 29.

[18] James McCullough and Roger Best, "Consumer Preference for Food Label Information: A Basis for Segmentation," *Journal of Consumer Affairs* 14 (Summer 1980), 180–192.

FIGURE 17.5
ENCOURAGING
CONSUMERS TO
EXAMINE PRODUCT
LABELS

It's time we stop taking yogurt for granted. Because while we've been peacefully eating what we thought was completely pure and natural, some yogurt makers have been adding things, like artificial flavorings, artificial colorings, agar, modified food starch and sorbic acid. Maybe it's time we start reading labels again.

NO ARTIFICIAL ANYTHING.

Source: Courtesy of The Dannon Company, Inc.

ratings meant.[19] The druggist remains an important information source on various aspects of health care and medication usage.[20]

Consumers' reliance on the opinions of salespeople should be considered in developing promotional strategy. A basic decision confronting marketers is the relative emphasis they should place on **push** versus **pull strategies.** A pull strategy involves the manufacturer creating product demand by appealing to the ultimate consumer, who, in turn, will encourage the channel to carry

---

[19] John D. Claxton and C. Dennis Anderson, "Energy Information at the Point of Sale: A Field Experiment," in Jerry C. Olson, ed., *Advances in Consumer Research* 7 (Ann Arbor: Association for Consumer Research, 1980), 277–282.

[20] "Public Goes on Strong 'Self-Medication Kick,'" *Marketing News* (June 27, 1980), 1.

the product. Under a push strategy, manufacturers focus their selling efforts on the channel, which is then responsible for attracting consumers. This latter strategy makes more sense when the salesperson represents an important source of information.

General Purpose Media. The mass media frequently contain items of interest to those in the midst of the decision process. Some purchasers of houseware items, for example, reported that editorial articles in magazines and newspapers proved helpful.[21] Governmental agencies also generate a wealth of consumer relevant information.

Various product-rating agencies have risen to the forefront in recent years, the most widely known being Consumers' Union, which publishes *Consumer Reports*. A number of manufacturers have found, frequently to their dismay, that ratings by such agencies can have a potent effect, especially if the ratings are negative.[22]

Social Others. As seen in Chapters 5 and 6, social others such as friends and family can serve as significant sources of information. In a 1984 survey by J. D. Power and Associates, an automotive market research firm, two-thirds of new car buyers reported that their decision concerning which make of car to buy was most strongly influenced by their social contacts.[23]

SEQUENCE OF SEARCH The final search dimension, sequence, focuses on the order of search activities. Researchers have been particularly interested in the order in which product-attribute information is acquired.[24] When confronted with a set of brands described along several attributes, consumers may follow a **brand search sequence** (often referred to as **processing by brand),** where each brand is examined along the various attributes before search proceeds to the next brand. Alternatively, an **attribute search sequence** (or **processing by attribute)** may occur, in which brand information is collected on an attribute-by-attribute basis. For example, a consumer might first examine

---

[21] "Study Tracks Housewares Buying, Information Sources."

[22] Mark G. Weinberger and William R. Dillon, "The Effects of Unfavorable Product Rating Information," in Jerry C. Olson, ed., *Advances in Consumer Research* 7 (Ann Arbor: Association for Consumer Research, 1980), 528–532.

[23] Cited in Bloch, Sherrell, and Ridgway, "Consumer Search: An Extended Framework," p. 121.

[24] See James R. Bettman and Jacob Jacoby, "Patterns of Processing in Consumer Information Processing," in Beverlee B. Anderson, ed., *Advances in Consumer Research* 3 (Ann Arbor: Association for Consumer Research, 1976), 315–320; James R. Bettman and Pradeep Kakkar, "Effects of Information Presentation Format on Consumer Information Acquisition Strategies," *Journal of Consumer Research* 3 (March 1977), 233–240; James R. Bettman and C. Whan Park, "Effects of Prior Knowledge and Experience and Phase of the Choice Process on Consumer Decision Processes: A Protocol Analysis," *Journal of Consumer Research* 7 (December 1980), 243–248; Itamar Simonson, Joel Huber, and John Payne, "The Relationship Between Prior Brand Knowledge and Information Acquisition Order," *Journal of Consumer Research* 14 (March 1988), 566–578.

each brand's price, followed by an inspection of each brand's warranty. The sequence in which product-attribute information is acquired is an important property of the choice rules we consider in the following chapter.

The information source consumers consult at the beginning of external search may partly determine consumption behavior. A study of consumers' appliance shopping behavior reports that those buying from Sears were most likely to begin their search process by consulting either newspaper ads or catalogs.[25] Purchases made at furniture stores, however, were most likely to start with discussing the situation with a friend or relative. Different sources can guide the consumer along different purchase paths.

DETERMINANTS OF SEARCH

A considerable amount of research has accumulated regarding the variety of factors that influence search. Some of these determinants are discussed next.

SITUATIONAL DETERMINANTS   The manner in which situational forces can affect consumer decision making is considered in Chapter 7. As we note there, the information environment will play a significant role in shaping consumer behavior. External search is obviously constrained by the availability and quantity of information in the marketplace. Even the format in which information is presented can alter search behavior, as reflected by consumers' greater use of unit price information when presented on lists (see *Consumer in Focus 7.2*).[26]

Time pressures are another source of situational influence.[27] A refrigerator stuffed with food that breaks down beyond repair affords the consumer little time to pursue an extensive and deliberate search.

PRODUCT DETERMINANTS   Features of the product can affect consumer search. The degree of product differentiation is very important. If consumers believe that all brands are essentially the same, then there is little need for extensive search. As brands become more distinct, then the potential payoff from search grows larger. However, such perceived differences must also be coupled with an uncertainty as to which brand is "best." For example, if consumers believe that a given brand offers the lowest prices, then they are

[25] William L. Wilkie and Peter R. Dickson, "Shopping for Appliances: Consumers' Strategies and Patterns of Information Search," Marketing Science Institute Working Paper No. 85–108, 1985.

[26] J. Edward Russo, "The Value of Unit Price Information," *Journal of Marketing Research* 14 (May 1977), 193–201; J. Edward Russo, Gene Krieser, and Sally Miyashita, "An Effective Display of Unit Price Information," *Journal of Marketing* 39 (April 1975), 11–19.

[27] Sharon E. Beatty and Scott M. Smith, "External Search Effort: An Investigation Across Several Product Categories," *Journal of Consumer Research* 14 (June 1987), 83–95; William L. Moore and Donald R. Lehmann, "Individual Differences in Search Behavior for a Nondurable," *Journal of Consumer Research* 7 (December 1980), 296–307.

unlikely to undertake price comparisons regardless of how much difference they perceive in the prices of competing brands.

Product price is another factor.[28] Higher prices will create greater concerns about the financial risks involved with the purchase, which in turn leads to greater search.

The stability of a product category may affect search. Experienced consumers can rely more heavily on their existing knowledge for categories (e.g., milk, garden hoses, cigarettes) that change little relatively over time. In contrast, unstable categories characterized by product innovations or price changes (e.g., personal computers, electronic games) may require consumers to "update" their knowledge through search.[29]

RETAIL DETERMINANTS   The retail environment will also influence consumer search. The distance between retail competitors can determine the number of stores consumers shop during decision making. Fewer stores will be visited as distance increases.

The similarity among retailers is another source of influence. Search is more likely when consumers perceive important differences across retailers.[30] This is particularly true when retailers differ in the prices charged for products.[31] Again, however, there must also be uncertainty about which store is best before perceptions of store differences will affect search.

CONSUMER DETERMINANTS   Characteristics of the consumer strongly determine search behavior. Some of the more important determinants are discussed subsequently.

Knowledge.   Knowledge can have both inhibiting and facilitating effects on search behavior. It can allow the consumer to rely more heavily on internal search during decision making, thereby lowering the need for prepurchase search. Consequently, knowledge or prior purchase experience is often found to have a negative relationship with external search.[32]

---

[28] Kiel and Layton, "Dimensions of Consumer Information Seeking Behavior."

[29] Joel E. Urbany and Peter R. Dickson, "Information Search in the Retail Grocery Market," working paper, The Ohio State University, 1987.

[30] Calvin P. Duncan and Richard W. Olshavsky, "External Search: The Role of Consumer Beliefs," *Journal of Marketing Research* 19 (February 1982), 32–43.

[31] Joel E. Urbany, "An Experimental Examination of the Economics of Information," *Journal of Consumer Research* 13 (September 1986), 257–271.

[32] Beatty and Smith, "External Search Effort: An Investigation Across Several Product Categories"; Kiel and Layton, "Dimensions of Consumer Information Seeking Behavior"; Moore and Lehmann, "Individual Differences in Search Behavior for a Nondurable"; Joseph W. Newman and Richard Staelin, "Prepurchase Information Seeking for New Cars and Major Household Appliances," *Journal of Marketing Research* 9 (August 1972), 249–257; Girish N. Punj and Richard Staelin, "A Model of Consumer Information Search Behavior for New Automobiles," *Journal of Consumer Research* 9 (March 1983), 366–380.

Alternatively, knowledge can enhance search, primarily by affording more effective utilization of newly acquired information. When consumers feel more confident about their ability to judge products, they will typically acquire more information.[33] Research has, therefore, found that knowledge may be related positively to external search.[34]

These positive and negative influences may combine to produce an inverted-U relationship between knowledge and external search.[35] Consumers possessing extremely limited knowledge (e.g., first-time buyers) may feel incompetent to undertake an elaborate search and analysis. Instead, they may try to solve their consumption problem by relying on others. For example, in the "purchase-pal" car buying segment described earlier in the chapter, these inexperienced and unconfident consumers depended very heavily on the opinions of others (e.g., dad) in making their decisions. Similarly, many first-time appliance buyers may decide to place their faith in the salesperson of a trusted retailer (e.g., Sears).

Greater prepurchase search should occur for moderately informed consumers. They will possess sufficient knowledge to explore and understand the information environment. However, their knowledge is not so great that they feel comfortable relying heavily on memory. In contrast, a stronger reliance on memory may take place for those possessing high levels of relevant knowledge. Internal search may uncover most, if not all, of the information desired for decision making, thus leading to little prepurchase search for very knowledgeable consumers.[36]

Involvement.   Search will also depend on the level of consumer involvement with the product and decision process. Product involvement, which reflects a more enduring interest in the product than that stimulated by purchase requirements, should exert a strong influence on ongoing search.[37] Prepurchase search, by contrast, will depend more heavily on consumers' involvement with the purchase decision stemming from their perceptions of the economic and psychological risks associated with product purchase. In both cases, higher involvement should lead to greater search.[38]

One tactic that consumers frequently employ for low-involvement pur-

---

[33] Duncan and Olshavsky, "External Search: The Role of Consumer Beliefs."

[34] Merrie Brucks, "The Effects of Product Class Knowledge on Information Search Behavior," *Journal of Consumer Research* 12 (June 1985), 1–16; Jacob Jacoby, Robert W. Chestnut, and William A. Fisher, "A Behavioral Process Approach to Information Acquisition in Nondurable Purchasing," *Journal of Marketing Research* 15 (November 1978), 532–544.

[35] Bettman and Park, "Effects of Prior Knowledge and Experience and Phase of the Choice Process on Consumer Decision Processes: A Protocol Analysis."

[36] Knowledge can also affect the sequence of search. See Simonson, Huber, and Payne, "The Relationship Between Prior Brand Knowledge and Information Acquisition."

[37] Block, Sherrell, and Ridgway, "Consumer Search: An Extended Framework."

[38] Beatty and Smith, "External Search Effort: An Investigation Across Several Product Categories"; Judith Lynne Zaichkowsky, "Measuring the Involvement Construct," *Journal of Consumer Research* 12 (December 1985), 341–352.

chases is the use of product trial as a "substitute" for prepurchase search. Such is the case for many of the new products that find their way onto the grocer's shelves. Given the relatively low cost of these items, consumers will often decide that the most efficient utilization of their resources is to simply "buy it and try it." However, when consumers are highly involved with the purchase decision, a substantial amount of search may be undertaken in order to develop the conviction desired by consumers that they are making a good choice.

Beliefs and Attitudes.   Search behavior, just like purchase behavior, is affected by consumers' beliefs and attitudes. Consumers engage in more search as their attitudes toward shopping become more favorable.[39] Moreover, search will tend to focus initially on brands with high prior attractiveness.[40]

The beliefs held by consumers are also important determinants.[41] Perceptions regarding the costs versus benefits of search play a major role in guiding search.[42] Consumers will usually invest more effort into search when the perceived benefits of this activity grow and the costs decline.

This cost–benefit view of search plays an important role in Wilkie and Dickson's model of appliance shopping behavior reproduced in Figure 17.6. Following need recognition (called "precipitating purchase circumstance" in their model), the consumer is seen as developing some preliminary specifications for the product purchase (e.g., must be under $400). A store is then visited, perhaps because it is currently promoting sale prices. At this point a salesperson might influence the consumer to modify his initial specifications. If the "best" alternative (i.e., the one coming closest to meeting the consumer's specifications) available at the store is exactly what the consumer wants, search will end and purchase takes place. If not, the consumer must then decide on the relative costs versus benefits of continued search.

Demographic Characteristics.   Research indicates that search may be related to several demographic characteristics.[43] Age is negatively related to search. Older consumers can call upon their greater experience. They may also be more brand loyal than their younger counterparts.

Higher-income consumers search less than lower-income consumers.

---

[39] Beatty and Smith, "External Search Effort: An Investigation Across Several Product Categories"; Punj and Staelin, "A Model of Consumer Information Search Behavior for New Automobiles."

[40] Simonson, Huber, and Payne, "The Relationship Between Prior Brand Knowledge and Information Acquisition Order."

[41] Duncan and Olshavsky, "External Search: The Role of Consumer Beliefs"; Deborah Roedder John, Carol A. Scott, and James R. Bettman, "Sampling Data for Covariation Assessment: The Effect of Prior Beliefs on Search Patterns," *Journal of Consumer Research* 13 (June 1986), 38–47.

[42] Urbany, "An Experimental Investigation of the Economics of Information."

[43] For a brief review of the literature concerning demographics and search, see Beatty and Smith, "External Search Effort: An Investigation Across Several Product Categories."

FIGURE 17.6
A DYNAMIC-ADAPTIVE MODEL OF APPLIANCE SHOPPING BEHAVIOR

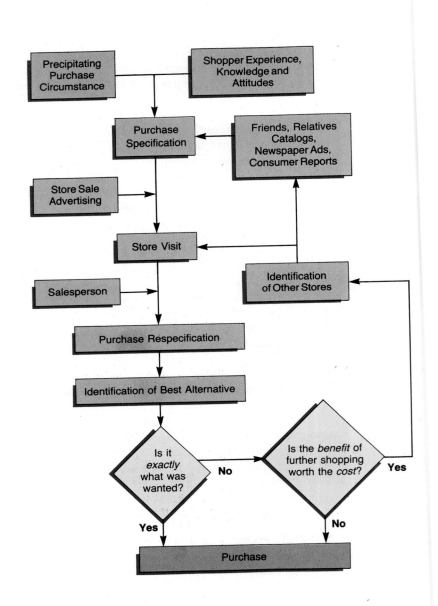

Source: William L. Wilkie and Peter R. Dickson, "Shopping for Appliances: Consumers' Strategies and Patterns of Information Search," Marketing Science Institute Working Paper No. 85–108, 1985, Figure 2. Used with permission.

Higher-income consumers presumably value their time more highly, which increases search costs. Higher costs will reduce search.[44]

A positive relationship usually occurs between education and search. More educated consumers seem likely to have greater confidence in their ability to use search effectively. Such confidence will enhance search behavior.[45]

MEASURING INFORMATION SEARCH

There are basically two main approaches to measuring consumer search: **retrospective questioning** and **observation.**

RETROSPECTIVE QUESTIONING   One of the most popular methods is simply to ask consumers to recall their search activities during decision making. This can be done through surveys and store exit interviews. Also, specifically designed warranty registration cards can be useful for this purpose.

Although this method finds widespread use, it suffers from the obvious limitation of reliance on recall. Unless the purchase is highly involving and recently made, it is probable that many details of the search process will be forgotten.

OBSERVATION   To a limited degree observation of information use has been tried in a retail setting.[46] It is nearly impossible to do in a home while preserving any degree of normality of behavior. Evidence thus far indicates that the incidences of actual information seeking are higher when they are observed than when indicated by a reliance on retrospective questioning.[47]

Summary

The decision process begins when a need is activated and recognized because of a discrepancy between the consumer's desired state and actual situation. Need recognition can be triggered by a number of factors. Changes in one's personal circumstances, such as the birth of a child, can activate new needs.

---

[44] John, Scott, and Bettman, "Sampling Data for Covariation Assessment: The Effect of Prior Beliefs on Search Patterns"; Urbany, "An Experimental Investigation of the Economics of Information."

[45] Duncan and Olshavsky, "External Search: The Role of Consumer Beliefs."

[46] Wayne D. Hoyer, "An Examination of Consumer Decision Making for a Common Repeat Purchase Product," *Journal of Consumer Research* 11 (December 1984), 822–829; Joseph W. Newman and Bradley D. Lockman, "Measuring Prepurchase Information Seeking," *Journal of Consumer Research* 11 (December 1975), 216–222.

[47] Newman and Lockman, "Measuring Prepurchase Information Seeking."

Marketers can also influence the likelihood of need activation through advertising and product innovations.

Search for potential need satisfiers will occur following need recognition. If an internal search of memory provides a satisfactory solution to the consumption problem, then it will be unnecessary for consumers to seek information from their environment. Often, however, some degree of external search will be necessary. Just how much search will occur varies across consumers and depends on a host of situational, marketplace, and consumer characteristics.

Not all external search is driven by an immediate purchase need. Indeed, some consumers continually engage in ongoing search activities as a result of their involvement with the product category.

Consumer search can serve as an important determinant of marketing strategy. How much consumers search and the particular sources consulted during search can help shape a firm's pricing, promotion, and distribution strategies.

REVIEW AND DISCUSSION QUESTIONS

1. Discuss how need recognition triggered your last soft drink purchase. Was this different from need recognition leading to purchase of new shoes? What role, if any, do you feel marketing efforts played in both situations?

2. How did need recognition underlie your decision to attend college or graduate school?

3. Referring again to question 2, describe how your institution could have influenced your need recognition through its marketing efforts.

4. Assume that you are a consultant to a national manufacturer of air conditioners. Your firm has 20 percent of the market. The remainder is divided among seven competitors. Your firm wants to stimulate need recognition among those who own second homes for vacation and weekend purposes. What are your recommendations concerning, first of all, the desirability of such a strategy and, secondly, the techniques that should be used for this purpose?

5. What effect do you believe ongoing search has on consumers' use of internal search during decision making?

6. Explain how each of the following factors might affect consumer search: (a) brand loyalty, (b) store loyalty, (c) uncertainty about which brand best meets consumers' needs, and (d) the importance consumers place on paying a low price.

7. Consider two alternative target segments that differ only in their propensity for information search. One segment undertakes a substantial amount of external search during decision making. In contrast, consumers in the remaining segment are far less active in their search behaviors. Which segment, if either, would be a better target market? Assuming both were targeted, how could marketing activities differ in pursuing each segment?

8. The results of a consumer research project have just arrived on your desk. This study examined whether target consumers' brand preferences at the time of need recognition carried over to actual purchase. Consumers just beginning their decision

process were asked about their preferences for the company's brand and two competitors. These results as well as each brand's share of purchase are presented below.

Brand	Consumers Preference at Time of Need Recognition	Share of Purchases
Company's brand	50%	30%
Competitor A	30%	50%
Competitor B	20%	20%
Total	100%	100%

What conclusions would you reach from this information?

ALTERNATIVE EVALUATION

C AUTO SAFETY: THE NEW SELLING POINT

an safety sell automobiles? For years the industry has said no. Support for this opinion could be found in Ford's unsuccessful 1956 advertising campaign stressing safety. That year, Ford watched as archrival Chevrolet, which went with a more traditional marketing approach, widened its sales lead from less than 70,000 cars in 1955 to nearly 200,000 in 1956.

Now, however, U.S. automakers are singing a different tune. "You won't hear any more beefs about air bags from me," crows a two-page newspaper ad from Chrysler Chairman Lee Iacocca, a one-time air-bag opponent who is now pledging to put them on all of his U.S.-built cars by 1990. General Motors is running ads playing up the formation of an in-house medical team dedicated to crash-injury research. Ford has launched a major ad campaign which depicts the company as a worldwide leader in automotive safety.

Automakers are also developing and testing a number of safety features that can be added to their products. Air bags, anti-lock brake systems, automatic seat belts, and four-wheel steering are options currently available for some cars. A limited-edition version of the 1989 Oldsmobile Cutlass Supreme will offer a digital readout of the car's speed onto the windshield (a technology borrowed from military fighter planes) so the driver can check it without looking away from the road. Meanwhile, Ford and GM are testing collision-avoidance systems that would warn a driver when vehicles behind the car get too close.

Why have automakers changed their tune? "Our research indicates that safety is the second most important consumer want," says James O'Connor, executive director of Ford's marketing staff. "The first is dependability-quality-reliability grouped together, but safety comes up second. So it's something that I think we should concentrate on."

The importance placed on safety by consumers is clearly reflected in Volkswagen's recent difficulties with its Audi 5000s automobiles. A number of complaints and lawsuits were filed by owners based on the claim that the car would suddenly accelerate on its own, even if the person's foot was on the brake. Fueled by a report on the CBS news program "60 Minutes," sales plummeted. In Audi's defense, a report by the National Highway Traffic Safety Administration suggests that the drivers probably stepped on the accelerator instead of the brake.

Adapted from: Joseph B. White, "U.S. Auto Makers Decide Safety Sells," *Wall Street Journal* (August 24, 1988), 17; Dave Zola, "Forget 1956; Ford Stresses Safety in New Ad Campaign," *Automotive News* (December 1, 1986), 14.
Additional Sources: Edward Giltenan, "Safer Driving," *Forbes* (February 9, 1987), 116–117; Ron Lietzke, "Audi Dealers 'Vindicated,' " *The Columbus Dispatch* (March 9, 1989), E1; "Can Audi Fix a Dented Image?" *Business Week* (November 17, 1986), 81–82; "Revving Without a Cause: When the Car Has a Mind of Its Own," *Business Week* (April 4, 1988), 66, 68.

The chapter opener aptly illustrates how the importance consumers place on product features in evaluating choice alternatives will affect a company's product offerings and marketing focus. This chapter examines the third stage of our consumer decision-making model, alternative evaluation. **Alternative evaluation** can be defined as the process by which a choice alternative is evaluated and selected to meet consumer needs. Although we have presented search and alternative evaluation as "separate" stages for pedagogical reasons, the reader should recognize that the two stages are intricately intertwined during decision making. The acquisition of product information from the environment, for instance, will normally lead to some evaluation that may then guide subsequent search.

The complexity of alternative evaluation will vary dramatically depending on the particular process consumers follow in making their consumption decisions. When decision making is habitual in nature, alternative evaluation will simply involve the consumer forming an intention to repurchase the same product as before. Similarly, consumers lacking the knowledge needed for selecting an appropriate medicinal product may rely on the pharmacist's recommendations rather than try to decide for themselves. Under this scenario, alternative evaluation consists of the rather simple decision rule, "Buy what the expert recommends."

Sometimes alternative evaluation will be quite complex, as in the case of an experienced car buyer wishing to purchase a second family car. Figure

FIGURE 18.1
BASIC
COMPONENTS OF
THE ALTERNATIVE
EVALUATION
PROCESS

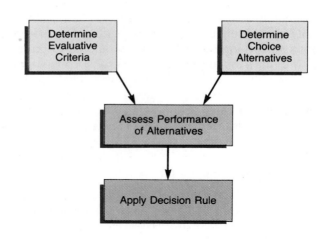

18.1 depicts the basic components of the alternative evaluation process. Decisions must be made initially about which choice alternatives to consider and the evaluative criteria (i.e., dimensions or attributes) to use in judging the alternatives. The relative performance of the considered alternatives along the evaluative criteria must then be judged. A decision rule is then applied to these judgments in order to select a particular alternative. In the following sections we examine more fully these components of the alternative evaluation process.

EVALUATIVE CRITERIA

Evaluative criteria are nothing more than the particular dimensions or attributes that are used in judging the choice alternatives. Evaluative criteria come in many forms. In purchasing a car, consumers may consider factors such as safety, reliability, price, brand name, country of origin (i.e., where it is made), warranty, and gas mileage. The consumer may also consider evaluative criteria more hedonic in nature, such as the feelings that come from owning (e.g., prestige, status) and driving (e.g., exhilaration, excitement) the car. Although it is beyond the scope of this text to provide a detailed review of the various evaluative criteria used by consumers, a couple deserve special comment.

PRICE

Certainly one of the more important evaluative criteria is price. Indeed, we have all experienced situations in which our product choice was heavily affected by pricing considerations. Nonetheless, there is considerable variation in the importance of price across both consumers and products.[1] Consequently, consumers' price sensitivity is often used as a basis for market segmentation.

Note, however, that the role of price is often overrated. Consumers are not always looking for the lowest possible price or even the best price-to-quality ratio; other factors such as convenience or brand name may assume greater importance.[2] In addition, consumers frequently reveal little consideration of price when making decisions. In one study, for example, 25 percent of those interviewed did not know the price of the brand of toothpaste they had just purchased relative to other brands.[3]

BRAND NAME

Brand name frequently emerges as a determinant criterion, as it did in a study of purchasing behavior involving dress shirts and suits.[4] It also proved to be significant in choosing over-the-counter drugs.[5] In these cases the brand name appears to serve as a surrogate indicator of product quality, and its importance seems to vary with the ease by which quality can be judged objectively. If it is difficult to judge quality, the consumer sometimes will perceive a high level of risk in the purchase.[6] Thus, reliance on a well-known brand name with a reputation of long-standing quality can be an effective way of reducing risk.

For example, in the case of headache and cold remedies, the average consumer cannot judge purity and quality. Consequently, brand name becomes especially crucial as a surrogate indicator of quality. It is such a dominant factor with many consumers that they will pay many times more for a brand name aspirin, even though they are aware that government regulations require all aspirin products to contain the same basic therapeutic formulation.[7]

---

[1] Andre Gabor and C. W. J. Granger, "Price Sensitivity of the Consumer," *Journal of Advertising Research* 4 (December 1964), 40–44; Joel Huber, Morris B. Holbrook, and Barbara Kahn, "Effects of Competitive Context and of Additional Information on Price Sensitivity," *Journal of Marketing Research* 23 (August 1986), 250–260.

[2] Huber, Holbrook, and Kahn, "Effects of Competitive Context and of Additional Information on Price Sensitivity"; Kent B. Monroe, "Buyer's Subjective Perceptions of Price," *Journal of Marketing Research* 10 (February 1973), 70–80.

[3] George Haines, "A Study of Why People Purchase New Products," in R. M. Haas, ed., *Science, Technology and Marketing* (Chicago: American Marketing Association, 1966), 665–685. Also see Peter R. Dickson and Alan G. Sawyer, "Point-of-Purchase Behavior and Price Perceptions of Supermarket Shoppers," Marketing Science Institute, Working Paper No. 86–102, 1986.

[4] David M. Gardner, "Is There a Generalized Price-Quality Relationship?" *Journal of Marketing Research* 8 (May 1971), 241–243.

[5] J. F. Engel, D. A. Knapp, and D. E. Knapp, "Sources of Influence in the Acceptance of New Products for Self-Medication: Preliminary Findings," in R. M. Haas, ed., *Science, Technology and Marketing* (Chicago: American Marketing Association, 1966), 776–782.

[6] Raymond A. Bauer, "Consumer Behavior as Risk Taking," in Robert S. Hancock, ed., *Dynamic Marketing in a Changing World* (Chicago: American Marketing Association, 1960), 389–398.

[7] Engel, Knapp, and Knapp, "Sources of Influence."

18.1   CONSIDERATION OF IMPORTS VERSUS AMERICAN IN NEW CAR BUYING

Are there differences in the likelihood that a car would be considered for purchase depending on its country-of-origin? The answer, based on a survey of 1,000 American households by Market Facts, a Chicago-based market research firm, is a definite yes. Nearly 90% of the respondents indicated that they would either definitely or probably consider an American-built car if they were shopping today. This percentage drops to 32% for Japanese autos and 27% for European cars.

Further analysis revealed that consumers' receptiveness to imports varied by age. Younger consumers were more likely to consider imports than their older counterparts. Whereas less than 10% of those 55 or older would consider a European auto, nearly 40% of those under 35 would do so. Similarly, Japanese cars registered a 17% consideration rate among the 55 and older segment, compared to 43% among consumers under 35. These demographic differences suggest that American manufacturers can anticipate even greater competition from imports as time passes due to the greater receptiveness of younger consumers.

Source: Larry Levin, "New Car Buying: Imports vs. American," *TeleNation Reports* (Fall 1987), 2.

COUNTRY OF ORIGIN

In this age of intensifying international competition and the loss of many manufacturing jobs to cheaper foreign labor, it is not surprising that the country in which a product is produced has become an important consideration among many American consumers.[8] *Consumer in Focus 18.1* describes the results of a recent study on the importance consumers would place on country of origin in buying a new car. Many companies have tried to capitalize upon this concern by emphasizing the fact that their product is "Made in the U.S.A." (see Figure 18.2).

THE SALIENCE OF EVALUATIVE CRITERIA

The concept of **salience** reflects the notion that evaluative criteria often differ in their influence on consumers' product selections. Some criteria will have a greater impact than others. Salience refers to the *potential* influence each dimension may exert during the comparison process and is often measured

---

[8] Johny K. Johansson, Susan P. Douglas, and Ikujiro Nonaka, "Assessing the Impact of Country of Origin on Product Evaluations: A New Methodological Perspective," *Journal of Marketing Research* 22 (November 1985), 388–396.

FIGURE 18.2
PROMOTING
THE PRODUCT'S
COUNTRY
OF ORIGIN

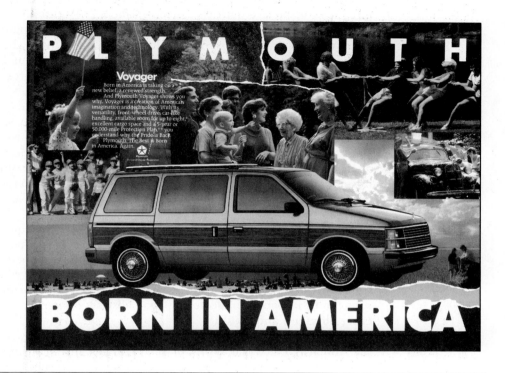

Source: Courtesy of Plymouth, Chrysler Corporation.

in terms of importance (e.g., How important is price in the purchase of a brand of toothpaste?).

Sometimes a salient evaluative criterion does not influence the evaluation process. This occurs when the alternatives under consideration perform equally well (or poorly) on this criterion. Consumers may rate price as a very important attribute, but if all brands cost the same amount, the impact of price essentially drops out. Salient attributes that actually influence the evaluation process (i.e., attributes on which alternatives differ) are known as **determinant attributes.**[9]

DETERMINANTS OF EVALUATIVE CRITERIA

The particular evaluative criteria used by consumers during decision making will depend on a number of factors. Some of these are discussed below.

[9] Mark I. Alpert, "Identification of Determinant Attributes: A Comparison of Methods," *Journal of Marketing Research* 8 (May 1971), 184–191.

SITUATIONAL INFLUENCES   Situational factors will often have an important influence on an evaluative criterion's salience.[10] Location convenience, for example, often assumes greater importance in the selection of a fast-food restaurant when the consumer is pressed for time than when time is not a factor. Similarly, many consumers will select a prestigious brand of liquor when it is to be served at a party but will opt for a less prestigious (and less expensive) brand for their own private use.

SIMILARITY OF CHOICE ALTERNATIVES   The similarity or comparability of alternatives from which consumers choose can vary substantially. A consumer deciding how to spend a tax refund may be considering such diverse alternatives as buying a new wardrobe, taking a vacation, or putting the money in the bank. Much greater similarity among choice alternatives will exist, on the other hand, for decisions about which brand to purchase within a product category.

Decisions involving noncomparable alternatives may require the consumer to employ more abstract evaluative criteria during alternative evaluation.[11] Consider, for instance, the consumer faced with choosing between a refrigerator, a television, and a stereo. These alternatives share few concrete attributes (price is an exception) along which comparisons can be made directly. Comparisons can be undertaken, however, using abstract dimensions such as necessity, entertainment, and status.

Consumers' reliance on price during decision making can be affected by the similarity of choice alternatives. If, for instance, consumers believe that all lawn care companies will provide essentially the same basic service and benefits, then they will depend much more heavily on price differences in making a choice. In general, price becomes more important in the absence of meaningful product differentiation.

MOTIVATION   As noted in Chapter 9, a basic distinction in understanding motivation is whether consumers are driven by utilitarian versus hedonic considerations. The presence of such motivations will determine the type of evaluative criteria likely to be used during alternative evaluation. Utilitarian motivations during the purchase of athletic shoes could lead to examination of a shoe's price and construction, whereas hedonic motivations might lead to consideration of the feelings that come from product ownership and usage (e.g., the person who buys Nike in order to project a desirable image).

---

[10] Peter R. Dickson, "Person-Situation: Segmentation's Missing Link," *Journal of Marketing* 6 (Fall 1982), 56–64; Kenneth E. Miller and James L. Ginter, "An Investigation of Situational Variation in Brand Choice Behavior and Attitude," *Journal of Marketing Research* 16 (February 1979), 111–123.

[11] James R. Bettman and Mita Sujan, "Effects of Framing on Evaluation of Comparable and Noncomparable Alternatives by Expert and Novice Consumers," *Journal of Consumer Research* 14 (September 1987), 141–154; Michael D. Johnson, "Consumer Choice Strategies for Comparing Noncomparable Alternatives," *Journal of Consumer Research* 11 (December 1984), 741–753.

INVOLVEMENT   Consumers' involvement with the decision will influence the number of evaluative criteria used in alternative evaluation. A greater number of evaluative criteria are likely to enter into the decision as involvement increases.[12]

Involvement may also influence the relative salience of evaluative criteria. A recent study of the evaluative criteria used by Iowa farmers in selecting a retail outlet for supplies found that highly involved decision makers were more concerned with service attributes, whereas those less involved focused on low price and a retailer's size and reputation.[13]

KNOWLEDGE   Knowledge can have several effects on consumers' use of evaluative criteria. Knowledgeable consumers will have information stored in memory about the dimensions useful for comparing choice alternatives. This information is much less likely to exist in the memory of novices. Consequently, novices will be much more susceptible to external influences that attempt to shape the particular criteria used during decision making.[14] For example, advertisements that suggest the evaluative criteria that consumers should consider, such as the Sony ad appearing in Figure 18.3, are likely to be more effective in this regard for first-time buyers.

Knowledge can also determine consumers' use of particular evaluative criteria. Consumers may rely much more heavily on brand name or others' recommendations, for instance, when they lack the knowledge necessary for directly evaluating product quality.

MEASURING EVALUATIVE CRITERIA

Because of the necessity for understanding the evaluative criteria used by consumers, the issue of measurement becomes quite important. Two important measurement objectives are (1) identifying salient evaluative criteria and (2) estimating the relative salience of each.

IDENTIFYING EVALUATIVE CRITERIA   The most obvious and popular approach for identifying salient criteria is to ask directly what considerations

---

[12] Michael L. Rothschild, "Advertising Strategies for High and Low Involvement Situations," in John C. Maloney and Bernard Silverman, eds., *Attitude Research Plays for High Stakes* (Chicago: American Marketing Association, 1979), 74–93; Michael L. Rothschild and Michael J. Houston, "The Consumer Involvement Matrix: Some Preliminary Findings," in Barnett A. Greenberg and Danny N. Bellenger, eds., *Contemporary Marketing Thoughts* (Chicago: American Marketing Association, 1977), 95–98.

[13] Dennis H. Gensch and Rajshekhar G. Javalgi, "The Influence of Involvement on Disaggregate Attribute Choice Models," *Journal of Consumer Research* 14 (June 1987), 71–82.

[14] Bettman and Sujan, "Effects of Framing on Evaluation of Comparable and Noncomparable Alternatives by Expert and Novice Consumers"; Peter Wright and Peter D. Rip, "Product Class Advertising Effects in First-Time Buyers' Decision Strategies," *Journal of Consumer Research* 7 (September 1980), 176–188.

**FIGURE 18.3
PROMOTING
PARTICULAR
EVALUATIVE
CRITERIA THROUGH
ADVERTISING**

Source: © 1984 Sony Corporation of America.

or product attributes are used during decision making. The assumption is made that the individual is aware of salient criteria and will state them when asked. Those attributes receiving the most frequent mention or highest ranking are considered to be the most important.

Sometimes, however, the consumer will not give the true reasons for a choice when asked directly.[15] People may distort their answers simply because of their concerns over what others may think of them. For instance, consumers may underreport their use of price as a criterion because they do not want to be perceived as cheap.

One proposed remedy is to elicit a third-person response through some

---

[15] See, for example, Ernest Dichter, *The Strategy of Desire* (New York: Doubleday, 1960).

type of projective question.[16] An example would be, "What product features do most of the people around here consider to be important in buying a dishwasher?" Response biases presumably are minimized by making respondents feel that they are not revealing their personal opinions. The underlying premise of the projective method has not been verified,[17] so it is seldom used.

MEASURING SALIENCE   The concept of salience is typically operationalized in marketing research as **importance.** That is, consumers are asked to rate the importance of the various evaluative criteria. There are a number of versions of this approach. The simplest version requires respondents only to give a "yes–no" response to questions such as, "Are a brand's nutritional properties important to you in selecting a breakfast cereal?" Such an approach, however, is probably too simplistic since it is typically desirable to understand the degree of importance attached to evaluative criteria.

Alternatively, consumers may be asked to rank order the evaluative criteria from most to least important. Respondents are presented with a list of attributes and are instructed to give a "1" to the most important attribute, a "2" to the next most important attribute, etc. Another popular approach is to have respondents rate each evaluative criterion on a 7-point scale ranging from 0 to 100. The greater the importance, the more points that should be assigned.

Measures of importance can sometimes provide an incomplete picture of consumer motivation. This is because some attributes can be important for very different reasons. An attribute may be important because consumers like or desire the product to have the attribute. In contrast, an attribute may be important because consumers dislike or do not wish the product to possess the attribute. For example, "carbonation" in a soft drink may be highly desirable for many consumers but highly undesirable for those preferring an uncarbonated drink. Both segments are likely to rate carbonation as "important," but for very different reasons.

Because of this potential limitation, measures assessing the **evaluation** or "goodness-badness" of an attribute are often more useful.[18] Rather than having consumers rate the importance of carbonation, they should be asked to evaluate buying a carbonated soft drink on a scale ranging from "very good" to "very bad." Importance is reflected by the extent to which responses deviate from the scale midpoint. Thus, measures of evaluation capture attribute importance as well as the "desirability" of the attribute.

---

[16] For an application of this technique, see Robert L. Thornton, "Selling the Hard Goods the Soft Way: American Versus Foreign Cars," *Journal of Consumer Marketing* 1 (1983), 35–44.

[17] James F. Engel and Hugh G. Wales, "Spoken versus Pictured Questions on Taboo Topics," *Journal of Advertising Research* 2 (March 1962), 11–17.

[18] Joel B. Cohen, Martin Fishbein, and Olli T. Ahtola, "The Nature and Uses of Expectancy-Value Models in Consumer Attitude Research," *Journal of Marketing Research* 9 (November 1972), 456–460.

DETERMINING CHOICE ALTERNATIVES

Not only must consumers decide on the criteria to use in alternative evaluation, they must also determine the alternatives from which choice is made. These alternatives define what is known as the **consideration set** (also known as the **evoked set**). In most cases, the consideration set will contain only a subset of the total number of alternatives available to the consumer. As an example, suppose you were asked which soft drink brands you would consider buying. Those of you who are extremely brand loyal might indicate only your preferred brand. Others might consider either Coke or Pepsi, while the consideration set for others may consist of noncola diet drinks.

Gaining entry into the consideration set is a top priority. Failure to do so means that a competitor's offering will be purchased. Marketers must, therefore, take steps to see that their products gain consideration during decision making. A common strategy is to offer incentives for such consideration. Auto manufacturers have sometimes offered consumers gifts and money to simply test-drive their cars. Similarly, a hot tub retailer has promised to pay consumers $100 if they buy from a competitor after checking out what the retailer has to offer (see Figure 18.4).

CONSTRUCTING THE CONSIDERATION SET

How does the consumer determine the alternatives that will receive consideration? The answer depends on both situational and individual factors. For example, suppose you were hungry and decided to go out for fast food. A search through memory is likely to yield a number of possibilities. In this situation, the consideration set would depend solely on your recall of alternatives from memory (i.e., the **retrieval set**).[19]

Suppose we change the setting to a drugstore, where you have decided to resume taking vitamin pills after getting out of the habit for a couple of years. Perhaps the easiest way to construct a consideration set would be to simply scan the shelving containing the vitamins and see if anything looks familiar. Choice might then be made from the brands you recognize. Note that recognition of alternatives available at the point of purchase will determine the consideration set.

A common element in both hypotheticals is the assumption of prior knowledge of at least some alternatives. Yet, in the case of first-time buyers for some product categories, consumers may lack knowledge about what alternatives are available to choose from. When this occurs, the consideration set may be developed in any one of a number of ways. The consumer might talk to others, search through the yellow pages, consider all brands available at the store, and so on. Thus, external factors such as the retail environment

---

[19] Joseph W. Alba and Amitava Chattopadhay, "Effects of Context and Part-Category Cues on Recall of Competing Brands," *Journal of Marketing Research* 22 (August 1985), 340–349.

FIGURE 18.4
GAINING
CONSIDERATION:
A NECESSARY
PREREQUISITE
FOR PURCHASE

have a greater opportunity to affect the consideration set of less knowledgeable consumers.[20]

The manner in which the consideration set is constructed can shape marketing strategy. Greater emphasis must be given to having consumers learn what the product packaging looks like when recognition at the point of purchase determines the consideration set. Conversely, brand name recall is the appropriate criterion when consumers rely on a recall retrieval process in selecting choice alternatives. There is also the possibility of undermining the competition by inhibiting the recall of competitive names (see Chapter 14).[21]

---

[20] Joseph W. Alba and J. Wesley Hutchinson, "Dimensions of Consumer Expertise," *Journal of Consumer Research* 13 (March 1987), 411–454.

[21] Alba and Chattopadhay, "Effects of Context and Part-Category Cues on Recall of Competing Brands"; Joseph W. Alba and Amitava Chattopadhay, "Salience Effects in Brand Recall," *Journal*

INFLUENCE OF THE CONSIDERATION SET

One area of recent research interest concerns how the evaluation and choice of a given alternative is affected by what other alternatives are included in the consideration set. Several studies have reported an attraction effect where a given alternative's attractiveness is enhanced when an inferior alternative is added to the set of choice alternatives.[22] Although the robustness of this effect is not well understood, it does suggest the possibility that a product might benefit from encouraging consumers to consider weaker offerings.

ASSESSING CHOICE ALTERNATIVES

Another component of the alternative evaluation process involves judging the performance of choice alternatives along salient evaluative criteria. There exists some rather interesting research, as reported in *Consumer in Focus 18.2,* which indicates that some consumers may be limited in their ability to "accurately" evaluate choice alternatives. Such findings are, of course, a cause for concern among those involved with consumer protection (see Chapter 25).

In many cases, consumers already have stored in memory judgments or beliefs about the performance of the choice alternatives under consideration. The ability to retrieve this information may strongly affect which alternative is eventually chosen.[23] On the other hand, consumers lacking such stored knowledge will need to rely on external information in forming beliefs about an alternative's performance.

---

of Marketing Research 23 (November 1986), 363–369. Also see Paul W. Miniard, H. Rao Unnava, and Sunil Bhatla, "Investigating the Recall Inhibition Effect: A Test of Practical and Theoretical Considerations," working paper, The Ohio State University, 1988.

[22] Joel Huber, John W. Payne, and Christopher Puto, "Adding Asymmetrically Dominated Alternatives: Violations of Regularity and the Similarity Hypothesis," *Journal of Consumer Research* 9 (June 1982), 90–98; Joel Huber and Christopher Puto, "Market Boundaries and Product Choice: Illustrating Attraction and Substitution Effects," *Journal of Consumer Research* 10 (June 1983), 31–44; Barbara Kahn, William L. Moore, and Rashi Glazer, "Experiments in Constrained Choice," *Journal of Consumer Research* 14 (June 1987), 96–113; Srinivasan Ratneshwar, Allan D. Shocker, and David W. Stewart, "Toward Understanding the Attraction Effect: The Implications of Product Stimulus Meaningfulness and Familiarity," *Journal of Consumer Research* 13 (March 1987), 520–533.

[23] Gabriel Biehal and Dipankar Chakravarti, "Information Accessibility as a Moderator of Consumer Choice," *Journal of Consumer Research* 10 (June 1983), 1–14; Gabriel Biehal and Dipankar Chakravarti, "Consumers' Use of Memory and External Information in Choice: Macro and Micro Perspectives," *Journal of Consumer Research* 12 (March 1986), 382–405; John G. Lynch, Jr., Howard Marmorstein, and Michael F. Weigold, "Choices from Sets Including Remembered Brands: Use of Recalled Attributes and Prior Overall Evaluations," *Journal of Consumer Research* 15 (September 1988), 169–184.

CONSUMER IN FOCUS

18.2 CAN CONSUMERS DETERMINE THE "BEST BUY"?

Suppose you were asked to decide which of two bottles of garlic powder, identical except in price and size, represented the "best buy." Powder weight in the first bottle is 2.37 ounces or 67 grams at a cost of 77 cents. The powder in the smaller bottle weighs 1.25 ounces or 35 grams. This bottle normally costs 51 cents, but is currently on sale at 41 cents. Which bottle is the "best buy"?

The answer is the larger bottle. Its unit price is 32.5 cents per ounce compared to 32.8 cents for the smaller bottle. Recognition of the need to estimate the relative unit price and the ability to do so would determine the accuracy of one's choice.

This problem was actually used in a study of consumer skills where subjects were given the incentive of having a chance to win $50 for making the correct choice. Of 100 female supermarket shoppers, 39 did not rely on a comparison of relative unit price in making their choice. Rather, they employed different decision rules, such as inferring that an item on sale would be a better buy. Highly educated shoppers were much more likely to consider relative unit price than those less educated.

Source: Noel Capon and Deanna Kuhn, "Can Consumer Calculate Best Buys?" *Journal of Consumer Research* 8 (March 1982), 449–453.

THE USE OF CUTOFFS

In judging how well an alternative performs, consumers may often employ **cutoffs**.[24] A cutoff is simply a restriction or requirement for acceptable attribute values. One example is price. Consumers are likely to have a fairly defined range of prices they are willing to pay. A price that falls outside of this range or zone will be viewed as unacceptable.[25]

Cutoffs are used for many evaluative criteria other than price. A consumer may refuse to consider generic soft drink brands. Another may reject any soft drink exceeding a certain number of calories. Still another may insist that the drink contain some amount of real fruit juices.

The cutoffs employed by consumers during decision making will obviously have a strong influence on the final choice. Consequently, it is important for marketers to understand the presence and nature of cutoffs. A brand

---

[24] For research on cutoff usage, see Barton Weitz and Peter Wright, "Retrospective Self-Insight on Factors Considered in Product Evaluations," *Journal of Consumer Research* 6 (December 1979), 280–294; Peter L. Wright and Barton Weitz, "Time Horizon Effects on Product Evaluation Strategies," *Journal of Marketing Research* 14 (November 1977), 429–443.

[25] Susan M. Petroshius and Kent B. Monroe, "Effects of Product-Line Pricing Characteristics on Product Evaluations," *Journal of Consumer Research* 13 (March 1987), 511–519.

that fails to meet a critical cutoff may be rejected regardless of how well it performs on other dimensions.

THE USE OF SIGNALS

Judgments about choice alternatives can depend on the presence of certain **cues** or **signals.** A classic illustration is the use of price as a signal of quality. One cosmetics manufacturer learned the hard way about price–quality relationships. The introduction of its new line of low-priced cosmetics was a failure in the marketplace. Subsequent reintroduction of essentially the same line, but with a higher price, produced greater sales. Why? Because consumers used price as a signal of quality and were unwilling to run the risk of wearing low-quality cosmetics.

The use of price as a signal of quality has been substantiated repeatedly.[26] Even so, price may have little influence on perceived quality in some situations and for some consumers. For instance, price may have little signaling power when consumers are able to easily judge product quality or rely on other signals (e.g., brand name, image of store carrying the product) to infer quality.

SELECTING A DECISION RULE

The final element of the alternative evaluation process to be considered is the decision rule. **Decision rules** represent the strategies consumers use to make a selection from the choice alternatives.[27] Decision rules can range from very simplistic procedures that require little time and effort to very elaborate ones that involve considerably more time and processing effort on the part of the consumer.

When choice is habituated, the decision rule is very simple: Buy the same brand as last time. Even when choice is not habituated, consumers may employ simplistic decision rules such as "buy the cheapest" or "buy the brand my spouse likes." This is because consumers continually make trade-offs between the quality of their choice (i.e., buying the "best" brand) and the amount of time and effort necessary to reach a decision. In many cases the consumer will follow decision rules that yield a satisfactory (as opposed

---

[26] Michael Etgar and Naresh K. Malhotra, "Determinants of Price Dependency: Personal and Perceptual Factors," *Journal of Consumer Research* 8 (September 1981), 217–222; Gary M. Erickson and Johny K. Johansson, "The Role of Price in Multi-Attribute Product Evaluations," *Journal of Consumer Research* 12 (September 1985), 195–199; Zarrel V. Lambert, "Product Perception: An Important Variable in Price Strategy," *Journal of Marketing* 34 (October 1970), 68–76; Irwin P. Levin, "Estimating Price-Quality Tradeoffs Using Comparative Judgments," *Journal of Consumer Research* 11 (June 1984), 593–600; Kent B. Monroe, "The Influence of Price Differences and Brand Familiarity on Brand Preferences," *Journal of Consumer Research* 3 (June 1976), 42–49; Petroshius and Monroe, "Effects of Product-Line Pricing Characteristics on Product Evaluations."
[27] For a detailed discussion of decision rules, see James R. Bettman, *An Information Processing Theory of Consumer Choice* (Reading, Massachusetts: Addison-Wesley, 1979), Chapter 7.

to optimal) choice while minimizing their time and effort. These simplistic decision rules are more likely to occur for repetitive product choices that are viewed as relatively low in importance or involvement.[28]

At other times, however, consumers are more highly motivated during decision making. Consequently, they will employ more elaborate or complex decision rules that require greater processing effort. A fundamental distinction between these more complex rules is whether they involve a compensatory versus a noncompensatory procedure.

NONCOMPENSATORY DECISION RULES

Noncompensatory decision rules are characterized by the fact that a weakness in one attribute *cannot* be offset by a strength in another attribute. The simplistic decision rules considered previously are examples of a noncompensatory strategy. For instance, a brand that is not the cheapest would not be chosen no matter how well it performs on other evaluative criteria when the decision rule is "buy the cheapest." That is, the brand's weakness in price is not compensated by its favorable performance in other attributes. Three additional types of noncompensatory rules are lexicographic, elimination by aspects, and conjunctive.[29]

LEXICOGRAPHIC   Under this decision strategy, brands are compared on the most important attribute. If one of the brands is perceived as superior based on that attribute, it is selected. If two or more brands are perceived as equally good, they are then compared on the second most important attribute. This process continues until the tie is broken.

To illustrate this rule, consider the information presented in Table 18.1. This table contains attribute-performance ratings (from excellent to poor) for four different food item brands and attribute-importance rankings (where "1" is the most important). Which brand would be chosen under the lexicographic rule?

The answer is brand A. A comparison on the most important attribute, taste, produces a tie between brands A, B, and D. This tie is broken on the next most important attribute, price, because brand A has the highest rating of the three brands. Notice, however, what would happen if the attribute-importance rankings were slightly different. For instance, if price were most important, brand C would then be chosen.

The concepts of processing by brand (PBB) and processing by attribute (PBA), originally introduced in the discussion of search sequence in Chapter 17, are also relevant here. Recall that in PBB, information is acquired for

---

[28] Wayne D. Hoyer, "An Examination of Consumer Decision Making for a Common Repeat Purchase Product," *Journal of Consumer Research* 11 (December 1984), 822–829.

[29] For a discussion of other forms of noncompensatory rules, see Bettman, *An Information Processing Theory of Consumer Choice*, 181–182.

TABLE 18.1	Attribute	Importance Ranking	Brand Performance Ratings			
HYPOTHETICAL RATINGS FOR ILLUSTRATING DECISION RULES			Brand A	Brand B	Brand C	Brand D
	Taste	1	Excellent	Excellent	Very Good	Excellent
	Price	2	Very Good	Good	Excellent	Fair
	Nutrition	3	Good	Good	Poor	Excellent
	Convenience	4	Fair	Good	Good	Excellent

one brand at a time. The person who learns all about one brand before learning about the next is processing by brand. PBA involves the acquisition of information about a particular attribute of the various brands. The person comparing brands on taste, then on price, and so forth, is processing by attribute.

Decision rules differ in whether they require PBB or PBA. The lexicographic procedure, for instance, involves PBA since brands are compared on one attribute at a time.

ELIMINATION BY ASPECTS   This rule closely resembles the lexicographic procedure. As before, brands are first evaluated on the most important attribute. Now, however, the consumer imposes cutoffs. The consumer may, for example, employ cutoffs such as "must be under $2" or "must be at least nutritious."

If only one brand meets the cutoff on the most important attribute, it is chosen. If several brands meet the cutoff, then the next most important attribute is selected and the process continues until the tie is broken. If none of the brands are acceptable, the consumer must revise the cutoffs, use a different decision rule, or postpone choice. Once again, processing by attribute is required.

Returning to Table 18.1, choice based on elimination by aspects would depend on the particular cutoff values imposed by the decision maker. Suppose the minimum acceptable values for taste and price were "excellent" and "very good," respectively. Brand A would again be chosen. But if the cutoff for taste was lowered to "very good" and the cutoff for price was raised to "excellent," then brand C would be selected.

CONJUNCTIVE   Cutoffs also play a prominent part in the **conjunctive decision rule.**[30] Cutoffs are established for each salient attribute. Each brand is compared, one at a time, against this set of cutoffs. Thus, processing by brand is required. If the brand meets the cutoffs for *all* the attributes, it is

---

[30] For a recent study of the conjunctive decision rule, see David Grether and Louis Wilde, "An Analysis of Conjunctive Choice: Theory and Experiments," *Journal of Consumer Research* 10 (March 1984), 373–385.

chosen. Failure to meet the cutoff for *any* attribute leads to rejection. As before, if none of the brands meet the cutoff requirements, then a change in either the cutoffs or the decision rule must occur. Otherwise, choice must be delayed.

To illustrate the conjunctive choice rule, assume that the consumer insists that the brand receive a rating of at least "good" on each attribute. In Table 18.1, brand A is rejected because of its inadequate rating (i.e., does not meet the cutoff requirement of "good") on convenience, whereas brand C is inadequate on nutrition. Brand D is eliminated by the unacceptable price rating. Only brand B meets all the cutoff requirements and therefore would be evaluated as an acceptable choice.

COMPENSATORY DECISION RULES

Did you notice the plight of poor brand D in Table 18.1? Despite its excellent ratings in three of the four salient attributes (including the most important attribute), brand D never emerged as the top brand. Why? Because of its poor price performance; that is, none of the noncompensatory strategies permitted the brand's poor rating on price to be offset by its otherwise excellent performance.

This is not the case for compensatory decision rules. Under a compensatory strategy, a perceived weakness of one attribute may be offset or compensated for by a perceived strength of another attribute. Two types of compensatory rules are the **simple** and **weighted additive.**

SIMPLE ADDITIVE   Under this rule, the consumer simply counts or adds the number of times each alternative is judged favorably in terms of the set of salient evaluative criteria. The alternative having the largest number of positive attributes is chosen. Research indicates that a simple additive rule is most likely when consumers' processing motivation or ability is limited.[31]

WEIGHTED ADDITIVE   A far more complex form of the compensatory rule is the weighted additive. The consumer now engages in more refined judgments about the alternatives' performance than simply whether it is favorable or unfavorable. The relative salience of relevant evaluative criteria is also incorporated into the decision rule. In essence, a weighted additive rule is equivalent to the multiattribute attitude models described in Chapter 11. Consequently, discussion of their mechanics is not needed here (although the reader may wish to refresh her or his memory with a brief review of this material).

---

[31] Joseph W. Alba and Howard Marmorstein, "The Effects of Frequency Knowledge on Consumer Decision Making," *Journal of Consumer Research* 14 (June 1987), 14–25.

PHASED DECISION STRATEGIES

Phased decision strategies involve the sequential use of at least two different decision rules as a means of coping with a large number of choice alternatives.[32] Phased strategies typically consist of a two-stage process. In the initial stage, one type of rule is used as a screening device to help narrow down the choice set to a more manageable number. A second decision rule is then applied to the remaining alternatives to make the final choice. For example, a consumer confronted with a very large number of brands might first eliminate those above a certain price from contention. The remaining brands would then be evaluated across a number of salient attributes.

CONSTRUCTIVE DECISION RULES

Many of the choice situations consumers encounter can be handled by simply retrieving the appropriate decision rule from memory. Stored rules are more likely to exist in memory as the consumer accumulates experience in making such choices. In other situations (e.g., novel or unfamiliar choices), however, consumers may find it necessary to construct their decision rules at the time of choice.[33] That is, consumers build a **constructive decision rule** using elementary processing operations (i.e., "fragments" of rules) available in memory that can accommodate the choice situation.

AFFECT REFERRAL

A special type of decision rule is known as **affect referral**.[34] This rule assumes that the consumer has previously formed overall evaluations of each choice alternative. Rather than judging alternatives on various evaluative criteria, the consumer simply retrieves these global evaluations from memory. The alternative having the highest affect is then chosen. In essence, overall evaluation serves as the single evaluative criterion used in decision making.

MARKETING IMPLICATIONS

At this point it is useful to stop and consider what all of this means for the practitioner. What value does knowledge about the particular decision rule

[32] Denis A. Lussier and Richard W. Olshavsky, "Task Complexity and Contingent Processing in Brand Choice," *Journal of Consumer Research* 6 (September 1979), 154–165.

[33] Biehal and Chakravarti, "Consumers' Use of Memory and External Information in Choice: Micro and Macro Perspectives"; James R. Bettman and Michel A. Zins, "Constructive Processes in Consumer Choice," *Journal of Consumer Research* 4 (September 1977), 75–85.

[34] Peter Wright, "Consumer Choice Strategies: Simplifying Vs. Optimizing," *Journal of Marketing Research* 12 (February 1975), 60–67. Also see Bettman, *An Information Processing Theory of Consumer Choice;* Amitava Chattopadhyay and Joseph W. Alba, "The Situational Importance of Recall and Inference in Consumer Decision Making," *Journal of Consumer Research* 15 (June 1988), 1–12.

consumers employ during alternative evaluation have for the development of marketing strategies?

Fundamentally speaking, marketers need to understand decision rules because these rules have an impact on consumer choice. An understanding of the decision rule (or rules) employed by current customers (i.e., the rule that leads to the choice of one's product) may suggest actions that maintain or facilitate customers' use of this rule. It may also indicate actions that should be avoided because of their potential to change the customer's decision rule (and, hence, choice). For example, when the customer's decision rule is simply "buy the same brand as last time" (i.e., choice is habituated), the marketer should avoid conditions that may trigger a change in the decision rule, such as a noticeable decline in product quality, significant price increases, or an out-of-stock situation. The manner in which attribute information is organized and presented may also be important.[35] Presenting information about the brands' performance on one attribute at a time, while conducive to decision rules that require processing by attribute, should discourage the use of rules requiring consumers to process by brand. Conversely, a brand-based presentation format should favor rules that involve processing by brand.

Even knowledge that consumers do not have a well-defined decision strategy (e.g., a constructive method is employed) can be useful. Consumers who are uncertain about how they should make their decision may be receptive to those offering some guidance. For this reason, ads such as the one presented in Figure 18.5 may be very effective.

Understanding consumers' decision rules is also important in the development of attitude-change strategies.[36] This can be demonstrated by returning to Table 18.1. Suppose that brand C improved its taste perception from "very good" to "excellent." This change makes considerable sense if consumers use a lexicographic process in making their evaluation, since it would lead to brand C being chosen. Suppose, however, that consumers employ a conjunctive rule with cutoffs of "good." Improving the product's taste would be of little value since its nutritional rating of "poor" is unacceptable. Instead, it would be critical to enhance the brand's nutritional performance.

Recognize that changing consumers' decision rules provides marketers with another mechanism for influencing consumer choice. In some cases, this might involve changing the relative importance of salient evaluative criteria. For instance, assuming a lexicographic rule, brand C in Table 18.1 might consider altering the relative importance consumers attach to taste and price. A lexicographic rule with price being the most important attribute would lead to the selection of brand C, whereas this type of rule with taste being most important results in brand A being chosen.

---

[35] For research relevant to this issue, see James R. Bettman and Michel A. Zins, "Information Format and Choice Task Effects in Decision Making," *Journal of Consumer Research* 6 (September 1979), 141–153.

[36] Peter L. Wright, "Use of Consumer Judgment Models in Promotion Planning," *Journal of Marketing* 37 (October 1973), 27–33.

FIGURE 18.5
ADS OFFERING
GUIDANCE APPEAL
TO CONSUMERS
LACKING A
DECISION
STRATEGY

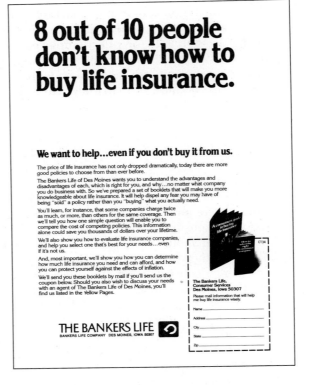

Source: Copyright Bankers Life Company. Reprinted by permission.

Changing the cutoffs is another mechanism for altering the decision rule. As illustrated by the example considered in our prior discussion of elimination by aspects, changes in the minimum acceptable values for taste and price resulted in the selection of different brands from Table 18.1.

It may sometimes be desirable to encourage a change in the type of decision rule. In Table 18.1, for instance, brand D would want consumers to switch from lexicographic to some other procedure such as compensatory. Unfortunately, little is known about the likelihood of getting consumers to switch their decision strategies.

SUMMARY

Alternative evaluation represents the decision-making stage in which consumers evaluate alternatives to make a choice. During this stage consumers must (1) determine the evaluative criteria to use for judging alternatives, (2) decide which alternatives to consider, (3) assess the performance of considered alternatives, and (4) select and apply a decision rule to make the final choice.

Consumers may employ a number of different evaluative criteria, including price, brand name, and country of origin, in making their decision. These criteria will usually vary in their relative importance or salience. Price may be a dominant dimension in some decisions and yet rather unimportant in others. The salience of evaluative criteria depends on a host of situational, product, and individual factors.

Attention was also given to the measurement of evaluative criteria. First, the evaluative criteria salient to consumers must be identified. Next, the relative salience of each criterion can be assessed by measures of importance or evaluation.

Consumers must determine the set of alternatives from which a choice will be made (i.e., the consideration set). Sometimes the consideration set will depend on the consumer's ability to recall from memory viable alternatives. On other occasions an alternative will be considered if it is recognized at the point of purchase. When consumers lack prior knowledge about choice alternatives, they must then turn to the environment for assistance in forming their consideration set.

Consumers may also rely on their existing knowledge for judging how well alternatives perform along the salient evaluative criteria. Otherwise, external search will be required to form these judgments. The cutoffs or ranges of acceptable values that consumers impose for evaluative criteria will strongly determine whether a given alternative is viewed as acceptable. In addition, consumers may often use certain signals or cues in forming their judgments. Such is the case when price is used to infer product quality.

Finally, the strategies or procedures used for making the final choice are called decision rules. These rules may be stored in memory and retrieved when needed. Alternatively, they may be constructed to fit situational contingencies.

Decision rules vary considerably in their complexity. They may be very simple (e.g., buy what I bought last time). They can also be quite complex, such as when the rule resembles a multiattribute attitude model. Another important distinction is between compensatory and noncompensatory decision rules. Noncompensatory rules, such as lexicographic, elimination by aspects, and conjunctive, do not permit product strengths to offset product weaknesses. In contrast, compensatory rules do allow product weaknesses to be compensated by product strengths.

REVIEW AND DISCUSSION QUESTIONS

1. What are evaluative criteria? What criteria did you use when you purchased your last pair of shoes? How did these differ, if at all, from those used by others in your family?

2. A recent survey using measures of attribute importance shows that "high price" was rated the most important of all attributes. Your boss asks you whether this means

consumers will avoid a high-priced brand. How would you respond? Would your answer be different if the survey had used a measure of attribute evaluation?

3. In the chapter we indicate that offering incentives is one way for a product to gain consideration during consumer decision making. How else might a product try to enter the consideration set?

4. A restaurant is trying to decide on the appropriate method for assessing consumers' consideration set in deciding where to eat out. One person has argued for a recall method where consumers are asked to remember without any memory cues. Another person recommends a recognition method in which consumers are given a list of local restaurants and asked to circle the appropriate names. Which method would you recommend? Would your answer change if consumers normally consulted the yellow pages in making the decision?

5. A company has been testing how price affects the perceived quality of the company's product. Consumers who participated in the study were split into two groups based on their performance on a test of product knowledge. Interestingly, those performing poorly (i.e., the low-knowledge group) used price as a signal of product quality. In contrast, price was not used as an indicator of product quality among those possessing a high level of product knowledge. How can you explain this difference?

6. Would you expect a price–quality relationship for each of the following product classes: hand soap, toilet paper, panty hose, men's shirts, china and glassware, and gasoline? Why?

7. Why is it important to understand the decision rules consumers use during alternative evaluation?

8. Identify which decision rule would lead to the selection of each of the brands below:

Attribute	Importance Ranking	Performance Ratings		
		Brand A	Brand B	Brand C
Price	1	Excellent	Very Good	Very Good
Quality	2	Poor	Very Good	Good
Convenience	3	Poor	Average	Good

PURCHASE AND ITS OUTCOMES

A PURCHASE-DECISION SCENARIO

t's early in August and Sue's attention turns once again to her back-to-college wardrobe. Two sweaters are at the top of her "must buy" list. So a shopping trip is planned to Marshall Fields, Lord & Taylor, and Saks in one of the large west-suburban-Chicago shopping malls.

Sue also has browsed through the many fashion catalogs she has received in the last couple of months. It seems to her as if everyone is taking advantage of her name, which has been acquired by buying or renting the subscribers' lists to *Elle, TAXI,* and other magazines. Some sweaters have caught her eye and she is seriously considering buying from a catalog. Certainly that would save shopping time.

Sue finally decides against the catalogs mostly because she really enjoys shopping, especially since two of her friends also need to replenish their wardrobes. Also, the options available in the catalogs seem much more limited, and she has some fear that sizes and colors might not be right. And there is some doubt that she would be able to return unwanted merchandise quickly and easily.

The act of purchase is the last major stage in our model of consumer behavior (Figure 19.1). The consumer now must make three decisions: (1) when to buy; (2) where to buy; and (3) how to pay.

Some products are bought mostly on a seasonal basis. Air conditioners in northern climates, Christmas gifts, and Caribbean cruises are examples.

FIGURE 19.1 A MODEL OF PURCHASE AND ITS OUTCOMES

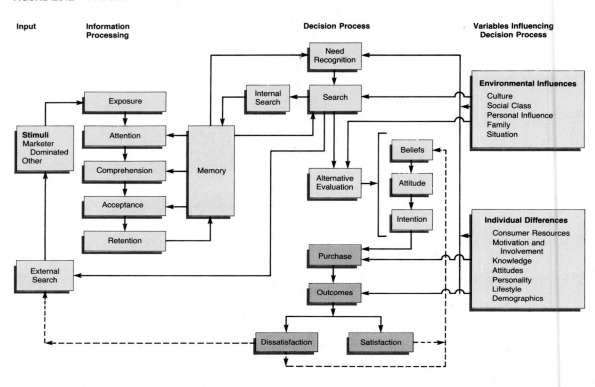

Others, such as detergents and frozen foods, are often purchased only when stock is depleted. Marketers can change these patterns by offering special rebates and other price incentives.

Consumers have changed shopping and buying preferences in the last decade. In-home shopping, for example, has seen remarkable growth in most of the developing countries of the world. Many retailing establishments have been forced into direct marketing to complement their normal activities. Also there are other trends affecting retailing, such as an increasing shift of cosmetic purchases away from department stores to supermarkets. Thus, it has been necessary to develop packaging that is both eye-catching and informative as retail display replaces the salesperson as a major persuasive influence.

Finally, the consumer must decide how to pay. Other chapters (especially Chapters 8 and 21) have demonstrated the relentless trend away from cash payment to use of credit cards and other forms of delayed payment.

The process does not stop once the purchase has been made, however. There often is substantial postpurchase evaluation, especially when high involvement has triggered extended problem solving. Sometimes buyers have doubts that the right choice was made. These doubts are designated in Figure 19.1 as *dissatisfaction*. The opposite response, of course, is one of *satisfaction*. Both depend upon the degree to which expectations have been fulfilled. The implications of buyer satisfaction for loyalty and word of mouth present a potent marketing challenge.

The focus of this chapter is on two of these issues: (1) where to buy and (2) consumer satisfaction and dissatisfaction. The discussion continues in Chapter 20, which explores how consumer research is utilized in retailing strategy.

THE PURCHASE PROCESS

The model in Figure 19.1 illustrates that purchase is a function of two determinants: (1) intentions and (2) environmental influences and/or individual differences. Of the many variables which fall into the latter category, *situation* stands out as being of special importance.

PURCHASE INTENTIONS

When asked to do so, it often is possible for consumers to articulate their purchase intentions, and these fall into two categories: (1) both product and brand and (2) product class only (e.g., there is an intention to buy ice cream, but additional decisions must be made on what type and what brand).

Category 1 intention is commonly referred to as a **fully planned purchase.** Often (although by no means always) it is the outcome of high involvement and extended problem solving. The consumer will be more willing to invest time and energy in shopping and buying. Hence, distribution can be more selective.

It also is correct to view category 2 (product only) as a planned purchase even though choice of brand is made at point of sale. Shopping now can become an important form of information search, especially when involvement is high. When involvement is low, on the other hand, the decision rule often is "buy one of the brands I already consider to be acceptable." The final decision now may hinge on promotional influences such as price reductions or special display and packaging.

But now we face a dilemma. Can we consider a purchase to be **unplanned** when a conscious intention was not articulated prior to the act of buying? Marketers have long recognized that this takes place.[1] In fact, a POPAI (Point-

---

[1] Dennis W. Rook, "The Buying Impulse," *Journal of Consumer Research* 14 (September 1987), 189–199.

of-purchase Advertising Institute) study showed that more than half of all 1987 retail transactions fell into this category.[2] Here is more current research on this topic:

> About 53% of groceries and 47% of hardware-store buys are spur of the moment, studies say. When Stillerman Jones & Co., a marketing-research firm, asked 34,300 mall shoppers across the country the primary reason for their visit, only 25% had come in pursuit of a specific item.[3]

It is important to note that a purchase can be planned in one sense even though a definite intention is not expressed verbally or in writing on a shopping list. This is because shoppers use products displayed on shelves in mass-merchandising outlets as a **surrogate shopping list.** In other words, display provides reminder of a need, and a purchase is triggered. This is often referred to as an **impulse purchase.**

Research has demonstrated that impulse buying actions can reflect a psychologically different type of behavior. Consider Rook's clarification:

> Impulse buying occurs when a consumer experiences a sudden, often powerful and persistent urge to buy something immediately. The impulse to buy is hedonically complex and may stimulate emotional conflict. Also, impulse buying is prone to occur with diminished regard to its consequences.[4]

When defined in this way, some impulse purchasing is not based on consumer problem solving and is best viewed from an hedonic or experiential perspective.[5] According to Rook's research, it can have one or more of these characteristics:

1. *Spontaneity.* It is unexpected and motivates the consumer to *buy now,* often in response to direct point-of-sale visual stimulation.

2. *Power, compulsion, and intensity.* There can be motivation to put all else aside and act immediately.

3. *Excitement and stimulation.* These sudden urges to buy are often accompanied by emotions characterized as "exciting," "thrilling," or "wild."

4. *Disregard for consequences.* The urge to buy can be so irresistible that potentially negative consequences are ignored.[6]

---

[2] Joe Agnew, "P-O-P Displays Are Becoming a Matter of Consumer Convenience," *Marketing News* (October 9, 1987), 14.

[3] Betsy Morris, "As a Favored Pastime, Shopping Ranks High with Most Americans," *The Wall Street Journal* (July 30, 1987), 13.

[4] Rook, "The Buying Impulse," 191.

[5] Morris B. Holbrook and Elizabeth C. Hirschman, "The Experiential Aspects of Consumer Behavior: Consumer Fantasies, Feelings, and Fun," *Journal of Consumer Research* 9 (September 1982), 132–140.

[6] Rook, "The Buying Impulse."

TABLE 19.1
A SUMMARY OF
SITUATIONAL
INFLUENCES ON
PURCHASING
BEHAVIOR
	1. The information environment.
	  a. Information availability both internal (stored in memory) and external.
	  b. Information load (or overload).
	  c. Information format.
	2. The retail environment.
	  a. Store atmospherics.
	  b. Layout and display.
	  c. Point-of-purchase (POP) materials.
	3. Time available for decision making.

SITUATIONAL INFLUENCE

You are familiar with the role played by situational influence from the discussion in Chapter 7, which was devoted entirely to this subject. The primary ways in which situational influences can affect purchase actions are summarized in Table 19.1.

Many situational factors, such as weather and temporary unemployment, are beyond the influence of the marketer or retailer, but this is not always the case by any means. Marketers have direct control over display, product promotion and exposure, price reductions, store atmospherics, and out-of-stock conditions, to mention only a few. The most important point here is to be aware of the manner in which these situational considerations can affect choice and to avoid such unfortunate situations as out of stock and inadequate display.[7]

RETAIL VERSUS IN-HOME SHOPPING AND BUYING

At one point in time a large percentage of shopping and buying was done at home through use of the itinerant peddler. As convenient and inexpensive transportation methods became commonplace, however, the retail store gained ascendancy. The pendulum has swung once again in recent years to the point where both retailing and in-home buying are vigorous competitors. An interesting marketing challenge is presented.

RETAIL SHOPPING AND PURCHASING

Although exact figures are difficult to come by, the best estimate is that 84 percent of all consumer purchases are made through visits to a retail outlet or catalog showroom or through a vending machine.[8] Around 70 percent of American adults visit a regional shopping mall each week. In turn, the

[7] For more detail see Gordon R. Foxall, *Consumer Choice* (London: Macmillan Press, 1983), 86–97.
[8] Arnold Fishman, "The 1986 Mail Order Guide," *Direct Marketing* (July 1987), 50.

19.1   SHOPPING — A FAVORED PASTIME

Why do so many people spend so much time shopping? According to shoppers and those who observe them, shopping can be all things to all people. It can alleviate loneliness and dispel boredom; it can be a sport and it can be imbued with the thrill of the hunt; it can provide escape, fulfill fantasies, relieve depression. A closer look at some of these categories follows.

Alleviating Loneliness: For a lot of people, "shopping appears to be a substitute for a relationship," says Jack Lesser, a marketing professor at Miami University in Ohio, who has found the most avid shoppers are the single, the widowed, and the divorced.

Dispelling Boredom: Shopping is tailor-made for a video generation that thrives on bright colors and visual distractions. "I shop when I'm feeling bored or when I feel like I need something new," says Brad Vroon, a 19-year-old Emory University student.

Shopping as a Sport: At Finale on Five, the discount paradise of Rich's downtown department store, the shoppers who cull through tangles of 90-percent-off belts and racks of half-price evening dresses are committed to beating the system.

Spoils of the Hunt: Some believe that shopping may be the modern manifestation of more primitive roles. One consultant explains, "Man, the provider, the big daddy, may not be able to bring home a mastodon, but he can sure bring home a VCR or a computer."

Shopping as an Escape: In focus groups, "I'm hearing [working] women more and more say, 'I can go into this home-decorating store and it's therapy. I can go into a trance,'" says Bill Huckabee, the president of C. W. Ress & Associates, a Columbus, Ohio, retail consulting firm.

Fantasy Fulfillment: Although Brad Clevenger visits Atlanta's Perimeter Mall twice weekly, he actually buys something only about once a month. The rest of the time, he fantasizes. "I usually come to get something to eat," says the 18-year-old data processor, "and then I look for what I'd like to have in the future. It gives me a goal, something to save my money for."

Relieving Depression: "Just the thought of going shopping makes me feel better," says a Nashville teacher. "I think about the clothes, the colors. I may not feel better in the long run, but it takes my mind off my problems."

Source: Adapted from Betsy Morris, "As a Favored Pastime, Shopping Ranks High with Most Americans," *The Wall Street Journal* (July 30, 1987), 1, 13.

majority of these people shop at neighborhood shopping centers twice weekly and visit grocery stores even more often. Furthermore, more men are shopping today, representing about one-third of shopping mall traffic, up from 25 percent in 1981.[9]

WHY DO PEOPLE SHOP?   One primary motivation for shopping is information acquisition.[10] For those who want to discover and evaluate a full range of options, there really is no other alternative. But the motivations for shopping are more diverse, as *Consumer in Focus 19.1* illustrates. Indeed, shopping has almost become a way of life in and of itself.

THE ANTI-SHOPPERS   Not everyone is totally enamored with shopping. In fact, McNeal and McKee found a substantial segment, consisting of 20 percent of the population, who will avoid the marketplace whenever possible.[11] Anti-shopping seems to be a part of a generally negative worldview. Moreover, such consumers are largely oblivious and nonresponsive to marketing efforts designed to lure them into the retailing net.

IN-HOME PURCHASING

A growing percentage of consumer shopping and buying activity now takes place in the home rather than in a retail store, through a vending machine, or in a catalog showroom. This type of buying exceeded an estimated $70 billion in 1986, 16 percent of all general merchandise sales.[12]

Strategies used to reach the consumer in his or her home are referred to as **direct marketing.**[13] Here is a useful definition from the Direct Mail Marketing Association (DMMA):

> *Direct [response] marketing is the total of activities by which products and services are offered to market segments in one or more media for information purposes or to solicit a direct response from a present or prospective customer or distributor by mail, telephone, or other access.*[14]

Direct Marketing magazine estimates that nearly two-thirds of U.S. advertising dollars are undertaken to generate a direct response, including home and retail sales.[15]

Direct marketing also is growing rapidly in most developing countries

---

[9] Morris, "As a Favored Pastime, Shopping Ranks High."

[10] Jack A. Lesser and Sanjay Jain, "A Preliminary Investigation of the Relationship Between Exploratory and Epistemic Shopping Behavior," in Robert F. Lusch et al., eds., *1985 AMA Educators' Proceedings* (Chicago: American Marketing Association, 1985), 75–81.

[11] James U. McNeal and Daryl McKee, "The Case of Antishoppers," in Lusch et al., *1985 AMA Educators' Proceedings*, 65–68.

[12] Fishman, "The 1986 Mail Order Guide," 50.

[13] See Stan Rapp and Thomas L. Collins, *Maximarketing* (New York: McGraw-Hill, 1987).

[14] Bob Stone, *Successful Direct Marketing Methods,* 2nd ed. (Chicago: Crain Books, 1979), 3.

[15] "Direct Marketing . . . An Aspect of Total Marketing," *Direct Marketing* (July 1987), 25.

of the world. Focusing only on mail-order statistics, 1986 sales in 14 countries in Europe and Asia totalled nearly $40 billion, as compared with almost $104 billion in the U.S. and Canada.[16]

THE IN-HOME BUYER   The Direct Marketing Association (DMA) commissioned Simmons Market Research Bureau to document the extent of telephone or direct-mail purchasing. Here are some of the major findings:

1. About half did some shopping at home during the month, and 65 percent intended to do so for Christmas purchases.
2. Apparel accounted for 18 percent of the orders, followed by magazines, home accessories, home maintenance and kitchen equipment, and home office supplies.
3. Direct-mail catalogs generated 24 percent of the orders, telephone and circulars 7 percent each, and newspaper ads 6 percent. In total, mail accounted for 64 percent and telephone for 27 percent.[17]

Who are the consumers who make at least some of their purchases in their home? Research shows that the majority are above average in both income and education but otherwise are similar demographically to in-store shoppers.[18] Also, most are active retail shoppers who shop at home for reasons other than deliberate avoidance of the store or shopping mall.[19]

Here are some of the factors which have contributed to the rapid growth of this phenomenon:

1. changing consumer lifestyles resulting from greater emphasis placed on leisure, the number of working wives, and demand for more services and conveniences in shopping;
2. the availability of credit, especially credit cards;
3. problems encountered when shopping (examples are congested parking lots, inadequate parking, uninformed sales personnel, long lines, and in-store congestion during peak hours).[20]

The in-home shopper offers a unique opportunity to the marketer, because there is evidence that people may be more likely to buy when they are most contented. Studies by Retail Planning Associates show, for example, that those

---

[16] Arnold Fishman, "International Mail Order Guide," *Direct Marketing* (July 1987), 167–171.

[17] "Direct Marketing Sales Far Outpace Estimates," *Marketing News* (November 23, 1984), 1 and 8.

[18] Paul I. Edwards, "Home Shopping Boom Forecast in Study," *Advertising Age* (December 15, 1986), 88.

[19] Peter L. Gillet, "In-Home Shoppers: An Overview," *Journal of Marketing* 40 (October 1976), 81–88.

[20] Stone, *Successful Direct Marketing*, 4.

who have just finished a meal at home are 25 percent more likely to buy clothing than a person who is hungry.[21]

DIRECT MARKETING METHODS

There are four primary ways in which consumers are reached to stimulate a direct response: (1) in-home personal selling; (2) direct-mail ads and catalogs; (3) other advertising media (especially telemarketing); and (4) interactive electronic media. All of these offer the unique benefit of precise segmentation.

IMPLICATIONS   While we devote Chapter 20 to an extensive review of distribution and retailing, two points should be stressed here. First, it is important to note that an inexplicable bias against direct marketing in some circles in the past is now rapidly changing. Many leading advertising agencies finally have entered this field. In part this is a belated recognition that many efforts to reach the prospective consumer, especially through media advertising, are little more than what Leo Bogart refers to as **background noise.**[22] It is increasingly difficult to reach a target audience without the interference of a barrage of competitive efforts.

Secondly, there is much to be gained from integration of direct marketing with normal retail-based strategies. For example, the venerable Fuller Brush Company is now opening retail stores targeted for the middle-to-upper-middle-income woman aged 35 to 55 who no longer can be found through house-to-house selling. This beefed-up strategy is backed by local newspaper advertising.[23]

Retailers, in turn, are finding that direct marketing is one key to restoring dwindling sales. Many historically have been reluctant to promote nonstore sales on the theory that this would detract from their regular business. Now some leaders, such as Saks and Neiman Marcus, are finding quite the opposite to be true. Failure to adapt strategies to consumer shopping preferences can be the worst kind of marketing myopia.

THE OUTCOMES OF PURCHASE

The marketing task does not cease once the sale has been made, because the buyer will evaluate the alternative after purchase as well as before. When involvement is high, it is not uncommon to experience an immediate and often transitory period of postdecision regret or doubt. This can have an impact on whether the buyer is satisfied or dissatisfied with the transaction

---

[21] "Home Shopping. Is It a Revolution in Retailing — or Just a Fad?" *Business Week* (December 16, 1986), 68.
[22] Leo Bogart, "Hitting the Right Consumer Target," *Advertising Age* (May 17, 1984), M-49–M-55.
[23] Susan Garland, "Stores Brush up Fuller's Image," *Advertising Age* (September 14, 1987), 107.

(see Figure 19.1). The beliefs and attitudes formed at this stage have a direct influence on future purchase intentions, word-of-mouth communication, and complaint behavior.

POSTDECISION REGRET

Have you ever come to a decision under high-involvement conditions, say the selection of a college or university, only to experience doubts that you did the right thing? You think perhaps of several other schools which also were good options and find yourself troubled.

You are now experiencing postdecision doubt (or dissonance), a common initial outcome under these circumstances:

1. a certain threshold of dissonance-motivated tension is surpassed;
2. the action is irrevocable;
3. there are other unchosen alternatives with qualitatively dissimilar but desirable attributes;
4. the choice is made entirely by free will or volition (i.e., you have not been constrained by social or parental pressures).[24]

You now are motivated to do something to reduce this dissonance, and you have two basic options: (1) confirmation of your choice or (2) conclusion that you have made an unwise decision.[25]

One of the best ways to underscore that you have done the right thing is to search for supportive information, especially that provided by the manufacturer through ads or new buyer instructions.[26] It makes marketing sense to recognize that buyer regret can occur and to take pains to reinforce the wisdom of choice by stressing product superiorities and other sources of uniqueness once again. A good place to do this is in owner manuals. Warranties also can be helpful for this purpose.

In other words, the buyer may need reassurance that he or she acted wisely. Doubts often can be counteracted if this can be put into their hands quickly. A personal letter or telephone call from manufacturer or dealer also is an effective strategy.

The other option, concluding that a bad choice has been made, is painful and can have negative consequences for the marketer. At the very least, a repurchase is unlikely, and it is quite possible that the product will be returned. Even more critical is the possibility of negative word of mouth.

---

[24] Jack W. Brehm and Arthur R. Cohen, *Explorations in Cognitive Dissonance* (New York: Wiley, 1962), 300.

[25] The literature here is dated. For an example, see Joel Cohen and Marvin E. Goldberg, "The Dissonance Model in Post-Decision Product Evaluation," *Journal of Marketing Research* 7 (1970), 315–321.

[26] For an early study on this subject see James F. Engel, "The Psychological Consequences of a Major Purchase Decision," in William S. Decker, ed., *Marketing in Transition* (Chicago: American Marketing Association, 1963), 462–475.

Bear in mind that these doubts usually are transitory and do not, as yet, signify dissatisfaction. They are an entirely normal consequence when there are attractive unchosen alternatives. There is no need for them to degenerate into dissatisfaction when it is so easy to provide reinforcement through a personal word or literature.

CONSUMER SATISFACTION/DISSATISFACTION (CS/D)

Everyone enters into purchase with certain expectations about what the product or service will do when it is used, and satisfaction is the hoped-for outcome. **Satisfaction** is defined here as a postconsumption evaluation that a chosen alternative at least meets or exceeds expectations. In short, it has done at least as well as you hoped it would. **Dissatisfaction,** of course, is the outcome of negatively confirmed expectations. The pressures of consumerism and growing public disdain for shoddy product quality have brought this subject to the forefront in consumer research in the past decade.

THE EXPECTANCY DISCONFIRMATION MODEL   Richard Oliver has spearheaded research on this subject with his **expectancy disconfirmation model.**[27] Consumers enter into purchase with *expectations* of how the product will actually perform once it is used. Researchers have identified three different types of expectations:

1. **Equitable performance**[28] — a normative judgment reflecting the performance one *ought* to receive given the costs and efforts devoted to purchase and use.

2. **Ideal performance**[29] — the optimum or hoped-for "ideal" performance level.

3. **Expected performance**[30] — what the performance probably will be.

Category 3, expected performance, is most often used in CS/D research, because this is the logical outcome of the alternative evaluation process discussed in Chapter 18.

---

[27] The basic source is Richard L. Oliver, "A Cognitive Model of the Antecedents and Consequences of Satisfaction Decisions," *Journal of Marketing Research* 17 (November 1980), 460–469. For a thorough current review of the evidence, see Richard L. Oliver and Wayne S. DeSarbo, "Response Determinants in Satisfaction Judgments," *Journal of Consumer Research* 14 (March 1988), 495–507; and David K. Tse and Peter C. Wilton, "Models of Consumer Satisfaction Formation: An Extension," *Journal of Marketing Research* 25 (May 1988) 204–212.

[28] Robert B. Woodruff, Ernest R. Cadotte, and Roger L. Jenkins, "Modeling Consumer Satisfaction Using Experience-Based Norms," *Journal of Marketing Research* 20 (August 1983), 296–304.

[29] Morris B. Holbrook, "Situation-Specific Ideal Points and Usage of Multiple Dissimilar Brands," in Jagdish N. Sheth, ed., *Research in Marketing* 7 (Greenwich, Connecticut: JAI Press, 1984), 93–112.

[30] M. Leichty and Gilbert A. Churchill, Jr., "Conceptual Insights into Consumer Satisfaction with Services," in Neil Beckwith *et al.*, eds., *Educators' Conference Proceedings* (Chicago: American Marketing Association, 1979), 509–515.

Once the product or service has been purchased and used, outcomes are compared against expectancies. Most researchers view this CS/D judgment as a subjective evaluation of the difference between expectancy and outcomes.[31] Others have shown that consumers also make use of objective product-performance evaluations in arriving at this judgment.[32]

The CS/D judgment takes one of three different forms:

1. **Positive disconfirmation** — performance is better than expected.
2. **Simple confirmation** — performance equals expectations.
3. **Negative disconfirmation** — performance is worse than expected.

Positive disconfirmation, of course, leads to a response of satisfaction, and the opposite takes place when disconfirmation is negative. Simple confirmation implies a more neutral response which is neither extremely positive nor negative. The outcome directly affects repurchase intentions; the greater the positive disconfirmation, the better.

To take an example, a young executive jogger develops knee pain that is diagnosed as a result of improper foot movement (pronation) and stride. He is given the choice of six different shoes that will minimize the problem. He has tried each on and makes a selection believing that the problem will be solved. His beliefs with respect to the chosen brand represent his prepurchase expectation, and it is positive. If actual running experience equals or exceeds that expectation, the outcome will be one of relative satisfaction. When this is not the case, there will be dissatisfaction.

It is interesting to note that high levels of satisfaction with a previously owned brand are often accompanied by some dissatisfaction following repurchase.[33] It appears that failure to exceed that high expectation can lead to mild dissatisfaction. At other times, however, those with poor prior

---

[31] William O. Bearden and Jesse E. Teel, "Selected Determinants of Consumer Satisfaction and Complaint Reports," *Journal of Marketing Research* 20 (February 1983), 21–28; Priscilla A. LaBarbera and David Mazursky, "A Longitudinal Assessment of Consumer Satisfaction/Dissatisfaction: The Dynamic Aspect of the Cognitive Process," *Journal of Marketing Research* 20 (November 1983), 393–404; and John E. Swan and I. Frederick Trawick, "Disconfirmation of Expectations and Satisfaction with a Retail Service," *Journal of Retailing* 57 (Fall 1981), 49–67.

[32] Gilbert A. Churchill, Jr., and Carol Suprenant, "An Investigation into the Determinants of Customer Satisfaction," *Journal of Marketing Research* 19 (November 1983), 491–504; Peter C. Wilton and David K. Tse, "A Model of Consumer Response to Communication and Product Experiences," in Larry Percy and Arch G. Woodside, eds., *Advertising and Consumer Psychology* (Lexington, Massachusetts: Lexington Books, 1983), 315–332; and Richard W. Olshavsky and John A. Miller, "Consumer Expectations, Product Performance, and Perceived Product Quality," *Journal of Marketing Research* 9 (February 1972), 19–21.

[33] Robert A. Westbrook and Joseph W. Newman, "An Analysis of Shopper Dissatisfaction for Major Household Appliances," *Journal of Marketing Research* 15 (August 1978), 456–466.

experience are pleasantly surprised and indicate even higher levels of satisfaction than do their previously satisfied counterparts.[34]

Westbrook has taken a different approach in CS/D research by challenging a sole reliance on cognitive (belief) measures.[35] He contends that it also is necessary to take account of feelings and emotions (affect) generated in purchase and use. His data suggest that satisfaction is better conceived as being a function of both cognitive and affective considerations. He rightly underscores the error of viewing the consumer only as a nonemotional information processor.

AN ATTRIBUTION THEORY PERSPECTIVE   Although the expectancy-disconfirmation model (and its modifications) has achieved wide acceptance, there have been some suggested alternatives, especially attribution theory.[36] Attribution theory postulates that there are three bases used to classify and understand why a product does not perform as expected:

1. *Stability.* Are the causes temporary or permanent?
2. *Locus.* Are the causes consumer or marketer related?
3. *Controllability.* Are these causes under volitional control or are they constrained by outside factors that cannot be influenced?

In one study, Folkes discovered that the stability and locus of product failure influenced expectancies regarding future failure and preferences for an outright refund rather than replacement.[37] Customers apparently expected the product to fail if purchased again when the cause was perceived to be stable. For that reason, a refund was preferred. When the cause was perceived as unstable, however, they were less likely to react in this way.

In a more recent study, Folkes and her colleagues found that airline passengers were more prone to complain about flight delays when the problem was attributed to airline negligence as opposed to constraints such as bad weather.[38] Also, passengers were affected by their perception of whether the cause was stable and recurring. If the problem was attributed to a recurring problem, future flying intentions were negatively affected.

---

[34] Stephen A. LaTour and Nancy C. Peat, "The Role of Situationally Produced Expectations, Others' Experiences, and Prior Experience in Determining Consumer Satisfaction," in Jerry C. Olson, ed., *Advances in Consumer Research* 7 (Ann Arbor: Association for Consumer Research, 1980), 588–592.

[35] Westbrook, "Product/Consumption-Based Affective Responses."

[36] Valerie S. Folkes, "Consumer Reactions to Product Failure: An Attributional Approach," *Journal of Consumer Research* 10 (March 1984), 398–409.

[37] Folkes, "Consumer Reactions."

[38] Valerie S. Folkes, Susan Kolestsky, and John L. Graham, "A Field Study of Causal Inferences and Consumer Reaction: The View from the Airport," *Journal of Consumer Research* 13 (March 1987), 534–539.

CONSUMER RESPONSE TO DISSATISFACTION

How extensive is dissatisfaction? What do consumers do when it occurs? Are complainers different from those who do not complain? These questions have been thoroughly researched in recent years.

CONSUMER COMPLAINT BEHAVIOR

Past evidence has shown dissatisfaction to range from about 20 percent[39] to around 50 percent of buyers depending on type of product,[40] with an average of approximately one-third.[41] A tally by Better Business Bureaus showed that the frequency of consumer gripes in 1986 did not change much from preceding years, with the majority involving order or delivery foul-ups, home improvement firms, and auto repair shops.[42]

A number of studies have showed the forms that consumer dissatisfaction can take,[43] and a recent study by Singh suggests three different categories:[44]

1. Voice responses — e.g., seeking redress from the seller.

2. Private responses — e.g., negative word-of-mouth communication.

3. Third-party responses — e.g., taking legal action.

"Once burned, twice shy" is a common reaction of Michigan consumers who no longer patronize businesses where they have had unpleasant experiences.[45]

These studies can be misleading, however, because they report only the complainers. There is solid evidence demonstrating that the majority never complain or seek redress.[46] In fact, Day and his colleagues have shown that only one-third do so and are more likely instead to boycott or to complain to others.[47]

---

[39] George B. Spokes and Loren V. Geistfeld, "Issues in Analyzing Consumer Satisfaction/Dissatisfaction with Clothing and Textiles," in H. Keith Hunt, ed., *Advances in Consumer Research* 5 (Ann Arbor: Association for Consumer Research, 1978), 383–391.

[40] John O. Summers and Donald H. Granbois, "Predictive and Normative Expectations in Consumer Dissatisfaction and Complaining Behavior," in William D. Perrault, ed., *Advances in Consumer Research* 4 (Atlanta, Georgia: Association for Consumer Research, 1977), 155–158.

[41] "More Than a Third of Michigan Consumers Have Been So 'Burned' That They Shy Away from Some Businesses," *Marketing News* (April 24, 1987), 20.

[42] *Research Recommendations*, National Institute of Business Management, July 31, 1987.

[43] Bearden and Teel, "Selected Determinants of Consumer Satisfaction"; Ralph L. Day, "Research Perspectives on Consumer Complaining Behavior," in Charles Lamb and Patrick Dunne, eds., *Theoretical Developments in Marketing* (Chicago: American Marketing Association, 1980), 211–215; and Ralph L. Day and E. Laird Landon, Jr., "Towards a Theory of Consumer Complaining Behavior," in Arch Woodside, Jagdish Sheth, and Peter Bennett, eds., *Consumer and Industrial Buying Behavior* (Amsterdam: North-Holland, 1977).

[44] Jagdip Singh, "Consumer Complaint Intentions and Behavior: Definition and Taxonomical Issues," *Journal of Marketing* 52 (January 1988), 93–107.

[45] "More Than a Third of Michigan Consumers."

[46] Bearden and Mason, "An Investigation of Influences."

[47] Ralph L. Day, Klaus Brabicke, Thomas Schaetzle, and Fritz Staubach, "The Hidden Agenda of Consumer Complaining," *Journal of Retailing* 57 (Fall 1981), 86–106.

Dissatisfaction often is a poor predictor of complaint behavior. Oliver has shown that the percentage of complaints among the dissatisfied directed toward the retailer range from 23 to 40 percent, and only 5 percent complain directly to the manufacturer.[48] In his research only 15 percent of variance in complaint behavior is explained by the satisfaction/dissatisfaction dimension.

Day and others have clarified the picture by demonstrating that attitude toward the act of complaining also must be taken into consideration.[49] Day has also shown that there are four additional factors that determine whether or not a complaint will be made:

1. significance of the consumption event — product importance, price, social visibility, time required in consumption;

2. knowledge and experience — number of previous purchases, product knowledge, perception of ability as a consumer, previous complaining experience;

3. difficulty of seeking redress — time, disruption of routine, costs;

4. chances for success in complaining.[50]

Nevin and George also have found that consumers will complain to the degree that there is some likelihood of positive outcomes.[51] For example, they will readily do so when a warranty is offered.

CHARACTERISTICS OF COMPLAINERS   The type of person who complains and seeks redress tends to be younger, with higher-than-average income and education.[52] Also, they are positive about consumerist activities in general,[53] prefer a lifestyle that demonstrates difference and individuality,[54] and experience little hesitancy in letting their problems be known.[55] They do not keep

---

[48] Richard L. Oliver, "An Investigation of the Interrelationship Between Consumer Dissatisfaction and Complaint Reports," in Melanie Wallendorf and Paul Anderson, eds., *Advances in Consumer Research* 14 (Provo, Utah: Association for Consumer Research, 1987), 218–222.

[49] Ralph L. Day, "Modeling Choices Among Alternative Responses to Dissatisfaction," in Thomas C. Kinnear, ed., *Advances in Consumer Research* 11 (Provo, Utah: Association for Consumer Research, 1984), 496–499; and Bearden and Mason, "An Investigation of Influences."

[50] Day, "Modeling Choices."

[51] George John and John R. Nevin, "The Role of Information Uncertainty, Disconfirmation and Disclosure Regulations as Determinants of Consumer Satisfaction and Complaint Behavior," in Terrance L. Shimp, ed., *1986 Educators' Proceedings* (Chicago: American Marketing Association, 1986), 68–73.

[52] Michelle N. Morganowsky and Hilda Mayer Buckley, "Complaint Behavior: Analysis by Demographics, Lifestyle, Consumer Values," in Wallendorf and Anderson, *Advances,* 223–226; and Bearden and Mason, "An Investigation of Influences."

[53] Bearden and Mason, "An Investigation of Influences."

[54] Kathy J. Cobb, Gary C. Walgren, and Mary Hollowed, "Differences in Organizational Responses to Consumer Letters of Satisfaction and Dissatisfaction," in Wallendorf and Anderson, *Advances,* 227.

[55] Marcia L. Richins, "An Investigation of Consumers' Attitudes Towards Complaining," in Andrew Mitchell, ed., *Advances in Consumer Research* 9 (Ann Arbor: Association for Consumer Research, 1982), 502–506.

these concerns to themselves. Over half share their experiences with friends and relatives, and evidence indicates that negative word of mouth can have a major influence on the buying behavior of others.[56]

RESPONSE TO COMPLAINTS   What type of response can be expected when a complaint is registered? Overall, research studies indicate that 55 to 60 percent are resolved to the consumer's satisfaction.[57] In a recent study, for example, Cobb, Walgren, and Hollowed found a 58-percent response rate to complaint letters.[58] The vast majority were in the form of a personal letter. The greatest response came from pizza and snack manufacturers, whereas only one-fourth of clothing firms replied.

Harmon and Resnik found that manufacturers responded positively about two-thirds of the time.[59] There was convincing evidence demonstrating that making a sincere effort to rectify problems increased consumer assurance that the firm really cares. Not surprisingly, satisfaction and intent to repurchase were notably strengthened.

RETAINING THE CUSTOMER

Customer retention should receive even greater priority than new customer solicitation. First, it generally is less expensive to hold onto present customers than to attract new ones. Furthermore, customer loss can be disastrous in mature markets that are experiencing little real growth. Therefore, customer loyalty based on genuine and ongoing satisfaction is one of the greatest assets a firm can acquire. Here are some of the ways in which marketers can strengthen their customer relationship.

ANALYZE LOST CUSTOMERS   The starting point lies in evaluation of overall sales growth. If sales are declining, then it is likely that problems exist in customer satisfaction and retention. This assumes, of course, that the overall market is not experiencing a corresponding sales decay.

The best diagnostic criterion is the **cancellation rate** — the proportion of customers who have not repurchased. This becomes most meaningful, of course, when it is viewed in comparison with previous years and the experience of competitors.

Cancellation rates indicate only *what* has happened, not *why*. Here is the crucial question: Are customers being *pushed away* by company actions (or

---

[56] Marcia L. Richins, "Word of Mouth Communication as Negative Information," in Kinnear, *Advances*, 697–702.

[57] Cynthia J. Grimm, "Understanding and Reaching the Consumer: A Summary of Recent Research. Part II — Complaint Response Satisfaction and Market Impact," *Mobius* (Fall 1987), 18.

[58] Cobb, Walgren, and Hollowed, "Differences in Organizational Responses."

[59] Robert R. Harmon and Alan J. Resnik, "Consumer Complaining: Exploring Expected and Desired Responses," in Bruce J. Walker *et al.*, eds., *An Assessment of Marketing Thought and Practice* (Chicago: American Marketing Association, 1982), 175–178.

CONSUMER IN FOCUS

19.2   AUTO MAKERS STRESS CONSUMER SATISFACTION

Auto marketers once determined how well a division or a dealer was doing just by analyzing the number of cars sold. The arithmetic isn't as simple now that consumers have more than 30 choices of car makes, many of them available in numerous models. Instead of just counting units sold, the industry is turning more to indices that indicate the number of customers satisfied.

The so-called Customer Satisfaction Index (CSI) has had a dramatic effect on nearly everyone in the industry, from product designers to the service desks at dealerships. The originator of the CSI and the most widely quoted CSI in the industry is the annual survey published since 1981 by J. D. Power & Associates, Agoura Hills, Calif. Power surveys 30,000 customers' satisfaction with technical aspects of the car and, separately, with dealer performance. The overall CSI averages how each make scores on both technical and dealer aspects.

And customer satisfaction, or dissatisfaction, affects more than just the odds that a customer will buy the same brand next time, says Jack Robbins, assistant general sales manager for General Motors Corp.'s Buick Division, Flint, Mich. Buick, which operates several programs aimed at improving customer relations from pre-sale to post-delivery, estimates that a satisfied customer will positively influence eight others and spur at least one more sale, while a soured customer will negatively affect 25 people.

Make	Rank	CSI
Acura	(1)	147
Mercedes-Benz	(2)	138
Honda	(3)	137
Toyota	(4)	134
Cadillac	(5)	131
Nissan	(6)	128
Subaru	(7)	126
Mazda	(8)	125
BMW	(9)	125
Buick	(10)	123
Plymouth	(11)	122
Audi	(12)	121
Volvo	(13)	121
Hyundai	(14)	119
Porsche	(15)	118
Mercury	(16)	118
Total Industry		**118**
Average of 16 other makes		**109**

Source: Raymond Serafin, "Auto Makers Stress Consumer Satisfaction," *Advertising Age* (February 23, 1987), S-12. CSI Data from *The Power Report*, August 1989, Vol. 11, No. 8, published by J. D. Power and Associates.

inaction), or are they being *pulled away* by competitors? If they are being pushed away by inadequate handling of complaints, a defective product, and so on, the problem obviously is an internal one. If they are pulled away, on the other hand, this is clear indication that some form of marketing overhaul is needed.

ANTICIPATE PROBLEMS IN CUSTOMER RETENTION   By the time a customer shows up as a cancellation, it normally is too late for retention measures to do much good. What is needed, then, is an "early warning system" that indicates problems with sufficient lead time for corrective actions to be taken. Ongoing surveys of consumer satisfaction lie at the heart of this warning system. *Consumer in Focus 19.2* provides an excellent example of how such data is collected and (hopefully) used in the American automobile industry.

This automobile-buyer satisfaction profile is replete with marketing implications. Let's take the example of Pontiac, which lies near the bottom of the pack. The median CSI index is 97, but Pontiac earned only 84. It was rated poorly by its own customers both on product quality as measured by the technical index and on satisfaction with dealer. If this rating has not already been translated into bad word of mouth and lower sales, it will be unless some immediate remedial actions are taken.

Incidentally, you may recall seeing the humorous TV ads for Isuzu featuring the outrageously exaggerated claims of dealer salesperson Joe Isuzu. There always would be a copy line saying, "He's lying." Given the low rating of Isuzu dealers on the CSI index, do you think this was a good strategy? Apparently a number of dealers thought to the contrary and cancelled their involvement in this campaign in Fall, 1987.

It also is helpful to undertake a "customer portfolio analysis" to provide an early warning of competitive problems. Table 19.2 provides an example of a portfolio analysis undertaken for a manufacturer of major household appliances. The focus here is on customer gain and loss relative to competitors for the current year as compared with the composite experience of previous years.

Notice, first of all, that the company is experiencing a decline overall in attracting customers from competitors, with the sole exception of brand A, where there has been a net gain this year. This is not a favorable indication. Even more ominous is the 6 percent decline in repeat buyers. Competitors B and C, in turn, are making some major inroads.

It is entirely possible that company actions are in some way causing customer alienation. Product quality could be slipping, prices may not be competitive, and so on. If this is the situation, then it is time for some remedial action in the marketing mix to remedy shortcomings. Further information obviously is required to detect where the problems lie.

There also is the possibility that competitors are making a more attractive offer to the consumer. If so, these losses could be permanent. It is necessary to make an immediate response based on further research into customer reactions and preferences.

A final possibility is that the problem lies in low consumer awareness of company distinctions. If this is the case, then the solution lies in revamped promotional strategy. Whatever the case, the early warning system has served its purpose.

These data also have their uses in an offensive rather than a defensive

TABLE 19.2		Customer Experience	
A CUSTOMER PORTFOLIO ANALYSIS FOR A MANUFACTURER OF MAJOR HOUSEHOLD APPLIANCES		Year-to-Date	Previous 5 Years
	First time buyers	31%	33%
	Switched from Brand A	7%	3%
	Switched from Brand B	2%	5%
	Switched from Brand C	3%	4%
	Switched from all other brands	9%	12%
	No previous buying history	10%	9%
	Repeat buyers	34%	40%
	Customers who switched brands	35%	27%
	Switched to Brand A	6%	6%
	Switched to Brand B	11%	7%
	Switched to Brand C	12%	7%
	All other brands	6	7%

strategy. The inroads into the share of Company A are encouraging. This is a good clue to a softening in its market position which can be further exploited once the reasons are clarified.

ENHANCE CUSTOMER RETENTION   While a certain level of customer loss is inevitable, it can be minimized if some simple precautions are observed in marketing strategy.

Build Realistic Expectations.   Remember that satisfaction is based on an assessment that prepurchase expectations were fulfilled. Consider what might happen if a consumer purchased a cellular car telephone on the basis of its offer of "clearest reception in the entire metropolitan area," only to find some real geographic limits on use. Even if all other brands have exactly the same problem, this company created an erroneous expectation through its promotion. Widespread dissatisfaction is altogether likely, and the blame lies with the advertising claim. The bottom line? Avoid exaggeration — the consumer might actually believe what you are saying and hold you accountable.

Make Sure That Product and Service Quality Meets Expectations.   The Strategic Planning Institute of Cambridge, Massachusetts, has analyzed the performance of nearly 2,600 businesses over a period of 15 years using such criteria as market share, return on investment, and asset turnover. Referred to as Profit Impact of Market Strategy (PIMS), this research led to one incontrovertible conclusion: *financial performance is tied directly to perceived quality of a company's goods and service.*[60]

More firms are importing a procedure called **Quality Function Deployment** (QFD) from Japan.[61] The concept itself is simple. To assure that products are perceived to be high quality, the voice of the customer is deployed throughout design, engineering, manufacturing, and distribution. Often for the first time engineers and designers are being forced to think about their customers and their needs. The overriding quality control criterion now becomes *conformity to customer specifications.*

This commitment to quality also must go beyond product and encompass service. The American Express Company provides an excellent example of what can happen when this is taken seriously.[62] Credit card operations expanded too quickly in the 1970s, and the number of complaints surged. A service tracking system was put in place to monitor success in processing new applications, sending accurate bills, and performing 100 other tasks. These reports are continually monitored, with rewards provided for meeting or exceeding standards of performance and corrective measures instituted when needed. The outcomes in terms of financial performance and market share have been impressive indeed.

Provide Realistic Guarantees.   "Quality comes first with us." This now is a common advertising message, but consumers often greet it with the bored response, "Oh yeah? Prove it!" Therefore, product guarantees are growing at "fever pitch."[63] It is easy to conclude that Lufthansa German Airlines fully intends an ontime arrival complete with checked baggage (see Figure 19.2), given their stringent guarantee to first class and business class passengers. There could be no better way to retain present customers, to say nothing of making competitive inroads.

Provide Information on Product Use.   Product designers should be aware of the ways in which the product fits into a consumer's lifestyle. How is it used? It should be designed and promoted in such a way that performance will be adequate under conditions actually experienced in the home. For example, buyers often use electric toasters for English muffins, rolls, and other types of baked goods as well as for bread. If the toaster will not properly handle these items, unconfirmed expectancies and dissatisfaction are likely.

---

[60] Bro Uttal, "Companies That Serve You Best," *Fortune* (December 7, 1987), 98–99.

[61] John R. Hauser and Robert L. Klein, "Without Good Research, Quality Is a Shot in Dark," *Marketing News* (January 4, 1988), 1–2.

[62] Uttal, "Companies That Serve You Best," 99.

[63] Sara E. Stern, "Guarantees at Fever Pitch," *Advertising Age* (October 26, 1987), 3.

FIGURE 19.2
**CUSTOMER
RETENTION AND
ATTRACTION
THROUGH USE
OF A GUARANTEE**

Source: Courtesy of Lufthansa German Airlines.

Reinforce Customer Loyalty.   Bergiel and Trosclair have demonstrated the benefits of a very simple application of instrumental learning theory.[64] You may recall from Chapter 14 how certain response patterns can be reinforced by reward. They found that the loyalty of insurance customers could be reinforced by occasional reminders that their company still is interested in them. All it takes is a periodic letter affirming the commitment of both the company and the broker.

Take Complaints Seriously and Act Responsibly.   You may remember the public furor over the Audi 5000 model which was given wide publicity

---

[64] Blaise Bergiel and Christine Trosclair, "Instrumental Learning: Its Application to Consumer Satisfaction," *Journal of Consumer Marketing* 2 (Fall 1985), 23–28.

FIGURE 19.3
POSITIVE
CORPORATE
RESPONSE TO A
QUALITY PROBLEM:
DELTA PLEDGES
COMPANY
RESPONSIBILITY

DELTA AIR LINES, INC.
HARTSFIELD ATLANTA INTERNATIONAL AIRPORT
ATLANTA, GEORGIA 30320

W. WHITLEY HAWKINS
SENIOR VICE PRESIDENT
MARKETING

August 14, 1987

Dear Frequent Flyer:

You have selected Delta for a substantial amount of your travels
and we sincerely appreciate it. By your making this selection,
we have always thought of you as part of the Delta family - a
matter we take very seriously.

We also take very seriously our responsibility to provide you
with the finest and safest air transportation in the world. In
keeping with this responsibility, we feel an obligation to share
with you the attached memo written to all Delta personnel by
Ron Allen on July 31, 1987, regarding the incidents involving
Delta between June 18 and July 12 which have received so much
media attention. (At the time the memo was written, Ron was
our President and Chief Operating Officer. He has since become
our Chairman and Chief Executive Officer.)

Your overwhelming support during this very trying period has
been extremely gratifying to all of us here at Delta. The cards,
letters, phone calls and comments many of you have made to the
media have sustained us through these very difficult times. It
is during times like these that people's true colors are shown
and when real friends become highly visible.

We are proud to have you as friends and customers, and we renew
our pledge to you to provide you the finest airline service
possible. All of the slashing comments, jokes, political cartoons
and questionable reporting cannot erase the fact that Delta has
the finest service record of any airline in the world. We owe it
to you to keep it that way, and we will.

Thank you for being so special.

Sincerely,

Whit Hawkins

Attachment

Source: Courtesy Delta Airlines, Inc.

by an exposé on the CBS "60 Minutes" program.[65] A number of owners of
the 5000 with automatic transmission complained that the engine would surge
unexpectedly, causing the car to go out of control. Many deaths and injuries
were reported. The consistent reponse of Audi management was that the
car was not at fault. They claimed instead that the blame is with the driver
who hits the accelerator instead of the brake.

---

[65] For a review of the Audi story, see Fannie Weinstein, "One Foot in the Junkyard," *Advertising
Age* (October 19, 1987), 92.

Although there was opinion and evidence to the contrary, management stuck to this position for a long period of time. Finally, a recall was ordered and a minor transmission modification was made. Unfortunately, public confidence in Audi plummeted, and the future of the Audi 5000 model was doomed. Later evidence exonerated the company, incidentally.

What is the problem here? It is entirely one of passing the buck to the consumer. What did the company have to gain by stonewalling on this issue? Absolutely nothing! An immediate and apologetic recognition that something was seriously wrong accompanied by a recall might have headed off the outrage. The point, of course, is that widespread dissatisfaction can prove fatal.

Notice the different tack taken by Chrysler Motors' Chairman, Lee Iacocca, when he publicly admitted that his management was grievously wrong in turning back the odometers on executive-driven cars, and apologized publicly. The issue was instantly and effectively defused.

Another good example of responsible action appears in Figure 19.3. After a series of lapses in flight safety procedures, Delta Airlines management admitted culpability and reassured its frequent-flier customers that everything possible was being done to restore public confidence. Once again the issue was addressed along with a pledge of company responsibility.

We wish we could be optimistic that business will accept the counsel given here. Unfortunately, data provided by Fornell and Westbrook argue to the contrary. After an extensive review of the way in which customer complaints are handled, they concluded that organizational willingness to listen and respond decreases as the numbers of complaints increase.[66] We have more to say about this distressing problem in Chapter 25.

SUMMARY

This chapter examines the act of purchase and its outcomes. First, it is pointed out, making use of the model of consumer behavior, that purchase is a function of two factors: (1) purchase intentions and (2) environmental influences and/or individual differences. Often purchases are fully planned in the sense that there is intention to purchase both product and brand. At other times, intention encompasses only the product, with the choice of brand reserved for further deliberation at point of sale.

The so-called "unplanned" purchase is discussed at length. It was stressed that a purchase intention is not always consciously articulated, in which case product display provides a "surrogate shopping list." But many items also are bought purely on the basis of impulse, which can be spontaneous and hedonic in motivation.

A purchase can be made either at a retail outlet of some type or in the

---

[66] Claes Fornell and Robert A. Westbrook, "The Vicious Cycle of Consumer Complaints," *Journal of Marketing* 48 (Summer 1984), 68–78.

home. Retail outlets prosper in part because shopping has instrinsic value in and of itself. But there is also a dramatic growth of buying through direct mail, telephone, catalogs, and other nonretail sources. Strategies designed to reach the in-home buyer are referred to as direct marketing.

Decision-process behavior does not cease once a purchase is consummated, however. Further evaluation takes place in the form of comparing product or service performance against expectations. The outcome is one of satisfaction or dissatisfaction. Satisfaction serves to reinforce buyer loyalty, whereas dissatisfaction can lead to complaints, negative word of mouth, and attempts to seek redress through legal means.

This means that customer retention becomes a crucial part of marketing strategy. We stress how this can be done through such tactics as creating realistic expectations, insuring that product and service quality meets expectations, monitoring satisfaction and customer-retention levels, offering guarantees, and meeting dissatisfaction head on by quick and appropriate response.

REVIEW AND DISCUSSION QUESTIONS

1. You are the marketing manager for a manufacturer of specialty electronic items such as tiny lamps which illuminate only the page of a book, and a line of watches designed for runners. Would you seek to sell these items through retail stores or would you be inclined to try direct marketing (either alone or in combination with retail distribution)? Why? Would your answer differ if the product line consisted mostly of costly "upscale" women's fashion accessories (e.g., gloves, scarves)?

2. Given the diverse reasons why many consumers genuinely enjoy shopping, how would you capitalize on this phenomenon if you are marketing a high-quality ice cream line?

3. Why would you say that many conventional marketers have been hesitant to enter into direct marketing? What case would you make for direct marketing to a book publisher? A distributor of French wines?

4. The brand manager for a laundry detergent has read about the phenomenon of buyer regret and asks the company marketing research department to undertake a survey to see if this happens when laundry products are purchased. Do you feel that research would disclose widespread buyer regret when purchasing and using this product? Would your answer be different if the product is a compact disc stereo system featuring an all-new speaker system design? Why?

5. Review the situation facing Audi Motors after the disclosure of widespread problems with engine surge in Audi 5000 models with automatic transmission. What might have been done differently to meet this problem? Make a case to management justifying your conclusions.

6. What influence do advertising and selling efforts have in forming buyer expectations? What advice can you give to an advertising manager if you are asked to suggest ways in which promotional strategy could help increase buyer satisfaction?

7. "Come to White Fence Farm where we offer the world's best chicken." This claim has been heard for many years on Chicago radio. Would you recommend its continuation from the perspective of consumer satisfaction? What are the possible dangers?

8. You are asked to recommend ways of getting small portable appliance designers and

engineers to take quality seriously from the consumer's perspective. What would you suggest?

9. A manufacturer of do-it-yourself lawn care items is interested in understanding what happens to former customers. The issue is what brands they are now using, and why. What kind of research would you undertake to answer this question?

10. Consider a company that has experienced an increase in both cancellation rates and customer satisfaction over the past 3 years. What implications can be drawn from these findings?

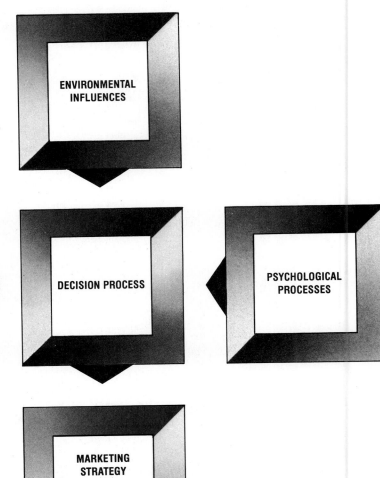

ENVIRONMENTAL
INFLUENCES

INDIVIDUAL
DIFFERENCES

DECISION PROCESS

PSYCHOLOGICAL
PROCESSES

MARKETING
STRATEGY
Product
Price
Promotion
Distribution

CONSUMER ANALYSIS AND MARKETING STRATEGY

We turn now to the final part of our overall model of consumer behavior shown on the facing page — *marketing strategy.* Traditionally, of course, marketing strategy is defined in terms of the four Ps — Product, Price, Promotion, and Place (distribution). Most readers have at least some grounding in marketing, so we do not feel it is necessary to provide an introductory discussion under these categories.

It has been our goal to stress marketing strategies in each chapter, and there will be little repetition here. Rather, we have chosen to highlight certain areas in which consumer research has special significance.

Chapter 19 opened the topic of consumer research as applied to distribution and retailing. There is much more to say, however, about the knowledge which has been gained in both retailing and direct marketing. This is the purpose of Chapter 20.

Chapter 21 broadens our earlier discussion on demographic and psychographic analysis and focuses on trends which are of greatest relevance to marketers. In a real sense, we enter the realms of *futurism,* but no one can avoid speculation on what will happen in the next decade.

Many chapters have referred to *market segmentation.* But we have not put this important type of marketing analysis into proper perspective. Therefore, Chapter 22 goes more deeply into this subject and summarizes and clarifies the discussion in earlier chapters.

Up to this point in time we have only referred occasionally to one area in which consumer research has had some of its greatest impact worldwide — *the diffusion of innovations.* There are thousands of published studies undergirding a solid body of theory and practical applications. This important subject is reviewed in Chapter 23 from the context of new product strategy.

Finally, Chapter 24 refers to the issue of global and international marketing. You were given a thorough introduction to cultural principles in Chapter 3, and this chapter both builds on and expands what has been said earlier, but from a cross-cultural perspective.

RETAILING

#1 AUTO DEALER IN THE NATION

n 1989, *Auto Age* magazine and *Automotive News* reported that Ricart Ford was the #1 Ford dealer in the world and the #1 Ford dealer in retail sales for the second year. With annual sales of over 16,000 cars, it might be expected that the #1 dealership would be in a major market such as New York or Los Angeles. Ricart Ford is in Canal Winchester, Ohio.

Ricart Ford was not always that successful. The average dealer in the U.S. sells about 500 cars in a year and in 1983, Ricart was below average. But during the early 1980's, they began to experiment with new forms of selling, training and advertising. The firm conducted over 500 consumer experiments, carefully observing the results of each.

Experiments involving careful observation and analysis to evaluate causation were nothing new to the President of the dealership, Fred Ricart. Ricart studied at Case Western Reserve University earning a bachelor's degree in biochemistry. During graduate study, he became a lab scientist spending years of research into the light-sensitive chemical necessary to transmit light patterns from the retina to the brain for translation into a visual image. Working hours in a darkened laboratory with only a dim safelight bulb for illumination, he turned to music to pass the time, singing to himself and playing the guitar. When the family business ran into a crisis, Fred Ricart left the lab to help his father but brought his scientist's approach to understanding consumer behavior — and his guitar — to the Ford dealership.

He spent years, along with his younger brother Rhett who is the accountant and information systems expert of the team, finding what works and what doesn't. They developed a training system for sales personnel that involves weeks of learning how "to sell yourself, instead of cars." They experimented with advertising media, learning what response could be expected if an ad was on the Bill Cosby show instead of Wheel of Fortune and the difference in response between 10 commercials ROS (run-of-schedule) on one channel versus more expensive commercials carefully placed on channels selected to match market targets.

They developed a system of selling whereby all visitors to the dealership are met with a parking plan as carefully orchestrated as parking at Disney World. Visitors are introduced to the well trained salespersons and the information system starts. At the beginning of each day, the computer displays the "close ratio" for each of the nearly 100 salespersons. The results: while the national average of 17% is considered good in many dealerships, Ricart Ford achieves a close ratio of 43%. You can afford to spend more on advertising to get a potential customer into the store when you are well prepared for them when they arrive.

With information systems that permit management to identify what every person in the firm is accomplishing, it is no wonder that independent rating services report the customer satisfaction with Ricart service area one of the highest of all dealerships in the nation. For both sales and service as well as other areas of the business, the Ricarts have detailed reports on the precise accomplishments of each person the preceding day. They don't threaten or intimidate employees with such information. Fred Ricart explains, "The advantage is derived simply from the fact that I know what our people are doing — and they know that I know."

Consumers are drawn from as far as Cleveland and Cincinnati. They see a friendly dealer having fun on TV, playing the guitar he picked up as a student and laboratory scientist, singing "We're dealing." The consumers may not see one of the most advanced training programs in the business, the careful design for the store and surrounding area, the cost-effective media plan, the computerized TV studio that allows changes in advertising (such as rebates or special service contracts) two to three weeks earlier than competitors or the state-of-the-art information system by which the firm is managed.

Advertising is the tip of the iceberg. It's the rest of the story that explains why Ricart Ford is the #1 Dealer in America.

Source: *The [Columbus] Daily Reporter,* December 16, 1987.

RETAILING: ULTIMATE TEST OF CONSUMER RESEARCH

In the last chapter, we examine the conceptual foundations of the purchase process — the final stage of decision making. This chapter "brings it home" with an applied analysis of the retailing environment. Here we examine questions such as: Where do consumers shop? In stores or in their own homes? Which stores do they choose? Which products and brands will be chosen as a result of in-store influences? How do the answers to these questions influence marketing strategy? How do consumers make decisions about retailers and retailing, and how is this related to the development of marketing strategy?

All of the material from preceding chapters is wasted unless consumer research can meet the ultimate test: Can retailers be persuaded to stock, price, service, and sell your product effectively? "Nothing happens of any value until someone sells something," the old adage states. And it's true. The best designed, produced, and advertised product is worthless unless retailers make it available to consumers in the format consumers are willing to buy.

Consumers have two places to buy: in stores or through nonstore retailing formats. Stores account for most of the sales, and therefore this chapter focuses on stores. Usually the term *retailing* refers to "store retailing" because of the dominance of stores over "nonstore" retailing. Therefore, when we speak of retailing, we usually are referring to in-store sales, even though the term *retailing* actually includes all forms of selling to consumers for their use.

Nonstore retailing is growing rapidly even though it is still the minority of total sales. New formats and innovative technologies are occurring, some of which are described in the latter part of the chapter. The chapter is divided into sections describing store and nonstore retailing, although most of the conclusions about consumer behavior apply to both formats of retailing.

THE POWER STRUGGLE

A massive power struggle is occurring between manufacturers and retailers for access to consumers. Increasingly, retailers are winning.

The struggle for channel control is not new. Only the winner is new. The period in American history following the Revolutionary War was the era of the traders, the forerunners of today's wholesalers. The wealthy and powerful businesses were those that could seek (mostly small, cottage-industry) manufacturers and match their goods with the small, decentralized retailers of the nation. In the era following the Civil War, the locus of power changed to large manufacturers, a condition that accelerated during the post–World War I era and continued until recently.

The emergence of massive mass merchants, often owned by a corporation with one or more billion-dollar chains, has put retailers in the driver's seat. Toys R Us recently announced that no manufacturer would be accepted as a supplier unless they conformed to the retailer's rules for packaging that, among other things, require information about what is inside the package on all four sides of the package. Why could the retailer dictate to the nation's largest toy manufacturers? Because Toys R Us accounts for 20 percent of the total market and is expected to double that market share during the 1990s.

When "power retailers" such as May, the Limited, or WalMart speak, manufacturers and distributors listen. Mergers and acquisitions within retailing also cause the shift. May Department Stores once was a fairly small chain of regional stores but, after acquisition of Gimbels and other chains, is a $10 billion department chain. Macy's bought Davisons. Federated bought Rich's. Macy's even tried to buy Federated but was outbid by a shopping center developer who understood the power of having "anchor stores" signed before breaking ground for new malls.

The concentration of volume among huge retail organizations is only part of the reason manufacturers are losing the power struggle to retailers. Among the best retail organizations, power is being concentrated internally as well. In the past, department organizations such as Federated, Macy's, and May were highly decentralized operations. Recent years have seen the development of centralized buying, national promotions, and sophisticated information and logistics systems that force manufacturers to conform to retailer requirements.

Retailing organizations such as the May Company aggressively recruit the brightest students from the nation's best business schools. Leading manufacturers have always done this. Retailers often were not competitive. But now when salespeople sit across from buyers and managers of the nation's best retailers, manufacturers are dealing with competent buyers backed with the power that arises from information systems and high-impact marketing programs to reach customers.

THE IMPACT OF RETAILING ON YOUR CAREER

The increasing power of retailers to impact consumers may interest you for two reasons. First, the most successful businesspersons are increasingly in the retailing sector rather than among manufacturing firms. The wealthiest person in the nation is reported to be Sam Walton, founder of WalMart, with personal assets of over $7.8 billion. If discount retailing does not appeal to you, maybe you would enjoy specialty retailing as much as Les Wexner, Chairman of the Limited, who made the list of the top five billionaires, with assets of over $2 billion.

More importantly, retailing is involved in innovative, sophisticated marketing programs. A career with top retailing organizations offers, or requires, as much sophistication in understanding consumer behavior as does any manufacturing organization.

Another reason for studying consumer behavior at the retailing level is the importance of the retailer to promotional decisions of consumer goods manufacturers. Resources are being shifted from advertising to programs that are more retailing oriented. Leo Bogart, one of the nation's most respected advertising analysts, explains this shift:

> *As companies expand into each other's traditional territories, the number of new brands and line extensions continues to grow, and competition intensifies for the limited amount of shelf and display space at the point of sale. Marketers' attention shifts from the struggle to influence the consumer to the primary battle to get products into the stores in the first place. Sheer presence and the visibility that can attract consumers count for a lot more than any amount of preconditioning through advertising. That is why a larger share of the marketing budget is going into promotion, much of it designed as a direct or indirect incentive to retailers to put the product where it can be bought. As the major retailers' market share expands, so does their power to dictate terms.* [1]

THE RETAILING REVOLUTION

A revolution began a few years ago and is exploding in the 1990s. The revolution is in retailing. Just as the Industrial Revolution dramatically affected the nature of manufacturing in the nineteenth century, so too the retailing revolution is affecting buying in the twentieth century. Retailers are pursuing innovations in effectiveness and productivity with aggressiveness and competitive fervor. Such competition requires more focus on how consumers buy. [2]

Two trends are especially dramatic. The first is the growth of the limited-line specialty store, which features narrow product lines but wide assortments. Hence, the service needs of customers can be met on a personalized basis. This is often tailored to specific lifestyle segments.

A second trend is the growth of mass merchandisers. They provide strong price appeal based on economies associated with self-service and operational efficiencies. They may also offer wide assortments to consumers. Caught in the middle are conventional outlets, which have increasing trouble competing and surviving.

The most successful firms in the retailing environment are increasingly building portfolios of retailing chains, each positioned to specific lifestyle segments. [2] Companies such as Dayton-Hudson, Melville Co., SCOA, W. R. Grace, and The Limited are examples of portfolio retailers.

The appeal of the specialty store is that everything it does is carefully tailored to meet a lifestyle segment with a unique product mix. [3] Such stores achieve inventory turnover rates often twice those of conventional stores.

---

[1] Leo Bogart, James Webb Young Fund Address, University of Illinois, April 7, 1988.

[2] Much of the following material is based upon Roger D. Blackwell and W. Wayne Talarzyk, "Life-Style Retailing: Competitive Strategies for the 1980's," *Journal of Retailing* 59 (Winter 1983), 7–27.

[3] A comparison of specialty shopping characteristics and conventional store characteristics is described in Daniel J. Sweeney and Richard C. Reizenstein, "Developing Retail Market Segmentation Strategy for a Women's Specialty Store Using Multiple Discriminate Analysis," in Boris Becker and Helmut Becker, eds., *1972 Combined Proceedings* (Chicago: American Marketing Association, 1972), 466–472.

Return on net worth follows suit. A good example is The Limited, which operates 780 Limited stores in carefully selected locations throughout the nation, maintains an ongoing program of consumer research to determine product and store criteria used by its market segments, and creates an exciting in-store atmosphere for presentation of high-fashion merchandise. Between 1980 and 1985, this approach yielded an average return on investment of 37 percent. The stock price in the same period rose 1,474 percent, more than any other on *Fortune's* list of 1,000 largest U.S. corporations, with a portfolio of over 3,400 Limited and other specialty stores by 1990.

At the other end of the spectrum are the mass merchandisers. These include discount department stores such as WalMart, one of the most successful retailers in the United States. Another successful example is Target, a division of Dayton-Hudson, which also operates major department stores. A number of newer forms are also emerging: warehouse stores such as Cub, Biggs, Warehouse Club, and supermarkets for commodities other than foods (examples are Toys R Us, Standard Brands Paint, and Herman's World of Sporting Goods).

The most dramatic and innovative of mass-merchandising forms is the **hypermarket.** These are stores in the 60,000- to 200,000-square-foot range that carry both convenience and shopping goods, with a heavy emphasis on general merchandise as well as on food. They have incorporated breakthrough technology in materials handling in a warehouse operating profile that provides both a warehouse feel for consumers as well as strong price appeal.

The hypermarket has been most successful in Europe, although Stein's in Montreal, Jewel in Chicago, WalMart in Dallas, and others have adapted some of the concepts to North America. Carrefour in France employs massive amounts of merchandise, total store graphics or graphics coordinated throughout the store, and classification dominance, all of which create excitement and price appeal. Hypermarkets also take advantage of operating economies involved in the technology of palletized product display and storage and the latest in scanning equipment at the cash registers.

These innovations underscore the rapidity of change in consumer purchasing and the consequent need for retailers to have a keen understanding of consumer research issues. How do consumers choose stores in which to shop? How important is location? How important is a store's image in determining store patronage? What factors determine image? What can be done to build store loyalty and to reduce shopper switching? These are topics discussed in this chapter.

WHERE WILL CONSUMERS SHOP?

Answering the questions about where consumers will shop involves several issues. How far will they travel to a retail location? Will they prefer regional shopping malls, neighborhood strip centers, or downtown shopping areas? After answering these questions, we can address the issue of which stores they will choose within acceptable categories. The strengths of individual stores will also influence consumer decisions about which shopping center may be chosen.

NUMBER OF LOCATIONS

Location strategies of retailers are one of the most important determinants of consumer behavior. More consumers buy fast food from McDonald's than any other organization, partially because McDonald's has two or three times more stores than its closest competitors. Attitude research may indicate consumers prefer Wendy's or taste tests may indicate consumers prefer Burger King's Whopper, but McDonald's, with over 10,000 stores, sells twice as much as the combined sales of both of its rivals.

Retailers with too few or too many stores often fail. So do retailers that locate on the wrong street, in the wrong shopping center, in the wrong city, or have the wrong parking spaces. An old adage says the three most important variables associated with retail success are: location, location, and location.

RETAILER STRATEGIES

Three levels of location decisions face marketing strategists: Market selection, area analysis, and site evaluation. This process is shown in Figure 20.1. Understanding how consumers decide where to buy is a critical input in each of these levels. Retailers need a clear understanding of the **value platform** of the firm — the manner in which the firm differentiates itself from its competitors in the minds of the consumers it intends to serve, allowing it to achieve a sustainable differential advantage over competitors.[4] The marketing strategy of a firm is then developed to select the quantity and specific locations of retail facilities.

A strategic approach relates location issues to the overall marketing plan of the firm. Management Horizons, a Division of Price Waterhouse, analyzed this process and formulated the following criteria for location decisions. Management Horizons concluded that location decisions for retailers and suppliers should be:

1. Broad-based — incorporating the exploration of new markets, the penetration of existing markets, and other long-term growth issues.

2. Proactive — helping to meet long-term corporate goals.

3. On-going — occurring at all levels of the strategic planning process from the development of corporate objectives to the monitoring of store location performance.

---

[4] Avijit Ghosh and Sara L. McLafferty, *Location Strategies for Retail and Service Firms* (Lexington, Massachusetts: Lexington Books, 1987), 16.

FIGURE 20.1   THREE LEVELS OF SPATIAL ANALYSIS IN SELECTING RETAIL LOCATIONS

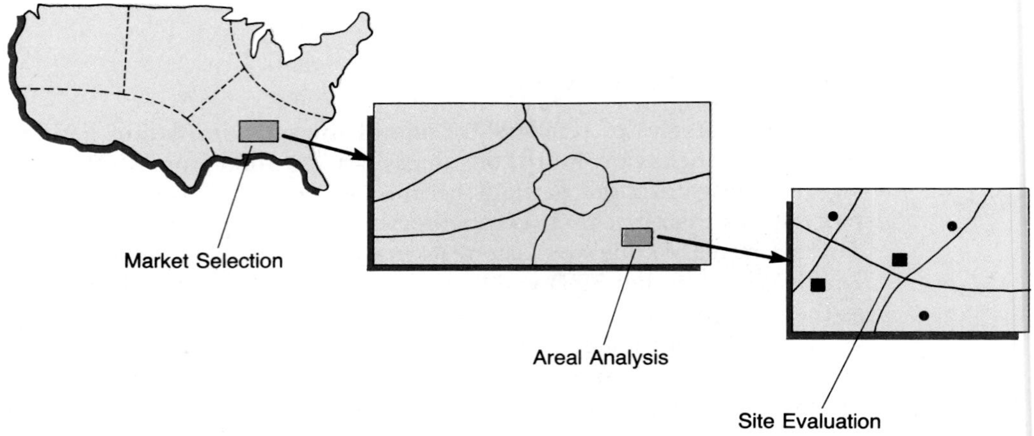

Market Selection

Areal Analysis

Site Evaluation

Source: Reprinted by permission of the publisher from *Location Strategies for Retail and Service Firms* by Avijit Ghosh and Sara L. McLafferty (Lexington, Mass.: Lexington Books, D. C. Heath and Company, 1987, 34, Copyright 1987; D. C. Heath and Company).

4. Consumer-oriented — based on a thorough knowledge of the target-market population, including their desire for convenience in time and space.

5. Whole-market — maximizing market coverage within a market.

6. Functionally integrated — providing input for merchandising, customer communications, and especially market share management.[5]

In Figure 20.1, the process of spatial analysis appears sequential. First, markets are selected, then areas within those markets and final specific sites. In actual practice, the process is interactive. Site selection may affect market selection as much as the converse.

As an example, a successful computer retailer based in one city wanted to expand its success to other cities. During the market selection process, they identified 15 cities with the geodemographic and competitive conditions that corresponded to the conditions of their current successful market. The firm did further analysis of the areas within those cities most likely to support the sales of personal computers. After completing the competitive and shopping center analysis, however, some cities contained much more attractive sites than did others. The final selection was made in the cities than ranked seventh, tenth, and eleventh on the original ranking of 15 cities.

---

[5] Peter A. Doherty, *Location Strategies to Support the Marketing Management Function* (Columbus: Management Horizons, 1984), 4.

CITIES AND TRADING AREAS

The marketing literature has a stream of studies attempting to explain the impact of the location of a town, city, or trading area. Foundational work by William J. Reilly postulated that two cities attract retail trade from an intermediate town in the vicinity of the **breaking point** (where 50 percent of the trade is attracted to each city) in direct proportion to their population and in inverse proportion to the square of the distance from the two cities to the intermediate town.[6]

Two decades later, Converse used the following modification of "Reilly's law" to explain intercity shopping patterns.[7]

$$\left(\frac{B_a}{B_b}\right) = \left(\frac{P_a}{P_b}\right)\left(\frac{D_b}{D_a}\right)$$

where

B_a = proportion of trade attracted from intermediate town by City A
B_b = proportion of trade attracted from intermediate town by City B
P_a = population of City A
P_b = population of City B
D_a = distance from intermediate town to City A
D_b = distance from intermediate town to City B.

These early models were useful but simplistic. They ignored relative incomes of the populations, merchandise assortments in the two cities, and consumer preferences. More recent research by Huff, Applebaum, Nakanishi, and Cooper and others incorporated other variables.[8] **Product category** also influences how far people will travel. Consumers will travel further for clothing than for household goods or products they feel need service locally.

What kind of person is the **outshopper** (one who shops outside a local trading area)? Socioeconomic status appears to be a big factor, especially in explaining the tendency of ghetto residents to shop in their neighborhood.[9] Outshoppers also have these psychographic characteristics:

1. They are significantly more exposed to nonlocal media and exhibit greater knowledge of the outside world.

2. They are more innovative, fashion conscious, gregarious, and socially active.

---

[6] William J. Reilly, *Methods for the Study of Retail Relationships* (Austin, Texas: Bureau of Business Research, University of Texas Press, 1929), 16.

[7] Paul D. Converse, "New Laws of Retail Gravitation," *Journal of Marketing* 13 (October 1949), 379–388.

[8] For a review of this literature, see Avijit Ghosh and G. Rushton, "Progress in Location Allocation Models," in A. Ghosh and G. Rushton, eds., *Spatial Analysis and Location Allocation Models* (New York: Van Nostrand Reinhold, 1987).

[9] Karen F. Stein, "Explaining Ghetto Consumer Behavior: Hypotheses from Urban Sociology," *The Journal of Consumer Affairs* 14 (Summer 1980), 232–242.

3. They invest a great deal of time and effort in shopping and consult all relevant sources of information to a greater extent than their counterparts do.

4. They are more mobile and more cosmopolitan in their outlook.[10]

Marketers can attract shoppers away from their neighborhood or local town by using regional media and offering strong variety of both product lines and shopping options, especially with unique specialty stores.

SHOPPING CENTERS

The shopping center selected by consumers is influenced by travel time and the size of shopping facility. The foundational research on this topic was conducted by Huff. Huff's model estimates the probability that consumers in each relatively homogeneous statistical unit (neighborhood) will go to a particular shopping center for a particular type of purchase.[11]

$$P_{ij} = \frac{\dfrac{S_j}{T_{ij}\lambda}}{\sum\limits_{j=1}^{n} (S/T_{ij}\lambda)}$$

where:

P_{ij} = probability that consumers from each of the ith statistical units will go to specific shopping center j

S_j = size of shopping center j

T_{ij} = travel time to shopping center j

λ = a parameter estimated empirically for each product category, for example, clothing, furniture.

Huff used this equation to plot isolines that are equiprobability contours that consumers will shop in center j. The probability of patronage declines as the distance to other centers becomes shorter and the distance to center j becomes longer.[12]

The willingness to go to a shopping center declines as driving time to the center increases. Bruner and Mason found 15 minutes to be the maximum

---

[10] William R. Darden, John L. Lennon, and Donna K. Darden, "Communicating with Interurban Shoppers," *Journal of Retailing* 42 (Spring 1978), 51–64.

[11] David L. Huff, "A Probabilistic Analysis of Consumer Spatial Behavior," in William S. Decker, ed., *Emerging Concepts in Marketing* (Chicago: American Marketing Association, 1962), 443–461.

[12] For an excellent discussion of other techniques for estimating shopping center patronage, see Bernard J. LaLonde, *Differentials in Super Market Drawing Power* (East Lansing, Michigan: Bureau of Business and Economic Research, Michigan State University, 1962). For dissenting findings about these types of models, see Joseph B. Mason and Charles T. Moore, "An Empirical Reappraisal of Behavioristic Assumptions in Trading Area Studies," *Journal of Retailing* (Winter 1970–1971), 31–37.

for approximately 75 percent of a center's patrons.[13] Other studies indicate wider variation depending on area of the country, normal traffic conditions, and other factors.

COGNITIVE MAPPING

Cognitive maps or consumer perceptions of store locations and shopping areas are more important than actual location.[14] Cognitive maps refer both to cognized distances and cognized traveling times. Consumers generally overestimate both functional (actual) distance and functional time.

Variations between cognitive and actual distance are related to factors such as ease of parking in the area, quality of merchandise offered by area stores, and display and presentation of merchandise by stores and ease of driving to an area. Other factors affecting the cognitive maps of consumers include price of merchandise and helpfulness of salespeople.[15]

INDIVIDUAL SITE LOCATION

Where people shop is influenced by very specific details of the retail site. For example, two restaurants may have similar offerings but the selection of a site a block or so away from the main artery may cause as much as 10 to 20 percent variation in sales between the otherwise identical restaurants. Retailers sometimes fail because they succumb to a short-term strategy of leasing cheaper space, with the consequence of long-term reduced profitability.

SITE LOCATION STUDIES   What variables affect consumer decisions about location and should therefore be considered in selecting a retail site? Some of the more important components of a site evaluation include the following items:

1. Site description (size, shape, etc.)
2. Lease requirements/land costs
3. Parking ratio
4. Pedestrian flow
5. Traffic flow (numbers and average speed)
6. Egress/Ingress
7. Public transportation access

---

[13] James A. Bruner and John L. Mason, "The Influence of Driving Time upon Shopping Center Preference," *Journal of Marketing* 32 (April 1968), 57–61.

[14] David B. Mackay and Richard W. Olshavsky, "Cognitive Maps of Retail Locations: An Investigation of Some Basic Issues," *Journal of Consumer Research* 2 (December 1975); and Edward M. Mazze, "Determining Shopper Movements by Cognitive Maps," *Journal of Retailing* 50 (Fall 1974), 43–48.

[15] R. Mittelstaedt et al., "Psychophysical and Evaluative Dimensions of Cognized Distance in an Urban Shopping Environment," in R. C. Curhan, ed., *Combined Proceedings* (Chicago: American Marketing Association, 1974), 190–193.

8. Visibility, signage, ambience
9. Affinities (neighbors)
10. Access to trade area [16]

COMPUTER ANALYSIS   Site location studies are usually done with a computer. A ring around the site is drawn at a distance of 1.5 miles, 3 miles, or 5 miles. A refinement of this process is to compute the circles on the basis of 5, 10, or 20 minutes driving time to the store. An example of such an analysis is shown in Figure 20.2. The market within 1.5 miles of a proposed site at Santa Monica Boulevard and Wilshire in Beverly Hills is shown in

FIGURE 20.2   COMPUTER ANALYSIS OF RETAIL SITE BASED ON DRIVING TIME

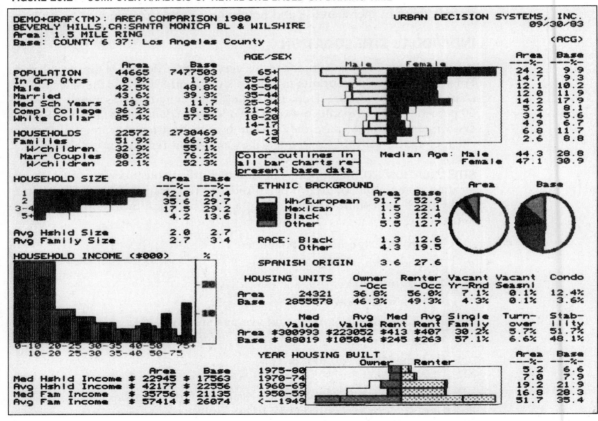

Source: Urban Decision Systems, Inc., Los Angeles, California.

---

[16] For additional details on store location decisions see William R. Davidson, Daniel J. Sweeney, and Ronald W. Stampfl, *Retailing Management,* 5th ed. (New York: John Wiley & Sons, 1984), 179–197.

this analysis, a computer printout by Urban Decision Systems. Note that Figure 20.2 shows the data (population, households, ethnic background, etc.) for both the primary area (1.5-mile ring) and the market base (Los Angeles County). Discriminant analysis or multiple regression models can be used to assess the probability of success in a specific site.

DENSITY   An important variable in site location is density of population. Demand may seem to be high because of income, ethnic characteristics, family size, or other variables. Lack of density negates many of these effects.

An example of the density problem can be seen in the case of the restaurant chain Max & Erma's. The firm has a varied menu but its specialty is gourmet hamburgers. They are large, very tasty, and served in a fun atmosphere that appeals to young, upscale, well-educated consumers. The restaurant chain opened a restaurant in Johnson County, Kansas (a suburb of Kansas City) because the market analysis showed that market area to have one of the highest incomes in the Midwest, with households that are young and well educated. The market profile seemed ideal for the restaurant's consumer profile, but Max & Erma's failed to consider that the area was so upscale that there were few houses per square mile. Density was too low, and the location was eventually closed. The firm learned that even though the product is excellent, consumer attitudes are favorable, service is good, and the socioeconomic profile of the market is excellent, a retailer still fails when the market area lacks the density required for success.

REGIONAL DENSITY   On a regional basis, retailing organizations sometimes fail by choosing regions with low density. Sun Belt markets may be growing rapidly but lack density. The best retailing sites may still be east of the Mississippi because 60 percent of retail sales are transacted in the 29 percent of continental land area east of the Mississippi. The top states in population density are New Jersey, Rhode Island, Massachusetts, Connecticut, Maryland, New York, Delaware, Pennsylvania, Ohio, Illinois, Michigan, Indiana, and the District of Columbia. It was not until recently that a Sun Belt state, Florida, even came close to matching the population densities of the top states. After analyzing these data, Cooke concluded, "In spite of ongoing population shifts to the South and West, the best retail markets are still located in the North and East, and will be for years to come."[17]

MICROSPECIALIZATION   Retail location decisions are increasingly made through **microspecialization** — identification of specific market targets and development of specialized retailing formats that provide a high level of satisfaction to those market targets. With microspecialization, most marketing organizations find it more efficient to access the data on-line by networking their own computer with private firms specializing in data bases specific enough to be useful to retailers. A list of some of these firms is displayed in Figure

---

[17] Ernest F. Cooke, "Why Most of the Retail Action Is East of the Mississippi," *American Demographics* 6 (November 1984), 20–23.

FIGURE 20.3   PROFILES OF ON-LINE DEMOGRAPHIC DATA BASE FOR RETAILERS AND OTHER MARKETING ORGANIZATIONS

Legend:
- □ Diaries are kept by cross section of the population.
- △ Includes sales reports from 20 different types of bullets including sales potential.
- ▲ Includes information on ten major U.S. markets.
- ○ U.S. household with incomes in the top 10%.

	SOURCES OF INFORMATION						DATABASE COVERAGE						SPECIAL FEATURES			INFORMATION ACCESSED BY						UPDATED	
	Census Data 1980	Census Data 1970	Demographic Reports	Projections/Estimates	Consumer Price Index	Census of Retail Trade	Total population	Number of size of households	Median income	Race, Age, Sex	Level of Education	Housing Value	Geo-demographics	Mapping software	Mailing label production	Zip Code	Counties	Census tracts	Entire U.S.	ADI	Geometric shapes	Annually	Daily
ACORN	●	●	●	●			●	●	●	●	●	●	●			●	●	●	●	●	●	●	
AMERICAN PROFILE	●	●		●			●	●	●	●	●	●				●	●		●	●		●	
ARBITRON RADIO & TV			●	●			□			●	●	●	●			□				●			
CENDATA	●		●				●	●	●	●	●	●											●
CENSUS REPORTING PROGRAM	●						●				●							●	●				
GRAPHIC PROFILE	●	●		●			●	●		●								●	●	●		●	
MARKETPOTENTIAL	●			●	●	●	△	●	●	●	●	●	●	●		●	●	●	●	●		●	
MAX	●	●	●	●	●	●	●	●	●	●	●	●	●	●		●	●	●	●	●		●	
MRI-MEDIAMARKETS							▲										●					●	
NPA/DEMOGRAPHIC				●			●										●					●	
ONSITE	●	●	●	●			●	●	●	●	●	●	●	●	●	●		●	●	●	●	●	
PRIZM	●	●		●			●	●	●	●	●	●	●	●	●	●		●	●	●	●	●	
SUPERSITE	●	●	●	●	●	●	●	●	●	●	●	●	●	●	●			●	●	●	●	●	
TARGETSCAN				●			●												●	●			
UPPER DECK—THE AFFLUENT				●			○			●	●	●	●						●			●	
VISION	●			●			●	●				●	●	●	●	●	●		●			●	

Source: "Tiny Targets: Pinpointing the Possibilities on Online Demographic Research," *Online Access 2* (November/December 1987), 29 and 44.

20.3, along with the geographical areas for which data can be accessed, the coverage of variables, and other features. Marketing analysts can obtain instant access to some of these data bases through networking services such as Compu-Serve. Any market analyst with a personal computer, a modem, and an account can find the data with which to make retail locations instantly at any time of the day or night.

THE COMPETITIVE BATTLE BETWEEN SHOPPING AREAS

A war is raging to decide which shopping area consumers will choose. The major competitors include regional shopping malls, neighborhood strip centers, or CBD (downtown Central Business Districts) shopping centers. Currently, regional malls are winning the war. A "flanking action" by some retailers is to locate stores in freestanding locations, usually near regional shopping malls. Innovative hybrids also arise such as "power centers" combining the convenience of neighborhood centers and the selection and attractiveness (although smaller) of regional malls.

THE MALLING OF AMERICA

Regional shopping malls have progressed dramatically since J. C. Nichols built the first one, Country Club Plaza, in Kansas City in 1922. That original shopping center is shown in Figure 20.4. Today it has changed so much that the Plaza is one of the most exciting collections of upscale retailers in the nation. The ultimate progression of the original shopping center is shown in the other portion of Figure 20.4, West Edmonton Mall in Edmonton, Alberta, Canada.

The West Edmonton Mall is generally recognized as the largest in the world, with 5.2 million square feet and 800 stores and services. One of the features is a 5-acre World Waterpark, the largest indoor waterpark in the world, shown in Figure 20.4. Other features include 19 movie theaters, a hotel, 110 food outlets, dozens of amusement rides, an ice rink, a miniature golf course, a chapel, a car dealership, and a zoo. Consumers arrive not only from nearby to shop; they arrive from all over North America to shop and play for a few days. West Edmonton Mall is a "destination shopping center," and developers are bringing a slightly smaller mega-mall to the United States, in suburban Minneapolis.

There are over 28,500 shopping centers in America, compared to only 2,000 in 1957. This has produced a serious overbuilding problem. Between 1974 and 1984, the retail footage increased 80 percent while population increased only 12 percent. As a consequence, only six new regional malls were built in 1986, down from an average of 14 per year in the early eighties and a high of 30 per year in the mid-seventies. Most of the new shopping centers are much smaller, sometimes called "mini-malls."

The competitive reality is that shopping centers are working as hard to attract consumers from other centers as are individual retailers competing with each other. The result is more emphasis on marketing. Southdale Center was opened in 1956 in suburban Minneapolis, described as the first enclosed

FIGURE 20.4
THE EVOLUTION OF SHOPPING MALLS FROM THE ORIGINAL IDEA TO THE NEWEST MEGA-MALL

Source: *The Evolution of Regional Shopping Centers* (Atlanta: Equitable Real Estate Investment Management Inc., 1987). Top photo courtesy of J. C. Nichols Company. Bottom photo courtesy of West Edmonton Mall.

CONSUMER IN FOCUS

20.1   DOWNTOWN IS FUN

The "big idea" of recent years has been the "festival marketplace." Of course, cities have always had markets and some specialized retail areas. The concept of recycling old buildings into a complex of shops and restaurants on a major scale was first done in the mid-1960's in Chirandelli Square and the Cannery in San Francisco. However, it was James Rouse who fully conceptualized and implemented the festival-marketplace concept with the development of Faneuil Hall Marketplace in Boston in 1976.

Other festival marketplaces and retail complexes already developed include Harborplace in Baltimore, the South Street Seaport in New York City, the Union Station project in St. Louis, the Waterside in Norfolk, Portside in Toledo, the 6th Street Marketplace in Richmond, and the Old Post Office in Washington, D.C. Almost every large city now has or is developing a marketplace.

While hugely successful as retail centers, the festival marketplaces have had a much more important role in creating new civic gathering places and in dramatically chang-

ing the image of American cities. A 1981 *Time* magazine cover story on James Rouse declared, "Cities Are Fun!" — a statement almost unthinkable in the atmosphere of the 1960s. The nurturing of this new spirit of fun and vitality at the core of cities has been a major factor in the resurgence of the American downtown in the past decade.

The success of the festival marketplace has spurred new interest in downtown retailing, which had been dormant or declining in most cities since the 1960s. Today, major retail complexes have been completed or are under construction in many cities, including development of new department stores. In many cases, the retail complexes connect existing stores. The Rouse Company has also been a pioneer in this movement, with the Gallery in Philadelphia, Grand Avenue Concourse in Milwaukee, The Shops in Washington, and the new Gallery at Harborplace in Baltimore.

Source: John Fondersmith, "Downtown 2040: Making Cities Fun," *Futurist* 22 (March–April 1988), 9–17.

mall. Today, not only has it been remodelled but it has a yearly marketing budget of about $424,000, with about 75 to 80 percent devoted to advertising and public relations.[18]

What can regional malls do to attract consumers? Many are adding the entertainment, merchandise, food, and ambiance required to be competitive since regional malls became the "Main Street of America."

MINI-MALLS AND STRIP CENTERS

The fastest growing shopping areas are small and medium-size centers of various formats, usually with less than 100,000 square feet. Some "strip"

---

[18] George R. Puskar, "Regional Malls: A Preferred Institutional Investment," *The Real Estate Finance Journal* (Summer 1987), 77–83.

centers are still being built, containing mostly mom-and-pop stores. Some are neighborhood shopping centers with a variety of convenience merchandise stores accompanied also by substantial traffic-flow problems, with concerns of the effects on neighboring residential areas.

A few of these are well planned and designed, sometimes in an enclosed or all-weather format, and are called **mini-malls** or **power malls.** Many older shopping centers have been "reformatted" by enclosing them and given a more contemporary appearance. Some have recaptured or maintained consumer patronage because of convenient location and density of population in the surrounding neighborhood.

CBD CENTERS

A major question about where consumers will shop is whether or not they will return downtown — to the **Central Business District** (CBD). There are many efforts to revitalize the downtown area as a place to shop as well as a

FIGURE 20.5   THE DOWNTOWN SHOPPING CENTER MAKES A COMEBACK

JVJ'S GALLERIA AT ERIEVIEW.

Downtown Dazzles Again. If you haven't seen Cleveland lately, you haven't seen it. There's a bold and optimistic new spirit that's personified in Jacobs, Visconsi & Jacobs Co.'s Galleria at Erieview. Almost overnight, city shopping, dining, and entertainment have taken on a whole new light.
...And The Light Keeps Getting Brighter. The Galleria is redefining not only downtown Cleveland, but what retailers can expect from urban shopping centers. And the results have been excellent. Clevelanders are shopping downtown again — even at night and on weekends — producing record-breaking results for Galleria shops and restaurants.

The brave new energy that built the Galleria is the driving force behind Jacobs, Visconsi & Jacobs Co. In its own hometown, JVJ has achieved the reputation as the company that gets things done. And it's the standard that JVJ brings to every one of its developments across the country.

JACOBS, VISCONSI & JACOBS CO.
25425 Center Ridge Road
Cleveland, Ohio 44145 · 216/871-4800

Source: Courtesy of Jacobs, Visconsi, & Jacobs Co., Cleveland, Ohio.

place to work. *Consumer in Focus 20.1* shows how **"festival marketplaces"** can be used to get people shopping downtown again. Figure 20.5, an ad for a shopping center developer, shows what CBD shopping centers are doing to attract people back downtown.

The consumer has many places to shop—downtown, neighborhood malls, regional shopping centers, even in other towns. Retailers have many decisions to make in responding to these choices — regarding markets, areas, and specific sites. Now we move from these decisions to how consumers choose specific retailers.

How CONSUMERS CHOOSE SPECIFIC RETAILERS

Consumer decisions to buy a product, brand, or from a specific retailer are closely related. The sequence of decisions is often thought to be product category, brand, store, but this is not always true. Sometimes consumers simply go shopping with no specific product or brand in mind. This may reflect a desire to get out of the house, to window shop, or to spend leisure time with the family. Whether the product or the retailer is foremost in consumers' minds, how people decide to enter specific stores and what they do in those stores is of enormous consequence in analyzing consumer behavior.

Consumers shop for both personal and social motives. These motives are described in Table 20.1. Examination of these motives indicates many things retailers can do to attract consumers. Consider, for example, the motive of "Sensory Stimulation" described in Table 20.1. Successful grocery stores place a bakery near the front of the store, greeting people with the aroma of fresh-baked products. The Limited has been a leader in attracting consumers with an array of visual and auditory stimuli in the Limited and Limited Express stores. Their newest addition to the sensory array is in Victoria's Secret, where attractive scents whiff through the store, enhancing the appeal of entering and lingering in the store.

THE STORE-CHOICE DECISION PROCESS

Choosing a store is a process of interaction between retailers' marketing strategies and individual and situational characteristics of buyers. This process is described by Monroe and Guiltinan.[19] Store choice is similar to the general model of decision making used throughout this book.

Individual characteristics (such as lifestyles) cause general outlooks on and activities involved in shopping and search behavior. Retailers influence these activities with advertising and promotional strategies. Buyer characteristics also affect store image. Store image, in turn, affects store choice and the eventual product or brand purchase. If past experiences have been satisfactory,

---

[19] Kent B. Monroe and Joseph P. Guiltinan, "A Path-Analytic Exploration of Retail Patronage Influences," *Journal of Consumer Research* (June 1975), 19–28.

Personal Motives

Role Playing
Many activities are learned behaviors, traditionally expected or accepted as part of a certain position or role in society—mother, housewife, husband, or student.

Diversion
Shopping can offer an opportunity for diversion from the routine of daily life and thus represents a form of recreation.

Self-Gratification
Different emotional states or moods may be relevant for explaining why (and when) someone goes shopping. Some people report that often they alleviate depression by simply spending money on themselves. In this case, the shopping trip is motivated not by the expected utility of consuming, but by the utility of the buying *process* itself.

Learning about New Trends
Products are intimately entwined in one's daily activities and often serve as symbols reflecting attitudes and life-styles. An individual learns about trends and movements and the symbols that support them when the individual visits a store.

Physical Activity
Shopping can provide people with a considerable amount of exercise at a leisurely pace, appealing to people living in an urban environment. Some shoppers apparently welcome the chance to walk in centers and malls.

Sensory Stimulation
Retail institutions provide many potential sensory benefits for shoppers. Customers browse through a store looking at the merchandise and at each other; they enjoy handling the merchandise, the sounds of background music, the scents of perfume counters or prepared food outlets.

Social Motives

Social Experiences Outside the Home
The marketplace has traditionally been a center of social activity and many parts of the United States and other countries still have market days, country fairs, and town squares that offer a time and place for social interaction. Shopping trips may result in direct encounters with friends (e.g., neighborhood women at a supermarket) and other social contact.

Communications with Others Having a Similar Interest
Stores that offer hobby-related goods or products and services such as boating, collecting stamps, car customizing, and home decorating provide an opportunity to talk with others about their interests and with sales personnel who provide special information concerning the activity.

Peer Group Attraction
The patronage of a store sometimes reflects a desire to be with one's peer group or a reference group to which one aspires to belong. For instance, record stores may provide a meeting place where members of a peer group may gather.

Status and Authority
Many shopping experiences provide the opportunity for an individual to command attention and respect or to be waited on without having to pay for this service. A person can attain a feeling of status and power in this limited master-servant relationship.

Pleasure of Bargaining
Many shoppers appear to enjoy the process of bargaining or haggling, believing that with bargaining, goods can be reduced to a more reasonable price. An individual prides himself in his ability to make wise purchases or to obtain bargains.

Source: Excerpted from Edward M. Tauber, "Why Do People Shop?" *Journal of Marketing* 36 (October 1972), 46–59. Reprinted from the *Journal of Marketing* published by the American Marketing Association.

the choice will be fairly habitual, unless other factors have changed since the last visit.

SHOPPER PROFILES

Store choice is affected by specific characteristics of buyers. Thus, some stores have customers with a particular profile while other stores attract differing shopper profiles. Demographics and psychographics are useful in describing shopper profiles.

DEMOGRAPHIC PROFILES   Retailers are most successful when they appeal to specific market segments. When stores understand the profile of their core customers with demographic variables such as age, income, and place of residence, the outlet can maximize its appeal through its product and service mix.[20] The Limited makes a strong appeal to women 25 to 40. The parent corporation targets younger women with the Limited Express and slightly older women with its Lane Bryant chain.

Geography is also important. In a study of grocery shopping for coffee, Winn and Childers found geographic regions and central city size as important correlates explaining shopping concentrations. Also important were social status variables such as income, education, and occupation.[21] The on-line data sources described in Figure 20.3 can be used to profile customers whose addresses are known to the store. Other demographic variables such as race are correlated with type of store shopped, days of the week that shopping occurs, and degree of shopping activity.[22] Even religion has been found to have relevance in predicting purchase of certain types of furniture.[23]

Demographics and socioeconomic variables are also correlated with the amount of purchasing activity that consumers will undertake. A scale developed by Slama and Taschian measures purchasing involvement. It includes Likert-type statements such as "It is part of my value system to shop around for the best buy," and "Being a smart shopper is worth the extra time it takes." Building on prior research investigating consumer involvement and search activity by Kassarjian and other researchers, Slama and Taschian found that the consumers most likely to be involved in purchasing ac-

[20] A. Coskun Samli, "Use of Segmentation Index to Measure Store Loyalty," *Journal of Retailing* 51 (Spring 1975), 51–60.

[21] Paul R. Winn and Terry L. Childers, "Demographics and Store Patronage Concentrations: Some Promising Results," in Kenneth L. Bernhart, ed., *Marketing: 1776–1976 and Beyond* (Chicago: American Marketing Association, 1976), 82–86.

[22] Donald E. Sexton, Jr., "Differences in Food Shopping Habits by Area of Residence, Race, and Income," *Journal of Retailing* 50 (Spring 1974), 37–49.

[23] Howard A. Thompson and Jesse E. Raine, "Religious Denomination Preference as a Basis for Store Location," *Journal of Retailing* 52 (Summer 1976), 71–78.

tivity (including search activities beyond the retailing environment) are women who have children, moderate incomes, and relatively high educations.[24]

PSYCHOGRAPHIC PROFILES   Psychographics allow retailers to profile the lifestyles of heavy users. Microspecialization, adapting the formats of retailing to specific market targets, is done by adapting the product and service mix of the store to the activities, interests, and opinions of customer groups. Observe the appeal in *Consumer in Focus 20.2* to women who wear petite sizes.

RETAIL IMAGE

Patronage is determined both by evaluative criteria of consumers and their perception of store attributes. The overall perception is referred to as **store image.** This concept has been defined in various ways,[25] but no one has improved much on Martineau's idea of store personality as "the way in which a store is defined in the shopper's mind, partly by its functional qualities and partly by an aura of psychological attributes."[26] Since image is the reality upon which consumers rely when making choices, image measurement is an essential tool for consumer analysts.

RETAIL IMAGE MEASUREMENT   Retail image is measured across a number of dimensions reflecting salient attributes. Not surprisingly, almost the entire gamut of attitude-research methods is used, including semantic differential,[27] customer prototypes,[28] the Q-sort,[29] the Guttman scale,[30] multidimensional scaling,[31] and psycholinguistics.[32]

[24] Mark E. Slama and Armen Taschian, "Selected Socioeconomic and Demographic Characteristics Associated with Purchasing Involvement," *Journal of Marketing* 49 (Winter 1985), 72–82.

[25] See Jay D. Lindquist, "The Meaning of Image," *Journal of Retailing* 50 (Winter 1974–1975), 29–38; Robert A. Hansen and Terry Deutscher, "An Empirical Investigation of Attribute Importance in Retail Store Selection," *Journal of Retailing* 53 (Winter 1977–1978), 59–72; and Leon Arons, "Does Television Viewing Influence Store Image and Shopping Frequency?" *Journal of Retailing* 37 (Fall 1961), 1–13; Ernest Dichter, "What's In An Image," *Journal of Consumer Marketing* 2 (Winter 1985), 75–81.

[26] Pierre Martineau, "The Personality of the Retail Store," *Harvard Business Review* 36 (January–February 1958), 47.

[27] G. H. G. McDougall and J. N. Fry, "Combining Two Methods of Image Measurement," *Journal of Retailing* 50 (Winter 1974–1975), 53–61.

[28] W. B. Weale, "Measuring the Customer's Image of a Department Store," *Journal of Retailing* 37 (Spring 1961), 40–48.

[29] See, for example, William Stephenson, "Public Images of Public Utilities," *Journal of Advertising Research* 3 (December 1963), 34–39.

[30] Elizabeth A. Richards, "A Commercial Application of Guttman Attitude Scaling Techniques," *Journal of Marketing* 22 (October 1957), 166–173.

[31] Peter Doyle and Ian Fenwick, "How Store Image Affects Shopping Habits in Grocery Chains," *Journal of Retailing* 50 (Winter 1974–1975), 39–52.

[32] Richard N. Cardozo, "How Images Vary by Product Class," *Journal of Retailing* 50 (Winter 1974–1975), 85–98.

CONSUMER IN FOCUS

20.2   PETITE FASHION RETAILERS

Fifty million American women are 5 feet 4 inches tall or under in sizes 2 to 12. Petite fashions cater to these shorter shoppers.

In 1983, The United States Shoe Corporation of Enfield, CT added the chain to its divisions: Casual Corner, Ups N'Downs, Caren Charles, August Max, Cabaret and Sophisticated Woman. To date, there are 160 Petite Sophisticate stores in most of the 50 states, with plans to open 10 to 15 this year. A long-term goal is to have 400 units by the early 1990s.

Says Skurow, "No one understands or knows how to dress the petite woman better than we do. Now we're going to use that expertise to offer great fashion to the 50 million American women who look to us as the authority on petites." According to the company, 50 million women translate into 54 percent of the American female population, aged 18 and over, in the 5 feet 4 inches or under category.

Skurow says the company looks at the demographics of the mall when deciding on locations for the 1,500-square-foot to 4,000-square-foot stores. "Ninety-five percent are in regional malls," he says.

The stores carry career separates, dresses, suits, coats, evening clothes, and active and leisure wear. Prices range from moderate to designer. "Most of the major designers have a petite line today," says Skurow. "There are more vendors and a broader selection now."

That broader selection is what some shoppers enjoy about the stores. Petite Sophisticate offers Club 5'4", PS Sport, Petite Sophisticate and Lauren Cole as private labels, in addition to the name brand and designer lines.

Selection, coupled with service, fashion and fit are hallmarks of the chain. "There are so many factors that lead to success, I can't pinpoint one," Skurow says. Fit includes scaling down the clothes to proportion, by adjusting waistlines, hemlines, sleeve lengths and pant rises. Also, the details are appropriately sized by narrowing lapels, reducing pocket size and shortening cuff depth.

Source: Jane A. Black, "Focus on Retailing," *Monitor* 18 (May 1988), 94 and 111.

Attitude-measurement techniques you learned in Chapter 11 are equally applicable for retail measurement. A multiattribute approach is appropriate for retailing applications.[33] Many retailers develop their own proprietary image-measurement techniques.

An example of a multiattribute approach in retailing is presented in Table 20.2. This research focuses on men's clothing stores in a college town. Potential customers were asked to list attributes, characteristics, or terms that come to

---

[33] See, for example, Don L. James, Richard M. Durand, and Robert A. Dreves, "The Use of a Multi-Attribute Attribute Model in a Store Image Study," *Journal of Retailing* 52 (Summer 1976), 23–32; and Hansen and Deutscher, "An Empirical Investigation."

TABLE 20.2 BELIEF AND IMPORTANCE SCORES FOR RETAIL STORES

Attribute	Importance Scores	Store A	Store B	Store C	Store D	Store E	Store F	Store G	Store H
Price	6.13	3.71	3.91	4.48	5.14	3.93	4.11	3.92	4.06
Assortment	6.11	4.79	4.56	4.21	4.68	4.33	4.23	4.39	4.46
Personnel	5.15	4.70	4.56	4.31	4.40	4.39	4.34	4.34	4.43
Atmosphere	4.84	4.86	4.64	4.24	4.56	4.50	4.35	4.42	4.53
Service	5.63	4.89	4.67	4.23	4.47	4.62	4.47	4.49	4.50
Quality	6.37	5.15	5.02	3.97	4.35	4.80	4.65	4.71	4.69

Source: Don L. James, Richard M. Durand, and Robert A. Dreves, "The Use of a Multi-Attribute Attitude Model in a Store Image Study," *Journal of Retailing* 52 (Summer 1976), 23–32. Reprinted by permission.

mind when one thinks of men's clothing stores. From that list, the attributes perceived as having the most salience were found to be assortment, personnel, atmosphere, service, quality, and price. Then stores were rated on a 1-to-7 scale along with each attribute, providing useful information for diagnostic purposes.[34] Store C, for example, rated poorly on quality, the most salient attribute. This could be a major cause of low patronage.

DETERMINANT ATTRIBUTES IN STORE CHOICE

The process of choosing a specific store is a function of consumer characteristics and store characteristics. That is, each market segment as defined by shopper profiles will have an image of various stores. The process is shown in Figure 20.6. Consumers sort out or compare perceived characteristics of stores with evaluative criteria of the core customers.

Store choice is a function of four variables shown in Figure 20.6: (1) evaluative criteria; (2) perceived characteristics of stores; (3) comparison process; and (4) acceptable and unacceptable stores. These processes are complex but understandable.

Determinants of store choice decision vary by market segment and by product class. Salient or determinant attributes usually fall into the following categories: (1) location; (2) nature and quality of assortment; (3) price; (4) advertising and promotion; (5) sales personnel; (6) services offered; (7) physical store attributes; (8) nature of store clientele; (9) store atmosphere; and (10) posttransaction service and satisfaction. Since location has been discussed in the context of market, area, and site selection, we go on to discuss the rest of the variables.

---

[34] For a useful discussion, see Eleanor G. May, "Practical Applications of Recent Retail Image Research, *Journal of Retailing* 50 (Winter 1974–1975), 15–20.

FIGURE 20.6
STORE CHOICE
PROCESS IS A
FUNCTION OF FOUR
VARIABLES

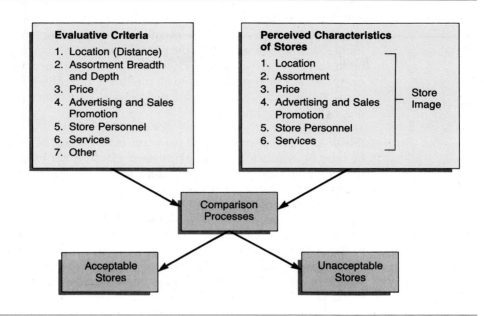

NATURE AND QUALITY OF ASSORTMENT   Depth, breadth, and quality of assortment are often determinant of store choice. This is especially true for department stores and other stores in shopping centers.[35] Specialty stores have risen rapidly in competitive ability because of their ability to assemble and present dominant assortments, whether defined on the basis of classification, end-use, or lifestyle.[36]

The importance of assortments of merchandise is also important to the increase in retailers known as **"category killers."** They carry a broad assortment in one category of merchandise. An example is Toys R Us. They have 313 stores in the United States and 37 in other countries and were adding 90 new units a year as of 1988, with total sales of over $3 billion. Other category killers include Tower Records, Circuit City, Block Buster Video, Home Depot, Sportsmart, and Lenscrafters.

Another method for capitalizing on consumers' desires for quality or depth of assortment is found among **niche retailers.** These include Benetton,

---

[35] Hansen and Deutscher, "An Empirical Investigation"; Lindquist, "The Meaning of Image"; Gentry and Burns, "How Important"; and John D. Claxton and J. R. Brent Ritchie, "Consumer Prepurchase Shopping Problems: A Focus on the Retailing Component," *Journal of Retailing,* 55 (Fall 1979), 24–43.

[36] Walter K. Levy, "Department Stores: The Next Generation," *Retailing Issues Letter* 1 (1987), 1.

the Gap, Aca Joe, Esprit, Judy's, the Limited, Banana Republic, and many others. They have narrow but deep assortments.

Category killers and niche retailers are competing effectively with department stores, which used to be the place for quality and quantity of assortments, because of the effect that narrow lines and disciplined merchandising have on turnover. In contrast, department stores typically have slower inventory turns along with higher operating expenses, lower sales per square foot, and bigger inventory losses.

PRICE The importance of price as a determinant of store patronage varies by type of product. Supermarkets have placed great emphasis on price since the 1930s although some research indicates that supermarkets that price below competitors are less profitable and achieve lower turnover rates.[37] At one time price was not important in selection of a department store[38] but it has become more important as department stores develop "sales mania" in their attempt to buy back market share from competitors. Constant sales may have undermined the credibility of department stores and the confidence of customers in store prices. The importance of price depends on the nature of the buyer. Some customers preferring other factors, such as convenience, will, in effect, trade off that consideration against higher prices.[39]

Price is a risky variable upon which to build a marketing program but some retailers do well with price as one of their attractions. The Price Club is a prime example. In 1988, they had 37 stores, 6 doing over $150 million per year and 2 doing over $200 million a year. For the $150 million stores, that is $1,550 per square foot turnover, an astounding achievement.

WalMart is another prime example of a retailer using price as one of its many excellent attributes. In addition to the many WalMart and Sam's Warehouse stores, the newest venture is their Hypermart in Garland, Texas, a suburb of Dallas. With 225,000 square feet (and even more in planned stores for Kansas City, St. Louis, and other cities), the stores carry high-end groceries, clothing, service shops, and a food court. The store has 48 checkout stands, most kept very busy. This store carries a wide assortment of goods, but each category is limited to only very high turnover items. Because of these and other policies and their logistics and other operating efficiencies, the Hypermarts are reported to be able to operate on 11 to 12 percent margin, in contrast to competitive but traditional forms of retailing requiring from 2½ to 3 times the margin of a Hypermart.

---

[37] L. Lynn Judd and John Beisel, "Do Price Level Strategies Affect Pricing Policy and Profitability?" in Robert L. King, ed., *Retailing: Theory and Practice for the 21st Century* (Charleston, South Carolina: Academy of Marketing Science, 1986), 42–46.

[38] Stuart U. Rich and Bernard D. Portis, "The Imageries of Department Stores," *Journal of Marketing* 28 (April 1964), 10–15.

[39] Robert H. Williams, John J. Painter, and Herbert R. Nicholas, "A Policy-Oriented Typology of Grocery Shoppers," *Journal of Retailing* 54 (Spring 1978), 27–42.

CONSUMER IN FOCUS

20.3   WHAT'S IN A NAME? ASK SUPERMARKET SHOPPERS

Generic and private-label supermarket products are losing the war against higher-priced, nationally advertised brands.

SAMI/Burke Inc., a market research firm, says generic and store brands' share of grocery store sales slid to 12.9% last year from 13.3% in 1986 and 16.8% in 1982. What's more, *Consumer Reports* magazine found in a recent survey that more than 80% of its readers prefer national brands for such products as detergent, toilet paper, soft drinks and ketchup, because they perceive them to be of higher quality.

"We feel that a major reason behind the downward trend is the tremendous amount of activity in coupons, which can bring the cost of the big, advertised brands below the level for private labels," says Alan Miller, a consultant at SAMI/Burke.

Despite the erosion, generic and private brands aren't insignificant. SAMI/Burke estimates they still account for sales of more than $17 billion a year. And they are holding up well in certain categories, such as disposable diapers and microwave popcorn, and in some grocery chains, such as Supermarkets General Corp.'s Pathmark stores.

"Our two-liter No Frills cola is the top-selling item in our stores," says Robert Wunderle, a vice president of Supermarkets General. "But to make generics succeed, you really have to establish product quality standards and police them carefully."

Source: *The Wall Street Journal*, May 9, 1988.

Price appears to be important from these examples. But of the 37 warehouse chains operating in 1988, only three made a profit. It is true that the two most profitable — WalMart and Price Club — were enormously successful, but many retailers — almost all in this category — bet on low price as a competitive weapon and lost.

The consumer's perception of price, or subjective price, is more important than actual price.[40] Price advertising of recognized products may create an image of low prices. Advertised specials that are unavailable or mispriced on the shelf may create skepticism and undermine store loyalty.

An area of price competition that generates considerable question about importance is **generic branding,** also called **no-name brands** in some countries or "no-frills" brands. *Consumer in Focus 20.3* describes the experiences of some retailers with generic brands.

---

[40] Kent B. Monroe, "Buyers' Subjective Perceptions of Price," *Journal of Marketing Research* 10 (February 1973), 73–80.

ADVERTISING AND PROMOTION   Advertising and promotion is an important, though controversial, variable associated with store choice. Its effectiveness varies by product category because some products and services are inherently more appealing than others. Men find restaurant ads and ads about tires and batteries most attention-getting, for example, while women look most at ads for restaurants, women's shoes, and women's apparel.[41] Advertising has proved useful for some retailers, with results as dramatic as those for Farm Fresh, which tripled volume in 5 years without increasing the number of outlets.[42] Their advertising stressed low prices. Managers conscientiously monitored competitive ads to guarantee that Farm Fresh prices were always on a par or lower. The impact on consumers was backed up by testimonials appearing in the ads. Food Lion, in the Southeastern portion of the United States, has become highly successful with an aggressive price policy.

The effectiveness of price promotions is questionable, despite their widespread use.[43] It may only shift demand from one time period to another for a store. It may shift from one brand to another without increasing a store's total sales, or it may shift market share from one competitor to the next without increasing total demand. Nevertheless, price advertising is frequently done to maintain competitive parity. Apparently, a segment of the population — as large as a third or more — is affected by price advertising. Still, loyalty may last only until the next set of advertised prices attracts that segment elsewhere.

The effects of price advertising are filtered by recipients through the dimensions of their overall image. Keiser and Krum concluded that "other information cues besides advertised low price would seem to influence consumer choice of retailers. These information cues are received from personal shopping experience, from friends, and from many other sources besides newspaper advertisements."[44]

Advertising, along with other forms of sales promotion, can affect store choice, but its impact is difficult to assess. It depends on the type of purchase and the nature of the store itself. For example, a study documenting the sources of awareness of a new dairy products outlet found that advertising accounted for only 16.9 percent of this awareness, compared with 50.5 percent

[41] Leo Bogart and B. Stuart Tolley, "The Search for Information in Newspaper Advertising," *Journal of Advertising Research* 28 (April–May 1988), 9–19.

[42] Ronald Tanner, "Building a Store Image with Careful Ad Planning," *Progressive Grocer* (March 1979), 35.

[43] Joseph N. Fry and Gordon H. McDougall, "Consumer Appraisal of Retail Price Advertisements," *Journal of Marketing* 38 (July 1974); V. Kumar and Robert P. Leone, "Measuring the Effect of Retail Store Promotions on Brand and Store Substitution," *Journal of Marketing Research*, 25 (May 1988), 178–185.

[44] Stephen K. Keiser and James R. Krum, "Consumer Perceptions of Retail Advertising with Overstated Price Savings," *Journal of Retailing*, 452 (Fall 1976), 27–36.

for visual notice and 32.6 percent for word of mouth.[45] Word of mouth, in turn, proved to be the most decisive influence on choice.

Questions about the relative effectiveness of price promotions, advertising, sales promotion, and so forth will be answered in the future due to the availability of scanner data. Specifically, it will be possible to examine more closely brand and store substitution effect, a situation that will further shift power in the channel from manufacturers to retailers. Research on this topic seems to indicate that price promotions and to a lesser degree displays have brand substitution effects but also store substitution effects on a retailer and its competitors.[46]

SALES PERSONNEL   "You win with people!" Woody Hayes titled his book. It is as true in retailing as in football. Knowledgeable and helpful salespeople were rated as an important consideration in choice of a shopping center by more than three-quarters of those interviewed in five major metropolitan areas.[47] The necessity of skillful personal selling was previously stressed under the discussion of search, so this finding is not surprising. But does performance match expectations?

Current evidence indicates that consumer confidence in retail salespeople is clearly ebbing.[48] Less than half of those interviewed in a nationwide survey said they believe what a salesperson tells them, down 10 percent from the previous year. Furthermore, they are not prone to switch brands because of selling efforts. If this trend continues, a substantial weeding out will occur at the retail level, with those who place proper emphasis on sales training and performance surviving while others fall farther and farther behind.

Leading retailers are beginning to put personal service back into their marketing program. Perhaps no one is more successful at this than Nordstrom's, the West Coast specialty department store with sales of over $2 billion. *Consumer In Focus 20.4* provides insights into the reasons for their success.

SERVICES OFFERED   Convenient self-service facilities, ease of merchandise return, delivery, credit, and overall good service have all been found to be considerations affecting store image.[49] This varies, of course, depending upon the type of outlet and consumer expectations. For instance, the 90 Giant supermarkets in the Washington, D.C., area began a nutrition education pro-

---

[45] Robert F. Kelly, "The Role of Information in the Patronage Decision: A Diffusion Phenomenon," in M. S. Moyer and R. E. Vosburgh, eds., *Marketing for Tomorrow . . . Today* (Chicago: American Marketing Association, 1967), 119–129.

[46] V. Kumar and Robert P. Leone, "Measuring the Effect of Retail Store Promotions on Brand and Store Substitution," *Journal of Marketing Research* 25 (May 1988), 178–185.

[47] "Service: Retail's No. 1 Problem," *Chain Store Age* (January 1987), 19.

[48] "7th National Consumer Survey," *Advertising Age.*

[49] Lindquist, "The Meaning of Image."

20.4 NORDSTROM'S GOOD VIBES

The secret of Nordstrom's success may be tied to a story that is probably apocryphal. Here it is: A retailer asked a sales person at Nordstrom's, "What can you be fired for?"

The person replied: "Number one, for not taking care of the customer. Number two, for stealing."

There is that sense about the specialty retailer that it has a handle, like nobody else, on customer service. Perception or fact? Most likely a halo effect has developed around the company's outstanding service. But the fact is, its service is excellent.

Larry Senn, of Senn-Delaney, expounds the theory about the company with: "They started in the shoe business. You fit shoes on people. You go get shoes for them. You put them on their feet. All this makes for a culture that personally serves people.

"As Nordstrom evolved into a specialty department store it maintained some of that personal attention. Nordstrom people run for the customer. Part of it comes from that. Part of it comes out of the family commitment to service.

"Nordstrom hasn't had a revolving door with executives with 10 different philosophies. It has a consistent philosophy. And that gets communicated when hiring people."

Source: *Stores* (September 1986), 83.

---

gram in cooperation with the National Heart, Lung, and Blood Institute with good effects. The program is called "Foods for Health," and various tips are presented through shelf-talkers, posters, and other forms of display.[50] Similarly, a *Chain Store Age Executive* survey of managers revealed that the presence of in-store banking facilities such as automated teller machines raised traffic levels by 10 to 15 percent annually.[51] In-store restaurants increase sales in the range of 5 to 6 percent. Hardware and home supply stores that service their products increase sales. Grocery stores sell products such as stamps as a service because of the increase in traffic. Other stores add technology, personnel, and training in order to increase service and decrease the time consumers spend in waiting at the checkout or other places in the store.[52] These are just a few examples of the variety of services that warrant experimentation because of their high potential payout.

---

[50] Jo-Ann Zbtniewski, "Just-the-Facts-Ma'am on Health and Nutrition Posted in Giant Stores," *Progressive Grocer* (February 1979), 29.

[51] "Retailers Asking: Is There Money in In-Store Banking?" *Chain Store Age Executive* 54 (October 1978), 35–39.

[52] John V. Hummell and Ronald Savitt, "Customer Service in Retailing: A Temporal Approach," in Robert L. King, ed., *Retailing: Its Present and Future* (Charleston, South Carolina: Academy of Marketing Science, 1988), 50–55.

PHYSICAL STORE ATTRIBUTES   Facilities such as elevators, lighting, air conditioning, convenient and visible washrooms, layout, aisle placement and width, carpeting, and architecture have been found to be factors in and of themselves in store image, and choice.[53] In a recent study, 61 percent of shoppers said convenient parking and 52.8 percent of shoppers said quick checkout would influence their decision about where to shop. Another physical store attribute of great importance was women's rest rooms, rated by 50.7 percent of the women in the study as factors influencing where they shop.[54]

STORE CLIENTELE   The type of person who shops in a store affects choice because of the pervasive tendency to attempt to match one's self-image with that of the store. The clientele of a restaurant makes it attractive or not so to customers who want to see or be seen by others. Some customers may avoid a restaurant because of the type of people who are generally there, such as the instance when adults avoid restaurants that are believed to attract children.

STORE ATMOSPHERE   An important determinant of store choice is store atmosphere. Its importance is recognized in the term **store atmospherics,** the conscious designing of space to create certain effects in buyers.[55] Intense competition between stores for young, upscale consumers has caused stores to discard their dowdy old formats for colorful, well-designed, image-enhanced selling environments. Even the masses of consumers want some class in their stores.

The major department stores and chains must manage atmospherics to survive and prosper. Sears, Roebuck and Co. has invested over $1.7 billion in a 5-year remodeling and expansion program. Their first "Store of the Future" was built in King of Prussia, Pennsylvania, patterned after the lifestyles of its customers.

Even supermarkets need revitalization of their atmospherics. Byerly's in Minneapolis has one of the most attractive stores in the United States. In Canada, Loblaws is an outstanding example of a store with coordinated graphics. The exterior signing invites people to come inside. When inside, customers are faced with super graphics as signing, clean and contemporary displays, and lighting and colors that encourage people to stay and shop. Products as ordinary as cookies can be exciting with the right atmospherics. Figure 20.7 shows a retail outlet for Cheryl & Co., a company that started with Cheryl Krueger making cookies in her kitchen for friends. The firm evolved into a successful entry in regional shopping malls, exciting not only because of the

---

[53] "Retailers Asking: Is There Money in In-Store Banking?", 35–39.
[54] "Service: Retail's No. 1 Problem," *Chain Store Age* (January 1987), 19.
[55] Philip Kotler, "Atmospherics as a Marketing Tool," *Journal of Retailing* 49 (Winter 1973–1974), 48–63.

FIGURE 20.7
ATMOSPHERICS OF
CHERYL & CO.: THE
CONSCIOUS DESIGN
OF SPACE TO
ATTRACT
CONSUMERS

Source: Courtesy of Cheryl & Co.

excellent taste of its cookies and other products but because of the bright red colors with designed-developed accents of black and white, and carefully coordinated displays.

POSTTRANSACTION SERVICE AND SATISFACTION   Customers want service and satisfaction after the sale. This is especially true for those who purchase such high-involvement products as furniture, appliances, and automobiles. More and more retailers and service firms are providing comment cards and other forms of feedback to insure that consumers are satisfied. Marriott Hotels go to great efforts to serve consumers well and to find out about unmet expectations.

Posttransaction service and satisfaction programs are more important in an era of slower growth in the total market. Successful retailers have found that the best source of new business is frequently present customers. As the population of industrialized countries slows or declines, it becomes more justifiable economically to implement programs that will satisfy present customers than to spend money to obtain new customers. Growing profits require more attention to meeting customer expectations for service.[56]

[56] For expansion of this concept, see Roger D. Blackwell, "The Consumer Affairs Role in an Era of Slow Growth Markets," *Mobius: Journal of Consumer Affairs Professionals in Business* 7 (Fall 1988), 1–7.

These are the reasons why consumers choose one store in preference to another. They help to understand some of the trends that are occurring in retailing and suggest implications for marketing strategy.

Marketing Strategies in Response to Consumer Decisions

The strategies of successful retailers interact with the decision processes of consumers to provide a satisfying and innovative interaction for both parties. A number of characteristics of firms most effective in this process were identified in research conducted by Management Horizons:

1. *Market-Driven* — These companies have identified pockets of high-growth opportunity in consumer, merchandise, and geographic markets and have well-defined marketing strategies geared to some form of dominance.

2. *Professional Entrepreneurial Management* — Managements have maintained a hands-on entrepreneurial approach to their businesses. The presence of an individual who is a professional manager, as well as the driving force behind the company's success, who has a vision for the company and whose personal satisfaction is tied to the company's performance, is seen in many of the retailers who are "stayers."

3. *Programmed Resource Relationships* — Higher-performance retailers tend to be the "captains" of their distribution channels, controlling the conditions under which they do business with suppliers. These companies have become powerful factors in the distribution channel because of an ability to deliver market share and/or through ownership of the source of supply.

4. *Productivity/Technology Leaders* — Technology represents a major commitment and a continuing investment for high-achievement retailers. Technological leadership contributes to efficiency in communications in marketing and operating activities, and often results in higher productivity.

5. *High-Value Offer* — The companies are high-value retailers, where value is defined as more for less. Such companies are compelling competitors because they greatly exaggerate the value equation in some way.[57]

LIFESTYLE RETAILING PORTFOLIOS

The wheel of retailing goes round and round but not necessarily in the same place. The old general store of original American retailing was a composite of items closely related to the lifestyles of the locality; a general store in a small town carried quite different items from those of the downtown or neigh-

---

[57] Robert E. O'Neill, "50 High Performance Retail Chains," *Monitor* 18 (May 1988), 55–66.

borhood stores of the cities. Store operators were essentially purchasing agents for the citizens of a specific locality, reflecting closely those customers' lifestyles, brand preferences, sizes, and preferred shopping hours. Without awareness of the concept of lifestyles and without psychographic research, the operators of those stores a hundred or more years ago were practitioners of both the "marketing concept" and what is now called lifestyle retailing.[58]

LIFESTYLE RETAILING   **Lifestyle retailing** may be defined as the policy of tailoring a retail offering closely to the lifestyles of specific target market groups of consumers. This contrasts with what might be called **supplier-style retailing,** in which the key to success in recent decades has been a focus on homogeneity in retailing operations.

A & P stores in a New Jersey city and Midwestern suburb varied little in size, personnel, product line, or promotional methods. Similarly, K-Mart achieved its market dominance because of the tremendous distributional, promotional, and operational efficiencies brought about by market homogeneity.

While A & P may have been the best (or, more correctly, the worst) example of homogeneity with its emphasis upon supplier-style retailing, Sears, Woolworth, Western Auto, and many other major retailers were different from A & P only in degree. Managers could be moved from store to store (and frequently were), and with the exception of physical size, they would find little difference in products carried, advertising used, or any other significant area of operations. Even department stores, traditionally the finest "purchasing agents" of consumers, followed the same strategy, in most instances, by building suburban stores that were little more than miniature carbon copies of the downtown stores. Minimal, if any, recognition was given to the fundamentally different lifestyles of suburban customers compared with those of traditional or downtown customers.

Lifestyle retailers, conversely, base their strategy and operations on unique living patterns of their target customers rather than on demographics or merchandise strength. The most successful of lifestyle retailers often emphasize lifestyle strength over demographic and merchandise strengths to find a differential advantage.

PORTFOLIOS OF RETAILING CHAINS   In the 1990s, success requirements are increasingly for movement beyond a chain that is lifestyle based and more toward a **portfolio** of such chains. Figure 20.8 shows how Woolworth has converted its previous 10,000-foot Woolworth stores — which tried to

---

[58] For additional details on this concept, see Roger D. Blackwell and W. Wayne Talarzyk, "Life-Style Retailing: Competitive Strategies for the 1980s," *Journal of Retailing* 59 (Winter 1983), 7–26.

FIGURE 20.8
THE WOOLWORTH
EVOLUTION FROM A
"DIME STORE" TO A
PORTFOLIO

Source: Courtesy Woolworth, Inc.

appeal to everyone and as a consequence appealed very little to anyone — to a portfolio of stores such as Brookstone, Eddie Bauer, and Ki Clayton, each programmed for specific lifestyles.

The Limited provides a premier example of a portfolio of lifestyle retailing groups. When men found the fashions in Limited Express more attractive than those available in men's stores, the Limited started new stores for men and also for kids. For the expanding leisure markets, the company added Abercrombie & Fitch to its portfolio and expanded its offering of clothing.

INTEGRATED MARKETING COMMUNICATIONS

The search for productivity in retailing is leading in new directions. One direction is the integration of marketing communications of retailing organizations in a closely coordinated program relating to consumer behavior. Such programs can be described as **Integrated Marketing Communications** or IMC.[59]

Marketing communications of retailers, defined as shared meanings between retailing organizations and persons, with exchange as their objective, are of increasing importance to retailing as well as other marketing organizations. The increased importance is due to the nature of the competitive environment as well as the enormous resources required to compete in contemporary retailing environments. One solution to the problem is an IMC.

Integrated marketing communications of retailers or other organizations differ from traditionally programmed communications in several ways:

1. IMC programs are comprehensive. Advertising, personal selling, retail atmospherics and in-store programs, behavioral modification programs, public relations, investor relations programs, employee communications, and other forms are all considered in the planning of an IMC.

2. IMC programs are unified. The messages delivered by all media, including such diverse influences as employee recruiting and the atmospherics of retailers, are the same or supportive of a unified theme.

3. IMC programs are targeted. The public relations program, advertising programs, in-store and point-of-purchase programs, all have the same or related target markets.

4. IMC programs have coordinated execution of all the communications components of the organization.

5. IMC programs emphasize productivity in reaching the designated targets when selecting communication channels and allocating resources to marketing media. One of the best examples of an IMC is the Limited.

MARKET TARGETING   The Limited started in 1963 with a single store targeted to young, fashion-conscious, moderately affluent women. Unlike other retailers, who often define their targets in terms of merchandise carried, the Limited focused on the consumer. It organized all aspects of store operations and communications toward that consumer. When retailers define their target in terms of products rather than consumers, they must constantly win the loyalty of new consumers as the previous ones mature and move to other product lines over the family life cycle. The Limited moved with the target market, and today's Limited is far different than 20 years ago.

UNIFIED MESSAGE   The Limited has achieved a unified message directed to a specific market target. The visual, auditory, and interpersonal environment is managed to provide a unified appeal. A market research firm selects exactly

---

[59] This section is based upon Roger D. Blackwell, "Integrated Marketing Communications," in Gary L. Frazier and Jagdish N. Sheth, eds., *Contemporary Views on Marketing Practice* (Lexington, Massachusetts: Lexington Books, 1987), 237–250.

the right music to be played in each store for the defined consumer segment. A shopper might walk from a Limited next door to a Limited Express, but the shopper's ears will tell her she has walked a decade away.

The most dramatic part of the in-store environment may be the Limited's high information content. Shoppers can walk into many competitive stores and fail to get help, personal or otherwise, in mixing and matching various items of apparel. That does not happen with the Limited. The information is on the walls. They are covered by carefully coordinated groups, assembled by expert designers. They are changed often; they are creative and persuasive as sale communications. The result is that shoppers may leave the Limited or its sister stores with several items rather than only one (as they might in competitive stores). Most importantly, the consumers probably are more satisfied because they have purchased items that truly do look better on them than if they had purchased mismatched items over time in a variety of stores.

COORDINATED PERSONAL SALES   The communications of the Limited are so integrated that they include specific criteria about the employees who are recruited to sell apparel and how they are trained. The employees are like the customers. They wear clothes the Limited sells and present the right image as they do their work, causing them to be effective opinion leaders to many of the customers.

At the Limited, sales associates are recruited to sell, trained to sell, given the time and opportunity to sell, and evaluated and compensated well when they do sell. This is not, however, "high pressure." Instead, sales communications are designed in the context of a philosophy that understands the best way to sell is to create customers so pleased they will be highly loyal. Even this philosophy is communicated simply and effectively at the Limited with the phrase, "No sale is ever final."

INFORMATION-BASED STRATEGIES   Changing demographics, especially more education, have created a consumer responsiveness to information-based marketing strategies. Understanding this can lead to higher margins as part of the IMC.

As the ratio of information increases relative to the physical mass of the product, the potential increases for higher-margin selling of goods by retailers. The process is also appropriate for other marketing organizations as well. Higher margins are possible because information increases the value of products and services to consumers. Higher margins are possible assuming, of course, that the marginal cost of producing the information is less than the marginal value created for consumers.[60]

Information-based strategies take many forms. Some include more information on packaging, special inserts or hangtags accompanying products,

---

[60] Paul Hawken, *The New Economy* (New York: Ballantine Books, 1983).

20.5 CLASSES TO UNSCRAMBLE COMPLEX INSTRUCTIONS

Palmer Stereo, a consumer electronics retailer specializing in quality more than low priced components, was chosen by an electronic association to develop classes to help consumers buy and hook up everything from music entertainment systems to stereo televisions. The Electronic Industries Association plans to develop the courses for possible use nationwide.

The free courses are offered on weekday evenings and Saturday mornings. Topics include how to buy and set up compact disc players, home entertainment centers, stereo televisions, telephone systems, audio/video setups, cable and satellite systems, videocassette recorders and cameras.

Bill Palmer, owner of the store located in Columbus, Ohio, states, "Japanese trans-lations are horrendous," speaking of instructions that are hard to understand when hooking up or integrating electronics systems. The purpose of the course is to help people get the best use out of their electronic systems and be better informed when they buy them.

In addition to the classes, Palmer Stereo, Ohio, mails as many as 40,000 brochures a week, providing details about components, how to choose and use them, and the availability of special clinics and other services to maximize customers' satisfaction with their audio and visual systems.

Source: *Columbus Dispatch*, May 28, 1988, 9D.

more attention to information contained in advertising, special training programs for salespeople and other workers who have contact with customers, enhanced point-of-purchase materials, including videotapes and computerized displays, and seminars or training programs for customers and potential customers. In the consumer electronics field, for example, many retailers rely on advertising strategies that feature little more than highly discounted prices. An information-based alternative for retailers and their suppliers is described in *Consumer in Focus 20.5*.

THE CORE STRATEGY

The key to long-term sustainable competitive advantage is to find a differential advantage that serves as a value platform for communicating the total product concept to customers. Retailing organizations with a long-term approach to markets take a process such as that portrayed in Figure 20.9. The first step is analysis of the environment — all of the types of information discussed in previous chapters of this book. The second step is to make decisions. These decisions are fundamental. Who will be our core customer? What will be our core merchandise? Who is likely to be among core competitors? Focusing on the really important or core aspects of the situation is more likely to produce a differential advantage than trying to be all things to all people.

FIGURE 20.9   DEVELOPING A CORE RETAILING STRATEGY: FINDING THE DIFFERENTIAL ADVANTAGE FOR A PARTICULAR PRODUCT

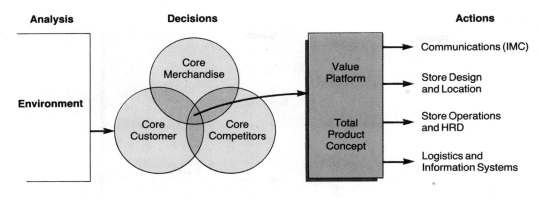

From the intersection of these core concepts should evolve the total product concept and the value platform that serves to make it specific and observable to the consumer. The final step is taking actions to implement this plan — communications (an IMC approach), store design and location, store operations and Human Relations Development (HRD), and the logistics management and information systems that are essential to highly profitable retailers in today's environment.

DIRECT MARKETING TO CONSUMERS

A total retailing strategy must include both store and nonstore formats. Some firms, such as Sharper Image, Banana Republic, and Victoria's Secret, are difficult to classify because they operate in both retail environments. Another example is Cheryl & Co. You may recall earlier in the chapter seeing a Cheryl's store in a regional shopping center. An even faster growing division of the company, however, is Cheryl's direct-marketing program, described in Figure 20.10.

IN-HOME PERSONAL SELLING

House-to-house personal selling accounted for 2 percent of general merchandise sales in 1986, and this percentage is declining.[61] The Fuller Brush Company, known for its door-to-door sales force, has been forced to change directions. Its 13,000 representatives still sell the same products for which the

---

[61] "1986 Mail Order Guide," 50.

FIGURE 20.10
CHERYL'S
GOURMET GIFTS:
SUCCESSFUL
DIRECT MARKETING

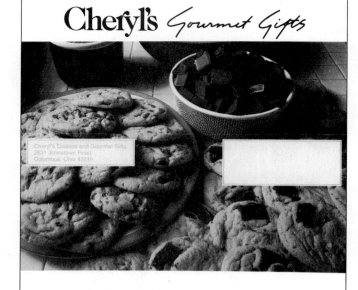

Source: Courtesy of Cheryl & Co.

company has achieved its popularity since 1906, but 80 percent of the contacts now are made by telephone; a direct visit to the home is confined to product delivery.[62] The reason is that changing demographics of two-income households have led to only a minority of women being at home during daytime hours.

The greatest market penetration of home personal selling (31 percent of all sales) is in cosmetics, with housewares and electronics (24 percent) being a close second.[63] As we discuss in Chapter 5, Mary Kay Cosmetics Incorporated has achieved a significant share of the cosmetics industry by concentrating exclusively on in-home presentations and sales.[64] All presenta-

---

[62] Susan Garland, "Stores Brush up Fuller's Image," *Advertising Age* (September 14, 1987), 107.
[63] "1986 Mail Order Guide," 50.
[64] "Mary Kay Cosmetics, Inc. (A)," in James F. Engel and W. Wayne Talarzyk, *Cases in Promotional Strategy,* rev. ed. (Homewood, Illinois: Richard D. Irwin, 1983), 3–10.

tions are made to groups invited by a hostess. This situation adds social influence to the powerful benefit of firsthand observation of the personal effects of skin care. A definite segment of the market prefers this method over a similar presentation in a department store.

DIRECT MAIL ADS AND CATALOGS

Direct-mail expenditures in all categories consistently average around 16 percent of all advertising dollars placed in a given year. In turn, 58 percent of all direct-response orders in July 1984 were triggered by direct mail (24 percent), catalogs (24 percent), circulars (7 percent), and bill inserts (3 percent).[65] The greatest mail penetration (2 percent or more) has occurred in clothing and jewelry, insurance, and business services.[66]

DIRECT MAIL Shopping in response to direct-mail appeals without catalog has been shown to meet real consumer needs. In a survey conducted by *Better Homes & Gardens* magazine, readers cited availability of merchandise (33 percent) and convenience (27 percent) as the two main reasons for responding. Other reasons given were "fun," "low price," and "better quality."[67]

College-educated readers often are skeptical of direct mail. They assume falsely that so-called "junk mail" is mostly disregarded and thrown away because that is what many of them do. A 1986 Gallup Poll showed that 56 percent of American adults open every envelope they receive, and an additional 20 percent do so occasionally.[68] Gallup also found that there are demographic differences in response. Those most likely to open their mail are women, people living in the East, those who buy through the mail, and individuals at either end of the age continuum (18 to 24 or over 50). Those with the most education and highest incomes, on the other hand, are less likely to pay attention to the mail they receive.

Direct-mail advertising *is read*. This is the invariable conclusion of numerous studies that appeared over the years in *Direct Marketing* magazine and other sources. One of the authors works extensively in direct-mail fund solicitation and can verify these data from unpublished proprietary research. The key is to segment the mailing list rigorously so that the direct-mail package is both personalized and relevant. When this is not done, the label of "junk mail" is appropriate.

CATALOGS Catalog buying is experiencing dramatic growth, and more than 10 billion are mailed each year. In a nationwide survey conducted for Spiegel Incorporated, Goldring & Company found that 73 percent of those

[65] Eileen Norris, "Alternative Media Try to Get Their Feet in the Door," *Advertising Age* (October 17, 1985), 58.
[66] "1986 Mail Order Guide," 45.
[67] Stone, *Successful Direct Marketing*, 4.
[68] Gallup Poll findings as cited in *Christian Marketing*.

surveyed made a catalog purchase during the preceding year.[69] Further, the study showed that consumers who made seven or more purchases represented about 20 percent of the total, whereas the dollar volume of their purchases exceeded 60 percent of all sales. The average number of purchases, in turn, was six.

The person who is most likely to buy from a catalog has these characteristics: a female with above average age, income, and education; married with children; a credit user; and an above average purchase frequency in the categories of housewares, appliances, men's clothing, and children's clothing.[70]

This type of purchasing has become so popular that some marketers now are offering their catalogs for sale at bookstores and newsstands for a price between $1 and $3. Moreover, it has been discovered that between 5 and 15 percent of those who buy a catalog actually order merchandise, versus only 2 percent who receive them through the mail.[71]

OTHER MEDIA

Direct-response marketing reaches far beyond direct mail into use of the telephone (telemarketing) and ads placed on television or in various print media.

TELEMARKETING   Seven percent of direct-response orders in 1984 were triggered by a telephone call (referred to as **outbound telemarketing**), but the percentage no doubt has increased since that time because of the sharp increase in telemarketing efforts. Homes can be targeted with great demographic precision using census data available within geographic zip codes. Also, real personalization can be achieved if the caller is skillful and sensitive.

Inbound telemarketing, on the other hand, refers to the use of an 800 number to place orders directly. A 1987 AT&T survey disclosed that the most frequently purchased items in the order of importance are clothing and accessories, records and tapes, housewares and cookware, and books and educational materials. The heaviest users are found among the younger and better educated families with higher incomes and children at home.[72]

[69] "Spiegel Attitude and Awareness Study," Goldring & Company, Marketing Research, November 1982. Cited in Roger D. Blackwell, James F. Engel, and W. Wayne Talarzyk, *Contemporary Cases in Consumer Behavior,* rev. ed. (Hinsdale, Illinois: Dryden Press, 1984), 351–355.

[70] James R. Lumpkin and John R. Hawes, "Retailing Without Stores: An Examination of Catalog Shoppers," *Journal of Business Research* 13 (1985), 139–151. Also Kenneth C. Gehrt, "Nonstore Retailing: Theoretically Based Selection of Household Predictor Variables and Consideration of Situational Predictor Variables," in Terrence L. Shimp et al., eds., *1986 AMA Educators' Proceedings* (Chicago: American Marketing Association, 1986), 172–176.

[71] "Behavior and Attitudes of Telephone Shoppers," *Direct Marketing* (September 1987), 50ff.

[72] "Behavior and Attitudes of Telephone Shoppers."

DIRECT RESPONSE ADS   Twenty-one percent of direct-response purchases in 1984 were stimulated by magazine ads (7 percent); newspaper ads (6 percent); yellow pages ads (5 percent); and TV commercials (3 percent).[73] These figures, however, do not reflect the recent upsurge in television home shopping. One authority estimates that sales through this medium will grow from $450 million in 1986 to $7.2 billion by 1991.[74]

In 1987, half of U.S. residents with TV, 50 million people, were able to tune into a television shopping program.[75] In that same year, 6 percent of cable TV subscribers purchased from home shopping services. Of these, 64 percent purchased once a month or more, 66 percent watched more than 1 hour per week, and 48 percent had household incomes of $25,000 or more. The vast majority spent more than $20 per purchase, and nearly half also had bought from a catalog in the past month.[76]

Home Shopping Network Inc. was the pioneer in television, starting its operations in July 1985. Its average club member places 15 orders a year, with a typical purchase of $32.[77] Because of its success, home shopping options on cable TV are burgeoning, although there are some initial signs that sales could plateau once viewer novelty wears off.[78]

Television home shopping efforts are also gaining rapidly around the world.[79] Fujisankel Communications International Inc., for example, has put together a 1-hour TV shopping program with American-made merchandise. It is broadcast live to Tokyo via international satellite. European marketers are turning the tables, however. A program entitled "Germany Today" can now be seen over video in 50 states, and it touts German-made products. Similarly, the French department store Galeries Lafayette will attempt to sell its products on Chicago area cable TV.

INTERACTIVE ELECTRONIC MEDIA

Most Americans and increasing numbers in Europe can now order a wide range of merchandise through video if they choose to subscribe to an interactive system. Referred to as **videotex,** anything that can be typed on a computer terminal keyboard can be transmitted to the home screen and even copied if the TV set has facsimile capability. The purchases are transmitted in the same manner.

The availability of nearly instantaneous two-way communication offers consumer benefits, including convenience and opportunity to plan purchases

[73] Norris, "Alternative Media Try to Get Their Feet in the Door."

[74] Joe Agnew, "Home Shopping: TV's Hit of the Season," *Marketing News* (March 13, 1987), 1, 20.

[75] Agnew, "Home Shopping: TV's Hit."

[76] Agnew, "Home Shopping: TV's Hit."

[77] Agnew, "Home Shopping: TV's Hit."

[78] "Viewers Start Tuning Out Home Shopping," *Business Week* (March 30, 1987), 30.

[79] Agnew, "Home Shopping: TV's Hit."

FIGURE 20.11
COMPUSERVE: AN
INTERACTIVE
MEDIUM

Source: Courtesy of CompuServe® Incorporated, an H&R Block Company.

through immediate access to needed information.[80] The disadvantage has been the necessity of purchasing specialized equipment which, until recently, appears to have been too costly for most consumers. Also, there has been some understandable reluctance from those who are not familiar with computer hardware and software.

Of the five major videotex services started since 1969, CompuServe is the major survivor. Figure 20.11 is an example of the CompuServe data base offering. All told, there are about 1 million videotex users, and growth has been slow. Yet, Sears and IBM have joined hands since 1984 and have invested $500 million in the new Prodigy service.[81] Prodigy is an on-line

[80] Pradeep K. Korgaonkar and Allan E. Smith, "Psychographic and Demographic Correlates of Electronic In-Home Shopping and Banking Service," in Shimp *et al., 1986 AMA Educators' Proceedings,* 167–170.
[81] Bill Saporito, "Are IBM and Sears Crazy? Or Canny?" *Fortune* (September 28, 1987), 73–80.

computer service that costs subscribers about $10 per month. The user, in turn, must own a modem, a color monitor, and a graphics card that allows the monitor to display illustrations. For best results, a very expensive high-resolution monitor is needed. This experiment is based on the assumptions that equipment costs will decline and home shopping will dramatically increase. By 1990, Sears and IBM had expanded the service into a number of cities with an investment of $600 million, which is predicted to eventually be $1 billion. Time will tell whether consumers will like the service enough to make it successful.

Videotex was started in France, however, where it is known as Minitel.[82] Over 2 million terminals have been distributed free, and it is not surprising that consumers have responded enthusiastically. This experience does provide some encouragement for the future elsewhere if costs can be reduced.

An alternative approach is interactive cable TV. The J. C. Penney Company is testing "Telaction," which allows consumers to communicate with their television monitor through a touchtone telephone. This allows pictures of items and their prices to appear on the screen. If this proves to be successful, the already dramatic growth of home shopping through cable programs may experience an even sharper increase.

Geodemographic marketing through direct mail offers especially intriguing possibilities.[83] In this procedure special attention is paid to geographic clustering of present customers. Using computer-stored census data, it is projected that others in the same area will be similar in terms of income and other measures of buying potential. Mailing or telemarketing is then directed to these homes in the expectation that most are qualified prospects.

COUNTERACTING BUYER RELUCTANCE

Some prospective buyers will perceive in-home shopping to be risky, voicing such concerns as, "Will the right order be received?" and, "Can I return it if it isn't right?" As Spiegel and others have found, great attention must be paid to informative ads and catalogs, facilitation of orders, credit arrangements, and liberal return policies.[84] Success demands continual monitoring of customer satisfaction on these dimensions.

Finally, some direct marketers, especially those confined to direct mail, are finding that they are falling victim to stiff competition in the mailboxes. ChemLawn was in this situation and discovered that competitive pieces often were nearly identical. To regain lost market position, the company began to feature a strong money-back guarantee in TV spots aired just before the spring season, backed up by direct mail featuring a strong offer and long

---

[82] George Nahon and Edith Pointeau, "Minitel Videotex in France: What We Have Learned," *Direct Marketing* (January 1987), 64–69.

[83] Dwight J. Shelton, "Birds of a Geodemographic Feather Flock Together," *Marketing News* (August 28, 1987), 13.

[84] "Spiegel, Inc. (A)," in Blackwell, Engel, and Talarzyk, *Contemporary Cases.*

body copy. The campaign reversed the decline and led to a 50 percent increase in response in 1985.[85]

SUMMARY

Purchasing processes is a term that refers to the interaction between consumers and retail outlets. Decisions about stores are fundamentally the same as decisions about products or brands. Need recognition leading to shopping behavior may be initiated by product problem recognition or by nonproduct-related motives such as the desire to get out of the house or engage in family-related leisure activity.

The fundamental questions facing retailers are where people will shop and which stores they will choose. Many options are now available to consumers to shop in their homes as well as in stores.

Store choice is a complex process consisting of four variables: (1) evaluative criteria; (2) perceived characteristics of stores; (3) comparison process; and (4) acceptable and unacceptable stores. In general, the determinants of store choice are location, nature and quality of assortment, price, advertising and promotion, sales personnel, services offered, physical attributes, store clientele, store atmosphere, and posttransaction service.

Store image is the perception of consumers about the objective characteristics of stores. Common methods of measuring store image include the semantic differential, multiattribute measures, multidimensional scaling, and other methods.

Shopper profiles are important for analyzing the comparison process by which consumers pick acceptable and unacceptable stores. Demographic variables, especially age, income, and place of residence, are often used to define patronage of a store, and many of these data are available from on-line computer data bases. Psychological variables such as psychographics and personality or perceived risk are sometimes used for store profiles, as are retailing-specific typologies such as the one developed by Stone.

REVIEW AND DISCUSSION QUESTIONS

1. Why is it important to understand purchasing processes as part of the decision-process approach to understanding consumer behavior?

2. Think of the last time you bought a product. How did you decide which store to patronize? How does your behavior compare with the conceptualization of the process as presented in this chapter?

3. Define the term *store image* and explain why it is important as a concept for retail management.

---

[85] "Direct Mail Nurtured ChemLawn Rebound," *Advertising Age* (September 2, 1985), 61.

4. What is the image of the two largest stores in your area? How do your perceptions of these stores compare with those of your friends? Your parents? Why do these differences exist?

5. Assume you are a consultant for a major department store. Describe how you would go about evaluating the type of competition faced by the department store in the next few years.

6. Assume that you are asked to measure the image of the dominant grocery chain in your area. How would you recommend this be done? Why?

7. Of what importance is location in analyzing the patronage of retail stores?

8. Several marketing responses to consumer decisions about retailing were described in this chapter. Briefly outline the salient characteristics of each and list some examples other than those mentioned in the chapter.

9. Describe the importance of price in the patronage decision for supermarkets.

10. Sears and IBM made a major investment in Prodigy. How successful will it be? What factors lead to your conclusion?

CONSUMER TRENDS

B

BMW FOLLOWS BABY-BOOMER MARKET INTO MIDDLE AGE

MW of North America, Inc. continues to sell what it calls "the ultimate driving machine" to a market it targeted 14 years ago — young, affluent, ambitious baby boomers not interested in the Buicks and Cadillacs that displayed their parents' success.

And as that market moves into middle age, BMW is confidently following along and carving a niche for itself with Mercedes-Benz, Porsche, Jaguar and Rolls-Royce at the top end of the luxury-car market.

BMW's most expensive car sells for about $69,000. While new customers are welcome, it is aimed directly at people who have been driving a less expensive BMW for several years and now want a little more elegance and prestige along with precise handling.

"When they were younger they chose BMW for its performance, but we are pointing out that BMW provides luxury and status as well," explained Martin Puris. His ads and TV commercials have aimed at the affluent young since 1975 and raised BMW's sales in the United States from 14,000 cars that year to a peak of nearly 97,000 in 1986. Puris slogans — "The Ultimate Driving Machine" and "Our symbol is under the hood, not on it" — focused on baby boomers' desire to buy the best quality product, not the glitziest.

Now that the leading edge of BMW's market has grown older, the trick for Puris is to show that customers don't have to give up the BMW experience to have a touch more luxury. To do that, his New York agency, Ammirati & Puris, has created a campaign unlike any thing BMW has tried before. In one new commercial, luxury cars drive by a town house in Washington's Georgetown district, discharging elegantly-dressed couples for a party.

Bobby Short, the cafe-society entertainer, is heard singing Cole Porter's *I Get a Kick Out of You.* Several partygoers have white hair. Print versions of the campaign resemble expressionist paintings. Copy is spare. They contrast with the way Puris has been marketing less expensive BMW's to younger buyers for 14 years — stark photos of the car and a lot of description. (See an example of new BMW ads in the color insert.)

Source: Associated Press, Columbus *Dispatch* (June 21, 1988), 16C.

Consumer Trends and Demographics

Unless management acts, the more successful a firm has been in the past, the more likely it is to fail in the future. Why? Because of the basic psychological principle that people tend to repeat behavior for which they have been rewarded. It is natural therefore for organizations to continue strategies that have made them successful in the past. The problem arises because the reality of successful strategies is that they must fit the environment. Consequently, marketing programs that have been successful will continue to be so only to the degree that the environment remains the same in the future as it has been in the past.

Consumer analysts are charged with the responsibility of monitoring and interpreting the environment and how it may change in the future. It is a role of increasing importance in most organizations. It is also a role of profound importance in understanding how the entire economy or society functions. These two roles are sometimes described as **micromarketing** and **macromarketing.**

Macroanalysis of Trends and Demographics

Will more food or less be required to feed the population of a country in the future? Will politicians of the future need to appeal to the affluent or to the poor in order to be elected? Will people support the use of nuclear power and its risk of nuclear disaster to meet their energy needs in the future? Or will they continue to support coal-fired energy and its atmospheric pollution that threatens flooding of coastal areas and droughts of inland areas due to the "greenhouse effect"? Will people spend their time in museums, at sporting events, or at home "cocooning" around their gardens and TV sets?

The answers to all of these questions will be provided by consumers. Finding those answers is the subject of macroanalysis of consumer behavior.

Macromarketing applications of consumer behavior focus upon determining the aggregate performance of marketing in society, evaluating marketing from society's perspective, and understanding the consequences in society of marketing actions and transactions. Marketing scholars generally agree that macromarketing issues also include comparison of the marketing systems of different nations, examining how marketing adapts to different cultures, and the impact of the marketing activities of influential firms such as General Motors on the quality of life in a society.[1]

The economic well-being of a country is directly related to the quantity and types of goods consumers decide to purchase. Consumers may decide to drive cars 2 or 3 years longer, which greatly affects employment and GNP in the country. A changed preference for Japanese or Korean cars has profound effects both domestically and globally, not only for managers and government officials but for labor leaders as well.

Many policy issues are related to macromarketing and trends in consumer decisions. If a tax cut is proposed by "supply-side" economists, what changes will result as consumers spend such reductions? What policies would cause consumers to save more and spend less on current consumption? When the average age of the population increases, will health prices increase for young working people who pay the bills or will prices decrease for young consumers because underutilized health care facilities are used more efficiently? If the white population of the United States has low birth rates in combination with high birth and immigration rates among minorities, what will be the effect on Social Security when most of the older (white) retirees are supported by young (black and Hispanic) members of the work force? When large numbers of people migrate to the Sun Belt, are consumers better served by the new but overcrowded facilities in the Sun Belt or by the older but less crowded (and possibly fully depreciated) facilities in the mature cities?

You will not find the answers to these questions in this chapter, unfortunately. The reason is that we don't know the answers. Consumer analysts have focused mostly on micromarketing research even though the field of consumer behavior had its birth in such questions in the pioneering work of George Katona.[2] Today, there is a reawakening of interest in what Katona called behavioral economics and what is now called psychological economics. But frankly, not much is yet known. Perhaps you, as a reader of this book, will generate research that will be included as answers to these questions in future editions.

---

[1] Shelby D. Hunt and John J. Burnett, "The Macromarketing/Micromarketing Dichotomy: A Taxonomical Model," *Journal of Marketing* 48 (Summer 1982), 11–26.
[2] George Katona, *Psychological Economics* (New York: Elsevier Scientific Publishing, 1975).

MICROAPPLICATIONS OF TREND ANALYSIS

Micromarketing analysis of consumer trends and demographics focuses on marketing programs of specific organizations. **Trend analysis** focuses on discovering marketing opportunities that arise as a result of changes in the environment. Such opportunities include developing new or modified products, changing distribution channels, and improving communications with consumers.

ESV AND THE CRITICALITY OF GROWING PROFITS

The chief financial goal of strong, well-managed corporations is **ESV — enhanced shareholder value.** The importance of long-term, consistent appreciation of shareholder value is observable in company annual reports and other communications with employees and the financial community.[3] If you have taken a financial management course, you will recognize that ESV is nothing new. What is new is the increased recognition that marketing personnel, especially consumer analysts, play a key role in discovering opportunities to grow profits and thus enhance shareholder value.

ESV reflects long-term strategies of a company—such things as investment in new products, joint ventures, and major capital investment.[4] Marketing objectives are much broader than market share, profits, sales increases, or other concepts that have traditionally been yardsticks by which marketing programs are evaluated. *The role of consumer research is to discover ways to increase profits in the future* rather than merely maintain profits. ESV occurs when financial markets believe a firm is well positioned for increasing its earnings in the future, often reflected in a high Price-Earnings (PE) ratio.

3 M'S OF PROFIT GROWTH

Three major ways of increasing profits exist in which the study of consumer trends plays a major role. The three ways of growing profits can be thought of as the 3 M's:

1. More markets
2. More market share
3. More margin

In this chapter we mainly examine the first M — markets. Much of the rest of this text focuses on the issue of the second M — gaining market share. The third M — margin — involves strategies to reduce costs or to increase

---

[3] For more information on this topic see Alfred Rappaport, *Creating Shareholder Value: The New Standard for Business Performance* (Glencoe, Illinois: Free Press, 1986).

[4] J. Randall Woolridge, "Competitive Decline: Is a Myopic Stock Market to Blame?" *Journal of Applied Corporate Finance* 1(Spring 1988), 26–36.

21.1 BUILDING TREND LINE EARNING POWER: CONAGRA'S STRATEGY

ConAgra concentrates on building trend line earning power to reward our stockholders over the long haul. ConAgra's most important objective is to average better than a 20-percent return on beginning common equity. ConAgra's five-year average return is about 22 percent. By contrast, the median return on equity for the Fortune 500 food companies is less than 16 percent. For all the Fortune 500 companies the figure is less than 12 percent.

One of the reasons Banquet has grown its volumes in a fairly flat industry is because the people at Banquet understand their equity better than anyone else in the industry. They understand price/value relationships — they fill consumer needs — they know what consumers are looking for from Banquet — and they deliver consistent quality that meets consumers' expectations.

A good example of Armour doing better what consumers *know* Armour does *well* is a successful line of lower-salt products. Armour is now the leader in the lower-salt category with a line that includes lower-salt ham, bacon, hot dogs, sausage, luncheon meats and cheeses.

Patio and Chun King are two more good examples. Our research helped us know they had good equity in the ethnic arena. We've found ways to build on it. We introduced Patio microwave burritos and Chun King microwave egg rolls.

The microwave oven, for example, has changed the lifestyles of many consumers — more than 60 percent of U.S. households now have microwave ovens. Many frozen foods today are "dual-oven," meaning you can prepare them in either a conventional oven or a microwave oven. So when we set out to restage the Dinner Classics line, our research showed us that consumers wanted microwavability. We produced the new Dinner Classics so that it would be superior when prepared in a microwave. The new Dinner Classics can also be prepared in a conventional oven, but it's best when microwaved. We did not compromise microwave performance to focus on "dual-ovenability."

Marketing is something that's been central to ConAgra's business philosophy for years. When we use the term, we are talking about marketing in its broadest sense; it's much more than the eye-catching packages and the memorable advertising campaigns that get so much attention. We focus on the entire marketing process of determining what our customers or consumers need, then providing the right product or service at an appropriate price/value relationship — and in a timely, consistent, and dependable manner.

Source: ConAgra *1988 Report of the Annual Meeting of Stockholders*, various pages.

the price that can be obtained for a product. Cost reduction is mostly outside the scope of our present study. Logistics or physical distribution management, which is often an important part of reducing costs, is closely related to consumer behavior, however, because of the need to define customer satisfaction standards. Increasing prices is closely related to consumer analysis, because consumer perceptions of value is directly related to pricing strategies.

21.2 **FINDING GROWING MARKETS IN RESPONSE TO TRENDS IN THE MARKETPLACE: HOW SERVICEMASTER GROWS**

The health care market in the United States continues to undergo transition. This is both a challenge and an opportunity. In 1987, we continued to demonstrate our leadership in serving our health care customers. For example, we secured a master agreement for the purchase and distribution of natural gas to ServiceMaster plan and maintenance customers that will reduce their energy costs by a range of 10 to 20 percent. We added the *Terminix*(r) pest control services to our housekeeping management program. Through our acquisition of Natking Energy Management, Inc., we are able to provide all required components of energy management in one service. We now service over 1,100 health care facilities with an average of 1.7 service contracts for each facility service. Our management services in the international health care market now extend to 43 hospitals in Japan and 15 hospitals in the Middle East.

In the education market, we now serve more than 400 school districts, colleges and universities with our combined program of custodial, plan operations and maintenance,

grounds care and food service. Our commitment is to provide a clean and safe environment, touching the learning experience of over a million students in America each day. We provide convenience and specialty services of carpet and furniture cleaning, janitorial, project cleaning, disaster restoration and lawn care services, provided through a network of over 3,700 franchises located in the United States, Canada, Japan, the United Kingdom and Europe.

We recently introduced *HomeBrite by ServiceMaster*(r), a new maid service to respond to the increasing demand for regular home cleaning. Because of the expanded number of two wage-earner households, there is a growing demand from consumers who will be purchasing services provided in and around the home. We offer a one-stop shop through a universal 800 number, as we seek to provide a truly "carefree" home.

Source: 1987 ServiceMaster Annual Report.

ConAgra is an example of a company that has achieved remarkable growth in mature industries often thought to have limited possibilities for growing earnings. ConAgra has grown by searching for market opportunities and exploiting them to their fullest. As you read *Consumer in Focus 21.1*, notice how ConAgra uses all three of the "M's" to enhance shareholder value.

MORE MARKETS   People and their ability to buy are the most basic determinants of markets. Thus, consumer analysts have a special responsibility of determining trends in population and buying power to *discover market segments that are growing*. Finding growth segments might include analysis of geographical growth areas, enlarging age groups, new sources of income, global opportunities to replace declining domestic markets, and other trends. Consumer trend analysis might also include methods of reaching growth segments more effectively or sooner than competitors.

Consumer trend analysis has an important application in industrial marketing because industrial demand is ultimately derived from consumer demand. Industrial firms (selling to other organizations) need to give attention to forecasting consumer markets likely to grow fastest. The purpose is to market industrial products and services needed by growth firms producing and marketing consumer goods.

Focusing on consumer trends helps firms avoid artificial separation of industrial and consumer markets. Firms that concentrate on products or services for one or the other may find growth opportunities by focusing on the overall trend and moving aggressively between industrial and consumer marketing, as is shown in *Consumer in Focus 21.2*. ServiceMaster is a rapidly growing service firm with sales of over $2 billion. Ten years ago the company received 93 percent of its revenues from business services and only 7 percent from consumer services. After a decade of responding to changing markets, the company receives 24 percent of its operating income from consumer services and products.

THE CHANGING STRUCTURE OF CONSUMER MARKETS

The search for growing profit opportunities leads to careful analysis of trends in the structure of markets. Markets are defined as having four major components:

1. People and their needs
2. Ability to buy
3. Willingness to buy
4. Authority to buy

Variables are examined in the following pages which help understand the first three of these components. First, we focus on people — forecasting how many are likely to exist as potential consumers and some understanding of their needs related to age and other demographic factors. Second, we focus on changes in buying power that have occurred and are likely to occur in the future. Third, we focus on the social and technological trends that affect willingness to buy some products more than others or favor particular marketers. Additionally, we examine some other trends that affect the development of marketing, especially trends in the geography of demand and the rise of an information society. The chapter concludes with discussion of how consumer analysts keep aware of these trends with a process called environmental scanning.

PEOPLE: FOUNDATION OF MARKET ANALYSIS

People are the foundation of market analysis. How many will there be? What will be the age distribution? Where will they live? These issues involve the study of demographics, defined as the size, structure, and distribution of a population. When combined with data on purchasing power or wealth, this type of analysis is called **economic demographics,** the study of the economic characteristics of a nation's population.

The most important application of economic demographics is market segmentation strategies, the process of dividing a total market into groups of people who have relatively similar characteristics and behavior. The next chapter describes how to reach those market segments. In this chapter, look for market segments that are growing either in size or in purchasing power. If a firm can market effectively to growing segments, the firm's profits will grow even when the total market is slowing in growth or declining.

Population is the foundation for market analysis because of its critical importance in determining demand. It is also reliably predictable. Population demographics move like celestial mechanics, a great advantage when compared to most variables studied by consumer analysts. There are unknowns, of course. Discontinuities include natural calamities, wars, and medical problems such as plagues in ancient times or AIDS in modern times. Ordinarily, though, populations of countries are reasonably predictable.

Births are the most important of the three variables (births, deaths, and net immigration) that determine the population of a country. Births are also the most volatile. Before looking at overall population projections, we need to examine the critical question of how many babies will be born in the future.

HOW MANY BABIES?

Slight changes in the birthrate have enormous impact on consumer demand. Whether families spend money on food and education of children or on luxury goods and travel is greatly influenced by average family size. Consumption decisions for both individual families and the larger society are impacted by birthrates.

CAUSES OF BABIES

Birthrates are determined by four variables. First is *age distribution* of the population. Second is *family structure.* What proportion are married? What proportion of the women are employed outside of the home? What is the average age when people get married? The third cause of births is *social attitudes* toward family and children. Finally, birthrates are affected by *technology,* such as availability and cost of contraception.

BASIC CONCEPTS

Several terms are used by consumer analysts and others when describing and projecting future populations.[5] The **birthrate** (also called **crude birthrate**) is the number of live births per 1,000 population in a given year. The **fertility rate** (also called **general fertility rate**) is the number of live births per 1,000 women of childbearing age (defined as 15 to 44). Fertility rates are sometimes stated as age-specific rates (such as age 30 to 39 women) to facilitate comparison over time or to see differences in fertility at different ages. **Completed fertility rate** is the total number of children ever born to women of a specific age group. In 1910, the completed fertility rate for women aged 50 to 54 was 4.1, but by 1980 that number had dropped to 3.0 and probably will be less in the 1990 Census.

The **total fertility rate** (TFR) is the average number of children that would be born alive to a woman during her lifetime if she were to pass through all her childbearing years conforming to the age-specific fertility rates of a given year. Although it is a synthetic number and might seem complex, TFR is the most useful indicator of fertility because it answers the simple question: How many children are women having currently? In many developing countries, the number is over 6.0. Currently in the United States it is about 1.8 children. As we see in Chapter 24, TFR is even lower in Europe and some other developed countries. A **replacement rate** is a fertility rate of 2.1 children, the number required for a couple to replace the current population, with allowance for some infant mortality.

The number of babies born in any year is a product of the fertility rate (generally declining in most countries) times the number of women of child-bearing age (generally increasing). The result is increasing population in the United States and most countries. The birthrate is as high as 52 per 1,000 in Kenya but as low as 10 per 1,000 in Denmark, where population is now decreasing annually. In the United States, the birthrate dropped from historical levels of 25 to 30 per 1,000 to about 15 or 16 in the latter part of the 1980s.

Birthrates should not be confused with **natural increase,** which is the surplus of births over deaths in a given time period. An even more important concept is **growth rate** of a population due to natural increase and net migration, expressed as a percentage of the base population. The growth rate takes into account all components of population growth. Although the world's growth rate is about 1.7 percent (or stated alternatively, an increase of 17 per 1,000 population per year), the United States is at .9 and with some projections of a decline to about .6 by the year 2000. If the rate of .9 were to continue, the U.S. population would double in about 78 years. Length of time required to double in size based on current growth rates is called the **doubling time.**

---

[5] Definitions in this section are based on Arthur Haupt and Thomas T. Kane, *Population Handbook* (Washington, D.C.: Population Reference Bureau, 1985).

FUTURE FERTILITY

Forecasting births in future decades is difficult. Although fecundity, the physiological capability of couples to reproduce, is fairly predictable, fertility, which is actual reproductive performance, is more difficult. Fertility is affected by fecundity but also by age at marriage or cohabitation, the availability and use of family planning, economic development, the status of women, and the age–sex structure.

The solution to the problem of forecasting babies born — and thus total population — adopted by the Census Bureau is to provide several projections based upon different fertility assumptions. Series I assumes 2.7 children per woman, Series II assumes 2.1 children per woman, and Series III assumes 1.7. Calculating the number of births that will occur under each assumption produces radically different estimates (Figure 21.1), anywhere between 3 and 4 million births per year by the year 2050.

Fertility rates declined from a high of 3.7 in 1960 to 1.8 in 1978. After 1978, a slight increase in fertility occurred, and the large number of women of childbearing age caused total births to increase in a "mini baby boom." However, fertility rates decreased in the latter part of the 1980s, and the picture for the future is uncertain. Greater labor force participation of females, later age of marriage, and increasing educational levels all are associated with lower fertility rate assumptions for the future. In 1987, women aged

FIGURE 21.1
BIRTHS AND DEATHS IN THE UNITED STATES

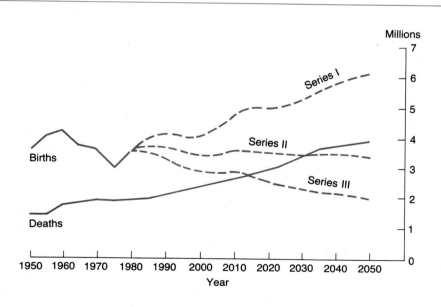

Source: Lowest, medium, and highest fertility series. U.S. Bureau of the Census.

18 to 34 expected to have an average of 2.1 children in their lifetime, although the actual rate is consistently lower than expectations.

Attitudes toward marriage and children are also changing. A study by *Better Homes & Gardens* of its readers — who presumably are among the more family-oriented consumers in the economy — investigated these attitudes. When asked the question, "Do you think a husband and wife must have children — either their own or adopted — in order to have a fulfilling and happy life?" 85 percent of the women responding and 74 percent of the men said "no."[6] If fertility rates continue at a low level and current trends in mortality rates also continue, there will come a time in the United States and other industrialized countries when deaths will outnumber births, as they already have in Germany and Scandinavian countries. Family size has been dramatically affected by attitudes and behavior toward contraception, a trend that is reasonably permanent considering that the leading method of contraception in the United States is now sterilization.[7]

ORDER EFFECTS

Order effects produce significant consumption differences between families even when the total number of babies is the same. **First-order** (first-born) babies generate more economic impact than **higher-order** (second, third, fourth, and so on) babies. First-order babies may generate $1,500 of retail sales, for example, compared to less than half of that for higher-order babies. In 1960, only one child in four was first-born, but by 1990 this figure was expected to be nearly 50 percent.

The marketing programs of some companies are especially impacted by order effects. Eastman Kodak benefits from first-order babies because their happy parents buy cameras and take massive quantities of pictures. Higher-order children may be lucky to get one picture at graduation. Families with one child can afford to eat at better restaurants and buy wanted products such as personal computers, extension phones in the child's room, new and better clothes instead of hand-me-downs, and services such as private education, ballet school, gymnastics or other sports lessons, and so forth.

Having one's first child at an older age—the trend for the foreseeable future — usually results in fewer children per family. Not only does this produce more money to spend on each child for a vast array of goods and services, but it also produces a slower-growing population base in the society, possibly even Zero Population Growth (ZPG) in some countries. The social effects of ZPG, or near-ZPG, include fewer people available to serve in the military and to pay for Social Security (at the same time that the number of

---

6 "Family Life Styles Changing," *Better Homes & Gardens* (July and August, 1983).
7 "Fertility of American Women," Series P-20, No. 427 (Washington, D.C.: U.S. Government Printing Office, 1988).

people receiving Social Security rises dramatically), less crime, higher productivity in offices and factories, lower unemployment rates, and other economic and social consequences.

Another factor affecting births is abortion. The Alan Guttmacher Institute in New York reports that abortions increased dramatically in the 1970s in the United States and other countries. The U.S. rate of abortion — 28.2 per 1,000 women — ranks about mid-range internationally. Canada's rate, 11.3 per 1,000, is very low. Among the highest are Cuba, with a rate of 52.1, and Bulgaria, with a rate of 68.3.

Childlessness has also become more prevalent. By the end of the 1980s, about 25 percent of college-educated working women were childless. In addition to college education and employment outside the home, other variables associated with childlessness tend to be marriage later in life, not actively religious, and urban residence. Some of the "baby busters" are those who have made a deliberate decision not to have children; others simply delay the decision for economic or other reasons until the opportunity to have children is greatly diminished. The practical consequence is more spending power available for travel, luxury products that pamper one's self, adult education and self-development services, and perhaps more need for savings and retirement planning.

ETHNIC VARIATIONS

A key variable in understanding the number of consumers in the future is ethnic variation in fertility. The fertility rate among Hispanic women aged 18 to 44 was 95.8 compared to about 83 births per 1,000 black women and 69 per 1,000 among white women in 1987. The key difference is among younger women, however. Among black and white women over 30, currently there are not statistically significant differences in fertility.

White women typically have babies at older ages than other ethnic groups. Therefore, white families have fewer babies in total. As of 1987, about 55 percent of births to black women were to women who were not married, a level about four times as high as that of white women (12 percent) and about twice as high as that reported by Hispanic women (26 percent). Approximately 11 percent of all births currently are to Hispanic women, although they constitute only 8 percent of all women 18 to 44 years old. Such ethnic variations markedly affect attractiveness of market segments as well as affecting total population in a country.

MOST LIKELY SCENARIOS

The variables described above will determine the population of the future. No one knows exactly what will occur. Since we don't know how many people

FIGURE 21.2
FEWER KIDS,
SMALLER FAMILIES
IN CANADA

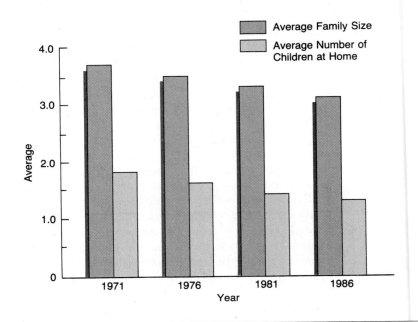

Source: *Statistics Canada,* The Daily, July 9, 1987.

will be born, one approach for consumer researchers is to examine the consequences of alternative scenarios. Based upon an understanding of the variations in fertility, it is possible to develop the most likely scenarios in making
projections. This is the approach reflected in Figure 21.2 and the following
pages in discussing future population trends and their marketing implications
in North America.

TRENDS IN THE POPULATION OF NORTH AMERICA

The population base in North America is expanding but at a decreasing
rate. In both Canada and the United States, the population is growing at
less than 1 percent a year. Projections of the populations for both countries
are presented in Tables 21.1 and 21.2 and Figure 21.2, which serve as the
basis for much of the following discussion. Differing years of census and
other problems make it difficult to present the projections in the same format,
but an examination of these tables reveals great similarities in changing age
distribution and growth rates of the two countries.

U.S.—CANADIAN MARKETS

Important changes in tariff restrictions began to take effect in 1990, allowing
freer access by Canadian and U.S. marketers to the consumers of the other

country. Canadian marketers were often more aware of the U.S. market in the past than were U.S. marketers of Canadian markets, but in the future consumer analysts must understand both countries.

Freer exchange of marketing programs between Canada and the United States will provide opportunities for growth. In some instances, increased competition will also occur. Canadian beers (as well as Mexican beers) have made significant penetration in the U.S. market, for example. Automobile production and marketing is highly integrated by North American manufacturers. Windsor plants supply all of Chrysler's minivan products for North America, as an example. Canada and the United States did $145 billion of merchandise trade in 1987, more than any other pair of nations, and the future promises even more.

Table 21.1 is a comprehensive and detailed description of the U.S. population in the year 2000. It also shows the effects of different scenarios about birthrates. Perhaps you will find it fascinating to look at all the numbers in that table, but don't be discouraged if it does not fascinate you. We explain the major trends contained in the table in the following pages. Since the Canadian population is smaller and the graphics less formidable, we examine Canadian trends first.

CANADIAN POPULATION

The population of Canada is currently almost 27 million persons, based upon the most recent (1986) Census. Figure 21.2 shows that Canadians are having fewer children and smaller families, causing the growth rate to drop to .84 percent annually, the lowest in history and down from a high of about 3 percent annually in the 1950s. An even more dramatic effect on population growth rate has been created by the drop in number of immigrants, from 135,000 in 1981–1982 to 85,000 by 1986. Women in Canada now average 1.6 births in their lifetimes. If present trends continue, Canada's population will peak at about 28 million sometime after the year 2000 and then begin to decrease in the next century.

The age structure of Canada is changing dramatically but in ways that are so similar to what is happening in the United States, we will not discuss them separately. Rather, as you read the following pages about the changing U.S. age structure, keep in mind that the same trends are occurring in Canada. This is also true with reference to the trends toward more education and the emerging importance of women in the labor force. Women make up the majority (about 52 percent) of all Canadian university students, as is true in the United States. The majority of Canadian families are also dual-earner families. In 1987, 53.9 percent of women aged 25 and over were in the labor force.

Average income in Canada has been on a roller coaster in recent years. Between 1980 and 1984, average real income (expressed in 1984 Canadian dollars) declined from $37,950 to $35,770. It began to rebound in the latter part of the 1980s to around $38,000 but still lagged behind the rapid growth

TABLE 21.1 PROJECTIONS OF THE TOTAL POPULATION BY AGE, SEX, RACE, AND SPANISH ORIGIN: 1990 TO 2000
(In thousands. As of July 1. Includes Armed Forces overseas.)

Age, Sex, Race, and Spanish Origin	Lowest Series			Middle Series			Highest Series		
	1990	1995	2000	1990	1995	2000	1990	1995	2000
Total population[1]	245,753	251,876	256,098	249,657	259,559	267,955	254,122	268,151	281,542
Under 5 years old	17,515	16,193	14,942	19,198	18,615	17,626	20,615	20,815	20,530
5–17 years old	44,486	46,125	44,951	45,139	48,518	49,763	46,055	50,990	54,434
18–24 years old	25,547	23,347	24,157	25,794	23,702	24,601	26,137	24,233	25,326
25–34 years old	43,147	39,887	35,596	43,529	40,520	36,415	44,329	41,672	37,850
35–44 years old	37,570	41,500	42,972	37,847	41,997	43,743	38,229	42,870	45,128
45–54 years old	25,226	31,044	36,533	25,402	31,397	37,119	25,578	31,763	37,813
55–64 years old	20,910	20,655	23,326	21,051	20,923	23,767	21,189	21,190	24,212
65 years old and over	31,353	33,127	33,621	31,697	33,887	34,921	31,989	34,618	36,246
16 years old and over	190,198	196,242	203,526	191,819	199,188	208,185	194,035	203,249	214,597
Male, total	119,620	122,608	124,671	121,518	126,368	130,491	123,698	130,577	137,163
Under 5 years old	8,964	8,288	7,647	9,827	9,529	9,022	10,550	10,653	10,508
5–17 years old	22,745	23,586	22,989	23,082	24,815	25,458	23,549	26,074	27,842
18–24 years old	13,016	11,904	12,314	13,127	12,072	12,530	13,283	12,325	12,881
25–34 years old	21,722	20,155	18,009	21,892	20,443	18,384	22,261	20,959	19,044
35–44 years old	18,598	20,649	21,508	18,732	20,879	21,866	18,927	21,322	22,537
45–54 years old	12,268	15,152	17,903	12,350	15,327	18,196	12,441	15,518	18,563
55–64 years old	9,804	9,733	11,046	9,871	9,865	11,272	9,936	10,000	11,511
65 years old and over	12,503	13,143	13,255	12,637	13,440	13,762	12,751	13,725	14,277
16 years old and over	91,205	94,152	97,779	91,929	95,480	99,906	92,964	97,378	102,913
Female, total	126,133	129,268	131,427	128,139	133,191	137,464	130,424	137,574	144,379
Under 5 years old	8,551	7,906	7,295	9,371	9,086	8,604	10,065	10,161	10,022
5–17 years old	21,741	22,539	21,962	22,056	23,703	24,305	22,506	24,915	26,592
18–24 years old	12,532	11,443	11,843	12,667	11,630	12,071	12,854	11,908	12,445
25–34 years old	21,426	19,731	17,586	21,637	20,077	18,031	22,068	20,713	18,806
35–44 years old	18,971	20,851	21,465	19,116	21,119	21,877	19,302	21,548	22,591
45–54 years old	12,958	15,891	18,630	13,051	16,071	18,923	13,137	16,245	19,251
55–64 years old	11,105	10,922	12,279	11,180	11,059	12,495	11,253	11,190	12,702
65 years old and over	18,850	19,984	20,366	19,061	20,447	21,158	19,238	20,893	21,969
16 years old and over	98,993	102,090	105,747	99,890	103,708	108,279	101,071	105,871	111,684

White, total	207,799	211,481	213,498	210,790	217,412	222,654	213,753	223,236	231,980
Under 5 years old	14,046	12,884	11,760	15,390	14,797	13,843	16,451	16,417	15,958
5–17 years old	36,028	37,062	35,876	36,523	38,941	39,667	37,149	40,716	43,061
18–24 years old	20,989	19,008	19,485	21,170	19,267	19,806	21,369	19,578	20,238
25–34 years old	36,027	32,867	29,009	36,289	33,312	29,590	36,768	33,998	30,442
35–44 years old	32,097	35,037	35,822	32,292	35,379	36,355	32,509	35,895	37,180
45–54 years old	21,868	26,822	31,239	21,994	27,077	31,662	22,090	27,286	32,071
55–64 years old	18,432	18,014	20,273	18,536	18,213	20,605	18,605	18,362	20,868
65 years old and over	28,313	29,787	30,032	28,596	30,424	31,126	28,810	30,984	32,162
16 years old and over	162,971	166,987	171,734	164,160	169,181	175,245	165,486	171,695	179,346
Male	101,518	103,352	104,369	102,979	106,266	108,879	104,460	109,175	113,536
Female	106,281	108,129	109,129	107,811	111,146	113,775	109,292	114,061	118,445
Black, total	30,836	32,506	33,957	31,412	33,651	35,753	31,974	34,780	37,602
Under 5 years old	2,948	2,771	2,620	3,215	3,165	3,079	3,440	3,525	3,570
5–17 years old	6,942	7,498	7,553	7,042	7,871	8,321	7,159	8,222	9,031
18–24 years old	3,766	3,495	3,715	3,798	3,542	3,773	3,849	3,620	3,865
25–34 years old	5,809	5,683	5,208	5,860	5,768	5,316	5,932	5,884	5,479
35–44 years old	4,254	5,096	5,701	4,295	5,169	5,811	4,339	5,261	5,954
45–54 years old	2,600	3,210	4,036	2,626	3,262	4,124	2,646	3,307	4,211
55–64 years old	1,978	2,035	2,292	1,998	2,073	2,355	2,013	2,103	2,407
65 years old and over	2,538	2,717	2,833	2,579	2,802	2,975	2,597	2,857	3,085
16 years old and over	21,922	23,230	24,996	22,138	23,618	25,613	22,372	24,055	26,317
Male	14,645	15,451	16,156	14,926	16,013	17,040	15,204	16,573	17,958
Female	16,191	17,055	17,802	16,485	17,638	18,714	16,769	18,207	19,644
Spanish origin, total[2]	19,148	21,149	23,065	19,887	22,550	25,223	22,053	26,475	31,208
Under 5 years old	2,047	2,039	2,033	2,282	2,412	2,496	2,690	3,129	3,510
5–17 years old	4,682	5,158	5,436	4,825	5,554	6,206	5,337	6,605	7,973
18–24 years old	2,289	2,376	2,602	2,386	2,511	2,766	2,811	3,069	3,499
25–34 years old	3,517	3,514	3,529	3,629	3,717	3,804	4,242	4,782	5,129
35–44 years old	2,721	3,309	3,602	2,788	3,430	3,803	2,900	3,771	4,590
45–54 years old	1,629	2,091	2,687	1,668	2,165	2,811	1,720	2,262	2,993
55–64 years old	1,160	1,297	1,547	1,183	1,341	1,619	1,209	1,394	1,709
65 years old and over	1,101	1,367	1,627	1,126	1,419	1,719	1,144	1,463	1,804
16 years old and over	13,070	15,663	16,434	13,453	15,322	17,419	14,763	17,597	20,807
Male	9,580	10,586	11,548	9,947	11,285	12,627	11,137	13,425	15,869
Female	9,568	10,562	11,516	9,940	11,265	12,596	10,916	13,050	15,339

[1] Includes other races not shown separately.
[2] Persons of Spanish origin may be of any race.
Source: U.S. Bureau of the Census, Current Population Reports, series P-25, No. 952.

FIGURE 21.3. APPEALS TO PARENTS OF FIRST-ORDER BABIES

World class charmers wear Weebok.

The best bib for your baby is one you'll never use again.

Introducing Playtex Disposable Bibs.

TABLE 21.2 CANADIAN POPULATION PROJECTIONS, 1981–2001	Year	Population as of June 1, 2000	Annual Rate of Population Growth	Distribution by Age			
				9–19	20–44	45–64	65+
	1981	24,041.4	1.1%	32.0%	39.6%	19.0%	9.4%
	1986	25,382.9	1.1	29.3	41.9	18.7	10.1
	1991	26,591.4	0.9	28.4	41.5	19.1	11.0
	1996	27,569.7	0.7	27.8	39.8	20.9	11.5
	2001	28,369.7	0.6	26.7	37.9	23.6	11.8

Source: Series C Projections, Statistics Canada.
(Series C assumes total fertility will change to 1.80 by 1985 and remain constant through 2001, net migration gain of 60,000 per year and expectation of life at birth will increase gradually to 70.2 years for males and 78.4 for females by 1986 and then remain constant through 2001.)

that had been seen in real income during the 1970s. Average income is highest in Alberta and Ontario and lowest in Newfoundland and Prince Edward Island. By age group, the young have not done so well, and the only families to gain purchasing power have been those headed by someone aged 65 or older.[8]

During the 1980s, caution and some lack of confidence occurred among Canadian consumers because of inflation, decreased purchasing power, the increased risk of unemployment, and slower economic growth. The latter

---

[8] "Canada Today — Results of the 1986 Census," *Consumer Markets Abroad* 6 (October 1987).

Sources: Courtesy of Johnson & Johnson. Kodak ad reprinted courtesy of Eastman Kodak Company.

part of the 1980s saw a reversal of some of these trends, leading to more willingness to buy and optimism about markets of the future.

As general trends, the Canadian market is characterized as one of slower growth population, an aging population, declining youth markets, maturing of the baby-boom generation, more working women, and a changed family structure that features later marriage, more single young adults, more common-law unions, and more well-educated dual-income households.

CHANGING AGES OF MARKETS

The changing age distribution in North America affects consumer behavior in many ways essential to understanding how to develop effective marketing programs. If you examine Table 21.1 carefully, you will notice that projections vary most among younger ages (not yet born at the time of the projection). Although less confidence exists about the number of children living in the future, there should be high confidence in their importance as markets.

CONSUMING CHILDREN

The number of young children may decline during the 1990s but not their importance as consumers. Using the low series of population projections, the number of children under 5 will decline from 17.5 million to 14.9 million between 1990 and 2000. The high proportion of first-order babies will generate high demand for quality products and services. In addition to higher-quality products, parents may expect more information about the product. Parents will pay for designer labels, shop more at specialty stores, and have higher expectations during usage of products.

Marketing programs emphasize style and attractiveness when clothing and other products are consumed by only one child. Attributes of durability and timelessness of style are not so important as when products are "handed down." JC Penney added designer clothes and discarded "hard lines" such as tires and auto supplies to create a fashion image that would appeal to children and parents who can afford and are willing to buy fashionable clothing.

Second-use stores and informal trading networks develop to achieve multiple use of beautiful and expensive products by multiple children — but in different families. Conversely, some products — such as diapers or other consumables — are more likely to be disposable.

The application of these strategies and tactics can be seen in the ads in Figure 21.3. Even infants deserve WEEBOK® shoes, just like their parents' REEBOK® shoes. Playtex provides a superior-design disposable bib for mothers who don't have time to wash dirty bibs. The Johnson & Johnson ad on Johnson's Baby Sunblock appeals to changing lifestyles and the concern of young parents about the sun's harmful effects. Eastman Kodak may be one of the companies that benefit most from first-order babies, as parents rush out to buy a camera and take thousands of pictures (with Kodacolor Gold) but take fewer pictures of subsequent children.

FALL AND RISE OF TEENAGERS

The tumultuous fall in number of teenagers that occurred during the 1980s should reverse in the 1990s with a rise of several million in the number of teenagers. During the decline, severe labor shortages occurred, as well as declining markets for fast food and other products appealing to teenagers. McDonald's changed its advertising that formerly featured teenagers to include mature individuals working in the restaurants. Salads and food appealing to young adults were added by McDonald's to compensate for a declining number of teenagers.

Marketers to teenagers can thrive by appealing to *spending power disproportionate to the number of teenagers*. In 1987, annual spending of teenagers was estimated at $234 billion and rising at the rate of $7 billion a year. Nearly $142 billion was created by the 75 percent of teenagers who claim that they urge their parents to buy products and services for the home.[9] Grocery marketers are now directing ads to teenagers, who are increasingly given the task of buying the family groceries in dual-income families. The Levi's® jeans ad in Figure 21.4 also shows the influence children and young teens may have on parents.

---

[9] "Teen Spenders," *American Demographics* 10 (June 1988), 21.

FIGURE 21.4
INFLUENCE OF
CHILDREN ON
PARENTAL
PURCHASING

Source: Courtesy of Levi Strauss & Co.

BABY BOOMERS AND OTHER YOUNG ADULTS

Baby Boomers is a term given to the cohort of people born in huge numbers following World War II. The soaring fertility lasted through 74 million births by 1964, which will continue to impact markets and all other aspects of society for decades. In the eighties, marketers focused on Yuppies — young urban professionals — because of their discretionary income and their influence on market trends. In the future, Yuppies will become Muppies — middle-aged, urban professionals creating different but even more profitable markets.

Baby Boomers delayed getting married and having children, but eventually they entered the trap and brought with them a permanent propensity to consume. They know what they want — quality products that are aesthetically pleasing, personally satisfying, natural, and if possible, noncaloric. The products and services must also be available in convenient and value-oriented distribution channels, such as off-price but quality retailers and catalogs. Baby Boomers buy more and save less than other generations, spending on products that past generations would have considered luxuries, such as consumer electronics, second cars, household services, and a wide range of other products.

The instrument of choice for purchases by Baby Boomers is the credit card. Nearly 1 billion pieces of plastic are now issued by financial and marketing institutions. Transactions of the 250 million Visa and MasterCard pieces of plastic total over $200 billion. Bank card marketers find Baby Boomers profitable not only because of their high usage but also because of the extended time payments required by consumers who need almost everything — home and everything for it, two cars, everything for children, clothing and much more — and who do their saving in the future by using credit cards now.[10] *Consumer in Focus 21.3* discloses consumption patterns of the most affluent of this cohort.

During the 1990s, it is the *aging* Baby Boomers who will grow. The age category of 25 to 34 will decline dramatically, while the 35 to 44 will increase dramatically. The lifestyle decisions of members of the baby-boom generation in large part determined trends in marriage, divorce and consumption during the 1980s.[11]

Trends created by Baby Boomers include more households headed by a female, smaller-size households, 47 percent home ownership, much higher proportion of women in the work force, rising education levels, and a permanent propensity for change. While they will mature in age and some may become "couch potatoes" as they "cocoon" in their homes, Landon Jones explains in *Great Expectations,* "There is no reason to think that the baby

---

[10] Roger D. Blackwell and Margaret Hanke, "The Credit Card and the Aging Baby Boomers," *Journal of Retail Banking* 9 (Spring 1987), 17–25.

[11] Paul Glick, "How American Families are Changing," *American Demographics* 6 (January 1984), 21–25. Also see Dale Blackwell and Roger Blackwell, "Yuppies, Muppies and Puppies: They Are Changing Real Estate Markets." *Ohio Realtor* (August 1989), 11–15.

CONSUMER IN FOCUS

21.3   **YUPPIE SPENDING GETS SERIOUS**

Since the Yuppies set the trends, what they are buying now will soon be taken up by the copycats. Today's prestige purchase is a house, and when it comes to his castle, this prince wants a palace. The homes that are moving fastest are in the 4,000-to-5,000-square-foot range. Says economist Michael Sumichrast, publisher of *Real Estate Perspectives:* "They are simply not satisfied with a house. They want a statement."

Furniture is the next spending priority. During the past three years sales have risen 23% to $161 billion — with most of the trade being in antiques and reproductions. "Affluent yuppies are very much influenced by instant tradition. That's why they like Ralph Lauren and Laura Ashley," explains Carl Levine, senior vice president of Bloomingdale's. Says Levine: "They say they are looking for their roots, but their ancestors probably lived much more simply."

So did their parents. All three boomer groups are springing for oversize bathrooms with whirlpool tubs, and lavish entertainment centers — that's the room Dad called the den — packed with CD players, tape decks, VCRs, stereo TVs, and electronic diaries. Kitchens bristle with automatic bread makers, pasta machines, food processors, and contraptions that dispense cappucino. Boomers who never baked a potato are buying industrial ranges with microwaves and restaurant-size freezers. Says Frederick Elkind, director of Ogilvy & Mather's Consumer TrendSights division: "Home has become the mother ship. It has all these exciting things to entertain and to sustain them."

Source: "Yuppie Spending Gets Serious," *Fortune* 119 (March 27, 1989), 147–149, at 148.

---

boomers will be any more docile or malleable in old age than they have been in youth and adulthood."[12]

Appealing to Baby Boomers often relies on subtle symbols that affected them when they were children, as Bob Green explains:

> If you ever needed final proof that the baby boom generation has, indeed, taken over America, you will find it in an ad currently running in many upscale national magazines.
>
> The ad is for Christian Brothers brandy. Most of the page is taken up by a picture of Chuck Berry, dressed all in orange and holding an orange guitar.
>
> The caption at the bottom reads: "C. B. in orange." And beneath that, in smaller letters: "With a little CB brandy and orange juice, Johnny B. very good indeed."
>
> The ad makes several assumptions: The first is that mainstream America will instantly recognize Chuck Berry — and his name never appears in the ad. The second is that the double meaning in the caption, "C. B. in orange" will be understandable to the reader — namely that C. B. (Chuck Berry) is dressed in orange, and that C. B. (Christian Brothers brandy) mixes well with orange juice. The third is that the

---

[12] Landon Y. Jones, *Great Expectations: America and the Baby-Boom Generation* (New York: Coward, McCann & Geoghegan, 1982).

phrase "Johnny B. very good indeed" will make sense — the reference being to the Berry song Johnny B. Goode.

All these assumptions are right on the mark: The ad is quite effective; and it is based on the knowledge that the country's adult purchasing power is now in the hands of the baby boom generation.[13]

ERA OF THE EMPTY-NESTERS

The 45 to 55 age group is projected to grow by 11 to 12 million during the 1990s, and the 55 to 64 category will also grow substantially. This may catch some marketers unprepared, since the 1980s experienced substantial declines in the 50 to 64 age group.

Empty-nesters, whose children have not only left home but have also left the university, provide opportunities to grow profits for firms that understand this segment. Not only are empty-nesters growing rapidly in numbers; they have more per capita discretionary income than any other age group. They have small families at home, are often at the height of their careers and earning power, and have low or no mortgages to pay and generally reduced family responsibilities.

The key to understanding the empty-nesters is freedom. They already have an adequate inventory of housing products, cars and clothing and such products. They not only have the freedom to *spend* on what they want; they have the *freedom to withhold* until they receive precisely what they want.

Empty-nesters indulge in luxury travel, restaurants, and the theatre — which often means they need more fashionable clothing, jewelry, and department stores. They watch their waistlines and diets, and are good prospects for spas, health clubs, and cosmetics and beauty parlors. As they approach retirement, they purchase condominiums and begin to take more frequent but less expensive vacations. They are a prime prospect for financial products oriented toward asset accumulation and retirement income.

MUSHROOMING MATURITY MARKET

The mushrooming maturity market is creating growth opportunities for empathetic marketing organizations. Several million additional consumers in the 65-plus category will be found during the 1990s.

Mature families are important to marketers because there are over 37 million households headed by people aged 50 and over compared to only 25 million under age 35. Additionally, households in the over-50 age group have $550 billion to spend compared to the $400 billion of young households. Because of smaller size, older families have a 30 percent higher per capita income.[14] Older families have more to spend, but they need to spend less.

---

[13] Bob Green, "Baby Boom Burst Into Mainstream," Tribune Media Services, September 24, 1987.

[14] Fabian Linden, "Older Markets," *American Demographics* 6 (August 1984), 4.

With home mortgages paid off or nearly so, no more college educations to finance, and an ample inventory of basic appliances and furnishings, mature families are especially good prospects for luxury goods, travel-related goods and services, health care, and a wide range of financial services.

Market segmentation is important in the maturity market. Often this is done by age, with marked differences in spending patterns between those who are "older" (55 to 64), "elderly" (65 to 74), "aged" (75 to 84), and the "very old" (85 and older).[15] But the most useful segmentation may be psychographic. Segmentation may be on the basis of engagement with society or internal versus external locus of control, similar to the inner- versus outer-directedness differentiation in the VALS typology.[16]

Mature market families may be divided into the young olds and the older olds. The young olds are characterized as "active retired" and participate heavily in the consumption of a wide variety of products. Only 16.7 percent of men over 65 were still in the work force in 1984 compared to about 63 percent in 1900. Despite the trend toward early retirement, large numbers are capable of working beyond 65, may need to do so financially, and may in the future seek to work at some kind of job longer than they now do.[17] In the 1990s, retirement may be just another work phase as people at 65 decide what job to do next, not what hobby to pursue.[18]

Women greatly outnumber men in the mature market because of greater life expectancy. Over 60 percent of women over 65 are not married. Many are widows who typically experience inability to earn an income, inadequate and often dangerous housing, and social and economic rejection.[19]

Older families tend to be careful in their shopping. Inflation may cause the prices of what they buy to increase but not necessarily their income. They also have the experience and ability to wait to find good value in their buying process. They may respond more to coupons and be willing to shift their buying to off-peak times if given an adequate incentive to do so.

Older families use the mass media more than younger consumers do and have less interpersonal contact. They may need special services such as delivery or telephone shopping, and they are more loyal to the firm that provides good service and value. In a comprehensive literature review of information processing among older consumers, Ross found many problems with the media because of declining sensory abilities. Older consumers are

---

[15] William Lazer and Eric H. Shaw, "How Older Americans Spend Their Money," *American Demographics* 9 (September 1988), 36–41.

[16] Ellen Day, Brian Davis, Rhonda Dove, and Warren French, "Reaching the Senior Citizen Market(s)," *Journal of Advertising Research* 27 (January 1988), 23–30.

[17] Harold A. Kieffer, *Gaining the Dividends of Longer Life: New Roles for Older Workers* (Boulder: Westview, 1984).

[18] Dede Ryan, *The Maturing Marketplace* (Silver Spring, Maryland: Business Publishers, 1987), 33.

[19] Benny Barak, "Elderly Solitary Survivors and Social Policy: The Case for Widows," in Andrew Mitchell, *Advances in Consumer Research* (1984), 27–30.

likely to be newspaper readers and AM radio listeners. They are more likely to shop at department or other traditional stores than in discount stores.[20]

Older markets are often affluent. World War II veterans who are now retiring have lived their lives in a 20-year economic expansion that has often given them a comfortable retirement. There are over 15 million people who are "comfortably retired," with incomes twice the poverty level but with lower spending needs. The **"pension elite"** consist of another 3 million older persons, mostly in the 65 to 74 age category, with enough income from multiple sources to support buying of products and services for an active, independent, and healthy lifestyle.[21] Some states, such as California, New York, and Florida, are home to over a million or more of these upscale retired consumers. Some cities, such as Fort Lauderdale, Palm Beach, San Diego, and Mobile Bay, have particularly large concentrations of such consumers, making these markets increasingly attractive as targets for segmented marketing offerings.

MARKETING TO THE MATURITY MARKET   Maturity markets are different from youthful markets in ways associated with their age but not limited to age. The maturity market currently reflects a cohort that was influenced by the Great Depression and World War II. The resulting emphasis was on saving and conservatism in consumption. The maturity market of the future, however, experienced mostly prosperity since World War II and willingness to spend as long as the credit cards were not over their limit. There exists the possibility that, in the future, the "new elderly" will have more of a consumption orientation, as well as the economic resources to support their habit.

Differences in consumption between older consumers and younger consumers go beyond attitudes. Some differences are physical. Eyes don't see as well, creating the need for larger print and bright colors rather than pastels or earth tones. Shiny paper in packaging or print ads should be avoided. TV commercials with visual changes every few seconds are annoying. Legs do not move as fast or as high, creating physical vulnerability that creates a booming home security market. Hands have less flexibility, causing doorknobs to be replaced with levers. Phones need larger buttons, as well as volume controls.

Maturity markets are "experience" markets rather than "things" markets. Mature consumers already have enough things, as well as the maturity of attitude that does not associate things with happiness. The maturity market therefore places more emphasis on experiences such as travel, activities with persons in similar situations, and staying in touch. Segmenting or predicting

---

[20] Ivan Ross, "Information Processing and the Older Consumer: Marketing and Public Policy Implications," in Mitchell, *Advances in Consumer Research* (1984), 31–39.
[21] Charles F. Longino, Jr., "The Comfortably Retired and the Pension Elite," *American Demographics* 10 (June 1988), 22–25.

FIGURE 21.5
POSITIONING TO
MATURE MARKETS:
THE OLDER MARKET
IS NOW MORE
CONSUMER
ORIENTED

Source: Courtesy of Carrington Perfumes Ltd.

purchase within the maturity market may not be so much based upon product/ service attributes as upon the amount of life satisfaction experienced by mature consumers and the relationship of life satisfaction with familiar concepts and product/service satisfaction.[22]

Three qualities are especially important in products purchased by mature markets: comfort, security, and convenience. Young people may stuff their feet into high-heeled shoes that are trendy. Older people want to be comfortable in their clothing, as well as in the furniture in their homes and in their feelings about the institutions handling their assets. They are less willing to take risks, whether they be physical, social, or financial. Thus, need for security is higher than with other markets and rewarding to the marketers who understand this need. Convenience is also a price for which the mature market

---

[22] Elaine Sherman and Philip Cooper, "Life Satisfaction: The Missing Focus of Marketing to Seniors," *Journal of Health Care Marketing* 9 (March 1988), 69–71.

will reward marketers. They want a computer that is easy to understand. They want to go to stores where they are sure they will find what they expect. They don't want to struggle with the frustration of automated teller machines too complex to operate. Some banks recognize these trends and provide personal assistance at teller machines with heavy concentrations of mature customers. Some stores and shopping malls provide convenient, dependable bus or van service between their facilities and concentrations of mature customers.

Positioning to older markets must be subtle. Figure 21.5 shows an ad based on recognizable actors who are recognizably not young. The headline talks about the continuation of romance rather than the beginning of romance, as an ad for younger targets might do. Examples of product positioning for the maturity market are also shown in *Consumer in Focus 21.4*.

Among the "young old" there is a sensitivity to revealing one's age. Consequently, an ad that blasts out in pictures or words that the product is for 60-year-olds won't work. Nor will advertising that is obviously directed to 30-year-olds. The most effective way to get around that problem is to create affinities between the product and some interest of the mature generation. Dychtwald, a gerontologist specializing in marketing, explains:

> *Quaker Oats is now very cleverly launching a campaign to get Quaker Oats viewed as a nutritious product for old people. They don't say, "Quaker Oats is good for you if you're old," What they say is, "Eating Quaker Oats lowers your cholesterol level." That's an affinity. That's an issue that anyone over the age of 50 is going to land right on. For 19-year-olds, it's invisible. They don't worry about their cholesterol levels.*[23]

THE CONSEQUENCES OF A SLOW GROWING, OLDER CONSUMER BASE

America and most other industrialized nations are becoming old; really old. While the United States has over 12 percent of its population above the age of 65 and Canada has 10.4 percent, that is young compared to Sweden, which has nearly 17 percent over age 65.[24] All European countries are older than the United States and Canada. The challenge for consumer analysts is to understand what this means, not only for products purchased by older consumers but for labor and retirement policies, political elections, family structures, health care, and many other areas of life.

The impact on the rest of consumers will also be substantial. As younger people are surrounded by older consumers and realize that life is going to last much longer than it used to, they may spend more money on health and appearance products and spend more time on healthier activities. As

[23] Ken Dychtwald, quoted in Curtis Hartman, "Redesigning America," *Inc.* 10 (June 1988), 59–69.
[24] Barbara Boyle Torrey, Kevin Kinsella, and Cynthia M. Taeuber, *An Aging World* (Washington, D.C.: Bureau of the Census, 1987), 7.

CONSUMER IN FOCUS

21.4 REDESIGNING PRODUCTS FOR THE MATURITY MARKET

Ken Dychtwald, gerontologist specializing in marketing, explains how currently successful firms might change their offering to meet the trend toward the aging of consumers.

Holiday Inns

"For any company that wants to serve the senior market, the first step is to claim it, to let seniors know they are a market the company wants to serve. Holiday Inns could be first. The relationship can be built by promoting Holiday Inns through networks such as the American Association of Retired Persons, senior centers, and social clubs. I'd also establish a 24-hour medical emergency hot line. For some people, that service alone would be a deciding factor."

"Most of all, though, I'd work on positioning. Bring back the original Holiday Inns marketing campaigns, the ones that said, No matter where you are in America, you can pull into a Holiday Inn and it will be the same. You can trust us. There are no surprises here. The sell is sameness, comfort, security; this is a serious and profound psychological theme on the minds of many older people when they travel."

Porsche

"Forty-eight percent of the luxury cars in America are already purchased by people over 55, so certainly the money is there to buy a car as expensive as a Porsche. But to sell them, Porsche has to understand that the mature market is interested in *experiences,* not *things.* They've already done enough accumulating; they'll purchase things if they become a means to an experience.

"What I'd do is build a special line — maybe a new product, maybe just an ergonomically modified version of an existing one. Chairs might swivel 90 degrees and tilt for getting in and out. The dash and instruments could be set higher, bigger. Simple stuff. Then: Market it. Turn the experience into something a 50-or-60-year-old can see himself doing. Convince older people that Porsches may be for them."

Source: Curtis Hartman, "Redesigning America," *Inc.* 10 (June 1988), 58–74.

Mickey Mantle is reported to have said, "If I'd known I was going to live so long, I'd have taken better care of myself."

The impact of slow growth in population is on the value of retaining customers rather than attaining new customers. When there are few new consumers to attract, marketing budgets shift from advertising to developing human resources to provide good service to current customers. Retailers such as Nordstrom have shown that good service can be a winning strategy.

More resources will be needed for consumer affairs departments or other programs for soliciting and handling complaints. **Defensive marketing** will be needed to encourage complaints. Higher economic value results from settling complaints quickly. The savings in offensive marketing may be high enough to justify additional costs associated with compensating dissatisfied

21.5 NETWORK MARKETING

Once upon a time, the marketing mix of an organization could be described as the four P's — product, promotion, price, and place. Increasingly, doing well with the four P's is not enough. Today, most marketing organizations need the four P's and an N — the N standing for a network.

Network marketing involves the development of one firm's marketing mix in close relationship to the marketing program of other firms, with the result of increased effectiveness of both programs. These synergistic programs go beyond the traditional relationships that firms have maintained with another, such as banks providing floor plans for auto dealers.

Network marketing depends upon a relationship to the customer that becomes central in the marketing of several organizations. The best example of network marketing is found currently in the travel industry, especially the frequent traveler programs. TWA, United, American, and all other major airlines have frequent flyer programs, possibly the most successful marketing innovation of the decade. Marriott has its "Honored Guest" program for frequent hotel guests. Many people who are the

prime target for airline programs are the same for Marriott, even though they are not direct competitors. In fact, it is just the opposite in the sense that the more a customer buys from TWA, the more likely the customer is to buy from Marriott. Other firms directly interested in this customer include car rental companies, restaurants, and providers of luggage and travel-related products. The list could be extended to include health clubs and other products and services that appeal to lifestyles of the frequent traveler.

Individual firms have their marketing mix, consisting of the four P's, but the big winners are organizations that establish a relationship with the customer that is synergistic with a common set of the potent marketing mixes of related firms. Thus, a firm's success in the marketplace is determined not only by how effective its own marketing program is but the quality of the network to which the firm belongs.

Source: Roger D. Blackwell and Margaret Hanke, "The Credit Card and the Aging Baby Boomers," *Journal of Retail Banking* 9 (Spring 1987), 21.

customers. Economic models have been developed to calculate these trade-offs.[25]

Businesses will need to develop **network marketing** as the value of an individual customer increases. *Consumer in Focus 21.5* describes how network marketing is implemented. Noncompetitive firms involved in a common network cooperate to find and satisfy the most valuable customers. Network marketing requires the ability to track target customers as they move through age, geographic, and economic groups.

[25] Claes Fornell and Birger Wernerfelt, "Defensive Marketing Strategy by Customer Complaint Management: A Theoretical Analysis," *Journal of Marketing Research,* 24 (November 1987), 337–346.

MONEY: SECOND REQUIREMENT FOR MARKETS

Willie Sutton, the infamous bank robber, said, "I go where the money is . . . and I go there often." So do marketers.

The search for growing market segments with ability to buy is essential for consumer analysts. Who has high income to spend on consumer products and services? Which segments are growing the fastest? What products and services do these segments value most? Where, when, and how do they buy?

These are critical questions for consumer analysts. Such questions are not meant to negate the macro issues or the social importance of studying people in poverty. For marketers, the simple reality lies in the truism that it is easier to sell to people with money than to people without money.

PROLIFERATION OF AFFLUENCE

What will consumer analysts primarily be studying in the future? At least half of their time will be spent in understanding what the affluent want to buy. The reason for this provocative statement is that the wealthiest 20 percent of U.S. families now command 50 percent of after-tax family income. Thus, assuming this trend continues, at least half of the activity of consumer analysts will have to be spent on studying the affluent. Perhaps more than half because the spending behavior of the poor is much more predictable and the financial rewards for serving the affluent, despite the difficulty of doing so, are so much greater.

Price increases are easier for marketers to achieve among the affluent than the poor. The Moet Index measures the cost of a market basket of a dozen luxury products — such things as a Rolls-Royce, Dom Perignon champagne, and Beluga caviar. When the CPI increased 4.4 percent per year, for example, the Moet Index of luxuries increased 9.0 percent.[26]

Trends in affluence are complicated by the relationship between income and other variables such as household composition, age, education, and temporal resources. Future consumers are likely to be better educated than those of earlier generations and will have a wide range of new technologies available for gaining access to information. On the other hand, the household composition reflects so many dual-income units that they may have less time to analyze information and make major decisions.

The trend toward affluence both in the United States and in some other industrialized countries is very important in understanding market opportunities. Table 21.3 displays this dramatic shift in income. A study released by the Congressional Budget Office in 1988 shows most of the increase in median family income concentrated in the top quintile. Inequality grew sharply. Most

---

[26] "Cost of the 'Good Life' Again Outpaces the CPI," *American Marketplace* 10 (March 16, 1989), 47.

TABLE 21.3 **AVERAGE AFTER-TAX FAMILY INCOME (IN 1987 DOLLARS)**	Income Group by Deciles	1977 Average Income	1988 Average Income	% Change	Dollar + or −
	First	$3,528	$3,157	− 10.5%	− $371
	Second	$7,084	$6,990	− 1.3%	− $94
	Third	$10,740	$10,614	− 1.2%	− $126
	Fourth	$14,323	$14,266	− 0.4%	− $57
	Fifth	$18,043	$18,076	+ 0.2%	+ $33
	Sixth	$22,009	$22,259	+ 1.1%	+ $250
	Seventh	$26,240	$27,038	+ 3.0%	+ $798
	Eighth	$31,568	$33,282	+ 5.4%	+ $1,714
	Ninth	$39,236	$42,323	+ 7.9%	+ $3,087
	Tenth	$70,459	$89,783	+ 27.4%	+ $19,324
	Top 5%	$90,756	$124,651	+ 37.3%	+ $33,895
	Top 1%	$174,498	$303,900	+ 74.2%	+ $129,402
	All groups	$24,184	$26,494	+ 9.6%	+ $2,310

Source: Congressional Budget Office.

of the gains arose from the entry of wives as second earners rather than from changes in incomes of established workers. Such changes are important for marketers of many goods and services, of course, but they are also important to analysts in the growing field of political marketing. The trend toward affluence has created an erosion in the voting power of the poor and the working class, with attendant effects on labor unions and the Democratic Party.

TARGETED AFFLUENTS   Affluent families increasingly are the targets for marketing programs. The number of over-$50,000 families is growing very rapidly. In 1980, only about 10 percent of families earned over $50,000, but the number, in constant dollars, is projected to be about 20 percent by 1995, nearly 15 million families to which to market goods and services.[27] Selling to affluents involves upscale products and retailers, as you recall from Chapter 8. Sometimes, however, the changes in positioning can be achieved for existing products as ordinary as paint, as *Consumer in Focus 21.6* discloses.

Even the dream of becoming a "millionaire" is more attainable for many Americans. In 1980, there were estimated to be 574,342 persons with net worth of over $1 million. Most of them made it themselves rather than inheriting it. Typically, they are entrepreneurs who own their own businesses. Many are physicians, dentists, or consultants. The average age is 57 years and most are likely to live in California, New York, Texas, or Illinois.

Millionaires are often considered to be the market for yachts, Rolls Royce's, and so forth, but, in fact, these products are more likely to be purchased by

---

[27] "Family Futures," *American Demographics* 8 (May 1984), 50. Also see "Money Income of Households, Families, and Persons," Series P-60, No. 162 (Washington, D.C.: U.S. Government Printing Office, 1989).

CONSUMER IN FOCUS

21.6   DUTCH BOY REPOSITIONS ITSELF TO REACH UPSCALE, FASHION-ORIENTED CONSUMERS

The Dutch Boy has gone upscale. Sherwin Williams Co., Cleveland, is targeting its Dutch Boy brand to a younger, more fashion-oriented consumer, which the company said accounts for the largest portion of major paint buyers.

The 18–34 age group buys nearly 38% of all paint, company research showed. Consumers in this group are not yet loyal to a particular brand and represent an untapped market, said Peter Balint, director of marketing and advertising.

To reach this group, Sherwin Williams came up with "The Look," a series of ads that seem more like music videos than commercials. Although the traditional selling points of paint — "scrubability," durability, and one-coat coverage — are important attributes, Balint said Dutch Boy's new campaign will emphasize fashion and the overall finished appearance of the painted surface.

Most of the commercials focus on modern consumers painting or enjoying the final appearance of their work. In one spot a young couple, looking as if they just stepped off the set of "thirtysomething," is shown working on their home. Interspersed with

this scene, vivid splashes of paint cross the screen. All of the action is set to fastpaced music.

Dutch Boy is not ignoring the older audience, however. One ad features a young woman with her child, relaxing on a bed. This ad features a slower, New Age soundtrack.

In addition to emphasizing consumers' personal lifestyles, the campaign stresses satin-finish paints to achieve the fashion trend of a higher-sheen surface. The campaign positions satin where it should be, Balint said, as part of an upscale trend that capitalizes on the popular European decorating style that's reaching the U.S.

Despite all the changes, the charming young Dutch Boy is still around, but now the slogan is "He Works Hard For Your Money" instead of "The Proof is in the Performance." The company has also reverted to the original 1907 illustration of the boy after research revealed that customers felt the portrait gave a feeling of quality.

Source: *Marketing News* 22 (July 4, 1988), 1.

corporations. Millionaires do not spend their fortunes on luxury goods; they are more likely to have a Sears credit card than American Express, Neiman-Marcus, Saks Fifth Avenue, or Lord and Taylor cards. They buy few home furnishings and appliances (because they already have them), but they do spend large amounts on services, travel, and college tuitions.[28]

---

[28] Thomas J. Stanley and George P. Moschis, "America's Affluent," *American Demographics* 6 (March 1984), 28–33.

CONSUMER BEHAVIOR IN A DEPRESSION

The affluent market is a major attraction for consumer analysts seeking growth opportunities. But what if there were to be a major depression, similar to the worldwise depression that occurred in the years following 1929? Edward Cornish, a noted futurist, describes some of the effects on consumers of such an event. Some marketing researchers project the possibility of such a depression,[29] but another value of considering such possibilities is to understand how marketing strategies may deal with less severe but more probable recession periods.

Cornish believes business failures will soar. Declining sales will lead to distress selling and eventually, to bankruptcies and liquidations. Workers who hang on to their jobs may also suffer, because their work weeks may be trimmed or their wages reduced. Cash will be king because people distrust financial institutions, causing stores to feature special "cash and carry" offers. People will decide it is smart to be thrifty, which will influence much of their saving and spending behavior. Born-again savers will save pieces of string, make baby blankets out of scraps of cloth, straighten and reuse nails, etc. People will mend their clothing, grow their own vegetables, and repair products instead of buying new ones. Buying things secondhand will become more popular. Sales of "big-ticket" goods such as cars and services will drop faster than those of less-expensive items. Cornish believes the depression will reduce the standard of living of both the rich and the poor, but the rich will be better able to maintain their usual lifestyles.[30]

TIME AND CHANGE IN SPENDING

Time and change will surely prove how firm a foundation is found in spending patterns. Knowing how consumers spend their money is basic to making major macroeconomic policy decisions, as well as to understanding the microeconomic implications of marketing opportunities for individual firms.

A major study by the Office of Technology Assessment (OTA) of the U.S. Government projects personal consumption expenditures in the year 2005, based upon important demographic, economic, lifestyle, and technological variables such as those discussed in this chapter.[31] This study discloses the close relationship between consumption and all economic variables, such as employment.

Early in the history of this country, Americans grew their own food. As manufacturing developed to reflect spending and production in the country, a specialized agricultural industry developed in which most of the nation derived their employment from either farming or manufacturing. Today,

---

[29] Ravi Batra, *The Great Depression of 1990* (New York: Random House, 1988).

[30] Edward Cornish, "Start of Another Depression?" *Futurist* 10 (January–February 1988), 2ff.

[31] Office of Technology Assessment, *Technology and the American Economic Transition: Choices for the Future* (Washington: U.S. Government Printing Office, 1988).

employment is much less derived from growing food and much more concentrated in its processing and serving. The OTA study shows, for example, that the number of scientists, lawyers, and computer professionals involved in supplying Americans with food is roughly equal to the number of farmers. In other areas, services that were once purchased, such as movies, are now provided at home through videocassette recorders. At the same time, services that once were provided at home are now purchased (care of children and the elderly, for example).

SCENARIO DEVELOPMENT   Projections of the future often involve scenario development. The future cannot be known by consumer analysts, but they can project the consequences of various alternative paths of development. For example, if GNP growth is 3 percent, the proportion of the nation's expenditures on food will be different than if GNP growth is 1.5 percent. If prices of inputs such as energy rise at the rate they have for the past 50 years, different spending will occur than if prices of energy rise at the rate they did during the 1970s. Estimates of the number of people in different age groups (a very reliable number to estimate) can be converted to estimates of household types, given assumptions about future marriage and divorce rates. With the aid of computerized models, estimates of future purchases can be developed, given the development of alternative growth rates and assumptions — or scenarios. The results of such an analysis are shown in Table 21.4 for the major types of personal consumption expenditures in the year 2005. This table displays the most likely scenario, although the source document contains alternative scenarios given other assumptions about demographic, income, and price changes. Marketing analysts can use such data to spot trends such as the rising importance of owner-occupied housing compared to the declining importance of renter housing, or the rising importance of clothing and personal care, or the enormous growth in the importance of recreation and leisure industries.

TABLE 21.4   THE EFFECTS OF DEMOGRAPHIC CHANGE, INCOME GROWTH, AND PRICE CHANGE ON U.S. PERSONAL CONSUMPTION IN 2005 (CHANGES IN PERCENT OF ALL SPENDING)

Amenity or Item Purchased	Percent Change from 1983 Due to Various Factors				
	All	**Demographic**	**Income**	**Price**	**Interactive**
Food	−5.26	0.07	−3.37	−1.87	−0.10
Food and beverages at home	−4.41	0.04	−4.05	−0.45	0.06
Food and beverages away from home	−0.15	0.03	1.31	−1.30	−0.19
Tobacco	−0.70	0.00	−0.63	−0.11	0.04
Housing	−0.48	0.40	−1.91	1.72	0.11
Owner occupied	0.28	0.19	0.00	0.47	0.00
Renters	−1.91	0.32	−1.81	0.19	0.03
Maintenance services	0.01	0.01	0.10	−0.07	−0.01
Maintenance commodities	−0.49	0.02	−0.30	−0.24	0.03
Tenants insurance	−0.02	0.04	0.02	−0.09	0.01

continued

TABLE 21.4   *continued*

Amenity or Item Purchased	Percent Change from 1983 Due to Various Factors				
	All	**Demographic**	**Income**	**Price**	**Interactive**
House furnishings	0.95	0.03	0.06	0.84	0.02
House appliances	0.71	0.01	0.17	0.47	0.06
Water and sewer	−0.01	0.01	−0.15	0.16	−0.03
Transportation	−0.51	0.06	0.38	−0.96	0.02
New vehicles	−0.33	0.03	−0.00	−0.33	−0.02
Used vehicles	−0.24	0.01	0.05	−0.29	0.01
Vehicle maintenance	−0.13	0.04	−0.06	−0.14	0.04
Other private transportation	−0.02	0.00	−0.01	−0.01	0.00
Air fare	0.37	0.00	0.37	−0.01	−0.00
Other public transportation	−0.17	0.00	0.02	−0.18	−0.00
Clothing and Personal Care	1.84	0.10	1.63	0.01	0.10
Personal care commodities	0.06	0.00	0.06	−0.00	0.00
Personal care services	0.11	0.01	−0.02	0.11	0.01
Men's and boys' clothing	0.39	0.02	0.38	−0.02	0.01
Women's and girls' clothing	0.94	0.06	0.87	−0.05	0.05
Other (including jewelry)	0.24	0.01	0.25	−0.01	0.01
Footwear	0.03	0.01	0.02	−0.01	0.01
Apparel services	0.06	0.00	0.06	−0.00	0.00
Personal Business and Communication	0.95	0.07	1.26	−0.16	−0.23
Telephone	0.17	0.02	−0.35	0.61	−0.08
Personal business	0.78	0.09	1.61	−0.77	−0.15
Recreation and Leisure	3.47	0.10	2.02	1.26	0.09
Entertainment services	1.26	0.06	1.43	−0.21	−0.02
Entertainment commodities	0.89	0.02	0.20	0.64	0.03
TV and sound	0.83	0.00	0.11	0.68	0.03
Lodging	0.49	0.02	0.28	0.14	0.06

How To Read This Table:

Assuming 3 percent annual economic growth through 2005, 2005 household distribution, and prices and incomes adjusted to this growth, the percentage of American spending on food eaten at home (as a share of the items listed here—roughly three-quarters of all personal spending) would decline by 4.41 percentage points. Changing incomes would account for a drop of 4.05 points and changing prices would account for a 0.45 point drop, while demographic changes would exert a slight positive trend of 0.04 percentage points; the effect of interaction between these factors would be a rise of 0.06.

NOTES: This table estimates how U.S. consumer spending on selected items and amenities could change, and attempts to isolate what factors may contribute to that change. The "All" column assumes 3 percent annual economic growth through 2005, 2005 household structure as developed earlier in this chapter, and a set of possible price changes for these items in 2005 as outlined in the appendix. Incomes are then raised by 35.5 percent, the level at which Americans will have enough purchasing power to satisfy the estimate of personal spending in 2005.

For individual components of change:

- For demographic changes in 2005: see table 2–4; price and income held at 1983 levels.
- For income changes in 2005: incomes raised by 35.5 percent; demographics and prices held at 1983 levels.
- For price changes in 2005: see the appendix; demographics and income held at 1983 levels.

The effects of these three components that cannot be traced individually but are rather the result of a combination of factors are captured in the "Interactive" column.

SOURCE: U.S. Congress, Office of Technology Assessment, "Consumer Expenditure Demand Projection Program," April 1986, based on data provided by the U.S. Department of Labor, Bureau of Labor Statistics; the U.S. Department of Commerce, Bureaus of Census and of Economic Analysis; and the U.S. Department of Health and Human Services, Social Security Administration.

CHANGING GEOGRAPHY OF DEMAND

People and money. They are certainly the foundation of consumer demand. Where those people live and earn their money is also critical to understanding demand, however, and we now turn our attention to an examination of the geography of demand in North American markets.

GEOGRAPHY: BASIS FOR IMPLEMENTING MARKETING PLANS

Marketing plans are usually implemented in geographical units, because of the ready availability of data on a geographic basis rather than its superiority as a unit of analysis in consumer behavior.

This is especially true for promotional programs. Advertising media such as television, radio, and newspapers are usually bought on a geographic basis — usually cities or the areas surrounding a city called **Area of Dominant Influence** (ADI) or **Designated Marketing Area** (DMA). Even national magazines such as *Time* or *Business Week* have regional advertising sections sold on a state or city basis. Print media are moving toward editions based on geographic divisions as specific as zip codes. As a consumer analyst, you are likely to be working with consumption and media data based on city, state, and regional units.

REGIONS AND ECONOMIC AREAS

Over 100 years ago, the Department of Commerce recognized the need to understand and classify the linkages between the natural environment of certain areas and the population statistics, economics, subcultures, and political characteristics of a primarily agricultural nation. Accordingly, U.S. geography was divided into physical regions that included lowlands, highlands, wetlands, drylands, woodlands, and grasslands.

Since 1910 these geographic areas have been combined into nine divisions frequently used for reporting census data. The divisions are fairly homogeneous in physical characteristics. The characteristics of their populations and their economic and social conditions differed originally from those of other divisions. These divisions of the United States are shown in Figure 21.6. Their greatest value is in the consistency of reporting over the years, even though considerable variation is found among markets within each division. Marketing research data are often collected or reported on the basis of these regions.

ECONOMIC AREAS

Another geographic unit of analysis is **Bureau of Economic Analysis** (BEA) **Economic Areas,** which are nodal functional areas delineated to facilitate regional economic analysis. Each area consists of an **economic node**—a metro-

FIGURE 21.6   CENSUS BUREAU DIVISIONS

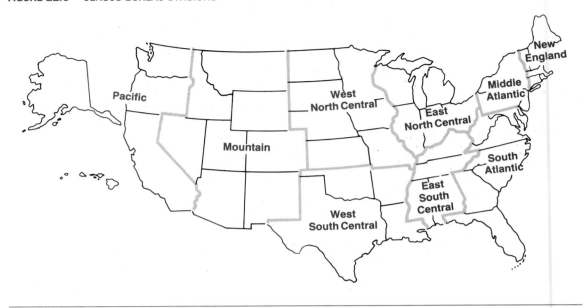

Source: U.S. Department of Commerce, Bureau of the Census

politan or similar area — that serves as a center of economic activity including the surrounding counties and smaller cities that are economically related to the center. The areas cover the entire United States, including both metropolitan areas (cities) and the nonmetropolitan areas that are neglected when only metropolitan data are analyzed. There are 183 economic areas, defined by journey-to-work data from the census; newspaper circulation data; and country commuting data developed from Social Security and Internal Revenue Service records.

Economic area data are superior to region data because they are specific and relatively homogeneous. They are superior to city or metropolitan area data because they cover the entire country. In addition, they give a much more accurate picture to marketing analysts of what is happening than is sometimes obtained from city data. For example, the Boston metropolitan statistical area lost population in recent years. The conclusion might be that the area should receive less emphasis in marketing plans. However, the "bedroom" metropolitan areas of Manchester, New Bedford, Portsmouth, and Worcester (treated as separate cities by the Census Bureau) grew almost as quickly as the nation as a whole did, and the nonmetropolitan areas surrounding Boston grew at an impressive rate, providing an overall growth rate for the Boston economic area.

STATE AND PROVINCIAL MARKETS

Market trends vary substantially between states and provinces. The states gaining the most population recently are California, Texas, and Florida. Florida passed Pennsylvania to become the fourth most populous state.

What will the future bring? These projections are shown in Table 21.5. Such projections are based upon the components of change: births, deaths, and net migration. California and Florida each gained more than 2 million persons through net immigration in the 1980s, and Texas gained more than 1.2 million. Those three states accounted for more than half of national population growth in the past decade.

TABLE 21.5   (TOTAL POPULATION IN THOUSANDS BY STATE, 1990 TO 2010; ABSOLUTE CHANGE AND PERCENT CHANGE FOR 1990 TO 2000, AND 2000 TO 2010)

	1990	2000	2010	1990–2000 Change	1990–2000 Percent	2000–2010 Change	2000–2010 Percent
U.S. Total	249,891	267,747	282,055	17,856	7.1%	14,308	5.3%
Alabama	4,181	4,410	4,609	229	5.5	199	4.5
Alaska	576	687	765	111	19.3	78	11.4
Arizona	3,752	4,618	5,319	866	23.1	701	15.2
Arkansas	2,427	2,529	2,624	102	4.2	95	3.8
California	29,126	33,500	37,347	4,374	15.0	3,847	11.5
Colorado	3,434	3,813	4,098	379	11.0	285	7.5
Connecticut	3,279	3,445	3,532	166	5.1	87	2.5
Delaware	666	734	790	68	10.2	56	7.6
District of Columbia	614	634	672	20	3.3	38	6.0
Florida	12,818	15,415	17,530	2,597	20.3	2,115	13.7
Georgia	6,663	7,957	9,045	1,294	19.4	1,088	13.7
Hawaii	1,141	1,345	1,559	204	17.9	214	15.9
Idaho	1,017	1,047	1,079	30	2.9	32	3.1
Illinois	11,612	11,580	11,495	−32	−0.3	−85	−0.7
Indiana	5,550	5,502	5,409	−48	−0.9	−93	−1.7
Iowa	2,758	2,549	2,382	−209	−7.6	−167	−6.6
Kansas	2,492	2,529	2,564	37	1.5	35	1.4
Kentucky	3,745	3,733	3,710	−12	−0.3	−23	−0.6
Louisiana	4,513	4,516	4,545	3	0.1	29	0.6
Maine	1,212	1,271	1,308	59	4.9	37	2.9
Maryland	4,729	5,274	5,688	545	11.5	414	7.8
Massachusetts	5,880	6,087	6,255	207	3.5	168	2.8
Michigan	9,293	9,250	9,097	−43	−0.5	−153	−1.7
Minnesota	4,324	4,490	4,578	166	3.8	88	2.0
Mississippi	2,699	2,877	3,028	178	6.6	151	5.2
Missouri	5,192	5,383	5,521	191	3.7	138	2.6
Montana	805	794	794	−11	−1.4	0	0.0
Nebraska	1,588	1,556	1,529	−32	−2.0	−27	−1.7
Nevada	1,076	1,303	1,484	227	21.1	181	13.9
New Hampshire	1,142	1,333	1,455	191	16.7	122	9.2
New Jersey	7,899	8,546	8,980	647	8.2	434	5.1
New Mexico	1,632	1,968	2,248	336	20.6	280	14.2

continued

TABLE 21.5 *continued*

	1990	2000	2010	1990–2000		2000–2010	
				Change	Percent	Change	Percent
New York	17,773	17,986	18,139	213	1.2	153	0.9
North Carolina	6,690	7,483	8,154	793	11.9	671	9.0
North Dakota	660	629	611	−31	−4.7	−18	−2.9
Ohio	10,791	10,629	10,397	−162	−1.5	−232	−2.2
Oklahoma	3,285	3,376	3,511	91	2.8	135	4.0
Oregon	2,766	2,877	2,991	111	4.0	114	4.0
Pennsylvania	11,827	11,503	11,134	−324	−2.7	−369	−3.2
Rhode Island	1,002	1,049	1,085	47	4.7	36	3.4
South Carolina	3,549	3,906	4,205	357	10.1	299	7.7
South Dakota	708	714	722	6	0.8	8	1.1
Tennessee	4,972	5,266	5,500	294	5.9	234	4.4
Texas	17,712	20,211	22,281	2,499	14.1	2,070	10.2
Utah	1,776	1,991	2,171	215	12.1	180	9.0
Vermont	562	591	608	29	5.2	17	2.9
Virginia	6,157	6,877	7,410	720	11.7	533	7.8
Washington	4,657	4,991	5,282	334	7.2	291	5.8
West Virginia	1,856	1,722	1,617	−134	−7.2	−105	−6.1
Wisconsin	4,808	4,784	4,713	−24	−0.5	−71	−1.5
Wyoming	502	489	487	−13	−2.6	−2	−0.4

Note: Numbers may not add to totals due to rounding.
Source: Bureau of the Census, *Current Population Reports*, Series P-25, No. 1017.

Marketers can find segments of growth even in states with declining population. Every state experienced large increases in the 25- to 44-year-old age cohort. This same group, which is about a third of the nation's population, will be the rapidly growing 35 to 44 age group during the 1990s.[32]

There are pitfalls associated with concentrating only on growth. Alaska was the fastest-growing state in the 1980s and is projected to grow rapidly during the 1990s. Alaska, along with Wyoming, is also one of the least populous states, with only 576,000 people in 1990. This illustrates the trap to avoid of chasing the trend but ignoring the substance. A 10-percent market share in a no-growth market such as Ohio or Michigan may be preferable to a high market share in a rapid growth but minuscule state such as Alaska or Nevada. Additionally, the costs of doing business in areas where the infrastructure is already paid for may be lower than in areas with rapidly expanding population.

The Water Belt may be a challenge to the Sun Belt for markets of the future, especially if the greenhouse effect causes widespread drought. Texas shipped valuable oil to northern states in the past, creating prosperity and

---

[32] "State Population and Household Estimates, with Age, Sex, and Components of Change: 1981–1987," Series P-25, No. 1024 (Washington, D.C.: U.S. Government Printing Office, 1988).

expanding markets. It may be the Great Lakes states that will ship valuable water to Texas and the Sun Belt in the future.[33]

CANADA

About 80 percent of all Canadians live within 200 kilometers of the United States–Canada border, creating a market about 4,000 miles long and 125 miles wide. The rural areas to the north contain 80 percent of Canada's land but only about 1 percent of the population. The largest market is a 750-mile megalopolis stretching from Quebec City southwestward through Montreal, Ottawa, Toronto, and the Niagara Peninsula to Windsor. The cities in this area contain about 40 percent of the population, income, and retail sales in Canada.

The fastest-growing areas of Canada in the past were Alberta, British Columbia, and the Northwest Territories, due to the rising value of energy. It is not expected that such rapid growth will continue in the future. Ontario is regaining momentum. About 36 percent of all Canadians now live in Ontario. The moderate climate and highly developed resource and service industries of British Columbia provide a good base for future growth. The eastern provinces continue to grow the slowest.

SUBURBANIZATION AND GENTRIFICATION

Population concentration is occurring in metropolitan areas throughout the world. Suburbs have been the big winners in the United States since World War II, with population growth increasing more than twice as fast as the total population and over five times as fast as that of central cities. People fled the sidewalk shops of the cities for the trees and grass of the suburbs. The shopping centers soon followed the people — in many cases becoming a magnet throughout the region.

SUBURBANIZATION   Suburbs have grown rapidly, but today **exurbs** — areas beyond the suburbs — are experiencing the fastest growth. Fast-growing counties are often nonmetropolitan or rural but adjacent to suburban or metropolitan areas.

Shopping centers and many businesses often "jumped" the suburbs to build on more desirable (and cheaper) land of the exurbs. Businesses that have failed to follow the trend are often in serious difficulty, despite the major investments required to keep up with consumer movements. Affluent cosmopolitans who live in the suburbs often know their city only from its airport, an infrequent evening out, and the crime reports on the local news.[34]

---

[33] Bruce Stokes, "Water Shortages: The Next Energy Crisis," *Futurist* 17 (April 1983), 37–47.
[34] Jane Newitt, "Where Do Suburbanites Come From?" *American Demographics* 3 (November 1981), 14–19.

GENTRIFICATION   **Gentrification** is a process in which people move back to the city in a renaissance of neighborhoods, often displacing low-income families who had occupied the neighborhood. Gentrification usually includes growth in retail trade and industry, housing improvement, and change in the number and composition (younger, more affluent, usually white) of residents. In spite of well-publicized examples of such rejuvenated neighborhoods, however, the numbers — which must be the basis for market analysis — are overwhelmingly in the direction of the suburbs and exurbs. Zip codes of gentrified areas may be attractive targets, however, for direct marketing, remodeling services, and household furnishings and for some forms of innovative and upscale retailing and service establishments.

Cities: Winners or Losers?

Cities are the most important unit of analysis in most marketing plans. They are fundamental in the analysis of micromarketing programs. Cities are also the fundamental unit in determining the prosperity of nations, according to economist Jane Jacobs. In her book, *Cities and the Wealth of Nations,* she describes the forces that transform regional economies originating in cities that are "import-replacing" (not dependent only on producing exports but having an economy of their own). The forces that create the health of cities are their markets, jobs, technology, transplants (of prosperity to suburbs and exurbs), and capital.[35]

DOWNTOWN

The future of the "downtown" of cities or Central Business Districts (CBD) is questionable. A number of innovations have occurred recently to indicate they might experience a revival in the 1990s and beyond. Innovative growth in the past was mainly in skyscrapers or office buildings, but developments such as Eaton Centre in Toronto, City Center in Columbus, and the Harborplace in Baltimore are more consumer-oriented.

The renaissance in CBD's emphasizes cities as a place to learn, to shop, to play, and perhaps even to live as well as a place to earn. The prototype for such projects is the festival marketplace known as Faneuil Hall Marketplace in Boston. Other projects include the Union Station in St. Louis, Portside in Toledo, and others. Historic preservation is a "big idea" that is creating excitement as well as cultural centers, open spaces, and waterfront developments. Events such as the Boston Marathon or the Columbus Red, White, and Boom attract people to cities. The success of such projects is closely related to improved transportation, security, and living projects.[36]

---

[35] Jane Jacobs, *Cities and the Wealth of Nations* (New York: Random House, 1984).
[36] John Fondersmith, "Downtown 2040: Making Cities Fun," *Futurist* 22 (March–April 1988), 9–17.

ANALYZING CITY DATA

The analysis of consumer trends by cities requires use of standardized definitions. The most affluent city, for example, is Bridgeport, Connecticut, with per capita income of $24,501 in contrast to the lowest per capita income, in McAllen, Texas, at $6,800.[37] Such comparisons of market attractiveness would not be useful without standardized definitions. For many years, data were collected on the basis of **Standard Metropolitan Statistical Areas** (SMSAs). They were counties of similar social and economic character surrounding a major central city.

SMSA has been replaced by several new terms. The **Metropolitan Statistical Area** (MSA) is the most direct descendant. MSA is defined as a freestanding metropolitan area, surrounded by nonmetropolitan counties and not closely related with other metropolitan areas. A **Primary Metropolitan Statistical Area** (PMSA) is a metropolitan area that is closely related to another city. A grouping of closely related PMSAs is a **Consolidated Metropolitan Statistical Area** (CMSA). CMSAs are classified as A areas when they have more than 1 million residents, B areas with 250,000 to 1 million, C areas with 100,000 to 250,000, and D areas with a population of less than 100,000.

When you are preparing market analyses, especially those comparing cities currently with past data, you may find most of the data reported on the basis of SMSAs, but remember that this term was deleted from usage in 1983, when it was replaced by MSAs, PMSAs, and CMSAs.

MEGALOPOLIS

More than one-third of the people in the United States live in the country's 22 **megalopolises** or CMSAs. The biggest of these are huge areas made up of many counties and two or more smaller metropolitan areas. The largest of them all is New York–Northern New Jersey–Long Island, with an estimated population of 17.9 million in 1990. Even though New York City itself has declined in population, the rest of the counties in the CMSA have grown.

The Los Angeles–Anaheim–Riverside CMSA gained more than 1 million people from 1980 to 1990, placing it ahead of third-ranking Chicago–Gary–Lake County. When implementing marketing strategies, it is useful to consider that reaching the New York–Newark–Jersey City CMSA is a market larger than Canada or six of the European Common Market countries.[38]

Who wins? Who loses? The cities that are winning the battle for population growth are mostly in the West and the South. During the past 15 years only one city east of the Mississippi and north of the Sun Belt increased consistently in population — Columbus, Ohio. Columbus has the technological and com-

---

[37] The Gap Grows," *American Demographics* 10 (December 1988), 16.
[38] "Megalopolis," *American Demographics* 6 (January 1984), 50–51.

puterized information economy described by John Naisbitt in *Megatrends* as more typical of the Sun Belt than the Northeast quadrant of the United States.[39] Some of the metropolitan areas of the Northeast grew, however, even though their central cities did not. In the future, most of the growing cities will be in the West and the South.

Cities are especially important for ethnic marketing. Most new immigrants settle in urban areas. New York is the most popular destination, but 37 other metropolitan areas in the United States receive at least 2,000 immigrants a year. Specific cities often attract immigrants from some countries more than others. Illinois has five times as many Polish immigrants as the rest of the United States.[40]

COLLECTING AND ANALYZING DEMOGRAPHIC DATA

You have now studied the major variables of economic demographics, the foundation of market analysis. But where do you find the data you need to make such analyses? At this point, you may be getting tired of studying so many tables and charts. Be assured that you won't have to do much more of this in this book. Demographic analysis, however, usually involves poring over numbers — questioning how they were collected and what they mean. You may have noted sources of data just by giving attention to the references for each figure in this chapter. There are so many that it is usually safe to assume data exist somewhere on the topic you need to analyze — if only you can figure out where!

CENSUS DATA

The first nationwide population census in the United States was conducted in 1770. In 1950, the Census Bureau introduced several sampling techniques as alternative methods to collecting census-required information. Today, many questions that are described as census data are really sampling data based on interviews of 5 to 20 percent of the population. Only a few basic questions needed for sensitive government allocation of funds are asked of 100 percent of the population queried.

The most important source of demographic data in Canada is Statistics Canada. In the United States, it is the Bureau of the Census of the U.S. Department of Commerce. The data collected change from decade to decade, with attempts to add or delete topics or terms that are obsolete.

---

[39] John Naisbitt, *Megatrends* (New York: Warner Books, 1982).
[40] James P. Allen and Eugene J. Turner, "Where to Find the New Immigrants," *American Demographics,* 10 (September 1988), 23–27.

ACCESSING CENSUS DATA

The Census Bureau has become "customer-oriented" in recent years to meet the needs of marketing and other organizations. In addition to the decennial census, the Census Bureau has an extensive program of sample-survey supplements on population, housing, and economic, agriculture, and government topics, issued through the Bureau's Data User Services Division.

Consumer analysts pay close attention to the Current Population Reports, known as the "P" series, based upon a monthly survey of 60,000 households. On a national basis, the "P-20" series provides reports on marital status, households and families, geographic residence and mobility, fertility, school enrollment, educational attainment, persons of Spanish origin, and other demographic topics. The "P-23" reports are special studies about such groups as blacks, youth, women, older people, and so forth. The "P-27" reports provide data about the farm population, and the "P-60" series reports on consumer income, classified by variables such as race, ethnic origin, age, sex, education, and so forth. The "P-25" series is of particular value to marketing planners because it provides projections of the future U.S. population. The U.S. Census Bureau also provides a considerable data base on international markets, although coverage is not as detailed as for U.S. markets.[41]

Census data are available in many forms. The most useful are increasingly computerized. Waiting for hard copy requires about 4 years after a census is completed, but the most valuable product is probably Summary Tape File 3, which contains data from the long census questionnaire administered in a sample about income and income type, residence, and transportation to work for specific geographic areas. Some census data not published in printed form are available in microfiche as well as computer tapes.[42]

CANADA   Statistics Canada provides more comprehensive market data than is generally available about U.S. markets from government services. *Canadian Social Trends* provides data on major social indicators as well as data for studying trends in income, population, crime, education, housing, and other variables. The most current data are reported in *Statistics Canada Daily* or on a weekly basis in Informat.

PRIVATE DATA FIRMS

Explosive growth has occurred among private firms providing analyses of demographic and economic data. Several of them have formed a consortium of firms to pay for assembly of census data by zip codes. These firms, in return, receive the right to use and sell census data in their form before it becomes available publicly.

---

[41] Martha Riche, "The Non-Census Bureau," *American Demographics* 6 (September 1984), 38–41.

[42] Martha Riche, "1980 Census Data Products," *American Demographics*, 6 (August 1984), 32–35.

FIGURE 21.7
ADAPTING
GEODEMOGRAPHIC
DATA TO SPECIFIC
MARKETING PLANS

We make more successful matches than any other geocoding system. No matter how unusual.

If you use geocodes to segment markets or to take advantage of postal discounts, you know the importance of consistently making correct matches. You also know how difficult that can be — especially when the unusual shows up. If your records contain the same inconsistencies commonly found in other files, the geocoding services of Urban Data Processing, Inc. will maximize your geocoding match rate.

Making a match is one thing. Making the right match is something else.

...and doing it consistently is another story. Our geocoding software achieves a higher percentage of accurate matches than conventional match code systems. The keys to this successful match rate are advanced logic, unparalleled flexibility, and the most accurate and complete census and postal directories available.

Whereas conventional systems use only a few portions of the address record for matching purposes, the system logic used by Urban Data fix — fields each component of

the address — including house number, primary and secondary directions, street name, street type, and apartment, floor, or suite designation — and standardizes these components in preparation for matching.

Nothing is unusual to us.

We've seen it all — misspellings, abbreviations, synonyms — you name it. Our matcher is designed to handle these and other

idiosyncrasies. It works on a scoring system that allows records which do not attain a 100% match to be geocoded — without compromising accuracy. Records can be matched which contain misspellings, two-letter transpositions, missing letters, extra characters, etc., as long as the matching scores do not fall below a certain threshold.

The census geocoding services available from Urban Data include Census Tract and Block Group/ED Coding — geographic designators that are the keys to cluster coding and creating segmented demographic profiles of your customer base. Postal geocoding services include Zip Coding, Zip+4 and Carrier Route.

Interested? Then give us a call, and we'll introduce you to the geocoding service that takes the unusual in stride.

URBAN DATA PROCESSING INC

A HARTE-HANKS
COMMUNICATIONS, INC. COMPANY.
For further information write or call:
Urban Data Processing, Inc.
25 Linnell Circle
Billerica, MA 01821-3961
(617) 663-9955

Source: Courtesy of Urban Data Processing, Inc.

Private firms provide specialized demographic analyses of great value to consumer analysts and marketing strategists. The goal is to match the general data with specific needs of marketers, as the ad for one of these firms communicates well in Figure 21.7. Some of these firms include Donnelly Marketing Information Services, Claritas, and National Data Systems. *American Demographics,* the "Bible" of marketers interested in demographics, is a valuable source of names and addresses of the many private firms that provide specialized demographic/economic analyses and marketing assistance.

A widely used source of demographic data is *Sales Management's* "Survey of Buying Power" (SBP). Published in July of each year, the SBP contains data on population; effective buying income; and retail sales for all metropolitan areas, states, counties, and cities in the United States and for most metropolitan areas, provinces, counties, and cities in Canada.

Another widely used source is the American Research Bureau, which compiles data on the areas of dominant influence or ADI, a geographic market area of contiguous counties defined by television viewing. For each ADI, information is available concerning the estimated number of television households by county, number of adult women and adult men, and number of teenagers and children.

DO-IT-YOURSELF ESTIMATES

Consumer analysts sometimes need to make their own estimates of the population in a market area. Four methods are used. The **Censal-Ratio method** compares the population of an area from the most recent census with a variable that changes as the size of the population changes. The **Housing-Unit method** estimates population by multiplying occupied housing units by the average household size. **Component methods** divide population into its components of change: births, deaths, and migration. The **ratio-correlation method** uses multiple regression to mathematically compute a population estimate.[43]

ENVIRONMENTAL SCANNING

Marketing organizations need systematic and timely information about the environment as it currently exists as well as projections of trends. This has given rise to the development of formal responsibility for such a function, usually called **environmental scanning.** Environmental scanning usually includes information internal to the organization, such as the cognitive maps used by executives in making decisions, as well as external variables. External variables include the following:

1. Descriptions of the *structural* properties of the environment.
2. Assumptions about the nature and sources of environmental *change*.
3. Proposed means for managers to gain *knowledge* of their environments.[44]

Environmental scanning is becoming a top priority with many firms in their search for the 3 M's of growing profits. Where should such responsibility be placed? Who should do environmental scanning? Some large corporations place such responsibility with staff departments, usually in marketing research or strategic planning. Research indicates, however, that environmental scanning is most effective when it is done by line managers who must also take responsibility for the decisions to be made with the scanning output.[45] Uncertainty about the environment is so important to line executives[46] that it makes

---

[43] James C. Raymondo, "How to Estimate Population," *American Demographics* 11 (January 1989), 46–49.

[44] R. T. Lenz and Jack L. Engledow, "Environmental Analysis: The Applicability of Current Theory," *Strategic Management Journal* 7 (1986), 329–346.

[45] Charles Stubbart, "Are Environmental Scanning Units Effective?" *Long Raement Review* 12 (1987), 133–143.

[46] A comprehensive review of these topics is found in The Conservation Foundation, *State of the Environment: A View Toward the Nineties* (New York: The Conference Board, 1978).

sense for line executives to be responsible for the scanning process, perhaps with technical assistance from centralized staff. Business planners focus on economic and customer variables, but scanning should include broader issues such as population growth, air quality, hazardous waste, land use, water quality, natural resources, and other biological and physical elements.

SALES FORECASTING AND CONSUMER ANALYSIS

An application of environmental scanning occurs in sales forecasting. The effectiveness of sales forecasting should be evaluated by the degree to which it improves the decisions of marketing managers. Even though sales forecasting was often self-contained in the sales or finance areas of responsibility, it is increasingly a planning and strategic activity. Thus, sales forecasts should involve all the elements of the environment about which managers must make decisions. A close relationship therefore exists between sales forecasting and decision support systems (DSS).[47]

The specific techniques of sales forecasting include judgmental methods, sales-force estimation, users' expectations, traditional and advanced time-series techniques, econometric or regression modeling, input-output analysis, and various other methods. A discussion of how to use these techniques is beyond the scope of this book, but there are many sources of information about these concepts and techniques.[48] Consumer researchers generally have data and methods useful in preparing sales forecasts.

CHANGING VALUES AND LIFESTYLES

Finally, the analysis of consumer trends should consider changes in values, lifestyles, and technologies discussed in earlier chapters. Futurists use a variety of methods to project these trends. It is the task of consumer analysts and marketing strategists to determine their possible effect on consumer behavior. One such projection is shown in Figure 21.8. Some trends in Figure 21.8 are demographically based. Others are interpersonal, technological, or social in nature. These trends are just that, changes over time, and thus will also be replaced in many instances by other trends. The thoughtful marketing analyst will find implications for both consumer and goods firms, whether the trends are considered as opportunities for growing profits or threats to existing strategies and profits.

---

[47] Essam Mahmoud, Gillian Rice, and Naresh Malhotra, "Emerging Issues in Sales Forecasting and Decision Support Systems," *Journal of the Academy of Marketing Science* 16 (Fall 1988), 47–61.

[48] Some sources which provide practical approaches to understanding these techniques include Lester Sartorious and N. Carroll Mohn, *Sales Forecasting Methods: A Diagnostic Approach* (Atlanta: Georgia State University, 1976); George C. Michael, *Sales Forecasting* (Chicago: American Marketing Association, 1979); Harry R. White, *Sales Forecasting: Timesaving and Profit-Making Strategies That Work* (Dallas: Scott, Foresman and Company, 1984.)

<table>
<tr><td>

FIGURE 21.8
LONG-TERM
TRENDS AFFECTING
THE UNITED STATES

</td><td>

General Long-Term Societal Trends

1. Ahead is a period of U.S. economic prosperity—affluence, low interest rates, low inflation rate.
2. Rise of knowledge industries and a knowledge-dependent society.
3. Fewer very poor or very wealthy in U.S. society.
4. Rise of the middle-class society.
5. Urbanization and suburbanization of rural land.
6. Cultural homogenization—the growth of a national society.
7. Continuation of a permanent military establishment.
8. Mobility: (A) personal, (B) physical, (C) occupational, (D) job.
9. International affairs and national security as a major societal factor.

Technology Trends

10. The centrality and increasing dominance of technology in the economy and society.
11. Integration of the U.S. economy.
12. Integration of the national with the international economy.
13. Growth of the international economy.
14. The growth of research and development as a factor in the economy.
15. High technological turnover rate.
16. The development of mass media in telecommunications and printing.
17. Major medical advances.

Educational Trends

18. Expanding education and training throughout society.
19. New technologies will greatly facilitate the training process.
20. Greater role of business in training and education.
21. Education costs will continue to rise.
22. Educational institutions will be more concerned with ways to assess outcomes and effectiveness of educational programs.
23. Improved pedagogy—the science of teaching—will revolutionize learning.
24. Universities will stress development of the whole student and how the university's total environment affects that development.
25. Reduction in the size of higher education institutions.

Trends in Labor Force and Work

26. Specialization.
27. Growth of the service sector.
28. Further decline in the manufacturing sector.
29. Growth of information industries, movement toward an information society.
30. More women will enter the labor force.
31. Women's salaries will be comparable to men's.
32. More blacks and other minority groups will enter the labor force.
33. Later retirement.
34. Decline of unionization.
35. Growth of pensions and pension funds.
36. Movement toward second and third careers and midlife changes in career.
37. Decline of the work ethic.
38. More two-income couples.
39. Shortage of low-wage workers.

Management Trends

40. More entrepreneurs.
41. The typical large business will be information-based, composed of specialists who guide themselves based on information from colleagues, customers, and headquarters.
42. The typical large business in 2010 will have less than half the levels of management of the typical large business today and about one-third the number of managers.
43. The command-and-control model of management will be a relic of the past as the information-based organization becomes the norm.
44. The actual work will be done by task-focused teams of specialists.

continued

</td></tr>
</table>

FIGURE 21.8
continued

Trends in Values and Concerns
45. General shift in societal values.
46. Diversity as a growing, explicit value.
47. Increasing aspirations and expectations of success.
48. Growth of tourism, vacationing, and travel (especially international).
49. General expectations of a high level of medical care.
50. Growth of physical culture and personal health movements.
51. General expectations of a high level of social service.
52. Growth of consumerism.
53. Growth of women's liberation movement.

Family Trends
54. Decline in birth rates.
55. Increase in rates of family formation and marriage.
56. Decrease in the number of divorces.
57. Growth of leisure.
58. Growth of the do-it-yourself movement.
59. Improved nutrition and the wellness movement will increase life expectancy.
60. Isolation of children from the world of adult concerns.
61. Protracted adolescence.
62. More single heads of households—the new poor.
63. Growth of the already large aged population.
64. The replacement of the extended family with other living arrangements.

Institutional Trends
65. Decrease in the size of the federal government—growth of state and local governments.
66. Growth of big business (deregulation).
67. Growth of multinational corporations.
68. Growth of futures studies and forecasting.
69. Growing demand for accountability in the expenditure of public resources.
70. Growing demand for social responsibility.
71. A phenomenon of "bimodal" distribution of institutions is emerging as the big get bigger, the small survive, and the middle-sized are squeezed out.

Source: Marvin J. Cetron, Wanda Rocha, and Rebecca Lucken, "Into the 21st Century," *The Futurist* 22 (July–August 1988), 29–40. Supporting materials for this article are also found in Marvin Cetron, *America At the Turn of the Century* (New York: St. Martin's Press, 1989).

Summary

Consumer analysts have responsibilities for monitoring the environment for both macromarketing and micromarketing reasons. Macromarketing applications focus upon determining the aggregate performance of marketing in society. Micromarketing analysis focuses on the marketing programs of specific organizations.

The primary financial goal of business firms is ESV — Enhanced Shareholder Value. The financial community attributes such value to a company's stock to the degree that the company is perceived to be able to increase profits in the future. Thus, a major role for consumer analysts is to determine trends that will allow a corporation to increase profits in the future. This can be achieved through the 3 M's — more markets, more market share, and more margin.

Consumer analysts focus upon finding markets that are growing. Markets involve people and their needs, ability to buy, willingness to buy, and authority to buy. Economic demographics involves the analysis of market trends and discovery of growing segments based upon changes in population and age distribution, buying power, geography of demand, and social and technological trends.

Population projections involve three variables: births, deaths, and net immigration. Of these, births is usually the most important determinant of population trends and the most difficult to forecast. Births are determined by four variables: age distribution, family structure, social attitudes toward family and children, and technology. All of these variables are contributing to declining fertility in industrialized countries such as the United States and Canada.

The population base of the United States and Canada is still growing but at a declining rate. It should peak at around 250 to 270 million in the United States sometime after the year 2000 and at around 28 million in Canada. During the 1990s, both countries will see fewer total but more first-order babies, more teenagers, more aging Baby Boomers (but less in the 24 to 35 age category), a new era of expanding empty-nesters, and an enormous increase in the mature or over-65 markets. Each of these categories can be attractive market opportunities for firms that recognize the specialized marketing programs required for success.

Much of the work of consumer analysts in the future will focus upon marketing to the affluent. Recognition should be given to the possibility, however, of marketing in a depression or recession.

A large part of consumer market analysis involves geodemography, the study of demand as it is related to geography. In the United States population is expanding rapidly in some states — notably California, Texas, and Florida, with slow growth in the Midwest. In Canada, the western provinces are experiencing the most growth, although not at the rate of the energy-induced boom times of the past. Ontario is recovering some of its growth, but growth of all provinces is slower as a result of decreased fertility and migration rates.

Analysis of demographic and trend data is essential for environmental scanning — the accumulation of systematic and timely information about trends. Such information focuses on the structural properties of the environment, the nature and sources of change, and the means for managers to gain knowledge of their environments. Line managers, sometimes assisted by staff, need to be involved in environmental scanning.

REVIEW AND DISCUSSION QUESTIONS

1. Distinguish between macromarketing and micromarketing. How does the work of consumer analysts vary between these two fields?

2. Is the concept of ESV (Enhanced Shareholder Value) a socially defensible objective for business corporations? Wouldn't society be better off by focusing on the needs of society and giving the money shareholders receive to poor consumers?

3. How does the concept of ESV compare with traditional goals such as market share, profitability, and sales?

4. "Analysis of consumer trends is obviously important for firms marketing consumer products but of limited value to industrial marketers." Evaluate this statement.

5. Will there be more or fewer births in the future in the United States? What variables should be considered in answering this question?

6. How should the answer to Question 5 affect government planning? How should it affect companies such as General Electric or Johnson & Johnson?

7. Assume a marketer of major appliances is interested in the effects of the Baby Boomers on demand for the company's products. What are your conclusions and what, if any, research should be conducted to answer the question more fully?

8. "Maturity markets are growing in number very rapidly but they are of little interest to marketers because they have little money compared to younger markets." Analyze this statement.

9. What are the major similarities and the major differences in the population structures of the United States and Canada? Why should consumer analysts in both countries have more interest since 1988 in understanding consumer markets in the other country?

10. "Cities are the key to marketing plans." How would you evaluate this statement?

11. Find and interview a firm that specializes in the analysis of consumer trend or demographic data. How are such analyses used by marketing organizations?

MARKET SEGMENTATION

WOMEN AND THE AUTO MARKET: UNLOCKING THE MYSTERY

Now that automotive marketers have a picture of the female consumer in mind, they're finding she has an enigmatic smile. What does she want? Economy or performance cars? Targeted, soft-sell promotions or low-cost financing? Ads addressed directly at her or a nonsegmented approach? The eventual winners among marketers might be those who gain women buyers' loyalty.

In addition to separate ad campaigns, car marketers are targeting women through media, special training and special promotions. These strategies are part of a pursuit of women buyers that has been accelerating every year since 1975, when women bought 29% of all vehicles.

A 249-page Conde Nast Publications' survey concludes that women play a role in 87.5% of all automotive purchases. The survey, by Significance Inc. of Ridgewood, N.J., reports that women buyers typically are employed fulltime, younger and more likely to be single than males who buy.

The Conde Nast report suggests that although women may buy the same cars as men do, their reasons frequently are different. They buy small cars for economy of maintenance and mileage, as well as purchase price. Because many women lack repair skills, they are concerned about dependability.

Women buy more imports than males largely because they perceive them as dependable and worry-free. And because they rely heavily on friends' advice, their influence extends beyond their own purchases. But one of the main tenets of the Conde Nast study is that female buyers cannot be viewed as a homogeneous group. The study, which divides women buyers into six categories, says auto marketers must employ segmentation in reaching these consumers.

Conde Nast says the largest group, the "value seekers," accounts for one of every five female car buyers. The other five groupings, in order of size, are the driving enthusiasts, domestic budget-minded comfort seekers, affluent luxury seekers and the voluntary minimalists.

The female automobile buyer is different from her male counterparts. There are six distinct segments within this market according to the Conde Nast study. The challenge to the manufacturers is to develop tactics capitalizing on these differences.

We have referred to market segmentation in many chapters. Market segmentation refers to a strategy in which separate products or marketing mixes are prepared for components (i.e., segments) of the market that differ in distinct and meaningful ways. The goal is to develop criteria that effectively identify the segments, offering the highest potential of response to marketing efforts.

Development of these criteria (or bases) is one of the most important roles for consumer research. Once segments are identified, the task then becomes one of designing marketing strategies to capitalize upon the market potential within each segment.

Our intent in this chapter is to elaborate further on the concept of segmentation and its strategic importance. Then our primary attention focuses on the many bases that can be used for segmentation and some of the ways in which marketers have found them to be of strategic significance.

THE CONCEPT OF SEGMENTATION

In a sense, each of us is a distinct market segment, because no two people are exactly alike in their motivations, needs, decision processes, and buying behavior. Such services as tailoring, beauty care, and landscaping take advantage of these differences by providing individualized attention. Obviously, this is not possible in larger-scale marketing. The objective there is to identify groups within the broader market that are sufficiently similar in characteristics and responses to warrant separate treatment.

CRITERIA OF USABLE SEGMENTS

For a segment to warrant special consideration in marketing strategy, four basic criteria must be met.

REACHABILITY   Do you recall our discussion in Chapter 5 of the important role played by influentials (or opinion leaders) whose endorsement can make the difference between marketing success and failure? Clearly, a case can be made for treating influentials as a prime market segment, but there is one major difficulty. Usually they cannot be isolated as a distinct segment and reached efficiently and economically through advertising media. The reason is that they most often are scattered throughout other market segments.

The goal of segmented strategy ideally is to fire a rifle shot, not a shotgun blast, at the market. If there is no good way to bring the target into focus and reach it economically, the benefits may not justify the effort.

IDENTIFICATION OF CAUSAL DIFFERENCES   When undertaking market segmentation it is important to distinguish between causal and descriptive **differences.** In other words, some consumer differences represent motivating influences or other factors that define and shape behavior. They would be considered causal, whereas others are merely descriptive. Unless causal differences are isolated, effective segmentation is impossible.

Referring back to our opening example, it is interesting to see the diversity within the broad category of female automobile purchasers. The importance of the Conde Nast study lies in the fact that these consumer differences are causal.[1] In other words, the basic designating variables represent factors that underlie and shape behavior and hence cannot be disregarded in strategy deliberations.

Let's take the driving enthusiasts as an example. These women love driving and prefer American-made performance cars. The underlying reasons for their preferences can be found in a lifestyle energized by interests in gambling, sports, and fast-paced activity. These are causal factors that lead them to favor the so-called "muscle cars." It is quite justifiable to consider marketing strategies designed to attract such women to high-performance cars.

The fact that driving enthusiasts are in their thirties, however, is probably not a causal consideration. The value seekers are in the same age bracket but are motivated differently. Hence, age is a helpful descriptor and not an underlying motivator in and of itself.

It should be noted, however, that descriptive factors find considerable use once the causal differences have been identified. The greatest value lies in expanding our understanding of the target consumer. If we know, for example, that she is under 35, living primarily in urban areas, this information

---

[1] Julie Candler, "Unlocking Mystery Surrounding Consumer Category," *Advertising Age* (September 15, 1986), S-3, S-4.

defines what can be done in advertising strategy. It obviously would be inappropriate to feature a women in her middle fifties enjoying her grandchildren.

Descriptive characteristics help in yet another important way. Research information is available on the audience characteristics of nearly all advertising media. The objective is to match target audience characteristics against media characteristics so that media choices can be made that minimize waste coverage.

ECONOMIC POTENTIAL   A leading manufacturer of paper products designed a crayon that was demonstrably different in both its concept and characteristics. Test marketing uncovered a segment which preferred its benefits over the more familiar competitive alternatives. But this segment totalled only 2 percent of a $30-million market and offered too little revenue payout to justify the effort. Hence, it did not meet the most basic of all criteria: *the revenue projection must offer a high potential of justifying the investment.*

POSSESSION OF REQUIRED MARKETING RESOURCES   A cable TV network designed and tested a new programming concept aimed at the nonchurch-going audience segment. The central theme was to demonstrate dramatically how lives can be changed by faith and answer to prayer. Even though all market tests, including on-air response, were positive, the program never went beyond the test stage. It soon became apparent that this program ideally should be a weekly series, but the costs of both production and air time were excessive.

The situation becomes even more critical when staff know-how and experience are lacking, even though the market opportunity is positive. As Peters and Waterman put it, an organization must "stick to its knitting" and not branch out beyond its basic mission and staff capabilities.[2]

THE MARKET TARGET DECISION

Once the market has been segmented properly in terms of the four criteria, the firm has three options:[3] (1) **concentrated marketing;** (2) **differentiated marketing;** and (3) **undifferentiated marketing.**

CONCENTRATED MARKETING   In concentrated marketing, the primary focus is on one segment. For years, Plough Inc. advertised its Coppertone line of tanning products by picturing a small dog pulling at the bathing briefs of a young girl, thereby revealing her tanning line. Such a message no longer appeals to a health-oriented public. Now Plough has dropped the term *tanning* in favor of *suncare* and has targeted the "tennis set." As of 1988, it is the "Official Suncare Product" of the Association of Tennis Professionals (ATP).[4]

---

[2] Tom Peters and Robert F. Waterman, Jr., *In Search of Excellence* (New York: Random House, 1982).

[3] Philip Kotler, *Principles of Marketing* (Englewood Cliffs, New Jersey: Prentice-Hall, 1980), 294.

[4] "Coppertone 'Suncare' Strategy Targets Tennis Set," *Marketing News* (April 25, 1988), 1.

The obvious danger of concentrated marketing is that a niche can evaporate sometimes with amazing rapidity, and the company is, in effect, eliminated as a competitor. Some diversification is always a good option, especially if there is continuing competitive turbulence.

DIFFERENTIATED MARKETING   An alternative approach is to concentrate on two or more segments, offering a differing marketing mix for each. There is a distinct trend toward multiple product offerings targeted at different segments. Most refrigerator manufacturers, for example, have added small units for use in offices, dormitory rooms, or other places where space is limited. These are in sharp contrast to large, split-door refrigerator/freezers designed for an entirely different segment.

There is no question that differentiated marketing offers the potential benefit of enhanced market position, but it is not without its disadvantages. One of the greatest dangers lies in loss of the core market unless precautions are taken.

The Chevrolet Division of General Motors is a case in point. At least two generations of North Americans were raised to identify the Chevrolet as one of three cars (Chevrolet, Ford, and Plymouth) made to provide safe, dependable, and affordable transportation for the "average family." The Chevy was quite different from other General Motors brands and had a clear identity.

The Chevrolet line was greatly expanded in the early 1980s, with models offered at nearly all price ranges. In so doing Chevrolet lost its traditional mass-market and low-price appeal and saw its core market dwindle because of inroads from the imports.[5] There is always the danger of blurring the established image in core markets unless precautions are taken. No product can be all things to all people.

UNDIFFERENTIATED MARKETING   Continuing with our earlier example of the female automobile purchaser, several manufacturers have concluded that the best approach is to include women in ads without creating a separate marketing strategy for them. This tactic worked well for Toyota, Nissan, Mazda, and Honda; and the net effect of their efforts has been to gain higher import penetration among women than among men.[6]

The problem with undifferentiated marketing, however, is that it is often exceedingly difficult to maintain market position if the needs of buyers are varied. Firms using this strategy become highly vulnerable to competitive inroads. The General Motors Corporation, for example, tried to broaden the appeal of the Cadillac Eldorado and Seville to attract young import-oriented buyers while, at the same time, retaining the loyal market core. In reality, they succeeded only in alienating core customers without attracting

---

[5] Robert Simison, "Chevy, GM's Leader, Sustains Worst Slump in U.S. Auto Industry," *The Wall Street Journal* (January 4, 1982), 1 and 4.
[6] Candler, "Unlocking Mystery."

many import buyers, and sales were less than half of projections.[7] Only rarely does this strategy work when there is rigorous competition.

UNDERTAKING SEGMENTATION ANALYSIS

There are two ways to proceed in segmentation analysis — the **a priori** or **post-hoc** approach.[8] Both strategies are very different in concept and procedure.

THE A PRIORI APPROACH

Often there is good reason to define the segmentation base in advance. We might be reasonably certain, for example, that the most frequent purchasers differ from occasional users. When this is the case, we establish purchase frequency as our basis for dividing the market and do research to determine ways in which frequent users differ from others in terms of demographic and psychographic characteristics, preferred product attributes, and so on.

Here is an example of what we mean. Table 22.1 provides a summary of segmentation research undertaken by the manufacturer of a special-purpose food condiment. Extent of usage was chosen a priori to be the segmentation base and serve as the dependent variable in the analysis which was to follow.

A nationwide survey was undertaken to differentiate between heavy users and occasional users. Each person interviewed responded to a series of questions on demographic and psychographic characteristics, usage and prefer-

TABLE 22.1 AN A PRIORI SEGMENTATION ANALYSIS FOR A FOOD CONDIMENT		Occasional Users (20%)	Heavy Users (41%)
	Demographics	35–54; large families; middle income; suburbs and farms; southern	20–45; well educated; small families; children under 5; southeast, urban, and suburban
	Usage	Mainly on holidays	At least weekly, year around
	Desired attributes	Interest in creative cookery; not interested in taking risks	Exotic and exciting taste, experimental cookery preferred
	Attitudes toward product	Favorable, but use only with one food category	Favorable; product is exciting and seen as asset in creative cooking
	Media exposure	Women's magazines, daytime TV	Shelter group magazines, FM radio
	Psychographics	Desire for self-expression constrained by maintenance of tradition; home-oriented	Contemporary; wants to express individuality; dislikes housework; not home-oriented
	Social	Desire to please family	Less desire to please family

[7] Russell Mitchell, "GM's New Luxury Cars: Why They're Not Selling," *Business Week* (January 19, 1987), 94ff.

[8] This section closely follows Yoram Wind, "Issues and Advances in Segmentation Research," *Journal of Marketing Research* 19 (August 1978), 321–322.

ences, and media exposure. Heavy users were separated from light users by cross-classification analysis, and the resulting differences appear in Table 22.1.

It is clear from the summary data that two distinctly different segments exist. If the goal is to increase frequency of use among the first segment, it will be necessary to position the product in a traditional home setting, showing how it will please the family if used creatively.

Such a strategy, however, could alienate the heavy user who more closely fits the stereotype of the "liberated woman." Fortunately, each segment can be reached efficiently through different media without much audience overlap. This allows maximum opportunity for differentiated marketing.

THE POST-HOC APPROACH

In post-hoc analysis, the base for segmentation is not decided in advance but, rather, is an outcome of the analysis itself. The first step is to cluster people into homogeneous segments on the basis of similarities in responses, as was done in the Conde Nast study of women automobile buyers. There is a family of multivariate statistical techniques that can be used for this purpose.[9] Once segments are isolated (e.g., the voluntary minimalist and

TABLE 22.2 **EIGHT MARKET** **SEGMENTS** **DEFINED BY POST** **HOC ANALYSIS**	1. *Traditionals.* Yield control, act first, and make fact-based decisions. Down-to-earth, practical, and conventional. Older, lower education and income, married, often retired. 2. *New Middle Americans.* Take control, act first, make fact-based decisions. Very sociable, achievement oriented, concerned with living standards, and are moderate risk takers. Somewhat younger, well educated, high family incomes, fewer children. 3. *Home and Community-Centered.* Yield control, think first, and are fact-based. Very conventional, prim, and proper. Exercise self-control, tend to go by acceptable rules of society, and are not gregarious. Somewhat older, better educated, higher incomes. 4. *Rising Stars.* Take control, think first, fact-based, intellectually curious but not socially gregarious. Has highest income and education and highest percentages of professionals, entrepreneurs, males, and singles. Oriented to cultural activities. 5. *Good Ol' Girls and Boys.* Yield control, act first, and are feeling-based. Practical, down-to-earth, no nonsense, sociable, yet cynical. Lower education and income. Like soap operas, game shows, and country and western music. 6. *Young Socials.* Take control, act first, and make decisions based on feelings. Outgoing, warm, and intuitive. Low self-control—if it feels good do it. Tend to be younger and less educated and have higher family incomes, and more females. 7. *Moralists.* Yield control, think first, and are feeling-based. Proper, detached, yet concerned. Older, lower education and income, factory workers, and homemakers. Attend church and are exposed to religious media. 8. *Aging Hippies.* Take control, think first, and are feeling-based. Sensitive, fanciful, unrealistic, and imaginative. Younger and better educated. Unconventional living arrangements.

Source: "Ad Agency Develops Eight New Market Segments," *Marketing News* (August 26, 1987), 12. Used by special permission from the American Marketing Association.

---

[9] See Girish Punj and David W. Stewart, "Cluster Analysis in Marketing Research: Review and Suggestions for Application," *Journal of Marketing Research* 20 (May 1983), 134–148.

others), the size, demographic and psychographic profile, and buying behavior are determined for each.

Eight market segments were identified by Valentine-Radford Advertising from survey responses focusing on dimensions of the consumer decision-making process. Referred to as **CUBE (Comprehensive Understanding of Buyer Environments),** segments were built post hoc from this information:

1. How people get control of their circumstances — takes control, yields control, creates own rules, accepts existing rules.
2. Method of action — acts first or thinks first.
3. Judgment of information — fact-based or feeling-based.[10]

Eight primary segments have been isolated (see Table 22.2). Each then is correlated with brand use, desired benefits, and other information to provide clues on the best market target for specific products and services.

BASES FOR SEGMENTATION

A variety of factors (or bases) can be used to segment a market, and these fall into the following categories; (1) geographic; (2) demographic; (3) psychographic; (4) behavioristic; and (5) usage situation.

GEOGRAPHIC

For most of its history, Campbell Soup Company has epitomized undifferentiated marketing with its standardized red-and-white cans sold nearly everywhere. Now it is tailoring its marketing mix to fit different regions of the country and even individual neighborhoods within a city.[11] Its nacho cheese soup is spicier in Texas and California, for example.

From Chapter 21 you learn the impact of changing geographic differences in terms of region, size of city or metropolitan area, density (urban, suburban, rural), and climate. All of these geographic factors have found their use in segmentation for many decades.

A more recent addition, however, is **geodemography.** As you may recall from earlier chapters, demographic census lifestyle profiles can be generated for households in clusters as small as the local neighborhood. Using geodemography, customer penetration can be mapped within these clusters, providing a good clue both to the characteristics of present customers and the extent of penetration in such segments as "educated, affluent executives and professionals in elite metro suburbs."

This type of geodemographic information was used by Haagen-Dazs Shoppe Company, an upscale ice cream marketer, to evaluate penetration

---

[10] "Ad Agency Develops Eight New Market Segments," *Marketing News* (August 28, 1987), 12.
[11] "Marketing's New Look," *Business Week* (January 26, 1987), 64ff.

in each of 40 possible clusters. It then proved possible to develop localized programs designed to increase both distribution and penetration.[12]

DEMOGRAPHIC

Market potential for any product is equivalent to the number of people who want or need it and also have the necessary resources to buy it. Hence, it is necessary to evaluate the demographic characteristics of both present and potential buyers.

Demographic information also can serve as a **proxy variable** for motivation, interests, and preferences. A proxy variable "stands in" or substitutes for something else. If you uncover a market segment described as "upper-middle-class teenagers," you already know a great deal about what makes such people "tick," from observation and published research.

The most widely used demographic factors are age, sex, family size, family life cycle, income, occupation, education, religion, race, nationality, and social class. Often two or more factors are used in tandem. A good example is the discovery of and capitalization upon strong interest in fragrances and grooming aids by males between the ages of 18 and 24.[13]

You have studied the implications of these variables for marketing strategy in many chapters in this book. Therefore, only several illustrative examples are given here.

AGE   Age is one of the variables most often used in segmentation for two reasons. First, age is one of the most helpful proxy variables for determination of motivation and interest because of extensive secondary research on this subject. Another reason age segmentation is so popular is that it is quite feasible to reach various age groups precisely and economically with mass media targeted specifically to them.

Here are two examples of age segmentation. At one time pickup trucks were rarely owned except by farmers, construction workers, and others who require utility vehicles for their livelihood. Today the scene is quite different. About half of sales of compact trucks are among persons under 35, 90 percent of whom are male.[14] There is particular growth among college students. According to one marketing authority:

> College students are by nature more active and more out-doorsy. Trucks fit the self-image of being a bit of a rebel. Add to that the price value of pickups, and you can see why they're a good growth category.[15]

---

[12] Dwight J. Shelton, "Birds of a Geodemographic Feather Flock Together," *Marketing News* (August 28, 1987), 13.

[13] "No Surprise: Modern Men Care About How They Look," *Marketing News* (September 11, 1987), 18.

[14] Raymond Serafin, "Pickups Deliver a Ton of First-Time Buyers," *Advertising Age* (February 2, 1987), S-14.

[15] A comment by Jim Omastiak, Vice President and Publisher of Campus Voice Network, as quoted in Serafin, "Pickups Deliver."

Also, the ready-to-eat cereal industry also has moved far beyond its traditional age niche and is targeting young adults. The Kellogg Company recognized that many in this age group place high priority on nutrition and physical fitness. It spent $30 million to introduce Pro Grain, a presweetened toasted oat cereal positioned as offering "high-performance nutrition for a high-performance body."[16] It is advertised as "Ironman Food," using the name of the annual championship triathlon held in Hawaii.

SOCIAL CLASS   You learned in Chapter 4 that social classes are very present in supposedly classless societies in the western world. At one time art collecting was largely a phenomenon confined to the upper class, but now wealthy businessmen a step down the social scale are becoming avid collectors. According to one art gallery proprietor, "Ownership separates people from the masses, and is a visible sign of upward mobility and good times."[17]

FAMILY LIFE CYCLE   As you learned in Chapter 6, families change over time, passing through a series of stages. This process is referred to as the family life cycle. Buying behavior often varies sharply from one stage to the next.

The Consumer Market Matrix designed by Management Horizons is a helpful analytical tool. The heavy buyers of Kentucky Fried Chicken were found to fall into this life cycle category: younger parents (head under age 45) with children at home, second-highest income quartile. It is highly likely that time is at a premium for these customers. No doubt most are willing to part with the extra money required to buy prepared food in return for gains in leisure time.

WORKING WOMEN   Often there is much to be gained by investigating the potential in segments beyond the core market. Jewelers have recently discovered that working women are a responsive target for expensive jewelry traditionally marketed to mid-life families and households (head aged 45 to 65) in the "Up Market" income quartile. See *Consumer in Focus 22.1.*

PSYCHOGRAPHIC

Psychographics is another term for lifestyle — those patterns by which people live and spend time and money. Personality also is a part of lifestyle, but, as we demonstrated in Chapter 12, it rarely has proved to be of much use in and of itself in segmentation analysis. Much greater use is made of AIO (Activities, Interests, and Opinion) profiles. In fact, the terms *AIO* and *psychographics* are often used synonymously.

---

[16] Julie Franz, "Cereals Growing Up," *Advertising Age* (February 9, 1987), 22.
[17] Joe Agnew, "National Art Gallery Chain Targets 'Upscale Masses,'" *Marketing News* (June 19, 1987), 8.

CONSUMER IN FOCUS

22.1   JEWELERS WOO THE WORKING WOMAN

Spin through the revolving door at Tiffany & Co. these days and you may be surprised by who's standing at the counter, handing over a credit card to buy that $1,500 brooch or $3,900 watch. A woman. The card does not belong to her husband or boyfriend, and she isn't buying the costly bauble as a gift. She's getting it for herself, and with her own money.

A new breed of working woman sees fine jewelry — gold, silver, and precious stones — as a necessary part of her office wardrobe and a just reward for achievement. Typically in her 30s or 40s, she holds down a management job or owns a business, earns over $50,000 a year, and, married or not, spends her own money. Market researchers estimate there are 560,000 of these top-drawer female consumers.

"Women are not asking for pieces encrusted with stones," reports Frank Arcaro,

manager of Tiffany's Boston store. "The jewelry they want is not frilly." It's not cheap either, but most of it sells for less than the five figures that trinkets from high-end jewelers usually command. Competitors who have successfully wooed working women find that they become regular buyers, accounting for 30% to 40% of a store's business.

But many women are intimidated by the traditional jewelry salon, with its hushed, exclusive ambiance and its snooty salespeople. They feel more comfortable at department store counters, where they can try on whatever catches the eye without feeling bulldozed into buying it.

Source: Susan Caminiti, "Jewelers Woo the Working Woman," *Fortune* (June 8, 1987), 71–72. © 1987 Time Inc. All rights reserved.

Here are the AIO responses given by males aged 18 to 24 who both drink and drive:

It seems like no matter what my friends and I do on a weekend, we almost always end up at a bar getting smashed.

A party wouldn't be a party without some liquor.

I've been drunk at least five times this month.

Being drunk is fun.

The chances of an accident or losing a driver's license from drinking and driving are low.

Drinking helps me to have fun and do better with girls.

A few drinks will have no noticeable effect on my coordination and self-control.[18]

---

[18] John L. Lastovicka, John P. Murry, Jr., Erich A. Joachimsthaler, Gaurav Bhalla, and Jim Scheurich, "A Lifestyle Typology to Model Young Male Drinking and Driving," *Journal of Consumer Research* 14 (September 1987), 257–263. Used by special permission of the American Marketing Association.

The heavy drinkers in this study were designated as the *Good Timers* based on this profile and represented 23 percent of the total.[19] They are not dissatisfied or troubled but are motivated by partying and sensation seeking. Hence, fear appeals and threat of injury are not likely to be a deterrent to drinking and driving. A campaign was designed instead to demonstrate that partying can be more fun without excessive alcohol consumption and that a "real man's" control of himself is threatened by too much alcohol.

There also is growing use of post-hoc segmentation with lifestyle data. The objective is to isolate lifestyle bases and segments through research and then discover ways to position new products or better position existing products.[20]

One of the most widely cited sources of data for lifestyle segmentation, VALS (SRI International's Values and Lifestyles) is discussed in Chapter 12. One of the most famous marketing examples mentioned there is the change in advertising strategy for Merrill Lynch when it was discovered that the prime customer is an upwardly mobile and self-motivated achiever. Formerly the "Bullish on America" theme depicted a thundering herd of cattle. This was shifted to the lone bull designed as a "breed apart" seeking the aid of Merrill Lynch in the canyons of Wall Street.

BEHAVIORISTIC

Some of the most productive forms of segmentation can be classified under the generic heading of **behavioristic variables.** These include (1) extent of use and loyalty; (2) benefit; and (3) usage situation.

EXTENT OF USE AND LOYALTY

Segmentation on the basis of usage usually requires extensive survey research covering a broad cross section of both present and hopefully potential users. Focus is on usage of both product and brand.

Nonusers of Product Category.   Young professional people between the ages of 21 and 40 have turned away from traditional distilled spirits to wine and lighter mixed drinks. The manufacturers of Chivas Regal scotch are understandably concerned and are committed to reversing this downturn.

Why is this taking place? Is it lack of awareness of Chivas Regal and other leading scotch whiskeys? If so, the solution probably lies in beefed-up promotion. Or is it because the product has not been correctly positioned for the young professional? This too can be corrected. A third possibility is conflict between lifestyle and product benefits. A person with alcoholic addicts in his or her family understandably may choose to avoid all forms of alcohol, regardless of marketing efforts.

---

[19] Lastovicka et al., "A Lifestyle Typology."
[20] For an example see "Projective Profiling Helps Reveal Buying Habits of 'Power Segments,'" *Marketing News* (August 26, 1987), 10.

Chivas Regal is tackling this problem by positioning the brand as a symbol of success for the upwardly mobile young professional.[21] Status symbols are important to those in this segment, and Chivas Regal may be able to position itself on this dimension. Ultimately, however, the nature and direction of reference group influence determining "correct and acceptable behavior" may hold the key to success.

Users of Product but Not Brand.   Here the objective is to make inroads into competitors' market segments. Some may be vulnerable because of inability to keep up with changes in demand and stay current with consumer preferences. Others may have alienated buyers with shoddy quality or poor customer service. The best strategy usually is to appeal to the **waverers** whose commitment is diminishing, rather than to attack entrenched competitors head-on.

The American Motors Corporation has experienced steady erosion in its sale of compact cars and has been bathed in red ink as a result. Therefore, it moved up to the compact segment with its new Medalion line in 1987 and backed this launch with a $10-million advertising investment.[22] Did the Medalion have much chance of drawing sales away from such popular competitors as the Ford Escort or Honda Civic? If a competitor is to succeed with this strategy, it must offer both high credibility and significant product improvement on attributes that are important to the consumer. Disappointing sales results underscored that a head-on attack was attempted without these advantages. Shortly thereafter, the American Motors brand disappeared from the North American market.

Regardless of competitive considerations, many recommend targeting the heavy users of the product, often referred to as the **heavy half.** For example, about 20 percent of the beer market consumes around 90 percent of the total. Because of strong propensity to consume, appealing to the heavy half may be the most practical and cost-effective way of establishing a foothold. This is especially likely if there is low involvement and little brand loyalty. When involvement and brand loyalty are high, however, the probability of inroads is much less.

Users of Product and Brand.   Now our objective is to increase brand loyalty. It is here where research making use of multiattribute models (discussed in Chapter 11) is particularly helpful. The most useful data are those that document consumer evaluation of various brands along the most important desired attributes. From such an analysis it is possible to detect early warnings of a decline in company brand ratings while there is still time to take remedial action.

---

[21] "Youthful Spirits," *Frequent Flier* (November 1987), 12.

[22] Raymond Serafin, "Renault Repositioning," *Advertising Age* (February 2, 1987), 60.

22.2 THE UPGRADING OF KITTY LITTER

Edward Lowe Industries is beating Clorox Co. to the punch in the $400 million cat-box filler market by introducing nationally an upgraded version of its Kitty Litter containing germ-inhibiting ingredients.

South Bend, Ind.-based Lowe is backing the rollout of Kitty Litter with Healthguard with an $8 million-to-$10 million TV and print campaign created by Campbell-Mithun, Chicago.

Ads, playing up the product's technological edge, describe Kitty Litter with Healthguard as the "Ultimate Odor Fighter."

Stan Beals, Lowe VP-advertising, described Kitty Litter with Healthguard as an innovation. Other odor-controlling cat-box products by Lowe and other marketers include perfumes to mask the smell, Mr. Beals said. Kitty Litter with Healthguard contains ingredients that inhibit the growth of germs that cause odor.

Lowe also claims the product is 99% dust-free, another point it believes separates it from the competition.

At the same time, Oakland, Calif.-based Clorox Co. is testing a product with similar odor-controlling properties (AA, Sept. 21).

The company is promoting, via print and TV, Control cat-box litter with a germ-inhibiting ingredient it calls Sanatac. The product is available in Maine, Massachusetts, New Hampshire and Vermont.

"Only cats have this kind of control," the advertising says. Young & Rubicam, San Francisco, handles Control.

A Clorox spokesman declined to comment on industry speculation it may accelerate the Control test or quickly take the brand national in light of the Lowe rollout.

With its Kitty Litter and Tidy Cat III brands, Lowe still dominates the business with an estimated 35% combined share, but Clorox is coming on strong.

Clorox's Fresh Step, a clay-base product featuring a microencapsulated fragrance that's released whenever a cat steps on or scratches the litter, has a 15% market share nationally. It was rolled out nationally three years ago.

In contrast, Litter Green, an alfalfa-base cat litter marketed by Clorox, has been steadily losing share since Fresh Step's introduction. The brand receives little advertising, and industry sources speculate Clorox eventually may dump it, but Clorox denies that.

Source: Jennifer Pendleton, "Lowe Rolls Upgraded Kitty Litter." Reprinted with permission from *Advertising Age* (October 5, 1987), 49. Copyright Crain Communications, Inc. All rights reserved.

BENEFIT SEGMENTATION   The strategy which capitalizes upon unmet consumer needs is referred to as **benefit segmentation.** At times this calls for a completely new product design, but in other situations such minor changes as package modification may prove sufficient.

In 1987 General Foods attempted to shore up the market share of its Sanka brand decaffeinated coffee by switching to a natural decaffeinating process as opposed to use of chemicals. Ad copy showed a woman speaking directly to a growing controversy over the decaffeinating process:

They say decaffeinated coffee is good for you. Then they turn around and get you wondering about the way it is decaffeinated. Well, the people who make Sanka want you to know that you can enjoy cup after cup without a drop of worry.[23]

The success of this attempt all depends upon the extent to which the natural decaffeination is perceived as a consumer benefit.

Benefit segmentation is a widely used competitive weapon. *Consumer in Focus 22.2* describes a real "David and Goliath" battle between Edward Lowe Industries and Procter & Gamble. The outcome depends on which company is perceived as the winner on odor and dust control in the cat-box filler market.

USAGE SITUATION

Usage situation, first discussed in Chapter 7, is useful for purposes of segmentation when it is combined with information on consumer characteristics or expected product benefits.[24] As Dickson has noted, the "product not targeted for particular people in particular usage situations is probably the exception rather than the rule."[25]

USES OF SEGMENTATION IN MARKETING STRATEGY

Segmentation analysis plays an essential role in all phases of the marketing mix. Here is an overview of the major implications.

One of the most common uses of segmentation is in **product positioning,** which refers to the ways in which consumers identify a product with a defined set of attributes such as power, sportiness, caffeine, or color. Products can be positioned or repositioned to capitalize upon untapped benefits, new uses or applications, or competitive weaknesses.

Segmentation also shapes advertising and promotion as we have noted earlier. The basic appeal must be designed to show how the company offering delivers expected benefits. The segment profile also provides a picture of the consumer in terms of demographic characteristics and lifestyle. Without such information it is difficult to speak meaningfully to a target segment. Finally, the demographic profile is used to obtain the closest possible match between market and media audience characteristics.

Distribution strategy takes account of segmentation in many ways. Lifestyle affects how and where the consumer prefers to buy. Busy working women may prefer in-home purchase and respond to direct marketing. Retailing outlets, in turn, are designed to appeal to increasingly narrow segments, as is demonstrated by the expansion of The Limited to encompass lower price

---

[23] Patricia Winters, "Sanka Going Natural; Decaf War Perks Up," *Advertising Age* (January 12, 1987), 1ff.

[24] Peter F. Dickson, "Person-Situation: Segmentation's Missing Link," *Journal of Marketing* 46 (Fall 1982).

[25] Dickson, "Person-Situation," 57.

offerings (The Gap) and clothing designed for a more downscale, older segment (Lerner Stores).

Finally, price policy is similarly affected. Income affects ability to pay. Lifestyle has an impact in that some consumers are more value- and low-price-conscious than others. At other times, lower price adversely affects perceptions of quality and is to be avoided.

SUMMARY

Market segmentation is a procedure whereby a market is divided into meaningful groups or subsets which merit separate marketing approaches. There are a number of bases or criteria used for this purpose, many of which are discussed in preceding chapters, including demographic and psychographic characteristics, geographic location, situation, and preferred benefits.

Marketers face three strategic options. One is undifferentiated marketing, in which the same mix is offered to everyone regardless of their differences. This is far less successful in today's competitive environment than it was in earlier years.

Another strategy is differentiated marketing, where two or more segments are targeted using different marketing mixes for each. The last option, concentrated marketing, focuses on one segment out of many possibilities.

In most situations some form of segmentation is a necessity rather than an option. Consumer research is essential, and the payouts can be substantial.

REVIEW AND DISCUSSION QUESTIONS

1. Ideally, each person is a market segment. Since individualized marketing can be done only on a limited basis, what is the objective of market segmentation?

2. A regional soft drink manufacturer has marketed under one brand name since 1904 and still has the original product line consisting of root beer and orange soda. The CEO is being pressed by his board chairman to consider market segmentation. You are asked to comment on this request. How would you define market segmentation? Under what conditions would you recommend it for this manufacturer?

3. You are the brand manager for a manufacturer of music systems. You have just received a research study which suggests that those who spend the most on new stereo products are more venturesome than other people. If this proves to be true, how could you capitalize on this in marketing strategy?

4. What is a proxy variable? In what ways do you think age could be a proxy variable to explain clothing preferences?

5. Many are saying that psychographic segmentation is more helpful than demographic segmentation. Why do you think this might be the case?

6. How would you describe the market segments who would be interested in upscale, expensive imported cars? Fully automatic single-lens reflex cameras? Canned soups? Motor oil?

7. Distinguish between undifferentiated, differentiated, and concentrated marketing. Under which circumstances could each be used with effectiveness?

8. In what ways does the a priori approach differ from the post-hoc approach to segmentation?

9. You have been asked by a major Protestant church denomination to discover why church attendance is declining. Some suspect that the market has become quite segmented. Would you agree? What segments do you think might exist?

10. You have now been asked to do segmentation research for this denomination. How would you tackle this request?

DIFFUSION OF INNOVATIONS

P WINNERS AND LOSERS IN PRODUCT INNOVATION

op Rocks, a carbonated candy that crackled and popped when eaten, was introduced by General Foods, stirring a short-lived sensation. The candy was so effervescent that rumors swelled that children who swallowed the granules too quickly would have a carbonated stomach. The new product apparently was nothing children could sink their teeth into and eventually lost its fizz.

The first automatic teller machine (ATM) was introduced by Bankone in an upscale suburb of Columbus, Ohio, in 1970. Today, almost every city in North America has adopted the ATM. In Columbus, bank customers stand in line to use the machine rather than deal with tellers.

Phillips, the Dutch electronics firm, developed the compact disc (CD), a technological innovation in audio and visual products that produced as much difference compared to current records and tapes as the difference between color and black-and-white television. In 1983 consumers purchased a mere 35,000 players. By 1986, sales reached nearly 2 million.

Proctor & Gamble introduced Certain, a new brand of lotion-laced toilet paper. Consumers did not buy it in sufficient quantities to exit test markets. Undaunted, the company later introduced Puffs Special Touch, a line extension of Puffs facial tissues, hoping that consumers would like lotion in their facial tissue better than in their toilet paper.

At the same time that Proctor & Gamble was introducing Puffs Special Touch, the company was also launching Liquid Tide, new "soft" cookies under the Duncan Hines brand, Ivory shampoo, and Home Fresh margarine made of a sucrose polyester that looks and tastes like fat but is not absorbed by the body (not only does it have no calories, but it actually cuts blood cholesterol levels by 20 percent or more).

In recent years new spackling compounds have been developed that contain air in tiny glass spheres. These compounds have many advantages over the previous wall patching products. They do not sag, which means holes can be patched with one application. The glass spheres provide dimensional stability so that the patch has very little cracking and shrinking. Most patches can be finished so that the wall can be painted without sanding.

Off-line, electronic banking was introduced on a widespread basis in 1989 by Checkfree. The system allows consumers to pay any bill from any banking institution on a home computer and upload the information instantly, potentially saving billions of pieces of paper as well as time and money for consumers. Will consumers with a computer and a modem also buy the software and monthly service to implement this fundamental change in the way they pay bills and transact financial services?

NEW PRODUCTS IN THE MARKETPLACE

As the opening scenario to this chapter indicates, consumers are bombarded with new products which they must decide to buy or reject. In Naples, New York, there is an art gallery exhibiting some of the 75,000 new products introduced in recent years.

Some new products succeed, bought by enough customers to achieve profitability. Most new products fail. This chapter discusses why some succeed and why some fail. The chapter also shows how to increase the number that succeed.

THE CRITICALITY OF NEW PRODUCT MANAGEMENT

Successful introduction of new products is a critical component of contemporary marketing programs. It is also one of the most misunderstood. About 5,000 new products appear each year on supermarket shelves, but as many as 80 percent are commercial duds. Both macromarketing and micromarketing reasons exist for concern about this situation.

MACROMARKETING   First, at the macromarketing level, much of the nation's technological and other resources are devoted to developing new products that are rejected. This causes two concerns: Valuable resources are wasted that might have been channeled toward more productive uses; and products that might have helped people do things more productively or attain higher levels in their quality of life fail to be used. Perhaps the rejected products should never have been developed because they were inferior to existing products and benefits. Perhaps the rejected products failed because of ineffective communication and diffusion processes. In either instance, society is harmed by the failure to understand why and how people adopt new products.

Second, at the moral or ethical level, the introduction of new products involves the attempt to change the behavior of human beings, often in rather fundamental ways. The changes usually involve more than simply switching from one brand to another, as is true in much of the material you have studied in this book. Sometimes the changes have profound effects on the people who buy the new product—as was true when some tampons produced adverse effects compared to the existing form of sanitary napkins. Sometimes the changes have profound effects on the people who do not adopt the product—as may be true among those who fail to adopt usage of microcomputers. More than any other area of marketing, perhaps, the ability to introduce new products effectively is the ability to change how society is organized.

The desire in most diffusion research is to persuade people to accept new products or practices. The "products" have been as diverse as birth control methods, sanitation techniques, computers, and hybrid seed corn. The motivation for research on these topics stems from the notion that people should change to what is good for them or society. With microcomputers, as an example, the technology has often been urged on consumers with little concern about the underlying value of the benefit or the information that consumers would derive from microcomputers.[1] People and organizations are agents for change in the behavior of other people. In a market economy, consumers are sovereign in their acceptance or rejection of products and practices, but there remain important moral and ethical questions about who should have the ability to be effective change agents.

MICROMARKETING   There is also major reason for concern about new products at the microeconomic level, which is the major focus of this chapter. New products are the lifeblood of most firms in the contemporary business environment. Firms must develop and gain acceptance of new products to survive and maintain adequate profitability.

A primary reason for new product development is slow growth or declining population in industrialized countries. Firms formerly could grow profits by selling the same products to an increasing number of customers. Now firms often grow profits by developing and selling additional new products to customers.

A second reason for new product development is the role market leadership plays in a firm's profitability. Research indicates that firms that are market

---

[1] Douglass K. Hawes, "The Role of Marketing in Facilitating the Diffusion of Microcomputers and The Information Society," *Journal of the Academy of Marketing Science* 15 (Summer 1987), 83–89.

leaders, as measured by market share, generally have the highest Return on Investment (ROI) and Enhanced Shareholder Value (ESV). The **PIMS (Profit Impact of Market Strategy)** research indicates that market leaders achieve average rates of return three times greater than firms with low market share.[2] The PIMS data also indicate that perceived product quality is highly associated with ROI and ESV. Successful new product development is an important element in achieving long-term competitive superiority and profitability.

A successful new product can also be the beginning of a whole new company. Edison's invention of electricity was the beginning of GE. Today new entrepreneurial activity is often based upon new products rather than on attempts to compete with marketers of existing products. Thus, the path to asset accumulation for individuals often leads through a single new product. Examples include computer products of Silicon Valley entrepreneurs, new packages such as Soft Soap, and new services such as the automatic debit service of Checkfree that allows people to pay bills without writing checks each month.

Large corporations usually require a portfolio of products, some of which are new but many of which are not so new. Such a portfolio often derives the most sales not from new products but from rapid growth from products that are recent introductions. While the BCG (Boston Consulting Group) matrix of "cash cows," "dogs," and other barnyard animals has been challenged as overly simplistic,[3] most corporations do maintain a variety of products at various stages of their life cycle and with varying rates of growth and return on investment.

Proctor & Gamble makes most of its sales and profits from detergents, coffee, peanut butter, and other products that have been in kitchen pantries for decades or longer. The focus is on brand strategies and product extensions for success. The company also devotes substantial resources to developing products that initially are miniscule but have the potential for attracting huge markets. Proctor & Gamble hoped that Pampers would become such a product and it did. It hoped Pringles would become such a product. It did not. By 1990, however, P & G was able to reposition Pringles to flavor "niches" using a successful segmentation strategy.

Existing products sometimes can be changed so they are perceived as new. Tom Peters, in lectures to business executives, makes the point that no marketing manager should accept the premise that he or she markets a "commodity." If you think such a goal is unrealistic, consider the case of Frank Perdue in *Consumer in Focus 23.1*. He changed consumer perceptions of "dead chickens" into a highly profitable, billion-dollar corporation. Even today, Perdue continues this progression with new packages, new methods of cooking, and new species of poultry.

---

[2] Robert D. Buzzell and Bradley T. Gale, *The PIMS Principles* (New York: Free Press, 1987).

[3] Buzzell and Gale, *The PIMS Principles*.

23.1 PERDUE: CHANGING A COMMODITY INTO A NEW PRODUCT

Before Frank Perdue took over the chicken business from his father it was the quintessential commodity business. Chickens had as strong a claim to commodity status as pork bellies or crude oil. The performance of each competitor was the same on each product and service attribute. This placed Perdue and his representative competitor at the 50th percentile on relative quality, neither ahead nor behind. With no differences in performance on product and service attributes, the customer bought basically on price.

After Frank Perdue took over the chicken business, he pulled ahead on almost every non-price attribute that counts in the purchase decision. His research showed that customers in his served market prefer their chickens plump and yellow. Careful breeding and the judicious use of feed additives enabled Frank to produce meatier, yellower chickens than competitors. His actions also produced a higher, more consistent meat-to-bone ratio.

To prevent wet pinfeathers from slipping past the torching process that's supposed to burn them off, he purchased a turbine engine to blow-dry his chickens just before they reach the torching station. This didn't get him to zero defects, but it did mean that fewer pinfeathers wound up in supermarkets or in family dining rooms.

Notice that his particular investment in capital equipment did not expand capacity and it did not take out labor costs. It just improved the perceived quality of Perdue's chickens! Most capital appropriation requests have difficulty quantifying the justification for expenditures to improve perceived quality.

To make sure that the customer perceived and remembered his quality improvements, Perdue utilized catchy slogans in audacious media advertising: "It takes a tough man to make a tender chicken"; "Buy Perdue chickens—you get an extra bite in every breast." (Would *you* have spent millions trying to differentiate chickens?) Perdue developed a favorable difference, he made sure that it was perceived, and as a result he gets a substantial premium for what certainly *had been* a commodity. As Perdue himself says, "Customers will go out of their way to buy a superior product, and you can charge them a toll for the trip." Is your product, with all its potential associated services, really harder to differentiate than a dead chicken?

Source: Robert D. Buzzell and Bradley T. Gale, *The PIMS Principles* (New York: Free Press, 1987), 119–120.

PRODUCT LIFE CYCLE

The product life cycle (PLC) is a key concept for understanding the criticality of new products. You probably studied the PLC similar to that shown in Figure 23.1 in a basic marketing course. This figure shows that just as products grow and mature, so do they decline and fail. As the process evolves, major changes are necessary in the marketing strategies and mix: price, product, place, and promotion. For the consumer as well as for marketing managers,

FIGURE 23.1   IMPACT OF THE PRODUCT LIFE CYCLE ON MARKETING

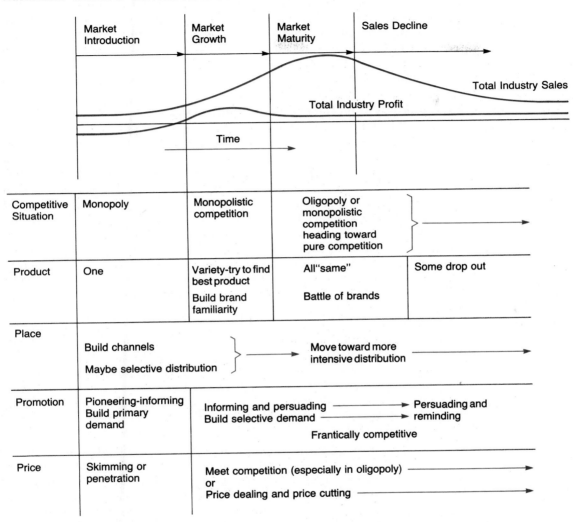

Source: Adapted by permission from Jerome McCarthy and William Perrault, *Basic Marketing: A Managerial Approach* (Homewood, Illinois: Richard D. Irwin, 1985).

the role of advertising may be different at varying stages of the life cycle.[4]

Profit margins vary greatly during the product life cycle, usually peaking during the latter stage of the growth phase and declining during subsequent

---

[4] Gerald J. Tellis and Claes Fornell, "The Relationship Between Advertising and Product Quality Over the Product Life Cycle: A Contingency Theory," *Journal of Marketing Research* 25 (February 1988), 64–71.

stages. Therefore, firms systematically introduce new products not only to maintain sales volume but also to command adequate margins and profits. Firms need a portfolio of products in various stages of the PLC to achieve the growth, profitability, and capital objectives of the firm. The problem increases because of what Olshavsky and others show to be an increasing rate of adoption of innovations, causing a rapidly shortened product life cycle.[5] Shortened PLCs, caused by rapidly changed technologies and improved mass communications, create the need for shorter amounts of time in management approval of movement between phases of product introduction.[6]

The diffusion of innovations and the acceptance (and rejection) of new products is one of the most researched topics in marketing. Inadequate market research is a major obstacle to the successful introduction of new products. This conclusion is shown in Figure 23.2, summarizing research by the consulting firm of Booz-Allen & Hamilton. That study also shows that major obstacles in introducing new products include lack of attention by management and delays in making decisions. Ideally, a firm and its managers would have plenty of time to perform new product research. Instead, managers must often rely on what is already known about how new products are accepted, based upon other products and theory. Fortunately, there is a great deal of both. This chapter describes both so that when you are making decisions about new products, you will have a thorough, immediate information base to help guide your decisions.

In addition to formal research, marketing managers need "grass roots" ways of understanding consumer reaction to new products. Campbell Soup Company has a constant need for new products in its many divisions, which include Le Menu and Swanson frozen foods, Prego spaghetti sauces, Pepperidge Farm baked products, Mrs. Paul's frozen foods, Vlasic pickles, and even Godiva chocolates. In addition to pursuing sophisticated marketing research, the president of Campbell insists that his managers do their own grocery shopping. The board of directors meets in the back room of a supermarket after roaming the store aisles and probing shoppers for comments on Campbell products. The Campbell chief executive officer spends Saturday mornings in the neighborhood supermarket getting to know consumers. The result in one recent year was 42 successful new products for Campbell.[7] You will find many useful principles in the following pages to guide you in understanding how new products become successful. The best understanding may occur, however, because of the time you spend in the marketplace, talking to customers and reflecting on their comments.

---

[5] Richard Olshavsky, "Time and the Rate of Adoption of Innovations," *Journal of Consumer Research* (March 1980), 425–428.

[6] Milton D. Rosenau, Jr., "Speeding Your New Product to Market," *Journal of Consumer Marketing* 5 (Spring 1988), 23–35.

[7] Christopher S. Eklund, "Campbell Soup's Recipe for Growth: Offering Something for Every Palate," *Business Week* (December 14, 1984), 66–67.

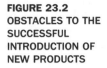

FIGURE 23.2
OBSTACLES TO THE
SUCCESSFUL
INTRODUCTION OF
NEW PRODUCTS

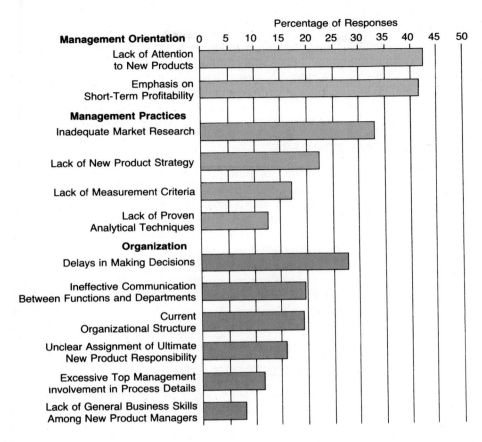

Source: *New Products Management for the 1980's* (New York: Booz-Allen & Hamilton, Inc., 1982), 5. Reprinted by permission.

The Growing Competitive Challenge.   Contemporary firms are being attacked competitively on every dimension and from every direction. The only way to survive this onslaught, Michael Porter has convincingly argued, is to create a "value chain" to serve the customer, which will serve to differentiate the successful firm from its competitors; which will provide competitive superiority on the critical attributes of importance to the customer.[8] A product that will "delight the customer" is the foundational variable of marketing strategy. The challenge is to understand which new products will do that.

Innovation is not limited to new products. Innovative ideas, innovative people, and innovative processes are characteristic of the business firms and

---

[8] Michael E. Porter, *Competitive Advantage* (New York: Free Press, 1985).

other organizations that are surviving and thriving. After careful research of over 115 innovations in major coporations, Kanter concluded that winners generate "idea power" that provides the competitive advantage, not only in new products but also in new ideas in every area: better packaging, more efficient invoicing techniques, new planning systems, and lower-cost manufacturing. The winners today are better users, adaptors, and incorporators of technology.[9]

THE DIFFUSION PROCESS

The criticality of new product adoption is clear, but, you might be asking, why should consumer decisions about new products be studied any differently from decisions about other products? Why not simply consider the elements of decision making and psychological and environmental variables that have been discussed in the text previously as they apply to new products rather than existing products?

The major distinction in traditional analyses of the diffusion of innovations is the emphasis on *communications within the social structure* rather than individual information processing. The **relational approach** analyzes communication networks and how social-structural variables affect diffusion flows in the system, in contrast to a **monodic approach,** which focuses upon the personal and social characteristics of individual consumers.

A MAJOR RESEARCH STREAM

A further reason for a separate chapter on new product diffusion is the great quantity of research on the topic and the diversity of disciplines from which the research is drawn. Over 3,000 studies and discussions of diffusion processes have been published in at least 12 identifiable disciplines. These include anthropology, sociology, rural sociology, education, marketing, psychology, and geography. The most important contribution to the study of diffusion of innovations was a book of the same name, written by Everett Rogers in 1962 and updated in 1983.[10] According to Rogers, **diffusion** is defined as the process by which an innovation (new idea) is communicated through certain channels over time among the members of a social system.

Consumer researchers and marketing analysts have been important contributors to the study of diffusion of innovations. An enumeration by Rogers of the research studies on diffusion indicates that marketing has conducted over 10 percent of all the studies in this field, surpassed only by the disciplines of rural sociology, communication, and education. The bulk of consumer

---

[9] Rosabeth Moss Kanter, "Highlights" from *The Change Masters: Innovation and Entrepreneurship in the American Corporation* (New York: Free Press), 1987.

[10] Everett M. Rogers, *Diffusion of Innovations,* 3rd ed. (New York: Free Press, 1983), 5.

behavior research, however, is on the adoption process of consumers rather than on the social structure and process variables.

The disciplines involved in diffusion studies include general sociology, anthropology, geography, and public health as well as rural sociology, communication and education. Marketing strategists should use care when applying diffusion research. Many of the studies were conducted in primitive societies where government or some other agency had the ability to contact every member of the community. In marketing programs, effective communication with all members of the community is much more limited.

Also, many of the products involved in sociological or anthropological studies have been high-involvement and more personal products. The consistency between disciplines is one of the basic reasons, however, for the impact diffusion research has achieved. In this chapter, the important conclusions are summarized that cut across the disciplines, and have applications for marketing.[11]

DIFFUSION VARIABLES

The variables that have emerged from over 3,000 studies on diffusion can be clustered to identify the critical determinants of the success of a new product. The main elements in the diffusion of innovations include:

1. the innovation (new product, service, idea, etc.)
2. the communication (through certain channels)
3. time (at which certain individuals decide to adopt the product relative to others)
4. the social system (interrelated people, groups, or other systems)

Each of these topics is a focus of discussion in the following pages.

The result of this process shows that some members of the social system are **adopters**—people who have made a decision to continue using a new product. Other people are **nonadopters,** and their decision not to adopt may occur for many reasons. Some will not be exposed to information about the product or will wait until other people have tried the product before doing so themselves. Some consumers will quickly decide a new product is not what they want, perhaps because of brand loyalty and satisfaction with current products. Other consumers may want a product but may not buy it for a variety of reasons.[12]

An early decision not to adopt is apparently what occurred when Gerber brought out a new product called Singles, small servings of beef burgundy and other foods that should appeal to the growing number of single households. The product was targeted to people such as college students who

---

[11] An excellent source for application materials is Thomas Robertson, *Innovative Behavior and Communication* (New York: Holt, Rinehart, and Winston, 1971).

[12] John O'Shaugnessy, *Why People Buy* (New York: Oxford University Press, 1987), 25–38.

need a simple-to-fix, inexpensive, nutritious meal without cooking or other complications. Gerber placed the product in the same type of glass jar in which consumers had purchased baby food and identified the manufacturer as Gerber. The product was a bomb. Apparently, many consumers did not like to be identified as singles eating alone. They also associated the product with baby food even though it tasted good and was very convenient.

In the following pages, let us look closely at the four elements of diffusion that cause some people to be early or late adopters, or nonadopters.

THE INNOVATION: WHICH PRODUCTS ARE WINNERS?

An **innovation** can be defined in a variety of ways. The most commonly accepted definition is that an innovation is any idea or product perceived by the potential adopter to be new. This is a subjective definition of innovation, since it is derived from the thought structure of a particular individual.

Innovations can also be defined objectively based on criteria external to the adopter. According to this definition, new products are ideas, behaviors, or things that are qualitatively different from existing forms. This definition also has its problems because of disagreement about what constitutes a qualitative difference. Certainly TV is qualitatively different from existing communication forms, but is Liquid Tide a new product compared to the existing form of Tide? Does the addition of "blue crystals" or an improved package make a product new?

Marketing studies often define new products in relation to market acceptance. Sometimes a simple approach is used by calling any product that has recently become available in a market "new." The Federal Trade Commission sanctions such an approach but limits the use of "new" in advertising to products available in the marketplace less than 6 months.

Academic researchers have often defined a new product as any recently introduced product that has achieved less than x percent of market penetration. Innovations frequently are operationally defined as recently introduced products that have not attained 10 percent of their ultimate market share. All these definitions have problems, pointing to the need for a classification system for various types of innovations.

TYPES OF INNOVATIONS

One system of classifying innovations is based on the impact of the innovation on behavior in the social structure. This taxonomy was described by Robertson and has been used extensively in marketing. It classifies innovations as (1) continuous, (2) dynamically continuous, and (3) discontinuous.[13]

---

[13] Thomas S. Robertson, "The Process of Innovation and the Diffusion of Innovation," *Journal of Marketing* (January 1967), 14–19.

A **continuous innovation** is the modification of an existing product rather than the establishment of a totally new one. It has the least disrupting influence on established patterns of behavior. Examples include adding fluoride to toothpaste, introducing new-model automobile changeovers, adding menthol to cigarettes or changing their length, and replacing dot-matrix printers with daisy wheels or laser printers.

A **dynamically continuous innovation** may involve the creation of either a new product or the alteration of an existing one but does not generally alter established patterns of customer buying and product use. Examples include electric toothbrushes, front-wheel-drive cars, compact discs, natural foods, and oversized tennis racquets.

A **discontinuous innovation** involves the introduction of an entirely new product that causes buyers to alter significantly their behavior patterns. Examples include television, computers, videocassette recorders, videotext products such as computerized data bases for shopping, and microwave ovens.

Most new products are of the continuous form. Examine Table 23.1

TABLE 23.1 **TOP 10 NEW PRODUCTS OF THE YEAR**	Convenience and indulgence characterize the top 10 new products of 1987 as chosen by the AMA's Marketing & Sales Management Division and the AMA's New York Chapter, judged on marketplace success and innovativeness. "This year," said Calvin Hadock, cochairman of the event, "we've had products that were technological breakthroughs and being at the cutting edge before it crests is what counts. Several are structured into tapping into life-style trends and consumer patterns." The ten best are described below.

- *Certified Stainmaster Carpet by E. I. du Pont de Nemours & Co.* DuPont developed the product based on research that showed consumers wanted more stain resistance in their carpets.
- *Bull's-Eye Barbecue Sauce by Kraft Inc.* Kraft market research indicated high consumer interest in a stronger, spicier barbecue sauce as a result of the Cajun food trend.
- *O.N.E. Dry Dog Food by Ralson-Purina Co.* O.N.E. is a successful introduction in the dry dog food category which has been flat for the last three years and is a super-premium product sold across product classes in grocery stores.
- *Optima Card by American Express.* Optima is a low interest revolving credit card with an annual fee of $15, giving American Express a marketing weapon to counter Visa and MasterCard.
- *Sundance Natural Juice Sparkler by Stroh Brewery.* The product capitalizes on the fast growth in natural sodas and juice-based soft drinks. It is 100% natural, geared to consumers looking for healthier mainstream beverages.
- *The Acura Legend by American Honda.* Honda's marketing strategy was based on the attributes that contributed to its success: engineering, quality and value, presented to upscale buyers in a fresh alternative to the world-class luxury car and sporty automobiles previously available only from Europe.
- *Lunch Buckets by Dial Corp.* Lunch Buckets pioneer a new category of shelf-stable microwavable meals, a major growth area offering a convenient alternative to frozen and canned goods. Packaged in a plastic microwave container, they provide a hot and convenient half-pound meal in 75 seconds.
- *American Collection Cookies by Pepperidge Farm Inc.* American Collection Cookies bring a boutique-quality cookie at an affordable price to supermarket shelves.
- *Cherry 7Up by the Seven-Up Co.* A product line extension which successfully tapped into teen markets with TV commercials in black and white and pink, because pink is popular with teens.
- *Fab 1 Shot by Colgate-Palmolive Co.* Fab 1 Shot are packets containing laundry detergent, fabric softener and an antistatic in a technical breakthrough, stunning competition because it was rolled out nationally without a test market.

Source: "AMA Names 10 Best New Products of 1987," *Marketing News* 22 (March 28, 1988), 1ff. Reprinted with permission of the American Marketing Association.

and you will note that most of the "best" new products in a recent year were modifications or extensions of existing products, with little change in basic behavior patterns required by consumers. The one exception is Lunch Buckets, which does require completely different technology (microwave) for some consumers and, more importantly, a changed perception that shelf-stable foods can be as good as ones previously prepared from refrigerated or frozen materials.

PRODUCTS MOST LIKELY TO SUCCEED

New products most likely to be adopted by consumers have some common basic characteristics. Innovations include both a hardware component and a software component. **Hardware** refers to the physical or tangible aspects of a product. **Software** is the information base that accompanies the hardware component. Just as with computers, a new product that is functionally excellent in its hardware may fail to be adopted because of inadequate software or information base. A frequent mistake is spending resources on research and development to perfect the physical attributes of the product but failing to provide adequate resources for the software necessary for success with the product. Understanding consumers' values and lifestyles in developing the software may determine success of the new product just as much as the technical R & D.

As an example, RCA devoted millions to technical perfection of the video disc, which delivered a picture quality superior to that of videocassettes. RCA later wrote off the entire new product costs (reportedly over $150 million) because the product was never accepted by consumers. For consumers, the software component of the activity—the ability to copy materials from TV or other videocassettes—apparently was more valued than the hardware component of the product.

On the other hand, Mindset Corporation wanted to develop a home computer to stand out from the competitors'. It hired GVO, an industrial design and engineering firm, to create a visually distinctive profile for the computer which would provide psychological benefits to the user. Through research, GVO discovered such features that could be incorporated into the computer's design. One such feature was semicircular cutouts, which not only made it easier to remove disks and software cartridges but also gave the computer a softer look and connoted friendliness. The Mindset computer was selected in 1985 for the permanent industrial design collection of New York's Museum of Modern Art.[14]

Total Product Concept.   *New products are often rejected because of failure to adopt a* **total product concept.** Ted Levitt makes the point that products

---

[14] Robert A. Adler, "The Value-Added of Design," *Business Marketing* (September 1986), 96–103.

FIGURE 23.3
THE TOTAL
PRODUCT CONCEPT

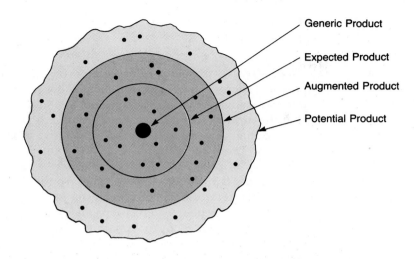

Generic Product

Expected Product

Augmented Product

Potential Product

Note: The dots inside each ring represent specific activities or tangible attributes. For example, inside the "Expected Product" are delivery conditions, installation services, postpurchase services, maintenance, spare parts, training, packaging convenience, and the like.
Source: Theodore Levitt, *The Marketing Imagination* (New York: Free Press, 1986), 79.

have little opportunity for profit when viewed only as *tangible attributes* or attributes (generic products). The total product concept defines the *expectations* of consumers about tangible and other attributes, such as delivery conditions, postpurchase service, and so forth. The **augmented product** includes what the customer perceives the product to do to *provide more* than what is expected (and thereby provides extra "value" beyond what would be justified to pay the price of the product). All of these produce the **product potential** or everything potentially feasible that will attract and hold customers.[15] The total product concept is shown graphically in Figure 23.3. When introducing new products, marketers may be so enamored with the "new" qualities of the product (tangible attributes) that they ignore the success requirements identified by understanding the total product concept.

What are some of the attributes or expectations and augmentations of a total product? Research by Rogers and other investigators indicates five characteristics that are associated with success with new products. They include the following:

1. relative advantage
2. compatibility

---

[15] Theodore Levitt, *The Marketing Imagination* (New York: Free Press, 1986), 74–93.

3. complexity
4. trialability
5. observability

RELATIVE ADVANTAGE   The most important question to ask in evaluating the potential success of a new product is, "Will it be perceived to offer substantially greater advantage than the product it supersedes?" The issue is not whether the product is objectively better than the existing product but whether or not consumers are likely to perceive a **relative advantage.** To what degree will the new product be a substitute for existing ones or complementary with the array of products already in consumers' inventories?

New products most likely to succeed are those that *appeal to strongly felt needs.* One marketer asked consumers about their problems around home and found that many people perceive problems with collection of their garbage. Existing garbage bags were too small and too easily broken. The company brought out a new line of strong, large garbage bags, and the product was diffused quickly. Garbage disposals appeal to similar felt needs and have been one of the most widely diffused new products for homes.

Campbell, on the other hand, introduced a new instant soup consisting of single servings of highly concentrated soup. The consumer merely added boiling water. Response by consumers was tepid. They perceived it to be scarcely more instant than Campbell's regular soup, to which consumers simply add water and then boil. Although the dry product was physically quite different from liquid soup and offered many advantages to the marketers (because dry products are much more efficient to ship and store than liquid ones), the product failed because it lacked perceived relative advantage to consumers.

In banking, ATMs diffused through the social system quickly because they offer high perceived relative advantage to consumers who want 24-hour availability. Point-of-sale (POS) systems, in contrast, have been slow to diffuse. Although POS may offer advantages to banks and retailers, consumers perceive little relative advantage over checks or credit cards.

COMPATIBILITY   **Compatibility** is an important determinant of new product acceptance. Compatibility refers to the degree to which the product is consistent with existing values and past experiences of the potential adopters. Clairol introduced a new shampoo called A Touch of Yogurt. It was unsuccessful, apparently because people found the idea of putting yogurt into their hair incompatible with their value systems, despite the fact that yogurt may be good for hair. Perhaps if the product had been called A Touch of Glamour, with Yogurt, it might have succeeded. Glamour is part of the norm of the target market even though yogurt in the hair is not.

As another example, Radio Shack was successful in introducing personal computers to America because of its existing distribution system of thousands of stores. Customers whose normal behavior favored technologically innovative products were already in the stores buying products. Computers, although technically very different in function, were related to consumers' product interests. The combination of distribution, personal service, and related product interests was compatible with the existing values and experiences of early adopters of computers.

COMPLEXITY   **Complexity** is the degree to which an innovation is perceived as difficult to understand and use. The more complex the new product, the more difficult it will be to gain acceptance. Microwave ovens represent a discontinuous or dynamically continuous innovation, but they diffused rapidly because they are easy to use. The complexity principle makes it advantageous to build products less than as sophisticated as possible during initial introduction in order to achieve simplicity in understanding and operation for consumers.

Apple Computer followed such a strategy with great success. Even the apple as a symbol communicates simplicity and a product that can be understood by all ages. IBM also used a symbol—"Charlie"—to personalize its technological image. Charlie bridged the gap to consumers who might have perceived "International Business Machines" as too complex for personal use, even though the IBM personal computer is relatively simple to use. IBM chose readily accessible software in the introduction of its personal computers, rather than less well known software of its own. Software that is "user friendly" is initially more successful, even though complex software might be more efficient.

Products can be designed to minimize perceived complexity. When consumers read instructions for assembly or use of a new product, will such instructions be perceived as simple or complex? The more complex, the less likely the product is to succeed.

TRIALABILITY   New products are more apt to succeed when consumers can try or experiment with the idea on a limited basis. Sampling is an effective method of inducing trial of new products. Companies such as Proctor & Gamble and General Foods give millions of new products away each year to make trial easy and without economic risk.

Enhancing the trialability of new products can be accomplished through sampling in continuous innovations, especially for low-unit-value, consumer-packaged goods. How can marketers do something similar for expensive, complex, and high-involvement, discontinuous innovations? The same principles apply, but it takes more creativity.

Leasing is a strategy for such products. When computers were first introduced, IBM and other firms used leases to reduce the perceived risk for innovators. After Lincoln changed the Town Car so drastically that it could be called a new product (downsized, fuel efficient, digital readouts, etc.), it used this strategy to reach a market target that might not ordinarily try a new luxury car. Lincoln conducted an "associative marketing" program with Budget Rent-a-Car. Budget gave away luggage and featured low prices for rental of Lincoln Town Cars. Sales increased for Lincoln even in an era of recession as people in the prime market target tried the new luxury car as a rental. Later they bought it for business or personal use.

New recipes and products are introduced through programs in supermarkets that demonstrate how to prepare these products. They also offer taste samples. Even communication programs can enhance the trialability of products by urging people to "Try it—you'll like it!"

The effectiveness of such programs is greatest when the trial is induced in settings likely to contain innovative consumers. An example was a new type of snack food consisting of nuts coated with honey, called Eagle Snacks. Anheuser-Busch introduced Eagle Snacks by providing small packages of the product on airlines. This setting contained large numbers of upscale consumers able to afford the relatively expensive snack food.

OBSERVABILITY   **Observability** and **communicability** reflect the degree to which results from using a new product are visible to friends and neighbors. It influences the acceptance of new products. For instance, when room air conditioners were first introduced, it was found that adoption often occurred within concentrated areas rather than throughout the city. Neighbors from next door or across the back fence saw the results of an air-conditioned room and wanted one for themselves.

Marketers can sometimes employ strategies to enhance the visibility of products by inducing celebrities to use them. Thus the visibility of the celebrity makes the new product visible. LaCoste used this strategy with its alligator sporting products. It gave them to celebrities for their own use. Visible use of a new product in very successful movies or TV shows can also be an effective device for obtaining the adoption of new products. Madonna and other recording stars influence adoption of new clothing styles and other products.

RESEARCHING NEW PRODUCT ATTRIBUTES

Developing a new product that will be a winner requires attention to the details of the total product concept. The complication with new products, compared to researching attributes of existing products, is the difficulty consumers have in thinking about products with which they have no experience. Often new product research investigates only tangible attributes and market segmentation variables rather than the lifestyle or other software details that determine the success or failure of the product.

Focus groups are a technique that can be helpful in the investigation of specific details that determine the fate of the products. Focus groups can even be used to spot the trends that indicate needs that lead to a new product development. Products most likely to succeed are those which solve problems of consumers. Where do problems come from? From life; therefore consumer analysts need good methods to study lifestyles. New products, however, often must be based on lifestyles which are emerging, and these are difficult to measure with quantitative techniques. Emerging lifestyles and trends usually are uncovered through qualitative research. A popular method of qualitative research is focus groups to indicate consumer acceptance of items that adapt to their wants, needs, and behavior. Two approaches are inferred insights and cross-study insights.[16]

Inferred insights are observations drawn from product-specific studies, revealing whether consumers feel certain products fits their lives. Cross-study insights are observations based on a wide variety of product-specific studies. They help uncover demographic groups, psychographic groups, changing values, and shopping habits, as well as feelings about advertising, service, and health.

Judith Langer, president of a New York research firm, usually begins lifestyle studies by asking consumers this question, "Thinking about yourself and the people you know, how is your lifestyle different today from a few years ago?" Focusing on change by having respondents describe ways in which their lives have been altered, gains clues about where they are heading.

COMMUNICATIONS ABOUT NEW PRODUCTS

Communication is the process by which consumers and marketing organizations share information with one another to reach a mutual understanding. Communication is critical to the widespread acceptance of new products. Communication about new products follows principles discussed throughout this book. Some of these principles are especially applicable to new product decisions of consumers, however, and are described subsequently.

Two models have been used by marketers in attempts to gain acceptance of new products. One is called the **hypodermic needle model.** It proposes that media have direct, immediate, and powerful effects on the acceptance of new products by a mass audience.

The mass media are important in brand preference or attitude formation concerning existing products and may also be important in the acceptance of continuous innovations. As new products approach higher levels of discontinuity (i.e., more fundamental behavioral changes are required of adopters), however, the media appear to be limited in effectiveness. For innovations, the media are considered to be less important than interpersonal communications, especially those of opinion leaders.

The **two-step flow model** provides another view of the role of media and personal communications. A more valid approach may be to extend the concept of two-step to a multi-stage approach. In the two-step flow model, ideas flow from the media to opinion leaders and from those opinion leaders to the mass markets. The mass media accomplish the transfer of information to opinion leaders, but influence is transferred by opinion leaders to the rest of the population.

---

[16] The information in this and the next two paragraphs is adapted from "Researcher: Focus Groups Are the Best Way to Spot Trends," *Marketing News*, 22 (March 28, 1988).

WORD OF MOUTH: KEY TO SUCCESS FOR NEW PRODUCTS

Word of Mouth (WOM), or interpersonal communications, plays a critical role in the adoption of new products. WOM is most important when the product is perceived to have substantial social, psychological, or economic risk involved in its purchase. WOM is also important when the choice between products is ambiguous. At later stages of the decision process to buy a new product—when people are evaluating products or confirming their decision—and when consumers have substantial experience with a product category, they may be more willing to rely upon the media. But the more innovative the product, the more likely consumers will be influenced by an existing user of the product or someone they consider an "expert" on the subject.

SPEED OF DIFFUSION   Although Word of Mouth is very important to the innovation diffusion process, marketers have little control over this variable. Marketers have more control over some factors, such as product characteristics, pricing, and resource allocations, which contribute to the speed of diffusion. Robertson and Gatignon compiled the diffusion literature into several propositions which affect the speed of diffusion.[17]

It is believed that the greater the **competitive intensity** of the supplier, the more rapid the diffusion and the higher the diffusion level. Highly competitive firms have more aggressive pricing strategies and allocate greater resources to the product introduction. Intense competition frequently leads to price wars and an increase in demand due to the more price-sensitive customers entering the market. High competitive intensity is likely to reduce the market penetration level for any given firm within an industry, however.

The better the reputation of the supplier (breeding confidence among potential adopters), the faster the initial diffusion, even though the final shape of the diffusion curve may depend on the actual technology incorporated into the product. A good reputation leads to source credibility, which in turn may reduce uncertainty and risk in the purchase decision.

Products diffuse more rapidly when the technology is **standardized.** This is particularly true with products dependent upon auxiliary components, such as personal computers. Consumers may believe a purchase to be more risky if they are unsure which technology will become standard. When this risk is reduced or avoided, more consumers are likely to adopt the product. High-resolution television (HRT), for example, offers readily perceived benefits to consumers but was delayed until the 1990s in the United States because of difficulty in agreeing on the European or Japanese standards.

Vertical coordination, which refers to a high degree of vertical dependence and an interlocking relationship among channel members, is also related to diffusion. As coordination increases, the information flow from supplier

---

[17] Thomas S. Robertson and Hubert Gatignon, "Competitive Effects on Technology Diffusion," *Journal of Marketing* 50 (July 1986), 1–12.

to consumer increases. As a result, diffusion increases. A corollary to this idea is that as information flows back up the channel—from consumer to supplier—innovative customers and opinion leaders can help identify new product opportunities.

Resource commitments are also important to the diffusion process. Greater research and development expenditures are positively related to innovations. As technologies become enhanced and more alternatives become available, diffusion will become broader and more rapid. As advertising, personal selling, sales promotion activities, and distribution support increase, diffusion also increases. Marketing research allocations can help guide R & D expenditures as well as develop a positioning strategy for the new technology; both of these areas are instrumental in the diffusion process.

HOMOPHILY–HETEROPHILY: WHOM DO YOU TRUST?   Consumers tend to trust a homophilous person when they need information about new products. Homophily is the degree to which pairs of individuals who interact are similar in important attributes such as beliefs, education, and social status. When people share common meanings, beliefs, and a mutual language, communication between them is more likely to be effective. Heterophilous communications may cause cognitive dissonance because individuals are exposed to messages that are inconsistent with their own beliefs and values. Homophily and effective communication, in contrast, breed each other.

Perhaps you are beginning to understand why so many new products fail. Marketing strategies rely heavily on advertising and personal selling—messages transmitted with a definite bias in their opinion ("buy our product") from people and organizations who exist outside the interpersonal communications network. Keep in mind that the homophily principle also means that people tend to trust people of similar socioeconomic status to themselves when deciding to buy new products. Many times, advertising spokespeople and sales personnel are heterophilous with the potential buyers of the new products.

Everett Rogers reviewed thousands of empirical studies concerning the diffusion of innovations, and many of these dealt with the issue of effective communications. He summarized his conclusions from this research in 17 generalizations. These, along with the number and percentage of studies that support each, are presented in Table 23.2.

MARKETING MANAGEMENT OF WOM (WORD OF MOUTH)   It is not enough for marketing managers to understand the importance of interpersonal communications in new product acceptance. Marketing organizations function as change agents—stimulating the adoption of the new product. They need to find ways to manage WOM. Public relations and sales promotion are programs that stimulate WOM.

Among business or industrial firms, there is an increasing practice of bringing the key opinion leaders in an industry together for a party, seminar, laser show, or other event in which these leaders become aware of, experience,

TABLE 23.2   A SUMMARY OF RESEARCH EVIDENCE SUPPORTING AND NOT SUPPORTING GENERALIZATIONS ABOUT OPINION LEADERSHIP AND DIFFUSION NETWORKS

Generalization	Support for the Generalization (Number of Research Studies)		Percentage of Research Studies Supporting the Generalization
	Supporting	Not Supporting	
8–1: Interpersonal diffusion networks are mostly homophilous.	22	13	62
8–2: When interpersonal diffusion networks are heterophilous, followers seek opinion leaders of higher socioeconomic status.	11	0	100
8–3: When interpersonal diffusion networks are heterophilous, followers seek opinion leaders with more education.	6	2	75
8–4: When interpersonal diffusion networks are heterophilous, followers seek opinion leaders with greater mass media exposure.	5	0	100
8–5: When interpersonal diffusion networks are heterophilous, followers seek opinion leaders who are more cosmopolite.	1	0	100
8–6: When interpersonal diffusion networks are heterophilous, followers seek opinion leaders with greater change agent contact.	2	0	100
8–7: When interpersonal diffusion networks are heterophilous, followers seek opinion leaders who are more innovative.	10	1	91
8–8: Opinion leaders have greater exposure to mass media than their followers.	9	1	90
8–9: Opinion leaders are more cosmopolite than their followers.	10	3	77
8–10: Opinion leaders have greater change agent contact than their followers.	10	3	77
8–11: Opinion leaders have greater social participation than their followers.	11	4	73
8–12: Opinion leaders have higher socioeconomic status than their followers.	20	7	74
8–13: Opinion leaders are more innovative than their followers.	24	4	86
8–14: When a social system's norms favor change, opinion leaders are more innovative, but when the norms do not favor change, opinion leaders are not especially innovative.	7	2	78
8–15: The interconnectedness of an individual in a social system is positively related to the individual's innovativeness.	4	0	100
8–16: The information-exchange potential of communication network links is negatively related to their degree of (1) communication proximity, and (2) homophily.	2	0	100
8–17: Individuals tend to be linked to others who are close to them in physical distance and who are relatively homophilous in social characteristics.	9	0	100

Source: Everett M. Rogers, *Diffusion of Innovations,* 3rd ed. (New York: Free Press, 1983), 308–309.

and evaluate the new product. They return home and tell opinion followers about it. This has become standard practice when firms such as IBM, Xerox, Apple, and others introduce new products. Such mega-events as methods of managing WOM not only are effective ways of introducing new products

CONSUMER IN FOCUS

23.2   CONSUMER EXPERIENCES AT MEGA-EVENTS

Polaroid Corp. hired Radio City Music Hall to help celebrate its 50th anniversary. Surprisingly, the party didn't include a single leggy Rockette, and it wasn't even held in New York's landmark art deco auditorium.

Instead, 25,000 Polaroid employees, retirees and their families assembled one Saturday night in August at a stadium in Boston. The evening featured 15 acts of entertainment as well as three giant video screens, which at one point showed Polaroid employees in six countries singing "Happy Birthday." For the grand finale, the Pointer Sisters performed their high energy music act, ending with their hit song "Jump" as torch-waving sky-divers jumped from an airplane. Now Polaroid just has to write the check: Nearly $1 million to Radio City Music Hall Productions, which pieced together the one-night extravaganza.

But for the Polaroid job as well as others, Radio City is finding it must bid against a growing number of competitors. Recently, a new industry trade group—the International Special Events Society—was formed in San Diego, California. There are 100 members so far.

Many people credit Walt Disney with the birth of the special event, and many of the kingpins of the event business today started at Walt Disney Co. Lesa Ukman, editor of Special Events Report, a newsletter published in Chicago, comments, "With the Olympics, the Statue of Liberty, Hands Across America, Live Aid, and so on, it has been one mega-event after another, brought to you by this corporation or that."

Polaroid, which spent two years planning an anniversary that includes scientific and artistic programs and giving Polaroid cameras to every elementary school in the country, told Radio City that it just wanted employees to leave the stadium thinking: "Good time, good company."

Source: Meg Cox, "Let's Put on a Show," *The Wall Street Journal* (September 10, 1987), 33.

but they may also be used to revitalize existing products to generate positive affective response and a new vitality. *Consumer in Focus 23.3* describes how **event marketing** is accomplished.

Stimulating Opinion Leaderhip.   When LaCoste was a small, unknown marketer of premium shirts, they developed a new concept of selling quality sports apparel for everyday usage. To achieve diffusion of this concept, LaCoste gave shirts bearing their logo—a distinctive alligator—to tennis and media celebrities. Following the careful placement of these shirts with key opinion leaders who were encouraged to wear them in places other than the tennis courts, there was widespread diffusion of the concept of wearing "Alligators" in settings far removed from tennis courts. Evaluation of the diffusion literature suggests that mass media can create awareness and even interest in new products or new usages of old products, but that personal communications are more effective in persuading people to try new products.

Sales Promotion.   When Owens-Corning introduced a new fabric made of Fiberglas, the company developed a total promotional program that emphasized the interpersonal communications that might occur among homeowners. Among other things, the company knew that the people in the "back rooms" of fabric departments often talked with customers when they measured and installed the draperies. To insure that even these people said good things and were supportive of good WOM, Owens-Corning promoted a contest featuring a luxurious vacation for the "back room" that installed the most draperies made of the new Fiberglas product.

Public Relations.   Managing WOM well requires attention to public relations as an important marketing function. Too often, the public relations function has been involved mostly with the financial community, industrial relations, or other areas of the firm. Publicity and public relations, however, should be viewed as a major communications priority, especially among marketing managers working on new product introduction. Trade shows are often effective in introducing new products, for example, because of the media presence and interest in the "latest and newest." Consumer electronics shows, toy shows, and clothing fashion shows are typical examples where firms make extensive use of publicity to stimulate WOM about their new products.

There are also cases in which unfavorable interpersonal communications can kill a new product. As an example, Anheuser-Busch introduced a soft drink called Chelsea, which contained a very small amount of alcohol, so low that labeling requirements did not even require mention of the alcohol. The word got around about the alcohol, however, and even though teenagers could drink two cases without becoming intoxicated, they would drink two or three bottles and pretend to be drunk. Parents went through the roof, forcing the withdrawal of the product from the market. The advertising was great, but that was irrelevant. WOM killed the product.

THE ADOPTION-DECISION PROCESS OVER TIME

Adoption of a new product is a decision process, in many ways similar to the general decision process described throughout this book. Not only does an individual consumer move through the stages of adopting the product through time, but other consumers are also moving through the process, probably at different rates and with different starting points in time. Thus, adoption of new products must be understood in a temporal context. Avoid any illusion that acceptance occurs instantly, either for an individual or a society.

Understanding the temporal process of adoption is very important. Otherwise, a firm might introduce a product, advertise it heavily, and commit large amounts of resources to the project, only to see it "fail." In actuality, the

FIGURE 23.4   MODELS OF THE ADOPTION/DIFFUSION PROCESS

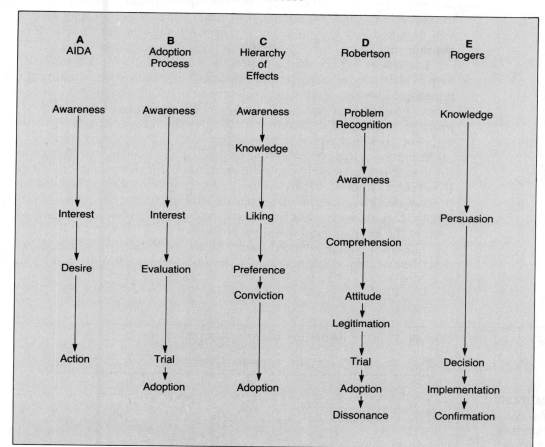

Source: John H. Antil, "New Product or Service Adoption: When Does It Happen?," *Journal of Consumer Marketing* 5 (Spring 1988), 7. Used with permission.

product may not have had enough time to move through the early stages that must inevitably be passed before arriving at the action—purchase—desired by the marketer. Frequently firms fail when introducing new products because they underestimate the time required for new products to diffuse through the market.

Business firms sometimes act as if individual consumers or markets simply decide to buy or not buy. When this fallacious assumption is made, the firm is likely not to budget properly, calculate return correctly, or plan promotional activity effectively. A further complication may arise because of confusing adoption of the physical product with the product concept or idea. People may move through the entire process of adoption but, due to situations such as their current inventory of goods or inadequate income, not buy the product until later. All elements of the firm's marketing program may have been well designed and executed, but the firm will fail if it does not understand the time and situations required for new product adoption.

Understanding the time and process required for adoption to occur may help explain why so many new products fail, especially when they are discontinuous innovations. Too many firms appear to believe that if they just develop a new product that fits an important need recognized by consumers and promote, price, and distribute it well, sales should result. Unfortunately, it does not work that way.

Adoption as a process over time has been understood by marketing scholars for a long time. An early conceptualization of this process was called **AIDA** (Awareness, Interest, Desire, Action). Alternative conceptualizations of this process use different terminology but are attempts to describe the same process. Figure 23.4 shows models or alternative conceptualizations that are widely used in the adoption and diffusion literature.

The most widely adopted model is that of Rogers, in which stages are described as knowledge, persuasion, decision, implementation, and confirma-

FIGURE 23.5 THE ROGERS MODEL OF THE INNOVATION–DECISION PROCESS

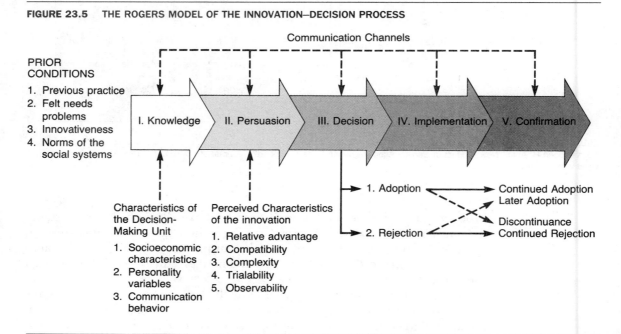

Source: Reprinted with permission of The Free Press, a Division of Macmillan, Inc. from *Diffusion of Innovation,* third edition by Everett M. Rogers (New York: The Free Press, 1983), 165. Copyright © 1962, 1971, 1983 by The Free Press.

tion. The Rogers model of innovation decisions is compared with alternatives in Figure 23.4 and the variables associated with movement through the process are elaborated in Figure 23.5.

KNOWLEDGE

The **knowledge stage** begins when a consumer receives physical or social stimuli that give exposure and attention to the new product and how it works. In this stage, consumers are aware of the product but have made no judgment concerning the relevance of the product to a problem or recognized need. Knowledge of the new product is usually thought to be a result of selective perception. It is more likely to occur through the mass media than in later stages, which are more influenced by opinion leaders.

A new brand of perfume by Christian Dior illustrates some of these principles. Figure 23.6 shows how Poison was introduced. The name is designed to break the selection-perception barrier. Is there any way to avoid noticing a brand with the name of Poison? The hope is that the person wearing or

**FIGURE 23.6
GETTING ATTENTION
FOR A NEW
PRODUCT**

Source: Courtesy of Christian Dior Perfumes, Inc.

giving Poison will also be noticed. The mass media can bring the new perfume to the attention of a person, but interpersonal communication will probably also be needed to consummate the hidden meaning of "le nouveau parfum" reserved for the person who can weave a spell over the other.

PERSUASION

Persuasion, in the Rogers paradigm, refers to the formation of favorable or unfavorable attitudes toward the innovation. The consumer may mentally imagine how satisfactory the new product might be in some anticipated future use situation, perhaps giving the product a "vicarious trial" in the consumer's mind.

Persuasiveness is related to perceived risk in the new product or an evaluation of the consequences of using the product. When an individual considers a new product, she or he must weigh the potential gains from adopting the

FIGURE 23.7
PERSUASION TO TRY A NEW PRODUCT: CATALOGS PROVIDE SPACE FOR INFORMATION COPY

Source: Courtesy of Impact 2000 Inc., Toms River, New Jersey.

product against the potential losses of switching from the product now used. If the new product is adopted, it may be inferior to a present product or the cost may be greater than the increased value gained by using the new product.

Consumers can reduce perceived risk in adopting the new product—and consequently the uncertainty that retards buying—by acquiring additional information. A person may seek out news stories, pay particular attention to advertising for the product, subscribe to product-rating services, talk with individuals who have already tried the product, talk with experts on the subject, or in some instances, try the product on a limited basis. Each of these information-search and evaluation strategies has an economic and/or psychological cost. Moreover, they are unlikely to yield information that will completely reduce uncertainty.

Catalogs are often used to introduce new products. The reason for their effectiveness includes the ability to provide more information than the typical retail setting. Figure 23.7 provides an example. This ad for a "hair zapper" is graphic and large enough to gain attention. The copy addresses several needs and attempts to show the relative advantages over present solutions to hair problems. The endorsement in the upper right corner includes an "M.D." Attempts are made to reduce perceived risk by references to physical safety and a 30-day money-back guarantee. This quantity of information would not be available in a retail store or affordable in most advertising media, but direct marketing firms such as Impact 2000, Sharper Image, and Land's End have been very successful in persuading consumers to buy new products. Using an "800" number and bank cards also makes the decision as easy as possible.

DECISION

The decision stage involves activities that lead to a choice between adopting or rejecting the innovation. **Adoption** can be defined as a decision to make full use of an innovation as the best course of action. Adoption involves both psychological and behavioral commitment to a product over time.[18] Ordinarily, this means continued use of the product unless situational variables (lack of availability, etc.) prevent usage. **Rejection** is a decision not to adopt an innovation. **Active rejection** consists of considering adoption of an innovation, perhaps even a trial, but then deciding not to adopt it. **Passive rejection** (or **nonadoption**) consists of never really considering use of the innovation.

IMPLEMENTATION

Implementation occurs when the consumer puts an innovation into use. Until the implementation stage, the process has been a strictly mental exercise, but now behavioral change is required. The strength of the marketing plan

---

[18] John M. Antil, "New Product or Service Adoption: When Does It Happen?" *Journal of Consumer Marketing* 5 (Spring 1988), 5–15.

may be the critical determinant in whether a good product that has been communicated effectively actually results in a sale.

The marketing mix should make purchase easy. To do so requires careful coordination of the channels of distribution with the new product introduction and communication process. Price is also an important ingredient. In the introduction of microcomputers, software availability, sales demonstrations in nonthreatening environments, price concessions, and educational seminars may be as important in the success of the innovation as the product itself—perhaps more so.

The importance of the marketing program in affecting implementation is illustrated by Post-it Notes, a new product consisting of simple notepaper with a special adhesive strip on the back. The product was introduced by 3M and has diffused throughout the world as a replacement for paper clips, notepads, and loose pieces of paper. Initially, the product was introduced with conventional marketing programs through office supply stores in Richmond and Tampa, but in Denver and Tulsa the dealers ran promotions and through sampling put the product in consumers' hands. Sales clicked and led to a market test in Boise, where the product was hand-sampled and mailed to every office in the city.

The test was successful and extended with a marketing program based upon sampling, direct mail, and advertising.[19] Most importantly, because the samples were "free," employees in many offices apparently took the Post-it Notes home and other family members began asking for them, creating the demand for widespread distribution. The product has become enormously successful, but if the company had not used sampling and direct-mail giveaways so extensively, it is possible that Post-it Notes would have taken many years to achieve much market penetration. Perhaps without the unconventional marketing program, this new product would have joined the majority of new products that are rejected by consumers.

CONFIRMATION

Confirmation is the process through which consumers seek reinforcement for the innovation decision. Consumers sometimes reverse previous decisions, especially when exposed to conflicting messages about the innovation, causing dissonance.

Discontinuance is a serious concern to marketers. The rate of discontinuance may be just as important as the rate of adoption, with a corresponding need for marketing strategies to devote attention to preventing its occurrence. Pringles was introduced by Proctor & Gamble as a new potato snack and was successful in attracting many adopters. The product eventually failed in

---

[19] Graydon E. Thompson, "Post-it Notes Click Thanks to Entrepreneurial Spirit," *Marketing News* (August 31, 1984), 21.

its original form, however, because the level of discontinuers was so high, a condition the company had not observed until too late.

People who adopt the product later than early adopters appear to be more likely to discontinue adoption. This creates a need for marketing organizations to work hard with follow-up service and feedback as sales of a new product expand. Offutt, in her study of videotex products, found that discontinuance is most likely to occur when the new product is not integrated into the practices and ways of life of the purchasers, or when the new product conflicts with other aspects of consumer lifestyles.[20]

Consumers Most Likely to Buy New Products

Which consumers are most likely to buy new products? If you knew the answer to that question, consider how helpful it would be in concentrating the firm's resources on those people as primary targets for the marketing program of new products.

ADOPTER CLASSES

Consumers can be classified according to the time they adopt a new product relative to other consumers. In the decision to buy a specific new product, some people are innovators. Others are **early adopters.** Others can be classified as **early** or **later majority.** The ones who are last to adopt the product are called **laggards.** The distribution of people has been described as a normal distribution or, when describing the cumulative total of adopters, as an S-curve. These distributions are shown in the top portion of Figure 23.8. Both curves represent the same data. The S-shaped curve represents the adoption of the innovation over time by the members of a social system, whereas the bell-shaped curves present these data in terms of individuals adopting each year. The shaded area marks the time period during which the S-curve of diffusion "takes off"—the critical interval between failure or success for most marketers.

The pattern shown in Figure 23.8 displays what is sometimes described as an **imitation effect.** That is, the rate of adoption increases as the number of adopters increases.[21] An idea is transmitted to a few innovators who must pass through various stages to acceptance or rejection. After some innovators have adopted the product, others may follow, depending on the value of the innovation and other characteristics of the product.

Figure 23.8 vividly emphasizes the point that acceptance of a new product does not come all at once in a social system. Usually it comes much slower

---

[20] Nancy Offutt, Perception of Product Attributes and the Innovation Decision Process (Ph.D. dissertation, The Ohio State University, Columbus, 1981).

[21] Ram C. Rao and Frank M. Bass, "Competition, Strategy, and Price Dynamics: A Theoretical and Empirical Investigation," *Journal of Marketing Research* 22 (August 1985), 283–296, at 284.

FIGURE 23.8
CLASSIFYING
ADOPTER
CATEGORIES

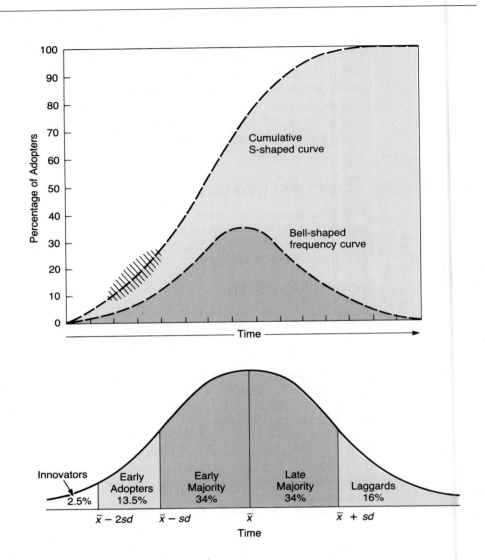

The bell-shaped frequency curve and the S-shaped cumulative curve for an adopter distribution

Adopter categorization on the basis of innovativeness

The innovativeness dimension, as measured by the time at which an individual adopts an innovation or innovations, is continuous. This variable, however, may be partitioned into five adopter categories by laying off standard deviations from the average time of adoption.

Source: Reprinted with permission of The Free Press, a division of Macmillan Inc. from *Diffusion of Innovations*, third edition by Everett M. Rogers (New York: The Free Press, 1983), 343 and 347. Copyright © 1962, 1971, 1983 by The Free Press.

than marketers wish it did. The process continues throughout the social system, and its speed as well as eventual penetration of the system will be determined by many factors. Not everyone falls into these categories, of course. Some consumers may actively reject the new product from the very beginning. It is not proper to call them laggards, as the Rogers classification suggests, since they might properly be considered early rejectors. For that reason and others adoption may be less than the 100 percent shown in Figure 23.8.

A key conclusion is possible from the phenomena expressed in Figure 23.8. Marketers must focus their attention on the innovators and early adopters, if they can be identified. If marketers do not succeed in winning adoption of the new product by these people, there is not much hope for the rest of the population.

INNOVATIVENESS

Innovativeness is the degree to which an individual adopts an innovation relatively earlier than other members in the system do. A goal of marketing strategies is to understand innovativeness in order to target innovators.

The construct of innovativeness typically is measured in one of two ways in marketing studies. The first measure is based upon time of adoption, such as for those individuals who purchase in the first x weeks, months, and so on. The second is a count of how many of a prespecified list of new products a particular individual has purchased at the time of the study.

Everyone has some degree of innovativeness. Hirschman explains the importance of understanding this principle:

> *Few concepts in the behavioral sciences have as much immediate relevance to consumer behavior as innovativeness. The propensities of consumers to adopt novel products, whether they are ideas, goods, or services, can play an important role in theories of brand loyalty, decision making, preference, and communication. If there were not such characteristics as innovativeness, consumer behavior would consist of a series of routine buying responses to a static set of products. The inherent willingness of a consuming population to innovate is what gives the market place its dynamic nature. On an individual basis, every consumer is, to some extent, an innovator; all of us over the course of our lives adopt some objects or ideas that are new in our perception.*[22]

Three major types of variables have been studied to determine their correlation with innovativeness: socioeconomic, personality, and communication behavior. The results of studies about these variables and the conclusions about their relationships (positive, negative, or not related) are shown in Table 23.3, which summarizes years of research on the diffusion process.

SOCIOECONOMIC VARIABLES   Analysis of socioeconomic variables indicates that people of high social status, who are upwardly mobile, educated,

---

[22] Elizabeth C. Hirschman, "Innovativeness, Novelty Seeking, and Consumer Creativity," *Journal of Consumer Research* (December 1980), 283–295, at 283.

TABLE 23.3 A SUMMARY OF THE RESEARCH EVIDENCE SUPPORTING AND NOT SUPPORTING GENERALIZATIONS ABOUT THE CHARACTERISTICS OF ADOPTER CATEGORIES

Generalization	Direction in Which the Independent Variable Is Related to Innovativeness	Support for the Generalization (Number of Research Studies)		Percentage of Research Studies Supporting the Generalization
		Supporting	Not Supporting	
I. Socioeconomic Characteristics				
7–2	Age (not related)	108	120*	48
7–3	Education (positive)	203	72	74
7–4	Literacy (positive)	24	14	63
7–5	Higher social status (positive)	275	127	68
7–6	Upward social mobility (positive)	5	0	100
7–7	Larger-sized units (positive)	152	75	67
7–8	A commercial, rather than a subsistence, economic orientation (positive)	20	8	71
7–9	A more favorable attitude toward credit (positive)	19	6	76
7–10	More specialized operations (positive)	9	6	60
II. Personality Variables				
7–11	Empathy (positive)	9	5	64
7–12	Dogmatism (negative)	17	19	47
7–13	Ability to deal with abstractions (positive)	5	3	63
7–14	Rationality (positive)	11	3	79
7–15	Intelligence (positive)	5	0	100
7–16	A more favorable attitude toward change (positive)	43	14	75
7–17	Ability to cope with uncertainty (positive)	27	10	73
7–18	A more favorable attitude toward education (positive)	25	6	81
7–19	A more favorable attitude toward science (positive)	20	7	74
7–20	Fatalism (negative)	14	3	82
7–21	Achievement motivation (positive)	14	9	61
7–22	Higher aspirations for education, occupations, etc. (positive)	29	10	74
III. Communication Behavior				
7–23	Social participation (positive)	109	40	73
7–24	Interconnectedness with the social system (positive)	6	0	100
7–25	Cosmopoliteness (positive)	132	42	76
7–26	Change agent contact (positive)	135	21	87
7–27	Mass media exposure (positive)	80	36	69
7–28	Exposure to interpersonal communication channels (positive)	46	14	77
7–29	More active information seeking (positive)	12	2	86
7–30	Knowledge of innovations (positive)	61	19	76
7–31	Opinion leadership (positive)	42	13	76
7–32	Belonging to highly interconnected systems (positive)	8	7	53

* Of these 120 studies, 44 show that earlier adopters are younger and 76 show that earlier adopters are older.

Source: Reprinted with permission of The Free Press, a Division of Macmillan, Inc. from *Diffusion of Innovation,* third edition by Everett M. Rogers (New York: The Free Press, 1983), 260–261. Copyright © 1962, 1971, 1983 by The Free Press.

and/or literate, and who are privileged relative to others in the social system are likely to be high in innovativeness. Income is almost always useful in profiling innovativeness. Higher-income people not only have the ability to buy more new products but they also have the ability to take the risk of trying new products. For low-priced products, this relationship may not be as important, however.

PERSONALITY AND ATTITUDE   Personality and attitudinal variables associated with innovativeness in consumers include venturesomeness or openmindedness, intelligence, higher aspirations for themselves and their children, rationality, and ability to deal with abstractions or to be creative. Dogmatism and rigidity, however, are likely to be negatively associated.

Consumers may react to new products based on their cognitive style of problem solving. Kirton indicates people can be placed on a continuum between two extremes: Adaptors or innovators. Extreme adaptors will adopt solutions that improve technical efficiency but involve practices and objects similar to those previously employed for the same purpose. Innovators are less likely to seek solutions within the context of previous solutions to the problem. They tend to produce different ways of organizing, deciding, and behaving which entail radical change and the incorporation of novel activities, techniques, and objects.[23]

Using the Kirton Adaption-Innovation Inventory (KAI), Foxall and Hawkins found relationships between this measure of personality and innovative brand choice.[24]

COMMUNICATION VARIABLES   Communication behavior variables include cosmopolitanism, social participation, contact with change agents, mass media exposure, higher amounts of interpersonal communication, active information seeking, knowledge of innovations, opinion leadership, and other variables. As you can see in Table 23.3, there are many studies (as is also true of socioeconomic variables) that indicate the association of communication variables, some of which can be influenced directly by marketing, and the adoption of new products. In the past, it was felt that innovators and early adopters use the mass media more but that later adopters used interpersonal sources more. Recent research indicates that earlier adopters use both mass media and interpersonal sources more than later adopters.[25]

---

[23] M. J. Kirton, "Adaptors and Innovators: A Theory of Cognitive Style," in K. Gronhaug and M. Kaufman, eds., *Innovation: A Crossdisciplinary Perspective* (New York: John Wiley & Sons, 1986).

[24] Gordon Foxall and Christopher G. Hawkins, "Cognitive Style and Consumer Innovativeness: An Empirical Test of Kirton's Adaption-Innovation Theory in the Context of Food Purchasing," *European Journal of Marketing* 20 (1986), 63–80.

[25] Linda Price, Lawrence Feick, and Daniel Smith, "A Re-Examination of Communication Channel Usage by Adopter Categories," in Richard Lutz, ed., *Advances in Consumer Research* 13 (Provo, Utah: Association for Consumer Research, 1986), 409–412.

POLYMORPHISM   **Polymorphism** is the degree to which the innovators and early adopters for one product are likely to be innovators for other products. Consumers who are innovators for many products are said to be polymorphic, whereas those for only one product are **monomorphic.** If innovativeness is monomorphic, the process of finding innovators for a specific new product may not be worth the cost, but if it is polymorphic, the search would be more justified.

Findings are conflicting in this area, but a position may be emerging that identifies categories of products that have the same innovators. For example, perhaps the people who are the first buyers of component stereo systems are likely to be innovators for microcomputers or a wide range of consumer electronics but are unlikely to be innovators for fashion clothing, food, or other products.

DEVELOPING MARKETING STRATEGIES

The innovation-adoption literature and the diffusion process can be used to develop strategies for introducing new products whether or not specific research is conducted on that new product. When a bank introduced automated teller machines to its city, the bank first carefully studied findings from the diffusion research tradition. Marketing officers of the bank made predictions from the literature about the economic, social, personal, and communication characteristics most likely to be associated with trial and adoption of ATMs. The introductory site was chosen to match the characteristics of innovators, as described in the literature. A communications program was developed on the basis of mass media to create awareness and interest, and of personal influence to induce trial, with a series of special meetings at clubs and organizations where opinion leaders could be shown the new bank machines. The introduction was a huge success, and the city eventually attained one of the highest penetration levels of ATMs in the nation.

PREDICTING DIFFUSION AND ADOPTION SUCCESS

Marketing strategies often have a need for predicting the ultimate sales that will be achieved for new products in future time periods. There are a number of mathematical approaches that are used for this purpose.[26]

The fundamental diffusion models are called **penetration models.** These

---

[26] Space does not permit more detailed discussion of these models. If you are interested, you will find them described, along with appropriate citations to source materials, in earlier editions of this text. See James Engel and Roger Blackwell, *Consumer Behavior*, 4th ed. (Homewood, Illinois: Dryden Press, 1982), 401–409. For a review of these models, see C. Naqrasimhan and S. K. Sen, "Test Market Models for New Product Introduction," in Yoram Wind, Vijay Mahjan, and Richard Cardozo, eds., *New Product Forecasting: Models and Applications* (Lexington, Massachusetts: Lexington Books, 1981).

predict the level of penetration by a new product in a given time period based upon early sales results. **Epidemiological models** predict acceptance based upon the view that new product diffusion is a process of social interaction in which the innovators and early adopters "infect" the rest of the people, similar to disease epidemics that move through a population. These models are stochastic in nature. Analysis in the marketing literature has generally focused on the structural or mathematical properties of the models rather than on a comparison of their ability to generate forecasts of new product sales in empirical studies. An excellent review of these models is available in Mahajan and Peterson.[27]

Adoption models are deterministic. They include internal variables that describe consumer decision making concerning the new product and the effects of external variables that may affect the penetration rates and timing of acceptance. These models, and hybrids that relate external variables to diffusion models, can be useful to show effects of marketing mix variables. Horsky and Simon, for example, show that advertising can accelerate the diffusion process. The optimal effects on profitability occur when a firm advertises heavily when the product is introduced and reduces advertising as the product moves through its life cycle and interpersonal communications take effect.[28]

Many adoption models, incorporating market structure variables, are used by advertising agencies and other organizations heavily involved in new product introductions. One of the foundational models for these approaches was the DEMON model, later revised to the NEWS (new product, early warning system) models, developed by the advertising agency of Batten, Barton, Durstine, and Osborne. The variables involved in DEMON are shown in Figure 23.9.

Both DEMON and NEWS are recursive, which means that each variable is first the dependent and then the independent variable. Thus, trial depends on awareness but, once activated, trial becomes the independent variable for prediction of usage. Each of these variables is influenced in turn by variables (such as advertising) that are marketing-dominated. Awareness is important and is predicted by measuring the ratio of advertising dollars spent to the number of delivered gross impressions and the ratio of impressions to the level of attained reach and frequency.

N. W. Ayer Advertising's model includes recall of advertising claims as an important determinant of initial purchases of new products. SPRINTER, developed by Glen Urban, simulates new product adoption. It is based upon an assumption of buying activity leading to trial in the following stages: (1) awareness; (2) interest; (3) search; (4) selection; (5) postpurchase behavior.

[27] Vijay Mahajan and Robert A. Peterson, *Innovation Diffusion: Models and Applications* (Beverly Hills: Sage Publications, 1985).
[28] Dan Horsky and Leonard S. Simon, "Advertising and the Diffusion of New Products," *Marketing Science* 2 (Winter 1983), 1–17.

FIGURE 23.9
DEMON MODEL OF
NEW PRODUCT
ACCEPTANCE

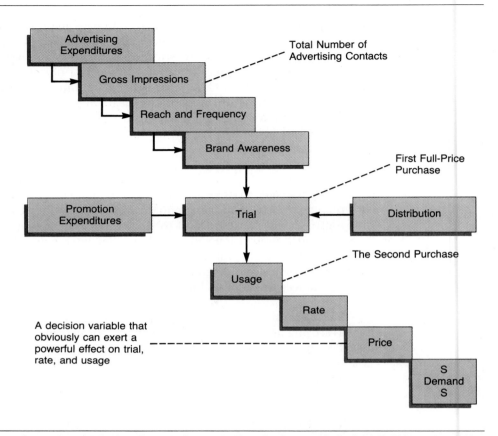

Source: James K. DeVoe, "Plans, Profits, and the Marketing Program," in Frederick E. Webster, Jr., ed. *New Directions in Marketing* (Chicago: American Marketing Association, 1965).

There are many other models, usually drawing upon test-market data that can be used with the simulation model, which combined with early returns in the marketplace are used to forecast future sales and profitability of the new product. Most of these models are the proprietary work of marketing organizations. Although they may be very useful in managing marketing programs, they are not generally published for scholarly examination. A fair conclusion, however, is that models to forecast new product performance have evolved from the academic interest of a few management scientists to standard practice in many good marketing organizations.[29] The increasing availability of scanner data in some markets should allow more development

---

[29] Robert S. Shulman and Kevin J. Clancy, "Refinements Improve New Product Models' Predictions," *Marketing News* (August 31, 1984), 15.

of models that predict ultimate market acceptance based upon early information about the new product.

THE DIFFUSION OF DIFFUSION

Information about the diffusion process has been circulated widely through academic and business organizations. Perhaps no topic of discussion has been affected by, and affected, so many diverse disciplines. Marketing managers could greatly improve the introduction of new products by simply reviewing plans on the basis of principles that are well established in the diffusion literature as it has been described in this chapter.

There is still room for improvement. Much of the diffusion research was conducted in social systems that are much more controlled than those faced by marketing managers. Many of the studies were conducted with discontinuous, high-involvement products that are different from the more mundane products marketing managers often must introduce. There is much more to be learned, therefore, about diffusion research by those involved in the study of marketing. Robertson reviewed the literature of marketing and the literature of diffusion and prepared a summary of the most critical needs. Although we do not have the luxury of space to discuss all of these, they are neatly summarized in Table 23.4. If you want to go further in your study of the

TABLE 23.4 NEW DIRECTIONS FOR CONSUMER DIFFUSION THEORY	**Extant Theory and Assumptions**	**Needed Conceptual Developments**
	The Innovation	*The Innovation*
	Generally assumed to be important and can be classified as to its: relative advantage, compatibility, complexity, trialability, observability	A broader framework for classifying and assessing innovations from high technology to line extensions
	Value of the innovation can be measured with a rational yardstick and scientific authority is often available	A framework for consumer evaluation of innovations when value cannot be measured by a rational yardstick and when there is no scientific authority
	Expectations on innovation performance are well developed and assumed to be an extension of the consumer's existing experience base	A framework for assessing innovations when consumers are required to develop new patterns of experience
	The Diffusion Process	*The Diffusion Process*
	Generally assumed to be an S-shaped (logistic) pattern	Specification of diffusion process to be expected as a function of:
	A single curve assumed for the entire market	innovation characteristics
		marketing variables
		competitive variables
		social contagion effect
		environmental factors
		Recognition of varying diffusion processes by market segment

continued

	Extant Theory and Assumptions	Needed Conceptual Developments
TABLE 23.4 *continued*	*The Adoption Process* Assumed to follow a single hierarchical process from awareness to knowledge, evaluation, trial, and adoption Generally assumed to be an individual consumer adoption decision Measures only initial adoption Ignores effect of adoption on the consumption system or innovator.	*The Adoption Process* Recognition of multiple models: hierarchical, low involvement, dissonance/attribution and specification of variables (including marketing program design) which determine the form of the adoption process Further development of organizational adoption and family adoption models Development of concepts and methods as to the width and depth of usage and adoption Assessment of adoption potential conditional on current consumer inventory of goods and services and consumption system
	The Communication Process Change agent is assumed to be non-self-serving Information is generally available — often from impartial sources Mass media and personal selling information sources are accorded limited attention	*The Communication Process* Research needed on marketing-controlled sources which are biased and self-serving Research needed when information is lacking or when impartial standards are non-existent An enriched conceptualization needed on the role of mass media in diffusion
	Opinion Leadership and Personal Influence Assumed important for all innovations Assumed to occur in a two-step manner Assumed to occur within the boundaries of social systems	*Opinion Leadership and Personal Influence* A better delineated model for when personal influence will occur Recognition of the multiflow nature of consumer influence and the lesser importance of opinion leaders More explicit research on the interaction of mass media influence and personal influence beyond social systems

Source: Thomas S. Robertson, "Marketing's Potential Contribution to Consumer Behavior Research: The Case of Diffusion Theory," in Thomas C. Kinnear, *Advances in Consumer Research* 11 (Provo, Utah: Association for Consumer Research, 1984), 485.

diffusion of innovations, this table will provide a number of good suggestions.[30]

NEW PRODUCT DIFFUSION AND ESV

As a concluding perspective to this chapter on Diffusion of Innovations, study *Consumer in Focus 23.3*. It provides a realistic application of many of the materials in this chapter. Perhaps it will suggest some of the things that

---

[30] Also see Hubert Gatignon and Thomas S. Robertson, "A Propositional Inventory for New Diffusion Research," *Journal of Consumer Research* 11 (March 1985), 849–867.

CONSUMER IN FOCUS

23.3 FORD TAURUS COPYCAT STUFF? HARDLY!

When Ford Motor Co. set out to design the Taurus, it looked hard at the competition: Let's see what we can learn from those guys. But the way they went about it was different, intriguing, and a focus-forcer.

Under Vice-President Lew Veraldi's direction, Team Taurus identified some 40 cars in the rough class category they were talking about (midsize, four-door). The idea was to pick the best cars they thought they could learn from—the "best of class"—and see what rival companies and vehicles from all over the world had to teach Ford.

Of the 40, they selected about a dozen cars (most of them foreign), which were then subjected to the indignity of what they call the "layered stripdown." They took them apart piece by piece to see how the cars were made.

They learned a lot. The stripdown helped them identify 400 features that went on their Taurus wish list—items they

thought they might be able to beat, or at least, emulate. The feature might be something as visible to the customer as a better lumbar support system in the seats, or as innocent and invisible as an engine part designed to be more accessible to the mechanic.

Of the 400, Ford reckons it either met or bettered the competition of 360 of them. It sounds like copycat stuff. Maybe that's why companies don't look at competition in this way more often. But Ford people will tell you that this is the first time in a long while that they *haven't* felt like imitators following a me-too strategy. It's a paradox—by taking little pieces of others, you become a better version of yourself.

Source: Robert H. Waterman, Jr., *The Renewal Factor: How the Best Get and Keep the Competitive Edge* (New York: Bantam Books, 1987).

must be done to manage the development of new products, a topic that space does not permit discussion of here.[31]

Ford Taurus is the most successful introduction of a new car by an American manufacturer in recent years. When it was first introduced in 1986, it received little mass acceptance. The innovators and early adopters who first bought it were probably thought a bit weird. The car was thought to be a bit weird—a jelly bean, some called it. Yet advertising communicated the idea to a relatively upscale, educated market target augmented by favorable publicity in consumer and auto magazines. The innovators "tried" it, and their decisions were confirmed sufficiently that they became opinion leaders, evangelizing others about the relative advantage, simplicity, and other attributes of the car. From *Consumer in Focus 23.3* you can see why the product was so well received. Market research in the auto industry had often asked consumers what they wanted (attitudes), but Taurus research asked consumers

---

[31] This topic is addressed well in William E. Souder, *Managing New Product Innovations* (New York: Lexington Books, 1987).

about their behavior—what they liked and disliked about their present behavior in buying and using cars.

The second year Taurus (and its Mercury sister, Sable) had only one change—a substantial price increase. The price did not cause a decline in sales; just the opposite, as both sales and status of the car soared. So did margins. The consequence of all of this—which reflected a radically improved approach to introducing new products at Ford—was to make Taurus the largest-selling nameplate in America and Ford Motor more profitable than GM.

The long-run effect? Ford Motor had a market value of $22.0 billion, about the same as GM, with $3 billion more in sales. Ford's 25 percent return on equity was nearly 2½ times that of GM's 10.8 percent.[32] The result was ESV; the cause was successful management of a new product that diffused through society just the way the textbooks say it should!

Summary

The diffusion of innovations, a topic of study and research that has grown rapidly in the past few decades, deals with how a new product is adopted in a society. It is of high importance to marketing organizations because new products must be brought out continuously in order for firms to survive.

The elements of the diffusion process include the innovation, the communication of the innovation, time, and the social system. The most commonly accepted definition of an innovation is any idea or product perceived by the potential innovator to be new.

Everett Rogers is the most influential change agent in the diffusion of the diffusion research. He has identified the types of consumers adopting a new product classified by the time of adoption as innovators, adopters, early majority, late majority, and laggards. Consumers who have a high amount of innovativeness can be identified in terms of socioeconomic (privileged), personality (venturesome), and communication behavior (contact with the mass media and other people) variables.

REVIEW AND DISCUSSION QUESTIONS

1. What are the major differences in perspective on diffusion of innovations of those who are studying macromarketing issues compared to micromarketing issues?

2. Sun Tzu, the famous Chinese strategist, once said, "He who occupies the field of battle first and awaits his enemy is at ease; he who comes later to the scene and rushes into the fight is weary." Does this quotation apply to the study of diffusion of innovations? Explain.

3. How would you define innovation? How does the choice of your definition affect research that might be conducted on the topic?

---

[32] "The Top 1000 U.S. Companies Ranked by Industry," *Business Week* (April 15, 1988).

4. Explain as precisely as possible the differences between continuous, dynamically continuous, and discontinuous innovations. Give some examples of each, other than those mentioned in the text.

5. What are the major competitive challenges facing firms in which understanding of diffusion of innovations might be helpful?

6. Prepare a short essay that explains how to pick winners from the many candidates for new product introduction.

7. Assume that a firm is introducing a new car. How would you suggest they manage Word of Mouth for this introduction?

8. The manufacturer of a new product is attempting to determine who the innovators for the product might be. The product is a game that requires players to answer each other with phrases from various foreign languages. Whom would you identify as the most likely innovators? What appeals would you suggest to be used in promoting the product?

9. A large manufacturer of drug and personal grooming products wants to introduce a new toothpaste brand in addition to the three already marketed. Evaluate for the firm what information might be used for innovation studies to guide introduction of the product.

10. How would you justify ESV (Enhanced Shareholder Value) as a firm's primary financial goal? What should be the role of new product development in this goal?

GLOBAL CONSUMER MARKETS

WINNING THE FOREIGN MARKET

Mead Corp., in the largest capital project in its history, is investing $500 million in a new mill in Alabama to make coated paperboard for consumer packaging. It is counting on selling $100 million worth a year in Japan within five years. "We have to be a major exporter," says Thomas H. Johnson, president of Mead's Coated Board Div.

—Chrysler Corp., after selling its overseas operations eight years ago, will export $750 million worth of Jeeps and minivans this year to Europe and Asia. Although the company is still a net importer to the tune of $750 million, Michael N. Hammes, vice-president for international operations, figures that exports will outpace imports within three years.

—Some small U.S. companies have become very successful by *customizing* products for foreign markets. Adolph Hertrich, who owns a small lumber mill in Boring, Ore., switched to metric sizing for his lumber and mastered Japan's complicated grading system. He even stacks his Japan-bound wood to suit the market there — with only vertical grain surfaces exposed. He generates 70% of his sales in Japan.

Source: "Made in the USA," *Business Week* (February 29, 1988), 60–65.

GLOBAL MARKETING STRATEGY

Perhaps no manager should be promoted to a position of major responsibility in contemporary business organizations if that individual cannot "think globally." Thinking globally involves the ability to understand markets beyond one's own country of origin with respect to sources of demand, sources of supply, and methods of effective management and marketing.

The globalization of marketing requires managers of all types, but especially those dealing with consumer behavior, to understand the broad forces that characterize contemporary markets. The forces affecting globalization of markets and international competition have been identified by Michael Porter to include the following:

1. Growing similarity of countries in terms of available infrastructure, distribution channels, and marketing approaches;

2. Fluid global capital markets — national capital markets are growing into global capital markets because of the large flow of funds between countries;

3. Technological restructuring — the reshaping of competition globally as a result of technological revolutions such as in microelectronics;

4. The integrating role of technology — reduced cost and increased impact of products have made them accessible to more global consumers;

5. New global competitors — a shift in competitors from traditional country competitors to emerging global competitors.[1]

An example of a "global company" is Ford Motor, far more at least than General Motors. When the U.S. auto market was under siege from Japanese imports, Chrysler and GM were in dismal shape. Ford had its troubles also but was "saved" by Ford of Europe, a subsidiary operating with considerable autonomy and innovation in developing cars with appeal that cuts across national boundaries. Ford developed "world class cars," such as the Escort and later the Taurus/Sable, that could sell in multiple countries. Another such car was the Scorpio, developed by Ford of Europe but also sold in the United States. Look at Figure 24.1 to see how the car is the same, although the appeals in ads vary for the German compared to the U.S. market.

IMPORTANCE OF GLOBAL THINKING IN MARKETING

Emergence of the Multi-National Enterprise (MNE) makes it essential that managers have the ability to "think globally." Corporations such as Coca-Cola, IBM, Gillette, Nestle, Sony, Phillips, and Unilever derive over 50 percent of their sales outside their country of domicile. So do many small, relatively

---

[1] Michael E. Porter, ed., *Competition in Global Industries* (Cambridge, Massachusetts: Harvard Business School Press, 1986).

FIGURE 24.1
SCORPIO — A CAR
FOR GERMAN AND
U.S. MARKETS: THE
SAME PRODUCT
REQUIRES
DIFFERENT
MARKETING
TECHNIQUES IN
DIFFERENT
COUNTRIES

CONSUMER IN FOCUS

24.1   MCDONALD'S OPENS THE 10,000TH RESTAURANT

McDonald's Corporation opened its 10,000th location, marking yet another "McMilestone" in the firm's 33-year history, during which it grew from a single hamburger joint in Des Plaines, Illinois to a household word across the country and around the world. In recent years, McDonald's has concentrated on expanding its marketing efforts to foreign countries, and now there are more than 2,340 restaurants outside the U.S., reaching a total of 49 markets worldwide. Of systemwide sales that reached $14.3 billion last year, international sales represented 26% of that total. Overall, sales in markets outside the U.S. have more than tripled since 1980.

Among other reasons for its success, McDonald's executives point to the firm's commitment to local communities, which it demonstrates in two ways. First, McDonald's depends on local businesses — local contractors, food suppliers, financial institution — to operate the restaurants. Sec-

ond, the company actively supports local charities and community programs. The *key to worldwide growth* has been in developing markets as a long-term investment and cultivating reliable local suppliers, said a firm spokesperson.

One of the biggest questions facing McDonald's as it considered its expansion overseas was "whether or not the Big Mac could make it in another culture," said Mike Gordon, director of public relations. With the answer a resounding yes, the firm has *continued to explore new markets* abroad and will open its first location in Hungary — but it has modified its product line to suit tastes and preferences as required. E.g., in the Philippines, "McSpaghetti," has been added because it was discovered that Filipinos consider this a treat.

Source: *American Marketplace* 9, (March 31, 1988), 49, and McDonald's Corporation 1987 Annual Report.

obscure companies with specialized "niches" that transcend national boundaries.

Today's consumers choose not only from products made in many countries. Consumers must also choose from ideas, advertisements, and friends representing a diversity of nations and cultures. Consumer analysts must therefore be global thinkers to design strategies to reach today's consumers.

The corporate cultures of today's successful organizations also are increasingly global. Volkswagen in Germany recently appointed a new President from the United States. The President of Coca-Cola came from Cuba. IBM for the first time recently appointed an American to head its far-flung European Division, which includes Africa and the Middle East. Caterpillar in the United States recruited its head of manufacturing from Austria. Global managers must be able to learn a new language quickly, understand the structure and culture of any country in the world, and work effectively with people from any country. Consumer analysts can play a key role in this process. *Consumer in Focus 24.1* shows the importance of this process and offers insights into how it is done at McDonald's. Growth in global marketing is one reason McDonald's has prospered while its competitors have stagnated in their attempt to grow. McDonald's now sells more hamburgers in Japan alone than major competitors do in the United States.

"Sourcing" for marketers increasingly involves global markets. Resource capabilities may emphasize labor costs in one country, raw materials in another, and information technologies in still others. The ability to sell, source, and manage on a global basis requires understanding of the structural, cultural, and ethnic variables discussed in this chapter.

Global market analysis starts with understanding the structure of markets on a global basis — people, their needs, and the ability to buy. Global market analysis also involves willingness to buy — often affected by cultural, ethnic, and motivation variables. The following pages discuss how to analyze these variables using a cross-cultural perspective. In the last part of the chapter, these variables are considered as well as marketing institutions to examine marketing opportunities in some specific countries of the world other than North America.

STRUCTURE OF GLOBAL MARKETS

The world population is nearly 5 billion and growing at the rate of about 1.7 percent annually. That represents a decline from a 2.04 percent growth rate in the 1960s and a reversal of two centuries of increasing growth rates. Demographers expect the growth rate to continue to decline to between 1.4 and 1.5 percent in 2000 and zero toward the end of the twenty-first century. Even though the *rate* is declining, the *numbers added* are still growing at about 83 million people each year and will increase to about 86 million people added each year in the 1990s, peaking at 89 million added in the year 2000 when the world's population is estimated by the United Nations to be about 6.1 billion. After that, the numbers added each year are projected to decline but will still produce a world population of 10.2 billion by the last decade of the twenty-first century, when population in absolute numbers should begin to decline.[2]

Fertility is declining in industrialized nations. The primary reasons are higher educational attainment, urbanization, rising standards of living, legal abortion, more effective methods of contraception, widespread sterilization, increased labor force participation of women, high divorce rates, and delayed marriage and childbearing.

The population of a country is affected by migration rates as well as by the natural growth variables of fertility and death rates. Emigration from developing countries to developed countries is increasing rapidly. The best-

---

[2] Thomas W. Merrick, "World Population in Transition," *Population Bulletin* 41 (April 1986), 3.

educated and relatively affluent segments of the population are often the ones who emigrate.

Strategic planning involves committing corporate resources and efforts to the most promising areas of the world. This requires accurate projection of world population trends over the next few decades. Table 24.1 displays current and projected population for major countries of the world by age distribution. This table serves as a reference point for many of the global trends discussed in this chapter, so you may want to study it closely, looking for the changes occurring in specific countries.

The important trends in global population can be summarized as the following:

1. prolonged below-replacement fertility in developed nations
2. rapid growth despite falling fertility in developing nations
3. rapid urbanization in less developed countries, with unprecedented migration from poor LDCs to more affluent industrialized nations.

FAST AND SLOW GROWTH MARKETS

Growth-oriented firms, striving for ESV (Enhanced Shareholder Value), need to find growth markets. Consumer analysts have a responsibility for the process of doing so. Let's examine where the growth markets are — and are not, focusing on the variables of population and ability to buy.

BIRTH DEARTH   Affluent countries are experiencing decline or small increases in population. Ability to buy has been concentrated historically in North America, Europe, and Japan. The industrialized countries (North America, Europe, Israel, Japan, Australia) are projected, however, to decline from 15 percent of the world's population in 1985 to barely 5 percent in the year 2100.[3] In Table 24.2 you can see that population in the European Common Market is expected to increase less than 3 percent between 1982 and 2000. Actual decline in population is projected in countries such as the Federal Republic of Germany and Scandinavian countries. In that same time period, Japan is projected to increase about 8 percent. It is not difficult to see why MNEs have been pouring their capital into the United States, why Europeans are developing a Single Market in 1992, and why there is intense interest in opening up the Russian market for economic development.

FAST-GROWTH POPULATIONS   Some countries are projected to grow rapidly. These countries can be identified in Table 24.1. Relative changes are easier to observe by identifying the changing rank of countries, as is done in Table 24.3.

---

[3] Ben J. Wattenberg, *Birth Dearth* (New York: Pharos Books, 1987).

TABLE 24.1 WORLD POPULATION TRENDS, BY AGE: 1985 AND 2025 (Numbers in thousands)

Country	Total all ages¹	1985 0 to 24 years	25 to 54 years	55 to 59 years	60 to 64 years	65 to 69 years	70 to 74 years	75 to 79 years	80 years and over
United States	238,631	91,578	96,256	11,245	10,943	9,214	7,641	5,556	6,198
WESTERN EUROPE									
Austria	7,502	2,643	2,953	420	425	256	319	256	228
Belgium	9,903	3,402	4,007	593	571	352	392	299	287
Denmark	5,122	1,747	2,081	262	268	235	205	161	162
France	54,621	20,093	21,789	3,086	2,905	1,594	1,769	1,644	1,741
Germany, Federal Republic	60,877	19,410	25,662	3,618	3,374	2,133	2,539	2,189	1,951
Greece	9,878	3,626	3,865	625	463	382	372	284	261
Italy	57,300	20,249	22,908	3,459	3,243	1,982	2,324	1,701	1,436
Luxembourg	363	119	157	23	18	13	14	11	8
Norway	4,142	1,483	1,578	208	230	207	173	131	133
Sweden	8,351	2,714	3,291	446	485	434	381	305	295
United Kingdom	56,125	19,901	21,520	3,069	3,171	2,543	2,367	1,824	1,732
EASTERN EUROPE									
Bulgaria	9,071	3,266	3,651	586	544	301	328	228	167
Hungary	10,697	3,663	4,436	650	614	363	420	310	240
Poland	37,187	14,669	15,379	2,000	1,655	980	1,017	837	650
OTHER DEVELOPED COUNTRIES									
Australia	15,698	6,385	6,279	757	686	559	454	310	268
Canada	25,426	9,732	10,734	1,196	1,113	896	731	511	513
Japan	120,742	43,445	52,896	6,920	5,356	4,164	3,522	2,439	2,000
New Zealand	3,318	1,415	1,268	150	140	118	98	70	59
DEVELOPING COUNTRIES									
Bangladesh	101,147	66,246	27,807	2,262	1,712	1,262	959	623	275
Brazil	135,564	76,932	45,799	3,909	3,098	2,283	1,718	1,037	790
China	1,043,204	545,766	378,000	36,697	29,851	22,340	15,471	9,381	5,697
Guatemala	7,963	5,197	2,198	191	143	97	66	38	34
Hong Kong	5,548	2,383	2,289	252	204	167	120	76	56
India	758,927	428,856	254,102	24,135	19,137	14,380	9,824	5,581	2,913
Indonesia	166,440	97,940	54,277	4,827	3,495	2,529	1,808	1,047	517
Israel	4,252	2,088	1,484	154	147	129	97	89	64
Mexico	78,996	49,882	23,166	1,715	1,436	1,008	798	532	459
Philippines	54,498	33,158	17,179	1,297	990	780	571	304	219
Singapore	2,559	1,148	1,125	88	65	52	40	25	15
Uruguay	3,012	1,296	1,091	163	139	109	94	62	57

United States	301,394	91,851	113,153	18,071	19,547	18,352	14,836	11,235	14,348
WESTERN EUROPE									
Austria	7,279	2,041	2,671	562	570	473	364	287	311
Belgium	10,054	3,000	3,659	691	717	654	539	408	387
Denmark	4,690	1,144	1,785	367	352	303	268	237	235
France	58,431	17,242	22,141	3,917	3,858	3,531	3,123	2,508	2,111
Germany, Federal Republic	53,490	13,862	18,460	4,522	4,628	3,827	3,088	2,247	2,855
Greece	10,789	3,357	4,136	726	648	583	482	400	457
Italy	57,178	16,268	21,271	4,292	4,126	3,441	2,868	2,427	2,485
Luxembourg	339	93	124	25	25	24	20	14	14
Norway	4,261	1,186	1,598	323	291	266	229	192	175
Sweden	7,707	2,048	2,842	576	532	466	433	405	404
United Kingdom	55,919	16,894	20,608	4,030	3,949	3,263	2,654	2,309	2,211
EASTERN EUROPE									
Bulgaria	10,070	3,342	3,914	579	549	513	459	367	347
Hungary	10,598	3,196	4,189	647	550	615	610	401	391
Poland	45,286	14,997	17,836	2,311	2,406	2,663	2,320	1,510	1,243
OTHER DEVELOPED COUNTRIES									
Australia	22,575	7,167	9,011	1,460	1,351	1,206	985	745	649
Canada	33,261	10,376	12,410	1,997	2,238	2,069	1,672	1,264	1,235
Japan	132,082	40,389	49,052	8,348	7,451	6,700	6,940	6,671	6,531
New Zealand	4,202	1,266	1,665	299	287	237	182	144	123
DEVELOPING COUNTRIES									
Bangladesh	219,383	103,492	92,273	8,114	6,119	4,463	2,559	1,472	892
Brazil	245,809	99,425	100,520	11,982	11,038	8,635	6,383	4,154	3,672
China	1,388,431	449,084	558,616	113,599	88,981	64,697	56,554	31,691	25,208
Guatemala	21,668	11,293	8,108	667	530	403	298	189	181
Hong Kong	7,617	2,361	2,866	493	560	517	375	245	199
India	1,228,829	441,190	540,386	69,710	58,574	46,980	33,989	21,564	16,435
Indonesia	272,744	103,677	118,444	14,971	11,989	9,700	6,612	4,027	3,324
Israel	6,865	2,578	2,770	380	318	269	227	179	144
Mexico	154,085	62,898	65,604	7,671	6,063	4,609	3,280	2,066	1,894
Philippines	102,787	41,350	44,598	5,025	4,127	3,230	2,263	1,298	896
Singapore	3,323	1,028	1,232	218	252	236	173	112	73
Uruguay	3,875	1,422	1,569	209	200	163	120	89	104

[1] The sum of the age groups may not add to the total because of rounding.

Source: Bureau of the Census, *An Aging World*, International Population Reports Series P-95, No. 78 (Washington, D.C.: U.S. Department of Commerce, 1987), 48–49.

TABLE 24.2		1982–2000		
POPULATION GROWTH IN EUROPEAN COMMON MARKET AND SOME OTHER COUNTRIES		1982	1990	2000	Percentage Change
F.R. Germany	61,638	60,640	59,143	–4.0%
France	54,219	56,139	58,573	8.0
Italy	56,639	57,258	57,925	2.3
Netherlands	14,313	14,973	15,643	9.3
Belgium	9,856	9,887	9,972	1.2
Luxembourg	366	370	373	1.9
United Kingdom	56,341	56,785	57,902	2.8
Ireland	3,483	3,765	4,123	18.4
Denmark	5,118	5,061	4,940	–3.5
Greece	9,792	9,880	10,435	6.6
Europe (Total of above)	271,763	274,758	279,029	2.7
Spain	37,935	40,541	43,362	14.3
Portugal	10,033	10,755	11,506	14.7
U.S.S.R.	269,994	291,637	311,817	15.5
U.S.A.	232,057	243,513	260,378	12.2
Japan	118,449	122,769	128,901	8.8
World Total	4,586,000	5,273,000	6,196,000	35.1

Source: Statistical Office of the European Communities, *Eurostat* (Luxembourg: Office des Publications Officielles des Commununautes Europeennes, 1984).

The fastest-growing country in the world is India. If current trends continue, India will surpass China as the largest country in the world in the next century. Kenya is the fastest growing country by percentage increase, rising at the rate of 4.2 percent annually. Kenya is not shown in Table 24.1 because of its relatively small size, but its 1988 population of 23 million is expected to quadruple by 2025. Kenya is a land of economic potential because of export commodities such as coffee and tea. It also has relative political stability, freedom, and increasing prosperity. The problems of Kenya as a consumer market are described, however, in this demographic analysis:

> The total fertility rate — or the average number of children a woman will bear in her lifetime — is well above 2.6 to 5 children per woman, the figure considered necessary to indicate that a country may be a good potential market. With the average woman bearing about eight children in her lifetime and with little prospect for change in the near future, the country shows small promise as a consumer market in this century. Just keeping up with the basic needs of a surging population will strain already limited resources. And Kenya's record-high population growth of about 4.2 percent per year is far above the 1.5 to 2.5 percent considered indicative of a good potential market.[4]

Another fast-growing country is Bangladesh, the eighth most populous nation in the world and growing rapidly. Between 1983 and 2000, 52 million people are projected to be added to Bangladesh's population. That is roughly

---

[4] *Trends & Opportunities Abroad, 1988* (Ithaca, New York: American Demographics, Inc., 1988), 1.

TABLE 24.3	1950	1987	2025	2050
COUNTRIES RANKED BY POPULATION SIZE: 1950, 1987, 2025, AND 2050	1. China	1. China	1. China	1. India
	2. India	2. India	2. India	2. China
	3. Soviet Union	3. Soviet Union	3. Soviet Union	3. Nigeria
	4. United States	4. United States	4. Indonesia	4. Pakistan
	5. Japan	5. Indonesia	5. Nigeria	5. Soviet Union
	6. Indonesia	6. Brazil	6. United States	6. Brazil
	7. Brazil	7. Japan	7. Brazil	7. Indonesia
	8. United Kingdom	8. Nigeria	8. Pakistan	8. United States
	9. West Germany	9. Bangladesh	9. Bangladesh	9. Bangladesh
	10. Italy	10. Pakistan	10. Iran	10. Iran
	11. Bangladesh	11. Mexico	11. Ethiopia	11. Ethiopia
	12. France	12. Vietnam	12. Mexico	12. Philippines
	13. Nigeria	13. Philippines	13. Philippines	13. Mexico
	14. Pakistan	14. West Germany	14. Vietnam	14. Vietnam
	15. Mexico	15. Italy	15. Japan	15. Kenya
	16. Spain	16. United Kingdom	16. Egypt	16. Zaire
	17. Vietnam	17. France	17. Turkey	17. Egypt
	18. Poland	18. Thailand	18. Zaire	18. Tanzania
	19. Egypt	19. Turkey	19. Kenya	19. Turkey
	20. Philippines	20. Egypt	20. Thailand	20. Japan
	21. Turkey	21. Iran	21. Tanzania	21. Saudi Arabia
	22. South Korea	22. Ethiopia	22. Burma	22. Thailand
	23. Ethiopia	23. South Korea	23. South Africa	23. Uganda
	24. Thailand	24. Spain	24. Sudan	24. Sudan
	25. Burma	25. Burma	25. South Korea	25. Burma
	26. East Germany	26. Poland	26. France	26. South Africa
	27. Argentina	27. South Africa	27. United Kingdom	27. Syria
	28. Iran	28. Zaire	28. Italy	28. Morocco
	29. Yugoslavia	29. Argentina	29. West Germany	29. Algeria
	30. Romania	30. Colombia	30. Uganda	30. Iraq

Note: Developing countries are shown in boldface.
Source: Bureau of the Census, *World Population Profile, 1987* (Washington, D.C.: U.S. Department of Commerce, 1987), 5.

equivalent to a country with the population of France being added to a state the size of Georgia.[5]

The difference between growth rates of developed and developing countries is dramatically indicated in Table 24.3. In 1950, only 8 of the top 15 countries were developing countries. Currently the number is 10, and by 2050, it is projected to rise to 13.

The changing rank of developing countries produces some dramatic changes over the next few decades. By 2025, Iran and Ethiopia will join the list of 15 largest countries while West Germany is expected to move off the list (to 29th). Japan also is expected to drop from 7th to 20th. Perhaps the greatest changes for consumer analysts to monitor are countries such as Nigeria

---

[5] Bryant Robey, "Some Numbing Numbers," *American Demographics* 6 (April 1984), 11. For additional discussion on world population trends, see Rafael M. Salas, "Beyond 2000: State of the World Population," *Populi: Journal of the U.S. Fund for Population Activities* 8 (1981), 3–11.

and Pakistan, which were 13th and 14th in 1950 but which are expected to move to 3rd and 4th place by the year 2050. Among Latin American countries, Brazil is expected to retain its rank as one of the 10 largest countries in the future.

From a market perspective, the greatest challenge for the "rich" countries that hope to have growing markets for their products in the future is to assist the "poor" countries in developing themselves to where they also are rich enough to be economically strong markets.

ECONOMIC RESOURCES AND MARKET ATTRACTIVENESS

The most attractive markets are countries that are growing both in population and in economic resources. An important task of consumer analysis is to identify such countries.

Economic resources, or ability to buy, is measured by consumer analysts in various ways. Per capita income is an important indicator, although there are problems, such as the currency with which it will be measured and the purchasing power of income within a country. One of the most valid indicators is "hours required to purchase" standard consumer goods. For example, consumers might require 11 hours at an average wage to purchase a standard television receiver in the United States but as much as 11 months in some developing countries. Unfortunately, such data are not readily available for market analysis purposes.

A useful indicator of "ability to buy" is Gross National Product (GNP) per capita in a country. Even though the statistic does not reflect variations in distribution between countries, per capita GNP is a commonly accepted indicator of market attractiveness. These data for some major countries are presented in Table 24.4.

Three other indicators of market attractiveness are: *Natural increase* (percentage increase in population each year considering births and deaths), *life expectancy,* and *urban population* (as a percentage of total population). The market indicators are also shown in Table 24.4. Data are presented for the same countries as population statistics in Table 24.1. Data for additional countries are available from the Population Reference Bureau.[6]

PACIFIC RIM

The search for both population growth and ability to buy increasingly takes consumer analysts to the Pacific Rim. Hong Kong, Singapore, Malaysia, and South Korea have much faster population growth than Europe, and relatively high income. China and India currently have low per capita GNP but attract the interest of world marketers because of the enormousness of the population base and the rapidity of their growth. Additionally, the forecast is for substantial

---

[6] World Population Data Sheet (published annually) (Washington, D.C.: Population Reference Bureau, Inc.). Data presented in Table 24.4 are from 1987.

TABLE 24.4 MARKET DATA FOR SELECTED MAJOR COUNTRIES, 1987 Country	Natural Increase %/Yr	Life Expectancy (Years)	Urban GNP (US$)	Per Capita
United States	.7	75	74	16,400
EUROPE	*.3*	*74*	*73*	*7,280*
Austria	.0	74	55	9,150
Belgium	.0	73	95	8,450
Denmark	−.1	75	84	11,240
France	.4	75	73	9,550
West Germany	−.2	74	85	10,940
Greece	.2	74	70	3,550
Italy	.1	75	72	6,520
Luxembourg	.0	73	78	13,380
Norway	.2	76	70	13,890
Sweden	.1	77	83	11,890
United Kingdom	.2	74	90	8,390
EASTERN EUROPE	*.4*	*71*	*63*	*n.a.*
Bulgaria	.1	72	66	n.a.
Hungary	−.2	70	56	1,940
Poland	.8	71	60	2,120
OTHER DEVELOPED COUNTRIES				
Australia	.2	76	86	10,840
Canada	.8	76	76	13,670
Japan	.6	77	76	1,330
New Zealand	.8	74	84	7,310
DEVELOPING COUNTRIES				
Bangladesh	2.7	50	13	150
Brazil	2.1	65	71	1,640
China	1.3	66	32	310
Guatemala	3.2	60	39	1,240
Hong Kong	.9	75	92	6,220
India	2.1	55	25	250
Indonesia	2.1	58	22	530
Israel	2.5	67	70	2,080
Mexico	1.7	75	90	4,920
Philippines	2.8	65	40	600
Singapore	1.1	71	100	7,420
Uruguay	.8	71	85	1,660

Source: *World Population Data Sheet* (Washington, D.C.: Population Reference Bureau, Inc., 1987).

improvement in per capita GNP. We take a closer look at some of these countries later in the chapter.

FUTURE GROWTH

Where will the growth be in future markets? Using a combination of demographic factors and technological structure of economies, Bouvier estimated that global markets will be of the following types and size:

1. Service/information societies (4 percent of global population), where immigration balances low fertility to prevent population decline.

2. Industrialized nations (38 percent of population), with fertility close to or at replacement level and growth slowing.

3. Developing nations (43 percent), in sight of replacement-level fertility.

4. Least developed nations (15 percent), with still-critical demographic problems.[7]

The challenge for MNE's is to develop a portfolio of products and marketing programs that will be effective in reaching the global portfolio of markets.

CULTURAL ANALYSIS OF GLOBAL MARKETS

After the structure of markets is examined, the next major area of understanding that must be developed by consumer analysts involves **cultural analysis.** This involves the ability to understand and be effective in communicating with the core values of a society. Ethnographic analysis of marketing focuses on the interactive processes of exchange with particular attention on the subtle nuances and orderliness of the selling process.[8]

Marketing practitioners need **cultural empathy,** defined as the ability to understand the inner logic and coherence of other ways of life. Cultural empathy includes restraint not to judge the value of other ways of life. Consumer analysis focuses on "meaning systems" of consumers in a nation which are intelligible within the cultural context of that country.

Global strategies need to be adapted to meaning systems of the market rather than attempting to change the market to the customary marketing programs of the firm. This includes **inter-environmental considerations** or consideration of the characteristic ways a culture responds to marketing.[9] Examples of inter-environmental considerations are shown in *Consumer in Focus 24.2.*

Consumer analysis also focuses on **intra-environmental considerations** or the methods of marketing that are characteristic of a firm in its own culture. For example, firms in the United States typically spend about 3 percent of sales on advertising. In nations such as Australia, the advertising/sales ratio is typically between 7 and 8 percent, in Sweden about 5 percent, in Mexico a little over 5 percent, and in Canada between 4 and 5 percent.[10] Thus, a

---

[7] Leon F. Bouvier, "Planet Earth 1984–2034: A Demographic Vision," *Population Bulletin* 39 (February 1984).

[8] Robert Prus, *Pursuing Customers: An Ethnography of Marketing Activities* (Newbury Park, California: Sage Publications, 1989).

[9] Tom Griffin, "International Marketing Communication Planning — A Focus on Substructure," World Congress of the Academy of Marketing Sciences, Barcelona, 1987.

[10] Charles F. Keown, Nicolas Synodinos, Laurence Jacobs, and Reginald Worthley, "Can International Advertising Be Standardized?" World Congress of the Academy of Marketing Sciences, Barcelona, 1987. For a macroeconomic perspective on this issue, see Seymour Banks, "Cross-National Analysis of Advertising Expenditures," *Journal of Advertising Research* 26 (April/May 1986), 11–23.

24.2 CULTURAL INFLUENCES ON MARKETING

Ego, a new deodorant, was advertised in an African country with a television commercial showing a short, fumbling man failing to be successful sexually with a harem full of women. After he applied Ego deodorant, the women pulled him inside the tent and overpowered him. This ad was successful with white consumers but was totally rejected by black consumers. Do you know the reason for this difference in reaction?

In Europe, McCain Foods distributes a highly successful brand of frozen French fried potatoes. Television commercials seen in Germany show the potatoes served at the dinner table with a glass of beer nearby. If the same ad were shown in France, consumers would probably find it offensive and ineffective. Why?

Both scenarios have the same explanation. They differ only in specifics. In each case, marketers were unaware of or failed to consider the effects of specific cultures.

In the African culture, deodorant did not have the same sexual connotation for blacks as for whites. Within the black African culture, there is a belief that men who are weak are not respected. Blacks who saw the ad featuring a man being overpowered by women interpreted it to mean that using Ego deodorant made a person weak — not a very good sales appeal!

In the case of McCain Foods, an ad for food in Germany would properly include a glass of beer, but this ad would be ineffective in France, where wine is the usual drink with meals.

U.S. or Canadian firm might seriously underbudget for advertising when entering the Australian market even though developing culturally appropriate appeals in the ads. More likely, the firm might also make a mistake in the creative appeals since the type of appeals vary considerably between countries, as Table 24.5 shows.

Cultural analysis provides an approach to understanding the consumer behavior not only of diverse nations but of diverse groups within a nation. In Africa, for example, tribal cultures within countries such as Zambia, Nigeria, Zimbabwe, and South Africa may be more influential than differences that exist between countries. Many of the tribal influences cut across national boundaries established by white colonists with little regard for cultural or tribal boundaries. In Europe people to the south of Switzerland may have more cultural similarity to France than to the north of Switzerland. Cross-cultural analysis provides an approach for understanding such situations and is likely to be even more important as Europe moves toward a "single market."

CROSS-CULTURAL ANALYSIS

Cross-cultural analysis is the systematic comparison of similarities and differences in the material and behavioral aspects of cultures. Anthropologists have developed techniques to catalog similarities and differences among peoples

TABLE 24.5
CREATIVE
APPROACHES USED
IN PRINT MEDIA

		Major Differences	
Creative Approach	**Mean %***	**Countries < than average**	**Countries > than average**
Product identification	61	Australia (42%)	Sweden (82%)
Benefit awareness	51	Sweden (0%) Argentina (28%)	Denmark (74%)
Dominant photo	37	Australia (12%) Argentina (24%) Canada (24%)	Sweden (58%) Denmark (54%) Finland (50%) Mexico (48%)
Testimonial	14	Singapore (5%) Finland (5%) Britain (5%) W. Germany (6%) Brazil (8%)	Denmark (31%) Sweden (24%) Mexico (23%)
Slice of life	12	Brazil (0%) Singapore (0%) Britain (3%)	Denmark (41%) Sweden (21%)
Reminder	11	Australia (0%) Israel (0%)	
Competitive demonstration	10	Argentina (0%) Australia (0%) W. Germany (0%)	Mexico (41%) Israel (19%) Sweden (18%)
Humor	7		Britain (22%) Denmark (18%) Israel (13%)
Spokesperson	5		Sweden (15%) Canada (11%)
Animation	5		Mexico (14%) Denmark (10%)
Interview	4		Mexico (16%)
Singing message	3		Mexico (11%)
Other	8		

* Totals exceed 100% since respondents checked all approaches that were used.
Source: C. Keown, N. Synodinos, L. Jacobs, and R. Worthley, "Can International Advertising Be Standardized?" World Congress of the Academy of Marketing Sciences, Barcelona, Spain, 1987.

of various cultures. Remarkable similarities are found in the methods they use to handle common problems among societies located so far apart that they could not possibly have come into contact with each other.

Cross-cultural research methodology involves standard research tech-

TABLE 24.6 OUTLINE OF CROSS-CULTURAL ANALYSIS OF CONSUMER BEHAVIOR	*Determine Relevant Motivations in the Culture:* What needs are fulfilled with this product in the minds of members of the culture? How are these needs presently fulfilled? Do members of this culture readily recognize these needs? *Determine Characteristic Behavior Patterns:* What patterns are characteristic of purchasing behavior? What forms of division of labor exist within the family structure? How frequently are products of this type purchased? What size packages are normally purchased? Do any of these characteristic behaviors conflict with behavior expected for this product? How strongly ingrained are the behavior patterns that conflict with those needed for distribution of this product? *Determine What Broad Cultural Values Are Relevant to This Product:* Are there strong values about work, morality, religion, family relations, and so on, that relate to this product? Does this product connote attributes that are in conflict with these cultural values? Can conflicts with values be avoided by changing the product? Are there positive values in this culture with which the product might be identified? *Determine Characteristic Forms of Decision Making:* Do members of the culture display a studied approach to decisions concerning innovations or an impulsive approach? What is the form of the decision process? Upon what information sources do members of the culture rely? Do members of the culture tend to be rigid or flexible in the acceptance of new ideas? What criteria do they use in evaluating alternatives? *Evaluate Promotion Methods Appropriate to the Culture:* What roles does advertising occupy in the culture? What themes, words, or illustrations are taboo? What language problems exist in present markets that cannot be translated into this culture? What types of salesmen are accepted by members of the culture? Are such salesmen available? *Determine Appropriate Institutions for This Product in the Minds of Consumers:* What types of retailers and intermediary institutions are available? What services do these institutions offer that are expected by the consumer? What alternatives are available for obtaining services needed for the product but not offered by existing institutions? How are various types of retailers regarded by consumers? Will changes in the distribution structure be readily accepted?

niques adapted to the special requirements of different languages, structural characteristics of the societies, and values of the investigator. Cross-cultural studies in anthropology often focus upon social organization, child rearing, belief systems, and similar topics. In marketing, the elements studied are more likely to be distribution systems, beliefs about sales and pricing activities, and communications channels.

An outline for conducting cross-cultural studies from a marketing perspective is shown in Table 24.6. This outline can be used by a marketing organization to discover if unmet needs exist for which a company might adapt or develop new products. The information gathered by use of this outline also helps develop a successful marketing program to meet those needs.

Cross-cultural studies may be **descriptive** or **analytical.** Descriptive studies describe structural components and are used to contrast or compare societies.

Analytical or functional studies attempt to deduce general principles of behavior that apply in one or more cultures.[11]

Cross-cultural studies often involve collection of attitudinal data from several countries, permitting statistical description. As an example, Plummer considered the role of hygiene across cultures. It appears that Americans may be obsessed with cleanliness from the percentages found in each nation agreeing with the statement, "Everyone should use a deodorant."[12]

United States	89%
French Canada	81%
English Canada	77%
United Kingdom	71%
Italy	69%
France	59%
Australia	53%

An alternative interpretation of these data, however, might be that Americans simply need a deodorant more than do people in other countries! Or at least that Americans *believe* they need a deodorant.

CAN MARKETING BE STANDARDIZED?

Can one marketing program be used in all or at least many countries? Or must marketing programs be modified for each country? If marketing programs must be modified to each culture, firms will fail if they do not develop specific products, promotions, and organizations for each country. Enormous economies are achieved, however, if the marketing program is standardized.

Is consumer behavior subject to cultural universals? Erik Elinder answered this question affirmatively and advanced the position that advertising can be standardized.[13] Elinder's question and the validity of his answer have intrigued marketers since Elinder first raised the issue. It was a major topic addressed in the first edition of this text over 20 years ago.

The issue of standardization has become more important because of increased global competition facing marketers. The debate was intensified by

---

[11] An introduction to cross-cultural methods is R. W. Bristin, W. J. Lonner, and R. M. Thorndike, *Cross-Cultural Research Methods* (New York: John Wiley & Sons, 1973) and Walter J. Lonner and John W. Berry, *Field Methods in Cross-Cultural Research* (Beverly Hills: Sage Publications, 1986).

[12] Joseph Plummer, "Consumer Focus in Cross-National Research," *Journal of Marketing* (November 1977), 5–15.

[13] Erik Elinder, "How International Can European Advertising Be?" *Journal of Marketing* 29 (April 1965), 7–11.

a controversial article by Ted Levitt describing the globalization of the marketplace.[14]

The need for globalized marketing strategies arises not only from market characteristics but also from technological and organizational characteristics. To compete, a firm must use technology that is not limited to national borders and people operating in worldwide organizations. Measures of marketing efficiency must now include global market share, requiring firms to understand their market niche in terms of customer types, not geodemographic segments.[15] As Europe moves toward the 1992 goal of a single market, firms are increasingly defining market segments to consist of similar types of customers and cultures throughout Europe rather than groups within a specific country.

STANDARDIZATION BASED ON SIMILARITIES

Standardization should be based on a solid understanding of the similarities as well as the differences between countries. Marketing organizations want such standardization in international marketing programs.[16] A study of 27 MNEs, including companies such as General Foods, Nestle, Coca-Cola, Proctor & Gamble, Unilever, and Revlon, found that 63 percent of the total marketing programs could be rated as "highly standardized." The authors of that study describe the need for cross-cultural (or "cross-border") analysis:

> *Management of multi-nationals should give high priority to developing the ability to conduct systematic cross-border analysis, if they are not already doing so. Such analysis can help management avoid the mistake of standardizing when markets are significantly different. At the same time, systematic cross-border analysis can help avoid the mistake of excessive custom-tailoring when markets are sufficiently similar to make standardized programs feasible.[17]*

PEOPLE ARE BASICALLY THE SAME AROUND THE GLOBE   They vary in specific traits, often influenced by structural elements such as economic resources, urbanization, age of the population, and other variables. The chal-

---

[14] Theodore Levitt, "The Globalization of Markets," *Harvard Business Review* 61 (May–June 1983), 92–102. For the contrasting perspective see Yoram Wind, "The Myth of Globalization," *Journal of Consumer Marketing* 3 (Spring 1986), 23–26.

[15] James Leontiades, "Going Global — Global Strategies vs. National Strategies," *Long Range Planning* 19 (1986), 96–104.

[16] Robert D. Buzzell, "Can You Standardize Multinational Marketing?" *Harvard Business Review* 46 (November–December 1986), 102–113; Theodore Levitt, "The Globalization of Markets," *Harvard Business Review* 61 (May–June 1983), 92–102; "Multinationals Tackle Global Marketing," *Advertising Age* (June 25, 1984), 50ff. Also see "Marketers Turn Sour on Global Sales Pitch Harvard Guru Makes," *The Wall Street Journal* (May 11, 1988), 1.

[17] Ralph Z. Sorenson and Ulrich E. Wiechmann, "How Multinationals View Marketing Standardization," *Harvard Business Review* 53 (May–June 1975), 38–56. Also see William H. Davidson and Philippe Haspeslagh, "Shaping a Global Product Organization," *Harvard Business Review* 60 (July–August 1982), 125–132.

24.3 NESTLE'S GLOBAL STRATEGY

Nestle is a huge worldwide company whose historic roots put it toward decentralization on the global continuum. Because of its early international start over a hundred years ago, long before intercontinental communications and travel were improved — and when wars often disturbed Swiss control — strong local managerial authority was a way of life at Nestle. Only recently has Vevey headquarters moved toward tighter global coordination. But Nestle does it globally with its Nescafe brand, despite the fact that *what coffee* means varies according to the local culture. Do you have a tea culture like Japan? Or, like the United Kingdom, a tea culture that has also become an instant coffee culture? Or, ground coffee cultures like France, Germany, and Brazil? It's a con-

fusing and steadily changing advertising environment, but Nescafe has given it one common emotional link: "Whatever good coffee means to you and however you like to serve it, Nescafe has a coffee for you." So wherever you sell Nescafe, you sell coffee-ness. The ingredients, the appetite appeal, the warmth of the shared moment — stir the mixture to suit the context. In fact, whatever consumers want their coffee to be, that coffee is Nescafe. This broad approach overcomes cultural differences and links Nescafe advertising today in 50 countries.

Source: Gordon L. Link, "Global Advertising: An Update," *Journal of Consumer Marketing* 5 (Spring 1988), 69–74, at 72.

lenge is to build the core of the marketing strategy on the *universals* rather than on the differences.

An example of standardization based on universals would be the desire to be beautiful. In a sense, young women in Tokyo and those in Berlin are sisters not only "under the skin" but on their skin, lips, fingernails, and even in their hairstyles. Consequently, Fatt states, they are likely to buy similar cosmetics with similar appeals. If they could, Fatt believes, the women of Moscow would follow suit, and some of them do.[18] Appeals to such images as mother and child, freedom from pain, glow of health, and so forth may cut across many boundaries. Avon found, for example, that its program of selling cosmetics door to door in the United States could be extended to countries such as Japan, where affluent women with high usage of beauty products are typically still at home during the day.

THE GLOBALIZATION CONTINUUM

A realistic approach to the issue of standardization-localization is that some elements must be localized and some can be standardized. The more a marketing manager can learn about the cultures targeted, the more likely the stan-

---

[18] Arthur Fatt, "The Danger of 'Local' International Advertising," *Journal of Marketing* 31 (January 1967), 60–62.

dardized approach can be used by avoiding elements that would be ineffective in one or more of the target countries. Some firms, such as Nestle in *Consumer in Focus 24.3,* are highly decentralized. Other firms, such as Coca-Cola, are highly standardized (still maintaining variations between countries, however) and this diversity of approaches forms a continuum of effective global strategies.

Success at any part of this globalization continuum requires certain basic elements. Gordon Link describes four key rules:

1. There is no one ideal approach to global marketing and advertising. It must be tailored to the specific needs of each product category. Flexibility is the name of the game.

2. Globalization is best approached as an evolutionary process. A revolutionary approach is often too disruptive to local marketing personnel. Time and patience are of the essence. There are no overnight successes in global branding.

3. Companies can begin the process at quite different points on a broad spectrum. The process can be visualized as a continuum from left to right. On the left are companies with highly decentralized, multi-domestic operations and products. Toward the middle are companies that have increasingly centralized product and brand positionings, adapted to local differences. On the right we find the totally integrated, globally marketed and advertised brands or companies. Consider where your own company and/or its brands already fit or might find a point of entry along this broad range of possibilities.

4. Whatever the company's stage of brand development, the move toward global advertising is greatly abetted by the right kind of agency structure: This means strong local agencies working in concert with the centralized creative, account, and media management resources of a major global advertising agency.[19]

OVERCOMING LANGUAGE PROBLEMS

The ability to standardize marketing programs must conquer language problems.

General Motors used the phrase "Body by Fisher" in its marketing. Some problems occurred, however, when it was translated into Flemish and took on the meaning of "Corpse by Fisher." The phrase "Come alive with Pepsi" experienced problems when it was translated in German ads as "Come alive out of the grave," and in Chinese as "Pepsi brings your ancestors back from the grave."[20] Linguistics techniques borrowed from cross-cultural methodologies are helpful to marketers in overcoming such problems.

---

[19] Gordon L. Link, "Global Advertising: An Update," *Journal of Consumer Marketing* 5 (Spring 1988), 69–74.

[20] Kevin Lynch, "Adplomancy Faux Pas Can Ruin Sales," *Advertising Age* (January 15, 1979), S-2ff.

BACK-TRANSLATION   A useful technique for overcoming language problems is back-translation. In this procedure, a message (word or a series of words) is translated from its original language to the translated language and back to the original by a number of translators. This process may be repeated several times, with the translated versions being interchanged with the original among the translators. The purpose of the iterations is an attempt to achieve conceptual equivalency in meaning by controlling the various translation biases of translators.[21]

Marketing research questionnaires often need to be translated into additional languages. This process can be more reliable with back-translation. Sometimes, however, it is necessary to use scales other than verbal or quantitative. Figure 24.2 shows an example from Holiday Inn in which questions are given in English and Afrikaans. Responses are given with smiling or unhappy faces.

BRAND NAMES

Brand names should be evaluated from a cross-cultural perspective even when they are currently used only in domestic markets. "Thinking globally" includes considering the possibility that the brand will someday be extended to other countries, as well as making it more appealing to diverse cultures within the current country.

The steps that should be used for a cross-cultural approach, in addition to legal search, in finding an English name acceptable on a global basis include the following:

1. Does the English name of the product have another meaning, perhaps unfavorable, in one or more of the countries where it might be marketed?

2. Can the English name be pronounced everywhere? For example, Spanish and some other languages lack a *k* in their alphabets, an initial letter in many popular U.S. brand names.

3. Is the name close to that of a foreign brand, or does it duplicate another product sold in English-speaking countries?

4. If the product is distinctly American, will national pride and prejudice work against the acceptance of the product?[22]

---

[21] Richard W. Brislin, "Back-Translation for Cross-Cultural Research," *Journal of Cross-Cultural Psychology* 1 (September 1970); Oswald Werner and Donald T. Campbell, "Translating, Working Through Interpreters and the Problems of Decentering," in Raoul Naroll and Ronald Cohen, eds., *A Handbook of Method in Cultural Anthropology* (Garden City, New York: National History Press, 1970), 298–420.

[22] Walter P. Margulies, "Why Global Marketing Requires a Global Focus on Product Design," *Business Abroad* 94 (January 1969), 22.

Consumer Analysis and Marketing Strategy

Part VI provides further testimony to the importance of understanding behavior in developing sound marketing strategy. The following full-color ads, as explained by the short description accompanying each, illustrate the role of consumer analysis in developing marketing strategy and action.

Successful marketers monitor shifts in age distribution and population characteristics. This advertisement illustrates how the Frye Company seeks to satisfy the needs of the aging baby-boom generation, a large and affluent market segment.

Source: Courtesy of The Frye Company, Union, New York.

THE BMW 7-SERIES. IT BRINGS
NEW BLOOD TO A CLASS OF AUTOMOBILE
THAT CAN CERTAINLY BENEFIT FROM IT.

THE ULTIMATE DRIVING MACHINE.

The analysis of trends and demographics helps marketers develop strategies that meet changing consumer needs and wants. To position its 7-series as an alternative to other luxury cars, BMW changed the focus of its advertising from the car's performance features to lifestyle portraits of its target audience.

Source: Courtesy of BMW of North America, Inc./Ammirati & Puris Ad Agency, Copywriter: Martin Puris; Art Directors: Marcus Kemp, Clem McCarthy; Photographer: Cheryl Koralik.

Age and sex are demographic variables frequently used in market segmentation. L'eggs increased the market potential of its pantyhose line by introducing new products targeted at 2-to-11-year-old girls.

Source: Courtesy of L'eggs Products, Inc./Ad Agency: Maged & Behar, New York.

The Balinese use a flag to keep their ducks in a row, all the way to the market.

All over the island of Bali you will see neat rows of ducks following flags on a bamboo pole.

This is how the duck shepherd guides his flock to feed at the nearby rice fields.

And at dusk the ducks huddle around the flag waiting for the duck shepherd to guide them back.

So, when it comes time to sell the flock, they happily follow the flag all the way to the markets.

Bali, nestling on the edge of the warm Indian Ocean, is rich with such ancient village traditions.

And yet with all this undiscovered beauty, the hotels here rival any in the world.

When you fly here with Garuda Indonesia you will discover another of our attractions.

The people who look after you have a gentle concern for you that belongs in another world.

For information about our flights and holiday packages, call Garuda Indonesia or your travel agent.

Garuda Indonesia
Proud to welcome you aboard.

Global advertising strategies work well for products and services with universal appeal. By highlighting exotic sights on the island of Bali, Garuda Indonesia airline created an international advertising campaign for consumers in Europe and the United States.

Source: Courtesy of Garuda Indonesia, Los Angeles/Advertising Agency: Foote, Cone & Belding, Australia.

**FIGURE 24.2
CROSS-CULTURAL
QUESTIONNAIRE
FOR HOLIDAY INN**

The "Faces" game

Die „Gesiggies"speletjie

Dear guest, to round off your stay we'd like you to play a "Faces" game. Indicate the face which corresponds most closely to your own expression in each of the situations mentioned below. Please hand this in at Reception (or if you prefer, mail to the Public Relations Officer, Holiday Inns, P.O. Box 4280, Johannesburg 2000).

Beste gas, om u kuiertjie af te rond, wil ons graag hê dat u die „Gesiggies"-speletjie speel. Dui die gesiggie aan met die uitdrukking wat naaste kom aan u eie in elk van die situasies hieronder. Gee dit asseblief by Ontvangs in (of, as u verkies, pos dit aan die Skakelbeampte, Holiday Inns, Posbus 4280, Johannesburg 2000).

What was your facial reaction to the following aspects of your stay?

Wat was u gesig se reaksie op elk van die volgende aspekte van u verblyf?

Making your reservation			Bespreking
Reception desk service			Die diens by die ontvangstoonbank
Standard of room			Gehalte van die kamer
Food			Kos
Restaurant service			Restourantdiens
Bar service			Kroegdiens
Hospitality			Gasvryheid

Other remarks/Ander opmerkings

Name/Naam

Address/Adres

Room No./Kamer No.   Date/Datum

Holiday Inn stayed at/Holiday Inn verblyf in

Source: Courtesy of the South African division of Holiday Inns. Reprinted by permission.

RESEARCH METHODOLOGY FOR CROSS-CULTURAL ANALYSIS

Consumer behavior and marketing have borrowed from disciplines such as anthropology, linguistics, and sociology to obtain needed methodology for cross-cultural studies. Increasingly, the marketing literature contains reports that show how standard marketing research techniques can be used on a cross-cultural basis.

Multiattribute methodology has dominated recent consumer behavior literature, as we see in earlier chapters. Berger, Stern, and Johansson have demonstrated that it can be used across cultures in comparing American and Japanese car buyers.[23] Japanese respondents tend to answer more in intermediate ranges of the scales, whereas Americans respond more at the extreme ends of scales.

Psychographic studies are important in many domestic marketing programs. Boote demonstrated their usefulness in a cross-cultural study in the United Kingdom, Germany, and France.[24] Using an approach based upon Rokeach's instrumental value scales, Boote found the methodology (coupled with Z-Methodology factor analysis) useful in discovering substantial differences between those three countries, belying what some believe to be a homogeneous Common Market. Germans scored high on an "appearance conscious" segment, whereas the French scored high on an "outside interest" in the environment segment. The British were more directed toward home interests.

Family purchasing roles have also been studied on a cross-cultural basis by numerous researchers. Green and his colleagues reviewed many of these studies and administered questionnaires in English and other languages in major cities of the United States, France, Holland, Venezuela, and Gabon. The researchers found a substantial range in purchase roles along lines that family decision-making theory had suggested.[25]

PARTICIPANT-OBSERVER STUDIES

Participant-observer studies involve an investigator or team of investigators living in intimate contact with a culture. The investigator makes careful and comprehensive notes of observations about the culture. Data collection includes records of what is observed, interviews with "key" informants, and perhaps structured questionnaires, attitude scales, and projective tests.

---

[23] Karen A. Berger, Barbara B. Stern, and J. K. Johansson, "Strategic Implications of a Cross-Cultural Comparison of Attribute Importance: Automobiles in Japan and the United States," in *Proceedings of the American Marketing Association Educators' Conference* (Chicago: American Marketing Association, 1983), 327–332.

[24] Alfred S. Boote, "Psychographic Segmentation in Europe," *Journal of Advertising Research* 22 (December 1982), 19–25.

[25] Robert T. Green, Jean-Paul Leonardi, Jean-Louis Chandon, Isabella C. M. Cunningham, Bronis Verhage, and Alain Strazzieri, "Societal Development and Family Purchasing Roles: A Cross-National Study," *Journal of Consumer Research* 9 (March 1983), 436–442.

CONTENT ANALYSIS

Content analysis is a technique for determining the values, themes, role prescriptions, norms of behavior, and other elements of culture. Analysis is based on objective materials produced by the people of a culture in the ordinary course of events.[26] Usually the content studied is verbal in nature, such as newspaper or magazine stories. It could be derived from advertisements or any other objective material, such as art, products, or even the garbage discarded by consumers. Some of the more interesting of these approaches are described in Webb's *Unobtrusive Measures.*[27]

Content analysis is used in domestic marketing studies as well as cross-nationally, often concerned with advertising themes. Kassarjian analyzed occupational roles of blacks in America, discovering some changes in occupational roles but the continuation of many stereotypes.[28] Pollay conducted a content-analytic study of American advertising during the past 80 years. He found that American advertising has become more focused, is more forceful, and attempts fewer total value appeals.[29] One study based on content analysis, John Naisbitt's book *Megatrends,* became a best-seller.[30]

While many of the methodologies described here are not fundamentally different from routine marketing research, the consumer analyst or marketing researcher equipped for the future can be expected to understand how to conduct research on a global basis, including the specific techniques involved in cross-cultural analysis.

GLOBAL MARKETING STRATEGIES

Business without borders will not be the reality, but global relationships between MNEs will be in the future environment facing consumer analysts and marketing strategists. It is not possible here to discuss the processes and techniques for managing international marketing but instead to discuss the responsibilities that consumer analysis has in this process.[31] It is the responsibility of consumer analysts, perhaps more than other individuals in an organization, to be on the "cutting edge" of knowledge about how global markets are changing, including the inter-environmental elements as well as the intra-environmental elements.

---

[26] For details of this methodology see Bernald Berelson, *Content Analysis in Communications Research* (New York: Free Press, 1952); and Klaus Krippendorff, *Content Analysis* (Beverly Hills: Sage Publications, 1980).

[27] Eugene J. Webb et al., *Unobtrusive Measures* (Chicago: Rand McNally, 1966).

[28] Harold H. Kassarjian, "The Negro and American Advertising, 1946–1965," *Journal of Marketing* 6 (February 1969), 29–39.

[29] Richard W. Pollay, "The Identification and Distribution of Values Manifest in Print Advertising 1900–1980," in Robert E. Pitts, Jr. and Arch G. Woodside, eds., *Personal Values and Consumer Psychology* (Lexington, Massachusetts: Lexington Books, 1984), 111–135.

[30] John Naisbitt, *Megatrends* (New York: Warner Books, 1982).

[31] For such information see Michael R. Czinkota and Ilkka A. Ronkainen, *International Marketing* (Chicago: Dryden Press, 1988).

FIGURE 24.3
INTERNATIONAL
GESTURE
DICTIONARY

International Gesture Dictionary

Gestures Using the Face

Eyebrow Raise: In Tonga, a gesture meaning "yes" or "I agree." In Peru, means "money" or "Pay me."

Blink: In Taiwan, blinking the eyes at someone is considered impolite.

Wink: Winking at women, even to express friendship, is considered improper in Australia.

Eyelid Pull: In Europe and some Latin American countries, means "Be alert" or "I am alert."

Ear Flick: In Italy, signifies that a nearby gentleman is effeminate.

Ear Grasp: Grasping one's ears is a sign of repentance or sincerity in India. A similar gesture in Brazil—holding the lobe of one's ear between thumb and forefinger—signifies appreciation.

Nose Circle: The classic American "okay" sign—the fingers circle—is placed over the nose in Colombia to signify that the person in question is homosexual.

Nose Tap: In Britain, secrecy or confidentiality. In Italy, a friendly warning.

Nose Thumb: One of Europe's most widely known gestures, signifying mockery. May be done double-handed for greater effect.

Nose Wiggle: In Puerto Rico, "What's going on?"

Cheek Screw: Primarily an Italian gesture of praise.

Cheek Stroke: In Greece, Italy, and Spain, means "attractive." In Yugoslavia, "success." Elsewhere, it can mean "ill" or "thin."

Source: Reprinted from the book "Do's and Taboos Around the World — A Guide to International Gift-Giving" published by Parker Pen U.S.A. Limited. To obtain a copy of the complete book contact John Wiley and Sons, Inc., 608 Third Ave., New York, New York 10158.

What are some of the specifics of how consumer analysts and their knowledge of cultural aspects can benefit an organization? Look at Figure 24.3, which displays the meaning of some common gestures. After you have read each one, ask yourself if this is the meaning you intend to communicate when you are in that country.

Network marketing is increasingly global. News reports indicate that corporate alliances between firms in different countries increased 47 percent *annually* during the past decade, and a survey of U.S.-based companies reported some 12,000 in which American firms owned 10 to 50 percent equity position in a foreign firm.[32] These networks are required for access to markets as

---

[32] "Business Without Borders," *U.S. News & World Report* 104 (June 20, 1988), 48–53.

well as resources. Such alliances may be essential for global dominance. This was apparently the motivation in an alliance between Du Pont, the largest American chemical firm, and Phillips, the largest Dutch electronics firm, but they needed each other in a joint venture to develop optical-disc products expected to be a $4 billion market by 1990. In centrally planned economies such as China, a local partner may be legally required to do business in the alien system.

In this final section of the chapter, we briefly spotlight some of the opportunities for consumer analysts seeking growth opportunities for organizations that are increasingly global in their operations.

CONSUMER BEHAVIOR IN DEVELOPING COUNTRIES

Population is growing rapidly in Africa, some Asian countries, and in Latin America. But most also have low income. Great care must therefore be used to design effective marketing strategies for developing countries.

What are the most important attributes of the developing countries? Youthfulness is one, specifically a large number of babies. In some developing countries, women bear seven or eight children. Infant mortality is high. The ten countries with the highest birth rates in the world (in order) are Kenya, Pakistan, Saudi Arabia, Egypt, the Philippines, Peru, South Africa, India, Venezuela, and Brazil.

Most developing countries are predominantly rural. In spite of the rural nature, consumers are usually dependent upon other countries for food supplies. Often other countries are also responsible for educating the nation's youth.

Observe how Johnson & Johnson has positioned its marketing strategy in Figure 24.4 for the African market. The photograph communicates the love and concern of a mother for her baby without the need for words. The copy, however, features an economy appeal by saving 20 cents. Additionally, however, Johnson & Johnson has positioned itself as concerned about all children in the culture by donating 20 cents to the Child Welfare Fund with each purchase. Figure 24.4 provides a useful example of effective strategy based upon an understanding of the economic and cultural realities of the African market.

Cultural sensitivity is especially needed in developing countries because pictures may be much more important than words. As an example, one marketer attempted to export his firm's detergent to a Middle Eastern country. Advertising for the detergent featured dirty clothes piled on the left and clean clothes stacked on the right. Reading right to left, as consumers in the Middle East frequently do, the message was clear: Soap soiled the clothes.

CONSUMER BEHAVIOR IN THE PACIFIC RIM

The Pacific Rim provides some of the most attractive markets for growth-oriented marketing strategies. The area includes many low-income but fast-growing population bases in Southeast Asia, as well as some of the most

FIGURE 24.4
ADVERTISING
APPEALS BASED ON
AFRICAN CULTURE

Source: Johnson & Johnson Company, Africa.

affluent markets in the world, such as Japan, Singapore, and Australia. (Refer to Tables 24.1 and 24.4.) Because of their importance, China and Japan will be examined in separate sections.

INDIA   As a country projected to become the largest in the world, India is attracting worldwide interest among marketers. Although poor by western standards, the attractiveness of India is based upon its infrastructure, well-developed legal system, and large numbers of well-educated doctors, engineers, and others needed for growth of a thriving middle class.

The middle class is the key to understanding India's consumer markets. Although the government does not publish statistics on this politically sensitive subject, some economists estimate the number at 7 to 12 percent of the population or a market range from 60 million to 100 million, larger, for example, than that of West Germany and France.[33] Consequently, the demand for consumer goods is rising rapidly. Yearly car sales have tripled since 1980, sales of motorbikes and scooters have more than tripled in recent years,

[33] Anthony Spaeth, "A Thriving Middle Class Is Changing the Face of India," *The Wall Street Journal* (May 19, 1988), 22.

and production of consumer durables in general is rising at the rate of 20 percent annually. Movie theaters have doubled in the past decade. The middle-class family with a yearly income of about $1,400 does not live in luxury but may be buying a television, a radio, appliances such as an electric iron, clocks, and so forth, with a respectable wardrobe of shoes, jewelry, and silk saris.[34] There are more than 14 million television sets in middle-class homes. Consumer purchases are often deliberate, with the wife acting as information gatherer but with long discussions and interaction about the best choice.[35]

SOUTH KOREA   Ability to buy has increased at an astounding rate in South Korea. Annual per capita GNP soared from $120 in 1965 to $2,150 in 1988. Private consumption in recent years has been growing at an annual rate of 5.5 percent. Soaring income and plummeting birth rates (from 5.4 lifetime births in the 1960s to 2.2 in 1988), good health care, a high regard for religious values, and a young, increasingly well-educated population give South Korea many strengths upon which to build.

A key element in the success of Korea has been export capabilities, strongly assisted by governmental policies. The most successful auto ever to be imported into the North American market is Hyundai, first in Canada and later in the United States. Consumers in North America might not have heard of Korean firms such as Daewoo, a massive industrial firm, but their recent ads in the United States designed to correct that situation appear to have done so.[36] For an example, see Figure 24.5.

AUSTRALIA   Australia is a market similar in characteristics to European and North American markets. High income, an older population, and fewer basics are characteristics shared with other industrialized economies.[37]

Australia has a well-developed infrastructure and plenty of room to grow. At one time, immigration was mostly European, but in recent years nearly 50 percent of immigration has been Asian. Marketers find the nation attractive because it also has a well-developed advertising and marketing research support system and, as sailing enthusiasts and *Crocodile Dundee* fans both can attest, the influence of Australia on the rest of the world is considerable.

CHINA   China is the largest nation in the world. The pent-up demand of a billion consumers excites marketers all over the world. In the past, most of China's imports have been industrial goods, but new government priorities caused marketers to begin to consider the potential for consumer markets,

---

[34] Spaeth, "A Thriving Middle Class Is Changing the Face of India."

[35] K. Ambarish Kumar and C. P. Rao, "Problems of Researching Household Consumer Behavior in India," World Congress of the Academy of Marketing Sciences, Barcelona, 1987.

[36] Inder Khera, "The Broadening Base of U.S. Consumer Acceptance of Korean Products," World Congress of the Academy of Marketing Science, Barcelona, 1987.

[37] Grame Hugo, *Australia's Changing Population: Trends and Implications* (Oxford: Oxford University Press, 1987).

FIGURE 24.5
ADVERTISING FOR A
MAJOR SOUTH
KOREAN FIRM

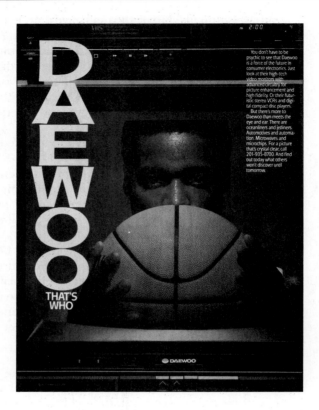

at least prior to the political instabilities and tragic demonstrations that occurred in 1989.

Private consumption makes up 70 percent of all final demand in China,
so that when consumers increase their demand for food, this initially puts
money in the pockets of agriculture. Suppliers to agriculture and food manufacturers then place orders with their suppliers, and the demand for any
consumer good multiplies throughout the economy. While most of the demand
in China for imports from other nations will be producer goods for many
years, the internal demand for consumer goods is so high that joint ventures
to produce them may present substantial opportunities for foreign marketers
to provide as well a broad range of industrial goods related to the production
of consumer goods.[38] This process is expected to double per capita consump-

---

[38] Jeffrey R. Taylor and Karen A. Hardee, *Consumer Demand in China* (Boulder: Westview Press,
1986).

tion by the year 2000. If government policies favoring market incentives continue, a growth in the 4.7 to 5.0 percent range is projected by the World Bank.

What do Chinese consumers want to buy most? Refrigerators top the list in a study made in two of China's largest cities, Beijing (with a population of 9.5 million) and Guyangzhou (with a population of 7 million).[39] Washing machines are equally wanted, although television sets are the electrical appliance most often owned. Chinese consumers are also interested in cameras and radio/cassette recorders, according to the study. With the results of the sixth Five-Year Plan producing an increase of salaries of urban workers by 68 percent and farmers by 109 percent, many more are now able to consider a broader array of consumer goods.[40]

Proctor & Gamble entered into a joint venture with three China-based organizations in 1988 to produce and sell dishwashing detergents, shampoo, bath foam, and other personal care products in China. Until then, P & G sold small quantities of their products through "friendship stores," which exist mostly to serve foreign visitors. The joint venture included provisions for manufacturing the products in China.

The shift toward deregulation and more of a market-driven system is producing enormous change and conflict in China. There are major issues about the proper role of marketing activities however.[41]

JAPAN   Japan is smaller in land area than California, and smaller in population than other nations. Yet its 123 million people consume more goods and services than every other country in the world, except one. The population of Japan is also aging more rapidly than in any other country.

Land is perhaps the most scarce and valuable resource in Japan. Japan also lacks petroleum and other natural resources. Japan's major assets are its culture and its people, which have both contributed to the development of its powerhouse economy.

Opportunities for non-Japanese firms will increase in the future perhaps as never before because of the emphatic shift in the Japanese economy to consumer goods. Wealth and economic power have been accumulated by efforts to stimulate export of goods, but a combination of accumulated affluence, world pressure to encourage more imports by Japan, and the relative inefficiency of consumer goods distributed in Japan is creating the opportunity for European and North American consumer goods firms to export more

---

[39] Doris L. Walsh, "Refrigerators Top List in China," *American Demographics* 9 (October 1986), 49.
[40] Jerry Stafford, "Vast China Market Just Waiting to Be Researched," *Marketing News* 20 (September 12, 1986), 1.
[41] Richard Semenik, Nan Zhou, and William Moore, "Chinese Managers' Attitude Toward Advertising in China," *Journal of Advertising* 15 (1986).

to Japan in the future. Space does not permit close examination of the Japanese market. Japanese culture has received widespread distribution in other places.[42] We can only look at how advertising is affected by consumer behavior in Japan.

Japanese Advertising.   The purpose of advertising is the same in Japan as it is in the West — to stimulate consumption. In Japan, however, one tries not to upset people. Outspoken opinions are not welcome. Advertising reflects a concern for harmony to the extent that Westerners often fail to understand the message of a particular advertisement. The underlying desire in the advertisement is to please the customer. Rather than pushing for a sale, the underlying idea is that the more the advertisement pleases customers, the more likely it is to move the product.

Japanese consumers react more to beautiful background scenery, a star of the entertainment world, or the development of a story than to product recommendations. Japanese viewers dislike garrulous and argumentative sales talk. Product information should be short and conveyed with a song that sets a mood. The great majority of Japanese TV commercials are directed toward affective rather than cognitive components of attitude. This is an important point for foreign manufacturers more accustomed to the American hard-sell advertisements. Japanese advertising is more likely to develop a story, describe the expression of people, and enhance poetically the mood of the product. The product message comes at the end of the commercial, almost as an afterthought to the rest of the commercial.

Commercials in Japan constructed around a comparison of products are virtually nonexistent. Commercial practices are based, at least at the visible level, on the principle of respect for one another. Attacking and putting down a rival openly is scrupulously avoided. Comparative advertising is not permitted by the Advertising Code, which explains, "Let us avoid slandering, defaming and attacking others."[43] Marketing programs in Japan are strongly influenced by Confucianism, which places high value on self-esteem, reciprocity, and harmony. Rudeness is intolerable even to the point that polite lies are acceptable rather than the expression of contradictory opinions. From Buddhism, values are also derived leading to a need for simplicity and a dominant aesthetic sense as well as loyalty and satisfaction in interpersonal relationships.[44]

---

[42] The classic book to understand Japanese culture for business persons is probably William Ouchi, *Theory Z* (New York: Addison-Wesley, 1981).

[43] This section abstracted from Dentsu Incorporated, *Marketing Opportunity in Japan* (London: McGraw-Hill, 1978), 84–114. Dentsu is one of the largest advertising agencies in the world.

[44] Walter A. Henry, "Impact of Cultural Value Systems on Japanese Distribution Systems," in Robert E. Pitts, Jr., and Arch G. Woodside, *Personal Values and Consumer Psychology* (Lexington, Massachusetts: Lexington Books, 1984), 255–270.

USSR AND OTHER COMMUNIST MARKETS

The Union of Soviet Socialist Republics is one of the most exciting markets in the world. It is a huge market, industrially developed, and with enough spending power to represent one of the great growth markets of the future. The "iffy" part of the market is whether or not that spending power will be mostly directed toward industrial and defense goods or whether consumer goods and services will become significantly more important.

The change in direction, if it truly happens, is directly associated with changes in policy advocated by Mikhail Gorbachev and his advocacy of *glasnost* and *perestroika* — the opening up of the society.[45] His plan to restructure the economy places much more emphasis on market-directed production — and it is clear that consumers desire to direct that production toward more consumer goods. People will be motivated to earn more by working harder and smarter. Business decisions will be made in response to market demand and profit prospects.

The market structure of the USSR is complicated. There are two, or more, Russias. European Russia has, up to this point, provided the majority of the population but will become a minority because of the tremendous rise in the Moslem republics of Central Asia and their high birth rates. In the USSR and most Eastern European countries, a high proportion of women is employed in the labor force, often in the professions. That fact, and the traditional system of labor-intensive distribution (reflecting a political philosophy that emphasizes labor rather than capital), has created a massive demand for labor-saving appliances and services. Shopping is often an arduous and time-consuming activity. Shortages and high prices are characteristics of the buying environment. Coffee has gone from $3 a pound to $15. Toilet paper is chronically in short supply, requiring consumers to use substitutes such as newspaper ripped in square pieces. Laundry soap has virtually disappeared except for a few luxury brands.[46]

About 65 percent of Soviet households have a refrigerator, 55 percent have a washing machine, 38 percent have a television, and 40 percent have a radio.[47] With one of the lowest ownership levels of refrigerators of any country in the world, and one of the most advanced technological capacities, significant opportunities exist for growth in joint ventures and other market development strategies for firms from other countries.

The receptivity to Western marketing techniques appears to be substantial. In 1988, Russian television began carrying commercials on an experimental basis, with the first companies in line Sony, Pepsi (featuring Michael Jackson, of course), and MasterCard. Perhaps one of the most revolutionary marketing

---

[45] Mikhail Gorbachev, *Perestroika: New Thinking for Our Country and the World* (New York: Harper & Row, 1988).

[46] "Why the Bear's Cupboards Are Bare," *Time* (January 16, 1989), 33–36.

[47] *Trends and Opportunities Abroad, 1988,* 190.

24.4 SOVIET PUZZLED BY U.S. AD TECHNIQUES

A Soviet public relations executive tried to get a handle on U.S. promotional techniques during a recent visit to this country.

First, he wanted to know why Americans have different beers for different times of the day. The official explained that he had seen an ad on U.S. television where people were expected to drink Michelob beer at night. And another thing, he asked: "Why is K Mart America's favorite store?"

Any advertising or public relations effort in the Soviet Union is "done very slowly, with much care and deliberation," he said. He described the American media as fast, colorful and timely. "There is much to learn about the methods here," he said. "In our country, it isn't so important to explain everything."

The official said interest in public relations methodology is increasing in the Soviet Union because the country, under Communist Party leader Mikhail Gorbachev, is taking a hard look at its traditions. "We have not only successes, we have mistakes," he said. "There is a need for us to explain our mistakes in history and modern life. There is the need to understand truths."

Source: Excerpted from *Marketing News* (April 11, 1988), 26.

actions was to begin the issue of bank credit cards, such as MasterCard, to Soviet citizens — and as consumer analysts know, that opens the door to a lot more activity. Read *Consumer in Focus 24.4*, however, to understand some of the problems of communications that exist when Western marketing techniques are transferred to the Russian market.

Other Eastern European economies are opening up for trade with the rest of the world. Hungary's "goulash communism" has been among the most receptive, especially for tourism and other markets that bring hard currency. Poland has suffered from sweeping price hikes, and in Romania, electricity is sometimes on for only a few hours a day. *Glasnost* has stimulated interest in many of the countries in consumer behavior and more market-oriented strategies.

EUROPEAN SINGLE MARKET

The European Community, formerly called the Common Market, set 1992 as the year when its 12 members become a free internal market. People, money, and goods are supposed to move across borders without passports, exchange controls, or customs. If this is accomplished, Europe may be a larger "single" market than the United States.

European factories are scheduled to become more efficient as a result of 1992 reforms. Consumer prices are expected to fall. As Europeans can open bank accounts and buy products sold and used throughout Europe, markets are expected to become more dynamic. A total of 320 million people are expected to purchase $4 trillion of goods and services. The result is expected to be:

— greater efficiencies and greater economic growth for Europe

— tougher competition in the EC, as companies take a Europe-wide approach to marketing

— harmonizing business regulations and eliminating national nontariff barriers will lower costs and increase internal EC trade.[48]

TOTAL MARKET GROWTH

The purpose of consumer analysis of global markets is to find opportunities for marketers to grow. Growth requires a total market perspective — on population, ability to buy, product development, channels of distribution systems, and consumer decision making and other variables.

The fastest growth in recent years provides clues to the future. For U.S. firms, the fastest-growing export product categories have been motion pictures, and phono and tape recordings, with 72.4 percent growth between 1983 and 1987. Other fast-growing categories include paper-making materials, data processing and office machines, aircraft and spacecraft, and electrical machinery equipment. The fastest growth markets (over $3 billion in total sales) for U.S. companies included Taiwan, PRC, Mexico, Canada, Brazil, Hong Kong, Italy, Australia, West Germany, and South Korea.[49] The opportunities for the future will be identified with the variables you have learned in this chapter.

Summary

Analysts of consumer behavior must be able to understand consumption decisions on a global basis if they are to be prepared for the contemporary world and the emerging future. Population growth is slowing so rapidly in industrialized countries that consumer analysts must find and understand the cultures of new markets that have both population vitality and ability.

The fastest-growing country in the world population is India. African countries such as Kenya and Nigeria have rapid population growth, but India is considered more attractive as a market. Not only is India projected to become the largest country in the world but it is also expected to have perhaps as many as 100 million middle-class families that can buy a wide range of consumer products.

---

[48] C. William Verity, "U.S. Business Needs to Prepare Now for Europe's Single Internal Market," *Business America* 109 (August 1, 1988), 2–6.

[49] Joel Kotkin, "Hot Spots," *Inc.'s Guide to International Business* (New York: INC., 1988), 40–44.

Cross-cultural analysis is the systematic comparison of similarities and differences in the behavioral and physical aspects of cultures. Cross-cultural analysis provides an approach to understanding market segments both across national boundaries and between groups within a society. The process of analyzing markets on a cross-cultural basis is particularly helpful in deciding which elements of a marketing program can be standardized in multiple nations and which elements must be localized.[50]

REVIEW AND DISCUSSION QUESTIONS

1. Is it really necessary to "think globally" in the study of consumer behavior? Why?
2. Which countries of the world will provide the best consumer markets in the next 5 to 10 years? In the next 10 to 30 years? Why?
3. How do you reconcile the belief that India represents an attractive market when Table 24.4 reports such a low per capita GNP?
4. Assume that a soft drink marketer wanted to enter the Russian market. Prepare a set of recommendations for doing so.
5. Assume that a manufacturer of shoes wishes a market analysis on how to enter the most profitable markets in Africa. What should be included in the report?
6. Assume that a French manufacturer of women's apparel is seeking to expand markets by exporting to Canda or the United States. What would you recommend for maximum effectiveness?
7. What is meant by the term *cross-cultural analysis?* Why is it important for marketers?
8. What is meant by *perestroika?* Why is it significant to marketing analysts?

---

[50] For an in-depth description of what can go wrong in global market situations see David Ricks, *Big Business Blunders: Mistakes in Multinational Marketing* (Homewood, Illinois: Dow Jones-Irwin, 1983). A valuable guide to avoiding global blunders is Vern Terpstra and Kenneth David, *The Cultural Environment of International Business* (Cincinnati: South-Western Publishing, 1985).

**ENVIRONMENTAL
INFLUENCES**
Culture
Social Class
Personal Influence
Family
Situation

**INDIVIDUAL
DIFFERENCES**
Consumer Resources
Motivation & Involvement
Knowledge
Attitudes
Personality, Lifestyle,
Demographics

DECISION PROCESS
Need Recognition
▼
Search for Information
▼
Alternative Evaluation
▼
Purchase
▼
Outcomes

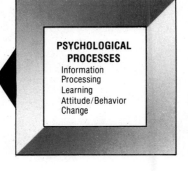

**PSYCHOLOGICAL
PROCESSES**
Information
Processing
Learning
Attitude/Behavior
Change

**MARKETING
STRATEGY**
Product
Price
Promotion
Distribution

EPILOGUE

N o study of consumer behavior would be complete without careful reflection from the broader perspective of consumer rights and interests. Chapter 25 looks at four basic consumer rights: (1) safety; (2) information; (3) choice; and (4) redress. These must be guaranteed and affirmed by an economic system that takes consumer interests seriously.

There are many implications. We challenge you to think seriously about your own sense of ethics and moral values. The choice you make can have far-reaching implications.

CONSUMERISM AND SOCIAL RESPONSIBILITY

BACK TO THE BASICS

n November 1986, as the company was preparing to enter its sesquicentennial year, Proctor & Gamble employees gathered at the Cincinnati Coliseum. President John E. Pepper introduced to them a formally adopted Statement of Purpose.

The first paragraph: "We'll provide products of superior quality and value that best fill the needs of the world's consumers." As Mr. Pepper put it, "When we're doing that, when we're really providing superior quality and superior value, then we don't have problem brands. If we have a problem brand, it's because of our failure to live up to this position."

The second paragraph begins and ends: "We will achieve that purpose through an organization and working environment which . . . maintains the company's historic principles of integrity and doing the right thing."

"When you have a problem brand that's not achieving the degree or share and profit progress we'd like, then," Mr. Pepper alleges, "what's usually at the root of it is you are not doing right—or as right as you need to be—by the consumer. You are not offering a competitive advantage to the consumer . . . [Or] you are not communicating [a benefit] well enough. . . . or you have a pricing—a value—issue."

In most cases, he believes, "The key to improving [it] gets right back to the fundamentals: knowing the consumer better, what they want; delivering that better than competition; communicating that . . . in our advertising . . . [and] having a competitive price."

Source: Larry Edwards, "Back to Basics," *Advertising Age* (August 20, 1987), 1ff. Reproduced by special permission.

In the past several decades, a social movement has arisen to ensure that the voice of the consumer is heard and responded to. This has become known as **consumerism,** defined here as policies and activities designed to protect consumer interests and rights as they are involved in an exchange relationship with any type of organization.

This definition is deliberately all-encompassing, following the lead of Aaker and Day,[1] to reflect the fact that the consumer receives exchanges from many organizations other than businesses. Hospitals, libraries, and governmental agencies are examples. According to former Illinois Senator Charles H. Percy, also an ex-president of Bell & Howell, consumerism, in the final analysis, "is a broad public reaction against bureaucratic neglect and corporate disregard of the public."[2]

Our concern in this chapter lies with business's social responsibility to the consumer. As Robin and Reidenbach put it, there is a social contract between business and society. Inherent within this contract is the responsibility to take seriously a set of " 'generally accepted relationships, obligations and duties' that relate to the corporate impact on the welfare of society."[3]

The late United States President John F. Kennedy enumerated four basic consumer rights that have been generally accepted as lying at the heart of this social contract:

1. The right to safety
2. The right to be informed
3. The right to choose
4. The right to be heard (redress)

Two more have been added by social consensus in the ensuing decades, making a total of six:

5. The right to enjoy a clean and healthful environment
6. The right of the poor and other minorities to have their interests protected

Although such eminent management authorities as Peter Drucker[4] have long stressed the centrality of social responsibility, most evidence indicates that this is usually not a primary consideration in business policy.[5] Fortunately,

---

[1] David A. Aaker and George S. Day, *Consumerism: Search for the Consumer Interest,* 2nd ed. (New York: Free Press, 1974), 17.

[2] Quoted in William T. Kelly, *New Consumerism: Selected Readings* (Columbus, Ohio: Grid Publishing, 1973), 2.

[3] Donald P. Robin and R. Eric Reidenbach, "Social Responsibility, Ethics, and Marketing Strategy: Closing the Gap Between Concept and Application," *Journal of Marketing* 51 (January 1987), 44–58.

[4] See Peter F. Drucker, *An Introductory View of Management* (New York: Harper & Row, 1977), Part Four.

[5] William F. Glueck, *Business Policy and Strategic Management,* 3rd ed. (New York: McGraw-Hill, 1980), 87.

there are firms such as Proctor & Gamble which, as you have seen, are refreshing exceptions.

It is the purpose of this chapter, first of all, to give an overview of the historical and sociological context in which consumerism has arisen. Only then is it possible to fully grasp its contemporary significance. Then we discuss the basic dimensions of a proper organizational response to consumer interests. The subject of corporate and individual ethics is basic in this context.

THE DEVELOPMENT OF CONSUMERISM

Consumerism has roots reaching far beyond the last two decades, when this name was assigned to the activities of such well-known leaders as Ralph Nader. The Bible, especially the Book of Proverbs, has many references to deceptive and irresponsible business practices. In their time, Thomas Aquinas, Martin Luther, John Calvin, and other reformers also represented a kind of consumerism. Specific attacks were made on deceptive selling practices. The concept of "just price," for example, was put forth as a contrast to pricing based on what the market would bear.[6]

A historical analysis reveals that consumerism increases most sharply when an era of rapidly rising income is followed by decrease in real purchasing power coming from rising prices.[7] In addition, the environment must be conducive to the rise of leadership for the movement, which normally centers among those with greater-than-average wealth and income.

Alienation is a major triggering factor.[8] It arises when the basic causes fueling consumer discontent are not dealt with satisfactorily or relief is only transitory. Feelings of powerlessness, alienation, and isolation lead to essentially defensive responses in the forms of boycotts, pressures for legislation, and so on.

The socially conscious consumer is usually an activist on many fronts, such as women's rights and politics.[9] Interestingly, it has been found that consumerists tend to enjoy shopping less than the average person does, are less exposed to broadcast media but more exposed to national and international sections of newspapers, consider themselves to be opinion leaders in many areas of life, and express high interest on a variety of other social issues.[10]

The rise and fall of consumerism pressures throughout history may be

---

[6] Leon Garry, "Consumerism Began with Cyrus of Persia," *Business and Society Review* (Winter 1972–1973), 62–64.

[7] Robert O. Herrman, "Consumerism: Its Goals, Organizations and Future," *Journal of Marketing* 35 (October 1970), 55–60.

[8] W. Thomas Anderson, Jr., and William H. Cunningham, "The Socially Conscious Consumer," *Journal of Marketing* 37 (July 1972), 23–31.

[9] Jacques C. Bourgeois and James G. Barnes, "Viability and Profile of the Consumerist Segment," *Journal of Consumer Research* 6 (March 1979), 217–228.

[10] Bourgeois and Barnes, "Viability and Profile."

explained by the theory of diffusion of innovations discussed in Chapter 23. Hendon contends that the innovation (consumerism) moves through phases of introduction (initial impact) and widespread acceptance of regulatory and remedial actions that quiet things down until the cycle begins again.[11] Therefore, it is possible to predict the likely path of such social movements, avoiding seemingly inevitable confrontations and social disruptions.

As we briefly summarize the history of consumerism since the early 1900s,[12] do not fail to grasp the essential lesson: Consumerism arises because of the failure of business or other organizations in the exchange relationship to meet and respond to legitimate consumer demands. Socially responsive business practice could have anticipated these movements and responded before alienation became widespread. Unfortunately, however, one basic law of history seems to be that its lessons are not heeded until it is too late.[13]

THE EARLY 1900s

Consumer activism in the early part of this century resulted in genuine progress in protective legislation before it gradually subsided. Upton Sinclair published *The Jungle* in 1906, exposing the filth surrounding the Chicago meat-packing industry. It created such substantial public outcry that Congress was compelled to act, even though it failed to enact pure food legislation in the 1890s and again in 1902.

The Meat Inspection Act was passed in 1906 to meet the specific issues Sinclair raised, and the Pure Food and Drug Act was passed in that same year. It created the Food and Drug Administration, an agency charged with preventing the appearance of misbranded and adulterated food and drugs in interstate commerce.

A few years later, in 1914, the Federal Trade Commission (FTC) was established to curb monopoly and trade practices that have the potential to be unfair to competitive businesses. The business community, however, remained largely indifferent to consumer protection, as it has throughout much of history, and the consumer movement gradually abated and remained quiescent until the 1930s.

THE 1930s

New and unfamiliar consumer products flooded the market during the buoyant years of the 1920s. Consumers, in turn, were deluged by ads in that new phenomenon, radio, as well as in rapidly burgeoning consumer magazines.

The consumerism fires were lit upon publication of *Your Money's Worth*

---

[11] Donald Hendon, "Toward a Theory of Consumerism," *Business Horizons* (August 1975), 16–24.

[12] For more details on the history of consumerism, see Joel R. Evans, *Consumerism in the United States: An Interindustry Analysis* (New York: Praeger, 1980).

[13] For a sobering analysis on this point see Will and Ariel Durant, *The Lessons of History* (New York: Simon and Schuster, 1968).

by Stuart Chase and J. J. Schlink. The book attacked alleged manipulation and deceit in advertising practices. It called for scientific testing and publication of product standards to provide consumer information for use in making wise decisions. This resulted in the foundation of Consumer's Research Incorporated, which was the forerunner of today's Consumer's Union, publishers of *Consumer's Reports.*

The stock market crash of 1929 forestalled a widespread consumer movement. Instead, efforts were focused mostly on consumer education. Budgeting and money management were the subjects emphasized to help the consumer identify the best buys at lowest cost.

There was considerable regulatory activity, however, triggered, at least in part, by Schlink and Kallet's book entitled *100,000,000 Guinea Pigs.* The authors pointed to loopholes in the 1906 Pure Food and Drug Act that allowed consumers to be forced into the role of guinea pigs as they purchased dangerous medications, unsafe cosmetics, and adulterated foods. Further outcry was generated by the sulfanilamide scandal of 1937, which led to 107 deaths. A new Food, Drug, and Cosmetic Act was passed in 1938, but many were dissatisfied, claiming that it had been emasculated after years of hearings and controversy.

A major step forward was passage of the Wheeler-Lea amendment to the Federal Trade Commission Act in 1938. Under this act the FTC became a consumer watchdog rather than just a regulator. In particular, it was empowered to prosecute unlawful, deceptive, or unfair trade practices.

There is no question that consumerism pressures grew in the late 1930s. The eyes of business leaders were opened by a Gallup survey indicating that the consumerism movement was likely to increase. World War II, however, diverted national attention away from these issues.

THE 1960s

The current consumerism movement really had its foundation in the 1960s, although the earlier decades were antecedents. Once again, an influential book served as a trigger. This time it was *The Hidden Persuaders* by Vance Packard, published in 1957. Delving into motivation research, which had begun about this time, Packard argued that the consumer was being manipulated largely unconsciously by advertising. The reaction to this book revealed that public interest in consumer problems had not abated but had taken a more sophisticated form.

The problem of drug safety continued as a pertinent issue just as it had been in prior eras. Senator Estes Kefauver's Antitrust and Monopoly Subcommittee launched investigations into the prescription drug industry in 1959, which heightened public awareness and concern. The thalidomide scandal finally triggered public reaction that resulted in passage of tougher testing standards in the Kefauver-Harris Amendment to the Food, Drug, and Cosmetic Act.

The so-called **new consumerism** (i.e., consumerism as it is known today) generally is attributed to President John F. Kennedy's message to Congress on March 15, 1962, in which he put forth the consumer bill of rights listed at the beginning of this chapter. Kennedy was explicit that government is the ultimate guarantor of these rights and hence built the foundation for much of the role federal consumerism plays today.

Other well-known issue advocates galvanized a movement that was to have many facets: women's liberation, Gray Panthers, and so on. Ralph Nader was one major catalyst with his book on the automobile industry, *Unsafe at Any Speed*. Rachael Carson polarized the pollution issue with *Silent Spring*. And these are only two examples from a large group.

Government took Kennedy seriously and began an activist role. False and misleading advertising was a major target of the FTC, leading to the onset of corrective advertising discussed later. Product safety became a major issue, especially in the automobile industry, which became characterized by government-ordered recalls. Products were withdrawn from the market because of pollution and public health danger — DDT being a leading example.

THE 1980s

History often records a moderating trend or pendulum swing after a period of extensive activism. Many came to feel that governmental regulation was more of a hindrance than a help. This conservatism was expressed in the election of both Jimmy Carter and Ronald Reagan, although it was to achieve its full expression under the latter president. The outcome was substantial deregulation in many industries, or, more precisely, a return to reliance on regulation by the marketplace through its own corrective influences.

This new climate resulted in deregulation of the airline and other industries. The Federal Trade Commission experienced a sharp reduction in its budget and influence. And there were a number of statements such as, "Parents, not government, should control the television viewing of their children." The outcome was a much lower profile at all levels of government, from federal to local.

One should not assume, however, that consumerism concerns have abated, for that is not the case. A major study by Lewis Harris and Associates revealed that the public is even more concerned today than previously, but few are taking any kind of activist role.[14] The greatest worries are high prices and interest rates, low product quality, and deficient after-sale service. About 60 percent of respondents, for example, felt that the quality of most products and services has deteriorated.

The consumer protection activities of federal and state agencies and private industry are held in low esteem, in contrast to the favorable evaluation of such agencies as Consumer's Union and Better Business Bureaus.[15] It is inter-

---

[14] Lewis Harris and Associates, Inc., "Consumerism in the Eighties" (Study Number 822047, 1983).

[15] Harris, "Consumerism in the Eighties."

esting, however, that the consumer movement and its impact is far better evaluated than its leadership. There is no public sentiment for increasing regulation, other than protective intervention such as approval of new drugs.[16]

Taken together, studies show that public attitudes toward consumerism in general are favorable and should remain strong.[17] Policy-makers in government are negatively evaluated, although the consumerism movement is widely appreciated.

How should businesses respond to the new market-regulated consumerism of the late 1980s and 1990s? This issue is yet to be resolved as a balance is sought between regulatory and market forces.

UNDERSTANDING AND RESPONDING TO CONSUMER RIGHTS

Consumer research is essential if disparate views of diverse groups are to be resolved. All parties, especially business and government, need the objectivity that well-designed research can provide in problem identification, problem clarification, and evaluation of proposed solutions.

THE IMPORTANCE OF A RESEARCH PERSPECTIVE

Few disagree with the need for objectivity, but there are inevitable difficulties in the use and interpretation of research. Differing values and resulting self-interest can lead to varying agendas from one party to the next.[18]

How, for example, do we interpret and use a finding that 11 percent of consumers misunderstood an ad and formed beliefs about the advertised product that contradict actual fact? An ardent consumer advocate could label this as a blatant indication of deception. The advertiser, on the other hand, could contend, with some merit, that a certain amount of misperception will occur regardless of the wording that is used.

It is precisely at this point that the propositions developed over the years in consumer research as a discipline and field of study find fruitful application.[19] As you have seen throughout this book, it is now possible to state with a fairly high degree of confidence how consumers process and use information. Therefore, there is an increasingly firm basis of theory and evidence on which to resolve disagreements more objectively. The resolution

---

[16] Harris, "Consumerism in the Eighties." Also see the results of a Middle Atlantic State Poll cited in Darlene Brannigan Smith and Paul N. Bloom, "Is Consumerism Dead or Alive? Some New Evidence," in Thomas C. Kinnear, ed., *Advances in Consumer Research* 11 (Provo, Utah: Association for Consumer Research, 1984), 469–473.

[17] Smith and Bloom, "Is Consumerism Dead?"

[18] Thomas Stanley and Larry Robinson, "Opinions on Consumer Issues: A Preview of Recent Studies of Executives and Consumers," *Journal of Consumer Affairs* 14 (Summer 1980), 217–220.

[19] For helpful examples on the role of consumer research, see William L. Wilkie, *Consumer Behavior* (New York: John Wiley & Sons, 1986), Chapter 21.

now relies less on theories of what consumers *ought to do* and shifts instead to *actual responses* to current or contemplated strategies.[20]

Consumer research also offers the benefit of test marketing proposed consumerism programs, just as it is used in all phases of marketing practices. Often there is need for sophisticated experimental designs.[21] Agencies such as the Federal Trade Commission (FTC) are increasingly research-sensitive, and this is an encouraging trend.

As a case in point, the FTC proposed that ads for over-the-counter drugs such as Alka-Seltzer or Rolaids contain specific warnings about contraindications (potential dangers in use), rather than the traditional "use as directed" warning on the label. Controversy quickly surfaced over the issue of the extent to which a brief insertion in TV ads would be heeded.

Houston and Rothschild demonstrated in a carefully controlled laboratory study that those exposed to the new warning had significantly higher recall of the contraindications than they would if the present "use as directed" approach is continued.[22] Those for whom the product was contraindicated, however, did not reduce their purchases as the FTC had hoped. Perhaps learning did not occur with so few low-level exposures, or perhaps the wording itself was at fault. Whatever the case, valuable information was provided.

THE RIGHT TO SAFETY

The first plank in the Consumer Bill of Rights put forward by President John F. Kennedy read, "Consumers have the right to be protected against products or services that are hazardous to health and life."[23] The right to safety has been made specific under the Consumer Product Safety Act, which established the Consumer Product Safety Commission (CPSC).

The CPSC has the mandate to protect consumers against unreasonable risk of injuries caused by hazardous household products. Manufacturers have always had some safety liability under common law, but now the manufacturer must assume explicit responsibility for designing the product in accordance with safety considerations.

Since 1980, however, the activity of the CPSC has been cut back, reflecting the move toward voluntary industry self-regulation. When enforcement and redress are necessary, increasing use has been made of cost/benefit criteria,

---

[20] Consumer research can be used to determine what consumers believe sellers or regulators should do about problems. See, for example, Roger D. Blackwell and W. Wayne Talarzyk, *Consumer Attitudes Toward Health Care and Medical Malpractice* (Columbus, Ohio: Grid Publishing, 1977), Chapter 6.

[21] Lynn Phillips and Bobby Calder, "Evaluating Consumer Protection Laws, Promising Methods," *Journal of Consumer Affairs* 14 (Summer 1980), 9–36.

[22] Michael Houston and Michael Rothschild, "Policy-Related Experiments on Information Provision: A Normative Model and Explication," *Journal of Marketing Research* 17 (November 1980), 432–449.

[23] "The Consumer Bill of Rights," in *Consumer Advisory Council, First Report* (Washington, D.C.: U.S. Government Printing Office, 1963).

assessing whether or not the benefits of a proposed remedial action are justified by its costs. This is not an easy issue to resolve.

There are two other regulatory agencies that focus on the issue of safety. The FTC has the specific mandate to regulate ad claims from the perspective of hazardous product use. In a more specific context, the Traffic Safety Administration is empowered to require automobile manufacturers to remedy safety defects. Millions of cars have been recalled because of specific orders which this agency has issued.

Consumer research has two specific functions here. The first is to document product-usage patterns, especially unexpected safety hazards. The second is to establish the expected probability of injuries or levels of safety.

USAGE PATTERNS AND SAFETY   A particular doctrine, **foreseeability,** is often a matter of contention between manufacturer and government. This doctrine holds that the manufacturer should be able to anticipate and evaluate risks inherent in product use and find out ways to avoid them.

Complaints about safety and poor performance often arise, of course, because of incorrect consumer usage. This is especially common with laundry equipment; for example, when people overload a machine with both clothing and detergent. Usage studies should be able to isolate the expected frequency of such usage errors and provide clues for how they can be prevented with proper warnings and information.

The real difficulty, however, lies in anticipating and minimizing the problems arising when so-called "normal" people use the product in a distinctly abnormal way. The manufacturer often is held liable in such situations.[24] Therefore, extensive usage testing may be required.

At times consumer research also proves useful in identifying needed safety features, even if they are not wanted by the buyer. The federal government has long wrestled with the issue of whether air bags should be mandatory on all cars sold in the United States. Air bags are not necessarily safer than properly used seat belts in minimizing potential injuries from accidents. Consumer research has consistently revealed, however, that large numbers do not use seat belts even when they are required by state laws. Here is a situation where the regulators can contend with some validity that air bags should be required to overcome consumer laxity with respect to seat-belt usage.

THE ISSUE OF COSTS VERSUS BENEFITS   What should be done if an automobile manufacturer predicts three potential fatalities for each 100,000 cars sold, resulting from rear-end skids caused by defective braking mechanisms? Perhaps fatalities can be cut to one per 1 million cars through mandatory installation of computerized braking systems, but the extra cost per

---

[24] Robert Larsen and Louis Marchese, *Product Liability* (Washington, D.C.: National Association of Wholesaler-Distributors, 1979).

25.1   THE DECISION WAS EASY: THE RELY WITHDRAWAL

To the marketing world, it seemed a shocking, stunning blow. After a terrible series of consequences, the late Edward G. Harness, then chairman–ceo of Procter & Gamble Co., made the decision: withdraw the company's highly successful new Rely tampons from sale nationwide. He would later call it one of the easiest decisions he ever made.

Fortune summed up Rely's marketing success. "It was P&G's first entry into a U.S. market for sanitary products (called catamenials) that is . . . around $1 billion in size and not given to fads. . . . Market research showed that Rely . . . was significantly preferred by women over other tampons and sales seemed to validate that finding. By September . . . Rely was getting about 25% of the tampon market, a remarkable share for a product so new. Rely may have been on its way . . . to 'driving Tampax right out of business.' "

In May 1980, the federal Centers for Disease Control in Atlanta issued a report noting the incidence of 55 cases of TSS [toxic shock syndrome] and their association with menstruating women. Follow-up CDC surveys—and news reports—went further and made a statistical link not only with menstruation but, tampon use.

Although CDC itself and other scientific groups said the evidence did not show Rely was causing TSS, there was a "statistically significant difference" that made Rely stand out. Even though the Denver doctor who first reported TSS cases was quoted as saying that "65% of victims . . . were not using Rely," P&G announced that it was suspending the sale of Rely tampons.

On September 26, 1980, P&G voluntarily signed an agreement with the federal Food & Drug Administration that called for extensive advertising informing consumers of the symptoms and risk of TSS and asking them to return boxes of Rely tampons for full refund.

At the October shareholders meeting, Mr. Harness said the company was taking a $75 million after-tax writeoff on Rely. "The financial cost to the company of Rely's voluntary suspension will be high," he told shareholders, "but we believe we have done what is right and that our action is consistent with the long-held Procter & Gamble view that the company and the company alone is responsible for the safety of our products."

"To sacrifice this principle could over the years ahead be a far greater cost than the monetary losses we face on the Rely brand."

Source: Larry Edwards, "The Decision Was Easy." Reprinted with permission from *Advertising Age* (August 26, 1987), 106ff. Copyright Crain Communications, Inc. All rights reserved.

car is $750. It is possible that 38 to 40 lives will be saved. Should the manufacturer make this change, which also will result in higher prices?

Everyone feels uneasy when a monetary value is placed on human life in this way. Many would not hesitate to recommend the change regardless of its cost. Others would be more hesitant, because matters of this type are never as simple as they seem. What effect will this have on lower-income buyers? Is the increased price justified if it is demonstrated that potential buyers with lower incomes are, in effect, priced out of the market? While research can be of value in clarifying the issues, policies can be established only on the basis of corporate and personal ethics.

The Procter & Gamble Company was forced to face exactly this type of dilemma when its highly successful Rely brand tampon was found to create toxic shock in some users. This story is detailed in *Consumer in Focus 25.1*.

AN ETHICAL DILEMMA IN MULTICULTURAL MARKETING   It has been illegal for more than two decades to advertise cigarettes on TV in the United States. Print ads are allowed only if there is a prominent warning, also appearing on each package, that cigarette smoking may be dangerous for your health. Growing antipathy toward smoking has led to a decrease in the number of smokers.

Cigarette manufacturers have more than made up for these lost sales by turning to developing countries in Africa, Asia, and South America. Ads are everywhere, and smoking is sharply increasing. Manufacturers, of course, are ignoring medical findings considered by most authorities as presenting conclusive and damaging evidence of health defects which can result from smoking. Furthermore, cigarettes are much more expensive proportionally in these countries, and their use limits already meager disposable income. Thus, it can be argued that the marketing of cigarettes has adverse effects on both personal health and standards of living.

The cigarette manufacturers are not alone in pursuing such marketing policies in the so-called "Third World." Cosmetics and self-medication products now abound. "So what's the problem?" is the frequent response. "After all, there is no law against it, and people are just exercising their freedom when they make the purchase."

The result, of course, is a stalemate that can be resolved only on the basis of what decision makers consider to be right or wrong. Our point in raising such dilemmas is not to proclaim an easy solution but to highlight how profoundly individual and corporate ethics ultimately affect consumer outcomes.

THE RIGHT TO BE INFORMED

The Kennedy Bill of Consumer Rights advocated that the consumer has the right "to be protected against fraudulent, deceitful, or grossly misleading information, advertising, labeling, or other practices, and to be given the facts he [or she] needs to make an informed choice."[25] The major issues evolving in this context are **information adequacy** and **veracity.**

---

[25] "The Consumer Bill of Rights."

FIGURE 25.1   WHICH AD IS MORE INFORMATIVE?

Source: Courtesy Colgate–Palmolive East Africa and China Airlines

INFORMATION ADEQUACY   As Hans Thorelli puts it, "Informed consumers are protected consumers—more than that, they are liberated consumers."[26] But how much information does the consumer want and need? How should it be provided? Can we provide too much information?

A Definitional Problem.   There is disagreement on what the word *informative* means. Contrast the two ads appearing in Figure 25.1. The Colgate ad was aimed at middle-class Kenyan families, whereas the China Airlines ad was designed for English speakers in Asian countries. Which do you think is most informative?

---

[26] Hans Thorelli, "The Future for Consumer Information Systems," in Jerry C. Olson, ed., *Advances in Consumer Research* 8 (Ann Arbor: Association for Consumer Research, 1980), 222.

Most probably will vote for the Colgate ad because of the product-feature demonstration and endorsement by the Kenya Dental Association. Empirical studies show, however, that less than half of all ads are informative in the sense that focus is on such objective features as price, quality, performance, and availability.[27]

But what about the China Airlines appeal? Would you say that it is noninformative because of its decidedly subjective (i.e., more emotional) message? We would seriously caution against such an interpretation, because the focus on Chinese tradition and ambiance is a benefit in and of itself, even though it cannot be quantified or objectified. It is entirely possible that the decision process of an Asian consumer is enhanced far more by the psychological and emotional associations than in any other way.

The issue comes down to this important point: *only the consumer can decide whether useful information has been provided.* It can be a serious mistake to allege, following some consumerists, that valid information is confined only to the factual and objective.

How Much Is Enough?   It has been made clear in many chapters that both the amount and type of information needed will depend upon the degree of involvement and resulting extended problem solving. Furthermore, there are individual differences in desire to search and willingness to act on limited information. Therefore, it is impossible to give a simple answer to the question of how much is enough. It can only be resolved on the basis of research that verifies actual information acquisition and use. If there are deficiencies resulting in unwise buying decisions, then action can be taken in the form of revamped promotion or consumer education efforts.

The Problem of Overload.   You will remember from our discussion of information processing that provision of too much information can cause overload and impair decision making. There are distinct limits on information-processing capacity. Many well-meaning consumer advocates mistakenly assume that "more is better" and wind up hindering rather than helping the consumer.

The Impact of Special Informational Strategies.   There has been a good deal of published research on policies and marketing practices designed to provide greater amounts of relevant information. Examples are unit pricing (price expressed in terms of a unit of measure) and open dating (highly visible printing of an expiration date).

Day and Brandt's conclusion regarding these well-intended efforts has stood the test of time:

---

[27] Alan J. Resnik and Bruce L. Stern, "An Analysis of Information Content in Television Advertising," *Journal of Marketing* (January 1977), 50–53.

What is clear . . . is that it is not enough to simply provide consumers with more information. That is simply the first step in a major educational task of getting consumers to understand the information, and persuading them to use it. Consumer researchers can make a significant contribution to both these tasks.[28]

INFORMATION VERACITY   No issue has given rise to greater concern over the years than deception and misrepresentation, because such practices materially interfere with the consumer's legitimate rights. What is deception? In its 1983 policy statement, the Federal Trade Commission defined deception as "a representation, omission, or practice that is likely to mislead the consumer acting reasonably in the circumstances, to the consumer's detriment."[29] Its current standard of deception requires that the representation, omission, or practice be "material." The representation becomes "material," in turn, when it is likely to affect consumer decision processes.[30]

The issue thus becomes resolved on the basis of the effect on consumers. In recent actions courts have ruled that this impact comes from what can be reasonably inferred by the consumer, as well as what is literally said.[31] Also, for a claim to be judged misleading, there generally must be evidence that more than 22 percent of actual or prospective buyers have been misled.[32]

An evaluation of the deception issue also must take into account that all forms of mass media content will be misperceived at times. According to Jacoby's findings, the incidence of misperception may run as high as 35 percent.[33] Therefore, we agree with Shimp and Preston that the following conditions should be demonstrated before arriving at a conclusion regarding deception:

1. The claim is *attended to* by the consumer.
2. The claim (or its implication) *affects beliefs.*
3. The claim (or its implication) is *important to the consumer.*
4. The claim (or its implication) becomes *represented in long-term memory.*
5. The claim (or its implication) is *objectively false.*
6. *Behavior* is influenced as a result of either the claim itself or implications which can reasonably be derived from it.[34]

---

[28] See George S. Day, "Assessing the Effects of Information Disclosure Requirements," *Journal of Marketing* (April 1976), 42–52.

[29] Resnik and Stern, "An Analysis of Information Content."

[30] Dorothy Cohen, "Legal Interpretations of Deception Are Deceiving," *Marketing News* (September 26, 1986), 12.

[31] Cohen, "Legal Interpretations."

[32] Cyndee Miller, "Ads Must Back up Their Claims—or Pay the Legal Price," *Marketing News* (February 1, 1988), 22.

[33] Jacob Jacoby, Wayne D. Hoyer, and David A. Sheluga, *Misperception of Televised Communications* (New York: American Association of Advertising Agencies, 1980).

[34] Terence A. Shimp and Ivan L. Preston, "Deceptive and Nondeceptive Consequences of Evaluative Advertising," *Journal of Marketing* (Winter 1981), 22–32.

FIGURE 25.2
TEXT OF A
CORRECTIVE AD
FOR OCEAN SPRAY
CRANBERRY JUICE
COCKTAIL

If you've wondered what some of our earlier advertising meant when we said Ocean Spray Cranberry Juice Cocktail has more food energy than orange juice or tomato juice, let us make it clear: we didn't mean vitamins and minerals. Food energy means calories. Nothing more.

Food energy is important at breakfast since many of us may not get enough calories, or food energy, to get off to a good start. Ocean Spray Cranberry Juice Cocktail helps because it contains more food energy than most other breakfast drinks.

And Ocean Spray Cranberry Juice Cocktail gives you and your family Vitamin C plus a great wake-up taste. It's . . . the other breakfast drink."

(To be run in one of every four ads for a year.)

Source: William L. Wilkie, Dennis L. McNeill, and Michael B. Mazis, "Marketing's 'Scarlet Letter': The Theory and Practice of Corrective Advertising," *Journal of Marketing* 48 (Spring 1984), 13.

Corrective Advertising.   In the 1970s the FTC initiated a new policy in which a firm found guilty of deception could be required to rectify its deception in future ads. This has become known as **corrective advertising.** The text of an early corrective ad appears in Figure 25.2.

What has been the impact of corrective advertising? Wilkie, NcNeill, and Mazis have summarized the research evidence, and here are the major conclusions:

1. Corrective ads have potential to provide consumers with useful information which may change beliefs and modify purchasing action.
2. There is little impact on company image or image of the general product category.
3. A corrective ad is capable of modifying consumer views on key product attributes.
4. Minor message variations are not likely to have much effect, whereas major changes will.[35]

The overall consensus is that "Corrective advertising has 'worked' but not nearly well enough to even approach correcting the misimpression levels in the marketplace."[36]

The Impact of Anti-Deception Efforts.   During the 1960s and 1970s the FTC was vigorous in its pursuit of advertising truthfulness. This abated substantially under the Reagan administration in the belief that a free market

---

[35] William L. Wilkie, Dennis L. McNeill, and Michael B. Mazis, "Marketing's 'Scarlet Letter': The Theory and Practice of Corrective Advertising," *Journal of Marketing* 48 (Spring 1984), 11–31.

[36] Wilkie *et al.,* "Marketing's 'Scarlet Letter.' "

CONSUMER IN FOCUS

25.2 **SOUR GRAPES FROM SWEET RAISINS**

A federal judge soon will be hearing from Kellogg Co. and General Foods about raisins, specifically about the fact there's a sugar-coating on the raisins in Kellogg's Raisin Bran and no sugar on the raisins in Post Natural Raisin Bran. But he'll also be hearing that there *is* sugar in the Post cereal, even though it doesn't happen to be on the raisins.

According to GF's own Consumer Nutrition Center, there are nine grams of sugar per 1-oz. serving of Post Natural Raisin Bran. That happens to be the same amount of sugar in the Kellogg's cereal. Does John Denver know that? There he is, wholesomely pitching Post's "naturally sweet" raisins in TV commercials, but failing to mention that the cereal itself is unnaturally sweet because it has added sugar.

A lot of people who aren't sitting around on a Rocky Mountain peak now do know of this advertising weasel. It has become part of a public squabble between two major advertisers. Unfortunately, we don't have to wait to find out what the judge thinks about all this.

The advertising business has already been found guilty. Consumer respect and trust is lost because Post and its ad agency sought to create the impression that Post Natural Raisin Bran doesn't contain sugar.

This is another example of an ad claim blowing up in our faces. It was supposed to set one product apart from a competitor's, but because the claim was strained and artificial, it boomeranged. Consumers who insist "you can't believe advertising" sure are going to make a hot three-course meal out of this cold breakfast cereal controversy.

Source: "Sour Grapes From Sweet Raisins." Reprinted with permission from *Advertising Age* (September 7, 1987), 16. Copyright Crain Communications, Inc. All rights reserved.

will provide correctives if left alone. The FTC also relaxed its standards for ad substantiation in that less evidence now is required to prove the veracity of claims.[37]

Traditionally the FTC and other agencies have performed the function of providing a "well-lighted street." The theory is that the threat of enforcement will deter violations. It seems that this light is being dimmed in favor of free-market correctives.[38]

Will businesses police themselves as expected? The evidence so far is not encouraging. Here are a few examples:

1. The claim "new and improved" actually related to modified graphics on the package.

---

[37] Debra L. Scammon and Mary Jane Scheffer, "Regulation in the Eighties: What's the Role of Consumer Researchers?" in Kinnear, *Advances*, 463–465.

[38] For a helpful review of voluntary regulation practices, see Gordon E. Miracle and Terence Nevett, *Voluntary Regulation of Advertising* (New York: Lexington Books, 1987).

2. A bonus package offer (i.e., 150 vitamins for the price of 100) was featured as lasting only a short time period, whereas the same labeling appeared for many consecutive seasons.

3. The offer of an "instant coupon" actually required extensive and time-consuming proof of prior purchase.[39]

The skepticism of the advertising community on the efficacy of self-regulation is amply underscored by the *Advertising Age* editorial in *Consumer in Focus 25.2*. To assume that advertisers and marketers will solve the misrepresentation problem by voluntary efforts requires a measure of faith.

THE RIGHT TO CHOOSE

"Consumers have the right to assured access, whenever possible, to a variety of products and services at competitive prices. In those industries in which competition is not workable, government regulation is substituted to assure satisfactory quality and service at fair prices."[40] So reads the third plank in the Consumer Bill of Rights.

BARRIERS TO ENTRY   Traditionally, the laws of market-based economies embody the principle of laissez-faire, which contends that the consumer is best served when firms freely compete, offering an unrestrained choice. Anti-trust legislation has long been a potent weapon against monopolies that allegedly curb this freedom—hence, the well-publicized breakup of AT&T into smaller, independent competitive units.

Anti-trust activity abated to less than 50 percent of its normal historic levels in the Reagan administration. In fact, former President Reagan vocally favored taking the FTC out of the anti-trust field. While we do not condone this action, it must, in fairness, also be pointed out that monopoly abuses did not seem to increase significantly during his tenure.

Consumerists usually do not make monopoly power into an issue because of the adequacy of both legislation and enforcement machinery. Enforcement lessened in the Reagan era, however. Hopefully the pendulum will swing toward more active enforcement in the future.

Even if there is no evidence of intent to create a monopoly, there is no denying the fact that entrenched firms with marketing muscle are often difficult and even impossible to dislodge. As a case in point, how many upstart airlines have been absorbed by the "big four" in the past few years? We no longer see People Express, Britt Air, or Frontier, just to mention a few, because the price of being competitive simply proved to be too high.

Fortunately, such barriers to entry rarely are permanent because of competitive counterattack. Just compare the lists of the top firms in any product

---

[39] Figures quoted by Summary Scan!, a division of the Advertising Checking Bureau, 1986.
[40] "The Consumer Bill of Rights."

field from one decade to the next and you will see substantial variation. The crumbling of the General Motors empire and the diminished market share of each of its divisions is ample evidence of competitive vulnerability.

In fact, there is growing evidence that smaller and more aggressive marketers often gain a competitive edge over their larger and more inflexible counterparts. Who would have believed that upstart Hyundai Motors would be listed in the top six for 1987? Many other examples can be given.

THE PROBLEM OF UNWISE CHOICE   Does the buyer have a right to choose even if there is evidence that actions are unwise? Should choice be regulated and restricted in such situations? This has been an unresolved issue since the very onset of consumerism nearly a century ago.

Some have doubts that people can make a sound, reasoned choice given the plethora of product alternatives and promotional claims. Others contend that consumers should be forced to do what is best for them, regardless of personal preferences. Both points of view, if enacted, inevitably lead to some restriction of choice. The auto seat-belt laws in many states are a case in point. Even though usage is mandated by statute, compliance is less than 50 percent in Illinois and other states.

In many ways this is a "no-win" issue. On the one hand, certain clearly unwise and destructive behaviors, such as heroin or cocaine use, must be regulated. Few would have any quarrel with this position, given extensive documentation of disastrous personal and social outcomes of addiction.

But what if similar legal limits were placed on the consumption of whole milk, which is known to produce allergies in some adults? Or chocolate? Now we have entered into the domain where any position taken inevitably will be arbitrary. Where is the line between wise and unwise buying and consumption behavior? In its most general sense, the principle of free choice must remain at the bedrock of a market economy, although some restraints always will be mandated by public consensus.

A more popular approach in the late 1980s is to move away from regulation and restriction toward education designed to bring about a more intelligent choice.[41] The goal is to enhance the ability to cope with complex choice processes in a mass consumption society, and programs should cover these elements:

1. Formal knowledge about criteria used to evaluate complex technical products, and ways to choose logically.

2. Consumer managerial and decision-making skills comparable to those developed in professional education.

3. Increased consumer knowledge of the workings of business, government, and the marketplace.

---

[41] Marilyn Kourilsky and Trudy Murray, "The Use of Economic Reasoning to Increase Satisfaction with Family Decision-Making," *Journal of Consumer Research* (September 1981), 183–188.

TABLE 25.1	Act	Purposes
SELECTED FEDERAL CONSUMER PROTECTION LAWS	**Pure Food and Drug Act (1906)**	Prohibits adulteration and misbranding of foods and drugs sold in interstate commerce
	Food, Drug, and Cosmetic Act (1938)	Prohibits the adulteration and sale of foods, drugs, cosmetics, or therapeutic devices that may endanger public health; allows the Food and Drug Administration to set minimum standards and to establish guides for food products
	Wool Products Labeling Act (1940)	Protects producers, manufacturers, distributors, and consumers from undisclosed substitutes and mixtures in all types of manufactured wool products
	Fur Products Labeling Act (1951)	Protects consumers and others against misbranding, false advertising, and false invoicing of furs and fur products
	Flammable Fabrics Act (1953)	Prohibits interstate transportation of dangerously flammable wearing apparel and fabrics
	Automobile Information Disclosure Act (1958)	Requires automobile manufacturers to post suggested retail prices on all new passenger vehicles
	Textile Fiber Products Identification Act (1958)	Guards producers and consumers against misbranding and false advertising of fiber content of textile fiber products
	Cigarette Labeling Act (1965)	Requires cigarette manufacturers to label cigarettes as hazardous to health
	Fair Packaging and Labeling Act (1966)	Declares unfair or deceptive packaging or labeling of certain consumer commodities illegal
	Child Protection Act (1966)	Excludes from sale potentially harmful toys; allows the FDA to remove dangerous products from the market
	Truth-in-Lending Act (1968)	Requires full disclosure of all finance charges on consumer credit agreements and in advertisements of credit to allow consumers to be better informed regarding their credit purchases
	Child Protection and Toy Safety Act (1969)	Protects children from toys and other products that contain thermal, electrical or mechanical hazards
	Fair Credit Reporting Act (1970)	Ensures that a consumer's credit report will contain only accurate, relevant, and recent information and will be confidential unless requested for an appropriate reason by a proper party
	Consumer Product Safety Act (1972)	Created an independent agency to protect consumers from unreasonable risk of injury arising from consumer products; agency is empowered to set safety standards
	Magnuson-Moss Warranty-Improvement Act (1975)	Provides for minimum disclosure standards for written consumer product warranties; defines minimum content standards for written warranties; allows the FTC to prescribe interpretive rules and policy statements regarding unfair or deceptive practices.

Source: William M. Pride and O. C. Ferrell, *Marketing: Basic Concepts and Decisions,* 4th ed., p. 481. Copyright © 1985 by Houghton Mifflin Company. Used by permission.

4. Values and consciousness which will encourage respect and concern for others in their pursuit of collective consumption.

THE RIGHT TO BE HEARD (REDRESS)

The fourth plank of the Kennedy Bill of Consumer Rights reads, "Consumers have the right to be assured that consumer interests will receive full and sympathetic consideration in the formulation of government policy and fair and expeditious treatment in its administrative tribunals."[42] Its focus unfortunately is entirely on regulatory behavior, and it must be broadened to encompass responsible marketing actions as well.

Redress can be achieved in three ways: prevention, restitution, and punishment. The main components of the body of legislation controlling restitution and punishment are detailed in Table 25.1, and the major avenues of consumer redress are summarized in Table 25.2.

PREVENTION   Ideally, the consumer voice needs to be heard before problems develop and redress becomes necessary. One possible answer lies in industry codes of conduct that are both observed and enforced. Hopefully, these codes then will become translated into high product quality backed by generous guarantees.

Codes of Ethics.   An example of an industry conduct code is given in Table 25.3. We recognize that such creeds are often little more than window dressing because of the lack of enforcement mechanisms. We contend subsequently, however, that consumerism problems will diminish if such standards are internalized and enforced by top management.

Quality and Guarantees.   As we have mentioned throughout the book, consumer dissatisfaction levels are increasing. In fact, one consumer researcher sees "almost the Naderistic feel of the '60s" in a "fight-back trend" that is making consumers "more conscious about getting ripped off."[43] During the first half of 1987, for example, the U.S. Department of Transportation experienced a 144-percent increase in complaint levels about airlines over the preceding year. Greatest numbers of complaints were registered for flight cancellations and delays, misplaced or lost baggage, difficulty in obtaining refunds, and rude or unhelpful service.[44]

Consumer rebellion inevitably will be felt in lost sales and bad word of mouth. The business solution lies in recognition that *quality is a marketing problem, not just a production problem.* When quality levels are improved and

---

[42] "The Consumer Bill of Rights."

[43] Faith Popcorn as quoted in Janet Neiman, "Values-Added Marketing," *ADWEEK* (April 6, 1987), 19.

[44] Lynn G. Coleman, "No Silver Lining Expected to Brighten Airline's Stormy Skies," *Marketing News* (September 25, 1987), 1 and 9.

TABLE 25.2 REMEDIES FOR CONSUMER PROTECTION	Prevention	Restitution	Punishment
	Codes of conduct	Affirmative disclosure	Fines and incarceration
	Disclosure of information requirements	Corrective advertising	Loss of profits
		Refunds	Class action suits
	Substantiation of claims	Limitations on contracts	
		Arbitration	

Source: Dorothy Cohen, "Remedies for Consumer Protection: Prevention, Restitution, or Punishment," *Journal of Marketing* 39 (October 1975), 25. Reprinted from the *Journal of Marketing* published by the American Marketing Association.

backed by stringent guarantees, it is possible to regain or solidify market position while, at the same time, contributing to legitimate consumer interests. Notice the wisdon of Lufthansa Airlines' strategy, as detailed in *Consumer in Focus 25.3*

RESTITUTION   Legal restitution for wrongs can be made many ways, as Table 25.2 indicates. Among the most visible is the almost daily incidence of mandatory automobile recalls ordered to remedy safety defects. You may recall our previous discussion of the initial resistance of management when such an order was issued to rectify engine surge problems with the Audi 5000 model. Here is a clear case, in our opinion, of disregard of social responsibility.

Issues of restitution should not have to reach the point where legal authori-

TABLE 25.3 THE ADVERTISING CODE OF AMERICAN BUSINESS	1. **Truth.** Advertising shall tell the truth, and shall reveal significant facts, the concealment of which would mislead the public.
	2. **Responsibility.** Advertising agencies and advertisers shall be willing to provide substantiation of claims made.
	3. **Taste and Decency.** Advertising shall be free of statements, illustrations, or implications which are offensive to good taste or public decency.
	4. **Disparagement.** Advertising shall offer merchandise or service on its merits, and refrain from attacking competitors unfairly or disparaging their products, services, or methods of doing business.
	5. **Balt Advertising.** Advertising shall offer only merchandise or services which are available for purchase at the advertised price.
	6. **Guarantees and Warranties.** Advertising of guarantees and warranties shall be explicit. Advertising of any guarantee or warranty shall clearly and conspicuously disclose its nature and extent, the manner in which the guarantor or warrantor will perform and the identity of the guarantor or warrantor.
	7. **Price Claims.** Advertising shall avoid price or savings claims which are false or misleading, or which do not offer provable bargains or savings.
	8. **Unprovable Claims.** Advertising shall avoid the use of exaggerated or unprovable claims.
	9. **Testimonials.** Advertising containing testimonials shall be limited to those of competent witnesses who are reflecting a real and honest choice.

Note: This code was part of a program of industry self-regulation pertaining to national consumer advertising announced jointly on September 18, 1971, by the American Advertising Federation, the American Association of Advertising Agencies, the Association of National Advertisers, and the Council of Better Business Bureaus, Inc.

25.3   LUFTHANSA AIRLINES GUARANTEES QUALITY

To distinguish itself from the competition, as the most dependable and punctual airline, Lufthansa German Airlines recently announced their new Quality Guarantee program for First Class and Business Class passengers.

The guarantee program offers three specific guarantees for First Class and Business Class passengers, and backs the guarantees with a cash compensation of $200, or with free and upgraded transportation.

Guarantee 1

If a First Class or Business Class passenger misses a connecting Lufthansa flight to destinations within Germany or to more than 130 Lufthansa destinations worldwide because of an operational problem, Lufthansa will pay the passenger $200 in compensation.

Guarantee 2

Lufthansa guarantees that the passenger's baggage will arrive at their Lufthansa desti-

nation at the same time. If the baggage isn't there, Lufthansa will pay $200 over and above any legal claim.

Guarantee 3

If a confirmed transatlantic reservation in First Class is unavailable, the passenger will fly Business Class at no charge. If a confirmed transatlantic reservation in Business Class is unavailable, the passenger will be upgraded to First Class at no extra charge. And if First Class is also full, the client will fly in Tourist Class free of charge.

Lufthansa has planned an intensive campaign drive to promote public awareness of the Quality Guarantee program. According to Hans Diessel, spokesperson for the airline, "the exclusive Quality Guarantee will be Lufthansa's major sales tool in the business travel market in 1987."

Source: As cited in *Services Marketing Newsletter* 4 (Summer 1987), 2.

ties must step in. The consumer has every right to expect response from the manufacturer or retailer when complaints are made. History has proven time and time again that the gains in consumer loyalty far offset costs. But this type of lesson does not seem to sink in as it should, if complaint levels are any indication.[45]

PUNISHMENT   If nothing else works, it is possible to take more extreme action in the form of fines and incarceration, loss of profits, and class action suits. Various members of the security and exchange industry have discovered to their dismay that fraudulent stock manipulation can lead to a stint behind

---

[45] Claes Fornell and Robert A. Westbrook, "The Vicious Cycle of Consumer Complaints," *Journal of Marketing* 48 (Summer 1984), 68–78.

bars. However, state and local authorities often have the greatest impact, especially in cases of outright fraud. Unfortunately, such legal proceedings can be extremely costly and time-consuming.

THE RIGHT TO ENJOY A CLEAN AND HEALTHFUL ENVIRONMENT

Environmental pollution is an unfortunate byproduct of a high and rising standard of living in a technological age. As of this writing there is frightening evidence that sharply increasing levels of carbon dioxide and chlorofluorocarbons (CFCs) in the atmosphere are depleting the ozone layer that shields the earth from dangerous radiation.[46]

If unchecked, the so-called "greenhouse" effect will raise temperatures throughout the earth and materially alter climatic patterns. The only solutions lie in drastic reductions in usage of fossil fuels and CFC-producing refrigerants. This inevitably has major impacts on standards of living.

Are we willing to pay this price? It may become necessary for firms to engage in **demarketing**—a deliberate attempt to induce consumers to buy *less* in product classes where environmental impacts are most severe. It requires quite a measure of faith to believe that this ever would take place voluntarily if it means sacrifice of potential profit, but is there any other choice short of regulative action?

RESPONSIBILITIES TO MINORITIES AND THE POOR

Even the most developed economies have not overcome the problems of poverty and disadvantaged minorities. These become especially acute in urban areas which are burgeoning around the world. Nairobi, Kenya, for example, must generate *1,000 new jobs* each day to cope with urban population growth.[47] Businesses in general and consumer researchers specifically cannot avoid playing a role in determination of the kind of urban environment to be built for the future and the ways in which greater equality can be achieved.

Consumer researchers have investigated the problems of how those who have been most subject to discrimination can more efficiently allocate their limited resources. The goal has been to determine whether a unique set of problems exists among minorities and the poor toward which special regulative and informational efforts should be directed.

A second contribution of consumer research is improvement of marketing efficiency among firms and organizations that serve disadvantaged segments. Minority-owned businesses, for example, are being helped to achieve greater market penetration.

A third contribution is made when research evidence documents the ways

---

[46] "Special Report: The Greenhouse Effect," *Newsweek* (July 11, 1988), 16–23.
[47] Comments made by the Hon. B. L. Kiplagat, Permanent Secretary of State, The Republic of Kenya, March 6, 1988.

in which those who are not disadvantaged enhance the problems of those who are. A case in point is the potent curb on upward mobility when those who are white rapidly sell their homes as blacks move in.

ORGANIZATIONAL ETHICS AND CONSUMERISM

Contemporary enterprises—business and nonbusiness—are faced with changing realities. The need is for *preventive* approaches to consumerism rather than *reactive* ones. Consumerism, after all, is not anti-business per se. It is, as we have stressed, a natural countervailing force in response to alienation. If abuses were not present, it would not exist.

Any market-controlled free enterprise system is built on an assumption that individual entrepreneurs and managers will act on the basis of *enlightened self-interest*. This premise recognizes that profit and material gain will be the guiding motive but introduces the constraint that the market must be truly served with focus on long-run consumer interest.

This doctrine presupposes a set of managerial ethics, a code of right and wrong, that is both workable and actively followed. What happens, however, when short-term financial gain becomes the guiding consideration? Ethical mandates quickly fall by the wayside, as economic history (and indeed the entire history of mankind) so amply reveals. It is the purpose of this section to explore some ways in which ethics can move beyond pious written codes into responsible business action.

ETHICAL FOUNDATIONS

Evidence is rapidly accumulating that today's competitive atmosphere is generating real pressures to compromise personal ethics.[48] Corporate decision makers are facing this dilemma on a continuing basis.[49] Unfortunately, the public only becomes aware of the most flagrant instances of resulting compromise behavior. Small wonder that *Business Week* reports "Businesses are Signing Up for Ethics 101."[50] This subject has become so popular that nearly 5,000 published works appeared between 1981 and 1985, more than twice the number published in the preceding 4 years.[51]

The diagram in Figure 25.3 shows that responsible managerial behavior is shaped by a five-dimensional foundation. The absolute floor is composed

---

[48] This section closely follows the writings of Lantos and Dickson. See Geoffrey P. Lantos, "An Ethical Base for Decision Making," *Journal of Consumer Research* (Fall, 1986), and "Ethics Has Its Roots in Judeo-Christian Morality," *Marketing News* (July 18, 1986).

[49] Daniel E. Maltby, "The One-Minute Ethicist," *Christianity Today* (February 19, 1988), 26–29.

[50] John A. Byrne, "Businesses are Signing Up for Ethics 101," *Business Week* (February 15, 1988), 56–57.

[51] Maltby, "The One-Minute Ethicist," 26.

FIGURE 25.3
THE FOUNDATIONS
OF ETHICAL
STANDARDS:
RESPONSIBLE
MANAGERIAL
BEHAVIOR

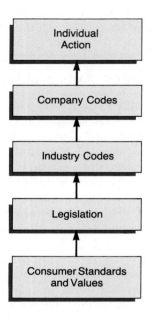

of the values and beliefs of the consumer public. Law builds on that foundation and defines and codifies the ethical baseline.

As we move from that foundation, each level becomes more specific. The third is industry-wide codes of ethics such as that appearing in Table 25.3. Even greater specificity appears in company codes, an example being that of IBM reproduced in Table 25.4. But it all becomes operational (or nonoperational) ultimately at the level of the individual decision maker.

TABLE 25.4
IBM'S GUIDELINES
FOR BUSINESS
CONDUCT

- Do not make misrepresentations to anyone you deal with.
- Do not use IBM's size unfairly to intimidate or threaten.
- Treat all buyers and sellers equitably.
- Do not engage in reciprocal dealing.
- Do not disparage competitors.
- Do not make premature disclosure of unannounced offerings.
- Do not engage in further selling after competitor has the firm order.
- Contact with the competition must be minimal.
- Do not make any illegal use of confidential information.
- Do not steal or obtain information by willfull deceit.
- Do not engage in violation of patents or copyrights.
- No bribes, gifts or entertainment that might be seen as creating an obligation should be accepted or given.

Source: Gene R. Laczniak and Patrick E. Murphy, *Marketing Ethics: Guidelines for Managers* (Lexington, Massachusetts: Lexington Books, 1985), pp. 117–123.

TABLE 25.5 **A PERSONAL** **ETHICS** **CHECKLIST**	1. Am I violating the law? If yes, why? 2. Are the values and ethics that I am applying in business lower than those I use to guide my personal life? If yes, why? 3. Am I doing to others as I would have them do to me? If not, why not? 4. Am I willfully risking the life and limb of consumers and others by my action? If yes, why? 5. Am I willfully exploiting children, the very elderly, the illiterate, the feeble minded, naive or the poor? If yes, why? 6. Am I keeping my promises? If not, why not? 7. Am I telling the truth — all the truth? If not, why not? 8. Am I exploiting a confidence or a trust? If yes, why? 9. Am I misrepresenting my true intentions to others? If yes, why? 10. Am I loyal to those who have been loyal to me? If not, why not? 11. Have I set up others to take responsibility for any negative consequences of my action? If yes, why? 12. When it comes to a marginal call am I fair and considerate or ruthless and greedy? 13. Am I prepared to redress wrongs and fairly compensate for damages? If not, why not? 14. Are my values and ethics as expressed in my strategy offensive to certain groups? If yes, why? 15. Am I being as efficient as I can? If not, why not?

Source: Peter Dickson (unpublished manuscript. The Ohio State University, 1988).

THE ISSUE OF RIGHT VERSUS WRONG

The ultimate dilemma faced in constructing any ethical philosophy is determining *what is right and what is wrong.* How can I decide? There are two ways in which issues of morality are attacked—through **individualized standards** (situation ethics) or **absolute standards** (moral revelation). Each marketer must resolve these issues for himself or herself.

We like the way in which Peter Dickson has fleshed out a personal ethics checklist for managers. We present this checklist for your consideration in Table 25.5.

PHASING ETHICS AND SOCIAL RESPONSIBILITY INTO MARKETING PLANNING

Corporate values of profit and efficiency will dominate unless there is the addition of counterbalancing ethical values. Robin and Reidenbach have diagrammed how this might look (see Figure 25.4).

A CONSUMERISM MANAGEMENT SYSTEM   Consumerism obviously is not going away, and it must be managed in the same way as every other environmental challenge. Here are the steps in a management system that is both workable and responsible:

1. Orienting top management to the consumer's world.

2. Organizing for responsive action.

3. Improving customer contact.

FIGURE 25.4
PARALLEL
PLANNING
SYSTEMS FOR
INTEGRATING
ETHICAL AND
SOCIALLY
RESPONSIBLE
PLANS INTO
STRATEGIC
MARKETING
PLANNING

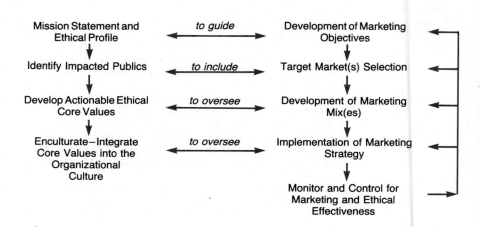

Source: Donald P. Robin and R. Eric Reidenbach, "Social Responsibility, Ethics, and Marketing Strategy: Closing the Gap between Concept and Application," *Journal of Marketing* 51 (January 1987), 52.

4. Redressing grievances.

5. Providing consumer information and education.

Top Management Orientation. There now is a consensus that the first step is to insure that both the board of directors and top management are acquainted with the realities of the consumer world, including economic and financial fears, negative attitudes toward business practice, and perceived grievances. This level of knowledge also must be backed consistently by a commitment to take responsible action when needed.[52]

As Peters and Austin have pointed out, managerial isolation is no longer tenable:

The number one managerial productivity problem in America is, quite simply, managers who are out of touch with their people and out of touch with their customers. And the alternative, "being in touch," does not come via computer printouts or the endless stream of overhead transparencies viewed in the thousand darkened meeting rooms stretching across the continent. Being in touch means tangible, visceral ways of being informed.[53]

Peters and Austin go on to note that a major factor differentiating effective firms from their counterparts is **Management by Wandering Around** (MBWA), a continuing commitment to maintain a direct, personal listening ear at the

---

[52] Esther Peterson, "Consumerism Then and Now," *Mobius* (Fall 1986), 8–9; Stephen A. Greyser, "Consumer Affairs: The Challenge Continues," *Mobius* (Fall 1986), 4–6; and Maltby, "The One-Minute Ethicist."

[53] Tom Peters and Nancy Austin, *A Passion for Excellence* (New York: Random House, 1985), 8.

FIGURE 25.5
THE AMERICAN
EXPRESS
CONSUMER
AFFAIRS OFFICE

Consumer Affairs is responsible for improving the Company's relations and communications with consumers, and for making the Company more responsive to consumers' needs. This mission is accomplished in three ways:

Monitoring consumer needs, trends, and issues; communicating consumer concerns to management.

Evaluating Company policies, products, and services; recommending changes or improvements to better serve the consumer while enhancing our competitive position.

Providing consumer information and education related to Company's products, services, and policies which are of particular benefit to consumers, as well as general information which will benefit the public or selected target audiences.

Source: Joyce Bryant, "Mission Statement for the Consumer Affairs Department," *Mobius* (Fall 1986), 10.

grass roots.[54] If this philosophy is not implemented and *enforced throughout the organization*, we are afraid that social responsibility and ethics will degenerate to meaningless buzzwords.

Organizing for Responsible Action.   A logical starting point is a written consumer rights policy specifying in detail what the company is prepared to do in the way of implementation when shortcomings arise. We also recommend the establishment of a consumer affairs department which is empowered to have a real voice in marketing decision making and responsibility to provide redress. A good example of how such a department functions appears in Figure 25.5.

The head person of the consumer affairs department, in turn, should be a member of top management assigned responsibility and authority to assure that product quality and safety are maintained, that promotional strategies are truthful and not misleading, and that there is no deception in other phases of the marketing program. If this position is seen as merely advisory without management power and sanctions, it will be little more than window dressing.

Improving Customer Contact.   One of the greatest challenges for any management team is to create customer credibility. Some logical steps include community involvement, soft-sell institutional ads, and just plain human friendliness and decency in all dealings. The intent is to break down and hopefully eliminate barriers.

---

[54] For more on MBWA, see Peters and Austin, *A Passion for Excellence,* Chapter 2.

One of the best strategies is a continual customer satisfaction monitoring program. For example, Bell South (Southern Bell and South Central Bell) Companies are committed by corporate mission to put the "customer first," and surveys are conducted continuously to monitor satisfaction.[55] This provides an ongoing evaluation of service as opposed to an occasional "snapshot," thus allowing immediate remedial action when needed.

Monitoring programs are undertaken in full recognition that most dissatisfied customers will not complain but, rather, will switch their business elsewhere. The Disney Cable TV Channel, for example, attributes its rapid growth and strong market position to wise use of information from its satisfaction-monitoring system.[56] Many other firms also are seeing the benefits. As Donald A. Kunstler, Executive Vice President of Elrick and Lavidge, San Francisco, puts it:

> *Top management should not expect "perfect scores," but should use the results in positive ways.*
>
> *Reward* good performance.
>
> *Motivate* sales and/or service contact personnel to do better.
>
> *Correct* poor performance by individuals (or entire organizations) by strengthening training programs.
>
> *Convert* companies to satisfied customers with appropriate follow-up programs.[57]

Providing for Redress.   It is essential to respond to grievances and injuries. This requires prompt and direct means of reacting to complaints and inquiries through a consumer affairs department.[58] There must be a clear recognition that commitment to information feedback and postsale communication is an ethical mandate, to say nothing of the extent to which this response is significant in building long-term consumer loyalty, a phenomenon that is becoming increasingly rare.

PROVIDING CONSUMER INFORMATION AND EDUCATION

Bloom and Silver have identified a true consumer education movement in some firms, and we find this response to be encouraging indeed.[59] The focus lies on moving beyond the usual forms of promotion, as important as these are, to efforts which clearly are designed to help the consumer buy wisely.

---

[55] Elridge and Lavidge, *Marketing Today* 14 (1987), 1–2.

[56] Wayne Walley, "Disney Channel no Fantasy," *Advertising Age* (December 1, 1986), S-10ff.

[57] *Marketing Today*, 2.

[58] For a detailed description of how the consumer affairs department at Procter & Gamble works, see Lenore Skenazy, "Heeding the Call," *Advertising Age* (August 20, 1987), 38.

[59] Paul N. Bloom and Mark J. Silver, "Consumer Education: Marketers Take Heed," *Harvard Business Review* 54 (January–February 1976), 32–42.

One noteworthy example is the J. C. Penney Company.[60] Among its consumer education activities are teaching materials for consumer education classes, buying guides containing objective product information, a staff of home economists who present educational programs in local stores, and cooperative consumer education ventures in universities. J. C. Penney and others have found that the gains in consumer loyalty can offset the costs of such programs.

CONCLUSION

We have noticed a disturbing trend since the first edition of this book in 1968. The majority of students of that generation developed a high sense of moral outrage over political and economic shortcomings. For a period, of course, this was expressed through campus protest, but a large percentage carried a commitment to ethically responsible action into their professional lives. Consumerism is a central part of the social agenda of that generation of business managers, and many of the most laudable corporate actions have come from their initiative.

It seems, however, that this moral outrage has given way to quite an opposite feeling of individualistic opportunism. A study of American university students has demonstrated conclusively that the central value of today is "me first," expressed as a single-minded commitment to wealth and position.[61] Social and moral issues are not seen negatively; rather such concerns are at the distinct periphery of life. Our belief is that each individual should consider the best interests of consumers when studying consumer behavior.

SUMMARY

The consumer has the right to safety, the right to be informed, the right to choose, and the right to be heard. These tenets have been reaffirmed by decree and administrative action ever since they were declared in 1962 by President John F. Kennedy. Yet, there is ample evidence that these rights are consistently violated, creating a rising interest in consumerism.

Consumerism is not a recent phenomenon. A historical review showed some ancient antecedents as well as specific activity that began in the United States around the turn of the century. Consumerism as we now know it, however, received its greatest impetus from the Kennedy declarations. The 1960s and 1970s were characterized by a frenzy of activity on many fronts, but there has been a pendulum swing toward a return to market forces as opposed to regulation as a corrective during the 1980s.

Our focus throughout is that consumer research plays the unique role

---

[60] Bloom and Silver, "Consumer Education."

[61] Unpublished study undertaken by Management Development Associates, Wheaton, Illinois.

of providing facts for policy and activity. Otherwise, there often is recourse to normative authoritarianism based on opinion and arbitrary fiat. In a sense, then, a research approach has the potential of becoming a boundary-spanning agent between the conflicting interests of business, government, and consumer advocacy groups.

This chapter covered relevant research, much of it fairly recent, directed to understanding consumer rights and needs. This was reviewed under the headings of consumer safety, information, choice, environmental protection, responsibilities to minorities and the poor, and the right of redress.

Consumerism is just an interesting textbook topic, however, unless recognized as a legitimate force and responded to by business accordingly. A number of suggestions were given in the spirit that responsible action is needed if a free-market economy is to function in the best interests of all parties.

REVIEW AND DISCUSSION QUESTIONS

1. Once deregulation began under the Reagan administration, it was not uncommon to hear executives express their conviction that consumerism is now a dead issue. Do you agree?

2. Examine your own experiences as a consumer in the past year. Have you experienced feelings of alienation? From what sources? What might have been done by the offending organizations to have prevented this?

3. Is the consumerism of the 1970s and 1980s fundamentally different from that of earlier eras? Why or why not?

4. *Unsafe at Any Speed* was the title of Nader's book castigating the automobile industry, and he alleges that things have not improved to any degree. Following a research approach, how would you go about substantiating his claim? What types of safety standards could legitimately be proposed, taking cost-benefit analysis into account?

5. "That advertisement is deceptive." If such a legal complaint were to reach your desk as advertising manager of a major consumer goods manufacturer, what would your response be? How would you define the term *deception?* What research would you undertake as a response? Be specific.

6. There has been a debate on "how much consumer information is enough." You are called in as an expert on consumer behavior. What would your response be?

7. Is corrective advertising an effective form of consumer redress? Why or why not?

8. William Lazer, a former President of the American Marketing Association, advocated during the 1960s that marketing should work toward the end of helping the consumer to accept self-indulgence, luxurious surroundings, and nonutilitarian products. Do you agree?

9. The president of Hunt-Wesson Foods proposes that business must divert some of its profits to help solve social problems and issues such as consumerism. However, this might reduce stockholders' financial returns, thus giving rise to potential conflict of interest. Can this be resolved?

10. "Get government out of the business of regulating automotive safety. The industry will police itself." What is your response?

11. This is not the typical end-of-chapter question, but we leave it with you anyway.

You are selling a name brand headache remedy containing only pure aspirin. You are fully aware that generic or distributor brands containing exactly the same ingredients sell for half the price or less. Yet, your brand is marketing with such claims as "purity," "a name you can trust," "speed of relief." Examine your own code of ethics carefully, and answer this question. Can you justify this marketing strategy? What would your answer be to the charge that the advertising is deceptive from a belief-claim interaction perspective? Is it justifiable to continue selling as long as people keep buying? Try to make explicit the ethical principles underlying your initial responses.

GLOSSARY

absolute standards categorical moral revelations and religious laws used as the basis for ethical decision making.

absolute threshold the amount of stimulus energy or intensity necessary for sensation to occur.

abstract elements intangible elements of culture, such as values, attitudes, ideas, personality types, and summary constructs, such as religion.

abstract words those that express a quality apart from an object (e.g., justice, equality).

acceptance a stage of information processing representing the degree to which a stimulus influences the person's knowledge and/or attitudes.

active rejection the decision not to adopt an innovation.

Actual State Types consumers in whom need recognition results from changes in the actual state.

adaptation level the level at which an individual becomes so habituated to a stimulus that it is no longer noticed.

adopter one who makes the decision to continue using a new product.

adoption the decision to make full use of an innovation.

advertising wearout the reduction of advertising effectiveness as a result of excessive ad repetition.

affective responses the feelings and emotions that are elicited by a stimulus.

affect referral a decision rule that assumes that a consumer has previously formed overall evaluations of each choice alternative, rather than judging them on various evaluative criteria.

AIDA an early conceptualization of the adoption process, including Awareness, Interest, Desire, Action.

aided recall measures measures that provide cues for retrieving learned information.

AIO measures measures of activities, interests, and opinions.

alienation feelings of powerlessness and isolation which, when experienced in regard to the business world, often results in consumerism.

alternative evaluation the third stage of the nonhabitual decision-making process in which a choice alternative is evaluated and selected to meet consumer needs.

analytical cross-cultural studies studies that attempt to deduce general principles of behavior that apply in one or more cultures.

anomie social instability resulting from a weakened respect for social norms and values.

approach in motivation, the theory that some forces promote or produce movement toward a goal object.

a priori segmentation analysis defining the segmentation base in advance.

Area of Dominant Influence an area for which advertising media is purchased, usually cities or areas surrounding them.

argument a message element relevant to forming a rational, reasoned opinion.

arousal a person's degree of alertness along a continuum ranging from extreme drowsiness to extreme wakefulness.

aspirational group a reference group whose members wish to adopt the norms, values, and behaviors of others.

association measures *see* evaluated participation studies

associative network a conceptualization according to which memory consists of a series of nodes (representing concepts) and links (which represent associations between nodes).

attention a stage of information processing representing the allocation of cognitive capacity. *see also* direction of attention and intensity of attention

attitude an overall evaluation that can range from extremely positive to extremely negative.

attitude change a term used to characterize conditions under which a person holds a preexisting attitude that is changed subsequently.

attitude formation a term used to characterize conditions under which a person has yet to develop an attitude.

attraction effect a phenomenon in which a given alternative's attractiveness is enhanced when an inferior alternative is added to the set of choice alternatives.

attribute a characteristic or property of a product; generally refers to a characteristic that serves as an evaluative criterion during decision making.

attribute evaluation measures measures used to assess the goodness or badness of an attribute.

attribute importance measures measures used to assess the concept of salience or potential influence of product attributes.

attribute search sequence brand information is collected on an attribute-by-attribute basis.

attribution theory a theory stating that an individual encountering a situation is motivated to ascertain whether the causal influence on the person is internal or external (e.g., if a product fails, is the failure in the product or in an adjunct system, such as wiring?).

augmented product the tangible attributes of a product

plus its additional value to the consumer.

avoidance in motivation, the theory that some forces promote or produce movement away from a goal object.

awareness analysis a technique for assessing brand awareness by asking consumers to recall or recognize brand names.

awareness set the set of brand familiar to a consumer.

baby boomer one of the cohort of 77 million Americans born between 1946 and 1964.

background noise a description of the way in which advertising may strike the consumer.

backward conditioning classical conditioning in which the conditioned stimulus follows the unconditioned stimulus.

behavioral consistency a phenomenon that exists when the purchase behavior of individuals in a submarket remains constant over time.

behavioral intention measures measures of the perceived likelihood that a particular behavior will be undertaken by the person.

behaviorist approach an approach to learning in which learning is demonstrated by changes in behavior and the role of mental processes is ignored.

behavioristic variables variables used for segmentation, including extent of use, loyalty, benefit, and usage situations.

belief a link between two nodes in an associate network, such as "IBM is an expensive brand."

benefit segmentation a marketing strategy oriented toward meeting a benefit or felt need in a target market segment.

birthrate the number of live births per 1,000 population in a given year.

brand loyalty a motivated, difficult-to-change habit of purchasing the same item or service, often rooted in high involvement.

brand personality the attributes of a product and the profile of perceptions received by consumers about a specific brand.

brand search sequence brand information is collected on a brand-by-brand basis.

breaking point in location analysis, the point at which 50 percent of the market trade is attracted to each of two locations.

Bureau of Economic Analysis Economic Area an area of geographic analysis designated by the Bureau of Economic Analysis and consisting of an "economic node" and the surrounding counties.

cancellation rate the proportion of customers who do not repurchase.

capacity the cognitive resources that an individual has available at any given time for processing information.

category killer a retailer that carries a broad assortment in one category of merchandise.

causal differences consumer differences that represent motivating influences or other factors that define and shape behavior.

Censal-Ratio method a population estimate method comparing an area's population from the most recent census with a variable that changes as the size of population changes.

Central Business District the traditional "downtown" shopping district.

central route a form of persuasion in which issue relevant thinking is high and message elements or arguments relevant to forming a reasoned opinion are influential.

chunk a grouping or combination of information that can be processed as a unit.

classical conditioning a form of learning in which a conditioned stimulus (e.g., the sound of a bell) is paired with an existing unconditioned stimulus (e.g., the sight of food) until the conditioned stimulus alone is sufficient to elicit a previously unconditioned response (e.g., salivation), which is now a conditioned response.

classification dominance the state a retailer achieves when giving the customer the impression that the merchandise assortment contains virtually any item that could be desired.

closure the tendency to develop a complete picture or perception even when elements in the perceptual field are missing.

cognitive approach an approach to learning in which learning is seen as reflected in changes in knowledge, and emphasis is on understanding the mental processes that determine how people learn information.

cognitive consistency theories theories, such as balance theory and congruity theory, that propose that people strive to maintain a consistent set of beliefs and attitudes.

cognitive map consumer perceptions of store locations and shopping areas, as opposed to actual locations.

cognitive responses the thoughts that occur to an individual during the comprehension stage of information processing.

cohesion the emotional bonding that family members have toward one another.

cohort any group of individuals linked in some way, usually by age.

cohort analysis a method of investigating the changes in patterns of behavior or attitudes of groups called cohorts.

communicability the degree to which results from using a new product are visible to friends and neighbors.

communication a facilitating dimension, critical to movement on the other family dimensions of cohesion and family adaptability.

communication situation the setting in which the consumer is exposed to either personal or nonpersonal communications.

comparative advertising advertising that makes comparisons between products.

compatibility the degree to which a product is consistent with the existing values and past experiences of a potential adopter.

compensatory strategy a strategy in alternative evaluation in which a perceived weakness on one attribute may be compensated for or offset by strength on others.

competitive intensity the degree of a firm's competition.

completed fertility rate the total number of children ever born to women of a specific age group.

complexity the degree to which an innovation is perceived as difficult to understand and use.

component method a population estimate method that divides population into its components of change: births, deaths, and migration.

comprehension a stage of information processing in which interpretation of a stimulus occurs.

concentrated marketing marketing in which the primary focus is on one segment.

concrete words those that name a real thing or class of things.

conditioned response (CR) *see* classical conditioning

conditioned stimulus (CS) *see* classical conditioning

confidence the degree of conviction with which an attitude is held.

confirmation the process through which consumers seek reinforcement for the innovation decision.

conjunctive decision rule a noncompensatory decision rule involving processing by brand in which cutoffs are established for each salient attribute and each brand is compared to this set of cutoffs.

consideration set the set of alternatives from which choice is made.

Consolidated Metropolitan Statistical Area a grouping of closely related PMSAs.

constructive decision rule a decision rule that a consumer builds using elementary processing operations (fragments of rules) available in memory that can accommodate the choice situation.

consumer behavior those actions directly involved in obtaining, consuming, and disposing of products and services, including the decision processes that precede and follow these actions.

consumerism policies and activities designed to protect consumer interests and rights as they are involved in an exchange relationship with any type of organization.

consumer knowledge information relevant to the functioning of consumers in the marketplace.

consumer satisfaction/ dissatisfaction (CS/D) a judgment as to whether purchase outcomes meet expectations.

consumer socialization the acquisition of consumption-related cognitions, attitudes, and behavior.

content analysis a technique for determining the values, themes, role prescriptions, norms of behavior, and other elements of culture.

contextualized marketing a marketing strategy designed to take into account cultural differences in consumer motivation and behavior by adapting marketing efforts in such a way that they are perceived as culturally relevant.

continuous innovation the modification of an existing product.

core merchandise the basic group of products essential to a store's traffic, customer loyalty, and profits.

core values values that are basic to understanding human behavior.

corrective advertising advertising used to rectify deception that occurred in previous advertising.

counterargument a cognitive response that opposes the claims made in a communication.

credence claims claims that a consumer cannot evaluate or verify (e.g., "Millions of research dollars are behind this product").

credit an amount or sum placed at a person's disposal by a bank or other financial institution, which extends the income resource, at least temporarily.

cross-cultural analysis the systematic comparison of similarities and differences in the material and behavioral aspects of cultures.

crude birthrate *see* birthrate

CUBE (Comprehensive Understanding of Buyer Environment) post-hoc segmentation analysis identifying eight primary segments.

cultural analysis studies whose goal is to create the ability to understand and be effective in addressing the core values of a society.

cultural artifacts *see* material components

cultural empathy the ability to understand without judging the inner logic and coherence of other ways of life.

cultural functionalist an anthropologist holding the view that culture is an entity that serves humans in their efforts to meet the basic biological and social needs of the society.

culture the values, ideas, artifacts, and other meaningful symbols that help individuals communicate, interpret, and evaluate as members of society.

customer satisfaction monitoring program a policy of using ongoing customer surveys to continually monitor and evaluate service.

cutoff a restriction or requirement for acceptable attribute values, used in alternative evaluation.

decay theory a theory positing that the strength of a memory trace will fade over time.

decision rule a strategy that a consumer uses to make a selection from the choice alternatives.

declarative knowledge knowledge of information facts, which are subjective in that they need not correspond to objective reality.

defensive marketing marketing that encourages and resolves consumer complaints.

deference the granting of social honor.

degree of search a dimension of search indicating the total amount of search.

demarketing a deliberate attempt to induce consumers to buy less in a product class.

demographics the characteristics of human

populations, such as size, growth, density, distribution, and vital statistics; used in consumer research to describe segments of consumers in such terms as age, income, and education.

demographic segmentation directing marketing efforts toward differing segments as defined by demographic characteristics.

demography the study of demographics.

demonstrated recall measure a measure utilizing a survey to determine what percentage of viewers can recall the name of the advertised product and one point from the advertising copy.

depth interview the interviewing of a small sample (50 or fewer), one at a time, in a lengthy, unstructured session.

descriptive cross-cultural studies studies that describe structural components and are used to contrast or compare societies.

descriptive differences consumer differences that are merely descriptive, as opposed to causal.

Designated Marketing Area *see* Area of Dominant Influence

Desired State Types consumers in whom need recognition results from changes in the desired state.

determinant attribute a salient attribute on which choice alternatives differ in their performance.

dialectical materialism the view that culture moves in a determined direction through a process of exchange and social interaction in competition for scarce resources.

difference threshold the smallest change in stimulus intensity that will be noticed by an individual.

differentiated marketing marketing that concentrates on two or more segments, offering a differing marketing mix for each.

diffusion the process by which an innovation is communicated through certain channels over time among the members of a social system.

directed learning learning that occurs when learning is the primary objective during information processing (i.e., motivation is high).

direction of attention a dimension of attention representing the focus of cognitive capacity.

direction of search a dimension of search representing the specific content of search.

direct marketing activities by which products and services are offered for information purposes or to solicit a direct response from a present or prospective customer or distributor by mail, telephone, or other access.

discontinuance ceasing to use a previously adopted innovation.

discontinuous innovation an entirely new product that causes buyers to significantly alter their behavior patterns.

discrimination in classical conditioning, the process whereby an organism learns to emit a response to one stimulus but avoids making the same response to a similar stimulus.

discriminative stimuli stimuli that serve as cues about the likelihood that performing a

particular behavior will lead to reinforcement.

dissatisfaction the outcome of purchase when the consumer perceives the choice as falling short of expectations.

dissociative group a reference group whose members are motivated to avoid association.

door-in-the-face a multiple-request procedure under which compliance with a critical request is increased if this request is preceded by an even more demanding request which is refused.

doubling rate the length of time required for the population to double in size based on current growth rates.

drive a condition of arousal that occurs when there is sufficient discrepancy between a present state and a desired or preferred state of being.

dynamically continuous innovation either the creation of a new product or the alteration of an existing one; either way, there is no alteration in established patterns of customer buying and product use.

early adopter a consumer who adopts an innovation later than innovators.

early majority consumers who adopt an innovation after early adopters.

echoic the term used to describe auditory processing at the sensory-memory stage.

economic demographics the study of the economic characteristics of a nation's population.

economic node a metropolitan or similar area that serves as a center of economic activity.

economic role *see* instrumental role

elaboration the amount of integration between new information and existing knowledge stored in memory (or, the number of personal connections made between the stimulus and one's life experiences and goals).

Elaboration Likelihood Model the theory of persuasion which proposes that the influence exerted by various communication elements will depend on the elaboration that occurs during processing.

elimination by aspects decision rule a noncompensatory decision rule involving processing by attribute in which cutoffs are established for each salient attribute and brands are compared on the most important attribute; if several brands meet the cutoff, the next most important attribute is selected until the tie is broken.

empty-nester an older adult whose children have left home and the university.

enhanced shareholder value long-term, consistent appreciation of shareholder value.

entrepreneurship organizing, managing, and assuming the risks of a business or enterprise. Refers not only to the traditional small business, but also to the value of individual effort and accomplishment in large corporations.

environmental scanning analysis of the current environment and projected trends, including internal and external variables.

epidemiological model a diffusion-prediction model assuming that diffusion is a process of social interaction in which innovators and early adopters "infect" other consumers.

episodic knowledge knowledge involving information that is bound by the passage of time (e.g., knowing when one last purchased clothing).

equitable performance in purchase expectations, a normative judgment reflecting the performance one ought to receive.

ergonomics the study of the human factors involved with product design.

ethnic patterns the norms and values of specific groups within the larger society.

evaluation the measure used to assess the "goodness-badness" of an attribute or product.

evaluative criteria the standards and specifications used by consumers to compare different products and brands.

evaluative participation studies studies in which researchers count the number and nature of personal contacts in people's informal relationships, using data collected from respondents as well as their own observations of the community and its formal and informal networks.

event marketing creating events at which opinion leaders are brought together to experience and evaluate a new or existing product.

evoked set *see* consideration set

executional elements elements in a communication other than the message content, such as visuals, sounds, colors, and pace.

expectancy disconfirmation model a theory of the process by which performance of a product or service is evaluated and a satisfaction/dissatisfaction outcome is reached.

expected performance in purchase expectations, a normative judgment reflecting what the performance probably will be.

experience claims claims that a consumer can fully evaluate only after product consumption.

experiential benefits the symbolic value of a consumption object in terms of emotional response, sensory pleasure, daydreams, or aesthetic considerations.

exposure physical proximity to a stimulus that allows the opportunity for one or more senses to be activated.

expressive role role behavior involving support to other family members in the decision-making process and expression of the family's aesthetic or emotional needs.

extended family nuclear family plus such other relatives as grandparents, uncles and aunts, cousins, and in-laws.

extended problem solving detailed and rigorous decision-making behavior, including need recognition, search for information, alternative evaluation, purchase, and outcomes. Often used in making major or critical purchases.

external search a stage of the consumer decision process in which relevant information is acquired.

extinction   in classical conditioning, when the conditioned stimulus no longer evokes the conditioned response.

exurbs   areas beyond the suburbs.

family   a group of two or more persons related by blood, marriage, or adoption who reside together.

family adaptability   the ability of a family or marital system to change its power structure, role relationships, and relationship rules in response to situational and developmental stress.

family branding   the strategy of placing the same brand name on various company products to encourage generalization.

family life cycle (FLC)   the stages a family passes through during its lifetime.

family of orientation   the family into which an individual is born.

family of procreation   the family which is established by marriage.

favorability   the degree of negativeness or positiveness of an attitude.

fertility rate   the number of live births per 1,000 women of childbearing age (15 to 44).

festival marketplace   a large complex of shops and restaurants, such as Boston's Faneuil Hall Marketplace or New York City's South Street Seaport.

figure   those elements within a perceptual field that receive the most attention (*see also* ground).

first-order child   first-born child

focus group   a group of about 10 individuals, brought together with a trained leader for about 1 hour to discuss motivations and behavior.

foot-in-the-door   a multiple-request procedure under which compliance with a critical request is increased if the person first agrees to an initial smaller request.

forced-choice recognition measures   measures that require respondents to choose among a set of fixed answers (as in a multiple-choice instrument) to demonstrate their memory of specific ad and brand elements.

foreseeability   the doctrine that a manufacturer should be able to anticipate and evaluate risks inherent in product use and find out ways to avoid them.

formal group   a reference group characterized by a defined, known list of members and an organization and structure codified in writings.

forward conditioning   conditioning in which the conditioned stimulus precedes the unconditioned stimulus.

framed ad   one in which the message relates the picture to the product.

fully planned purchase   a purchase in which both the product and the brand are selected as intended.

functionality   the degree to which a product's features meet a consumer's needs.

functional role   *see* instrumental role

general fertility rate   *see* fertility rate

generalization   in classical conditioning, when a new stimulus similar to the existing one elicits the same response.

generic branding   descriptive labeling of products that sell at lower prices than nationally advertised brands.

generic need recognition   the activation of a need for a particular product category; the need is not brand specific as in selective need recognition.

gentrification   a process in which people move back to revitalized city neighborhoods, often displacing low-income families.

geodemography   the analysis of demographic lifestyle profiles for areas as small as a neighborhood.

geographic segmentation   analysis of geographic differences in terms of region, size of metropolitan area, and density.

Gestalt psychology   a theory that focuses on how people organize or combine stimuli into a meaningful whole.

global marketing   the technique of using the same marketing strategy in all cultural contexts.

global thinking   the ability to understand markets beyond one's own country of origin with respect to sources of demand, sources of supply, and methods of effective management and marketing.

ground   the elements, other than figure, that comprise the background in a perceptual field.

group norms   stable expectations arrived at by consensus concerning behavioral rules for individual members.

growth rate the increase in population due to natural increase and net migration, expressed as a percentage of base population.

habitual decision making decision making based on habits of repeat purchasing, often formed to simplify decision-process activity.

hardware the physical or tangible aspects of a product.

heavy half the heavy users of a product.

hedonic benefits *see* experiential benefits

higher-order child any child born after a first-born child.

historicalist *see* structuralist

homophilous influence influence brought about by information transmission between people similar in social class, age, education, and other demographic characteristics.

household all the persons, related and unrelated, who occupy a housing unit.

Housing-Unit method a population estimate method that multiplies occupied housing units by the average household size.

hypermarket a retail store in the 60,000- to 200,000-square-foot range that carries both convenience and shopping goods, with a heavy emphasis on general merchandise as well as on food.

hypodermic needle model a theory of marketing communications proposing that media have direct, immediate, and powerful effects on new product acceptance.

iconic the terms used to describe visual processing at the sensory-memory stage.

ideal performance in purchase expectations, a normative judgment reflecting the optimum or ideal performance level.

ideology of consumption the social meaning attached to and communicated by products.

image analysis the examination of consumers' knowledge or beliefs about a product's properties.

imagery a process by which sensory information and experiences are represented in working memory.

imitation effect a phenomenon in which the rate of adoption increases as the number of adopters increases.

implementation the process by which a consumer puts a product into use.

importance the measure used to operationalize the concept of salience.

impulse purchase a spur-of-the-moment purchase triggered by product display or point-of-sale promotion.

inbound telemarketing use of the telephone to place orders for goods or services.

incentive an anticipated reward from a course of action that offers need-satisfying potential.

incidental learning learning that occurs even when learning is not the primary objective during information processing.

individualized standards situational or individual ethic strategies used as the basis for ethical decision making.

inertia a motivation that leads to habitual decision making due to a lack of sufficient incentive to consider alternative brands.

influential a transmitter of opinions about products and services.

informal group a loosely structured reference group based on friendship or collegial associations. Norms, even when stringent, seldom appear in writing.

information adequacy the degree to which a consumer has the facts needed to make an informed choice.

informational advertising advertising that attempts to influence consumers' product knowledge and attitudes by providing information that elicits favorable cognitive responses.

informational influence the influence of friends or spokespeople, which consumers often accept as providing credible and needed evidence about reality.

information environment the entire array of product-related data available to the consumer.

information overload a situation that occurs when the amount of information in a choice environment exceeds cognitive capacity.

information processing the process by which a stimulus is received, interpreted, stored in memory, and later retrieved.

information veracity the degree to which advertising is free of deception and misrepresentation.

inner-directed consumers consumers whose lives are directed more toward their individual needs than toward values oriented to externals.

innovation   any idea or product perceived by the potential adopters to be new.

innovativeness   the degree to which an individual adopts an innovation relatively earlier than other members in the system do.

innovator   a consumer who adopts a new product early.

instrumental learning a form of learning in which the consequences of a behavior affect the frequency or probability of the behavior being performed again.

instrumental role   role behavior based on knowledge of functional attributes, such as financial aspects, performance characteristics, or conditions of purchase.

Integrated Marketing Communications (IMC)   a comprehensive, unified marketing program emphasizing the same theme or themes in advertising, public relations, investor relations, and other communications, with a targeted market.

intensity   the strength of an attitude.

intensity of attention   the amount of attention focused in a particular direction.

interactive picture   one in which both the product class and brand name are represented visually.

inter-environmental considerations   the concept, important in global marketing strategy, of considering the characteristic ways a culture responds to marketing.

interference theory   according to this theory, forgetting is due to the learning of new information.

internal search   retrieval of knowledge from memory.

intra-environmental considerations   the methods of marketing that are characteristic of a firm in its own culture.

involvement   strong motivation, as reflected in high perceived personal relevance of a stimulus in a particular context.

key-informant method   a research method in which knowledgeable people are used to identify the influentials within a social system.

knowledge   the information stored within memory.

knowledge stage   the first Rogers innovation-decision stage, in which a consumer receives physical or social stimuli that give exposure and attention to the new product.

labeling   a behavior modification technique in which attaching a label or description to a person increases the likelihood of her or him behaving in a manner that is consistent with the label.

laddering   in-depth probing directed toward uncovering higher-level meanings both at the benefit (attribute) level and at the value level.

laggard   consumers who are the last to adopt a new product.

later majority   consumers who adopt an innovation after the early majority.

learning   the process by which experience leads to changes in knowledge, attitudes, and/or behavior resulting from experience.

leisure   discretionary or uncommitted time.

lexicographic decision rule   a noncompensatory rule involving processing by attribute in which brands are compared on the most important attribute; if more than one brand qualifies, the next most important attribute is selected until the tie is broken.

life chances   the fundamental aspects of a person's future possibilities.

lifestyle   patterns by which people live and spend time and money.

lifestyle retailing   the policy of tailoring a retail offer closely to the lifestyles of specific target market groups of consumers.

limited problem solving limited decision-making behavior using a reduced number and variety of information sources, alternatives, and evaluation criteria.

lowballing   the behavior modification technique of citing a low price to gain customer commitment, then raising the price.

lower threshold   *see* absolute threshold

macroculture   the set of values and symbols that apply to an entire society.

macromarketing   macroanalysis of consumer behavior focused on determining the aggregate performance of marketing in society.

Management by Wandering Around   the practice of keeping open channels of communication with subordinates and customers by direct personal contact.

market-driven a firm using a strategy that involves identifying high-growth opportunities in consumer, merchandise, and geographic markets, and having well-defined marketing strategies geared to some form of dominance.

marketing the process of planning and executing the conception, pricing, promotion, and distribution of ideas, goods, and services to create exchanges that satisfy individual and organizational objectives.

marketing communications shared meanings between retailing organizations and persons, with exchange as their objective.

marketing mix a marketing strategy integrating product, price, promotion, and distribution.

market segment one of various groupings of buyers who expect benefits from a given transaction.

market segmentation a marketing strategy involving viewing each segment as a distinct target with its own requirements for product, price, distribution, and promotion.

market types classifications of products, including consumer package goods, consumer durable goods, industrial support consumables, industrial process consumables (commodities), make-or-buy consumables, and industrial capital goods.

massification theory the theory that social class

distinctions among the working and middle classes are disappearing.

material components the physical components of culture, such as books, computers, tools, buildings, and specific products.

megalopolis *see* Consolidated Metropolitan Statistical Area

me-too product one whose packaging mimics that of a highly successful brand.

Metropolitan Statistical Area a freestanding metropolitan area, surrounded by nonmetropolitan counties and not closely related with other metropolitan areas.

microculture the set of values and symbols of a restrictive group, such as a religious, ethnic, or other subdivision of the social whole.

micromarketing microanalysis of consumer trends and demographics that focuses on the marketing programs of specific organizations.

microspecialization the identification of specific market targets and the development of specialized retailing formats that provide a high level of satisfaction to those market targets.

mid-range problem solving decision-making behavior falling between extended problem solving and limited problem solving on the problem-solving continuum.

mini-mall small and medium-size shopping centers of various formats, usually with less than 100,000 square feet. Some are fully enclosed or have an all-weather format.

modeling a form of learning in which an individual observes the

behaviors of others and the consequences of those behaviors.

monodic approach in innovation-diffusion research, a focus upon the personal and social characteristics of industrial consumers.

monomorphic describes consumers who are innovative for only one product.

monomorphic influence influence that relates to one product only.

motivation research research into the classification of consumer motives and whether they are conscious or unconscious.

motive an enduring predisposition that arouses and directs behavior toward certain goals. Motives can be rational (utilitarian) or emotional (hedonic).

multiattribute attitude models models that propose that overall attitude depends on beliefs about the attitude object's attributes weighted by the salience of these attributes.

multi-stage interaction a theory of personal influence that holds that both influentials and information seekers are affected by the media.

natural increase the surplus of births over deaths in a given time period.

need a perceived difference between an ideal state and the present state, sufficient to activate behavior.

need-driven consumers consumers who exhibit spending driven by need rather than preference.

need for cognition a personality trait representing an individual's tendency to undertake and enjoy thinking.

need recognition perception of a difference between the desired state of affairs and the actual situation sufficient to arouse and activate the decision process; the first stage of the decision-making process.

negative disconfirmation a CS/D judgment that performance is worse than expected.

negative reinforcement in operant conditioning, a behavior leading to the removal of some adverse stimulus which increases the odds of the behavior being repeated.

network marketing the development of a firm's marketing mix in close relationship to the marketing program of other firms.

new consumerism contemporary consumerism, generally thought to begin with President Kennedy's 1962 address on the consumer bill of rights.

niche retailer a retailer offering a narrow but deep assortment, such as Banana Republic.

nonadopter one who makes the decision not to adopt a new product.

nonadoption *see* passive rejection

no-name brand *see* generic branding

noncompensatory strategy a strategy in alternative evaluation in which a brand's weakness on one attribute cannot be offset by a strength on another attribute.

noninteractive pictures pictures in which either product class or brand name, but not both, are shown visually.

normative influence *see* utilitarian influence

norms beliefs held by consensus of a group concerning the behavior rules for individual members.

nuclear family immediate group of father, mother, and children living together.

objective knowledge measures measures that assess the knowledge actually stored in memory.

objective research methods assigning status to respondents on the basis of a stratified variable such as occupation, income, or education.

observability *see* communicability

observation a measure for observing consumer search based on how much people seek information before making a decision.

one-sided message a communication presenting only the pros of the advocated position.

ongoing search a type of external search in which information acquisition occurs on a relatively regular basis regardless of sporadic purchase needs.

operant conditioning *see* instrumental learning

opinion leader person from whom a consumer seeks consumer-related advice.

order effects the differences in consumption between families caused by birth order (first-order babies generate more economic impact than higher-order babies).

outbound telemarketing marketing telephone contact by the seller to the consumer.

outcomes the fifth stage in decision making, in which the consumer evaluates whether or not the chosen alternative meets needs and expectations once it is used.

outer-directed consumers consumers who generally buy with awareness of what other people will attribute to their consumption of the purchased product.

outshopper a consumer who shops outside a local trading area.

PAD paradigm a categorization of emotional responses including the dimensions of pleasure, arousal, and dominance.

parody display the mockery of status symbols and behavior, as in the wearing of "work clothes" by upper-class youth.

partial reinforcement a schedule of reinforcement in which the desired response is reinforced only part of the time; it may be systematic (e.g., every third response) or random.

passive rejection never really considering use of an innovation.

penetration model model that predicts the level of penetration by a new product in a given time period based on early sales results.

pension elite 3 million older adults, mostly between 65 and 74, with enough income from multiple sources to support an active, independent, and healthy lifestyle.

peripheral cues elements in a communication that are irrelevant to developing a reasoned opinion.

peripheral route a form of persuasion in which issue relevant thinking is low and peripheral cues become influential.

personal determinants of attention the characteristics of an individual that influence attention.

personality the consistent responses of an individual to environmental stimuli.

person-situation segmentation a segmentation strategy that takes into account the fact that different consumers seek different product benefits, which can change across different usage situations.

persuasion the formation of favorable or unfavorable attitudes toward an innovation.

phased decision strategy a process using one decision rule as a screening device to help narrow the choice set to a more manageable number, and a different rule or rules to make the final choice.

piece part and tooling costs a reflection of whether a product is designed to be produced with processes and materials suited to the manufacturer's product levels and target costs as well as the product's actual purpose.

polymorphic influence influence that relates to several product areas.

polymorphism describes consumers who are innovators for many products.

positive disconfirmation a CS/ D judgment that performance is better than expected.

positive reinforcement in operant conditioning, a behavior leading to receiving some positive stimulus which increases the odds of the behavior being repeated.

post-hoc segmentation analysis defining the segmentation base as an outcome of analysis.

power mall *see* mini-mall

prepotency the theory that needs are organized in such a way as to establish priorities and hierarchies of importance.

prepurchase search a type of external search that is motivated by an upcoming purchase decision.

primacy an order effect wherein stimuli appearing at the beginning of a sequence are given more weight in the resulting interpretation.

primary group a social aggregation (reference group) sufficiently small to permit and facilitate unrestricted face-to-face interaction.

Primary Metropolitan Statistical Area a metropolitan area closely related to another city.

proactive inhibition a form of interference in which prior learning hinders the learning and retrieval of new information.

problem solving thoughtful, reasoned action undertaken to bring about need satisfaction.

procedural knowledge the understanding of how the facts of declarative knowledge can be used.

processing by attribute *see* attribute search sequence

processing by brand *see* brand search sequence

producibility the degree to which a product can be made with a firm's normal capabilities.

product category the category of goods (e.g., clothing, appliances).

product knowledge information stored in memory about a product category, such as the brands within it, product terminology, product attributes, and beliefs about the product category and specific brands.

product life cycle the cycle of introduction, growth, and decline of a product. Marketing strategy and mix must be adapted to the changing stages of the life cycle.

product positioning the ways in which consumers identify a product with a defined set of attributes such as power, sportiness, caffeine, or color.

product potential the tangible attributes, augmented product, and consumer expectations for the product, all combined to incorporate every factor that might attract and hold customers.

product semantics *see* semiotics

Profit Impact of Market Strategy Research research into how market strategy affects practitioners economically; it indicates that market leaders achieve average rates of return three times greater than firms with low market share.

programmed resource relationship a retailer-supplier relationship in which the retailer is a powerful controlling factor.

projective test a questioning technique that allows the respondent to reply in the third person.

prompting   a behavior modification technique in which consideration of product purchase is gained by a simple request (e.g., offering or suggesting a side dish in a restaurant).

proposition   *see* belief

proxy variable   a variable that stands in for another (e.g., demographic data can serve as a proxy variable for motivation and interests).

psychoanalytic theory   a personality theory that posits that the human personality system consists of the id (the source of psychic energy), the superego (representing societal or personal norms), and the ego (which mediates the hedonistic demands of the id and the moralistic prohibitions of the superego).

psychographics   research into psychological profiles of groups or individuals, especially regarding personality traits, values, beliefs, preferences, and behavior patterns.

psychographic segmentation   analysis of lifestyle factors for segmentation purposes.

psycholinguistics   the study of psychological factors involved in the perception of and response to linguistic phenomena.

pull strategy   a marketing strategy for creating product demand by appealing to the ultimate consumers, who, in turn, encourage the channel to carry the product.

punishment   in operant conditioning, a behavior leading to the appearance of an adverse stimulus which decreases the odds of the behavior being repeated.

purchase   the fourth stage in the decision-making process, in which the consumer acquires the preferred alternative or an acceptable substitute.

purchase knowledge   information stored in memory that is germane to acquiring products.

purchase situation   those settings in which consumers acquire products and services.

push strategy   a marketing strategy that involves focusing selling efforts on the channel, which is then responsible for attracting consumers.

Quality Function Deployment   the use of customer input throughout the design, engineering, manufacturing, and distribution of a product.

ratio-correlation method   a population estimation method that uses multiple regression to mathematically compute a population estimate.

rational decision making   problem solving based on the careful weighing and evaluation of utilitarian or functional product attributes.

recall measures   measures of cognitive learning that do not provide cues to prompt memory.

recency   an order effect wherein stimuli appearing at the end of a sequence are given more weight in the resulting interpretation.

reciprocity   a principle that states that we should try to repay what others have done for us.

recognition measures   measures of cognitive learning that provide cues to prompt memory.

reference group   a person or group of people that significantly influences an individual's behavior and attitudes.

rehearsal   the mental repetition of information (i.e., the recycling of information through short-term memory).

rejection   the decision not to adopt an innovation.

relational approach   in innovation-diffusion research, a focus on communication networks and how social-structural variables affect diffusion flows in the system.

relative advantage   the degree to which consumers perceive a relative advantage of a new product over the existing product.

repeated problem solving   decision-making dynamics that lead the consumer to buy a different brand than previously purchased.

replacement rate   the fertility rate required to replace the current population, with allowance for some infant mortality.

reputational research methods   methods utilizing people's rankings of the social position or prestige of other people.

resource commitments   the degree to which research and development, advertising, personal selling, sales promotion, and distribution support are devoted to the diffusion process.

retail image   the way a store is defined in a shopper's mind, partly by its functional qualities and partly by an aura of psychological attributes.

retail image measurement measures of image include many attitude-measurement techniques, including semantic differential and psycholinguistics.

retailing portfolio a group of specialty stores, each programmed for a specific lifestyle, owned by one retailer.

retention the transfer of information to long-term memory.

retrieval the process by which knowledge stored in long-term memory is activated.

retrieval set a consideration set obtained by recall of alternatives from memory.

retroactive inhibition a form of interference in which recently learned information inhibits the retrieval of previously learned information.

retrospective questioning a measure for consumer search based on recall of search activities during decision making.

role what the typical occupant of a given position is expected to do in that position in a particular social context.

role overload a situation in which the total demands on time and energy associated with the prescribed activities of multiple roles are too great to allow an individual to perform the roles adequately or comfortably.

salience the potential influence that a criterion exerts during the alternative evaluation process, often measured in terms of importance.

satisfaction a postconsumption evaluation that a chosen alternative meets or exceeds expectations.

schema a high-order knowledge structure made up of a combination of propositions or beliefs.

script one type of schema, which contains knowledge about the temporal action sequences that occur during an event.

search the motivated activation of knowledge stored in memory or acquisition of information from the environment; the second stage of the decision-making process.

search claims claims that a consumer can accurately evaluate before purchase through external search.

secondary group a reference group exhibiting face-to-face behavior that is more sporadic, less comprehensive, and less influential in shaping thought and behavior than that of a primary group.

selective need recognition the activation of a need for a specific brand within a product category.

self-actualization the desire to know, understand, systematize, prioritize, and construct a system of values.

self-concept an organized configuration of perceptions of the self which are admissible to awareness, including perceptions of one's characteristics, values, and relationships.

self-designation method a research method by which people are asked to evaluate the extent to which they are sought out for advice.

self-monitoring a personality trait representing the degree of

sensitivity to situational and interpersonal considerations.

self-perception theory a theory stating that individuals come to know their own attitudes, emotions, and other internal states by inferring them from observations of their own behavior.

self-referencing relating information to one's own self and experiences.

self-serving strategy a technology-development strategy in which a firm develops innovations but waits to introduce them until sales of its current products decline.

semantic knowledge generalized knowledge that gives meaning to an individual's world.

semiotics the study of the symbolic qualities of products in the context of their use.

sensation the activation of sensory receptors, following which the encoded information about the stimulus is transmitted along nerve fibers to the brain.

sensation seeker an individual motivated by the need for continued high-level stimulation.

sequence of search a dimension of search representing the order in which search activities occur.

shaping the reinforcement of successive approximations of a desired behavior pattern or of behaviors that must be performed before the desired response can be emitted.

simple additive decision rule a compensatory decision rule under which the consumer counts the number of times each alternative is judged favorably in terms of the set of salient evaluative criteria.

simple confirmation a CS/D judgment that performance equals expectations.

simple recognition measures measures that involve presenting ads to people and asking whether they remember seeing them previously.

simultaneous conditioning classical conditioning in which the conditioned stimulus and unconditioned stimulus are presented at the same time.

situational influence the influence arising from factors that are particular to a specific time and place and are independent of consumer and object characteristics.

social class divisions within society composed of individuals sharing similar values, interests, and behavior.

socialization the process of absorbing a culture and all of its values and symbols.

sociometric measures *see* evaluative participation studies

sociometric method a research method in which individuals are asked to identify others they seek out for advice or information for decision making.

socio-psychological theory a personality theory that posits that social variables (not biological instincts) shape personality and that behavioral motivation is directed to shape those needs created by the social variables.

software the information base that accompanies a product's hardware component.

standardized technology technology that has become standardized among firms; its presence encourages diffusion.

Standard Metropolitan Statistical Area the old term for Metropolitan Statistical Area.

status group a group that reflects a community's expectations for style of life among each class as well as the positive or negative social estimation of honor given each class.

stimulus categorization the classifying of a stimulus during the comprehension stage of information processing using concepts stored in memory.

stimulus determinants of attention the characteristics of a stimulus that influence attention.

store atmospherics the physical properties of the retail environment.

store image *see* retail image

structuralist an anthropologist who believes that culture follows a logic based on the patterns of the human mind.

subjective knowledge measures measures that assess a person's perception of the amount of knowledge he or she possesses, which may or may not correspond to her or his actual knowledge.

subjective research methods methods assigning status to individuals based on the perceptions of other people and the subjective insights or theories of the researchers.

subliminal persuasion the theory that stimuli below the lower or absolute threshold can influence attitudes and behavior.

supplier-style retailing in contrast to lifestyle retailing, supplier-side retailing emphasizes homogeneity and

gives little or no recognition to customer differences.

support argument a cognitive response that is favorable to the claims of a communication.

surrogate shopping list a list of products obtained in response to product display rather than through cognitive planning.

terminal threshold the point at which additional increases in stimulus intensity have no effect on sensation.

time goods products and services classified by their time properties.

time guarantee a promise by the seller that the customer will not have to devote an unreasonable amount of time to getting product and service problems resolved.

total fertility rate the average number of children that would be born alive to a woman if she were to pass through all her childbearing years conforming to the age specific fertility rates of a given year.

total product concept the combination of the generic product, expected product, augmented product, and potential product; successful introduction of new products requires understanding of this concept.

total reinforcement a schedule of reinforcement in which the desired response is always reinforced.

trait any distinguishable, relatively enduring way in which one individual differs from another.

trait-factor theory a personality theory that

postulates that an individual's personality is composed of definite predispositional attributes called traits.

transformational advertising advertising that attempts to influence consumers' perceptions of a product's emotional and symbolic features by eliciting favorable affective responses.

trend analysis the analysis of marketing opportunities that arise as a result of changes in the environment.

trend following a technology-development strategy in which a firm capitalizes on the developments of other firms in the industry while minimizing its own research and development expenses.

trend setting a technology-development strategy in which a firm continuously develops innovations for current and future product developments, and introduces these innovations as soon as feasible.

trickle-down theory a theory of personal influence that holds that lower classes emulate the behavior of their high-class counterparts.

two-sided message a communication presenting the pros and cons of the advocated position.

two-step flow model a theory of personal influence that holds that new ideas first flow to influentials, who then pass them on to the rest of the population.

unaided recall measures measures that do not provide cues for retrieving information from memory.

unconditioned response see classical conditioning

unconditioned stimulus see classical conditioning

undifferentiated marketing marketing that targets all available segments.

unframed ad one in which the message does not relate the picture to the product.

unplanned purchase a purchase for which a conscious intention was not articulated in advance.

usage knowledge information in memory about how a product can be used and what is required to actually use it.

usage situation the setting where consumption occurs.

usage situation segmentation segmentation derived from information on product usage.

utilitarian benefits benefits resulting from purchase or other consumer decisions that are objective, functional product attributes.

utilitarian influence pressure that the reference group applies to the individual to comply with group norms.

value an enduring belief that a specific mode of conduct or end-state of existence is personally or socially preferable to an opposite or converse made of conduct or end-state of existence.

value-expressive influence the pressure to experience psychological association with a group by conforming to its norms, values, or behaviors, even if membership is not sought.

value platform the manner in which a firm differentiates itself from its competitors in the minds of the consumers it intends to serve.

values shared beliefs or group norms that have been internalized by individuals.

variety seeking switching of brands simply in the interest of variety; often used when many similar alternatives are available.

vertical coordination the flow of information from supplier to consumer that affects the diffusion of information.

vicarious learning see modeling

videotex interactive electronic media used for in-home shopping and information.

waverer a consumer whose commitment to the product is diminishing.

wealth net worth or assets, in consumer terms correlated with income.

Weber's Law a rule stating that the amount of change necessary to reach the difference threshold will depend on the initial starting point; e.g., as stimulus intensity increases, a greater amount of change is required to produce a just noticeable difference.

weighted additive decision rule a compensatory decision rule in which judgments about an alternative's performance on evaluative criteria are weighted by the relative salience of the evaluative criteria.

SUBJECT INDEX

Note: Page numbers in *italics* indicate illustrations.